ST/ESA/STAT/SER.R/42

Department of Economic and Social Affairs
Département des affaires économiques et sociales

2012

Demographic Yearbook
Annuaire démographique

Sixty-third issue/Soixante-troisième édition

United Nations/Nations Unies
New York, 2013

The Department of Economic and Social Affairs of the United Nations Secretariat is a vital interface between global policies in the economic, social and environmental spheres and national action. The Department works in three main interlinked areas: (i) it compiles, generates and analyses a wide range of economic, social and environmental data and information on which States Members of the United Nations draw to review common problems and to take stock of policy options; (ii) it facilitates the negotiations of Member States in many intergovernmental bodies on joint courses of action to address ongoing or emerging global challenges; and (iii) it advises interested Governments on the ways and means of translating policy frameworks developed in United Nations conferences and summits into programmes at the country level and, through technical assistance, helps build national capacities.

Le Département des affaires économiques et sociales du Secrétariat de l'Organisation des Nations Unies sert de relais entre les orientations arrêtées au niveau international dans les domaines économiques, sociaux et environnementaux et les politiques exécutées à l'échelon national. Il intervient dans trois grands domaines liés les uns aux autres : i) il compile, produit et analyse une vaste gamme de données et d'éléments d'information sur des questions économiques, sociales et environnementales dont les États Membres de l'Organisation se servent pour examiner des problèmes communs et évaluer les options qui s'offrent à eux; ii) il facilite les négociations entre les États Membres dans de nombreux organes intergouvernementaux sur les orientations à suivre de façon collective afin de faire face aux problèmes mondiaux existants ou en voie d'apparition; iii) il conseille les gouvernements intéressés sur la façon de transposer les orientations politiques arrêtées à l'occasion des conférences et sommets des Nations Unies en programmes exécutables au niveau national et aide à renforcer les capacités nationales au moyen de programmes d'assistance technique.

NOTE

Symbols of United Nations documents are composed of capital letters combined with figures. Mention of such a symbol indicates reference to a United Nations document.

The designations employed and the presentation of material in this publication do not imply the expression of any opinion whatsoever on the part of the Secretariat of the United Nations concerning the legal status of any country, territory, city or area, or of its authorities, or concerning the delimitation of its frontiers or boundaries.

Where the designation "country or area" appears in the headings of tables, it covers countries, territories, or areas.

NOTE

Les cotes des documents de l'Organisation des Nations Unies se composent de lettres majuscules et de chiffres. La simple mention d'une cote dans un texte signifie qu'il s'agit d'un document de l'Organisation.

Les appellations employées dans cette publication et la présentation des données qui y figurent n'impliquent de la part du Secrétariat de l'Organisation des Nations Unies aucune prise de position quant au statut juridique des pays, territoires, villes ou zones, ou de leurs autorités, ni quant au tracé de leurs frontières ou limites.

L'appellation "pays ou zone" figurant dans les titres des rubriques des tableaux désigne des pays, des territoires, ou des zones.

ST/ESA/STAT/SER.R/42

UNITED NATIONS PUBLICATION
Sales number: B.14.XIII.1 H

PUBLICATION DES NATIONS UNIES
Numéro de vente: B.14.XIII.1 H

ISBN 978-92-1-051106-3
eISBN 978-92-1-056251-5
ISSN 0082-8041

Topics of the Demographic Yearbook series: 1948 - 2012

Sujets des diverses éditions de l'Annuaire démographique : 1948 - 2012

Year Année	Sales No. - Numéro de vente	Issue - Edition	Special topic - Sujet spécial
1948	49.XIII.1	First-Première	General demography-Démographie générale
1949-50	51.XIII.1	Second-Deuxième	Natality statistics-Statistiques de la natalité
1951	52.XIII.1	Third-Trosième	Mortality statistics-Statistiques de la mortalité
1952	53.XIII.1	Fourth-Quatrième	Population distribution-Répartition de la population
1953	54.XIII.1	Fifth-Cinquième	General demography-Démographie générale
1954	55.XIII.1	Sixth-Sixième	Natality statistics -Statistiques de la natalité
1955	56.XIII.1	Seventh-Septième	Population censuses-Recensement de population
1956	57.XIII.1	Eighth-Huitième	Ethnic and economic characteristics of population-Caractéristiques ethniques et économiques de la population
1957	58.XIII.1	Ninth-Neuvième	Mortality statistics- Statistiques de la mortalité
1958	59.XIII.1	Tenth-Dixième	Marriage and divorce statistics- Statistiques de la nuptialité et de la divortialité
1959	60.XIII.1	Eleventh-Onzième	Natality statistics- Statistiques de la natalité
1960	61.XIII.1	Twelfth-Douzième	Population trends- l' évolution de la population
1961	62.XIII.1	Thirteenth-Treizième	Mortality Statistics- Statistiques de la mortalité
1962	63.XIII.1	Fourteenth-Quatorzième	Population census statistics I- Statistiques des recensements de population I
1963	64.XIII.1	Fifteenth-Quinzième	Population census statistics II- Statistiques des recensements de population II
1964	65.XIII.1	Sixteenth-Seizième	Population census statistics III- Statistiques des recensements de population III
1965	66.XIII.1	Seventeenth-Dix-septième	Natality statistics- Statistiques de la natalité
1966	67.XIII.1	Eighteenth-Dix-huitième	Mortality statistics I- Statistiques de la mortalité I
1967	E/F.68.XIII.1	Nineteenth-Dix-neuvième	Mortality statistics II - Statistiques de la mortalité II
1968	E/F.69.XIII.1	Twentieth-Vingtième	Marriage and divorce statistics-Statistiques de la nuptialité et de la divortialité
1969	E/F.70.XIII.1	Twenty-first-Vingt et unième	Natality statistics-Statistiques de la natalité
1970	E/F.71.XIII.1	Twenty-second-Vingt-deuxième	Population trends-l' évolution de la population
1971	E/F.72.XIII.1	Twenty-third-Vingt-troisième	Population census statistics I- Statistiques de recensements de population I
1972	E/F.73.XIII.1	Twenty-fourth-Vingt-quatrième	Population census statistics II- Statistiques des recensements de population II
1973	E/F.74.XIII.1	Twenty-fifth-Vingt-cinquième	Population census statistics III- Statistiques des recensements de population III
1974	E/F.75.XIII.1	Twenty-sixth-Vingt-sixième	Mortality statistics - Statistiques de la mortalité
1975	E/F.76.XIII.1	Twenty-seventh-Vingt-septième	Natality statistics- Statistiques de la natalité
1976	E/F.77.XIII.1	Twenty-eighth-Vingt-huitième	Marriage and divorce statistics- Statistiques de la nuptialité et de la divortialité
1977	E/F.78.XIII.1	Twenty-ninth-Vingt-neuvième	International Migration Statistics- internationales
1978	E/F.79.XIII.1	Thirtieth-Trentième	General tables- Tableaux de caractère général
1978	E/F.79.XIII.8	Special issue-Edition spéciale	Historical supplement-Supplément rétrospectif
1979	E/F.80.XIII.1	Thirty-first-Trente et unième	Population census statistics-Statistiques des recensements de population
1980	E/F.81.XIII.1	Thirty-second-Trente-deuxième	Mortality statistics- Statistiques de la mortalité
1981	E/F.82.XIII.1	Thirty-third-Trente-troisième	Natality statistics-Statistiques de la natalité

Topics of the Demographic Yearbook series: 1948 - 2012

Sujets des diverses éditions de l'Annuaire démographique : 1948 - 2012

Year Année	Sales No. - Numéro de vente	Issue - Edition	Special topic - Sujet spécial
1982	E/F.83.XIII.1	Thirty-fourth- Trente-quatrième	Marriage and divorce statistics- Statistiques de la nuptialité et de la divortialité
1983	E/F.84.XIII.1	Thirty fifth- Trente-cinquième	Population census statistics I- Statistiques des recensements de population I
1984	E/F.85.XIII.1	Thirty-sixth- Trente-sixième	Population census statistics II- Statistiques des recensements de population II
1985	E/F.86.XIII.1	Thirty-seventh- Trente-septième	Mortality statistics- Statistiques de la mortalité
1986	E/F.87.XIII.1	Thirty-eighth- Trente-huitième	Natality statistics- Statistiques de la natalité
1987	E/F.88.XIII.1	Thirty-ninth- Trente-neuvième	Household composition- Les éléments du ménage
1988	E/F.89.XIII.1	Fortieth- Quarantième	Population census statistics- Statistiques des recensements de population
1989	E/F.90.XIII.1	Forty-first- Quarante-et-unième	International Migration Statistics- Statistiques des migration internationales
1990	E/F.91.XIII.1	Forty-second- Quarante-deuxième	Marriage and divorce statistics- Statistiques de la nuptialité et de la divortialité
1991	E/F.92.XIII.1	Forty-third- Quarante-troisième	General tables- Tableaux de caractère général
1991	E/F.92.XIII.9	Special Issue	Population Ageing and the Situation of Elderly Persons Vieillissement de la population et situation des personnes âgées
1992	E/F.94.XIII.1	Forty-fourth- Quarante-quatrième	Fertility and mortality statistics- Statistiques de la fecondité et de la mortalité
1993	E/F.95.XIII.1	Forty-fifth- Quarante-cinquième	Population census statistics I- Statistiques des recensements de population I
1994	E/F.96.XIII.1	Forty-sixth- Quarante-sixième	Population census statistics II- Statistiques des recensements de population II
1995	E/F.97.XIII.1	Forty-seventh- Quarante-septième	Household composition-Les éléments du ménage
1996	E/F.98.XIII.1	Forty-eighth- Quarante-huitième	Mortality statistics- Statistiques de la mortalité
1997	E/F.99.XIII.1	Forty-ninth- Quarante-neuvième	General tables- Tableaux de caractère général
1997	E/F.99.XIII.12	Special issue- Edition spéciale (CD)	Historical supplement- Supplément rétrospectif
1998	E/F.00.XIII.1	Fiftieth- Cinquantième	General tables- Tableaux de caractère général
1999	E/F.01.XIII.1	Fifty-first- Cinquante-et-unième	General tables- Tableaux de caractère général
1999	E/F.02.XIII.6	Special issue- Edition spéciale (CD)	Natality Statistics- Statistiques de la natalité
2000	E/F.02.XIII.1	Fifty-second- Cinquante-deuxième	General tables- Tableaux de caractère général
2001	E/F.03.XIII.1	Fifty-third- Cinquante- troisième	General tables- Tableaux de caractère général
2002	E/F.05.XIII.1	Fifty-fourth- Cinquante-quatrième	General tables- Tableaux de caractère général
2003	E/F.06.XIII.1	Fifty-fifth- Cinquante-cinquième	General tables- Tableaux de caractère général
2004	E/F.07.XIII.1	Fifty-sixth- Cinquante-sixième	General tables- Tableaux de caractère général
2005	E/F.08.XIII.1	Fifty-seventh- Cinquante-septième	General tables- Tableaux de caractère général
2006	E/F.09.XIII.1	Fifty-eighth- Cinquante-huitième	General tables- Tableaux de caractère général
2007	E/F.10.XIII.1	Fifty-ninth- Cinquante-neuvième	General tables- Tableaux de caractère général

Topics of the Demographic Yearbook series: 1948 - 2012

Sujets des diverses éditions de l'Annuaire démographique : 1948 - 2012

Year Année	Sales No. - Numéro de vente	Issue - Edition	Special topic - Sujet spécial
2008	E/F.11.XIII.1	Sixtieth- Soixantième	General tables- Tableaux de caractère général
2009 - 2010	B.12.XIII.1 H	Sixty-first Soixante-et-unième	General tables- Tableaux de caractère général
2011	B.13.XIII.1 H	Sixty-second Soixante- deuxième	General tables- Tableaux de caractère général
2012	B.14.XIII.1 H	Sixty-third Soixante- troisième	General tables- Tableaux de caractère général

CONTENTS - TABLE DES MATIERES

EXPLANATIONS OF SYMBOLS

Category not applicable ....

Data not available... ...

Magnitude zero or less than half of unit employed .... -

Provisional .... *

Data tabulated by year of registration rather than occurrence .... +

Based on less than specified minimum .... ◆

Relatively reliable data .... Roman type

Data of lesser reliability .... *Italics*

EXPLICATION DES SIGNES

Sans objet ....

Données non disponibles ....

Néant ou chiffre inférieur à la moitié de l'unité employée .... -

Données provisoires .... *

Donnée exploitées selon l'année de l'enregistrement et non l'année de l'événement +

Rapport fondé sur un nombre inférieur à celui spécifié.. ◆

Données relativement sûres.. Caractères romains

Données dont l'exactitude est moindre .... *Italiques*

INTRODUCTION

The *Demographic Yearbook* is an international compendium of national demographic statistics provided by national statistical authorities to the Statistics Division of the United Nations Department of Economic and Social Affairs. The *Demographic Yearbook* is part of the set of coordinated and interrelated publications issued by the United Nations and its specialized agencies, designed to supply statistical data for such users as demographers, economists, public-health workers and sociologists. Through the co-operation of national statistical services, available official demographic statistics are compiled in the *Demographic Yearbook* for more than 230 countries or areas throughout the world.

The *Demographic Yearbook 2012* is the sixty-third issue in a series published by the United Nations since 1948. It contains tables on a wide range of demographic statistics, including a world summary of selected demographic statistics, statistics on the size, distribution and trends in national populations, fertility, foetal mortality, infant and maternal mortality, general mortality, nuptiality and divorce. Data are shown by urban/rural residence, as available. In addition, the volume provides Technical Notes, a synoptic table, a historical index and a listing of the issues of the *Demographic Yearbook* published to date. This issue of *Demographic Yearbook* contains data as available including reference year 2012.

The Technical Notes on the Statistical Tables are provided to assist the reader in using the tables. Table A, the synoptic table, provides an overview of the completeness of data coverage of the current *Demographic Yearbook*. The cumulative historical index is a guide on content and coverage of all sixty-three issues, and indicates, for each of the topics that have been published, the issues in which they are presented and the years covered. A list of the *Demographic Yearbook* issues, with their corresponding sales numbers and the special topics featured in each issue are shown on pages iii and iv.

Until the 48th issue (1996), each issue consisted of two parts, the general tables and special topic tables, published in the same volume[1]. Beginning with the 49th issue (1997), the special topic tables were being disseminated in digital format as supplements to the regular issues. Two CD-ROMs have been issued: the *Demographic Yearbook Historical Supplement*, which presents a wide panorama of basic demographic statistics for the period 1948 to 1997, and the *Demographic Yearbook*: *Natality Statistics*, which contains a series of detailed tables dedicated to natality and covering the period from 1980 to 1998. Later on, three volumes of *Demographic Yearbook* Special Census Topics for the 2000 round of censuses, covering the period from 1995 to 2004, were published on-line at http://unstats.un.org/unsd/demographic/products/dyb/dybcens.htm. Current *Demographic Yearbook* census topics datasets for the reference years 1995 to the present, as available, are presented at http://unstats.un.org/unsd/demographic/products/dyb/dybcensusdata.htm. These datasets cover basic population characteristics, educational, household, ethnocultural and economic characteristics, and also foreign-born and foreign population.

Population statistics are not available for all countries or areas, for a variety of reasons. In an effort to provide estimates of mid-year population and of selected vital statistics for all countries and areas, two annexes are presented. Annex I presents United Nations population estimates for the period 2003-2012 and Annex II presents the medium variant estimates of crude birth and death rates, infant mortality and total fertility rates, as well as life expectancy at birth over the period 2010-2015. These data were produced by the United Nations Population Division and are published in the *2012 Revision of World Population Prospects*[2].

Demographic statistics shown in this issue of the *Demographic Yearbook* are available online at the *Demographic Yearbook* website http://unstats.un.org/unsd/demographic/products/dyb/dyb2012.htm. Information about the Statistics Division's data collection and dissemination programme is also available on the same website. Additional information can be made available by contacting the Statistics Division of the United Nations Department of Economic and Social Affairs at demostat@un.org.

TECHNICAL NOTES ON THE STATISTICAL TABLES

1. GENERAL REMARKS

1.1 Arrangement of Technical Notes

These Technical Notes are designed to provide the reader with relevant information related to the statistical tables. Information pertaining to the *Demographic Yearbook* in general is presented in the sections dealing with geographical aspects, population and vital statistics. In addition, preceding each table are notes describing the variables, remarks on the reliability and limitation of the data, countries and areas covered, and information on the presentation of earlier data. When appropriate, details on computation of rates, ratios or percentages are presented.

1.2 Arrangement of tables

The numbering of tables from one issue of *Demographic Yearbook* to the next is preserved to the extent possible. However, since for some of the tables the numbering may not correspond exactly to those in previous issues, the reader is advised to use the historical index that appears at the end of this book to find the reference to data in earlier issues.

1.3 Source of data

The statistics presented in the *Demographic Yearbook* are national data provided by official statistical authorities unless otherwise indicated. The primary source of data for the *Demographic Yearbook* is a set of questionnaires sent annually by the United Nations Statistics Division to over 230 national statistical services. Data reported on these questionnaires are supplemented, to the extent possible, with data taken from official national publications, official websites and through correspondence with national statistical services. In the interest of comparability, rates, ratios and percentages have been calculated by the Statistics Division of the United Nations, except for the life table functions, the total fertility rate, and also crude birth rate and crude death rate for some countries or areas as appropriately noted. The methods used by the Statistics Division to calculate these rates and ratios are described in the Technical Notes for each table. The population figures used for these computations are those pertaining to the corresponding years published in this or previous issues of the *Demographic Yearbook*.

In cases when data in this issue of the *Demographic Yearbook* differ from those published in earlier issues or related publications, statistics in this issue may be assumed to reflect revisions to the data received by June 2013.

2. GEOGRAPHICAL ASPECTS

2.1 Coverage

Data are shown for all individual countries or areas that provided information. Table 3 is the most comprehensive in geographical coverage, presenting data on population and surface area for all countries or areas with a population of at least 50 persons. Not all of these countries or areas appear in subsequent tables. In many cases the data required for a particular table are not available. In general, the more detailed the data required for a table, the fewer the number of countries or areas that can provide them.

In addition, rates and ratios are presented only for countries or areas reporting at least a minimum number of relevant events. The minimums are stated in the Technical Notes to individual tables.

Except for summary data shown for the world and by major areas and regions in tables 1 and 2 and data shown for capital cities and cities with a population of 100 000 or more in table 8, all data are presented at the national level. The number of countries shown in each table is provided in table A, the synoptic table.

2.2 Territorial composition

To the extent possible, all data, including time series data, relate to the territory within 2012 boundaries. Exceptions are footnoted in individual tables. Relevant clarifications are specified below.

Data relating to **Denmark** exclude Faeroe Islands and Greenland, which are shown separately.

Data relating to **Finland** include Åland Islands, unless otherwise indicated by a footnote.

Data relating to **France** exclude Overseas Departments, namely, French Guiana, Guadeloupe, Martinique and Réunion, which are shown separately, unless otherwise indicated by a footnote.

Data relating to **United Kingdom of Great Britain and Northern Ireland** exclude Guernsey, Isle of Man and Jersey which are shown separately.

Data relating to **Western Sahara** comprise the Northern Region (former Saguia el Hamra) and Southern Region (former Rio de Oro).

2.3 Nomenclature

Because of space limitations, the country or area names listed in the tables are generally the commonly employed short titles currently in use[3] in the United Nations, the full titles being used only when a short form is not available. The latest version of the *Standard Country or Area Codes for Statistics Use* can be accessed at http://unstats.un.org/unsd/methods/m49/m49alpha.htm.

2.3.1 Order of presentation

Countries or areas are listed in English alphabetical order within the following continents: Africa, North America, South America, Asia, Europe and Oceania.

The designations and presentation of the material in this publication were adopted solely for the purpose of providing a convenient geographical basis for the accompanying statistical series. The same qualification applies to all notes and explanations concerning the geographical units for which data are presented.

2.4 Surface area data

Surface area data, shown in tables 1 and 3, represent the total surface area, comprising land area and inland waters (assumed to consist of major rivers and lakes) and excluding only Polar Regions and uninhabited islands. The surface area given is the most recent estimate available. They are presented in square kilometres, a conversion factor of 2.589988 having been applied to surface areas originally reported in square miles.

2.4.1 Comparability over time

Comparability over time in surface area estimates for any given country or area may be affected by changes in the surface area estimation procedures, increases in actual land surface by reclamation, boundary changes, changes in the concept of "land surface area" used or a change in the unit of measurement used. In most cases it was possible to ascertain the reason for a revision; otherwise, the latest figures have generally been accepted as correct and substituted for those previously on file.

2.4.2 International comparability

    Lack of international comparability between surface area estimates arises primarily from differences in definition. In particular, there is considerable variation in the treatment of coastal bays, inlets and gulfs, rivers and lakes. International comparability is also impaired by the variation in methods employed to estimate surface area. These range from surveys based on modern scientific methods to conjectures based on diverse types of information. Some estimates are recent while others may not be.   Since neither the exact method of determining the surface area nor the precise definition of its composition and time reference is known for all countries or areas, the estimates in table 3 should not be considered strictly comparable from one country or area to another.

3. POPULATION

    Population statistics, that is, those pertaining to the size, geographical distribution and demographic characteristics of the population, are presented in a number of tables of the *Demographic Yearbook*.

    Summary estimates of the mid-year population of the world, major areas and regions for selected years and of its age and sex distribution in 2012 are set forth in tables 1 and 2, respectively.

    Data for countries or areas include population census figures, estimates based on results of sample surveys (in the absence of a census), postcensal or intercensal estimates and those derived from continuous population registers. In the present issue of the *Demographic Yearbook* , the latest available census figure of the total population of each country or area and mid-year estimates for 2005 and 2012 are presented in table 3. Mid-year estimates of total population for ten years (2003-2012) are shown in table 5 and mid-year estimates of urban and total population by sex for ten years (2003-2012) are shown in table 6. The latest available data on population by age, sex and urban/rural residence are given in table 7. The latest available figures on the population of capital cities and of cities or urban agglomerations of 100 000 or more inhabitants are presented in table 8.

    The statistics on total population, population by age, sex, or urban/rural distribution are used for the calculation of rates in the *Demographic Yearbook*. Vital rates by residence (urban/rural), age or sex were calculated using data presented in tables 6 or 7 in this issue or the corresponding tables of previous issues of the *Demographic Yearbook*.

3.1 Sources of variation of data

    The comparability of data is affected by several factors, including (1) the definition of total population; (2) the definition used to classify the population into its urban/rural components; (3) the accuracy of age reporting; (4) the extent of over-enumeration or under-enumeration in the most recent census or other source of benchmark population statistics; and (5) the quality of population estimates. These five factors will be discussed in some detail in sections 3.1.1 to 3.2 below. Other relevant problems are discussed in the technical notes to the individual tables. Readers interested in more detail, relating in particular to the basic concepts of population size, distribution and characteristics as elaborated by the United Nations, should consult the *Principles and Recommendations for Population and Housing Censuses, Revision 2*[4].

3.1.1 Total population

    The most important impediment to comparability of total populations is the difference between the concept of a *de facto* and *de jure* population. A *de facto* population includes all persons physically present in the country or area at the reference date. The *de jure* population, by contrast, includes all usual residents of the given country or area, whether or not they were physically present in the area at the reference date. By definition, therefore, a *de facto* total and a *de jure* total are not entirely comparable.

    Comparability of even two *de facto* or *de jure* totals is often affected by the fact that strict conformity to either of these concepts is rare. For example, some so-called *de facto* counts do not include foreign military, naval and diplomatic personnel present in the country or area on official duty, and their accompanying family and household members; some do not include foreign visitors in transit through the country or area or transients on ships in harbours. On the other hand, they may include such persons as merchant seamen and fishermen who are temporarily out of the country or area working at their trade.

The *de jure* population figure presents even greater variations in comparability, in part because it depends in the first place on the concept of "usual residence", which varies from one country or area to another and is difficult to apply consistently in a census or survey enumeration. For example, non-national civilians temporarily in a country or area as short-term workers may officially be considered residents after a stay of a specified period of time or they may be considered as non-residents throughout the duration of their stay; at the same time, these individuals may be officially considered as residents or non-residents of the country or area from which they came, depending on the duration and/or purpose of their absence. Furthermore, regardless of the official treatment, individual respondents may apply their own interpretation of residence in responding to the inquiry. In addition, there may be considerable differences in the accuracy with which countries or areas are informed about the number of their residents temporarily out of the country or area.

As far as possible, the population statistics presented in the tables of the *Demographic Yearbook* refer to the *de facto* population. Those reported to have been based on the *de jure* concept are identified as such. Figures not otherwise qualified may, therefore, be assumed to have been reported by countries or areas as being based on a *de facto* definition of the population. In an effort to overcome, to the extent possible, the effect of the lack of strict conformity to either the *de facto* or the *de jure* concept given above, significant exceptions with respect to inclusions and exclusions of specific population groups, are footnoted when they are known.

It should be remembered, however, that the necessary detailed information has not been available in many cases. It cannot, therefore, be assumed that figures not thus qualified reflect strict *de facto* or *de jure* definitions.

A possible source of variation within the statistics of a single country or area may arise from the fact that some countries or areas collect information on both the *de facto* and the *de jure* population in, for example, a census, but prepare detailed tabulations for only the *de jure* population. Hence, even though the total population shown in table 3 is de facto, the figures shown in the tables presenting various characteristics of the population, for example, urban/rural distribution, age and sex distribution, may be on the *de jure* concept.

3.1.2 Urban/rural classification

International comparability of urban/rural distributions is seriously impaired by the wide variation among national definitions of the concept of "urban". The definitions used by individual countries or areas and their implications are shown at the end of technical notes for table 6.

3.1.3 Age distribution

The classification of population by age is a core element of most analyses, estimation and projection of population statistics. Unfortunately, age data are subject to a number of sources of error and non-comparability. Accordingly, the reliability of age data should be of concern to users of these statistics.

3.1.3.1 Collection and compilation of age data

Age is the estimated or calculated interval of time between the date of birth and the date of the census or survey, expressed in completed solar years[5]. There are two methods of collecting information on age. The first is to obtain the date of birth for each member of the population in a census or survey and then to calculate the completed age of the individual by subtracting the date of birth from the date of enumeration[6]. The second method is to record the individual's completed age at the time of the census or survey, that is to say, age at last birthday.

The recommended method is to calculate age at last birthday by subtracting the exact date of birth from the date of the census. Some practices, however, do not use this method but instead calculate the difference between the year of birth and the year of the census. Classifications of this type are footnoted whenever possible. They can be identified to a certain extent by a smaller than expected population under one year of age. However, an irregular number of births from one year to the next or age selective omission of infants may also obscure the expected population under one year of age.

3.1.3.2 Errors in age data

Errors in age data may be due to a variety of causes, including ignorance of the correct age; reporting years of age in terms of a calendar concept other than completed solar years since birth[7]; carelessness in reporting and recording age; a general tendency to state age in figures ending in certain digits (such as zero, two, five and eight); a tendency to exaggerate length of life at advanced ages; a subconscious aversion to certain numbers; and wilful misrepresentations.

These reasons for errors in reported age data are common to most investigations of age and to most countries or areas, and they may significantly impair comparability of the data.

As a result of the above-mentioned difficulties, the age-sex distribution of population in many countries or areas shows irregularities which may be summarized as follows: (1) a deficiency in the number of infants and young children; (2) a concentration at ages ending with zero and five (that is, 5, 10, 15, 20, ...); (3) heaping at even ages (for example, 10, 12, 14, ...) relative to odd ages (for example, 11, 13, 15, ...); (4) unexpectedly large differences between the frequency of males and females at certain ages; and (5) unaccountably large differences between the frequencies in adjacent age groups. Comparing of identical age-sex cohorts from successive censuses, as well as studying the age-sex composition of each census, may reveal these and other inconsistencies, some of which in varying degree are characteristic of even the most modern censuses.

3.2 Methods used to indicate quality of published statistics

To the extent possible, efforts have been made to give the reader an indication of reliability of the statistics published in the *Demographic Yearbook*. This has been approached in several ways. Any information regarding a possible under-enumeration or over-enumeration, coming from a postcensal survey, for example, has been noted in the footnotes to table 3. Any deviation from full national coverage, as explained in section 2.1 under Geographical Aspects, has also been noted. In addition, national statistical offices have been asked to evaluate the estimates of total population they submit to the Statistics Division of the United Nations.

Estimates of the age-sex distribution of population may be constructed by two major methods: (1) by applying the specific components of population change to each age-sex group of the population as enumerated at the time of the census, and (2) by distributing the total estimated for a postcensal year proportionately according to the age-sex structure at the time of the census.

Estimated age-sex distributions are categorized as "reliable" or otherwise, according to the method of construction established for the latest estimates of total mid-year population as well as population by age and sex. Hence, the quality designation of the total figure, as indicated by the code, is considered to apply also to the whole distribution by age and sex, and the data are set in *italic* or roman type, as appropriate, on this basis alone. Further evaluation of detailed age structure data has not been undertaken to date.

4. VITAL STATISTICS

For purposes of the *Demographic Yearbook*, vital statistics have been defined as statistics of live birth, death, foetal death, marriage and divorce.

This volume of the *Demographic Yearbook* presents tables on fertility, nuptiality and divorce as well as tables on mortality referring to foetal mortality, infant and maternal mortality and general mortality.

4.1 Sources of variation of data

Most of the vital statistics data published in this *Demographic Yearbook* come from national civil registration systems. The completeness and the accuracy of the data that these systems produce vary from one country or area to another.

The provision for a national civil registration system is not universal, and in some cases, the registration system covers only certain vital events. For example, in some countries or areas only births and deaths are registered. There are also differences in the effectiveness with which national laws pertaining to civil registration operate in the various countries or areas. The manner in which the law is implemented and the degree to which the public complies with the legislation determine the reliability of vital statistics obtained from the civil registers.

It should be noted that some statistics on marriage and divorce are obtained from sources other than civil registers. For example, in some countries or areas, the only source for data on marriages is church registers. Divorce statistics, on the other hand, are obtained from court records and/or civil registers according to national practice. The actual compilation of these statistics may be the responsibility of the civil registrar, the national statistical office or other government offices.

Other factors affecting international comparability of vital statistics are much the same as those that must be considered in evaluating the variations in other population statistics. Differences in statistical definitions of vital events, differences in geographical and ethnic coverage of the data and diverse tabulation procedures may also influence comparability.

In addition to vital statistics from civil registers, some vital statistics published in the *Demographic Yearbook* are official estimates. These estimates are frequently from population censuses and sample surveys. As such, their comparability may be affected by the national completeness of reporting in population censuses and household surveys, whether a *de facto* or *de jure* based census, non-sampling and sampling errors and other sources of bias.

Readers interested in more detailed information on standards for vital statistics should consult the *Principles and Recommendations for a Vital Statistics System Revision 2*[8]; *Handbook on Civil Registration and Vital Statistics Systems: Preparation of a Legal Framework*[9]; *Handbook on Civil Registration and Vital Statistics Systems: Management, Operation and Maintenance*[10]; *Handbook on Civil Registration and Vital Statistics Systems: Developing Information, Education and Communication*[11]; *Handbook on Civil Registration and Vital Statistics Systems: Policies and Protocols for the Release and Archiving of Individual Records*[12]; and *Handbook on Civil Registration and Vital Statistics Systems: Computerization*[13]. The *Handbook on the Collection of Fertility and Mortality Data*[14] provides information in collection and evaluation of data on fertility and mortality collected in population censuses and household surveys. These publications are also available on the website at http://unstats.un.org/unsd/demographic/standmeth/handbooks/default.htm.

4.1.1 Statistical definition of events

An important source of variation lies in the statistical definition of each vital event. The *Demographic Yearbook* attempts to collect data on vital events, using the standard definitions put forth in paragraph 57 of *Principles and Recommendations for a Vital Statistics System Revision 2*[8]. These definitions are as follows:

LIVE BIRTH is the complete expulsion or extraction from its mother of a product of conception, irrespective of the duration of pregnancy, which after such separation breathes or shows any other evidence of life such as beating of the heart, pulsation of the umbilical cord, or definite movement of voluntary muscles, whether or not the umbilical cord has been cut or the placenta is attached; each product of such a birth is considered live-born regardless of gestational age.

DEATH is the permanent disappearance of all evidence of life at any time after live birth has taken place (postnatal cessation of vital functions without capability of resuscitation). This definition therefore excludes foetal deaths.

FOETAL DEATH is death prior to the complete expulsion or extraction from its mother of a product of conception, irrespective of the duration of pregnancy; the death is indicated by the fact that after such separation the foetus does not breathe or show any other evidence of life, such as beating of the heart, pulsation of the umbilical cord, or definite movement of voluntary muscles. Late foetal deaths are those of twenty-eight or more completed weeks of gestation. These are synonymous with the events reported under the pre-1950 term stillbirth.

MARRIAGE is an act, ceremony or process by which the legal relationship of husband and wife is constituted. The legality of the union may be established by civil, religious or other means as recognized by the laws of each country or area.

DIVORCE is a final legal dissolution of a marriage, that is, that separation of husband and wife which confers on the parties the right to remarriage under civil, religious and/or other provisions, according to the laws of each country.

In addition to these internationally recommended definitions, the *Demographic Yearbook* collects and presents data on abortions, defined as:

ABORTION is defined, with reference to the woman, as any interruption of pregnancy before 28 weeks of gestation with a dead foetus. There are two major categories of abortion: spontaneous and induced. Induced abortions are those initiated by deliberate action undertaken with the intention of terminating pregnancy; all other abortions are considered spontaneous.

4.1.2 Problems relating to standard definitions

A basic problem affecting international comparability of vital statistics is deviations from the standard definitions of vital events. An example of this can be seen in the cases of live births and foetal deaths. In some countries or areas, an infant must survive for at least 24 hours, to be inscribed in the live-birth register. Infants who die before the expiration of the 24-hour period are classified as late foetal deaths and, barring special tabulation procedures, they would not be counted either as live births or as deaths. Similarly, in several other countries or areas, those infants who are born alive but die before registration of their birth, are also considered late foetal deaths.

Unless special tabulation procedures are adopted in such cases, the live-birth and death statistics will both be deficient by the number of these infants, while the incidence of late foetal deaths will be increased by the same amount. Hence the infant mortality rate is underestimated. Although both components (infant deaths and live births) are deficient by the same absolute amount, the deficiency is proportionately greater in relation to the infant deaths, causing greater errors in the infant mortality rate than in the birth rate.

Moreover, the practice exaggerates the late foetal death ratios. Some countries or areas make provision for correcting this deficiency (at least in the total frequencies) at the tabulation stage. Data for which the correction has not been made are indicated by a footnote whenever possible.

The definitions used for marriage and divorce also present problems for international comparability. Unlike birth and death, which are biological events, marriage and divorce are defined only in terms of law and custom and as such are less amenable to universally applicable statistical definitions. They have therefore been defined for statistical purposes in general terms referring to the laws of individual countries or areas. Laws pertaining to marriage and particularly to divorce, vary from one country or area to another. With respect to marriage, the most widespread requirement relates to the minimum age at which persons may marry but frequently other requirements are specified.

When known the minimum legal age of men and women at which marriage can occur with or without parental consent is presented in table 23-1. Laws and regulations relating to the dissolution of marriage by divorce range from total prohibition, through a wide range of grounds upon which divorces may be granted, to the granting of divorce in response to a simple statement of desire or intention by spouses.

4.1.3 Fragmentary geographical or ethnic coverage

Ideally, vital statistics for any given country or area should cover the entire geographical area and include all ethnic groups. Fragmentary coverage is, however, not uncommon. In some countries or areas, registration is compulsory for only a small part of the population, limited to certain ethnic groups, for example. In other places there is no national provision for compulsory registration, but only municipal or state ordinances that do not cover the entire geographical area. Still others have developed a registration area that comprises only a part of the country or area, the remainder being excluded because of inaccessibility or for economic and cultural considerations that make regular registration practically impossible.

4.1.4 Tabulation procedures

4.1.4.1 By place of occurrence

Vital statistics presented at the national level relate to the de facto, that is, the present-in-area population. Thus, unless otherwise noted, vital statistics for a given country or area cover all the events that occur within its present boundaries and among all segments of the population therein. They may be presumed to include events among nomadic tribes and indigenous peoples, and among nationals and foreigners. When known, deviations from the *de facto* concept are footnoted.

Urban/rural differentials in vital rates for some countries may vary considerably depending on whether the relevant vital events were tabulated on the basis of place of occurrence or place of usual residence. For example, if a substantial number of women residing in rural areas near major urban centres travel to hospitals or maternity homes located in a city to give birth, urban fertility and neo-natal and infant mortality rates will usually be higher (and the corresponding rural rates will usually be lower) if the events are tabulated on the basis of place of occurrence rather than on the basis of place of usual residence. A similar process will affect general mortality differentials if substantial numbers of persons residing in rural areas use urban health facilities when seriously ill.

4.1.4.2 By date of occurrence versus by date of registration

To the extent possible, the vital statistics presented in the *Demographic Yearbook* refer to events that occurred during the specified year, rather than to those that were registered during that period. However, a considerable number of countries or areas tabulate their vital statistics not by date of occurrence, but by date of registration. Because such statistics can be misleading, the countries or areas known to tabulate vital statistics by date of registration are identified in the tables by a plus sign "+". Since information on the method of tabulating vital statistics is not available for all countries and areas, tabulation by date of registration may be more prevalent than the symbols on the vital statistics tables would indicate.

Because quality of data is inextricably related to the timeliness of registration, this must always be considered in conjunction with the quality code description in section 4.2.1 below. If registration of births is complete and timely (code "C"), the ill effects of tabulating by date of registration, are, for all practical purposes, nullified. Similarly, with respect to death statistics, the effect of tabulating events by date of registration may be minimized in many countries or areas in which the sanitary code requires that a death must be registered before a burial permit can be issued, and this regulation tends to make registration prompt. With respect to foetal death, registration is usually done right away or not at all. Therefore, if registration is prompt, the difference between statistics tabulated by date of occurrence and those tabulated by date of registration may be negligible. In many cases, the length of the statutory time period allowed for registering various vital events plays an important part in determining the effects of tabulation by date of registration on comparability of data.

With respect to marriage and divorce, the practice of tabulating data by date of registration does not generally pose serious problems. In many countries or areas marriage is a civil legal contract which, to establish its legality, must be celebrated before a civil officer. It follows that for these countries or areas registration would tend to be almost automatic at the time of, or immediately following, the marriage ceremony. Because the registration of a divorce in many countries or areas is the responsibility solely of the court or the authority which granted it, and since the registration record in such cases is part of the records of the court proceedings, it follows that divorces are likely to be registered soon after the decree is granted.

On the other hand, if registration is not prompt, vital statistics by date of registration will not produce internationally comparable data. Under the best circumstances, statistics by date of registration will include primarily events that occurred in the immediately preceding year; in countries or areas with less developed systems, tabulations will include some events that occurred many years in the past. Examination of available information reveals that delays of many years are not uncommon for birth registration, though the majority is recorded between two to four years after birth.

As long as registration is not prompt, statistics by date of registration will not be internationally comparable either among themselves or with statistics by date of occurrence.

It should also be mentioned that lack of international comparability is not the only limitation introduced by date-of-registration tabulation. Even within the same country or area, comparability over time may be lost by the practice of counting registrations rather than occurrences. If the number of events registered from year to year fluctuates because of *ad hoc* incentives to stimulate registration, or to the sudden need, for example, for proof of (unregistered) birth or death to meet certain requirements, vital statistics tabulated by date of registration are not useful in measuring and analyzing demographic levels and trends. All they can give is an indication of the fluctuations in the need for a birth, death or marriage certificate and the work-load of the registrars. Therefore, statistics tabulated by date of registration may be of very limited use for either national or international studies.

4.2 Methods used to indicate quality of published vital statistics

The quality of vital statistics can be assessed in terms of a number of factors. Most fundamental is the completeness of the civil registration system on which these statistics are based. In some cases, the incompleteness of the data obtained from civil registration systems is revealed when these events are used to compute rates. However, this technique applies only where the data are markedly deficient, where they are tabulated by date of occurrence and where the population base is correctly estimated. Tabulation by date of registration will often produce rates which appear correct, simply because the numerator is artificially inflated by the inclusion of delayed registration and, conversely, rates may be of credible magnitude because the population at risk has been underestimated. Moreover, it should be remembered that knowledge of what is credible in regard to levels of fertility, mortality and nuptiality is extremely scant for many parts of the world, and borderline cases, which are the most difficult to appraise, are frequent.

4.2.1 Quality code for vital statistics from registers.

In the *Demographic Yearbook* annual "Questionnaire on Vital Statistics" national statistical offices are asked to provide their own estimates of the completeness of the births, deaths, late foetal deaths, marriages and divorces recorded in their civil registers.

On the basis of information from the questionnaires, from direct correspondence and from relevant official publications, it has been possible to classify current national statistics from civil registers of birth, death, infant death, late foetal death, marriage and divorce into three broad quality categories, as follows:

C: Data estimated to be virtually complete, that is, representing at least 90 per cent of the events occurring each year.

U: Data estimated to be incomplete, that is representing less than 90 per cent of the events occurring each year.

|: Data not derived from civil registration systems but considered reliable, such as estimates derived from projections, other estimation techniques or population and housing censuses.

...: Data for which no specific information is available regarding completeness.

These quality codes appear in the first column of the tables which show total frequencies and crude rates (or ratios) over a period of years for all tables on live births, late foetal deaths, infant deaths, deaths, marriages, and divorces. Reliability of maternal mortality statistics is provided by the World Health Organisation.

The classification of countries and areas in terms of these quality codes may not be uniform. Nevertheless, it was felt that national statistical offices were in the best position to judge the quality of their data. It was considered that even the very broad categories that could be established on the basis of the available information would provide useful indicators of the quality of the vital statistics presented in this *Demographic Yearbook*.

Among the countries or areas indicating that the registration of live births was estimated to be 90 per cent or more complete (and hence classified as "C" or "+C" in table 9), the following countries or areas provided information on the method used to evaluate the completeness estimate:

(a) Demographic analysis -- Argentina, Austria, Bulgaria, Chile, China - Hong Kong SAR, Croatia, Egypt, Estonia, Italy, Latvia, Lithuania, Malta, Mauritius, Mexico, Republic of Korea, Republic of Moldova, Romania, Seychelles and Sweden.

(b) Dual record check -- Austria, Cuba, Estonia, Hungary, Israel, Italy, Malaysia, Montserrat, Norway, Qatar, Republic of Korea, Romania and Switzerland.

(c) Other specified methods -- Aruba, Austria, Bahrain, Curaçao, Denmark, Dominican Republic, France, Guatemala, Ireland, Kyrgyzstan, Liechtenstein, Luxembourg, Mexico, Panama, Poland, Puerto Rico, Singapore, Slovenia, Spain, State of Palestine and Sweden.

Among the countries or areas indicating that the registration of late foetal-deaths was estimated to be 90 per cent or more complete (and hence classified as "C" or "+C" in table 12), the following countries or areas provided information on the method used to evaluate the completeness estimate:

(a) Demographic analysis -- Argentina, Austria, Bulgaria, Croatia, Egypt, Estonia, Italy, Latvia, Lithuania, Malta, Mauritius, Mexico, Romania and Sweden.

(b) Dual record check -- Austria, Cuba, Estonia, Hungary, Israel, Italy, Lithuania, Montserrat, Norway, Qatar, Romania and Switzerland.

(c) Other specified methods -- Austria, Bahrain, Denmark, Kyrgyzstan, Luxembourg, Poland, Puerto Rico, Slovenia, Spain and Sweden.

Among the countries or areas indicating that the registration of infant deaths was estimated to be 90 per cent or more complete (and hence classified as "C" or "+C" in table 15), the following countries or areas provided information on the method used to evaluate the completeness estimate:

(a) Demographic analysis -- Argentina, Austria, Bulgaria, Chile, China - Hong Kong SAR, Croatia, Egypt, Estonia, Israel, Italy, Latvia, Lithuania, Malta, Mauritius, Mexico, Republic of Korea, Republic of Moldova, Romania, Seychelles and Sweden.

(b) Dual record check -- Austria, Cuba, Cyprus, Estonia, Hungary, Ireland, Israel, Italy, Lithuania, Montserrat, Norway, Qatar, Republic of Korea, Romania and Switzerland.

(c) Other specified methods -- Austria, Bahrain, Curaçao, Cayman Islands, Denmark, Kyrgyzstan, Liechtenstein, Luxembourg, Poland, Puerto Rico, Singapore, Slovenia, Spain and Sweden.

Among the countries or areas indicating that the registration of deaths was estimated to be 90 per cent or more complete (and hence classified as "C" or "+C" in table 18), the following countries or areas provided information on the method used to evaluate the completeness estimate:

(a) Demographic analysis -- Argentina, Austria, Bulgaria, Chile, China - Hong Kong SAR, Croatia, Egypt, Estonia, Israel, Italy, Latvia, Lithuania, Malta, Mauritius, Mexico, Republic of Korea, Republic of Moldova, Romania, Seychelles and Sweden.

(b) Dual record check -- Austria, Cuba, Cyprus, Estonia, Hungary, Israel, Italy, Lithuania, Mexico, Montserrat, Norway, Qatar, Republic of Korea, Romania and Switzerland.

(c) Other specified methods -- Aruba, Austria, Bahrain, Curaçao, Denmark, Dominican Republic, France, Kyrgyzstan, Liechtenstein, Luxembourg, Malaysia, Poland, Puerto Rico, Singapore, Slovenia, Spain and Sweden.

Among the countries or areas indicating that the registration of marriages was estimated to be 90 per cent or more complete (and hence classified as "C" or "+C" in table 22), the following countries or areas provided information on the method used to evaluate the completeness estimate:

(a) Demographic analysis -- Argentina, Austria, Bulgaria, Chile, China - Hong Kong SAR, Croatia, Egypt, Estonia, Italy, Latvia, Lithuania, Malta, Mauritius, Mexico, Republic of Korea, Republic of Moldova, Romania, Seychelles, State of Palestine and Sweden.

(b) Dual record check -- Cuba, Estonia, Hungary, Israel, Italy, Mexico, Norway, Qatar, Republic of Korea, Romania and Switzerland.

(c) Other specified methods -- Aruba, Austria, Australia, Curaçao, Cyprus, Denmark, Dominican Republic, France, Kyrgyzstan, Liechtenstein, Luxembourg, Mexico, Poland, Puerto Rico, Slovenia, Spain, Sweden and Tajikistan.

Among the countries or areas indicating that the registration of divorces was estimated to be 90 per cent or more complete (and hence classified as "C" or "+C" in table 24), the following countries or areas provided information on the method used to evaluate the completeness estimate:

(a) Demographic analysis -- Austria, Bulgaria, Croatia, Egypt, Estonia, Italy, Latvia, Lithuania, Mexico, Republic of Korea, Republic of Moldova, Romania, Seychelles, State of Palestine and Sweden.

(b) Dual record check -- Cuba, Estonia, Hungary, Israel, Italy, Mexico, Norway, Qatar, Republic of Korea, Romania and Switzerland.

(c) Other specified methods -- Aruba, Austria, Curaçao, Cyprus, Denmark, Dominican Republic, Kyrgyzstan, Liechtenstein, Luxembourg, Mauritius, Mexico, Poland, Puerto Rico, Slovenia, Sweden and Tajikistan.

4.2.2 Treatment of vital statistics from registers

On the basis of the quality code described above, the vital statistics shown in all tables of the *Demographic Yearbook* are treated as either reliable or unreliable. Data coded "C" are considered reliable and appear in roman type. Data coded "U" or "..." are considered unreliable and appear in *italics*. Although the quality code itself appears only in certain tables, the indication of reliability (that is, the use of *italics* to indicate unreliable data) is shown in all tables presenting vital statistics data.

It should be noted that the indications of reliability used for infant mortality rates, maternal mortality ratios and late foetal death ratios (all of which are calculated using the number of live births in the denominator) are determined on the basis of the quality codes for infant deaths, deaths and late foetal deaths respectively. To evaluate these rates and ratios more precisely, one would have to take into account the quality of the live-birth data used in the denominator of these rates and ratios. The quality codes for live births are shown in table 9 and described more fully in the text of the technical notes for that table.

4.2.3 Treatment of time series of vital statistics from registers

The quality of a time series of vital statistics is more difficult to determine than the quality of data for a single year. Since a time series of vital statistics is usually generated only by a system of continuous civil registration, it was assumed that the quality of the entire series was the same as that for the latest year's data obtained from the civil register. The entire series is treated as described in section 4.2.2 above. That is, if the quality code for the latest registered data is "C", the frequencies and rates for earlier years are also considered reliable and appear in roman type. Conversely, if the latest registered data are coded as "U" or "..." then data for earlier years are considered unreliable and appear in *italics*. It is recognized that this method is not entirely satisfactory because it is known that data from earlier years in many of the series were considerably less reliable than the current code implies. Efforts are being made to gradually move away from this method and code the registered data of each year or range of years separately.

4.2.4 Treatment of estimated vital statistics

In addition to data from vital registration systems, estimated frequencies and rates of the events, usually *ad hoc* official estimates that have been derived either from the results of a population census or sample survey or by demographic analyses, also appear in the *Demographic Yearbook*. Estimated frequencies and rates have been included in the tables because it is assumed that they provide information that is more accurate than that from existing civil registration systems. By implication, they are assumed to be reliable and as such they are set in roman type.

In tables showing the quality code, the code applies only to data from civil registers. Estimated data are denoted by the symbol "|".

4.3 Cause of death

World Health Organization (WHO) Member States are bound by the International Nomenclature Regulations to provide the Organization with cause of death data coded in accordance with the current revision of the International Statistical Classification of Diseases and Related Health Problems (ICD). In order to promote international comparability of cause of death statistics, the World Health Organization organizes and conducts an international conference for the revision of the ICD on a regular basis in order to ensure that the Classification is kept current with the most recent clinical and statistical concepts. The data are now usually submitted to WHO at the full four-character level of detail provided by the ICD and are compiled and stored in the WHO Mortality Database at the level of detail as provided by the country. Data from the WHO Mortality Database are available in electronic format at http://www3.who.int/whosis/menu.cfm.

Although revisions provide an up-to-date version of the ICD, such revisions create several problems related to the comparability of cause of death statistics. The first is the lack of comparability over time that inevitably accompanies the use of a new classification. The second problem affects comparability between countries and areas because they may adopt a new classification at different times. The more refined the classification becomes the greater is the need for expert clinical diagnosis of cause of death. In many countries or areas, few of the deaths occur in the presence of an attendant, who is medically trained, i.e., most deaths are certified by a lay attendant. Because the ICD contains many diagnoses that cannot be identified by a non-medical person, the ICD is not always accurately or precisely used, which affects international comparability particularly between countries and areas where the level of medical services differ widely.

The chapters of the tenth revision[15], the latest revision of the ICD, consist of an alphanumeric coding scheme of one letter followed by three numbers at the four-character level. Chapter one contains infectious and parasitic diseases, chapter two refers to all neoplasms, chapter three to disorders of the immune mechanism including diseases of the blood and blood-forming organs; and chapter four to endocrine, nutritional and metabolic diseases. The remaining chapters group diseases according to the anatomical site affected, except for chapters that refer to mental disorders; complications of pregnancy, childbirth and the puerperium; congenital malformations; and conditions originating in the perinatal period. Finally, an entire chapter is devoted to symptoms, signs, and abnormal findings.

4.3.1 Maternal mortality

According to the tenth revision of the ICD, "Maternal death" is defined as the death of a woman while pregnant or within 42 days of termination of pregnancy, irrespective of the duration and the site of the pregnancy, from any cause related to or aggravated by the pregnancy or its management but not from accidental or incidental causes.

"Maternal deaths" should be subdivided into direct and indirect obstetric deaths. Direct obstetric deaths are those resulting from obstetric complications of the pregnant state (pregnancy, labour and puerperium), from interventions, omissions, incorrect treatment, or from a chain of events resulting from any of the above. Indirect obstetric deaths are those resulting from previous existing disease or disease that developed during pregnancy and which was not due to direct obstetric causes, but which was aggravated by physiologic effects of pregnancy.

While the denominator for the maternal mortality ratio theoretically should be the number of pregnant women, it is impossible to determine the number of pregnant women. A further recommendation by the tenth revision is therefore that maternal mortality ratios be expressed per 100,000 live births or per 100,000 total births (live births and foetal deaths). The maternal mortality ratio calculated here is expressed per 100,000 live births. Although live births do not represent an unbiased estimate of pregnant women, this figure is more reliable than other estimates, in particular, live births are more accurately registered than live births plus foetal deaths.

---

[1]   There are two exceptions – the 1978 and 1991 issues, which were disseminated in separate volumes from the respective regular issues.

[2]   United Nations, Department of Economic and Social Affairs, Population Division (2013). *World Population Prospects: The 2012 Revision. Extended dataset in Excel and ASCII formats, DVD-ROM edition* (United Nations publication, ST/ESA/SER.A/334).

[3]   ST/ESA/STAT/SER.M/49/Rev.4/WWW ; http://unstats.un.org/unsd/methods/m49/m49.htm; see also Standard Country or Area Codes for Statistical Use, Sales No. M.98.XVII.9, United Nations, New York, 1999.

[4]   Sales No. E.07.XVII.8, United Nations, New York, 2007. The publication is available online at : http://unstats.un.org/unsd/demographic/standmeth/principles/Series_M67Rev2en.pdf

[5]   Ibid, para. 2.135.

[6]   Alternatively, if a population register is used, completed ages are calculated by subtracting the date of birth of individuals listed in the register from a reference date to which the age data pertain.

[7]   A source of non-comparability may result from differences in the method of reckoning age, for example, the Western versus the Eastern or, as it is usually known, the English versus the Chinese system. By the latter, a child is considered one year old at birth and advances an additional year at each Chinese New Year. The effect of this system is most obvious at the beginning of the age span, where the frequencies in the under-one-year category are markedly understated. The effect on higher age groups is not so apparent. Distributions constructed on this basis are often adjusted before publication, but the possibility of such aberrations should not be excluded when census data by age are compared.

[8]   Sales No. E.01.XVII.10, United Nations, New York, 2001.

[9]   Sales No. E.98.XVII.7, United Nations, New York, 1998.

[10]   Sales No. E.98.XVII.11, United Nations, New York, 1998.

[11]   Sales No. E.98.XVII.4, United Nations, New York, 1998.

[12]   Sales No. E.98.XVII.6, United Nations, New York, 1998.

[13]   Sales No. E.98.XVII.10, United Nations, New York, 1998.

[14]   Sales No. E.03.XVII.11, United Nations, New York, 2004.

[15]   *International Statistical Classification of Diseases and Related Health Problems*, Tenth Revision, Volume 2, World Health Organization, Geneva, 1992.

INTRODUCTION

L'*Annuaire démographique* est un recueil de statistiques démographiques internationales qui est établi par la Division de statistique du Département des affaires économiques et sociales de l'Organisation des Nations Unies. Il fait partie d'un ensemble de publications complémentaires publiées par l'Organisation des Nations Unies et les institutions spécialisées, qui ont pour objet de fournir des statistiques aux démographes, aux économistes, aux spécialistes de la santé publique et aux sociologues. Grâce à la coopération des services nationaux de statistique, il a été possible de faire figurer dans la présente édition de l'*Annuaire démographique* les statistiques officielles disponibles pour plus de 230 pays ou zones du monde entier.

L'*Annuaire démographique 2012* est la soixante-troisième édition d'une série que publie l'ONU depuis 1948. Le présent volume comprend un aperçu mondial des statistiques démographiques de base et des tableaux qui regroupent des statistiques sur la dimension, la répartition et les tendances de la population, la natalité, la mortalité fœtale, la mortalité infantile et la mortalité liée à la maternité, la mortalité générale, la nuptialité et la divortialité. Des données classées selon le lieu de résidence (zone urbaine ou rurale) sont présentées dans un grand nombre de tableaux. En outre, l'*Annuaire démographique* contient des notes techniques, un tableau synoptique, un index historique et une liste des éditions de l'*Annuaire démographique* publiées jusqu'à présent. Cette édition de l'*Annuaire démographique* contient les données disponibles couvrant les année de référence jusqu'à 2012.

Les notes techniques sur les tableaux statistiques sont destinées à aider le lecteur. Le tableau A, qui correspond au tableau synoptique, donne un aperçu de l''exhaustivité des données publiées dans la présente édition de l'*Annuaire démographique*. Un index cumulatif donne des renseignements sur les matières traitées dans chacune des 63 éditions et sur les années sur lesquelles portent les données. Les numéros de vente des éditions antérieures et une liste des sujets spéciaux traités dans les différentes éditions sont indiqués aux pages iii et iv.

Jusqu'à la 48e édition (1996), chaque édition se composait de deux parties : les tableaux de caractère général et ceux sur des sujets spéciaux, publiés dans le même volume[1]. À partir de 49e édition (1997), les tableaux sur les sujets spéciaux ont été publiés dans un format numérique en tant que suppléments à l'*Annuaire démographique*. Deux CD-ROM ont été produits : l'*Annuaire démographique : Supplément historique*, qui présente un grand nombre de statistiques démographiques pour la période allant de 1948 à 1997, et l'*Annuaire démographique : Statistiques de la natalité*, qui contient des tableaux détaillés sur la natalité pour la période allant de 1980 à 1998. Par la suite, trois volumes concernant l'*Annuaire démographique* consacrés à des thèmes de recensement spéciaux pour le cycle de recensements de 2000 ont été publiés en ligne à l'adresse suivante : http://unstats.un.org/unsd/demographic/products/dyb/dybcens.htm. Les données actuelles sur les thèmes du recensement de l'*Annuaire démographique* pour les années de référence entre 1995 et aujourd'hui, lorsqu'elles sont disponibles, sont présentées sur http://unstats.un.org/unsd/demographic/products/dyb/dybcensusdata.htm. Ils comprennent des données sur la population selon les principales caractéristiques démographiques, scolaires, ethnoculturelles et économiques, les caractéristiques des ménages ainsi que des données sur les étrangers dans le pays ou les personnes nées à l'étranger.

Les statistiques sur la population ne sont pas disponibles pour tous les pays et zones pour plusieurs raisons. Deux annexes sont présentées afin d'offrir des estimations sur la population en milieu d'année et un aperçu des statistiques de l'état civil pour chaque pays ou zone. La première porte sur des estimations concernant la population pour la période 2003-2012. La seconde présente les estimations des variantes moyennes concernant les taux bruts de natalité et de mortalité, la mortalité infantile, les indicateurs synthétiques de fécondité et l'espérance de vie à la naissance pour la période 2010-2015. Ces données ont été établies par la Division de la population de l'ONU et publiées dans les *Perspectives de la population mondiale : La révision de 2012*[2].

Les statistiques démographiques figurant dans la présente édition de l'*Annuaire démographique* sont disponibles en ligne sur les pages Web consacrées à l'*Annuaire démographique* : http://unstats.un.org/unsd/demographic/products/dyb/dyb2012.htm. On trouvera également des renseignements sur le programme de collecte et de diffusion des données de la Division de statistique sur le même site. Il est possible de se procurer d'autres données en contactant la Division de statistique du Département des affaires économiques et sociales de l'Organisation des Nations Unies à l'adresse suivante : demostat@un.org.

NOTES TECHNIQUES SUR LES TABLEAUX STATISTIQUES

1. REMARQUES D'ORDRE GÉNÉRAL

1.1 Notes techniques

Les notes techniques ont pour but de donner au lecteur des informations pertinentes en lien avec les tableaux statistiques. Les renseignements qui concernent l'*Annuaire démographique* en général sont présentés dans des sections portant sur diverses considérations géographiques, sur la population et sur les statistiques de natalité et de mortalité. Les tableaux sont ensuite commentés séparément et l'on trouvera pour chacun une description des variables et des observations sur la fiabilité et les lacunes des données ainsi que sur les pays et zones visés et sur les données publiées antérieurement. Des détails sont également donnés, le cas échéant, sur le mode de calcul des taux, quotients et pourcentages.

1.2 Tableaux

Dans la mesure du possible, la numérotation des tableaux dans les éditions successives de l'*Annuaire démographique* est préservée. Comme la numérotation des tableaux ne correspond pas exactement à celle des éditions précédentes, il est recommandé de se reporter à l'index qui figure à la fin du présent ouvrage pour trouver les données publiées dans les précédentes éditions.

1.3 Origine des données

Sauf indication contraire, les statistiques présentées dans l'*Annuaire démographique* sont des données nationales fournies par les organismes de statistique officiels. Elles sont recueillies essentiellement au moyen de questionnaires qui sont envoyés tous les ans à plus de 230 services nationaux de statistique. Les données communiquées en réponse à ces questionnaires sont complétées, dans toute la mesure possible, par des données tirées de publications nationales officielles et des sites web d'organismes officiels et des renseignements communiqués par les services nationaux de statistique à la demande de l'ONU. Pour que les données soient comparables, les taux, rapports et pourcentages ont été calculés par la Division de statistique de l'ONU, à l'exception des paramètres des tables de mortalité et des indicateurs synthétiques de fécondité ainsi que des taux bruts de natalité et de mortalité pour certains pays et zones, qui ont été dûment signalés en note. Les méthodes suivies par la Division pour le calcul des taux et rapports sont décrites dans les notes techniques relatives à chaque tableau. Les chiffres de population utilisés pour ces calculs sont ceux qui figurent dans la présente édition de l'*Annuaire démographique* ou qui ont paru dans des éditions antérieures.

Chaque fois que l'on constatera des différences entre les données du présent volume et celles des éditions antérieures de l'*Annuaire démographique*, ou de certaines publications apparentées, on pourra en conclure que les statistiques publiées cette année sont des chiffres révisés communiqués à la Division de statistique avant juin 2013.

2. CONSIDÉRATIONS GÉOGRAPHIQUES

2.1 Portée

Des données sont présentées sur tous les pays ou zones qui en ont communiquées. Le tableau 3, le plus complet, contient des données sur la population et la superficie de chaque pays ou zone ayant une population d'au moins 50 habitants. Ces pays ou zones ne figurent pas tous dans les tableaux qui suivent. Dans bien des cas, les données requises pour un tableau particulier n'étaient pas disponibles. En général, les pays ou zones qui peuvent fournir des données sont d'autant moins nombreux que les données demandées sont plus détaillées.

De plus les taux et rapports ne sont présentés que pour les pays ou zones ayant communiqué des chiffres correspondant à un nombre minimal de faits considérés. Les minimums sont indiqués dans les notes techniques relatives à chacun des tableaux.

À l'exception des données récapitulatives présentées dans les tableaux 1 et 2 pour l'ensemble du monde et les grandes zones et régions et des données relatives aux capitales et aux villes de 100 000 habitants ou plus dans le tableau 8, toutes les données se rapportent aux pays. Le nombre de pays sur lequel porte chacun des tableaux est indiqué dans le tableau A.

2.2 Composition territoriale

Autant que possible, toutes les données, y compris les séries chronologiques, se rapportent au territoire de 2011. Les exceptions à cette règle sont signalées en note à la fin des tableaux. Des clarifications importantes sont présentées ci-dessous.

Les données relatives au **Danemark** ne comprennent pas les Iles Féroé et le Groenland, qui font l'objet de rubriques distinctes.

Les données relatives à la **Finlande** comprennent les Îles d'Åland, sauf indication contraire en note de bas de page.

Les données relatives à la **France** ne comprennent pas les départements d'outre-mer, à savoir, la Guyane française, Guadeloupe, la Martinique et La Réunion, qui font l'objet de rubriques distinctes, sauf indication contraire en note de bas de page.

Les données relatives au **Royaume-Uni de Grande-Bretagne et d'Irlande du Nord** ne comprennent pas la Guernesey, l'île de Man et Jersey, qui font l'objet de rubriques distinctes.

Les données relatives au **Sahara Occidental** comprennent la région septentrionale (ancien Saguia-el-Hamra) et la région méridionale (ancien Rio de Oro).

2.3 Nomenclature

En règle générale, pour gagner de la place, on a jugé commode de désigner dans les tableaux les pays ou zones par les noms abrégés couramment utilisés par l'Organisation des Nations Unies[3], les désignations complètes n'étant utilisées que lorsqu'il n'existait pas de forme abrégée. La liste des désignations des pays ou zones est disponible à l'adresse suivante : http://unstats.un.org/unsd/methods/m49/m49alphaf.htm.

2.3.1 Ordre de présentation

Les pays ou zones sont classés dans l'ordre alphabétique anglais et regroupés par continent comme ci-après : Afrique, Amérique du Nord, Amérique du Sud, Asie, Europe et Océanie.

Les appellations employées dans la présente édition et la présentation des données qui y figurent n'ont d'autre objet que de donner un cadre géographique commode aux séries statistiques. La même observation vaut pour toutes les notes et précisions concernant les unités géographiques pour lesquelles des données sont présentées.

2.4 Superficie

Les données relatives à la superficie qui figurent dans les tableaux 1 et 3 représentent la superficie totale, c'est-à-dire qu'elles englobent les terres émergées et les eaux intérieures (qui sont censées comprendre les principaux lacs et cours d'eau), mais excluent les régions polaires et les îles inhabitées. Les données relatives à la superficie correspondent aux chiffres estimatifs les plus récents. Les superficies sont toutes exprimées en kilomètres carrés ; les chiffres qui avaient été communiqués en miles carrés ont été convertis au moyen d'un coefficient de 2,589988.

2.4.1 Comparabilité dans le temps

La révision des estimations antérieures de la superficie, des augmentations effectives de la superficie terrestre due par exemple à des travaux d'assèchement, à des rectifications de frontières, à des changements d'interprétation du concept de « terres émergées » ou à l'utilisation de nouvelles unités de mesure peut avoir des incidences sur la comparabilité dans le temps des estimations relatives à la superficie d'un pays ou d'une zone donnés. Dans la plupart des cas, il a été possible de déterminer la raison de ces révisions; toutefois, même lorsque la raison n'était pas connue, on a remplacé les anciens chiffres par les nouveaux et on a généralement admis que ce sont ces derniers qui sont exacts.

2.4.2 Comparabilité internationale

Le manque de comparabilité internationale entre les données relatives à la superficie est dû principalement à des différences de définition. En particulier, la définition des golfes, baies et criques, lacs et cours d'eau varie sensiblement d'un pays à l'autre. La diversité des méthodes employées pour estimer les superficies nuit elle aussi à la comparabilité internationale. Certaines données proviennent de levés effectués selon des méthodes scientifiques modernes ; d'autres ne représentent que des conjectures reposant sur diverses catégories de renseignements. Certains chiffres sont récents, d'autres pas. Étant donné que ni la méthode de calcul de la superficie ni la composition du territoire et la date à laquelle se rapportent les données ne sont connues avec précision pour tous les pays ou zones, les estimations figurant dans le tableau 3 ne doivent pas être considérées comme rigoureusement comparables d'un pays ou d'une zone à une autre.

3. POPULATION

Les statistiques de la population, c'est-à-dire celles qui se rapportent à la dimension, à la répartition géographique et aux caractéristiques démographiques de la population, sont présentées dans un certain nombre de tableaux de *l'Annuaire démographique*.

Les tableaux 1 et 2 présentent respectivement des estimations récapitulatives de milieu d'année de la population du monde, des grandes zones et régions, pour certaines années présélectionnées, ainsi que de sa répartition selon l'âge et le sexe pour l'année 2012.

Les données concernant les pays ou les zones représentent les résultats de recensements de population, des estimations fondées sur les résultats d'enquêtes par sondage (s'il n'y a pas eu recensement), des estimations postcensitaires ou intercensitaires, ou des estimations établies à partir de données provenant des registres permanents de population. Dans la présente édition, le tableau 3 indique pour chaque pays ou zone le chiffre le plus récent de la population totale issu du dernier recensement et des estimations établies au milieu de l'année 2005 et de l'année 2012. Le tableau 5 contient des estimations de la population totale au milieu de chaque année pendant 10 ans (2003-2012), et le tableau 6 des estimations de la population urbaine et de la population totale, par sexe, au milieu de chaque année pendant 10 ans (2003-2012). Les dernières données disponibles sur la répartition de la population selon l'âge, le sexe et le lieu de résidence (zone urbaine ou rurale) sont présentées dans le tableau 7. Les derniers chiffres disponibles sur la population des capitales et des villes de 100 000 habitants ou plus sont regroupés dans le tableau 8.

On a utilisé pour le calcul des taux les statistiques de la population totale et de la population répartie selon l'âge, le sexe ou le lieu de résidence (zone urbaine ou rurale). Les taux démographiques selon la résidence (urbaine/rurale), l'âge ou le sexe ont été calculés à partir des données présentées dans les tableaux 6 ou 7 de la présente édition ou dans les tableaux correspondants d'éditions précédentes de *l'Annuaire démographique*.

3.1 Sources de variation des données

Plusieurs facteurs influent sur la comparabilité des données : 1) la définition de la population totale ; 2) les définitions utilisées pour faire la distinction entre population urbaine et population rurale ; 3) les difficultés liées aux déclarations d'âge ; 4) l'étendue du surdénombrement ou du sous-dénombrement dans le recensement le plus récent ou dans une autre source de statistiques de référence sur la population ; 5) la qualité des estimations relatives à la population. Ces cinq facteurs sont analysés en détail aux sections 3.1.1 à 3.2 ci-après. D'autres questions seront traitées dans les notes techniques relatives à chaque tableau. Pour plus de précisions concernant, notamment, les notions fondamentales de dimension, de répartition et de caractéristiques de la population qui ont été élaborées par l'Organisation des Nations Unies, le lecteur est invité à se reporter aux *Principes et recommandations concernant les recensements de la population et de l'habitat, Révision 2*[4].

3.1.1 Population totale

Le principal obstacle à la comparabilité des données relatives à la population totale est la différence qui existe entre population de fait et population de droit. La population de fait comprend toutes les personnes présentes dans le pays ou la zone à la date de référence, tandis que la population de droit comprend toutes celles qui résident habituellement dans le pays ou la zone, qu'elles y aient été ou non présentes à la date de référence. Par définition, la population totale de fait et la population totale de droit ne sont donc pas rigoureusement comparables entre elles.

Même lorsque l'on veut comparer deux totaux qui se rapportent à des populations de fait ou deux totaux qui se rapportent à des populations de droit, on risque souvent de faire des erreurs pour cette raison qu'il est rare que l'une et l'autre notions soient appliquées strictement. Pour citer quelques exemples, certains chiffres qui sont censés porter sur la population de fait ne tiennent pas compte du personnel militaire, naval et diplomatique étranger en fonction dans le pays ou la zone, ni des membres de leurs familles et de leurs ménages; d'autres ne comprennent pas les visiteurs étrangers de passage dans le pays ou la zone ni les personnes à bord de navires ancrés dans des ports. En revanche, il arrive que l'on compte des personnes, inscrits maritimes et marins pêcheurs par exemple, qui, en raison de leur activité professionnelle, se trouvent hors du pays ou de la zone de recensement.

Les risques de disparités sont encore plus grands quand il s'agit de comparer des populations de droit, car les comparaisons dépendent au premier chef de la définition que l'on donne à l'expression « lieu de résidence habituel », qui varie d'un pays ou d'une zone à l'autre et qu'il est, de toute façon, difficile d'appliquer uniformément pour le dénombrement lors d'un recensement ou d'une enquête. Par exemple, les civils étrangers qui se trouvent temporairement dans un pays ou une zone comme travailleurs à court terme peuvent officiellement être considérés comme résidents après un séjour d'une durée déterminée, mais ils peuvent aussi être considérés comme non-résidents pendant toute la durée de leur séjour ; ailleurs, ces mêmes personnes peuvent être considérées officiellement comme résidents ou comme non-résidents du pays ou de la zone d'où elles viennent, selon la durée et, éventuellement, la raison de leur absence. Qui plus est, quel que soit son statut officiel, chacun des recensés peut, au moment de l'enquête, interpréter à sa façon la notion de résidence. De plus, les autorités nationales ou les entités responsables des zones ne savent pas toutes avec la même précision combien de leurs résidents se trouvent temporairement à l'étranger.

Les chiffres de population présentés dans les tableaux de l'*Annuaire démographique* représentent, autant qu'il a été possible, la population de fait. Sauf indication contraire, on peut supposer que les chiffres présentés ont été communiqués par les pays ou les zones comme se rapportant à la population de fait. Les chiffres qui ont été communiqués comme se rapportant à la population de droit sont indiqués comme tels. Lorsque l'on savait que les données avaient été recueillies selon une définition de la population de fait ou de la population de droit qui s'écartait sensiblement de celle exposée plus haut, on l'a signalé en note, de manière à compenser dans toute la mesure possible les conséquences des divergences.

Il ne faut pas oublier néanmoins que l'on ne disposait pas toujours de renseignements détaillés à ce sujet. On ne peut donc partir du principe que les chiffres qui ne sont pas accompagnés d'une note signalant une divergence correspondent exactement aux définitions de la population de fait ou de la population de droit.

Il peut y avoir hétérogénéité dans les statistiques d'un même pays ou d'une même zone dans le cas des pays ou zones qui ne font une exploitation statistique détaillée des données que pour la population de droit alors qu'ils recueillent des données sur la population de droit et sur la population de fait à l'occasion d'un recensement, par exemple. Ainsi, tandis que les chiffres relatifs à la population totale qui figurent au tableau 3 se rapportent à la population de fait, ceux des tableaux qui présentent des données sur diverses caractéristiques de la population, par exemple le lieu de résidence (zone urbaine ou rurale), l'âge et le sexe, peuvent être basés sur le concept de la population de droit.

3.1.2 Lieu de résidence (zone urbaine ou rurale)

L'hétérogénéité des définitions nationales du terme « urbain » nuit considérablement à la comparabilité internationale des données concernant la répartition selon le lieu de résidence. Les définitions utilisées par les différents pays ou zones et leurs implications sont exposées à la fin des notes techniques correspondant au tableau 6.

3.1.3 Répartition par âge

La répartition de la population selon l'âge est un paramètre fondamental de la plupart des analyses, estimations et projections relatives aux statistiques de la population. Malheureusement, ces données sont sujettes à un certain nombre d'erreurs et difficilement comparables. C'est pourquoi pratiquement tous les utilisateurs de ces statistiques doivent considérer ces répartitions avec la plus grande circonspection.

3.1.3.1 Collecte et exploitation des données sur l'âge

L'âge est l'intervalle de temps déterminé par calcul ou par estimation qui sépare la date de naissance de la date du recensement et qui est exprimé en années solaires révolues[5]. Les données sur l'âge peuvent être recueillies selon deux méthodes : la première consiste à obtenir la date de naissance de chaque personne à l'occasion d'un recensement ou d'un sondage, puis à calculer l'âge en années révolues en soustrayant la date de naissance de celle du dénombrement[6]. La seconde consiste à enregistrer l'âge en années révolues au moment du recensement, c'est-à-dire l'âge au dernier anniversaire.

La méthode recommandée consiste à calculer l'âge au dernier anniversaire en soustrayant la date exacte de la naissance de la date du recensement. Toutefois, on n'a pas toujours recours à cette méthode ; certains pays ou zones calculent l'âge en faisant la différence entre l'année du recensement et l'année de la naissance. Lorsque les données sur l'âge ont été établies de cette façon, on l'a signalé chaque fois que possible par une note. On peut d'ailleurs s'en rendre compte dans une certaine mesure, car les chiffres dans la catégorie des moins d'un an sont plus faibles qu'ils ne devraient l'être. Cependant, un nombre irrégulier de naissances d'une année à l'autre ou l'omission de certains âges parmi les moins d'un an peut aussi fausser les chiffres de la population de moins d'un an.

3.1.3.2 Erreurs dans les données sur l'âge

Les causes d'erreurs dans les données sur l'âge sont diverses : on peut citer notamment l'ignorance de l'âge exact, la déclaration d'années d'âge correspondant à un calendrier différent de celui des années solaires révolues depuis la naissance[7], la négligence dans les déclarations et dans la façon dont elles sont consignées, la tendance générale à déclarer des âges se terminant par certains chiffres tels que 0, 2, 5 ou 8, la tendance pour les personnes âgées à exagérer leur âge, une aversion subconsciente pour certains nombres, et les fausses déclarations faites délibérément.

Les causes d'erreurs mentionnées ci-dessus, communes à la plupart des enquêtes sur l'âge et à la plupart des pays ou zones, peuvent nuire sensiblement à la comparabilité.

À cause des difficultés indiquées ci-dessus, les répartitions par âge et par sexe de la population d'un grand nombre de pays ou de zones font apparaître les irrégularités suivantes : 1) sous-estimation des groupes d'âge correspondant aux enfants de moins d'un an et aux jeunes enfants ; 2) polarisation des déclarations sur les âges se terminant par les chiffres 0 ou 5 (c'est-à-dire 5, 10, 15, 20...) ; 3) prépondérance des âges pairs (par exemple 10, 12, 14...) au détriment des âges impairs (par exemple 11, 13, 15...) ; 4) écart considérable et surprenant entre le rapport masculin/féminin à certains âges ; 5) différences importantes et difficilement explicables entre les données concernant des groupes d'âge voisins. En comparant les statistiques provenant de recensements successifs pour des cohortes identiques sur le plan de l'âge et de la répartition par sexe et en étudiant la répartition par âge et par sexe de la population à chaque recensement, on peut déceler l'existence de ces incohérences et de quelques autres, un certain nombre d'entre elles se retrouvant à des degrés divers même dans les recensements les plus modernes.

3.2 Méthodes utilisées pour indiquer la qualité des statistiques publiées

On a cherché dans toute la mesure possible à donner au lecteur une indication du degré de fiabilité des statistiques publiées dans *l'Annuaire démographique*. Pour ce faire, on a procédé de diverses façons. Chaque fois que l'on savait, grâce par exemple à une enquête post censitaire, qu'il y avait eu sousdénombrement ou surdénombrement, on l'a signalé dans les notes qui accompagnent le tableau 3. Comme on l'a indiqué à la section 2.1 sous la rubrique « Considérations géographiques », chaque fois que les données ne portaient pas sur la totalité du pays, on l'a également signalé en note. De plus, les services nationaux de statistique ont été invités à fournir une évaluation des estimations de la population totale qu'ils communiquaient à la Division de statistique de l'ONU.

Des estimations de la répartition de la population par âge et par sexe peuvent être obtenues selon deux grandes méthodes : 1) en appliquant les composantes spécifiques du mouvement de la population, pour chaque groupe d'âge et pour chaque sexe, à la population dénombrée lors du recensement ; 2) en répartissant proportionnellement le chiffre total estimé pour une année postcensitaire d'après la composition par âge et par sexe au moment du recensement.

Les séries estimatives selon l'âge et le sexe sont classées en deux catégories, « fiable » ou autrement, selon la méthode retenue pour le plus récent calcul estimatif de la population totale en milieu d'année ainsi que de la population par âge et par sexe. Ainsi, l'appréciation de la qualité du chiffre total, telle qu'elle ressort des signes de code, est censée s'appliquer aussi à l'ensemble de la répartition par âge et par sexe, et c'est sur cette seule base que les données figurent en caractères italiques ou romains. On n'a pas encore procédé à une évaluation plus poussée des données détaillées concernant la composition par âge.

4. STATISTIQUES DE L'ÉTAT CIVIL

Aux fins de *l'Annuaire démographique*, on entend par statistiques de l'état civil les statistiques des naissances vivantes, des décès, des morts fœtales, des mariages et des divorces.

Dans le présent volume de l'*Annuaire démographique*, on a présenté des tableaux sur la natalité, la mortalité, la nuptialité et la divortialité. Les tableaux consacrés à la mortalité sont groupés sous les rubriques suivantes : mortalité fœtale, mortalité infantile, mortalité liée à la maternité et mortalité générale.

4.1 Sources de variations des données

La plupart des statistiques de l'état civil publiées dans le présent volume de l'*Annuaire démographique* émanent des systèmes nationaux d'enregistrement des faits d'état civil. Le degré d'exhaustivité et d'exactitude de ces données varie d'un pays ou d'une zone à l'autre.

Il n'existe pas partout de système national d'enregistrement des faits d'état civil et, dans quelques cas, seuls certains faits sont enregistrés. Par exemple, dans certains pays ou zones, seuls les naissances et les décès sont enregistrés. Il existe également des différences quant au degré d'efficacité avec lequel les lois relatives à l'enregistrement des faits d'état civil sont appliquées dans les divers pays ou zones. La fiabilité des statistiques provenant des registres d'état civil dépend des modalités d'application de la loi et de la mesure dans laquelle le public s'y soumet.

Il est à signaler que dans certains cas les statistiques de la nuptialité et de la divortialité sont tirées d'autres sources que les registres d'état civil. Dans certains pays ou zones, par exemple, les seules données disponibles sur la nuptialité proviennent des registres des églises. Selon la pratique suivie par chaque pays, les statistiques de la divortialité sont tirées des actes des tribunaux et/ou des registres d'état civil. L'officier de l'état civil, le service national de statistique ou d'autres services administratifs peuvent être chargés d'établir ces statistiques.

Les autres facteurs qui influent sur la comparabilité internationale des statistiques de l'état civil sont à peu près les mêmes que ceux qu'il convient de prendre en considération pour interpréter les variations observées dans les statistiques de la population. La définition des faits d'état civil aux fins de statistique, la portée des données du point de vue géographique et ethnique ainsi que les méthodes d'exploitation des données sont autant d'éléments qui peuvent influer sur la comparabilité.

En plus des statistiques tirées des registres d'état civil, l'*Annuaire démographique* présente des statistiques de l'état civil qui sont des estimations officielles nationales, fondées souvent sur les résultats de sondages ou des recensements de la population. Aussi leur comparabilité varie-t-elle en fonction du degré d'exhaustivité des déclarations recueillies lors des recensements de la population ou d'enquêtes sur les ménages, des erreurs d'échantillonnage ou autres, et des distorsions d'origines diverses.

Pour plus de détails sur les normes d'établissement des statistiques d'état civil, le lecteur pourra se reporter aux : *Principes et recommandations pour un système de statistiques de l'état civil, deuxième révision*[8] ; *Manuel des systèmes d'enregistrement des faits d'état civil et de statistiques de l'état civil : Élaboration d'un cadre juridique*[9] ; *Manuel des systèmes d'enregistrement des faits d'état civil et de statistiques de l'état civil : Gestion, fonctionnement et tenue*[10]; *Manuel des systèmes d'enregistrement des faits d'état civil et de statistiques de l'état civil : Élaboration de programmes d'information, d'éducation et de communication*[11] ; *Manuel des systèmes d'enregistrement des faits d'état civil et de statistiques de l'état civil : Principes et protocoles concernant la communication et l'archivage des documents individuels*[12]; *Manuel des systèmes d'enregistrement des faits d'état civil et de statistiques de l'état civil : Informatisation*[13]. Le *Manuel de collecte de données sur la fécondité et la mortalité*[14] fournit des informations ayant trait à la collecte et à l'évaluation des données sur la fécondité, sur la mortalité et sur d'autres faits d'état civil, qui ont été recueillies au cours des enquêtes sur les ménages. Ces publications sont également disponibles sur le Web à partir de l'adresse suivante : http://unstats.un.org/unsd/demographic/standmeth/handbooks/default.htm.

4.1.1 Définition des faits d'état civil aux fins de la statistique

Une cause importante d'hétérogénéité dans les données est le manque d'uniformité des définitions des différents faits d'état civil. Aux fins de l'*Annuaire démographique*, il est recommandé de recueillir les données relatives aux faits d'état civil en utilisant les définitions établies au paragraphe 57 des *Principes et recommandations pour un système de statistiques de l'état civil, deuxième révision*[8]. Ces définitions sont les suivantes :

La NAISSANCE VIVANTE est l'expulsion ou l'extraction complète du corps de la mère, indépendamment de la durée de la gestation, d'un produit de la conception qui, après cette séparation, respire ou manifeste tout autre signe de vie, tel que battement de cœur, pulsation du cordon ombilical ou contraction effective d'un muscle soumis à l'action de la volonté, que le cordon ombilical ait été coupé ou non et que le placenta soit ou non demeuré attaché ; tout produit d'une telle naissance est considéré comme « enfant né vivant ».

Le DÉCÈS est la disparition permanente de tout signe de vie à un moment quelconque postérieur à la naissance vivante (cessation des fonctions vitales après la naissance sans possibilité de réanimation). Cette définition ne comprend donc pas les morts fœtales.

La MORT FŒTALE est le décès d'un produit de la conception lorsque ce décès est survenu avant l'expulsion ou l'extraction complète du corps de la mère, indépendamment de la durée de la gestation; le décès est indiqué par le fait qu'après cette séparation le fœtus ne respire ni ne manifeste aucun signe de vie, tel que battement de cœur, pulsation du cordon ombilical ou contraction effective d'un muscle soumis à l'action de la volonté. Les morts fœtales tardives sont celles qui sont survenues après 28 semaines de gestation ou plus. Il n'y a aucune différence entre ces « morts fœtales tardives » et les faits désignés, avant 1950, par le terme « mortinatalité ».

Le MARIAGE est l'acte, la cérémonie ou la procédure qui établit un rapport légal entre mari et femme. L'union peut être rendue légale par une procédure civile ou religieuse, ou par toute autre procédure, conformément à la législation du pays.

Le DIVORCE est la dissolution légale et définitive des liens du mariage, c'est-à-dire la séparation de l'époux et de l'épouse qui confère aux parties le droit de se remarier civilement ou religieusement, ou selon toute autre procédure, conformément à la législation du pays.

En plus de ces notions définies internationalement, l'*Annuaire démographique* recueille et met à disposition ces données sur les avortements :

Par référence à la femme, l'AVORTEMENT se définit comme toute interruption de grossesse qui est survenue avant 28 semaines de gestation et dont le produit est un fœtus mort. Il existe deux grandes catégories d'avortement : l'avortement spontané et l'avortement provoqué. L'avortement provoqué a pour origine une action délibérée entreprise en vue d'interrompre une grossesse. Tout autre avortement est considéré comme spontané.

4.1.2 Problèmes posés par les définitions établies

Les variations par rapport aux définitions établies des faits d'état civil sont le principal obstacle à la comparabilité internationale des statistiques de l'état civil. Un exemple en est fourni par le cas des naissances vivantes et celui des morts fœtales. Dans certains pays ou zones, il faut que le nouveau-né ait vécu 24 heures pour pouvoir être inscrit sur le registre des naissances vivantes. Les décès d'enfants qui surviennent avant l'expiration du délai de 24 heures sont classés parmi les morts fœtales tardives et, en l'absence de méthodes spéciales d'exploitation des données, ne sont comptés ni dans les naissances vivantes ni dans les décès. De même, dans plusieurs autres pays ou zones, les décès d'enfants nés vivants et décédés avant l'enregistrement de leur naissance sont également comptés parmi les morts fœtales tardives.

À moins que des méthodes spéciales n'aient été adoptées pour l'exploitation de ces données, les statistiques des naissances vivantes et des décès ne tiendront pas compte de ces cas, qui viendront en revanche accroître d'autant le nombre des morts fœtales tardives. Le taux de mortalité infantile sera donc sous-estimé. Bien que les éléments constitutifs du taux (décès d'enfants de moins d'un an et naissances vivantes) accusent exactement la même insuffisance en valeur absolue, les lacunes sont proportionnellement plus fortes pour les décès de moins d'un an, ce qui cause des erreurs plus importantes dans les taux de mortalité infantile.

De plus, cette pratique augmente les rapports de mortinatalité. Quelques pays ou zones effectuent les ajustements nécessaires pour corriger cette anomalie (du moins dans les fréquences totales) au moment de l'établissement des tableaux. Si aucun ajustement n'a été effectué, cela est indiqué dans les notes chaque fois que possible.

Les définitions du mariage et du divorce posent aussi un problème du point de vue de la comparabilité internationale. Contrairement à la naissance et au décès, qui sont des faits biologiques, le mariage et le divorce sont uniquement déterminés par la législation et la coutume et, de ce fait, il est moins facile d'en donner une définition statistique qui ait une application universelle. À des fins statistiques, ces notions ont donc été définies de manière générale par référence à la législation de chaque pays ou zone. La législation relative au mariage et plus particulièrement au divorce varie d'un pays ou d'une zone à l'autre. En ce qui concerne le mariage, l'âge de nubilité est la condition la plus fréquemment requise, mais il arrive souvent que d'autres conditions soient exigées.

Lorsqu'il est connu, l'âge minimum auquel le mariage peut avoir lieu avec le consentement des parents (et dans certains cas sans le consentement des parents) est indiqué au tableau 23-1. Les lois et règlements relatifs à la dissolution du mariage par le divorce vont de l'interdiction absolue, en passant par diverses conditions requises pour l'obtention du divorce, jusqu'à la simple déclaration, par l'épouse, de son désir ou de son intention de divorcer.

4.1.3 Couverture géographique ou ethnique fragmentaire

En principe, les statistiques de l'état civil devraient s'étendre à l'ensemble du pays ou de la zone auxquels elles se rapportent et englober tous les groupes ethniques. En fait, il n'est pas rare que les données soient fragmentaires. Dans certains pays ou zones, l'enregistrement n'est obligatoire que pour une petite partie de la population, par exemple pour certains groupes ethniques. Dans d'autres, il n'existe pas de disposition qui prescrive l'enregistrement obligatoire sur le plan national, mais seulement des règlements ou décrets des municipalités ou des États, qui ne s'appliquent pas à l'ensemble du territoire. Il en est encore autrement dans d'autres pays ou zones où les autorités ont institué une zone d'enregistrement comprenant seulement une partie du territoire, le reste étant exclu en raison des difficultés d'accès ou parce qu'il est pratiquement impossible, pour des raisons d'ordre économique ou culturel, d'y procéder à un enregistrement régulier.

4.1.4 Méthodes de présentation des données

4.1.4.1 Selon le lieu de l'événement

Les statistiques de l'état civil qui sont présentées pour l'ensemble du territoire national se rapportent à la population de fait ou population présente. En conséquence, sauf indication contraire, les statistiques de l'état civil relatives à une zone ou à un pays donné portent sur tous les faits survenus dans l'ensemble de la population, à l'intérieur des frontières actuelles de la zone ou du pays considéré. On peut donc estimer qu'elles englobent les faits d'état civil survenus dans les tribus nomades et parmi les populations autochtones ainsi que parmi les ressortissants du pays et les étrangers. Des notes signalent les exceptions lorsque celles-ci sont connues.

Pour certains pays, les écarts entre les taux démographiques pour les zones urbaines et pour les zones rurales peuvent varier notablement selon que les faits d'état civil ont été exploités sur la base du lieu de l'événement ou du lieu de résidence habituel. Par exemple, si un nombre appréciable de femmes résidant dans des zones rurales proches de grands centres urbains accouchent dans les hôpitaux ou maternités d'une ville, les taux de fécondité ainsi que les taux de mortalité néo-natale et infantile seront généralement plus élevés dans les zones urbaines (et par conséquent plus faibles dans les zones rurales) si les faits sont exploités en se fondant sur le lieu de l'événement et non sur le lieu de résidence habituel. Le phénomène sera le même dans le cas de la mortalité générale si un bon nombre de personnes résidant dans des zones rurales font appel aux services de santé des villes lorsqu'elles sont gravement malades.

4.1.4.2 Selon la date de l'événement ou la date de l'enregistrement

Autant que possible, les statistiques de l'état civil figurant dans l'Annuaire démographique se rapportent aux faits survenus pendant l'année considérée et non aux faits enregistrés au cours de ladite année. Bon nombre de pays ou zones, toutefois, exploitent leurs statistiques de l'état civil selon la date de l'enregistrement et non selon la date de l'événement. Comme ces statistiques risquent d'induire en erreur, les pays ou zones dont on sait qu'ils établissent leurs statistiques d'après la date de l'enregistrement sont signalés dans les tableaux par un signe plus « + ». On ne dispose toutefois pas pour tous les pays ou zones de renseignements complets sur la méthode d'exploitation des statistiques de l'état civil et les données sont peut-être exploitées selon la date de l'enregistrement plus souvent que ne le laisserait supposer l'emploi des signes.

Étant donné que la qualité des données est inextricablement liée aux retards dans l'enregistrement, il faudra toujours considérer en même temps le code de qualité qui est décrit à la section 4.2.1 ci-après. Évidemment, si l'enregistrement des naissances est complet et effectué en temps voulu (code « C »), les effets perturbateurs de la méthode consistant à exploiter les données selon la date de l'enregistrement seront pratiquement annulés. De même, s'agissant des statistiques des décès, les effets pourront bien souvent être réduits au minimum dans les pays ou zones où le code sanitaire subordonne la délivrance du permis d'inhumer à l'enregistrement du décès, ce qui tend à hâter l'enregistrement. Quant aux morts fœtales, elles sont généralement déclarées immédiatement ou ne sont pas déclarées du tout. En conséquence, si l'enregistrement se fait dans un délai très court, la différence entre les statistiques établies selon la date de l'événement et celles qui sont établies selon la date de l'enregistrement peut être négligeable. Dans bien des cas, la durée des délais légaux accordés pour l'enregistrement des faits d'état civil est un facteur dont dépend dans une large mesure l'incidence sur la comparabilité de l'exploitation des données selon la date de l'enregistrement.

En ce qui concerne le mariage et le divorce, la pratique consistant à exploiter les statistiques selon la date de l'enregistrement ne pose généralement pas de graves problèmes. Le mariage étant, dans de nombreux pays ou zones, un contrat juridique civil qui, pour être légal, doit être conclu devant un officier de l'état civil, il s'ensuit que dans ces pays ou zones l'enregistrement a lieu presque systématiquement au moment de la cérémonie ou immédiatement après. De même, dans de nombreux pays ou zones, le tribunal ou l'autorité qui a prononcé le divorce est seul habilité à enregistrer cet acte, et comme l'acte d'enregistrement figure alors sur les registres du tribunal l'enregistrement suit généralement de peu le jugement.

En revanche, si l'enregistrement n'a lieu qu'avec un certain retard, les statistiques de l'état civil établies selon la date de l'enregistrement ne sont pas comparables sur le plan international. Au mieux, les statistiques par date de l'enregistrement prendront surtout en considération des faits survenus au cours de l'année précédente ; dans les pays ou zones où le système d'enregistrement n'est pas très développé, il y entrera des faits datant de plusieurs années. Il ressort des documents dont on dispose que des retards de plusieurs années dans l'enregistrement des naissances ne sont pas rares, encore que, dans la majorité des cas, les retards ne dépassent pas deux à quatre ans.

Tant que l'enregistrement se fera avec retard, les statistiques fondées sur la date d'enregistrement ne seront comparables sur le plan international ni entre elles ni avec les statistiques établies selon la date de fait d'état civil.

Il convient également de noter que l'exploitation des données selon la date de l'enregistrement ne nuit pas seulement à la comparabilité internationale des statistiques. Même à l'intérieur d'un pays ou d'une zone, le procédé qui consiste à compter les enregistrements et non les faits peut compromettre la comparabilité des chiffres sur une longue période. Si le nombre des faits d'état civil enregistrés varie d'une année à l'autre (par suite de l'application de mesures visant tout particulièrement à encourager l'enregistrement ou parce qu'il est subitement devenu nécessaire de produire le certificat d'une naissance ou d'un décès non enregistré pour l'accomplissement de certaines formalités), les statistiques de l'état civil établies d'après la date de l'enregistrement ne permettent pas de quantifier ni d'analyser l'état et l'évolution de la population. Tout au plus peuvent-elles révéler l'évolution des conditions d'exigibilité de l'acte de naissance, de décès ou de mariage et les fluctuations du volume de travail des bureaux d'état civil. Les statistiques établies selon la date de l'enregistrement peuvent donc ne présenter qu'une utilité très réduite pour des études nationales ou internationales.

4.2 Méthodes utilisées pour indiquer la qualité des statistiques de l'état civil qui sont publiées

La qualité des statistiques de l'état civil peut être évaluée en se fondant sur plusieurs facteurs. Le facteur essentiel est la complétude du système d'enregistrement des faits d'état civil d'après lequel ces statistiques sont établies. Dans certains cas, on constate que les données tirées de l'enregistrement ne sont pas complètes lorsque l'on les utilise pour le calcul des taux. Toutefois, cette observation est valable uniquement lorsque les statistiques présentent des lacunes évidentes, qu'elles sont exploitées d'après la date de l'événement et que l'estimation du chiffre de population pris pour base est exacte. L'exploitation des données d'après la date de l'enregistrement donne souvent des taux qui paraissent exacts, tout simplement parce que le numérateur est artificiellement gonflé par suite de l'inclusion d'enregistrements tardifs ; inversement, il arrive que des taux paraissent vraisemblables parce que l'on a sous-évalué la population étudiée. Il ne faut pas non plus oublier que les renseignements dont on dispose sur les taux de fécondité, de mortalité et de nuptialité considérés comme normaux sont extrêmement sommaires dans un grand nombre de régions du monde et que les cas limites, qui sont les plus difficiles à évaluer, sont fréquents.

4.2.1 Codage qualitatif des statistiques provenant des registres de l'état civil

Dans le questionnaire relatif au mouvement de la population qui leur est envoyé chaque année dans le cadre de l'établissement de l'*Annuaire démographique*, les services nationaux de statistique sont invités à donner leur propre évaluation du degré de complétude des données sur les naissances, les décès, les décès d'enfants de moins d'un an, les morts fœtales tardives, les mariages et les divorces figurant dans leurs registres d'état civil.

D'après les renseignements directement communiqués par les gouvernements ou extraits des questionnaires ou de publications officielles pertinentes, il a été possible de classer les statistiques de l'enregistrement des faits d'état civil (naissances, décès, décès d'enfants de moins d'un an, morts fœtales tardives, mariages et divorces) en trois grandes catégories, selon leur qualité :

C : Données jugées pratiquement complètes, c'est-à-dire représentant au moins 90 % des faits d'état civil survenant chaque année.
U : Données jugées incomplètes, c'est-à-dire représentant moins de 90 % des faits survenant chaque année.

| : Données ne provenant pas des systèmes nationaux d'enregistrement des faits d'état civil, mais jugées fiables, telles que les estimations dérivées des projections, d'autres techniques d'estimation ou recensements de population ou du logement.

... : Données dont le degré de complétude ne fait pas l'objet de renseignements précis.

Ces codes de qualité figurent dans la première colonne des tableaux qui présentent, pour un nombre d'années déterminé les chiffres absolus et les taux (ou rapports) bruts concernant les naissances vivantes, les morts fœtales tardives, les décès d'enfants de moins d'un an, les décès, les mariages et les divorces. Les niveaux de fiabilité des statistiques de mortalité maternelle sont transmis par l'Organisation mondiale de la santé.

La classification des pays ou zones selon ces codes de qualité peut ne pas être uniforme. On a estimé néanmoins que les services nationaux de statistique étaient les mieux placés pour juger de la qualité de leurs données. On a pensé que les catégories que l'on pouvait distinguer sur la base des renseignements disponibles, bien que très larges, permettaient cependant de se faire une idée de la qualité des statistiques de l'état civil publiées dans l'*Annuaire démographique*.

Sur les pays ou zones qui ont estimé à 90 % ou plus le degré d'exhaustivité de leur enregistrement des naissances vivantes (classé « C » ou « +C » dans le tableau 9), les pays ou zones suivants ont communiqué des renseignements concernant les bases sur lesquelles leur estimation reposait :

a) Analyse démographique : Argentine, Autriche, Bulgarie, Chili, Chine - Hong Kong RAS, Croatie, Égypte, Estonie, Italie, Lettonie, Lituanie, Malte, Maurice, Mexique, République de Corée, République de Moldova, Roumanie, Seychelles et Suède.

b) Double contrôle des registres : Autriche, Cuba, Estonie, Hongrie, Israël, Italie, Malaisie, Montserrat, Norvège, Qatar, République de Corée, Roumanie et Suisse.

c) Autre méthode : Aruba, Autriche, Bahreïn, Curaçao, Danemark, Espagne, État de Palestine, France, Guatemala, Irlande, Kirghizstan, Liechtenstein, Luxembourg, Mexique, Panama, Pologne, Porto Rico, République dominicaine, Singapour, Slovénie et Suède.

Sur les pays ou zones qui ont estimé à 90 % ou plus le degré d'exhaustivité de leur enregistrement des morts fœtales tardives (classé « C » ou « +C » dans le tableau 12), les pays ou zones suivants ont communiqué des renseignements concernant les bases sur lesquelles leur estimation reposait :

a) Analyse démographique : Argentine, Autriche, Bulgarie, Croatie, Égypte, Estonie, Italie, Lettonie, Lituanie, Malte, Maurice, Mexique, Roumanie et Suède.

b) Double contrôle des registres : Autriche, Cuba, Estonie, Hongrie, Israël, Italie, Lituanie, Montserrat, Norvège, Qatar, Roumanie et Suisse.

c) Autre méthode : Autriche, Bahreïn, Danemark, Espagne, Kirghizstan, Luxembourg, Pologne, Porto Rico, Slovénie et Suède.

Sur les pays ou zones qui ont estimé à 90 % ou plus le degré d'exhaustivité de leur enregistrement des décès à moins d'un an (classé « C » ou « +C » dans le tableau 15), les pays ou zones suivants ont donné des indications touchant la base de cette estimation :

a) Analyse démographique : Argentine, Autriche, Bulgarie, Chili, Chine - Hong Kong RAS, Croatie, Égypte, Estonie, Israël, Italie, Lettonie, Lituanie, Malte, Maurice, Mexique, République de Corée, République de Moldova, Roumanie, Seychelles et Suède.

b) Double contrôle des registres : Autriche, Cuba, Chypre, Estonie, Hongrie, Irlande, Israël, Italie, Lituanie, Montserrat, Norvège, Qatar, République de Corée, Roumanie et Suisse.

c) Autre méthode : Autriche, Bahreïn, Curaçao, Danemark, Espagne, Îles Caïmans, Kirghizstan, Liechtenstein, Luxembourg, Pologne, Porto Rico, Singapour, Slovénie et Suède.

Sur les pays ou zones qui ont estimé à 90 % ou plus le degré d'exhaustivité de leur enregistrement des décès (classé « C » ou « +C » dans le tableau 18), les pays ou zones suivants ont donné des indications touchant la base de cette estimation :

a) Analyse démographique : Argentine, Autriche, Bulgarie, Chili, Chine - Hong Kong RAS, Croatie, Égypte, Estonie, Israël, Italie, Lettonie, Lituanie, Malte, Maurice, Mexique, République de Corée, République de Moldova, Roumanie, Seychelles et Suède.

b) Double contrôle des registres : Autriche, Cuba, Chypre, Estonie, Hongrie, Israël, Italie, Lituanie, Mexique, Montserrat, Norvège, Qatar, République de Corée, Roumanie et Suisse.

c) Autre méthode : Aruba, Autriche, Bahreïn, Curaçao, Danemark, Espagne, France, Kirghizstan, Liechtenstein, Luxembourg, Malaisie, Pologne, Porto Rico, République dominicaine, Singapour, Slovénie et Suède.

Sur les pays ou zones qui ont estimé à 90 % ou plus le degré d'exhaustivité de leur enregistrement des mariages (classé « C » ou « +C «» dans le tableau 22), les pays ou zones suivants ont communiqué des renseignements concernant les bases sur lesquelles leur estimation reposait :
a) Analyse démographique : Argentine, Autriche, Bulgarie, Chili, Chine - Hong Kong RAS, Croatie, Égypte, Estonie, État de Palestine, Italie, Lettonie, Lituanie, Malte, Maurice, Mexique, République de Corée, République de Moldova, Roumanie et Seychelles.

b) Double contrôle des registres : Cuba, Estonie, Hongrie, Israël, Italie, Mexique, Norvège, Qatar, République de Corée, Roumanie et Suisse.

c) Autre méthode : Aruba, Australie, Autriche, Chypre, Curaçao, Danemark, Espagne, France, Kirghizstan, Liechtenstein, Luxembourg, Mexique, Pologne, Porto Rico, République dominicaine, Slovénie, Suède et Tadjikistan.

Sur les pays ou zones qui ont estimé à 90 % ou plus le degré d'exhaustivité de leur enregistrement des divorces (classé « C » ou « +C » dans le tableau 24), les pays ou zones suivants ont communiqué des renseignements concernant les bases sur lesquelles leur estimation reposait :

a) Analyse démographique : Autriche, Bulgarie, Croatie, Égypte, Estonie, État de Palestine, Italie, Lettonie, Lituanie, Mexique, République de Corée, République de Moldova, Roumanie, Seychelles et Suède.

b) Double contrôle des registres : Cuba, Estonie, Hongrie, Israël, Italie, Mexique, Norvège, Qatar, République de Corée, Roumanie et Suisse.

c) Autre méthode : Aruba, Autriche, Chypre, Curaçao, Danemark, Kirghizstan, Liechtenstein, Luxembourg, Maurice, Mexique, Pologne, Porto Rico, République dominicaine, Slovénie, Suède et Tadjikistan.

4.2.2 Traitement des statistiques tirées des registres d'état civil

Dans tous les tableaux de l'*Annuaire démographique*, on a indiqué le degré de fiabilité des statistiques de l'état civil en se fondant sur le codage qualitatif décrit ci-dessus. Les statistiques codées « C », jugées sûres, sont imprimées en caractères romains. Celles qui sont codées « U » ou « ... », jugées douteuses, sont reproduites en *italique*. Bien que le codage qualitatif proprement dit n'apparaisse que dans certains tableaux, l'indication du degré de fiabilité (c'est-à-dire l'emploi des caractères italiques pour désigner les données douteuses) se retrouve dans tous les tableaux présentant des statistiques de l'état civil.

Il convient de noter que, pour les taux de mortalité infantile, les taux de mortalité maternelle et les rapports de morts fœtales tardives (calculées en utilisant au dénominateur le nombre de naissances vivantes), les indications relatives à la fiabilité sont déterminées sur la base des codes de qualité utilisés pour les décès d'enfants de moins d'un an, les décès totaux et les morts fœtales tardives, respectivement. Pour évaluer ces taux et rapports de façon plus précise, il faudrait tenir compte de la qualité des données relatives aux naissances vivantes, utilisées au dénominateur dans leur calcul. Les codes de qualité pour les naissances vivantes figurent au tableau 9 et sont décrits plus en détail dans les notes techniques se rapportant à ce tableau.

4.2.3 Traitement des séries chronologiques de statistiques tirées des registres d'état civil

Il est plus difficile de déterminer la qualité des séries chronologiques de statistiques de l'état civil que celle des données pour une seule année. Étant donné qu'une série chronologique de statistiques de l'état civil ne peut généralement avoir pour source qu'un système permanent d'enregistrement des faits d'état civil, on a arbitrairement supposé que le degré d'exactitude de la série tout entière était le même que celui de la dernière tranche annuelle de données tirées du registre d'état civil. La série tout entière est traitée de la manière décrite à la section 4.2.2 ci-dessus : lorsque le code de qualité relatif aux données d'enregistrement les plus récentes est « C », les fréquences et les taux relatifs aux années antérieures sont eux aussi considérés comme sûrs et figurent en caractères romains. Inversement, si les données d'enregistrement les plus récentes sont codées « U » ou «...», les données des années antérieures sont jugées douteuses et figurent en italique. Cette méthode n'est certes pas entièrement satisfaisante, car les données des premières années de la série sont souvent beaucoup moins sûres que le code actuel ne le laisse supposer. On s'efforce d'abandonner progressivement cette méthode et de coder les données enregistrées pour chaque année séparément.

4.2.4 Traitement des estimations fondées sur les statistiques de l'état civil

En plus des données provenant des systèmes d'enregistrement des faits d'état civil, *l'Annuaire démographique* contient aussi des estimations relatives aux fréquences et aux taux. Il s'agit d'estimations officielles, généralement calculées à partir des résultats d'un recensement de la population ou d'un sondage ou par analyse démographique. Si des estimations concernant les fréquences et les taux figurent dans les tableaux, c'est parce que l'on considère qu'elles fournissent des renseignements plus exacts que les systèmes existants d'enregistrement des faits d'état civil. En conséquence, elles sont également jugées sûres et sont donc imprimées en caractères romains.

Dans les tableaux qui indiquent le code de qualité, ce code ne s'applique qu'aux données tirées des registres d'état civil. Les données estimatives sont dénotées par le «|».

4.3 Causes de décès

Les États membres de l'Organisation mondiale de la santé (OMS) sont tenus de communiquer à celle-ci les données sur les causes de décès codifiées selon la révision en vigueur de la Classification internationale des maladies et des problèmes de santé connexes (CIM). Pour assurer la comparabilité internationale des statistiques des causes de décès, l'OMS organise régulièrement des conférences internationales de révision de la Classification internationale des maladies afin de suivre, au fur et à mesure, les progrès les plus récents de la médecine clinique et de la statistique. Les données sont généralement présentées à l'OMS selon le degré de détail à tous les quatre caractères requis par la CIM et sont compilées et archivées dans la Base de données sur la mortalité de l'OMS au degré de détail présenté par le pays. Les données de la Base de données sur la mortalité de l'OMS sont disponibles sur le site Internet suivant : http://www3.who.int/whosis/menu.cfm.

Les révisions de la CIM permettent certes de disposer d'une version actualisée, mais elles posent plusieurs problèmes de comparabilité des statistiques des causes de décès. Le premier tient au manque de comparabilité dans le temps, qui accompagne inévitablement la mise en œuvre d'une classification nouvelle. Le deuxième est celui de la comparabilité entre pays ou zones, car les différents pays peuvent adopter la nouvelle classification à des époques différentes. Établir la cause des décès exige des compétences de plus en plus poussées à mesure que la classification devient plus précise. Or, dans beaucoup de pays ou zones, il est rare que les décès se produisent en présence d'un témoin possédant une formation médicale et le certificat de décès est le plus souvent établi par quelqu'un qui n'est pas qualifié sur le plan médical. Étant donné que la CIM répertorie de nombreux diagnostics qu'il est impossible d'établir si l'on n'a pas de formation en médecine, la CIM n'est pas toujours exactement ou précisément utilisée ce qui affecte la comparabilité internationale, notamment entre pays ou zones où la qualité des services médicaux est très disparate.

La dixième révision[15] est la dernière qu'ait connue la CIM. Les chapitres de la dixième révision se fondent sur un système de codification alphanumérique à une lettre suivie de trois chiffres pour les catégories à quatre caractères. Le chapitre 1 concerne les maladies infectieuses et parasitaires et le chapitre 2 l'ensemble des néoplasmes. Le chapitre 3 a trait aux troubles du système immunitaire, aux maladies du sang et aux organes hématopoïétiques. Le chapitre 4 porte sur les maladies du système endocrinien, de la nutrition et du métabolisme. Les autres chapitres groupent les maladies selon leur site anatomique, à l'exception de ceux qui concernent les affections mentales, les complications de la grossesse, de l'accouchement et des suites de couches, les malformations congénitales et les affections de la période périnatale. Enfin, un chapitre entier est consacré aux symptômes, manifestations et résultats anormaux.

4.3.1 Mortalité liée à la maternité

D'après la dixième révision de la CIM, la « mortalité liée à la maternité » est définie comme le décès d'une femme survenu au cours de la grossesse ou dans un délai de 42 jours après sa terminaison, quelle qu'en soit la durée et la localisation, pour une cause quelconque déterminée ou aggravée par la grossesse ou les soins qu'elle a motivés, mais ni accidentelle ni fortuite.

Les « décès liés à la maternité » doivent se répartir en décès par cause obstétricale directe et indirecte. Les décès par cause obstétricale directe sont ceux qui résultent de complications obstétricales de l'état de grossesse (grossesse, travail et suites de couches), d'interventions, d'omissions, d'un traitement incorrect ou d'un enchaînement d'événements de l'un quelconque des facteurs ci-dessus. Les décès par cause obstétricale indirecte sont ceux qui résultent d'une maladie préexistante ou d'une affection apparue au cours de la grossesse, sans qu'elle soit due à des causes obstétricales directes, mais qui a été aggravée par les effets physiologiques de la grossesse.

En théorie, le nombre de femmes enceintes aurait dû être pris comme dénominateur pour le taux de mortalité maternelle, mais il est impossible de déterminer ce nombre. En conséquence, il est en outre recommandé dans la dixième révision d'exprimer les taux de mortalité maternelle sur la base de 100 000 naissances vivantes ou 100 000 naissances totales (naissances vivantes et morts fœtales). Le taux de mortalité maternelle est ici calculé par 100 000 naissances vivantes. Bien que les naissances vivantes ne permettent pas d'évaluer sans distorsion le nombre des femmes enceintes, leur nombre est plus fiable que d'autres estimations car le nombre des naissances vivantes est plus exactement enregistré que celui des naissances vivantes et des morts fœtales.

---

[1] Les éditions de 1978 et de 1991 font exception à la règle, puisque les tableaux sur des sujets spéciaux ont été publiés séparément.

[2] Organisation des Nations Unies, Département des affaires économiques et sociales, Division de la population (2013). *Perspectives de la population mondiale : La révision de 2012. Ensemble de données étendues en formats Excel et ASCII, edition DVD-ROM* (publication des Nations Unies, ST/ESA/SER.A/334).

[3] ST/ESA/STAT/SER.M/49/Rev.4/WWW ; http://unstats.un.org/unsd/methods/m49/m49frnch.htm; voir également *Code standard des pays et des zones à usage statistique*, numéro de vente : M.98.XVII.9, Nations Unies, New

York, 1999.

[4] Numéro de vente : F.07.XVII.8, Nations Unies, New York, 2007. Cette publication est disponible en ligne à l'adresse : http://unstats.un.org/unsd/demographic/standmeth/principles/Series_M67Rev2en.pdf

[5] Ibid., par. 2.135.

[6] Lorsque l'on utilise un registre de la population, on peut également calculer l'âge en années révolues en soustrayant la date de naissance de chaque personne inscrite sur le registre de la date de référence à laquelle se rapportent les données sur l'âge.

[7] L'emploi de méthodes différentes de calcul de l'âge, par exemple la méthode occidentale et la méthode orientale, ou, comme on les désigne plus communément, la méthode anglaise et la méthode chinoise, représente une cause de non-comparabilité. Selon la méthode chinoise, on considère que l'enfant est âgé d'un an à sa naissance et qu'il avance d'un an à chaque nouvelle année chinoise. Les répercussions de cette méthode sont particulièrement apparentes dans les données pour le premier âge : les données concernant les enfants de moins d'un an sont nettement inférieures à la réalité. Les effets sur les chiffres relatifs aux groupes d'âge suivants sont moins visibles. Les séries ainsi établies sont souvent ajustées avant d'être publiées, mais il ne faut pas exclure la possibilité d'aberrations de ce genre lorsque l'on compare des données censitaires sur l'âge.

[8] Numéro de vente : F.01.XVII.10, publication des Nations Unies, New York, 2001.

[9] Numéro de vente : F. 98.XVII.7, publication des Nations Unies, New York, 1998.

[10] Numéro de vente : F.98.XVII.11, publication des Nations Unies, New York, 1998.

[11] Numéro de vente : F.98.XVII.4, publication des Nations Unies, New York, 1998.

[12] Numéro de vente : F.98.XVII.6, publication des Nations Unies, New York, 1998.

[13] Numéro de vente : F.98.XVII.10, publication des Nations Unies, New York, 1998.

[14] Numéro de vente : F.03.XVII.11, United Nations, New York, 2004.

[15] Organisation mondiale de la santé, *Classification statistique internationale des maladies et problèmes de santé connexes,* dixième révision, vol. 2, Genève, 1992.

Table A. Demographic Yearbook 2012 synoptic table: Availability of data by country/area, table and sex, where applicable
Tableau A. Tableau synoptique de l'Annuaire démographique 2012 : Disponibilité des données par pays ou zone, tableau et le sexe, si disponible

General topic and table number - Sujet général et numéro de tableau

Continent and country or area / Continent et pays ou zone	Table totals	Summary - Aperçu 3 Total	3 M/F	4	5	Population 6 Total¹	6 M/F	7 Total	7 M/F	8 Total	8 M/F	Fertility - Natalité 9	10 Total	10 M/F	11	Foetal mortality - Mortalité foetale 12	13	14
Total number of countries or areas - Total des pays ou zones	..	234	225	171	218	221	217	205	201	199	155	158	147	123	90	84	70	49

AFRICA - AFRIQUE

Continent and country or area	Table totals	3 Total	3 M/F	4	5	6 Total¹	6 M/F	7 Total	7 M/F	8 Total	8 M/F	9	10 Total	10 M/F	11	12	13	14
Algeria - Algérie	16	•	•	•	•	•	•	•	•	•	...	•	...	...	...	•	...	...
Angola	4	•	•	...	...	...	...	...	...	•	•	...	...	...	...	...	...	...
Benin - Bénin	10	•	•	...	...	•	...	•	...	•	•	...	...	...	...	...	...	...
Botswana	17	•	•	•	•	•	•	•	•	•	...	•	...	...	•	•	...	...
Burkina Faso	13	•	•	...	•	•	•	•	•	•	•	•	...	...	...	...	...	...
Burundi	9	•	•	...	•	•	•	•	•	•	...	...	...	...	...	...	...	...
Cabo Verde	14	•	•	•	•	•	•	•	•	•	•	•	...	...	...	...	...	...
Cameroon - Cameroun	7	•	•	...	•	•	•	...	•	•	...	...	...	...	...	...	...	...
Central African Republic - République centrafricaine	5	•	•	...	•	•	•	...	...	...	...	...	...	...	...	...	...	...
Chad - Tchad	3	•	•	...	...	...	•	...	...	...	...	...	...	...	...	...	...	...
Comoros - Comores	2	•	...	...	...	•	...	...	...	...	...	...	...	...	...	...	...	...
Congo	7	•	•	...	...	•	•	•	...	...	...	...	...	...	...	...	...	...
Côte d'Ivoire	6	•	•	...	...	•	•	...	...	...	...	...	...	...	...	...	...	...
Democratic Republic of the Congo - République démocratique du Congo	2	•	•	...	...	...	...	...	...	...	...	...	...	...	...	...	...	...
Djibouti	4	•	•	...	•	...	...	...	...	...	...	...	...	...	...	...	...	...
Egypt - Égypte	27	•	•	•	•	•	•	•	•	•	•	•	•	•	•	•	...	...
Equatorial Guinea - Guinée équatoriale	2	•	•	...	...	...	...	...	...	...	...	...	...	...	...	...	...	...
Eritrea - Érythrée	2	•	•	...	...	...	...	...	...	...	...	...	...	...	...	...	...	...
Ethiopia - Éthiopie	10	•	•	...	•	•	•	•	•	•	...	...	...	...	...	...	...	...
Gabon	6	•	•	...	•	•	•	•	•	...	...	...	...	...	...	...	...	...
Gambia - Gambie	6	•	...	•	•	•	•	•	...	...	...	...	...	...	...	...	...	...
Ghana	13	•	•	•	•	•	•	•	•	•	...	•	...	...	...	...	...	...
Guinea - Guinée	8	•	•	...	•	•	•	•	•	•	...	...	...	...	...	...	...	...
Guinea-Bissau - Guinée-Bissau	6	•	•	...	•	•	•	•	...	...	...	...	...	...	...	...	...	...
Kenya	18	•	•	•	•	•	•	•	•	•	...	•	•	•	•	...	...	...
Lesotho	10	•	•	...	•	•	•	•	•	•	...	...	•	•	...	...	...	...
Liberia - Libéria	10	•	•	•	...	•	•	•	•	•	...	•	•	•	...	...	...	...
Libya - Libye	12	•	•	•	•	•	•	•	•	•	...	•	...	...	...	...	...	...
Madagascar	7	•	•	...	•	•	•	•	•	...	...	...	...	...	...	...	...	...
Malawi	16	•	•	•	•	•	•	•	•	•	...	•	•	...	...	...	...	...
Mali	5	•	•	...	•	•	•	...	...	...	...	...	...	...	...	...	...	...
Mauritania - Mauritanie	9	•	•	...	•	•	•	•	•	•	...	...	...	...	...	...	...	...
Mauritius - Maurice	27	•	•	•	•	•	•	•	•	•	•	•	•	•	...	•	...	...
Mayotte	5	•	...	...	...	•	•	•	...	...	...	...	...	...	...	...	...	...
Morocco - Maroc	11	•	•	...	...	•	•	•	...	•	...	...	...	...	...	...	...	...
Mozambique	9	•	•	...	•	•	•	•	•	•	...	...	...	...	...	...	...	...
Namibia - Namibie	10	•	•	...	•	•	•	•	•	•	...	...	...	...	...	...	...	...
Niger	9	•	•	...	•	•	•	•	•	•	...	...	...	...	...	...	...	...
Nigeria - Nigéria	8	•	•	...	•	•	•	•	...	...	...	•	...	...	...	...	...	...
Republic of South Sudan - République de Soudan du Sud	10	•	•	•	...	•	•	•	...	•	...	...	...	...	...	...	...	...
Réunion	23	•	...	•	•	•	•	•	•	•	...	•	...	...	...	•	...	...
Rwanda	14	•	•	...	•	•	•	•	•	•	...	•	...	...	...	...	...	...
Saint Helena ex. dep. - Sainte-Hélène sans dép.	20	•	•	•	•	•	•	•	•	•	...	•	...	...	...	...	...	...
Saint Helena: Ascension - Sainte-Hélène: Ascension	7	•	•	...	•	•	•	•	...	...	...	...	...	...	...	...	...	...
Saint Helena: Tristan da Cunha - Sainte-Hélène: Tristan da Cunha	5	•	•	...	•	•	•	...	...	...	...	...	...	...	...	...	...	...
Sao Tome and Principe - Sao Tomé-et-Principe	10	•	•	...	•	•	•	•	•	•	...	...	...	...	...	...	...	...
Senegal - Sénégal	14	•	•	...	•	•	•	•	•	•	...	...	...	...	...	...	...	...
Seychelles	24	•	•	•	•	•	•	•	•	•	...	•	•	•	...	•	...	...
Sierra Leone	16	•	•	•	•	•	•	•	•	•	...	...	...	...	...	...	...	...
Somalia - Somalie	3	•	•	...	...	•	...	...	...	...	...	...	...	...	...	...	...	...
South Africa - Afrique du Sud	26	•	•	...	•	•	•	•	•	•	•	•	•	•	...	•	...	...
Sudan - Soudan	0	...	...	...	...	...	...	...	...	...	...	...	...	...	...	...	...	...
Swaziland	12	•	•	...	•	•	•	•	•	•	...	...	•	•	...	...	...	...
Togo	7	•	•	...	•	•	•	•	...	...	...	...	...	...	...	...	...	...
Tunisia - Tunisie	17	•	•	•	•	•	•	•	•	•	...	•	•	...	...	•	...	...

Table A. Demographic Yearbook 2012 synoptic table: Availability of data by country/area, table and sex, where applicable
Tableau A. Tableau synoptique de l'Annuaire démographique 2012 : Disponibilité des données par pays ou zone, tableau et le sexe, si disponible

Continent and country or area / Continent et pays ou zone	General topic and table number - Sujet général et numéro de tableau												
	Infant and maternal mortality - Mortalité infantile et mortalité liée à la maternité				General mortality - Mortalité générale					Nuptiality and divorces - Nuptialité et divortialité			
	15	16		17	18	19		20	21	22	23	24	25
		Total	M/F			Total	M/F						
Total number of countries or areas - Total des pays ou zones	121	112	107	118	154	151	146	64	174	133	110	111	83
AFRICA - AFRIQUE													
Algeria - Algérie	•	...	...	...	•	...	...	...	•	•	...	...	...
Angola	...	...	...	...	...	...	...	...	...	...	...	...	...
Benin - Bénin	...	...	...	...	...	...	...	...	•	...	...	...	...
Botswana	...	...	...	...	•	•	...	...	•	•	•	...	...
Burkina Faso	...	...	...	...	•	...	...	...	•	...	...	...	...
Burundi	...	...	...	...	...	...	...	...	...	...	...	...	...
Cabo Verde	•	•	...	...	•	...	...	...	...	...	...	...	...
Cameroon - Cameroun	...	...	...	...	...	...	...	...	...	...	...	...	...
Central African Republic - République centrafricaine	...	...	...	...	...	...	...	...	...	...	...	...	...
Chad - Tchad	...	...	...	...	...	...	...	...	...	...	...	...	...
Comoros - Comores	...	...	...	...	...	...	...	...	...	...	...	...	...
Congo	...	...	...	...	...	...	...	...	...	...	...	...	...
Côte d'Ivoire	...	...	...	...	...	...	...	...	•	...	...	...	...
Democratic Republic of the Congo - République démocratique du Congo	...	...	...	...	...	...	...	...	...	...	...	...	...
Djibouti	...	...	...	...	...	...	...	...	•	...	...	...	...
Egypt - Égypte	•	•	•	•	•	•	•	...	•	•	•	•	•
Equatorial Guinea - Guinée équatoriale	...	...	...	...	...	...	...	...	...	...	...	...	...
Eritrea - Érythrée	...	...	...	...	...	...	...	...	...	...	...	...	...
Ethiopia - Éthiopie	...	...	...	...	...	...	...	...	•	...	...	...	...
Gabon	...	...	...	...	...	...	...	...	...	...	...	...	...
Ghana	•	...	...	...	...	...	...	...	•	...	...	...	...
Guinea - Guinée	...	...	...	...	...	...	...	...	•	...	...	...	...
Guinea-Bissau - Guinée-Bissau	...	...	...	...	...	...	...	...	•	...	...	...	...
Kenya	•	...	...	...	•	•	•	...	•	...	...	...	...
Lesotho	...	...	...	...	...	...	...	...	•	•	...	•	...
Liberia - Libéria	...	...	...	...	...	...	...	...	...	...	...	...	...
Libya - Libye	...	...	...	...	•	...	...	...	...	•	...	•	...
Madagascar	...	...	...	...	...	...	...	...	•	...	...	...	...
Malawi	...	...	...	...	•	•	•	...	•	...	...	...	...
Mali	...	...	...	...	...	...	...	...	...	...	...	...	...
Mauritania - Mauritanie	...	...	...	...	...	...	...	...	...	...	...	...	...
Mauritius - Maurice	•	•	•	•	•	•	•	...	•	•	•	•	•
Mayotte	...	...	...	...	...	...	...	...	...	...	...	...	...
Morocco - Maroc	...	...	...	•	•	•	...	...	...	...	...	...	...
Mozambique	...	...	...	...	...	...	...	...	...	...	...	•	...
Namibia - Namibie	...	...	...	...	...	...	...	...	•	...	...	...	...
Niger	...	...	...	...	...	...	...	...	...	...	...	...	...
Nigeria - Nigéria	...	...	...	...	...	...	...	...	...	...	...	...	...
Republic of South Sudan - République de Soudan du Sud	...	...	...	...	•	•	•	...	...	...	...	...	...
Réunion	...	•	•	•	•	•	•	...	•	•	•	...	...
Rwanda	•	...	...	...	•	...	...	...	•	...	...	...	...
Saint Helena ex. dep. - Sainte-Hélène sans dép.	•	•	•	...	•	•	•	...	•	•	...	•	...
Saint Helena: Ascension - Sainte-Hélène: Ascension	...	...	...	...	...	...	...	...	...	...	...	...	...
Saint Helena: Tristan da Cunha - Sainte-Hélène: Tristan da Cunha	...	...	...	...	...	...	...	...	...	...	...	...	...
Sao Tome and Principe - Sao Tomé-et-Principe	...	...	...	...	...	...	...	...	•	...	...	...	...
Senegal - Sénégal	•	...	...	...	...	...	...	...	•	...	...	...	...
Seychelles	•	•	•	•	•	...	...	...	•	•	•	•	...
Sierra Leone	•	...	...	...	•	...	...	...	...	...	...	...	...
South Africa - Afrique du Sud	•	•	•	•	•	•	•	...	•	•	•	...	•
Sudan - Soudan	...	...	...	...	...	...	...	...	...	...	...	...	...
Swaziland	...	...	...	...	•	•	•	...	...	...	...	...	...
Togo	...	...	...	...	...	...	...	...	...	...	...	...	...
Tunisia - Tunisie	...	...	...	...	•	...	...	...	•	•	•	•	...

General topic and table number - Sujet général et numéro de tableau

Continent and country or area / Continent et pays ou zone	Table totals	Summary - Apercu 3 Total	3 M/F	4	5	Population 6 Total[1]	6 M/F	7 Total	7 M/F	8 Total	8 M/F	9	Fertility - Natalité 10 Total	10 M/F	11	Foetal mortality - Mortalité foetale 12	13	14
AFRICA - AFRIQUE																		
Uganda - Ouganda	10	•	•	•	•	•	•	...	•	•	...	...	...	...	...	...	...	...
United Republic of Tanzania - République Unie de Tanzanie	10	•	•	•	•	•	•	•	•	...	•	...	•	...	...	...	...	...
Western Sahara - Sahara occidental	3	•	•	...	...	...	...	...	•	•	...	...	...	...	...	...	...	...
Zambia - Zambie	7	•	•	...	•	•	•	•	•	•	...	...	...	...	...	...	...	...
Zimbabwe	11	•	•	...	•	•	•	•	•	•	...	...	...	...	...	...	...	...
AMERICA, NORTH - AMÉRIQUE DU NORD																		
Anguilla	17	•	•	•	•	...	•	•	•	•	...	•	•	•	...	...	•	...
Antigua and Barbuda - Antigua-et-Barbuda	13	•	•	•	•	•	•	•	•	•	...	•	•	•	...	...	...	...
Aruba	24	•	•	•	•	•	•	•	•	•	•	•	•	•	...	...	...	...
Bahamas	26	•	•	•	•	•	•	•	•	•	•	•	•	•	•	...	...	...
Barbados - Barbade	13	•	•	...	•	•	•	•	•	•	•	•	•	•	...	•	...	...
Belize	10	•	•	...	•	•	•	•	•	•	•	...	...	...	...	...	...	...
Bermuda - Bermudes	28	•	•	•	•	•	•	•	•	•	•	•	•	•	•	...	...	•
Bonaire, Saba and Sint Eustatius - Bonaire, Saba et Saint-Eustache	0	...	...	...	...	...	...	...	...	...	...	...	...	...	...	...	...	...
British Virgin Islands - Îles Vierges britanniques	5	•	...	...	...	•	•	•	•	•	...	...	...	...	...	...	...	...
Canada	29	•	•	•	•	•	•	•	•	•	•	•	•	•	•	•	•	•
Cayman Islands - Îles Caïmanes	21	•	•	•	•	•	•	•	•	•	...	•	•	•	...	•	•	...
Costa Rica	29	•	•	•	•	•	•	•	•	•	•	•	•	•	...	•	•	•
Cuba	29	•	•	•	•	•	•	•	•	•	...	•	•	•	...	•	•	•
Curaçao	22	•	•	•	•	•	•	•	•	•	...	•	•	•	...	...	...	...
Dominica - Dominique	16	•	•	•	•	•	•	•	•	•	...	•	•	•	...	•	•	...
Dominican Republic - République dominicaine	27	•	•	•	•	•	•	•	•	•	•	•	•	•	...	•	•	...
El Salvador	27	•	•	•	•	•	•	•	•	•	•	•	•	•	•	•	•	...
Greenland - Groenland	24	•	•	•	•	•	•	•	•	•	•	•	•	•	•	•	•	...
Grenada - Grenade	4	•	•	...	•	...	...	...	...	...	...	...	...	...	...	...	...	...
Guadeloupe	23	•	...	•	•	•	•	•	•	•	•	•	•	•	•	•	•	•
Guatemala	25	•	•	•	•	•	•	•	•	•	•	•	•	•	•	•	•	•
Haiti - Haïti	12	•	•	•	•	•	•	•	•	•	•	•	...	...	...	...	...	...
Honduras	12	•	•	•	•	•	•	•	•	•	•	•	...	...	...	...	...	...
Jamaica - Jamaïque	23	•	•	•	•	•	•	•	•	•	•	•	•	•	...	•	•	•
Martinique	24	•	...	•	•	•	•	•	•	•	•	•	•	•	•	•	•	•
Mexico - Mexique	30	•	•	•	•	•	•	•	•	•	•	•	•	•	•	•	•	•
Montserrat	21	•	•	•	•	•	•	•	•	•	...	...	•	•	...	•	•	...
Nicaragua	22	•	•	•	•	•	•	•	•	•	•	•	•	•	...	...	•	...
Panama	28	•	•	•	•	•	•	•	•	•	•	•	•	•	...	•	•	...
Puerto Rico - Porto Rico	27	•	•	•	•	•	•	•	•	•	•	•	•	•	...	•	•	•
Saint Kitts and Nevis - Saint-Kitts-et-Nevis	5	•	•	...	...	•	•	•	...	...	...	...	...	...	...	...	...	...
Saint Lucia - Sainte-Lucie	14	•	•	...	•	•	•	•	•	•	•	•	•	•	...	...	...	...
Saint Pierre and Miquelon - Saint Pierre-et-Miquelon	8	•	...	...	...	•	•	•	•	•	•	•	...	...	...	...	...	...
Saint Vincent and the Grenadines - Saint-Vincent-et-les Grenadines	21	•	•	•	•	•	•	•	•	•	...	...	•	•	...	...	...	...
Sint Maarten (Dutch part) - Saint-Martin (partie néerlandaise)	6	...	...	•	•	•	•	•	...	...	•	•	...	...	...	...	...	...
Trinidad and Tobago - Trinité-et-Tobago	17	•	•	...	•	•	•	•	•	•	•	•	•	•	...	...	...	...
Turks and Caicos Islands - Îles Turques et Caïques	24	•	•	•	•	•	•	•	•	...	•	•	•	•	...	•	•	•
United States of America - États-Unis d'Amérique	25	•	•	•	•	•	•	•	•	•	•	•	•	•	•	...	...	...
United States Virgin Islands - Îles Vierges américaines	14	•	•	•	•	•	•	•	•	•	•	•	•	•	...	...	...	...
AMERICA, SOUTH - AMÉRIQUE DU SUD																		
Argentina - Argentine	20	•	•	•	•	•	•	•	•	•	•	...	...	•	•	...	...	...
Bolivia (Plurinational State of) - Bolivie (État plurinational de)	12	•	•	•	•	•	•	•	•	•	•	...	...	...	...	...	...	...

Continent and country or area Continent et pays ou zone	General topic and table number - Sujet général et numéro de tableau												
	Infant and maternal mortality - Mortalité infantile et mortalité liée à la maternité				General mortality - Mortalité générale					Nuptiality and divorces - Nuptialité et divortialité			
	15	16 Total	16 M/F	17	18	19 Total	19 M/F	20	21	22	23	24	25
AFRICA - AFRIQUE													
Uganda - Ouganda	...	...	...	...	...	...	...	...	•	...	...	...	...
United Republic of Tanzania - République Unie de Tanzanie	...	...	...	...	•	...	...	...	...	...	...	...	...
Western Sahara - Sahara occidental	...	...	...	...	...	...	...	...	...	...	...	...	...
Zambia - Zambie	...	...	...	...	...	...	...	...	...	...	...	...	...
Zimbabwe	...	...	...	...	...	...	...	•	•	...	...	...	...
AMERICA, NORTH - AMÉRIQUE DU NORD													
Anguilla	•	...	...	•	•	•	•	...	•	•	•	•	...
Antigua and Barbuda - Antigua-et-Barbuda	•	...	...	•	•	•	•	...	•	...	...	...	...
Aruba	•	•	•	•	•	•	•	...	•	•	•	•	•
Bahamas	•	•	•	•	•	•	•	...	•	•	•	•	...
Barbados - Barbade	...	•	•	•	•	•	•	...	•	•	•	•	...
Belize	...	...	•	•	•	•	•	...	•	•	•	•	•
Bermuda - Bermudes	•	•	•	•	•	•	•	...	•	•	•	•	•
Bonaire, Saba and Sint Eustatius - Bonaire, Saba et Saint-Eustache	...	...	...	...	...	...	...	...	...	...	...	...	...
British Virgin Islands - Îles Vierges britanniques	...	...	...	•	...	...	...	...	•	...	...	...	...
Canada	•	•	•	•	•	•	•	•	•	•	•	•	...
Cayman Islands - Îles Caïmanes	•	•	•	•	•	•	•	...	•	•	•	•	...
Costa Rica	•	•	•	•	•	•	•	•	•	•	•	•	...
Cuba	•	•	•	•	•	•	•	•	•	•	•	•	•
Curaçao	•	•	•	...	•	•	•	•	•	•	•	•	...
Dominica - Dominique	...	...	...	•	...	...	...	...	...	...	...	...	...
Dominican Republic - République dominicaine	•	•	•	•	•	•	•	...	•	•	•	•	•
El Salvador	•	•	•	•	•	•	•	...	•	•	•	•	•
Greenland - Groenland	•	•	•	•	•	•	•	...	•	...	...	...	...
Grenada - Grenade	...	...	...	•	...	...	...	...	•	...	...	...	...
Guadeloupe	...	•	•	•	•	•	•	...	•	•	•	•	...
Guatemala	•	•	•	•	•	•	•	...	•	•	•	•	...
Haiti - Haïti	...	...	...	•	•	•	•	...	...	...	...	...	...
Honduras	...	...	...	...	•	...	...	...	...	...	...	...	...
Jamaica - Jamaïque	...	•	•	•	•	•	•	...	•	•	•	•	•
Martinique	...	•	•	•	•	•	•	...	•	•	•	•	•
Mexico - Mexique	•	•	•	•	•	•	•	•	•	•	•	•	•
Montserrat	•	•	•	•	•	•	•	...	•	•	•	•	•
Nicaragua	•	•	•	•	•	•	•	...	•	...	•	•	...
Panama	•	•	•	•	•	•	•	•	•	•	•	•	•
Puerto Rico - Porto Rico	•	•	•	•	•	•	•	...	•	•	•	•	•
Saint Kitts and Nevis - Saint-Kitts-et-Nevis	...	...	...	•	...	...	...	...	•	...	...	...	...
Saint Lucia - Sainte-Lucie	...	...	...	•	•	•	•	...	•	...	...	...	...
Saint Pierre and Miquelon - Saint Pierre-et-Miquelon	...	...	...	...	...	...	...	...	...	...	...	...	...
Saint Vincent and the Grenadines - Saint-Vincent-et-les Grenadines	•	•	•	•	•	•	•	...	•	•	•	•	...
Sint Maarten (Dutch part) - Saint-Martin (partie néerlandaise)	...	...	...	•	...	...	...	...	•	...	•	...	...
Trinidad and Tobago - Trinité-et-Tobago	...	...	...	•	•	•	•	...	•	•	•	•	•
Turks and Caicos Islands - Îles Turques et Caïques	•	...	...	•	•	•	•	...	•	•	•	•	•
United States of America - États-Unis d'Amérique	•	•	•	•	•	•	•	•	•	•	•	•	...
United States Virgin Islands - Îles Vierges américaines	...	...	...	•	...	•	•	...	...	...	...	...	...
AMERICA, SOUTH - AMÉRIQUE DU SUD													
Argentina - Argentine	•	•	•	•	•	•	•	...	•	•	•	•	...
Bolivia (Plurinational State of) - Bolivie (État plurinational de)	...	...	...	...	...	...	...	...	•	•	...	...	...

General topic and table number - Sujet général et numéro de tableau

Continent and country or area / Continent et pays ou zone	Table totals	Summary - Aperçu 3 Total	3 M/F	4	5	Population 6 Total[1]	6 M/F	7 Total	7 M/F	8 Total	8 M/F	Fertility - Natalité 9	10 Total	10 M/F	11	Foetal mortality - Mortalité foetale 12	13	14
AMERICA, SOUTH - AMÉRIQUE DU SUD																		
Brazil - Brésil	25	•	•	•	•	•	•	•	•	•	•	•	•	•	•	...	...	...
Chile - Chili	29	•	•	•	•	•	•	•	•	•	•	•	•	•	•	...	•	...
Colombia - Colombie	23	•	•	•	•	•	•	•	•	•	•	•	•	•	•	...	...	...
Ecuador - Équateur	26	•	•	•	•	•	•	•	•	•	•	•	•	•	•	...	...	...
Falkland Islands (Malvinas) - Îles Falkland (Malvinas)	7	•	•	...	...	•	•	•	•	...	...	...	...	...	•	•	...	...
French Guiana - Guyane française	24	...	•	•	•	•	•	•	•	•	•	•	•	•	•	...	...	...
Guyana	15	•	•	•	•	•	•	•	•	•	•	...	...	•	•	...	...	...
Paraguay	23	•	•	•	•	•	•	•	•	•	•	•	•	•	•	...	•	...
Peru - Pérou	24	•	•	•	•	•	•	•	•	•	•	•	•	•	•	...	...	...
Suriname	17	...	•	•	•	•	•	•	•	•	•	•	•	•	•	...	...	...
Uruguay	20	•	•	•	•	•	•	•	•	•	•	•	•	•	•	...	...	...
Venezuela (Bolivarian Republic of) - Venezuela (République bolivarienne du)	25	•	•	•	•	•	•	•	•	•	•	•	•	•	•	...	...	...
ASIA - ASIE																		
Afghanistan	11	•	•	•	•	•	•	•	•	•	•	...	...	•	•	...	...	...
Armenia - Arménie	29	•	•	•	•	•	•	•	•	•	•	•	•	•	•	•	...	•
Azerbaijan - Azerbaïdjan	30	•	•	•	•	•	•	•	•	•	•	•	•	•	•	•	•	•
Bahrain - Bahreïn	28	•	•	•	•	•	•	•	•	•	•	•	•	•	•	•	•	...
Bangladesh	20	•	•	•	•	•	•	•	•	•	•	•	•	•	•	...	...	...
Bhutan - Bhoutan	14	•	•	...	•	•	•	•	•	•	•	...	•	•	•	...	...	...
Brunei Darussalam - Brunéi Darussalam	24	•	•	•	•	•	•	•	•	•	•	•	•	•	•	•	...	...
Cambodia - Cambodge	11	•	•	•	•	•	•	•	•	•	•	...	•	...	•	...	...	...
China - Chine[2]	17	•	•	•	•	•	•	•	•	•	•	•	•	•	•	...	...	...
China, Hong Kong SAR - Chine, Hong Kong RAS	29	•	•	•	•	•	•	•	•	•	•	•	•	•	•	•	•	•
China, Macao SAR - Chine, Macao RAS	27	•	•	•	•	•	•	•	•	•	•	•	•	•	•	•	•	•
Cyprus - Chypre	25	•	•	•	•	•	•	•	•	•	•	...	•	•	•	•	...	...
Democratic People's Republic of Korea - République populaire démocratique de Corée	18	•	•	•	•	•	•	•	•	•	•	...	•	•	•	...	...	...
Georgia - Géorgie	27	•	•	•	•	•	•	•	•	•	•	...	•	•	•	•	...	...
India - Inde[3]	14	•	•	•	•	•	•	•	•	•	•	...	...	•	•	...	...	...
Indonesia - Indonésie	13	•	•	•	•	•	•	•	•	•	•	...	...	•	•	...	...	...
Iran (Islamic Republic of) - Iran (République islamique d')	21	•	•	•	•	•	•	•	•	•	•	•	•	•	•	...	...	...
Iraq	9	•	•	...	•	•	•	•	...	...	...	...	...	•	•	...	...	...
Israel - Israël[4]	30	•	•	•	•	•	•	•	•	•	•	•	•	•	•	•	...	•
Japan - Japon	30	•	•	•	•	•	•	•	•	•	•	•	•	•	•	•	•	•
Jordan - Jordanie	17	•	•	•	•	•	•	•	•	•	•	•	•	•	•	...	...	...
Kazakhstan	28	•	•	•	•	•	•	•	•	•	•	•	•	•	•	•	...	...
Kuwait - Koweït	26	•	•	•	•	•	•	•	•	•	•	•	•	•	•	•	...	...
Kyrgyzstan - Kirghizstan	30	•	•	•	•	•	•	•	•	•	•	•	•	•	•	•	•	•
Lao People's Democratic Republic - République démocratique populaire lao	10	•	•	•	•	•	•	•	•	•	•	...	...	•	•	...	...	...
Lebanon - Liban	13	•	•	•	...	•	•	•	•	•	•	...	...	•	•	...	...	...
Malaysia - Malaisie	22	•	•	•	•	•	•	•	•	•	•	•	•	•	•	...	...	...
Maldives	23	•	•	•	•	•	•	•	•	•	•	•	•	•	•	...	...	...
Mongolia - Mongolie	23	•	•	•	•	•	•	•	•	•	•	•	•	•	•	•	...	...
Myanmar	15	•	•	•	•	•	•	•	•	...	...	...	...	•	•	...	...	...
Nepal - Népal	11	•	•	•	•	•	•	•	•	•	•	...	...	•	•	...	...	...
Oman	25	•	•	•	•	•	•	•	•	•	•	•	•	•	•	...	...	...
Pakistan[5]	16	•	•	...	•	•	•	•	•	•	•	...	•	•	•	...	...	...
Philippines	24	•	•	•	•	•	•	•	•	•	•	•	•	•	•	...	...	...
Qatar	29	•	•	•	•	•	•	•	•	•	•	•	•	•	•	•	•	...
Republic of Korea - République de Corée	28	•	•	•	•	•	•	•	•	•	•	•	•	•	•	•	...	...
Saudi Arabia - Arabie saoudite	19	•	•	•	•	•	•	•	•	•	•	•	•	•	•	...	...	...
Singapore - Singapour	29	•	•	•	•	•	•	•	•	•	•	...	•	•	•	•	...	•
Sri Lanka	20	•	•	•	•	•	•	•	•	•	•	•	•	•	•	...	...	...
State of Palestine - État de Palestine	18	•	•	•	•	•	•	•	•	•	•	...	...	•	•	...	...	...
Syrian Arab Republic - République arabe syrienne	14	•	•	•	•	•	•	•	•	•	•	...	...	•	•	...	...	...

Table A. Demographic Yearbook 2012 synoptic table: Availability of data by country/area, table and sex, where applicable
Tableau A. Tableau synoptique de l'Annuaire démographique 2012 : Disponibilité des données par pays ou zone, tableau et le sexe, si disponible (continued - suite)

Continent and country or area / Continent et pays ou zone	Infant and maternal mortality - Mortalité infantile et mortalité liée à la maternité				General mortality - Mortalité générale					Nuptiality and divorces - Nuptialité et divortialité			
	15	16 Total	16 M/F	17	18	19 Total	19 M/F	20	21	22	23	24	25
AMERICA, SOUTH - AMÉRIQUE DU SUD													
Brazil - Brésil	•	•	•	•	•	•	•	•	•	•	•	...	•
Chile - Chili	•	•	•	•	•	•	•	•	•	•	•	•	•
Colombia - Colombie	•	•	•	•	•	•	...	•	...	...	...	...	...
Ecuador - Équateur	•	•	•	•	•	•	...	•	•	•	•	•	•
Falkland Islands (Malvinas) - Îles Falkland (Malvinas)	...	...	...	...	...	...	...	...	...	...	...	...	...
French Guiana - Guyane française	...	•	...	...	...	•	...	...	•	...	...	•	...
Guyana	...	...	•	•	•	•	...	•	•	•	•	•	...
Paraguay	•	•	...	•	•	•	...	•	•	•	•	•	...
Peru - Pérou	•	•	•	•	•	•	•	•	•	•	•	•	...
Suriname	•	•	•	•	•	•	•	•	•	•	•	•	•
Uruguay	•	•	•	•	•	•	...	•	•	•	•	•	•
Venezuela (Bolivarian Republic of) - Venezuela (République bolivarienne du)	...	•	•	•	•	•	...	•	•	•	•	•	•
ASIA - ASIE													
Afghanistan	...	...	...	...	...	...	...	•	...	...	...	...	...
Armenia - Arménie	•	•	•	•	•	•	•	•	•	•	•	•	•
Azerbaijan - Azerbaïdjan	•	•	•	•	•	•	•	•	•	•	•	•	•
Bahrain - Bahreïn	•	•	•	•	•	•	•	•	•	•	•	•	•
Bangladesh	•	•	•	•	•	•	•	...	•	•	•	•	...
Bhutan - Bhoutan	...	...	...	...	•	•	•	•	•	...	...	...	...
Brunei Darussalam - Brunéi Darussalam	•	...	...	•	•	•	•	•	•	•	•	•	•
Cambodia - Cambodge	...	...	...	•	•	•	•	•	•	•	•	•	...
China - Chine[2]	•	...	...	•	•	•	•	•	•	•	•	•	•
China, Hong Kong SAR - Chine, Hong Kong RAS	•	•	•	•	•	•	•	•	•	•	•	•	•
China, Macao SAR - Chine, Macao RAS	•	•	•	...	•	•	•	•	•	•	•	•	•
Cyprus - Chypre	•	•	•	•	•	•	•	...	•	•	•	•	•
Democratic People's Republic of Korea - République populaire démocratique de Corée	•	...	...	...	•	•	•	•	...	...	...	...	...
Georgia - Géorgie	•	•	•	•	•	•	•	•	•	•	•	•	•
India - Inde[3]	•	...	...	•	...	...	...	•	•	•	•	•	...
Indonesia - Indonésie	...	...	...	...	...	...	...	•	•	•	...	•	...
Iran (Islamic Republic of) - Iran (République islamique d')	...	...	...	...	•	•	•	•	•	•	•	•	•
Iraq	...	...	...	•	...	...	...	•	...	•	•	•	...
Israel - Israël[4]	•	•	•	•	•	•	•	•	•	•	•	•	•
Japan - Japon	•	•	•	•	•	•	•	•	•	•	•	•	•
Jordan - Jordanie	...	...	...	•	•	•	•	•	•	•	•	•	•
Kazakhstan	•	•	•	•	•	•	•	•	•	•	•	•	•
Kuwait - Koweït	•	•	•	•	•	•	•	•	•	•	•	•	•
Kyrgyzstan - Kirghizstan	•	•	•	•	•	•	•	•	•	•	•	•	•
Lao People's Democratic Republic - République démocratique populaire lao	...	...	...	...	...	...	...	•	...	...	...	•	...
Lebanon - Liban	...	...	...	...	•	...	...	...	...	...	...	•	...
Malaysia - Malaisie	•	•	•	•	•	•	...	...	•	...	...	•	...
Maldives	•	•	•	•	•	•	•	...	•	...	...	•	...
Mongolia - Mongolie	•	...	...	...	•	•	•	...	•	•	•	•	•
Myanmar	•	...	...	...	•	•	•	...	•	...	...	...	...
Nepal - Népal	...	...	...	•	•	•	•	...	•	•	•	•	...
Oman	•	•	•	•	•	•	•	...	•	•	•	•	•
Pakistan[5]	...	•	•	•	•	•	...	...	•	•	•	•	...
Philippines	•	•	•	•	•	•	•	...	•	•	•	•	•
Qatar	•	•	•	•	•	•	•	•	•	•	•	•	•
Republic of Korea - République de Corée	•	•	•	•	•	•	•	•	•	•	•	•	•
Saudi Arabia - Arabie saoudite	•	•	•	•	•	•	•	...	•	•	•	•	...
Singapore - Singapour	•	•	•	•	•	•	•	...	•	•	•	•	•
Sri Lanka	•	...	...	•	•	•	•	...	•	•	•	•	•
State of Palestine - État de Palestine	...	•	•	•	...	•	•	•	•	•	•	•	•
Syrian Arab Republic - République arabe syrienne	...	...	...	...	•	...	...	...	...	•	•	•	...

Table A. Demographic Yearbook 2012 synoptic table: Availability of data by country/area, table and sex, where applicable
Tableau A. Tableau synoptique de l'Annuaire démographique 2012 : Disponibilité des données par pays ou zone, tableau et le sexe, si disponible (continued - suite)

General topic and table number - Sujet général et numéro de tableau

Continent and country or area / Continent et pays ou zone	Table totals	Summary - Apercu 3 Total	3 M/F	4	5	Population 6 Total¹	6 M/F	7 Total	7 M/F	8 Total	8 M/F	9	Fertility 10 Total	10 M/F	11	Foetal mort. 12	13	14
ASIA - ASIE																		
Tajikistan - Tadjikistan	26	•	•	•	•	•	•	•	•	•	•	•	...	...	•	•	•	•
Thailand - Thaïlande	24	•	•	•	•	•	•	•	•	•	•	•	•	...	•	...	•	...
Timor-Leste	9	•	•	...	•	•	...	•	•	...	•	...	•	...	•	...	•	...
Turkey - Turquie	23	•	•	•	•	•	•	•	•	...	•	•	•	•	•	•	•	...
Turkmenistan - Turkménistan	8	•	•	...	•	•	•	•	...	...	•	...	•	...	•	...	...	...
United Arab Emirates - Émirats arabes unis	20	•	•	•	•	•	•	•	•	•	•	•	...	•	...	•	...	...
Uzbekistan - Ouzbékistan	14	•	•	•	•	...	...	•	•	•	•	•	...	•	...	•	...	...
Viet Nam	10	•	•	•	•	•	•	•	...	...	...	•	...	•	...	...	...	...
Yemen - Yémen	13	•	•	•	•	•	•	•	•	•	•	...	•	...	•	...	...	...
EUROPE																		
Åland Islands - Îles d'Åland	27	•	•	•	•	•	•	•	•	•	•	•	•	•	•	•	•	•
Albania - Albanie	25	•	•	•	•	•	•	•	•	•	•	•	•	•	•	•	...	...
Andorra - Andorre	21	•	•	•	•	•	•	•	•	•	•	•	•	•	•	•	...	...
Austria - Autriche	28	•	•	•	•	•	•	•	•	•	•	•	•	•	•	•	...	...
Belarus - Bélarus	30	•	•	•	•	•	•	•	•	•	•	•	•	•	•	•	•	...
Belgium - Belgique	30	•	•	•	•	•	•	•	•	•	•	•	•	•	•	•	•	•
Bosnia and Herzegovina - Bosnie-Herzégovine	24	•	•	•	•	•	•	•	•	...	...	•	•	•	•	•	•	•
Bulgaria - Bulgarie	30	•	•	•	•	•	•	•	•	•	•	•	•	•	•	•	•	•
Croatia - Croatie	28	•	•	•	•	•	•	•	•	•	•	•	•	•	•	•	•	•
Czech Republic - République tchèque	30	•	•	•	•	•	•	•	•	•	•	•	•	•	•	•	•	•
Denmark - Danemark	30	•	•	•	•	•	•	•	•	•	•	•	•	•	•	•	•	•
Estonia - Estonie	30	•	•	•	•	•	•	•	•	•	•	•	•	•	•	•	•	•
Faeroe Islands - Îles Féroé	19	•	•	•	•	•	•	•	•	•	•	•	•	•	...	...	•	•
Finland - Finlande	30	•	•	•	•	•	•	•	•	•	•	•	•	•	•	•	•	•
France	29	•	•	•	•	•	•	•	•	•	...	•	•	•	•	•	•	•
Germany - Allemagne	30	•	•	•	•	•	•	•	•	•	•	•	•	•	•	•	•	•
Gibraltar	15	•	•	•	•	...	...	•	•	•	•	...	...	...	•	...	...	...
Greece - Grèce	30	•	•	•	•	•	•	•	•	•	...	•	•	•	•	•	•	•
Guernsey - Guernesey	12	•	•	•	•	•	•	•	•	...	...	•	•	•	•	•	•	•
Holy See - Saint-Siège	7	•	•	...	•	•	•	•	•	...	...	•	•	•	...	•	•	•
Hungary - Hongrie	30	•	•	•	•	•	•	•	•	•	•	•	•	•	•	•	•	•
Iceland - Islande	30	•	•	•	•	•	•	•	•	•	•	•	•	•	•	•	•	•
Ireland - Irlande	27	•	•	•	•	•	•	•	•	•	•	•	•	•	•	•	...	...
Isle of Man - Île de Man	15	•	•	...	•	•	•	•	•	•	•	...	•	•	•	•	•	...
Italy - Italie	30	•	•	•	•	•	•	•	•	•	•	•	•	•	•	•	•	•
Jersey	14	•	•	•	•	•	•	•	•	•	•	•	•	•	•	...	•	...
Latvia - Lettonie	30	•	•	•	•	•	•	•	•	•	•	•	•	•	•	•	•	•
Liechtenstein	23	•	•	•	•	•	•	•	•	•	•	•	•	•	•	•	•	•
Lithuania - Lituanie	30	•	•	•	•	•	•	•	•	•	•	•	•	•	•	•	•	•
Luxembourg	27	•	•	•	•	•	•	•	•	•	...	•	•	•	•	•	•	...
Malta - Malte	28	•	•	•	•	•	•	•	•	•	•	•	•	•	•	•	•	...
Monaco	9	•	•	...	•	•	•	•	•	•	•	...	...	...	•	•	•	•
Montenegro - Monténégro	28	•	•	•	•	•	•	•	•	•	•	•	•	•	•	•	•	•
Netherlands - Pays-Bas	27	•	•	•	•	•	•	•	•	•	•	•	•	•	•	•	•	•
Norway - Norvège	28	•	...	•	•	•	•	•	•	...	•	•	•	•	•	•	•	•
Poland - Pologne	30	•	•	•	•	•	•	•	•	•	•	•	•	•	•	•	•	•
Portugal	29	•	•	•	•	•	•	•	•	•	•	•	•	•	•	•	•	...
Republic of Moldova - République de Moldova	29	•	•	•	•	•	•	•	•	•	•	•	•	•	•	•	...	•
Romania - Roumanie	30	•	•	•	•	•	•	•	•	•	•	•	•	•	•	•	•	•
Russian Federation - Fédération de Russie	30	•	•	•	•	•	•	•	•	•	•	•	•	•	•	•	•	•
San Marino - Saint-Marin	26	•	•	•	•	•	•	•	•	•	•	•	•	•	•	•	...	...
Serbia - Serbie	30	•	•	•	•	•	•	•	•	•	•	•	•	•	•	•	•	•
Slovakia - Slovaquie	30	•	•	•	•	•	•	•	•	•	•	•	•	•	•	•	•	•
Slovenia - Slovénie	30	•	•	•	•	•	•	•	•	•	•	•	•	•	•	•	•	•
Spain - Espagne	30	•	•	•	•	•	•	•	•	•	•	•	•	•	•	•	•	•
Svalbard and Jan Mayen Islands - Îles Svalbard et Jan Mayen	3	•	•	...	•	...	•	•	...	...	...	...	...	...	•	•	•	•
Sweden - Suède	30	•	•	•	•	•	•	•	•	•	•	•	•	•	•	•	•	•
Switzerland - Suisse	30	•	•	•	•	•	•	•	•	•	•	•	•	•	•	•	•	•

Table A. Demographic Yearbook 2012 synoptic table: Availability of data by country/area, table and sex, where applicable
Tableau A. Tableau synoptique de l'Annuaire démographique 2012 : Disponibilité des données par pays ou zone, tableau et le sexe, si disponible (continued - suite)

Continent and country or area / Continent et pays ou zone	Infant and maternal mortality - Mortalité infantile et mortalité liée à la maternité				General mortality - Mortalité générale					Nuptiality and divorces - Nuptialité et divortialité			
	15	16 Total	16 M/F	17	18	19 Total	19 M/F	20	21	22	23	24	25
ASIA - ASIE													
Tajikistan - Tadjikistan	•	•	•	•	•	•	•	...	•	•	•	•	•
Thailand - Thaïlande	•	•	•	•	•	•	•	•	•	...	•	...	
Timor-Leste	...	...	...	...	...	...	...	...	...	...	...	...	...
Turkey - Turquie	•	•	•	...	•	•	•	...	...	•	•	...	•
Turkmenistan - Turkménistan	...	...	...	...	...	...	...	...	...	...	...	...	...
United Arab Emirates - Émirats arabes unis	...	...	...	...	•	•	•	...	...	...	...	...	...
Uzbekistan - Ouzbékistan	...	...	...	•	•	•	•	...	...	...	•	...	
Viet Nam	...	...	...	...	...	...	...	•	...	...	...	...	
Yemen - Yémen	...	...	...	...	•	...	...	...	...	...	...	...	
EUROPE													
Åland Islands - Îles d'Åland	•	•	•	...	•	•	•	...	•	•	•	•	...
Albania - Albanie	•	•	...	•	•	•	...	•	•	•	...		
Andorra - Andorre	•	•	•	•	•	•	•	...	•	•	•	•	...
Austria - Autriche	•	•	•	•	•	•	•	•	•	•	•	•	•
Belarus - Bélarus	•	•	•	•	•	•	•	•	•	•	•	•	•
Belgium - Belgique	•	•	•	•	•	•	•	•	•	•	•	•	•
Bosnia and Herzegovina - Bosnie-Herzégovine	•	•	•	...	•	•	•	...	•	•	•	...	
Bulgaria - Bulgarie	•	•	•	•	•	•	•	•	•	•	•	•	•
Croatia - Croatie	•	•	•	•	•	•	•	•	•	•	•	•	•
Czech Republic - République tchèque	•	•	•	•	•	•	•	•	•	•	•	•	•
Denmark - Danemark	•	•	•	•	•	•	•	•	•	•	•	•	•
Estonia - Estonie	•	•	•	•	•	•	•	•	•	•	•	•	•
Faeroe Islands - Îles Féroé	...	...	...	...	•	•	•	...	...	...	...	...	...
Finland - Finlande	•	•	•	•	•	•	•	•	•	•	•	•	•
France	•	•	•	•	•	•	•	•	•	•	•	•	•
Germany - Allemagne	•	•	•	•	•	•	•	•	•	•	•	•	•
Gibraltar	...	•	•	•	...	...	•	...	...	...	...	...	...
Greece - Grèce	•	•	•	•	•	•	•	•	•	•	•	•	•
Guernsey - Guernesey	...	...	...	...	•	•	•	...	...	...	...	...	...
Holy See - Saint-Siège	...	...	...	...	...	...	...	...	...	...	...	...	...
Hungary - Hongrie	•	•	•	•	•	•	•	•	•	•	•	•	•
Iceland - Islande	•	•	•	•	•	•	•	•	•	•	•	•	•
Ireland - Irlande	•	•	•	•	•	•	•	•	•	•	•	•	...
Isle of Man - Île de Man	...	•	•	...	•	•	•	...	•	•	•	•	•
Italy - Italie	•	•	•	•	•	•	•	•	•	•	•	•	•
Jersey	...	...	...	...	•	...	...	...	...	...	...	...	...
Latvia - Lettonie	•	•	•	•	•	•	•	•	•	•	•	•	•
Liechtenstein	•	•	•	•	•	•	•	...	...	•	•	•	•
Lithuania - Lituanie	•	•	•	•	•	•	•	•	•	•	•	•	•
Luxembourg	•	•	•	•	•	•	•	•	•	•	•	•	•
Malta - Malte	•	•	•	•	•	•	•	•	•	•	•	•	•
Monaco	...	...	...	...	...	...	...	...	...	...	...	...	...
Montenegro - Monténégro	•	•	•	•	•	•	•	•	•	•	•	•	•
Netherlands - Pays-Bas	•	•	•	•	•	•	•	•	•	•	•	•	•
Norway - Norvège	•	•	•	•	•	•	•	•	•	•	•	•	•
Poland - Pologne	•	•	•	•	•	•	•	•	•	•	•	•	•
Portugal	•	•	•	•	•	•	•	•	•	•	•	•	•
Republic of Moldova - République de Moldova	•	•	•	•	•	•	•	•	•	•	•	•	•
Romania - Roumanie	•	•	•	•	•	•	•	•	•	•	•	•	•
Russian Federation - Fédération de Russie	•	•	•	•	•	•	•	•	•	•	•	•	•
San Marino - Saint-Marin	•	•	•	•	•	•	•	...	•	•	•	•	•
Serbia - Serbie	•	•	•	•	•	•	•	•	•	•	•	•	•
Slovakia - Slovaquie	•	•	•	•	•	•	•	•	•	•	•	•	•
Slovenia - Slovénie	•	•	•	•	•	•	•	•	•	•	•	•	•
Spain - Espagne	•	•	•	•	•	•	•	•	•	•	•	•	•
Svalbard and Jan Mayen Islands - Îles Svalbard et Jan Mayen	...	...	...	...	...	...	...	...	...	...	...	...	...
Sweden - Suède	•	•	•	•	•	•	•	•	•	•	•	•	•
Switzerland - Suisse	•	•	•	•	•	•	•	•	•	•	•	•	•

Table A. Demographic Yearbook 2012 synoptic table: Availability of data by country/area, table and sex, where applicable
Tableau A. Tableau synoptique de l'Annuaire démographique 2012 : Disponibilité des données par pays ou zone, tableau et le sexe, si disponible (continued - suite)

Continent and country or area / Continent et pays ou zone	Table totals	Summary - Apercu				Population						Fertility - Natalité				Foetal mortality - Mortalité foetale		
		3 Total	3 M/F	4	5	6 Total¹	6 M/F	7 Total	7 M/F	8 Total	8 M/F	9	10 Total	10 M/F	11	12	13	14
EUROPE																		
TFYR of Macedonia - L'ex-R. y. de Macédoine	28	•	•	•	•	•	•	•	•	•	•	•	•	•	•	•	...	...
Ukraine	29	•	•	•	•	•	•	•	•	•	•	•	•	•	...	•	•	...
United Kingdom of Great Britain and Northern Ireland - Royaume-Uni de Grande-Bretagne et d'Irlande du Nord	30	•	•	•	•	•	•	•	•	•	•	•	•	•	•	•	•	•
OCEANIA - OCÉANIE																		
American Samoa - Samoas américaines	15	•	•	•	•	•	•	•	•	•	•	•	•	...	...	...	...	...
Australia - Australie	28	•	•	•	•	•	•	•	•	•	•	•	•	•	•	•	•	...
Cook Islands - Îles Cook	17	•	•	•	•	•	•	•	...	•	•	•	•	...	•	...	...	...
Fiji - Fidji	19	•	•	•	•	•	•	•	•	•	•	•	•	•	•	...	...	...
French Polynesia - Polynésie française	15	•	•	•	•	•	•	•	•	•	•	•	•	...	•	...	...	...
Guam	23	•	•	•	•	•	•	•	•	•	•	•	•	...	•	•	•	...
Kiribati	8	•	•	...	...	•	•	•	•	...	...	...	...	...	•	...	...	...
Marshall Islands - Îles Marshall	13	•	•	...	•	•	•	•	•	...	...	...	...	...	•	...	...	...
Micronesia (Federated States of) - Micronésie (États fédérés de)	11	•	•	...	•	•	•	•	•	•	•	...	•	...	...	...	...	...
Nauru	2	•	...	...	...	...	...	...	...	...	...	...	...	...	...	...	...	...
New Caledonia - Nouvelle-Calédonie	23	•	•	•	•	•	•	•	•	•	•	•	•	...	•	•	...	...
New Zealand - Nouvelle-Zélande	30	•	•	•	•	•	•	•	•	•	•	•	•	•	•	•	•	•
Niue - Nioué	17	•	•	•	•	•	•	•	•	•	•	...	•	...	•	...	...	...
Norfolk Island - Île Norfolk	12	•	•	•	•	•	•	•	•	•	•	...	•	...	...	...	...	...
Northern Mariana Islands - Îles Mariannes septentrionales	16	•	•	•	•	•	•	•	•	•	•	...	•	...	•	...	...	...
Palau - Palaos	14	•	•	...	•	•	•	•	•	•	•	...	•	...	•	•	...	...
Papua New Guinea - Papouasie-Nouvelle-Guinée	7	•	•	...	...	•	•	•	...	•	•	...	•	...	...	...	...	...
Pitcairn	12	•	•	...	...	•	•	•	•	•	•	...	•	...	...	...	...	...
Samoa	19	•	•	•	•	•	•	•	•	•	•	...	•	•	•	...	...	...
Solomon Islands - Îles Salomon	9	•	•	...	•	•	•	•	•	•	•	...	•	...	...	...	...	...
Tokelau - Tokélaou	6	•	•	...	...	•	•	•	•	...	...	...	...	...	•	...	...	...
Tonga	14	•	•	•	•	•	•	•	•	•	•	•	•	...	•	...	...	...
Tuvalu	11	•	•	...	•	•	•	•	•	•	•	•	•	•	•	...	...	...
Vanuatu	9	•	•	...	•	•	•	...	...	•	•	...	•	...	...	...	...	...
Wallis and Futuna Islands - Îles Wallis et Futuna	14	•	•	•	...	•	•	...	...	•	•	...	•	•	...	...	...	...

Table A. Demographic Yearbook 2012 synoptic table: Availability of data by country/area, table and sex, where applicable
Tableau A. Tableau synoptique de l'Annuaire démographique 2012 : Disponibilité des données par pays ou zone, tableau et le sexe, si disponible (continued - suite)

Continent and country or area Continent et pays ou zone	General topic and table number - Sujet général et numéro de tableau												
	Infant and maternal mortality - Mortalité infantile et mortalité liée à la maternité				General mortality - Mortalité générale				Nuptiality and divorces - Nuptialité et divortialité			
	15	16 Total	16 M/F	17	18	19 Total	19 M/F	20	21	22	23	24	25
EUROPE													
TFYR of Macedonia - L'ex-R. y. de Macédoine	•	•	•	•	•	•	•	•	•	•	•	•	•
Ukraine	•	•	•	•	•	•	•	•	•	•	•	•	•
United Kingdom of Great Britain and Northern Ireland - Royaume-Uni de Grande-Bretagne et d'Irlande du Nord	•	•	•	•	•	•	•	•	•	•	•	•	•
OCEANIA - OCÉANIE													
American Samoa - Samoas américaines	...	...	...	...	...	•	•	...	•	...	...	...	...
Australia - Australie	•	•	•	•	•	•	•	•	•	•	•	...	...
Cook Islands - Îles Cook	•	...	...	...	•	•	•	...	•	...	•	...	...
Fiji - Fidji	•	...	...	•	•	•	•	...	•	...	•	...	...
French Polynesia - Polynésie française	•	•	...	...	•	...	...	...	•	...	•	...	...
Guam	•	...	...	...	•	•	•	...	•	...	...	...	...
Kiribati	...	...	...	...	...	•	...	...	•	...	...	...	...
Marshall Islands - Îles Marshall	...	...	...	...	•	•	•	...	•	...	...	...	...
Micronesia (Federated States of) - Micronésie (États fédérés de)	...	...	...	...	...	•	...	...	•	...	...	...	...
Nauru	...	...	...	...	...	•	...	...	•	...	...	...	...
New Caledonia - Nouvelle-Calédonie	•	•	•	...	•	•	•	...	•	•	•	...	...
New Zealand - Nouvelle-Zélande	•	•	•	•	•	•	•	•	•	•	•	•	•
Niue - Nioué	•	...	...	•	•	•	•	...	•	•	•	...	...
Norfolk Island - Île Norfolk	...	...	...	...	•	...	...	...	•	...	...	...	...
Northern Mariana Islands - Îles Mariannes septentrionales	•	...	...	...	•	•	•	...	•	...	...	...	...
Palau - Palaos	...	...	...	...	•	•	•	...	•	...	...	...	...
Papua New Guinea - Papouasie-Nouvelle-Guinée	...	...	...	...	...	...	...	...	•	...	...	...	...
Pitcairn	...	...	...	...	...	•	...	...	...	...	...	...	...
Samoa	...	...	...	...	•	•	•	...	•	•	•	•	•
Solomon Islands - Îles Salomon	...	...	...	...	•	•	•	...	•	...	...	...	...
Tokelau - Tokélaou	...	...	...	...	...	•	...	...	•	...	...	...	...
Tonga	...	...	...	...	...	•	•	...	•	...	...	...	...
Tuvalu	...	...	...	...	...	•	•	...	•	...	...	...	...
Vanuatu	...	...	...	...	...	•	...	...	•	...	...	...	...
Wallis and Futuna Islands - Îles Wallis et Futuna	...	...	...	•	•	•	...	...	•	•	•	...	...

FOOTNOTES - NOTES

* Data presented in the table. - Les données présentées dans le tableau.

... Data not available. - Données non disponibles.

[1] Including countries with data on total population only and without data on urban population. The number of countries with data on urban population for both sexes and also by sex presented in this issue of the Demographic Yearbook is 138 and 123 respectively. - Y compris les pays avec des données sur la population totale mais pas sur la population urbaine. Le nombre de pays disposant de données sur la population urbaine pour les deux sexes et aussi par sexe présentées dans cette édition de l'Annuaire démographique est de 138 et 123 respectivement.

[2] For statistical purposes, the data for China do not include those for the Hong Kong Special Administrative Region (Hong Kong SAR), Macao special Administrative Region (Macao SAR) and Taiwan province of China. - Pour la présentation des statistiques, les données pour Chine ne comprennent pas la Région Administrative Spéciale de Hong Kong (Hong Kong RAS), la Région Administrative Spéciale de Macao (Macao RAS) et Taïwan province de Chine.

[3] Including data for the Indian-held part of Jammu and Kashmir, the final status of which has not yet been determined. - Y compris les données pour la partie du Jammu et du Cachemire occupée par l'Inde dont le statut définitif n'a pas encore été déterminé.

[4] Including data for East Jerusalem and Israeli residents in certain other territories under occupation by Israeli military forces since June 1967. - Y compris les données pour Jérusalem-Est et les résidents israéliens dans certains autres territoires occupés depuis 1967 par les forces armées israéliennes.

[5] Excluding data for the Pakistan-held part of Jammu and Kashmir, the final status of which has not yet been determined. - Non compris les données concernant la partie du Jammu et Cachemire occupée par le Pakistan dont le statut définitif n'a pas été déterminé.

Table 1 – *Demographic Yearbook 2012*

Table 1 presents for the world and major areas and regions estimates of the order of magnitude of population size, rates of population increase, crude birth and death rates, surface area as well as population density.

Description of variables: Estimates of world population by major areas and by regions are presented for 1960, 1970, 1980, 1990, 2000, 2010 and 2012. Average annual percentage rates of population growth, crude birth and crude death rates are shown for the period from 2010 to 2015. Surface area in square kilometers and population density estimates relate to 2012.

All population estimates and rates presented in this table were prepared by the Population Division of the United Nations Department of Economic and Social Affairs, and have been published in the *2012 Revision of World Population Prospects*[1].

The scheme of regionalization used for these estimates is described below. Although some continental totals are given, and all can be derived, this table presents six major areas that are so drawn as to obtain greater homogeneity in sizes of population, types of demographic circumstances and accuracy of demographic statistics. Five of the major areas are subdivided into a total of 20 regions, which are arranged within the major areas; these regions together with Northern America, which is not subdivided, make a total of 21 regions.

The major areas of Northern America and Latin America and the Caribbean are distinguished, rather than the conventional continents of North America and South America, because population trends in the middle American mainland and the Caribbean region more closely resemble those of South America than those of America north of Mexico. Data for the traditional continents of North and South America can be obtained by adding Central America and Caribbean region to Northern America and deducting from Latin America. Latin America, as defined here, has somewhat wider limits than it would be if defined only to include the Spanish-speaking, French-speaking and Portuguese-speaking countries.

The average annual percentage rates of population growth are calculated by the Population Division of the United Nations using an exponential rate of increase.

Crude birth and crude death rates are expressed in terms of the average annual number of births and deaths, respectively, per 1 000 mid-year population. These rates are estimated.

Surface area totals are estimated by the Population Division of the United Nations.

Computation: Density, calculated by the Statistics Division of the United Nations, is the number of persons in the 2012 total population per square kilometer of total surface area.

Reliability of data: With the exception of surface area, all data are set in *italic* type to indicate their conjectural quality.

Limitations: The estimated orders of magnitude of population and surface area are subject to all the basic limitations set forth in connection with table 3, and to the same qualifications set forth for population and surface area statistics in sections 3 and 2.4 of the Technical Notes, respectively.

Likewise, rates of population increase and density index are affected by the limitations of the original figures. However, it may be noted that, in compiling data for regional and major areas totals, errors in the components may tend to compensate each other and the resulting aggregates may be more reliable than the quality of the individual components would imply.

Because of their estimated character, many of the birth and death rates shown should also be considered only as orders of magnitude, and not as measures of the true level of fertility or mortality.

In interpreting the population densities, one should consider that some of the regions include large segments of land that are uninhabitable or barely habitable, and density values calculated as described make no allowance for this, nor for differences in patterns of land settlement.

Composition of major areas and regions

AFRICA

Eastern Africa
Burundi
Comoros
Djibouti
Eritrea
Ethiopia
Kenya
Madagascar
Malawi
Mauritius
Mayotte
Mozambique
Réunion
Rwanda
Seychelles
Somalia
South Sudan
Uganda
United Republic of Tanzania
Zambia
Zimbabwe

Middle Africa
Angola
Cameroon
Central African Republic
Chad
Congo
Democratic Republic of the
  Congo
Equatorial Guinea
Gabon
Sao Tome and Principe

Northern Africa
Algeria
Egypt
Libyan Arab Jamahiriya
Morocco
Sudan
Tunisia
Western Sahara

Southern Africa
Botswana
Lesotho
Namibia
South Africa
Swaziland

Western Africa
Benin
Burkina Faso
Cabo Verde
Côte d'Ivoire
Gambia

Ghana
Guinea
Guinea-Bissau
Liberia
Mali
Mauritania
Niger
Nigeria
Saint Helena
Senegal
Sierra Leone
Togo

ASIA

Eastern Asia
China
China, Hong Kong SAR
China, Macao SAR
Democratic People's
  Republic of Korea
Japan
Mongolia
Republic of Korea

South-Central Asia
Afghanistan
Bangladesh
Bhutan
India
Iran (Islamic Republic of)
Kazakhstan
Kyrgyzstan
Maldives
Nepal
Pakistan
Sri Lanka
Tajikistan
Turkmenistan
Uzbekistan

South-Eastern Asia
Brunei Darussalam
Cambodia
Indonesia
Lao People's Democratic
  Republic
Malaysia
Myanmar
Philippines
Singapore
Thailand
Timor Leste
Viet Nam

Western Asia
Armenia
Azerbaijan

Bahrain
Cyprus
Georgia
Iraq
Israel
Jordan
Kuwait
Lebanon
Oman
Qatar
Saudi Arabia
State of Palestine
Syrian Arab Republic
Turkey
United Arab Emirates
Yemen

EUROPE

Eastern Europe
Belarus
Bulgaria
Czech Republic
Hungary
Poland
Republic of Moldova
Romania
Russian Federation
Slovakia
Ukraine

Northern Europe
Åland Islands
Denmark
Estonia
Faeroe Islands
Finland
Guernsey
Iceland
Ireland
Isle of Man
Jersey
Latvia
Lithuania
Norway
Sweden
United Kingdom of Great Britain
  and Northern Ireland

Southern Europe
Albania
Andorra
Bosnia and Herzegovina
Croatia
Gibraltar
Greece
Holy See

Italy
Malta
Montenegro
Portugal
San Marino
Serbia
Slovenia
Spain
TFYR of Macedonia

Western Europe
Austria
Belgium
France
Germany
Liechtenstein
Luxembourg
Monaco
Netherlands
Switzerland

**LATIN AMERICA
  and the CARIBBEAN**

Caribbean
Anguilla
Antigua and Barbuda
Aruba
Bahamas
Barbados
Bonaire, Saba and Sint Eustatius
British Virgin Islands
Cayman Islands
Cuba
Curaçao
Dominica
Dominican Republic
Grenada
Guadaloupe
Haiti
Jamaica
Martinique

Montserrat
Puerto Rico
Saint Kitts and Nevis
Saint Lucia
Saint Vincent and the
  Grenadines
Sint Maarten (Dutch part)
Trinidad and Tobago
Turks and Caicos Islands
United States Virgin
  Islands

Central America
Belize
Costa Rica
El Salvador
Guatemala
Honduras
Mexico
Nicaragua
Panama

South America
Argentina
Bolivia (Plurinational State of)
Brazil
Chile
Colombia
Ecuador
Falkland Islands (Malvinas)
French Guiana
Guyana
Paraguay
Peru
Suriname
Uruguay
Venezuela (Bolivarian Republic of)

NORTHERN AMERICA

Bermuda

Canada
Greenland
Saint Pierre and Miquelon
United States of America

OCEANIA

Australia and New Zealand
Australia
New Zealand
Norfolk Island

Melanesia
Fiji
New Caledonia
Papua New Guinea
Solomon Islands
Vanuatu

Micronesia
Guam
Kiribati
Marshall Islands
Micronesia (Federated States of)
Nauru
Northern Mariana Islands
Palau

Polynesia
American Samoa
Cook Islands
French Polynesia
Niue
Pitcairn
Samoa
Tokelau
Tonga
Tuvalu
Wallis and Futuna Islands

---

[1] United Nations, Department of Economic and Social Affairs, Population Division (2013). *World Population Prospects: The 2012 Revision. Extended dataset in Excel and ASCII formats, DVD-ROM edition* (United Nations publication, ST/ESA/SER.A/334).

Tableau 1 – *Annuaire démographique 2012*

Le tableau 1 présente, pour l'ensemble du monde et les grandes zones et régions, des estimations concernant l'ordre de grandeur de la population, les taux d'accroissement démographique, les taux bruts de natalité et de mortalité, la superficie et la densité de peuplement.

Description des variables : des estimations de la population mondiale par grandes zones et régions sont présentées pour 1960, 1970, 1980, 1990, 2000 et 2010 ainsi que pour 2012. Les taux annuels moyens d'accroissement de la population et les taux bruts de natalité et de mortalité portent sur la période allant de 2010 à 2015. Les indications concernant la superficie exprimée en kilomètres carrés et les estimations de la densité de population se rapportent à 2012.

Toutes les estimations de population et les taux de natalité, taux de mortalité et taux annuels d'accroissement de la population qui sont présentés dans le tableau 1 ont été établis par la Division de la population du Département des affaires économiques et sociales de l'Organisation des Nations Unies, et ont été publiés dans les *Perspectives de la population mondiale : La révision de 2012*[1].

Bien que l'on ait donné certains totaux pour les continents (tous les autres pouvant être calculés), on a réparti le monde en six grandes zones qui ont été découpées de manière à obtenir une plus grande homogénéité du point de vue des dimensions de population, des types de situations démographiques et de l'exactitude des statistiques démographiques.

Cinq de ces six grandes zones ont été subdivisées en 20 régions. Avec l'Amérique septentrionale, qui n'est pas subdivisée, on arrive à un total de 21 régions.

Au lieu de faire la distinction classique entre l'Amérique du Nord et l'Amérique du Sud, on a choisi d'opérer une comparaison entre l'Amérique septentrionale et l'Amérique latine et Caraïbes, parce que les tendances démographiques dans la partie continentale de l'Amérique centrale et dans la région des Caraïbes se rapprochent davantage de celles de l'Amérique du Sud que de celles de l'Amérique au nord du Mexique. On obtient les données pour les continents traditionnels de l'Amérique du Nord et de l'Amérique du Sud en extrayant les données concernant l'Amérique centrale et les Caraïbes de celles relatives à l'Amérique latine et en les regroupant avec celles relatives à l'Amérique septentrionale. L'Amérique latine ainsi définie a par conséquent des limites plus larges que celles des pays ou zones de langues espagnole, portugaise et française qui constituent l'Amérique latine au sens le plus strict du terme.

Les taux annuels moyens d'accroissement de la population sont calculés par la Division de la population de l'Organisation des Nations Unies en appliquant un taux d'accroissement exponentiel.

Les taux bruts de natalité et de mortalité représentent respectivement le nombre annuel moyen de naissances et de décès par millier d'habitants en milieu d'année. Ces taux sont estimatifs.

La superficie totale a été estimée par la Division de la population de l'Organisation des Nations Unies.

Calculs : la densité, calculée par la Division de statistique de l'Organisation des Nations Unies, est égale au rapport entre l'effectif total de la population en 2012 et la superficie totale exprimée en kilomètres carrés.

Fiabilité des données : á l'exception des données concernant la superficie, toutes les données sont reproduites en *italique* pour en faire ressortir le caractère conjectural.

Insuffisance des données : les estimations concernant l'ordre de grandeur de la population et la superficie reposent en partie sur les données du tableau 3 ; elles appellent donc toutes les réserves fondamentales formulées à propos de ce tableau, et celles qui ont été respectivement formulées aux sections 3 et 2.4 des Notes techniques en ce qui concerne les statistiques relatives à la population et à la superficie.

Les taux d'accroissement et les indices de densité de la population se ressentent eux aussi des insuffisances inhérentes aux données de base. Toutefois, il est à noter que, lorsque l'on additionne des données par territoire pour obtenir des totaux régionaux et par grandes zones, les erreurs qu'elles comportent arrivent parfois à s'équilibrer, de sorte que les agrégats obtenus peuvent être un peu plus exacts que chacun des éléments dont on est parti.

Vu leur caractère estimatif, nombre des taux de natalité et de mortalité du tableau 1 doivent être considérés uniquement comme des ordres de grandeur et ne sont pas censés mesurer exactement le niveau de la natalité ou de la mortalité.

Pour interpréter les valeurs de la densité de population, on se souviendra qu'il existe dans certaines des régions de vastes étendues de terres inhabitables ou à peine habitables et que les chiffres calculés selon la méthode indiquée ne tiennent compte ni de ce fait ni des différences de dispersion de la population selon le mode d'habitat.

Composition des grandes zones et régions

AFRIQUE

Afrique orientale
Burundi
Comores
Djibouti
Érythrée
Éthiopie
Kenya
Madagascar
Malawi
Maurice
Mayotte
Mozambique
Ouganda
République-Unie de Tanzanie
Réunion
Rwanda
Seychelles
Somalie
Soudan du Sud
Zambie
Zimbabwe

Afrique centrale
Angola
Cameroun
Congo
Gabon
Guinée équatoriale
République centrafricaine
République démocratique du Congo
Sao Tomé-et-Principe
Tchad

Afrique septentrionale
Algérie
Égypte
Jamahiriya arabe libyenne
Maroc
Sahara occidental
Soudan
Tunisie

Afrique australe
Afrique du Sud
Botswana
Lesotho
Namibie
Swaziland

Afrique occidentale
Bénin
Burkina Faso
Cabo Verde
Côte d'Ivoire
Gambie
Ghana
Guinée
Guinée-Bissau
Libéria
Mali
Mauritanie
Niger
Nigéria
Sainte-Hélène
Sénégal
Sierra Leone
Togo

AMÉRIQUE LATINE ET CARAÏBES

Caraïbes
Anguilla
Antigua-et-Barbuda
Aruba
Bahamas
Barbade
Bonaire, Saint-Eustache et Saba
Cuba
Curaçao
Dominique
Grenade
Guadeloupe
Haïti
Îles Caïmanes
Îles Turques et Caïques
Îles Vierges américaines
Îles Vierges britanniques
Jamaïque
Martinique
Montserrat
Porto Rico
République dominicaine
Saint-Kitts-et-Nevis
Sainte-Lucie
Saint-Martin
(partie néerlandaise)

Saint-Vincent-et-les Grenadines
Trinité-et-Tobago

Amérique centrale
Belize
Costa Rica
El Salvador
Guatemala
Honduras
Mexique
Nicaragua
Panama

Amérique du Sud
Argentine
Bolivie (État plurinational de)
Brésil
Chili
Colombie
Équateur
Guyana
Guyane française
Îles Falkland (Malvinas)
Paraguay
Pérou
Suriname
Uruguay
Venezuela (République bolivarienne du)

AMÉRIQUE SEPTENTRIONALE

Bermudes
Canada
États-Unis d'Amérique
Groenland
Saint-Pierre-et-Miquelon

ASIE

Asie orientale
Chine
Chine, Région administrative spéciale de Hong Kong
Chine, Région administrative spéciale de Macao
Japon
Mongolie
République de Corée

République populaire démocratique de Corée

Asie centrale et Asie du Sud
Afghanistan
Bangladesh
Bhoutan
Inde
Iran (République Islamique d')
Kazakhstan
Kirghizistan
Maldives
Népal
Ouzbékistan
Pakistan
Sri Lanka
Tadjikistan
Turkménistan

Asie du Sud-Est
Brunéi Darussalam
Cambodge
Indonésie
Malaisie
Myanmar
Philippines
République démocratique populaire lao
Singapour
Thaïlande
Timor-Leste
Viet Nam

Asie occidentale
Arabie saoudite
Arménie
Azerbaïdjan
Bahreïn
Chypre
Émirats arabes unis
État de Palestine
Géorgie
Iraq
Israël
Jordanie
Koweït
Liban
Oman
Qatar
République arabe syrienne

Turquie
Yémen

EUROPE

Europe orientale
Bélarus
Bulgarie
Fédération de Russie
Hongrie
Pologne
République de Moldova
République tchèque
Roumanie
Slovaquie
Ukraine

Europe septentrionale
Danemark
Estonie
Finlande
Guernesey
Île de Man
Îles d'Åland
Îles Féroé
Îles Svalbard et Jan Mayen
Irlande
Islande
Jersey
Lettonie
Lituanie
Norvège
Royaume-Uni de Grande-Bretagne et d'Irlande du Nord
Suède

Europe méridionale
Albanie
Andorre
Bosnie-Herzégovine
Croatie
Espagne
Gibraltar
Grèce
Italie
L'ex-R. y. de Macédoine
Malte
Monténégro
Portugal

Saint-Marin
Saint-Siège
Serbie
Slovénie

Europe occidentale
Allemagne
Autriche
Belgique
France
Liechtenstein
Luxembourg
Monaco
Pays-Bas
Suisse

OCÉANIE

Australie et Nouvelle-Zélande
Australie
Île Norfolk
Nouvelle-Zélande

Mélanésie
Fidji
Îles Salomon
Nouvelle-Calédonie
Papouasie-Nouvelle-Guinée
Vanuatu

Micronésie
Guam
Îles Mariannes septentrionales
Îles Marshall
Kiribati
Micronésie (États fédérés de)
Nauru
Palaos

Polynésie
Îles Cook
Îles Wallis et Futuna
Nioué
Pitcairn
Polynésie française
Samoa
Samoa américaines
Tokélaou
Tonga
Tuvalu

NOTE

[1] Organisation des Nations Unies, Département des affaires économiques et sociales, Division de la population (2013). *Perspectives de la population mondiale : La révision de 2012. Ensemble de données étendues en formats Excel et ASCII, edition DVD-ROM* (publication des Nations Unies, ST/ESA/SER.A/334).

1. Population, rate of increase, birth and death rates, surface area and density for the world, major areas and regions: selected years
Population, taux d'accroissement, taux de natalité et taux de mortalité, superficie et densité pour l'ensemble du monde, les régions macro géographiques et les composantes géographiques : diverses années

Major areas and regions Régions macro géographiques et composantes	Mid-year population estimates - Estimations de population au milieu de l'année (millions)							Annual rate of increase - Taux d'accroissement annuel (%)	Crude birth rate - Taux bruts de natalité	Crude death rate - Taux bruts de mortalité	Surface area (km2) - Superficie (km2) (000s)	Density - Densité[1]
	1960	1970	1980	1990	2000	2010	2012	2010-2015			2012	
WORLD TOTAL - ENSEMBLE DU MONDE	3 026.0	3 691.2	4 449.0	5 320.8	6 127.7	6 916.2	7 080.1	1.1	20	8	136 162	52
AFRICA - AFRIQUE	285.3	366.5	478.5	630.0	808.3	1 031.1	1 083.5	2.5	36	10	30 311	36
Eastern Africa - Afrique orientale	84.4	110.5	147.7	198.4	260.0	342.6	362.7	2.8	37	9	7 005	52
Middle Africa - Afrique centrale	31.9	40.5	52.6	70.0	93.8	125.0	132.1	2.7	42	14	6 613	20
Northern Africa - Afrique septentrionale	64.5	84.3	108.2	139.9	169.3	199.6	206.5	1.7	25	7	7 880	26
Southern Africa - Afrique méridionale	19.7	25.5	33.0	42.1	51.4	58.8	59.9	0.8	22	13	2 675	22
Western Africa - Afrique occidentale	84.7	105.7	137.0	179.7	233.8	305.1	322.3	2.7	40	12	6 138	53
LATIN AMERICA AND CARIBBEAN - AMÉRIQUE LATIN ET CARAÏBES	220.4	287.6	364.2	445.2	526.3	596.2	609.8	1.1	18	6	20 546	30
Caribbean - Caraïbes	20.7	25.3	29.7	34.3	38.4	41.6	42.2	0.7	18	8	234	180
Central America - Amérique centrale	51.9	70.7	93.4	115.1	139.6	160.5	165.1	1.4	20	5	2 480	67
South America - Amérique méridionale..................	147.8	191.6	241.0	295.8	348.2	394.0	402.5	1.0	17	6	17 832	23
NORTHERN AMERICA - AMÉRIQUE SEPTENTRIONALE...	204.4	231.4	254.8	282.3	315.4	346.5	352.5	0.8	13	8	21 776	16
ASIA - ASIE	1 694.6	2 128.6	2 634.2	3 213.1	3 717.4	4 165.4	4 254.5	1.0	18	7	31 915	133
Eastern Asia - Asie orientale	794.4	984.0	1 179.6	1 379.4	1 506.6	1 593.6	1 611.9	0.5	13	7	11 799	137
South Central Asia - Asie centrale méridionale......	619.3	777.6	984.5	1 241.7	1 502.9	1 743.1	1 789.9	1.3	21	7	10 791	166
South Eastern Asia - Asie méridionale orientale	214.9	281.1	356.6	443.7	524.4	597.1	611.5	1.2	18	6	4 495	136
Western Asia - Asie occidentale............................	66.1	85.9	113.5	148.2	183.5	231.7	241.2	1.9	22	5	4 831	50
EUROPE	605.5	657.4	694.5	723.2	729.1	740.3	742.0	0.1	11	12	23 049	32
Eastern Europe - Europe orientale........................	253.6	276.2	295.1	310.8	304.5	296.2	294.9	-0.3	11	14	18 814	16
Northern Europe - Europe septentrionale	81.9	87.4	89.9	92.1	94.4	98.8	99.9	0.5	12	10	1 810	55
Southern Europe - Europe méridionale..................	117.7	127.1	138.1	143.4	145.6	154.7	155.6	0.2	10	10	1 317	118
Western Europe - Europe occidentale....................	152.3	166.7	171.3	177.0	184.5	190.6	191.6	0.2	10	10	1 108	173
OCEANIA - OCÉANIA	15.8	19.7	23.0	27.0	31.2	36.7	37.8	1.4	17	7	8 564	4
Australia and New Zealand - Australie et Nouvelle Zélande	12.7	15.7	17.9	20.5	23.1	26.8	27.5	1.3	13	7	8 012	3
Melanesia - Melanésie	2.6	3.3	4.3	5.5	7.0	8.7	9.1	2.0	28	7	541	17
Micronesia	0.2	0.2	0.3	0.4	0.5	0.5	0.5	0.9	20	5	3	168
Polynesia - Polynésie..	0.3	0.4	0.5	0.5	0.6	0.7	0.7	0.7	21	6	8	84

FOOTNOTES - NOTES

[1] Population per square kilometre of surface area. Figures are estimates of population divided by surface area and are not to be considered as either reflecting density in the urban sense or as indicating the supporting power of a territory's land and resources. - Habitants par kilomètre carré. Il s'agit simplement du quotient calculé en divisant la population par la superficie et n'est par considéré comme indiquant la densité au sens urbain du terme ni l'effectif de population que les terres et les ressources du territoire sont capables de nourrir.

Table 2 - *Demographic Yearbook 2012*

Table 2 presents estimates of population and the percentage distribution by age and sex as well as the sex ratio for all ages; data are presented for the world, the six major areas and the twenty regions for 2012.

Description of variables: All population estimates presented in this table are prepared by the Population Division of the United Nations Department of Economic and Social Affairs. These estimates are published (using more detailed age groups) in the *2012 Revision of World Population Prospects*[1].

The scheme of regionalization used for these estimates is discussed in detail in the technical notes for table 1. Age groups presented in this table are: 0-14 years, 15-64 years, and 65 years or over. Sex ratio refers to the number of males per 100 females of all ages.

The percentage distributions and the sex ratios that appear in this table were calculated by the Statistics Division of the United Nations Department of Economic and Social Affairs using the Population Division of the United Nations estimates.

Reliability of data: All data are set in *italic* type to indicate their conjectural quality.

Limitations: The data presented in this table are from the same series of estimates, prepared by the Population Division of the United Nations, presented in table 1. The estimated orders of magnitude of population are subject to all the basic limitations set forth for population statistics in section 3 of the Technical Notes. In brief, because they are estimates, these distributions by broad age groups and sex should be considered only as orders of magnitude. However, in compiling data for regional and major areas' totals, errors in the components tend to compensate each other and the resulting aggregates may be somewhat more reliable than the quality of the individual components would imply.

In addition, data in this table are limited by factors affecting data by age. These factors are described in the technical notes for table 7. Because the age groups presented in this table are so broad, these problems are minimized.

NOTES

[1] United Nations, Department of Economic and Social Affairs, Population Division (2013). *World Population Prospects: The 2012 Revision. Extended dataset in Excel and ASCII formats, DVD-ROM edition* (United Nations publication, ST/ESA/SER.A/334).

Tableau 2 – *Annuaire démographique 2012*

Le tableau 2 présente, pour l'ensemble du monde, les six grandes zones et les vingt régions, des estimations concernant la population en 2012 ainsi que sa répartition en pourcentage selon l'âge et le sexe, et le rapport de masculinité pour tous les âges.

Description des variables : toutes les données figurant dans le tableau 2 ont été établies par la Division de la population du Département des affaires économiques et sociales de l'Organisation des Nations Unies, et ont été publiés dans les *Perspectives de la population mondiale : La révision de 2012*[1].

La classification géographique utilisée pour établir ces estimations est exposée en détail dans les notes techniques relatives au tableau 1. Les groupes d'âge présentés dans ce tableau sont définis comme suit : de 0 à 14 ans, de 15 à 64 ans et 65 ans ou plus. Le rapport de masculinité correspond au nombre d'individus de sexe masculin pour 100 individus de sexe féminin sans considération d'âge.

Les pourcentages et les rapports de masculinité qui sont présentés dans le tableau 2 ont été calculés par la Division de statistique du Département des affaires économiques et sociales de l'Organisation des Nations Unies à partir des estimations établies par la Division de la population de l'Organisation des Nations Unies.

Fiabilité des données : toutes les données figurant dans ce tableau sont reproduites en *italique* pour en faire ressortir le caractère conjectural.

Insuffisance des données : les données de ce tableau appartiennent à la même série d'estimations, établie par la Division de la population de l'Organisation des Nations Unies, que celles qui figurent au tableau 1. Les estimations concernant l'ordre de grandeur de la population appellent donc toutes les réserves fondamentales qui ont été formulées à la section 3 des Notes techniques à propos des statistiques relatives à la population. Sans entrer dans le détail, il convient de préciser que les données relatives à la répartition par grand groupe d'âge et par sexe doivent être considérées uniquement comme des ordres de grandeur en raison de leur caractère estimatif. Toutefois, il est à noter que, lorsque l'on additionne des données par territoire pour obtenir des totaux régionaux et par grandes zones, les erreurs qu'elles comportent arrivent parfois à s'équilibrer, de sorte que les agrégats obtenus peuvent être un peu plus exacts que chacun des éléments dont on est parti.

En outre, les donnés figurant dans le tableau 2 comportent certaines imprécisions en raison des facteurs influant sur les données par âge (voir à ce propos les notes techniques relatives au tableau 7). Ces imprécisions sont cependant atténuées du fait de l'étendue des groupes d'âge présentés dans le tableau 2.

NOTE

[1] Organisation des Nations Unies, Département des affaires économiques et sociales, Division de la population (2013). *Perspectives de la population mondiale : La révision de 2012. Ensemble de données étendues en formats Excel et ASCII, edition DVD-ROM* (publication des Nations Unies, ST/ESA/SER.A/334).

2. Estimates of population and its percentage distribution, by age and sex and sex ratio for all ages for the world, major areas and regions: 2012
Estimations de la population et pourcentage de répartition selon l'âge et le sexe et rapport de masculinité pour l'ensemble du monde, les grandes régions et les régions géographiques : 2012

Major areas and regions / Grandes régions et régions	Population (millions)												Sex ratio - Rapport de masculinité[1]
	Both sexes - Les deux sexes				Male - Masculin				Female - Féminin				
	All ages - Tous âges	0-14	15-64	65+	All ages - Tous âges	0-14	15-64	65+	All ages - Tous âges	0-14	15-64	65+	
WORLD TOTAL - ENSEMBLE DU MONDE													
Number - Nombre	7 080	1 865	4 659	556	3 569	965	2 357	247	3 511	901	2 301	309	
Percent - Pourcentage	100.0	26.3	65.8	7.9	100.0	27.0	66.0	6.9	100.0	25.7	65.5	8.8	101.6
AFRICA - AFRIQUE													
Number - Nombre	1 084	444	602	37	542	225	300	17	542	219	302	21	
Percent - Pourcentage	100.0	41.0	55.5	3.5	100.0	41.5	55.4	3.1	100.0	40.5	55.7	3.8	99.9
Eastern Africa - Afrique orientale													
Number - Nombre	363	160	192	11	181	81	95	5	182	79	97	6	
Percent - Pourcentage	100.0	44.1	52.8	3.0	100.0	44.6	52.6	2.8	100.0	43.6	53.1	3.3	99.3
Middle Africa - Afrique centrale													
Number - Nombre	132	60	69	4	66	30	34	2	66	30	35	2	
Percent - Pourcentage	100.0	45.2	51.9	2.9	100.0	45.6	51.8	2.6	100.0	44.8	52.0	3.2	99.0
Northern Africa - Afrique septentrionale													
Number - Nombre	206	65	131	10	103	33	66	5	103	32	66	6	
Percent - Pourcentage	100.0	31.4	63.6	5.0	100.0	32.0	63.6	4.4	100.0	30.8	63.6	5.6	100.4
Southern Africa - Afrique méridionale													
Number - Nombre	60	18	39	3	29	9	19	1	31	9	20	2	
Percent - Pourcentage	100.0	30.4	64.4	5.2	100.0	31.4	64.6	4.0	100.0	29.4	64.2	6.4	94.6
Western Africa - Afrique occidentale													
Number - Nombre	322	141	172	9	163	72	86	4	160	69	85	5	
Percent - Pourcentage	100.0	43.9	53.3	2.9	100.0	44.3	53.1	2.6	100.0	43.4	53.5	3.1	101.8
LATIN AMERICA AND CARIBBEAN - AMÉRIQUE LATIN ET CARAÏBES													
Number - Nombre	610	166	400	43	300	85	196	19	310	81	204	24	
Percent - Pourcentage	100.0	27.3	65.6	7.1	100.0	28.3	65.4	6.3	100.0	26.3	65.9	7.8	96.9
Caribbean - Caraïbes													
Number - Nombre	42	11	28	4	21	6	14	2	21	5	14	2	
Percent - Pourcentage	100.0	25.9	65.3	8.7	100.0	26.7	65.3	8.0	100.0	25.2	65.4	9.4	98.4
Central America - Amérique centrale													
Number - Nombre	165	50	105	10	80	26	50	4	85	25	55	6	
Percent - Pourcentage	100.0	30.5	63.5	6.0	100.0	32.0	62.5	5.5	100.0	29.0	64.5	6.5	94.8
South America - Amérique méridionale													
Number - Nombre	403	105	268	30	199	54	132	13	204	52	135	17	
Percent - Pourcentage	100.0	26.1	66.5	7.3	100.0	27.0	66.6	6.5	100.0	25.3	66.5	8.2	97.6
NORTHERN AMERICA - AMÉRIQUE SEPTENTRIONALE													
Number - Nombre	352	68	236	48	174	35	118	21	179	33	118	27	
Percent - Pourcentage	100.0	19.3	66.9	13.7	100.0	20.0	67.7	12.2	100.0	18.6	66.2	15.2	97.0
ASIA - ASIE													
Number - Nombre	4 255	1 063	2 893	299	2 177	556	1 482	139	2 077	506	1 410	161	
Percent - Pourcentage	100.0	25.0	68.0	7.0	100.0	25.5	68.1	6.4	100.0	24.4	67.9	7.7	104.8
Eastern Asia - Asie orientale													
Number - Nombre	1 612	283	1 167	162	829	151	601	76	783	131	566	86	
Percent - Pourcentage	100.0	17.5	72.4	10.1	100.0	18.3	72.6	9.2	100.0	16.8	72.2	11.0	105.8
South Central Asia - Asie centrale méridionale													
Number - Nombre	1 790	539	1 161	90	919	281	595	43	871	257	566	48	
Percent - Pourcentage	100.0	30.1	64.8	5.1	100.0	30.6	64.8	4.6	100.0	29.6	64.9	5.5	105.5
South Eastern Asia - Asie méridionale orientale													
Number - Nombre	612	168	409	34	304	86	203	15	308	82	206	20	
Percent - Pourcentage	100.0	27.5	66.8	5.6	100.0	28.4	66.8	4.9	100.0	26.7	66.9	6.4	98.8
Western Asia - Asie occidentale													
Number - Nombre	241	73	156	12	126	37	83	5	115	35	73	7	
Percent - Pourcentage	100.0	30.2	64.8	5.1	100.0	29.7	65.9	4.4	100.0	30.6	63.5	5.8	108.9
EUROPE													
Number - Nombre	742	115	503	124	357	59	249	49	385	56	255	74	
Percent - Pourcentage	100.0	15.5	67.8	16.7	100.0	16.5	69.6	13.9	100.0	14.6	66.2	19.3	92.8
Eastern Europe - Europe orientale													
Number - Nombre	295	44	209	41	138	23	101	14	157	22	108	27	
Percent - Pourcentage	100.0	15.1	70.9	14.1	100.0	16.5	73.2	10.3	100.0	13.8	68.8	17.3	88.3
Northern Europe - Europe septentrionale													
Number - Nombre	100	18	65	17	49	9	33	7	51	9	33	10	
Percent - Pourcentage	100.0	17.6	65.4	17.0	100.0	18.3	66.6	15.1	100.0	16.9	64.3	18.9	96.7
Southern Europe - Europe méridionale													
Number - Nombre	156	23	104	29	76	12	52	12	79	11	52	17	
Percent - Pourcentage	100.0	14.9	66.5	18.5	100.0	15.7	68.2	16.1	100.0	14.2	64.9	20.8	95.9

2. Estimates of population and its percentage distribution, by age and sex and sex ratio for all ages for the world, major areas and regions: 2012

Estimations de la population et pourcentage de répartition selon l'âge et le sexe et rapport de masculinité pour l'ensemble du monde, les grandes régions et les régions géographiques : 2012 (continued - suite)

| Major areas and regions | Population (millions) | | | | | | | | | | | | Sex ratio - |
| | Both sexes - Les deux sexes | | | | Male - Masculin | | | | Female - Féminin | | | | Rapport de |
Grandes régions et régions	All ages - Tous âges	0-14	15-64	65+	All ages - Tous âges	0-14	15-64	65+	All ages - Tous âges	0-14	15-64	65+	masculinité[1]
Western Europe - Europe occidentale													
Number - Nombre	192	30	125	36	94	15	63	16	98	15	63	21	
Percent - Pourcentage	100.0	15.6	65.5	19.0	100.0	16.3	67.1	16.6	100.0	14.9	63.9	21.2	95.6
OCEANIA - OCÉANIA													
Number - Nombre	37.77	9.03	24.54	4.21	18.89	4.65	12.31	1.93	18.88	4.38	12.23	2.27	
Percent - Pourcentage	100.0	23.9	65.0	11.1	100.0	24.6	65.2	10.2	100.0	23.2	64.8	12.0	100.1
Australia and New Zealand - Australie et Nouvelle Zélande													
Number - Nombre	27.51	5.30	18.38	3.83	13.66	2.72	9.18	1.77	13.85	2.58	9.20	2.07	
Percent - Pourcentage	100.0	19.3	66.8	13.9	100.0	19.9	67.2	12.9	100.0	18.6	66.4	14.9	98.7
Melanesia - Melanésie													
Number - Nombre	9.09	3.38	5.41	0.30	4.63	1.75	2.75	0.14	4.46	1.63	2.66	0.17	
Percent - Pourcentage	100.0	37.2	59.5	3.3	100.0	37.8	59.3	2.9	100.0	36.6	59.7	3.8	104.0
Micronesia													
Number - Nombre	0.50	0.15	0.32	0.03	0.26	0.08	0.16	0.01	0.25	0.07	0.16	0.01	
Percent - Pourcentage	100.0	30.1	64.5	5.4	100.0	30.6	64.6	4.9	100.0	29.6	64.4	6.0	102.8
Polynesia - Polynésie													
Number - Nombre	0.67	0.20	0.42	0.04	0.34	0.11	0.22	0.02	0.33	0.10	0.21	0.02	
Percent - Pourcentage	100.0	30.5	63.3	6.2	100.0	30.9	63.4	5.7	100.0	30.1	63.2	6.7	103.9

FOOTNOTES - NOTES

[1] Males per 100 females of all ages - Hommes pour 100 femmes de tous âges

Table 3 - *Demographic Yearbook 2012*

Table 3 presents for each country or area of the world the total, male and female population enumerated at the latest population census, estimates of the mid-year total population for 2005 and 2012, the average annual exponential rate of population increase (or decrease) for the period 2005 to 2012, the surface area and the population density for 2012.

Description of variables: The total, male and female population is the population enumerated at the most recent census for which data are available. The date of this census is given. Population census data are usually the results of a nation-wide gathering of individual information through full field enumeration. Alternatively other approaches for generating reliable statistics on population and housing can be used by countries, such as the use of population registers. Data that are the result of such an alternative approach are also coded as census and are footnoted accordingly. Also, the results of sample surveys, essentially national in character, may be presented showing the appropriate code. However, results of surveys referring to less than 50 percent of the total territory or population are not included.

Mid-year population estimates refer to the population on 1 July. Otherwise, a footnote is appended. Mid-year estimates of the total population are those provided by national statistical offices.

Surface area, expressed in square kilometres, refers to the total surface area, comprising land area and inland waters (assumed to consist of major rivers and lakes) and excluding polar regions as well as uninhabited islands. Exceptions to this are noted. Surface areas, originally reported in square miles by the country or area, have been converted to square kilometres using a conversion factor of 2.589988.

Computation: The annual rate of population increase is the average annual exponential rate of population growth between 2005 and 2012, computed by the Statistics Division of the United Nations Department of Economic and Social Affairs using the unrounded mid-year estimates of 2005 and 2012. This rate is expressed as percentage.

Density is the number of persons in the 2012 total population per square kilometre of total surface area.

Reliability of data: Reliable mid-year population estimates are those that are based on a complete census (or a sample survey) and have been adjusted by a continuous population register or on the basis of the calculated balance of births, deaths and migration. Mid-year estimates of this type are considered reliable and appear in roman type. Mid-year estimates not calculated on this basis are considered less reliable and are shown in italics.

Census data and sample survey results are considered reliable and, therefore, appear in roman type.

Rates of population increase that were calculated using population estimates considered less reliable, as described above, are set in italics rather than roman type.

All surface area data are assumed to be reliable and therefore appear in roman type.

Population density data, however, are considered reliable or less reliable on the basis of the reliability of the 2012 population estimates used as the numerator.

Limitations: Statistics on the total population enumerated at the time of the census, estimates of the mid-year total population and surface area data are subject to the same qualifications as have been set forth for population and surface area statistics in sections 3 and 2.4 of the Technical Notes, respectively.

Regarding the limitations of census data, it should be noted that although census data are considered reliable, and therefore appear in roman type, the actual quality of census data varies widely from one country or area to another. When known, an estimate of the extent of over-enumeration or under-enumeration is given in footnotes.

Rates of population increase are subject to all the qualifications of the population estimates mentioned above. In some cases, they simply reflect the rate calculated or assumed in constructing the estimates themselves when adequate measures of natural increase and net migration were not available. Despite their shortcomings, these rates provide a useful index for studying population change and can be also useful in evaluating the accuracy of vital and migration statistics.

Population density data as shown in this table give only an indication of actual population density as they do not take account of the dispersion or concentration of population within countries or areas nor the proportion of habitable land. They should not be interpreted as reflecting density in the urban sense or as indicating the supporting power of a territory's land and resources.

Tableau 3 – *Annuaire démographique 2012*

Le tableau 3 indique pour chaque pays ou zone du monde la population totale selon le sexe d'après les derniers recensements effectués, les estimations concernant la population totale au milieu de l'année 2005 et de l'année 2012, le taux moyen d'accroissement annuel exponentiel positif ou négatif de la population pour la période allant de 2005 à 2012, ainsi que la superficie et la densité de population en 2012.

Description des variables : la population masculine et féminine totale est, la population enregistrée lors du recensement le plus récent sur lequel on dispose de données. La date de ce recensement est indiquée. Les données des recensements de la population sont habituellement le résultat d'un collecte à l'échelle nationale des données individuelles obtenues au moyen d'un dénombrement complet. Les pays peuvent recourir à d'autres moyens pour établir des statistiques fiables sur la population et le logement, tels que des registres de la population. Les données obtenues par ce moyen sont présentées comme celles d'un recensement et sont annotées en conséquence. Par ailleurs, les résultats des enquêtes par sondage, réalisées habituellement à l'échelle nationale, peuvent être présentés à l'aide du code correspondant. En revanche, les résultats des enquêtes portant sur moins de 50 % du territoire total ou de la population ne sont pas indiqués.

Les estimations de la population en milieu d'année sont celles de la population au 1er juillet. Lorsque la date est différente, cela est signalé par une note. Les estimations de la population totale en milieu d'année sont celles qui ont été communiquées par les services nationaux de statistique.

La superficie - exprimée en kilomètres carrés - représente la superficie totale, c'est-à-dire qu'elle englobe les terres émergées et les eaux intérieures (qui sont censées comprendre les principaux lacs et cours d'eau) mais exclut les régions polaires et certaines îles inhabitées. Les exceptions à cette règle sont signalées en note. Les superficies initialement exprimées en miles carrés par les pays ou les zones ont été transformées en kilomètres carrés au moyen d'un coefficient de conversion de 2,589988.

Calculs : le taux d'accroissement annuel est le taux exponentiel annuel moyen de variation (en pourcentage) de la population entre 2005 et 2012, calculé par la Division de statistique du Département des affaires économiques et sociales de l'Organisation des Nations Unies à partir des estimations en milieu d'année non arrondies pour les années 2005 et 2012.

La densité est égale au rapport de l'effectif total de la population en 2012 à la superficie totale, exprimée en kilomètres carrés.

Fiabilité des données : les estimations en milieu d'année qui sont considérées sûres sont fondées sur un recensement complet (ou sur une enquête par sondage) et ont été ajustées en fonction des données provenant d'un registre permanent de population ou en fonction de la balance établie par le calcul des naissances, des décès et des migrations. Les estimations de ce type sont considérées comme sûres et apparaissent en caractères romains. Les estimations en milieu d'année dont le calcul n'a pas été effectué sur cette base sont considérées comme moins sûres et apparaissent en italique.

Les données de recensements ou les résultats d'enquêtes par sondage sont considérés comme sûrs et apparaissent par conséquent en caractères romains.

Les taux d'accroissement de la population, calculés à partir d'estimations jugées moins sûres d'après les normes décrites ci-dessus, sont indiqués en italique plutôt qu'en caractères romains.

Toutes les données de superficie sont présumées sûres et apparaissent par conséquent en caractères romains. En revanche, les données relatives à la densité de la population sont considérées plus ou moins sûres en fonction de la fiabilité des estimations de la population en 2012 ayant servi de numérateur.

Insuffisance des données : les statistiques portant sur la population totale dénombrée lors d'un recensement, les estimations de la population totale en milieu d'année et les données de superficie appellent les mêmes réserves que celles formulées aux sections 3 et 2.4 des Notes techniques à propos des statistiques relatives à la population et à la superficie.

S'agissant de l'insuffisance des données obtenues par recensement, il convient d'indiquer que, bien que ces données soient considérées comme sûres et apparaissent par conséquent en caractères romains, leur qualité réelle varie considérablement d'un pays ou d'une région à l'autre. Lorsque l'on possédait les renseignements voulus, on a donné une estimation du degré de sur-dénombrement ou de sous-dénombrement.

Les taux d'accroissement appellent toutes les réserves formulées plus haut à propos des estimations concernant la population. Dans certains cas, ils représentent seulement le taux calculé ou que l'on a pris pour base pour établir les estimations elles-mêmes lorsque l'on ne disposait pas de mesures appropriées de l'accroissement naturel et des migrations nettes. Malgré leurs imperfections, ces taux fournissent des indications intéressantes pour l'étude du mouvement de la population et, utilisés avec les précautions nécessaires, ils peuvent également servir à évaluer l'exactitude des statistiques de l'état civil et des migrations.

Les données relatives à la densité de population figurant dans le tableau 3 n'ont qu'une valeur indicative en ce qui concerne la densité de population effective, car elles ne tiennent compte ni de la dispersion ou de la concentration de la population à l'intérieur des pays ou zones, ni de la proportion du territoire qui est habitable. Il ne faut donc y voir d'indication ni de la densité au sens urbain du terme ni du nombre d'habitants qui pourraient vivre sur les terres et avec les ressources naturelles du territoire considéré.

3. Population by sex, annual rate of population increase, surface area and density
Population selon le sexe, taux d'accroissement annuel de la population, superficie et densité

Continent, country or area and census date / Continent, pays ou zone et date du recensement	Census type[a]	Population at the latest available census / Population d'après le dernier recensement disponible (in units — en unités)			Estimate type[a]	Mid-year estimates Estimations au milieu de l'année (in thousands — en milliers)		Annual rate of increase Taux d'accrois sement annuel 2005-12	Surface area Superficie (km²) 2012	Density Densité 2012[b]
		Both sexes Les deux sexes	Male Masculin	Female Feminin		2005	2012			

AFRICA - AFRIQUE

Algeria - Algérie										
16 IV 2008	DJ	*34 452 759	*17 428 500	*17 024 259	DJ	32 906	*37 495[1]	1.9	2 381 741	16
Angola										
15 XII 1970	DF	5 646 166	2 943 974	2 702 192		...	...	...	1 246 700	...
Benin - Bénin										
11 II 2002	DJ	6 769 914	3 284 119	3 485 795	DF	7 447[2]	...	...	114 763	...
Botswana										
9 VIII 2011	DF	2 024 904	989 128	1 035 776	DJ	1 708	...	...	582 000	...
Burkina Faso										
9 XII 2006	DF	14 196 259	6 842 560	7 353 699	DJ	13 374	...	...	272 967	...
Burundi										
16 VIII 2008	DF	7 877 728	3 838 045	4 039 683		...	...	...	27 834	...
Cabo Verde										
16 VI 2010	DJ	491 683	243 401	248 282	DF	475	...	...	4 033	...
Cameroon - Cameroun										
11 XI 2005	DF	17 052 134	8 408 495	8 643 639	DJ	...	20 387[3]	...	475 650	43
Central African Republic - République centrafricaine										
8 XII 2003	DF	3 151 072	1 569 446	1 581 626		...	...	...	622 984	...
Chad - Tchad										
8 IV 1993	DF	6 158 992	2 950 415	3 208 577		...	...	...	1 284 000	...
Comoros - Comores										
1 IX 2003	DF	575 660[4]	...	...					2 235	
Congo										
28 IV 2007	DF	3 697 490	1 821 357	1 876 133	DF	3 488[2]	...	...	342 000	...
Côte d'Ivoire										
21 XI 1998	DF	15 366 672	7 844 621	7 522 050	DF	*19 097[2]	...	...	322 463	...
Democratic Republic of the Congo - République démocratique du Congo										
1 VII 1984	DF	29 916 800	14 543 800	15 373 000		...	...	...	2 344 858	...
Djibouti										
29 V 2009	DF	*818 159	...	...				...	23 200	
Egypt - Égypte										
21 XI 2006	DF	72 798 031	37 219 056	35 578 975	DF	70 653	82 541	2.2	1 002 000	82
Equatorial Guinea - Guinée équatoriale										
1 II 2002	DF	1 014 999	501 387	513 612		...	...	...	28 051	...
Eritrea - Érythrée										
9 V 1984	DF	2 748 304	1 374 452	1 373 852		...	...	...	117 600	...
Ethiopia - Éthiopie										
29 V 2007	DF	73 750 932	37 217 130	36 533 802	DF	73 044[5]	...	...	1 104 300	...
Gabon										
1 XII 2003	DF	*1 269 000	...	...	DF	1 313[6]	...	...	267 668	...
Gambia - Gambie										
15 IV 2003	DF	1 360 681	...	...	DF	1 436	...	...	11 295	...
Ghana										
26 IX 2010	DF	24 658 823	12 024 845	12 633 978	DF	21 367	...	...	238 533	...
Guinea - Guinée										
1 XII 1996	DF	7 156 406	3 497 979	3 658 427		...	...	...	245 857	...
Guinea-Bissau - Guinée-Bissau										
15 III 2009	DF	1 520 830	737 634	783 196	DF	1 326[2]	...	...	36 125	...
Kenya										
24 VIII 2009	DF	38 610 097	19 192 458	19 417 639	DF	35 267[7]	42 436[7]	2.6	591 958	72
Lesotho										
13 IV 2006	DF	1 741 406	818 379	923 027		...	...	...	30 355	...
Liberia - Libéria										
21 III 2008	DF	3 476 608	1 739 945	1 736 663		...	...	...	111 369	...
Libya - Libye										
15 IV 2006	DF	*5 657 692	*2 934 452	*2 723 240		...	...	...	1 759 540	...
Madagascar										
1 VIII 1993	DF	12 238 914	6 088 116	6 150 798	DF	17 550	...	...	587 295	...
Malawi										
8 VI 2008	DF	13 077 160	6 358 933	6 718 227	DF	12 341[2]	...	...	118 484	...

3. Population by sex, annual rate of population increase, surface area and density
Population selon le sexe, taux d'accroissement annuel de la population, superficie et densité (continued - suite)

Continent, country or area and census date / Continent, pays ou zone et date du recensement	Census type[a]	Population at the latest available census / Population d'après le dernier recensement disponible (in units — en unités)			Estimate type[a]	Mid-year estimates Estimations au milieu de l'année (in thousands — en milliers)		Annual rate of increase Taux d'accrois sement annuel 2005-12	Surface area Superficie (km²) 2012	Density Densité 2012[b]
		Both sexes Les deux sexes	Male Masculin	Female Feminin		2005	2012			

AFRICA - AFRIQUE

Mali										
1 IV 2009 .... DJ	DJ	*14 517 176	*7 202 744	*7 314 432	DF	11 732[8]	...	...	1 240 192	...
Mauritania - Mauritanie										
1 XI 2000 .... DF	DF	2 508 159	1 241 712	1 266 447	DF	2 906[2]	...	...	1 030 700	...
Mauritius - Maurice[9]										
4 VII 2011 .... DF	DF	1 237 000	611 053	625 947	DJ	1 243	*1 291	0.5	1 969	656
Mayotte										
21 VIII 2012 .... DJ	DJ	212 645	...	...	...	...	...	...	...	...
Morocco - Maroc										
1 IX 2004 .... DF	DF	29 680 069	14 640 662	15 039 407	DF	30 172[10]	32 597[10]	1.1	446 550	73
Mozambique										
1 VIII 2007 .... DF	DF	20 252 223	9 746 690	10 505 533	DF	19 420[2]	...	...	801 590	...
Namibia - Namibie										
28 VIII 2011 .... DF	DF	*2 104 900	*1 021 600	*1 083 300	DF	1 957[2]	...	...	824 268	...
Niger										
20 V 2001 .... DJ	DJ	11 060 291	5 516 588	5 543 703	DJ	12 628[2]	16 275[2]	3.6	1 267 000	13
Nigeria - Nigéria										
21 III 2006 .... DF	DF	140 431 790	71 345 488	69 086 302	DF	133 767[2]	...	...	923 768	...
Republic of South Sudan - République de Soudan du Sud										
21 IV 2008 .... DF	DF	8 260 490	4 287 300	3 973 190		...	...	...	...	...
Réunion										
1 I 2010 .... DJ	DJ	829 903	...	...	DJ	777	...	...	2 513	...
Rwanda										
15 VIII 2012 .... DJ	DJ	*10 537 222	*5 074 942	*5 462 280	DF	9 225[2]	11 033[2]	2.6	26 338	419
Saint Helena ex. dep. - Sainte-Hélène sans dép.										
10 II 2008 .... DF	DF	4 257	2 165	2 092	DF	...	4	...	122	33
Saint Helena: Ascension - Sainte-Hélène: Ascension										
8 III 1998 .... DJ	DJ	712	458	254		...	...	...	88	...
Saint Helena: Tristan da Cunha - Sainte-Hélène: Tristan da Cunha										
31 XII 1988 .... DF	DF	296	139	157		...	...	...	98	...
Sao Tome and Principe - Sao Tomé-et-Principe										
13 V 2012 .... DF	DF	187 356	93 735	93 621	DF	149	*187	3.3	964	194
Senegal - Sénégal										
8 XII 2002 .... DF	DF	9 555 346	4 672 015	4 883 331	DJ	10 901[11]	13 208[12]	2.7	196 712[13]	67
Seychelles										
26 VIII 2010 .... DF	DF	90 945	46 912	44 033	DF	83	88	0.9	456	194
Sierra Leone										
4 XII 2004 .... DF	DF	4 976 871	2 420 218	2 556 653	DF	5 095	6 038	2.4	72 300	84
Somalia - Somalie										
15 II 1987 .... DF	DF	7 114 431	3 741 664	3 372 767		...	...	...	637 657	...
South Africa - Afrique du Sud										
10 X 2011 .... DF	DF	51 770 560	25 188 791	26 581 769	DF	47 177[14]	...	...	1 221 037	...
Swaziland										
11 III 2007 .... DF	DF	844 223	405 868	438 355	DF	1 126	1 080	-0.6	17 363	62
Togo										
6 XI 2010 .... DJ	DJ	6 191 155	3 009 095	3 182 060	DF	5 212	...	...	56 785	...
Tunisia - Tunisie										
28 IV 2004 .... DF	DF	9 910 872	4 965 435	4 945 437	DF	10 029	10 778	1.0	163 610	66
Uganda - Ouganda										
12 IX 2002 .... DF	DF	24 442 084	11 929 803	12 512 281	DF	26 741	34 131	3.5	241 550	141
United Republic of Tanzania - République Unie de Tanzanie										
26 VIII 2012 .... DF	DF	44 928 923	21 869 990	23 058 933	DF	37 083[12]	45 798[12]	3.0	947 303	48

3. Population by sex, annual rate of population increase, surface area and density
Population selon le sexe, taux d'accroissement annuel de la population, superficie et densité (continued - suite)

Continent, country or area and census date / Continent, pays ou zone et date du recensement	Census type[a]	Population at the latest available census / Population d'après le dernier recensement disponible (in units — en unités) Both sexes / Les deux sexes	Male / Masculin	Female / Feminin	Estimate type[a]	Mid-year estimates Estimations au milieu de l'année (in thousands — en milliers) 2005	2012	Annual rate of increase Taux d'accrois sement annuel 2005-12	Surface area Superficie (km²) 2012	Density Densité 2012[b]
AFRICA - AFRIQUE										
Western Sahara - Sahara occidental[15]										
31 XII 1970 .... DF	DF	76 425	43 981	32 444		...	...	...	266 000	...
Zambia - Zambie										
16 X 2010 .... DF	DF	*13 046 508	*6 394 455	*6 652 053	DF	11 441[2]	...	...	752 612	...
Zimbabwe										
17 VIII 2012 .... DF	DF	*12 973 808	*6 234 931	*6 738 877	DF	11 830[12]	...	...	390 757	...
AMERICA, NORTH - AMÉRIQUE DU NORD										
Anguilla										
9 V 2001 .... DF	DF	11 430[16]	5 628[16]	5 802[16]	DF	14	...	...	91	...
Antigua and Barbuda - Antigua-et-Barbuda										
27 V 2011 .... DF	DF	*83 278	*40 007	*43 271	DF	83	...	...	442	...
Aruba										
29 IX 2010 .... DJ	DJ	101 484	48 241	53 243	DJ	101	...	...	180	...
Bahamas										
3 V 2010 .... DJ	DJ	351 461	170 257	181 204	DF	325[2]	...	...	13 943	...
Barbados - Barbade										
1 V 2000 .... DF	DF	250 010	119 926	130 084	DF	273	...	...	430	...
Belize										
12 V 2010 .... DF	DF	*312 698	*157 935	*154 763	DF	292	...	...	22 966	...
Bermuda - Bermudes										
20 V 2010 .... DJ	DJ	64 237[17]	30 858[17]	33 379[17]	DJ	64	65	0.3	53	1 224
British Virgin Islands - Îles Vierges britanniques										
21 V 2001 .... DF	DF	20 647	10 627	10 020		...	...	...	151	...
Canada										
2 V 2011 .... DJ	DJ	33 476 685	16 414 225	17 062 460	DJ	32 245[18]	*34 880[19]	1.1	9 984 670	3
Cayman Islands - Îles Caïmanes										
10 X 2010 .... DJ	DJ	55 036[20]	27 218[20]	27 818[20]	DJ	48	57[21]	2.3	264	215
Costa Rica										
30 V 2011 .... DJ	DJ	4 301 712	2 106 063	2 195 649	DJ	4 266	4 667	1.3	51 100	91
Cuba										
7 IX 2002 .... DJ	DJ	11 177 743	5 597 233	5 580 510	DJ	11 243	...	...	109 884	...
Curaçao										
26 III 2011 .... DF	DF	150 563	68 848	81 715	DJ	137	151[8]	1.5	444	341
Dominica - Dominique										
14 V 2011 .... DF	DF	*71 293	*36 411	*34 882	DF	71	...	...	751	...
Dominican Republic - République dominicaine										
1 XII 2010 .... DJ	DJ	9 445 281	4 739 038	4 706 243	DF	9 226[2]	10 135[2]	1.3	48 192	210
El Salvador										
12 V 2007 .... DJ	DJ	5 744 113	2 719 371	3 024 742	DF	6 049[22]	6 251[22]	0.5	21 041[23]	297
Greenland - Groenland										
1 I 2008 .... DJ	DJ	56 462[24]	29 885[24]	26 577[24]	DJ	57[24]	57[24]	0.0	2 166 086	0
Grenada - Grenade										
25 V 2001 .... DF	DF	102 632	50 481	52 151		...	...	...	344	...
Guadeloupe										
1 I 2010 .... DJ	DJ	409 905[25]	...	...	DJ	446	...	...	1 705	...
Guatemala										
24 XI 2002 .... DJ	DJ	11 237 196	5 496 839	5 740 357	DF	12 701[12]	...	...	108 889	...
Haiti - Haïti										
11 I 2003 .... DJ	DJ	8 373 750	4 039 272	4 334 478	DJ	9 292[26]	10 413[26]	1.6	27 750	375
Honduras										
28 VII 2001 .... DF	DF	6 071 200	3 000 530	3 070 670	DF	7 197[27]	...	...	112 492	...
Jamaica - Jamaïque										
4 IV 2011 .... DJ	DJ	2 697 983	1 334 533	1 363 450	DJ	2 650	*2 708	0.3	10 991	246
Martinique										
1 I 2010 .... DJ	DJ	400 535	...	...	DJ	396[8]	...	...	1 128	...

3. Population by sex, annual rate of population increase, surface area and density
Population selon le sexe, taux d'accroissement annuel de la population, superficie et densité (continued - suite)

Continent, country or area and census date / Continent, pays ou zone et date du recensement	Census type[a]	Population at the latest available census / Population d'après le dernier recensement disponible (in units — en unités)			Estimate type[a]	Mid-year estimates / Estimations au milieu de l'année (in thousands — en milliers)		Annual rate of increase / Taux d' accrois sement annuel 2005-12	Surface area / Superficie (km²) 2012	Density / Densité 2012[b]
		Both sexes / Les deux sexes	Male / Masculin	Female / Feminin		2005	2012			
AMERICA, NORTH - AMÉRIQUE DU NORD										
Mexico - Mexique										
12 VI 2010 .... DF		112 336 538[28]	54 855 231[28]	57 481 307[28]	DJ	*103 947*	...	...	1 964 375	...
Montserrat										
12 V 2011 .... DJ		4 922	2 546	2 376	DF	5	5	0.4	103	48
Nicaragua										
4 VI 2005 .... DJ		5 142 098	2 534 491	2 607 607	DJ	*5 450*	*6 071*	*1.5*	130 373	*47*
Panama										
16 V 2010 .... DF		3 405 813	1 712 584	1 693 229	DF	*3 228[29]*	*3 788[30]*	2.3	75 417	*50*
Puerto Rico - Porto Rico										
1 IV 2010 .... DJ		3 725 789[31]	1 785 171[31]	1 940 618[31]	DJ	*3 912[31]*	3 667[32]	-0.9	8 870	413
Saint Kitts and Nevis - Saint-Kitts-et-Nevis										
14 V 2001 .... DF		45 841	22 784	23 057	DF	*49	...	...	261	...
Saint Lucia - Sainte-Lucie										
10 V 2010 .... DF		*173 720	*86 595	*87 125	DF	164	...	...	539[33]	...
Saint Pierre and Miquelon - Saint Pierre-et-Miquelon										
1 I 2010 .... DJ		6 312	...	...		...	...	...	242	...
Saint Vincent and the Grenadines - Saint-Vincent-et-les Grenadines										
14 V 2001 .... DF		109 022[34]	55 456[34]	53 566[34]	DF	104	...	...	389	...
Saint-Barthélemy										
1 I 2010 .... DJ		9 072	...	...		...	...	...	...	...
Saint-Martin (French part) - Saint-Martin (partie française)										
1 I 2010 .... DJ		37 630	...	...		...	...	...	...	...
Sint Maarten (Dutch part) - Saint-Martin (partie néerlandaise)[8]										
....		...	...	...	DJ	36	...	...	...	...
Trinidad and Tobago - Trinité-et-Tobago										
9 I 2011 .... DF		*1 324 699	*665 119	*659 580	DF	1 294[35]	...	...	5 130	...
Turks and Caicos Islands - Îles Turques et Caïques										
10 IX 2001 .... DF		19 886	9 897	9 989	DJ	*31*	...	...	948[36]	...
United States of America - États-Unis d'Amérique										
1 IV 2010 .... DJ		308 745 538[37]	151 781 326[37]	156 964 212[37]	DJ	295 753[37]	*313 914[37]	0.9	9 629 091	33
United States Virgin Islands - Îles Vierges américaines										
1 IV 2010 .... DJ		106 405[31]	50 854[31]	55 551[31]	DJ	110[31]	...	...	347	...
AMERICA, SOUTH - AMÉRIQUE DU SUD										
Argentina - Argentine										
27 X 2010 .... DF		40 117 096	19 523 766	20 593 330	DF	38 592[27]	41 282[27]	1.0	2 780 400	15
Bolivia (Plurinational State of) - Bolivie (État plurinational de)										
5 IX 2001 .... DF		8 274 325	4 123 850	4 150 475	DF	*9 427*	...	...	1 098 581[38]	...
Brazil - Brésil										
31 VII 2010 .... DJ		190 755 799	93 406 990	97 348 809	DF	*183 383[39]*	*193 947[39]*	0.8	8 514 877	23
Chile - Chili										
9 IV 2012 .... DF		*16 572 475	*8 059 148	*8 513 327	DF	16 267	17 403	1.0	756 102	23
Colombia - Colombie										
22 V 2005 .... DF		41 468 384	20 336 117	21 132 267	DJ	*42 889[40]*	*46 582[40]*	*1.2*	1 141 748	*41*

3. Population by sex, annual rate of population increase, surface area and density
Population selon le sexe, taux d'accroissement annuel de la population, superficie et densité (continued - suite)

Continent, country or area and census date / Continent, pays ou zone et date du recensement	Census type[a]	Population at the latest available census / Population d'après le dernier recensement disponible (in units — en unités)			Estimate type[a]	Mid-year estimates Estimations au milieu de l'année (in thousands — en milliers)		Annual rate of increase Taux d' accrois sement annuel 2005-12	Surface area Superficie (km²) 2012	Density Densité 2012[b]
		Both sexes Les deux sexes	Male Masculin	Female Feminin		2005	2012			
AMERICA, SOUTH - AMÉRIQUE DU SUD										
Ecuador - Équateur										
28 XI 2010 .... DF	DF	14 483 499	7 177 683	7 305 816	DF	13 215[41]	15 495[41]	2.3	256 369	60
Falkland Islands (Malvinas) - Îles Falkland (Malvinas)[42]										
8 X 2006 .... DF	DF	2 955	1 569	1 386		...	...	...	12 173	...
French Guiana - Guyane française										
1 I 2010 .... DJ	DJ	231 167	...	...	DJ	199[8]	...	...	83 534	...
Guyana										
15 IX 2002 .... DF	DF	751 223	376 034	375 189	DF	758	*796	0.7	214 969	4
Paraguay										
28 VIII 2002 .... DF	DF	5 163 198	2 603 242	2 559 956	DF	5 899[12]	6 673[12]	1.8	406 752	16
Peru - Pérou										
21 X 2007 .... DF	DF	27 412 157	13 622 640	13 789 517	DF	27 811	30 136[22]	1.1	1 285 216	23
Suriname										
13 VIII 2012 .... DJ	DJ	*534 189	...	...	DJ	499	...	...	163 820	...
Uruguay										
4 X 2011 .... DJ	DJ	3 286 314	1 577 725[43]	1 708 481[43]	DF	3 306[2]	*3 381[2]	0.3	176 215	19
Venezuela (Bolivarian Republic of) - Venezuela (République bolivarienne du)										
1 IX 2011 .... DF	DF	27 227 930	13 549 752	13 678 178	DF	26 577[27]	29 718[27]	1.6	912 050	33
ASIA - ASIE										
Afghanistan										
23 VI 1979 .... DF	DF	13 051 358[44]	6 712 377[44]	6 338 981[44]	DF	22 098[45]	25 500[45]	2.0	652 864	39
Armenia - Arménie										
12 X 2011 .... DF	DF	2 871 771	1 346 729	1 525 042	DJ	3 218	3 274[8]	0.2	29 743	110
Azerbaijan - Azerbaïdjan										
13 IV 2009 .... DJ	DJ	8 922 447	4 414 398	4 508 049	DF	8 500[46]	9 296	1.3	86 600	107
Bahrain - Bahreïn										
27 IV 2010 .... DJ	DJ	1 234 571	768 414	466 157	DJ	889	1 235	4.7	767	1 610
Bangladesh										
15 III 2011 .... DF	DF	*149 772 364	*74 980 386	*74 791 978	DF	138 600	...	...	147 570	...
Bhutan - Bhoutan										
30 V 2005 .... DF	DF	634 982	333 595	301 387	DF	...	721[47]	...	38 394	19
Brunei Darussalam - Brunéi Darussalam										
20 VI 2011 .... DF	DF	393 372	203 149	190 223	DF	370	...	...	5 765	...
Cambodia - Cambodge										
3 III 2008 .... DF	DF	13 395 682[48]	6 516 054[48]	6 879 628[48]	DF	13 807[49]	14 741[50]	0.9	181 035	81
China - Chine										
1 XI 2010 .... DJ	DJ	1 339 724 852[51]	686 852 572[51]	652 872 280[51]	DF	1 307 560[52]	1 350 695[53]	0.5	9 596 961	141
China, Hong Kong SAR - Chine, Hong Kong RAS										
30 VI 2011 .... DJ	DJ	7 071 576	3 303 015	3 768 561	DJ	6 813	7 155	0.7	1 104	6 481
China, Macao SAR - Chine, Macao RAS										
12 VIII 2011 .... DF	DF	625 674	305 398	320 276	DJ	473	568	2.6	30	18 930
Cyprus - Chypre										
1 X 2011 .... DJ	DJ	840 407[54]	408 780[54]	431 627[54]	DJ	738[54]	*862[55]	2.2	9 251	93
Democratic People's Republic of Korea - République populaire démocratique de Corée										
1 X 2008 .... DJ	DJ	24 052 231	11 721 838	12 330 393		...	...	...	120 538	...
Georgia - Géorgie										
17 I 2002 .... DF	DF	4 355 673	2 049 786	2 305 887	DF	4 361	4 491	0.4	69 700	64
India - Inde										
9 II 2011 .... DF	DF	*1 210 193 422[56]	*623 724 248[56]	*586 469 174[56]	DF	1 101 318[57]	1 213 370[57]	1.4	3 287 263	369

3. Population by sex, annual rate of population increase, surface area and density
Population selon le sexe, taux d'accroissement annuel de la population, superficie et densité (continued - suite)

Continent, country or area and census date / Continent, pays ou zone et date du recensement	Census type[a]	Population at the latest available census / Population d'après le dernier recensement disponible (in units — en unités)			Estimate type[a]	Mid-year estimates Estimations au milieu de l'année (in thousands — en milliers)		Annual rate of increase Taux d' accrois sement annuel 2005-12	Surface area Superficie (km²) 2012	Density Densité 2012[b]
		Both sexes Les deux sexes	Male Masculin	Female Feminin		2005	2012			

ASIA - ASIE

Indonesia - Indonésie										
1 V 2010 .... DJ	DJ	237 641 326	119 630 913	118 010 413	DJ	*220 926*	*247 214*	1.6	1 910 931	129
Iran (Islamic Republic of) - Iran (République islamique d')										
24 X 2011 .... DJ	DJ	75 149 669	37 905 669	37 244 000	DJ	69 390[58]	76 725[58]	1.4	1 628 750	47
Iraq										
16 X 1997 .... DF	DF	19 184 543[59]	9 536 570[59]	9 647 973[59]	DF	27 963	33 913	2.8	435 244	78
Israel - Israël										
27 XII 2008 .... DF	DF	7 412 180[60]	3 663 910[60]	3 748 270[60]	DJ	6 930[61]	*7 901[61]	1.9	22 072	358
Japan - Japon										
1 X 2010 .... DJ	DJ	128 057 352[62]	62 327 737[62]	65 729 615[62]	DJ	127 773[62]	127 561[63]	0.0	377 930[64]	338
Jordan - Jordanie										
1 X 2004 .... DF	DF	5 103 639[65]	2 626 287[65]	2 477 352[65]	DF	5 473[66]	6 388[66]	2.2	89 328	72
Kazakhstan										
25 II 2009 .... DF	DF	16 009 597	7 712 224	8 297 373	DF	15 147	16 673[8]	1.4	2 724 900	6
Kuwait - Koweït										
20 IV 2011 .... DF	DF	*3 065 850	*1 738 372	*1 327 478	DF	2 245	3 268	5.4	17 818	183
Kyrgyzstan - Kirghizstan										
24 III 2009 .... DJ	DJ	5 362 793	2 645 921	2 716 872	DF	5 007[67]	5 352[67]	1.0	199 949	27
Lao People's Democratic Republic - République démocratique populaire lao										
1 III 2005 .... DJ	DJ	5 621 982	2 800 551	2 821 431	DF	5 651[68]	6 549[68]	2.1	236 800	28
Lebanon - Liban										
3 III 2007 .... SDF	SDF	3 759 134[69]	1 857 659[69]	1 901 475[69]		...	...	...	10 452	...
Malaysia - Malaisie										
6 VII 2010 .... DJ	DJ	28 334 135[70]	14 562 638[70]	13 771 497[70]	DJ	26 046[71]	29 337[72]	1.7	330 803	89
Maldives										
21 III 2006 .... DF	DF	298 968[73]	151 459[73]	147 509[73]	DF	294	331	1.7	300	1 102
Mongolia - Mongolie										
11 XI 2010 .... DF	DF	2 647 199	1 314 246	1 332 953	DF	2 548	...	...	1 564 116	...
Myanmar										
31 III 1983 .... DF	DF	35 307 913	17 518 255	17 789 658	DF	55 396[74]	60 976[74]	1.4	676 578	90
Nepal - Népal										
22 VI 2011 .... DJ	DJ	26 494 504	12 849 041	13 645 463	DJ	25 343	29 129	2.0	147 181	198
Oman										
12 XII 2010 .... DF	DF	2 773 479	1 612 408	1 161 071	DF	2 509	...	...	309 500	...
Pakistan										
2 III 1998 .... DF	DF	130 579 571[75]	67 840 137[75]	62 739 434[75]	DJ	144 367[76]	...	...	796 095	...
Philippines										
1 V 2010 .... DJ	DJ	92 335 113[77]	46 634 257[77]	45 700 856[77]	DJ	85 261[29]	...	...	300 000	...
Qatar										
21 IV 2010 .... DF	DF	1 699 435	1 284 739	414 696	DF	906	...	...	11 607	...
Republic of Korea - République de Corée										
1 XI 2010 .... DJ	DJ	48 580 293[78]	24 167 098[78]	24 413 195[78]	DJ	48 138	50 345	0.6	100 148	503
Saudi Arabia - Arabie saoudite										
28 IV 2010 .... DF	DF	*27 136 977	*15 306 793	*11 830 184	DF	*23 330[79]	*29 196[79]	3.2	2 206 714	13
Singapore - Singapour										
30 VI 2010 .... DJ	DJ	3 771 721[80]	1 861 133[80]	1 910 588[80]	DJ	4 266[81]	5 312[81]	3.1	716	7 422
Sri Lanka										
27 II 2012 .... DJ	DJ	20 263 723	9 832 401	10 431 322	DF	19 644	*20 328	0.5	65 610	310
State of Palestine - État de Palestine										
1 XII 2007 .... DF	DF	*3 761 646[82]	*1 908 432[82]	*1 853 214[82]	DF	3 508	4 293	2.9	6 020	713
Syrian Arab Republic - République arabe syrienne										
22 IX 2004 .... DF	DF	*17 921 000[83]	*9 161 000[83]	*8 760 000[83]	DF	18 138[83]	...	...	185 180	...
Tajikistan - Tadjikistan										
21 IX 2010 .... DF	DF	7 564 502	3 817 004	3 747 498	DF	6 850	...	...	143 100	...
Thailand - Thaïlande										
1 IX 2010 .... DJ	DJ	65 981 659	32 355 032	33 626 627	DJ	64 839[2]	67 912[2]	0.7	513 120	132

3. Population by sex, annual rate of population increase, surface area and density
Population selon le sexe, taux d'accroissement annuel de la population, superficie et densité (continued - suite)

Continent, country or area and census date / Continent, pays ou zone et date du recensement	Census type[a]	Population at the latest available census / Population d'après le dernier recensement disponible (in units — en unités)			Estimate type[a]	Mid-year estimates / Estimations au milieu de l'année (in thousands — en milliers)		Annual rate of increase Taux d' accrois sement annuel 2005-12	Surface area Superficie (km²) 2012	Density Densité 2012[b]
		Both sexes Les deux sexes	Male Masculin	Female Feminin		2005	2012			

ASIA - ASIE

Timor-Leste										
11 VII 2010 ...... DF		*1 066 582	*541 147	*525 435	DF	983[2]	...	...	14 919	...
Turkey - Turquie										
31 XII 2008 ...... DJ		71 517 100[84]	35 901 154[84]	35 615 946[84]	DF	72 065	75 176	0.6	783 562	96
Turkmenistan - Turkménistan										
10 I 1995 ...... DF		4 483 251	2 225 331	2 257 920		...	...	...	488 100	...
United Arab Emirates - Émirats arabes unis										
5 XII 2005 ...... DF		4 106 427[85]	2 806 141[85]	1 300 286[85]	DF	4 041[85]	...	...	83 600	...
Uzbekistan - Ouzbékistan										
12 I 1989 ...... DJ		19 810 077	9 784 156	10 025 921	DF	*26 021	*29 555	1.8	447 400	66
Viet Nam										
1 IV 2009 ...... DJ		85 846 997	42 413 143	43 433 854	DF	82 394[86]	88 773	1.1	330 957	268
Yemen - Yémen										
16 XII 2004 ...... DF		19 685 161	10 036 953	9 648 208	...	20 283[21]	24 527[2]	...	527 968	46

EUROPE

Åland Islands - Îles d'Åland										
31 XII 2000 ...... DJ		25 776[87]	12 700[87]	13 076[87]	DJ	27[24]	28[24]	0.9	1 580	18
Albania - Albanie										
1 X 2011 ...... DJ		2 800 138	1 403 059	1 397 079	DF	2 993	2 802	-0.9	28 748	97
Andorra - Andorre										
31 XII 2000 ...... DJ		65 844[24]	34 268[24]	31 576[24]	DJ	79[24]	77[24]	-0.3	468	165
Austria - Autriche										
15 V 2001 ...... DJ		8 032 926	3 889 189	4 143 737	DJ	8 225	8 466	0.4	83 871	101
Belarus - Bélarus										
14 X 2009 ...... DJ		9 503 807	4 420 039	5 083 768	DF	9 775	9 465[8]	-0.5	207 600	46
Belgium - Belgique										
1 X 2001 ...... DJ		10 296 350	5 035 446	5 260 904	DJ	10 473	11 139	0.9	30 528	365
Bosnia and Herzegovina - Bosnie-Herzégovine										
31 III 1991 ...... DJ		4 377 033	2 183 795	2 193 238	DF	3 843	*3 837	0.0	51 209	75
Bulgaria - Bulgarie										
1 II 2011 ...... DJ		7 364 570	3 586 571	3 777 999	DJ	7 740	7 305	-0.8	110 900	66
Croatia - Croatie										
1 IV 2011 ...... DF		4 284 889	2 066 335	2 218 554	DJ	4 442	*4 268	-0.6	56 594	75
Czech Republic - République tchèque										
25 III 2011 ...... DJ		10 436 560	5 109 766	5 326 794	DJ	10 234	10 511	0.4	78 866	133
Denmark - Danemark[88]										
1 I 2001 ...... DJ		5 349 212[24]	2 644 319[24]	2 704 893[24]	DJ	5 416[24]	5 587[24]	0.4	43 094	130
Estonia - Estonie										
31 XII 2011 ...... DJ		1 294 455	600 526	693 929	DJ	1 346	1 340[8]	-0.1	45 227	30
Faeroe Islands - Îles Féroé										
1 I 2008 ...... DJ		48 433[24]	25 174[24]	23 259[24]	DJ	48	48[8]	0.0	1 393	35
Finland - Finlande										
31 XII 2010 ...... DJ		5 375 276	2 638 416	2 736 860	DJ	5 246[24]	5 401[89]	0.4	336 852[90]	16
France										
1 I 2006 ...... DJ		61 399 541[91]	29 714 539[91]	31 685 002[91]	DJ	61 181[91]	*63 556[91]	0.5	551 500	115
Germany - Allemagne										
28 III 2004 ...... SDJ		82 491 000[92]	40 330 000[92]	42 161 000[92]	DJ	82 464	81 932	-0.1	357 137	229
Gibraltar										
12 XI 2001 ...... DF		27 495[93]	13 644[93]	13 851[93]	DF	29[94]	...	...	6	...
Greece - Grèce										
9 V 2011 ...... DF		*10 815 197	*5 302 703	*5 512 494	DF	11 104[95]	*11 290[96]	0.2	131 957	86
Guernsey - Guernesey										
29 IV 2001 ...... DJ		59 807	29 138	30 669	DF	...	63[97]	...	63	995
Holy See - Saint-Siège[98]										
1 VII 2000 ...... DF		*798[99]	*529[99]	*269[99]	DF	...	0[100]	...	0[101]	1 025
Hungary - Hongrie										
1 X 2011 ...... DF		9 937 628	4 718 479	5 219 149	DJ	10 087	*9 919	-0.2	93 026	107

Continent, country or area and census date Continent, pays ou zone et date du recensement	Census type[a]	Population at the latest available census Population d'après le dernier recensement disponible (in units — en unités)			Estimate type[a]	Mid-year estimates Estimations au milieu de l'année (in thousands — en milliers)		Annual rate of increase Taux d' accrois sement annuel 2005-12	Surface area Superficie (km²) 2012	Density Densité 2012[b]
		Both sexes Les deux sexes	Male Masculin	Female Feminin		2005	2012			
EUROPE										
Iceland - Islande										
1 VII 2000	DJ	281 154[24]	140 718[24]	140 436[24]	DJ	296[24]	321[102]	1.2	103 000	3
Ireland - Irlande										
10 IV 2011	DF	4 588 252	2 272 699	2 315 553	...	4 160	4 585[103]	...	69 825	66
Isle of Man - Île de Man										
27 III 2011	DJ	*84 497	*41 971	*42 526	DJ	79[104]	...	...	572	...
Italy - Italie										
21 X 2001	DF	57 110 144	27 617 335	29 492 809	DF	58 607	60 851[8]	0.5	301 339	202
Jersey										
27 III 2011	DF	97 857	48 296	49 561	DJ	91	...	...	116	...
Latvia - Lettonie										
1 III 2011	DJ	2 070 371	946 102	1 124 269	DJ	2 301	*2 032	-1.8	64 562	31
Liechtenstein										
31 XII 2010	DF	36 149	17 886	18 263	DJ	35	*36[8]	0.7	160	228
Lithuania - Lituanie										
1 III 2011	DJ	3 483 972	1 629 148	1 854 824	DJ	3 414	3 008[8]	-1.8	65 300	46
Luxembourg										
1 II 2011	DJ	512 353	254 967	257 386	DJ	465	525[8]	1.7	2 586	203
Malta - Malte										
20 XI 2011	DJ	*416 055	*207 185	*208 870	DJ	404[105]	418[106]	0.5	316	1 321
Monaco										
9 VI 2008	DJ	31 109	15 076[107]	15 914[107]		...	...	...	2	...
Montenegro - Monténégro										
1 IV 2011	DJ	620 029	306 236	313 793	DJ	623	622	0.0	13 812	45
Netherlands - Pays-Bas										
1 I 2002	DJ	16 105 285[108]	7 971 967[108]	8 133 318[108]	DJ	16 320	16 730[8]	0.4	37 354	448
Norway - Norvège										
19 XI 2011	DJ	4 979 955[109]	...	...	DJ	4 623[110]	4 986[111]	1.1	323 787	15
Poland - Pologne										
31 III 2011	DJ	38 512 000[112]	18 644 000[112]	19 868 000[112]	DJ	38 161[112]	38 538[113]	0.1	311 888	124
Portugal										
21 III 2011	DF	10 282 306	4 868 755	5 413 551	DJ	10 549	*10 542[8]	0.0	92 212	114
Republic of Moldova - République de Moldova										
5 X 2004	DF	3 386 673[114]	1 629 689[114]	1 756 984[114]	DJ	3 595[114]	3 560[115]	-0.1	33 846	105
Romania - Roumanie										
18 III 2002	DJ	21 680 974	10 568 741	11 112 233	DJ	21 624	*21 356[8]	-0.2	238 391	90
Russian Federation - Fédération de Russie										
14 X 2010	DF	143 436 145	66 457 074	76 979 071	DJ	143 519	143 056[8]	0.0	17 098 246	8
San Marino - Saint-Marin										
1 VII 2000	DF	26 941[24]	13 185[24]	13 756[24]	DF	30[24]	33[89]	1.6	61	548
Serbia - Serbie										
1 X 2011	DJ	7 186 862[116]	3 499 176[116]	3 687 686[116]	DJ	7 441[116]	7 241[117]	-0.4	88 361	82
Slovakia - Slovaquie										
21 V 2011	DJ	5 397 036	2 627 772	2 769 264	DJ	5 387	5 408[8]	0.1	49 036[118]	110
Slovenia - Slovénie										
1 I 2011	DF	2 058 051	1 019 826	1 038 225	DJ	2 001	2 057	0.4	20 273	101
Spain - Espagne										
1 XI 2011	DJ	46 815 916	23 104 303	23 711 613	DJ	43 398	46 163	0.9	505 992	91
Svalbard and Jan Mayen Islands - Îles Svalbard et Jan Mayen										
1 XI 1960	DF	3 431[119]	2 545[119]	886[119]	DF	2[120]	...	...	62 422	...
Sweden - Suède										
31 XII 2003	DJ	8 975 670[24]	4 446 656[24]	4 529 014[24]	DJ	9 030[24]	9 519[24]	0.8	450 295	21
Switzerland - Suisse										
5 XII 2000	DF	7 288 010	3 567 567	3 720 443	DJ	7 437	*7 996	1.0	41 285	194
TFYR of Macedonia - L'ex-R. y. de Macédoine										
31 X 2002	DJ	2 022 547	1 015 377	1 007 170	DF	2 037	2 061	0.2	25 713	80
Ukraine										
5 XII 2001	DF	48 240 902	22 316 317	25 924 585	DF	47 105	45 634[8]	-0.5	603 500	76

3. Population by sex, annual rate of population increase, surface area and density
Population selon le sexe, taux d'accroissement annuel de la population, superficie et densité (continued - suite)

Continent, country or area and census date Continent, pays ou zone et date du recensement	Census type[a]	Population at the latest available census Population d'après le dernier recensement disponible (in units — en unités)			Estimate type[a]	Mid-year estimates Estimations au milieu de l'année (in thousands — en milliers)		Annual rate of increase Taux d' accrois sement annuel 2005-12	Surface area Superficie (km²) 2012	Density Densité 2012[b]
		Both sexes Les deux sexes	Male Masculin	Female Feminin		2005	2012			
EUROPE										
United Kingdom of Great Britain and Northern Ireland - Royaume-Uni de Grande-Bretagne et d'Irlande du Nord[121]										
27 III 2011	DJ	63 182 000	31 028 000	32 154 000	DF	60 235	63 244	0.7	242 495	261
OCEANIA - OCÉANIE										
American Samoa - Samoas américaines										
1 IV 2010	DJ	55 519[31]	28 164[31]	27 355[31]	DJ	66[31]	...	...	199	...
Australia - Australie										
9 VIII 2011	DF	21 727 158[122]	10 737 148[122]	10 990 010[122]	DJ	20 395[123]	*22 684[124]	1.5	7 692 024	3
Cook Islands - Îles Cook[125]										
1 XII 2006	DF	19 342	9 816	9 526	DF	22	...	...	236	...
Fiji - Fidji										
16 IX 2007	DF	837 271	427 176	410 095	DF	825	...	...	18 272	...
French Polynesia - Polynésie française										
20 VIII 2007	DJ	259 706	133 109	126 597	DF	*253*	...	...	4 000	...
Guam										
1 IV 2010	DJ	159 358	81 568	77 790	DJ	158[126]	160[126]	0.1	549	291
Kiribati										
10 X 2010	DF	103 058	50 796	52 262		...	...	...	726[127]	...
Marshall Islands - Îles Marshall										
1 VI 1999	DF	50 848	26 034	24 814		...	...	...	181	...
Micronesia (Federated States of) - Micronésie (États fédérés de)										
1 IV 2000	DJ	107 008	54 191	52 817	DJ	*108*[2]	...	...	702	...
Nauru										
31 X 2011	DF	*10 086	...	...		...	...	...	21	...
New Caledonia - Nouvelle-Calédonie										
27 VII 2009	DF	245 580	124 524	121 056	DF	*234*	...	...	18 575	...
New Zealand - Nouvelle-Zélande										
7 III 2006	DF	4 143 282[128]	2 021 277[128]	2 122 005[128]	DJ	4 134[129]	4 433[129]	1.0	270 467	16
Niue - Nioué										
9 IX 2006	DF	1 625	802	823	DJ	2	...	...	260	...
Norfolk Island - Île Norfolk										
9 VIII 2011	DF	2 302	1 082	1 220	DF	2	...	...	36	...
Northern Mariana Islands - Îles Mariannes septentrionales										
1 IV 2010	DF	53 883	27 746	26 137	DF	71	...	...	457	...
Palau - Palaos										
1 IV 2005	DJ	19 907	10 699	9 208		...	...	...	459	...
Papua New Guinea - Papouasie-Nouvelle-Guinée										
10 VII 2011	DF	*7 059 653	*3 663 249	*3 396 404		...	...	...	462 840	...
Pitcairn										
10 VIII 2012	DF	48	22	26		...	...	...	5	...
Samoa										
7 XI 2011	DF	187 820	96 990	90 830	DF	*183*	...	...	2 842	...
Solomon Islands - Îles Salomon										
22 XI 2009	DF	*515 870	*264 455	*251 415	DF	*471*[2]	*554*[2]	2.3	28 896	*19*
Tokelau - Tokélaou										
18 X 2011	DF	1 205	600	605		...	...	...	12	...

3. Population by sex, annual rate of population increase, surface area and density
Population selon le sexe, taux d'accroissement annuel de la population, superficie et densité (continued - suite)

Continent, country or area and census date / Continent, pays ou zone et date du recensement	Census type[a]	Population at the latest available census / Population d'après le dernier recensement disponible (in units — en unités)			Estimate type[a]	Mid-year estimates / Estimations au milieu de l'année (in thousands — en milliers)		Annual rate of increase / Taux d' accrois sement annuel 2005-12	Surface area / Superficie (km²) 2012	Density / Densité 2012[b]
		Both sexes / Les deux sexes	Male / Masculin	Female / Feminin		2005	2012			
OCEANIA - OCÉANIE										
Tonga										
30 XI 2011 .... DJ		*103 036	*52 001	*51 035	DF	*102*[130]	...	...	747	...
Tuvalu										
1 XI 2002 .... DF		9 561	4 729	4 832	DF	*10*	...	...	26	...
Vanuatu										
16 XI 2009 .... DJ		234 023	119 091	114 932		...	...	...	12 189	...
Wallis and Futuna Islands - Îles Wallis et Futuna										
21 VII 2008 .... DF		13 445	6 669	6 776		...	...	...	142	...

FOOTNOTES - NOTES

Italics: estimates which are less reliable. - Italiques : estimations moins sûres.

* Provisional. - Données provisoires.

a 'Code' indicates the source of data, as follows:
DF - De facto
DJ - De jure
SDF - Sample survey, de facto
SDJ - Sample survey, de jure

Le 'Code' indique la source des données, comme suit :
DF - Population de fait
DJ - Population de droit
SDF - Enquête par sondage, population de fait
SDJ - Enquête par sondage, Population de droit

b Population per square kilometre of surface area. Figures are estimates of population divided by surface area and are not to be considered either as reflecting density in the urban sense or as indicating the supporting power of a territory's land and resources. - Nombre d'habitants au kilomètre carré. Il s'agit simplement d'éstimations de la population divisé par celui de la superficie: il ne faut pas y voir d'indication de la densité au sens urbain du terme ni de l'effectif de population que les terres et les ressources du territoire sont capables de nourrir.

1 Data based on 2008 Population Census. - Données fondées sur le recensement de population de 2008.
2 Data refer to national projections. - Les données se réfèrent aux projections nationales.
3 Data refer to national projections. Data refer to 1 January. - Les données se réfèrent aux projections nationales. Données se raportent au 1 janvier.
4 Excluding Mayotte. - Non compris Mayotte.
5 Projections based on the 1994 Population Census. - Projections fondées sur le recensement de la population de 1994.
6 Based on the results of the Gabonese Survey for the Evaluation and Tracking of Poverty. - Sur base des résultats de l'enquête gabonaise sur l'évaluation et le suivi de la pauvreté.
7 Post-censal estimates based on the 1999 Population Census. - Les estimations post-censitaire fondées sur le recensement de la population de 1999.
8 Data refer to 1 January. - Données se raportent au 1 janvier.
9 Excludes the islands of St. Brandon and Agalega. - Non compris les îles St. Brandon et Agalega.
10 Based on the results of the 2004 Population Census. - D'après des résultats du recensement de la population de 2004.
11 Projections based on the 2002 Population Census. Data refer to 31 December. - Projections fondées sur le recensement de la population de 2002. Données se raportent au 31 décembre.
12 Projections based on the 2002 Population Census. - Projections fondées sur le recensement de la population de 2002.

13 Surface area is based on the 2002 population and housing census. - La superficie est fondée sur les données provenant du recensement de la population et du logement de 2002.
14 Mid-year estimates have been adjusted for underenumeration at latest census. - Les estimations au millieu de l'année tiennent compte d'un ajustement destiné à compenser les lacunes du dénombrement lors du dernier recensement.
15 Comprising the Northern Region (former Saguia el Hamra) and Southern Region (former Rio de Oro). - Comprend la région septentrionale (ancien Saguia-el-Hamra) et la région méridionale (ancien Rio de Oro).
16 Excluding persons who were not contacted at the time of the census. - La population non comprend pas les personnes qui n'ont pas été contactées à l'heure du recensement.
17 Bermuda is 100% urban. - 100 % de la population des Bermudes est urbaine.
18 Final intercensal estimates. Estimates adjusted for census net undercoverage (including adjustment for incompletely enumerated Indian reserves). - Estimations inter-censitaires definitives. Ajusté pour la sous-estimation du recensement (y compris les réservations en Inde incomplètement énumérées).
19 Estimates adjusted for census net undercoverage (including adjustment for incompletely enumerated Indian reserves). Preliminary postcensal estimates. - Ajusté pour la sous-estimation du recensement (y compris les réservations en Inde incomplètement énumérées). Estimations post censitaires préliminaires.
20 Excludes the institutional population. - Non compris la population dans les institutions.
21 Data refer to 31 December. - Données se raportent au 31 décembre.
22 Estimates based on the 2007 Population Census. - Estimations fondées sur le recensement de la population de 2007.
23 The total surface is 21040.79 square kilometers, without taking into account the last ruling of The Hague. - La superficie totale est égale à 21040.79 km2, sans tenir compte de la dernière décision de la Haye.
24 Population statistics are compiled from registers. - Les statistiques de la population sont compilées à partir des registres.
25 Excluding data for Saint Barthélémy and Saint Martin. - Non compris les données pour Saint Barthélémy et Saint Martin.
26 Projections produced by l'Institut Haïtien de Statistique et d'Informatique (IHSI) and the Latin American and Caribbean Demographic Centre (CELADE) - Population Division of ECLAC. - Les données sont projections produits par l'Institut Haïtien de Statistique et d'Informatique (IHSI) et le centre démographique de l'Amérique latine et les Caraïbes - Division de la population de la CEPALC.
27 Data refer to projections based on the 2001 Population Census. - Les données se référent aux projections basées sur le recensement de la population de 2001.
28 Including an estimation of 1 334 585 persons corresponding to 448 195 housing units without information of the occupants. - Y compris une estimation de 1 334 585 personnes correspondant aux 448 195 unités d'habitation sans information sur les occupants.
29 Data refer to projections based on the 2000 Population Census. - Les données se référent aux projections basées sur le recensement de la population de 2000.

[30] Data refer to projections based on the 2010 Population Census. - Les données se réfèrent aux projections basées sur le recensement de la population de 2010.

[31] Including armed forces stationed in the area. - Y compris les militaires en garnison sur le territoire.

[32] Including armed forces stationed in the area. Data based on the 2010 Population Census results. - Y compris les militaires en garnison sur le territoire. D'après le résultats du recensement de la population de 2010.

[33] Refers to habitable area. Excludes St. Lucia's Forest Reserve. - S'applique à la zone habitable. Exclut la réserve forestière de Sainte-Lucie.

[34] Excluding residents of institutions. - À l'exclusion de personnes en établissements de soins.

[35] Based on the results of the 2000 Population Census. - Basé sur les résultats du recencement de la population de 2000.

[36] Including low water level for all islands (area to shoreline). - Incluent le niveau de basses eaux pour toutes les îles.

[37] Excluding armed forces overseas and civilian citizens absent from the country for an extended period of time. - Non compris les militaires à l'étranger, et les civils hors du pays pendant une période prolongée.

[38] Data updated according to "Superintendencia Agraria". Interior waters correspond to natural or artificial bodies of water or snow. - Données actualisées d'après la « Superintendencia Agraria ». Les eaux intérieures correspondent aux étendues d'eau naturelles ou artificielles et aux étendues neigeuses.

[39] Data include persons in remote areas, military personnel outside the country, merchant seamen at sea, civilian seasonal workers outside the country, and other civilians outside the country, and exclude nomads, foreign military, civilian aliens temporarily in the country, transients on ships and Indian jungle population. - Y compris les personnes vivant dans des régions éloignées, le personel militaire en dehors du pays, les marins marchands, les ouvriers saisonniers en dehors du pays, et autres civils en dehors du pays, et non compris les nomades, les militaires étrangers, les étrangers civils temporairement dans le pays, les transiteurs sur des bateaux et les Indiens de la jungle.

[40] Data are revised projections taking into consideration also the results of 2005 census. - Les données sont des projections révisées tenant compte également des résultats du recensement de 2005.

[41] Excludes nomadic Indian tribes. Data refer to national projections. - Non compris les tribus d'Indiens nomades. Les données se réfèrent aux projections nationales.

[42] A dispute exists between the governments of Argentina and the United Kingdom of Great Britain and Northern Ireland concerning sovereignty over the Falkland Islands (Malvinas). - La souveraineté sur les îles Falkland (Malvinas) fait l'objet d'un différend entre le Gouvernement argentin et le Gouvernement du Royaume-Uni de Grande-Bretagne et d'Irlande du Nord.

[43] Figures for male and female population do not add up to the figure for total population, since they do not include 108 homeless people. - Les chiffres relatifs à la population masculine et féminine ne correspondent pas au chiffre de la population totale, parce que l'on en a exclu 108 personnes sans toit.

[44] Excluding nomad population. - Non compris les nomades.

[45] Data refer to the settled population based on the 1979 Population Census and the latest household prelisting. The refugees of Afghanistan in Iran, Pakistan, and an estimated 1.5 million nomads, are not included. - Les données se rapportent à la population stationnaire sur la base du recensement de 1979 et du recensement préliminaire des logements le plus récent. Sont exclus les réfugiés d'Afghanistan en Iran et au Pakistan et les nomades estimés à 1,5 million.

[46] Intercensal estimates. - Estimations inter-censitaires.

[47] Data refer to projections based on the 2005 Population Census. - Les données se réfèrent aux projections basées sur le recensement de la population de 2005.

[48] Excluding foreign diplomatic personnel and their dependants. - Non compris le personnel diplomatique étranger et les membres de leur famille les accompagnant.

[49] Excluding foreign diplomatic personnel and their dependants. Based on 1998 census results. - Non compris le personnel diplomatique étranger et les membres de leur famille les accompagnant. A partir des résultats de recensement de l'année 1998.

[50] Data based on 2008 Population Census. Excluding foreign diplomatic personnel and their dependants. - Données fondées sur le recensement de population de 2008. Non compris le personnel diplomatique étranger et les membres de leur famille les accompagnant.

[51] For statistical purposes, the data for China do not include those for the Hong Kong Special Administrative Region (Hong Kong SAR), Macao Special Administrative Region (Macao SAR) and Taiwan province of China. Data are from Communique of the National Bureau of Statistics of the People's Republic of China on Major Figures of the 2010 Population Census (No.1). - Pour la présentation des statistiques, les données pour la Chine ne comprennent pas la Région Administrative Spéciale de Hong Kong (Hong Kong RAS), la Région Administrative Spéciale de Macao (Macao RAS) et Taïwan province de Chine.

Données issues du communiqué du Bureau national de la statistique de la République populaire de Chine sur les chiffres importants du recensement de 2010 (n° 1).

[52] For statistical purposes, the data for China do not include those for the Hong Kong Special Administrative Region (Hong Kong SAR), Macao Special Administrative Region (Macao SAR) and Taiwan province of China. Data have been estimated on the basis of the annual National Sample Survey on Population Changes. - Pour la présentation des statistiques, les données pour la Chine ne comprennent pas la Région Administrative Spéciale de Hong Kong (Hong Kong RAS), la Région Administrative Spéciale de Macao (Macao RAS) et Taïwan province de Chine. Les données ont été estimées sur la base de l'enquête annuelle "National Sample Survey on Population Changes".

[53] For statistical purposes, the data for China do not include those for the Hong Kong Special Administrative Region (Hong Kong SAR), Macao Special Administrative Region (Macao SAR) and Taiwan province of China. Data have been adjusted on the basis of the Population Census of 2010. - Pour la présentation des statistiques, les données pour la Chine ne comprennent pas la Région Administrative Spéciale de Hong Kong (Hong Kong RAS), la Région Administrative Spéciale de Macao (Macao RAS) et Taïwan province de Chine. Les données ont été ajustées à partir des résultats du recensement de la population de 2010.

[54] Data refer to government controlled areas. - Les données se rapportent aux zones contrôlées par le Gouvernement.

[55] Data refer to government controlled areas. Data refer to 1 January. Data have been adjusted on the basis of the Population Census of 2011. - Les données se rapportent aux zones contrôlées par le Gouvernement. Données se raportent au 1 janvier. Les données ont été calculées sur la base du recensement de population de 2011.

[56] Includes data for the Indian-held part of Jammu and Kashmir, the final status of which has not yet been determined. - Y compris les données pour la partie du Jammu et du Cachemire occupée par l'Inde dont le statut définitif n'a pas encore été déterminé.

[57] Includes data for the Indian-held part of Jammu and Kashmir, the final status of which has not yet been determined. Data refer to projections based on the 2001 Population Census. - Y compris les données pour la partie du Jammu et du Cachemire occupée par l'Inde dont le statut définitif n'a pas encore été déterminé. Les données se réfèrent aux projections basées sur le recensement de la population de 2001.

[58] Data refer to the Iranian Year which begins on 21 March and ends on 20 March of the following year. - Les données concernent l'année iranienne, qui commence le 21 mars et se termine le 20 mars de l'année suivante.

[59] Excluding the population in three autonomous provinces in the north of the country. - La population des trois provinces autonomes dans le nord du pays est exclue.

[60] Includes data for East Jerusalem and Israeli residents in certain other territories under occupation by Israeli military forces since June 1967. Data are rounded for confidentiality reasons. - Y compris les données pour Jérusalem-Est et les résidents israéliens dans certains autres territoires occupés depuis 1967 par les forces armées israéliennes. Chiffres arrondis pour des raisons de confidentialité.

[61] Includes data for East Jerusalem and Israeli residents in certain other territories under occupation by Israeli military forces since June 1967. - Y compris les données pour Jérusalem-Est et les résidents israéliens dans certains autres territoires occupés depuis 1967 par les forces armées israéliennes.

[62] Excluding diplomatic personnel outside the country and foreign military and civilian personnel and their dependants stationed in the area. - Non compris le personnel diplomatique hors du pays ni les militaires et agents civils étrangers en poste sur le territoire et les membres de leur famille les accompagnant.

[63] Excluding diplomatic personnel outside the country and foreign military and civilian personnel and their dependants stationed in the area. Estimates based on the complete counts of the 2010 Population Census. - Non compris le personnel diplomatique hors du pays ni les militaires et agents civils étrangers en poste sur le territoire et les membres de leur famille les accompagnant. Estimations basées sur le dénombrement complet du recensement de la population de 2010.

[64] Data refer to 1 October 2007. - Les données se réfèrent au 1er octobre 2007.

[65] Excluding data for Jordanian territory under occupation since June 1967 by Israeli military forces. Including registered Palestinian refugees and Jordanians abroad. - Non compris les données pour le territoire jordanien occupé depuis juin 1967 par les forces armées israéliennes. Y compris les réfugiés palestiniens enregistrés et les Jordaniens à l'étranger.

[66] Data refer to 31 December. Excluding data for Jordanian territory under occupation since June 1967 by Israeli military forces. Excluding foreigners, including registered Palestinian refugees. - Données se raportent au 31 décembre. Non compris les données pour le territoire jordanien occupé depuis

juin 1967 par les forces armées israéliennes. Non compris les étrangers, mais y compris les réfugiés de Palestine enregistrés.

[67] Data are calculated from the results of the Population and Housing Census of 2009. - Les données sont calculées à partir des résultats du recensement de la population et de l'habitat de 2009.

[68] Based on the results of the 2005 Population and Housing Census. - Données fondées sur les résultats du recensement de la population et de l'habitat de 2005.

[69] Based on the results of a household survey. - D'après les résultats d'une enquête des ménages.

[70] Data have been adjusted for underenumeration. - Les données ont été ajustées pour compenser les lacunes du dénombrement.

[71] Intercensal Mid-Year Population Estimates based on the adjusted Population and Housing Census of 2000 and 2010. - Les estimations inter-censitaires au millieu de l'année sont fondée sur les résultats ajustées des recensements de la population et de l'habitat de 2000 et 2010.

[72] Estimates based on the adjusted Population and Housing Census of 2010. - Les estimations sont fondée sur les résultats ajustées du recensement de la population et de l'habitat de 2010.

[73] Total Population is taken as de facto and de jure together. - Population totale considérée comme de fait et de droit.

[74] Data refer to 1 October. - Données se raportent au 1 octobre.

[75] Excluding data for the Pakistan-held part of Jammu and Kashmir, the final status of which has not yet been determined. - Non compris les données concernant la partie du Jammu et Cachemire occupée par le Pakistan dont le statut définitif n'a pas été déterminé.

[76] Excluding data for the Pakistan-held part of Jammu and Kashmir, the final status of which has not yet been determined. Based on the results of the Pakistan Demographic Survey (PDS 2005). These estimates do not reflect completely accurately the actual population and vital events of the country. - Non compris les données concernant la partie du Jammu et Cachemire occupée par le Pakistan dont le statut définitif n'a pas été déterminé. D'après les résultats de l'enquête démographique effectuée par le Pakistan en 2005. Ces estimations ne dénotent pas d'une manière complètement ponctuelle la population actuelle et les statistiques de l'état civil du pays.

[77] Excluding 2739 Filipinos in Philippine Embassies, Consulates and Mission Abroad. - Excepté 2739 Philippins travaillant dans les ambassades, les consulats et les missions des Philippines à l'étranger.

[78] Excluding usual residents not in the country at the time of census. - À l'exclusion des résidents habituels qui ne sont pas dans le pays au moment du recensement.

[79] Data based on the preliminary results of the 2010 Population and Housing Census. - D'après les résultats préliminaires du recensement de la population et des logements de 2010.

[80] Urban and rural breakdown not applicable as Singapore is a city-state. Data are based on the latest register-based population estimates for 2010. Data refer to resident population which comprises Singapore citizens and permanent residents. - La ventilation entre zones urbaines et zones rurales ne s'applique pas à Singapour, puisqu'il s'agit d'une ville État. Données basées sur les estimations démographiques les plus récentes fondées sur les registres de 2010. Les données se rapportent à la population résidente composé des citoyens de Singapour et des résidents permanents.

[81] Data refer to total population, which comprises Singapore residents and non-residents. Data refer to 30 June. - Les données se rapportent à la population totale composé des résidents de Singapour et les non résidents. Données se raportent au 30 juin.

[82] Data have been adjusted for underenumeration, estimated at 2.70 per cent. - Les données ont été ajustées pour compenser les lacunes du dénombrement, estimées à 2,70 p. 100.

[83] Including Palestinian refugees. - Y compris les réfugiés de Palestine.

[84] Data based on Address Based Population Registration System. - Les données sont basées sur le registre national de la population basé sur l'adresse.

[85] Data include non-national population. - Les données comprennent les non-nationaux.

[86] Data are adjusted according to the results of the 1999 and 2009 censuses. - Les données ont été ajustées à partir des résultats des recensements de la population de 1999 et 2009.

[87] Statistics are compiled from registers. - Les statistiques sont compilées à partir des registres.

[88] Excluding Faeroe Islands and Greenland shown separately, if available. - Non compris les Iles Féroé et le Groenland, qui font l'objet de rubriques distinctes, si disponible.

[89] Data refer to 1 January. Population statistics are compiled from registers. - Données se raportent au 1 janvier. Les statistiques de la population sont compilées à partir des registres.

[90] Excluding Åland Islands. - Non compris les Îles d'Åland.

[91] Excluding diplomatic personnel outside the country and including members of alien armed forces not living in military camps and foreign diplomatic personnel not living in embassies or consulates. - Non compris le personnel diplomatique hors du pays et y compris les militaires étrangers ne vivant pas dans des camps militaires et le personnel diplomatique étranger ne vivant pas dans les ambassades ou les consulats.

[92] Data of the microcensus - a 1 per cent household sample survey - refer to a single reference week in spring (usually last week in April). Excluding homeless persons. Excluding foreign military personnel and foreign diplomatic and consular personnel and their family members in the country. - Les données du microrecensement (enquête sur les ménages, réalisée sur un échantillon de 1 pour cent) concernent une seule semaine de référence au printemps (habituellement la dernière semaine d'avril). Non compris les personnes sans domicile fixe. Non compris le personnel militaire étranger, le personnel diplomatique et consulaire étranger et les membres de leur famille se trouvant dans le pays.

[93] Excluding families of military personnel, visitors and transients. - Non compris les familles des militaires, ni les visiteurs et transients.

[94] Data refer to 31 December. Excluding military personnel, visitors and transients. - Données se raportent au 31 décembre. Non compris les militaires, ni les visiteurs et transients.

[95] Excluding armed forces stationed outside the country, but including alien armed forces stationed in the area. - Non compris les militaires en garnison hors du pays, mais y compris les militaires étrangers en garnison sur le territoire.

[96] Excluding armed forces stationed outside the country, but including alien armed forces stationed in the area. Data refer to 1 January. - Non compris les militaires en garnison hors du pays, mais y compris les militaires étrangers en garnison sur le territoire. Données se raportent au 1 janvier.

[97] Data refer to 31 March. - Données se raportent au 31 mars.

[98] Data refer to the Vatican City State. - Les données se rapportent à l'Etat de la Cité du Vatican.

[99] Population statistics are compiled from registers. Including nationals outside the country. - Les statistiques de la population sont compilées à partir des registres. Y compris les nationaux hors du pays.

[100] Data refer to 21 June. - Données se raportent au 21 juin.

[101] Surface area is 0.44 Km2. - Superficie: 0,44 Km2.

[102] Population statistics are compiled from registers. Definition of localities was revised from 2011 causing a break with the previous series. - Les statistiques de la population sont compilées à partir des registres. La rupture par rapport aux séries précédentes s'explique par le fait que la définition des localités a été révisée depuis 2011.

[103] Data refer to 15 April. - Données se raportent au 15 avril.

[104] Data refer to 30 April. - Données se raportent au 30 avril.

[105] Including civilian nationals temporarily outside the country. - Y compris les civils nationaux temporairement hors du pays.

[106] Including civilian nationals temporarily outside the country. Data refer to 1 January. - Y compris les civils nationaux temporairement hors du pays. Données se raportent au 1 janvier.

[107] Figures for male and female population do not add up to the figure for total population, because they exclude 119 persons of unknown sex. - Les chiffres relatifs à la population masculine et féminine ne correspondent pas au chiffre de la population totale, parce que l'on en a exclu 119 personnes de sexe inconnu.

[108] Census results based on compilation of continuous accounting and sample surveys. - Le résultat du recensement, d'après les résultats des dénombrements et enquêtes par sondage continue.

[109] Including residents temporarily outside the country. Population statistics are compiled from registers. - Y compris les résidents se trouvant temporairement hors du pays. Les statistiques de la population sont compilées à partir des registres.

[110] Including residents temporarily outside the country. - Y compris les résidents se trouvant temporairement hors du pays.

[111] Including residents temporarily outside the country. Data refer to 1 January. - Y compris les résidents se trouvant temporairement hors du pays. Données se raportent au 1 janvier.

[112] Excluding civilian aliens within country, but including civilian nationals temporarily outside country. - Non compris les civils étrangers dans le pays, mais y compris les civils nationaux temporairement hors du pays.

[113] Excluding civilian aliens within country, but including civilian nationals temporarily outside country. Data refer to 1 January. - Non compris les civils étrangers dans le pays, mais y compris les civils nationaux temporairement hors du pays. Données se raportent au 1 janvier.

[114] Excluding Transnistria and the municipality of Bender. - Les données ne tiennent pas compte de l'information sur la Transnistria et la municipalité de Bender.

[115] Excluding Transnistria and the municipality of Bender. Data refer to 1 January. - Les données ne tiennent pas compte de l'information sur la Transnistria et la municipalité de Bender. Données se raportent au 1 janvier.

[116] Excludes data for Kosovo and Metohia. - Sans les données pour le Kosovo et Metohie.

[117] Excludes data for Kosovo and Metohia. Data refer to 1 January. - Sans les données pour le Kosovo et Metohie. Données se raportent au 1 janvier.

[118] Excluding inland water. - Exception faite des eaux intérieures.

[119] Inhabited only during the winter season. Census data are for total population while estimates refer to Norwegian population only. Included also in the de jure population of Norway. - N'est habitée que pendant la saison d'hiver. Les données de recensement se rapportent à la population totale, mais les estimations ne concernent que la population norvégienne, comprise également dans la population de droit de la Norvège.

[120] Data refer to 1 January. Data refer to Svalbard only. - Données se raportent au 1 janvier. Données ne concernant que le Svalbard.

[121] Excluding Channel Islands (Guernsey and Jersey) and Isle of Man, shown separately, if available. - Non compris les îles Anglo-Normandes (Guernesey et Jersey) et l'île de Man, qui font l'objet de rubriques distinctes, si disponible.

[122] This data has been randomly rounded to protect confidentiality. Individual figures may not add up to totals, and values for the same data may vary in different tables. Including population in off-shore, migratory and shipping. - Ces données ont été arrondies de façon aléatoire afin d'en préserver la confidentialité. La somme de certains chiffres peut ne pas correspondre aux totaux indiqués et les valeurs des mêmes données peuvent varier d'un tableau à un autre. Y compris les populations extraterritoriales, les populations nomades et les populations maritimes.

[123] Data are based on Australian Standard Geographical Classification boundaries. Intercensal estimates. - Les données réfèrent au découpage de la nomenclature géographique normalisée d'Australie. Estimations inter-censitaires.

[124] Data are based on Australian Standard Geographical Classification boundaries. These estimates are preliminary revised. - Les données réfèrent au découpage de la nomenclature géographique normalisée d'Australie. Ces estimations sont des estimations préliminaires révisées.

[125] Excluding Niue, shown separately, which is part of Cook Islands, but because of remoteness is administered separately. - Non compris Nioué, qui fait l'objet d'une rubrique distincte et qui fait partie des îles Cook, mais qui, en raison de son éloignement, est administrée séparément.

[126] Including armed forces stationed in the area. Data refer to projections based on the 2010 Population Census. - Y compris les militaires en garnison sur le territoire. Les données se réfèrent aux projections basées sur le recensement de la population de 2010.

[127] Land area only. Excluding 84 square km of uninhabited islands. - La superficie des terres seulement. Exclut des îles inhabitées d'une superficie de 84 kilomètres carrés.

[128] This data has been randomly rounded to protect confidentiality. Individual figures may not add up to totals, and values for the same data may vary in different tables. - Ces données ont été arrondies de façon aléatoire afin d'en préserver la confidentialité. La somme de certains chiffres peut ne pas correspondre aux totaux indiqués et les valeurs des mêmes données peuvent varier d'un tableau à un autre.

[129] Based on the census, updated for residents missed or counted more than once by the census (net census undercount); residents temporarily overseas on census night, and births, deaths and net migration between the census night and the date of the estimate. Because of rounding, totals are not in all cases the sum of the respective components. - D'après le recensement, mise à jour pour les résidents omis ou dénombrés plus d'une fois par le recensement (sous-dénombrement net); résidents temporairement à l'étranger la nuit du recensement, et naissances, décès et migration nette entre la nuit du recensement et la date de l'estimation. Les chiffres étant arrondis, les totaux ne correspondent pas toujours rigoureusement à la somme des composants respectifs.

[130] Data refer to national projections. Based on the results of the 1996 population census. - Les données se réfèrent aux projections nationales. À partir des résultats du recensement de la population de 1996.

Table 4 - *Demographic Yearbook 2012*

Table 4 presents, for each country or area of the world, basic vital statistics for the period 2008 - 2012: live births, crude birth rate, deaths, crude death rate, rate of natural increase, infant deaths, infant death rate, life expectancy at birth by sex and total fertility rate.

Description of variables: The vital events and rates shown in this table are defined as follows[1]:

Live birth is the complete expulsion or extraction from its mother of a product of conception, irrespective of the duration of pregnancy, which after such separation breathes or shows any other evidence of life such as beating of the heart, pulsation of the umbilical cord, definite movement of voluntary muscles, whether or not the umbilical cord has been cut or the placenta is attached. Each product of such a birth is considered live-born regardless of gestational age.

Death is the permanent disappearance of all evidence of life at any time after live birth has taken place (post-natal cessation of vital functions without capability of resuscitation).

Infant deaths are deaths of live-born infants under one year of age.

Life expectancy at birth is defined as the average number of years of life for males and females if they continued to be subject to the same mortality experienced in the year(s) to which these life expectancies refer.

The total fertility rate is the average number of children that would be born alive to a hypothetical cohort of women if, throughout their reproductive years, the age-specific fertility rates remained unchanged. The standard method of calculating the total fertility rate is the sum of the age-specific fertility rates.

Crude birth rates and crude death rates presented in this table are calculated using the number of live births and the number of deaths obtained from civil registers. These civil registration data are used only if they are considered reliable (estimated completeness of 90 per cent or more).

Similarly, infant mortality rates presented in this table are calculated using the number of live births and the number of infant deaths obtained from civil registers. If, however, the registration of births or infant deaths for any given country or area is estimated to be less than 90 per cent complete, the rates are not calculated.

For some countries, the data and rates presented in this table are based on vital statistics data sourced from censuses or demographic surveys.

Rate computation: The crude birth and death rates are the annual number of each of these vital events per 1 000 mid-year population.

Infant mortality rate is the annual number of deaths of infants under one year of age per 1 000 live births in the same year.

Rates of natural increase are the difference between the crude birth rate and the crude death rate. It should be noted that the rates of natural increase presented here may differ from the population growth rates presented in table 3 as rates of natural increase do not take net international migration into account while the population growth rates do.

Rates that appear in this table have been calculated by the Statistics Division of the United Nations Department of Economic and Social Affairs, unless otherwise noted. Exceptions include official estimated rates for Bangladesh and India, which were based on sample registration systems in these countries.

Rates calculated by the Statistics Division of the United Nations presented in this table have been limited to those countries or areas having a minimum number of 30 events (for life births and deaths) or 100 events (for infant deaths) in a given year.

Reliability of data: Rates calculated on the basis of registered vital statistics which are considered unreliable (estimated to be less than 90 per cent complete) are not calculated. Estimated rates, prepared by individual countries or areas, are presented whenever applicable.

The designation of vital statistics as being either reliable or unreliable is discussed in general in section 4.2 of the Technical Notes. The technical notes for tables 9, 15 and 18 provide specific information on reliability of statistics on live births, infant deaths and deaths, respectively.

The values shown for life expectancy in this table come from official life tables. It is assumed that, if necessary, the basic data (population and deaths classified by age and sex) have been adjusted for deficiencies before their use in constructing the life tables.

Limitations: Statistics on births, deaths and infant deaths are subject to the same qualifications as have been set forth for vital statistics, in general, in section 4 of the Technical Notes and in the technical notes for individual tables presenting detailed data on these events (table 9, live births; table 15, infant deaths; table 18, deaths).

In assessing comparability it is important to take into account the reliability of the data used to calculate the rates, as discussed above.

The problem of obtaining precise correspondence between numerator (births and deaths) and denominator (population for crude birth and death rates) as regards the inclusion or exclusion of armed forces, refugees, displaced persons and other special groups is particularly difficult where vital rates are concerned. This is the case for Japan, where births and deaths refer to Japanese nationals only while the population include foreigners except foreign military and civilian personnel and their dependants stationed in the area.

It should also be noted that crude rates are particularly affected by the age-sex structure of the population. Infant mortality rates, and to a much lesser extent crude birth rates and crude death rates, are affected by the variation in the definition of a live birth and tabulation procedures.

NOTES

[1] *Principles and Recommendations for a Vital Statistics System, Revision 2,* United Nations publication, Sales No. E.01.XVII.10, United Nations, New York, 2001.

Tableau 4 – *Annuaire démographique 2012*

Le tableau 4 présente, pour chaque pays ou zone du monde, des statistiques de base de l'état civil pour les années 2008 – 2012 : les naissances vivantes, le taux brut de natalité, les décès, le taux brut de mortalité et le taux d'accroissement naturel de la population, les décès d'enfants de moins d'un an et le taux de mortalité infantile, l'espérance de vie à la naissance par sexe et l'indice synthétique de fécondité.

Description des variables : les faits d'état civil utilisés aux fins du calcul des taux présentés dans le tableau 4 sont définis comme suit[1] :

La naissance vivante est l'expulsion ou l'extraction complète du corps de la mère, indépendamment de la duré de la gestation, d'un produit de la conception qui après cette séparation, respire ou manifeste tout autre signe de vie, tel que battement de cœur, pulsation du cordon ombilical ou contraction effective d'un muscle soumis à l'action de la volonté, que le cordon ombilical ait été coupé ou non et que le placenta soit ou non demeuré attaché ; tout produit d'une telle naissance est considéré comme « enfant né vivant ».

Le décès est la disparition permanente de tout signe de vie à un moment quelconque postérieur à la naissance vivante (cessation des fonctions vitales après la naissance sans possibilité de réanimation).

Il convient de préciser que les chiffres relatifs aux décès d'enfants de moins d'un an se rapportent aux naissances vivantes.

L'espérance de vie à la naissance est le nombre moyen d'années que vivraient les individus de sexe masculin et de sexe féminin s'ils continuaient d'être soumis aux mêmes conditions de mortalité que celles qui existaient pendant les années auxquelles se rapportent les valeurs indiquées.

L'indice synthétique de fécondité représente le nombre moyen d'enfants que mettrait au monde une cohorte hypothétique de femmes qui seraient soumises, tout au long de leur vie, aux mêmes conditions de fécondité par âge que celles auxquelles sont soumises les femmes, dans chaque groupe d'âge, au cours d'une année ou d'une période donnée. La méthode standard pour calculer l'indice synthétique de fécondité consiste à additionner les taux de fécondité par âge simple.

Les taux bruts de natalité et de mortalité ont été établis sur la base du nombre de naissances vivantes et du nombre de décès inscrits sur les registres de l'état civil. Ces données n'ont été utilisées que lorsqu'elles étaient considérées comme sûres (degré estimatif de complétude égal ou supérieur à 90 p. 100).

De même, les taux de mortalité infantile présentés dans le tableau 4 ont été établis à partir du nombre de naissances vivantes et du nombre de décès d'enfants de moins d'un an inscrits sur les registres de l'état civil. Toutefois, lorsque les données relatives aux naissances ou aux décès d'enfants de moins d'un an pour un pays ou zone quelconque n'étaient pas considérées complètes à 90 p. 100 au moins, les indices n'ont pas été calculés.

Pour quelques pays, les données et les taux présentés dans ce tableau ont été extraites des recensements de la population ou des enquêtes démographiques.

Calcul des taux : les taux bruts de natalité et de mortalité, représentent le nombre annuel de chacun de ces faits d'état civil pour 1 000 habitants au milieu de l'année considérée.

Les taux de mortalité infantile correspondent au nombre annuel de décès d'enfants de moins d'un an pour 1 000 naissances vivantes survenues pendant la même année.

Le taux d'accroissement naturel est égal à la différence entre le taux brut de natalité et le taux brut de mortalité. Il y a lieu de noter que les taux d'accroissement naturel indiqués dans le tableau 4 peuvent différer des taux d'accroissement de la population figurant dans le tableau 3, les taux d'accroissement naturel ne tenant pas compte des taux nets de migration internationale, alors que ceux-ci sont inclus dans les taux d'accroissement de la population.

Sauf indication contraire, les taux figurant dans le tableau 4 ont été calculés par la Division de statistique du Département des affaires économiques et sociales de l'Organisation des Nations Unies. Les exceptions comprennent le Bangladesh et l'Inde, pour lesquels les taux estimatifs officiels ont été fournis sur la base d'un système d'enregistrement par échantillonnage.

Les taux calculés par la Division de statistique de l'Organisation des Nations Unies qui sont présentés dans le tableau 4 se rapportent aux seuls pays ou zones où l'on a enregistré au moins 30 événements (pour les naissances vivantes et les décès) ou 100 événements (pour les décès d'enfants de moins d'un an) au cours d'une année donnée.

Fiabilité des données : les taux n'ont pas été calculés lorsque les statistiques de l'état civil issues de systèmes d'enregistrement d'état civil étaient jugées douteuses (degré estimatif de complétude inférieur à 90 p.100) et des taux estimatifs, calculés par les pays ou zones, ont été présentés lorsqu'ils étaient disponibles.

On trouve à la section 4.2 des Notes techniques des explications générales concernant la façon dont les statistiques de l'état civil ont été classées selon leur degré de fiabilité. Les notes techniques relatives aux tableaux 9, 15 et 18 ont trait respectivement à la fiabilité des statistiques des naissances vivantes, des décès d'enfants de moins d'un an et des décès.

Les valeurs relatives à l'espérance de vie figurant dans le tableau 4 proviennent de tables officielles de mortalité. On présume que les données de base (la population et les décès par sexe et âge) ont été rectifiées d'éventuelles insuffisances avant d'être utilisées pour construire les tables de mortalité.

Insuffisance des données : les statistiques des naissances, décès et décès d'enfants de moins d'un an appellent toutes les réserves qui ont été formulées à propos des statistiques de l'état civil en général à la section 4 des Notes techniques et dans les notes techniques relatives aux différents tableaux présentant des données détaillées sur ces événements [tableau 9 (naissances vivantes), tableau 15 (décès d'enfants de moins d'un an) et tableau 18 (décès)].

Pour évaluer la comparabilité des divers taux, il importe de tenir compte de la fiabilité des données utilisées pour calculer ces taux, comme il a été indiqué précédemment.

Le calcul des taux est particulièrement affecté par la difficulté à obtenir une correspondance parfaite entre le numérateur (naissances et décès) et le dénominateur (population, pour les taux bruts de natalité et de mortalité) en raison de l'inclusion ou non dans la population des forces armées, des réfugiés, des personnes déplacées ou d'autres groupes sociaux. C'est le cas pour le Japon, où les naissances et les décès se réfèrent aux seuls nationaux japonais tandis que la population inclus les étrangers, à l'exception toutefois des militaires étrangers ainsi que des personnels civils et leurs familles stationnés sur le territoire.

Il y a lieu de noter que la structure par âge et par sexe de la population influe de façon particulière sur les taux bruts. Le manque d'uniformité dans la définition des naissances vivantes et dans les procédures de mise en tableaux a une incidence sur les taux de mortalité infantile et, à un moindre degré, sur les taux bruts de natalité et les taux bruts de mortalité.

NOTE

[1] *Principes et recommandations pour un système de statistiques de l'état civil, deuxième révision,* numéro de vente : F.01.XVII.10, publication des Nations Unies, New York, 2001.

4. Vital statistics summary and life expectancy at birth: 2008 - 2012
Aperçu des statistiques de l'état civil et de l'espérance de vie à la naissance : 2008 - 2012

Continent, country or area and year / Continent, pays ou zone et année	Live births / Naissances vivantes Code[a]	Number Nombre	Crude birth rate Taux brut de natalité	Deaths / Décès Code[a]	Number Nombre	Crude death rate Taux brut de mortalité	Rate of natural increase Taux d'accroissement naturel	Infant deaths / Décès d'enfants de moins d'un an Code[a]	Number Nombre	Rate (per 1000 births) Taux (par 1000 naissances)	Life expectancy at birth / Espérance de vie à la naissance Male[b] Masculin[b]	Female[b] Féminin[b]	Total fertility rate L'indice synthétique de fécondité
AFRICA - AFRIQUE													
Algeria - Algérie													
2008	C	817 000[1]	23.6	U	153 000[1]	...	...	U	20 793[1]	...	74.9[2]	76.6[2]	2.840
2009	C	849 000[1]	24.1	U	159 000[1]	...	...	U	21 076[1]	...	74.7[2]	76.3[2]	...
2010	C	887 810[1]	24.7	U	157 000[1]	...	...	U	21 046[1]	...	75.6[2]	77.0[2]	2.870
2011	C	910 000[1]	24.8	U	162 000[1]	...	...	U	21 055[1]	...	...	...	2.870
2012	C	977 992[1]	26.1	U	170 000[1]	...	...	U	22 088[1]	...	...	...	3.020
Botswana[3]													
2008		...	...		...	...	...		...	...	...	...	2.791
2009		...	...		...	...	...		...	...	...	...	2.791
2010		...	...		...	...	...		...	...	...	...	2.791
2011		...	...		...	...	...		...	...	...	...	2.689
Burkina Faso[3]													
2008	I	679 200	46.1	I	174 800	11.9	34.2		...	...	...	...	...
Cabo Verde													
2008	C	12 697	25.4	C	2 873	5.7	19.7	C	316	24.9	...	...	...
2009	C	13 044	25.6	C	2 897	5.7	19.9		...	...	...	...	...
2010	C	13 415	25.9	C	2 917	5.6	20.3		...	...	...	...	...
Egypt - Égypte													
2008	+C	2 050 704	27.3	C	461 934	6.1	21.1	C	32 174	15.7	...	...	3.000
2009	+C	2 217 409	28.8	C	476 592	6.2	22.6	C	25 760	11.6	...	...	...
2010	+C	2 261 409	28.7	C	483 385	6.1	22.6	C	31 698	14.0	68.2	70.9	...
2011	+C	2 442 094	30.4	C	493 086	6.1	24.2	C	35 997	14.7	68.6	71.4	...
Ghana													
2008	+U	553 119[4]	...		...	...	...	+U	52 038	...	...	...	4.000
Kenya													
2008	U	660 383	...	U	219 477	...	...	U	46 565	...	...	...	4.600
2009	U	698 447	...	U	178 352	...	...	U	40 190	...	...	...	...
2010	U	747 576	...	U	175 760	...	...		...	...	...	...	...
2011	U	746 643	...	U	174 487	...	...	U	23 167	...	...	...	...
2012	U	754 429	...	U	173 912	...	...		...	...	...	...	...
Liberia - Libéria[5]													
2008	I	63 171	18.2		...	...	...		...	...	...	...	...
Libya - Libye[6]													
2008	+U	132 826	...	+U	21 481	...	...		...	...	...	...	...
2009	+U	134 682	...	+U	22 859	...	...		...	...	...	...	...
Malawi[7]													
2008	I	516 629	37.9	I	135 865	10.0	27.9		...	...	...	...	...
Mauritius - Maurice[8]													
2008	+C	16 372	12.9	+C	9 004	7.1	5.8	+C	236	14.4	[III]69.2	76.1	1.582
2009	+C	15 344	12.0	+C	9 224	7.2	4.8	+C	205	13.4	[III]69.4	76.6	1.502
2010	+C	15 005	11.7	+C	9 131	7.1	4.6	+C	187	12.5	[III]69.5	76.7	1.466
2011	+C	14 701	11.4	+C	9 170	7.1	4.3	+C	189	12.9	[III]69.7	77.0	1.446
2012	+C*	14 494	11.2	+C*	9 343	7.2	4.0		...	...	...	...	...
Republic of South Sudan - République de Soudan du Sud[9]													
2008		...	...	I	165 897	20.1	...		...	...	...	...	...
Réunion													
2008	C	14 927[10]	18.5	C	4 115	5.1	13.4		...	...	...	...	...
2009	C	14 299[10]	17.5	C	4 109	5.0	12.5		...	...	74.9	82.7	...
2010	C	14 146[10]	17.1	C	4 221	5.1	12.0		...	...	...	...	...
Rwanda													
2008	U	407 157	...	U	141 640	...	...		...	...	49.0	52.8	5.460
2009	U	408 353	...	U	141 648	...	...		...	...	49.4	53.3	5.420
2010	U	408 267	...	U	141 256	...	...	U	27	...	...	...	5.380
2011	U	406 838	...	U	140 519	...	...		...	...	...	...	5.340
2012	U	404 067	...	U	139 499	...	...		...	...	...	...	5.300

Continent, country or area and year / Continent, pays ou zone et année	Live births / Naissances vivantes			Deaths / Décès			Rate of natural increase / Taux d'accroissement naturel	Infant deaths / Décès d'enfants de moins d'un an			Life expectancy at birth / Espérance de vie à la naissance		Total fertility rate / L'indice synthétique de fécondité
	Code[a]	Number / Nombre	Crude birth rate / Taux brut de natalité	Code[a]	Number / Nombre	Crude death rate / Taux brut de mortalité		Code[a]	Number / Nombre	Rate (per 1000 births) / Taux (par 1000 naissances)	Male[b] / Masculin[b]	Female[b] / Féminin[b]	
AFRICA - AFRIQUE													
Saint Helena ex. dep. - Sainte-Hélène sans dép.													
2008	C	36	9.0	C	44	11.1	-2.0	C	-	...	X71.1	77.6	...
2009	C	35	8.5	C	41	9.9	-1.5	C	-	...	X72.5	79.2	...
2010	C	34	8.0	C	53	12.5	-4.5	C	-	...	...	...	...
2011	C	34	8.0	C	49	11.5	-3.5	C	-	...	...	...	...
2012	C	32	7.9	C	62	15.3	-7.4	C	1	...	X72.0	79.7	...
Senegal - Sénégal													
2008	I	488 754[11]	41.3	I	136 839[11]	11.6	29.7	I	31 889[11]	65.2	...	...	4.970[3]
2009	I	498 714[11]	41.0	I	138 182[11]	11.4	29.6	I	32 094[11]	64.4	...	...	4.910[3]
2010	I	509 230[11]	40.7	I	139 651[11]	11.2	29.5	I	32 314[11]	63.5	...	...	4.860[3]
2011		...	...		...	...	...		...	...	56.9[3]	59.8[3]	...
Seychelles													
2008	+C	1 546	17.8	+C	662	7.6	10.2	+C	20	...	68.4	78.0	2.300
2009	+C	1 580	18.1	+C	684	7.8	10.3	+C	17	...	...	...	2.380
2010	+C	1 504	16.8	+C	664	7.4	9.4	+C	21	...	...	...	2.170
2011	+C	1 625	18.6	+C	691	7.9	10.7	+C	16	...	67.7	78.1	2.380
Sierra Leone													
2008	+...	114 823	...	+...	14 045	...	...	+...	2 895	...	...	...	6.100
2009	+...	107 947	...	+...	11 819	...	...	+...	3 137	...	...	...	5.820
2010	+...	101 185	...	+...	10 847	...	...	+...	1 935	...	...	...	5.820
2011	+...	117 207	...	+...	13 674	...	...	+...	1 289	...	...	...	5.820
2012	+...	147 958	...	+...	12 767	...	...	+...	2 135	...	...	...	5.820
South Africa - Afrique du Sud													
2008	U	1 062 689	...	U	592 073	...	...	...	45 316	...	53.3	57.2	2.410
2009	U	1 000 741	...	U	572 673	...	...		...	...	53.5	57.2	2.380
2010	U	939 646	...		...	...	...		...	...	...	...	...
2011	U	1 059 417	...	I	604 545[12]	12.0	...		...	...	...	...	...
Swaziland													
2008		...	...		...	...	...		...	...	...	...	3.900
2009		...	...		...	...	...		...	...	...	...	3.800
2010		...	...		...	...	...		...	...	...	...	3.800
2011		...	...		...	...	...		...	...	...	...	3.700
2012		...	...		...	...	...		...	...	...	...	3.600
Tunisia - Tunisie													
2008	C	182 990	17.7	U	59 975	...	...		...	...	72.4	76.3	2.060
2009	C	184 282	17.7	U	59 499	...	...		...	...	72.5	76.5	2.050
2010	C	196 039	18.6	U	60 438	...	...		...	...	72.7	76.6	2.130
2011	C	201 120	18.8	U	63 258	...	...		...	...	72.9	76.9	2.150
Uganda - Ouganda[13]													
2011		...	...		...	...	...		...	...	...	...	6.200
United Republic of Tanzania - République Unie de Tanzanie													
2008	...	1 656 216	...	...	576 705	...	...		...	...	...	...	5.300
2009	...	1 667 889	...	...	577 393	...	...		...	...	...	...	5.200
2010	...	1 678 325	...	...	573 213	...	...		...	...	...	...	5.100
2011	...	1 687 203	...	...	565 099	...	...		...	...	...	...	5.000
2012	...	1 694 943	...	...	555 975	...	...		...	...	...	...	4.900
AMERICA, NORTH - AMÉRIQUE DU NORD													
Anguilla													
2008	+C	154	9.9	+C	52[14]	3.3	6.6	+C	...	...	...	...	...
2009	+C	181	11.3	+C	59[14]	3.7	7.6		...	...	...	...	...
2010	+C	182	11.1	+C	66[14]	4.0	7.1		...	...	...	...	...
2011	+C	185	11.1	+C	57[14]	3.4	7.7		...	...	...	...	...

4. Vital statistics summary and life expectancy at birth: 2008 - 2012
Aperçu des statistiques de l'état civil et de l'espérance de vie à la naissance : 2008 - 2012 (continued - suite)

Continent, country or area and year / Continent, pays ou zone et année	Code[a]	Live births - Naissances vivantes Number Nombre	Crude birth rate Taux brut de natalité	Code[a]	Deaths - Décès Number Nombre	Crude death rate Taux brut de mortalité	Rate of natural increase Taux d'accroissement naturel	Code[a]	Infant deaths - Décès d'enfants de moins d'un an Number Nombre	Rate (per 1000 births) Taux (par 1000 naissances)	Life expectancy at birth - Espérance de vie à la naissance Male[b] Masculin[b]	Female[b] Féminin[b]	Total fertility rate L'indice synthétique de fécondité
AMERICA, NORTH - AMÉRIQUE DU NORD													
Antigua and Barbuda - Antigua-et-Barbuda													
2008	+C	1 452	16.6	+C	531	6.1	10.5	+C	14	...	71.6	78.1	...
2009	+C	1 418	15.9	+C	507	5.7	10.2	+C	7	...	72.9	78.7	...
2010	+C	1 255	13.8	+C	491	5.4	8.4	+C	11	...	74.0	79.7	...
Aruba													
2008	C	1 218	11.6	C	523	5.0	6.6		...	...	...	...	2.000
2009	C	1 213	11.3	C	623	5.8	5.5		...	...	...	...	1.900
2010	C	1 141	11.2	C	610	6.0	5.2		...	...	...	...	1.900
2011		...	...		...	...							1.700
Bahamas													
2008	+U	5 124	...	+C	1 863	5.5	...	+C	71	...	...	...	1.995
2009	+U	5 027	...	+C	2 021	5.9	...	+C	71	...	...	...	2.025
2010	+U	4 915	...	+C*	2 023	5.8	...	+C*	67	...	...	...	1.825
2011	+U	4 747	...	+C*	2 117	6.0	...	+C*	48	...	...	...	1.977
Bermuda - Bermudes													
2008	C	821[15]	12.8	C	443[15]	6.9	5.9	C	4	...	76.8	82.1	1.765
2009	C	819[15]	12.7	C	471[15]	7.3	5.4	C	1	...	...	...	1.765
2010	C	769[15]	11.9	C	475[15]	7.4	4.6	C	1	...	76.9	82.3	1.764
2011	C	670[15]	10.4	C	429[15]	6.6	3.7	C	-	...	76.6	82.1	1.768
2012		...	...		...	...	...				77.2	82.4	1.763
Canada													
2008	C	377 886[16]	11.3	C	238 617[16]	7.2	4.2	C	1 911[16]	5.1	III78.5	83.2	1.681
2009	C	380 863[16]	11.3	C	238 418[16]	7.1	4.2		...	...	...	...	1.668
2010	C	377 213[16]	11.1	C	240 075[16]	7.0	4.0		...	...	...	...	...
2011	C	377 636[16]	11.0	C	242 074[16]	7.0	3.9		...	...	...	...	...
Cayman Islands - Îles Caïmanes													
2008	C	793[17]	14.2	C	166	3.0	11.2		...	...	...	...	...
2009	C	824[17]	15.6	C	152	2.9	12.7	C	3	...	...	...	...
2010	C	821[17]	15.0	C	152	2.8	12.2	C	2	...	...	...	...
2011	C	800[17]	14.5	C	176	3.2	11.3		...	...	...	...	...
2012	C*	759[17]	13.4	C*	172	3.0	10.3		...	...	...	...	...
Costa Rica													
2008	C	75 187	16.9	C	18 021	4.0	12.8	C	673	9.0	...	...	1.900
2009	C	75 000	16.6	C	18 560	4.1	12.5	C	663	8.8	76.8	81.8	1.974
2010	C*	70 922	15.5	C*	19 077	4.2	11.4	C*	671	9.5	76.8	81.8	1.810
2011	C*	73 459	15.9	C*	18 801	4.1	11.8	C*	666	9.1	...	...	...
2012	C*	73 326	15.7	C*	19 200	4.1	11.6	C*	624	8.5	...	...	...
Cuba													
2008	C	122 569	10.9	C	86 423	7.7	3.2	C	579	4.7	...	...	1.590
2009	C	130 036	11.6	C	86 940	7.7	3.8	C	626	4.8	...	...	1.704
2010	C	127 746	11.4	C	91 065	8.1	3.3	C*	581	4.5	...	...	1.687
2011	C	133 067	11.8	C*	87 040	7.7	4.1	C*	653	4.9	...	...	1.771
Curaçao													
2008	C	2 001	13.8	C	1 209	8.3	5.5	C	13	...	...	...	2.193
2009	C	1 898	13.0	C	1 114	7.6	5.4	C	20	...	...	...	2.084
2010	C	2 032	13.6	C	1 246	8.3	5.3	C	26	...	III72.0[18]	78.8[18]	2.231
2011	C	1 974	13.1	C	1 276	8.5	4.6	C	15	...	...	...	2.070[19]
Dominica - Dominique													
2008	+C	964	13.5	+C	545	7.6	5.9		...	...	73.8	78.2	...
2009	+C	943	13.2	+C	559	7.8	5.4		...	...	...	...	...
2010	+C	933	...	+C	588	...	...		...	...	...	...	...
Dominican Republic - République dominicaine													
2008	U	141 702	...	U	33 017	...	...	U	491	...	...	...	2.670
2009	U	141 184	...	U	32 856	...	...	U	473	...	69.3	75.7	2.632
2010	U	138 753	...	U	35 269	...	...	U	491	...	VI69.2	75.5	2.594

4. Vital statistics summary and life expectancy at birth: 2008 - 2012
Aperçu des statistiques de l'état civil et de l'espérance de vie à la naissance : 2008 - 2012 (continued - suite)

Continent, country or area and year / Continent, pays ou zone et année	Live births - Naissances vivantes Code[a]	Number Nombre	Crude birth rate Taux brut de natalité	Deaths - Décès Code[a]	Number Nombre	Crude death rate Taux brut de mortalité	Rate of natural increase Taux d'accrois-sement naturel	Infant deaths - Décès d'enfants de moins d'un an Code[a]	Number Nombre	Rate (per 1000 births) Taux (par 1000 naiss-ances)	Life expectancy at birth - Espérance de vie à la naissance Male[b] Masculin[b]	Female[b] Féminin[b]	Total fertility rate L'indice synthétique de fécondité
AMERICA, NORTH - AMÉRIQUE DU NORD													
Dominican Republic - République dominicaine													
2011	U	128 836	...	U	34 006	...	...	U	672	...	...	...	2.556
2012		...	...		...	...	...		...	...	...	...	2.518
El Salvador													
2008	C	111 278[20]	18.2	C	31 594	5.2	13.0	C	947[21]	8.5	...	...	...
2009	C	107 880[20]	17.5	C	32 872	5.3	12.2	C	888[21]	8.2	...	...	...
2010	C	104 939[20]	17.0	C	32 586	5.3	11.7	C	749[21]	7.1	...	...	...
2011	C	109 384[20]	17.6	C	33 211	5.3	12.3	C	826[21]	7.6	...	...	...
Greenland - Groenland													
2008	C	834	14.8	C	428	7.6	7.2	C	8	...	V66.6	71.6	2.217
2009	C	895	15.9	C	437	7.8	8.1	C	4	...			2.394
2010	C	869	15.4	C	504	8.9	6.5	C	6	...	V67.8	72.8	2.259
2011	C	821	14.5	C	476	8.4	6.1	C	9	...	V68.2	72.9	2.100
2012	C	786	13.8	C	453	8.0	5.9	C	7	...			
Guadeloupe[10]													
2008	C	5 758	14.3	C	2 786	6.9	7.4		...	...	...	...	...
2009	C	5 487	13.7	C	2 857	7.1	6.5		...	...	...	...	...
2010	C	5 341	13.3	C	2 963	7.4	5.9		...	...	...	...	...
Guatemala													
2008	C	369 769	27.0	C	70 233	5.1	21.9		...	...	...	...	...
2009	C	351 628	25.1	C	71 707	5.1	20.0		...	...	...	...	...
2010	C	361 906	25.2	C	72 748	5.1	20.1	C	7 562	20.9	...	...	...
2011	C	373 692	...	C	72 354	...	...	C	7 413	19.8	...	...	...
Honduras													
2008	+U	223 390	...	+U	36 260	...	...		...	...	...	...	...
2009	+U	223 483	...	+U	36 536	...	...		...	...	...	...	...
2010	+U	223 345	...	+U	36 812	...	...		...	...	...	...	...
2011	+U	224 409	...	+U	37 211	...	...		...	...	...	...	...
Jamaica - Jamaïque													
2008	C	43 112[22]	16.0	U	19 966[23]	...	...		...	...	...	...	...
2009	C	42 782[22]	15.9	U	18 855[23]	...	...		...	...	...	...	...
2010	C	40 508[22]	15.0	U	21 503[23]	...	...		...	...	...	...	...
2011	C	39 673[22]	14.7	U	16 926[23]	...	...		...	...	...	...	...
2012	C	39 348[22]	14.5	U	16 998[23]	...	...		...	...	...	...	...
Martinique[10]													
2008	C	5 333	13.4	C	2 793	7.0	6.4		...	...	...	...	...
2009	C	5 174	13.1	C	2 771	7.0	6.1		...	...	...	...	...
2010	C	4 889	12.3	C	2 844	7.2	5.2		...	...	...	...	...
Mexico - Mexique													
2008	+U	2 243 145[24]	...	+C	538 288[25]	5.0	...	+U	29 519[25]	...	72.8	77.5	2.104
2009	+U	2 252 786[24]	...	+C	563 516[25]	5.2	...	+U	28 983[25]	...			
2010	+U	2 643 908[24]	...	+C	590 886[25]	5.3	...	+U	28 861[25]	...			
2011	+U	2 586 287[24]	...	+C	589 646[25]	...	...	+U	29 037[25]	...			
Montserrat													
2008	+C	72	14.8	+C	45	9.2	5.5	+C	-	...	...	...	...
2009	+C	50	9.9	+C	44	8.7	1.2	+C	-	...	...	...	...
2010	+C	62	12.4	+C	40	8.0	4.4	+C	1	...	...	...	...
2011	+C	46	9.3	+C	55	11.2	-1.8	+C	-	...	...	...	...
Nicaragua													
2008	+U	125 028	...	+U	18 079	...	...	+U	1 932	...	...	...	...
2010		...	...		...	...	...		...	...	VI63.4	68.9	...
Panama													
2008	C	68 759	20.3	U	15 115	...	...	U	877	...	...	...	2.500
2009	C	68 364	19.8	U	15 498	...	...	U	837	...	...	...	2.500
2010	C	67 955	19.4	U	16 542	...	...	U	910	...	73.4[26]	78.7[26]	2.400
2011	C*	73 292	20.1	U	16 367	...	...		...	...	...	...	...
2012		...	...		...	...	...		...	...	74.1[26]	80.4[26]	...

4. Vital statistics summary and life expectancy at birth: 2008 - 2012
Aperçu des statistiques de l'état civil et de l'espérance de vie à la naissance : 2008 - 2012 (continued - suite)

Continent, country or area and year Continent, pays ou zone et année	Live births Naissances vivantes			Deaths Décès			Rate of natural increase Taux d'accrois-sement naturel	Infant deaths Décès d'enfants de moins d'un an			Life expectancy at birth Espérance de vie à la naissance		Total fertility rate L'indice synthétique de fécondité
	Co-de[a]	Number Nombre	Crude birth rate Taux brut de natalité	Co-de[a]	Number Nombre	Crude death rate Taux brut de mortalité		Co-de[a]	Number Nombre	Rate (per 1000 births) Taux (par 1000 naiss-ances)	Male[b] Masculin[b]	Female[b] Féminin[b]	
AMERICA, NORTH - AMÉRIQUE DU NORD													
Puerto Rico - Porto Rico													
2008	C	45 675	11.6	C	29 100	7.4	4.2	C	400	8.8	...	...	...
2010	C	42 153	11.3		...	...	...		...	...	...	...	...
Saint Vincent and the Grenadines - Saint-Vincent-et-les Grenadines													
2008	+C	1 901	19.2	+C	848	8.6	10.6	+C	34	17.9	...	...	...
2009	+C	1 905	18.9	+C	765	7.6	11.3	+C	32	16.8	...	...	...
Sint Maarten (Dutch part) - Saint-Martin (partie néerlandaise)													
2008	+C	526	13.1	+C	152	3.8	9.3		...	...	...	...	...
Turks and Caicos Islands - Îles Turques et Caïques													
2008	C	453[27]	12.4	C	65	1.8	10.6	C	3	...	...	...	...
United States of America - États-Unis d'Amérique													
2008	C	4 247 694	14.0	C	2 471 984	8.1	5.8	C	28 059	6.6	75.6	80.6	2.085
2009	C	4 130 665	13.5	C	2 437 163	7.9	5.5	C	26 412	6.4	...	...	2.007
2010	C	3 999 386	12.9	C	2 465 936	8.0	5.0	C*	24 548	6.1	...	...	1.932
2011	C	3 953 590	12.7	C*	2 513 171	8.1	4.6		...	...	...	...	...
United States Virgin Islands - Îles Vierges américaines													
2010	C	1 600	14.5		...	...	...		...	...	...	...	...
AMERICA, SOUTH - AMÉRIQUE DU SUD													
Argentina - Argentine													
2008	C	746 066	18.8	C	301 801	7.6	11.2	C	9 326	12.5	...	...	2.409
2009	C	745 336	18.6	C	304 525	7.6	11.0	C	9 013	12.1	...	...	2.380
2010	C	756 176	18.7	C	318 602	7.9	10.8	C	8 961	11.9	V71.6[3]	79.1[3]	2.392
2011	C	758 042	18.5	C	319 059	7.8	10.7	C	8 878	11.7	...	...	2.379
Bolivia (Plurinational State of) - Bolivie (État plurinational de)													
2008		...	...		...	...	...		...	...	...	...	3.456
2009		...	...		...	...	...		...	...	...	...	3.371
2010		...	...		...	...	...		...	...	...	...	3.287
2011		...	...		...	...	...		...	...	64.6	68.9	3.207
Brazil - Brésil													
2008	U	2 789 820	...	U	1 060 365	...	...	U	34 375[28]	...	69.1[26]	76.7[26]	1.863
2009	U	2 752 401	...	U	1 079 228	...	...	U	33 713[28]	...	69.7[26]	77.3[26]	1.806
2010	U	2 760 961[29]	...	U	1 117 675[28]	...	...	U	31 733[28]	...	...	...	1.755
2011	U	2 824 776[29]	...	U	1 148 165[28]	...	...	U	32 184[28]	...	...	...	...
Chile - Chili													
2008	C	246 581	14.7	C	90 168	5.4	9.3	C	1 948	7.9	...	...	1.918
2009	C	252 240	14.9	C	91 965	5.4	9.5	C	1 997	7.9	75.4	80.9	1.940
2010	C	250 643	14.7	C	97 930	5.7	8.9	C	1 862	7.4	VI75.5	81.5	1.910
2011		...	...		...	...	...		...	...	75.7	81.0	...
Colombia - Colombie													
2008	U	715 453	...	U	196 943	...	...	U	10 560	...	...	...	...
2009	U	699 775	...	U	196 933	...	...	U	9 580	...	...	...	...
2010	U	654 627	...	U	200 524	...	...	U	8 355	...	VI70.7[30]	77.5[30]	...
2011	U*	621 901	...	U*	162 706	...	...	U*	7 060	...	...	...	...
2012	U*	662 554	...	U*	179 646	...	...		...	...	...	...	2.350[31]

4. Vital statistics summary and life expectancy at birth: 2008 - 2012
Aperçu des statistiques de l'état civil et de l'espérance de vie à la naissance : 2008 - 2012 (continued - suite)

Continent, country or area and year / Continent, pays ou zone et année	Live births / Naissances vivantes Code[a]	Number Nombre	Crude birth rate Taux brut de natalité	Deaths / Décès Code[a]	Number Nombre	Crude death rate Taux brut de mortalité	Rate of natural increase Taux d'accrois-sement naturel	Infant deaths / Décès d'enfants de moins d'un an Code[a]	Number Nombre	Rate (per 1000 births) Taux (par 1000 naiss-ances)	Life expectancy at birth / Espérance de vie à la naissance Male[b] Masculin[b]	Female[b] Féminin[b]	Total fertility rate L'indice synthétique de fécondité
AMERICA, SOUTH - AMÉRIQUE DU SUD													
Ecuador - Équateur													
2008	+U	291 055	...	U	60 023[32]	...	...	U	3 380[32]	...	...	...	2.580[3]
2009	+U	215 906	...	U	59 714[32]	...	...	U	3 279[32]	...	...	...	2.580[3]
2010	+U	219 162	...	U	61 681[32]	...	...	U	3 204[32]	...	VI72.1[33]	78.0[33]	1.898[3]
French Guiana - Guyane française[10]													
2008	C	6 247	28.5	C	762	3.5	25.0		...	...	...	...	...
2009	C	6 171	27.5	C	699	3.1	24.4		...	...	...	...	...
2010	C	6 083	26.4	C	773	3.4	23.0		...	...	...	...	...
Guyana													
2008		...	...	+C	5 003	6.5	...		...	...	...	...	...
2009		...	...	+C	3 849	5.0	...		...	...	...	...	...
2010		...	...	+C	4 649	5.9	...		...	...	...	...	...
Paraguay													
2008	+U	99 674	...	+U	24 417	...	...	+U	1 674				
2010		...	...		...	...	...		...	...	VI69.7	73.9	...
Peru - Pérou													
2008	+U	359 140[34]	...	+U	91 277[34]	...	...	+U	5 581[35]	...	...	...	2.580
2009	+U	396 616[34]	...	+U	95 722[34]	...	...	+U	5 993[35]	...	...	...	2.530
2010	+U	402 493[34]	...	+U	99 334[34]	...	...	+U	5 287[35]	...	...	...	2.490
2011	+U	396 839[34]	...	+U	96 852[34]	...	...	+U	4 569[35]	...	...	...	2.440
2012		...	...		...	...	...		...	...	...	...	2.400
Suriname													
2008	C	10 097[36]	19.5	C	3 357[37]	6.5	13.0		...	...	...	...	...
2009	C	9 792[36]	18.7	C	3 293[37]	6.3	12.4		...	...	...	...	...
Uruguay													
2008	C	53 199	16.0	C	31 363	9.4	6.5	C	504	9.5	72.4	79.7	2.008
2009	C	47 152	14.1	C	32 179	9.6	4.5	C	451	9.6	...	...	...
2010	C	47 420	14.1	C	33 474	10.0	4.2	C	364	7.7	...	...	...
2011	C	46 699	13.9	C*	32 807	9.7	4.1	C*	417	8.9	...	...	...
2012	C	48 200	14.3	C*	33 002	9.8	4.5		...	...	...	...	...
Venezuela (Bolivarian Republic of) - Venezuela (République bolivarienne du)													
2008	C	581 480	20.8	C	124 062	4.4	16.4		...	...	...	...	2.550[38]
2009	C	593 845	20.9	C	123 530	4.4	16.6		...	...	...	...	...
2010	C	591 303	20.5	C	130 597	4.5	16.0		...	...	...	...	...
2011	C	615 132	21.0	C	136 803	4.7	16.3		...	...	...	...	...
ASIA - ASIE													
Afghanistan[39]													
2008		...	...		...	...	...		...	...	...	...	6.300
2009		...	...		...	...	...		...	...	...	...	6.300
Armenia - Arménie													
2008	C	41 185	12.7	C	27 412[40]	8.5	4.3	C	442[40]	10.7	...	...	1.444
2009	C	44 413	13.7	C	27 560[40]	8.5	5.2	C	454[40]	10.2	...	...	1.551
2010	C	44 825	13.8	C	27 921[40]	8.6	5.2	C	512[40]	11.4	...	...	...
2011	C	43 340	13.3	C	27 963[40]	8.6	4.7	C	507[40]	11.7	...	...	...
2012	C*	42 333	12.9	C*	27 514[40]	8.4	4.5		...	...	...	...	...
Azerbaijan - Azerbaïdjan													
2008	+C	152 086[40]	17.2	+C	52 710[40]	6.0	11.2	+C	1 715[40]	11.3	69.9	75.4	2.251
2009	+C	152 139[40]	17.0	+C	52 514[40]	5.9	11.1	+C	1 731[40]	11.4	71.0	76.1	2.260
2010	+C	165 643[40]	18.3	+C	53 580[40]	5.9	12.4	+C	1 843[40]	11.1	70.9	76.1	...
2011	+C	176 072[40]	19.2	+C	53 762[40]	5.9	13.3	+C	1 903[40]	10.8	...	...	...
2012	+C	174 469[40]	18.8	+C	55 017[40]	5.9	12.9	+C	1 884[40]	10.8	...	...	...

Continent, country or area and year / Continent, pays ou zone et année	Live births / Naissances vivantes Code[a]	Number Nombre	Crude birth rate Taux brut de natalité	Deaths / Décès Code[a]	Number Nombre	Crude death rate Taux brut de mortalité	Rate of natural increase Taux d'accroissement naturel	Infant deaths / Décès d'enfants de moins d'un an Code[a]	Number Nombre	Rate (per 1000 births) Taux (par 1000 naissances)	Life expectancy at birth / Espérance de vie à la naissance Male[b] Masculin[b]	Female[b] Féminin[b]	Total fertility rate L'indice synthétique de fécondité
ASIA - ASIE													
Bahrain - Bahreïn													
2008	C	17 022	15.4	C	2 390	2.2	13.3	C	127	7.5	...	...	1.920
2009	C	17 841	15.1	C	2 387	2.0	13.1	C	128	7.2	...	...	1.951
2010	C	17 791	14.5	C	2 388	1.9	12.5		...	...	...	...	1.877
2011	C	17 213	14.4	C	2 513	2.1	12.3		...	...	...	...	1.940
2012	C*	18 725	15.2	C*	2 299	1.9	13.3		...	...	...	...	...
Bangladesh													
2008		...	...		...	...	...		...	...	...	...	2.300
2009		...	...		...	...	...		...	...	...	...	2.150
2010	U	2 868 494	...	U	842 095	...	...	U	104 591	...	66.7	68.8	2.120
2011	U	2 891 000	...	U	828 000	...	...	U	100 751	...	67.9	70.3	2.110
Brunei Darussalam - Brunéi Darussalam													
2008	+C	6 424	16.1	+C	1 091	2.7	13.4	+C	45	7.0	76.6	79.8	1.700
Cambodia - Cambodge													
2008		...	...		...	...	...		...	...	...	...	3.300
China - Chine[41]													
2008	I	16 080 000[42]	12.1	I	9 350 000[42]	7.1	5.1		...	...	...	...	...
2009	I	16 190 396[42]	12.2	I	9 449 959[42]	7.1	5.1		...	...	...	...	...
2010	I	15 920 000[42]	11.9	I	9 510 000[42]	7.1	4.8		...	...	66.8	70.5	...
2011	I	16 040 000[42]	11.9	I	9 600 000[42]	7.1	4.8		...	...	...	...	...
2012	I	16 350 000[42]	12.1	I	9 660 000[42]	7.2	5.0		...	...	...	...	...
China, Hong Kong SAR - Chine, Hong Kong RAS													
2008	C	78 822	11.3	C	41 796	6.0	5.3	C	145	1.8	79.3	85.5	1.064[43]
2009	C	82 095	11.8	C	41 175	5.9	5.9	C	136	1.7	79.7	85.9	1.055[43]
2010	C	88 584	12.6	C	42 194	6.0	6.6	C	149	1.7	...	...	1.127[43]
2011	C	95 451	13.5	C	42 346	6.0	7.5	C	127	1.3	80.3	86.7	1.204[43]
2012	C*	91 600	12.8	C*	43 200	6.0	6.8	C*	127	1.4	...	...	...
China, Macao SAR - Chine, Macao RAS													
2008	C	4 717	8.7	C	1 756	3.2	5.5	C	15	...	...	...	0.979
2009	C	4 764	8.9	C	1 664	3.1	5.8	C	10	...	IV79.4	85.2	1.004
2010	C	5 114	9.5	C	1 774	3.3	6.2	C	15	...	IV79.5	85.4	1.070
2011	C	5 852	10.6	C	1 845	3.4	7.3	C	17	...	...	...	1.150
2012	C	7 315	12.9	C	1 841	3.2	9.6	C	18	...	IV79.1	85.7	1.357
Cyprus - Chypre[44]													
2008	C	9 205	11.7	C	5 194	6.6	5.1	C	32	3.5	...	...	1.460
2009	C	9 608	11.9	C	5 182	6.4	5.5	C	32	3.3	...	...	1.510
2010	C	9 801	11.8	C	5 103	6.2	5.7	C	31	3.2	...	...	1.437
2011	C	9 622	11.3	C	5 504	6.5	4.9	C	30	3.1	II79.0	82.9	1.349
Democratic People's Republic of Korea - République populaire démocratique de Corée													
2008	I	345 630[12]	14.4	I	216 616[12]	9.0	5.4	I	6 686[12]	19.3	65.6	72.7	2.000
Georgia - Géorgie													
2008	C	56 565	12.9	C	43 011[40]	9.8	3.1	C	959[40]	17.0	69.3	79.0	1.670
2009	C	63 377	14.4	C	46 625[40]	10.6	3.8	C	945[40]	14.9	69.9	78.7	...
2010	C	62 585	14.1	C	47 864[40]	10.7	3.3	C	701[40]	11.2	70.2	78.6	1.830
2011	C	58 014	12.9	C	49 818[40]	11.1	1.8	C	703[40]	12.1	...	...	1.690
2012	C	57 031	12.7	C	49 348[40]	11.0	1.7	C	715[40]	12.5	...	...	...
India - Inde[45]													
2008	I	...	22.8[46]	I	...	7.4[46]	...	I	...	53.0[46]	...	...	2.600
2009	I	...	22.5[46]	I	...	7.3[46]	...	I	...	50.0[46]	...	...	2.600
2010	I	...	22.1[46]	I	...	7.2[46]	...	I	...	47.0[46]	...	...	2.500

4. Vital statistics summary and life expectancy at birth: 2008 - 2012
Aperçu des statistiques de l'état civil et de l'espérance de vie à la naissance : 2008 - 2012 (continued - suite)

Continent, country or area and year / Continent, pays ou zone et année	Live births / Naissances vivantes Code[a]	Number Nombre	Crude birth rate Taux brut de natalité	Deaths / Décès Code[a]	Number Nombre	Crude death rate Taux brut de mortalité	Rate of natural increase Taux d'accroissement naturel	Infant deaths / Décès d'enfants de moins d'un an Code[a]	Number Nombre	Rate (per 1000 births) Taux (par 1000 naissances)	Life expectancy at birth Male[b] Masculin[b]	Female[b] Féminin[b]	Total fertility rate L'indice synthétique de fécondité
ASIA - ASIE													
Indonesia - Indonésie													
2008		...	...		...	...	...		...	...	...	...	2.170
2009		...	...		...	...	...		...	...	...	...	2.160
2010		...	...		...	...	...		...	...	68.7	72.6	2.150
Iran (Islamic Republic of) - Iran (République islamique d')[47]													
2008	+C	1 300 166	18.0	+U	417 798	...	...		...	...	...	...	...
2009	C	1 348 546	18.4	C	393 514	5.4	13.0		...	...	...	...	...
2010	C	1 363 542	18.3	C	441 042	5.9	12.4		...	...	...	...	...
2011	C	1 382 229	18.3	C	422 133	5.6	12.7		...	...	...	...	...
Israel - Israël[48]													
2008	C	156 923	21.5	C	39 484[49]	5.4	16.1	C	602[49]	3.8	79.1	83.0	2.962
2009	C	161 042	21.5	C	38 812[49]	5.2	16.3	C	619[49]	3.8	79.7	83.5	2.962
2010	C	166 255	21.8	C	39 613[49]	5.2	16.6	C	618[49]	3.7	79.7	83.6	3.029
2011	C	166 296	21.4	C	40 835[49]	5.3	16.2	C	585[49]	3.5	79.9	83.6	3.004
2012	C*	168 654	21.3	C	40 736[49]	5.2	16.2	C	563[49]	3.3	...	...	...
Japan - Japon[50]													
2008	C	1 091 156	8.7	C	1 142 407	9.1	-0.4	C	2 798	2.6	79.3	86.1	1.367
2009	C	1 070 035	8.4	C	1 141 865	8.9	-0.6	C	2 556	2.4	79.6	86.4	1.368
2010	C	1 071 304	8.4	C	1 197 012	9.3	-1.0	C	2 450	2.3	79.6	86.4	1.387
2011	C	1 050 806	8.2	C	1 253 066	9.8	-1.6	C	2 463	2.3	79.4	85.9	1.393
Jordan - Jordanie[51]													
2008	C	181 328	31.0	U	19 403	...	...		...	...	...	...	3.800
2009	C	179 872	30.1	U	20 251	...	...		...	...	...	...	3.800
2010	C	183 948	30.1	U	21 550	...	...		...	...	...	...	3.800
2011	C	178 435	28.6	U	21 730	...	...		...	...	71.6	74.4	3.800
Kazakhstan													
2008	C	356 575[40]	22.7	C	152 706[40]	9.7	13.0	C	7 322[40]	20.5	61.9	72.4	2.680
2009	C	357 552[40]	22.2	C	142 780[40]	8.9	13.3		...	...	...	...	...
2010	C	367 752[40]	22.5	C	145 875[40]	8.9	13.6		...	...	...	...	...
2011	C	372 544[40]	22.5	C	144 213[40]	8.7	13.8		...	...	...	...	...
Kuwait - Koweït													
2008	C	54 571	21.9	C	5 701	2.3	19.6	C	494	9.1	...	...	2.678
2009	C	56 503	20.3	C	6 266	2.3	18.1	C	596	10.5	...	...	2.690
2010	C	57 533	19.6	C	5 448	1.9	17.8	C	496	8.6	...	...	...
2011	C	58 198	18.8	C	5 339	1.7	17.1	C	484	8.3	...	...	...
Kyrgyzstan - Kirghizstan													
2008	C	127 332	25.1	C	37 710	7.4	17.7	C	3 453	27.1	64.5	72.6	2.757[52]
2009	C	135 494	26.4	C	35 898	7.0	19.4	C	3 393	25.0	65.2	73.2	2.876
2010	C	146 123	28.1	C	36 174	7.0	21.2	C	3 337	22.8	65.3	73.5	3.062
2011	C	149 612	28.4	C	35 941	6.8	21.6	C	3 150	21.1	65.7	73.7	3.085
Lao People's Democratic Republic - République démocratique populaire lao[53]													
2010		...	...		...	...	...		...	...	...	...	3.200
Lebanon - Liban													
2008	C	84 823	...	C	21 048	...	...		...	...	...	...	...
2009	C	90 388	...	C	22 260	...	...		...	...	...	...	...
2010	C	95 218	...	C	22 926	...	...		...	...	...	...	...
2011	C	98 569	...	C	26 070	...	...		...	...	...	...	...
2012	C	94 842	...	C	23 452	...	...		...	...	...	...	...
Malaysia - Malaisie													
2008	C	487 346	17.7	C	124 857	4.5	13.1	C	3 045	6.2	71.6	76.4	2.326
2009	C	496 313	17.7	C	130 135	4.6	13.0	C	3 404	6.9	71.6	76.5	2.329
2010	C*	475 816	16.6	C*	129 327	4.5	12.1	C*	3 251	6.8	...	...	2.200*
2011	C*	494 600	17.1	C*	133 400	4.6	12.5		...	...	...	...	...

Continent, country or area and year / Continent, pays ou zone et année	Live births / Naissances vivantes			Deaths / Décès			Rate of natural increase / Taux d'accrois-sement naturel	Infant deaths / Décès d'enfants de moins d'un an			Life expectancy at birth / Espérance de vie à la naissance		Total fertility rate / L'indice synthétique de fécondité
	Code[a]	Number Nombre	Crude birth rate Taux brut de natalité	Code[a]	Number Nombre	Crude death rate Taux brut de mortalité		Code[a]	Number Nombre	Rate (per 1000 births) Taux (par 1000 naiss-ances)	Male[b] Masculin[b]	Female[b] Féminin[b]	
ASIA - ASIE													
Maldives													
2008	C	6 989	22.6	C	1 083	3.5	19.1	C	76	10.9	...	...	...
2009	C	7 423	23.6	C	1 163	3.7	19.9	C	81	10.9	72.5	74.2	...
2010	C	7 115	22.3	C	1 105	3.5	18.8	C	78	11.0	72.6	74.4	...
2011	C	7 180	22.1	C	1 137	3.5	18.6	C	65	9.1	72.8	74.8	...
Mongolia - Mongolie													
2008	+C	63 768	24.0	+C	15 413	5.8	18.2	+C	1 240	19.4	[X]63.7	71.0	2.595
2009	+C	69 167	25.5	+C	16 911	6.2	19.3	+C	1 386	20.0	64.3	71.8	2.695
2010	+C	63 270	22.9	+C	18 293	6.6	16.3	+C	1 275	20.2	64.9	72.3	2.390
Myanmar													
2008	+U	890 034	...	+U	483 373	...	...	+U	26 265	...	64.3[54]	68.3[54]	2.050[54]
2009	+U	948 106	...	+U	325 343	...	...	+U	25 782	...	65.5[54]	70.7[54]	2.040[54]
2010	+U	965 937	...	+U	346 205	...	...	+U	26 206	...	64.6[54]	68.6[54]	2.030[54]
2011	+U*	1 007 039	...	+U*	342 420	...	...	...	...	...	...	...	...
Nepal - Népal													
2008		...	...		...	...	...		...	...	63.6	64.5	...
2011		...	...		...	...	...		...	...	...	...	2.600
Oman													
2008	U	58 280[55]	...	U	7 298[55]	...	...	U	534[55]	...	72.2	75.7	2.610
2009	U	64 735[55]	...	U	7 098[55]	...	...	U	676[55]	...	...	...	3.300
2010	U	65 528[55]	...	U	6 974[55]	...	...	U	600[55]	...	73.6	78.7	3.000
2011	U	67 922[55]	...	U	7 667[55]	...	...	U	598[55]	...	73.1	77.7	2.900
Philippines													
2008	C	1 784 316	19.7	C	461 581	5.1	14.6	C	22 351	12.5	...	...	...
2009	C	1 745 585	18.9	C	480 820	5.2	13.7	C	21 659	12.4	...	...	...
2010	C*	1 782 981	19.0	C*	488 265	5.2	13.8		...	...	...	...	...
Qatar													
2008	C	17 210	11.9	C	1 942	1.3	10.5	C	132	7.7	77.9	78.1	2.428
2009	C	18 351	11.2	C	2 008	1.2	10.0	C	130	7.1	...	...	2.282
2010	C	19 504	11.4	C	1 970	1.1	10.2	C	132	6.8	78.0	78.8	2.076
2011	C*	14 879	8.6	C	1 949	1.1	7.5	C	156	10.5	76.5	81.0	2.118
Republic of Korea - République de Corée													
2008	C	465 892[56]	9.4	C	246 113[57]	5.0	4.4	C	1 580[57]	3.4	76.5	83.3	1.192[57]
2009	C	444 849[56]	9.0	C	246 942[57]	5.0	4.0	C	1 415[57]	3.2	77.0	83.8	1.149[57]
2010	C	470 171[56]	9.4	C	255 405[57]	5.1	4.3	C	1 508[57]	3.2	77.2	84.1	1.226[57]
2011	C	471 265[56]	9.4	C	257 396[57]	5.1	4.3	C	1 435[57]	3.0	77.7	84.5	1.244[57]
Saudi Arabia - Arabie saoudite[58]													
2008	...	598 126	...	...	96 641	...	...	...	10 576	...	...	...	3.100
2009	...	601 949	...	...	98 289	...	...	...	10 409	...	72.5	74.7	3.040
2010		...	...		100 073	...	...		10 219	...	...	...	2.980
2011		...	...		102 066	...	...		10 023	...	...	...	2.930
2012		...	...		104 195	...	...		9 843	...	72.8	75.2	2.870
Singapore - Singapour													
2008	C	39 826	10.9	+C	17 222	4.7	6.2	+C	104	2.6	78.4[59]	83.3[59]	1.280[60]
2009	C	39 570	10.6	+C	17 101	4.6	6.0	+C	102	2.6	78.9[59]	83.7[59]	1.220[60]
2010	C	37 967	10.1	+C	17 610	4.7	5.4	+C	100	2.6	79.2[59]	84.0[59]	1.150[60]
2011	C	39 654	10.5	+C	18 027	4.8	5.7	+C	97	2.4	79.5[59]	84.1[59]	1.200[60]
2012	C	42 663	11.2	+C	18 481	4.8	6.3	+C	98	2.3	79.9[61]	84.5[61]	1.290[60]
Sri Lanka													
2008	+C	373 575[62]	18.5	+C	123 814[62]	6.1	12.4	+C	3 362[62]	9.0	...	...	2.260
2009	+C*	376 843	18.4	+C*	120 085	5.9	12.6		...	...	...	...	...
2010	+C*	364 565	17.7	+C*	128 603	6.2	11.4		...	...	...	...	...
2011	+C*	363 415	17.4	+C*	123 261	5.9	11.5		...	...	...	...	...
State of Palestine - État de Palestine													
2008		...	...		...	...	...		...	...	70.2	72.9	...
2010		...	...		...	...	...		...	...	...	...	4.400

4. Vital statistics summary and life expectancy at birth: 2008 - 2012
Aperçu des statistiques de l'état civil et de l'espérance de vie à la naissance : 2008 - 2012 (continued - suite)

Continent, country or area and year / Continent, pays ou zone et année	Live births Naissances vivantes			Deaths Décès			Rate of natural increase Taux d'accrois-sement naturel	Infant deaths Décès d'enfants de moins d'un an			Life expectancy at birth Espérance de vie à la naissance		Total fertility rate L'indice synthétique de fécondité
	Code[a]	Number Nombre	Crude birth rate Taux brut de natalité	Code[a]	Number Nombre	Crude death rate Taux brut de mortalité		Code[a]	Number Nombre	Rate (per 1000 births) Taux (par 1000 naiss-ances)	Male[b] Masculin[b]	Female[b] Féminin[b]	
ASIA - ASIE													
State of Palestine - État de Palestine													
2011		...	...		...	...	...		...	...	71.0	73.9	...
2012		...	...		...	...	...		...	...	71.3	74.1	...
Syrian Arab Republic - République arabe syrienne[63]													
2008	+U	750 321	...	+U	85 811	...	...		...	...	...	...	...
2009	+U	721 587	...	+U	86 642	...	...		...	...	...	...	...
2010	+U	870 100	...	+U	91 981	...	...		...	...	...	...	...
Tajikistan - Tadjikistan													
2008	U	203 332[64]	...	U	30 743[40]	...	...	U	2 480[40]	...	69.7	74.8	...
2009	U	199 826[64]	...	U	30 895[40]	...	...	U	2 814[40]	...	70.5	75.3	...
2010	U	239 805[64]	...	U	31 937[40]	...	...	U	3 092[40]	...	...	...	...
2011	U	224 178[64]	...	U	32 909[40]	...	...	U	3 131[40]	...	70.9	74.1	...
Thailand - Thaïlande													
2008	+U	784 256	...	+U	397 327	...	...	+U	5 721	...	...	...	...
2009	+U	765 047	...	+U	393 916	...	...	+U	5 416	...	...	...	...
2010	+U	761 689	...	+U	411 331	...	...	+U	5 357	...	...	...	...
2011	+U	795 031	...	+U	414 670	...	...	+U	5 275	...	...	...	...
Turkey - Turquie													
2008	C	1 292 839	18.2	U	454 000	...	...	U	18 968	...	71.4	75.8	2.140
2009	C	1 261 299	17.5	U	368 390	...	...	U	17 388	...	71.5	76.1	2.120
2010	C	1 253 309	17.1	U	365 190	...	...	U	15 049	...	...	...	2.110
2011	C	1 237 172	16.7	U	465 000	...	...	U	16 103	...	72.0	77.1	2.090
2012	C	1 279 864	17.0	U	374 855	...	...	U	14 845	...	...	...	...
United Arab Emirates - Émirats arabes unis[65]													
2008	...	68 779	...	...	7 755	...	...		...	...	...	...	...
2009	...	76 366	...	...	7 789	...	...		...	...	...	...	...
2010	...	79 625	...	...	7 414	...	...		...	...	...	...	...
2011	...	83 950	...	...	7 350	...	...		...	...	...	...	...
Uzbekistan - Ouzbékistan													
2008	C	646 096	23.9	C	138 792[40]	5.1	18.7		...	...	...	...	...
2009	C	651 320	23.7	C	133 610[40]	4.9	18.8		...	...	...	...	...
2010	C	634 810	22.7	C	138 411[40]	4.9	17.7		...	...	...	...	...
2011	C	622 835	21.4	C	143 253[40]	4.9	16.5		...	...	...	...	...
2012	C	625 106	21.2	C	145 988[40]	4.9	16.2		...	...	...	...	...
Viet Nam													
2008		...	...		...	...	...		...	...	70.6	76.0	2.080
2009		...	...		...	...	...		...	...	70.2	75.6	2.030
2010		...	...		...	...	...		...	...	...	...	2.000
2011		...	...		...	...	...		...	...	70.4	75.8	1.990
2012		...	...		...	...	...		...	...	70.4	75.8	2.050
Yemen - Yémen													
2008	U	309 373	...	U	30 463	...	...		...	...	...	...	...
2009	U	271 269	...	U	31 914	...	...		...	...	...	...	...
2010	U	318 936	...	U	28 494	...	...		...	...	...	...	...
2011	U	239 980	...	U	23 662	...	...		...	...	...	...	...
2012	U	279 719	...	U	28 596	...	...		...	...	...	...	...
EUROPE													
Åland Islands - Îles d'Åland													
2008	C	294	10.8	C	250	9.2	1.6	C	1	...	...	...	1.881
2009	C	267	9.7	C	247	9.0	0.7	C	-	...	79.4	84.1	1.694
2010	C	286	10.3	C	233	8.4	1.9	C	1	...	81.2	84.2	1.834
2011	C	285	10.1	C	277	9.8	0.3	C	-	...	79.5	84.8	1.801
2012	C*	293	10.3	C*	313	11.0	-0.7		...	...	...	...	...

4. Vital statistics summary and life expectancy at birth: 2008 - 2012
Aperçu des statistiques de l'état civil et de l'espérance de vie à la naissance : 2008 - 2012 (continued - suite)

Continent, country or area and year — Continent, pays ou zone et année	Live births — Naissances vivantes Code[a]	Number Nombre	Crude birth rate Taux brut de natalité	Deaths — Décès Code[a]	Number Nombre	Crude death rate Taux brut de mortalité	Rate of natural increase Taux d'accrois-sement naturel	Infant deaths — Décès d'enfants de moins d'un an Code[a]	Number Nombre	Rate (per 1000 births) Taux (par 1000 naiss-ances)	Life expectancy at birth — Espérance de vie à la naissance Male[b] Masculin[b]	Female[b] Féminin[b]	Total fertility rate L'indice synthétique de fécondité
EUROPE													
Albania - Albanie													
2008	C	36 251	12.4	C	16 143	5.5	6.9	C	217	6.0	...	...	...
2011	C	32 628	11.5	C	19 636	6.9	4.6		...	...	...	...	...
Andorra - Andorre													
2008	C	875	10.4	C	237	2.8	7.6	C	3	...	...	...	1.263
2009	C	838	9.8	C	272	3.2	6.6	C	1	...	...	...	1.232
2010	C	828	9.8	C	239	2.8	7.0	C	-	...	...	...	1.246
2011	C	793	10.0	C	275	3.5	6.5		...	...	...	...	...
2012	C	737	9.5	C	303	3.9	5.6	C	4	...	...	...	...
Austria - Autriche													
2008	C	77 752	9.3	C	75 083	9.0	0.3	C	287	3.7	77.6	83.0	1.414
2009	C	76 344	9.1	C	77 381[66]	9.3	-0.1	C	289	3.8	77.4	82.9	1.392
2010	C	78 742	9.4	C	77 199[66]	9.2	0.2	C	307	3.9	77.7	83.2	1.440
2011	C	78 109	9.3	C	76 479[66]	9.1	0.2	C	281	3.6	78.1	83.4	1.430
2012	C	78 952	9.3	C	79 436[66]	9.4	-0.1	C	252	3.2	...	...	...
Belarus - Bélarus													
2008	C	107 876	11.1	C	133 879	13.8	-2.7	C	483	4.5	64.7	76.5	1.424
2009	C	109 263	11.4	C	135 097	14.1	-2.7	C	511	4.7	64.7	76.4	1.442
2010	C	108 050	11.4	C	137 132	14.5	-3.1	C	429	4.0	64.6	76.5	...
2011	C	109 147	11.5	C	135 090	14.3	-2.7	C	420	3.8	64.7	76.7	1.515
2012	C	115 893	12.2	C	126 531	13.4	-1.1	C	386	3.3	...	...	...
Belgium - Belgique													
2008	C	127 205[67]	11.9	C	104 587[67]	9.8	2.1	C	478[67]	3.8	...	...	...
2009	C	127 297[67]	11.8	C	104 509[67]	9.7	2.1	C	439[67]	3.4	...	...	...
2010	C	129 909[67]	11.9	C	105 094[67]	9.6	2.3	C	463[67]	3.6	...	...	1.845
2011	C	128 678[67]	11.7	C*	106 000[67]	9.6	2.1	C*	426[67]	3.3	...	...	1.810
2012	C*	127 000[67]	11.4	C*	103 500[67]	9.3	2.1	C*	415[67]	3.3	...	...	...
Bosnia and Herzegovina - Bosnie-Herzégovine													
2008	C	34 176	8.9	C	34 026	8.9	0.0	C	235	6.9	...	...	...
2009	C	34 550	9.0	C	34 904	9.1	-0.1	C	224	6.5	...	...	1.303
2010	C	33 528	8.7	C	35 118	9.1	-0.4	C	216	6.4	...	...	1.266
2011	C	31 875	8.3	C	35 522	9.2	-0.9		...	...	...	...	...
2012	C*	32 072	8.4	C*	35 692	9.3	-0.9	C*	161	5.0	...	...	...
Bulgaria - Bulgarie													
2008	C	77 712	10.2	C	110 523	14.5	-4.3	C	668	8.6	III69.5	76.6	1.478
2009	C	80 956	10.7	C	108 068	14.2	-3.6	C	729	9.0	III69.9	77.1	1.565
2010	C	75 513	10.0	C	110 165	14.6	-4.6	C	708	9.4	III70.0	77.2	1.486
2011	C	70 846	9.6	C	108 258	14.7	-5.1	C	601	8.5	III70.4	77.4	1.508
2012	C	69 121	9.5	C	109 281	15.0	-5.5	C	536	7.8	...	...	...
Croatia - Croatie													
2008	C	43 753	9.9	C	52 151	11.8	-1.9	C	195	4.5	...	...	1.472
2009	C	44 577	10.1	C	52 414	11.8	-1.8	C	235	5.3	...	...	1.497
2010	C	43 361	9.8	C	52 096	11.8	-2.0	C	192	4.4	...	...	1.460
2011	C	41 197	9.4	C	51 019	11.6	-2.2	C	192	4.7	...	...	1.407
Czech Republic - République tchèque													
2008	C	119 570[68]	11.5	C	104 948	10.1	1.4	C	338	2.8	74.0	80.1	1.497
2009	C	118 348[68]	11.3	C	107 421	10.2	1.0	C	341	2.9	74.2	80.1	1.492
2010	C	117 153[68]	11.1	C	106 844	10.2	1.0	C	313	2.7	74.4	80.6	1.493
2011	C	108 673[68]	10.4	C	106 848	10.2	0.2	C	298	2.7	74.7	80.7	1.426
2012	C	108 576[68]	10.3	C	108 189	10.3	0.0	C	285	2.6	...	...	...
Denmark - Danemark[69]													
2008	C	65 038	11.8	C	54 591	9.9	1.9	C	262	4.0	II76.3	80.7	1.892
2009	C	62 818	11.4	C	54 872	9.9	1.4	C	193	3.1	II76.5	80.8	1.842
2010	C	63 411	11.4	C	54 368	9.8	1.6	C	216	3.4	II77.1	81.2	1.875
2011	C	58 998	10.6	C	52 516	9.4	1.2	C	208	3.5	II77.3	81.6	1.756
2012	C	57 916	10.4	C	52 325	9.4	1.0	C	197	3.4	...	...	...

Continent, country or area and year / Continent, pays ou zone et année	Live births Naissances vivantes			Deaths Décès			Rate of natural increase Taux d'accrois-sement naturel	Infant deaths Décès d'enfants de moins d'un an			Life expectancy at birth Espérance de vie à la naissance		Total fertility rate L'indice synthétique de fécondité
	Code[a]	Number Nombre	Crude birth rate Taux brut de natalité	Code[a]	Number Nombre	Crude death rate Taux brut de mortalité		Code[a]	Number Nombre	Rate (per 1000 births) Taux (par 1000 naiss-ances)	Male[b] Masculin[b]	Female[b] Féminin[b]	
EUROPE													
Estonia - Estonie													
2008	C	16 028	12.0	C	16 675	12.4	-0.5	C	80	5.0	68.6	79.2	1.661
2009	C	15 763	11.8	C	16 081	12.0	-0.2	C	57	3.6	69.8	80.2	1.630
2010	C	15 825	11.8	C	15 790	11.8	0.0	C	53	3.3	70.6	80.7	1.636
2011	C	14 679	11.0	C	15 244	11.4	-0.4	C	36	2.5	71.2	81.3	1.524
2012	C	14 056	10.5	C	15 450	11.5	-1.0	C	50	3.6	...	...	...
Faeroe Islands - Îles Féroé													
2008	C	665	13.7	C	378	7.8	5.9		...	...	76.8	82.3	...
2009	C	614	12.6	C	387	8.0	4.7		...	...	...	...	...
2010	C	639	13.2	C	348	7.2	6.0		...	...	...	...	...
2011	C	576	11.9	C	364	7.5	4.4		...	...	...	...	...
2012	C	617	12.8	C	407	8.4	4.3		...	...	...	...	...
Finland - Finlande													
2008	C	59 530	11.2	C	49 094	9.2	2.0	C	157	2.6	76.3	83.0	1.846
2009	C	60 163[70]	11.3	C	49 636[70]	9.3	2.0	C	158[70]	2.6	76.5	83.1	1.864
2010	C	60 694[70]	11.4	C	50 654[70]	9.5	1.9	C	139[70]	2.3	76.7[70]	83.2[70]	1.870
2011	C	59 676[70]	11.1	C	50 308[70]	9.4	1.7	C	143	2.4	...	...	1.827
2012	C	59 493	11.1	C	51 707	9.6	1.4	C	141	2.4	...	...	...
France													
2008	C	796 044[71]	12.8	C	532 131[71]	8.5	4.2	C	2 856[71]	3.6	III77.4	84.3	1.998
2009	C	793 420[71]	12.7	C	538 116[71]	8.6	4.1	C	2 903[71]	3.7	III77.6	84.4	...
2010	C	802 224[71]	12.7	C	540 469[71]	8.6	4.2	C	2 785[71]	3.5	III77.8	84.5	1.997
2011	C	792 996[71]	12.5	C	534 795[71]	8.4	4.1	C	2 604[71]	3.3	...	...	1.997
2012	C*	792 000[71]	12.5	C*	560 000[71]	8.8	3.7	C*	2 626[71]	3.3	...	...	...
Germany - Allemagne													
2008	C	682 514	8.3	C	844 439	10.3	-2.0	C	2 414	3.5	...	...	1.376
2009	C	665 126	8.1	C	854 544	10.4	-2.3	C	2 334	3.5	...	...	...
2010	C	677 947	8.3	C	858 768	10.5	-2.2	C	2 322	3.4	III77.5	82.6	1.393
2011	C	662 685	8.1	C	852 328	10.4	-2.3	C	2 408	3.6	III77.7	82.7	1.364
2012	C*	671 000	8.2	C*	863 000	10.5	-2.3	C*	2 300	3.4	...	...	...
Gibraltar													
2008	+C	400[72]	13.7	+C	227[73]	7.8	5.9		...	...	...	...	...
2009	+C	417[72]	14.2	+C	234[73]	8.0	6.2		...	...	...	...	...
2010	+C	493[72]	16.7	+C	231[73]	7.8	8.9		...	...	...	...	...
2011	+C	442[72]	14.9	+C	241[73]	8.1	6.8		...	...	...	...	...
Greece - Grèce													
2008	C	118 302	10.5	C	107 979	9.6	0.9	C	314	2.7	77.5	82.5	1.506
2009	C	117 933	10.5	C	108 316	9.6	0.9	C	371	3.1	77.7	82.8	1.522
2010	C	114 766	10.1	C	109 084	9.6	0.5	C	436	3.8	...	...	...
2011	C	106 428	9.4	C	111 099	9.8	-0.4	C	357	3.4	78.3	83.1	1.423
Guernsey - Guernesey													
2008	C	603	9.8	C	495	8.0	1.7		...	...	...	...	...
2009	C	646	10.4	C	535	8.6	1.8		...	...	...	...	...
2010	C	613	9.8	C	497	8.0	1.9		...	...	...	...	...
2011	C	650	10.3	C	535	8.5	1.8		...	...	...	...	...
2012	C	674	10.7	C	547	8.7	2.0		...	...	...	...	...
Hungary - Hongrie													
2008	C	99 149	9.9	C	130 027	13.0	-3.1	C	553	5.6	69.8	77.8	1.352
2009	C	96 442	9.6	C	130 414	13.0	-3.4	C	495	5.1	70.1	77.9	1.327
2010	C	90 335	9.0	C	130 456	13.0	-4.0	C	481	5.3	70.5	78.1	1.256
2011	C	88 049	8.8	C	128 795	12.9	-4.1	C	433	4.9	70.9	78.2	1.238
2012	C*	90 300	9.1	C*	129 500	13.1	-4.0	C*	440	4.9	...	...	...
Iceland - Islande													
2008	C	4 835	15.1	C	1 987	6.2	8.9	C	12	...	II79.6	81.3	2.140
2009	C	5 026	15.7	C	2 002	6.3	9.5	C	9	...	...	...	2.221
2010	C	4 907	15.4	C	2 020	6.4	9.1	C	11	...	II79.5	83.5	2.197
2011	C	4 492[74]	14.1	C	1 986[74]	6.2	7.9	C	4[74]	...	II79.9	82.8	2.017
2012	C*	4 533	14.1	C*	1 952	6.1	8.0		...	...	...	...	...

Continent, country or area and year / Continent, pays ou zone et année	Live births / Naissances vivantes			Deaths / Décès			Rate of natural increase / Taux d'accrois-sement naturel	Infant deaths / Décès d'enfants de moins d'un an			Life expectancy at birth / Espérance de vie à la naissance		Total fertility rate / L'indice synthétique de fécondité
	Code[a]	Number Nombre	Crude birth rate Taux brut de natalité	Code[a]	Number Nombre	Crude death rate Taux brut de mortalité		Code[a]	Number Nombre	Rate (per 1000 births) Taux (par 1000 naiss-ances)	Male[b] Masculin[b]	Female[b] Féminin[b]	
EUROPE													
Ireland - Irlande													
2008	C	75 173[75]	17.0[75]	C	28 274[75]	6.4[75]	10.6	C	284[75]	3.8[75]	...	...	2.100
2009	C	75 554[75]	16.9[75]	C	28 380[75]	6.4[75]	10.6	C	247[75]	3.3[75]	...	...	2.000
2010	+C	74 976	16.8	+C	27 565	6.2	10.6	+C	282	3.8	...	...	2.070
2011	+C	74 650	16.6	+C	28 995	6.5	10.2	+C	258	3.5	...	...	2.040
2012	+C*	72 291	15.8	+C*	29 365	6.4	9.4		...	...	...	...	...
Italy - Italie													
2008	+C	576 659	9.6	C	578 192	9.7	0.0	C	1 896	3.3	78.8	84.1	1.414
2009	+C	568 857	9.5	C	585 182	9.7	-0.3	C	1 947	3.4	79.0	84.1	1.411
2010	+C	561 944	9.3	C	581 307	9.6	-0.3	C	1 887	3.4	...	...	1.410
2011	+C*	546 607	9.0	C*	593 404	9.8	-0.8	C	1 762	3.2	...	...	1.420
2012		...	...		...	...	...	C*	1 786		...	...	...
Jersey													
2008	+C	973[24]	10.3	+C	743	7.8	2.4		...	...	...	...	...
Latvia - Lettonie													
2008	C	23 948	10.6	C	31 006	13.7	-3.1	C	161	6.7	67.2	77.9	1.453
2009	C	21 677	9.6	C	29 897	13.3	-3.6	C	168	7.8	68.3	78.1	1.319
2010	C	19 219	8.6	C	30 040	13.4	-4.8	C	110	5.7	68.8	78.4	1.180
2011	C	18 825	9.1	C	28 540	13.8	-4.7	C	124	6.6	...	...	1.341
2012	C	19 897	9.8	C	29 025	14.3	-4.5	C	125	6.3	...	...	...
Liechtenstein													
2008	C	350	9.9	C	205	5.8	4.1	C	-	...	...	...	1.400
2009	C	406	11.3	C	229	6.4	4.9	C	1	...	...	...	1.728
2010	C	329	9.1	C	238	6.6	2.5	C	1	...	...	...	1.402
2011	C	395	10.9	C	248	6.8	4.1	C*	1	...	...	...	1.688
2012	C	356	9.8	C	224	6.1	3.6	C*	3	...	...	...	...
Lithuania - Lituanie													
2008	C	35 065	10.4	C	43 832	13.1	-2.6	C	172	4.9	66.3	77.6	1.470
2009	C	36 682	11.0	C	42 032	12.6	-1.6	C	181	4.9	67.5	78.6	1.546
2010	C	35 626	10.8	C	42 120	12.8	-2.0	C	153	4.3	68.0	78.8	1.550
2011	C	34 385	11.3	C	41 037	13.5	-2.2	C	144	4.2	68.1	79.1	...
2012	C	30 459	9.6	C	40 938	12.9	-3.3	C	118	3.9	...	...	...
Luxembourg													
2008	C	5 596	11.5	C	3 595	7.4	4.1	C	10	...	...	...	1.605
2009	C	5 638	11.3	C	3 655	7.3	4.0	C	14	...	...	...	1.586
2010	C	5 874	11.6	C	3 760	7.4	4.2	C	20	...	...	...	1.625
2011	C	5 639	10.9	C	3 819	7.4	3.5	C	24	...	...	...	1.513
2012	C	6 026	11.3	C	3 876	7.3	4.0	C	15	...	...	...	...
Malta - Malte													
2008	C	4 126	10.1	C	3 243	7.9	2.2	C	34	8.2	76.7	82.3	1.430
2009	C	4 143	10.0	C	3 221	7.8	2.2	C	22	...	77.7	82.2	1.440
2010	C	4 008	9.7	C	3 010	7.2	2.4	C	22	...	78.9	83.1	1.370
2011	C	4 283	10.3	C	3 290	7.9	2.4	C	27	...	78.4	82.7	1.488
Montenegro - Monténégro													
2008	C	8 258	13.1	C	5 708	9.1	4.1	C	62	7.5	...	...	1.772
2009	C	8 642	13.7	C	5 862	9.3	4.4	C	49	5.7	...	...	...
2010	C	7 418	12.0	C	5 633	9.1	2.9	C	50	6.7	...	...	...
2011	C	7 215	11.6	C	5 847	9.4	2.2	C	32	4.4	...	...	1.652
2012	C	7 459	12.0	C	5 922	9.5	2.5	C*	33	4.4	...	...	...
Netherlands - Pays-Bas													
2008	C	184 634[76]	11.2	C	135 136[76]	8.2	3.0	C	698[76]	3.8	78.3	82.3	1.775
2009	C	184 915[76]	11.2	C	134 235[76]	8.1	3.1	C	711[76]	3.8	78.5	82.7	1.790
2010	C	184 397[76]	11.1	C	136 058[76]	8.2	2.9	C	695[76]	3.8	78.8	82.7	1.800
2011	C	180 060[76]	10.8	C	135 741[76]	8.1	2.7	C	654[76]	3.6	79.2	82.8	1.760
2012	C	175 959[76]	10.5		...	...	...		...	...	...	...	...
Norway - Norvège													
2008	C	60 497	12.7	C	41 712[77]	8.7	3.9	C	163[77]	2.7	78.3	83.0	1.960
2009	C	61 807	12.8	C	41 449[77]	8.6	4.2	C	192[77]	3.1	78.6	83.1	1.980
2010	C	61 442	12.6	C	41 499[77]	8.5	4.1	C	171[77]	2.8	78.9	83.2	1.950

4. Vital statistics summary and life expectancy at birth: 2008 - 2012
Aperçu des statistiques de l'état civil et de l'espérance de vie à la naissance : 2008 - 2012 (continued - suite)

Continent, country or area and year / Continent, pays ou zone et année	Live births / Naissances vivantes Code[a]	Number Nombre	Crude birth rate Taux brut de natalité	Deaths / Décès Code[a]	Number Nombre	Crude death rate Taux brut de mortalité	Rate of natural increase Taux d'accrois-sement naturel	Infant deaths / Décès d'enfants de moins d'un an Code[a]	Number Nombre	Rate (per 1000 births) Taux (par 1000 naiss-ances)	Life expectancy at birth / Espérance de vie à la naissance Male[b] Masculin[b]	Female[b] Féminin[b]	Total fertility rate L'indice synthétique de fécondité
EUROPE													
Norway - Norvège													
2011	C	60 220	12.2	C	41 393[77]	8.4	3.8	C	142[77]	2.4	79.0	83.5	1.880
2012	C	60 255	12.0	C	41 992[77]	8.4	3.6	C	150[77]	2.5	...	...	...
Poland - Pologne													
2008	C	414 499	10.9	C	379 399	10.0	0.9	C	2 338	5.6	...	...	1.390
2009	C	417 589	10.9	C	384 940	10.1	0.9	C	2 327	5.6	71.5	80.1	1.398
2010	C	413 300	10.7	C	378 478	9.8	0.9	C	2 057	5.0	72.1	80.6	1.382
2011	C	388 416	10.1	C	375 501	9.7	0.3	C	1 836	4.7	72.4	80.9	1.301
2012	C	386 257	10.0	C	384 788	10.0	0.0	C	1 791	4.6	...	...	...
Portugal													
2008	C	104 594[24]	9.8	C	104 280[25]	9.8	0.0	C	340[25]	3.3	III75.5	81.7	1.374
2009	C	99 491[24]	9.4	C	104 434[25]	9.8	-0.5	C	362[25]	3.6	III75.8	81.8	1.323
2010	C	101 381[24]	9.5	C	105 954[25]	10.0	-0.4	C	256[25]	2.5	III76.1	82.1	...
2011	C	96 856[24]	9.2	C	102 848[78]	9.7	-0.6	C	301[25]	3.1	III76.4	82.3	1.356
2012	C	89 841[24]	8.5	C	107 598[25]	10.2	-1.7	C	303[25]	3.4	...	...	...
Republic of Moldova - République de Moldova[79]													
2008	C	39 018	10.9	C	41 948	11.7	-0.8	C	473	12.1	...	...	1.277
2009	C	40 803	11.4	C	42 139	11.8	-0.4	C	492	12.1	65.3	73.4	1.326
2010	C	40 474	11.4	C	43 631	12.2	-0.9	C	476	11.8	65.0	73.4	1.309
2011	C	39 182	11.0	C	39 249	11.0	0.0	C	431	11.0	...	...	1.266
2012	C	39 435	11.1	C	39 560	11.1	0.0	C	387	9.8	...	...	...
Romania - Roumanie													
2008	C	221 900	10.3	C	253 202	11.8	-1.5	C	2 434	11.0	III69.5	76.7	1.350
2009	C	222 388	10.4	C	257 213	12.0	-1.6	C	2 250	10.1	III69.7	77.1	1.371
2010	C	212 199	9.9	C	259 723	12.1	-2.2	C	2 078	9.8	III69.8	77.3	1.327
2011	C	196 242	9.2	C	251 439	11.8	-2.6	C	1 850	9.4	III70.1	77.5	1.251
2012	C	201 104	9.4	C	255 539	12.0	-2.5	C	1 812	9.0	...	...	...
Russian Federation - Fédération de Russie													
2008	C	1 713 947[40]	12.0	C	2 075 954[40]	14.5	-2.5	C	14 436[40]	8.4	61.8	74.2	1.494
2009	C	1 761 687[40]	12.3	C	2 010 543[40]	14.1	-1.7	C	14 271[40]	8.1	62.8	74.7	1.537
2010	C	1 788 948[40]	12.5	C	2 028 516[40]	14.2	-1.7	C	13 405[40]	7.5	...	...	...
2011	C	1 796 629[40]	12.6	C	1 925 720[40]	13.5	-0.9	C	13 168[40]	7.3	64.0	75.6	...
2012	C*	1 896 263[40]	13.3	C*	1 898 836[40]	13.3	0.0		...	...	...	...	...
San Marino - Saint-Marin													
2008	+C	349	11.0	+C	190	6.0	5.0		...	...	...	...	...
2009	+C	306	9.3	+C	233	7.1	2.2		...	...	...	...	...
2010	+C	334	10.5	+C	222	7.0	3.5		...	...	...	...	...
2011	+C	325	9.7	+C	222	6.7	3.1	+C	1	...	...	...	...
2012	+C	292	8.7	+C	237	7.1	1.6	+C	-	...	...	...	...
Serbia - Serbie[80]													
2008	+C	69 083	9.4	+C	102 711	14.0	-4.6	+C	460	6.7	71.1	76.3	1.406
2009	+C	70 299	9.6	+C	104 000	14.2	-4.6	+C	492	7.0	71.1	76.4	1.437
2010	+C	68 304	9.4	+C	103 211	14.2	-4.8	+C	460	6.7	71.4	76.6	1.410
2011	+C	65 598	9.0	+C	102 935	14.2	-5.1	+C	414	6.3	71.6	76.8	1.360
2012	+C	67 257	9.3	+C	102 400	14.1	-4.9	+C	415	6.2	...	...	...
Slovakia - Slovaquie													
2008	C	57 360	10.6	C	53 164	9.8	0.8	C	336	5.9	70.9	78.7	1.320
2009	C	61 217	11.3	C	52 913	9.8	1.5	C	346	5.7	71.3	78.7	1.411
2010	C	60 410	11.1	C	53 445	9.8	1.3	C	344	5.7	71.6	78.8	1.398
2011	C	60 813	11.3	C	51 903	9.6	1.7	C	300	4.9	72.2	79.4	1.447
2012	C	55 535	10.3	C	52 437	9.7	0.6	C	321	5.8	...	...	...
Slovenia - Slovénie													
2008	C	21 817	10.8	C	18 308	9.1	1.7	C	52	2.4	75.8	82.3	1.528
2009	C	21 856	10.7	C	18 750	9.2	1.5	C	52	2.4	...	...	1.534
2010	C	22 343	10.9	C	18 609	9.1	1.8	C	56	2.5	76.3	82.7	1.574
2011	C	21 947	10.7	C	18 699	9.1	1.6	C	64	2.9	76.6	82.9	1.562
2012	C*	21 711	10.6	C*	19 189	9.3	1.2	C*	35	1.6	...	...	...

Continent, country or area and year / Continent, pays ou zone et année	Live births Naissances vivantes			Deaths Décès			Rate of natural increase Taux d'accroissement naturel	Infant deaths Décès d'enfants de moins d'un an			Life expectancy at birth Espérance de vie à la naissance		Total fertility rate L'indice synthétique de fécondité
	Code[a]	Number Nombre	Crude birth rate Taux brut de natalité	Code[a]	Number Nombre	Crude death rate Taux brut de mortalité		Code[a]	Number Nombre	Rate (per 1000 births) Taux (par 1000 naissances)	Male[b] Masculin[b]	Female[b] Féminin[b]	
EUROPE													
Spain - Espagne													
2008	C	518 503	11.4	C	384 198	8.4	2.9	C	1 741	3.4	78.2	84.3	1.459
2009	C	493 717	10.7	C	383 209	8.3	2.4	C	1 578	3.2	78.5	84.6	1.393
2010	C	485 252	10.5	C	381 409	8.3	2.3	C	1 531	3.2	78.9	84.9	1.382
2011	C	470 553	10.2	C	386 017	8.4	1.8	C	1 477	3.1	79.2	85.0	1.360
2012	C*	456 778	9.9	C*	410 966	8.9	1.0	C*	1 620	3.5	...	...	...
Sweden - Suède													
2008	C	109 301	11.9	C	91 449	9.9	1.9	C	272	2.5	79.1	83.2	1.907
2009	C	111 801	12.0	C	90 080	9.7	2.3	C	278	2.5	79.4	83.4	1.935
2010	C	115 641	12.3	C	90 487	9.6	2.7	C	294	2.5	79.5	83.5	1.985
2011	C	111 770	11.8	C	89 938	9.5	2.3	C	235	2.1	79.8	83.7	1.900
2012	C	113 177	11.9	C	91 938	9.7	2.2	C	293	2.6	...	...	...
Switzerland - Suisse													
2008	C	76 691	10.0	C	61 233	8.0	2.0	C	308	4.0	[II]79.5	84.2	1.480
2009	C	78 286	10.1	C	62 476	8.1	2.0	C	337	4.3	[II]79.7	84.3	1.497
2010	C	80 290	10.3	C	62 649	8.0	2.3	C	307	3.8	[II]79.9	84.4	1.540
2011	C	80 808	10.2	C	62 091	7.8	2.4	C	305	3.8	[II]80.2	84.5	...
2012	C*	82 164	10.3	C*	64 174	8.0	2.2	C*	296	3.6	...	...	...
TFYR of Macedonia - L'ex-R. y. de Macédoine													
2008	C	22 945	11.2	C	18 982	9.3	1.9	C	223	9.7	72.1	76.3	1.471
2009	C	23 684	11.5	C	19 060	9.3	2.3	C	278	11.7	72.5	76.7	1.520
2010	C	24 296	11.8	C	19 113	9.3	2.5	C	185	7.6	...	...	1.553
2011	C	22 770	11.1	C	19 465	9.5	1.6	C*	174	7.6	...	...	1.458
2012	C	23 568	11.4	C	20 134	9.8	1.7	C	230	9.8	...	...	...
Ukraine													
2008	+C	510 589[81]	11.0	+C	754 460[82]	16.3	-5.3	+C	5 049[82]	9.9	[II]62.5	74.3	1.390
2009	+C	512 525[81]	11.1	+C	706 739[82]	15.3	-4.2	+C	4 801[82]	9.4	...	...	...
2010	+C	497 689[81]	10.9	+C	698 235[82]	15.3	-4.4	+C	4 564[82]	9.2	[II]65.3	75.5	1.430
2011	+C	502 595[81]	11.0	+C	664 588[82]	14.6	-3.6	+C	4 511[82]	9.0	66.0	75.9	1.459
2012	+C	520 705[81]	11.4	+C	663 139[82]	14.6	-3.1	+C	4 371[82]	8.4	...	...	...
United Kingdom of Great Britain and Northern Ireland - Royaume-Uni de Grande-Bretagne et d'Irlande du Nord[83]													
2008	C	794 383[84]	12.9	+C	579 697	9.4	3.5	+C	3 745	4.7	[III]77.5	81.7	1.958
2009	C	790 204[84]	12.8	+C	559 617	9.1	3.7	+C	3 677	4.7	...	...	...
2010	C*	807 272[84]	13.0	+C	561 666	9.0	3.9	+C	3 416	4.2	...	...	...
2011	C	807 776[84]	12.9	+C	552 232	8.8	4.1	+C	3 386	4.2	...	...	1.913
OCEANIA - OCÉANIE													
American Samoa - Samoas américaines													
2010	C	1 234	18.7		...	...	...		...	...	...	...	...
Australia - Australie													
2008	+C	296 621	13.9	+C	143 946	6.7	7.1	+C	1 226	4.1	[III]79.2	83.7	1.956
2009	+C	295 738	13.6	+C	140 760	6.5	7.1	+C	1 261	4.3	[III]79.3	83.9	1.903
2010	+C	297 903	13.5	+C	143 473	6.5	7.0	+C	1 229	4.1	[III]79.5	84.0	1.886
2011	+C	301 617	13.5	+C	146 932	6.6	6.9	+C	1 140	3.8	[III]79.8	84.2	1.884
Cook Islands - Îles Cook[85]													
2008	+C	261	11.9	+C	56	2.6	9.4	+C	1	...	...	...	...
2009	+C	255	11.3	+C	67	3.0	8.3	+C	2	...	...	...	...
2010	+C	279	11.8	+C	95	4.0	7.8	+C	2	...	...	...	...
2011	+C*	262	12.6	+C*	72	3.5	9.1	+C*	2	...	...	...	...
2012	+C*	259	...	+C*	104	...	...	+C*	1	...	...	...	...

4. Vital statistics summary and life expectancy at birth: 2008 - 2012
Aperçu des statistiques de l'état civil et de l'espérance de vie à la naissance : 2008 - 2012 (continued - suite)

Continent, country or area and year / Continent, pays ou zone et année	Live births / Naissances vivantes			Deaths / Décès			Rate of natural increase / Taux d'accrois-sement naturel	Infant deaths / Décès d'enfants de moins d'un an			Life expectancy at birth / Espérance de vie à la naissance		Total fertility rate / L'indice synthétique de fécondité
	Code[a]	Number / Nombre	Crude birth rate / Taux brut de natalité	Code[a]	Number / Nombre	Crude death rate / Taux brut de mortalité		Code[a]	Number / Nombre	Rate (per 1000 births) / Taux (par 1000 naiss-ances)	Male[b] / Masculin[b]	Female[b] / Féminin[b]	
OCEANIA - OCÉANIE													
Fiji - Fidji													
2008	+C	18 944	...		...	...	...		...	...	...	...	...
2009	+C	18 166	21.5		...	...	...		...	...	...	...	...
French Polynesia - Polynésie française													
2008	C	4 627	17.6	C	1 166	4.4	13.2	C	23	...	73.2	78.2	...
2009	C	4 544	17.1	C	1 261	4.8	12.4	C	26	...	73.3	77.6	...
2010	C	4 579	17.1	C	1 261	4.7	12.4	C	25	...	73.2	78.3	...
Guam													
2008	C	3 466[86]	21.8	C	787	4.9	16.8	C	31[86]	8.9	75.9	82.2	...
2009	C	3 423[86]	21.5	C	850[86]	5.3	16.1		...	...	...	...	...
2010	C	3 419[86]	21.5	C	872[86]	5.5	16.0		...	...	...	...	...
2011	C	3 298[86]	20.7	C	842[86]	5.3	15.4		...	...	...	...	...
New Caledonia - Nouvelle-Calédonie													
2008	C	4 015	16.6	C	1 169	4.8	11.7	C	20	...	...	...	...
2009	C	4 103	16.7	C	1 261	5.1	11.6	C	23	...	...	...	...
2010	C	4 178	16.7	C	1 191	4.8	11.9	C	19	...	74.4	80.7	...
New Zealand - Nouvelle-Zélande													
2008	+C	64 343	15.1	+C	29 188[25]	6.8	8.2	+C	322[25]	5.0	III78.2	82.2	2.183
2009	+C	62 543	14.5	+C	28 964[25]	6.7	7.8	+C	308[25]	4.9	III78.4	82.4	2.116
2010	+C	63 897	14.6	+C	28 438[25]	6.5	8.1	+C	325[25]	5.1	...	...	2.148
2011	+C	61 403	13.9	+C	30 082[25]	6.8	7.1	+C	290[25]	4.7	III79.1	82.8	2.060
2012	+C	61 178	13.8	+C	30 099[25]	6.8	7.0	+C	256[25]	4.2	III79.3	83.0	2.050
Niue - Nioué													
2008	C	20[87]	...	C	13[88]	...	...		...	...	...	...	...
2009	C	31[87]	20.0	C	12[88]	...	...		...	...	...	...	...
Norfolk Island - Île Norfolk[89]													
2008	+C	22	...	+C	20	...	...		...	...	...	...	...
Northern Mariana Islands - Îles Mariannes septentrionales													
2008	U	1 260[90]	...	U	176[90]	...	...	U	4[90]	...	...	...	2.300
2009	U	1 110[91]	...		...	...	...		...	...	74.5	79.9	2.200
2010	U	1 072[91]	...		...	...	...		...	...	...	...	2.200
Pitcairn													
2008	C	1	...		...	...	...		...	...	...	...	...
Samoa													
2008	C	2 371	13.0	U	409	...	...		...	...	...	...	...
2009	C	1 602	8.7	U	561	...	...		...	...	...	...	...
2011	I	5 703[92]	30.8	I	812[92]	4.4	26.5		...	...	...	...	...
Wallis and Futuna Islands - Îles Wallis et Futuna													
2008	C	185	13.8	C	90	6.7	7.1		...	...	...	...	...

FOOTNOTES - NOTES

Italics: data from civil registers which are incomplete or of unknown completeness. - Italiques : données incomplètes ou dont le degré d'exactitude n'est pas connu, provenant des registres de l'état civil.

* Provisional. - Données provisoires.

[a] 'Code' indicates the source of data, as follows:
C - Civil registration, estimated over 90% complete
U - Civil registration, estimated less than 90% complete
| - Other source, estimated reliable
+ - Data tabulated by date of registration rather than occurence

... - Information not available

Le 'Code' indique la source des données, comme suit :
C - Registres de l'état civil considérés complets à 90 p. 100 au moins
U - Registres de l'état civil qui ne sont pas considérés complets à 90 p. 100 au moins
| - Autre source, considérée fiable
+ - Données exploitées selon la date de l'enregistrement et non la date de l'événement
... - Information non disponible

[b] A Roman number in front of the data for males specifies the range of the reference period of life expectancy for males and females presented on the

row. For example, a reference year of 2005 and a range of V years means that the reference period for the life expectancy is 2001 - 2005. The absence of a Roman number means the reference period is one year and the reference period therefore coincides with the reference year. - Un chiffre romain devant la donnée relative aux hommes indique l'étendue de la période de référence concernant l'espérance de vie des hommes et des femmes présentée dans la ligne. Par exemple, une année de référence 2005 et une étendue de V signifie que la période de référence pour l'espérance de vie est 2001-2005. L'absence de chiffre romain signifie que la période de référence est d'un an et donc coïncide avec l'année de référence.

[1] Excluding live-born infants who died before their birth was registered. Data refer to Algerian population only. - Non compris les enfants nés vivants décédés avant l'enregistrement de leur naissance. Les données ne concernent que la population algérienne.

[2] Data refer to Algerian population only. - Les données ne concernent que la population algérienne.

[3] Data refer to national projections. - Les données se réfèrent aux projections nationales.

[4] Excluding data for November and December. Coverage of live births is below 60 per cent. - Ne comprend pas les données pour novembre et décembre. La couverture des naissances vivantes est inférieure à 60 pour cent.

[5] Data refer to the 12 months preceding the census in March. - Les données se rapportent aux 12 mois précédant le recensement de mars.

[6] Data refer to Libyan nationals only. - Les données se raportent aux nationaux libyens seulement.

[7] Data refer to the 12 months preceding the census in June. - Les données se raportent aux 12 mois précédant le recensement de juin.

[8] Excludes the islands of St. Brandon and Agalega. - Non compris les îles St. Brandon et Agalega.

[9] Data refer to the 12 months preceding the census in April. The figures in this table are derived from survey data. They are representative only of private households, internally displaced persons, refugees and nomads, and do not include cattle camps, institutional households, homeless people or overnight travelers. - Les données se rapportent aux douze mois précédant le recensement d'avril. Les chiffres de ce tableau proviennent de données d'enquête. Ils représentent exclusivement les ménages privés et les déplacés, réfugiés et nomades; ils ne comprennent ni les personnes se trouvant dans des camps pastoraux et des établissements collectifs, ni les sans-abri, ni les voyageurs.

[10] Excluding live-born infants who died before their birth was registered. - Non compris les enfants nés vivants décédés avant l'enregistrement de leur naissance.

[11] Based on estimates and projections from 'Agence Nationale de la Statistique et de la Démographie'. - Données fondées sur des estimations et des projections provenant de l'Agence Nationale de la Statistique et de la Démographie.

[12] Data refer to the 12 months preceding the census in October. - Les données se rapportent aux 12 mois précédant le recensement de octobre.

[13] Based on preliminary findings of 2011 Uganda Demographic and Health Survey. - D'après les résultats préliminaires de l'enquête de 2011 sur la démographie et la santé en Ouganda.

[14] Excluding visitors. - Ne comprend pas les visiteurs.

[15] Excluding non-residents and foreign service personnel and their dependants. - À l'exclusion des non-résidents et du personnel diplomatique et de leurs charges de famille.

[16] Including Canadian residents temporarily in the United States, but excluding United States residents temporarily in Canada. - Y compris les résidents canadiens se trouvant temporairement aux Etats-Unis, mais ne comprennent pas les résidents des Etats-Unis se trouvant temporairement au Canada.

[17] Resident births outside the islands are excluded. - Non compris les naissances de résidents hors des îles.

[18] Because of the small population and the resulting small numbers of deaths, the data for the calendar years 2008-2010 have been aggregated to construct a more reliable life table. - La population étant peu élevée et, par conséquent, le nombre de décès aussi, les données des années civiles 2008, 2009 et 2010 ont été agrégées afin d'améliorer la fiabilité de la table de mortalité.

[19] Data refer to births to women aged 15-49. - Les données concernent les enfants nés de femmes âgées de 15 à 49 ans.

[20] Excluding children born in the country of non-resident mothers. - Exceptés les enfants nés dans le pays des mères non-résidentes.

[21] Excluding infant deaths to mothers living abroad. - Exception faite des décès d'enfants en bas âge survenus lorsque la mère résidait à l'étranger.

[22] Data have been adjusted for underenumeration. - Les données ont été ajustées pour compenser les lacunes du dénombrement.

[23] Data have been adjusted for undercoverage of infant deaths and sudden and violent deaths. - Ajusté pour la sous-estimation de la mortalité infantile, du nombre de morts soudaines et de morts violentes.

[24] Data refer to births to resident mothers. - Ces données concernent les enfants nés de mères résidentes.

[25] Data refer to resident population only. - Pour la population résidante seulement.

[26] Excluding Indian jungle population. - Non compris les Indiens de la jungle.

[27] Excluding births of nationals outside the country. - Non compris les naissances de nationaux hors du pays.

[28] Including deaths abroad and deaths of unknown residence. - Y compris les décès à l'étranger et les décès dont on ignore la résidence.

[29] Including births abroad and births of unknown residence. - Y compris les naissances survenues à l'étranger et les naissances d'enfants dont la résidence n'était pas connue.

[30] Data refer to projections based on the 2005 Population Census. - Les données se réfèrent aux projections basées sur le recensement de la population de 2005.

[31] Estimate for 2010 – 2015. - Estimation pour la période 2010-2015.

[32] Excludes nomadic Indian tribes. - Non compris les tribus d'Indiens nomades.

[33] Excludes nomadic Indian tribes. Data refer to national projections. - Non compris les tribus d'Indiens nomades. Les données se réfèrent aux projections nationales.

[34] Source: Reports of the Ministry of Health. - Source: Rapports du Ministère de la Santé.

[35] Source: Reports of the Ministry of Health. Completeness of coverage estimated at 40 per cent. - Source: Rapports du Ministère de la Santé. Degré de complétude évalué à 40 pour cent.

[36] Including births to non-resident mothers. - Y compris les naissances de femmes non résidentes.

[37] Including non-residents. - Y compris les non-résidents.

[38] Indicators based on projected or estimated fertility from the 2001 Population Census. - Les indicateurs sont fondés sur la fécondité projetée ou estimée à partir du recensement de population de 2001.

[39] Estimated rate. - Taux estimatif.

[40] Excluding infants born alive of less than 28 weeks' gestation, of less than 1 000 grams in weight and 35 centimeters in length, who die within seven days of birth. - Non compris les enfants nés vivants après moins de 28 semaines de gestations, pesant moins de 1 000 grammes, mesurant moins de 35 centimètres et décédés dans les sept jours qui ont suivi leur naissance.

[41] For statistical purposes, the data for China do not include those for the Hong Kong Special Administrative Region (Hong Kong SAR), Macao Special Administrative Region (Macao SAR) and Taiwan province of China. - Pour la présentation des statistiques, les données pour la Chine ne comprennent pas la Région Administrative Spéciale de Hong Kong (Hong Kong RAS), la Région Administrative Spéciale de Macao (Macao RAS) et Taïwan province de Chine.

[42] Data have been estimated on the basis of the annual National Sample Survey on Population Changes. - Les données ont été estimées sur la base de l'enquête annuelle "National Sample Survey on Population Changes".

[43] The fertility rates have been compiled using a population denominator which has excluded female foreign domestic helpers. - Les taux de fécondité ont été compilés pour une population (en dénominateur) ne comprenant pas les domestiques étrangères.

[44] Data refer to government controlled areas. - Les données se rapportent aux zones contrôlées par le Gouvernement.

[45] Includes data for the Indian-held part of Jammu and Kashmir, the final status of which has not yet been determined. - Y compris les données pour la partie du Jammu et du Cachemire occupée par l'Inde dont le statut définitif n'a pas encore été déterminé.

[46] Rates were obtained by the Sample Registration System of India, which is a large demographic survey. - Les taux ont été obtenus par le Système de l'enregistrement par échantillon de l'Inde qui est une large enquête démographique.

[47] Data refer to the Iranian Year which begins on 21 March and ends on 20 March of the following year. - Les données concernent l'année iranienne, qui commence le 21 mars et se termine le 20 mars de l'année suivante.

[48] Includes data for East Jerusalem and Israeli residents in certain other territories under occupation by Israeli military forces since June 1967. - Y compris les données pour Jérusalem-Est et les résidents israéliens dans certains autres territoires occupés depuis 1967 par les forces armées israéliennes.

[49] Including deaths abroad of Israeli residents who were out of the country for less than a year. - Y compris les décès à l'étranger de résidents israéliens qui ont quitté le pays depuis moins d'un an.

[50] Data refer to Japanese nationals in Japan only. - Les données se raportent aux nationaux japonais au Japon seulement.

[51] Excluding data for Jordanian territory under occupation since June 1967 by Israeli military forces. Excluding foreigners, including registered Palestinian refugees. - Non compris les données pour le territoire jordanien occupé depuis juin 1967 par les forces armées israéliennes. Non compris les étrangers, mais y compris les réfugiés de Palestine enregistrés.

52 Data are calculated from the results of the Population and Housing Census of 2009. - Les données sont calculées à partir des résultats du recensement de la population et de l'habitat de 2009.

53 Based on the results of the 2005 Population and Housing Census. - Données fondées sur les résultats du recensement de la population et de l'habitat de 2005.

54 Data refer to urban areas only. - Données ne concernant que les zones urbaines.

55 Data from Births and Deaths Notification System (Ministry of Health and all health care providers). - Les données proviennent du système de notification des naissances et des décès (Ministère de la santé et tous prestataires de soins de santé).

56 Data refer to residence of child. Excluding alien armed forces, civilian aliens employed by armed forces, and foreign diplomatic personnel and their dependants. - Les données correspondent à la résidence de l'enfant. Non compris les militaires étrangers, les civils étrangers employés par les forces armées ni le personnel diplomatique étranger et les membres de leur famille les accompagnant.

57 Excluding alien armed forces, civilian aliens employed by armed forces, and foreign diplomatic personnel and their dependants. - Non compris les militaires étrangers, les civils étrangers employés par les forces armées ni le personnel diplomatique étranger et les membres de leur famille le accompagnant.

58 Projections based on the final results of the 2004 Population and Housing Census. - Projections basées sur les résultats définitifs du recensement de la population et de l'habitat de 2004.

59 Data refer to resident population which comprises Singapore citizens and permanent residents. - Les données se rapportent à la population résidente composé des citoyens de Singapour et des résidents permanents.

60 Data refer to resident total fertility rate. - Les données se rapportent aux indices synthétique de fécondité de la population résidante.

61 Data refer to resident population which comprises Singapore citizens and permanent residents. Provisional. - Les données se rapportent à la population résidente composé des citoyens de Singapour et des résidents permanents. Données provisoires.

62 Excluding data from Mulative and Killnochchi districts. - À l'exclusion des données des districts de Mulative et Killnochchi.

63 Excluding live-born infants who died before their birth was registered. Excluding nomad population and Palestinian refugees. - Non compris les enfants nés vivants décédés avant l'enregistrement de leur naissance. Non compris la population nomade et les réfugiés de Palestine.

64 Excluding infants born alive of less than 28 weeks' gestation, of less than 1 000 grams in weight and 35 centimeters in length, who die within seven days of birth. Data have been adjusted for under-registration. - Non compris les enfants nés vivants après moins de 28 semaines de gestations, pesant moins de 1 000 grammes, mesurant moins de 35 centimètres et décédés dans les sept jours qui ont suivi leur naissance. Y compris un ajustement pour sous-enregistrement.

65 The registration of births and deaths is conducted by the Ministry of Health. An estimate of completeness is not provided. - L'enregistrement des naissances et des décès est mené par le Ministère de la Santé. Le degré estimatif de complétude n'est pas fourni.

66 Including deaths of nationals abroad. - Y compris les décès des nationaux survenus à l'étranger.

67 Including armed forces stationed outside the country, but excluding alien armed forces stationed in the area. - Y compris les militaires nationaux hors du pays, mais non compris les militaires étrangers en garnison sur le territoire.

68 A live-born child is a child fully expelled or removed out of the mother's body, who gives a sign of life and whose birth weight is (a) 500 g or more, or (b) lower than 500 g, if it survives 24 hours after delivery. - Un enfant né vivant est un enfant qui a été entièrement expulsé ou retiré du corps de la mère, qui présente des signes de vie et dont le poids à la naissance est : a) soit égal ou supérieur à 500 grammes; b) soit inférieur à 500 grammes s'il survit plus de 24 heures après l'accouchement.

69 Excluding Faeroe Islands and Greenland shown separately, if available. - Non compris les Iles Féroé et le Groenland, qui font l'objet de rubriques distinctes, si disponible.

70 Excluding Åland Islands. - Non compris les Îles d'Åland.

71 Including armed forces stationed outside the country. - Y compris les militaires nationaux hors du pays.

72 Including live births by military personnel and their dependants. - Y compris les naissances vivantes parmi les membres du personnel militaire et leurs personnes à charge.

73 Excluding armed forces. - Non compris les militaires en garnison.

74 Definition of localities was revised from 2011 causing a break with the previous series. - La rupture par rapport aux séries précédentes s'explique par le fait que la définition des localités a été révisée depuis 2011.

75 Data refer to events registered within one year of occurrence. - Les données portent sur des événements enregistrés dans l'année pendant laquelle ils sont survenus.

76 Including residents outside the country if listed in a Netherlands population register. - Englobe les résidents se trouvant à l'étranger à condition qu'ils soient inscrits sur le registre de population des Pays-Bas.

77 Including residents temporarily outside the country. - Y compris les résidents se trouvant temporairement hors du pays.

78 Data refer to resident population only. Including unknown sex. - Pour la population résidante seulement. Y compris le sexe inconnu.

79 Excluding Transnistria and the municipality of Bender. - Les données ne tiennent pas compte de l'information sur la Transnistria et la municipalité de Bender.

80 Excludes data for Kosovo and Metohia. - Sans les données pour le Kosovo et Metohie.

81 Data refer to births with weight 500g and more (if weight is unknown - with length 25 centimeters and more, or with gestation during 22 weeks or more). - Données concernant les nouveau-nés de 500 grammes ou plus (si le poids est inconnu – de 25 centimètres de long ou plus, ou après une grossesse de 22 semaines ou plus).

82 Data includes deaths resulting from births with weight 500g and more (if weight is unknown - with length 25 centimeters and more, or with gestation during 22 weeks or more). - Y compris les décès de nouveau-nés de 500 grammes ou plus (si le poids est inconnu – de 25 centimètres de long ou plus, ou après une grossesse de 22 semaines ou plus).

83 Excluding Channel Islands (Guernsey and Jersey) and Isle of Man, shown separately, if available. - Non compris les îles Anglo-Normandes (Guernesey et Jersey) et l'île de Man, qui font l'objet de rubriques distinctes, si disponible.

84 Data tabulated by date of occurrence for England and Wales, and by date of registration for Northern Ireland and Scotland. - Données exploitées selon la date de l'événement pour l'Angleterre et le pays de Galles, et selon la date de l'enregistrement pour l'Irlande du Nord et l'Ecosse.

85 Excluding Niue, shown separately, which is part of Cook Islands, but because of remoteness is administered separately. - Non compris Nioué, qui fait l'objet d'une rubrique distincte et qui fait partie des îles Cook, mais qui, en raison de son éloignement, est administrée séparément.

86 Including United States military personnel, their dependants and contract employees. - Y compris les militaires des Etats-Unis, les membres de leur famille les accompagnant et les agents contractuels des Etats-Unis.

87 Includes children born in New Zealand to women resident in Niue who chose to travel to New Zealand to give birth. - Y compris les enfants nés en Nouvelle-Zélande de femmes résidant à Nioué qui ont choisi de se rendre en Nouvelle-Zélande pour accoucher.

88 Includes deaths occurred in New Zealand but buried in Niue and deaths occurred in Niue but buried elsewhere. - Y compris les personnes décédées en Nouvelle-Zélande qui sont enterrées à Nioué et les personnes décédées à Nioué qui sont enterrées ailleurs.

89 Data cover the period from 1 July of the previous year to 30 June of the present year. - Pour la période allant du 1er juillet de l'année précédente au 30 juin de l'année en cours.

90 Source: Commonwealth Health Center - Vital Statistics Office - Source : Centre de Santé du Commonwealth - Bureau des statistiques d'État civil

91 Source: U.S. National Center for Health Statistics, National Vital Statistics Reports (NVSR). - Source : US National Center for Health Statistics, National Vital Statistics Reports (NVSR).

92 Data refer to the 12 months preceding the census in November. - Données se rapportant aux 12 mois précédant le recensement de novembre.

Table 5 - *Demographic Yearbook 2012*

Table 5 presents national estimates of mid-year population for all available years between 2003 and 2012.

Description of variables: Mid-year estimates of the total population are those provided by national statistical offices. They refer to the *de facto* or *de jure* population on 1 July of the reference year. Exceptions to this are footnoted accordingly. The data are presented in thousands, rounded by the Statistics Division of the United Nations Department of Economic and Social Affairs.

For some countries or areas the figures presented in this table and the figures used to calculate rates in subsequent tables are not the same, as these countries have provided a reference population for vital events that is different than the total population.

Unless otherwise indicated, all estimates relate to the population within present geographical boundaries. Major exceptions to this principle are explained in footnotes.

Reliability of data: Reliable mid-year population estimates are those that are based on a complete census (or on a sample survey) and have been adjusted on a basis of a continuous population register or on the balance of births, deaths and migration. Reliable mid-year estimates appear in roman type. Mid-year estimates that are not calculated on this basis are considered less reliable and are shown in *italics*.

Limitations: Statistics on estimates of the mid-year total population are subject to the same qualifications as have been set forth for population statistics in general in section 3 of the Technical Notes.

International comparability of mid-year population estimates is also affected by the fact that some of these estimates refer to the *de jure*, and not the *de facto*, population. These are indicated in the column titled "Code". The difference between the *de facto* and the *de jure* population is discussed in section 3.1.1 of the Technical Notes.

Earlier data: Estimates of mid-year population have been shown in previous issues of the *Demographic Yearbook*. Information on the years and specific topics covered is presented in the Historical Index.

Tableau 5 – *Annuaire démographique 2012*

Le tableau 5 présente des estimations nationales de la population en milieu d'année pour le plus grand nombre possible d'années entre 2003 et 2012.

Description des variables : les estimations de la population totale en milieu d'année sont celles qui ont été communiquées par les services nationaux de statistique. Elles correspondent à la population de fait ou se réfèrent à la population de droit, au 1er juillet de l'année de référence. Lorsque la date est différente, cela est signalé par une note. Sauf indication contraire, tous les chiffres sont exprimés en milliers. Les données ont été arrondies par la Division de statistique du Département des affaires économiques et sociales de l'Organisation des Nations Unies.

Pour certains pays ou territoires, les données présentées dans ce tableau sont différentes des données utilisées pour calculer les taux dans les tableaux suivants, parce que ces pays ont fourni une population de référence pour les événements démographiques différente de la population totale.

Sauf indication contraire, toutes les estimations se rapportent à la population présente sur le territoire actuel des pays ou zones considérés. Les principales exceptions à cette règle sont expliquées en note.

Fiabilité des données : les estimations de la population en milieu d'année sont considérées sûres quand elles sont fondées sur un recensement complet (ou sur une enquête par sondage) et ont été ajustées en fonction des données provenant d'un registre permanent de population ou en fonction des naissances, décès et mouvements migratoires qui ont eu lieu pendant la période. Les estimations considérées comme sûres apparaissent en caractères romains. Les estimations dont le calcul n'a pas été effectué sur cette base sont considérées comme moins sûres et apparaissent en italique.

Insuffisance des données : les statistiques concernant les estimations de la population totale en milieu d'année appellent toutes les réserves qui ont été formulées à la section 3 des Notes techniques à propos des statistiques de la population en général.

Le fait que certaines des estimations concernant la population en milieu d'année se réfèrent à la population de droit et non à la population de fait influe sur la comparabilité internationale. Ces cas ont été signalés dans la colonne « Code ». La différence entre la population de fait et la population de droit est expliquée à la section 3.1.1 des Notes techniques.

Données publiées antérieurement : des estimations de la population en milieu d'année ont été publiées dans des éditions antérieures de l'*Annuaire démographique*. Pour plus de précisions concernant les années et les sujets pour lesquels des données ont été publiées, se reporter à l'index.

5. Estimates of mid-year population: 2003 - 2012
Estimations de la population au milieu de l'année : 2003 - 2012

Continent and country or area / Continent et pays ou zone	Code[a]	Population estimates (in thousands) - Estimations (en milliers)									
		2003	2004	2005	2006	2007	2008	2009	2010	2011	2012

AFRICA - AFRIQUE

Algeria - Algérie	DJ	31 848	32 364	32 906	33 481	34 096	*34 591[1]	*35 268[1]	*35 978[1]	*36 717[1]	*37 495[1]
Benin - Bénin[2]	DF	6 983	7 209	7 447	7 700	7 959	8 225	8 498	8 779	9 067	...
Botswana	DJ	1 673	1 693	1 708	1 720	1 736	1 755	1 776	1 823	1 850	...
Burkina Faso	DJ	12 567	12 963	13 374	...	14 252[2]	14 731[2]	15 225[2]	15 731[2]	...	...
Burundi	DF	7 211	7 384	...	...	...	...	...	...	...	...
Cabo Verde	DF	461	468	475	483	491	500	509	518	527	...
Cameroon - Cameroun[2]	DF	16 626	17 000	...	...	...	...	...	...	...	...
	DJ	...	...	...	...	...	...	18 928[3]	19 406[3]	19 865[3]	20 387[3]
Central African Republic - République centrafricaine	DF	3 151	...	...	...	...	...	...	...	...	...
Congo[2]	DF	3 241	3 344	3 488	3 589	3 616	3 790	3 884	...	...	...
Côte d'Ivoire[2]	DF	*18 001	*18 546	*19 097	*19 658	*20 228	*20 807	*21 395	...	...	...
Djibouti	DF	...	632	...	...	...	...	...	...	...	...
Egypt - Égypte	DF	67 965	69 304	70 653	72 009	73 644	75 194	76 925	78 685	80 410	82 541
Ethiopia - Éthiopie[4]	DF	69 127	71 066	73 044	75 067	77 127	79 221	...	...	...	...
Gabon	DF	*1 300	...	1 313[5]	...	...	...	...	...	...	...
Gambia - Gambie	DF	...	...	1 436	1 510	...	...	...	...	...	...
Ghana	DF	20 371	20 859	21 367	21 876	22 388	22 901	23 417	...	...	...
Guinea - Guinée	DF	...	9 214	...	...	...	10 183[2]	10 218[2]	10 537[2]	...	...
Guinea-Bissau - Guinée-Bissau[2]	DF	1 267	1 296	1 326	1 357	1 389	...	...	1 558	...	...
Kenya[6]	DF	33 142	34 191	35 267	36 433	37 184	38 300	...	40 124	41 745	42 436
Lesotho[2]	DF	...	...	...	1 878	1 880	1 884	1 887	1 892	1 897	...
Libya - Libye[7]	DF	...	...	...	5 298	...	...	...	5 702	...	...
Madagascar	DF	16 585	17 062	17 550	18 048	18 556	19 072	19 601	20 142	20 696	...
Malawi[2]	DF	11 549	11 938	12 341	12 758	13 188	13 630	14 085	14 553	15 034	...
Mali[3]	DF	11 111	11 419	11 732	12 051	12 378	12 706	...	...	...	...
Mauritania - Mauritanie[2]	DF	2 702	2 823	2 906	2 990	3 075	3 162	3 251	3 341	3 297	...
Mauritius - Maurice[8]	DJ	1 223	1 233	1 243	1 253	1 260	1 269	1 275	1 281	1 286	*1 291
Morocco - Maroc	DF	30 088	29 840[9]	30 172[9]	30 509[9]	30 850[9]	31 195[9]	31 543[9]	31 894[9]	32 245[9]	32 597[9]
Mozambique[2]	DF	18 514	18 962	19 420	19 889	20 367	20 854	21 350	21 854	...	...
Namibia - Namibie[2]	DF	1 891	1 923	1 957	1 992	2 028	2 065	2 104	2 143	...	...
Niger[2]	DJ	11 834	12 225	12 628	13 045	13 716	14 198	14 693	15 204	15 731	16 275
Nigeria - Nigéria	DF	126 153[2]	129 175[2]	133 767[2]	*140 004[10]	...	...	...	...	...	...
Réunion	DJ	756	767	777	786	794[3]	806[3]	816[3]	*828[3]	*839[3]	...
Rwanda[2]	DF	8 879	9 032	9 225	9 468	9 557	9 832	10 117	10 413	10 718	11 033
Saint Helena ex. dep. - Sainte-Hélène sans dép.	DF	...	...	...	...	4	4	4	4	4	4
Saint Helena: Ascension - Sainte-Hélène: Ascension	DJ	...	...	...	...	...	1	...	...	...	...
Saint Helena: Tristan da Cunha - Sainte-Hélène: Tristan da Cunha[11]	DF	...	...	...	...	0	0	0	...	...	...
Sao Tome and Principe - Sao Tomé-et-Principe	DF	143	146	149	152	155	158	161	164	167	*187
Senegal - Sénégal[12]	DJ	10 317[13]	10 605[13]	10 901[13]	11 206[13]	11 519[13]	11 841[13]	12 171[13]	12 509[13]	12 842[13]	13 208
Seychelles	DF	83	82	83	85	85	87	87	90	87	88
Sierra Leone	DF	5 280	...	5 095	5 217	5 343	5 474	5 608	5 747	5 890	6 038
South Africa - Afrique du Sud[14]	DF	45 997	46 589	47 177	47 760	48 337	48 909	49 475	50 034	50 587	...
Swaziland	DF	1 081	1 105	1 126	1 146	1 020	1 032	1 044	1 056	1 068	1 080
Togo	DF	4 970	5 090	5 212	5 337	5 465	5 596	5 731	...	...	...
Tunisia - Tunisie	DF	9 840	9 932	10 029	10 128	10 225	10 329	10 440	10 547	10 674	10 778
Uganda - Ouganda	DF	25 089	25 896	26 741	27 629	28 581	29 593	30 661	31 785	32 940	34 131
United Republic of Tanzania - République Unie de Tanzanie[12]	DF	34 860	35 944	37 083	38 251	39 446	40 668	41 916	43 188	44 485	45 798
Zambia - Zambie[2]	DF	10 744	11 090	11 441	11 799	12 161	12 526	12 897	...	...	...
Zimbabwe[12]	DF	11 640	11 730	11 830	11 930	12 040	12 150	13 668	...	...	...

AMERICA, NORTH - AMÉRIQUE DU NORD

Anguilla	DF	12	13	14	14	15	16	16	16	17	...
Antigua and Barbuda - Antigua-et-Barbuda	DF	80	81	83	84	86	88	89	91	...	...
Aruba	DJ	95	98	101	103	104	105	107	102	103	...

Continent and country or area / Continent et pays ou zone	Code[a]	Population estimates (in thousands) - Estimations (en milliers)									
		2003	2004	2005	2006	2007	2008	2009	2010	2011	2012
AMERICA, NORTH - AMÉRIQUE DU NORD											
Bahamas[2]	DF	317	321	325	330	334	338	342	347	351	...
Barbados - Barbade	DF	272	272	273	273	274	275	...	276[13]	...	...
Belize	DF	*274*	*283*	*292*	*301*	*311*	*322*	*333*	...	...	...
Bermuda - Bermudes	DJ	63	63	64	64	64	64	64	65	65	65
British Virgin Islands - Îles Vierges britanniques	DF	21	22	...	...	...	...	...	...	...	...
Canada[15]	DJ	31 640[16]	31 941[16]	32 245[16]	32 576[17]	32 930[17]	33 319[17]	33 730[18]	34 126[18]	*34 483[19]	*34 880[19]
Cayman Islands - Îles Caïmanes	DJ	44	44	48	52	54	56	53	55	56[13]	57[13]
Costa Rica	DJ	4 089	4 179	4 266	4 354	4 443	4 451	4 509	4 564	4 616	4 667
Cuba	DJ	11 215	11 236	11 243	11 241	11 238	11 236	11 239	11 242	11 245	...
Curaçao	DJ	130	133	137	140	143	145	146	149	151	151[3]
Dominica - Dominique	DF	70	70	71	71	71	71	72	...	69	...
Dominican Republic - République dominicaine[2]	DF	*8 958*	*9 093*	*9 226*	*9 360*	*9 493*	*9 625*	*9 756*	*9 884*	*10 011*	*10 135*
El Salvador	DF	6 638	6 757	6 049[20]	6 074[20]	6 099[20]	6 125[20]	6 153[20]	6 183[20]	6 216[20]	6 251[20]
Greenland - Groenland[21]	DJ	57	57	57	57	57	56	56	57	57	57
Grenada - Grenade	DF	...	...	...	...	107	109	111	...	...	...
Guadeloupe	DJ	439	445	446	458	401[22]	402[22]	402[22]	*402[22]	*402[22]	...
Guatemala	DF	12 084[14]	12 390[14]	12 701[12]	13 019[12]	13 345[12]	13 678[12]	14 017[12]	14 362[12]	...	...
Haiti - Haïti[23]	DJ	*9 001*	*9 145*	*9 292*	*9 445*	*9 602*	*9 762*	*9 923*	*10 085*	*10 248*	*10 413*
Honduras[24]	DF	6 861	7 028	7 197	7 367	7 537	7 707	7 877	8 046	8 215	...
Jamaica - Jamaïque	DJ	2 626	2 638	2 650	2 663	2 676	2 687	2 696	2 702	2 700	*2 708
Martinique[3]	DJ	392	394	396	398	398	398	396	*396	*396	...
Mexico - Mexique	DJ	*102 000*	*103 002*	*103 947*	*104 874*	*105 791*	*106 683*	*107 551*	*112 337*	...	...
Montserrat	DF	4	5	5	5	5	5	5	5	5	5
Nicaragua	DJ	*5 313*	*5 381*	*5 450*	*5 523*	*5 596*	*5 669*	*5 742*	*5 816*	*5 889*	*6 071*
Panama	DF	*3 116[25]*	*3 172[25]*	*3 228[25]*	*3 284[25]*	*3 340[25]*	*3 395[25]*	*3 450[25]*	*3 504[25]*	*3 643[26]*	*3 788[26]*
Puerto Rico - Porto Rico[27]	DJ	3 879	3 895	3 912	3 928	3 942	3 954	3 967	3 721[28]	3 694[28]	3 667[28]
Saint Kitts and Nevis - Saint-Kitts-et-Nevis	DF	*48	*49	*49	*50	*51	*51	*52	...	...	...
Saint Lucia - Sainte-Lucie	DF	161	162	164	166	168	170	172	...	...	...
Saint Vincent and the Grenadines - Saint-Vincent-et-les Grenadines	DF	105	105	104	101	100	99	101	...	...	...
Sint Maarten (Dutch part) - Saint-Martin (partie néerlandaise)[3]	DJ	33	34	36	38	39	40	41	...	...	...
Trinidad and Tobago - Trinité-et-Tobago[29]	DF	1 282	1 291	1 294	1 298	1 303	1 309	1 310	1 318	...	...
Turks and Caicos Islands - Îles Turques et Caïques	DJ	*25*	*27*	*31*	*33*	*35*	*37	*38*	*40*	...	...
United States of America - États-Unis d'Amérique[30]	DJ	290 326	293 046	295 753	298 593	301 580	304 375	307 007	*309 051	*311 592	*313 914
United States Virgin Islands - Îles Vierges américaines[27]	DJ	109	109	110	110	110	110	*110	*110	...	...
AMERICA, SOUTH - AMÉRIQUE DU SUD											
Argentina - Argentine[24]	DF	37 870	38 226	38 592	38 971	39 356	39 746	40 134	40 519	40 900	41 282
Bolivia (Plurinational State of) - Bolivie (État plurinational de)	DF	*9 025*	*9 227*	*9 427*	*9 627*	*9 828*	*10 028*	*10 227*	*10 426*	*10 624*	...
Brazil - Brésil[31]	DF	*178 741*	*181 106*	*183 383*	*185 564*	*187 642*	*189 613*	*191 481*	*193 253*	*192 376*	*193 947*
Chile - Chili	DF	15 919	16 093	16 267	16 433	16 598	16 763	16 929	17 094	17 248	17 403
Colombia - Colombie[32]	DJ	*41 849*	*42 368*	*42 889*	*43 406*	*43 927*	*44 451*	*44 979*	*45 510*	*46 045*	*46 582*
Ecuador - Équateur[33]	DF	*12 843*	*13 027*	*13 215*	*13 408*	*13 605*	*13 805*	*14 005*	*15 005*	*15 248*	*15 495*
French Guiana - Guyane française	DJ	181	193[3]	199[3]	206[3]	213[3]	219[3]	224[3]	*230[3]	...	...
Guyana	DF	753	756	758	761	763	766	777	785	*790	*796
Paraguay[12]	DF	*5 677*	*5 788*	*5 899*	*6 009*	*6 120*	*6 230*	*6 341*	*6 451*	*6 562*	*6 673*
Peru - Pérou	DF	*27 103*	*27 460*	*27 811*	*28 151*	*28 482[20]*	*28 807[20]*	*29 132[20]*	*29 462[20]*	*29 798[20]*	*30 136[20]*
Suriname	DJ	483	487	499	506	510	517	524	531	540	...
Uruguay[2]	DF	3 304	3 302	3 306	3 314	3 324	3 334	3 345	3 357	*3 369	*3 381

5. Estimates of mid-year population: 2003 - 2012
Estimations de la population au milieu de l'année : 2003 - 2012 (continued - suite)

Continent and country or area / Continent et pays ou zone	Code[a]	Population estimates (in thousands) - Estimations (en milliers)									
		2003	2004	2005	2006	2007	2008	2009	2010	2011	2012
AMERICA, SOUTH - AMÉRIQUE DU SUD											
Venezuela (Bolivarian Republic of) - Venezuela (République bolivarienne du)[24]	DF	25 674	26 127	26 577	27 031	27 483	27 935	28 384	28 834	29 278	29 718
ASIA - ASIE											
Afghanistan	DF	20 691[34]	21 678[34]	22 098[34]	22 576[35]	23 039[34]	23 511[34]	23 994[36]	24 486[37]	24 988[34]	25 500[34]
Armenia - Arménie	DJ	3 211	3 214	3 218	3 221	3 227	3 234	3 244	3 256	3 268	3 274[3]
Azerbaijan - Azerbaïdjan	DF	8 309[38]	8 398[38]	8 500[38]	8 610[38]	8 723[38]	8 839[38]	8 947	9 054	9 173	9 296
Bahrain - Bahreïn	DJ	765	824	889	960	1 039	1 103	1 178	1 229	1 195	1 235
Bangladesh	DF	134 800	136 700	138 600	140 600	142 600	144 500	146 600	148 620	150 611	...
Bhutan - Bhoutan	DF	613	624	...	647[39]	659[39]	671[39]	683[39]	696[39]	708[39]	721[39]
Brunei Darussalam - Brunéi Darussalam	DF	350	360	370	383	390	398	406	...	...	...
Cambodia - Cambodge[40]	DF	13 287[41]	13 542[41]	13 807[41]	14 081[41]	14 364[41]	13 868[1]	14 085[1]	14 303[1]	14 521[1]	14 741[1]
China - Chine[42]	DF	1 292 270[43]	1 299 880[43]	1 307 560[43]	1 314 480[43]	1 317 900[43]	1 324 700[43]	1 331 300[43]	1 337 700[43]	1 344 100[44]	1 350 695[44]
China, Hong Kong SAR - Chine, Hong Kong RAS	DJ	6 731	6 784	6 813	6 857	6 916	6 958	6 973	7 024	7 072	7 155
China, Macao SAR - Chine, Macao RAS	DJ	444	455	473	499	521	541	535	537	550	568
Cyprus - Chypre[45]	DJ	718	728	738	750	766	786	807	828	849	*862[46]
Democratic People's Republic of Korea - République populaire démocratique de Corée	DF	23 464	23 612	...	...	...	...	...	...	...	...
Georgia - Géorgie	DF	4 329	4 318	4 361	4 398	4 388	4 384	4 411	4 453	4 483	4 491
India - Inde[47]	DF	1 068 065	1 084 757	1 101 318	1 117 734	1 134 023	1 150 196	1 166 228	1 182 105	1 197 813	1 213 370
Indonesia - Indonésie	DJ	214 468	217 673	220 926	224 228	227 579	230 980	234 432	...	236 954	*247 214
Iran (Islamic Republic of) - Iran (République islamique d')[48]	DJ	67 315	68 345	69 390	70 603	71 279	72 182	73 202	74 340	75 591	76 725
Iraq	DF	26 340	27 139	27 963	28 810	29 682	31 895	32 105	...	33 402	33 913
Israel - Israël[49]	DJ	6 690	6 809	6 930	7 054	7 180	7 309	7 486	7 624	7 766	*7 901
Japan - Japon[50]	DJ	127 718	127 761	127 773	127 854[51]	128 001[51]	128 063[51]	128 047[51]	128 070[51]	127 817[51]	127 561[51]
Jordan - Jordanie[52]	DF	5 230	5 350	5 473	5 600	5 723	5 850	5 980	6 113	6 249	6 388
Kazakhstan	DF	14 909	15 013	15 147	15 308	15 484	15 674	16 093	16 323	16 559	16 673[3]
Kuwait - Koweït	DF	2 093	2 167	2 245	2 328	2 411	2 496	2 778	2 933	3 099[53]	3 268
Kyrgyzstan - Kirghizstan[54]	DF	4 944	4 977	5 007	5 034	5 056	5 078	5 128	5 193	5 260	5 352
Lao People's Democratic Republic - République démocratique populaire lao	DF	5 679[55]	5 836[55]	5 651[56]	5 778[56]	5 904[56]	6 032[56]	6 160[56]	6 289[56]	6 419[56]	6 549[56]
Malaysia - Malaisie	DJ	25 038[57]	25 541[57]	26 046[57]	26 550[57]	27 058[57]	27 568[57]	28 081[57]	28 589[58]	28 964[58]	29 337[58]
Maldives	DF	285	289	294	...	305	310	315	320	325	331
Mongolia - Mongolie	DF	2 490	2 519	2 548	2 579	2 615	2 659	2 710	2 758	*2 781	...
Myanmar[59]	DF	53 224	54 299	55 396	56 515	57 504	58 377	59 130	59 780	60 384	60 976
Nepal - Népal	DJ	24 250	24 797	25 343	25 887	26 427	26 967	27 504	28 044	28 585	29 129
Oman	DF	...	2 416	2 509	2 577	2 743	2 867	3 174	...	3 295	...
Pakistan[60]	DF	...	151 090	...	...	...	166 410	169 940	173 510	177 100	...
	DJ	138 979[61]	...	144 367[62]	147 100	149 860[63]	...	...	...	...	...
Philippines[25]	DJ	81 878	83 559	85 261	86 973	88 706	90 457	92 227	94 013	...	...
Qatar	DF	714	798	906	1 043	1 218	1 448	1 639	1 715	1 733	...
Republic of Korea - République de Corée	DJ	47 859	48 039	48 138	48 372	48 598	48 949	49 182	49 410	50 111	50 345
Saudi Arabia - Arabie saoudite	DF	22 023	22 564	*23 330[64]	*24 122[64]	*24 941[64]	*25 787[64]	*26 661[64]	*27 563[64]	*28 376[64]	*29 196[64]
Singapore - Singapour[65]	DJ	4 115	4 167	4 266	4 401	4 589	4 839	4 988	5 077	5 184	5 312
Sri Lanka	DF	19 252	19 435	19 644	19 858	20 039	20 216	*20 450	*20 653	*20 869	*20 328
State of Palestine - État de Palestine	DF	3 315	3 407	3 508	3 612	3 719	3 826	3 935	4 048	4 169	4 293
Syrian Arab Republic - République arabe syrienne[66]	DF	17 550	17 829	18 138	18 717	19 172	19 644	20 125	20 619	21 124	...
Tajikistan - Tadjikistan	DF	6 573	6 710	6 850	6 992	7 140	7 295	7 334	7 519	7 714	...
Thailand - Thaïlande[2]	DJ	64 019	64 177	64 839	65 306	66 042	66 480	66 903	67 312	67 599	67 912
Timor-Leste[2]	DF	...	952	983	1 015	1 048	1 081	1 115	1 066	...	...
Turkey - Turquie	DF	70 231	71 151	72 065	72 971	70 138	71 052	72 039	73 142	74 224	75 176
Turkmenistan - Turkménistan	DF	5 124	...	...	...	...	...	...	...	...	...

5. Estimates of mid-year population: 2003 - 2012
Estimations de la population au milieu de l'année : 2003 - 2012 (continued - suite)

Continent and country or area / Continent et pays ou zone	Code[a]	Population estimates (in thousands) - Estimations (en milliers)									
		2003	2004	2005	2006	2007	2008	2009	2010	2011	2012

ASIA - ASIE

United Arab Emirates - Émirats arabes unis[67]	DF	*3 551*	*3 761*	*4 041*	*5 012*[13]	*6 219*[13]	*8 074*[13]	*8 200*[13]	*8 264*	...	...
Uzbekistan - Ouzbékistan	DF	25 568	*25 707	*26 021	*26 313	*26 664	*27 072	*27 533	*28 001	*29 123	*29 555
Viet Nam	DF	*80 468*[68]	*81 438*[68]	*82 394*[68]	*83 313*[68]	*84 221*[68]	*85 122*[68]	*86 025*	*86 933*	*87 840*	*88 773*
Yemen - Yémen	DF	*19 104*[13]	...	*20 283*[13]	*20 901*[13]	*21 539*[13]	*22 198*[13]	...	...	...	...
	DJ	...	...	...	...	...	...	*22 492*[2]	*23 154*[2]	*23 833*[2]	*24 527*[2]

EUROPE

Åland Islands - Îles d'Åland[21]	DJ	26	26	27	27	27	27	28	28	28	28
Albania - Albanie	DF	3 034	3 015	2 993	2 968	2 941	2 913	2 884	2 857	2 829	2 802
Andorra - Andorre[21]	DJ	70	75	79	80	82	84	85	85	79[69]	77
Austria - Autriche	DJ	8 118	8 169	8 225	8 268	8 301	8 337	8 365	8 388	8 423	8 466
Belarus - Bélarus	DF	9 874	9 825	9 775	9 733	9 702	9 681	9 576	9 481	...	9 465[3]
	DJ	...	...	...	...	...	...	...	...	9 473	...
Belgium - Belgique	DJ	10 372	10 417	10 473	10 542	10 623	10 710	10 796	10 896	10 996	11 139
Bosnia and Herzegovina - Bosnie-Herzégovine	DF	3 832	3 843	3 843	3 843	3 843	3 842	3 843	3 843	3 841	*3 837
Bulgaria - Bulgarie	DJ	7 824	7 781	7 740	7 699	7 660	7 623	7 585	7 534	7 348	7 305
Croatia - Croatie	DJ	4 440	4 439	4 442	4 440	4 436	4 435	4 429	4 418	4 412[3]	*4 268
Czech Republic - République tchèque	DJ	10 202	10 207	10 234	10 267	10 323	10 430	10 491	10 517	10 497	10 511
Denmark - Danemark[70]	DJ	5 387	5 401	5 416	5 435	5 457	5 489	5 519	5 545	5 567	5 587
Estonia - Estonie	DJ	1 354	1 349	1 346	1 344	1 342	1 341	1 340	1 340	1 340	1 340[3]
Faeroe Islands - Îles Féroé	DJ	48	48	48	48	48	49	49	49	48	48[3]
Finland - Finlande[21]	DJ	5 213	5 228	5 246	5 266	5 289	5 313	5 311[71]	5 335[71]	5 360[71]	5 401[3]
France[72]	DJ	60 304	60 734	61 181	61 597	61 965	62 300	*62 628	*62 959	*63 294	*63 556
Germany - Allemagne	DJ	82 520	82 501	82 464	82 366	82 263	82 120	81 875	81 757	81 779	81 932
Gibraltar[73]	DF	29	29	29	29	29	29	29	29	30	...
Greece - Grèce[74]	DF	11 024	11 062	11 104	11 149	11 193	11 237	11 283	11 308	11 300	*11 290[3]
Guernsey - Guernesey	DF	...	60	...	61[75]	61[75]	62[75]	62[75]	62[75]	63[75]	63[75]
Holy See - Saint-Siège[76]	DF	...	...	...	...	...	...	0	0[77]	...	0[78]
Hungary - Hongrie	DJ	10 130	10 107	10 087	10 071	10 056	10 038	10 023	10 000	9 972	*9 919
Iceland - Islande[21]	DJ	289	293	296	304	311	319	319	318	319[79]	321[79]
Ireland - Irlande[21]	DF	3 997	4 070	4 160	4 260	4 357	4 426	4 459	4 471[80]	4 484[80]	...
	DJ	...	...	...	...	...	...	...	...	...	4 585[80]
Isle of Man - Île de Man[81]	DJ	77	78	79	...	81	82	82	...	...	...
Italy - Italie	DJ	57 605	58 175	58 607	58 941	59 375	59 832	60 193	60 483	60 626[3]	60 851[3]
Jersey	DJ	89	90	91	92	93	95	96	97	98	...
Latvia - Lettonie	DJ	2 325	2 313	2 301	2 288	2 276	2 266	2 255	2 239	2 075[3]	*2 032
Liechtenstein	DJ	34	34	35	35	35	35	36	36	36	*36[3]
Lithuania - Lituanie	DJ	3 454	3 436	3 414	3 394	3 376	3 358	3 339	3 287	3 030	3 008[3]
Luxembourg	DJ	452	458	465	473	480	489	498	507	512[3]	525[3]
Malta - Malte[82]	DJ	399	401	404	406	408	410	413	415	417	418[3]
Monaco	DJ	...	...	...	...	...	...	35	36	36	...
Montenegro - Monténégro	DJ	620	622	623	624	626	629	632	617	621	622
Netherlands - Pays-Bas	DJ	16 225	16 282	16 320	16 346	16 382	16 446	16 530	16 615	16 693	16 730[3]
Norway - Norvège[83]	DJ	4 565	4 592	4 623	4 661	4 709	4 768	4 829	4 889	4 953	4 986[3]
Poland - Pologne[84]	DJ	38 195	38 180	38 161	38 132	38 116	38 116	38 153	38 517	38 526	38 538[3]
Portugal	DJ	10 441	10 502	10 549	10 584	10 608	10 622	10 632	10 637	*10 557	*10 542[3]
Republic of Moldova - République de Moldova[85]	DJ	3 613	3 604	3 595	3 585	3 577	3 570	3 566	3 562	3 560	3 560[3]
Romania - Roumanie	DJ	21 734	21 673	21 624	21 584	21 538	21 504	21 470	21 431	*21 354	*21 356[3]
Russian Federation - Fédération de Russie	DJ	144 649	144 067	143 519	143 050	142 805	142 742	142 785	142 849	142 961	143 056[3]
San Marino - Saint-Marin[21]	DF	29	29	30	30	31	32	33[3]	33[3]	33[3]	33[3]
Serbia - Serbie[86]	DJ	7 481	7 463	7 441	7 412	7 382	7 350	7 321	7 291	7 259	7 241[3]
Slovakia - Slovaquie	DJ	5 379	5 383	5 387	5 391	5 398	5 407	5 418	5 431	5 398	5 408[3]
Slovenia - Slovénie	DJ	1 997	1 997	2 001	2 009	2 019	2 023	2 042	2 049	2 052	2 057
Spain - Espagne	DJ	42 005	42 692	43 398	44 068	44 874	45 593	45 929	46 073	46 125	46 163
Svalbard and Jan Mayen Islands - Îles Svalbard et Jan Mayen[87]	DF	2	2	2	...	2	2	...	...	...	...
Sweden - Suède[21]	DJ	8 958	8 994	9 030	9 081	9 148	9 220	9 299	9 378	9 449	9 519
Switzerland - Suisse	DJ	7 339	7 390	7 437	7 484	7 551	7 648	7 744	7 825	7 912	*7 996

Continent and country or area Continent et pays ou zone	Code[a]	Population estimates (in thousands) - Estimations (en milliers)									
		2003	2004	2005	2006	2007	2008	2009	2010	2011	2012
EUROPE											
TFYR of Macedonia - L'ex-R. y. de Macédoine	DF	2 027	2 033	2 037	2 040	2 044	2 047	2 051	2 055	2 059	2 061
Ukraine	DF	47 813	47 452	47 105	46 788	46 509	46 258	46 053	45 963[3]	45 779[3]	45 634[3]
United Kingdom of Great Britain and Northern Ireland - Royaume-Uni de Grande-Bretagne et d'Irlande du Nord[88]	DF	59 552	59 842	60 235	60 584	60 986	61 398	61 792	62 262	62 752	63 244
OCEANIA - OCÉANIE											
American Samoa - Samoas américaines[27]	DJ	63	64	66	67	64	65	66	66	...	...
Australia - Australie[89]	DJ	19 895[38]	20 127[38]	20 395[38]	20 698[38]	*21 016[90]	*21 384[90]	*21 779[90]	*22 065[90]	*22 324[90]	*22 684[90]
Cook Islands - Îles Cook[91]	DF	18	20	22	24	21	22	23	24	*21	...
Fiji - Fidji	DF	816	822	825	830	834	...	843	857	...	...
French Polynesia - Polynésie française	DF	247	250	253	256	259	262	265	269	270[3]	...
Guam[92]	DJ	158	158	158	159	159	159	159	...	160	160
Marshall Islands - Îles Marshall[93]	DF	...	55	...	52	53	53	54	54	...	...
Micronesia (Federated States of) - Micronésie (États fédérés de)[2]	DJ	108	108	108	108	108	108	108	108	...	...
New Caledonia - Nouvelle-Calédonie	DF	226	230	234	238	242	242	...	250	252[3]	...
New Zealand - Nouvelle-Zélande[94]	DJ	4 027	4 088	4 134	4 185	4 228	4 269	4 316	4 368	4 405	4 433
Niue - Nioué	DJ	2	2	2	2	2	...	2	1	...	...
Norfolk Island - Île Norfolk	DF	3	3	2	2	...	...	...	...	...	...
Northern Mariana Islands - Îles Mariannes septentrionales	DF	77	79	71	61	59	55	51	48	46	...
Palau - Palaos	DF	20	21	...	22	21	21	...	...	...	...
Pitcairn[95]	DF	...	...	...	...	0	0	...	...	...	...
Samoa	DF	180	182	183	185	182	182	183	184	185	...
Solomon Islands - Îles Salomon[2]	DF	448	460	471	483	495	507	518	531	542	554
Tonga[96]	DF	101	102	102	103	103	104	...	...	...	...
Tuvalu	DF	9	10	10	11	11	...	...	...	11	...
Vanuatu[2]	DF	...	216	...	221	...	...	...	...	...	...

FOOTNOTES - NOTES

Italics: estimates which are less reliable. - Italiques : estimations moins sûres.

* Provisional. - Données provisoires.

[a] 'Code' indicates source of data, as follows: - Le 'Code' indique la source des données, comme suit :
DF: Population de facto - Population de fait
DJ : Population de jure - Population de droit

[1] Data based on 2008 Population Census. - Données fondées sur le recensement de population de 2008.
[2] Data refer to national projections. - Les données se réfèrent aux projections nationales.
[3] Data refer to 1 January. - Données se raportent au 1 janvier.
[4] Projections based on the 1994 Population Census. - Projections fondées sur le recensement de la population de 1994.
[5] Based on the results of the Gabonese Survey for the Evaluation and Tracking of Poverty. - Sur base des résultats de l'enquête gabonaise sur l'évaluation et le suivi de la pauvreté.
[6] Post-censal estimates based on the 1999 Population Census. - Les estimations post-censitaire fondées sur le recensement de la population de 1999.

[7] Data refer to Libyan nationals only. - Les données se raportent aux nationaux libyens seulement.
[8] Excludes the islands of St. Brandon and Agalega. - Non compris les îles St. Brandon et Agalega.
[9] Based on the results of the 2004 Population Census. - D'après des résultats du recensement de la population de 2004.
[10] Based on the results of the 2006 Population Census. - D'après des résultats du recensement de la population de 2006.
[11] Data refer to 31 December. Based on the results of a population count. The population figures are 264, 263 and 262 persons for 2007, 2008 and 2009 respectively. - Données se raportent au 31 décembre. D'après les résultats d'un comptage de la population. La population est respectivement égale à 264, 263 et 262 personnes pour les années 2007, 2008 et 2009.
[12] Projections based on the 2002 Population Census. - Projections fondées sur le recensement de la population de 2002.
[13] Data refer to 31 December. - Données se raportent au 31 décembre.
[14] Mid-year estimates have been adjusted for underenumeration at latest census. - Les estimations au millieu de l'année tiennent compte d'un ajustement destiné à compenser les lacunes du dénombrement lors du dernier recensement.
[15] Estimates adjusted for census net undercoverage (including adjustment for incompletely enumerated Indian reserves). - Ajusté pour la sous-estimation du recensement (y compris les réservations en Inde incomplètement énumérées).
[16] Final intercensal estimates. - Estimations inter-censitaires definitives.
[17] Final postcensal estimates. - Estimations postcensitaires definitives.

[18] Updated postcensal estimates. - Estimations post censitaires mises à jour.

[19] Preliminary postcensal estimates. - Estimations post censitaires préliminaires.

[20] Estimates based on the 2007 Population Census. - Estimations fondées sur le recensement de la population de 2007.

[21] Population statistics are compiled from registers. - Les statistiques de la population sont compilées à partir des registres.

[22] Data refer to 1 January. Excluding data for Saint Barthélémy and Saint Martin. - Données se raportent au 1 janvier. Non compris les données pour Saint Barthélémy et Saint Martin.

[23] Projections produced by l'Institut Haïtien de Statistique et d'Informatique (IHSI) and the Latin American and Caribbean Demographic Centre (CELADE) - Population Division of ECLAC. - Les données sont projections produits par l'Institut Haïtien de Statistique et d'Informatique (IHSI) et le centre démographique de l'Amérique latine et les Caraïbes - Division de la population de la CEPALC.

[24] Data refer to projections based on the 2001 Population Census. - Les données se réfèrent aux projections basées sur le recensement de la population de 2001.

[25] Data refer to projections based on the 2000 Population Census. - Les données se réfèrent aux projections basées sur le recensement de la population de 2000.

[26] Data refer to projections based on the 2010 Population Census. - Les données se réfèrent aux projections basées sur le recensement de la population de 2010.

[27] Including armed forces stationed in the area. - Y compris les militaires en garnison sur le territoire.

[28] Data based on the 2010 Population Census results. - D'après le résultats du recensement de la population de 2010.

[29] Based on the results of the 2000 Population Census. - Basé sur les résultats du recencement de la population de 2000.

[30] Excluding armed forces overseas and civilian citizens absent from the country for an extended period of time. - Non compris les militaires à l'étranger, et les civils hors du pays pendant une période prolongée.

[31] Data include persons in remote areas, military personnel outside the country, merchant seamen at sea, civilian seasonal workers outside the country, and other civilians outside the country, and exclude nomads, foreign military, civilian aliens temporarily in the country, transients on ships and Indian jungle population. - Y compris les personnes vivant dans des régions éloignées, le personel militaire en dehors du pays, les marins marchands, les ouvriers saisonniers en dehors du pays, et autres civils en dehors du pays, et non compris les nomades, les militaires étrangers, les étrangers civils temporairement dans le pays, les transiteurs sur des bateaux et les Indiens de la jungle.

[32] Data are revised projections taking into consideration also the results of 2005 census. - Les données sont des projections révisées tenant compte également des résultats du recensement de 2005.

[33] Excludes nomadic Indian tribes. Data refer to national projections. - Non compris les tribus d'Indiens nomades. Les données se réfèrent aux projections nationales.

[34] Data refer to the settled population based on the 1979 Population Census and the latest household prelisting. The refugees of Afghanistan in Iran, Pakistan, and an estimated 1.5 million nomads, are not included. - Les données se rapportent à la population stationnaire sur la base du recensement de 1979 et du recensement préliminaire des logements le plus récent. Sont exclus les réfugiés d'Afghanistan en Iran et au Pakistan et les nomades estimés à 1,5 million.

[35] Data refer to the settled population based on the 1979 Population Census and the latest household prelisting. The refugees of Afghanistan in Iran, Pakistan, and an estimated 1.5 million nomads, are not included. The so adjusted total population of the country for 2006 is 24.1 million (12.3 million males and 11.8 million females). - Les données se rapportent à la population stationnaire sur la base du recensement de 1979 et du recensement préliminaire des logements le plus récent. Sont exclus les réfugiés d'Afghanistan en Iran et au Pakistan et les nomades estimés à 1,5 million. La population totale du pays ainsi ajustée pour 2006 comprend 24,1 millions de personnes (12,3 millions d'hommes et 11,8 millions de femmes).

[36] The adjusted total population of the country is 25.5 million. Data refer to the settled population based on the 1979 Population Census and the latest household prelisting. The refugees of Afghanistan in Iran, Pakistan, and an estimated 1.5 million nomads, are not included. - La population totale ajustée du pays comprend 25,5 millions de personnes. Les données se rapportent à la population stationnaire sur la base du recensement de 1979 et du recensement préliminaire des logements le plus récent. Sont exclus les réfugiés d'Afghanistan en Iran et au Pakistan et les nomades estimés à 1,5 million.

[37] The adjusted total population of the country is 26 million (13.3 million males and 12.7 million females). Data refer to the settled population based on the 1979 Population Census and the latest household prelisting. The refugees of Afghanistan in Iran, Pakistan, and an estimated 1.5 million nomads, are not

included. - La population totale ajustée du pays comprend 26 millions de personnes (13.3 millions d'homes et 12.7 millions de femmes). Les données se rapportent à la population stationnaire sur la base du recensement de 1979 et du recensement préliminaire des logements le plus récent. Sont exclus les réfugiés d'Afghanistan en Iran et au Pakistan et les nomades estimés à 1,5 million.

[38] Intercensal estimates. - Estimations inter-censitaires.

[39] Data refer to projections based on the 2005 Population Census. - Les données se réfèrent aux projections basées sur le recensement de la population de 2005.

[40] Excluding foreign diplomatic personnel and their dependants. - Non compris le personnel diplomatique étranger et les membres de leur famille les accompagnant.

[41] Based on 1998 census results. - A partir des résultats de recensement de l'année 1998.

[42] For statistical purposes, the data for China do not include those for the Hong Kong Special Administrative Region (Hong Kong SAR), Macao Special Administrative Region (Macao SAR) and Taiwan province of China. - Pour la présentation des statistiques, les données pour la Chine ne comprennent pas la Région Administrative Spéciale de Hong Kong (Hong Kong RAS), la Région Administrative Spéciale de Macao (Macao RAS) et Taïwan province de Chine.

[43] Data have been estimated on the basis of the annual National Sample Survey on Population Changes. - Les données ont été estimées sur la base de l'enquête annuelle "National Sample Survey on Population Changes".

[44] Data have been adjusted on the basis of the Population Census of 2010. - Les données ont été ajustées à partir des résultats du recensement de la population de 2010.

[45] Data refer to government controlled areas. - Les données se rapportent aux zones contrôlées par le Gouvernement.

[46] Data refer to 1 January. Data have been adjusted on the basis of the Population Census of 2011. - Données se raportent au 1 janvier. Les données ont été calculées sur la base du recensement de population de 2011.

[47] Includes data for the Indian-held part of Jammu and Kashmir, the final status of which has not yet been determined. Data refer to projections based on the 2001 Population Census. - Y compris les données pour la partie du Jammu et du Cachemire occupée par l'Inde dont le statut définitif n'a pas encore été déterminé. Les données se réfèrent aux projections basées sur le recensement de la population de 2001.

[48] Data refer to the Iranian Year which begins on 21 March and ends on 20 March of the following year. - Les données concernent l'année iranienne, qui commence le 21 mars et se termine le 20 mars de l'année suivante.

[49] Includes data for East Jerusalem and Israeli residents in certain other territories under occupation by Israeli military forces since June 1967. - Y compris les données pour Jérusalem-Est et les résidents israéliens dans certains autres territoires occupés depuis 1967 par les forces armées israéliennes.

[50] Excluding diplomatic personnel outside the country and foreign military and civilian personnel and their dependants stationed in the area. - Non compris le personnel diplomatique hors du pays ni les militaires et agents civils étrangers en poste sur le territoire et les membres de leur famille les accompagnant.

[51] Estimates based on the complete counts of the 2010 Population Census. - Estimations basées sur le dénombrement complet du recensement de la population de 2010.

[52] Data refer to 31 December. Excluding data for Jordanian territory under occupation since June 1967 by Israeli military forces. Excluding foreigners, including registered Palestinian refugees. - Données se raportent au 31 décembre. Non compris les données pour le territoire jordanien occupé depuis juin 1967 par les forces armées israéliennes. Non compris les étrangers, mais y compris les réfugiés de Palestine enregistrés.

[53] Estimates based on population census data of 2005 and 2011. - Estimations basées sur les données des recensements de la population de 2005 et 2011.

[54] Data are calculated from the results of the Population and Housing Census of 2009. - Les données sont calculées à partir des résultats du recensement de la population et de l'habitat de 2009.

[55] Population estimates for 2000 to 2004 are based on the age-sex distribution of 1995 population census and growth rate at year 2000. - Pour les années 2000 à 2004, on a pris pour base la répartition par âge et sexe du recensement de population de 1995 et le taux de croissance de 2000.

[56] Based on the results of the 2005 Population and Housing Census. - Données fondées sur les résultats du recensement de la population et de l'habitat de 2005.

[57] Intercensal Mid-Year Population Estimates based on the adjusted Population and Housing Census of 2000 and 2010. - Les estimations inter-censitaires au millieu de l'année sont fondée sur les résultats ajustés des recensements de la population et de l'habitat de 2000 et 2010.

[58] Estimates based on the adjusted Population and Housing Census of 2010. - Les estimations sont fondée sur les résultats ajustées du recensement de la population et de l'habitat de 2010.

[59] Data refer to 1 October. - Données se raportent au 1 octobre.

60 Excluding data for the Pakistan-held part of Jammu and Kashmir, the final status of which has not yet been determined. - Non compris les données concernant la partie du Jammu et Cachemire occupée par le Pakistan dont le statut définitif n'a pas été déterminé.

61 Based on the results of the Pakistan Demographic Survey (PDS 2003). These estimates do not reflect completely accurately the actual population and vital events of the country. - D'après les résultats de l'enquête démographique effectuée par le Pakistan en 2003. Ces estimations ne dénotent pas d'une manière complètement ponctuelle la population actuelle et les statistiques de l'état civil du pays.

62 Based on the results of the Pakistan Demographic Survey (PDS 2005). These estimates do not reflect completely accurately the actual population and vital events of the country. - D'après les résultats de l'enquête démographique effectuée par le Pakistan en 2005. Ces estimations ne dénotent pas d'une manière complètement ponctuelle la population actuelle et les statistiques de l'état civil du pays.

63 Based on the results of the Pakistan Demographic Survey (PDS 2007). - D'après les résultats de l'enquête démographique effectuée par le Pakistan en 2007.

64 Data based on the preliminary results of the 2010 Population and Housing Census. - D'après les résultats préliminaires du recensement de la population et des logements de 2010.

65 Data refer to 30 June. Data refer to total population, which comprises Singapore residents and non-residents. - Données se raportent au 30 juin. Les données se rapportent à la population totale composé des résidents de Singapour et les non résidents.

66 Including Palestinian refugees. - Y compris les réfugiés de Palestine.

67 Data include non-national population. - Les données comprennent les non-nationaux.

68 Data are adjusted according to the results of the 1999 and 2009 censuses. - Les données ont été ajustées à partir des résultats des recensements de la population de 1999 et 2009.

69 Decrease in population due to revision in administrative registers. - Diminution de la population due à la révision des registres administratifs.

70 Excluding Faeroe Islands and Greenland shown separately, if available. Population statistics are compiled from registers. - Non compris les Iles Féroé et le Groenland, qui font l'objet de rubriques distinctes, si disponible. Les statistiques de la population sont compilées à partir des registres.

71 Excluding Åland Islands. - Non compris les Îles d'Åland.

72 Excluding diplomatic personnel outside the country and including members of alien armed forces not living in military camps and foreign diplomatic personnel not living in embassies or consulates. - Non compris le personnel diplomatique hors du pays et y compris les militaires étrangers ne vivant pas dans des camps militaires et le personnel diplomatique étranger ne vivant pas dans les ambassades ou les consulats.

73 Data refer to 31 December. Excluding military personnel, visitors and transients. - Données se raportent au 31 décembre. Non compris les militaires, ni les visiteurs et transients.

74 Excluding armed forces stationed outside the country, but including alien armed forces stationed in the area. - Non compris les militaires en garnison hors du pays, mais y compris les militaires étrangers en garnison sur le territoire.

75 Data refer to 31 March. - Données se raportent au 31 mars.

76 Data refer to the Vatican City State. - Les données se rapportent à l'Etat de la Cité du Vatican.

77 Data refer to 26 February. - Données se rapportent au 26 février.

78 Data refer to 21 June. - Données se raportent au 21 juin.

79 Definition of localities was revised from 2011 causing a break with the previous series. - La rupture par rapport aux séries précédentes s'explique par le fait que la définition des localités a été révisée depuis 2011.

80 Data refer to 15 April. - Données se raportent au 15 avril.

81 Data refer to 30 April. - Données se raportent au 30 avril.

82 Including civilian nationals temporarily outside the country. - Y compris les civils nationaux temporairement hors du pays.

83 Including residents temporarily outside the country. - Y compris les résidents se trouvant temporairement hors du pays.

84 Excluding civilian aliens within country, but including civilian nationals temporarily outside country. - Non compris les civils étrangers dans le pays, mais y compris les civils nationaux temporairement hors du pays.

85 Excluding Transnistria and the municipality of Bender. - Les données ne tiennent pas compte de l'information sur la Transnistria et la municipalité de Bender.

86 Excludes data for Kosovo and Metohia. - Sans les données pour le Kosovo et Metohie.

87 Data refer to 1 January. Data refer to Svalbard only. - Données se raportent au 1 janvier. Données ne concernant que le Svalbard.

88 Excluding Channel Islands (Guernsey and Jersey) and Isle of Man, shown separately, if available. - Non compris les îles Anglo-Normandes (Guernesey et Jersey) et l'île de Man, qui font l'objet de rubriques distinctes, si disponible.

89 Data are based on Australian Standard Geographical Classification boundaries. - Les données réfèrent au découpage de la nomenclature géographique normalisée d'Australie.

90 These estimates are preliminary revised. - Ces estimations sont des estimations préliminaires révisées.

91 Excluding Niue, shown separately, which is part of Cook Islands, but because of remoteness is administered separately. - Non compris Nioué, qui fait l'objet d'une rubrique distincte et qui fait partie des îles Cook, mais qui, en raison de son éloignement, est administrée séparément.

92 Including armed forces stationed in the area. Data refer to projections based on the 2010 Population Census. - Y compris les militaires en garnison sur le territoire. Les données se réfèrent aux projections basées sur le recensement de la population de 2010.

93 Projections are prepared by the Secretariat of the Pacific Community based on 1999 census of population and housing. - Les projections sont preparées par le Secrétariat de la Communauté du Pacifique à partir des résultats du recensement de la population et de l'habitat de 1999.

94 Because of rounding, totals are not in all cases the sum of the respective components. Based on the census, updated for residents missed or counted more than once by the census (net census undercount); residents temporarily overseas on census night, and births, deaths and net migration between the census night and the date of the estimate. - Les chiffres étant arrondis, les totaux ne correspondent pas toujours rigoureusement à la somme des composants respectifs. D'après le recensement, mise à jour pour les résidents omis ou dénombrés plus d'une fois par le recensement (sous-dénombrement net); résidents temporairement à l'étranger la nuit du recensement, et naissances, décès et migration nette entre la nuit du recensement et la date de l'estimation.

95 Data refer to 31 December. The population figures are 64 and 58 persons for 2007 and 2008 respectively. - Données se raportent au 31 décembre. La population est respectivement égale à 64 et 58 personnes pour les années 2007 et 2008.

96 Data refer to national projections. Based on the results of the 1996 population census. - Les données se réfèrent aux projections nationales. À partir des résultats du recensement de la population de 1996.

Table 6 - *Demographic Yearbook 2012*

Table 6 presents total population by sex for as many years as possible between 2003 and 2012, as well as urban population as available.

Description of variables: Data are from nation-wide population censuses or are estimates, some of which are based on sample surveys of population carried out among all segments of the population. This characteristic of the data is indicated in the column "Code". The codes used are explained at the end of the table.

Urban is defined according to the national census definition. The definition for each country is set forth at the end of the technical notes to this table.

Percentage computation: Percentages urban are the number of persons residing in an area defined as "urban" per 100 total population. They are calculated by the Statistics Division of the United Nations Department of Economic and Social Affairs. In very few cases the data for total population have been revised but the data for the urban and rural population have not been. These data are footnoted accordingly. In these cases, particular caution should be used in interpreting the figures for percentage urban.

Reliability of data: Estimates that are believed to be less reliable are set in *italics* rather than in roman type. Classification in terms of reliability is based on the method of construction of the total population estimate discussed in the technical notes for table 3.

Limitations: Statistics on urban population by sex are subject to the same qualifications as have been set forth for population statistics in general, as discussed in section 3 of the Technical Notes.

The basic limitations imposed by variations in the definition of the total population and in the degree of under-enumeration are perhaps more important in relation to urban/rural than to any other distributions. The classification by urban and rural is affected by variations in defining usual residence for purposes of sub-national tabulations. Likewise, the geographical differentials in the degree of under-enumeration in censuses affect the comparability of these categories throughout the table. The distinction between *de facto* and *de jure* population is also very important with respect to urban/rural distributions. The difference between the *de facto* and the *de jure* population is discussed at length in section 3.1.1 of the Technical Notes.

A most important and specific limitation, however, lies in the national differences in the definition of urban. Because the distinction between urban and rural areas is made in so many different ways, the definitions have been included at the end of this table. The definitions are necessarily brief and, where the classification of urban involves administrative civil divisions, they are often given in the terminology of the particular country or area. As a result of variations in terminology, it may appear that differences between countries or areas are greater than they actually are. On the other hand, similar or identical terms (for example, town, village, district) as used in different countries or areas may have quite different meanings.

It will be seen from an examination of the definitions that they fall roughly into three major types: (1) classification of localities as urban based on size; (2) classification of administrative centres of minor civil divisions as urban and the remainder of the division as rural; and (3) classification of minor civil divisions on a set of criteria, which may include type of local government, number of inhabitants or proportion of population engaged in agriculture.

The designation of areas as urban or rural is so closely bound to historical, political, cultural, and administrative considerations that the process of developing uniform definitions and procedures moves very slowly. Not only do the definitions differ from one country or area to the other, but, they may also no longer reflect the original intention for distinguishing urban from rural. The criteria once established on the basis of administrative subdivisions (as most of these are) become fixed and resistant to change. For this reason, comparisons of time-series data may be severely affected because the definitions used become outdated. Special care must be taken in comparing data from censuses with those from sample surveys because the definitions of urban used may differ.

Despite their shortcomings, however, statistics on urban and rural population are useful in describing the diversity of population distribution within a country or area.

The definition of urban/rural areas is based on both qualitative and quantitative criteria that may include any combination of the following: size of population, population density, distance between built-up areas, predominant type of economic activity, conformity to legal or administrative status and urban characteristics such as specific services and facilities[1]. Although statistics classified by urban/rural areas are widely available, no international standard definition appears to be possible at this time since the meaning differs from one country or area to another. The urban/rural classification of population used here is reported according to the national definition.

Earlier data: Urban and total population by sex have been shown in previous issues of the Demographic Yearbook. For information on specific years covered, readers should consult the Historical Index.

DEFINITION OF "URBAN"

AFRICA

Algeria: The urban/rural delimitation is performed after the census operation based on the classification of built-up areas. Groupings of 100 or more constructions, distant less than 200 metres from one another are considered urban.

Botswana: Agglomeration of 5 000 or more inhabitants where 75 per cent of the economic activity is non-agricultural.

Burundi: Commune of Bujumbura.

Burkina Faso: All administrative centres of provinces (total of 45) plus 4 medium-sized towns are considered as urban areas.

Comoros: Every locality or administrative centre of an island, region or prefecture that has the following facilities: asphalted roads, electricity, a medical centre, telephone services, etc.

Egypt: Governorates of Cairo, Alexandria, Port Said, Ismailia, Suez, frontier governorates and capitals of other governorates, as well as district capitals (Markaz). The definition of urban areas for the November 2006 census is "SHIAKHA", a part of a district.

Equatorial Guinea: District centres and localities with 300 dwellings and/or 1 500 inhabitants or more.

Ethiopia: Localities of 2 000 or more inhabitants.

Kenya: Areas having a population of 2 000 or more inhabitants that have transport systems, build-up areas, industrial/manufacturing structures and other developed structures.

Lesotho: All administrative headquarters and settlements of rapid growth.

Liberia: Localities of 2 000 or more inhabitants.

Malawi: All townships and town planning areas and all district centres.

Mauritius: The five Municipal Council Areas which are subdivided into twenty Municipal Wards defined according to proclaimed boundaries.

Namibia: Proclaimed urban areas for which cadastral data is available and other unplanned squatter areas.

Niger: Capital city, capitals of the departments and districts.

Rwanda: All administrative areas recognized as urban by the law. These are all administrative centres of provinces, and the cities of Kigali, Nyanza, Ruhango and Rwamagana.

Senegal: Agglomerations of 10 000 or more inhabitants.

South Africa: Places with some form of local authority.

Sudan: Localities of administrative and/or commercial importance or with population of 5 000 or more inhabitants.

Swaziland: A geographical area constituting of a city or town, characterized by higher population density and vast human features in comparison to areas surrounding it.

Tunisia: Population living in communes.

Uganda: Gazettes, cities, municipalities and towns.

United Republic of Tanzania: 16 gazetted townships.

Zambia: Localities of 5 000 or more inhabitants, the majority of whom all depend on non-agricultural activities.

AMERICA, NORTH

Canada: Places of 1 000 or more inhabitants, having a population density of 400 or more per square kilometre.

Costa Rica: Administrative centres of cantons.

Cuba: Towns that fulfil a political or administrative function, or that have a population of 2 000 or more and definite urban characteristics.

Dominican Republic: Administrative centres of municipalities and municipal districts, some of which include suburban zones of rural character.

El Salvador: Administrative centres of municipalities.

Greenland: Localities of 200 or more inhabitants.

Guatemala: Municipality of Guatemala Department and officially recognized centres of other departments and municipalities.

Haiti: Administrative centres of communes.

Honduras: Localities of 2 000 or more inhabitants, having essentially urban characteristics.

Jamaica: Localities of 2 000 or more inhabitants, having urban characteristics.

Mexico: Localities of 2 500 or more inhabitants.

Nicaragua: Administrative centres of municipalities and localities of 1 000 or more inhabitants or with more than 150 dwellings, with streets, electric light, water service, school and health centre.

Panama: Localities of 1 500 or more inhabitants having essentially urban characteristics. Beginning 1970, localities of 1 500 or more inhabitants with such urban characteristics as streets, water supply systems, sewerage systems and electric light.

Puerto Rico: Agglomerations of 2 500 or more inhabitants, generally having population densities of 1 000 persons per square mile or more. Two types of urban areas: urbanized areas of 50 000 or more inhabitants and urban clusters of at least 2 500 and less than 50 000 inhabitants.

United States of America: Agglomerations of 2 500 or more inhabitants, generally having population densities of 1 000 persons per square mile or more. Two types of urban areas: urbanized areas of 50 000 or more inhabitants and urban clusters of at least 2 500 and less than 50 000 inhabitants.

United States Virgin Islands: Agglomerations of 2 500 or more inhabitants, generally having population densities of 1 000 persons per square mile or more. Two types of urban areas: urbanized areas of 50 000 or more inhabitants and urban clusters of at least 2 500 and less than 50 000 inhabitants. (As of Census 2000, no urbanized areas are identified in the United States Virgin Islands.)

AMERICA, SOUTH

Argentina: Populated centres with 2 000 or more inhabitants.

Bolivia: Localities of 2 000 or more inhabitants.

Brazil: Urban and suburban zones of administrative centres of municipalities and districts.

Chile: Areas of concentrated housing units with more than 2 000 inhabitants, or between 1 001 and 2 000 inhabitants having 50 per cent or more of its economically active population doing secondary or tertiary activities. As an exception, centres of tourism and recreation with more than 250 housing units that do not satisfy the population requirement are nevertheless considered urban.

Colombia: Areas composed of groups of buildings and adjacent structures grouped into blocks with, in general, provision of essential services such as water, sewage, electricity, hospitals and schools, among others. This category includes the capital city and other municipal capitals.

Ecuador: Capitals of provinces and cantons.

Falkland Islands (Malvinas): Town of Stanley.

Paraguay: Cities, towns and administrative centres of departments and districts.

Peru: Populated centres with 100 or more dwellings.

Suriname: The districts of Paramaribo and Wanica.

Uruguay: Towns established as cities, villages, towns and other populated centers by legislation under the Law of Population Centers.

Venezuela (Bolivarian Republic of): Centres with a population of 2 500 or more inhabitants.

ASIA

Armenia: Cities and urban-type localities, officially designated as such, usually according to the criteria of number of inhabitants and predominance of agricultural, or number of non-agricultural workers and their families.

Azerbaijan: An administrative division which covers more than 15 000 population, engaging mainly in industrial and other economic and social activities and which include administrative and cultural centers.

Bahrain: Communes or villages of 2 500 or more inhabitants.

Cambodia: Areas at the commune level satisfying the following three conditions: (1) Population Density exceeding 200 per square Km, (2) Percentage of male employed in agriculture below 50 per cent, (3) Total population of the commune exceeds 2 000 inhabitants.

China: Cities only refer to the cities proper of those designated by the State Council. In the case of cities with district establishment, the city proper refers to the whole administrative area of the district if its population density is 1 500 people per kilometre or higher; or the seat of the district government and other areas of streets under the administration of the district if the population density is less than 1 500 people per kilometre. In the case of cities without district establishment, the city proper refers to the seat of the city government and other areas of streets under the administration of the city. For the city district with the population density below 1 500 people per kilometre and the city without district establishment, if the urban construction of the district or city government seat has extended to some part of the neighboring designated town(s) or township(s), the city proper does include the whole administrative area of the town(s) or township(s).

Cyprus: As determined by the Department of Town Planning and Housing of the Ministry of Interior.

Georgia: Cities and urban-type localities, officially designated as such, usually according to the criteria of number of inhabitants and predominance of agricultural, or number of non-agricultural workers and their families.

India: Towns (places with municipal corporation, municipal area committee, town committee, notified area committee or cantonment board); also, all places having 5 000 or more inhabitants, a density of not less than 1 000 persons per square mile or 400 per square kilometre, pronounced urban characteristics and at least three fourths of the adult male population employed in pursuits other than agriculture.

Indonesia: Area which satisfies certain criteria in terms of population density, percentage of agricultural households, and a number of urban facilities such as roads, formal education facilities, public health services, etc.

Iran (Islamic Republic of): Every district with a municipality.

Israel: Localities with 2 000 or more residents.

Japan: City (shi) having 50 000 or more inhabitants with 60 per cent or more of the houses located in the main built-up areas and 60 per cent or more of the population (including their dependants) engaged in manufacturing, trade or other urban type of business.

Jordan: Localities of 5 000 or more inhabitants.

Kazakhstan: Cities and urban-type localities, officially designated as such, usually according to the criteria of number of inhabitants and predominance of agricultural, or number of non-agricultural workers and their families.

Kyrgyzstan: Cities and urban-type localities, officially designated as such, usually according to the criteria of number of inhabitants and predominance of agricultural, or number of non-agricultural workers and their families.

Lao People's Democratic Republic: Areas or villages that satisfy at least three of the following five conditions: located in metropolitan areas of district or province, there is access to road in dry and rainy seasons, about 70 per cent or 2/3 of the population has access to piped water, about 70 per cent or 2/3 of the population has access to public electricity, there is a market operating every day.

Malaysia: Gazetted areas with their adjoining built-up areas which have a combined population of 10 000 or more. Built-up areas are defined as areas contiguous to a gazetted area and have at least 60 per cent of their population (aged 15 years and over) engaged in non-agricultural activities. The definition of urban areas also takes into account the special development area which is not gazetted and can be indentified and separated from the gazetted area or built-up area of more than 5km and a population of at least 10 000 with 60 per cent of the population (aged 15 years and over) engaged in non-agricultural activities.

Maldives: Malé, the capital.

Mongolia: Capital and district centres.

Nepal: As declared by the government municipalities.

Pakistan: Places with municipal corporation, town committee or cantonment.

Philippines: Cities and municipalities and their central districts with a population density of at least 500 persons per square km. Urban areas are considered other districts regardless of population size that have streets, at least six establishments (commercial, manufacturing, recreational and/or personal services), and at least three public structures such as town hall, church, public park, school, hospital, library, etc.

Republic of Korea: For estimates: Places with 50 000 or more inhabitants. For census: the figures are composed in the basis of the minor administrative divisions such as Dongs (mostly urban areas) and Eups or Myeons (rural areas).

Sri Lanka: Urban sector comprises of all municipal and urban council areas.

State of Palestine: Any locality where the population amounts to 10 000 persons or more. This applies to all governorates/districts regardless of their size, and to all localities whose populations vary from 4 000 to 9 999 persons provided they have at least four of the following elements: public electricity network, public water network, post office, health center with a full time physician and a school offering a general secondary education certificate.

Syrian Arab Republic: Cities, Mohafaza centres and Mantika centres, and communities with 20 000 or more inhabitants.

Tajikistan: Cities and urban-type localities, officially designated as such, usually according to the criteria of number of inhabitants and predominance of agricultural, or number of non-agricultural workers and their families.

Thailand: Municipal areas.

Turkey: Province and district centres.

Turkmenistan: Cities and urban-type localities, officially designated as such, usually according to the criteria of number of inhabitants and predominance of agricultural, or number of non-agricultural workers and their families.

Uzbekistan: Cities and urban-type localities, officially designated as such, usually according to the criteria of number of inhabitants and predominance of agricultural, or number of non-agricultural workers and their families.

Viet Nam: Urban areas include inside urban districts of cities, urban quarters and towns. All other local administrative units (communes) belong to rural areas.

EUROPE

Albania: Towns and other industrial centres of more than 400 inhabitants.

Austria: Urban areas are localities with 2 000 or more inhabitants. The delineation of localities goes back to 1991.

Belarus: Urban settlements are settlements authorized under the law as towns, urban-type settlements, workers settlements and health resort areas.

Bulgaria: All towns and cities according to the Territorial and Administrative-Territorial Division of the country.

Czech Republic: Localities with 2 000 or more inhabitants.

Estonia: Urban settlements include cities, cities without municipal status and towns.

Finland: Urban communes including those municipalities in which at least 90 per cent of the population lives in urban settlements or in which the population of the largest urban settlement is at least 15 000.

France: Communes containing an agglomeration of more than 2 000 inhabitants living in contiguous houses or with not more than 200 metres between houses, also communes of which the major portion of the population is part of a multi-communal agglomeration of this nature.

Greece: Urban is considered every municipal or communal department of which the largest locality has 2 000 inhabitants and over.

Hungary: Localities recognized by the President of the Republic with the title of town, on the basis of specific (economic, commercial, institutional, cultural etc.) criteria.

Iceland: Localities of 200 or more inhabitants.

Ireland: Cities and towns including suburbs of 1 500 or more inhabitants.

Latvia: Cities and urban-type localities, officially designated as such, usually according to the criteria of number of inhabitants and predominance of agricultural, or number of non-agricultural workers and their families.

Lithuania: Urban population refers to persons who live in cities and towns, i.e., the population areas with closely built permanent dwellings and with the resident population of more than 3 000 of which 2/3 of employees work in industry, social infrastructure and business. In a number of towns the population may be less than 3 000 since these areas had already the status of "town" before the law was enforced (July 1994)

Malta: Areas with population density of 150 persons or more per square km.

Montenegro: According to the current law of territorial division of Montenegro. This means that each local community has the obligation to decide which settlements are urban and which are rural.

Netherlands: Urban: Municipalities with a population of 2 000 and more inhabitants. Semi-urban: Municipalities with a population of less than 2 000 but with not more than 20 per cent of their economically active male population engaged in agriculture, and specific residential municipalities of commuters.

Norway: A hub of buildings inhabited by at least 200 people and where the distance between the buildings does not exceed 50 metres. The boundaries are dynamic and may be changed due to developments and population changes.

Poland: Towns and settlements of urban type, e.g. workers' settlements, fishermen's settlements, health resorts.

Portugal: Localities with 2 000 or more inhabitants.

Republic of Moldova: Cities and urban-type localities, officially designated as such, usually according to the criteria of number of inhabitants and predominance of agricultural, or number of non-agricultural workers and their families.

Romania: Cities, municipalities and other towns.

Russian Federation: Cities and urban-type localities, officially designated as such, usually according to the criteria of number of inhabitants and predominance of agricultural, or number of non-agricultural   workers and their families.

Serbia: Municipalities, cities and the city of Belgrade.

Slovakia: The municipalities with the status of a town having 5 000 inhabitants or more.

Slovenia: Settlements of 3 000 or more inhabitants, settlements that serve as seats of municipalities with at least 1 400 inhabitants, and sub-urban areas that are being gradually integrated with an urban settlement of 5 000 or more inhabitants.

Spain: For the purposes of publishing comparable results at the European level, Eurostat proposes to consider as urban, intermediate and rural, areas formed by municipalities with respectively a population over 10 000 inhabitants, 2 001 to 10 000 inhabitants, and 2 000 or less inhabitants.

Switzerland: Agglomerations and isolated towns (towns not attached to a cluster and with at least 10,000 inhabitants) are the urban space.

Ukraine: Cities and urban-type localities, officially designated as such, usually according to the criteria of number of inhabitants and predominance of agricultural, or number of non-agricultural workers and their families.

United Kingdom of Great Britain and Northern Ireland: Built-up areas (of at least 20 hectares of built-up land) with 10 000 or more people living in them.

OCEANIA

Australia: An urban centre is generally defined as a population cluster of 1 000 or more people.

American Samoa: Agglomerations of 2 500 or more inhabitants, generally having population densities of 1 000 persons per square mile or more. Two types of urban areas: urbanized areas of 50 000 or more inhabitants and urban clusters of at least 2 500 and less than 50 000 inhabitants. (As of Census 2000, no urbanized areas are identified in American Samoa.)

Cook Islands: Raratonga, the most populous island.

Guam: Agglomerations of 2 500 or more inhabitants, generally having population densities of 1 000 persons per square mile or more, referred to as "urban clusters".

New Caledonia: Nouméa and communes of Païta, Nouvel Dumbéa and Mont-Dore.

New Zealand: All cities, plus boroughs, town districts, townships and country towns with a population of 1 000 or more usual residents.

Northern Mariana Islands: Agglomerations of 2 500 or more inhabitants, generally having population densities of 1 000 persons per square mile or more. Two types of urban areas: urbanized areas of 50 000 or more inhabitants and urban clusters of at least 2 500 and less than 50 000 inhabitants.

Tokelau: All of Tokelau's population is considered to be rural.
Tonga: Nuku'alofa.
Vanuatu: Luganville centre and Vila urban.

NOTES

[1]   For further information, see *Social and Demographic Statistics: Classifications of Size and Type of Locality and Urban/Rural Areas.* E/CN.3/551, United Nations, New York, 1980.

Tableau 6 – *Annuaire démographique 2012*

Le tableau 6 présente des données sur la population totale selon le sexe pour le plus grand nombre possible d'années entre 2003 et 2012, ainsi que la population urbaine si disponible.

Description des variables : les données proviennent de recensements de la population ou sont des estimations fondées, dans certains cas, sur des enquêtes par sondage portant sur toute la population. Le code qui figure dans la colonne « Code » du tableau indique comment les données ont été obtenues. Les codes utilisés sont expliqués à la fin du tableau.

Le sens donné au terme « urbain » est conforme aux définitions utilisées dans les recensements nationaux. La définition pour chaque pays figure à la fin des présentes notes technique.

Calcul des pourcentages : les pourcentages de la population urbaine sont calculés par la Division de statistique du Département des affaires économiques et sociales de l'Organisation des Nations Unies et représentent le nombre de personnes qui vivent dans des régions considérées comme urbaines pour 100 personnes de la population totale. Dans de très rares cas, les données pour la population totale ont été révisées mais les données pour la population urbaine et la population rurale ne l'ont pas été. Ces données sont indiquées en note. Dans ces cas, les proportions de population urbaine ou rurale sont à interpréter avec précaution.

Fiabilité des données : les estimations considérées comme moins sûres sont indiquées en italique plutôt qu'en caractères romains. Le classement du point de vue de la fiabilité est fondé sur la méthode utilisée pour établir l'estimation de la population totale qui figure au tableau 3 (voir les explications dans les notes techniques relatives à ce même tableau).

Insuffisance des données : les statistiques de la population urbaine selon le sexe appellent toutes les réserves qui ont été formulées à la section 3 des Notes techniques à propos des statistiques de la population en général.

Les limitations fondamentales imposées par les variations de la définition de la population totale et par les lacunes du recensement se font peut-être sentir davantage dans la répartition de la population en population urbaine et population rurale que dans sa répartition suivant toute autre caractéristique. De fait, des différences dans la définition du lieu de résidence habituel utilisée pour l'exploitation des données à l'échelon sous-national influent sur la classification en population urbaine et en population rurale. De même, les différences de degré de sous-dénombrement suivant la zone, à l'occasion des recensements, ont une incidence sur la comparabilité de ces deux catégories dans l'ensemble du tableau. La distinction entre population de fait et population de droit est également très importante du point de vue de la répartition de la population en population urbaine et en population rurale. Cette distinction est expliquée en détail à la section 3.1.1 des Notes techniques.

Toutefois, la difficulté la plus importante tient aux différences de définition du terme « urbain » selon le pays. Les distinctions faites entre « zone urbaine » et « zone rurale » varient tellement que les définitions utilisées ont été reproduites à la fin des notes techniques du tableau 6. Les définitions sont forcément brèves et, lorsque le classement en « zone urbaine » repose sur des divisions administratives, on a souvent désigné celles-ci par le nom qu'elles portent dans la zone ou le pays considéré. Par suite des variations dans la terminologie, les différences entre pays ou zones peuvent sembler plus grandes qu'elles ne le sont réellement. Il se peut aussi que des termes similaires ou identiques, tels que ville, village ou district, aient des significations très différentes selon les pays ou zones.

On constatera, en examinant les définitions adoptées par les différents pays ou zones, qu'elles peuvent être ramenées à trois types principaux : 1) les localités dépassant certaines dimensions sont classées parmi les zones urbaines ; 2) les centres administratifs de petites circonscriptions administratives sont classées parmi les zones urbaines, le reste de la circonscription étant considéré comme zone rurale ; 3) les petites divisions administratives sont classées parmi les zones urbaines selon un critère déterminé, qui peut être soit le type d'administration locale, soit le nombre d'habitants, soit le pourcentage de la population exerçant une activité agricole.

La distinction entre régions urbaines et régions rurales est si étroitement liée à des considérations d'ordre historique, politique, culturel et administratif que l'on ne peut progresser que très lentement vers des définitions et des méthodes uniformes. Non seulement les définitions sont différentes d'une zone ou d'un pays à un autre, mais on n'y retrouve parfois même plus l'intention originale de distinguer les régions rurales des régions urbaines. Lorsque la classification est fondée, en particulier, sur le critère des circonscriptions administratives (comme la plupart le sont), elle a tendance à devenir rigide avec le temps et à décourager toute modification. Pour cette raison, la comparaison des données appartenant à des séries chronologiques risque d'être gravement faussée du fait que les définitions employées sont désormais périmées. Il faut être particulièrement prudent lorsque l'on compare des données issues de recensements avec des données provenant d'enquêtes par sondage, car il se peut que les définitions du terme « urbain » auxquelles ces données se réfèrent respectivement soient différentes.

Malgré leurs insuffisances, les statistiques sur la population urbaine et rurale permettent de mettre en évidence la diversité de la répartition de la population au sein d'un pays ou d'une zone.

La distinction entre « zone urbaine » et « zone rurale » repose sur une série de critères qualitatifs aussi bien que quantitatifs, notamment l'effectif de la population, la densité de peuplement, la distance entre îlots d'habitations, le type prédominant d'activité économique, le statut juridique ou administratif, et les caractéristiques d'une agglomération urbaine, c'est-à-dire l'existence de services publics et d'équipements collectifs[1]. Bien que les statistiques différenciant les zones urbaines des zones rurales soient très répandues, il ne paraît pas possible pour le moment d'adopter une classification internationale type de ces zones, vu la diversité des interprétations nationales. La classification de la population en population urbaine et population rurale retenue ici est celle qui correspond aux définitions nationales.

Données publiées antérieurement : des statistiques concernant la population urbaine et la population totale selon le sexe ont été publiées dans des éditions antérieures de l'*Annuaire démographique*. Pour plus de précisions concernant les années pour lesquelles ces données ont été publiées, se reporter à l'index historique.

DÉFINITIONS DU TERME « URBAIN »

AFRIQUE

Algérie : La délimitation des zones urbaines et rurales se font après l'opération du recensement sur la base de la classification des agglomérations. Regroupement de 100 constructions ou plus distantes l'une à l'autre de moins de 200m ont été considérées comme zones urbaines.

Afrique du Sud : Zones dotées d'une administration locale.

Botswana : Agglomération de 5 000 habitants ou plus dont 75 p. 100 de l'activité économique n'est pas de type agricole.

Burkina Faso : Tous les chefs-lieux de province (45 au total) plus 4 villes moyennes ont été considérées comme zones urbaines.

Burundi : Commune de Bujumbura.

Comores : Toute localité ou chef-lieu d'une île, région/préfecture disposant des infrastructures suivantes : route bitumée, électricité, centre hospitalier, téléphone, etc.

Égypte : Chefs-lieux des gouvernorats du Caire, d'Alexandrie, de Port Saïd, d'Ismaïlia, de Suez ; chefs-lieux des gouvernorats frontaliers, autres chefs-lieux de gouvernorat et chefs-lieux de district (Markaz). La définition des zones urbaines pour le recensement de novembre 2006 est celle de « SHIAKHA », une partie d'un district.

Éthiopie : Localités de 2 000 habitants ou plus.

Guinée équatoriale : Chefs-lieux de district et localités comprenant 300 habitations et/ou 1 500 habitants ou plus.

Kenya : Zone ayant une population de 2 000 habitants ou plus qui dispose de réseaux de transport, comporte des zones bâties, des structures industrielles ou manufacturières et d'autres équipements modernes.

Lesotho : Tous les chefs-lieux administratifs et établissements urbains en forte croissance.

Libéria : Localités de 2 000 habitants ou plus.

Malawi : Toutes les villes et zones urbanisées et tous les chefs-lieux de district.

Maurice : Les cinq circonscriptions municipales, divisées en vingt arrondissements municipaux dont les limites ont été officiellement définies.

Namibie : Zones urbaines déclarées pour lesquelles il existe des données cadastrales et autres zones d'habitat non planifié.

Niger : Ville capital, villes capitales de départements ou de districts.

Ouganda : «Gazettes», villes, municipalités et bourgs.

République-Unie de Tanzanie : 16 townships érigées en communes.

Rwanda : Toutes les zones administratives reconnues comme urbaines par la loi. Il s'agit de tous les chefs-lieux des provinces, de la ville de Kigali ainsi que des villes de Nyanza, Ruhango et Rwamagana.

Sénégal : Agglomérations de 10 000 habitants ou plus.

Soudan : Centres administratifs et/ou commerciaux ou localités ayant une population de 5 000 habitants ou plus.

Swaziland : Zone géographique qui constitue une ville et se caractérise par une densité de population et de constructions humaines plus élevée que dans les zones qui l'entourent.

Tunisie : Population vivant dans les communes.

Zambie : Localités de 5 000 habitants ou plus dont l'activité économique prédominante n'est pas de type agricole.

AMÉRIQUE DU NORD

Canada : Agglomérations de 1 000 habitants ou plus ayant une densité de population d'au moins 400 habitants au kilomètre carré.

Costa Rica : Chefs-lieux de canton.

Cuba : Villes ayant une fonction politique ou administrative, ou une population supérieure à 2 000 habitants et présentant des traits urbains.

El Salvador : Chefs-lieux de municipios.

États-Unis d'Amérique : Agglomérations de 2 500 habitants ou plus ayant généralement une densité de population d'au moins 1 000 habitants au mile carré. Deux types de zones urbaines : zones urbanisées de 50 000 habitants ou plus et groupements urbains comptant au moins 2 500 habitants mais moins de 50 000.

Groenland : Localités d'au moins 200 habitants.

Guatemala : Municipio du département de Guatemala et centres administratifs officiels d'autres départements et municipios.

Haïti : Chefs-lieux de communes.

Honduras : Localités d'au moins 2 000 habitants ayant des caractéristiques essentiellement urbaines.

Îles Vierges américaines : Agglomérations de 2 500 habitants ou plus ayant généralement une densité de population d'au moins 1 000 habitants au mile carré. Deux types de zones urbaines : zones urbanisées de 50 000 habitants ou plus et groupements urbains comptant au moins 2 500 habitants mais moins de 50 000. (D'après les résultats du recensement de 2 000, les Îles Vierges américaines ne comptent aucune zone urbanisée.)

Jamaïque : Localités de 2 000 habitants ou plus présentant des traits urbains.

Mexique : Localités d'au moins 2 500 habitants.

Nicaragua : Centres administratifs des municipalités et localités d'au moins 1 000 habitants ou d'au moins 150 logements, possédant des rues, un éclairage électrique, un réseau de distribution d'eau, une école et un dispensaire.

Panama : Localités d'au moins 1 500 habitants ayant des caractéristiques essentiellement urbaines. À partir de 1970, localités de 1 500 habitants ou plus présentant des caractéristiques urbaines, telles que rues, éclairage électrique, systèmes d'approvisionnement en eau et réseaux d'égouts.

Porto Rico : Agglomérations de 2 500 habitants ou plus ayant généralement une densité de population d'au moins 1 000 habitants au mile carré. Deux types de zones urbaines : zones urbanisées de 50 000 habitants ou plus et groupements urbains comptant au moins 2 500 habitants mais moins de 50 000.

République dominicaine : Chefs-lieux de municipios et districts municipaux, dont certains comprennent des zones suburbaines ayant des caractéristiques rurales.

AMÉRIQUE DU SUD

Argentine : Centres comptant au moins 2 000 habitants.

Bolivie : Localités de 2 000 habitants ou plus.

Brésil : Zones urbaines et suburbaines des chefs lieux de municipalités et de districts.

Chili : Zones d'habitat concentré comptant 2 000 habitants ou plus, ou comptant entre 1 001 et 2 000 habitants dont 50 pour cent au moins de la population active a une activité secondaire ou tertiaire. Par dérogation, les centres qui ont une fonction touristique ou récréative et plus de 250 unités de logement mais n'atteignent pas le critère de population sont néanmoins considérés comme zones urbaines.

Colombie : Zone où l'on trouve des ensembles de bâtiments et des structures adjacentes regroupés en pâtés de maison et, en général, des services essentiels comme l'eau courante, l'évacuation des eaux usées, l'électricité et des hôpitaux et des écoles. Cette catégorie comprend la capitale du pays et des chefs-lieux de divisions administratives.

Équateur : Capitales des provinces et chefs-lieux de canton.

Îles Falkland (Malvinas) : Ville de Stanley.

Paraguay : Grandes villes, villes et chefs-lieux des départements et des districts.

Pérou : Centres de peuplement comptant plus de 100 logements.

Suriname : Les districts de Paramaribo et de Wanica.

Uruguay : Les villes, villages et autres zones habitées répondant aux définitions de la loi sur les agglomérations.

Venezuela (République bolivarienne du) : Centres de 2 500 habitants ou plus.

ASIE

Arménie : Grandes villes et localités de type urbain, officiellement désignées comme telles, généralement sur la base du nombre d'habitants et de la prédominance des travailleurs agricoles ou non agricoles avec leur famille.

Azerbaïdjan : Division administrative regroupant plus de 15 000 habitants se livrant principalement à des activités industrielles et autres activités économiques et sociales et comprenant des centres administratifs et culturels.

Bahreïn : Communes ou villages comptant au moins 2 500 habitants.

Cambodge : Zones au niveau de la commune répondant aux trois conditions suivantes: 1) Densité démographique supérieure à 200 habitants au km carré, 2) pourcentage d'hommes travaillant dans l'agriculture inférieur à 50 pour cent, 3) population totale de la commune supérieure à 2 000 habitants.

Chine : Villes désignées comme telles par le Conseil d'État. Dans le cas de villes ayant rang de district, la ville s'entend comme l'ensemble de la zone administrative qui relève du district si sa densité est d'au moins 1 500 habitants au kilomètre carré ou comme le siège des autorités du district et les rues qui relèvent du district si sa densité est inférieure à 1 500 habitants au kilomètre carré. Dans le cas des villes qui n'ont pas rang de district, la ville s'entend comme le siège des autorités de la commune et les rues qui relèvent des autorités de la commune. Dans le cas des villes ayant rang de district qui comptent moins de 1 500 habitants au kilomètre carré et des villes n'ayant pas rang de district, si l'urbanisation du siège du district ou du siège des autorités de la commune a empiété sur une partie de la ou des localités voisines, la ville inclut alors l'ensemble de la zone administrative desdites localités.

Chypre : Selon la définition du Département de l'urbanisme et du logement du Ministère de l'intérieur.

État de Palestine : Localités peuplées de plus de 10 000 personnes. L'expression désigne tous les gouvernorats (districts), quelle qu'en soit la taille, ainsi que toutes les villes dont la population est comprise entre 4 000 et 9 999 personnes qui disposent d'au moins quatre des éléments suivants : réseau public de distribution d'électricité, réseau public de distribution d'eau, bureau de poste, centre médical doté d'un médecin à temps plein et école préparant les élèves au certificat général de l'enseignement secondaire.

Géorgie : Grandes villes et localités de type urbain, officiellement désignées comme telles, généralement sur la base du nombre d'habitants et de la prédominance des travailleurs agricoles ou non agricoles avec leur famille.

Inde : Villes [localités dotées d'une charte municipale, d'un comité de zone municipale, d'un comité de zone déclarée urbaine ou d'un comité de zone de regroupement (cantonnement)] ; également toutes les localités qui ont une population de 5 000 habitants au moins, une densité de population d'au moins 1 000 habitants au mile carré ou 400 au kilomètre carré, des caractéristiques urbaines prononcées et où les trois quarts au moins des adultes de sexe masculin ont une occupation non agricole.

Indonésie : Zones qui répondent à certains critères de densité démographique et de pourcentage des ménages agricoles et possèdent un certain nombre d'équipements urbains tels que routes, écoles, services de santé publique, etc.

Iran (République islamique d') : Tous les districts comptant une municipalité.

Israël : Tous les lieux comptant au moins 2 000 résidents.

Japon : Villes (shi), comptant au moins 50 000 habitants, où 60 p. 100 au moins des logements sont situés dans les principales zones bâties, et dont 60 p. 100 au moins de population (y compris les personnes à charge) exercent un métier dans l'industrie, le commerce et d'autres branches d'activités essentiellement urbaines.

Jordanie : Localités comptant 5 000 habitants ou plus.

Kazakhstan : Grandes villes et localités de type urbain, officiellement désignées comme telles, généralement sur la base du nombre d'habitants et de la prédominance des travailleurs agricoles ou non agricoles avec leur famille.

Kirghizistan : Grandes villes et localités de type urbain, officiellement désignées comme telles, généralement sur la base du nombre d'habitants et de la prédominance des travailleurs agricoles ou non agricoles avec leur famille.

Malaisie : Zone ayant le statut de centre urbain et dont la population totale dépasse 10 000 habitants. On nomme périphérie toute zone contiguë à un centre urbain dont au moins 60 % de la population (âgée de 15 ans et plus) a une activité non agricole. La définition des zones urbaines couvre également les zones spéciales de développement qui n'ont pas officiellement le statut de centre urbain, se trouvent à 5 kilomètres ou plus d'un tel centre ou de sa périphérie et comptent au moins 10 000 habitants dont 60 % (parmi les plus de 15 ans) ont une activité non agricole.

Maldives : Malé (capitale).

Mongolie : Capitale et chefs-lieux de district.

Népal : Zones déclarées telles par les municipalités.

Ouzbékistan : Grandes villes et localités de type urbain, officiellement désignées comme telles, généralement sur la base du nombre d'habitants et de la prédominance des travailleurs agricoles ou non agricoles avec leur famille.

Pakistan : Localités dotées d'une charte municipale ou d'un comité municipal et regroupements (cantonments).

Philippines : Villes et municipalités et leurs quartiers centraux dont la densité démographique est d'au moins 500 habitants au km carré. Sont considérés comme zones urbaines les autres quartiers quelle que soit leur population qui sont équipés de routes et possèdent au moins six établissements (commerce, industrie manufacturière, équipements récréatifs ou services aux personnes), et au moins trois équipements publics tels que hôtel de ville, église, parc public, école, hôpital, bibliothèque, etc.

République arabe syrienne : Villes, chefs-lieux de district (Mohafaza) et chefs-lieux de sous district (Mantika), et communes d'au moins 20 000 habitants.

République de Corée : Pour les estimations : localités de 50 000 habitants ou plus. Pour recensements, les données sont établies sont la base des divisions administratives mineures comme les Dongs (principalement en zone urbaines) et des Eups ou Myeons (en zones rurales).

République démocratique populaire lao : Zones ou villages répondant à au moins trois des cinq conditions suivantes: situés dans l'aire métropolitaine du district ou de la province, accessibles par la route en toute saison, quelque 70 pour cent ou deux tiers de la population ayant accès à de l'eau distribuée par canalisation, quelque 70 pour cent ou deux tiers de la population ayant accès au réseau d'électricité et existence d'un marché ouvert tous les jours.

Sri Lanka : Secteur urbain composé de toutes les zones municipales et zones dotées d'un conseil urbain.

Tadjikistan : Grandes villes et localités de type urbain, officiellement désignées comme telles, généralement sur la base du nombre d'habitants et de la prédominance des travailleurs agricoles ou non agricoles avec leur famille.

Thaïlande : Zones municipales.

Turkménistan : Grandes villes et localités de type urbain, officiellement désignées comme telles, généralement sur la base du nombre d'habitants et de la prédominance des travailleurs agricoles ou non agricoles avec leur famille.

Turquie : Chefs-lieux des provinces et des districts.

Viet Nam : Zones urbaines comprises à l'intérieur des districts urbains des villes ainsi que des quartiers urbains et des localités. Toutes les autres unités administratives locales (communes) sont considérées comme zones rurales.

EUROPE

Albanie : Villes et autres centres industriels de plus de 400 habitants.

Autriche : Les zones urbaines sont les localités comptant 2 000 habitants ou plus. Leur délimitation remonte à 1991.

Bélarus : Les établissements urbains sont des établissements autorisés en vertu de la loi comme les villes, les agglomérations de type urbain, les cités ouvrières et les zones de villégiature de santé.

Bulgarie : Toutes les zones considérées comme villes et bourgs selon la Division territoriale et administrative du pays.

Espagne : Aux fins de la publication de résultats qui soient comparables au niveau européen, Eurostat propose de considérer comme zones urbaines, intermédiaires et rurales les communes comptant respectivement plus de 10 000 habitants, de 2 001 à 10 000 habitants et moins de 2 000 habitants.

Estonie : Les établissements urbains comprennent les villes et les agglomérations n'ayant pas de statut municipal.

Fédération de Russie : Grandes villes et localités de type urbain, officiellement désignées comme telles, généralement sur la base du nombre d'habitants et de la prédominance des travailleurs agricoles ou non agricoles avec leur famille.

Finlande : Communes urbaines (communes où au moins 90 % de la population vit en milieu urbain ou dont le plus grand centre urbain compte au moins 15 000 habitants).

France : Communes comprenant une agglomération de plus de 2 000 habitants vivant dans des habitations contiguës ou qui ne sont pas distantes les unes des autres de plus de 200 mètres et communes où la majeure partie de la population vit dans une agglomération regroupant plusieurs communes de cette nature.

Grèce : Est considérée comme zone urbaine toute municipalité ou commune dont la plus grande localité compte 2 000 habitants ou plus.

Hongrie : Localités dont le statut de ville a été reconnu par le Président de la République compte tenu de critères spécifiques (économiques, commerciaux, institutionnels, culturels, etc.).

Irlande : Localités, y compris leur banlieues, comptant 1 500 habitants ou plus.

Islande : Localités de 200 habitants ou plus.

Lettonie : Grandes villes et localités de type urbain, officiellement désignées comme telles, généralement sur la base du nombre d'habitants et de la prédominance des travailleurs agricoles ou non agricoles avec leur famille.

Lituanie : Par population urbaine, on entend les personnes qui vivent dans des villes ou des localités, à savoir les zones habitées comportant des logements permanents proches les uns des autres et dont la population est d'au moins 3 000 habitants, les deux tiers desquels étant employés dans le secteur industriel, l'infrastructure sociale ou le commerce. Un certain nombre de villes peuvent compter moins de 3 000 habitants dans la mesure où elles avaient acquis le statut de ville avant l'entrée en vigueur de la nouvelle loi en juillet 1994.

Malte : Zones ayant une densité démographique supérieure ou égale à 150 habitants au kilomètre carré.

Monténégro : D'après la législation actuelle relative à l'organisation territoriale du Monténégro, qui oblige chaque collectivité à déterminer quelles sont ses zones urbaines et rurales.

Norvège : Ensemble construit habité par au moins 200 personnes, où les bâtiments ne sont pas éloignés de plus de 50 mètres les uns des autres. Les limites en sont évolutives et peuvent être redéfinies pour tenir compte de l'urbanisation et de l'évolution de la population.

Pays Bas : Zones urbaines : municipalités comptant au moins 2 000 habitants. Zones semi-urbaines : municipalités comptant moins de 2 000 habitants, mais où 20 p. 100 au maximum de la population active de sexe masculin pratiquent l'agriculture, et certaines municipalités de caractère résidentiel dont les habitants travaillent ailleurs.

Pologne : Villes et zones de type urbain, par exemple groupements de travailleurs ou de pêcheurs et stations climatiques.

Portugal : Localités comptant 2 000 habitants ou davantage.

République de Moldova : Grandes villes et localités de type urbain, officiellement désignées comme telles, généralement sur la base du nombre d'habitants et de la prédominance des travailleurs agricoles ou non agricoles avec leur famille.

République tchèque : Localités d'au moins 2 000 habitants.

Roumanie : Grandes villes, municipalités et autres villes.

Royaume-Uni de Grande-Bretagne et d'Irlande du Nord : Zones construites (d'au moins 20 hectares) où vivent 10 000 personnes ou plus.

Serbie : Municipalités, villes et Belgrade.

Slovaquie : Municipalités ayant le statut ville ayant 5 000 habitants ou plus.

Slovénie : Établissements de 3 000 habitants ou plus, chefs-lieux de municipalités comptant au moins 1 400 habitants, et quartiers suburbains qui s'intègrent progressivement dans une ville de 5 000 habitants ou plus.

Suisse : L'espace urbain comprend les agglomérations et les villes isolées (n'appartenant pas à une agglomération et ayant au moins 10 000 habitants à elles seules).

Ukraine : Grandes villes et localités de type urbain, officiellement désignées comme telles, généralement sur la base du nombre d'habitants et de la prédominance des travailleurs agricoles ou non agricoles avec leur famille.

OCÉANIE

Australie : Un regroupement de population de 1 000 personnes ou plus est généralement considéré comme un centre urbain.

Guam : Agglomérations de 2 500 habitants ou plus ayant généralement une densité de population d'au moins 1 000 habitants au mile carré et considérées comme étant des groupements urbains.

Îles Cook : Rarotonga, île la plus peuplée.

Îles Mariannes septentrionales : Agglomérations de 2 500 habitants ou plus ayant généralement une densité de population d'au moins 1 000 habitants au mile carré. Deux types de zones urbaines : zones urbanisées de 50 000 habitants ou plus et groupements urbains comptant au moins 2 500 habitants mais moins de 50 000.

Nouvelle-Calédonie : Nouméa et communes de Païta, Dumbéa et Mont-Dore.

Nouvelle-Zélande : Toutes les villes et les quartiers, districts et bourgs ayant 1 000 habitants permanents ou plus.

Samoa américaines : Agglomérations de 2 500 habitants ou plus ayant généralement une densité de population d'au moins 1 000 habitants au mile carré. Deux types de zones urbaines : zones urbanisées de 50 000 habitants ou plus et groupements urbains comptant au moins 2 500 habitants mais moins de 50 000. (D'après les résultats du recensement de 2000, les Samoa américaines ne comptent aucune zone urbanisée.)

Tokélaou : L'ensemble de la population est considéré comme vivant en milieu rural.

Tonga : Nuku'alofa.

Vanuatu : Centre de Luganville et Port-Vila.

NOTES

[1] Pour plus de précisions, voir *Social and Demographic Statistics: Classifications of Size and Type of Locality and Urban/Rural Areas*, E/CN.3/551, publication des Nations Unies, New York, 1980.

Continent, country or area, and date / Continent, pays ou zone et date	Code[a]	Both sexes - Les deux sexes			Male - Masculin			Female - Féminin		
		Total	Urban - Urbaine		Total	Urban - Urbaine		Total	Urban - Urbaine	
			Number Nombre	Percent P.100		Number Nombre	Percent P.100		Number Nombre	Percent P.100

AFRICA - AFRIQUE

Algeria - Algérie										
1 VII 2003 ....ESDJ		31 847 995	...	...	16 090 568	...	...	15 757 427	...	...
16 IV 2008* ....CDJC		34 452 759	...	...	17 428 500	...	...	17 024 259	...	...
Benin - Bénin[1]										
1 VII 2003 ....ESDF		6 982 711	2 740 221	39.2	3 392 055	1 335 810	39.4	3 590 656	1 404 411	39.1
1 VII 2004 ....ESDF		7 208 552	2 863 952	39.7	3 506 558	1 397 974	39.9	3 701 994	1 465 978	39.6
1 VII 2005 ....ESDF		7 447 454	3 002 229	40.3	3 627 613	1 467 342	40.4	3 819 841	1 534 887	40.2
1 VII 2006 ....ESDF		7 699 697	3 156 172	41.0	3 755 408	1 544 515	41.1	3 944 289	1 611 657	40.9
1 VII 2007 ....ESDF		7 958 813	3 324 220	41.8	3 886 596	1 628 650	41.9	4 072 217	1 695 570	41.6
1 VII 2008 ....ESDF		8 224 642	3 499 506	42.5	4 021 094	1 716 411	42.7	4 203 548	1 783 095	42.4
1 VII 2009 ....ESDF		8 497 827	3 682 496	43.3	4 159 291	1 808 057	43.5	4 338 536	1 874 439	43.2
1 VII 2010 ....ESDF		8 778 648	3 873 462	44.1	4 301 224	1 903 683	44.3	4 477 424	1 969 779	44.0
1 VII 2011 ....ESDF		9 067 076	4 072 574	44.9	4 446 877	2 003 366	45.1	4 620 199	2 069 208	44.8
Botswana										
1 VII 2003 ....ESDJ		1 673 184	...	...	809 278	...	...	863 906	...	...
1 VII 2004 ....ESDJ		1 692 731	...	...	820 577	...	...	872 155	...	...
1 VII 2005 ....ESDJ		1 708 327	...	...	829 850	...	...	878 477	...	...
1 VII 2006 ....ESDJ		1 719 996	...	...	837 114	...	...	882 882	...	...
1 VIII 2006[2] ....SSDJ		1 773 240	1 000 443	56.4	851 670	473 136	55.6	921 570	527 307	57.2
1 VII 2007 ....ESDJ		1 736 396	...	...	847 539	...	...	888 857	...	...
1 VII 2008 ....ESDJ		1 755 246	...	...	859 167	...	...	896 079	...	...
1 VII 2009 ....ESDJ		1 776 494	...	...	871 964	...	...	904 530	...	...
1 VII 2010 ....ESDJ		1 822 859	...	...	895 007	...	...	927 852	...	...
1 VII 2011 ....ESDJ		1 849 692	...	...	910 404	...	...	939 288	...	...
9 VIII 2011 ....CDFC		2 024 904	...	...	989 128	...	...	1 035 776	...	...
Burkina Faso										
1 VII 2003 ....ESDJ		12 566 683	1 958 013[3]	15.6	6 064 260	992 431[3]	16.4	6 502 423	965 582[3]	14.8
1 VII 2004 ....ESDJ		12 962 750	2 015 546[3]	15.5	6 256 552	1 021 683[3]	16.3	6 706 198	993 863[3]	14.8
1 VII 2005 ....ESDJ		13 373 670	2 074 879[3]	15.5	6 456 103	1 051 853[3]	16.3	6 917 567	1 023 026[3]	14.8
9 XII 2006 ....CDFC		14 196 259	3 230 504	22.8	6 842 560	1 609 349	23.5	7 353 699	1 621 155	22.0
1 VII 2007[1] ....ESDJ		14 252 012	3 322 360	23.3	6 880 824	1 629 956	23.7	7 371 188	1 692 404	23.0
1 VII 2008[1] ....ESDJ		14 731 167	3 520 744[3]	23.9	7 110 097	1 699 313[3]	23.9	7 621 070	1 821 431[3]	23.9
1 VII 2009[1] ....ESDJ		15 224 780	...	...	7 346 835	...	...	7 877 945	...	...
1 VII 2010[1] ....ESDJ		15 730 977	...	...	7 590 133	...	...	8 140 844	...	...
Burundi										
1 VII 2003 ....ESDF		7 211 356	...	...	3 515 469	...	...	3 695 887	...	...
1 VII 2004 ....ESDF		7 384 423	...	...	3 599 838	...	...	3 784 585	...	...
16 VIII 2008 ....CDFC		7 877 728	799 802	10.2	3 838 045	432 442	11.3	4 039 683	367 360	9.1
Cabo Verde										
1 VII 2003 ....ESDF		460 601	263 791	57.3	222 911	...	...	237 690	...	...
1 VII 2004 ....ESDF		468 164	271 415	58.0	226 560	...	...	241 604	...	...
1 VII 2005 ....ESDF		475 465	278 947	58.7	230 063	...	...	245 402	...	...
1 VII 2006 ....ESDF		483 090	286 687	59.3	233 729	...	...	249 361	...	...
1 VII 2007 ....ESDF		491 419	295 046	60.0	237 842	...	...	253 577	...	...
1 VII 2008 ....ESDF		499 796	303 512	60.7	241 914	...	...	257 882	...	...
1 VII 2009 ....ESDF		508 633	310 958	61.1	246 219	...	...	262 414	...	...
16 VI 2010 ....CDJC		491 683	303 673	61.8	243 401	151 217	62.1	248 282	152 456	61.4
1 VII 2010 ....ESDF		517 831	320 111	61.8	250 710	...	...	267 121	...	...
1 VII 2011 ....ESDF		527 269	328 177	62.2	255 327	...	...	271 942	...	...
Cameroon - Cameroun										
1 VII 2003[1] ....ESDF		16 626 000	8 779 000	52.8	...	...	...	...	...	...
1 VII 2004[1] ....ESDF		17 000 000	9 086 000	53.4	...	...	...	...	...	...
11 XI 2005 ....CDFC		17 052 134	...	...	8 408 495	...	...	8 643 639	...	...
1 I 2010[1] ....ESDJ		19 406 100	10 091 172	52.0	9 599 224	5 029 993	52.4	9 806 876	5 061 179	51.6
Central African Republic - République centrafricaine										
8 XII 2003 ....CDFC		3 151 072	1 194 851	37.9	1 569 446	598 880	38.2	1 581 626	595 969	37.7
Comoros - Comores										
1 IX 2003 ....CDFC		575 660[4]	160 865	27.9	...	...	...	...	...	...
Congo										
28 IV 2007 ....CDFC		3 697 490	...	...	1 821 357	...	...	1 876 133	...	...
Côte d'Ivoire[1]										
1 VII 2003* ....ESDF		18 000 876	...	...	9 185 371	...	...	8 815 505	...	...
1 VII 2004* ....ESDF		18 545 968	...	...	9 461 594	...	...	9 084 374	...	...

Continent, country or area, and date / Continent, pays ou zone et date	Code[a]	Both sexes - Les deux sexes			Male - Masculin			Female - Féminin		
		Total	Urban - Urbaine		Total	Urban - Urbaine		Total	Urban - Urbaine	
			Number Nombre	Percent P.100		Number Nombre	Percent P.100		Number Nombre	Percent P.100
AFRICA - AFRIQUE										
Côte d'Ivoire[1]										
1 VII 2005* .... ESDF		19 096 988	...	...	9 740 427	...	...	9 356 561	...	...
1 VII 2006* .... ESDF		19 657 738	...	...	10 023 964	...	...	9 633 774	...	...
1 VII 2007* .... ESDF		20 227 876	...	...	10 312 061	...	...	9 915 815	...	...
1 VII 2008* .... ESDF		20 807 216	...	...	10 604 596	...	...	10 202 620	...	...
1 VII 2009* .... ESDF		21 395 198	...	...	10 901 322	...	...	10 493 876	...	...
Egypt - Égypte										
1 VII 2003 .... ESDF		67 965 096	29 130 214	42.9	34 720 973	...	...	33 244 123	...	...
1 VII 2004 .... ESDF		69 303 902	29 652 904	42.8	35 379 626	...	...	33 924 276	...	...
1 VII 2005 .... ESDF		70 653 326	30 187 331	42.7	36 037 030	...	...	34 616 296	...	...
1 VII 2006 .... ESDF		72 008 900	30 699 375	42.6	36 725 501	...	...	35 283 399	...	...
21 XI 2006 .... CDFC		72 798 031	31 370 925	43.1	37 219 056	16 013 864	43.0	35 578 975	15 357 061	43.2
1 VII 2007 .... ESDF		73 643 587	31 719 927	43.1	37 643 353	16 186 484	43.0	36 000 234	15 533 443	43.1
1 VII 2008 .... ESDF		75 193 567	32 248 476	42.9	38 413 404	16 437 464	42.8	36 780 163	15 811 012	43.0
1 VII 2009 .... ESDF		76 925 139	33 082 770	43.0	39 327 098	16 887 176	42.9	37 598 041	16 195 594	43.1
1 VII 2010 .... ESDF		78 684 622	33 804 181	43.0	40 228 119	17 255 735	42.9	38 456 503	16 548 446	43.0
1 VII 2011 .... ESDF		80 410 017	34 515 708	42.9	41 110 578	17 619 110	42.9	39 299 439	16 896 598	43.0
1 VII 2012 .... ESDF		82 541 354	35 372 091	42.9	42 199 843	18 056 137	42.8	40 341 511	17 315 954	42.9
Ethiopia - Éthiopie										
1 VII 2003[5] .... ESDF		69 127 000	10 745 000	15.5	34 653 000	5 347 000	15.4	34 474 000	5 398 000	15.7
1 VII 2004[5] .... ESDF		71 066 000	11 199 000	15.8	35 618 000	5 568 000	15.6	35 448 000	5 631 000	15.9
1 VII 2005[5] .... ESDF		73 043 510	11 674 521	16.0	36 604 591	5 802 931	15.9	36 438 919	5 871 590	16.1
1 VII 2006[5] .... ESDF		75 067 000	12 172 000	16.2	37 615 000	6 050 000	16.1	37 452 000	6 122 000	16.3
29 V 2007 .... CDFC		73 750 932	11 862 821	16.1	37 217 130	5 895 916	15.8	36 533 802	5 966 905	16.3
1 VII 2007[5] .... ESDF		77 127 000	12 689 000	16.5	38 644 000	6 307 000	16.3	38 483 000	6 382 000	16.6
1 VII 2008[5] .... ESDF		79 221 000	13 225 000	16.7	39 691 000	6 575 000	16.6	39 530 000	6 650 000	16.8
Gabon[6]										
1 VII 2005 .... ESDF		1 312 500	...	...	645 700	...	...	666 700	...	...
Gambia - Gambie										
15 IV 2003* .... CDFC		1 364 507	...	...	676 726	...	...	687 781	...	...
Ghana										
1 VII 2003 .... ESDF		20 370 643	...	...	10 083 283	...	...	10 287 360	...	...
1 VII 2004 .... ESDF		20 859 482	...	...	10 326 358	...	...	10 533 124	...	...
1 VII 2005 .... ESDF		21 367 006	...	...	10 579 368	...	...	10 787 638	...	...
1 VII 2006 .... ESDF		21 876 031	...	...	10 833 033	...	...	11 042 998	...	...
1 VII 2007 .... ESDF		22 387 911	...	...	11 088 060	...	...	11 299 851	...	...
1 VII 2008 .... ESDF		22 900 927	...	...	11 343 581	...	...	11 557 346	...	...
1 VII 2009 .... ESDF		23 416 518	10 243 312	43.7	11 600 326	5 006 198	43.2	11 816 192	5 237 114	44.3
26 IX 2010 .... CDFC		24 658 823	12 545 229	50.9	12 024 845	6 016 059	50.0	12 633 978	6 529 170	51.7
Guinea - Guinée[1]										
1 VII 2008 .... ESDF		10 182 926	2 851 219	28.0	...	...	...	...	...	...
1 VII 2009 .... ESDF		10 217 591	...	...	5 038 823	...	...	5 178 768	...	...
Guinea-Bissau - Guinée-Bissau										
15 III 2009 .... CDFC		1 520 830	...	...	737 634	...	...	783 196	...	...
1 VII 2010[1] .... ESDF		1 558 090	...	...	802 384	...	...	755 706	...	...
Kenya										
1 VII 2003[7] .... ESDF		33 141 617	5 809 612	17.5	16 372 798	3 443 644	21.0	16 768 819	2 365 968	14.1
1 VII 2004[7] .... ESDF		34 191 382	6 009 718	17.6	16 908 648	3 564 746	21.1	17 282 734	2 444 972	14.1
1 VII 2005[7] .... ESDF		35 267 222	6 213 505	17.6	17 457 906	3 688 113	21.1	17 809 316	2 525 392	14.2
1 VII 2006[7] .... ESDF		36 432 866	...	...	18 052 944	...	...	18 379 922	...	...
1 VII 2007[7] .... ESDF		37 183 923	...	...	18 440 822	...	...	18 743 102	...	...
24 VIII 2009 .... CDFC		38 610 097	12 487 375	32.3	19 192 458	6 278 811	32.7	19 417 639	6 208 564	32.0
1 VII 2010[7] .... ESDF		40 124 000	...	...	19 860 438	...	...	20 263 562	...	...
1 VII 2011[7] .... ESDF		41 745 193	...	...	20 382 914	...	...	21 362 279	...	...
1 VII 2012[7] .... ESDF		42 435 603	...	...	20 792 155	...	...	21 643 448	...	...
Lesotho										
13 IV 2006 .... CDFC		1 741 406	403 104	23.1	818 379	181 351	22.2	923 027	221 753	24.0
Liberia - Libéria										
21 III 2008 .... CDFC		3 476 608	1 633 719	47.0	1 739 945	802 092	46.1	1 736 663	831 627	47.9
Libya - Libye										
15 IV 2006* .... CDFC		5 657 692	...	...	2 934 452	...	...	2 723 240	...	...
1 VII 2006[8] .... ESDF		5 298 000	...	...	2 687 000	...	...	2 610 000	...	...
1 VII 2010[8] .... ESDF		5 702 000	...	...	2 890 000	...	...	2 812 000	...	...

Continent, country or area, and date / Continent, pays ou zone et date	Code[a]	Both sexes - Les deux sexes			Male - Masculin			Female - Féminin		
		Total	Urban - Urbaine		Total	Urban - Urbaine		Total	Urban - Urbaine	
			Number Nombre	Percent P.100		Number Nombre	Percent P.100		Number Nombre	Percent P.100
AFRICA - AFRIQUE										
Madagascar										
1 VII 2003 ....ESDF		16 584 801	4 544 000	27.4	...	...	...	...	...	...
1 VII 2004 ....ESDF		17 062 131	4 232 745	24.8	...	...	...	...	...	...
Malawi										
1 VII 2003[1].................ESDF		11 548 841	1 453 771	12.6	5 672 569	752 544	13.3	5 876 272	701 227	11.9
1 VII 2004[1].................ESDF		11 937 934	1 533 930	12.8	5 866 462	792 661	13.5	6 071 472	741 269	12.2
1 VII 2005[1].................ESDF		12 341 170	1 616 169[9]	13.1	6 067 563	833 812[9]	13.7	6 273 607	782 357[9]	12.5
1 VII 2006[1].................ESDF		12 757 883	1 700 379	13.3	6 275 533	875 943	14.0	6 482 350	824 436	12.7
1 VII 2007[1].................ESDF		13 187 632	1 786 434	13.5	6 490 146	918 991	14.2	6 697 486	867 443	13.0
8 VI 2008 ....CDFC		13 077 160	2 003 309	15.3	6 358 933	1 014 477	16.0	6 718 227	988 832	14.7
1 VII 2008[1].................ESDF		13 630 164	1 874 199[9]	13.8	6 711 263	962 887[9]	14.3	6 918 901	911 312[9]	13.2
Mali										
1 I 2003 ....ESDF		11 111 219	3 344 066	30.1	5 499 912	1 674 538	30.4	5 611 305	1 669 528	29.8
1 I 2004 ....ESDF		11 419 483	3 522 033	30.8	5 652 867	1 763 554	31.2	5 766 615	1 758 478	30.5
1 I 2005 ....ESDF		11 732 416	3 707 315	31.6	5 808 166	1 856 224	32.0	5 924 252	1 851 091	31.2
1 I 2006 ....ESDF		12 051 021	3 900 404	32.4	5 966 339	1 952 802	32.7	6 084 681	1 947 601	32.0
1 I 2007 ....ESDF		12 377 542	4 102 223	33.1	6 128 544	2 053 767	33.5	6 248 999	2 048 456	32.8
1 IV 2009* ....CDJC		14 517 176	...	...	7 202 744	...	...	7 314 432	...	...
Mauritania - Mauritanie[1]										
1 VII 2005 ....ESDF		2 905 727	...	...	1 450 418	...	...	1 455 309	...	...
1 VII 2008 ....ESDF		3 162 338	...	...	1 584 913	...	...	1 577 425	...	...
1 VII 2010 ....ESDF		3 340 627	...	...	1 678 324	...	...	1 662 303	...	...
1 VII 2011 ....ESDF		3 296 958	...	...	1 644 572	...	...	1 652 386	...	...
Mauritius - Maurice[10]										
1 VII 2003 ....ESDJ		1 222 811	518 368	42.4	605 084	255 077	42.2	617 727	263 291	42.6
1 VII 2004 ....ESDJ		1 233 386	521 588	42.3	610 108	256 542	42.0	623 278	265 046	42.5
1 VII 2005 ....ESDJ		1 243 253	524 318	42.2	614 786	257 785	41.9	628 467	266 533	42.4
1 VII 2006 ....ESDJ		1 252 698	527 138	42.1	619 243	259 028	41.8	633 455	268 110	42.3
1 VII 2007 ....ESDJ		1 260 403	528 961	42.0	622 926	259 800	41.7	637 477	269 161	42.2
1 VII 2008 ....ESDJ		1 268 565	531 097	41.9	626 556	260 675	41.6	642 009	270 422	42.1
1 VII 2009 ....ESDJ		1 275 032	532 591	41.8	629 157	261 041	41.5	645 875	271 550	42.0
1 VII 2010 ....ESDJ		1 280 924	533 771	41.7	631 692	261 489	41.4	649 232	272 282	41.9
1 VII 2011 ....ESDJ		1 286 051	534 842	41.6	633 724	261 755	41.3	652 327	273 087	41.9
4 VII 2011 ....CDFC		1 237 000	...	...	611 053	...	...	625 947	...	...
Mayotte										
31 VII 2007 ....CDJC		186 387	...	...	91 405	...	...	94 982	...	...
Morocco - Maroc										
1 VII 2003 ....ESDF		30 088 000	17 244 000	57.3	14 972 000	8 438 000	56.4	15 116 000	8 806 000	58.3
1 VII 2004[11] ....ESDF		29 840 000	16 433 000	55.1	14 820 000	8 126 000	54.8	15 020 000	8 307 000	55.3
1 IX 2004 ....CDFC		29 680 069	16 339 561	55.1	14 640 662	8 022 273	54.8	15 039 407	8 317 288	55.3
1 VII 2005[11] ....ESDF		30 172 000	16 755 000	55.5	14 981 000	8 275 000	55.2	15 190 000	8 480 000	55.8
1 VII 2006[11] ....ESDF		30 509 000	17 082 000	56.0	15 146 000	8 426 000	55.6	15 363 000	8 656 000	56.3
1 VII 2007[11] ....ESDF		30 850 000	17 415 000	56.5	15 314 000	8 579 000	56.0	15 536 000	8 836 000	56.9
1 VII 2008[11] ....ESDF		31 195 000	17 753 000	56.9	15 484 000	8 734 000	56.4	15 711 000	9 019 000	57.4
1 VII 2009[11] ....ESDF		31 543 000	18 097 000	57.4	15 657 000	8 891 000	56.8	15 886 000	9 205 000	57.9
1 VII 2010[11] ....ESDF		31 894 046	18 446 241	57.8	15 831 463	9 051 145	57.2	16 062 583	9 395 096	58.5
1 VII 2011[11] ....ESDF		32 245 120	18 802 208	58.3	16 010 979	9 212 763	57.5	16 234 141	9 589 444	59.1
1 VII 2012[11] ....ESDF		32 596 997	19 157 539	58.8	16 190 815	9 373 546	57.9	16 406 182	9 783 993	59.6
Mozambique										
1 VII 2003[1].................ESDF		18 513 826	...	...	8 915 639	...	...	9 598 187	...	...
1 VII 2004[1].................ESDF		18 961 503	5 828 150	30.7	9 139 205	2 909 903	31.8	9 822 298	2 918 247	29.7
1 VII 2005[1].................ESDF		19 420 036	6 022 319	31.0	9 368 425	3 009 531	32.1	10 051 611	3 012 788	30.0
1 VII 2006[1].................ESDF		19 888 701	...	...	9 603 031	...	...	10 285 670	...	...
1 VII 2007[1].................ESDF		20 366 795	...	...	9 842 760	...	...	10 524 035	...	...
1 VIII 2007 ....CDFC		20 252 223	6 151 974	30.4	9 746 690	3 021 756	31.0	10 505 533	3 130 218	29.8
1 VII 2008[1].................ESDF		20 854 057	...	...	10 087 479	...	...	10 766 578	...	...
1 VII 2009[1].................ESDF		21 350 008	...	...	10 336 944	...	...	11 013 064	...	...
1 VII 2010[1].................ESDF		21 854 387	...	...	10 591 020	...	...	11 263 367	...	...
Namibia - Namibie										
1 VII 2003[1].................ESDF		1 891 098	...	...	919 031	...	...	972 067	...	...
1 VII 2004[1].................ESDF		1 923 346	...	...	935 590	...	...	987 756	...	...
1 VII 2005[1].................ESDF		1 956 900	...	...	952 788	...	...	1 004 112	...	...
1 VII 2006[1].................ESDF		1 991 747	...	...	970 617	...	...	1 021 130	...	...
1 VII 2007[1].................ESDF		2 027 871	...	...	989 067	...	...	1 038 804	...	...
1 VII 2008[1].................ESDF		2 065 226	...	...	1 008 115	...	...	1 057 111	...	...

Continent, country or area, and date / Continent, pays ou zone et date	Code[a]	Both sexes - Les deux sexes			Male - Masculin			Female - Féminin		
		Total	Urban - Urbaine		Total	Urban - Urbaine		Total	Urban - Urbaine	
			Number Nombre	Percent P.100		Number Nombre	Percent P.100		Number Nombre	Percent P.100
AFRICA - AFRIQUE										
Namibia - Namibie										
1 VII 2009[1]	ESDF	2 103 761	...	...	1 027 736	...	...	1 076 025	...	...
1 VII 2010[1]	ESDF	2 143 410	...	...	1 047 900	...	...	1 095 510	...	...
28 VIII 2011*	CDFC	2 104 900	...	...	1 021 600	...	...	1 083 300	...	...
Niger[1]										
1 VII 2003	ESDJ	11 834 290	1 925 288	16.3	5 902 639	963 194	16.3	5 931 651	962 094	16.2
1 VII 2004	ESDJ	12 224 822	1 988 822	16.3	6 097 426	994 979	16.3	6 127 396	993 843	16.2
1 VII 2005	ESDJ	12 628 241	2 054 453	16.3	6 298 641	1 027 814	16.3	6 329 600	1 026 640	16.2
1 VII 2006	ESDJ	13 044 973	2 184 605	16.7	6 506 496	1 092 927	16.8	6 538 477	1 091 678	16.7
1 VII 2007	ESDJ	13 716 233	2 556 499	18.6	6 851 314	1 280 155	18.7	6 864 919	1 276 344	18.6
1 VII 2008	ESDJ	14 197 601	2 728 541	19.2	7 088 858	1 366 304	19.3	7 108 743	1 362 237	19.2
1 VII 2009	ESDJ	14 693 112	2 911 006	19.8	7 339 392	1 458 250	19.9	7 353 720	1 452 756	19.8
1 VII 2010	ESDJ	15 203 822	3 104 574	20.4	7 594 565	1 555 187	20.5	7 609 257	1 549 387	20.4
1 VII 2011	ESDJ	15 730 754	...	...	7 857 845	...	...	7 872 909	...	...
1 VII 2012	ESDJ	16 274 738	3 527 852	21.7	8 129 650	1 767 255	21.7	8 145 088	1 760 597	21.6
Nigeria - Nigéria										
1 VII 2003[1]	ESDF	126 152 844	...	...	63 241 808	...	...	62 911 036	...	...
1 VII 2004[1]	ESDF	129 175 000	...	...	64 459 000	...	...	64 716 000	...	...
1 VII 2005[1]	ESDF	133 767 000	...	...	67 111 000	...	...	66 656 000	...	...
21 III 2006	CDFC	140 431 790	...	...	71 345 488	...	...	69 086 302	...	...
Republic of South Sudan - République de Soudan du Sud										
21 IV 2008	CDFC	8 260 490	1 405 186	17.0	4 287 300	754 086	17.6	3 973 190	651 100	16.4
Réunion										
1 VII 2003	ESDJ	756 235	...	...	368 715	...	...	387 521	...	...
1 VII 2004	ESDJ	767 269	...	...	373 532	...	...	393 737	...	...
1 VII 2005	ESDJ	777 435	...	...	377 593	...	...	399 842	...	...
1 I 2006	CDJC	781 962	...	...	379 176	...	...	402 786	...	...
1 VII 2006	ESDJ	786 231	...	...	381 030	...	...	405 202	...	...
1 I 2007	ESDJ	794 107	...	...	385 335	...	...	408 772	...	...
1 I 2008	ESDJ	805 500	...	...	390 645	...	...	414 855	...	...
1 I 2009	ESDJ	816 364	...	...	395 688	...	...	420 676	...	...
1 I 2010*	ESDJ	828 054	...	...	399 728	...	...	428 326	...	...
Rwanda										
1 VII 2003[1]	ESDF	8 879 000	...	...	4 350 710	...	...	4 528 290	...	...
1 VII 2004[1]	ESDF	9 032 000	...	...	4 434 712	...	...	4 597 288	...	...
1 VII 2005[1]	ESDF	9 225 000	1 476 000	16.0	4 372 650	...	...	4 852 350	...	...
1 VII 2006[1]	ESDF	9 468 000	1 514 880	16.0	4 487 832	...	...	4 980 168	...	...
1 VII 2007[1]	ESDF	9 556 669	1 726 613	18.1	4 597 277	812 148	17.7	4 959 393	914 465	18.4
1 VII 2008[1]	ESDF	9 831 501	...	...	4 736 104	...	...	5 095 397	...	...
1 VII 2009[1]	ESDF	10 117 029	...	...	4 880 233	...	...	5 236 796	...	...
1 VII 2010[1]	ESDF	10 412 820	1 541 097	14.8	5 029 450	...	...	5 383 371	...	...
1 VII 2011[1]	ESDF	10 718 379	1 564 883	14.6	5 183 505	...	...	5 534 874	...	...
1 VII 2012[1]	ESDF	11 033 141	...	...	5 342 112	...	...	5 691 029	...	...
15 VIII 2012*	CDJC	10 537 222	...	...	5 074 942	...	...	5 462 280	...	...
Saint Helena ex. dep. - Sainte-Hélène sans dép.										
10 II 2008	CDFC	4 257	...	...	2 165	...	...	2 092	...	...
1 VII 2008	ESDF	3 981	...	...	2 022	...	...	1 959	...	...
Saint Helena: Ascension - Sainte-Hélène: Ascension										
1 VII 2008	ESDJ	702	...	...	397	...	...	305	...	...
Saint Helena: Tristan da Cunha - Sainte-Hélène: Tristan da Cunha[12]										
31 XII 2009	ESDF	262[13]	...	...	123	...	...	139	...	...
Sao Tome and Principe - Sao Tomé-et-Principe										
1 VII 2003	ESDF	143 186	...	...	70 821	...	...	72 365	...	...
1 VII 2004	ESDF	146 056	...	...	72 153	...	...	73 903	...	...
1 VII 2005	ESDF	148 968	...	...	73 506	...	...	75 462	...	...
1 VII 2006	ESDF	151 912	...	...	74 876	...	...	77 036	...	...

Continent, country or area, and date / Continent, pays ou zone et date	Code[a]	Both sexes - Les deux sexes			Male - Masculin			Female - Féminin		
			Urban - Urbaine			Urban - Urbaine			Urban - Urbaine	
		Total	Number Nombre	Percent P.100	Total	Number Nombre	Percent P.100	Total	Number Nombre	Percent P.100
AFRICA - AFRIQUE										
Sao Tome and Principe - Sao Tomé-et-Principe										
1 VII 2007 .... ESDF		154 875	...	...	76 256	...	...	78 619	...	...
1 VII 2008 .... ESDF		157 847	...	...	77 641	...	...	80 206	...	...
1 VII 2009 .... ESDF		160 820	...	...	79 027	...	...	81 794	...	...
1 VII 2010 .... ESDF		163 783	...	...	80 409	...	...	83 375	...	...
1 VII 2011 .... ESDF		166 728	...	...	81 783	...	...	84 945	...	...
13 V 2012 .... CDFC		187 356	...	...	93 735	...	...	93 621	...	...
Senegal - Sénégal[14]										
31 XII 2003 .... ESDJ		10 317 339	4 195 560	40.7	5 078 633	2 080 007	41.0	5 238 706	2 115 553	40.4
31 XII 2004 .... ESDJ		10 604 970	4 312 525	40.7	5 220 217	2 137 994	41.0	5 384 753	2 174 531	40.4
31 XII 2005 .... ESDJ		10 901 006	4 432 909	40.7	5 365 938	2 197 676	41.0	5 535 068	2 235 233	40.4
31 XII 2006 .... ESDJ		11 205 774	4 556 843	40.7	5 515 959	2 259 118	41.0	5 689 815	2 297 725	40.4
31 XII 2007 .... ESDJ		11 519 242	4 684 315	40.7	5 670 261	2 322 314	41.0	5 848 981	2 362 001	40.4
31 XII 2008 .... ESDJ		11 841 137	4 815 214	40.7	5 828 711	2 387 209	41.0	6 012 426	2 428 005	40.4
31 XII 2009 .... ESDJ		12 171 264	4 949 461	40.7	5 991 214	2 453 764	41.0	6 180 050	2 495 697	40.4
31 XII 2010 .... ESDJ		12 509 434	5 086 978	40.7	6 157 675	2 521 940	41.0	6 351 759	2 565 038	40.4
31 XII 2011 .... ESDJ		12 841 702	6 086 966	47.4	6 350 673	3 010 218	47.4	6 491 029	3 076 748	47.4
Seychelles										
1 VII 2003 .... ESDF		82 781	...	...	40 859	...	...	41 922	...	...
1 VII 2004 .... ESDF		82 475	...	...	40 652	...	...	41 823	...	...
1 VII 2005 .... ESDF		82 852	...	...	41 233	...	...	41 619	...	...
1 VII 2006 .... ESDF		84 600	...	...	42 875	...	...	41 725	...	...
1 VII 2007 .... ESDF		85 032	...	...	43 160	...	...	41 872	...	...
1 VII 2008 .... ESDF		86 956	...	...	44 999	...	...	41 957	...	...
1 VII 2009 .... ESDF		87 298	...	...	45 022	...	...	42 276	...	...
1 VII 2010 .... ESDF		89 770	...	...	45 907	...	...	43 863	...	...
26 VIII 2010 .... CDFC		90 945	...	...	46 912	...	...	44 033	...	...
1 VII 2011 .... ESDF		87 441	...	...	43 127	...	...	44 314	...	...
1 VII 2012 .... ESDF		88 303	...	...	43 313	...	...	44 990	...	...
Sierra Leone										
1 VII 2003 .... ESDF		5 280 406	1 910 779	36.2	...	...	...	...	...	...
4 XII 2004 .... CDFC		4 976 871	...	...	2 420 218	...	...	2 556 653	...	...
1 VII 2005 .... ESDF		5 094 500	1 934 235	38.0	2 468 832	955 441	38.7	2 625 668	978 794	37.3
1 VII 2006 .... ESDF		5 216 890	1 999 707	38.3	2 528 430	987 782	39.1	2 688 460	1 011 925	37.6
1 VII 2007 .... ESDF		5 343 200	2 069 160	38.7	2 589 965	1 022 089	39.5	2 753 235	1 047 071	38.0
1 VII 2008 .... ESDF		5 473 530	2 142 918	39.2	2 653 490	1 058 523	39.9	2 820 040	1 084 395	38.5
1 VII 2009 .... ESDF		5 607 930	2 221 331	39.6	2 719 034	1 097 256	40.4	2 888 896	1 124 075	38.9
1 VII 2010 .... ESDF		5 746 800	2 304 955	40.1	2 786 797	1 138 563	40.9	2 960 003	1 166 392	39.4
1 VII 2011 .... ESDF		5 890 080	2 394 041	40.6	2 856 755	1 182 568	41.4	3 033 325	1 211 473	39.9
1 VII 2012 .... ESDF		6 037 660	2 489 123	41.2	2 928 862	1 229 535	42.0	3 108 798	1 259 588	40.5
South Africa - Afrique du Sud										
1 VII 2003[15] .... ESDF		45 997 199	...	...	22 119 800	...	...	23 877 399	...	...
1 VII 2004[15] .... ESDF		46 589 258	...	...	22 425 202	...	...	24 164 056	...	...
1 VII 2005[15] .... ESDF		47 176 877	...	...	22 729 279	...	...	24 447 598	...	...
1 VII 2006[15] .... ESDF		47 759 650	...	...	23 031 829	...	...	24 727 821	...	...
1 VII 2007[15] .... ESDF		48 337 174	...	...	23 332 664	...	...	25 004 510	...	...
1 VII 2008[15] .... ESDF		48 909 051	...	...	23 631 605	...	...	25 277 446	...	...
1 VII 2009[15] .... ESDF		49 474 880	...	...	23 928 439	...	...	25 546 441	...	...
1 VII 2010[15] .... ESDF		50 034 236	...	...	24 222 976	...	...	25 811 260	...	...
1 VII 2011[15] .... ESDF		50 586 757	...	...	24 515 036	...	...	26 071 721	...	...
10 X 2011 .... CDFC		51 770 560	...	...	25 188 791	...	...	26 581 769	...	...
Swaziland										
11 III 2007 .... CDFC		844 223	186 890	22.1	405 868	93 918	23.1	438 355	92 972	21.2
1 VII 2007 .... ESDF		1 020 102	225 700	22.1	482 209	108 264	22.5	537 893	117 436	21.8
1 VII 2008 .... ESDF		1 031 747	229 516	22.2	488 132	109 937	22.5	543 615	119 579	22.0
1 VII 2009 .... ESDF		1 043 509	233 504	22.4	494 061	111 704	22.6	549 448	121 800	22.2
1 VII 2010 .... ESDF		1 055 506	237 641	22.5	500 070	113 554	22.7	555 436	124 087	22.3
1 VII 2011 .... ESDF		1 067 773	241 947	22.7	506 186	115 493	22.8	561 587	126 454	22.5
1 VII 2012 .... ESDF		1 080 337	246 441	22.8	512 432	117 528	22.9	567 905	128 913	22.7

Continent, country or area, and date / Continent, pays ou zone et date	Code[a]	Both sexes - Les deux sexes			Male - Masculin			Female - Féminin		
		Total	Urban - Urbaine		Total	Urban - Urbaine		Total	Urban - Urbaine	
			Number Nombre	Percent P.100		Number Nombre	Percent P.100		Number Nombre	Percent P.100
AFRICA - AFRIQUE										
Togo										
6 XI 2010 .... CDJC		6 191 155	2 334 495	37.7	3 009 095	...	...	3 182 060	...	...
Tunisia - Tunisie										
1 VII 2003 .... ESDF		9 839 800	...	...	4 933 600	...	...	4 906 200	...	...
28 IV 2004 .... CDFC		9 910 872	6 429 461	64.9	4 965 435	...	...	4 945 437	...	...
1 VII 2004 .... ESDF		9 932 400	...	...	4 976 200	...	...	4 956 200	...	...
1 VII 2005 .... ESDF		10 029 000	...	...	5 020 000	...	...	5 009 000	...	...
1 VII 2006 .... ESDF		10 127 900	...	...	5 062 100	...	...	5 065 800	...	...
1 VII 2007 .... ESDF		10 225 100	...	...	5 105 100	...	...	5 120 000	...	...
1 VII 2008 .... ESDF		10 328 900	...	...	5 156 300	...	...	5 172 600	...	...
1 VII 2009 .... ESDF		10 439 600	...	...	5 207 200	...	...	5 232 400	...	...
1 VII 2010 .... ESDF		10 547 100	...	...	5 261 700	...	...	5 285 400	...	...
1 VII 2011 .... ESDF		10 673 800	...	...	5 316 900	...	...	5 356 800	...	...
Uganda - Ouganda										
1 VII 2003 .... ESDF		25 089 400	3 708 800	14.8	12 146 100	1 775 300	14.6	12 943 300	1 933 500	14.9
1 VII 2004 .... ESDF		25 895 700	3 829 000	14.8	12 532 100	1 830 600	14.6	13 363 600	1 998 400	15.0
1 VII 2005 .... ESDF		26 741 300	3 953 200	14.8	12 944 800	1 889 800	14.6	13 796 500	2 063 400	15.0
1 VII 2006 .... ESDF		27 629 300	4 084 700	14.8	13 386 100	1 953 300	14.6	14 243 200	2 131 400	15.0
1 VII 2007 .... ESDF		28 581 300	4 223 800	14.8	13 866 700	2 022 200	14.6	14 714 600	2 201 600	15.0
1 VII 2008 .... ESDF		29 592 600	4 372 000	14.8	14 383 200	2 095 700	14.6	15 209 400	2 276 300	15.0
1 VII 2009 .... ESDF		30 661 300	4 524 900	14.8	14 933 900	2 171 400	14.5	15 727 400	2 353 500	15.0
1 VII 2010 .... ESDF		31 784 600	...	...	15 516 600	...	...	16 268 000	...	...
1 VII 2011 .... ESDF		32 939 800	...	...	16 118 600	...	...	16 821 200	...	...
1 VII 2012 .... ESDF		34 131 400	...	...	16 741 400	...	...	17 390 000	...	...
United Republic of Tanzania - République Unie de Tanzanie										
1 VII 2003[14] .... ESDF		34 859 582	8 280 739	23.8	17 043 465	4 078 071	23.9	17 816 117	4 202 668	23.6
1 VII 2004[14] .... ESDF		35 944 015	8 675 470	24.1	17 588 980	4 273 459	24.3	18 355 035	4 402 011	24.0
1 VII 2005[14] .... ESDF		37 083 346	9 090 703	24.5	18 161 261	4 478 982	24.7	18 922 085	4 611 721	24.4
1 VII 2006[14] .... ESDF		38 250 927	9 518 688	24.9	18 748 743	4 691 158	25.0	19 502 184	4 827 530	24.8
1 VII 2007[14] .... ESDF		39 446 061	9 962 731	25.3	19 352 480	4 911 847	25.4	20 093 581	5 050 884	25.1
1 VII 2008[14] .... ESDF		40 667 794	10 419 287	25.6	19 970 944	5 139 187	25.7	20 696 850	5 280 100	25.5
1 VII 2009[14] .... ESDF		41 915 880	10 892 350	26.0	20 604 730	5 375 260	26.1	21 311 150	5 517 090	25.9
1 VII 2010[14] .... ESDF		43 187 823	11 378 015	26.3	21 252 423	5 618 133	26.4	21 935 400	5 759 882	26.3
1 VII 2011[14] .... ESDF		44 484 857	11 875 395	26.7	21 914 229	5 867 287	26.8	22 570 628	6 008 108	26.6
1 VII 2012[14] .... ESDF		45 798 475	12 386 841	27.0	22 585 634	6 123 839	27.1	23 212 841	6 263 002	27.0
26 VIII 2012 .... CDFC		44 928 923	13 305 004	29.6	21 869 990	6 407 396	29.3	23 058 933	6 897 608	29.9
Zambia - Zambie										
16 X 2010* .... CDFC		13 046 508	5 068 234	38.8	6 394 455	...	...	6 652 053	...	...
Zimbabwe										
1 VII 2003[14] .... ESDF		11 640 000	4 032 597	34.6	5 638 152	1 989 577	35.3	6 001 848	2 043 019	34.0
1 VII 2004[14] .... ESDF		11 730 000	4 063 777	34.6	5 681 745	2 004 961	35.3	6 048 255	2 058 816	34.0
1 VII 2005[14] .... ESDF		11 830 000	4 098 422	34.6	5 730 183	2 022 053	35.3	6 099 817	2 076 367	34.0
1 VII 2006[14] .... ESDF		11 930 000	4 133 066	34.6	5 778 621	2 039 146	35.3	6 151 379	2 093 919	34.0
1 VII 2007[14] .... ESDF		12 040 000	4 171 175	34.6	5 831 902	2 057 948	35.3	6 208 098	2 113 226	34.0
1 VII 2008[14] .... ESDF		12 150 000	3 495 205	28.8	5 885 184	1 691 434	28.7	6 264 816	1 803 752	28.8
1 VII 2009[14] .... ESDF		13 667 894	...	...	6 642 551	...	...	7 025 344	...	...
17 VIII 2012* .... CDFC		12 973 808	...	...	6 234 931	...	...	6 738 877	...	...
AMERICA, NORTH - AMÉRIQUE DU NORD										
Antigua and Barbuda - Antigua-et-Barbuda										
1 VII 2003 .... ESDF		79 781	...	...	37 467	...	...	42 314	...	...
1 VII 2004 .... ESDF		81 270	...	...	38 166	...	...	43 104	...	...
1 VII 2005 .... ESDF		82 786	...	...	38 878	...	...	43 908	...	...
1 VII 2006 .... ESDF		84 330	...	...	39 603	...	...	44 727	...	...
1 VII 2007 .... ESDF		85 903	...	...	40 342	...	...	45 561	...	...
27 V 2011* .... CDFC		83 278	...	...	40 007	...	...	43 271	...	...
Aruba										
1 VII 2003 .... ESDJ		95 076	...	...	45 461	...	...	49 615	...	...
1 VII 2004 .... ESDJ		97 658	...	...	46 657	...	...	51 001	...	...

Continent, country or area, and date Continent, pays ou zone et date	Code[a]	Both sexes - Les deux sexes			Male - Masculin			Female - Féminin		
		Total	Urban - Urbaine		Total	Urban - Urbaine		Total	Urban - Urbaine	
			Number Nombre	Percent P.100		Number Nombre	Percent P.100		Number Nombre	Percent P.100
AMERICA, NORTH - AMÉRIQUE DU NORD										
Aruba										
1 VII 2005 .... ESDJ		100 644	...	...	48 038	...	...	52 606	...	...
1 VII 2006 .... ESDJ		102 833	...	...	49 063	...	...	53 770	...	...
1 VII 2007 .... ESDJ		104 005	...	...	49 614	...	...	54 391	...	...
1 VII 2008 .... ESDJ		105 287	...	...	50 304	...	...	54 983	...	...
1 VII 2009 .... ESDJ		106 925	...	...	51 227[16]	...	...	55 697[16]	...	...
29 IX 2010 .... CDJC		101 484	...	...	48 241	...	...	53 243	...	...
1 VII 2011 .... ESDJ		102 711	...	...	48 754	...	...	53 957	...	...
Bahamas										
1 VII 2003[1] .... ESDF		316 900	...	...	154 100	...	...	162 800	...	...
1 VII 2004[1] .... ESDF		320 800	...	...	155 900	...	...	164 900	...	...
1 VII 2005[1] .... ESDF		325 200	...	...	158 000	...	...	167 200	...	...
1 VII 2006[1] .... ESDF		329 500	...	...	160 100	...	...	169 400	...	...
1 VII 2007[1] .... ESDF		334 000	...	...	162 300	...	...	171 700	...	...
1 VII 2008[1] .... ESDF		338 300	...	...	164 800	...	...	173 500	...	...
1 VII 2009[1] .... ESDF		342 400	...	...	166 800	...	...	175 600	...	...
3 V 2010 .... CDJC		351 461	...	...	170 257	...	...	181 204	...	...
1 VII 2010[1] .... ESDF		346 900	...	...	169 200	...	...	177 700	...	...
1 VII 2011[1] .... ESDF		351 100	...	...	171 500	...	...	179 600	...	...
Barbados - Barbade										
1 VII 2003 .... ESDF		271 646	...	...	130 887	...	...	140 759	...	...
1 VII 2004 .... ESDF		272 436	...	...	131 418	...	...	141 018	...	...
1 VII 2005 .... ESDF		273 018	...	...	131 721	...	...	141 297	...	...
1 VII 2006 .... ESDF		273 428	...	...	131 916	...	...	141 512	...	...
1 VII 2007 .... ESDF		274 197	...	...	132 413	...	...	141 784	...	...
1 VII 2008 .... ESDF		274 937	...	...	132 839	...	...	142 098	...	...
Belize										
1 VII 2003 .... ESDF		*273 700*	*135 600*	*49.5*	*138 300*	*67 000*	*48.4*	*135 400*	*68 600*	*50.7*
1 VII 2004 .... ESDF		*282 600*	*141 000*	*49.9*	*142 700*	*69 500*	*48.7*	*139 900*	*71 500*	*51.1*
1 VII 2005 .... ESDF		*291 800*	*146 600*	*50.2*	*147 400*	*72 200*	*49.0*	*144 400*	*74 400*	*51.5*
1 VII 2006 .... ESDF		*301 386*	*152 583*	*50.6*	*149 676*	*73 495*	*49.1*	*151 710*	*79 089*	*52.1*
1 VII 2008 .... ESDF		*322 100*	...	...	*160 900*	...	...	*161 200*	...	...
1 VII 2009 .... ESDF		*333 200*	...	...	*166 500*	...	...	*166 700*	...	...
12 V 2010* .... CDFC		312 698	138 796	44.4	157 935	67 896	43.0	154 763	70 900	45.8
Bermuda - Bermudes										
1 VII 2003 .... ESDJ		63 042	...	...	30 205	...	...	32 837	...	...
1 VII 2004 .... ESDJ		63 320	...	...	30 323	...	...	32 997	...	...
1 VII 2005 .... ESDJ		63 571	...	...	30 424	...	...	33 147	...	...
1 VII 2006 .... ESDJ		63 797	...	...	30 504	...	...	33 293	...	...
1 VII 2007 .... ESDJ		64 009	...	...	30 577	...	...	33 432	...	...
1 VII 2008 .... ESDJ		64 209	...	...	30 644	...	...	33 565	...	...
1 VII 2009 .... ESDJ		64 395	...	...	30 704	...	...	33 691	...	...
20 V 2010[17] .... CDJC		64 237	64 237	100.0	30 858	30 858	100.0	33 379	33 379	100.0
1 VII 2010 .... ESDJ		64 566	...	...	30 755	...	...	33 811	...	...
1 VII 2011 .... ESDJ		64 722	...	...	30 798	...	...	33 924	...	...
1 VII 2012 .... ESDJ		64 867	...	...	30 833	...	...	34 034	...	...
Canada										
1 VII 2003[18] .... ESDJ		31 639 670	...	...	15 675 460	...	...	15 964 210	...	...
1 VII 2004[18] .... ESDJ		31 940 676	...	...	15 825 754	...	...	16 114 922	...	...
1 VII 2005[18] .... ESDJ		32 245 209	...	...	15 979 800	...	...	16 265 409	...	...
16 V 2006[19] .... CDJC		31 612 895	25 350 585	80.2	15 475 970	12 289 025	79.4	16 136 930	13 061 560	80.9
1 VII 2006[20] .... ESDJ		32 576 074	...	...	16 147 873	...	...	16 428 201	...	...
1 VII 2007[20] .... ESDJ		32 929 733	...	...	16 324 732	...	...	16 605 001	...	...
1 VII 2008[20] .... ESDJ		33 319 098	...	...	16 520 442	...	...	16 798 656	...	...
1 VII 2009[21] .... ESDJ		33 729 690	...	...	16 727 239	...	...	17 002 451	...	...
1 VII 2010[21] .... ESDJ		34 126 181	...	...	16 925 006	...	...	17 201 175	...	...
2 V 2011 .... CDJC		33 476 685	27 147 190	81.1	16 414 225	13 190 225	80.4	17 062 460	13 956 960	81.8
1 VII 2011*[22] .... ESDJ		34 482 779	...	...	17 104 098	...	...	17 378 681	...	...
1 VII 2012*[22] .... ESDJ		34 880 491	...	...	17 309 143	...	...	17 571 348	...	...
Cayman Islands - Îles Caïmanes										
1 IV 2007 .... SSDJ		54 100	...	...	27 281[3]	...	...	26 011[3]	...	...
31 XII 2009 .... ESDJ		52 830	...	...	26 255	...	...	26 575	...	...
10 X 2010[23] .... CDJC		55 036	55 036	100.0	27 218	27 218	100.0	27 818	27 818	100.0

6. Total and urban population by sex: 2003 - 2012
Population totale et population urbaine selon le sexe : 2003 - 2012 (continued - suite)

Continent, country or area, and date / Continent, pays ou zone et date	Code[a]	Both sexes - Les deux sexes			Male - Masculin			Female - Féminin		
		Total	Urban - Urbaine		Total	Urban - Urbaine		Total	Urban - Urbaine	
			Number Nombre	Percent P.100		Number Nombre	Percent P.100		Number Nombre	Percent P.100
AMERICA, NORTH - AMÉRIQUE DU NORD										
Cayman Islands - Îles Caïmanes										
31 XII 2010 .... ESDJ		55 036	...	...	27 219	...	...	27 817	...	...
31 XII 2011 .... ESDJ		55 517	...	...	27 454	...	...	28 063	...	...
31 XII 2012 .... ESDJ		56 732	...	...	27 753	...	...	28 979	...	...
Costa Rica										
1 VII 2003 .... ESDJ		4 088 773	2 412 542	59.0	2 017 467	1 167 617	57.9	2 071 306	1 244 925	60.1
1 VII 2004 .... ESDJ		4 178 755	2 465 255	59.0	2 062 468	1 191 560	57.8	2 116 287	1 273 695	60.2
1 VII 2005 .... ESDJ		4 266 185	2 516 602	59.0	2 116 648	1 231 912	58.2	2 149 537	1 284 690	59.8
1 VII 2006 .... ESDJ		4 353 843	2 567 797	59.0	2 146 610	1 243 202	57.9	2 207 233	1 324 595	60.0
1 VII 2007 .... ESDJ		4 443 100	2 619 591	59.0	2 195 652	1 273 998	58.0	2 247 448	1 345 593	59.9
1 VII 2008 .... ESDJ		4 451 205	...	...	2 258 500	...	...	2 192 705	...	...
1 VII 2009 .... ESDJ		4 509 290	...	...	2 287 405	...	...	2 221 885	...	...
1 VII 2010 .... ESDJ		4 563 539	...	...	2 314 293	...	...	2 249 246	...	...
30 V 2011 .... CDJC		4 301 712	3 130 871	72.8	2 106 063	1 509 161	71.7	2 195 649	1 621 710	73.9
1 VII 2011 .... ESDJ		4 615 518	...	...	2 339 975	...	...	2 275 543	...	...
1 VII 2012 .... ESDJ		4 667 096	...	...	2 365 425	...	...	2 301 671	...	...
Cuba										
1 VII 2003 .... ESDJ		11 215 229	8 501 628	75.8	5 616 275	4 181 234	74.4	5 598 954	4 320 394	77.2
1 VII 2004 .... ESDJ		11 235 687	8 503 738	75.7	5 626 690	4 183 047	74.3	5 608 997	4 320 691	77.0
1 VII 2005 .... ESDJ		11 242 519	8 497 885	75.6	5 629 843	4 180 296	74.3	5 612 676	4 317 589	76.9
1 VII 2006 .... ESDJ		11 241 439	8 490 165	75.5	5 629 233	4 176 609	74.2	5 612 206	4 313 556	76.9
1 VII 2007 .... ESDJ		11 237 916	8 478 510	75.4	5 627 694	4 171 388	74.1	5 610 222	4 307 122	76.8
1 VII 2008 .... ESDJ		11 236 444	8 468 168	75.4	5 627 687	4 167 421	74.1	5 608 757	4 300 747	76.7
1 VII 2009 .... ESDJ		11 239 363	8 469 528	75.4	5 629 345	4 169 181	74.1	5 610 018	4 300 347	76.7
1 VII 2010 .... ESDJ		11 241 894	8 469 602	75.3	5 629 874	4 169 518	74.1	5 612 020	4 300 084	76.6
1 VII 2011 .... ESDJ		11 244 543	8 464 392	75.3	5 630 955	4 167 382	74.0	5 613 587	4 297 010	76.5
Curaçao										
1 I 2003 .... ESDJ		130 617	...	...	60 318	...	...	70 299	...	...
1 I 2004 .... ESDJ		131 893	...	...	60 492	...	...	71 401	...	...
1 I 2005 .... ESDJ		134 849	...	...	61 793	...	...	73 056	...	...
1 I 2006 .... ESDJ		138 593	...	...	63 394	...	...	75 199	...	...
1 I 2007 .... ESDJ		141 860	...	...	64 907	...	...	76 953	...	...
1 I 2008 .... ESDJ		144 201	...	...	65 899	...	...	78 301	...	...
1 I 2009 .... ESDJ		145 574	...	...	66 512	...	...	79 062	...	...
1 I 2010 .... ESDJ		146 347	...	...	67 007	...	...	79 340	...	...
26 III 2011 .... CDFC		150 563	...	...	68 848	...	...	81 715	...	...
1 VII 2011 .... ESDJ		150 843	...	...	68 914	...	...	81 929	...	...
1 I 2012 .... ESDJ		151 336	...	...	69 099	...	...	82 237	...	...
Dominica - Dominique										
1 VII 2003 .... ESDF		70 352	...	...	35 442	...	...	34 910	...	...
1 VII 2004 .... ESDF		70 417	...	...	35 645	...	...	34 772	...	...
1 VII 2005 .... ESDF		70 665	...	...	35 991	...	...	34 675	...	...
1 VII 2006 .... ESDF		71 008	...	...	36 169	...	...	34 839	...	...
14 V 2011* .... CDFC		71 293	...	...	36 411	...	...	34 882	...	...
Dominican Republic - République dominicaine										
1 VII 2003[1] .... ESDF		8 958 206	5 512 122	61.5	4 484 683	2 730 026	60.9	4 473 523	2 782 096	62.2
1 VII 2004[1] .... ESDF		9 092 778	5 664 035	62.3	4 550 204	2 805 678	61.7	4 542 574	2 858 357	62.9
1 VII 2005[1] .... ESDF		9 226 449	5 817 419	63.1	4 615 274	2 882 076	62.4	4 611 175	2 935 343	63.7
1 VII 2006[1] .... ESDF		9 359 706	5 965 957	63.7	4 680 145	2 955 948	63.2	4 679 561	3 010 009	64.3
1 VII 2007[1] .... ESDF		9 492 876	6 116 273	64.4	4 744 960	3 030 711	63.9	4 747 916	3 085 562	65.0
1 VII 2008[1] .... ESDF		9 625 207	6 267 880	65.1	4 809 337	3 106 114	64.6	4 815 870	3 161 766	65.7
1 VII 2009[1] .... ESDF		9 755 954	6 420 260	65.8	4 872 903	3 181 903	65.3	4 883 051	3 238 357	66.3
1 VII 2010[1] .... ESDF		9 884 371	6 572 893	66.5	4 935 282	3 257 817	66.0	4 949 089	3 315 076	67.0
1 XII 2010 .... CDJC		9 445 281	7 013 575	74.3	4 739 038	3 449 122	72.8	4 706 243	3 564 453	75.7
1 VII 2011[1] .... ESDF		10 010 590	6 719 108	67.1	4 996 533	3 330 394	66.7	5 014 057	3 388 714	67.6
1 VII 2012[1] .... ESDF		10 135 105	6 865 739	67.7	5 056 917	3 403 176	67.3	5 078 188	3 462 563	68.2
El Salvador										
1 VII 2003 .... ESDF		6 638 168	3 932 569	59.2	3 261 938	1 891 429	58.0	3 376 230	2 041 140	60.5
1 VII 2004 .... ESDF		6 757 408	4 020 878	59.5	3 321 564	1 934 445	58.2	3 435 844	2 086 433	60.7
1 VII 2005[24] .... ESDF		6 049 412	3 646 537	60.3	2 874 929	1 701 356	59.2	3 174 483	1 945 181	61.3
1 VII 2006[24] .... ESDF		6 073 859	3 706 525	61.0	2 881 162	1 726 983	59.9	3 192 697	1 979 542	62.0

119

Continent, country or area, and date / Continent, pays ou zone et date	Code[a]	Both sexes - Les deux sexes			Male - Masculin			Female - Féminin		
		Total	Urban - Urbaine		Total	Urban - Urbaine		Total	Urban - Urbaine	
			Number Nombre	Percent P.100		Number Nombre	Percent P.100		Number Nombre	Percent P.100
AMERICA, NORTH - AMÉRIQUE DU NORD										
El Salvador										
12 V 2007 ....CDJC		5 744 113	3 598 836	62.7	2 719 371	1 676 313	61.6	3 024 742	1 922 523	63.6
1 VII 2007[24] ....ESDF		6 098 714	3 766 800	61.8	2 887 804	1 752 851	60.7	3 210 910	2 013 949	62.7
1 VII 2008[24] ....ESDF		6 124 705	3 828 004	62.5	2 895 210	1 779 210	61.5	3 229 495	2 048 794	63.4
1 VII 2009[24] ....ESDF		6 152 558	3 890 523	63.2	2 903 737	1 806 310	62.2	3 248 821	2 084 213	64.2
1 VII 2010[24] ....ESDF		6 183 002	3 954 803	64.0	2 913 743	1 834 400	63.0	3 269 259	2 120 404	64.9
1 VII 2011[24] ....ESDF		6 216 143	4 019 742	64.7	2 925 284	1 862 924	63.7	3 290 858	2 156 818	65.5
1 VII 2012[24] ....ESDF		6 251 495	4 086 880	65.4	2 938 123	1 892 642	64.4	3 313 372	2 194 238	66.2
Greenland - Groenland[25]										
1 VII 2003 ....ESDJ		56 766	46 746	82.3	30 292	24 771	81.8	26 474	21 975	83.0
1 VII 2004 ....ESDJ		56 912	46 989	82.6	30 327	24 860	82.0	26 585	22 129	83.2
1 VII 2005 ....ESDJ		56 935	47 080	82.7	30 251	24 837	82.1	26 685	22 243	83.4
1 VII 2006 ....ESDJ		56 775	47 037	82.8	30 094	24 763	82.3	26 681	22 274	83.5
1 VII 2007 ....ESDJ		56 555	47 056	83.2	29 945	24 746	82.6	26 610	22 310	83.8
1 I 2008 ....CDJC		56 462	...	...	29 885	...	...	26 577	...	...
1 VII 2008 ....ESDJ		56 328	47 103	83.6	29 847	24 790	83.1	26 481	22 313	84.3
1 VII 2009 ....ESDJ		56 323	47 230	83.9	29 873	24 865	83.2	26 451	22 366	84.6
1 VII 2010 ....ESDJ		56 534	47 646	84.3	29 939	25 045	83.7	26 595	22 601	85.0
1 VII 2011 ....ESDJ		56 682	48 045	84.8	29 992	25 233	84.1	26 690	22 812	85.5
1 VII 2012 ....ESDJ		56 840	48 224	84.8	30 123	25 331	84.1	26 717	22 897	85.7
Guadeloupe[26]										
1 I 2003 ....ESDJ		394 881	...	...	187 151	...	...	207 730	...	...
1 I 2004 ....ESDJ		396 992	...	...	187 603	...	...	209 389	...	...
1 I 2005 ....ESDJ		399 178	...	...	188 158	...	...	211 020	...	...
1 I 2006 ....CDJC		400 736	...	...	188 720	...	...	212 016	...	...
1 I 2007 ....ESDJ		400 584	...	...	188 325	...	...	212 259	...	...
1 I 2008 ....ESDJ		401 784	...	...	188 385	...	...	213 399	...	...
1 I 2009 ....ESDJ		401 554	...	...	187 867	...	...	213 687	...	...
1 I 2010* ....ESDJ		401 784	...	...	186 946	...	...	214 838	...	...
Guatemala[14]										
1 VII 2008 ....ESDF		13 677 815	...	...	6 673 533	...	...	7 004 282	...	...
1 VII 2009 ....ESDF		14 017 057	...	...	6 836 849	...	...	7 180 208	...	...
1 VII 2010 ....ESDF		14 361 666	...	...	7 003 337	...	...	7 358 328	...	...
Haiti - Haïti										
11 I 2003 ....CDJC		8 373 750	...	...	4 039 272	...	...	4 334 478	...	...
1 VII 2003[27] ....ESDJ		9 001 471	...	...	4 452 024	...	...	4 549 447	...	...
1 VII 2004[27] ....ESDJ		9 144 533	...	...	4 523 032	...	...	4 621 501	...	...
1 VII 2005[27] ....ESDJ		9 292 282	...	...	4 596 593	...	...	4 695 689	...	...
1 VII 2006[27] ....ESDJ		9 445 410	...	...	4 673 089	...	...	4 772 321	...	...
1 VII 2007[27] ....ESDJ		9 602 304	...	...	4 751 622	...	...	4 850 682	...	...
1 VII 2008[27] ....ESDJ		9 761 927	...	...	4 831 621	...	...	4 930 306	...	...
1 VII 2009[27] ....ESDJ		9 923 243	...	...	4 912 515	...	...	5 010 728	...	...
1 VII 2010[27] ....ESDJ		10 085 214	4 817 666	47.8	4 993 731	2 321 608	46.5	5 091 483	2 496 059	49.0
1 VII 2011[27] ....ESDJ		10 248 306	...	...	5 075 517	...	...	5 172 789	...	...
1 VII 2012[27] ....ESDJ		10 413 211	5 154 940	49.5	5 158 254	2 495 108	48.4	5 254 957	2 659 832	50.6
Honduras[28]										
1 VII 2003 ....ESDF		6 860 842	3 260 934	47.5	3 388 874	1 555 369	45.9	3 471 968	1 705 565	49.1
1 VII 2004 ....ESDF		7 028 389	3 382 254	48.1	3 470 259	1 614 104	46.5	3 558 130	1 768 150	49.7
1 VII 2005 ....ESDF		7 197 303	3 504 730	48.7	3 552 360	1 673 434	47.1	3 644 943	1 831 296	50.2
1 VII 2006 ....ESDF		7 367 021	3 628 228	49.2	3 634 900	1 733 290	47.7	3 732 121	1 894 938	50.8
1 VII 2007 ....ESDF		7 536 952	3 752 579	49.8	3 717 577	1 793 588	48.2	3 819 375	1 958 991	51.3
1 VII 2008 ....ESDF		7 706 907	...	...	3 800 300	...	...	3 906 607	...	...
1 VII 2009 ....ESDF		7 876 662	...	...	3 882 957	...	...	3 993 705	...	...
1 VII 2010 ....ESDF		8 045 990	...	...	3 965 430	...	...	4 080 560	...	...
Jamaica - Jamaïque										
1 VII 2003 ....ESDJ		2 625 708	1 364 719	52.0	1 293 121	651 243	50.4	1 332 587	713 476	53.5
1 VII 2004 ....ESDJ		2 638 074	1 371 144	52.0	1 299 406	654 407	50.4	1 338 668	716 736	53.5
1 VII 2005 ....ESDJ		2 650 402	1 377 546	52.0	1 305 639	657 546	50.4	1 344 763	720 000	53.5
1 VII 2006 ....ESDJ		2 663 106	1 384 145	52.0	1 312 025	660 763	50.4	1 351 081	723 383	53.5
1 VII 2007 ....ESDJ		2 675 831	1 390 754	52.0	1 318 444	663 995	50.4	1 357 387	726 759	53.5
1 VII 2008 ....ESDJ		2 687 241	1 396 470	52.0	1 324 277	666 761	50.3	1 362 964	729 709	53.5
1 VII 2009 ....ESDJ		2 695 583	...	...	1 328 124	...	...	1 367 460	...	...
1 VII 2010 ....ESDJ		2 702 314	...	...	1 324 134	...	...	1 378 180	...	...
4 IV 2011 ....CDJC		2 697 983	1 454 153	53.9	1 334 533	700 957	52.5	1 363 450	753 196	55.2

Continent, country or area, and date / Continent, pays ou zone et date	Code[a]	Both sexes - Les deux sexes			Male - Masculin			Female - Féminin		
		Total	Urban - Urbaine		Total	Urban - Urbaine		Total	Urban - Urbaine	
			Number Nombre	Percent P.100		Number Nombre	Percent P.100		Number Nombre	Percent P.100
AMERICA, NORTH - AMÉRIQUE DU NORD										
Jamaica - Jamaïque										
1 VII 2011	ESDJ	2 699 838	...	...	1 335 466	...	...	1 364 372	...	...
1 VII 2012*	ESDJ	2 707 805	...	...	1 339 740	...	...	1 368 065	...	...
Martinique										
1 . 2003	ESDJ	391 676	...	...	183 735	...	...	207 941	...	...
1 I 2004	ESDJ	393 852	...	...	184 303	...	...	209 549	...	...
1 I 2005	ESDJ	395 982	...	...	184 841			211 141	...	...
1 I 2006	CDJC	397 732	355 189	89.3	185 604	165 012	88.9	212 128	190 177	89.7
1 I 2007	ESDJ	397 730	...	...	184 970			212 760	...	...
1 I 2008	ESDJ	397 693	...	...	184 404	...	...	213 289	...	...
1 I 2009	ESDJ	396 404	...	...	183 655	...	...	212 749	...	...
1 I 2010*	ESDJ	396 308	...	...	182 644	...	...	213 664	...	...
Mexico - Mexique										
1 VII 2003	ESDJ	101 999 555	77 303 384	75.8	50 361 179	...	...	51 638 376	...	...
1 VII 2004	ESDJ	103 001 867	78 436 582	76.2	50 814 580	...	...	52 187 287	...	...
1 VII 2005	ESDJ	103 946 866	79 467 885	76.5	51 238 427	...	...	52 708 439	...	...
17 X 2005	CDJC	103 263 388	78 986 852	76.5	50 249 955	38 300 417	76.2	53 013 433	40 686 435	76.7
1 VII 2006	ESDJ	104 874 282	80 373 543	76.6	51 654 642	...	...	53 219 640	...	...
1 VII 2007	ESDJ	105 790 725	81 288 078	76.8	52 066 743	...	...	53 723 982	...	...
1 VII 2008	ESDJ	106 682 518	82 179 785	77.0	52 466 262	...	...	54 216 256	...	...
1 VII 2009	ESDJ	107 550 697	83 088 985	77.3	52 853 788	...	...	54 696 909	...	...
12 VI 2010[29]	CDFC	112 336 538	86 287 410	76.8	54 855 231	41 946 540	76.5	57 481 307	44 340 870	77.1
Montserrat										
1 VII 2003	ESDF	4 482	...	...	2 421	...	...	2 061	...	...
1 VII 2004	ESDF	4 681	...	...	2 480	...	...	2 201	...	...
12 V 2011	CDJC	4 922	...	...	2 546	...	...	2 376	...	...
Nicaragua										
1 VII 2003	ESDJ	5 312 750	...	...	2 641 869	...	...	2 670 881	...	...
1 VII 2004	ESDJ	5 380 510	...	...	2 674 138	...	...	2 706 372	...	...
4 VI 2005	CDJC	5 142 098	2 875 550	55.9	2 534 491	1 368 622	54.0	2 607 607	1 506 928	57.8
1 VII 2005	ESDJ	5 450 387	3 047 740	55.9	2 707 309	1 462 218	54.0	2 743 078	1 585 522	57.8
1 VII 2006	ESDJ	5 522 606	3 099 918	56.1	2 741 414	1 488 694	54.3	2 781 192	1 611 224	57.9
1 VII 2007	ESDJ	5 595 541	3 152 807	56.3	2 775 638	1 515 432	54.6	2 819 903	1 637 375	58.1
1 VII 2008	ESDJ	5 668 866	3 206 205	56.6	2 809 918	1 542 386	54.9	2 858 948	1 663 819	58.2
1 VII 2009	ESDJ	5 742 316	3 259 955	56.8	2 844 244	1 569 555	55.2	2 898 072	1 690 400	58.3
Panama										
1 VII 2003[30]	ESDF	3 116 277	1 964 517	63.0	1 572 850	967 537	61.5	1 543 427	996 980	64.6
1 VII 2004[30]	ESDF	3 172 360	2 007 892	63.3	1 600 879	989 709	61.8	1 571 481	1 018 183	64.8
1 VII 2005[30]	ESDF	3 228 186	2 020 965	62.6	1 628 720	1 011 700	62.1	1 599 466	1 009 265	63.1
1 VII 2006[30]	ESDF	3 283 959	2 093 871	63.8	1 656 469	1 033 634	62.4	1 627 490	1 060 237	65.1
1 VII 2007[30]	ESDF	3 339 781	2 136 637	64.0	1 684 189	1 055 455	62.7	1 655 592	1 081 182	65.3
1 VII 2008[30]	ESDF	3 395 346	2 179 118	64.2	1 711 735	1 077 090	62.9	1 683 611	1 102 028	65.5
1 VII 2009[30]	ESDF	3 450 349	2 221 211	64.4	1 738 965	1 098 484	63.2	1 711 384	1 122 727	65.6
16 V 2010	CDFC	3 405 813	...	...	1 712 584	...	...	1 693 229	...	...
1 VII 2010[30]	ESDF	3 504 483	2 262 765	64.6	1 765 734	1 119 546	63.4	1 738 749	1 143 219	65.7
Puerto Rico - Porto Rico[31]										
1 VII 2003	ESDJ	3 878 532	...	...	1 865 170	...	...	2 013 362	...	...
1 VII 2004	ESDJ	3 894 855	...	...	1 871 657	...	...	2 023 198	...	...
1 VII 2005	ESDJ	3 912 054	...	...	1 879 236	...	...	2 032 818	...	...
1 VII 2006	ESDJ	3 927 776	...	...	1 886 031	...	...	2 041 745	...	...
1 VII 2007	ESDJ	3 942 375	...	...	1 892 503	...	...	2 049 872	...	...
1 VII 2008	ESDJ	3 954 037	...	...	1 897 396	...	...	2 056 641	...	...
1 VII 2009	ESDJ	3 967 288	...	...	1 903 370	...	...	2 063 918	...	...
1 IV 2010	CDJC	3 725 789	3 493 256	93.8	1 785 171	...	...	1 940 618	...	...
1 VII 2010[32]	ESDJ	3 721 208	...	...	1 782 619	...	...	1 938 589	...	...
1 VII 2011[32]	ESDJ	3 694 093	...	...	1 769 033	...	...	1 925 060	...	...
1 VII 2012[32]	ESDJ	3 667 084	...	...	1 755 479	...	...	1 911 605	...	...
Saint Lucia - Sainte-Lucie										
1 VII 2003	ESDF	160 673	...	...	78 618	...	...	82 055	...	...
1 VII 2004	ESDF	162 434	...	...	79 407	...	...	83 027	...	...
1 VII 2005	ESDF	164 330	...	...	80 440	...	...	83 890	...	...
1 VII 2006	ESDF	166 387	...	...	81 558	...	...	84 829	...	...

Continent, country or area, and date / Continent, pays ou zone et date	Code[a]	Both sexes - Les deux sexes			Male - Masculin			Female - Féminin		
		Total	Urban - Urbaine		Total	Urban - Urbaine		Total	Urban - Urbaine	
			Number Nombre	Percent P.100		Number Nombre	Percent P.100		Number Nombre	Percent P.100
AMERICA, NORTH - AMÉRIQUE DU NORD										
Saint Lucia - Sainte-Lucie										
1 VII 2007 .... ESDF		168 338	...	...	82 426	...	...	85 912	...	...
1 VII 2008 .... ESDF		170 331	...	...	83 478	...	...	86 853	...	...
1 VII 2009 .... ESDF		172 370	...	...	84 465	...	...	87 905	...	...
10 V 2010* .... CDFC		173 720	...	...	86 595	...	...	87 125	...	...
Saint Pierre and Miquelon - Saint Pierre-et-Miquelon										
19 I 2006 .... CDFC		6 125	...	...	3 034	...	...	3 091	...	...
Saint Vincent and the Grenadines - Saint-Vincent-et-les Grenadines										
1 VII 2003 .... ESDF		105 158	42 063	40.0	53 073	...	...	52 085	...	...
1 VII 2004 .... ESDF		104 555	41 822	40.0	52 769	...	...	51 786	...	...
1 VII 2005 .... ESDF		103 751	...	...	52 363	...	...	51 388	...	...
1 VII 2006 .... ESDF		101 402	...	...	51 178	...	...	50 224	...	...
1 VII 2007 .... ESDF		100 130	...	...	50 536	...	...	49 594	...	...
1 VII 2008 .... ESDF		99 086	...	...	50 009	...	...	49 077	...	...
Trinidad and Tobago - Trinité-et-Tobago										
1 VII 2003[33] .... ESDF		1 282 447	...	...	642 037	...	...	640 410	...	...
1 VII 2004[33] .... ESDF		1 290 646	...	...	647 259	...	...	643 387	...	...
1 VII 2005[33] .... ESDF		1 294 494	...	...	649 189	...	...	645 305	...	...
1 VII 2006[33] .... ESDF		1 297 944	...	...	650 919	...	...	647 025	...	...
1 VII 2007[33] .... ESDF		1 303 188	...	...	653 549	...	...	649 639	...	...
1 VII 2008[33] .... ESDF		1 308 587	...	...	656 257	...	...	652 330	...	...
1 VII 2010[33] .... ESDF		1 317 714	...	...	656 892	...	...	660 822	...	...
9 I 2011* .... CDFC		1 324 699	...	...	665 119	...	...	659 580	...	...
Turks and Caicos Islands - Îles Turques et Caïques										
1 VII 2003 .... ESDJ		*25 143*	...	...	*12 513*	...	...	*12 630*	...	...
1 VII 2004 .... ESDJ		*27 496*	...	...	*13 684*	...	...	*13 812*	...	...
1 VII 2005 .... ESDJ		*30 602*	...	...	*15 230*	...	...	*15 372*	...	...
1 VII 2006 .... ESDJ		*33 202*	...	...	*16 524*	...	...	*16 678*	...	...
1 VII 2007 .... ESDJ		*34 862*	...	...	*18 023*	...	...	*16 839*	...	...
United States of America - États-Unis d'Amérique[34]										
1 VII 2003 .... ESDJ		290 326 418	...	...	142 676 927	...	...	147 649 491	...	...
1 VII 2004 .... ESDJ		293 045 739	...	...	144 137 674	...	...	148 908 065	...	...
1 VII 2005 .... ESDJ		295 753 151	...	...	145 560 767	...	...	150 192 384	...	...
1 VII 2006 .... ESDJ		298 593 212	...	...	147 060 702	...	...	151 532 510	...	...
1 VII 2007 .... ESDJ		301 579 895	...	...	148 612 102	...	...	152 967 793	...	...
1 VII 2008 .... ESDJ		304 374 846	...	...	150 074 226	...	...	154 300 620	...	...
1 VII 2009 .... ESDJ		307 006 550	...	...	151 449 490	...	...	155 557 060	...	...
1 IV 2010 .... CDJC		308 745 538	249 253 271	80.7	151 781 326	121 698 595	80.2	156 964 212	127 554 676	81.3
United States Virgin Islands - Îles Vierges américaines[31]										
1 VII 2003 .... ESDJ		109 148	...	...	51 954	...	...	57 194	...	...
1 VII 2004 .... ESDJ		109 354	...	...	52 007	...	...	57 347	...	...
1 VII 2005 .... ESDJ		109 600	...	...	52 081	...	...	57 519	...	...
1 VII 2006 .... ESDJ		109 764	...	...	52 113	...	...	57 651	...	...
1 VII 2007 .... ESDJ		109 821	...	...	52 089	...	...	57 732	...	...
1 VII 2008 .... ESDJ		109 840	...	...	52 045	...	...	57 795	...	...
1 IV 2010 .... CDJC		106 405	...	...	50 854	...	...	55 551	...	...

Continent, country or area, and date / Continent, pays ou zone et date	Code[a]	Both sexes - Les deux sexes Total	Urban - Urbaine Number Nombre	Urban - Urbaine Percent P.100	Male - Masculin Total	Urban - Urbaine Number Nombre	Urban - Urbaine Percent P.100	Female - Féminin Total	Urban - Urbaine Number Nombre	Urban - Urbaine Percent P.100
AMERICA, SOUTH - AMÉRIQUE DU SUD										
Argentina - Argentine										
1 VII 2003[28] .... ESDF		37 869 730	34 101 536	90.0	18 546 570	16 559 682	89.3	19 323 160	17 541 854	90.8
1 VII 2004[28] .... ESDF		38 226 051	34 493 965	90.2	18 719 869	16 758 540	89.5	19 506 182	17 735 425	90.9
1 VII 2005[28] .... ESDF		38 592 150	34 894 057	90.4	18 898 472	16 961 698	89.8	19 693 678	17 932 359	91.1
1 VII 2006[28] .... ESDF		38 970 611	35 304 205	90.6	19 083 828	17 170 659	90.0	19 886 783	18 133 546	91.2
1 VII 2007[28] .... ESDF		39 356 383	35 719 891	90.8	19 273 494	17 383 239	90.2	20 082 889	18 336 652	91.3
1 VII 2008[28] .... ESDF		39 745 613	36 137 648	90.9	19 465 305	17 597 280	90.4	20 280 308	18 540 368	91.4
1 VII 2009[28] .... ESDF		40 134 425	36 553 965	91.1	19 657 086	17 810 843	90.6	20 477 339	18 743 122	91.5
1 VII 2010[28] .... ESDF		40 518 951	36 965 313	91.2	19 846 671	18 023 080	90.8	20 672 280	18 942 233	91.6
27 X 2010 .... CDFC		40 117 096	...	...	19 523 766	...	...	20 593 330	...	...
1 VII 2011[28] .... ESDF		40 900 496	37 372 872	91.4	20 034 781	...	...	20 865 715		
1 VII 2012[28] .... ESDF		41 281 631	37 778 989	91.5	20 222 859	...	...	21 058 772	...	...
Bolivia (Plurinational State of) - Bolivie (État plurinational de)										
1 VII 2003 .... ESDF		9 024 922	5 712 138	63.3	4 495 426	2 780 137	61.8	4 529 495	2 932 001	64.7
1 VII 2004 .... ESDF		9 226 511	5 883 724	63.8	4 597 081	2 863 378	62.3	4 629 430	3 020 347	65.2
1 VII 2005 .... ESDF		9 427 219	6 055 392	64.2	4 698 293	2 946 725	62.7	4 728 926	3 108 667	65.7
1 VII 2006 .... ESDF		9 627 269	6 227 367	64.7	4 799 178	3 030 290	63.1	4 828 091	3 197 077	66.2
1 VII 2007 .... ESDF		9 827 522	6 400 366	65.1	4 900 162	3 114 403	63.6	4 927 360	3 285 963	66.7
1 VII 2008 .... ESDF		10 027 643	6 574 048	65.6	5 001 071	3 198 900	64.0	5 026 572	3 375 148	67.1
1 VII 2009 .... ESDF		10 227 299	6 748 075	66.0	5 101 733	3 283 616	64.4	5 125 566	3 464 459	67.6
1 VII 2010 .... ESDF		10 426 154	6 922 107	66.4	5 201 974	3 368 384	64.8	5 224 180	3 553 722	68.0
1 VII 2011 .... ESDF		10 624 495	7 096 464	66.8	5 301 942	...	...	5 322 553	...	...
Brazil - Brésil										
1 VII 2003[35] .... ESDF		178 741 412	...	...	87 923 721	...	...	90 817 691	...	...
1 VII 2004[35] .... ESDF		181 105 601	...	...	89 051 847	...	...	92 053 754	...	...
1 VII 2005[35] .... ESDF		183 383 216	...	...	90 135 967	...	...	93 247 249	...	...
1 VII 2006[35] .... ESDF		185 564 212	...	...	91 171 295	...	...	94 392 917	...	...
1 VII 2007[35] .... ESDF		187 641 714	...	...	92 154 636	...	...	95 487 078	...	...
1 VII 2008[35] .... ESDF		189 612 814	...	...	93 084 588	...	...	96 528 226	...	...
1 VII 2009[35] .... ESDF		191 480 630	...	...	93 962 767	...	...	97 517 863	...	...
1 VII 2010[35] .... ESDF		193 252 604	...	...	94 792 952	...	...	98 459 652	...	...
31 VII 2010 .... CDJC		190 755 799	160 925 804	84.4	93 406 990	77 710 179	83.2	97 348 809	83 215 625	85.5
Chile - Chili										
1 VII 2003 .... ESDF		15 919 479	13 808 880	86.7	7 879 658	6 754 181	85.7	8 039 821	7 054 699	87.7
1 VII 2004 .... ESDF		16 093 378	13 966 203	86.8	7 966 110	6 832 205	85.8	8 127 268	7 133 998	87.8
1 VII 2005 .... ESDF		16 267 278	14 123 527	86.8	8 052 564	6 910 230	85.8	8 214 714	7 213 297	87.8
1 VII 2006 .... ESDF		16 432 674	14 272 454	86.9	8 134 314	6 983 850	85.9	8 298 360	7 288 604	87.8
1 VII 2007 .... ESDF		16 598 074	14 421 386	86.9	8 216 068	7 057 476	85.9	8 382 006	7 363 910	87.9
1 VII 2008 .... ESDF		16 763 470	14 570 311	86.9	8 297 819	7 131 097	85.9	8 465 651	7 439 214	87.9
1 VII 2009 .... ESDF		16 928 873	14 719 246	86.9	8 379 571	7 204 720	86.0	8 549 302	7 514 526	87.9
1 VII 2010 .... ESDF		17 094 275	14 868 172	87.0	8 461 327	7 278 342	86.0	8 632 948	7 589 830	87.9
1 VII 2011 .... ESDF		17 248 450	15 006 226	87.0	8 536 904	7 346 185	86.1	8 711 546	7 660 041	87.9
9 IV 2012* .... CDFC		16 572 475	...	...	8 059 148	...	...	8 513 327	...	...
1 VII 2012 .... ESDF		17 402 630	15 144 277	87.0	8 612 483	7 414 026	86.1	8 790 147	7 730 251	87.9
Colombia - Colombie										
1 VII 2003[36] .... ESDJ		41 848 959	30 879 056	73.8	20 653 560	14 865 895	72.0	21 195 399	16 013 161	75.6
1 VII 2004[36] .... ESDJ		42 368 489	31 385 655	74.1	20 913 566	15 114 250	72.3	21 454 923	16 271 405	75.8
22 V 2005 .... CDFC		41 468 384	31 510 379	76.0	20 336 117	15 086 536	74.2	21 132 267	16 423 843	77.7
1 VII 2005[36] .... ESDJ		42 888 592	31 889 299	74.4	21 169 835	15 356 383	72.5	21 718 757	16 532 916	76.1
1 VII 2006[36] .... ESDJ		43 405 956	32 386 530	74.6	21 426 954	15 605 323	72.8	21 979 002	16 781 207	76.4
1 VII 2007[36] .... ESDJ		43 926 929	32 888 860	74.9	21 683 071	15 850 700	73.1	22 243 858	17 038 160	76.6
1 VII 2008[36] .... ESDJ		44 451 147	33 396 380	75.1	21 942 355	16 100 320	73.4	22 508 792	17 296 060	76.8
1 VII 2009[36] .... ESDJ		44 978 832	33 892 634	75.4	22 203 708	16 343 820	73.6	22 775 124	17 548 814	77.1
1 VII 2010[36] .... ESDJ		45 509 584	34 388 013	75.6	22 466 660	16 587 100	73.8	23 042 924	17 800 913	77.3
1 VII 2011[36] .... ESDJ		46 044 601	34 883 399	75.8	22 731 299	16 830 795	74.0	23 313 302	18 052 604	77.4
1 VII 2012[36] .... ESDJ		46 581 823	35 377 138	75.9	22 997 087	17 073 806	74.2	23 584 736	18 303 332	77.6
Ecuador - Équateur										
1 VII 2003[37] .... ESDF		12 842 578	8 001 231	62.3	6 444 656	3 963 574	61.5	6 397 920	4 037 657	63.1
1 VII 2004[37] .... ESDF		13 026 891	8 187 908	62.9	6 535 564	4 057 642	62.1	6 491 327	4 130 266	63.6
1 VII 2005[37] .... ESDF		13 215 089	8 378 469	63.4	6 628 368	4 153 605	62.7	6 586 721	4 224 864	64.1
1 VII 2006[37] .... ESDF		13 408 270	8 580 090	64.0	6 723 629	4 254 974	63.3	6 684 641	4 325 116	64.7
1 VII 2007[37] .... ESDF		13 605 486	8 785 745	64.6	6 820 842	4 358 292	63.9	6 784 644	4 427 453	65.3

Continent, country or area, and date / Continent, pays ou zone et date	Code[a]	Both sexes - Les deux sexes			Male - Masculin			Female - Féminin		
		Total	Urban - Urbaine		Total	Urban - Urbaine		Total	Urban - Urbaine	
			Number Nombre	Percent P.100		Number Nombre	Percent P.100		Number Nombre	Percent P.100
AMERICA, SOUTH - AMÉRIQUE DU SUD										
Ecuador - Équateur										
1 VII 2008[37] .... ESDF		13 805 092	8 993 796	65.1	6 919 185	4 462 739	64.5	6 885 907	4 531 057	65.8
1 VII 2009[37] .... ESDF		14 005 449	9 202 590	65.7	7 017 839	4 567 499	65.1	6 987 610	4 635 091	66.3
1 VII 2010[37] .... ESDF		15 004 674	9 410 481[3]	62.7	7 439 794	4 671 748[3]	62.8	7 564 880	4 738 733[3]	62.6
28 XI 2010 .... CDFC		14 483 499	9 090 786	62.8	7 177 683	4 451 434	62.0	7 305 816	4 639 352	63.5
1 VII 2011[37] .... ESDF		15 248 459	...	...	7 558 210	...	...	7 690 249	...	...
1 VII 2012[37] .... ESDF		15 495 016	...	...	7 678 696	...	...	7 816 320	...	...
Falkland Islands (Malvinas) - Îles Falkland (Malvinas)[38]										
8 X 2006 .... CDFC		2 955	...	...	1 569	...	...	1 386	...	...
French Guiana - Guyane française										
1 I 2003 .... ESDJ		184 792	...	...	92 273	...	...	92 519	...	...
1 I 2004 .... ESDJ		193 167	...	...	96 300	...	...	96 867	...	...
1 I 2005 .... ESDJ		199 206	...	...	99 223	...	...	99 983	...	...
1 I 2006 .... CDJC		205 954	167 454	81.3	101 930	81 888	80.3	104 023	85 565	82.3
1 I 2006 .... ESDJ		205 954	...	...	102 032	...	...	103 922	...	...
1 I 2007 .... ESDJ		213 031	...	...	105 546	...	...	107 485	...	...
1 I 2008 .... ESDJ		219 266	...	...	108 662	...	...	110 604	...	...
1 I 2009 .... ESDJ		224 469	...	...	111 201	...	...	113 268	...	...
1 I 2010* .... ESDJ		230 441	...	...	113 824	...	...	116 617	...	...
Guyana										
1 VII 2003 .... ESDF		753 196	...	...	377 019	...	...	376 177	...	...
1 VII 2004 .... ESDF		755 685	...	...	378 265	...	...	377 420	...	...
1 VII 2005 .... ESDF		758 183	...	...	379 515	...	...	378 668	...	...
1 VII 2006 .... ESDF		760 689	...	...	380 770	...	...	379 919	...	...
1 VII 2007 .... ESDF		763 203	...	...	382 028	...	...	381 175	...	...
1 VII 2008 .... ESDF		766 183	...	...	383 522	...	...	382 661	...	...
1 VII 2009 .... ESDF		777 237	...	...	390 230	...	...	387 007	...	...
1 VII 2010 .... ESDF		784 894	...	...	393 059	...	...	391 835	...	...
Paraguay[14]										
1 VII 2003 .... ESDF		5 677 448	3 183 160	56.1	2 872 186	1 553 561	54.1	2 805 262	1 629 599	58.1
1 VII 2004 .... ESDF		5 788 088	3 265 346	56.4	2 927 657	1 594 161	54.5	2 860 430	1 671 185	58.4
1 VII 2005 .... ESDF		5 898 651	3 347 793	56.8	2 983 123	1 634 869	54.8	2 915 528	1 712 924	58.8
1 VII 2006 .... ESDF		6 009 143	3 430 619	57.1	3 038 590	1 675 752	55.1	2 970 553	1 754 868	59.1
1 VII 2007 .... ESDF		6 119 642	3 513 944	57.4	3 094 044	1 716 874	55.5	3 025 598	1 797 070	59.4
1 VII 2008 .... ESDF		6 230 143	3 597 588	57.7	3 149 475	1 758 138	55.8	3 080 668	1 839 450	59.7
1 VII 2009 .... ESDF		6 340 641	...	...	3 681 376	...	...	2 659 265	...	...
1 VII 2010 .... ESDF		6 451 122	...	...	3 260 223	...	...	3 190 899	...	...
1 VII 2011 .... ESDF		6 561 785	...	...	3 315 636	...	...	3 246 149	...	...
1 VII 2012 .... ESDF		6 672 631	...	...	3 371 117	...	...	3 301 514	...	...
Peru - Pérou										
1 VII 2003 .... ESDF		27 103 457	18 953 109	69.9	13 597 121	9 384 413	69.0	13 506 336	9 568 696	70.8
1 VII 2004 .... ESDF		27 460 073	19 368 782	70.5	13 774 414	9 588 293	69.6	13 685 659	9 780 489	71.5
1 VII 2005 .... ESDF		27 810 540	19 782 408	71.1	13 948 639	9 791 272	70.2	13 861 901	9 991 136	72.1
18 VII 2005*[39] .... CDFC		26 152 265	...	...	13 061 026	...	...	13 091 239	...	...
1 VII 2006 .... ESDF		28 151 443	20 191 318	71.7	14 118 112	9 991 965	70.8	14 033 331	10 199 353	72.7
1 VII 2007[24] .... ESDF		28 481 901	20 594 600	72.3	14 282 346	10 189 918	71.3	14 199 555	10 404 682	73.3
21 X 2007 .... CDFC		27 412 157	20 810 288	75.9	13 622 640	10 226 205	75.1	13 789 517	10 584 083	76.8
1 VII 2008[24] .... ESDF		28 807 034	20 995 699	72.9	14 443 858	10 386 799	71.9	14 363 176	10 608 900	73.9
1 VII 2009[24] .... ESDF		29 132 013	21 398 222	73.5	14 605 206	10 584 348	72.5	14 526 807	10 813 874	74.4
1 VII 2010[24] .... ESDF		29 461 933	21 805 837	74.0	14 768 901	10 784 345	73.0	14 693 032	11 021 492	75.0
1 VII 2011[24] .... ESDF		29 797 694	22 219 201	74.6	14 935 396	10 987 090	73.6	14 862 298	11 232 111	75.6
1 VII 2012[24] .... ESDF		30 135 875	22 635 742	75.1	15 103 003	11 191 332	74.1	15 032 872	11 444 410	76.1
Suriname										
31 III 2003* .... CDJC		481 146[40]	...	...	241 837	...	...	239 292	...	...
1 VII 2003 .... ESDJ		482 769	...	...	242 662	...	...	240 107	...	...
2 VIII 2004 .... CDJC		492 829	328 932[41]	66.7	248 046	164 444[41]	66.3	244 783	164 488[41]	67.2
1 VII 2007 .... ESDJ		509 970	...	...	257 181	...	...	252 789	...	...
1 VII 2008 .... ESDJ		517 052	...	...	260 898	...	...	256 154	...	...
Uruguay										
1 VII 2003[1] .... ESDF		3 303 540	3 078 812	93.2	1 597 362	1 469 246	92.0	1 706 177	1 609 565	94.3
1 VI 2004[42] .... CDFC		3 241 003	2 974 714	91.8	1 565 533	1 415 362	90.4	1 675 470	1 559 352	93.1

6. Total and urban population by sex: 2003 - 2012
Population totale et population urbaine selon le sexe : 2003 - 2012 (continued - suite)

Continent, country or area, and date / Continent, pays ou zone et date	Code[a]	Both sexes - Les deux sexes			Male - Masculin			Female - Féminin		
		Total	Urban - Urbaine		Total	Urban - Urbaine		Total	Urban - Urbaine	
			Number Nombre	Percent P.100		Number Nombre	Percent P.100		Number Nombre	Percent P.100

AMERICA, SOUTH - AMÉRIQUE DU SUD

Uruguay
1 VII 2004[1] ....ESDF		3 301 732	3 083 096	93.4	1 595 635	1 471 098	92.2	1 706 097	1 611 998	94.5
1 VII 2005[1] ....ESDF		3 305 723	3 089 988	93.5	1 597 040	1 474 638	92.3	1 708 683	1 615 350	94.5
1 VII 2006[1] ....ESDF		3 314 466	3 101 685	93.6	1 601 024	1 480 779	92.5	1 713 442	1 620 906	94.6
1 VII 2007[1] ....ESDF		3 323 906	3 114 125	93.7	1 605 466	1 487 391	92.6	1 718 440	1 626 734	94.7
1 VII 2008[1] ....ESDF		3 334 052	3 127 318	93.8	1 610 356	1 494 470	92.8	1 723 696	1 632 848	94.7
1 VII 2009[1] ....ESDF		3 344 938	3 141 299	93.9	1 615 709	1 502 032	93.0	1 729 229	1 639 267	94.8
1 VII 2010[1] ....ESDF		3 356 584	...	...	1 621 528	...	...	1 735 056	...	...
4 X 2011 ....CDJC		3 286 314	3 110 701	94.7	1 577 725[43]	1 478 967[43]	93.7	1 708 481[43]	1 631 626[43]	95.5
1 VII 2012*[1] ....ESDF		3 380 544	3 186 429	94.3	1 633 728	1 526 761	93.5	1 746 816	1 659 668	95.0

Venezuela (Bolivarian Republic of) - Venezuela (République bolivarienne du)
1 VII 2003[28] ....ESDF		25 673 550	22 570 794	87.9	12 901 999	11 221 668	87.0	12 771 551	11 349 126	88.9
1 VII 2004[28] ....ESDF		26 127 351	22 977 915	87.9	13 125 804	11 421 991	87.0	13 001 547	11 555 924	88.9
1 VII 2005[28] ....ESDF		26 577 423	23 381 277	88.0	13 347 732	11 620 413	87.1	13 229 691	11 760 864	88.9
1 VII 2006[28] ....ESDF		27 030 656	23 786 937	88.0	13 570 418	11 819 341	87.1	13 460 238	11 967 596	88.9
1 VII 2007[28] ....ESDF		27 483 208	24 191 525	88.0	13 792 761	12 017 754	87.1	13 690 447	12 173 771	88.9
1 VII 2008[28] ....ESDF		27 934 783	24 594 784	88.0	14 014 614	12 215 477	87.2	13 920 169	12 379 307	88.9
1 VII 2009[28] ....ESDF		28 384 132	...	...	14 235 351	...	...	14 148 781	...	...
1 VII 2010[28] ....ESDF		28 833 845	25 396 369	88.1	14 456 287	12 608 398	87.2	14 377 558	12 787 971	88.9
1 VII 2011[28] ....ESDF		29 277 736	25 791 535	88.1	14 673 402	12 801 370	87.2	14 604 334	12 990 165	88.9
1 IX 2011 ....CDFC		27 227 930	...	...	13 549 752	...	...	13 678 178	...	...
1 VII 2012[28] ....ESDF		29 718 357	...	...	14 888 876	...	...	14 829 481	...	...

ASIA - ASIE

Afghanistan
1 VII 2003[44] ....ESDF		20 691 400	4 629 500	22.4	10 657 000	2 419 700	22.7	10 034 400	2 209 800	22.0
1 VII 2004[44] ....ESDF		21 677 700	4 668 700	21.5	11 086 400	2 403 500	21.7	10 591 300	2 265 200	21.4
1 VII 2005[44] ....ESDF		22 097 900	4 759 200	21.5	11 301 300	2 450 100	21.7	10 796 600	2 309 100	21.4
1 VII 2006[45] ....ESDF		22 575 900	4 862 100	21.5	11 545 800	2 503 100	21.7	11 030 100	2 359 000	21.4
1 VII 2007[44] ....ESDF		23 038 900	5 159 200	22.4	11 783 600	2 656 200	22.5	11 255 300	2 503 000	22.2
1 VII 2008[44] ....ESDF		23 511 400	5 330 200	22.7	12 025 700	2 744 400	22.8	11 485 700	2 585 800	22.5
1 VII 2009[44] ....ESDF		23 993 500[46]	5 507 300	23.0	12 272 900	2 835 900	23.1	11 720 600	2 671 400	22.8
1 VII 2010[44] ....ESDF		24 485 600[47]	5 690 300	23.2	12 524 700[47]	2 929 900	23.4	11 960 900[47]	2 760 400	23.1
1 VII 2011[44] ....ESDF		24 987 700	5 879 200	23.5	12 782 000	3 027 400	23.7	12 205 700	2 851 800	23.4
1 VII 2012[44] ....ESDF		25 500 100	6 074 200	23.8	13 044 400	3 127 700	24.0	12 455 700	2 946 500	23.7

Armenia - Arménie
1 VII 2003 ....ESDJ		3 211 267	2 061 952	64.2	1 545 168	975 356	63.1	1 666 099	1 086 596	65.2
1 VII 2004 ....ESDJ		3 214 030	2 061 984	64.2	1 548 713	976 728	63.1	1 665 317	1 085 256	65.2
1 VII 2005 ....ESDJ		3 217 535	2 062 472	64.1	1 552 382	978 396	63.0	1 665 153	1 084 076	65.1
1 VII 2006 ....ESDJ		3 221 094	2 064 268	64.1	1 555 755	980 272	63.0	1 665 339	1 083 996	65.1
1 VII 2007 ....ESDJ		3 226 520	2 067 650	64.1	1 559 978	982 632	63.0	1 666 542	1 085 018	65.1
1 VII 2008 ....ESDJ		3 234 031	2 071 942	64.1	1 565 411	985 913	63.0	1 668 620	1 086 029	65.1
1 VII 2009 ....ESDJ		3 243 729	2 077 181	64.0	1 572 046	989 609	63.0	1 671 683	1 087 572	65.1
1 VII 2010 ....ESDJ		3 256 066	...	...	1 579 705	...	...	1 676 361	...	...
1 VII 2011 ....ESDJ		3 268 468	...	...	1 586 935	...	...	1 681 533	...	...
12 X 2011 ....CDFC		2 871 771	1 847 124	64.3	1 346 729	851 475	63.2	1 525 042	995 649	65.3
1 I 2012 ....ESDJ		3 274 285	...	...	1 590 285	...	...	1 684 000	...	...

Azerbaijan - Azerbaïdjan
1 VII 2003[48] ....ESDF		8 309 200	4 298 000	51.7	4 080 100	2 099 100	51.4	4 229 100	2 198 900	52.0
1 VII 2004[48] ....ESDF		8 398 300	4 390 900	52.3	4 129 200	2 148 200	52.0	4 269 100	2 242 700	52.5
1 VII 2005[48] ....ESDF		8 500 300	4 462 900	52.5	4 184 900	2 186 100	52.2	4 315 400	2 276 800	52.8
1 VII 2006[48] ....ESDF		8 609 600	4 533 300	52.7	4 244 200	2 223 100	52.4	4 365 400	2 310 200	52.9
1 VII 2007[48] ....ESDF		8 723 000	4 608 200	52.8	4 305 800	2 262 400	52.5	4 417 200	2 345 800	53.1
1 VII 2008[48] ....ESDF		8 838 500	4 690 000	53.1	4 368 600	2 304 800	52.8	4 469 900	2 385 200	53.4
13 IV 2009 ....CDJC		8 922 447	4 739 123	53.1	4 414 398	2 330 527	52.8	4 508 049	2 408 596	53.4
1 VII 2009 ....ESDF		8 947 300	4 751 400	53.1	4 427 900	2 337 100	52.8	4 519 400	2 414 300	53.4
1 VII 2010 ....ESDF		9 054 300	4 802 200	53.0	4 486 300	2 364 400	52.7	4 568 000	2 437 800	53.4

Continent, country or area, and date / Continent, pays ou zone et date	Code[a]	Both sexes - Les deux sexes Total	Urban - Urbaine Number Nombre	Urban - Urbaine Percent P.100	Male - Masculin Total	Urban - Urbaine Number Nombre	Urban - Urbaine Percent P.100	Female - Féminin Total	Urban - Urbaine Number Nombre	Urban - Urbaine Percent P.100
ASIA - ASIE										
Azerbaijan - Azerbaïdjan										
1 VII 2011 .... ESDF		9 173 082	...	...	4 550 270	...	...	4 622 812	...	...
1 VII 2012 .... ESDF		9 295 784	...	...	4 616 139	...	...	4 679 646	...	...
Bahrain - Bahreïn										
1 VII 2003 .... ESDJ		764 519	...	...	452 900	...	...	311 619	...	...
1 VII 2004 .... ESDJ		823 744	...	...	491 195	...	...	332 549	...	...
1 VII 2005 .... ESDJ		888 824	...	...	533 501	...	...	355 323	...	...
1 VII 2006 .... ESDJ		960 425	...	...	580 285	...	...	380 141	...	...
1 VII 2007 .... ESDJ		1 039 297	...	...	632 074	...	...	407 223	...	...
1 VII 2008 .... ESDJ		1 103 496	...	...	676 590	...	...	426 906	...	...
1 VII 2009 .... ESDJ		1 178 415	...	...	731 997	...	...	446 418	...	...
27 IV 2010 .... CDJC		1 234 571	...	...	768 414	...	...	466 157	...	...
1 VII 2010 .... ESDJ		1 228 543	...	...	764 357	...	...	464 186	...	...
1 VII 2011 .... ESDJ		1 195 020	...	...	741 483	...	...	453 537	...	...
Bangladesh										
1 VII 2003 .... ESDF		134 800 000	31 300 000	23.2	69 100 000	...	...	65 700 000	...	...
1 VII 2004 .... ESDF		136 700 000	32 400 000	23.7	70 100 000	...	...	66 600 000	...	...
1 VII 2005 .... ESDF		138 600 000	33 600 000	24.2	71 000 000	...	...	67 600 000	...	...
1 VII 2006 .... ESDF		140 600 000	34 600 000	24.6	72 000 000	...	...	68 600 000	...	...
1 VII 2007 .... ESDF		142 600 000	35 700 000	25.0	73 100 000	...	...	69 500 000	...	...
1 VII 2008 .... ESDF		144 500 000	36 700 000	25.4	74 000 000	...	...	70 500 000	...	...
1 VII 2010 .... ESDF		148 620 000	38 540 000	25.9	76 120 000	20 427 000	26.8	72 500 000	18 113 000	25.0
15 III 2011* .... CDFC		149 772 364	...	...	74 980 386	...	...	74 791 978	...	...
1 VII 2011 .... ESDF		150 611 000	39 000 000	25.9	77 101 062	20 560 587	26.7	73 509 938	18 439 413	25.1
Bhutan - Bhoutan										
1 VII 2003 .... ESDF		612 515	...	...	370 805[3]	...	...	363 535[3]	...	...
1 VII 2004 .... ESDF		623 647	...	...	380 090[3]	...	...	372 610[3]	...	...
30 V 2005 .... CDFC		634 982	196 111	30.9	333 595	105 559	31.6	301 387	90 552	30.0
1 VII 2006[49] .... ESDF		646 851	204 691	31.6	339 403	109 920	32.4	307 448	94 771	30.8
1 VII 2007[49] .... ESDF		658 888	213 571	32.4	345 298	114 593	33.2	313 590	98 978	31.6
1 VII 2008[49] .... ESDF		671 083	222 753	33.2	351 269	119 342	34.0	319 814	103 411	32.3
1 VII 2009[49] .... ESDF		683 407	232 232	34.0	357 305	124 246	34.8	326 102	107 986	33.1
1 VII 2010[49] .... ESDF		695 823	242 001	34.8	363 384	129 298	35.6	332 439	112 703	33.9
1 VII 2011[49] .... ESDF		708 265	252 038	35.6	369 476	134 484	36.4	338 789	117 554	34.7
1 VII 2012[49] .... ESDF		720 679	262 325	36.4	375 554	139 798	37.2	345 125	122 530	35.5
Brunei Darussalam - Brunéi Darussalam										
1 VII 2003 .... ESDF		349 600	...	...	182 500	...	...	167 100	...	...
1 VII 2004 .... ESDF		359 700	...	...	189 400	...	...	170 300	...	...
1 VII 2005 .... ESDF		370 100	...	...	195 300	...	...	174 800	...	...
1 VII 2006 .... ESDF		383 000	...	...	203 300	...	...	179 700	...	...
1 VII 2007 .... ESDF		390 000	...	...	206 900	...	...	183 100	...	...
1 VII 2008 .... ESDF		398 000	...	...	211 000	...	...	187 000	...	...
1 VII 2009 .... ESDF		406 200	...	...	215 000	...	...	191 200	...	...
20 VI 2011 .... CDFC		393 372	...	...	203 149	...	...	190 223	...	...
Cambodia - Cambodge[50]										
1 VII 2003[51] .... ESDF		13 287 053	...	...	6 437 037	...	...	6 850 016	...	...
1 VII 2004[52] .... SSDF		12 824 170	1 920 752	15.0	6 197 128	932 126	15.0	6 627 042	988 626	14.9
1 VII 2004[51] .... ESDF		13 542 410	...	...	6 565 556	...	...	6 976 854	...	...
1 VII 2005[51] .... ESDF		13 806 923	...	...	6 698 783	...	...	7 108 140	...	...
1 VII 2006[51] .... ESDF		14 080 653	...	...	6 836 759	...	...	7 243 894	...	...
1 VII 2007[51] .... ESDF		14 363 519	...	...	6 979 452	...	...	7 384 067	...	...
3 III 2008 .... CDFC		13 395 682	2 614 027	19.5	6 516 054	1 255 570	19.3	6 879 628	1 358 457	19.7
1 VII 2008[53] .... ESDF		13 868 227	2 707 240	19.5	6 745 592	1 299 799	19.3	7 122 635	1 407 441	19.8
1 VII 2009[53] .... ESDF		14 085 324	2 814 943	20.0	6 859 756	1 351 939	19.7	7 225 568	1 463 004	20.2
1 VII 2010[53] .... ESDF		14 302 779	2 926 810	20.5	6 973 994	1 406 183	20.2	7 328 785	1 520 627	20.7
1 VII 2011[53] .... ESDF		14 521 275	3 042 794	21.0	7 088 691	1 462 518	20.6	7 432 584	1 580 276	21.3
1 VII 2012[53] .... ESDF		14 741 414	3 165 683	21.5	7 204 166	1 520 722	21.1	7 537 248	1 644 961	21.8
China - Chine[54]										
1 VII 2003[55] .... ESDF		1 292 270 000	523 760 000[56]	40.5	665 560 000	...	...	626 710 000	...	...
1 VII 2004[55] .... ESDF		1 299 880 000	542 830 000[56]	41.8	669 760 000	...	...	630 120 000	...	...
1 VII 2005[55] .... ESDF		1 307 560 000	562 120 000[56]	43.0	673 750 000	...	...	633 810 000	...	...
1 VII 2006[55] .... ESDF		1 314 480 000	577 060 000[56]	43.9	677 280 000	...	...	637 200 000	...	...
1 VII 2007[55] .... ESDF		1 317 900 000	606 330 000[57]	46.0	680 480 000[19]	...	...	640 810 000[19]	...	...
1 VII 2008[55] .... ESDF		1 324 700 000	624 030 000[57]	47.1	683 570 000[19]	...	...	644 450 000[19]	...	...

Continent, country or area, and date / Continent, pays ou zone et date	Code[a]	Both sexes - Les deux sexes			Male - Masculin			Female - Féminin		
		Total	Urban - Urbaine		Total	Urban - Urbaine		Total	Urban - Urbaine	
			Number Nombre	Percent P.100		Number Nombre	Percent P.100		Number Nombre	Percent P.100
ASIA - ASIE										
China - Chine[54]										
1 VII 2009[55] ....ESDF		1 331 300 000	645 120 000[57]	48.5	686 470 000[19]	...	...	648 030 000[19]	...	...
1 VII 2010[55] ....ESDF		1 337 700 000	669 780 000[57]	50.1	687 480 000[19]	...	...	653 430 000[19]	...	...
1 XI 2010[58] ....CDJC		1 339 724 852	665 575 306	49.7	686 852 572	...	...	652 872 280	...	...
1 VII 2011[59] ....ESDF		1 344 100 000	691 000 000[57]	51.4	691 000 000[19]	...	...	657 000 000[19]	...	...
1 VII 2012[59] ....ESDF		1 350 695 000	701 305 000[56]	51.9	692 315 000	...	...	658 380 000	...	...
China, Hong Kong SAR - Chine, Hong Kong RAS										
1 VII 2003 ....ESDJ		6 730 800	...	...	3 259 100	...	...	3 471 700	...	...
1 VII 2004 ....ESDJ		6 783 500	...	...	3 266 800	...	...	3 516 700	...	...
1 VII 2005 ....ESDJ		6 813 200	...	...	3 264 000	...	...	3 549 200	...	...
1 VII 2006 ....ESDJ		6 857 100	...	...	3 270 100	...	...	3 587 000	...	...
14 VII 2006[60] ....CDJC		6 864 346	...	...	3 272 956	...	...	3 591 390	...	...
1 VII 2007 ....ESDJ		6 916 300	...	...	3 283 900	...	...	3 632 400	...	...
1 VII 2008 ....ESDJ		6 957 800	...	...	3 290 200	...	...	3 667 600	...	...
1 VII 2009 ....ESDJ		6 972 800	...	...	3 284 800	...	...	3 688 000	...	...
1 VII 2010 ....ESDJ		7 024 200	...	...	3 294 300	...	...	3 729 900	...	...
30 VI 2011 ....CDJC		7 071 576	...	...	3 303 015	...	...	3 768 561	...	...
1 VII 2011 ....ESDJ		7 071 600	...	...	3 303 000	...	...	3 768 600	...	...
1 VII 2012 ....ESDJ		7 154 600	...	...	3 327 300	...	...	3 827 300	...	...
China, Macao SAR - Chine, Macao RAS										
1 VII 2003 ....ESDJ		443 600	...	...	212 866	...	...	230 734	...	...
1 VII 2004 ....ESDJ		454 661	...	...	218 122	...	...	236 539	...	...
1 VII 2005 ....ESDJ		473 457	...	...	227 600	...	...	245 857	...	...
1 VII 2006 ....ESDJ		498 852	...	...	243 009	...	...	255 843	...	...
19 VIII 2006 ....CDJC		502 113	...	...	245 167	...	...	256 946	...	...
1 VII 2007 ....ESDJ		520 900	...	...	256 500	...	...	264 400	...	...
1 VII 2008 ....ESDJ		540 700	...	...	264 900	...	...	275 800	...	...
1 VII 2009 ....ESDJ		535 000	...	...	257 900[19]	...	...	277 200[19]	...	...
1 VII 2010 ....ESDJ		537 000	...	...	257 200[19]	...	...	279 700[19]	...	...
1 VII 2011 ....ESDJ		549 600	...	...	263 500	...	...	286 100	...	...
12 VIII 2011 ....CDFC		625 674	...	...	305 398	...	...	320 276	...	...
1 VII 2012 ....ESDJ		567 900	...	...	274 300	...	...	293 600	...	...
Cyprus - Chypre[61]										
1 VII 2003 ....ESDJ		717 836	...	...	352 136	...	...	365 700	...	...
1 VII 2004 ....ESDJ		727 517	...	...	356 685	...	...	370 832	...	...
1 VII 2005 ....ESDJ		738 157	...	...	361 721	...	...	376 436	...	...
1 VII 2006 ....ESDJ		750 331	...	...	367 789	...	...	382 542	...	...
1 VII 2007 ....ESDJ		766 392	...	...	375 696	...	...	390 696	...	...
1 VII 2008 ....ESDJ		785 680	...	...	384 786	...	...	400 894	...	...
1 VII 2009 ....ESDJ		807 144	...	...	394 417	...	...	412 727	...	...
1 VII 2010 ....ESDJ		827 697	...	...	403 422	...	...	424 275	...	...
1 VII 2011 ....ESDJ		848 964	...	...	413 050	...	...	435 914	...	...
1 X 2011 ....CDJC		840 407	566 191	67.4	408 780	273 065	66.8	431 627	293 126	67.9
1 I 2012*[62] ....ESDJ		862 011	...	...	418 993	...	...	443 018	...	...
Democratic People's Republic of Korea - République populaire démocratique de Corée										
1 X 2008 ....CDJC		24 052 231	...	...	11 721 838	...	...	12 330 393	...	...
Georgia - Géorgie										
1 VII 2003 ....ESDF		4 328 900	2 259 700	52.2	2 039 300	...	...	2 289 600	...	...
1 VII 2004 ....ESDF		4 318 300	2 255 000	52.2	2 034 400	...	...	2 283 900	...	...
1 VII 2005 ....ESDF		4 361 400	2 284 000	52.4	2 060 300	...	...	2 301 100	...	...
1 VII 2006 ....ESDF		4 398 000	2 309 700	52.5	2 081 700	...	...	2 316 300	...	...
1 VII 2007 ....ESDF		4 388 400	2 306 400	52.6	2 079 000	...	...	2 309 400	...	...
1 VII 2008 ....ESDF		4 383 800	2 306 500	52.6	2 079 600	...	...	2 304 200	...	...
1 VII 2009 ....ESDF		4 410 900	2 332 700	52.9	2 094 800	...	...	2 316 100	...	...
1 VII 2010 ....ESDF		4 452 800	2 360 900	53.0	2 118 100	...	...	2 334 700	...	...
1 VII 2011 ....ESDF		4 483 400	2 381 500	53.1	2 135 600	...	...	2 347 800	...	...
1 VII 2012 ....ESDF		4 490 700	...	...	2 141 300	...	...	2 349 400	...	...
India - Inde[63]										
1 VII 2003[64] ....ESDF		1 068 065 117	302 416 034	28.3	552 616 508	159 117 861	28.8	515 448 609	143 298 173	27.8
1 VII 2004[64] ....ESDF		1 084 756 558	309 506 730	28.5	561 281 181	162 846 812	29.0	523 475 376	146 659 918	28.0

Continent, country or area, and date / Continent, pays ou zone et date	Code[a]	Both sexes - Les deux sexes			Male - Masculin			Female - Féminin		
		Total	Urban - Urbaine		Total	Urban - Urbaine		Total	Urban - Urbaine	
			Number Nombre	Percent P.100		Number Nombre	Percent P.100		Number Nombre	Percent P.100
ASIA - ASIE										
India - Inde[63]										
1 VII 2005[64] ....ESDF		1 101 317 709	316 648 000	28.8	569 882 367	166 604 533	29.2	531 435 342	150 043 467	28.2
1 VII 2006[64] ....ESDF		1 117 733 826	323 827 490	29.0	578 411 677	170 384 885	29.5	539 322 149	153 442 605	28.5
1 VII 2007[64] ....ESDF		1 134 023 232	331 060 644	29.2	586 879 523	174 195 527	29.7	547 143 709	156 865 117	28.7
1 VII 2008[64] ....ESDF		1 150 196 000	338 356 000	29.4	595 291 000	178 041 000	29.9	554 905 000	160 315 000	28.9
9 II 2011* ....CDFC		1 210 193 422	...	...	623 724 248	...	...	586 469 174	...	...
1 VII 2011*[64] ....ESDF		1 192 503 000	...	...	617 315 000	...	...	575 188 000	...	...
Indonesia - Indonésie										
1 VII 2003 ....ESDJ		214 467 613	...	...	107 550 230	...	...	106 917 383	...	...
1 VII 2004 ....ESDJ		217 672 800	...	...	109 157 552	...	...	108 515 248	...	...
1 VII 2005 ....ESDJ		220 925 888	...	...	110 788 896	...	...	110 136 992	...	...
31 X 2005[65] ....SSDF		213 375 287	92 005 069	43.1	107 274 528	46 055 993	42.9	106 100 759	45 949 076	43.3
1 VII 2006 ....ESDJ		224 227 593	...	...	112 444 620	...	...	111 782 973	...	...
1 VII 2007 ....ESDJ		227 578 641	...	...	114 125 088	...	...	113 453 553	...	...
1 VII 2008 ....ESDJ		230 979 770	...	...	115 830 670	...	...	115 149 100	...	...
1 VII 2009 ....ESDJ		234 431 729	...	...	117 561 743	...	...	116 869 986	...	...
1 V 2010 ....CDJC		237 641 326	118 320 256	49.8	119 630 913	59 559 622	49.8	118 010 413	58 760 634	49.8
1 VII 2011 ....ESDJ		236 954 100	...	...	118 591 100	...	...	118 363 000	...	...
Iran (Islamic Republic of) - Iran (République islamique d')										
1 VII 2003[66] ....ESDJ		67 314 814	44 834 988	66.6	34 233 497	22 849 043	66.7	33 081 317	21 985 945	66.5
1 VII 2004[66] ....ESDJ		68 344 730	45 966 432	67.3	34 761 738	23 419 649	67.4	33 582 992	22 546 783	67.1
1 VII 2005[66] ....ESDJ		69 390 405	47 095 882	67.9	35 298 812	23 989 204	68.0	34 091 593	23 106 678	67.8
28 X 2006 ....CDJC		70 495 782	48 259 964[67]	68.5	35 866 362	24 576 442[67]	68.5	34 629 420	23 683 522[67]	68.4
1 VII 2007[66] ....ESDJ		71 278 952	48 874 656	68.6	36 247 296	24 891 876	68.7	35 031 392	23 982 780	68.5
1 VII 2008[66] ....ESDJ		72 181 632	49 576 146	68.7	36 691 780	25 253 132	68.8	35 489 488	24 323 014	68.5
1 VII 2009[66] ....ESDJ		73 202 096	50 365 184	68.8	37 198 776	25 660 500	69.0	36 003 320	24 704 684	68.6
1 VII 2010[66] ....ESDJ		74 339 576	51 242 546	68.9	37 767 220	26 114 342	69.1	36 572 356	25 128 204	68.7
1 VII 2011[66] ....ESDJ		75 590 952	52 208 496	69.1	38 395 536	26 614 762	69.3	37 195 416	25 593 734	68.8
24 X 2011 ....CDJC		75 149 669	53 646 661	71.4	37 905 669	27 023 638	71.3	37 244 000	26 623 023	71.5
1 VII 2012[66] ....ESDJ		76 725 160	53 085 228	69.2	38 959 784[68]	27 066 664[68]	69.5	37 765 226[68]	26 018 414[68]	68.9
Iraq										
1 VII 2003 ....ESDF		26 340 000	...	...	13 216 000	...	...	13 124 000	...	...
1 VII 2004 ....ESDF		27 139 000	...	...	13 629 000	...	...	13 510 000	...	...
1 VII 2005 ....ESDF		27 963 000	...	...	14 055 000	...	...	13 908 000	...	...
1 VII 2006 ....ESDF		28 810 441	19 226 476	66.7	14 493 207	9 698 293	66.9	14 317 234	9 528 183	66.6
1 VII 2007 ....ESDF		29 682 081	19 752 833	66.5	14 943 516	9 970 074	66.7	14 738 565	9 782 759	66.4
1 VII 2008 ....ESDF		31 895 000	...	...	16 058 000	...	...	15 837 000	...	...
1 VII 2009 ....ESDF		32 105 000	...	...	15 942 000	...	...	16 163 000	...	...
Israel - Israël[69]										
1 VII 2003 ....ESDJ		6 689 700	6 122 400	91.5	3 301 800	3 010 900	91.2	3 387 900	3 111 600	91.8
1 VII 2004 ....ESDJ		6 809 000	6 226 900	91.5	3 362 000	3 063 600	91.1	3 447 000	3 163 300	91.8
1 VII 2005 ....ESDJ		6 930 128	6 359 940	91.8	3 423 132	3 131 229	91.5	3 506 996	3 228 711	92.1
1 VII 2006 ....ESDJ		7 053 707	6 475 600[70]	91.8	3 485 501	3 189 511[70]	91.5	3 568 206	3 286 089[70]	92.1
1 VII 2007 ....ESDJ		7 180 115	6 589 632[70]	91.8	3 549 216	3 247 280[70]	91.5	3 630 899	3 342 352[70]	92.1
1 VII 2008 ....ESDJ		7 308 795	6 701 217[70]	91.7	3 614 125	3 303 732[70]	91.4	3 694 671	3 397 485[70]	92.0
27 XII 2008[71] ....CDFC		7 412 180	6 799 340[19]	91.7	3 663 910	3 350 610[19]	91.4	3 748 270	3 448 730[19]	92.0
1 VII 2009 ....ESDJ		7 485 565	6 865 023	91.7	3 701 384	3 384 556	91.4	3 784 181	3 480 467	92.0
1 VII 2010 ....ESDJ		7 623 561	6 987 218	91.7	3 771 321	3 446 830	91.4	3 852 240	3 540 388	91.9
1 VII 2011 ....ESDJ		7 765 832	7 109 718	91.6	3 841 121	3 506 773	91.3	3 924 711	3 602 945	91.8
Japan - Japon[72]										
1 VII 2003 ....ESDJ		127 718 000	...	...	62 370 000	...	...	65 348 000	...	...
1 VII 2004 ....ESDJ		127 761 000	...	...	62 355 000	...	...	65 406 000	...	...
1 VII 2005 ....ESDJ		127 773 000	...	...	62 332 000	...	...	65 441 000	...	...
1 X 2005 ....CDJC		127 767 994	110 264 324	86.3	62 348 977	53 886 000	86.4	65 419 017	56 378 324	86.2
1 VII 2006[73] ....ESDJ		127 854 000	...	...	62 357 000	...	...	65 497 000	...	...
1 VII 2007[73] ....ESDJ		128 001 000	...	...	62 401 000[19]	...	...	65 599 000[19]	...	...
1 VII 2008[73] ....ESDJ		128 063 000	...	...	62 409 000	...	...	65 654 000	...	...
1 VII 2009[73] ....ESDJ		128 047 000	...	...	62 354 000	...	...	65 693 000	...	...
1 VII 2010[73] ....ESDJ		128 070 000	...	...	62 330 000	...	...	65 740 000	...	...
1 X 2010 ....CDJC		128 057 352	116 156 631	90.7	62 327 737	56 569 051	90.8	65 729 615	59 587 580	90.7
1 VII 2011[73] ....ESDJ		127 817 000	...	...	62 189 000	...	...	65 628 000	...	...
1 VII 2012[73] ....ESDJ		127 561 000	...	...	62 041 000	...	...	65 520 000	...	...

Continent, country or area, and date / Continent, pays ou zone et date	Code[a]	Both sexes - Les deux sexes			Male - Masculin			Female - Féminin		
		Total	Urban - Urbaine		Total	Urban - Urbaine		Total	Urban - Urbaine	
			Number Nombre	Percent P.100		Number Nombre	Percent P.100		Number Nombre	Percent P.100
ASIA - ASIE										
Jordan - Jordanie										
31 XII 2003[74] ....ESDF		5 230 000	4 320 600	82.6	2 693 500	...	...	2 536 500	...	...
1 X 2004[75] ....CDFC		5 103 639	3 997 383	78.3	2 626 287	2 055 431	78.3	2 477 352	1 941 952	78.4
31 XII 2004[74] ....ESDF		5 350 000	4 419 000	82.6	2 757 700	...	...	2 592 300	...	...
31 XII 2005[74] ....ESDF		5 473 000	4 520 600	82.6	2 821 100	...	...	2 651 900	...	...
31 XII 2006[74] ....ESDF		5 600 000	4 625 600	82.6	2 886 600	...	...	2 713 400	...	...
31 XII 2007[74] ....ESDF		5 723 000	4 727 100	82.6	2 950 000	...	...	2 773 000	...	...
31 XII 2008[74] ....ESDF		5 850 000	4 832 100	82.6	3 015 000	...	...	2 835 000	...	...
31 XII 2009[74] ....ESDF		5 980 000	4 939 400	82.6	3 082 000	...	...	2 898 000	...	...
31 XII 2010[74] ....ESDF		6 113 000	5 049 300	82.6	3 151 000	...	...	2 962 000	...	...
31 XII 2011[74] ....ESDF		6 249 000	5 161 600	82.6	3 221 100	...	...	3 027 900	...	...
31 XII 2012[74] ....ESDF		6 388 000	5 276 400	82.6	3 293 000	...	...	3 095 000	...	...
Kazakhstan										
1 VII 2003 ....ESDF		14 909 018	8 487 697	56.9	7 179 583	3 971 520	55.3	7 729 435	4 516 177	58.4
1 VII 2004 ....ESDF		15 012 985	8 566 447	57.1	7 227 960	4 005 199	55.4	7 785 025	4 561 248	58.6
1 VII 2005 ....ESDF		15 147 029	8 655 586	57.1	7 290 852	4 044 092	55.5	7 856 177	4 611 494	58.7
1 VII 2006 ....ESDF		15 308 084	8 764 884	57.3	7 367 032	4 094 572	55.6	7 941 052	4 670 312	58.8
1 VII 2007 ....ESDF		15 484 192	8 195 389	52.9	7 450 418	3 815 422	51.2	8 033 774	4 379 967	54.5
1 VII 2008 ....ESDF		15 674 000	8 331 030	53.2	7 541 053	3 877 559	51.4	8 132 947	4 453 471	54.8
25 II 2009 ....CDFC		16 009 597	8 662 432	54.1	7 712 224	4 055 341	52.6	8 297 373	4 607 091	55.5
Kuwait - Koweït										
1 VII 2003 ....ESDF		2 093 396	...	...	1 232 781	...	...	860 615	...	...
1 VII 2004 ....ESDF		2 167 467	...	...	1 278 865	...	...	888 602	...	...
20 IV 2005 ....CDFC		2 193 651	...	...	1 300 347	...	...	893 304	...	...
1 VII 2005 ....ESDF		2 244 995	...	...	1 326 871	...	...	918 124	...	...
1 VII 2006 ....ESDF		2 328 116	...	...	1 378 341	...	...	949 775	...	...
1 VII 2007 ....ESDF		2 410 829	...	...	1 430 584	...	...	980 245	...	...
1 VII 2008 ....ESDF		2 495 851	...	...	1 484 422	...	...	1 011 429	...	...
1 VII 2009 ....ESDF		2 777 861	...	...	1 597 843	...	...	1 180 018	...	...
1 VII 2010 ....ESDF		2 933 268	...	...	1 674 156	...	...	1 259 112	...	...
20 IV 2011* ....CDFC		3 065 850	...	...	1 738 372	...	...	1 327 478	...	...
1 VII 2011[76] ....ESDF		3 098 892	...	...	1 754 248	...	...	1 344 644	...	...
Kyrgyzstan - Kirghizstan										
1 VII 2003[77] ....ESDF		4 943 770	1 749 780	35.4	2 426 226	827 820	34.1	2 517 544	921 960	36.6
1 VII 2004[77] ....ESDF		4 976 881	1 773 667	35.6	2 439 845	836 840	34.3	2 537 036	936 827	36.9
1 VII 2005[77] ....ESDF		5 006 514	1 788 181	35.7	2 450 975	841 960	34.4	2 555 539	946 221	37.0
1 VII 2006[77] ....ESDF		5 033 953	1 790 295	35.6	2 460 578	841 414	34.2	2 573 375	948 881	36.9
1 VII 2007[77] ....ESDF		5 055 671	1 791 267	35.4	2 467 458	839 913	34.0	2 588 213	951 354	36.8
1 VII 2008[77] ....ESDF		5 077 722	1 794 620	35.3	2 475 331	839 873	33.9	2 602 391	954 747	36.7
24 III 2009 ....CDJC		5 362 793	1 827 136	34.1	2 645 921	863 002	32.6	2 716 872	964 134	35.5
1 VII 2009[77] ....ESDF		5 128 124	1 809 738	35.3	2 499 977	846 861	33.9	2 628 147	962 877	36.6
1 VII 2010[77] ....ESDF		5 192 806	1 828 955	35.2	2 532 547	856 262	33.8	2 660 259	972 693	36.6
1 VII 2011[77] ....ESDF		5 259 601	1 847 757	35.1	2 566 031	865 260	33.7	2 693 570	982 497	36.5
1 VII 2012[77] ....ESDF		5 352 358	1 856 305	34.7	2 613 586	869 564	33.3	2 738 772	986 741	36.0
Lao People's Democratic Republic - République démocratique populaire lao										
1 VII 2003[78] ....ESDF		5 679 000	...	...	2 807 000	...	...	2 872 000	...	...
1 VII 2004[78] ....ESDF		5 836 000	...	...	2 884 000	...	...	2 952 000	...	...
1 III 2005 ....CDJC		5 621 982	1 522 137[79]	27.1	2 800 551	763 043[79]	27.2	2 821 431	759 094[79]	26.9
1 VII 2005[80] ....ESDF		5 651 497	...	...	2 815 254	...	...	2 836 244	...	...
1 VII 2006[80] ....ESDF		5 777 797	...	...	2 879 511	...	...	2 898 285	...	...
1 VII 2007[80] ....ESDF		5 904 453	...	...	2 943 941	...	...	2 960 512	...	...
1 VII 2008[80] ....ESDF		6 031 881	...	...	3 008 754	...	...	3 023 128	...	...
1 VII 2009[80] ....ESDF		6 160 083	...	...	3 073 951	...	...	3 086 131	...	...
1 VII 2010[80] ....ESDF		6 289 042	...	...	3 139 533	...	...	3 149 508	...	...
1 VII 2011[80] ....ESDF		6 418 577	...	...	3 205 405	...	...	3 213 173	...	...
1 VII 2012[80] ....ESDF		6 548 633	...	...	3 271 538	...	...	3 277 095	...	...
Lebanon - Liban[81]										
3 III 2004 ....SSDF		3 755 034	...	...	1 868 322	...	...	1 886 712	...	...
3 III 2007 ....SSDF		3 759 134	...	...	1 857 659	...	...	1 901 475	...	...
Malaysia - Malaisie										
1 VII 2003[82] ....ESDJ		25 038 075	...	...	12 808 230	...	...	12 229 845	...	...
1 VII 2004[82] ....ESDJ		25 541 494	...	...	13 078 746	...	...	12 462 748	...	...

Continent, country or area, and date / Continent, pays ou zone et date	Code[a]	Both sexes - Les deux sexes			Male - Masculin			Female - Féminin		
		Total	Urban - Urbaine		Total	Urban - Urbaine		Total	Urban - Urbaine	
			Number Nombre	Percent P.100		Number Nombre	Percent P.100		Number Nombre	Percent P.100

ASIA - ASIE

Malaysia - Malaisie

1 VII 2005[82] .... ESDJ		26 045 529	...	...	13 353 253	...	...	12 692 276	...	...
1 VII 2006[82] .... ESDJ		26 549 855	...	...	13 627 408	...	...	12 922 447	...	...
1 VII 2007[82] .... ESDJ		27 058 427	...	...	13 903 701	...	...	13 154 726	...	...
1 VII 2008[82] .... ESDJ		27 567 636	...	...	14 179 116	...	...	13 388 520	...	...
1 VII 2009[82] .... ESDJ		28 081 496	...	...	14 456 939	...	...	13 624 557	...	...
1 VII 2010[83] .... ESDJ		28 588 637	...	...	14 730 542	...	...	13 858 095	...	...
6 VII 2010[84] .... CDJC		28 334 135	20 124 970	71.0	14 562 638	10 298 698	70.7	13 771 497	9 826 272	71.4
1 VII 2011[83] .... ESDJ		28 964 292	...	...	14 912 034	...	...	14 052 258	...	...
1 VII 2012[83] .... ESDJ		29 336 795	...	...	15 093 673	...	...	14 243 122	...	...

Maldives

1 VII 2003 .... ESDF		285 066	78 173	27.4	144 599	...	...	140 467	...	...
1 VII 2004 .... ESDF		289 480	79 383	27.4	146 799	...	...	142 681	...	...
1 VII 2005 .... ESDF		293 746	...	...	148 929	...	...	144 817	...	...
21 III 2006[85] .... CDFC		298 968	103 693	34.7	151 459	51 992	34.3	147 509	51 701	35.0
1 VII 2007 .... ESDF		304 869	...	...	154 391	...	...	150 478	...	...
1 VII 2008 .... ESDF		309 575	...	...	156 714	...	...	152 861	...	...
1 VII 2009 .... ESDF		314 542	...	...	159 159	...	...	155 383	...	...
1 VII 2010 .... ESDF		319 738	...	...	161 708	...	...	158 030	...	...
1 VII 2011 .... ESDF		325 135	...	...	164 349	...	...	160 786	...	...
1 VII 2012 .... ESDF		330 655	...	...	167 058	...	...	163 597	...	...

Mongolia - Mongolie

1 VII 2003 .... ESDF		2 489 702	1 442 589	57.9	1 235 164	705 367	57.1	1 254 538	737 222	58.8
1 VII 2004 .... ESDF		2 518 573	1 481 205	58.8	1 249 487	723 856	57.9	1 269 086	757 349	59.7
1 VII 2005 .... ESDF		2 547 751	1 520 763	59.7	1 263 962	741 689	58.7	1 283 789	779 074	60.7
1 VII 2006 .... ESDF		2 578 587	1 561 417	60.6	1 268 249	756 004	59.6	1 310 338	805 413	61.5
1 VII 2007 .... ESDF		2 614 981	1 590 253	60.8	1 274 852	764 608	60.0	1 340 128	825 645	61.6
1 VII 2008 .... ESDF		2 659 347	1 630 116	61.3	1 297 153	784 189	60.5	1 362 194	845 927	62.1
1 VII 2009 .... ESDF		2 709 652	1 686 266	62.2	1 323 779	811 966	61.3	1 385 874	874 300	63.1
1 VII 2010 .... ESDF		2 758 269	1 736 861	63.0	1 344 689	831 770	61.9	1 413 580	905 091	64.0
11 XI 2010 .... CDFC		2 647 199	1 797 338	67.9	1 314 246	869 827	66.2	1 332 953	927 511	69.6

Myanmar

1 X 2003 .... ESDF		53 224 361	15 964 481	30.0	26 467 378	7 799 035	29.5	26 756 983	8 165 446	30.5
1 X 2004 .... ESDF		54 299 493	16 416 487	30.2	27 000 086	8 016 044	29.7	27 299 407	8 400 443	30.8
1 X 2005 .... ESDF		55 396 343	16 828 570	30.4	27 539 748	8 195 258	29.8	27 856 595	8 633 312	31.0
1 X 2006 .... ESDF		56 515 349	17 239 318	30.5	28 096 895	8 425 026	30.0	28 418 454	8 814 292	31.0
1 X 2007 .... ESDF		57 504 368	17 567 506	30.5	28 585 910	8 582 809	30.0	28 918 458	8 984 697	31.1
1 X 2008 .... ESDF		58 376 839	17 894 194	30.7	29 025 480	8 798 657	30.3	29 351 359	9 095 537	31.0
1 X 2009 .... ESDF		59 129 900	18 133 654	30.7	29 399 744	8 888 838	30.2	29 730 156	9 244 816	31.1
1 X 2010 .... ESDF		59 780 329	18 342 824	30.7	29 723 184	8 992 226	30.3	30 057 145	9 350 598	31.1
1 X 2011 .... ESDF		60 384 144	18 572 481	30.8	29 846 846	9 186 385	30.8	30 537 298	9 386 096	30.7
1 X 2012 .... ESDF		60 975 993	18 754 944	30.8	30 139 447	9 276 256	30.8	30 836 546	9 478 688	30.7

Nepal - Népal

1 VII 2003 .... ESDJ		24 249 996	...	...	12 126 262	...	...	12 123 734	...	...
1 VII 2004 .... ESDJ		24 797 059	...	...	12 406 222	...	...	12 390 837	...	...
1 VII 2005 .... ESDJ		25 342 638	...	...	12 685 375	...	...	12 657 263	...	...
1 VII 2006 .... ESDJ		25 886 736	...	...	12 963 722	...	...	12 923 014	...	...
1 VII 2007 .... ESDJ		26 427 399	...	...	13 240 233	...	...	13 187 166	...	...
1 VII 2008 .... ESDJ		26 966 581	...	...	13 515 938	...	...	13 450 643	...	...
1 VII 2009 .... ESDJ		27 504 280	...	...	13 790 836	...	...	13 713 444	...	...
1 VII 2010 .... ESDJ		28 043 744	...	...	14 066 638	...	...	13 977 106	...	...
22 VI 2011 .... CDJC		26 494 504	4 523 820	17.1	12 849 041	2 306 049	17.9	13 645 463	2 217 771	16.3
1 VII 2011 .... ESDJ		28 584 975	...	...	14 343 343	...	...	14 241 632	...	...
1 VII 2012 .... ESDJ		29 128 517	...	...	14 621 285	...	...	14 507 232	...	...

Oman

7 XII 2003 .... CDFC		2 340 815[86]	1 673 480	71.5	1 313 239	950 471	72.4	1 027 576	723 009	70.4
1 VII 2004 .... ESDF		2 415 576	1 732 701	71.7	1 360 891	988 163	72.6	1 054 685	744 538	70.6
1 VII 2005 .... ESDF		2 508 837	1 804 995	71.9	1 458 845	1 063 202	72.9	1 049 992	741 793	70.6
1 VII 2006 .... ESDF		2 577 062	1 857 263	72.1	1 498 143	1 093 546	73.0	1 078 919	763 717	70.8
1 VII 2007 .... ESDF		2 743 499	1 984 158	72.3	1 622 119	1 188 537	73.3	1 121 380	795 621	71.0
1 VII 2008 .... ESDF		2 867 428	2 077 862	72.5	1 687 414	1 238 527	73.4	1 180 014	839 335	71.1
1 VII 2009 .... ESDF		3 173 917	2 314 865	72.9	1 971 115	1 457 197	73.9	1 202 802	857 668	71.3
12 XII 2010 .... CDFC		2 773 479	2 091 320	75.4	1 612 408	1 227 680	76.1	1 161 071	863 640	74.4
1 VII 2011 .... ESDF		3 295 298	...	...	2 090 883	...	...	1 204 415	...	...

Continent, country or area, and date / Continent, pays ou zone et date	Code[a]	Both sexes - Les deux sexes Total	Urban - Urbaine Number Nombre	Urban - Urbaine Percent P.100	Male - Masculin Total	Urban - Urbaine Number Nombre	Urban - Urbaine Percent P.100	Female - Féminin Total	Urban - Urbaine Number Nombre	Urban - Urbaine Percent P.100
ASIA - ASIE										
Pakistan[87]										
1 VII 2003[88]	ESDJ	138 979 270	49 640 104	35.7	71 741 403	25 819 279	36.0	67 237 867	23 820 825	35.4
1 VII 2004	ESDF	151 090 000	50 800 000	33.6	78 410 000	...	...	72 690 000	...	...
1 VII 2005[89]	ESDJ	144 367 293	51 408 193	35.6	74 247 400	26 556 848	35.8	70 119 893	24 851 345	35.4
1 VII 2006	ESDJ	147 099 534	...	...	75 582 494	...	...	71 517 040	...	...
1 VII 2007[90]	ESDJ	149 860 388	52 807 585	35.2	76 857 737	27 178 203	35.4	73 002 651	25 629 382	35.1
1 VII 2008	ESDF	166 410 000	...	...	86 130 000	...	...	80 280 000	...	...
1 VII 2009	ESDF	169 940 000	...	...	87 940 000	...	...	82 010 000	...	...
1 VII 2010	ESDF	173 510 000	...	...	89 760 000	...	...	83 750 000	...	...
1 VII 2011	ESDF	177 100 000	...	...	91 590 000	...	...	85 510 000	...	...
Philippines										
1 VII 2003[30]	ESDJ	81 877 700	...	...	41 200 600	...	...	40 677 100		
1 VII 2004[30]	ESDJ	83 558 700	...	...	42 037 200	...	...	41 521 500		
1 VII 2005[30]	ESDJ	85 261 000	...	...	42 887 300	...	...	42 373 700		
1 VII 2006[30]	ESDJ	86 972 500	...	...	43 742 100	...	...	43 230 400		
1 VII 2007[30]	ESDJ	88 706 300	...	...	44 608 300	...	...	44 098 000		
1 VII 2008[30]	ESDJ	90 457 200	...	...	45 483 100	...	...	44 974 100		
1 VII 2009[30]	ESDJ	92 226 600	...	...	46 368 900	...	...	45 857 700		
1 V 2010[91]	CDJC	92 335 113	...	...	46 634 257	...	...	45 700 856		
1 VII 2010[30]	ESDJ	94 013 200	...	...	47 263 600	...	...	46 749 600		
Qatar										
1 VII 2003	ESDF	713 858	...	...	476 508	...	...	237 350		
16 III 2004	CDFC	744 029	...	...	496 382	...	...	247 647		
1 VII 2004	ESDF	798 059	...	...	546 116	...	...	251 943		
1 VII 2005	ESDF	906 123	...	...	637 070	...	...	269 053		
1 VII 2006	ESDF	1 042 947	...	...	754 298	...	...	288 649		
1 VII 2007	ESDF	1 218 250	...	...	905 747	...	...	312 503		
1 VII 2008	ESDF	1 448 479	...	...	1 111 176	...	...	337 303		
1 VII 2009	ESDF	1 638 626	...	...	1 265 146	...	...	373 480		
21 IV 2010	CDFC	1 699 435	...	...	1 284 739	...	...	414 696		
1 VII 2010	ESDF	1 715 010	...	...	1 296 107	...	...	418 903		
1 VII 2011	ESDF	1 732 717	...	...	1 288 590	...	...	444 127		
Republic of Korea - République de Corée										
1 VII 2003	ESDJ	47 859 311	...	...	24 089 703	...	...	23 769 608	...	...
1 VII 2004	ESDJ	48 039 415	...	...	24 165 488	...	...	23 873 927	...	...
1 VII 2005	ESDJ	48 138 077	...	...	24 190 906	...	...	23 947 171	...	...
1 XI 2005[79]	CDJC	47 278 951	38 514 753	81.5	23 623 954	19 258 840	81.5	23 654 997	19 255 913	81.4
1 VII 2006	ESDJ	48 371 946	...	...	24 302 796	...	...	24 069 150	...	...
1 VII 2007	ESDJ	48 597 652	...	...	24 410 110	...	...	24 187 542	...	...
1 VII 2008	ESDJ	48 948 698	...	...	24 576 155	...	...	24 372 543	...	...
1 VII 2009	ESDJ	49 182 038	...	...	24 664 502	...	...	24 517 536	...	...
1 VII 2010	ESDJ	49 410 366	...	...	24 757 776	...	...	24 652 590	...	...
1 XI 2010[79]	CDJC	48 580 293	39 822 647	82.0	24 167 098	19 798 739	81.9	24 413 195	20 023 908	82.0
1 VII 2011	ESDJ	50 111 476	40 655 913	81.1	25 081 788	20 287 967	80.9	25 029 688	20 367 947	81.4
1 VII 2012	ESDJ	50 345 325	40 892 751	81.2	25 187 494	20 394 084	81.0	25 157 831	20 498 667	81.5
Saudi Arabia - Arabie saoudite										
1 VII 2003	ESDF	22 022 864	...	...	12 206 825	...	...	9 816 039	...	...
1 VII 2004	ESDF	22 563 886	...	...	12 493 910	...	...	10 069 976	...	...
15 IX 2004	CDFC	22 678 262	...	...	12 557 240	...	...	10 121 022	...	...
1 VII 2005*[92]	ESDF	23 329 584	...	...	12 959 625	...	...	10 369 959	...	...
1 VII 2006*[92]	ESDF	24 121 890	...	...	13 444 010	...	...	10 677 880	...	...
1 VII 2007*[92]	ESDF	24 941 298	...	...	13 947 610	...	...	10 993 688	...	...
1 VII 2008*[92]	ESDF	25 787 025	...	...	14 470 381	...	...	11 316 644	...	...
1 VII 2009*[92]	ESDF	26 660 857	...	...	15 013 600	...	...	11 647 257	...	...
28 IV 2010*	CDFC	27 136 977	...	...	15 306 793	...	...	11 830 184	...	...
1 VII 2010*[92]	ESDF	27 563 432	...	...	15 578 015	...	...	11 985 417	...	...
1 VII 2011*[92]	ESDF	28 376 355	...	...	16 041 361	...	...	12 334 994	...	...
1 VII 2012*[92]	ESDF	29 195 895	...	...	16 543 836	...	...	12 652 059	...	...
Singapore - Singapour[93]										
30 VI 2003	ESDJ	3 366 900	...	...	1 673 400	...	...	1 693 500	...	...
30 VI 2004	ESDJ	3 413 300	...	...	1 695 000[19]	...	...	1 718 200[19]	...	...
30 VI 2005	ESDJ	3 467 814	...	...	1 721 139	...	...	1 746 675	...	...
30 VI 2006	ESDJ	3 525 900	...	...	1 748 200	...	...	1 777 700	...	...

Continent, country or area, and date / Continent, pays ou zone et date	Code[a]	Both sexes - Les deux sexes Total	Urban - Urbaine Number Nombre	Urban - Urbaine Percent P.100	Male - Masculin Total	Urban - Urbaine Number Nombre	Urban - Urbaine Percent P.100	Female - Féminin Total	Urban - Urbaine Number Nombre	Urban - Urbaine Percent P.100
ASIA - ASIE										
Singapore - Singapour[93]										
30 VI 2007	ESDJ	3 583 100	...	...	1 775 500	...	...	1 807 600	...	...
30 VI 2008	ESDJ	3 642 700	...	...	1 803 000	...	...	1 839 700	...	...
30 VI 2009	ESDJ	3 733 900	...	...	1 844 700[19]	...	...	1 889 100[19]	...	...
30 VI 2010[94]	CDJC	3 771 721	...	...	1 861 133	...	...	1 910 588	...	...
30 VI 2010	ESDJ	3 771 721	...	...	1 861 133	...	...	1 910 588	...	...
30 VI 2011	ESDJ	3 789 300	...	...	1 868 200	...	...	1 921 100	...	...
30 VI 2012	ESDJ	3 818 200	...	...	1 880 000	...	...	1 938 200	...	...
Sri Lanka										
1 VII 2003	ESDF	19 252 000	...	...	9 510 000	...	...	9 742 000	...	...
1 VII 2004	ESDF	19 435 000	...	...	9 678 000	...	...	9 757 000	...	...
1 VII 2005	ESDF	19 644 000	...	...	9 782 000	...	...	9 862 000	...	...
1 VII 2006	ESDF	19 858 000	...	...	9 889 000	...	...	9 969 000	...	...
1 VII 2007	ESDF	20 039 000	...	...	9 956 000	...	...	10 083 000	...	...
1 VII 2008	ESDF	20 216 000	...	...	9 980 000	...	...	10 236 000	...	...
1 VII 2009*	ESDF	20 450 000	...	...	10 148 000	...	...	10 302 000	...	...
1 VII 2010*	ESDF	20 653 000	...	...	10 249 000	...	...	10 404 000	...	...
1 VII 2011*	ESDF	20 869 000	...	...	10 357 000	...	...	10 512 000	...	...
27 II 2012	CDJC	20 263 723	...	...	9 832 401	...	...	10 431 322	...	...
1 VII 2012*	ESDF	20 328 000	...	...	9 864 000	...	...	10 464 000	...	...
State of Palestine - État de Palestine										
1 VII 2003	ESDF	3 314 509	2 369 874[95]	71.5	1 682 238	...	...	1 632 271	...	...
1 VII 2004	ESDF	3 407 417	2 436 303[95]	71.5	1 729 392	...	...	1 678 025	...	...
1 VII 2005	ESDF	3 508 126	2 508 310[95]	71.5	1 780 506	...	...	1 727 620	...	...
1 VII 2006	ESDF	3 611 998	2 582 579[95]	71.5	1 833 225	...	...	1 778 773	...	...
1 VII 2007	ESDF	3 719 189	3 086 102[95]	83.0	1 887 628	...	...	1 831 561	...	...
1 XII 2007*[96]	CDFC	3 761 646	...	...	1 908 432	...	...	1 853 214	...	...
1 VII 2008	ESDF	3 825 512	3 175 546[95]	83.0	1 941 742	...	...	1 883 770	...	...
1 VII 2009	ESDF	3 935 249	3 267 977[95]	83.0	1 997 625	...	...	1 937 624	...	...
1 VII 2010	ESDF	4 048 403	3 363 385[95]	83.1	2 055 211	...	...	1 993 192	...	...
1 VII 2011	ESDF	4 168 860	3 465 483[95]	83.1	2 116 782	...	...	2 052 078	...	...
1 VII 2012	ESDF	4 293 313	3 571 037[95]	83.2	2 180 386	...	...	2 112 927	...	...
Syrian Arab Republic - République arabe syrienne[97]										
1 VII 2003	ESDF	17 550 000	8 806 000	50.2	8 979 000	4 541 000	50.6	8 571 000	4 265 000	49.8
1 VII 2004	ESDF	17 829 000	9 539 000	53.5	9 150 000	4 916 000	53.7	8 679 000	4 623 000	53.3
22 IX 2004*	CDFC	17 921 000	...	...	9 161 000	...	...	8 760 000	...	...
1 VII 2005	ESDF	18 138 000	9 705 000	53.5	9 268 000	4 977 000	53.7	8 870 000	4 728 000	53.3
1 VII 2006	ESDF	18 717 000	10 013 000	53.5	9 563 000	5 139 000	53.7	9 154 000	4 874 000	53.2
1 VII 2007	ESDF	19 172 000	10 257 000	53.5	9 798 000	5 265 000	53.7	9 374 000	4 992 000	53.3
1 VII 2008	ESDF	19 644 000	10 511 000	53.5	10 042 000	5 394 000	53.7	9 602 000	5 117 000	53.3
1 VII 2009	ESDF	20 125 000	10 769 000	53.5	10 287 000	5 526 000	53.7	9 838 000	5 243 000	53.3
1 VII 2010	ESDF	20 619 000	11 033 000	53.5	10 539 000	5 661 000	53.7	10 080 000	5 372 000	53.3
1 VII 2011	ESDF	21 124 000	11 297 000	53.5	10 794 000	5 795 000	53.7	10 330 000	5 502 000	53.3
Tajikistan - Tadjikistan										
1 VII 2003	ESDF	6 573 224	1 738 838	26.5	3 296 211	868 890	26.4	3 277 013	869 948	26.5
1 VII 2004	ESDF	6 710 161	1 774 799	26.4	3 365 832	888 087	26.4	3 344 329	886 712	26.5
1 VII 2005	ESDF	6 850 324	1 808 339	26.4	3 436 922	906 229	26.4	3 413 402	902 110	26.4
1 VII 2006	ESDF	6 992 066	1 841 258	26.3	3 508 345	923 963	26.3	3 483 721	917 295	26.3
1 VII 2007	ESDF	7 139 772	1 877 203	26.3	3 581 930	943 032	26.3	3 557 842	934 171	26.3
1 VII 2008	ESDF	7 294 747	1 918 996	26.3	3 659 238	965 220	26.4	3 635 510	953 776	26.2
1 VII 2009	ESDF	7 334 083	1 944 038	26.5	3 699 641	979 510	26.5	3 634 442	964 528	26.5
1 VII 2010	ESDF	7 519 280	1 996 961	26.6	3 794 467	1 007 796	26.6	3 724 813	989 165	26.6
21 IX 2010	CDFC	7 564 502	...	...	3 817 004	...	...	3 747 498	...	...
1 VII 2011	ESDF	7 714 198	2 042 660	26.5	3 893 798	1 032 106	26.5	3 820 401	1 010 554	26.5
Thailand - Thaïlande										
1 VII 2003[1]	ESDJ	64 018 857	20 990 626	32.8	31 883 154	10 188 273	32.0	32 135 703	10 802 353	33.6
1 VII 2004[1]	ESDJ	64 177 484	19 300 414	30.1	31 574 765	9 261 252	29.3	32 602 719	10 039 162	30.8
1 VII 2005[1]	ESDJ	64 838 628	19 538 420	30.1	31 848 905	9 360 642	29.4	32 989 723	10 177 778	30.9
1 VII 2006[1]	ESDJ	65 305 736	19 792 296	30.3	32 060 034	9 474 510	29.6	33 245 702	10 317 786	31.0
1 VII 2007[1]	ESDJ	66 041 512	20 117 497	30.5	32 467 223	9 733 251	30.0	33 574 289	10 384 246	30.9
1 VII 2008[1]	ESDJ	66 480 004	20 471 816	30.8	32 671 831	9 802 741	30.0	33 808 173	10 669 075	31.6
1 VII 2009[1]	ESDJ	66 903 277	21 133 663	31.6	32 872 931	10 112 852	30.8	34 030 346	11 020 811	32.4

Continent, country or area, and date / Continent, pays ou zone et date	Code[a]	Both sexes - Les deux sexes			Male - Masculin			Female - Féminin		
		Total	Urban - Urbaine		Total	Urban - Urbaine		Total	Urban - Urbaine	
			Number Nombre	Percent P.100		Number Nombre	Percent P.100		Number Nombre	Percent P.100
ASIA - ASIE										
Thailand - Thaïlande										
1 VII 2010[1]...........ESDJ		67 311 917	23 096 811	34.3	33 067 359	11 070 161	33.5	34 244 558	12 026 650	35.1
1 IX 2010 ....CDJC		65 981 659	29 133 829	44.2	32 355 032	14 120 842	43.6	33 626 627	15 012 987	44.6
1 VII 2011[1]...........ESDJ		67 598 735	23 309 100	34.5	33 190 193	11 167 094	33.6	34 408 542	12 142 006	35.3
1 VII 2012[1]...........ESDJ		67 911 720	23 430 180	34.5	33 328 645	11 219 175	33.7	34 583 075	12 211 005	35.3
Timor-Leste										
1 VII 2004[1]...........ESDF		952 000	...	...	484 000	...	...	468 000	...	...
11 VII 2004 ....CDFC		923 198	...	...	469 919	...	...	453 279	...	...
1 VII 2005[1]...........ESDF		983 000	...	...	500 000[19]	...	...	484 000[19]	...	...
1 VII 2006[1]...........ESDF		1 015 000	...	...	515 000	...	...	500 000	...	...
1 VII 2007[1]...........ESDF		1 048 000	...	...	532 000	...	...	516 000	...	...
1 VII 2008[1]...........ESDF		1 080 742	...	...	549 000[19]	...	...	532 000[19]	...	...
11 VII 2010*..........CDFC		1 066 582	315 140	29.5	541 147	164 780	30.5	525 435	150 360	28.6
Turkey - Turquie										
1 VII 2003 ....ESDF		70 231 018	...	...	35 439 247	...	...	34 791 771	...	...
1 VII 2004 ....ESDF		71 151 009	...	...	35 895 750	...	...	35 255 259	...	...
1 VII 2005 ....ESDF		72 064 992	...	...	36 349 233	...	...	35 715 759	...	...
1 VII 2006 ....ESDF		72 971 474	...	...	36 796 216	...	...	36 175 258	...	...
1 VII 2007 ....ESDF		70 137 756	...	...	35 158 437	...	...	34 979 319	...	...
1 VII 2008 ....ESDF		71 051 678	...	...	35 638 843	...	...	35 412 835	...	...
31 XII 2008[98] ....CDJC		71 517 100	...	...	35 901 154	...	...	35 615 946	...	...
1 VII 2009 ....ESDF		72 039 206	...	...	36 181 812	...	...	35 857 394	...	...
1 VII 2010 ....ESDF		73 142 150	...	...	36 752 826	...	...	36 389 324	...	...
1 VII 2011 ....ESDF		74 223 629	...	...	37 288 068	...	...	36 935 561	...	...
1 VII 2012 ....ESDF		75 175 827	...	...	37 744 561	...	...	37 431 266	...	...
Turkmenistan - Turkménistan										
1 VII 2003 ....ESDF		5 123 940	...	...	2 571 866[19]	...	...	2 552 073[19]	...	...
United Arab Emirates - Émirats arabes unis[99]										
5 XII 2005 ....CDFC		4 106 427	3 384 839	82.4	2 806 141	...	...	1 300 286	...	...
31 XII 2006 ....ESDF		5 012 384	...	...	3 533 564	...	...	1 478 820	...	...
31 XII 2007 ....ESDF		6 219 006	...	...	4 533 281	...	...	1 685 725	...	...
31 XII 2008 ....ESDF		8 073 626	...	...	6 039 971	...	...	2 033 655	...	...
31 XII 2009 ....ESDF		8 199 996	...	...	6 120 885	...	...	2 079 111	...	...
1 VII 2010 ....ESDF		8 264 070	...	...	6 161 820	...	...	2 102 250	...	...
Viet Nam										
1 VII 2003[100].............ESDF		80 468 422	20 725 128	25.8	39 535 505	...	...	40 932 917	...	...
1 VII 2004[100].............ESDF		81 437 728	21 601 403	26.5	40 042 598	...	...	41 395 130	...	...
1 VII 2005[100].............ESDF		82 393 519	22 332 173	27.1	40 522 211	...	...	41 871 308	...	...
1 VII 2006[100].............ESDF		83 312 993	23 046 110	27.7	40 999 887	...	...	42 313 106	...	...
1 VII 2007[100].............ESDF		84 221 105	23 746 705	28.2	41 448 572	...	...	42 772 533	...	...
1 VII 2008[100].............ESDF		85 122 271	24 673 681	29.0	41 957 844	...	...	43 164 427	...	...
1 IV 2009 ....CDJC		85 846 997	25 436 896	29.6	42 413 143	12 349 995	29.1	43 433 854	13 086 901	30.1
1 VII 2009 ....ESDF		86 024 979	25 584 740	29.7	42 523 416	...	...	43 501 563	...	...
1 VII 2010 ....ESDF		86 932 527	26 515 940	30.5	42 986 075	...	...	43 946 452	...	...
1 VII 2011 ....ESDF		87 840 038	27 888 152	31.7	43 444 777	...	...	44 395 261	...	...
1 VII 2012 ....ESDF		88 772 884	28 356 363	31.9	43 907 154	...	...	44 865 730	...	...
Yemen - Yémen										
16 XII 2004 ....CDFC		19 685 161	5 637 756	28.6	10 036 953	3 012 256	30.0	9 648 208	2 625 500	27.2
31 XII 2005 ....ESDF		20 282 944	5 849 749	28.8	...	...	...	...	...	...
31 XII 2006 ....ESDF		20 900 532	6 070 613	29.0	...	...	...	...	...	...
31 XII 2007 ....ESDF		21 538 995	6 256 462	29.0	...	...	...	...	...	...
1 VII 2008[1]...........ESDJ		21 843 554	...	...	11 127 218	...	...	10 716 336	...	...
1 VII 2009[1]...........ESDJ		22 492 035	...	...	11 454 963	...	...	11 037 072	...	...
1 VII 2010[1]...........ESDJ		23 153 982	...	...	11 789 814	...	...	11 364 168	...	...
1 VII 2011[1]...........ESDJ		23 833 000	6 876 000	28.9	12 133 000	...	...	11 699 000	...	...
1 VII 2012[1]...........ESDJ		24 527 000	7 076 000	28.8	12 485 000	...	...	12 042 000	...	...

Continent, country or area, and date / Continent, pays ou zone et date	Code[a]	Both sexes - Les deux sexes			Male - Masculin			Female - Féminin		
		Total	Urban - Urbaine		Total	Urban - Urbaine		Total	Urban - Urbaine	
			Number Nombre	Percent P.100		Number Nombre	Percent P.100		Number Nombre	Percent P.100

EUROPE

Åland Islands - Îles d'Åland[25]

1 VII 2003 .... ESDJ		26 302	10 629	40.4	12 945	5 011	38.7	13 358	5 619	42.1
1 VII 2004 .... ESDJ		26 439	10 669	40.4	13 030	5 036	38.7	13 409	5 633	42.0
1 VII 2005 .... ESDJ		26 648	10 746	40.3	13 174	5 087	38.6	13 475	5 660	42.0
1 VII 2006 .... ESDJ		26 845	10 802	40.2	13 299	5 123	38.5	13 546	5 680	41.9
1 VII 2007 .... ESDJ		27 038	10 863	40.2	13 407	5 151	38.4	13 631	5 712	41.9
1 VII 2008 .... ESDJ		27 305	10 954	40.1	13 552	5 189	38.3	13 753	5 765	41.9
1 VII 2009 .... ESDJ		27 595	11 064	40.1	13 724	5 264	38.4	13 871	5 800	41.8
1 VII 2010 .... ESDJ		27 871	11 157	40.0	13 880	5 327	38.4	13 991	5 830	41.7
1 VII 2011 .... ESDJ		28 181	11 227	39.8	14 045	5 364	38.2	14 137	5 863	41.5
1 VII 2012 .... ESDJ		28 429	11 305	39.8	14 172	5 408	38.2	14 257	5 897	41.4

Albania - Albanie

1 VII 2003 .... ESDF		3 033 658	1 353 693	44.6	1 514 117	669 214	44.2	1 519 541	684 479	45.0
1 VII 2004 .... ESDF		3 014 578	1 375 341	45.6	1 505 246	680 144	45.2	1 509 332	695 197	46.1
1 VII 2005 .... ESDF		2 992 724	1 395 896	46.6	1 495 033	690 505	46.2	1 497 691	705 391	47.1
1 VII 2006 .... ESDF		2 968 027	1 413 294	47.6	1 483 509	700 088	47.2	1 484 518	713 206	48.0
1 VII 2007 .... ESDF		2 940 879	1 430 878	48.7	1 470 715	709 114	48.2	1 470 164	721 764	49.1
1 VII 2008 .... ESDF		2 912 559	1 449 081	49.8	1 457 037	717 565	49.2	1 455 522	731 516	50.3
1 VII 2009 .... ESDF		2 884 301	1 465 663	50.8	1 443 417	725 868	50.3	1 440 884	739 795	51.3
1 VII 2010 .... ESDF		2 856 672	1 482 270	51.9	1 430 368	734 329	51.3	1 426 304	747 941	52.4
1 VII 2011 .... ESDF		2 829 337	1 498 679	53.0	1 417 403	742 677	52.4	1 411 934	756 002	53.5
1 X 2011 .... CDJC		2 800 138	1 498 508	53.5	1 403 059	742 671	52.9	1 397 079	755 837	54.1
1 VII 2012 .... ESDF		2 801 682	1 514 746	54.1	1 404 175	750 821	53.5	1 397 507	763 925	54.7

Andorra - Andorre[25]

1 VII 2003 .... ESDJ		69 840	...	...	36 258	...	...	33 582	...	...
1 VII 2004 .... ESDJ		74 885	...	...	38 990	...	...	35 895	...	...
1 VII 2005 .... ESDJ		78 607	...	...	41 097	...	...	37 510	...	...
1 VII 2006 .... ESDJ		80 104	...	...	41 876	...	...	38 228	...	...
1 VII 2007 .... ESDJ		82 392	...	...	43 100	...	...	39 292	...	...
1 VII 2008 .... ESDJ		83 884	...	...	43 911	...	...	39 973	...	...
1 VII 2009 .... ESDJ		85 116	...	...	44 444	...	...	40 672	...	...
1 VII 2010 .... ESDJ		84 549	...	...	43 992	...	...	40 557	...	...
1 VII 2011[101] .... ESDJ		79 280	...	...	40 529	...	...	38 751	...	...
1 VII 2012 .... ESDJ		77 181	...	...	39 351	...	...	37 830	...	...

Austria - Autriche

1 VII 2003 .... ESDJ		8 118 245	...	...	3 940 285	...	...	4 177 960	...	...
1 VII 2004 .... ESDJ		8 169 441	...	...	3 967 701	...	...	4 201 740	...	...
1 VII 2005 .... ESDJ		8 225 278	...	...	3 998 952	...	...	4 226 326	...	...
1 VII 2006 .... ESDJ		8 267 948	...	...	4 022 516	...	...	4 245 432	...	...
1 VII 2007 .... ESDJ		8 300 954	...	...	4 040 089	...	...	4 260 865	...	...
1 VII 2008 .... ESDJ		8 336 549	...	...	4 058 635	...	...	4 277 914	...	...
1 VII 2009 .... ESDJ		8 365 275	...	...	4 073 570	...	...	4 291 705	...	...
1 VII 2010 .... ESDJ		8 387 742	...	...	4 086 434	...	...	4 301 308	...	...
1 VII 2011 .... ESDJ		8 423 136	...	...	4 107 033	...	...	4 316 103	...	...
1 VII 2012 .... ESDJ		8 465 765	...	...	4 131 420	...	...	4 334 345	...	...

Belarus - Bélarus

1 VII 2003 .... ESDF		9 873 826	7 040 950	71.3	4 623 963	3 297 535	71.3	5 249 863	3 743 415	71.3
1 VII 2004 .... ESDF		9 824 568	7 050 685	71.8	4 596 633	3 296 800	71.7	5 227 935	3 753 885	71.8
1 VII 2005 .... ESDF		9 775 307	7 057 463	72.2	4 569 189	3 294 851	72.1	5 206 118	3 762 612	72.3
1 VII 2006 .... ESDF		9 732 501	7 066 903	72.6	4 545 164	3 294 559	72.5	5 187 337	3 772 344	72.7
1 VII 2007 .... ESDF		9 702 116	7 091 407	73.1	4 528 222	3 302 285	72.9	5 173 894	3 789 122	73.2
1 VII 2008 .... ESDF		9 680 842	...	...	4 516 518	...	...	5 164 324	...	...
1 VII 2009 .... ESDF		9 576 046	...	...	4 464 268	...	...	5 111 778	...	...
14 X 2009 .... CDJC		9 503 807	7 064 529	74.3	4 420 039	3 271 014	74.0	5 083 768	3 793 515	74.6
1 VII 2010 .... ESDJ		9 480 686	...	...	4 412 536	...	...	5 068 150	...	...
1 VII 2011 .... ESDJ		9 473 172	7 148 636	75.5	4 403 227	3 303 932	75.0	5 069 945	3 844 704	75.8
1 I 2012 .... ESDF		9 465 150	...	...	4 398 293	...	...	5 066 857	...	...

Belgium - Belgique

1 VII 2003 .... ESDJ		10 372 469	10 223 221	98.6	5 075 268	5 000 466	98.5	5 297 201	5 222 755	98.6
1 VII 2004 .... ESDJ		10 417 122	10 267 298	98.6	5 097 709	5 022 559	98.5	5 319 413	5 244 739	98.6
1 VII 2005 .... ESDJ		10 472 842	10 322 099	98.6	5 125 387	5 049 822	98.5	5 347 455	5 272 277	98.6
1 VII 2006 .... ESDJ		10 541 893	10 389 801	98.6	5 159 947	5 083 829	98.5	5 381 946	5 305 972	98.6
1 VII 2007 .... ESDJ		10 622 604	10 469 341	98.6	5 201 670	5 125 007	98.5	5 420 934	5 344 334	98.6
1 VII 2008 .... ESDJ		10 709 973	10 555 681	98.6	5 246 480	5 169 223	98.5	5 463 493	5 386 458	98.6
1 VII 2009 .... ESDJ		10 796 493	10 641 089	98.6	5 290 436	5 212 557	98.5	5 506 057	5 428 532	98.6

6. Total and urban population by sex: 2003 - 2012
Population totale et population urbaine selon le sexe : 2003 - 2012 (continued - suite)

Continent, country or area, and date / Continent, pays ou zone et date	Code[a]	Both sexes - Les deux sexes			Male - Masculin			Female - Féminin		
		Total	Urban - Urbaine		Total	Urban - Urbaine		Total	Urban - Urbaine	
			Number Nombre	Percent P.100		Number Nombre	Percent P.100		Number Nombre	Percent P.100

EUROPE

Belgium - Belgique										
1 VII 2010 .... ESDJ		10 895 586	...	...	5 341 228	...	...	5 554 358	...	...
1 VII 2011 .... ESDJ		10 996 266	...	...	5 393 484	...	...	5 602 782	...	...
1 VII 2012 .... ESDJ		11 139 100	...	...	5 475 268	...	...	5 663 833	...	...
Bosnia and Herzegovina - Bosnie-Herzégovine										
1 VII 2003 .... ESDF		3 832 301	...	...	1 877 827	...	...	1 954 474	...	...
1 VII 2004 .... ESDF		3 842 527	...	...	1 882 838	...	...	1 959 689	...	...
1 VII 2005 .... ESDF		3 842 537	...	...	1 882 843	...	...	1 959 694	...	...
1 VII 2006 .... ESDF		3 842 762	...	...	1 882 953	...	...	1 959 809	...	...
1 VII 2007 .... ESDF		3 842 562	...	...	1 877 309	...	...	1 965 253	...	...
1 VII 2008 .... ESDF		3 842 265	...	...	1 877 165	...	...	1 965 100	...	...
1 VII 2009 .... ESDF		3 842 566	...	...	1 877 312	...	...	1 965 254	...	...
1 VII 2010 .... ESDF		3 843 126	...	...	1 877 587	...	...	1 965 539	...	...
1 VII 2011 .... ESDF		3 841 224	...	...	1 876 546	...	...	1 964 678	...	...
1 VII 2012* .... ESDF		3 837 455	...	...	1 874 608	...	...	1 962 848	...	...
Bulgaria - Bulgarie										
1 VII 2003 .... ESDJ		7 823 557	5 459 344	69.8	3 803 501	2 636 908	69.3	4 020 056	2 822 436	70.2
1 VII 2004 .... ESDJ		7 781 161	5 440 536	69.9	3 779 224	2 624 031	69.4	4 001 937	2 816 505	70.4
1 VII 2005 .... ESDJ		7 739 900	5 424 661	70.1	3 755 469	2 613 346	69.6	3 984 431	2 811 315	70.6
1 VII 2006 .... ESDJ		7 699 020	5 428 388	70.5	3 732 130	2 613 030	70.0	3 966 890	2 815 358	71.0
1 VII 2007 .... ESDJ		7 659 764	5 414 260	70.7	3 710 315	2 604 175	70.2	3 949 449	2 810 085	71.2
1 VII 2008 .... ESDJ		7 623 395	5 405 147	70.9	3 690 485	2 597 929	70.4	3 932 910	2 807 218	71.4
1 VII 2009 .... ESDJ		7 585 131	5 408 330	71.3	3 670 296	2 598 442	70.8	3 914 835	2 809 888	71.8
1 VII 2010 .... ESDJ		7 534 289	5 388 142	71.5	3 644 560	2 587 844	71.0	3 889 729	2 800 298	72.0
1 II 2011 .... CDJC		7 364 570	5 338 261	72.5	3 586 571	2 580 734	72.0	3 777 999	2 757 527	73.0
1 VII 2011 .... ESDJ		7 348 328	5 336 366	72.6	3 577 847	2 579 205	72.1	3 770 481	2 757 161	73.1
1 VII 2012 .... ESDJ		7 304 633	...	...	3 555 187	...	...	3 749 446	...	...
Croatia - Croatie										
1 VII 2003 .... ESDJ		4 440 290	...	...	2 137 037	...	...	2 303 253	...	...
1 VII 2004 .... ESDJ		4 439 353	...	...	2 136 887	...	...	2 302 466	...	...
1 VII 2005 .... ESDJ		4 441 989	...	...	2 138 663	...	...	2 303 326	...	...
1 VII 2006 .... ESDJ		4 440 022	...	...	2 138 934	...	...	2 301 088	...	...
1 VII 2007 .... ESDJ		4 435 982	...	...	2 137 984	...	...	2 297 998	...	...
1 VII 2008 .... ESDJ		4 434 508	...	...	2 138 022	...	...	2 296 486	...	...
1 VII 2009 .... ESDJ		4 429 078	...	...	2 136 231	...	...	2 292 847	...	...
1 VII 2010 .... ESDJ		4 417 781	...	...	2 131 812	...	...	2 285 969	...	...
1 I 2011 .... ESDJ		4 412 137	...	...	2 129 701	...	...	2 282 436	...	...
1 IV 2011 .... CDFC		4 284 889	...	...	2 066 335	...	...	2 218 554	...	...
1 I 2012* .... ESDJ		4 398 150	...	...	2 123 180	...	...	2 274 970	...	...
Czech Republic - République tchèque										
1 VII 2003 .... ESDJ		10 201 651	7 533 782	73.8	4 968 189	3 640 805	73.3	5 233 462	3 892 977	74.4
1 VII 2004 .... ESDJ		10 206 923	7 526 698	73.7	4 971 730	3 637 603	73.2	5 235 193	3 889 095	74.3
1 VII 2005 .... ESDJ		10 234 092	7 552 515	73.8	4 991 439	3 655 100	73.2	5 242 653	3 897 415	74.3
1 VII 2006 .... ESDJ		10 266 646	7 566 774	73.7	5 013 040	3 666 038	73.1	5 253 606	3 900 736	74.2
1 VII 2007 .... ESDJ		10 322 689	7 607 487	73.7	5 048 101	3 691 647	73.1	5 274 588	3 915 840	74.2
1 VII 2008 .... ESDJ		10 429 692	7 697 774	73.8	5 113 332	3 746 004	73.3	5 316 360	3 951 770	74.3
1 VII 2009 .... ESDJ		10 491 492	7 731 056	73.7	5 150 509	3 767 819	73.2	5 340 983	3 963 237	74.2
1 VII 2010 .... ESDJ		10 517 247	7 733 130	73.5	5 160 782	3 765 654	73.0	5 356 465	3 967 476	74.1
25 III 2011 .... CDJC		10 436 560	7 650 450	73.3	5 109 766	3 712 348	72.7	5 326 794	3 938 102	73.9
1 VII 2011 .... ESDJ		10 496 672	7 686 532	73.2	5 153 009	3 742 874	72.6	5 343 663	3 943 658	73.8
1 VII 2012 .... ESDJ		10 510 785	...	...	5 161 280	...	...	5 349 506	...	...
Denmark - Danemark[102]										
1 VII 2003 .... ESDJ		5 387 174	...	...	2 664 526	...	...	2 722 648	...	...
1 VII 2004 .... ESDJ		5 401 177	...	...	2 671 907	...	...	2 729 270	...	...
1 VII 2005 .... ESDJ		5 415 978	...	...	2 679 857	...	...	2 736 121	...	...
1 VII 2006 .... ESDJ		5 434 567	...	...	2 690 179	...	...	2 744 388	...	...
1 VII 2007 .... ESDJ		5 457 415	...	...	2 702 894	...	...	2 754 521	...	...
1 VII 2008 .... ESDJ		5 489 022	...	...	2 720 016	...	...	2 769 006	...	...
1 VII 2009 .... ESDJ		5 519 441	...	...	2 735 983	...	...	2 783 458	...	...
1 VII 2010 .... ESDJ		5 545 039	...	...	2 748 439	...	...	2 796 600	...	...
1 VII 2011 .... ESDJ		5 566 856	...	...	2 760 140	...	...	2 806 716	...	...
1 VII 2012 .... ESDJ		5 587 085	...	...	2 771 208	...	...	2 815 877	...	...

Continent, country or area, and date / Continent, pays ou zone et date	Code[a]	Both sexes - Les deux sexes Total	Urban - Urbaine Number Nombre	Urban - Urbaine Percent P.100	Male - Masculin Total	Urban - Urbaine Number Nombre	Urban - Urbaine Percent P.100	Female - Féminin Total	Urban - Urbaine Number Nombre	Urban - Urbaine Percent P.100
EUROPE										
Estonia - Estonie										
1 VII 2003	ESDJ	1 353 557	937 201	69.2	623 705	421 604	67.6	729 852	515 597	70.6
1 VII 2004	ESDJ	1 349 290	934 665	69.3	621 525	420 309	67.6	727 765	514 356	70.7
1 VII 2005	ESDJ	1 346 097	932 985	69.3	619 949	419 513	67.7	726 148	513 472	70.7
1 VII 2006	ESDJ	1 343 547	931 855	69.4	618 772	419 103	67.7	724 775	512 752	70.7
1 VII 2007	ESDJ	1 341 672	931 163	69.4	617 828	418 873	67.8	723 844	512 290	70.8
1 VII 2008	ESDJ	1 340 675	930 866	69.4	617 354	418 863	67.8	723 321	512 003	70.8
1 VII 2009	ESDJ	1 340 271	930 774	69.4	617 311	419 001	67.9	722 960	511 773	70.8
1 VII 2010	ESDJ	1 340 160	930 683	69.4	617 540	419 227	67.9	722 620	511 456	70.8
1 VII 2011	ESDJ	1 339 928	930 427	69.4	617 809	419 448	67.9	722 119	510 979	70.8
31 XII 2011	CDJC	1 294 455	879 157	67.9	600 526	396 719	66.1	693 929	482 438	69.5
1 I 2012	ESDJ	1 339 662	...	...	617 862	...	...	721 800	...	...
Faeroe Islands - Îles Féroé										
1 VII 2003	ESDJ	47 923	...	...	24 873	...	...	23 051	...	...
1 VII 2004	ESDJ	48 258	...	...	25 070	...	...	23 188	...	...
1 VII 2005	ESDJ	48 260	...	...	25 074	...	...	23 187	...	...
1 VII 2006	ESDJ	48 373	17 537	36.3	25 127	8 828	35.1	23 246	8 709	37.5
1 VII 2007	ESDJ	48 424	17 469	36.1	25 160	8 815	35.0	23 264	8 654	37.2
1 I 2008[25]	CDJC	48 433	...	...	25 174	...	...	23 259	...	...
1 VII 2008	ESDJ	48 618	17 624	36.2	25 263	8 920	35.3	23 355	8 704	37.3
1 VII 2009	ESDJ	48 635	...	...	25 283	...	...	23 352	...	...
1 VII 2010	ESDJ	48 542	...	...	25 216	...	...	23 326	...	...
1 VII 2011	ESDJ	48 433	...	...	25 149	...	...	23 284	...	...
1 I 2012	ESDJ	48 351	...	...	25 114	...	...	23 237	...	...
Finland - Finlande										
1 VII 2003[25]	ESDJ	5 213 014	3 482 747	66.8	2 548 905	1 679 310	65.9	2 664 109	1 803 437	67.7
1 VII 2004[25]	ESDJ	5 228 172	3 501 888	67.0	2 557 485	1 689 778	66.1	2 670 687	1 812 110	67.9
1 VII 2005[25]	ESDJ	5 246 096	3 522 669	67.1	2 567 214	1 700 985	66.3	2 678 882	1 821 684	68.0
1 VII 2006[25]	ESDJ	5 266 268	3 545 913	67.3	2 578 046	1 713 341	66.5	2 688 222	1 832 572	68.2
1 VII 2007[25]	ESDJ	5 288 720	3 571 129	67.5	2 590 265	1 726 895	66.7	2 698 455	1 844 234	68.3
1 VII 2008[25]	ESDJ	5 313 399	3 601 321	67.8	2 604 220	1 743 503	66.9	2 709 179	1 857 819	68.6
1 VII 2009[103]	ESDJ	5 311 276	3 619 503	68.1	2 604 636	1 754 275	67.4	2 706 640	1 865 228	68.9
1 VII 2010[103]	ESDJ	5 335 481	3 637 706	68.2	2 617 862	1 764 711	67.4	2 717 620	1 872 995	68.9
31 XII 2010	CDJC	5 375 276	3 662 915	68.1	2 638 416	1 777 697	67.4	2 736 860	1 885 218	68.9
1 VII 2011[103]	ESDJ	5 360 091	3 666 940	68.4	2 631 431	1 780 188	67.7	2 728 660	1 886 752	69.1
1 I 2012[25]	ESDJ	5 401 267	...	...	2 652 534	...	...	2 748 733	...	...
France[104]										
1 VII 2003	ESDJ	60 303 631	...	...	29 221 986	...	...	31 081 645	...	...
1 VII 2004	ESDJ	60 734 343	...	...	29 416 938	...	...	31 317 405	...	...
1 VII 2005	ESDJ	61 181 499	...	...	29 616 894	...	...	31 564 605	...	...
1 I 2006	CDJC	61 399 541	...	...	29 714 539	...	...	31 685 002	...	...
1 VII 2006	ESDJ	61 597 486	...	...	29 815 995	...	...	31 781 491	...	...
1 VII 2007	ESDJ	61 965 052	...	...	30 001 162	...	...	31 963 890	...	...
1 VII 2008	ESDJ	62 300 288	...	...	30 166 091	...	...	32 134 197	...	...
1 VII 2009*	ESDJ	62 628 361	...	...	30 329 503	...	...	32 298 858	...	...
1 VII 2010*	ESDJ	62 959 391	...	...	30 495 509	...	...	32 463 882	...	...
1 VII 2011*	ESDJ	63 294 268	...	...	30 662 432	...	...	32 631 836	...	...
1 VII 2012*	ESDJ	63 556 191	...	...	30 797 116	...	...	32 759 076	...	...
Germany - Allemagne										
1 VII 2003	ESDJ	82 520 176	...	...	40 349 200	...	...	42 170 976	...	...
28 III 2004[105]	SSDJ	82 491 000	...	...	40 330 000	...	...	42 161 000	...	...
1 VII 2004	ESDJ	82 501 274	...	...	40 350 091	...	...	42 151 183	...	...
1 VII 2005	ESDJ	82 464 344	...	...	40 348 986	...	...	42 115 358	...	...
1 VII 2006	ESDJ	82 365 810	...	...	40 317 807	...	...	42 048 003	...	...
1 VII 2007	ESDJ	82 262 642	...	...	40 287 823	...	...	41 974 819	...	...
1 VII 2008	ESDJ	82 119 776	...	...	40 238 595	...	...	41 881 181	...	...
1 VII 2009	ESDJ	81 874 770	...	...	40 133 270	...	...	41 741 500	...	...
1 VII 2010	ESDJ	81 757 471	...	...	40 099 871	...	...	41 657 600	...	...
1 VII 2011	ESDJ	81 779 210	...	...	40 152 977	...	...	41 626 233	...	...
1 VII 2012	ESDJ	81 932 216	...	...	40 275 903	...	...	41 656 313	...	...
Gibraltar[106]										
31 XII 2003	ESDF	28 605	...	...	14 384	...	...	14 221	...	...
31 XII 2004	ESDF	28 759	...	...	14 426	...	...	14 333	...	...
31 XII 2005	ESDF	28 779	...	...	14 408	...	...	14 371	...	...

Continent, country or area, and date / Continent, pays ou zone et date	Code[a]	Both sexes - Les deux sexes			Male - Masculin			Female - Féminin		
		Total	Urban - Urbaine		Total	Urban - Urbaine		Total	Urban - Urbaine	
			Number Nombre	Percent P.100		Number Nombre	Percent P.100		Number Nombre	Percent P.100
EUROPE										
Gibraltar[106]										
31 XII 2006 .... ESDF		28 875	...	...	14 435	...	...	14 440	...	...
31 XII 2007 .... ESDF		29 257	...	...	14 655	...	...	14 602	...	...
31 XII 2008 .... ESDF		29 286	...	...	14 725	...	...	14 561	...	...
31 XII 2009 .... ESDF		29 431	...	...	14 820	...	...	14 611	...	...
31 XII 2010 .... ESDF		29 441	...	...	14 672	...	...	14 769	...	...
31 XII 2011 .... ESDF		29 752	...	...	14 883	...	...	14 869	...	...
Greece - Grèce										
1 VII 2003[107] .... ESDF		11 023 532	...	...	5 456 496	...	...	5 567 036	...	...
1 VII 2004[107] .... ESDF		11 061 735	...	...	5 475 529	...	...	5 586 206	...	...
1 VII 2005[107] .... ESDF		11 103 929	...	...	5 497 372	...	...	5 606 557	...	...
1 VII 2006[107] .... ESDF		11 148 533	...	...	5 520 164	...	...	5 628 369	...	...
1 VII 2007[107] .... ESDF		11 192 849	...	...	5 543 018	...	...	5 649 831	...	...
1 VII 2008[107] .... ESDF		11 237 068	...	...	5 565 281	...	...	5 671 787	...	...
1 VII 2009[107] .... ESDF		11 282 751	...	...	5 587 096	...	...	5 695 655	...	...
1 VII 2010[107] .... ESDF		11 307 557	...	...	5 598 793	...	...	5 708 764	...	...
9 V 2011* .... CDFC		10 815 197	...	...	5 302 703	...	...	5 512 494	...	...
1 VII 2011[107] .... ESDF		11 299 976	...	...	5 595 099	...	...	5 704 877	...	...
1 I 2012*[107] .... ESDF		11 290 067	...	...	5 590 131	...	...	5 699 936	...	...
Guernsey - Guernesey										
1 VII 2004 .... ESDF		60 382	...	...	29 841	...	...	30 541	...	...
31 III 2006 .... ESDF		61 029	...	...	30 034	...	...	30 995	...	...
31 III 2007 .... ESDF		61 175	...	...	30 022	...	...	31 153	...	...
31 III 2008 .... ESDF		61 726	...	...	30 405	...	...	31 321	...	...
31 III 2009 .... ESDF		62 274	...	...	30 777	...	...	31 497	...	...
31 III 2010 .... ESDF		62 431	...	...	30 695	...	...	31 736	...	...
31 III 2011 .... ESDF		62 915	...	...	31 025	...	...	31 890	...	...
31 III 2012 .... ESDF		63 085	...	...	31 147	...	...	31 938	...	...
Holy See - Saint-Siège[108]										
1 VII 2009 .... ESDF		466	...	...	320	...	...	146	...	...
Hungary - Hongrie										
1 VII 2003 .... ESDJ		10 129 552	6 568 539[109]	64.8	4 811 285	3 079 592[109]	64.0	5 318 268	3 488 947[109]	65.6
1 VII 2004 .... ESDJ		10 107 146	6 571 923[109]	65.0	4 798 614	3 078 582[109]	64.2	5 308 532	3 493 342[109]	65.8
1 VII 2005 .... ESDJ		10 087 065	6 670 187	66.1	4 788 847	3 125 833	65.3	5 298 218	3 544 354	66.9
1 VII 2006 .... ESDJ		10 071 370	6 749 388	67.0	4 781 829	3 163 716	66.2	5 289 541	3 585 673	67.8
1 VII 2007 .... ESDJ		10 055 780	6 737 792	67.0	4 774 320	3 156 954	66.1	5 281 460	3 580 839	67.8
1 VII 2008 .... ESDJ		10 038 188	6 810 173	67.8	4 766 306	3 191 030	66.9	5 271 882	3 619 143	68.6
1 VII 2009 .... ESDJ		10 022 650	6 861 432	68.5	4 759 975	3 215 749	67.6	5 262 675	3 645 683	69.3
1 VII 2010 .... ESDJ		10 000 023	6 953 071	69.5	4 750 401	3 260 344	68.6	5 249 623	3 692 727	70.3
1 VII 2011 .... ESDJ		9 971 727	6 945 873	69.7	4 737 813	3 256 796	68.7	5 233 914	3 689 077	70.5
1 X 2011 .... CDFC		9 937 628	6 903 858	69.5	4 718 479	3 241 911	68.7	5 219 149	3 661 947	70.2
1 I 2012* .... ESDJ		9 957 731	...	...	4 731 724	...	...	5 226 007	...	...
Iceland - Islande[25]										
1 VII 2003 .... ESDJ		289 272	267 957	92.6	144 713	133 340	92.1	144 559	134 617	93.1
1 VII 2004 .... ESDJ		292 587	270 931	92.6	146 697	134 827	91.9	145 890	136 104	93.3
1 VII 2005 .... ESDJ		295 864	275 017	93.0	148 449	137 003	92.3	147 415	138 014	93.6
1 VII 2006 .... ESDJ		304 334	281 961	92.6	154 287	141 673	91.8	150 047	140 288	93.5
1 VII 2007 .... ESDJ		311 396	289 119	92.8	158 866	146 168	92.0	152 530	142 951	93.7
1 VII 2008 .... ESDJ		319 355	298 024	93.3	163 176	151 378	92.8	156 179	146 646	93.9
1 VII 2009 .... ESDJ		319 246	298 890	93.6	161 548	150 604	93.2	157 698	148 286	94.0
1 VII 2010 .... ESDJ		318 006	297 432	93.5	159 838	148 901	93.2	158 168	148 531	93.9
1 VII 2011[110] .... ESDJ		319 014	314 413	98.6	160 185	157 797	98.5	158 829	156 616	98.6
1 VII 2012[110] .... ESDJ		320 716	...	...	160 901	...	...	159 815	...	...
Ireland - Irlande										
1 VII 2003 .... ESDF		3 996 521	...	...	1 986 195	...	...	2 010 327	...	...
1 VII 2004 .... ESDF		4 070 262	...	...	2 026 256	...	...	2 044 006	...	...
1 VII 2005 .... ESDF		4 159 914	...	...	2 076 400	...	...	2 083 515	...	...
23 IV 2006 .... CDFC		4 239 848	2 574 313	60.7	2 121 171	1 267 960	59.8	2 118 677	1 306 353	61.7
1 VII 2006 .... ESDF		4 260 341	...	...	2 130 565	...	...	2 129 776	...	...
1 VII 2007 .... ESDF		4 356 931	...	...	2 177 582	...	...	2 179 349	...	...
1 VII 2008 .... ESDF		4 425 683	...	...	2 206 165	...	...	2 219 518	...	...
1 VII 2009 .... ESDF		4 458 942	...	...	2 215 646	...	...	2 243 297	...	...
15 IV 2010 .... ESDF		4 470 700	...	...	2 216 000	...	...	2 254 700	...	...
10 IV 2011 .... CDFC		4 588 252	2 846 882	62.0	2 272 699	1 389 160	61.1	2 315 553	1 457 722	63.0

Continent, country or area, and date / Continent, pays ou zone et date	Code[a]	Both sexes - Les deux sexes			Male - Masculin			Female - Féminin		
		Total	Urban - Urbaine Number Nombre	Urban - Urbaine Percent P.100	Total	Urban - Urbaine Number Nombre	Urban - Urbaine Percent P.100	Total	Urban - Urbaine Number Nombre	Urban - Urbaine Percent P.100
EUROPE										
Ireland - Irlande										
15 IV 2011 ....ESDF		4 484 323	...	...	2 221 672	...	...	2 262 651	...	...
15 IV 2012 ....ESDJ		4 585 407	...	...	2 269 612	...	...	2 315 795	...	...
Isle of Man - Île de Man										
30 IV 2003 ....ESDJ		77 464	...	...	38 019	...	...	39 444	...	...
30 IV 2004 ....ESDJ		77 581	...	...	38 111	...	...	39 470	...	...
30 IV 2005 ....ESDJ		78 800	...	...	38 775	...	...	40 025	...	...
23 IV 2006 ....CDJC		80 058	...	...	39 523	...	...	40 535	...	...
30 IV 2007 ....ESDJ		80 885	...	...	39 995	...	...	40 889	...	...
30 IV 2008 ....ESDJ		81 722	...	...	40 472	...	...	41 250	...	...
30 IV 2009 ....ESDJ		82 371	...	...	40 849	...	...	41 522	...	...
27 III 2011* ....CDJC		84 497	...	...	41 971	...	...	42 526	...	...
Italy - Italie										
1 VII 2003 ....ESDJ		57 604 658	...	...	27 917 416	...	...	29 687 242	...	...
1 VII 2004 ....ESDJ		58 175 310	...	...	28 222 706	...	...	29 952 604	...	...
1 VII 2005 ....ESDJ		58 607 043	...	...	28 451 846	...	...	30 155 197	...	...
1 VII 2006 ....ESDJ		58 941 499	...	...	28 622 665	...	...	30 318 835	...	...
1 VII 2007 ....ESDJ		59 375 289	...	...	28 834 094	...	...	30 541 195	...	...
1 VII 2008 ....ESDJ		59 832 179	...	...	29 051 085	...	...	30 781 094	...	...
1 VII 2009 ....ESDJ		60 192 698	...	...	29 219 913	...	...	30 972 785	...	...
1 VII 2010 ....ESDJ		60 483 386	...	...	29 350 339	...	...	31 133 047	...	...
1 I 2011....................ESDJ		60 626 442	...	...	29 413 274	...	...	31 213 168	...	...
1 I 2012 ....ESDJ		60 850 782	...	...	29 517 237	...	...	31 333 545	...	...
Jersey										
27 III 2011 ....CDFC		97 857	...	...	48 296	...	...	49 561	...	...
Latvia - Lettonie										
1 VII 2003 ....ESDJ		2 325 342	1 576 965	67.8	1 070 697	709 024	66.2	1 254 645	867 941	69.2
1 VII 2004 ....ESDJ		2 312 819	1 570 406	67.9	1 065 627	706 082	66.3	1 247 192	864 324	69.3
1 VII 2005 ....ESDJ		2 300 512	1 563 372	68.0	1 060 101	702 490	66.3	1 240 411	860 882	69.4
1 VII 2006 ....ESDJ		2 287 948	1 554 766	68.0	1 054 159	697 812	66.2	1 233 789	856 954	69.5
1 VII 2007 ....ESDJ		2 276 100	1 545 560	67.9	1 048 969	693 369	66.1	1 227 131	852 191	69.4
1 VII 2008 ....ESDJ		2 266 094	1 536 826	67.8	1 045 012	689 602	66.0	1 221 082	847 224	69.4
1 VII 2009 ....ESDJ		2 254 834	1 526 930	67.7	1 040 286	685 170	65.9	1 214 549	841 760	69.3
1 VII 2010 ....ESDJ		2 239 008	1 513 343	67.6	1 033 421	679 286	65.7	1 205 587	834 057	69.2
1 I 2011....................ESDJ		2 074 605	...	...	947 939	...	...	1 126 666	...	...
1 III 2011 ....CDJC		2 070 371	...	...	946 102	...	...	1 124 269	...	...
1 I 2012*....................ESDJ		2 041 763	...	...	933 114	...	...	1 108 649	...	...
Liechtenstein										
1 VII 2003 ....ESDJ		34 022	...	...	16 725	...	...	17 297	...	...
1 VII 2004 ....ESDJ		34 477	...	...	16 974	...	...	17 503	...	...
1 VII 2005 ....ESDJ		34 734	...	...	17 100	...	...	17 634	...	...
1 VII 2006 ....ESDJ		35 010	...	...	17 256	...	...	17 754	...	...
1 VII 2007 ....ESDJ		35 322	...	...	17 426	...	...	17 896	...	...
1 VII 2008 ....ESDJ		35 446	...	...	17 508	...	...	17 938	...	...
1 VII 2009 ....ESDJ		35 789	...	...	17 716	...	...	18 073	...	...
1 VII 2010 ....ESDJ		36 010	...	...	17 817	...	...	18 193	...	...
31 XII 2010 ....CDFC		36 149	-	.0	17 886	-	.0	18 263	-	.0
1 VII 2011 ....ESDJ		36 281	...	...	17 950	...	...	18 331	...	...
1 I 2012* ....ESDJ		36 475	...	...	18 042	...	...	18 433	...	...
Lithuania - Lituanie										
1 VII 2003 ....ESDJ		3 454 205	2 307 326	66.8	1 612 996	1 058 108	65.6	1 841 209	1 249 218	67.8
1 VII 2004 ....ESDJ		3 435 591	2 289 399	66.6	1 603 421	1 048 397	65.4	1 832 170	1 241 002	67.7
1 VII 2005 ....ESDJ		3 414 304	2 275 118	66.6	1 592 402	1 040 296	65.3	1 821 902	1 234 822	67.8
1 VII 2006 ....ESDJ		3 394 082	2 264 535	66.7	1 581 807	1 034 128	65.4	1 812 275	1 230 407	67.9
1 VII 2007 ....ESDJ		3 375 618	2 255 508	66.8	1 571 979	1 028 619	65.4	1 803 639	1 226 889	68.0
1 VII 2008 ....ESDJ		3 358 114	2 245 653	66.9	1 563 120	1 022 903	65.4	1 794 994	1 222 750	68.1
1 VII 2009 ....ESDJ		3 339 455	2 235 033	66.9	1 553 499	1 016 639	65.4	1 785 956	1 218 394	68.2
1 VII 2010 ....ESDJ		3 286 820	2 200 376	66.9	1 527 510	998 907	65.4	1 759 310	1 201 469	68.3
1 III 2011 ....CDJC		3 483 972	2 332 098	66.9	1 629 148	1 071 986	65.8	1 854 824	1 260 112	67.9
1 VII 2011 ....ESDJ		3 030 173	2 022 926	66.8	1 396 447	908 817	65.1	1 633 726	1 114 109	68.2
1 I 2012 ....ESDJ		3 007 758	...	...	1 385 671	...	...	1 622 087	...	...
Luxembourg										
1 VII 2003 ....ESDJ		451 631	...	...	222 859	...	...	228 772	...	...
1 VII 2004 ....ESDJ		458 095	...	...	226 432	...	...	231 663	...	...
1 VII 2005 ....ESDJ		465 158	...	...	230 128	...	...	235 030	...	...
1 VII 2006 ....ESDJ		472 637	...	...	233 946	...	...	238 691	...	...

Continent, country or area, and date / Continent, pays ou zone et date	Code[a]	Both sexes - Les deux sexes			Male - Masculin			Female - Féminin		
		Total	Urban - Urbaine		Total	Urban - Urbaine		Total	Urban - Urbaine	
			Number Nombre	Percent P.100		Number Nombre	Percent P.100		Number Nombre	Percent P.100

EUROPE

Luxembourg
1 VII 2007 .... ESDJ		479 993	...	...	237 700	...	...	242 294	...	...
1 VII 2008 .... ESDJ		488 650	...	...	242 221	...	...	246 429	...	...
1 VII 2009 .... ESDJ		497 782	...	...	247 120	...	...	250 662	...	...
1 VII 2010 .... ESDJ		506 953	...	...	252 013	...	...	254 941	...	...
1 I 2011 .... ESDJ		511 840	...	...	254 619	...	...	257 221	...	...
1 II 2011 .... CDJC		512 353	...	...	254 967	...	...	257 386	...	...
1 I 2012 .... ESDJ		524 853	...	...	261 820	...	...	263 033	...	...

Malta - Malte
1 VII 2003[111] .... ESDJ		398 582	...	...	197 468	...	...	201 114	...	...
1 VII 2004[111] .... ESDJ		401 306	...	...	198 860	...	...	202 446	...	...
1 VII 2005[111] .... ESDJ		403 509	...	...	200 104	...	...	203 405	...	...
27 XI 2005 .... CDJC		404 962	404 544	99.9	200 819	200 611	99.9	204 143	203 933	99.9
1 VII 2006[111] .... ESDJ		405 951	...	...	201 559	...	...	204 392	...	...
1 VII 2007[111] .... ESDJ		407 726	...	...	202 657	...	...	205 069	...	...
1 VII 2008[111] .... ESDJ		410 213	...	...	204 011	...	...	206 202	...	...
1 VII 2009[111] .... ESDJ		413 240	...	...	205 692	...	...	207 548	...	...
1 VII 2010[111] .... ESDJ		415 275	...	...	206 625	...	...	208 650	...	...
1 VII 2011[111] .... ESDJ		416 725	...	...	207 257	...	...	209 468	...	...
20 XI 2011* .... CDJC		416 055	...	...	207 185	...	...	208 870	...	...
1 I 2012[111] .... ESDJ		417 520	...	...	207 677	...	...	209 843	...	...

Monaco
9 VI 2008 .... CDJC		31 109	...	...	15 076[112]	...	...	15 914[112]	...	...

Montenegro - Monténégro
1 VII 2003 .... ESDJ		620 279	385 205	62.1	305 745	187 299	61.3	314 534	197 906	62.9
31 X 2003 .... CDJC		620 145	383 808	61.9	305 225	186 437	61.1	314 920	197 371	62.7
1 VII 2004 .... ESDJ		622 118	387 501	62.3	306 428	188 266	61.4	315 690	199 235	63.1
1 VII 2005 .... ESDJ		623 277	389 678	62.5	306 839	189 222	61.7	316 439	200 456	63.3
1 VII 2006 .... ESDJ		624 241	391 884	62.8	307 271	190 286	61.9	316 970	201 598	63.6
1 VII 2007 .... ESDJ		626 104	394 653	63.0	308 267	191 692	62.2	317 836	202 961	63.9
1 VII 2008 .... ESDJ		628 804	397 747	63.3	309 787	193 393	62.4	319 018	204 354	64.1
1 VII 2009 .... ESDJ		631 536	400 928	63.5	311 258	195 088	62.7	320 278	205 840	64.3
1 VII 2010 .... ESDJ		617 304	...	...	304 861	...	...	312 443	...	...
1 IV 2011 .... CDJC		620 029	399 264	64.4	306 236	193 691	63.2	313 793	205 573	65.5
1 VII 2011 .... ESDJ		620 556	...	...	306 472	...	...	314 084	...	...
1 VII 2012 .... ESDJ		622 009	...	...	307 252	...	...	314 757	...	...

Netherlands - Pays-Bas
1 VII 2003 .... ESDJ		16 225 302	10 556 424	65.1	8 030 693	5 191 871	64.7	8 194 610	5 364 553	65.5
1 VII 2004 .... ESDJ		16 281 779	10 687 028	65.6	8 055 947	5 255 716	65.2	8 225 833	5 431 312	66.0
1 VII 2005 .... ESDJ		16 319 868	10 764 171	66.0	8 071 693	5 292 532	65.6	8 248 175	5 471 640	66.3
1 VII 2006 .... ESDJ		16 346 101	10 803 902	66.1	8 082 961	5 311 812	65.7	8 263 141	5 492 090	66.5
1 VII 2007 .... ESDJ		16 381 696	10 825 307	66.1	8 100 294	5 322 596	65.7	8 281 402	5 502 712	66.4
1 VII 2008 .... ESDJ		16 445 593	10 877 858	66.1	8 134 235	5 350 572	65.8	8 311 359	5 527 286	66.5
1 VII 2009 .... ESDJ		16 530 388	10 938 780	66.2	8 179 936	5 383 776	65.8	8 350 452	5 555 004	66.5
1 VII 2010 .... ESDJ		16 615 394	11 096 288	66.8	8 223 479	5 464 083	66.4	8 391 915	5 632 205	67.1
1 VII 2011 .... ESDJ		16 693 074	...	...	8 263 177	...	...	8 429 897	...	...
1 I 2012 .... ESDJ		16 730 348	...	...	8 282 871	...	...	8 447 477	...	...

Norway - Norvège[113]
1 VII 2003 .... ESDJ		4 564 855	...	...	2 262 578	...	...	2 302 277	...	...
1 VII 2004 .... ESDJ		4 591 910	...	...	2 276 560	...	...	2 315 351	...	...
1 VII 2005 .... ESDJ		4 623 291	...	...	2 293 026	...	...	2 330 266	...	...
1 VII 2006 .... ESDJ		4 660 677	...	...	2 313 885	...	...	2 346 792	...	...
1 VII 2007 .... ESDJ		4 709 153	...	...	2 342 739	...	...	2 366 414	...	...
1 VII 2008 .... ESDJ		4 768 212	...	...	2 377 372	...	...	2 390 840	...	...
1 VII 2009 .... ESDJ		4 828 726	...	...	2 410 903	...	...	2 417 823	...	...
1 VII 2010 .... ESDJ		4 889 252	...	...	2 443 801	...	...	2 445 452	...	...
1 VII 2011 .... ESDJ		4 953 088	...	...	2 479 860	...	...	2 473 228	...	...
1 I 2012 .... ESDJ		4 985 870	...	...	2 498 871	...	...	2 486 999	...	...

Poland - Pologne[114]
1 VII 2003 .... ESDJ		38 195 177	23 543 325	61.6	18 492 950	11 195 269	60.5	19 702 227	12 348 056	62.7
1 VII 2004 .... ESDJ		38 180 249	23 490 202	61.5	18 478 368	11 162 807	60.4	19 701 881	12 327 395	62.6
1 VII 2005 .... ESDJ		38 161 313	23 450 597	61.5	18 460 730	11 135 706	60.3	19 700 583	12 314 891	62.5
1 VII 2006 .... ESDJ		38 132 177	23 400 565	61.4	18 436 101	11 103 869	60.2	19 696 176	12 296 696	62.4
1 VII 2007 .... ESDJ		38 115 967	23 350 920	61.3	18 417 074	11 070 886	60.1	19 698 893	12 280 034	62.3

Continent, country or area, and date / Continent, pays ou zone et date	Code[a]	Both sexes - Les deux sexes			Male - Masculin			Female - Féminin		
		Total	Urban - Urbaine		Total	Urban - Urbaine		Total	Urban - Urbaine	
			Number Nombre	Percent P.100		Number Nombre	Percent P.100		Number Nombre	Percent P.100
EUROPE										
Poland - Pologne[114]										
1 VII 2008 ....ESDJ		38 115 909	23 305 018	61.1	18 408 405	11 041 359	60.0	19 707 504	12 263 659	62.2
1 VII 2009 ....ESDJ		38 153 389	23 293 906	61.1	18 423 343	11 032 562	59.9	19 730 046	12 261 344	62.1
1 VII 2010 ....ESDJ		38 516 689	23 448 497	60.9	18 647 604	11 136 164	59.7	19 869 085	12 312 333	62.0
31 III 2011..................CDJC		38 512 000	23 406 000	60.8	18 644 000	11 113 000	59.6	19 868 000	12 293 000	61.9
1 VII 2011 ....ESDJ		38 525 670	23 404 926	60.8	18 650 105	11 111 443	59.6	19 875 565	12 293 483	61.9
1 I 2012 ....ESDJ		38 538 447	...	...	18 654 577	...	...	19 883 870	...	...
Portugal										
1 VII 2003 ....ESDJ		10 441 075	...	...	5 048 278	...	...	5 392 798	...	...
1 VII 2004 ....ESDJ		10 501 970	...	...	5 080 324	...	...	5 421 647	...	...
1 VII 2005 ....ESDJ		10 549 424	...	...	5 105 041	...	...	5 444 383	...	...
1 VII 2006 ....ESDJ		10 584 344	...	...	5 122 840	...	...	5 461 504	...	...
1 VII 2007 ....ESDJ		10 608 335	...	...	5 134 372	...	...	5 473 963	...	...
1 VII 2008 ....ESDJ		10 622 413	...	...	5 140 687	...	...	5 481 726	...	...
1 VII 2009 ....ESDJ		10 632 482	...	...	5 145 385	...	...	5 487 097	...	...
1 VII 2010 ....ESDJ		10 637 346	...	...	5 147 423	...	...	5 489 923	...	...
21 III 2011..................CDFC		10 282 306	6 286 712	61.1	4 868 755	2 949 862	60.6	5 413 551	3 336 850	61.6
1 VII 2011*..................ESDJ		10 556 999	...	...	5 042 781	...	...	5 514 218	...	...
1 I 2012*.....................ESDJ		10 542 398	...	...	5 030 437	...	...	5 511 961	...	...
Republic of Moldova - République de Moldova[115]										
1 VII 2003 ....ESDJ		3 612 874	1 481 035	41.0	1 730 861	714 970	41.3	1 882 013	766 065	40.7
1 VII 2004 ....ESDJ		3 603 940	1 476 980	41.0	1 726 630	712 971	41.3	1 877 310	764 009	40.7
5 X 2004 ....CDFC		3 386 673	1 308 069	38.6	1 629 689	613 221	37.6	1 756 984	694 848	39.5
1 VII 2005 ....ESDJ		3 595 187	1 472 929	41.0	1 722 105	710 796	41.3	1 873 082	762 133	40.7
1 VII 2006 ....ESDJ		3 585 209	1 481 398	41.3	1 720 139	706 649	41.1	1 865 070	774 749	41.5
1 VII 2007 ....ESDJ		3 576 910	1 477 062	41.3	1 719 246	694 308	40.4	1 857 664	782 754	42.1
1 VII 2008 ....ESDJ		3 570 108	1 475 609	41.3	1 716 195	693 550	40.4	1 853 913	782 059	42.2
1 VII 2009 ....ESDJ		3 565 604	1 476 390	41.4	1 714 209	694 134	40.5	1 851 395	782 257	42.3
1 VII 2010 ....ESDJ		3 562 045	1 479 196	41.5	1 712 783	695 603	40.6	1 849 262	783 593	42.4
1 VII 2011 ....ESDJ		3 559 986	...	...	1 711 916	...	...	1 848 070	...	...
1 I 2012 ....ESDJ		3 559 541	...	...	1 711 725	...	...	1 847 816	...	...
Romania - Roumanie										
1 VII 2003 ....ESDJ		21 733 556	11 600 157	53.4	10 606 245	5 566 401	52.5	11 127 311	6 033 756	54.2
1 VII 2004 ....ESDJ		21 673 328	11 895 598	54.9	10 571 606	5 704 297	54.0	11 101 722	6 191 301	55.8
1 VII 2005 ....ESDJ		21 623 849	11 879 897	54.9	10 543 518	5 692 516	54.0	11 080 331	6 187 381	55.8
1 VII 2006 ....ESDJ		21 584 365	11 913 938	55.2	10 521 189	5 704 872	54.2	11 063 176	6 209 066	56.1
1 VII 2007 ....ESDJ		21 537 563	11 877 659	55.1	10 496 720	5 683 983	54.2	11 040 843	6 193 676	56.1
1 VII 2008 ....ESDJ		21 504 442	11 835 328	55.0	10 477 611	5 658 512	54.0	11 026 831	6 176 816	56.0
1 VII 2009 ....ESDJ		21 469 959	11 823 516	55.1	10 457 219	5 649 707	54.0	11 012 740	6 173 809	56.1
1 VII 2010 ....ESDJ		21 431 298	11 798 735	55.1	10 434 143	5 632 704	54.0	10 997 155	6 166 031	56.1
1 VII 2011*..................ESDJ		21 354 396	11 727 153	54.9	10 392 537	5 590 187	53.8	10 961 859	6 136 966	56.0
1 I 2012*.....................ESDJ		21 355 849	...	...	10 394 402	...	...	10 961 447	...	...
Russian Federation - Fédération de Russie										
1 VII 2003 ....ESDJ		144 648 618	106 180 380	73.4	67 281 081	48 956 250	72.8	77 367 537	57 224 130	74.0
1 VII 2004 ....ESDJ		144 067 316	105 610 817	73.3	66 883 860	48 573 353	72.6	77 183 456	57 037 464	73.9
1 VII 2005 ....ESDJ		143 518 814	105 000 366	73.2	66 498 963	48 169 679	72.4	77 019 851	56 830 687	73.8
1 VII 2006 ....ESDJ		143 049 637	104 775 157	73.2	66 176 725	47 967 026	72.5	76 872 912	56 808 131	73.9
1 VII 2007 ....ESDJ		142 805 114	104 798 401	73.4	66 013 796	47 923 326	72.6	76 791 318	56 875 075	74.1
1 VII 2008 ....ESDJ		142 742 366	104 890 297	73.5	65 968 338	47 938 815	72.7	76 774 028	56 951 482	74.2
1 VII 2009 ....ESDJ		142 785 349	104 988 448	73.5	65 988 356	47 969 474	72.7	76 796 993	57 018 974	74.2
1 VII 2010 ....ESDJ		142 849 468	105 241 319	73.7	66 033 070	48 081 267	72.8	76 816 398	57 160 052	74.4
14 X 2010 ....CDFC		143 436 145	...	...	66 457 074	...	...	76 979 071	...	...
1 VII 2011 ....ESDJ		142 960 908	105 581 615	73.9	66 113 269	48 243 022	73.0	76 847 639	57 338 593	74.6
San Marino - Saint-Marin[25]										
1 VII 2003 ....ESDF		28 992	...	...	14 207	...	...	14 785	...	...
1 VII 2004 ....ESDF		29 457	...	...	14 442	...	...	15 015	...	...
1 VII 2005 ....ESDF		29 836	...	...	14 625	...	...	15 212	...	...
1 VII 2006 ....ESDF		30 184	...	...	14 814	...	...	15 370	...	...
1 VII 2007 ....ESDF		31 211	...	...	15 664	...	...	15 547	...	...
1 VII 2008 ....ESDF		31 662	...	...	15 874	...	...	15 788	...	...
1 I 2009 ....ESDF		32 969	...	...	16 052	...	...	16 917	...	...
1 I 2010 ....ESDF		33 163	...	...	16 124	...	...	17 039	...	...

Continent, country or area, and date / Continent, pays ou zone et date	Code[a]	Both sexes - Les deux sexes Total	Urban - Urbaine Number Nombre	Urban - Urbaine Percent P.100	Male - Masculin Total	Urban - Urbaine Number Nombre	Urban - Urbaine Percent P.100	Female - Féminin Total	Urban - Urbaine Number Nombre	Urban - Urbaine Percent P.100
EUROPE										
San Marino - Saint-Marin[25]										
1 I 2011	ESDF	33 376	...	...	16 217	...	...	17 159	...	...
1 I 2012	ESDF	33 402	...	...	16 224	...	...	17 178	...	...
Serbia - Serbie[116]										
1 VII 2003	ESDJ	7 480 591	4 239 980	56.7	3 637 789	2 026 423	55.7	3 842 802	2 213 557	57.6
1 VII 2004	ESDJ	7 463 157	4 249 544	56.9	3 629 194	2 030 310	55.9	3 833 963	2 219 234	57.9
1 VII 2005	ESDJ	7 440 769	4 257 880	57.2	3 618 040	2 033 179	56.2	3 822 729	2 224 701	58.2
1 VII 2006	ESDJ	7 411 569	4 263 386	57.5	3 603 698	2 034 616	56.5	3 807 871	2 228 770	58.5
1 VII 2007	ESDJ	7 381 579	4 270 400	57.9	3 588 957	2 037 012	56.8	3 792 622	2 233 388	58.9
1 VII 2008	ESDJ	7 350 222	4 275 245	58.2	3 573 814	2 038 642	57.0	3 776 408	2 236 603	59.2
1 VII 2009	ESDJ	7 320 807	4 279 035	58.5	3 560 048	2 039 934	57.3	3 760 759	2 239 101	59.5
1 VII 2010	ESDJ	7 291 436	4 283 985	58.8	3 546 374	2 041 975	57.6	3 745 062	2 242 010	59.9
1 VII 2011	ESDJ	7 258 753	4 286 114	59.0	3 530 924	2 042 566	57.8	3 727 829	2 243 548	60.2
1 X 2011	CDJC	7 186 862	4 271 872	59.4	3 499 176	2 039 105	58.3	3 687 686	2 232 767	60.5
1 I 2012	ESDJ	7 241 295	...	...	3 522 675	...	...	3 718 620	...	...
Slovakia - Slovaquie										
1 VII 2003	ESDJ	5 378 950	3 001 619	55.8	2 610 872	1 442 117	55.2	2 768 078	1 559 502	56.3
1 VII 2004	ESDJ	5 382 574	2 994 284	55.6	2 612 313	1 438 019	55.0	2 770 261	1 556 265	56.2
1 VII 2005	ESDJ	5 387 285	2 989 291	55.5	2 614 912	1 435 469	54.9	2 772 373	1 553 822	56.0
1 VII 2006	ESDJ	5 391 184	2 989 769	55.5	2 616 924	1 435 472	54.9	2 774 260	1 554 297	56.0
1 VII 2007	ESDJ	5 397 766	2 985 680	55.3	2 621 095	1 433 808	54.7	2 776 671	1 551 872	55.9
1 VII 2008	ESDJ	5 406 972	2 980 828	55.1	2 626 895	1 432 161	54.5	2 780 077	1 548 667	55.7
1 VII 2009	ESDJ	5 418 374	2 978 004	55.0	2 633 428	1 430 928	54.3	2 784 946	1 547 076	55.6
1 VII 2010	ESDJ	5 431 024	2 975 976	54.8	2 639 896	1 429 637	54.2	2 791 128	1 546 339	55.4
21 V 2011	CDJC	5 397 036	2 937 735	54.4	2 627 772	1 412 818	53.8	2 769 264	1 524 917	55.1
1 VII 2011	ESDJ	5 398 384	2 938 053	54.4	2 628 463	1 412 966	53.8	2 769 922	1 525 087	55.1
1 I 2012	ESDJ	5 407 579	...	...	2 633 866	...	...	2 773 714	...	...
Slovenia - Slovénie										
1 VII 2003	ESDJ	1 996 773	971 513[117]	48.7	977 436[117]	460 811[117]	47.1	1 019 337[117]	510 702[117]	50.1
1 VII 2004	ESDJ	1 997 004	968 989[117]	48.5	977 092[117]	459 504[117]	47.0	1 019 912[117]	509 485[117]	50.0
1 VII 2005	ESDJ	2 001 114	965 538[117]	48.3	980 070[117]	457 869[117]	46.7	1 021 044[117]	507 669[117]	49.7
1 VII 2006	ESDJ	2 008 516	962 740[117]	47.9	985 876[117]	456 764[117]	46.3	1 022 640[117]	505 976[117]	49.5
1 VII 2007	ESDJ	2 019 406	1 006 767	49.9	995 125	490 610	49.3	1 024 281	516 157	50.4
1 VII 2008	ESDJ	2 022 629	1 012 477	50.1	996 969	491 605	49.3	1 025 660	520 872	50.8
1 VII 2009	ESDJ	2 042 335	1 024 087	50.1	1 011 767	500 253	49.4	1 030 568	523 834	50.8
1 VII 2010	ESDJ	2 049 261	1 024 812	50.0	1 014 716	500 063	49.3	1 034 545	524 749	50.7
1 I 2011	CDFC	2 058 051	1 030 172	50.1	1 019 826	503 083	49.3	1 038 225	527 089	50.8
1 VII 2011	ESDJ	2 052 496	1 023 650	49.9	1 015 430	498 490	49.1	1 037 066	525 160	50.6
1 VII 2012	ESDJ	2 057 159	...	...	1 017 896	...	...	1 039 263	...	...
Spain - Espagne										
1 VII 2003	ESDJ	42 004 575	...	...	20 626 192	...	...	21 378 383	...	...
1 VII 2004	ESDJ	42 691 751	...	...	20 987 670	...	...	21 704 081	...	...
1 VII 2005	ESDJ	43 398 190	...	...	21 367 297	...	...	22 030 893	...	...
1 VII 2006	ESDJ	44 068 244	...	...	21 725 232	...	...	22 343 012	...	...
1 VII 2007	ESDJ	44 873 567	...	...	22 155 286	...	...	22 718 281	...	...
1 VII 2008	ESDJ	45 593 385	...	...	22 512 354	...	...	23 081 031	...	...
1 VII 2009	ESDJ	45 929 476	...	...	22 670 863	...	...	23 258 614	...	...
1 VII 2010	ESDJ	46 072 831	...	...	22 697 679	...	...	23 375 152	...	...
1 VII 2011	ESDJ	46 125 154	...	...	22 683 725	...	...	23 441 429	...	...
1 XI 2011	CDJC	46 815 916	...	...	23 104 303	...	...	23 711 613	...	...
1 VII 2012	ESDJ	46 163 114	...	...	22 668 768	...	...	23 494 346	...	...
Sweden - Suède[25]										
1 VII 2003	ESDJ	8 958 229	...	...	4 436 882	...	...	4 521 348	...	...
31 XII 2003	CDJC	8 975 670	...	...	4 446 656	...	...	4 529 014	...	...
1 VII 2004	ESDJ	8 993 531	...	...	4 456 484	...	...	4 537 048	...	...
1 VII 2005	ESDJ	9 029 572	...	...	4 476 431	...	...	4 553 142	...	...
1 VII 2006	ESDJ	9 080 505	...	...	4 505 037	...	...	4 575 468	...	...
1 VII 2007	ESDJ	9 148 092	...	...	4 543 722	...	...	4 604 370	...	...
1 VII 2008	ESDJ	9 219 637	...	...	4 583 816	...	...	4 635 822	...	...
1 VII 2009	ESDJ	9 298 515	...	...	4 626 362	...	...	4 672 153	...	...
1 VII 2010	ESDJ	9 378 126	...	...	4 669 629	...	...	4 708 497	...	...
1 VII 2011	ESDJ	9 449 213	...	...	4 708 539	...	...	4 740 674	...	...
1 VII 2012	ESDJ	9 519 374	...	...	4 746 370	...	...	4 773 005	...	...

Continent, country or area, and date / Continent, pays ou zone et date	Code[a]	Both sexes - Les deux sexes			Male - Masculin			Female - Féminin		
		Total	Urban - Urbaine		Total	Urban - Urbaine		Total	Urban - Urbaine	
			Number Nombre	Percent P.100		Number Nombre	Percent P.100		Number Nombre	Percent P.100

EUROPE

Switzerland - Suisse

1 VII 2003 ....ESDJ		7 339 002	5 375 076	73.2	3 588 285	2 609 517	72.7	3 750 717	2 765 559	73.7
1 VII 2004 ....ESDJ		7 389 626	5 414 867	73.3	3 615 118	2 630 590	72.8	3 774 508	2 784 277	73.8
1 VII 2005 ....ESDJ		7 437 116	5 452 361	73.3	3 640 600	2 650 983	72.8	3 796 516	2 801 378	73.8
1 VII 2006 ....ESDJ		7 483 935	5 489 614	73.4	3 665 931	2 671 318	72.9	3 818 004	2 818 296	73.8
1 VII 2007 ....ESDJ		7 551 117	5 543 848	73.4	3 703 187	2 701 296	72.9	3 847 930	2 842 552	73.9
1 VII 2008 ....ESDJ		7 647 675	5 622 042	73.5	3 756 845	2 744 671	73.1	3 890 831	2 877 371	74.0
1 VII 2009 ....ESDJ		7 743 832	5 699 003	73.6	3 808 621	2 786 186	73.2	3 935 211	2 912 817	74.0
1 VII 2010 ....ESDJ		7 824 909	...	...	3 851 028	...	...	3 973 882	...	...
1 VII 2011 ....ESDJ		7 912 398	5 831 864	73.7	3 899 840	2 857 476	73.3	4 012 559	2 974 388	74.1
1 VII 2012* ....ESDJ		7 995 790	...	...	3 944 798	...	...	4 050 992	...	...

TFYR of Macedonia - L'ex-R. y. de Macédoine

1 VII 2003 ....ESDF		2 026 773	...	...	1 017 274	...	...	1 009 499	...	...
1 VII 2004 ....ESDF		2 032 544	...	...	1 019 903	...	...	1 012 641	...	...
1 VII 2005 ....ESDF		2 036 855	...	...	1 021 772	...	...	1 015 083	...	...
1 VII 2006 ....ESDF		2 040 228	...	...	1 023 069	...	...	1 017 159	...	...
1 VII 2007 ....ESDF		2 043 559	...	...	1 024 489	...	...	1 019 070	...	...
1 VII 2008 ....ESDF		2 046 898	...	...	1 026 022	...	...	1 020 876	...	...
1 VII 2009 ....ESDF		2 050 671	...	...	1 027 810	...	...	1 022 861	...	...
1 VII 2010 ....ESDF		2 055 004	...	...	1 029 848	...	...	1 025 156	...	...
1 VII 2011 ....ESDF		2 058 539	...	...	1 031 403	...	...	1 027 136	...	...
1 VII 2012 ....ESDF		2 061 044	...	...	1 032 532	...	...	1 028 512	...	...

Ukraine

1 VII 2003 ....ESDF		47 812 949	32 237 409	67.4	22 125 646	14 870 398	67.2	25 687 303	17 367 011	67.6
1 VII 2004 ....ESDF		47 451 626	32 077 893	67.6	21 946 375	14 778 929	67.3	25 505 251	17 298 965	67.8
1 VII 2005 ....ESDF		47 105 171	31 943 515	67.8	21 770 304	14 698 072	67.5	25 334 867	17 245 443	68.1
1 VII 2006 ....ESDF		46 787 786	31 827 539	68.0	21 610 648	14 628 495	67.7	25 177 138	17 199 044	68.3
1 VII 2007 ....ESDF		46 509 355	31 723 062	68.2	21 472 153	14 567 851	67.8	25 037 202	17 155 212	68.5
1 VII 2008 ....ESDF		46 258 189	31 627 980	68.4	21 347 279	14 512 344	68.0	24 910 910	17 115 637	68.7
1 VII 2009 ....ESDF		46 053 307	31 556 002	68.5	...	...	...	...	...	...
1 I 2010 ....ESDF		45 962 947	31 524 795	68.6	21 213 041	14 456 186	68.1	24 749 906	17 068 609	69.0
1 I 2011 ....ESDF		45 778 534	31 441 649	68.7	21 138 590	14 416 922	68.2	24 639 944	17 024 727	69.1
1 I 2012 ....ESDF		45 633 637	31 380 874	68.8	21 082 686	14 387 076	68.2	24 550 951	16 993 798	69.2

United Kingdom of Great Britain and Northern Ireland - Royaume-Uni de Grande-Bretagne et d'Irlande du Nord[118]

1 VII 2003 ....ESDF		59 552 182	...	...	29 104 342	...	...	30 447 840	...	...
1 VII 2004 ....ESDF		59 841 892	...	...	29 273 840	...	...	30 568 052	...	...
1 VII 2005 ....ESDF		60 235 498	...	...	29 493 020	...	...	30 742 478	...	...
1 VII 2006 ....ESDF		60 584 338	...	...	29 689 265	...	...	30 895 073	...	...
1 VII 2007 ....ESDF		60 985 677	...	...	29 917 938	...	...	31 067 739	...	...
1 VII 2008 ....ESDF		61 398 226	...	...	30 153 832	...	...	31 244 394	...	...
1 VII 2009 ....ESDF		61 791 956	...	...	30 374 010	...	...	31 417 946	...	...
1 VII 2010 ....ESDF		62 261 967	...	...	30 643 254	...	...	31 618 713	...	...
27 III 2011 ....CDJC		63 182 000	...	...	31 028 000	...	...	32 154 000	...	...
1 VII 2011 ....ESDF		62 752 472	...	...	30 914 792	...	...	31 837 680	...	...
1 VII 2012 ....ESDF		63 243 845	...	...	31 178 697	...	...	32 065 148	...	...

OCEANIA - OCÉANIE

American Samoa - Samoas américaines[31]

1 IV 2010 ....CDJC		55 519	...	...	28 164	...	...	27 355	...	...

Australia - Australie

1 VII 2003[119] ....ESDJ		19 895 435	16 183 448	81.3	9 874 412	7 987 391	80.9	10 021 023	8 196 057	81.8
1 VII 2004[119] ....ESDJ		20 127 363	16 395 358	81.5	9 992 728	8 096 009	81.0	10 134 635	8 299 349	81.9
1 VII 2005[119] ....ESDJ		20 394 791	16 626 325	81.5	10 128 064	8 213 288	81.1	10 266 727	8 413 037	81.9
1 VII 2006[119] ....ESDJ		20 697 880	16 890 471	81.6	10 282 433	8 348 198	81.2	10 415 447	8 542 273	82.0
8 VIII 2006[120] ....CDFC		20 061 646[121]	17 670 009	88.1	9 896 500[121]	8 651 811	87.4	10 165 146[121]	9 018 198	88.7
1 VII 2007*[122] ....ESDJ		21 015 936	17 186 008	81.8	10 444 803	8 498 794	81.4	10 571 133	8 687 214	82.2

Continent, country or area, and date / Continent, pays ou zone et date	Code[a]	Both sexes - Les deux sexes			Male - Masculin			Female - Féminin		
		Total	Urban - Urbaine		Total	Urban - Urbaine		Total	Urban - Urbaine	
			Number Nombre	Percent P.100		Number Nombre	Percent P.100		Number Nombre	Percent P.100
OCEANIA - OCÉANIE										
Australia - Australie										
1 VII 2008*[122] ....ESDJ		21 384 427	17 522 394	81.9	10 634 132	8 671 358	81.5	10 750 295	8 851 036	82.3
1 VII 2009*[122] ....ESDJ		21 778 845	17 880 298	82.1	10 836 468	8 854 848	81.7	10 942 377	9 025 450	82.5
1 VII 2010*[122] ....ESDJ		22 065 317	18 145 520	82.2	10 974 176	8 982 267	81.8	11 091 141	9 163 253	82.6
1 VII 2011*[122] ....ESDJ		22 323 933	18 389 594	82.4	11 099 615	9 101 034	82.0	11 224 318	9 288 560	82.8
9 VIII 2011[120] ....CDFC		21 727 158[121]	19 312 642	88.9	10 737 148[121]	9 471 918	88.2	10 990 010[121]	9 840 724	89.5
1 VII 2012*[122] ....ESDJ		22 683 573	...	...	11 280 804	...	...	11 402 769	...	...
Cook Islands - Îles Cook[123]										
1 XII 2006 ....CDFC		19 342	...	...	9 816	...	...	9 526	...	...
Fiji - Fidji										
1 VII 2004 ....ESDF		822 370	408 032	49.6	...	...	...	...	...	...
16 IX 2007 ....CDFC		837 271	424 846	50.7	427 176	212 454	49.7	410 095	212 392	51.8
1 VII 2010 ....ESDF		857 000	446 000	52.0	...	...	...	...	...	...
French Polynesia - Polynésie française										
20 VIII 2007 ....CDJC		259 706	...	...	133 109	...	...	126 597	...	...
1 I 2009 ....ESDF		264 000	...	...	135 200	...	...	128 800	...	...
1 I 2011 ....ESDF		269 989	...	...	138 127	...	...	131 862	...	...
Guam										
1 VII 2003[124] ....ESDJ		157 579	...	...	80 419	...	...	77 160	...	...
1 VII 2004[124] ....ESDJ		158 024	...	...	80 603	...	...	77 421	...	...
1 VII 2005[124] ....ESDJ		158 398	...	...	80 744	...	...	77 654	...	...
1 VII 2006[124] ....ESDJ		158 711	...	...	80 851	...	...	77 860	...	...
1 VII 2007[124] ....ESDJ		158 967	...	...	80 930	...	...	78 037	...	...
1 VII 2008[124] ....ESDJ		159 169	...	...	80 982	...	...	78 187	...	...
1 VII 2009[124] ....ESDJ		159 323	...	...	81 010	...	...	78 313	...	...
1 IV 2010 ....CDJC		159 358	149 918	94.1	81 568	...	...	77 790	...	...
1 VII 2011[124] ....ESDJ		159 600	...	...	81 053	...	...	78 547	...	...
1 VII 2012[124] ....ESDJ		159 914	...	...	81 165	...	...	78 749	...	...
Kiribati										
7 XII 2005 ....CDFC		92 533	40 311	43.6	45 612	19 435	42.6	46 921	20 876	44.5
10 X 2010 ....CDFC		103 058	...	...	50 796	...	...	52 262	...	...
Marshall Islands - Îles Marshall[125]										
1 VII 2004 ....ESDF		55 366	...	...	28 232	...	...	27 134	...	...
1 VII 2006 ....ESDF		52 163	...	...	26 746	...	...	25 417	...	...
1 VII 2007 ....ESDF		52 701	...	...	27 022	...	...	25 679	...	...
1 VII 2008 ....ESDF		53 236	...	...	27 297	...	...	25 939	...	...
1 VII 2009 ....ESDF		53 763	...	...	27 567	...	...	26 196	...	...
1 VII 2010 ....ESDF		54 305	...	...	27 843	...	...	26 462	...	...
Micronesia (Federated States of) - Micronésie (États fédérés de)[1]										
1 VII 2003 ....ESDJ		107 644	...	...	54 361	...	...	53 283	...	...
1 VII 2004 ....ESDJ		107 785	...	...	54 396	...	...	53 389	...	...
1 VII 2005 ....ESDJ		107 885	...	...	54 419	...	...	53 466	...	...
1 VII 2006 ....ESDJ		107 965	...	...	54 411	...	...	53 554	...	...
1 VII 2007 ....ESDJ		108 031	...	...	54 403	...	...	53 628	...	...
1 VII 2008 ....ESDJ		108 026	...	...	54 350	...	...	53 676	...	...
1 VII 2009 ....ESDJ		107 973	...	...	54 275	...	...	53 698	...	...
1 VII 2010 ....ESDJ		107 839	...	...	54 158	...	...	53 681	...	...
New Caledonia - Nouvelle-Calédonie										
1 I 2003 ....ESDF		223 592	...	...	113 320	...	...	110 272	...	...
1 VII 2004 ....ESDF		230 068	133 815	58.2	112 716	...	...	109 242	...	...
31 VIII 2004 ....CDFC		230 789	...	...	116 485	...	...	114 304	...	...
1 I 2005 ....ESDF		232 258	...	...	117 221	...	...	115 037	...	...
1 I 2006 ....ESDF		236 528	...	...	119 415	...	...	117 113	...	...
1 VII 2007 ....ESDF		242 400	...	...	122 261	...	...	120 139	...	...
1 VII 2008 ....ESDF		242 400	...	...	122 261	...	...	120 139	...	...
27 VII 2009 ....CDFC		245 580	...	...	124 524	...	...	121 056	...	...
1 VII 2010 ....ESDF		250 040	...	...	126 771	...	...	123 269	...	...

6. Total and urban population by sex: 2003 - 2012
Population totale et population urbaine selon le sexe : 2003 - 2012 (continued - suite)

Continent, country or area, and date / Continent, pays ou zone et date	Code[a]	Both sexes - Les deux sexes			Male - Masculin			Female - Féminin		
		Total	Urban - Urbaine		Total	Urban - Urbaine		Total	Urban - Urbaine	
			Number Nombre	Percent P.100		Number Nombre	Percent P.100		Number Nombre	Percent P.100
OCEANIA - OCÉANIE										
New Zealand - Nouvelle-Zélande										
1 VII 2003[126] ....ESDJ		4 027 200	3 467 200[127]	86.1	1 975 600	1 686 600[127]	85.4	2 051 700	1 780 600[127]	86.8
1 VII 2004[126] ....ESDJ		4 087 500	3 521 500[127]	86.2	2 003 800	1 712 100[127]	85.4	2 083 800	1 809 400[127]	86.8
1 VII 2005[126] ....ESDJ		4 133 900	3 562 300[127]	86.2	2 025 200	1 731 100[127]	85.5	2 108 700	1 831 200[127]	86.8
7 III 2006[120] ....CDFC		4 143 282	...	...	2 021 277	...	...	2 122 005	...	...
1 VII 2006[126] ....ESDJ		4 184 600	3 606 700[127]	86.2	2 048 300	1 751 400[127]	85.5	2 136 200	1 855 300[127]	86.9
1 VII 2007[126] ....ESDJ		4 228 300	3 646 400[127]	86.2	2 070 800	1 771 900[127]	85.6	2 157 600	1 874 400[127]	86.9
1 VII 2008[126] ....ESDJ		4 268 900	3 681 400[127]	86.2	2 092 200	1 790 600[127]	85.6	2 176 700	1 890 800[127]	86.9
1 VII 2009[126] ....ESDJ		4 315 800	3 721 600[127]	86.2	2 117 500	1 812 500[127]	85.6	2 198 300	1 909 100[127]	86.8
1 VII 2010[126] ....ESDJ		4 367 800	3 766 700[127]	86.2	2 144 600	1 836 200[127]	85.6	2 223 200	1 930 500[127]	86.8
1 VII 2011[126] ....ESDJ		4 405 200	3 796 400[127]	86.2	2 164 600	1 852 500[127]	85.6	2 240 600	1 943 900[127]	86.8
1 VII 2012[126] ....ESDJ		4 433 000	3 822 700[127]	86.2	2 180 100	1 867 400[127]	85.7	2 253 000	1 955 300[127]	86.8
Niue - Nioué										
1 VII 2004 ....ESDJ		1 761	...	...	866	...	...	895	...	...
1 VII 2005 ....ESDJ		1 746	...	...	849	...	...	896	...	...
1 VII 2006 ....ESDJ		1 679	...	...	815	...	...	864	...	...
9 IX 2006 ....CDFC		1 625	...	...	802	...	...	823	...	...
1 VII 2010 ....ESDJ		1 496	...	...	754	...	...	740	...	...
Norfolk Island - Île Norfolk										
8 VIII 2006 ....CDFC		2 523	...	...	1 218	...	...	1 305	...	...
9 VIII 2011 ....CDFC		2 302	...	...	1 082	...	...	1 220	...	...
Northern Mariana Islands - Îles Mariannes septentrionales										
1 VII 2003 ....ESDF		76 617	...	...	33 952	...	...	42 665	...	...
1 VII 2004 ....ESDF		78 889	...	...	34 550	...	...	44 339	...	...
1 VII 2005 ....ESDF		70 636	...	...	32 093	...	...	38 543	...	...
1 VII 2006 ....ESDF		60 662	...	...	29 071	...	...	31 591	...	...
1 VII 2007 ....ESDF		58 629	...	...	28 124	...	...	30 505	...	...
1 VII 2008 ....ESDF		55 244	...	...	26 524	...	...	28 720	...	...
1 VII 2009 ....ESDF		51 484	...	...	24 738	...	...	26 746	...	...
1 IV 2010 ....CDFC		53 883	...	...	27 746	...	...	26 137	...	...
1 VII 2010 ....ESDF		48 317	...	...	23 231	...	...	25 086	...	...
1 VII 2011 ....ESDF		46 050	...	...	22 153	...	...	23 897	...	...
Palau - Palaos										
1 IV 2005 ....CDJC		19 907	15 399	77.4	10 699	...	...	9 208	...	...
Papua New Guinea - Papouasie-Nouvelle-Guinée										
10 VII 2011* ....CDFC		7 059 653	...	...	3 663 249	...	...	3 396 404	...	...
Pitcairn										
31 XII 2007 ....ESDF		64[128]	...	...	37	...	...	27	...	...
31 XII 2008 ....ESDF		58[128]	...	...	30	...	...	28	...	...
10 VIII 2012 ....CDFC		48	...	...	22	...	...	26	...	...
Samoa										
1 VII 2003 ....ESDF		179 962	39 551	22.0	93 744	20 202	21.6	86 218	19 349	22.4
1 VII 2004 ....ESDF		181 611	39 913	22.0	94 603	20 387	21.6	87 008	19 526	22.4
1 VII 2005 ....ESDF		183 275	40 279	22.0	95 470	20 574	21.6	87 805	19 705	22.4
1 VII 2006 ....ESDF		184 955	40 648	22.0	96 345	20 763	21.6	88 610	19 885	22.4
5 XI 2006 ....CDFC		180 741	37 708	20.9	93 677	19 120	20.4	87 064	18 588	21.3
1 VII 2007 ....ESDF		181 588	37 878	20.9	94 101	19 206	20.4	87 458	18 672	21.3
1 VII 2008 ....ESDF		182 379	38 050	20.9	94 526	19 293	20.4	87 853	18 756	21.3
1 VII 2009 ....ESDF		183 204	38 222	20.9	94 953	19 381	20.4	88 250	18 841	21.3
1 VII 2010 ....ESDF		184 032	38 395	20.9	95 383	19 468	20.4	88 649	18 926	21.3
1 VII 2011 ....ESDF		184 864	38 568	20.9	95 814	19 556	20.4	89 050	19 012	21.3
7 XI 2011 ....CDFC		187 820	36 735	19.6	96 990	18 485	19.1	90 830	18 250	20.1
Solomon Islands - Îles Salomon										
1 VII 2003[1] ....ESDF		448 286	...	...	231 267	...	...	217 019	...	...
1 VII 2004[1] ....ESDF		460 110	...	...	237 626	...	...	222 484	...	...
1 VII 2005[1] ....ESDF		471 266	...	...	242 927	...	...	228 339	...	...
1 VII 2006[1] ....ESDF		483 083	...	...	248 944	...	...	234 139	...	...
1 VII 2007[1] ....ESDF		495 026	...	...	255 063	...	...	239 963	...	...

Continent, country or area, and date / Continent, pays ou zone et date	Code[a]	Both sexes - Les deux sexes			Male - Masculin			Female - Féminin		
		Total	Urban - Urbaine		Total	Urban - Urbaine		Total	Urban - Urbaine	
			Number Nombre	Percent P.100		Number Nombre	Percent P.100		Number Nombre	Percent P.100
OCEANIA - OCÉANIE										
Solomon Islands - Îles Salomon										
1 VII 2008[1]	ESDF	*506 992*	...	...	*261 214*	...	...	*245 778*	...	...
1 VII 2009[1]	ESDF	*518 321*	...	...	*267 704*	...	...	*250 617*	...	...
22 XI 2009*	CDFC	515 870	102 030	19.8	264 455	53 596	20.3	251 415	48 434	19.3
Tokelau - Tokélaou										
19 X 2006	CDFC	1 151	...	...	583	...	...	568	...	...
18 X 2011	CDFC	1 205	...	...	600	...	...	605	...	...
Tonga										
1 VII 2003[129]	ESDF	*101 405*	...	...	*51 710*	...	...	*49 694*	...	...
1 VII 2004[129]	ESDF	*101 866*	...	...	*51 975*	...	...	*49 890*	...	...
1 VII 2005[129]	ESDF	*102 371*	...	...	*52 261*	...	...	*50 109*	...	...
1 VII 2006[129]	ESDF	*102 907*	...	...	*52 561*	...	...	*50 346*	...	...
30 XI 2006	CDJC	101 991	23 658	23.2	51 772	11 860	22.9	50 219	11 798	23.5
1 VII 2007[129]	ESDF	*103 289*	...	...	*52 771*	...	...	*50 518*	...	...
1 VII 2008[129]	ESDF	*103 647*	...	...	*52 972*	...	...	*50 673*	...	...
30 XI 2011*	CDJC	103 036	...	...	52 001	...	...	51 035	...	...
Tuvalu										
1 VII 2011	ESDF	*11 206*	...	...	*5 582*	...	...	*5 625*	...	...
Vanuatu										
1 VII 2004[1]	ESDF	*215 541*	...	...	*110 141[130]*	...	...	*105 399[130]*	...	...
1 VII 2006[1]	ESDF	*221 417*	...	...	*113 034*	...	...	*108 383*	...	...
16 XI 2009	CDJC	234 023	57 195	24.4	119 091	29 618	24.9	114 932	27 577	24.0
Wallis and Futuna Islands - Îles Wallis et Futuna										
22 VII 2003	CDFC	14 944	...	...	7 494	...	...	7 450	...	...
21 VII 2008	CDFC	13 445	...	...	6 669	...	...	6 776	...	...

FOOTNOTES - NOTES

Italics: estimates which are less reliable. - Italiques : estimations moins sûres.

* Provisional. - Données provisoires.

[a] 'Code' indicates the source of data, as follows:
CDFC - Census, de facto, complete tabulation
CDFS - Census, de facto, sample tabulation
CDJC - Census, de jure, complete tabulation
CDJS - Census, de jure, sample tabulation
SSDF - Sample survey, de facto
SSDJ - Sample survey, de jure
ESDF - Estimates, de facto
ESDJ - Estimates, de jure

Le 'Code' indique la source des données, comme suit :
CDFC - Recensement, population de fait, tabulation complète
CDFS - Recensement, population de fait, tabulation par sondage
CDJC - Recensement, population de droit, tabulation complète
CDJS - Recensement, population de droit, tabulation par sondage
SSDF - Enquête par sondage, population de fait
SSDJ - Enquête par sondage, population de droit
ESDF - Estimations, population de fait
ESDJ - Estimations, population de droit

[1] Data refer to national projections. - Les données se réfèrent aux projections nationales.
[2] Based on the results of 2006 Demographic Survey. - D'après les résultats de l'enquête Démographique par Sondage de 2006.
[3] Unrevised data. - Les données n'ont pas été révisées.
[4] Excluding Mayotte. - Non compris Mayotte.
[5] Projections based on the 1994 Population Census. - Projections fondées sur le recensement de la population de 1994.

[6] Based on the results of the Gabonese Survey for the Evaluation and Tracking of Poverty. - Sur base des résultats de l'enquête gabonaise sur l'évaluation et le suivi de la pauvreté.
[7] Post-censal estimates based on the 1999 Population Census. - Les estimations post-censitaire fondées sur le recensement de la population de 1999.
[8] Data refer to Libyan nationals only. - Les données se raportent aux nationaux libyens seulement.
[9] Reason for discrepancy between these figures and corresponding figures shown elsewhere not ascertained. - On ne sait pas comment s'explique la divergence entre ces chiffres et les chiffres correspondants indiqués ailleurs.
[10] Excludes the islands of St. Brandon and Agalega. - Non compris les îles St. Brandon et Agalega.
[11] Based on the results of the 2004 Population Census. - D'après des résultats du recensement de la population de 2004.
[12] Based on the results of a population count. - D'après les résultats d'un comptage de la population.
[13] The population figures are 264, 263 and 262 persons for 2007, 2008 and 2009 respectively. - La population est respectivement égale à 264, 263 et 262 personnes pour les années 2007, 2008 et 2009.
[14] Projections based on the 2002 Population Census. - Projections fondées sur le recensement de la population de 2002.
[15] Mid-year estimates have been adjusted for underenumeration at latest census. - Les estimations au millieu de l'année tiennent compte d'un ajustement destiné à compenser les lacunes du dénombrement lors du dernier recensement.
[16] Male and female population don't add up to total due to rounding. - La somme des populations d'hommes et des femmes diffère de la population totale au raison des arrondis.
[17] Bermuda is 100% urban. - 100 % de la population des Bermudes est urbaine.
[18] Estimates adjusted for census net undercoverage (including adjustment for incompletely enumerated Indian reserves). Final intercensal estimates. - Ajusté pour la sous-estimation du recensement (y compris les réservations en Inde incomplètement énumérées). Estimations inter-censitaires definitives.

19 Because of rounding, totals are not in all cases the sum of the respective components. - Les chiffres étant arrondis, les totaux ne correspondent pas toujours rigoureusement à la somme des composants respectifs.

20 Final postcensal estimates. Estimates adjusted for census net undercoverage (including adjustment for incompletely enumerated Indian reserves). - Estimations postcensitaires definitives. Ajusté pour la sous-estimation du recensement (y compris les réservations en Inde incomplètement énumérées).

21 Estimates adjusted for census net undercoverage (including adjustment for incompletely enumerated Indian reserves). Updated postcensal estimates. - Ajusté pour la sous-estimation du recensement (y compris les réservations en Inde incomplètement énumérées). Estimations post censitaires mises à jour.

22 Preliminary postcensal estimates. Estimates adjusted for census net undercoverage (including adjustment for incompletely enumerated Indian reserves). - Estimations post censitaires préliminaires. Ajusté pour la sous-estimation du recensement (y compris les réservations en Inde incomplètement énumérées).

23 Excludes the institutional population. - Non compris la population dans les institutions.

24 Estimates based on the 2007 Population Census. - Estimations fondées sur le recensement de la population de 2007.

25 Population statistics are compiled from registers. - Les statistiques de la population sont compilées à partir des registres.

26 Excluding data for Saint Barthélémy and Saint Martin. - Non compris les données pour Saint Barthélémy et Saint Martin.

27 Projections produced by l'Institut Haïtien de Statistique et d'Informatique (IHSI) and the Latin American and Caribbean Demographic Centre (CELADE) - Population Division of ECLAC. - Les données sont projections produits par l'Institut Haïtien de Statistique et d'Informatique (IHSI) et le centre démographique de l'Amérique latine et les Caraïbes - Division de la population de la CEPALC.

28 Data refer to projections based on the 2001 Population Census. - Les données se réfèrent aux projections basées sur le recensement de la population de 2001.

29 Including an estimation of 1 334 585 persons corresponding to 448 195 housing units without information of the occupants. - Y compris une estimation de 1 334 585 personnes correspondant aux 448 195 unités d'habitation sans information sur les occupants.

30 Data refer to projections based on the 2000 Population Census. - Les données se réfèrent aux projections basées sur le recensement de la population de 2000.

31 Including armed forces stationed in the area. - Y compris les militaires en garnison sur le territoire.

32 Data based on the 2010 Population Census results. - D'après le résultats du recensement de la population de 2010.

33 Based on the results of the 2000 Population Census. - Basé sur les résultats du recencement de la population de 2000.

34 Excluding armed forces overseas and civilian citizens absent from the country for an extended period of time. - Non compris les militaires à l'étranger, et les civils hors du pays pendant une période prolongée.

35 Data include persons in remote areas, military personnel outside the country, merchant seamen at sea, civilian seasonal workers outside the country, and other civilians outside the country, and exclude nomads, foreign military, civilian aliens temporarily in the country, transients on ships and Indian jungle population. - Y compris les personnes vivant dans des régions éloignées, le personel militaire en dehors du pays, les marins marchands, les ouvriers saisonniers en dehors du pays, et autres civils en dehors du pays, et non compris les nomades, les militaires étrangers, les étrangers civils temporairement dans le pays, les transiteurs sur des bateaux et les Indiens de la jungle.

36 Data are revised projections taking into consideration also the results of 2005 census. - Les données sont des projections révisées tenant compte également des résultats du recensement de 2005.

37 Excludes nomadic Indian tribes. Data refer to national projections. - Non compris les tribus d'Indiens nomades. Les données se réfèrent aux projections nationales.

38 A dispute exists between the governments of Argentina and the United Kingdom of Great Britain and Northern Ireland concerning sovereignty over the Falkland Islands (Malvinas). - La souveraineté sur les îles Falkland (Malvinas) fait l'objet d'un différend entre le Gouvernement argentin et le Gouvernement du Royaume-Uni de Grande-Bretagne et d'Irlande du Nord.

39 The population for the year 2005 corresponds to the population actually enumerated in the census conducted between 18 July and 20 August 2005. The total (adjusted) population is 27 219 264 inhabitants. - La population pour 2005 correspond à la population effectivement dénombrée lors du recensement réalisé entre le 18 juillet et le 20 août 2005. La population totale (après ajustement) compte 27 219 264 habitants.

40 Including 17 diplomats. - La population totale indiquée comprend 17 diplomates.

41 The districts of Paramaribo and Wanica are considered urban areas, whereas all other districts are considered more or less rural areas. - Les districts de Paramaribo et de Wanica sont considérés comme des zones urbaines, les autres districts étant considérés comme des zones rurales à divers degrés.

42 Data refer to resident population in Uruguay according to Census Phase 1, carried out between the months of June and July 2004. - Les données se rapportent à la population résidente en Uruguay d'après la phase 1 du recensement, qui a eu lieu entre juin et juillet 2004.

43 Figures for male and female population do not add up to the figure for total population, since they do not include 108 homeless people. - Les chiffres relatifs à la population masculine et féminine ne correspondent pas au chiffre de la population totale, parce que l'on en a exclu 108 personnes sans toit.

44 Data refer to the settled population based on the 1979 Population Census and the latest household prelisting. The refugees of Afghanistan in Iran, Pakistan, and an estimated 1.5 million nomads, are not included. - Les données se rapportent à la population stationnaire sur la base du recensement de 1979 et du recensement préliminaire des logements le plus récent. Sont exclus les réfugiés d'Afghanistan en Iran et au Pakistan et les nomades estimés à 1,5 million.

45 Data refer to the settled population based on the 1979 Population Census and the latest household prelisting. The refugees of Afghanistan in Iran, Pakistan, and an estimated 1.5 million nomads, are not included. The so adjusted total population of the country for 2006 is 24.1 million (12.3 million males and 11.8 million females). - Les données se rapportent à la population stationnaire sur la base du recensement de 1979 et du recensement préliminaire des logements le plus récent. Sont exclus les réfugiés d'Afghanistan en Iran et au Pakistan et les nomades estimés à 1,5 million. La population totale du pays ainsi ajustée pour 2006 comprend 24,1 millions de personnes (12,3 millions d'hommes et 11,8 millions de femmes).

46 The adjusted total population of the country is 25.5 million. - La population totale ajustée du pays comprend 25,5 millions de personnes.

47 The adjusted total population of the country is 26 million (13.3 million males and 12.7 million females). - La population totale ajustée du pays comprend 26 millions de personnes (13.3 millions d'homes et 12.7 millions de femmes).

48 Intercensal estimates. - Estimations inter-censitaires.

49 Data refer to projections based on the 2005 Population Census. - Les données se réfèrent aux projections basées sur le recensement de la population de 2005.

50 Excluding foreign diplomatic personnel and their dependants. - Non compris le personnel diplomatique étranger et les membres de leur famille les accompagnant.

51 Based on 1998 census results. - A partir des résultats de recensement de l'année 1998.

52 Based on the results of the Cambodia Intercensal Population Survey. Data exclude institutional, homeless households and transient population. - Les données ne comprennent pas la population des institutions, les ménages sans abri et la population de passage.

53 Data based on 2008 Population Census. - Données fondées sur le recensement de population de 2008.

54 For statistical purposes, the data for China do not include those for the Hong Kong Special Administrative Region (Hong Kong SAR), Macao Special Administrative Region (Macao SAR) and Taiwan province of China. - Pour la présentation des statistiques, les données pour la Chine ne comprennent pas la Région Administrative Spéciale de Hong Kong (Hong Kong RAS), la Région Administrative Spéciale de Macao (Macao RAS) et Taïwan province de Chine.

55 Data have been estimated on the basis of the annual National Sample Survey on Population Changes. - Les données ont été estimées sur la base de l'enquête annuelle "National Sample Survey on Population Changes".

56 The military personnel are classified as urban population. - Le personnel militaire est classé dans la population urbaine.

57 The military personnel are classified as urban population. Because of rounding, totals are not in all cases the sum of the respective components. - Le personnel militaire est classé dans la population urbaine. Les chiffres étant arrondis, les totaux ne correspondent pas toujours rigoureusement à la somme des composants respectifs.

58 Data are from Communique of the National Bureau of Statistics of the People's Republic of China on Major Figures of the 2010 Population Census (No.1). - Données issues du communiqué du Bureau national de la statistique de la République populaire de Chine sur les chiffres importants du recensement de 2010 (n° 1).

59 Data have been adjusted on the basis of the Population Census of 2010. - Les données ont été ajustées à partir des résultats du recensement de la population de 2010.

60 Data are estimates from sample enquiry. - Les données sont des chiffres estimatifs dérivés d'une enquête par sondage.

61 Data refer to government controlled areas. - Les données se rapportent aux zones contrôlées par le Gouvernement.

62 Data have been adjusted on the basis of the Population Census of 2011. - Les données ont été calculées sur la base du recensement de population de 2011.

63 Includes data for the Indian-held part of Jammu and Kashmir, the final status of which has not yet been determined. - Y compris les données pour la partie du Jammu et du Cachemire occupée par l'Inde dont le statut définitif n'a pas encore été déterminé.

64 Data refer to projections based on the 2001 Population Census. - Les données se réfèrent aux projections basées sur le recensement de la population de 2001.

65 Data refer to the "Intercensal Population Survey". Excluding Province Nanggroe Aceh Darussalam, Regency Nias & Nias Selatan, Regency Boven Digul & Teluk Wondama. - Les données concernent l'enquête intercensitaire sur la population. En excluant les provinces de Nanggroe Aceh Darussalam, Regency Nias & Nias Selatan, Regency Boven Digul & Teluk Wondama.

66 Data refer to the Iranian Year which begins on 21 March and ends on 20 March of the following year. - Les données concernent l'année iranienne, qui commence le 21 mars et se termine le 20 mars de l'année suivante.

67 Differences between the total country figures and sum of urban and rural areas are due to the inclusion of unsettled population. - Les différences entre les chiffres pour l'ensemble du pays et la somme des zones urbaines et rurales s'expliquent par l'inclusion de la population non sédentaire.

68 Excluding unknown sex. - Non compris le sexe inconnu.

69 Includes data for East Jerusalem and Israeli residents in certain other territories under occupation by Israeli military forces since June 1967. - Y compris les données pour Jérusalem-Est et les résidents israéliens dans certains autres territoires occupés depuis 1967 par les forces armées israéliennes.

70 Excluding residents who had been registered in the Israeli localities (the Jewish localities) in the Gaza Area and northern Samaria, which were evacuated in August 2005, but did not notify the Ministry of Interior of their new address. These residents are included in total. - Hors résidents enregistrés dans les localités d'Israel (localités juives) de la Bande de Gaza (verfify) et du nord de la Samarie, qui ont été évacués en Août 2005, mais qui n'ont pas notifié leur nouvelle adresse au ministère de l'intérieur. Ces résidents sont inclus dans le total.

71 Data are rounded for confidentiality reasons. - Chiffres arrondis pour des raisons de confidentialité.

72 Excluding diplomatic personnel outside the country and foreign military and civilian personnel and their dependants stationed in the area. - Non compris le personnel diplomatique hors du pays ni les militaires et agents civils étrangers en poste sur le territoire et les membres de leur famille les accompagnant.

73 Estimates based on the complete counts of the 2010 Population Census. - Estimations basées sur le dénombrement complet du recensement de la population de 2010.

74 Excluding data for Jordanian territory under occupation since June 1967 by Israeli military forces. Excluding foreigners, including registered Palestinian refugees. - Non compris les données pour le territoire jordanien occupé depuis juin 1967 par les forces armées israéliennes. Non compris les étrangers, mais y compris les réfugiés de Palestine enregistrés.

75 Excluding data for Jordanian territory under occupation since June 1967 by Israeli military forces. Including registered Palestinian refugees and Jordanians abroad. - Non compris les données pour le territoire jordanien occupé depuis juin 1967 par les forces armées israéliennes. Y compris les réfugiés palestiniens enregistrés et les Jordaniens à l'étranger.

76 Estimates based on population census data of 2005 and 2011. - Estimations basées sur les données des recensements de la population de 2005 et 2011.

77 Data are calculated from the results of the Population and Housing Census of 2009. - Les données sont calculées à partir des résultats du recensement de la population et de l'habitat de 2009.

78 Population estimates for 2000 to 2004 are based on the age-sex distribution of 1995 population census and growth rate at year 2000. - Pour les années 2000 à 2004, on a pris pour base la répartition par âge et sexe du recensement de population de 1995 et le taux de croissance de 2000.

79 Excluding usual residents not in the country at the time of census. - À l'exclusion des résidents habituels qui ne sont pas dans le pays au moment du recensement.

80 Based on the results of the 2005 Population and Housing Census. - Données fondées sur les résultats du recensement de la population et de l'habitat de 2005.

81 Based on the results of a household survey. - D'après les résultats d'une enquête des ménages.

82 Intercensal Mid-Year Population Estimates based on the adjusted Population and Housing Census of 2000 and 2010. - Les estimations inter-censitaires au milieu de l'année sont fondée sur les résultats ajustées des recensements de la population et de l'habitat de 2000 et 2010.

83 Estimates based on the adjusted Population and Housing Census of 2010. - Les estimations sont fondée sur les résultats ajustées du recensement de la population et de l'habitat de 2010.

84 Data have been adjusted for underenumeration. - Les données ont été ajustées pour compenser les lacunes du dénombrement.

85 Total Population is taken as de facto and de jure together. - Population totale considérée comme de fait et de droit.

86 76% are Omani and the rest are Expatriates. - Le pourcentage d'Omanais atteint 76 %; le pourcentage restant correspond à des personnes expatriées.

87 Excluding data for the Pakistan-held part of Jammu and Kashmir, the final status of which has not yet been determined. - Non compris les données concernant la partie du Jammu et Cachemire occupée par le Pakistan dont le statut définitif n'a pas été déterminé.

88 Based on the results of the Pakistan Demographic Survey (PDS 2003). These estimates do not reflect completely accurately the actual population and vital events of the country. - D'après les résultats de l'enquête démographique effectuée par le Pakistan en 2003. Ces estimations ne dénotent pas d'une manière complètement ponctuelle la population actuelle et les statistiques de l'état civil du pays.

89 Based on the results of the Pakistan Demographic Survey (PDS 2005). These estimates do not reflect completely accurately the actual population and vital events of the country. - D'après les résultats de l'enquête démographique effectuée par le Pakistan en 2005. Ces estimations ne dénotent pas d'une manière complètement ponctuelle la population actuelle et les statistiques de l'état civil du pays.

90 Based on the results of the Pakistan Demographic Survey (PDS 2007). - D'après les résultats de l'enquête démographique effectuée par le Pakistan en 2007.

91 Excluding 2739 Filipinos in Philippine Embassies, Consulates and Mission Abroad. - Excepté 2739 Philippins travaillant dans les ambassades, les consulats et les missions des Philippines à l'étranger.

92 Data based on the preliminary results of the 2010 Population and Housing Census. - D'après les résultats préliminaires du recensement de la population et des logements de 2010.

93 Data refer to resident population which comprises Singapore citizens and permanent residents. - Les données se rapportent à la population résidente composé des citoyens de Singapour et des résidents permanents.

94 Data are based on the latest register-based population estimates for 2010. Urban and rural breakdown not applicable as Singapore is a city-state. - Données basées sur les estimations démographiques les plus récentes fondées sur les registres de 2010. La ventilation entre zones urbaines et zones rurales ne s'applique pas à Singapour, puisqu'il s'agit d'une ville État.

95 Data for urban include population in refugee camps. - Les données pour la population urbaine comprennent la population dans les camps réfugiés.

96 Data have been adjusted for underenumeration, estimated at 2.70 per cent. - Les données ont été ajustées pour compenser les lacunes du dénombrement, estimées à 2,70 p. 100.

97 Including Palestinian refugees. - Y compris les réfugiés de Palestine.

98 Data based on Address Based Population Registration System. - Les données sont basées sur le registre national de la population basé sur l'adresse.

99 Data include non-national population. - Les données comprennent les non-nationaux.

100 Data are adjusted according to the results of the 1999 and 2009 censuses. - Les données ont été ajustées à partir des résultats des recensements de la population de 1999 et 2009.

101 Decrease in population due to revision in administrative registers. - Diminution de la population due à la révision des registres administratifs.

102 Excluding Faeroe Islands and Greenland shown separately, if available. Population statistics are compiled from registers. - Non compris les Iles Féroé et le Groenland, qui font l'objet de rubriques distinctes, si disponible. Les statistiques de la population sont compilées à partir des registres.

103 Population statistics are compiled from registers. Excluding Åland Islands. - Les statistiques de la population sont compilées à partir des registres. Non compris les Îles d'Åland.

104 Excluding diplomatic personnel outside the country and including members of alien armed forces not living in military camps and foreign diplomatic personnel not living in embassies or consulates. - Non compris le personnel diplomatique hors du pays et y compris les militaires étrangers ne vivant pas dans des camps militaires et le personnel diplomatique étranger ne vivant pas dans les ambassades ou les consulats.

105 Data of the microcensus - a 1 per cent household sample survey - refer to a single reference week in spring (usually last week in April). Excluding homeless persons. Excluding foreign military personnel and foreign diplomatic and consular personnel and their family members in the country. - Les données du microrecensement (enquête sur les ménages, réalisée sur un échantillon de 1 pour cent) concernent une seule semaine de référence au printemps (habituellement la dernière semaine d'avril). Non compris les personnes sans

domicile fixe. Non compris le personnel militaire étranger, le personnel diplomatique et consulaire étranger et les membres de leur famille se trouvant dans le pays.

[106] Excluding military personnel, visitors and transients. - Non compris les militaires, ni les visiteurs et transients.

[107] Excluding armed forces stationed outside the country, but including alien armed forces stationed in the area. - Non compris les militaires en garnison hors du pays, mais y compris les militaires étrangers en garnison sur le territoire.

[108] Data refer to the Vatican City State. - Les données se rapportent à l'Etat de la Cité du Vatican.

[109] The regional grouping (urban/rural) was made from 1990 to 2000 according to the administrative division of 1 January 2000 and from 2001 according to the administrative division of 1 January 2004. - Pour les années 1990 à 2000, le découpage régional (zone urbaine/rurale) correspond au découpage administratif en vigueur au 1er janvier 2000; à partir de 2001, il correspond à celui en vigueur au 1er janvier 2004.

[110] Definition of localities was revised from 2011 causing a break with the previous series. - La rupture par rapport aux séries précédentes s'explique par le fait que la définition des localités a été révisée depuis 2011.

[111] Including civilian nationals temporarily outside the country. - Y compris les civils nationaux temporairement hors du pays.

[112] Figures for male and female population do not add up to the figure for total population, because they exclude 119 persons of unknown sex. - Les chiffres relatifs à la population masculine et féminine ne correspondent pas au chiffre de la population totale, parce que l'on en a exclu 119 personnes de sexe inconnu.

[113] Including residents temporarily outside the country. - Y compris les résidents se trouvant temporairement hors du pays.

[114] Excluding civilian aliens within country, but including civilian nationals temporarily outside country. - Non compris les civils étrangers dans le pays, mais y compris les civils nationaux temporairement hors du pays.

[115] Excluding Transnistria and the municipality of Bender. - Les données ne tiennent pas compte de l'information sur la Transnistria et la municipalité de Bender.

[116] Excludes data for Kosovo and Metohia. - Sans les données pour le Kosovo et Metohie.

[117] Excluding citizens temporarily residing abroad, the sum by urban and rural does not add up to the total. - Les nationaux se trouvant provisoirement à l'étranger ne sont pas pris en compte. La somme des chiffres disponibles pour les zones urbaines et rurales ne correspond donc pas au total.

[118] Excluding Channel Islands (Guernsey and Jersey) and Isle of Man, shown separately, if available. - Non compris les îles Anglo-Normandes (Guernesey et Jersey) et l'île de Man, qui font l'objet de rubriques distinctes, si disponible.

[119] Intercensal estimates. Data are based on Australian Standard Geographical Classification boundaries. - Estimations inter-censitaires. Les données réfèrent au découpage de la nomenclature géographique normalisée d'Australie.

[120] This data has been randomly rounded to protect confidentiality. Individual figures may not add up to totals, and values for the same data may vary in different tables. - Ces données ont été arrondies de façon aléatoire afin d'en préserver la confidentialité. La somme de certains chiffres peut ne pas correspondre aux totaux indiqués et les valeurs des mêmes données peuvent varier d'un tableau à un autre.

[121] Including population in off-shore, migratory and shipping. - Y compris les populations extraterritoriales, les populations nomades et les populations maritimes.

[122] Data are based on Australian Standard Geographical Classification boundaries. These estimates are preliminary revised. - Les données réfèrent au découpage de la nomenclature géographique normalisée d'Australie. Ces estimations sont des estimations préliminaires révisées.

[123] Excluding Niue, shown separately, which is part of Cook Islands, but because of remoteness is administered separately. - Non compris Nioué, qui fait l'objet d'une rubrique distincte et qui fait partie des îles Cook, mais qui, en raison de son éloignement, est administrée séparément.

[124] Including armed forces stationed in the area. Data refer to projections based on the 2010 Population Census. - Y compris les militaires en garnison sur le territoire. Les données se réfèrent aux projections basées sur le recensement de la population de 2010.

[125] Projections are prepared by the Secretariat of the Pacific Community based on 1999 census of population and housing. - Les projections sont préparées par le Secrétariat de la Communauté du Pacifique à partir des résultats du recensement de la population et de l'habitat de 1999.

[126] Based on the census, updated for residents missed or counted more than once by the census (net census undercount); residents temporarily overseas on census night, and births, deaths and net migration between the census night and the date of the estimate. Because of rounding, totals are not in all cases the sum of the respective components. - D'après le recensement, mise à jour pour les résidents omis ou dénombrés plus d'une fois par le recensement (sous-dénombrement net); résidents temporairement à l'étranger la nuit du

recensement, et naissances, décès et migration nette entre la nuit du recensement et la date de l'estimation. Les chiffres étant arrondis, les totaux ne correspondent pas toujours rigoureusement à la somme des composants respectifs.

[127] Population estimates by urban/rural residence exclude inland waters and oceanic areas. - Les estimations de la population par lieu de résidence urbaine ou rurale excluent les eaux intérieures et les zones océaniques.

[128] The population figures are 64 and 58 persons for 2007 and 2008 respectively. - La population est respectivement égale à 64 et 58 personnes pour les années 2007 et 2008.

[129] Data refer to national projections. Based on the results of the 1996 population census. - Les données se réfèrent aux projections nationales. À partir des résultats du recensement de la population de 1996.

[130] Figures for male and female do not add up to the total, reason for discrepancy not ascertained. - La some des données pour la population masculine et pour la population féminine n'est pas égale au total, les raisons de cette différence ne sont pas expliquées.

Table 7 - *Demographic Yearbook 2012*

Table 7 presents population by age, sex and urban/rural residence for the latest available year between 2003 and 2012.

Description of variables: Data in this table are either population census figures or estimates, some of which are based on sample surveys. The source of data is indicated by the 'code' explained at the end of the table.

The reference date of the census or estimate appears in the left-most column of the table. In general, the estimates refer to mid-year, i.e. 1 July.

Age is defined as age at last birthday, that is, the difference between the date of birth and the reference date of the age distribution expressed in completed solar years. The age classification used in this table is the following: under 1 year, 1-4 years, 5-year groups through 95-99 years, and 100 years or over.

Statistics are presented for one year, the most recent available. However, if more complete disaggregation is available for an earlier year, both are displayed.

The urban/rural classification of population is that provided by each country or area; it is presumed to be based on the national census definitions of urban population that have been set forth at the end of the technical notes to table 6.

Reliability of data: Estimates which are believed to be less reliable are set in *italics* rather than in roman type.

Limitations: Statistics on population by age and sex are subject to the same qualifications as have been set forth for population statistics in general and age distributions in particular, as discussed in sections 3 and 3.1.3, respectively, of the Technical Notes.

Comparability of population data classified by age and sex is limited by variations in the definition of total population, discussed in detail in section 3 of the Technical Notes, and by the accuracy of the original enumeration. Both factors are more important in relation to certain age groups than to others. For example, under-enumeration is known to be more prevalent among infants and young children than among older persons. Similarly, the exclusion from the total population of certain groups that tend to be of selected ages (such as the armed forces) can markedly affect the age structure and its comparability with that for other countries or areas. Consideration should be given to the implications of these basic limitations in using the data.

In addition to these general qualifications are the special problems of comparability that arise in relation to age statistics in particular. Age distributions of population are known to suffer from certain deficiencies that have their origin in irregularities in age reporting. Although some of the irregularities tend to be obscured or eliminated when data are tabulated in five-year age groups rather than by single years, precision still continues to be affected, though the degree of distortion is not always readily seen.

Another factor limiting comparability is the age classification employed by the various countries or areas. Age may be based on the year of birth rather than the age at last birthday, in other words, calculated using the day, month and year of birth. Distributions based only on the year of birth are footnoted when known.

The absence of data in the unknown age group does not necessarily indicate completely accurate reporting and tabulation of the age item. The unknowns may have been eliminated by assigning ages to them before tabulation, or by proportionately distributing the unknown category across the age groups after tabulation.

As noted in connection with table 5, intercensal estimates of total population are usually revised to accord with the results of a census of population if inexplicable discontinuities appear to exist. Postcensal age-sex distributions, however, are less likely to be revised in this way. When it is known that a total population estimate for a given year has been revised and the corresponding age distribution has not been, the age distribution is shown as provisional. Distributions of this type should be used with caution when studying trends over a period of years, though their utility for studying age structure for the specified year is probably unimpaired.

The comparability of data by urban/rural residence is affected by the national definitions of urban and rural used in tabulating these data. When known, the definitions of urban used in national population censuses are presented at the end of the technical notes for table 6. As discussed in detail in the technical notes for table 6, these definitions vary considerably from one country or area to another.

Earlier data: Population by age, sex and urban/rural residence has been shown in previous issues of the *Demographic Yearbook*. For more information on specific topics, and years for which data are reported, readers should consult the Historical Index. In addition, population data by single years of age, sex and urban/rural residence, for censuses conducted since 1995, are shown in the *Demographic Yearbook* webpage http://unstats.un.org/unsd/demographic/products/dyb/dybcensusdata.htm.

Tableau 7 – *Annuaire démographique 2012*

Le tableau 7 présente les données les plus récentes disponibles pour la période 2003-2012 sur la population selon l'âge, le sexe et le lieu de résidence (zone urbaine ou rurale).

Description des variables : les données de ce tableau proviennent de recensements de la population ou correspondent à des estimations, fondées dans certains cas, sur des enquêtes par sondage. Le 'code' indique comment les données ont été obtenues. Les codes utilisés sont expliqués à la fin du tableau.

La date du recensement ou de l'estimation figure dans la colonne de gauche du tableau. En général, les estimations se rapportent au milieu de l'année (1er juillet).

L'âge désigne l'âge au dernier anniversaire, c'est-à-dire la différence entre la date de naissance et la date de référence de la répartition par âge exprimée en années solaires révolues. La classification par âge utilisée dans ce tableau est la suivante : moins d'un an, 1 à 4 ans, groupes quinquennaux jusqu'à 95-99 ans et 100 ans ou plus.

Les statistiques portent sur une année, qui correspond à celle pour laquelle on dispose des statistiques les plus récentes. Toutefois, si l'on dispose de répartitions plus complètes pour des années antérieures, les statistiques sont alors présentées pour les deux années.

La classification par zones urbaines et rurales de la population est celle qui est communiquée par chaque pays ou zone ; on part du principe qu'elle repose sur les définitions de la population urbaine utilisées pour les recensements de la population nationaux telles qu'elles sont reproduites à la fin des notes techniques du tableau 6.

Fiabilité des données : les estimations considérées comme moins sûres sont indiquées en italique plutôt qu'en caractères romains.

Insuffisance des données : les statistiques de la population selon l'âge et le sexe appellent les mêmes réserves que celles qui ont été formulées aux sections 3 et 3.1.3 des Notes techniques à propos des statistiques de la population en général et des répartitions par âge en particulier.

La comparabilité des statistiques de la population selon l'âge et le sexe pâtit du manque d'uniformité dans la définition de la population totale (voir la section 3 des Notes techniques) et des lacunes des dénombrements. L'influence de ces deux facteurs varie selon les groupes d'âge. Ainsi, le dénombrement des enfants de moins d'un an et des jeunes enfants comporte souvent plus de lacunes que celui des personnes plus âgées. De même, le fait que certains groupes de personnes appartenant souvent à des groupes d'âge déterminés, par exemple les militaires, ne soient pas pris en compte dans la population totale peut influer sensiblement sur la structure par âge et sur la comparabilité des données avec celles d'autres pays ou zones. Il conviendra de tenir compte de ces facteurs fondamentaux lorsque l'on utilisera les données du tableau.

Outre ces difficultés d'ordre général, la comparabilité pose des problèmes particuliers lorsqu'il s'agit des données par âge. On sait que les répartitions de la population selon l'âge présentent certaines imperfections dues à l'inexactitude des déclarations d'âge. Certaines de ces anomalies ont tendance à s'estomper ou à disparaître lorsque l'on classe les données par groupes d'âge quinquennaux et non par années d'âge, mais une certaine imprécision subsiste, même s'il n'est pas toujours facile de voir à quel point il y a distorsion.

Le degré de comparabilité dépend également de la classification par âge employée dans les divers pays ou zones. L'âge retenu peut être défini par date exacte (jour, mois et année) de naissance ou par celle du dernier anniversaire. Lorsqu'elles étaient connues, les répartitions établies seulement d'après l'année de la naissance ont été signalées en note à la fin du tableau.

Si aucun nombre ne figure dans la rangée réservée aux âges inconnus, cela ne signifie pas nécessairement que les déclarations d'âge et l'exploitation des données par âge aient été tout à fait exactes. C'est souvent une indication que l'on a attribué un âge aux personnes d'âge inconnu avant l'exploitation des données ou qu'elles ont été réparties proportionnellement entre les différents groupes après cette opération.

Comme on l'a indiqué à propos du tableau 5, les estimations intercensitaires de la population totale sont d'ordinaire rectifiées d'après les résultats des recensements de population si l'on constate des discontinuités inexplicables. Les données postcensitaires concernant la répartition de la population par âge et par sexe ont toutefois moins de chance d'être rectifiées de cette manière. Lorsque l'on savait qu'une estimation de la population totale pour une année donnée avait été rectifiée sans qu'il en soit de même pour la répartition par âge correspondante, cette dernière a été indiquée comme ayant un caractère provisoire. Les répartitions de ce type doivent être utilisées avec prudence lorsque l'on étudie les tendances sur un certain nombre d'années, quoique leur utilité pour l'étude de la structure par âge de la population pour l'année visée reste probablement entière.

La comparabilité des données selon le lieu de résidence (zone urbaine ou rurale) peut être limitée par les définitions nationales des termes « urbain » et « rural » utilisées pour la mise en tableaux de ces données. Les définitions du terme « urbain » utilisées pour les recensements nationaux de population ont été présentées à la fin des notes techniques du tableau 6 lorsqu'elles étaient connues. Comme on l'a précisé dans les notes techniques relatives au tableau 6, ces définitions varient considérablement d'un pays ou d'une zone à l'autre.

Données publiées antérieurement : des statistiques concernant la population selon l'âge, le sexe et le lieu de résidence (zone urbaine ou rurale) ont été présentées dans des éditions antérieures de l'*Annuaire démographique*. Pour plus de précisions concernant les années et les sujets pour lesquels des données ont été publiées, se reporter à l'index historique. En plus, des statistiques disponibles concernant la « Population selon chaque année d'âge, le sexe et la résidence urbaine/rurale », pour les recensements depuis 1995, ont été présentées dans la page internet suivante de l'*Annuaire démographique* http://unstats.un.org/unsd/demographic/products/dyb/dybcensusdata.htm.

7. Population by age, sex and urban/rural residence: latest available year, 2003 - 2012
Population selon l'âge, le sexe et la résidence, urbaine/rurale : dernière année disponible, 2003 - 2012

Continent, country or area, date, code and age (in years) Continent, pays ou zone, date, code et âge (en annèes)	Total			Urban - Urbaine			Rural - Rurale		
	Both sexes Les deux sexes	Male Masculin	Female Féminin	Both sexes Les deux sexes	Male Masculin	Female Féminin	Both sexes Les deux sexes	Male Masculin	Female Féminin
AFRICA - AFRIQUE									
Algeria - Algérie[1]									
16 IV 2008* (CDJC)									
Total	34 080 030	17 232 747	16 847 283	...	...	...	...	...	...
0 - 4	3 404 918	1 750 097	1 654 821	...	...	...	...	...	...
5 - 9	2 888 376	1 475 674	1 412 702	...	...	...	...	...	...
10 - 14	3 258 774	1 662 260	1 596 513	...	...	...	...	...	...
15 - 19	3 635 170	1 847 311	1 787 859	...	...	...	...	...	...
20 - 24	3 763 506	1 895 704	1 867 802	...	...	...	...	...	...
25 - 29	3 422 377	1 730 409	1 691 968	...	...	...	...	...	...
30 - 34	2 740 995	1 379 085	1 361 910	...	...	...	...	...	...
35 - 39	2 342 778	1 167 249	1 175 529	...	...	...	...	...	...
40 - 44	2 018 327	1 007 683	1 010 644	...	...	...	...	...	...
45 - 49	1 629 435	817 004	812 432	...	...	...	...	...	...
50 - 54	1 346 695	682 357	664 337	...	...	...	...	...	...
55 - 59	1 062 579	547 181	515 398	...	...	...	...	...	...
60 - 64	711 482	354 694	356 788	...	...	...	...	...	...
65 - 69	631 303	314 958	316 345	...	...	...	...	...	...
70 - 74	504 926	248 672	256 254	...	...	...	...	...	...
75 - 79	363 843	181 478	182 364	...	...	...	...	...	...
80 - 84	187 130	93 472	93 657	...	...	...	...	...	...
85 +	132 445	62 141	70 304	...	...	...	...	...	...
Unknown - Inconnu	34 973	15 317	19 657	...	...	...	...	...	...
Benin - Bénin[2]									
1 VII 2011 (ESDF)									
Total	9 067 076	4 446 877	4 620 199	4 072 574	2 003 366	2 069 208	4 994 502	2 443 511	2 550 991
0 - 4	1 629 512	828 064	801 448	633 629	321 667	311 962	995 883	506 397	489 486
0	350 292	178 565	171 727	...	...	...	...	...	...
1 - 4	1 279 220	649 499	629 721	...	...	...	...	...	...
5 - 9	1 335 166	675 912	659 254	511 822	251 283	260 539	823 344	424 629	398 715
10 - 14	1 137 068	572 756	564 312	517 373	244 437	272 936	619 695	328 319	291 376
15 - 19	1 081 199	553 241	527 958	550 694	279 420	271 274	530 505	273 821	256 684
20 - 24	767 946	398 920	369 026	406 496	224 092	182 404	361 450	174 828	186 622
25 - 29	609 489	291 598	317 891	303 896	153 731	150 165	305 593	137 867	167 726
30 - 34	537 893	227 400	310 493	264 521	117 596	146 925	273 372	109 804	163 568
35 - 39	494 619	213 385	281 234	236 804	106 800	130 004	257 815	106 585	151 230
40 - 44	378 111	175 956	202 155	178 115	86 225	91 890	199 996	89 731	110 265
45 - 49	308 866	142 056	166 810	145 334	68 351	76 983	163 532	73 705	89 827
50 - 54	232 650	110 074	122 576	101 866	48 831	53 035	130 784	61 243	69 541
55 - 59	171 970	82 190	89 780	77 819	37 319	40 500	94 151	44 871	49 280
60 - 64	135 768	64 968	70 800	52 261	24 642	27 619	83 507	40 326	43 181
65 - 69	75 534	35 915	39 619	31 238	14 546	16 692	44 296	21 369	22 927
70 - 74	82 740	36 511	46 229	30 032	12 558	17 474	52 708	23 953	28 755
75 - 79	36 453	15 591	20 862	14 064	5 573	8 491	22 389	10 018	12 371
80 +	52 092	22 340	29 752	16 610	6 295	10 315	35 482	16 045	19 437
Botswana									
1 VIII 2006 (SSDJ)[3]									
Total	1 773 240	851 670	921 570	1 000 443	473 136	527 307	772 797	378 534	394 263
0	48 555	23 864	24 691	25 317	12 680	12 637	23 238	11 184	12 054
1 - 4	163 917	83 700	80 217	80 681	40 540	40 141	83 236	43 160	40 076
5 - 9	199 685	102 650	97 035	100 949	51 227	49 722	98 736	51 423	47 313
10 - 14	214 874	106 643	108 231	112 297	54 176	58 121	102 577	52 467	50 110
15 - 19	183 449	91 806	91 623	109 115	51 830	57 285	74 314	39 976	34 338
20 - 24	196 191	92 134	104 057	124 532	57 134	67 398	71 659	35 000	36 659
25 - 29	169 260	80 087	89 173	113 205	52 679	60 526	56 055	27 408	28 647
30 - 34	131 406	65 142	66 264	85 466	41 546	43 920	45 940	23 596	22 344
35 - 39	95 739	44 147	51 592	62 301	28 348	33 953	33 438	15 799	17 639
40 - 44	82 595	37 525	45 070	48 769	23 197	25 572	33 826	14 328	19 498
45 - 49	69 451	31 320	38 131	40 748	18 431	22 317	28 703	12 889	15 814
50 - 54	55 815	24 853	30 962	28 916	13 436	15 480	26 899	11 417	15 482
55 - 59	39 871	18 041	21 830	18 329	8 895	9 434	21 542	9 146	12 396
60 - 64	30 679	12 980	17 699	13 763	5 742	8 021	16 916	7 238	9 678
65 - 69	26 929	11 783	15 146	10 998	4 490	6 508	15 931	7 293	8 638
70 +	64 520	24 818	39 702	24 895	8 695	16 200	39 625	16 123	23 502
Unknown - Inconnu	324	177	147	162	90	72	162	87	75

7. Population by age, sex and urban/rural residence: latest available year, 2003 - 2012
Population selon l'âge, le sexe et la résidence, urbaine/rurale : dernière année disponible, 2003 - 2012 (continued - suite)

Continent, country or area, date, code and age (in years) / Continent, pays ou zone, date, code et âge (en années)	Total			Urban - Urbaine			Rural - Rurale		
	Both sexes Les deux sexes	Male Masculin	Female Féminin	Both sexes Les deux sexes	Male Masculin	Female Féminin	Both sexes Les deux sexes	Male Masculin	Female Féminin
AFRICA - AFRIQUE									
Botswana									
1 VII 2011 (ESDJ)[4]									
Total	1 849 692	910 404	939 288	...	...	...	...	...	...
0	49 540	24 892	24 648	...	...	...	...	...	...
1 - 4	165 847	83 569	82 278	...	...	...	...	...	...
5 - 9	193 918	97 806	96 112	...	...	...	...	...	...
10 - 14	217 062	109 426	107 636	...	...	...	...	...	...
15 - 19	204 292	102 971	101 321	...	...	...	...	...	...
20 - 24	201 918	101 885	100 033	...	...	...	...	...	...
25 - 29	181 814	93 334	88 480	...	...	...	...	...	...
30 - 34	153 759	79 862	73 897	...	...	...	...	...	...
35 - 39	116 506	60 504	56 002	...	...	...	...	...	...
40 - 44	81 745	41 205	40 540	...	...	...	...	...	...
45 - 49	59 165	26 240	32 925	...	...	...	...	...	...
50 - 54	51 197	19 308	31 889	...	...	...	...	...	...
55 - 59	43 415	16 707	26 708	...	...	...	...	...	...
60 - 64	33 882	13 686	20 196	...	...	...	...	...	...
65 - 69	27 086	11 107	15 979	...	...	...	...	...	...
70 - 74	21 226	9 003	12 223	...	...	...	...	...	...
75 +	47 320	18 899	28 421	...	...	...	...	...	...
Burkina Faso									
9 XII 2006 (CDJC)									
Total	14 017 262	6 768 739	7 248 523	3 181 967	1 588 895	1 593 072	10 835 295	5 179 844	5 655 451
0	466 516	235 090	231 426	87 021	44 072	42 949	379 495	191 018	188 477
1 - 4	1 970 397	995 520	974 877	333 623	169 737	163 886	1 636 774	825 783	810 991
5 - 9	2 315 710	1 176 473	1 139 237	401 898	200 004	201 894	1 913 812	976 469	937 343
10 - 14	1 746 588	900 103	846 485	369 532	178 639	190 893	1 377 056	721 464	655 592
15 - 19	1 475 285	710 323	764 962	411 383	192 566	218 817	1 063 902	517 757	546 145
20 - 24	1 185 378	530 425	654 953	366 029	178 980	187 049	819 349	351 445	467 904
25 - 29	1 009 285	448 431	560 854	296 420	150 350	146 070	712 865	298 081	414 784
30 - 34	794 820	363 408	431 412	228 658	122 850	105 808	566 162	240 558	325 604
35 - 39	656 824	298 236	358 588	172 705	92 889	79 816	484 119	205 347	278 772
40 - 44	549 287	250 143	299 144	136 961	71 800	65 161	412 326	178 343	233 983
45 - 49	427 739	195 016	232 723	99 671	52 052	47 619	328 068	142 964	185 104
50 - 54	358 810	166 281	192 529	78 866	41 122	37 744	279 944	125 159	154 785
55 - 59	273 563	132 254	141 309	56 234	29 228	27 006	217 329	103 026	114 303
60 - 64	238 962	111 176	127 786	45 740	21 983	23 757	193 222	89 193	104 029
65 - 69	163 609	80 542	83 067	29 765	14 189	15 576	133 844	66 353	67 491
70 - 74	136 282	63 727	72 555	23 129	10 103	13 026	113 153	53 624	59 529
75 - 79	77 113	37 186	39 927	12 366	5 449	6 917	64 747	31 737	33 010
80 - 84	50 317	21 791	28 526	8 171	2 957	5 214	42 146	18 834	23 312
85 - 89	21 694	9 645	12 049	3 512	1 230	2 282	18 182	8 415	9 767
90 - 94	11 529	4 480	7 049	1 898	619	1 279	9 631	3 861	5 770
95 +	13 067	4 727	8 340	1 956	467	1 489	11 111	4 260	6 851
Unknown - Inconnu	74 487	33 762	40 725	16 429	7 609	8 820	58 058	26 153	31 905
1 VII 2009 (ESDJ)[2]									
Total	15 224 780	7 346 835	7 877 945	...	...	...	...	...	...
0	652 074	332 861	319 213	...	...	...	...	...	...
1 - 4	2 262 278	1 166 932	1 095 346	...	...	...	...	...	...
5 - 9	2 416 407	1 236 776	1 179 631	...	...	...	...	...	...
10 - 14	1 973 815	988 126	985 689	...	...	...	...	...	...
15 - 19	1 577 324	774 081	803 243	...	...	...	...	...	...
20 - 24	1 309 638	579 080	730 558	...	...	...	...	...	...
25 - 29	1 045 616	455 063	590 553	...	...	...	...	...	...
30 - 34	878 095	389 101	488 994	...	...	...	...	...	...
35 - 39	679 903	308 106	371 797	...	...	...	...	...	...
40 - 44	589 777	263 840	325 937	...	...	...	...	...	...
45 - 49	453 094	206 387	246 707	...	...	...	...	...	...
50 - 54	382 895	172 330	210 565	...	...	...	...	...	...
55 - 59	280 518	133 841	146 677	...	...	...	...	...	...
60 - 64	254 972	118 221	136 751	...	...	...	...	...	...
65 - 69	167 320	81 902	85 418	...	...	...	...	...	...
70 - 74	138 614	64 975	73 639	...	...	...	...	...	...
75 - 79	75 664	37 101	38 563	...	...	...	...	...	...
80 +	86 776	38 112	48 664	...	...	...	...	...	...

7. Population by age, sex and urban/rural residence: latest available year, 2003 - 2012
Population selon l'âge, le sexe et la résidence, urbaine/rurale : dernière année disponible, 2003 - 2012 (continued - suite)

Continent, country or area, date, code and age (in years) / Continent, pays ou zone, date, code et âge (en annèes)	Total			Urban - Urbaine			Rural - Rurale		
	Both sexes Les deux sexes	Male Masculin	Female Féminin	Both sexes Les deux sexes	Male Masculin	Female Féminin	Both sexes Les deux sexes	Male Masculin	Female Féminin
AFRICA - AFRIQUE									
Burundi									
16 VIII 2008 (CDJC)									
Total	8 053 574	3 964 906	4 088 668	811 866	442 596	369 270	7 241 708	3 522 310	3 719 398
0 - 4	1 424 016	701 119	722 897	121 181	60 098	61 083	1 302 835	641 021	661 814
5 - 9	1 133 011	554 819	578 192	93 103	46 020	47 083	1 039 908	508 799	531 109
10 - 14	992 125	479 874	512 251	81 559	39 261	42 298	910 566	440 613	469 953
15 - 19	967 635	462 251	505 384	102 274	51 816	50 458	865 361	410 435	454 926
20 - 24	771 686	364 574	407 112	95 104	52 641	42 463	676 582	311 933	364 649
25 - 29	607 541	304 842	302 699	87 743	52 567	35 176	519 798	252 275	267 523
30 - 34	414 453	209 982	204 471	61 717	38 063	23 654	352 736	171 919	180 817
35 - 39	371 931	186 018	185 913	45 180	27 712	17 468	326 751	158 306	168 445
40 - 44	303 720	153 694	150 026	32 626	20 899	11 727	271 094	132 795	138 299
45 - 49	280 890	146 870	134 020	25 095	15 625	9 470	255 795	131 245	124 550
50 - 54	228 246	116 798	111 448	17 525	10 673	6 852	210 721	106 125	104 596
55 - 59	141 758	76 723	65 035	10 835	6 528	4 307	130 923	70 195	60 728
60 - 64	107 403	52 602	54 801	7 274	3 910	3 364	100 129	48 692	51 437
65 - 69	67 434	34 477	32 957	4 369	2 260	2 109	63 065	32 217	30 848
70 - 74	63 458	28 759	34 699	3 656	1 646	2 010	59 802	27 113	32 689
75 - 79	35 140	18 344	16 796	2 120	973	1 147	33 020	17 371	15 649
80 - 84	28 212	12 675	15 537	1 403	556	847	26 809	12 119	14 690
85 - 89	11 836	6 328	5 508	639	298	341	11 197	6 030	5 167
90 - 94	8 545	4 074	4 471	417	156	261	8 128	3 918	4 210
95 +	7 300	3 585	3 715	493	295	198	6 807	3 290	3 517
Unknown - Inconnu	87 234	46 498	40 736	17 553	10 599	6 954	69 681	35 899	33 782
Cabo Verde									
1 VII 2003 (ESDF)[5]									
Total	460 968	223 254	237 715	257 412	125 652	131 759	203 556	97 600	105 956
0 - 4	58 940	30 004	28 936	30 116	15 352	14 765	28 823	14 652	14 171
5 - 9	61 218	30 867	30 351	30 927	15 643	15 284	30 291	15 224	15 067
10 - 14	64 803	32 445	32 358	34 166	16 918	17 248	30 636	15 526	15 110
15 - 19	57 898	28 923	28 975	33 909	16 551	17 358	23 990	12 372	11 618
20 - 24	42 677	21 383	21 294	26 883	13 427	13 456	15 794	7 956	7 838
25 - 29	31 691	15 870	15 821	20 027	9 970	10 057	11 664	5 901	5 763
30 - 34	27 198	13 321	13 877	16 627	8 322	8 306	10 570	4 999	5 571
35 - 39	26 745	12 770	13 975	16 748	8 330	8 419	9 996	4 440	5 556
40 - 44	22 729	10 461	12 268	13 844	6 826	7 018	8 886	3 635	5 251
45 - 49	16 084	6 733	9 351	9 359	4 438	4 921	6 726	2 296	4 430
50 - 54	9 378	3 674	5 704	5 496	2 386	3 110	3 882	1 288	2 594
55 - 59	5 466	2 224	3 242	2 921	1 271	1 651	2 545	953	1 592
60 - 64	7 569	2 919	4 650	3 580	1 404	2 176	3 989	1 515	2 474
65 - 69	9 285	3 660	5 625	4 224	1 629	2 595	5 062	2 032	3 030
70 - 74	7 654	3 244	4 410	3 316	1 270	2 046	4 338	1 974	2 364
75 - 79	5 041	2 183	2 858	2 264	853	1 410	2 778	1 330	1 448
80 +	6 593	2 573	4 020	3 005	1 064	1 941	3 589	1 510	2 079
1 VII 2011 (ESDF)									
Total	527 269	255 327	271 942	...	...	...	...	...	...
0	13 460	6 778	6 682	...	...	...	...	...	...
1 - 4	50 678	25 438	25 240	...	...	...	...	...	...
5 - 9	57 789	28 923	28 866	...	...	...	...	...	...
10 - 14	57 177	28 773	28 404	...	...	...	...	...	...
15 - 19	60 912	30 486	30 426	...	...	...	...	...	...
20 - 24	61 465	30 479	30 986	...	...	...	...	...	...
25 - 29	48 416	23 782	24 634	...	...	...	...	...	...
30 - 34	35 452	17 379	18 073	...	...	...	...	...	...
35 - 39	27 130	13 085	14 045	...	...	...	...	...	...
40 - 44	26 081	12 350	13 731	...	...	...	...	...	...
45 - 49	24 501	11 490	13 011	...	...	...	...	...	...
50 - 54	19 163	8 591	10 572	...	...	...	...	...	...
55 - 59	13 045	5 240	7 805	...	...	...	...	...	...
60 - 64	6 603	2 691	3 912	...	...	...	...	...	...
65 - 69	5 293	2 140	3 153	...	...	...	...	...	...
70 - 74	7 492	2 838	4 654	...	...	...	...	...	...
75 - 79	6 261	2 425	3 836	...	...	...	...	...	...
80 +	6 351	2 439	3 912	...	...	...	...	...	...

7. Population by age, sex and urban/rural residence: latest available year, 2003 - 2012
Population selon l'âge, le sexe et la résidence, urbaine/rurale : dernière année disponible, 2003 - 2012 (continued - suite)

Continent, country or area, date, code and age (in years) / Continent, pays ou zone, date, code et âge (en années)	Total Both sexes Les deux sexes	Total Male Masculin	Total Female Féminin	Urban - Urbaine Both sexes Les deux sexes	Urban - Urbaine Male Masculin	Urban - Urbaine Female Féminin	Rural - Rurale Both sexes Les deux sexes	Rural - Rurale Male Masculin	Rural - Rurale Female Féminin
AFRICA - AFRIQUE									
Cameroon - Cameroun[2]									
1 VII 2010* (ESDJ)									
Total	19 406 100	9 599 224	9 806 876	...	...	...	...	...	...
0 - 4	3 287 234	1 662 298	1 624 936	...	...	...	...	...	...
5 - 9	2 783 459	1 412 467	1 370 992	...	...	...	...	...	...
10 - 14	2 394 671	1 227 470	1 167 201	...	...	...	...	...	...
15 - 19	2 170 035	1 068 509	1 101 526	...	...	...	...	...	...
20 - 24	1 837 289	855 334	981 955	...	...	...	...	...	...
25 - 29	1 525 816	712 550	813 266	...	...	...	...	...	...
30 - 34	1 209 607	588 210	621 397	...	...	...	...	...	...
35 - 39	942 713	460 394	482 319	...	...	...	...	...	...
40 - 44	793 846	388 539	405 307	...	...	...	...	...	...
45 - 49	640 247	323 507	316 740	...	...	...	...	...	...
50 - 54	521 910	261 626	260 284	...	...	...	...	...	...
55 - 59	337 988	178 876	159 112	...	...	...	...	...	...
60 - 64	315 879	155 208	160 671	...	...	...	...	...	...
65 - 69	227 290	110 645	116 645	...	...	...	...	...	...
70 - 74	189 571	88 969	100 602	...	...	...	...	...	...
75 - 79	98 078	47 173	50 905	...	...	...	...	...	...
80 - 84	71 585	31 609	39 976	...	...	...	...	...	...
85 - 89	26 564	12 109	14 455	...	...	...	...	...	...
90 - 94	15 715	6 942	8 773	...	...	...	...	...	...
95 +	16 603	6 789	9 814	...	...	...	...	...	...
Congo									
28 IV 2007 (CDFC)									
Total	3 697 490	1 821 357	1 876 133	...	...	...	...	...	...
0 - 4	557 500	278 342	279 158	...	...	...	...	...	...
5 - 9	458 151	230 099	228 052	...	...	...	...	...	...
10 - 14	412 363	205 101	207 262	...	...	...	...	...	...
15 - 19	379 365	183 295	196 070	...	...	...	...	...	...
20 - 24	355 500	164 340	191 160	...	...	...	...	...	...
25 - 29	334 397	163 098	171 299	...	...	...	...	...	...
30 - 34	289 481	147 570	141 911	...	...	...	...	...	...
35 - 39	238 628	124 027	114 601	...	...	...	...	...	...
40 - 44	180 456	93 830	86 626	...	...	...	...	...	...
45 - 49	137 033	70 361	66 672	...	...	...	...	...	...
50 - 54	102 641	49 171	53 470	...	...	...	...	...	...
55 - 59	74 467	35 307	39 160	...	...	...	...	...	...
60 - 64	57 975	26 655	31 320	...	...	...	...	...	...
65 - 69	46 793	20 882	25 911	...	...	...	...	...	...
70 - 74	34 675	14 704	19 971	...	...	...	...	...	...
75 - 79	21 044	8 401	12 643	...	...	...	...	...	...
80 - 84	9 657	3 494	6 163	...	...	...	...	...	...
85 - 89	5 188	1 864	3 324	...	...	...	...	...	...
90 +	2 176	816	1 360	...	...	...	...	...	...
Egypt - Égypte									
1 VII 2011 (ESDF)									
Total	80 410 017	41 110 578	39 299 439	34 515 708	17 619 110	16 896 598	45 894 309	23 491 468	22 402 841
0 - 4	8 526 674	4 370 269	4 156 405	3 215 324	1 645 898	1 569 426	5 311 350	2 724 371	2 586 979
5 - 9	8 444 066	4 353 223	4 090 843	3 290 584	1 691 089	1 599 495	5 153 482	2 662 134	2 491 348
10 - 14	8 528 333	4 420 078	4 108 255	3 260 778	1 682 584	1 578 194	5 267 555	2 737 494	2 530 061
15 - 19	9 433 512	4 837 291	4 596 221	3 834 360	1 951 128	1 883 232	5 599 152	2 886 163	2 712 989
20 - 24	8 696 396	4 451 881	4 244 515	3 816 625	1 920 777	1 895 848	4 879 771	2 531 104	2 348 667
25 - 29	7 061 124	3 486 398	3 574 726	3 114 438	1 523 932	1 590 506	3 946 686	1 962 466	1 984 220
30 - 34	5 229 190	2 671 664	2 557 526	2 386 274	1 209 471	1 176 803	2 842 916	1 462 193	1 380 723
35 - 39	5 145 076	2 554 033	2 591 043	2 291 059	1 148 718	1 142 341	2 854 017	1 405 315	1 448 702
40 - 44	4 519 659	2 286 131	2 233 528	2 135 237	1 072 465	1 062 772	2 384 422	1 213 666	1 170 756
45 - 49	4 058 422	2 074 515	1 983 907	1 920 349	979 583	940 766	2 138 073	1 094 932	1 043 141
50 - 54	3 378 499	1 703 894	1 674 605	1 705 393	866 825	838 568	1 673 106	837 069	836 037
55 - 59	2 500 283	1 340 259	1 160 024	1 215 051	652 311	562 740	1 285 232	687 948	597 284
60 - 64	1 881 168	991 751	889 417	979 633	535 336	444 297	901 535	456 415	445 120
65 - 69	1 317 296	707 193	610 103	595 711	338 377	257 334	721 585	368 816	352 769
70 - 74	872 692	444 815	427 877	405 778	215 839	189 939	466 914	228 976	237 938
75 +	817 627	417 183	400 444	349 114	184 777	164 337	468 513	232 406	236 107

7. Population by age, sex and urban/rural residence: latest available year, 2003 - 2012
Population selon l'âge, le sexe et la résidence, urbaine/rurale : dernière année disponible, 2003 - 2012 (continued - suite)

Continent, country or area, date, code and age (in years) / Continent, pays ou zone, date, code et âge (en annèes)	Total			Urban - Urbaine			Rural - Rurale		
	Both sexes Les deux sexes	Male Masculin	Female Féminin	Both sexes Les deux sexes	Male Masculin	Female Féminin	Both sexes Les deux sexes	Male Masculin	Female Féminin
AFRICA - AFRIQUE									
Egypt - Égypte									
1 VII 2012* (ESDF)									
Total	82 304 664	42 057 664	40 247 000	...	...	...	...	...	...
0 - 4	9 190 028	4 778 853	4 411 175	...	...	...	...	...	...
5 - 9	8 725 862	4 533 259	4 192 603	...	...	...	...	...	...
10 - 14	7 676 223	3 970 439	3 705 784	...	...	...	...	...	...
15 - 19	7 715 963	3 970 439	3 745 524	...	...	...	...	...	...
20 - 24	8 260 206	4 236 499	4 023 706	...	...	...	...	...	...
25 - 29	8 007 359	4 083 003	3 924 356	...	...	...	...	...	...
30 - 34	6 594 991	3 346 220	3 248 770	...	...	...	...	...	...
35 - 39	5 111 510	2 588 000	2 523 510	...	...	...	...	...	...
40 - 44	4 466 587	2 261 000	2 205 587	...	...	...	...	...	...
45 - 49	4 114 008	2 077 317	2 036 691	...	...	...	...	...	...
50 - 54	3 620 249	1 822 000	1 798 249	...	...	...	...	...	...
55 - 59	2 974 358	1 494 031	1 480 327	...	...	...	...	...	...
60 - 64	2 217 902	1 105 174	1 112 729	...	...	...	...	...	...
65 - 69	1 552 353	767 482	784 871	...	...	...	...	...	...
70 - 74	1 018 045	501 421	516 624	...	...	...	...	...	...
75 - 79	584 579	286 527	298 052	...	...	...	...	...	...
80 +	474 442	236 000	238 442	...	...	...	...	...	...
Ethiopia - Éthiopie[6]									
1 VII 2008 (ESDF)									
Total	79 221 000	39 691 000	39 530 000	13 225 000	6 575 000	6 650 000	65 996 000	33 116 000	32 880 000
0 - 4	12 634 128	6 381 651	6 252 477	1 608 103	837 115	770 988	11 027 607	5 545 365	5 482 242
5 - 9	11 375 406	5 742 553	5 632 853	1 572 449	796 842	775 606	9 804 015	4 946 304	4 857 711
10 - 14	9 860 705	4 983 414	4 877 291	1 510 467	746 491	763 976	8 350 671	4 237 207	4 113 464
15 - 19	8 178 673	4 146 348	4 032 325	1 390 318	679 466	710 851	6 788 253	3 466 879	3 321 374
20 - 24	7 442 221	3 777 710	3 664 510	1 433 539	700 859	732 680	6 008 054	3 076 545	2 931 509
25 - 29	6 446 813	3 269 384	3 177 429	1 326 898	654 980	671 918	5 119 126	2 613 980	2 505 146
30 - 34	5 337 998	2 677 364	2 660 634	1 100 820	556 544	544 276	4 236 510	2 120 406	2 116 104
35 - 39	4 293 830	2 112 022	2 181 807	871 216	440 672	430 544	3 422 119	1 671 022	1 751 097
40 - 44	3 447 552	1 663 907	1 783 644	658 160	328 837	329 322	2 789 134	1 334 886	1 454 248
45 - 49	2 727 580	1 292 456	1 435 124	491 450	241 120	250 330	2 236 012	1 051 240	1 184 772
50 - 54	2 194 347	1 045 893	1 148 454	378 827	183 526	195 301	1 815 478	862 329	953 149
55 - 59	1 740 176	844 895	895 281	291 867	142 040	149 828	1 448 305	702 849	745 456
60 - 64	1 322 620	649 306	673 314	220 967	103 852	117 115	1 101 659	545 471	556 189
65 - 69	951 626	471 805	479 820	159 064	72 250	86 814	792 569	399 578	392 991
70 - 74	639 657	318 537	321 119	106 400	46 747	59 653	533 265	271 814	261 451
75 +	627 670	313 753	313 917	104 457	43 659	60 798	523 224	270 126	253 098
Ghana									
26 IX 2010 (CDFC)									
Total	24 658 823	12 024 845	12 633 978	12 545 229	6 016 059	6 529 170	12 113 594	6 008 786	6 104 808
0 - 4	3 405 406	1 731 787	1 673 619	1 541 391	783 017	758 374	1 864 015	948 770	915 245
5 - 9	3 128 952	1 589 632	1 539 320	1 389 660	697 031	692 629	1 739 292	892 601	846 691
10 - 14	2 916 040	1 477 525	1 438 515	1 391 229	672 906	718 323	1 524 811	804 619	720 192
15 - 19	2 609 989	1 311 112	1 298 877	1 364 124	651 829	712 295	1 245 865	659 283	586 582
20 - 24	2 323 491	1 100 727	1 222 764	1 356 838	642 140	714 698	966 653	458 587	508 066
25 - 29	2 050 111	943 213	1 106 898	1 194 867	553 927	640 940	855 244	389 286	465 958
30 - 34	1 678 809	790 301	888 508	955 698	455 204	500 494	723 111	335 097	388 014
35 - 39	1 421 403	676 768	744 635	781 852	373 678	408 174	639 551	303 090	336 461
40 - 44	1 186 350	572 620	613 730	632 049	304 875	327 174	554 301	267 745	286 556
45 - 49	938 098	452 975	485 123	487 192	231 146	256 046	450 906	221 829	229 077
50 - 54	833 098	394 600	438 498	421 478	195 556	225 922	411 620	199 044	212 576
55 - 59	523 695	258 582	265 113	275 958	132 984	142 974	247 737	125 598	122 139
60 - 64	475 849	227 050	248 799	225 385	105 738	119 647	250 464	121 312	129 152
65 - 69	293 871	136 244	157 627	143 114	64 588	78 526	150 757	71 656	79 101
70 - 74	351 330	149 512	201 818	153 951	63 786	90 165	197 379	85 726	111 653
75 - 79	205 953	89 149	116 804	93 297	38 300	54 997	112 656	50 849	61 807
80 - 84	159 084	62 357	96 727	67 888	25 271	42 617	91 196	37 086	54 110
85 - 89	83 070	32 937	50 133	37 719	13 683	24 036	45 351	19 254	26 097
90 - 94	51 081	19 004	32 077	21 270	6 985	14 285	29 811	12 019	17 792
95 +	23 143	8 750	14 393	10 269	3 415	6 854	12 874	5 335	7 539

Continent, country or area, date, code and age (in years) / Continent, pays ou zone, date, code et âge (en annèes)	Total			Urban - Urbaine			Rural - Rurale		
	Both sexes Les deux sexes	Male Masculin	Female Féminin	Both sexes Les deux sexes	Male Masculin	Female Féminin	Both sexes Les deux sexes	Male Masculin	Female Féminin

AFRICA - AFRIQUE

Guinea - Guinée[2]
1 VII 2009 (ESDF)

Total	10 217 591	5 038 823	5 178 768	...	...	...	...	...	...
0 - 4	1 708 508	866 996	841 512	...	...	...	...	...	...
5 - 9	1 355 253	686 211	669 042	...	...	...	...	...	...
10 - 14	1 155 226	581 127	574 099	...	...	...	...	...	...
15 - 19	1 225 991	621 661	604 330	...	...	...	...	...	...
20 - 24	996 391	517 007	479 384	...	...	...	...	...	...
25 - 29	668 191	344 997	323 194	...	...	...	...	...	...
30 - 34	565 801	260 720	305 081	...	...	...	...	...	...
35 - 39	494 352	216 535	277 817	...	...	...	...	...	...
40 - 44	478 364	204 559	273 805	...	...	...	...	...	...
45 - 49	366 578	163 816	202 762	...	...	...	...	...	...
50 - 54	315 033	147 915	167 118	...	...	...	...	...	...
55 - 59	240 705	118 129	122 576	...	...	...	...	...	...
60 - 64	182 506	87 782	94 724	...	...	...	...	...	...
65 - 69	139 166	66 929	72 237	...	...	...	...	...	...
70 - 74	111 293	54 579	56 714	...	...	...	...	...	...
75 +	214 233	99 860	114 373	...	...	...	...	...	...

Kenya
24 VIII 2009 (CDFC)

Total	38 610 097	19 192 458	19 417 639	12 487 375	6 278 811	6 208 564	26 122 722	12 913 647	13 209 075
0 - 4	5 939 306	3 000 439	2 938 867	1 739 251	875 830	863 421	4 200 055	2 124 609	2 075 446
5 - 9	5 597 716	2 832 669	2 765 047	1 484 285	742 473	741 812	4 113 431	2 090 196	2 023 235
10 - 14	5 034 855	2 565 313	2 469 542	1 312 671	650 438	662 233	3 722 184	1 914 875	1 807 309
15 - 19	4 169 543	2 123 653	2 045 890	1 244 054	587 384	656 670	2 925 489	1 536 269	1 389 220
20 - 24	3 775 103	1 754 105	2 020 998	1 572 026	708 458	863 568	2 203 077	1 045 647	1 157 430
25 - 29	3 201 226	1 529 116	1 672 110	1 442 798	715 957	726 841	1 758 428	813 159	945 269
30 - 34	2 519 506	1 257 035	1 262 471	1 056 483	568 615	487 868	1 463 023	688 420	774 603
35 - 39	2 008 632	1 004 361	1 004 271	785 390	431 054	354 336	1 223 242	573 307	649 935
40 - 44	1 476 169	743 594	732 575	533 174	297 202	235 972	942 995	446 392	496 603
45 - 49	1 272 745	635 276	637 469	422 941	235 467	187 474	849 804	399 809	449 995
50 - 54	956 206	478 346	477 860	286 074	159 814	126 260	670 132	318 532	351 600
55 - 59	711 953	359 466	352 487	187 793	103 563	84 230	524 160	255 903	268 257
60 - 64	593 778	295 197	298 581	139 271	73 800	65 471	454 507	221 397	233 110
65 - 69	390 763	183 151	207 612	83 728	41 299	42 429	307 035	141 852	165 183
70 - 74	339 301	160 301	179 000	68 868	32 691	36 177	270 433	127 610	142 823
75 - 79	218 508	99 833	118 675	42 247	19 276	22 971	176 261	80 557	95 704
80 +	383 701	159 125	224 576	77 003	30 335	46 668	306 698	128 790	177 908
Unknown - Inconnu	21 086	11 478	9 608	9 318	5 155	4 163	11 768	6 323	5 445

Lesotho
13 IV 2006 (CDJC)

Total	1 862 860	904 392	958 468	421 105	194 097	227 008	1 441 755	710 295	731 460
0 - 4	201 995	101 397	100 598	39 245	19 604	19 641	162 750	81 793	80 957
5 - 9	211 947	106 695	105 252	40 208	20 051	20 157	171 739	86 644	85 095
10 - 14	220 938	110 778	110 160	42 546	20 751	21 795	178 392	90 027	88 365
15 - 19	229 389	114 800	114 589	48 783	21 971	26 812	180 606	92 829	87 777
20 - 24	207 062	101 385	105 677	52 026	21 394	30 632	155 036	79 991	75 045
25 - 29	164 867	82 202	82 665	49 796	21 948	27 848	115 071	60 254	54 817
30 - 34	119 530	60 107	59 423	36 708	17 327	19 381	82 822	42 780	40 042
35 - 39	93 490	45 645	47 845	28 605	13 639	14 966	64 885	32 006	32 879
40 - 44	83 299	39 596	43 703	22 742	10 805	11 937	60 557	28 791	31 766
45 - 49	72 621	34 102	38 519	17 782	8 461	9 321	54 839	25 641	29 198
50 - 54	63 084	28 723	34 361	13 153	6 037	7 116	49 931	22 686	27 245
55 - 59	50 148	23 225	26 923	9 367	4 266	5 101	40 781	18 959	21 822
60 - 64	37 699	16 724	20 975	6 325	2 851	3 474	31 374	13 873	17 501
65 - 69	32 028	13 369	18 659	4 794	1 977	2 817	27 234	11 392	15 842
70 - 74	35 609	13 380	22 229	4 158	1 569	2 589	31 451	11 811	19 640
75 - 79	18 141	6 327	11 814	2 281	742	1 539	15 860	5 585	10 275
80 - 84	10 498	3 251	7 247	1 336	380	956	9 162	2 871	6 291
85 +	10 515	2 686	7 829	1 250	324	926	9 265	2 362	6 903

Liberia - Libéria
21 III 2008 (CDFC)

Total	3 476 608	1 739 945	1 736 663	...	...	...	...	...	...
0 - 4	534 475	270 564	263 911	...	...	...	...	...	...

Continent, country or area, date, code and age (in years) / Continent, pays ou zone, date, code et âge (en annèes)	Total			Urban - Urbaine			Rural - Rurale		
	Both sexes Les deux sexes	Male Masculin	Female Féminin	Both sexes Les deux sexes	Male Masculin	Female Féminin	Both sexes Les deux sexes	Male Masculin	Female Féminin
AFRICA - AFRIQUE									
Liberia - Libéria									
21 III 2008 (CDFC)									
5 - 9	501 931	251 411	250 520	...	...	...	...	...	...
10 - 14	421 666	214 859	206 807	...	...	...	...	...	...
15 - 19	375 695	189 407	186 288	...	...	...	...	...	...
20 - 24	342 930	161 951	180 979	...	...	...	...	...	...
25 - 29	291 858	141 006	150 852	...	...	...	...	...	...
30 - 34	219 632	107 326	112 306	...	...	...	...	...	...
35 - 39	203 536	99 136	104 400	...	...	...	...	...	...
40 - 44	155 737	81 670	74 067	...	...	...	...	...	...
45 - 49	118 807	63 827	54 980	...	...	...	...	...	...
50 - 54	82 940	44 870	38 070	...	...	...	...	...	...
55 - 59	56 460	30 975	25 485	...	...	...	...	...	...
60 - 64	52 830	25 473	27 357	...	...	...	...	...	...
65 - 69	39 807	19 250	20 557	...	...	...	...	...	...
70 - 74	25 746	12 343	13 403	...	...	...	...	...	...
75 - 79	22 913	11 580	11 333	...	...	...	...	...	...
80 - 84	12 007	5 408	6 599	...	...	...	...	...	...
85 +	17 638	8 889	8 749	...	...	...	...	...	...
Libya - Libye[7]									
15 IV 2006* (CDFC)									
Total	5 298 152	2 687 513	2 610 639	4 670 858	2 372 379	2 298 479	627 294	315 134	312 160
0	117 479	60 167	57 312	103 670	53 129	50 541	13 809	7 038	6 771
1 - 4	457 866	234 512	223 354	403 509	206 639	196 870	54 357	27 873	26 484
5 - 9	527 595	269 079	258 516	465 506	237 468	228 038	62 089	31 611	30 478
10 - 14	542 893	277 270	265 623	476 896	243 693	233 203	65 997	33 577	32 420
15 - 19	573 026	290 568	282 458	501 444	254 266	247 178	71 582	36 302	35 280
20 - 24	573 287	289 663	283 624	502 229	253 539	248 690	71 058	36 124	34 934
25 - 29	566 458	287 101	279 357	497 522	252 364	245 158	68 936	34 737	34 199
30 - 34	492 828	248 875	243 953	434 821	220 019	214 802	58 007	28 856	29 151
35 - 39	390 800	195 328	195 472	347 316	174 078	173 238	43 484	21 250	22 234
40 - 44	281 849	140 872	140 977	251 876	126 302	125 574	29 973	14 570	15 403
45 - 49	199 142	100 653	98 489	178 471	90 336	88 135	20 671	10 317	10 354
50 - 54	132 619	64 677	67 942	119 463	58 576	60 887	13 156	6 101	7 055
55 - 59	122 277	61 439	60 838	109 004	55 174	53 830	13 273	6 265	7 008
60 - 64	95 127	51 295	43 832	84 339	45 822	38 517	10 788	5 473	5 315
65 - 69	80 018	42 724	37 294	70 241	37 786	32 455	9 777	4 938	4 839
70 - 74	57 851	30 325	27 526	50 282	26 511	23 771	7 569	3 814	3 755
75 - 79	45 675	23 125	22 550	39 337	19 978	19 359	6 338	3 147	3 191
80 - 84	24 576	12 158	12 418	20 930	10 332	10 598	3 646	1 826	1 820
85 +	16 786	7 682	9 104	14 002	6 367	7 635	2 784	1 315	1 469
Malawi									
8 VI 2008 (CDFC)									
Total	13 077 160	6 358 933	6 718 227	2 003 309	1 014 477	988 832	11 073 851	5 344 456	5 729 395
0	503 385	247 809	255 576	67 264	33 375	33 889	436 121	214 434	221 687
1 - 4	1 866 626	922 138	944 488	248 703	122 976	125 727	1 617 923	799 162	818 761
5 - 9	1 968 299	972 307	995 992	261 838	127 930	133 908	1 706 461	844 377	862 084
10 - 14	1 670 391	826 076	844 315	232 203	110 545	121 658	1 438 188	715 531	722 657
15 - 19	1 276 692	625 664	651 028	218 307	105 746	112 561	1 058 385	519 918	538 467
20 - 24	1 240 329	554 799	685 530	248 790	117 648	131 142	991 539	437 151	554 388
25 - 29	1 102 976	530 103	572 873	236 512	122 761	113 751	866 464	407 342	459 122
30 - 34	827 547	417 599	409 948	162 061	91 637	70 424	665 486	325 962	339 524
35 - 39	623 330	323 643	299 687	105 572	61 564	44 008	517 758	262 079	255 679
40 - 44	441 231	218 546	222 685	67 267	37 061	30 206	373 964	181 485	192 479
45 - 49	343 190	167 285	175 905	47 706	25 811	21 895	295 484	141 474	154 010
50 - 54	269 634	126 778	142 856	33 849	18 400	15 449	235 785	108 378	127 407
55 - 59	258 214	122 616	135 598	26 253	14 525	11 728	231 961	108 091	123 870
60 - 64	184 679	87 008	97 671	16 622	9 256	7 366	168 057	77 752	90 305
65 - 69	153 829	72 038	81 791	11 298	6 217	5 081	142 531	65 821	76 710
70 - 74	106 020	46 481	59 539	6 992	3 573	3 419	99 028	42 908	56 120
75 - 79	106 769	46 003	60 766	5 629	2 769	2 860	101 140	43 234	57 906
80 - 84	55 970	21 945	34 025	2 926	1 262	1 664	53 044	20 683	32 361
85 - 89	40 784	16 680	24 104	1 895	818	1 077	38 889	15 862	23 027
90 - 94	18 739	6 967	11 772	780	323	457	17 959	6 644	11 315
95 +	18 526	6 448	12 078	842	280	562	17 684	6 168	11 516

Continent, country or area, date, code and age (in years) / Continent, pays ou zone, date, code et âge (en annèes)	Total			Urban - Urbaine			Rural - Rurale		
	Both sexes Les deux sexes	Male Masculin	Female Féminin	Both sexes Les deux sexes	Male Masculin	Female Féminin	Both sexes Les deux sexes	Male Masculin	Female Féminin
AFRICA - AFRIQUE									
Mauritania - Mauritanie[2]									
1 VII 2011 (ESDF)									
Total	3 296 958	1 644 572	1 652 386	...	...	...	...	...	...
0 - 4	486 998	249 178	237 820	...	...	...	...	...	...
5 - 9	431 336	220 611	210 725	...	...	...	...	...	...
10 - 14	409 046	209 012	200 034	...	...	...	...	...	...
15 - 19	363 537	187 123	176 414	...	...	...	...	...	...
20 - 24	302 188	154 583	147 605	...	...	...	...	...	...
25 - 29	266 486	130 402	136 084	...	...	...	...	...	...
30 - 34	214 541	100 670	113 871	...	...	...	...	...	...
35 - 39	183 254	84 740	98 514	...	...	...	...	...	...
40 - 44	151 035	70 948	80 087	...	...	...	...	...	...
45 - 49	129 908	61 360	68 548	...	...	...	...	...	...
50 - 54	100 565	49 452	51 113	...	...	...	...	...	...
55 - 59	89 705	43 699	46 006	...	...	...	...	...	...
60 - 64	60 869	29 570	31 299	...	...	...	...	...	...
65 - 69	35 621	17 923	17 698	...	...	...	...	...	...
70 - 74	32 976	16 410	16 566	...	...	...	...	...	...
75 - 79	19 064	9 430	9 634	...	...	...	...	...	...
80 +	19 829	9 461	10 368	...	...	...	...	...	...
Mauritius - Maurice[8]									
4 VII 2011 (CDJC)									
Total	1 236 817	610 848	625 969	499 349	244 688	254 661	737 468	366 160	371 308
0 - 4	73 078	36 702	36 376	26 297	13 220	13 077	46 781	23 482	23 299
5 - 9	89 015	44 947	44 068	32 036	16 177	15 859	56 979	28 770	28 209
10 - 14	93 639	47 302	46 337	35 028	17 523	17 505	58 611	29 779	28 832
15 - 19	101 008	50 715	50 293	39 403	19 725	19 678	61 605	30 990	30 615
20 - 24	92 671	46 871	45 800	37 224	18 836	18 388	55 447	28 035	27 412
25 - 29	90 937	45 589	45 348	35 908	17 899	18 009	55 029	27 690	27 339
30 - 34	103 429	52 182	51 247	39 099	19 805	19 294	64 330	32 377	31 953
35 - 39	87 797	44 241	43 556	32 781	16 142	16 639	55 016	28 099	26 917
40 - 44	89 386	45 150	44 236	34 449	17 010	17 439	54 937	28 140	26 797
45 - 49	99 341	49 800	49 541	41 705	20 637	21 068	57 636	29 163	28 473
50 - 54	86 337	42 996	43 341	37 429	18 627	18 802	48 908	24 369	24 539
55 - 59	73 054	35 713	37 341	32 421	15 983	16 438	40 633	19 730	20 903
60 - 64	57 342	27 143	30 199	25 449	12 058	13 391	31 893	15 085	16 808
65 +	...	...	...	49 745	20 813	28 932	49 419	20 311	29 108
65 - 69	35 439	15 846	19 593	...	...	...	...	...	...
70 - 74	25 375	10 986	14 389	...	...	...	...	...	...
75 - 79	18 044	7 349	10 695	...	...	...	...	...	...
80 - 84	11 369	4 176	7 193	...	...	...	...	...	...
85 - 89	6 368	2 135	4 233	...	...	...	...	...	...
90 - 94	1 982	512	1 470	...	...	...	...	...	...
95 - 99	491	107	384	...	...	...	...	...	...
100 +	96	13	83	...	...	...	...	...	...
Unknown - Inconnu	619	373	246	375	233	142	244	140	104
Mayotte									
31 VII 2007 (CDJC)									
Total	186 387	91 405	94 982	...	...	...	...	...	...
0	6 424	3 255	3 169	...	...	...	...	...	...
1 - 4	25 429	12 948	12 481	...	...	...	...	...	...
5 - 9	27 239	13 739	13 500	...	...	...	...	...	...
10 - 14	23 403	11 483	11 920	...	...	...	...	...	...
15 - 19	18 724	9 144	9 580	...	...	...	...	...	...
20 - 24	13 660	5 789	7 871	...	...	...	...	...	...
25 - 29	14 987	6 262	8 725	...	...	...	...	...	...
30 - 34	14 376	6 651	7 725	...	...	...	...	...	...
35 - 39	12 390	6 468	5 922	...	...	...	...	...	...
40 - 44	8 375	4 385	3 990	...	...	...	...	...	...
45 - 49	6 133	3 261	2 872	...	...	...	...	...	...
50 - 54	4 763	2 508	2 255	...	...	...	...	...	...
55 - 59	3 566	1 948	1 618	...	...	...	...	...	...
60 - 64	2 522	1 329	1 193	...	...	...	...	...	...
65 - 69	1 621	833	788	...	...	...	...	...	...
70 - 74	1 266	671	595	...	...	...	...	...	...

Continent, country or area, date, code and age (in years) / Continent, pays ou zone, date, code et âge (en années)	Total			Urban - Urbaine			Rural - Rurale		
	Both sexes Les deux sexes	Male Masculin	Female Féminin	Both sexes Les deux sexes	Male Masculin	Female Féminin	Both sexes Les deux sexes	Male Masculin	Female Féminin

AFRICA - AFRIQUE

Mayotte
31 VII 2007 (CDJC)

75 - 79	689	348	341	...	...	...	...	...	...
80 - 84	459	234	225	...	...	...	...	...	...
85 - 89	199	89	110	...	...	...	...	...	...
90 - 94	101	35	66	...	...	...	...	...	...
95 +	61	25	36	...	...	...	...	...	...

Morocco - Maroc[9]
1 VII 2012 (ESDF)

Total	32 596 997	16 190 815	16 406 182	19 157 539	9 373 546	9 783 993	13 439 458	6 817 269	6 622 189
0 - 4	2 904 759	1 483 636	1 421 123	1 524 473	777 497	746 976	1 380 285	706 138	674 147
5 - 9	2 842 496	1 451 096	1 391 400	1 528 442	774 469	753 973	1 314 054	676 627	637 427
10 - 14	2 921 694	1 486 201	1 435 493	1 564 234	788 126	776 108	1 357 460	698 075	659 385
15 - 19	3 103 036	1 578 121	1 524 915	1 667 614	825 363	842 251	1 435 422	752 758	682 664
20 - 24	3 160 001	1 597 280	1 562 720	1 775 875	857 701	918 174	1 384 126	739 579	644 546
25 - 29	2 963 865	1 469 833	1 494 032	1 768 264	851 390	916 874	1 195 601	618 443	577 158
30 - 34	2 670 419	1 297 435	1 372 984	1 667 531	802 213	865 318	1 002 888	495 222	507 667
35 - 39	2 264 409	1 085 811	1 178 597	1 454 087	689 722	764 365	810 321	396 089	414 232
40 - 44	1 985 826	946 096	1 039 730	1 308 743	623 304	685 439	677 083	322 792	354 291
45 - 49	1 824 795	872 188	952 607	1 207 538	575 387	632 151	617 256	296 801	320 455
50 - 54	1 695 929	836 873	859 056	1 100 166	545 671	554 495	595 763	291 202	304 561
55 - 59	1 336 053	686 368	649 685	857 728	446 979	410 749	478 326	239 389	238 936
60 - 64	975 913	490 966	484 947	601 494	307 358	294 135	374 420	183 608	190 812
65 - 69	662 148	309 467	352 680	391 372	181 335	210 037	270 776	128 132	142 644
70 - 74	577 757	264 103	313 654	336 897	148 915	187 981	240 860	115 187	125 673
75 +	707 897	335 341	372 556	403 081	178 115	224 966	304 816	157 226	147 590

Mozambique
1 VIII 2007 (CDFC)

Total	20 252 223	9 746 690	10 505 533	6 151 974	3 021 756	3 130 218	14 100 249	6 724 934	7 375 315
0 - 4	3 881 454	1 917 794	1 963 660	975 719	484 625	491 094	2 905 735	1 433 169	1 472 566
5 - 9	3 202 546	1 587 302	1 615 244	854 269	419 428	434 841	2 348 277	1 167 874	1 180 403
10 - 14	2 406 607	1 222 668	1 183 939	771 954	380 380	391 574	1 634 653	842 288	792 365
15 - 19	1 917 052	925 729	991 323	707 479	353 094	354 385	1 209 573	572 635	636 938
20 - 24	1 760 939	774 413	986 526	673 354	319 552	353 802	1 087 585	454 861	632 724
25 - 29	1 549 019	707 603	841 416	534 662	261 595	273 067	1 014 357	446 008	568 349
30 - 34	1 251 554	583 689	667 865	396 532	191 636	204 896	855 022	392 053	462 969
35 - 39	1 037 587	481 396	556 191	314 888	151 166	163 722	722 699	330 230	392 469
40 - 44	755 605	366 518	389 087	247 154	125 016	122 138	508 451	241 502	266 949
45 - 49	649 896	321 236	328 660	201 248	105 420	95 828	448 648	215 816	232 832
50 - 54	514 520	231 232	283 288	150 346	75 258	75 088	364 174	155 974	208 200
55 - 59	402 668	194 011	208 657	106 176	54 038	52 138	296 492	139 973	156 519
60 - 64	299 703	140 146	159 557	75 555	36 842	38 713	224 148	103 304	120 844
65 - 69	241 634	113 840	127 794	55 906	26 286	29 620	185 728	87 554	98 174
70 - 74	153 617	72 288	81 329	37 666	16 950	20 716	115 951	55 338	60 613
75 - 79	116 460	55 448	61 012	26 084	11 270	14 814	90 376	44 178	46 198
80 - 84	50 695	22 417	28 278	11 090	4 394	6 696	39 605	18 023	21 582
85 - 89	36 024	16 576	19 448	7 222	2 698	4 524	28 802	13 878	14 924
90 - 94	10 686	4 803	5 883	1 896	664	1 232	8 790	4 139	4 651
95 +	13 957	7 581	6 376	2 774	1 444	1 330	11 183	6 137	5 046

Namibia - Namibie[2]
1 VII 2009 (ESDF)

Total	2 103 761	1 027 736	1 076 025	...	...	...	...	...	...
0	61 973	30 983	30 990	...	...	...	...	...	...
1 - 4	218 907	109 298	109 609	...	...	...	...	...	...
5 - 9	234 680	117 447	117 233	...	...	...	...	...	...
10 - 14	243 605	121 345	122 260	...	...	...	...	...	...
15 - 19	240 570	118 986	121 584	...	...	...	...	...	...
20 - 24	216 190	106 543	109 647	...	...	...	...	...	...
25 - 29	185 753	91 819	93 934	...	...	...	...	...	...
30 - 34	159 765	79 375	80 390	...	...	...	...	...	...
35 - 39	132 567	65 052	67 515	...	...	...	...	...	...
40 - 44	103 615	49 345	54 271	...	...	...	...	...	...
45 - 49	82 101	37 963	44 137	...	...	...	...	...	...
50 - 54	61 305	28 147	33 158	...	...	...	...	...	...
55 - 59	47 576	21 756	25 820	...	...	...	...	...	...

7. Population by age, sex and urban/rural residence: latest available year, 2003 - 2012
Population selon l'âge, le sexe et la résidence, urbaine/rurale : dernière année disponible, 2003 - 2012 (continued - suite)

Continent, country or area, date, code and age (in years) / Continent, pays ou zone, date, code et âge (en années)	Total			Urban - Urbaine			Rural - Rurale		
	Both sexes Les deux sexes	Male Masculin	Female Féminin	Both sexes Les deux sexes	Male Masculin	Female Féminin	Both sexes Les deux sexes	Male Masculin	Female Féminin
AFRICA - AFRIQUE									
Namibia - Namibie[2]									
1 VII 2009 (ESDF)									
60 - 64	35 662	16 126	19 536	...	...	...	...	...	...
65 +	79 492	33 552	45 940	...	...	...	...	...	...
Niger[2]									
1 VII 2008 (ESDJ)									
Total	14 197 601	7 088 858	7 108 743	2 728 541	1 366 304	1 362 237	11 469 060	5 722 554	5 746 506
0 - 4	2 772 294	1 398 479	1 373 815	415 380	206 784	208 597	2 356 913	1 191 695	1 165 219
5 - 9	2 371 488	1 215 095	1 156 392	423 476	213 989	209 486	1 948 012	1 001 106	946 906
10 - 14	1 943 445	992 731	950 714	431 778	219 501	212 278	1 511 667	773 230	738 437
15 - 19	1 423 793	709 730	714 063	335 882	169 492	166 390	1 087 912	540 238	547 673
20 - 24	1 065 568	516 559	549 009	219 299	110 883	108 415	846 269	405 675	440 594
25 - 29	897 791	424 031	473 760	179 185	88 607	90 578	718 606	335 424	383 182
30 - 34	775 516	362 941	412 575	157 712	75 184	82 528	617 805	287 757	330 047
35 - 39	685 244	332 962	352 282	138 488	68 225	70 263	546 756	264 737	282 019
40 - 44	592 064	296 644	295 420	116 797	60 420	56 377	475 267	236 224	239 042
45 - 49	454 577	230 338	224 239	88 522	45 663	42 859	366 055	184 674	181 380
50 - 54	345 072	175 779	169 293	66 726	32 219	34 507	278 345	143 560	134 786
55 - 59	283 989	140 750	143 240	54 282	25 466	28 815	229 708	115 283	114 424
60 - 64	222 706	107 899	114 807	41 492	21 912	19 581	181 213	85 987	95 226
65 - 69	139 748	69 004	70 745	24 598	13 189	11 409	115 151	55 815	59 336
70 - 74	83 512	42 509	41 003	13 466	6 517	6 949	70 046	35 992	34 054
75 - 79	56 491	29 140	27 350	8 220	2 655	5 565	48 271	26 485	21 786
80 +	84 303	44 268	40 035	13 238	5 598	7 640	71 066	38 671	32 395
Nigeria - Nigéria									
21 III 2006 (CDFC)									
Total	140 431 790	71 345 488	69 086 302	...	...	...	...	...	...
0 - 4	22 594 967	11 569 218	11 025 749	...	...	...	...	...	...
5 - 9	20 005 380	10 388 611	9 616 769	...	...	...	...	...	...
10 - 14	16 135 950	8 504 319	7 631 631	...	...	...	...	...	...
15 - 19	14 899 419	7 536 532	7 362 887	...	...	...	...	...	...
20 - 24	13 435 079	6 237 549	7 197 530	...	...	...	...	...	...
25 - 29	12 211 426	5 534 458	6 676 968	...	...	...	...	...	...
30 - 34	9 467 538	4 505 186	4 962 352	...	...	...	...	...	...
35 - 39	7 331 755	3 661 133	3 670 622	...	...	...	...	...	...
40 - 44	6 456 470	3 395 489	3 060 981	...	...	...	...	...	...
45 - 49	4 591 293	2 561 526	2 029 767	...	...	...	...	...	...
50 - 54	4 249 219	2 363 937	1 885 282	...	...	...	...	...	...
55 - 59	2 066 247	1 189 770	876 477	...	...	...	...	...	...
60 - 64	2 450 286	1 363 219	1 087 067	...	...	...	...	...	...
65 - 69	1 151 048	628 436	522 612	...	...	...	...	...	...
70 - 74	1 330 597	765 988	564 609	...	...	...	...	...	...
75 - 79	579 838	327 416	252 422	...	...	...	...	...	...
80 - 84	760 053	408 680	351 373	...	...	...	...	...	...
85 +	715 225	404 021	311 204	...	...	...	...	...	...
Republic of South Sudan - République de Soudan du Sud									
21 IV 2008 (CDFC)									
Total	8 260 490	4 287 300	3 973 190	1 405 186	754 086	651 100	6 855 304	3 533 214	3 322 090
0 - 4	1 304 131	689 427	614 704	218 276	114 126	104 150	1 085 855	575 301	510 554
5 - 9	1 297 816	688 385	609 431	196 136	101 760	94 376	1 101 680	586 625	515 055
10 - 14	1 057 390	569 537	487 853	160 054	84 981	75 073	897 336	484 556	412 780
15 - 19	889 829	462 902	426 927	153 683	81 602	72 081	736 146	381 300	354 846
20 - 24	739 006	360 788	378 218	148 237	78 336	69 901	590 769	282 452	308 317
25 - 29	698 011	335 398	362 613	141 623	76 445	65 178	556 388	258 953	297 435
30 - 34	536 915	258 531	278 384	101 597	56 705	44 892	435 318	201 826	233 492
35 - 39	475 813	238 985	236 828	87 844	49 346	38 498	387 969	189 639	198 330
40 - 44	339 704	173 493	166 211	58 645	33 444	25 201	281 059	140 049	141 010
45 - 49	276 100	149 941	126 159	45 605	26 316	19 289	230 495	123 625	106 870
50 - 54	197 265	104 812	92 453	31 870	17 548	14 322	165 395	87 264	78 131
55 - 59	121 795	67 845	53 950	18 520	10 557	7 963	103 275	57 288	45 987
60 - 64	115 631	64 236	51 395	16 523	8 849	7 674	99 108	55 387	43 721
65 +	211 084	123 020	88 064	26 573	14 071	12 502	184 511	108 949	75 562

7. Population by age, sex and urban/rural residence: latest available year, 2003 - 2012
Population selon l'âge, le sexe et la résidence, urbaine/rurale : dernière année disponible, 2003 - 2012 (continued - suite)

Continent, country or area, date, code and age (in years) / Continent, pays ou zone, date, code et âge (en années)	Total			Urban - Urbaine			Rural - Rurale		
	Both sexes Les deux sexes	Male Masculin	Female Féminin	Both sexes Les deux sexes	Male Masculin	Female Féminin	Both sexes Les deux sexes	Male Masculin	Female Féminin
AFRICA - AFRIQUE									
Réunion									
1 I 2010* (ESDJ)									
Total	828 054	399 728	428 326	...	...	...	...	...	...
0 - 4	68 137	35 044	33 093	...	...	...	...	...	...
5 - 9	71 223	36 404	34 819	...	...	...	...	...	...
10 - 14	70 827	36 292	34 535	...	...	...	...	...	...
15 - 19	71 254	35 775	35 479	...	...	...	...	...	...
20 - 24	56 332	28 067	28 265	...	...	...	...	...	...
25 - 29	50 540	22 922	27 618	...	...	...	...	...	...
30 - 34	55 239	24 936	30 303	...	...	...	...	...	...
35 - 39	60 586	28 029	32 557	...	...	...	...	...	...
40 - 44	67 780	32 311	35 469	...	...	...	...	...	...
45 - 49	62 291	30 352	31 939	...	...	...	...	...	...
50 - 54	49 960	24 261	25 699	...	...	...	...	...	...
55 - 59	42 397	20 577	21 820	...	...	...	...	...	...
60 - 64	31 315	15 588	15 727	...	...	...	...	...	...
65 - 69	24 247	11 380	12 867	...	...	...	...	...	...
70 - 74	18 441	7 912	10 529	...	...	...	...	...	...
75 - 79	12 549	5 036	7 513	...	...	...	...	...	...
80 - 84	8 243	2 948	5 295	...	...	...	...	...	...
85 - 89	4 641	1 438	3 203	...	...	...	...	...	...
90 - 94	1 523	350	1 173	...	...	...	...	...	...
95 +	529	106	423	...	...	...	...	...	...
Rwanda[2]									
1 VII 2012 (ESDF)									
Total	*11 033 141*	*5 342 112*	*5 691 029*	...	...	...	...	...	...
0	*430 920*	*218 488*	*212 432*	...	...	...	...	...	...
1 - 4	*1 499 630*	*754 959*	*744 672*	...	...	...	...	...	...
5 - 9	*1 534 001*	*770 292*	*763 709*	...	...	...	...	...	...
10 - 14	*1 230 213*	*608 836*	*621 378*	...	...	...	...	...	...
15 - 19	*1 120 730*	*552 629*	*568 101*	...	...	...	...	...	...
20 - 24	*1 075 971*	*525 485*	*550 486*	...	...	...	...	...	...
25 - 29	*1 049 712*	*508 839*	*540 872*	...	...	...	...	...	...
30 - 34	*782 772*	*366 700*	*416 072*	...	...	...	...	...	...
35 - 39	*532 702*	*241 362*	*291 340*	...	...	...	...	...	...
40 - 44	*425 733*	*197 005*	*228 728*	...	...	...	...	...	...
45 - 49	*358 499*	*165 096*	*193 402*	...	...	...	...	...	...
50 - 54	*333 839*	*153 080*	*180 759*	...	...	...	...	...	...
55 - 59	*239 433*	*107 200*	*132 234*	...	...	...	...	...	...
60 - 64	*164 223*	*71 924*	*92 299*	...	...	...	...	...	...
65 - 69	*96 710*	*38 125*	*58 585*	...	...	...	...	...	...
70 - 74	*75 521*	*29 285*	*46 236*	...	...	...	...	...	...
75 - 79	*45 293*	*17 736*	*27 557*	...	...	...	...	...	...
80 +	*37 239*	*15 071*	*22 168*	...	...	...	...	...	...
Saint Helena ex. dep. - Sainte-Hélène sans dép.[10]									
10 II 2008 (CDJC)									
Total	3 981	2 022	1 959	...	...	...	...	...	...
0 - 4	166	84	82	...	...	...	...	...	...
5 - 9	198	109	89	...	...	...	...	...	...
10 - 14	236	124	112	...	...	...	...	...	...
15 - 19	285	149	136	...	...	...	...	...	...
20 - 24	155	79	76	...	...	...	...	...	...
25 - 29	162	73	89	...	...	...	...	...	...
30 - 34	185	83	102	...	...	...	...	...	...
35 - 39	281	131	150	...	...	...	...	...	...
40 - 44	322	168	154	...	...	...	...	...	...
45 - 49	342	169	173	...	...	...	...	...	...
50 - 54	288	157	131	...	...	...	...	...	...
55 - 59	326	172	154	...	...	...	...	...	...
60 - 64	331	197	134	...	...	...	...	...	...
65 - 69	242	130	112	...	...	...	...	...	...
70 - 74	183	105	78	...	...	...	...	...	...
75 - 79	128	54	74	...	...	...	...	...	...
80 - 84	83	26	57	...	...	...	...	...	...

7. Population by age, sex and urban/rural residence: latest available year, 2003 - 2012

Population selon l'âge, le sexe et la résidence, urbaine/rurale : dernière année disponible, 2003 - 2012 (continued - suite)

Continent, country or area, date, code and age (in years) / Continent, pays ou zone, date, code et âge (en annèes)	Total			Urban - Urbaine			Rural - Rurale		
	Both sexes Les deux sexes	Male Masculin	Female Féminin	Both sexes Les deux sexes	Male Masculin	Female Féminin	Both sexes Les deux sexes	Male Masculin	Female Féminin
AFRICA - AFRIQUE									
Saint Helena ex. dep. - Sainte-Hélène sans dép.[10]									
10 II 2008 (CDJC)									
85 - 89	45	9	36	...	...	...	...	...	...
90 - 94	18	2	16	...	...	...	...	...	...
95 +	4	-	4	...	...	...	...	...	...
Unknown - Inconnu	1	1	-	...	...	...	...	...	...
Saint Helena: Ascension - Sainte-Hélène: Ascension									
1 VII 2008 (ESDJ)									
Total	702	397	305	...	...	...	...	...	...
0 - 4	32	16	16	...	...	...	...	...	...
5 - 9	19	9	10	...	...	...	...	...	...
10 - 14	41	20	21	...	...	...	...	...	...
15 - 19	30	19	11	...	...	...	...	...	...
20 - 24	63	29	34	...	...	...	...	...	...
25 - 29	73	42	31	...	...	...	...	...	...
30 - 34	76	41	35	...	...	...	...	...	...
35 - 39	92	58	34	...	...	...	...	...	...
40 - 44	85	42	43	...	...	...	...	...	...
45 - 49	65	36	29	...	...	...	...	...	...
50 - 54	51	32	19	...	...	...	...	...	...
55 - 59	43	29	14	...	...	...	...	...	...
60 - 64	21	15	6	...	...	...	...	...	...
65 - 69	10	9	1	...	...	...	...	...	...
70 - 74	-	-	-	...	...	...	...	...	...
75 - 79	-	-	-	...	...	...	...	...	...
80 +	1	-	1	...	...	...	...	...	...
Sao Tome and Principe - Sao Tomé-et-Principe									
1 VII 2006 (ESDF)									
Total	151 912	74 876	77 036	...	...	...	...	...	...
0 - 4	23 675	12 001	11 675	...	...	...	...	...	...
5 - 9	20 424	10 268	10 156	...	...	...	...	...	...
10 - 14	18 498	9 447	9 051	...	...	...	...	...	...
15 - 19	17 615	8 979	8 637	...	...	...	...	...	...
20 - 24	16 162	8 053	8 109	...	...	...	...	...	...
25 - 29	13 024	6 336	6 688	...	...	...	...	...	...
30 - 34	8 918	4 290	4 628	...	...	...	...	...	...
35 - 39	7 091	3 322	3 770	...	...	...	...	...	...
40 - 44	6 206	2 796	3 410	...	...	...	...	...	...
45 - 49	5 183	2 363	2 820	...	...	...	...	...	...
50 - 54	3 825	1 799	2 026	...	...	...	...	...	...
55 - 59	2 836	1 322	1 514	...	...	...	...	...	...
60 - 64	2 154	998	1 157	...	...	...	...	...	...
65 - 69	2 332	1 093	1 239	...	...	...	...	...	...
70 - 74	1 668	801	867	...	...	...	...	...	...
75 - 79	1 152	527	625	...	...	...	...	...	...
80 +	1 147	483	663	...	...	...	...	...	...
Senegal - Sénégal[11]									
31 XII 2011 (ESDJ)									
Total	12 841 702	6 350 673	6 491 029	...	...	...	...	...	...
0 - 4	2 107 821	1 064 142	1 043 679	...	...	...	...	...	...
5 - 9	1 743 172	883 929	859 243	...	...	...	...	...	...
10 - 14	1 475 980	756 283	719 697	...	...	...	...	...	...
15 - 19	1 426 306	721 900	704 406	...	...	...	...	...	...
20 - 24	1 251 215	627 044	624 171	...	...	...	...	...	...
25 - 29	1 078 097	522 097	556 000	...	...	...	...	...	...
30 - 34	822 785	398 478	424 307	...	...	...	...	...	...
35 - 39	674 509	319 435	355 074	...	...	...	...	...	...
40 - 44	548 517	253 917	294 600	...	...	...	...	...	...
45 - 49	431 928	196 833	235 095	...	...	...	...	...	...
50 - 54	353 258	167 190	186 068	...	...	...	...	...	...
55 - 59	278 483	138 092	140 391	...	...	...	...	...	...
60 - 64	228 524	103 582	124 942	...	...	...	...	...	...

7. Population by age, sex and urban/rural residence: latest available year, 2003 - 2012
Population selon l'âge, le sexe et la résidence, urbaine/rurale : dernière année disponible, 2003 - 2012 (continued - suite)

Continent, country or area, date, code and age (in years) / Continent, pays ou zone, date, code et âge (en annèes)	Total			Urban - Urbaine			Rural - Rurale		
	Both sexes Les deux sexes	Male Masculin	Female Féminin	Both sexes Les deux sexes	Male Masculin	Female Féminin	Both sexes Les deux sexes	Male Masculin	Female Féminin
AFRICA - AFRIQUE									
Senegal - Sénégal[11]									
31 XII 2011 (ESDJ)									
65 - 69	141 674	65 514	76 160	...	...	...	...	...	...
70 - 74	127 779	60 454	67 325	...	...	...	...	...	...
75 - 79	65 406	30 689	34 717	...	...	...	...	...	...
80 +	86 248	41 094	45 154	...	...	...	...	...	...
Seychelles									
1 VII 2012 (ESDF)									
Total	88 303	43 313	44 990	...	...	...	...	...	...
0	1 661	842	819	...	...	...	...	...	...
1 - 4	5 418	2 700	2 718	...	...	...	...	...	...
5 - 9	6 503	3 278	3 225	...	...	...	...	...	...
10 - 14	6 107	3 088	3 019	...	...	...	...	...	...
15 - 19	7 090	3 686	3 404	...	...	...	...	...	...
20 - 24	6 305	3 352	2 953	...	...	...	...	...	...
25 - 29	6 752	3 297	3 455	...	...	...	...	...	...
30 - 34	7 183	3 427	3 756	...	...	...	...	...	...
35 - 39	7 098	3 426	3 672	...	...	...	...	...	...
40 - 44	6 997	3 455	3 542	...	...	...	...	...	...
45 - 49	6 965	3 357	3 608	...	...	...	...	...	...
50 - 54	5 865	2 996	2 869	...	...	...	...	...	...
55 - 59	4 452	2 221	2 231	...	...	...	...	...	...
60 - 64	2 918	1 411	1 507	...	...	...	...	...	...
65 - 69	2 175	1 060	1 115	...	...	...	...	...	...
70 - 74	1 828	745	1 083	...	...	...	...	...	...
75 - 79	1 375	515	860	...	...	...	...	...	...
80 - 84	879	268	611	...	...	...	...	...	...
85 - 89	475	133	342	...	...	...	...	...	...
90 - 94	192	46	146	...	...	...	...	...	...
95 - 99	57	9	48	...	...	...	...	...	...
100 +	8	1	7	...	...	...	...	...	...
Sierra Leone									
1 VII 2010 (ESDF)									
Total	5 746 800	2 786 797	2 960 003	2 304 955	1 138 563	1 166 392	3 441 845	1 648 234	1 793 611
0 - 4	878 231	437 908	440 323	297 865	147 565	150 300	580 366	290 343	290 023
5 - 9	856 605	424 222	432 383	307 007	145 641	161 366	549 598	278 581	271 017
10 - 14	662 651	338 453	324 198	303 094	148 401	154 693	359 557	190 052	169 505
15 - 19	637 914	308 982	328 932	287 597	141 564	146 033	350 317	167 418	182 899
20 - 24	488 054	221 932	266 122	241 599	119 622	121 977	246 455	102 310	144 145
25 - 29	473 952	210 004	263 948	205 137	102 492	102 645	268 815	107 512	161 303
30 - 34	356 727	160 822	195 905	149 414	73 308	76 106	207 313	87 514	119 799
35 - 39	341 470	160 326	181 144	133 461	66 104	67 357	208 009	94 222	113 787
40 - 44	247 978	123 279	124 699	97 102	51 623	45 479	150 876	71 656	79 220
45 - 49	201 708	107 932	93 776	76 536	41 832	34 704	125 172	66 100	59 072
50 - 54	149 167	77 236	71 931	55 139	30 564	24 575	94 028	46 672	47 356
55 - 59	96 801	51 344	45 457	37 477	21 157	16 320	59 324	30 187	29 137
60 - 64	99 394	44 873	54 521	31 058	14 915	16 143	68 336	29 958	38 378
65 - 69	71 174	34 054	37 120	24 423	11 420	13 003	46 751	22 634	24 117
70 - 74	61 847	28 198	33 649	18 941	8 268	10 673	42 906	19 930	22 976
75 - 79	41 728	21 586	20 142	12 876	6 356	6 520	28 852	15 230	13 622
80 +	81 399	35 646	45 753	26 229	7 731	18 498	55 170	27 915	27 255
South Africa - Afrique du Sud									
10 X 2011 (CDFC)									
Total	51 770 560	25 188 791	26 581 769	...	...	...	...	...	...
0 - 4	5 685 452	2 867 585	2 817 867	...	...	...	...	...	...
5 - 9	4 819 751	2 425 181	2 394 570	...	...	...	...	...	...
10 - 14	4 594 886	2 344 275	2 250 611	...	...	...	...	...	...
15 - 19	5 003 477	2 498 572	2 504 905	...	...	...	...	...	...
20 - 24	5 374 542	2 694 646	2 679 896	...	...	...	...	...	...
25 - 29	5 059 317	2 542 682	2 516 635	...	...	...	...	...	...
30 - 34	4 029 010	2 036 206	1 992 804	...	...	...	...	...	...
35 - 39	3 467 767	1 709 347	1 758 420	...	...	...	...	...	...
40 - 44	2 948 619	1 402 328	1 546 291	...	...	...	...	...	...
45 - 49	2 620 283	1 195 740	1 424 543	...	...	...	...	...	...
50 - 54	2 218 289	1 011 349	1 206 940	...	...	...	...	...	...

Continent, country or area, date, code and age (in years) / Continent, pays ou zone, date, code et âge (en annèes)	Total			Urban - Urbaine			Rural - Rurale		
	Both sexes Les deux sexes	Male Masculin	Female Féminin	Both sexes Les deux sexes	Male Masculin	Female Féminin	Both sexes Les deux sexes	Male Masculin	Female Féminin
AFRICA - AFRIQUE									
South Africa - Afrique du Sud									
10 X 2011 (CDFC)									
55 - 59	1 797 408	811 950	985 458	...	...	...	...	...	...
60 - 64	1 385 768	612 364	773 404	...	...	...	...	...	...
65 - 69	957 804	401 548	556 256	...	...	...	...	...	...
70 - 74	748 330	293 498	454 832	...	...	...	...	...	...
75 - 79	481 267	165 283	315 984	...	...	...	...	...	...
80 - 84	322 916	100 694	222 222	...	...	...	...	...	...
85 +	255 673	75 543	180 130	...	...	...	...	...	...
Swaziland									
1 VII 2012 (ESDF)									
Total	1 080 337	512 432	567 905	246 441	117 528	128 913	833 896	394 904	438 992
0	31 392	15 910	15 482	5 209	2 645	2 564	26 213	13 295	12 918
1 - 4	113 168	57 724	55 444	18 479	9 405	9 074	94 689	48 319	46 370
5 - 9	127 820	64 684	63 136	21 428	10 759	10 669	106 392	53 925	52 467
10 - 14	130 169	64 303	65 866	21 696	10 143	11 553	108 473	54 160	54 313
15 - 19	126 990	61 642	65 348	23 352	10 223	13 129	103 638	51 419	52 219
20 - 24	114 112	54 488	59 624	28 246	12 515	15 731	85 866	41 973	43 893
25 - 29	97 265	44 671	52 594	31 959	14 829	17 130	65 306	29 842	35 464
30 - 34	80 146	35 515	44 631	27 399	13 236	14 163	52 747	22 279	30 468
35 - 39	61 398	26 609	34 789	20 936	10 355	10 581	40 462	16 254	24 208
40 - 44	48 904	20 997	27 907	16 023	7 910	8 113	32 881	13 087	19 794
45 - 49	37 936	16 542	21 394	11 075	5 625	5 450	26 861	10 917	15 944
50 - 54	30 300	13 373	16 927	7 913	4 049	3 864	22 387	9 324	13 063
55 - 59	23 978	10 659	13 319	5 278	2 611	2 667	18 700	8 048	10 652
60 - 64	18 812	8 420	10 392	3 361	1 595	1 766	15 451	6 825	8 626
65 - 69	14 579	6 569	8 010	1 884	815	1 069	12 695	5 754	6 941
70 - 74	10 382	4 719	5 663	1 152	474	678	9 230	4 245	4 985
75 - 79	6 500	2 942	3 558	599	229	370	5 901	2 713	3 188
80 +	6 456	2 635	3 821	452	110	342	6 004	2 525	3 479
Togo									
6 XI 2010 (CDJC)									
Total	6 191 155	3 009 095	3 182 060	...	...	...	...	...	...
0	190 136	96 043	94 093	...	...	...	...	...	...
1 - 4	711 135	360 481	350 654	...	...	...	...	...	...
5 - 9	951 700	482 501	469 199	...	...	...	...	...	...
10 - 14	747 726	390 477	357 249	...	...	...	...	...	...
15 - 19	606 401	313 257	293 144	...	...	...	...	...	...
20 - 24	545 245	252 807	292 438	...	...	...	...	...	...
25 - 29	496 822	214 803	282 019	...	...	...	...	...	...
30 - 34	424 380	199 636	224 744	...	...	...	...	...	...
35 - 39	352 008	166 528	185 480	...	...	...	...	...	...
40 - 44	291 584	139 731	151 853	...	...	...	...	...	...
45 - 49	228 446	112 191	116 255	...	...	...	...	...	...
50 - 54	178 233	82 969	95 264	...	...	...	...	...	...
55 - 59	115 950	54 936	61 014	...	...	...	...	...	...
60 - 64	102 694	44 431	58 263	...	...	...	...	...	...
65 - 69	66 324	26 700	39 624	...	...	...	...	...	...
70 - 74	61 756	24 127	37 629	...	...	...	...	...	...
75 - 79	33 574	13 250	20 324	...	...	...	...	...	...
80 +	73 591	27 960	45 631	...	...	...	...	...	...
Unknown - Inconnu	13 450	6 267	7 183	...	...	...	...	...	...
Tunisia - Tunisie[12]									
1 VII 2008 (ESDF)									
Total	10 328 900	5 156 300	5 172 600	...	...	...	...	...	...
0 - 4	832 300	425 600	406 800	...	...	...	...	...	...
5 - 9	806 900	416 500	390 400	...	...	...	...	...	...
10 - 14	867 000	444 700	422 300	...	...	...	...	...	...
15 - 19	1 011 800	518 800	493 000	...	...	...	...	...	...
20 - 24	1 053 600	531 600	522 000	...	...	...	...	...	...
25 - 29	964 100	476 500	487 600	...	...	...	...	...	...
30 - 34	828 500	397 700	430 800	...	...	...	...	...	...
35 - 39	714 000	343 700	370 400	...	...	...	...	...	...
40 - 44	702 000	338 400	363 600	...	...	...	...	...	...
45 - 49	623 300	311 200	312 000	...	...	...	...	...	...

7. Population by age, sex and urban/rural residence: latest available year, 2003 - 2012
Population selon l'âge, le sexe et la résidence, urbaine/rurale : dernière année disponible, 2003 - 2012 (continued - suite)

Continent, country or area, date, code and age (in years) / Continent, pays ou zone, date, code et âge (en annèes)	Total			Urban - Urbaine			Rural - Rurale		
	Both sexes Les deux sexes	Male Masculin	Female Féminin	Both sexes Les deux sexes	Male Masculin	Female Féminin	Both sexes Les deux sexes	Male Masculin	Female Féminin
AFRICA - AFRIQUE									
Tunisia - Tunisie[12]									
1 VII 2008 (ESDF)									
50 - 54	531 300	265 800	265 500	...	...	...	...	...	...
55 - 59	395 000	195 000	200 000	...	...	...	...	...	...
60 - 64	278 900	132 800	146 100	...	...	...	...	...	...
65 - 69	236 900	116 000	121 000	...	...	...	...	...	...
70 - 74	214 800	105 000	109 800	...	...	...	...	...	...
75 - 79	147 400	74 700	72 700	...	...	...	...	...	...
80 +	121 100	62 500	58 600	...	...	...	...	...	...
Uganda - Ouganda									
1 VII 2012 (ESDF)									
Total	34 131 400	...	...	...	...	...	...	...	...
0 - 4	7 220 700	...	...	...	...	...	...	...	...
5 - 9	5 930 300	...	...	...	...	...	...	...	...
10 - 14	4 160 000	...	...	...	...	...	...	...	...
15 - 19	3 661 100	...	...	...	...	...	...	...	...
20 - 24	3 033 800	...	...	...	...	...	...	...	...
25 - 29	2 468 500	...	...	...	...	...	...	...	...
30 - 34	1 969 300	...	...	...	...	...	...	...	...
35 - 39	1 549 200	...	...	...	...	...	...	...	...
40 - 44	1 206 400	...	...	...	...	...	...	...	...
45 - 49	927 600	...	...	...	...	...	...	...	...
50 - 54	695 700	...	...	...	...	...	...	...	...
55 - 59	501 900	...	...	...	...	...	...	...	...
60 - 64	344 400	...	...	...	...	...	...	...	...
65 - 69	221 300	...	...	...	...	...	...	...	...
70 - 74	130 300	...	...	...	...	...	...	...	...
75 - 79	67 800	...	...	...	...	...	...	...	...
80 +	43 100	...	...	...	...	...	...	...	...
United Republic of Tanzania - République Unie de Tanzanie									
26 VIII 2012 (CDFC)									
Total	44 928 923	21 869 990	23 058 933	13 305 004	6 407 396	6 897 608	31 623 919	15 462 594	16 161 325
0 - 4	7 273 832	3 637 982	3 635 850	1 764 292	883 170	881 122	5 509 540	2 754 812	2 754 728
5 - 9	6 659 037	3 333 835	3 325 202	1 574 812	777 161	797 651	5 084 225	2 556 674	2 527 551
10 - 14	5 792 587	2 892 583	2 900 004	1 490 658	714 627	776 031	4 301 929	2 177 956	2 123 973
15 - 19	4 608 836	2 238 976	2 369 860	1 541 643	688 648	852 995	3 067 193	1 550 328	1 516 865
20 - 24	3 954 039	1 793 053	2 160 986	1 506 206	673 146	833 060	2 447 833	1 119 907	1 327 926
25 - 29	3 392 494	1 548 762	1 843 732	1 302 946	602 715	700 231	2 089 548	946 047	1 143 501
30 - 34	2 909 678	1 380 068	1 529 610	1 082 032	526 965	555 067	1 827 646	853 103	974 543
35 - 39	2 440 952	1 182 651	1 258 301	849 359	427 265	422 094	1 591 593	755 386	836 207
40 - 44	1 899 114	944 033	955 081	614 918	320 553	294 365	1 284 196	623 480	660 716
45 - 49	1 505 919	718 372	787 547	466 083	226 670	239 413	1 039 836	491 702	548 134
50 - 54	1 211 027	607 361	603 666	343 871	182 099	161 772	867 156	425 262	441 894
55 - 59	773 840	392 104	381 736	218 786	116 805	101 981	555 054	275 299	279 755
60 - 64	770 717	380 223	390 494	193 428	100 996	92 432	577 289	279 227	298 062
65 - 69	492 836	238 972	253 864	111 749	57 158	54 591	381 087	181 814	199 273
70 - 74	477 830	226 484	251 346	98 546	46 418	52 128	379 284	180 066	199 218
75 - 79	292 132	144 643	147 489	57 162	27 512	29 650	234 970	117 131	117 839
80 +	474 053	209 888	264 165	88 513	35 488	53 025	385 540	174 400	211 140
Zimbabwe[11]									
1 VII 2009 (ESDF)									
Total	13 667 894	6 642 551	7 025 344	...	...	...	...	...	...
0	358 716	179 238	179 477	...	...	...	...	...	...
1 - 4	1 407 894	704 085	703 809	...	...	...	...	...	...
5 - 9	1 616 550	805 739	810 811	...	...	...	...	...	...
10 - 14	1 593 935	795 340	798 595	...	...	...	...	...	...
15 - 19	1 584 799	776 472	808 327	...	...	...	...	...	...
20 - 24	1 288 969	594 496	694 473	...	...	...	...	...	...
25 - 29	1 041 137	499 582	541 554	...	...	...	...	...	...
30 - 34	769 568	389 810	379 758	...	...	...	...	...	...
35 - 39	531 742	248 421	283 321	...	...	...	...	...	...
40 - 44	457 897	205 217	252 680	...	...	...	...	...	...
45 - 49	375 869	174 372	201 497	...	...	...	...	...	...

Population selon l'âge, le sexe et la résidence, urbaine/rurale : dernière année disponible, 2003 - 2012 (continued - suite)

Continent, country or area, date, code and age (in years) Continent, pays ou zone, date, code et âge (en années)	Total			Urban - Urbaine			Rural - Rurale		
	Both sexes Les deux sexes	Male Masculin	Female Féminin	Both sexes Les deux sexes	Male Masculin	Female Féminin	Both sexes Les deux sexes	Male Masculin	Female Féminin
AFRICA - AFRIQUE									
Zimbabwe[11]									
1 VII 2009 (ESDF)									
50 - 54	317 532	134 943	182 589	...	...	...	...	...	...
55 - 59	222 309	103 732	118 577	...	...	...	...	...	...
60 - 64	204 340	99 548	104 792	...	...	...	...	...	...
65 - 69	139 291	67 774	71 517	...	...	...	...	...	...
70 - 74	129 407	63 568	65 839	...	...	...	...	...	...
75 +	173 135	75 836	97 299	...	...	...	...	...	...
Unknown - Inconnu	46 910	20 292	26 619	...	...	...	...	...	...
AMERICA, NORTH - AMÉRIQUE DU NORD									
Antigua and Barbuda - Antigua-et-Barbuda									
1 VII 2005 (ESDF)									
Total	82 786	38 878	43 908	...	...	...	...	...	...
0	1 537	765	772	...	...	...	...	...	...
1 - 4	6 269	3 230	3 039	...	...	...	...	...	...
5 - 9	7 954	3 966	3 988	...	...	...	...	...	...
10 - 14	7 635	3 699	3 937	...	...	...	...	...	...
15 - 19	6 812	3 230	3 582	...	...	...	...	...	...
20 - 24	6 527	3 119	3 408	...	...	...	...	...	...
25 - 29	6 889	3 169	3 719	...	...	...	...	...	...
30 - 34	7 518	3 344	4 174	...	...	...	...	...	...
35 - 39	7 199	3 251	3 948	...	...	...	...	...	...
40 - 44	5 977	2 697	3 280	...	...	...	...	...	...
45 - 49	4 658	2 176	2 482	...	...	...	...	...	...
50 - 54	3 518	1 659	1 859	...	...	...	...	...	...
55 - 59	2 573	1 162	1 411	...	...	...	...	...	...
60 - 64	2 028	929	1 099	...	...	...	...	...	...
65 - 69	1 700	778	922	...	...	...	...	...	...
70 - 74	1 442	633	809	...	...	...	...	...	...
75 - 79	1 100	507	593	...	...	...	...	...	...
80 - 84	783	332	451	...	...	...	...	...	...
85 - 89	437	160	278	...	...	...	...	...	...
90 - 94	197	65	132	...	...	...	...	...	...
95 +	32	9	23	...	...	...	...	...	...
Aruba									
1 VII 2011 (ESDJ)									
Total	102 711	48 754	53 957	...	...	...	...	...	...
0 - 4	6 396	3 289	3 107	...	...	...	...	...	...
5 - 9	7 014	3 568	3 446	...	...	...	...	...	...
10 - 14	7 536	3 812	3 724	...	...	...	...	...	...
15 - 19	7 460	3 834	3 626	...	...	...	...	...	...
20 - 24	5 474	2 824	2 650	...	...	...	...	...	...
25 - 29	5 559	2 606	2 953	...	...	...	...	...	...
30 - 34	6 478	2 940	3 537	...	...	...	...	...	...
35 - 39	7 289	3 415	3 876	...	...	...	...	...	...
40 - 44	8 405	3 884	4 521	...	...	...	...	...	...
45 - 49	9 132	4 266	4 866	...	...	...	...	...	...
50 - 54	8 635	4 018	4 618	...	...	...	...	...	...
55 - 59	7 093	3 268	3 824	...	...	...	...	...	...
60 - 64	5 341	2 451	2 891	...	...	...	...	...	...
65 - 69	3 903	1 770	2 133	...	...	...	...	...	...
70 - 74	2 976	1 288	1 688	...	...	...	...	...	...
75 - 79	2 062	824	1 239	...	...	...	...	...	...
80 - 84	1 168	458	710	...	...	...	...	...	...
85 - 89	510	173	337	...	...	...	...	...	...
90 - 94	211	58	153	...	...	...	...	...	...
95 +	76	14	63	...	...	...	...	...	...

7. Population by age, sex and urban/rural residence: latest available year, 2003 - 2012
Population selon l'âge, le sexe et la résidence, urbaine/rurale : dernière année disponible, 2003 - 2012 (continued - suite)

Continent, country or area, date, code and age (in years) / Continent, pays ou zone, date, code et âge (en années)	Total			Urban - Urbaine			Rural - Rurale		
	Both sexes Les deux sexes	Male Masculin	Female Féminin	Both sexes Les deux sexes	Male Masculin	Female Féminin	Both sexes Les deux sexes	Male Masculin	Female Féminin
AMERICA, NORTH - AMÉRIQUE DU NORD									
Bahamas[13]									
1 VII 2011 (ESDF)									
Total	351 100	171 500	179 600	...	...	...	...	...	...
0 - 4	29 400	15 400	14 000	...	...	...	...	...	...
5 - 9	28 800	14 800	14 000	...	...	...	...	...	...
10 - 14	28 500	14 200	14 300	...	...	...	...	...	...
15 - 19	31 100	15 500	15 600	...	...	...	...	...	...
20 - 24	28 400	13 800	14 600	...	...	...	...	...	...
25 - 29	26 200	13 000	13 200	...	...	...	...	...	...
30 - 34	25 400	12 500	12 900	...	...	...	...	...	...
35 - 39	27 800	13 500	14 300	...	...	...	...	...	...
40 - 44	27 200	13 100	14 100	...	...	...	...	...	...
45 - 49	26 600	12 900	13 700	...	...	...	...	...	...
50 - 54	22 100	10 600	11 500	...	...	...	...	...	...
55 - 59	16 200	7 700	8 500	...	...	...	...	...	...
60 - 64	11 500	5 400	6 100	...	...	...	...	...	...
65 - 69	8 800	4 000	4 800	...	...	...	...	...	...
70 - 74	6 300	2 800	3 500	...	...	...	...	...	...
75 - 79	3 780	1 600	2 180	...	...	...	...	...	...
80 +	2 900	700	2 200	...	...	...	...	...	...
Belize									
1 VII 2006 (ESDF)[14]									
Total	*301 298*	*149 598*	*151 700*	*151 994*	*73 576*	*78 418*	*149 394*	*76 101*	*73 293*
0 - 4	*36 761*	*18 145*	*18 616*	*17 720*	*8 446*	*9 274*	*19 808*	*10 070*	*9 738*
5 - 9	*40 974*	*20 850*	*20 124*	*19 294*	*9 792*	*9 502*	*21 574*	*11 011*	*10 563*
10 - 14	*40 474*	*20 611*	*19 862*	*19 185*	*9 790*	*9 395*	*21 185*	*10 775*	*10 410*
15 - 19	*33 960*	*17 192*	*16 769*	*16 629*	*8 785*	*7 844*	*17 246*	*8 369*	*8 877*
20 - 24	*24 423*	*11 939*	*12 484*	*12 728*	*5 973*	*6 755*	*11 631*	*5 939*	*5 692*
25 - 29	*20 990*	*9 733*	*11 256*	*11 262*	*5 018*	*6 244*	*9 673*	*4 693*	*4 980*
30 - 34	*20 405*	*9 522*	*10 883*	*11 277*	*5 183*	*6 094*	*9 075*	*4 318*	*4 757*
35 - 39	*18 464*	*8 747*	*9 718*	*9 745*	*4 294*	*5 451*	*8 672*	*4 433*	*4 239*
40 - 44	*15 793*	*7 735*	*8 058*	*8 174*	*3 931*	*4 243*	*7 579*	*3 787*	*3 792*
45 - 49	*12 378*	*6 295*	*6 065*	*6 555*	*3 305*	*3 250*	*5 791*	*2 976*	*2 815*
50 - 54	*9 686*	*4 983*	*4 703*	*5 176*	*2 385*	*2 791*	*4 485*	*2 586*	*1 899*
55 - 59	*6 637*	*3 363*	*3 264*	*3 385*	*1 636*	*1 749*	*3 235*	*1 720*	*1 515*
60 - 64	*5 692*	*2 913*	*2 778*	*2 838*	*1 376*	*1 462*	*2 839*	*1 531*	*1 308*
65 - 69	*4 877*	*2 547*	*2 330*	*2 584*	*1 201*	*1 383*	*2 281*	*1 341*	*940*
70 - 74	*3 867*	*2 073*	*1 794*	*2 203*	*999*	*1 204*	*1 654*	*1 069*	*585*
75 - 79	*2 708*	*1 374*	*1 330*	*1 511*	*716*	*795*	*1 191*	*656*	*535*
80 - 84	*1 578*	*782*	*798*	*794*	*327*	*467*	*784*	*453*	*331*
85 +	*1 629*	*794*	*835*	*934*	*419*	*515*	*691*	*374*	*317*
1 VII 2009 (ESDF)									
Total	*333 200*	*166 500*	*166 700*	...	...	...	...	...	...
0 - 4	*35 400*	*18 000*	*17 400*	...	...	...	...	...	...
5 - 9	*43 500*	*21 900*	*21 600*	...	...	...	...	...	...
10 - 14	*43 800*	*22 700*	*21 100*	...	...	...	...	...	...
15 - 19	*38 700*	*19 700*	*19 000*	...	...	...	...	...	...
20 - 24	*27 100*	*13 600*	*13 500*	...	...	...	...	...	...
25 - 29	*22 700*	*10 500*	*12 200*	...	...	...	...	...	...
30 - 34	*21 500*	*9 900*	*11 600*	...	...	...	...	...	...
35 - 39	*20 600*	*9 700*	*10 900*	...	...	...	...	...	...
40 - 44	*19 000*	*9 200*	*9 800*	...	...	...	...	...	...
45 - 49	*16 200*	*8 200*	*8 000*	...	...	...	...	...	...
50 - 54	*12 000*	*6 000*	*6 000*	...	...	...	...	...	...
55 - 59	*8 900*	*4 700*	*4 200*	...	...	...	...	...	...
60 - 64	*6 800*	*3 600*	*3 200*	...	...	...	...	...	...
65 - 69	*5 500*	*3 000*	*2 500*	...	...	...	...	...	...
70 - 74	*4 300*	*2 200*	*2 100*	...	...	...	...	...	...
75 - 79	*3 300*	*1 700*	*1 600*	...	...	...	...	...	...
80 - 84	*2 000*	*1 000*	*1 000*	...	...	...	...	...	...
85 +	*1 900*	*900*	*1 000*	...	...	...	...	...	...

Continent, country or area, date, code and age (in years) / Continent, pays ou zone, date, code et âge (en années)	Total			Urban - Urbaine			Rural - Rurale		
	Both sexes Les deux sexes	Male Masculin	Female Féminin	Both sexes Les deux sexes	Male Masculin	Female Féminin	Both sexes Les deux sexes	Male Masculin	Female Féminin
AMERICA, NORTH - AMÉRIQUE DU NORD									
Bermuda - Bermudes									
20 V 2010 (CDJC)[15]									
Total	64 237	30 858	33 379	64 237	30 858	33 379	-	-	-
0 - 4	3 567	1 851	1 716	3 567	1 851	1 716	-	-	-
0	709	372	337	709	372	337	-	-	-
1 - 4	2 858	1 479	1 379	2 858	1 479	1 379	...	...	...
5 - 9	3 456	1 759	1 697	3 456	1 759	1 697	-	-	-
10 - 14	3 481	1 706	1 775	3 481	1 706	1 775	-	-	-
15 - 19	3 431	1 682	1 749	3 431	1 682	1 749	-	-	-
20 - 24	3 342	1 608	1 734	3 342	1 608	1 734	-	-	-
25 - 29	4 076	1 947	2 129	4 076	1 947	2 129	-	-	-
30 - 34	4 645	2 259	2 386	4 645	2 259	2 386	-	-	-
35 - 39	5 050	2 572	2 478	5 050	2 572	2 478	-	-	-
40 - 44	5 158	2 588	2 570	5 158	2 588	2 570	-	-	-
45 - 49	5 731	2 811	2 920	5 731	2 811	2 920	-	-	-
50 - 54	5 427	2 531	2 896	5 427	2 531	2 896	-	-	-
55 - 59	4 498	2 146	2 352	4 498	2 146	2 352	-	-	-
60 - 64	3 692	1 733	1 959	3 692	1 733	1 959	-	-	-
65 - 69	2 807	1 290	1 517	2 807	1 290	1 517	-	-	-
70 - 74	2 163	961	1 202	2 163	961	1 202	-	-	-
75 - 79	1 768	747	1 021	1 768	747	1 021	-	-	-
80 - 84	1 120	432	688	1 120	432	688	-	-	-
85 - 89	584	185	399	584	185	399	-	-	-
90 - 94	187	41	146	187	41	146	-	-	-
95 - 99	48	8	40	48	8	40	-	-	-
100 +	6	1	5	6	1	5	-	-	-
1 VII 2012 (ESDJ)									
Total	64 867	30 833	34 034	...	...	...	...	...	...
0	760	386	374	...	...	...	...	...	...
1 - 4	2 941	1 488	1 453	...	...	...	...	...	...
5 - 9	3 630	1 876	1 754	...	...	...	...	...	...
10 - 14	3 682	1 871	1 811	...	...	...	...	...	...
15 - 19	3 612	1 795	1 817	...	...	...	...	...	...
20 - 24	3 618	1 734	1 884	...	...	...	...	...	...
25 - 29	4 441	2 109	2 332	...	...	...	...	...	...
30 - 34	4 290	2 011	2 279	...	...	...	...	...	...
35 - 39	4 418	2 108	2 310	...	...	...	...	...	...
40 - 44	5 002	2 441	2 561	...	...	...	...	...	...
45 - 49	5 569	2 782	2 787	...	...	...	...	...	...
50 - 54	5 573	2 657	2 916	...	...	...	...	...	...
55 - 59	4 664	2 175	2 489	...	...	...	...	...	...
60 - 64	3 856	1 795	2 061	...	...	...	...	...	...
65 - 69	2 987	1 347	1 640	...	...	...	...	...	...
70 - 74	2 110	891	1 219	...	...	...	...	...	...
75 - 79	1 680	679	1 001	...	...	...	...	...	...
80 - 84	1 154	424	730	...	...	...	...	...	...
85 +	880	264	616	...	...	...	...	...	...
Canada									
2 V 2011 (CDJC)									
Total	33 476 685	16 414 230	17 062 460	27 147 190	13 190 225	13 956 965	6 329 495	3 224 005	3 105 500
0 - 4	1 877 095	961 150	915 945	1 531 620	784 165	747 460	345 480	176 985	168 490
5 - 9	1 809 895	925 960	883 935	1 455 570	743 510	712 060	354 325	182 450	171 875
10 - 14	1 920 355	983 990	936 365	1 526 165	781 760	744 410	394 185	202 230	191 955
15 - 19	2 178 135	1 115 845	1 062 290	1 745 370	890 940	854 430	432 765	224 900	207 860
20 - 24	2 187 450	1 108 780	1 078 670	1 858 035	935 265	922 765	329 415	173 510	155 900
25 - 29	2 169 585	1 077 275	1 092 310	1 879 840	930 835	949 005	289 745	146 445	143 305
30 - 34	2 162 900	1 058 810	1 104 095	1 838 125	897 275	940 855	324 775	161 535	163 235
35 - 39	2 173 930	1 064 195	1 109 735	1 814 025	884 235	929 785	359 910	179 965	179 945
40 - 44	2 324 875	1 141 715	1 183 155	1 908 095	933 115	974 980	416 780	208 605	208 175
45 - 49	2 675 130	1 318 715	1 356 420	2 142 125	1 050 625	1 091 500	533 005	268 085	264 915
50 - 54	2 658 965	1 309 025	1 349 940	2 091 050	1 021 340	1 069 700	567 920	287 680	280 235
55 - 59	2 340 635	1 147 300	1 193 335	1 809 810	876 210	933 600	530 825	271 090	259 735
60 - 64	2 052 670	1 002 685	1 049 980	1 573 340	754 910	818 430	479 330	247 780	231 550
65 - 69	1 521 715	738 010	783 700	1 163 785	549 495	614 290	357 930	188 515	169 415

Population selon l'âge, le sexe et la résidence, urbaine/rurale : dernière année disponible, 2003 - 2012 (continued - suite)

Continent, country or area, date, code and age (in years) / Continent, pays ou zone, date, code et âge (en annèes)	Total			Urban - Urbaine			Rural - Rurale		
	Both sexes Les deux sexes	Male Masculin	Female Féminin	Both sexes Les deux sexes	Male Masculin	Female Féminin	Both sexes Les deux sexes	Male Masculin	Female Féminin
AMERICA, NORTH - AMÉRIQUE DU NORD									
Canada									
2 V 2011 (CDJC)									
70 - 74	1 153 065	543 435	609 630	906 035	413 260	492 775	247 025	130 175	116 850
75 - 79	922 695	417 945	504 755	751 575	329 760	421 815	171 125	88 185	82 940
80 - 84	702 070	291 085	410 985	591 015	237 310	353 705	111 055	53 775	57 280
85 - 89	427 015	149 415	277 600	369 925	125 615	244 310	57 090	23 800	33 290
90 - 94	170 285	48 470	121 815	148 965	41 530	107 435	21 315	6 940	14 380
95 - 99	42 390	9 455	32 935	37 515	8 225	29 285	4 875	1 230	3 645
100 +	5 825	955	4 870	5 195	840	4 355	630	115	510
1 VII 2012* (ESDJ)[16]									
Total	34 880 491	17 309 143	17 571 348	...	...	...	...	...	...
0 - 4	1 928 762	988 702	940 060	...	...	...	...	...	...
5 - 9	1 857 086	955 026	902 060	...	...	...	...	...	...
10 - 14	1 877 315	964 740	912 575	...	...	...	...	...	...
15 - 19	2 162 960	1 108 238	1 054 722	...	...	...	...	...	...
20 - 24	2 441 086	1 254 222	1 186 864	...	...	...	...	...	...
25 - 29	2 452 285	1 246 818	1 205 467	...	...	...	...	...	...
30 - 34	2 406 319	1 203 520	1 202 799	...	...	...	...	...	...
35 - 39	2 307 219	1 155 226	1 151 993	...	...	...	...	...	...
40 - 44	2 384 574	1 199 401	1 185 173	...	...	...	...	...	...
45 - 49	2 681 337	1 350 108	1 331 229	...	...	...	...	...	...
50 - 54	2 703 198	1 352 288	1 350 910	...	...	...	...	...	...
55 - 59	2 428 528	1 199 013	1 229 515	...	...	...	...	...	...
60 - 64	2 063 000	1 010 196	1 052 804	...	...	...	...	...	...
65 - 69	1 645 143	797 942	847 201	...	...	...	...	...	...
70 - 74	1 190 654	563 820	626 834	...	...	...	...	...	...
75 - 79	924 085	418 918	505 167	...	...	...	...	...	...
80 - 84	718 825	303 603	415 222	...	...	...	...	...	...
85 - 89	450 986	164 114	286 872	...	...	...	...	...	...
90 - 94	196 109	58 642	137 467	...	...	...	...	...	...
95 - 99	51 738	12 429	39 309	...	...	...	...	...	...
100 +	9 282	2 177	7 105	...	...	...	...	...	...
Cayman Islands - Îles Caïmanes									
31 XII 2012 (ESDJ)									
Total	56 732	27 753	28 979	...	...	...	...	...	...
0 - 14	10 357	5 301	5 055	...	...	...	...	...	...
15 - 24	5 592	2 658	2 935	...	...	...	...	...	...
25 - 34	10 555	4 982	5 573	...	...	...	...	...	...
35 - 44	12 892	6 609	6 283	...	...	...	...	...	...
45 - 54	8 981	4 381	4 600	...	...	...	...	...	...
55 - 64	5 011	2 380	2 632	...	...	...	...	...	...
65 +	3 343	1 442	1 901	...	...	...	...	...	...
Costa Rica									
30 V 2011 (CDJC)									
Total	4 301 712	2 106 063	2 195 649	3 130 871	1 509 161	1 621 710	1 170 841	596 902	573 939
0 - 4	338 717	172 943	165 774	234 389	119 447	114 942	104 328	53 496	50 832
5 - 9	342 057	173 995	168 062	237 723	120 804	116 919	104 334	53 191	51 143
10 - 14	387 056	195 680	191 376	267 066	134 646	132 420	119 990	61 034	58 956
15 - 19	405 176	201 934	203 242	284 597	141 159	143 438	120 579	60 775	59 804
20 - 24	410 480	203 280	207 200	303 323	149 411	153 912	107 157	53 869	53 288
25 - 29	378 424	184 046	194 378	283 074	136 864	146 210	95 350	47 182	48 168
30 - 34	332 897	160 678	172 219	249 150	119 752	129 398	83 747	40 926	42 821
35 - 39	288 071	138 718	149 353	211 482	100 355	111 127	76 589	38 363	38 226
40 - 44	282 914	136 344	146 570	206 026	97 511	108 515	76 888	38 833	38 055
45 - 49	267 747	128 560	139 187	199 296	93 128	106 168	68 451	35 432	33 019
50 - 54	235 256	112 308	122 948	177 366	81 982	95 384	57 890	30 326	27 564
55 - 59	183 581	87 315	96 266	139 256	63 778	75 478	44 325	23 537	20 788
60 - 64	137 624	65 432	72 192	103 757	47 354	56 403	33 867	18 078	15 789
65 - 69	103 528	49 637	53 891	77 345	35 357	41 988	26 183	14 280	11 903
70 - 74	78 054	37 117	40 937	58 108	26 250	31 858	19 946	10 867	9 079
75 - 79	56 538	26 038	30 500	42 485	18 437	24 048	14 053	7 601	6 452
80 - 84	40 154	18 177	21 977	30 727	13 102	17 625	9 427	5 075	4 352
85 - 89	21 263	9 068	12 195	16 374	6 473	9 901	4 889	2 595	2 294

Continent, country or area, date, code and age (in years) / Continent, pays ou zone, date, code et âge (en années)	Total			Urban - Urbaine			Rural - Rurale		
	Both sexes Les deux sexes	Male Masculin	Female Féminin	Both sexes Les deux sexes	Male Masculin	Female Féminin	Both sexes Les deux sexes	Male Masculin	Female Féminin
AMERICA, NORTH - AMÉRIQUE DU NORD									
Costa Rica									
30 V 2011 (CDJC)									
90 - 94	8 719	3 473	5 246	6 702	2 429	4 273	2 017	1 044	973
95 - 99	2 947	1 117	1 830	2 259	791	1 468	688	326	362
100 +	509	203	306	366	131	235	143	72	71
1 VII 2012 (ESDJ)									
Total	4 667 096	2 365 425	2 301 671	...	...	...	...	...	...
0 - 4	340 900	174 507	166 393	...	...	...	...	...	...
5 - 9	361 868	185 522	176 346	...	...	...	...	...	...
10 - 14	393 529	201 953	191 576	...	...	...	...	...	...
15 - 19	419 717	215 653	204 064	...	...	...	...	...	...
20 - 24	437 425	224 256	213 169	...	...	...	...	...	...
25 - 29	425 048	217 415	207 633	...	...	...	...	...	...
30 - 34	382 828	195 936	186 892	...	...	...	...	...	...
35 - 39	325 247	166 265	158 982	...	...	...	...	...	...
40 - 44	306 596	155 874	150 722	...	...	...	...	...	...
45 - 49	307 993	155 967	152 026	...	...	...	...	...	...
50 - 54	270 682	136 492	134 190	...	...	...	...	...	...
55 - 59	213 126	106 675	106 451	...	...	...	...	...	...
60 - 64	156 292	77 369	78 923	...	...	...	...	...	...
65 - 69	111 803	54 303	57 500	...	...	...	...	...	...
70 - 74	81 849	39 163	42 686	...	...	...	...	...	...
75 - 79	59 311	27 026	32 285	...	...	...	...	...	...
80 - 84	40 331	17 675	22 656	...	...	...	...	...	...
85 - 89	21 331	8 937	12 394	...	...	...	...	...	...
90 - 94	8 083	3 230	4 853	...	...	...	...	...	...
95 +	3 137	1 207	1 930	...	...	...	...	...	...
Cuba[17]									
1 VII 2011 (ESDJ)									
Total	11 244 543	5 630 955	5 613 587	8 464 392	4 167 382	4 297 010	2 780 151	1 463 573	1 316 577
0	129 764	66 741	63 024	100 272	51 542	48 730	29 492	15 198	14 293
1 - 4	479 145	247 233	231 912	365 137	188 527	176 609	114 008	58 704	55 304
5 - 9	630 545	324 851	305 694	458 893	236 571	222 322	171 652	88 280	83 372
10 - 14	702 273	362 058	340 214	512 488	264 017	248 471	189 784	98 041	91 743
15 - 19	727 610	372 835	354 774	531 352	271 422	259 930	196 257	101 413	94 844
20 - 24	831 805	428 587	403 218	617 072	315 701	301 371	214 732	112 885	101 847
25 - 29	738 015	382 063	355 951	551 070	283 008	268 062	186 944	99 055	87 889
30 - 34	671 807	347 372	324 435	495 168	255 248	239 920	176 639	92 124	84 515
35 - 39	946 790	481 872	464 918	700 038	354 186	345 852	246 752	127 686	119 066
40 - 44	1 028 187	514 723	513 464	768 905	379 388	389 517	259 282	135 335	123 947
45 - 49	1 031 313	511 357	519 956	801 889	391 023	410 866	229 424	120 334	109 090
50 - 54	693 058	339 202	353 856	534 999	255 767	279 232	158 059	83 435	74 624
55 - 59	616 683	300 013	316 670	479 346	226 945	252 401	137 337	73 068	64 269
60 - 64	564 707	272 819	291 887	440 945	207 066	233 879	123 762	65 753	58 008
65 - 69	473 652	227 692	245 959	367 448	170 339	197 109	106 203	57 353	48 850
70 - 74	375 533	180 811	194 722	288 374	132 314	156 059	87 159	48 497	38 662
75 - 79	253 077	117 483	135 594	191 787	82 945	108 842	61 290	34 538	26 752
80 - 84	177 789	79 963	97 825	134 360	55 223	79 136	43 429	24 740	18 689
85 +	172 783	73 275	99 508	124 844	46 145	78 699	47 939	27 129	20 809
Curaçao									
1 VII 2011 (ESDJ)									
Total	150 843	68 914	81 929	...	...	...	...	...	...
0 - 4	8 998	4 556	4 442	...	...	...	...	...	...
5 - 9	9 739	5 000	4 739	...	...	...	...	...	...
10 - 14	10 629	5 540	5 089	...	...	...	...	...	...
15 - 19	11 333	5 738	5 595	...	...	...	...	...	...
20 - 24	8 021	3 858	4 163	...	...	...	...	...	...
25 - 29	7 739	3 449	4 290	...	...	...	...	...	...
30 - 34	8 027	3 369	4 658	...	...	...	...	...	...
35 - 39	9 812	4 242	5 570	...	...	...	...	...	...
40 - 44	11 228	4 930	6 298	...	...	...	...	...	...
45 - 49	12 730	5 574	7 156	...	...	...	...	...	...
50 - 54	12 046	5 222	6 824	...	...	...	...	...	...
55 - 59	10 405	4 555	5 850	...	...	...	...	...	...

Continent, country or area, date, code and age (in years) Continent, pays ou zone, date, code et âge (en annèes)	Total			Urban - Urbaine			Rural - Rurale		
	Both sexes Les deux sexes	Male Masculin	Female Féminin	Both sexes Les deux sexes	Male Masculin	Female Féminin	Both sexes Les deux sexes	Male Masculin	Female Féminin
AMERICA, NORTH - AMÉRIQUE DU NORD									
Curaçao									
1 VII 2011 (ESDJ)									
60 - 64	9 169	4 136	5 033	...	...	...	...	...	...
65 - 69	7 220	3 143	4 077	...	...	...	...	...	...
70 - 74	5 358	2 313	3 045	...	...	...	...	...	...
75 - 79	3 918	1 679	2 239	...	...	...	...	...	...
80 - 84	2 442	981	1 461	...	...	...	...	...	...
85 - 89	1 343	451	892	...	...	...	...	...	...
90 - 94	506	133	373	...	...	...	...	...	...
95 - 99	140	38	102	...	...	...	...	...	...
100 + ...	40	7	33	...	...	...	...	...	...
Dominica - Dominique									
31 XII 2006 (ESDF)									
Total............................	71 180	36 238	34 942	...	...	...	...	...	...
0 - 4	6 317	3 250	3 067	...	...	...	...	...	...
5 - 9	7 554	3 951	3 603	...	...	...	...	...	...
10 - 14	7 105	3 558	3 547	...	...	...	...	...	...
15 - 19	6 818	3 452	3 366	...	...	...	...	...	...
20 - 24	4 578	2 438	2 140	...	...	...	...	...	...
25 - 29	5 121	2 601	2 520	...	...	...	...	...	...
30 - 34	5 663	2 886	2 777	...	...	...	...	...	...
35 - 39	5 296	2 841	2 455	...	...	...	...	...	...
40 - 44	4 476	2 417	2 059	...	...	...	...	...	...
45 - 49	3 561	1 947	1 614	...	...	...	...	...	...
50 - 54	2 820	1 467	1 353	...	...	...	...	...	...
55 - 59	2 391	1 209	1 182	...	...	...	...	...	...
60 - 64	2 255	1 022	1 233	...	...	...	...	...	...
65 - 69	2 324	1 091	1 233	...	...	...	...	...	...
70 - 74	1 844	871	973	...	...	...	...	...	...
75 - 79	1 332	596	736	...	...	...	...	...	...
80 - 84	901	354	547	...	...	...	...	...	...
85 + ...	825	288	537	...	...	...	...	...	...
Dominican Republic - République dominicaine[2]									
1 VII 2012 (ESDF)									
Total............................	10 135 105	5 056 917	5 078 188	6 865 739	3 403 176	3 462 563	3 269 366	1 653 741	1 615 625
0 - 4	1 060 807	541 149	519 658	701 806	362 818	338 988	359 001	178 331	180 670
0	212 046	108 416	103 630	...	...	...	...	...	...
1 - 4	848 761	432 733	416 028	...	...	...	...	...	...
5 - 9	1 054 931	537 239	517 692	686 486	353 033	333 453	368 445	184 206	184 239
10 - 14	1 010 371	512 814	497 557	665 269	337 290	327 979	345 102	175 524	169 578
15 - 19	978 734	494 566	484 168	665 245	333 036	332 209	313 489	161 530	151 959
20 - 24	921 443	461 539	459 904	643 626	319 960	323 666	277 817	141 579	136 238
25 - 29	839 964	416 317	423 647	592 213	292 881	299 332	247 751	123 436	124 315
30 - 34	743 932	365 162	378 770	521 039	255 033	266 006	222 893	110 129	112 764
35 - 39	661 267	324 073	337 194	462 559	225 488	237 071	198 708	98 585	100 123
40 - 44	595 377	292 923	302 454	411 305	200 540	210 765	184 072	92 383	91 689
45 - 49	532 190	262 692	269 498	365 979	178 334	187 645	166 211	84 358	81 853
50 - 54	459 853	227 559	232 294	310 317	151 389	158 928	149 536	76 170	73 366
55 - 59	372 009	184 005	188 004	248 188	120 633	127 555	123 821	63 372	60 449
60 - 64	281 726	138 494	143 232	184 235	87 844	96 391	97 491	50 650	46 841
65 - 69	207 431	101 125	106 306	135 067	63 686	71 381	72 364	37 439	34 925
70 - 74	163 046	78 782	84 514	105 337	48 508	56 829	57 959	30 274	27 685
75 - 79	121 644	57 879	63 765	79 376	35 525	43 851	42 268	22 354	19 914
80 + ...	130 130	60 599	69 531	87 692	37 178	50 514	42 438	23 421	19 017
El Salvador									
12 V 2007 (CDJC)									
Total............................	5 744 113	2 719 371	3 024 742	3 598 836	1 676 313	1 922 523	2 145 277	1 043 058	1 102 219
0 - 4	555 893	283 272	272 621	324 299	165 397	158 902	231 594	117 875	113 719
5 - 9	684 727	349 150	335 577	390 873	199 184	191 689	293 854	149 966	143 888
10 - 14	706 347	359 523	346 824	404 755	205 222	199 533	301 592	154 301	147 291
15 - 19	600 565	298 384	302 181	355 376	174 488	180 888	245 189	123 896	121 293
20 - 24	486 542	228 001	258 541	309 107	143 779	165 328	177 435	84 222	93 213
25 - 29	457 890	206 963	250 927	306 456	138 320	168 136	151 434	68 643	82 791

Continent, country or area, date, code and age (in years) / Continent, pays ou zone, date, code et âge (en annèes)	Total			Urban - Urbaine			Rural - Rurale		
	Both sexes Les deux sexes	Male Masculin	Female Féminin	Both sexes Les deux sexes	Male Masculin	Female Féminin	Both sexes Les deux sexes	Male Masculin	Female Féminin
AMERICA, NORTH - AMÉRIQUE DU NORD									
El Salvador									
12 V 2007 (CDJC)									
30 - 34	402 249	178 400	223 849	274 037	121 278	152 759	128 212	57 122	71 090
35 - 39	353 147	156 514	196 633	242 566	106 882	135 684	110 581	49 632	60 949
40 - 44	303 631	132 218	171 413	209 958	90 559	119 399	93 673	41 659	52 014
45 - 49	252 122	109 957	142 165	170 464	73 027	97 437	81 658	36 930	44 728
50 - 54	215 734	95 275	120 459	143 882	62 014	81 868	71 852	33 261	38 591
55 - 59	183 075	81 718	101 357	119 193	51 574	67 619	63 882	30 144	33 738
60 - 64	151 864	68 207	83 657	97 101	41 821	55 280	54 763	26 386	28 377
65 - 69	125 157	55 781	69 376	79 690	33 492	46 198	45 467	22 289	23 178
70 - 74	97 457	43 449	54 008	62 075	25 726	36 349	35 382	17 723	17 659
75 - 79	75 984	33 658	42 326	48 760	20 096	28 664	27 224	13 562	13 662
80 - 84	46 870	20 401	26 469	30 578	12 261	18 317	16 292	8 140	8 152
85 +	44 859	18 500	26 359	29 666	11 193	18 473	15 193	7 307	7 886
1 VII 2011 (ESDF)[18]									
Total	6 216 143	2 925 284	3 290 858	...	...	...	...	...	...
0	123 924	63 285	60 639	...	...	...	...	...	...
1 - 4	482 293	246 501	235 791	...	...	...	...	...	...
5 - 9	602 535	308 052	294 483	...	...	...	...	...	...
10 - 14	710 343	362 232	348 111	...	...	...	...	...	...
15 - 19	703 389	352 598	350 791	...	...	...	...	...	...
20 - 24	581 668	276 109	305 559	...	...	...	...	...	...
25 - 29	470 955	209 615	261 340	...	...	...	...	...	...
30 - 34	415 609	180 198	235 412	...	...	...	...	...	...
35 - 39	387 835	168 638	219 197	...	...	...	...	...	...
40 - 44	344 907	149 955	194 952	...	...	...	...	...	...
45 - 49	295 565	127 846	167 719	...	...	...	...	...	...
50 - 54	249 692	108 714	140 978	...	...	...	...	...	...
55 - 59	213 593	93 682	119 911	...	...	...	...	...	...
60 - 64	179 525	78 899	100 625	...	...	...	...	...	...
65 - 69	148 295	65 846	82 450	...	...	...	...	...	...
70 - 74	119 928	52 993	66 934	...	...	...	...	...	...
75 - 79	88 281	38 678	49 603	...	...	...	...	...	...
80 +	97 806	41 443	56 363	...	...	...	...	...	...
Greenland - Groenland[19]									
1 VII 2012 (ESDJ)									
Total	56 840	30 123	26 717	48 224	25 331	22 893	8 616	4 792	3 824
0	791	394	397	683	343	340	108	51	57
1 - 4	3 300	1 755	1 545	2 787	1 483	1 304	513	272	241
5 - 9	4 050	2 056	1 994	3 350	1 702	1 648	700	354	346
10 - 14	4 203	2 119	2 084	3 492	1 778	1 714	711	341	370
15 - 19	4 416	2 203	2 213	3 700	1 843	1 857	716	360	356
20 - 24	4 723	2 419	2 304	4 020	2 041	1 979	703	378	325
25 - 29	4 124	2 111	2 013	3 545	1 762	1 783	579	349	230
30 - 34	3 783	1 981	1 802	3 253	1 679	1 574	530	302	228
35 - 39	3 211	1 776	1 435	2 744	1 517	1 227	467	259	208
40 - 44	4 148	2 250	1 898	3 525	1 899	1 626	623	351	272
45 - 49	5 476	2 960	2 516	4 712	2 512	2 200	764	448	316
50 - 54	4 685	2 626	2 059	3 998	2 198	1 800	687	428	259
55 - 59	3 445	1 949	1 496	2 896	1 616	1 280	549	333	216
60 - 64	2 367	1 404	963	2 025	1 186	839	342	218	124
65 - 69	1 838	1 048	790	1 562	876	686	276	172	104
70 - 74	1 119	584	535	936	483	453	183	101	82
75 - 79	684	319	365	575	266	309	109	53	56
80 - 84	358	134	224	319	119	200	39	15	24
85 - 89	100	32	68	84	25	59	16	7	9
90 - 94	16	3	13	15	3	12	1	-	1
95 - 99	3	-	3	3	-	3	-	-	-
Guadeloupe[20]									
1 I 2010* (ESDJ)									
Total	401 784	186 946	214 838	...	...	...	...	...	...
0 - 4	26 805	13 809	12 996	...	...	...	...	...	...
5 - 9	29 284	15 175	14 109	...	...	...	...	...	...
10 - 14	31 683	16 306	15 377	...	...	...	...	...	...

Continent, country or area, date, code and age (in years) Continent, pays ou zone, date, code et âge (en années)	Total			Urban - Urbaine			Rural - Rurale		
	Both sexes Les deux sexes	Male Masculin	Female Féminin	Both sexes Les deux sexes	Male Masculin	Female Féminin	Both sexes Les deux sexes	Male Masculin	Female Féminin
AMERICA, NORTH - AMÉRIQUE DU NORD									
Guadeloupe[20]									
1 I 2010* (ESDJ)									
15 - 19	30 792	15 755	15 037	...	...	...	...	...	...
20 - 24	21 089	10 649	10 440	...	...	...	...	...	...
25 - 29	18 090	7 826	10 264	...	...	...	...	...	...
30 - 34	21 380	8 654	12 726	...	...	...	...	...	...
35 - 39	29 401	12 372	17 029	...	...	...	...	...	...
40 - 44	32 077	13 848	18 229	...	...	...	...	...	...
45 - 49	32 798	15 179	17 619	...	...	...	...	...	...
50 - 54	27 579	13 007	14 572	...	...	...	...	...	...
55 - 59	24 015	10 979	13 036	...	...	...	...	...	...
60 - 64	21 626	9 991	11 635	...	...	...	...	...	...
65 - 69	16 370	7 342	9 028	...	...	...	...	...	...
70 - 74	13 298	5 914	7 384	...	...	...	...	...	...
75 - 79	10 578	4 505	6 073	...	...	...	...	...	...
80 - 84	7 355	2 931	4 424	...	...	...	...	...	...
85 - 89	4 757	1 844	2 913	...	...	...	...	...	...
90 - 94	1 940	605	1 335	...	...	...	...	...	...
95 +	867	255	612	...	...	...	...	...	...
Guatemala									
1 VII 2005 (ESDF)									
Total	12 699 780[21]	6 197 399	6 502 381	6 345 918	3 059 570	3 286 348	6 353 862	3 137 829	3 216 033
0 - 4	2 036 312	1 035 549	1 000 763	866 844	447 724	419 120	1 169 468	587 825	581 643
5 - 9	1 823 642	921 924	901 718	790 225	405 750	384 475	1 033 417	516 174	517 243
10 - 14	1 624 119	815 791	808 328	755 292	378 704	376 587	868 827	437 087	431 741
15 - 19	1 379 574	685 359	694 215	715 501	351 554	363 947	664 073	333 805	330 268
20 - 24	1 180 264	571 385	608 879	636 046	306 874	329 172	544 218	264 511	279 707
25 - 29	952 695	446 309	506 386	523 699	243 461	280 237	428 996	202 848	226 149
30 - 34	753 145	340 378	412 767	416 357	184 973	231 384	336 788	155 405	181 383
35 - 39	600 160	270 907	329 253	326 576	144 824	181 752	273 584	126 083	147 501
40 - 44	492 747	225 243	267 504	270 162	120 913	149 248	222 585	104 330	118 256
45 - 49	409 688	191 635	218 053	221 123	100 439	120 685	188 565	91 196	97 368
50 - 54	367 062	175 311	191 751	201 790	92 775	109 014	165 272	82 536	82 737
55 - 59	310 913	149 593	161 320	171 480	79 044	92 436	139 433	70 549	68 884
60 - 64	233 643	113 686	119 957	128 803	58 925	69 878	104 840	54 761	50 079
65 - 69	192 992	94 128	98 864	111 865	51 579	60 285	81 127	42 549	38 579
70 - 74	156 267	74 463	81 804	93 750	42 080	51 669	62 517	32 383	30 135
75 - 79	107 429	50 340	57 089	66 759	29 241	37 519	40 670	21 099	19 570
80 +	79 128	35 398	43 730	49 648	20 709	28 939	29 480	14 689	14 791
1 VII 2010 (ESDF)[11]									
Total	14 361 666	7 003 337	7 358 328	...	...	...	...	...	...
0 - 4	2 165 745	1 103 521	1 062 224	...	...	...	...	...	...
5 - 9	2 004 670	1 017 180	987 490	...	...	...	...	...	...
10 - 14	1 798 262	906 603	891 659	...	...	...	...	...	...
15 - 19	1 590 147	794 459	795 688	...	...	...	...	...	...
20 - 24	1 322 125	646 911	675 214	...	...	...	...	...	...
25 - 29	1 128 960	538 214	590 746	...	...	...	...	...	...
30 - 34	913 192	418 535	494 657	...	...	...	...	...	...
35 - 39	725 691	323 010	402 681	...	...	...	...	...	...
40 - 44	580 303	258 454	321 849	...	...	...	...	...	...
45 - 49	475 449	215 304	260 145	...	...	...	...	...	...
50 - 54	393 702	182 662	211 040	...	...	...	...	...	...
55 - 59	350 124	165 910	184 214	...	...	...	...	...	...
60 - 64	292 331	139 395	152 936	...	...	...	...	...	...
65 - 69	214 491	103 433	111 058	...	...	...	...	...	...
70 - 74	170 028	81 809	88 219	...	...	...	...	...	...
75 - 79	128 990	60 257	68 733	...	...	...	...	...	...
80 +	107 456	47 678	59 778	...	...	...	...	...	...
Haiti - Haïti[22]									
1 VII 2010 (ESDJ)									
Total	*10 085 214*	*4 993 731*	*5 091 483*	*4 817 666*	*2 321 608*	*2 496 059*	*5 267 548*	*2 672 123*	*2 595 424*
0 - 4	*1 263 322*	*644 550*	*618 772*	*532 352*	*274 597*	*257 755*	*730 970*	*369 953*	*361 017*
5 - 9	*1 195 479*	*608 495*	*586 984*	*493 368*	*249 982*	*243 386*	*702 111*	*358 513*	*343 598*
10 - 14	*1 158 478*	*588 618*	*569 860*	*532 573*	*255 002*	*277 571*	*625 905*	*333 616*	*292 289*

7. Population by age, sex and urban/rural residence: latest available year, 2003 - 2012
Population selon l'âge, le sexe et la résidence, urbaine/rurale : dernière année disponible, 2003 - 2012 (continued - suite)

Continent, country or area, date, code and age (in years) / Continent, pays ou zone, date, code et âge (en années)	Total			Urban - Urbaine			Rural - Rurale		
	Both sexes Les deux sexes	Male Masculin	Female Féminin	Both sexes Les deux sexes	Male Masculin	Female Féminin	Both sexes Les deux sexes	Male Masculin	Female Féminin
AMERICA, NORTH - AMÉRIQUE DU NORD									
Haiti - Haïti[22]									
1 VII 2010 (ESDJ)									
15 - 19	1 092 364	551 467	540 897	583 183	276 258	306 925	509 181	275 209	233 972
20 - 24	1 019 589	509 042	510 547	600 175	296 233	303 943	419 414	212 809	206 604
25 - 29	919 636	454 123	465 513	537 063	267 198	269 865	382 573	186 925	195 648
30 - 34	702 596	340 518	362 078	390 054	189 432	200 622	312 542	151 086	161 456
35 - 39	548 004	261 157	286 847	272 855	128 575	144 280	275 149	132 582	142 567
40 - 44	488 482	235 182	253 300	225 057	106 072	118 985	263 425	129 110	134 315
45 - 49	423 377	204 077	219 300	179 712	81 240	98 472	243 665	122 837	120 828
50 - 54	342 913	166 418	176 495	138 580	61 854	76 726	204 333	104 564	99 769
55 - 59	284 731	136 034	148 697	107 391	46 062	61 329	177 340	89 972	87 368
60 - 64	206 835	95 939	110 896	73 562	29 974	43 588	133 273	65 965	67 308
65 - 69	175 898	81 854	94 044	61 671	24 975	36 696	114 227	56 879	57 348
70 - 74	129 436	58 181	71 255	44 448	17 100	27 347	84 988	41 081	43 908
75 - 79	80 898	35 538	45 360	27 630	10 473	17 158	53 268	25 065	28 202
80 +	53 176	22 538	30 638	17 992	6 581	11 412	35 184	15 957	19 226
1 VII 2011 (ESDJ)									
Total	10 248 306	5 075 517	5 172 789	...	...	...	...	...	...
0 - 4	1 268 897	647 465	621 432	...	...	...	...	...	...
5 - 9	1 201 161	611 472	589 690	...	...	...	...	...	...
10 - 14	1 163 085	591 018	572 066	...	...	...	...	...	...
15 - 19	1 100 883	556 085	544 798	...	...	...	...	...	...
20 - 24	1 029 132	514 235	514 898	...	...	...	...	...	...
25 - 29	940 847	465 396	475 451	...	...	...	...	...	...
30 - 34	737 993	358 927	379 066	...	...	...	...	...	...
35 - 39	566 936	270 574	296 362	...	...	...	...	...	...
40 - 44	495 026	237 754	257 273	...	...	...	...	...	...
45 - 49	433 416	208 671	224 746	...	...	...	...	...	...
50 - 54	353 800	171 468	182 332	...	...	...	...	...	...
55 - 59	293 134	140 392	152 742	...	...	...	...	...	...
60 - 64	214 819	99 846	114 973	...	...	...	...	...	...
65 - 69	177 069	82 201	94 868	...	...	...	...	...	...
70 - 74	132 790	59 833	72 957	...	...	...	...	...	...
75 - 79	83 834	36 751	47 083	...	...	...	...	...	...
80 +	55 484	23 431	32 053	...	...	...	...	...	...
Honduras[4]									
1 VII 2007 (ESDF)									
Total	7 536 952	3 717 577	3 819 375	3 752 579	1 793 588	1 958 991	3 784 373	1 923 989	1 860 384
0 - 4	1 063 247	541 070	522 177	478 059	243 771	234 288	585 188	297 299	287 889
5 - 9	1 009 399	511 733	497 666	432 422	221 023	211 399	576 977	290 710	286 267
10 - 14	920 850	464 403	456 447	414 394	208 459	205 935	506 456	255 944	250 512
15 - 19	802 793	402 792	400 001	398 138	192 053	206 085	404 655	210 739	193 916
20 - 24	710 751	353 317	357 434	390 899	179 723	211 176	319 852	173 594	146 258
25 - 29	626 413	308 283	318 130	352 025	165 114	186 911	274 388	143 169	131 219
30 - 34	522 679	255 818	266 861	286 860	136 186	150 674	235 819	119 632	116 187
35 - 39	425 045	205 171	219 874	235 598	109 749	125 849	189 447	95 422	94 025
40 - 44	334 632	157 492	177 140	184 004	84 081	99 923	150 628	73 411	77 217
45 - 49	276 277	128 813	147 464	149 861	67 682	82 179	126 416	61 131	65 285
50 - 54	227 421	105 428	121 993	118 577	52 986	65 591	108 844	52 442	56 402
55 - 59	180 676	83 643	97 033	92 810	40 714	52 096	87 866	42 929	44 937
60 - 64	137 652	63 863	73 789	67 361	29 245	38 116	70 291	34 618	35 673
65 - 69	107 540	49 404	58 136	52 443	22 197	30 246	55 097	27 207	27 890
70 - 74	82 118	37 134	44 984	41 131	17 107	24 024	40 987	20 027	20 960
75 - 79	54 593	24 368	30 225	28 183	11 568	16 615	26 410	12 800	13 610
80 +	54 866	24 845	30 021	29 814	11 930	17 884	25 052	12 915	12 137
1 VII 2010 (ESDF)									
Total	8 045 990	3 965 430	4 080 560	...	...	...	...	...	...
0 - 4	1 079 289	549 179	530 110	...	...	...	...	...	...
5 - 9	1 035 077	525 938	509 139	...	...	...	...	...	...
10 - 14	973 613	492 090	481 523	...	...	...	...	...	...
15 - 19	866 193	434 856	431 337	...	...	...	...	...	...
20 - 24	747 514	371 818	375 696	...	...	...	...	...	...
25 - 29	663 903	326 377	337 526	...	...	...	...	...	...
30 - 34	577 561	282 042	295 519	...	...	...	...	...	...

7. Population by age, sex and urban/rural residence: latest available year, 2003 - 2012
Population selon l'âge, le sexe et la résidence, urbaine/rurale : dernière année disponible, 2003 - 2012 (continued - suite)

Continent, country or area, date, code and age (in years) / Continent, pays ou zone, date, code et âge (en années)	Total			Urban - Urbaine			Rural - Rurale		
	Both sexes Les deux sexes	Male Masculin	Female Féminin	Both sexes Les deux sexes	Male Masculin	Female Féminin	Both sexes Les deux sexes	Male Masculin	Female Féminin
AMERICA, NORTH - AMÉRIQUE DU NORD									
Honduras[4]									
1 VII 2010 (ESDF)									
35 - 39	474 884	230 506	244 378	...	...	...	...	...	...
40 - 44	381 715	181 554	200 161	...	...	...	...	...	...
45 - 49	301 565	140 031	161 534	...	...	...	...	...	...
50 - 54	251 618	116 240	135 378	...	...	...	...	...	...
55 - 59	203 187	93 205	109 982	...	...	...	...	...	...
60 - 64	157 317	72 071	85 246	...	...	...	...	...	...
65 - 69	117 790	53 835	63 955	...	...	...	...	...	...
70 - 74	90 125	40 470	49 655	...	...	...	...	...	...
75 - 79	62 138	27 381	34 757	...	...	...	...	...	...
80 +	62 501	27 837	34 664	...	...	...	...	...	...
Jamaica - Jamaïque									
4 IV 2011 (CDJC)									
Total	2 697 983	1 334 533	1 363 450	1 454 151	700 957	753 194	1 243 832	633 576	610 256
0 - 4	209 871	106 107	103 764	109 121	55 157	53 965	100 750	50 950	49 799
5 - 9	226 378	114 792	111 586	114 520	57 817	56 703	111 858	56 975	54 883
10 - 14	266 586	136 183	130 403	138 596	70 428	68 168	127 990	65 755	62 235
15 - 19	274 658	139 777	134 881	143 644	72 173	71 471	131 014	67 604	63 410
20 - 24	250 711	125 243	125 468	140 770	68 692	72 078	109 941	56 551	53 390
25 - 29	226 120	109 919	116 201	129 961	61 980	67 981	96 159	47 939	48 220
30 - 34	185 495	87 810	97 685	106 228	49 452	56 776	79 267	38 358	40 909
35 - 39	183 756	86 647	97 109	103 560	47 408	56 152	80 196	39 239	40 957
40 - 44	173 924	85 656	88 268	97 069	46 377	50 693	76 855	39 279	37 575
45 - 49	155 389	79 201	76 188	88 044	41 385	46 658	67 345	37 816	29 530
50 - 54	137 895	67 297	70 598	74 271	34 341	39 930	63 624	32 956	30 668
55 - 59	100 798	50 717	50 081	54 090	26 020	28 070	46 708	24 697	22 011
60 - 64	88 057	44 407	43 650	46 868	22 549	24 319	41 189	21 858	19 331
65 - 69	65 164	32 543	32 621	33 182	15 691	17 491	31 982	16 852	15 130
70 - 74	51 276	24 627	26 649	25 354	11 785	13 569	25 922	12 842	13 080
75 - 79	42 762	19 847	22 915	20 542	9 085	11 458	22 220	10 762	11 457
80 - 84	30 738	13 258	17 480	14 941	6 132	8 809	15 797	7 126	8 671
85 - 89	18 457	7 267	11 190	8 789	3 151	5 638	9 668	4 116	5 552
90 - 94	6 921	2 303	4 618	3 238	957	2 281	3 683	1 346	2 337
95 - 99	2 503	808	1 695	1 119	326	793	1 384	482	902
100 +	524	124	400	243	53	190	281	71	210
Martinique									
1 I 2010* (ESDJ)									
Total	396 308	182 644	213 664	...	...	...	...	...	...
0 - 4	23 686	12 113	11 573	...	...	...	...	...	...
5 - 9	26 410	13 174	13 236	...	...	...	...	...	...
10 - 14	27 636	14 074	13 562	...	...	...	...	...	...
15 - 19	29 421	14 763	14 658	...	...	...	...	...	...
20 - 24	22 587	11 099	11 488	...	...	...	...	...	...
25 - 29	18 188	7 989	10 199	...	...	...	...	...	...
30 - 34	19 910	8 326	11 584	...	...	...	...	...	...
35 - 39	27 580	11 585	15 995	...	...	...	...	...	...
40 - 44	32 091	14 036	18 055	...	...	...	...	...	...
45 - 49	33 120	15 044	18 076	...	...	...	...	...	...
50 - 54	28 690	13 186	15 504	...	...	...	...	...	...
55 - 59	24 930	11 376	13 554	...	...	...	...	...	...
60 - 64	21 653	10 057	11 596	...	...	...	...	...	...
65 - 69	16 961	7 816	9 145	...	...	...	...	...	...
70 - 74	15 415	7 038	8 377	...	...	...	...	...	...
75 - 79	11 423	4 898	6 525	...	...	...	...	...	...
80 - 84	8 464	3 461	5 003	...	...	...	...	...	...
85 - 89	5 093	1 785	3 308	...	...	...	...	...	...
90 - 94	2 125	593	1 532	...	...	...	...	...	...
95 +	925	231	694	...	...	...	...	...	...
Mexico - Mexique[23]									
12 VI 2010 (CDFC)									
Total	112 336 538	54 855 231	57 481 307	86 287 410	41 946 540	44 340 870	26 049 128	12 908 691	13 140 437
0 - 4	10 528 322	5 346 943	5 181 379	7 766 149	3 945 636	3 820 513	2 762 173	1 401 307	1 360 866
5 - 9	11 047 537	5 604 175	5 443 362	8 124 337	4 124 524	3 999 813	2 923 200	1 479 651	1 443 549

7. Population by age, sex and urban/rural residence: latest available year, 2003 - 2012
Population selon l'âge, le sexe et la résidence, urbaine/rurale : dernière année disponible, 2003 - 2012 (continued - suite)

Continent, country or area, date, code and age (in years) / Continent, pays ou zone, date, code et âge (en annèes)	Total			Urban - Urbaine			Rural - Rurale		
	Both sexes Les deux sexes	Male Masculin	Female Féminin	Both sexes Les deux sexes	Male Masculin	Female Féminin	Both sexes Les deux sexes	Male Masculin	Female Féminin
AMERICA, NORTH - AMÉRIQUE DU NORD									
Mexico - Mexique[23]									
12 VI 2010 (CDFC)									
10 - 14	10 939 937	5 547 613	5 392 324	7 974 649	4 041 649	3 933 000	2 965 288	1 505 964	1 459 324
15 - 19	11 026 112	5 520 121	5 505 991	8 191 229	4 097 876	4 093 353	2 834 883	1 422 245	1 412 638
20 - 24	9 892 271	4 813 204	5 079 067	7 725 598	3 775 245	3 950 353	2 166 673	1 037 959	1 128 714
25 - 29	8 788 177	4 205 975	4 582 202	6 985 279	3 354 569	3 630 710	1 802 898	851 406	951 492
30 - 34	8 470 798	4 026 031	4 444 767	6 719 047	3 188 789	3 530 258	1 751 751	837 242	914 509
35 - 39	8 292 987	3 964 738	4 328 249	6 642 253	3 160 713	3 481 540	1 650 734	804 025	846 709
40 - 44	7 009 226	3 350 322	3 658 904	5 633 205	2 676 230	2 956 975	1 376 021	674 092	701 929
45 - 49	5 928 730	2 824 364	3 104 366	4 739 911	2 241 753	2 498 158	1 188 819	582 611	606 208
50 - 54	5 064 291	2 402 451	2 661 840	4 051 487	1 904 317	2 147 170	1 012 804	498 134	514 670
55 - 59	3 895 365	1 869 537	2 025 828	3 043 924	1 443 868	1 600 056	851 441	425 669	425 772
60 - 64	3 116 466	1 476 667	1 639 799	2 403 645	1 119 077	1 284 568	712 821	357 590	355 231
65 - 69	2 317 265	1 095 273	1 221 992	1 719 078	794 137	924 941	598 187	301 136	297 051
70 - 74	1 873 934	873 893	1 000 041	1 338 906	603 945	734 961	535 028	269 948	265 080
75 - 79	1 245 483	579 689	665 794	892 237	399 026	493 211	353 246	180 663	172 583
80 - 84	798 936	355 277	443 659	576 855	244 082	332 773	222 081	111 195	110 886
85 - 89	454 164	197 461	256 703	322 844	132 826	190 018	131 320	64 635	66 685
90 - 94	164 924	68 130	96 794	116 950	45 123	71 827	47 974	23 007	24 967
95 - 99	65 732	25 920	39 812	44 084	16 122	27 962	21 648	9 798	11 850
100 +	18 475	7 228	11 247	10 451	3 753	6 698	8 024	3 475	4 549
Unknown - Inconnu	1 397 406	700 219	697 187	1 265 292	633 280	632 012	132 114	66 939	65 175
Montserrat									
12 V 2011 (CDJC)									
Total	4 922	2 546	2 376	...	...	...	...	...	...
0 - 4	301	157	144	...	...	...	...	...	...
5 - 9	311	146	165	...	...	...	...	...	...
10 - 14	359	187	172	...	...	...	...	...	...
15 - 19	319	179	140	...	...	...	...	...	...
20 - 24	269	152	117	...	...	...	...	...	...
25 - 29	299	154	145	...	...	...	...	...	...
30 - 34	298	138	160	...	...	...	...	...	...
35 - 39	368	172	196	...	...	...	...	...	...
40 - 44	406	189	217	...	...	...	...	...	...
45 - 49	381	196	185	...	...	...	...	...	...
50 - 54	331	183	148	...	...	...	...	...	...
55 - 59	314	181	133	...	...	...	...	...	...
60 - 64	275	165	110	...	...	...	...	...	...
65 - 69	231	130	101	...	...	...	...	...	...
70 - 74	145	75	70	...	...	...	...	...	...
75 - 79	116	61	55	...	...	...	...	...	...
80 - 84	94	44	50	...	...	...	...	...	...
85 +	105	37	68	...	...	...	...	...	...
Nicaragua									
1 VII 2009 (ESDJ)									
Total	5 742 316[12]	2 844 244	2 898 072	3 259 955	1 569 555	1 690 400	2 482 361	1 274 689	1 207 672
0 - 4	680 125[12]	347 205	332 920	335 635	172 875	162 760	344 490	174 330	170 160
5 - 9	660 096[12]	336 817	323 279	332 694	169 358	163 336	327 402	167 459	159 943
10 - 14	677 756[12]	344 831	332 925	359 316	180 457	178 859	318 440	164 374	154 066
15 - 19	660 608[12]	331 536	329 072	363 427	178 690	184 737	297 181	152 846	144 335
20 - 24	576 923[12]	286 484	290 439	332 187	160 315	171 872	244 736	126 169	118 567
25 - 29	511 402[12]	250 672	260 730	306 186	145 137	161 049	205 216	105 535	99 681
30 - 34	412 087[12]	197 120	214 967	251 145	115 523	135 622	160 942	81 597	79 345
35 - 39	337 317[12]	162 472	174 845	208 505	96 540	111 965	128 812	65 932	62 880
40 - 44	279 795[12]	136 223	143 572	177 594	83 709	93 885	102 201	52 514	49 687
45 - 49	239 942[12]	115 914	124 028	154 027	71 955	82 072	85 915	43 959	41 956
50 - 54	206 088[12]	98 355	107 733	130 198	59 417	70 781	75 890	38 938	36 952
55 - 59	154 329[12]	74 173	80 156	95 879	43 653	52 226	58 450	30 520	27 930
60 - 64	93 681[12]	45 221	48 460	57 189	25 734	31 455	36 492	19 487	17 005
65 - 69	89 351[12]	43 121	46 230	54 102	24 079	30 023	35 249	19 042	16 207
70 - 74	67 861[12]	32 418	35 443	41 515	18 145	23 370	26 346	14 273	12 073
75 - 79	48 205[12]	22 249	25 956	30 640	12 935	17 705	17 565	9 314	8 251
80 +	46 750[12]	19 433	27 317	29 716	11 033	18 683	17 034	8 400	8 634

7. Population by age, sex and urban/rural residence: latest available year, 2003 - 2012
Population selon l'âge, le sexe et la résidence, urbaine/rurale : dernière année disponible, 2003 - 2012 (continued - suite)

Continent, country or area, date, code and age (in years) / Continent, pays ou zone, date, code et âge (en années)	Total			Urban - Urbaine			Rural - Rurale		
	Both sexes Les deux sexes	Male Masculin	Female Féminin	Both sexes Les deux sexes	Male Masculin	Female Féminin	Both sexes Les deux sexes	Male Masculin	Female Féminin
AMERICA, NORTH - AMÉRIQUE DU NORD									
Panama[24]									
1 VII 2010 (ESDF)									
Total	3 504 483	1 765 734	1 738 749	2 262 765	1 119 546	1 143 219	1 241 718	646 188	595 530
0 - 4	351 221	179 371	171 850	208 269	106 475	101 794	142 952	72 896	70 056
5 - 9	341 709	174 456	167 253	205 648	105 111	100 537	136 061	69 345	66 716
10 - 14	329 340	168 137	161 203	190 973	97 407	93 566	138 367	70 730	67 637
15 - 19	307 769	156 928	150 841	183 791	93 422	90 369	123 978	63 506	60 472
20 - 24	298 800	151 900	146 900	193 108	97 226	95 882	105 692	54 674	51 018
25 - 29	277 505	140 612	136 893	191 549	94 536	97 013	85 956	46 076	39 880
30 - 34	263 334	132 845	130 489	189 011	93 774	95 237	74 323	39 071	35 252
35 - 39	259 755	130 366	129 389	182 595	90 863	91 732	77 160	39 503	37 657
40 - 44	236 952	118 777	118 175	165 600	81 805	83 795	71 352	36 972	34 380
45 - 49	201 998	100 644	101 354	141 013	68 336	72 677	60 985	32 308	28 677
50 - 54	165 538	81 908	83 630	113 611	54 248	59 363	51 927	27 660	24 267
55 - 59	134 094	66 304	67 790	90 029	42 678	47 351	44 065	23 626	20 439
60 - 64	106 753	53 121	53 632	68 245	32 196	36 049	38 508	20 925	17 583
65 - 69	84 013	41 413	42 600	51 441	23 860	27 581	32 572	17 553	15 019
70 - 74	60 678	29 519	31 159	35 148	15 728	19 420	25 530	13 791	11 739
75 - 79	43 317	20 618	22 699	25 559	10 990	14 569	17 758	9 628	8 130
80 +	41 707	18 815	22 892	27 175	10 891	16 284	14 532	7 924	6 608
Puerto Rico - Porto Rico[25]									
1 VII 2012 (ESDJ)									
Total	3 667 084	1 755 479	1 911 605	...	...	...	...	...	...
0 - 4	209 597	107 000	102 597	...	...	...	...	...	...
5 - 9	225 853	116 188	109 665	...	...	...	...	...	...
10 - 14	252 728	129 722	123 006	...	...	...	...	...	...
15 - 19	270 896	138 646	132 250	...	...	...	...	...	...
20 - 24	266 662	134 894	131 768	...	...	...	...	...	...
25 - 29	230 238	112 981	117 257	...	...	...	...	...	...
30 - 34	240 311	115 030	125 281	...	...	...	...	...	...
35 - 39	233 808	111 971	121 837	...	...	...	...	...	...
40 - 44	236 499	113 223	123 276	...	...	...	...	...	...
45 - 49	243 555	114 114	129 441	...	...	...	...	...	...
50 - 54	236 761	109 550	127 211	...	...	...	...	...	...
55 - 59	226 139	103 031	123 108	...	...	...	...	...	...
60 - 64	212 001	96 256	115 745	...	...	...	...	...	...
65 - 69	191 166	86 858	104 308	...	...	...	...	...	...
70 - 74	144 338	64 745	79 593	...	...	...	...	...	...
75 - 79	107 083	46 652	60 431	...	...	...	...	...	...
80 - 84	71 309	29 398	41 911	...	...	...	...	...	...
85 +	68 140	25 220	42 920	...	...	...	...	...	...
Saint Lucia - Sainte-Lucie									
1 VII 2009 (ESDF)									
Total	172 370	84 465	87 905	...	...	...	...	...	...
0 - 4	15 344	7 808	7 536	...	...	...	...	...	...
5 - 9	13 188	6 514	6 674	...	...	...	...	...	...
10 - 14	16 105	8 047	8 058	...	...	...	...	...	...
15 - 19	17 386	8 735	8 651	...	...	...	...	...	...
20 - 24	17 430	8 553	8 877	...	...	...	...	...	...
25 - 29	15 114	7 422	7 692	...	...	...	...	...	...
30 - 34	13 317	6 469	6 848	...	...	...	...	...	...
35 - 39	12 240	5 895	6 345	...	...	...	...	...	...
40 - 44	11 709	5 644	6 065	...	...	...	...	...	...
45 - 49	10 541	5 107	5 434	...	...	...	...	...	...
50 - 54	7 978	3 988	3 990	...	...	...	...	...	...
55 - 59	5 957	2 977	2 980	...	...	...	...	...	...
60 - 64	4 559	2 142	2 417	...	...	...	...	...	...
65 - 69	3 647	1 662	1 985	...	...	...	...	...	...
70 - 74	3 077	1 410	1 667	...	...	...	...	...	...
75 - 79	2 276	1 034	1 242	...	...	...	...	...	...
80 +	2 502	1 058	1 444	...	...	...	...	...	...

7. Population by age, sex and urban/rural residence: latest available year, 2003 - 2012

Population selon l'âge, le sexe et la résidence, urbaine/rurale : dernière année disponible, 2003 - 2012 (continued - suite)

Continent, country or area, date, code and age (in years) / Continent, pays ou zone, date, code et âge (en années)	Total			Urban - Urbaine			Rural - Rurale		
	Both sexes Les deux sexes	Male Masculin	Female Féminin	Both sexes Les deux sexes	Male Masculin	Female Féminin	Both sexes Les deux sexes	Male Masculin	Female Féminin
AMERICA, NORTH - AMÉRIQUE DU NORD									
Saint Pierre and Miquelon - Saint Pierre-et-Miquelon									
19 I 2006 (CDFC)									
Total	6 125	3 034	3 091	...	...	...	...	...	...
0 - 4	289	143	146	...	...	...	...	...	...
5 - 9	417	211	206	...	...	...	...	...	...
10 - 14	461	237	224	...	...	...	...	...	...
15 - 19	366	188	178	...	...	...	...	...	...
20 - 24	258	136	122	...	...	...	...	...	...
25 - 29	333	166	167	...	...	...	...	...	...
30 - 34	431	202	229	...	...	...	...	...	...
35 - 39	568	294	274	...	...	...	...	...	...
40 - 44	575	293	282	...	...	...	...	...	...
45 - 49	471	246	225	...	...	...	...	...	...
50 - 54	435	238	197	...	...	...	...	...	...
55 - 59	432	231	201	...	...	...	...	...	...
60 - 64	280	143	137	...	...	...	...	...	...
65 - 69	243	115	128	...	...	...	...	...	...
70 - 74	208	83	125	...	...	...	...	...	...
75 - 79	128	42	86	...	...	...	...	...	...
80 - 84	114	35	79	...	...	...	...	...	...
85 - 89	75	19	56	...	...	...	...	...	...
90 - 94	30	12	18	...	...	...	...	...	...
95 +	11	-	11	...	...	...	...	...	...
Saint Vincent and the Grenadines - Saint-Vincent-et-les Grenadines[12]									
1 VII 2008 (ESDF)									
Total	99 086	50 009	49 077	...	...	...	...	...	...
0 - 4	9 302	4 782	4 520	...	...	...	...	...	...
5 - 9	10 684	5 352	5 332	...	...	...	...	...	...
10 - 14	10 391	5 269	5 122	...	...	...	...	...	...
15 - 19	10 531	5 293	5 238	...	...	...	...	...	...
20 - 24	9 060	4 639	4 420	...	...	...	...	...	...
25 - 29	7 941	4 057	3 884	...	...	...	...	...	...
30 - 34	7 155	3 747	3 408	...	...	...	...	...	...
35 - 39	7 525	3 911	3 614	...	...	...	...	...	...
40 - 44	6 243	3 214	3 029	...	...	...	...	...	...
45 - 49	4 410	2 252	2 158	...	...	...	...	...	...
50 - 54	3 481	1 807	1 674	...	...	...	...	...	...
55 - 59	2 595	1 299	1 296	...	...	...	...	...	...
60 - 64	2 550	1 222	1 328	...	...	...	...	...	...
65 - 69	2 379	1 143	1 236	...	...	...	...	...	...
70 - 74	1 819	831	989	...	...	...	...	...	...
75 - 79	1 412	591	821	...	...	...	...	...	...
80 - 84	879	359	520	...	...	...	...	...	...
85 +	729	241	488	...	...	...	...	...	...
Trinidad and Tobago - Trinité-et-Tobago[26]									
1 VII 2010 (ESDF)									
Total	1 317 714	...	...	...	...	...	...	...	...
0 - 14	333 965	...	...	...	...	...	...	...	...
15 - 19	144 548	...	...	...	...	...	...	...	...
20 - 24	116 890	...	...	...	...	...	...	...	...
25 - 29	100 841	...	...	...	...	...	...	...	...
30 - 34	96 235	...	...	...	...	...	...	...	...
35 - 39	107 070	...	...	...	...	...	...	...	...
40 - 44	94 333	...	...	...	...	...	...	...	...
45 - 49	78 103	...	...	...	...	...	...	...	...
50 - 54	65 170	...	...	...	...	...	...	...	...
55 - 59	48 537	...	...	...	...	...	...	...	...
60 - 64	38 736	...	...	...	...	...	...	...	...
65 +	93 286	...	...	...	...	...	...	...	...

Continent, country or area, date, code and age (in years) / Continent, pays ou zone, date, code et âge (en années)	Total			Urban - Urbaine			Rural - Rurale		
	Both sexes Les deux sexes	Male Masculin	Female Féminin	Both sexes Les deux sexes	Male Masculin	Female Féminin	Both sexes Les deux sexes	Male Masculin	Female Féminin
AMERICA, NORTH - AMÉRIQUE DU NORD									
United States of America - États-Unis d'Amérique[27] 1 IV 2010 (CDJC)									
Total	308 745 538	151 781 326	156 964 212	249 253 271	121 698 595	127 554 676	59 492 267	30 082 731	29 409 536
0 - 4	20 201 362	10 319 427	9 881 935	16 838 001	8 597 234	8 240 767	3 363 361	1 722 193	1 641 168
5 - 9	20 348 657	10 389 638	9 959 019	16 597 127	8 464 939	8 132 188	3 751 530	1 924 699	1 826 831
10 - 14	20 677 194	10 579 862	10 097 332	16 576 171	8 466 809	8 109 362	4 101 023	2 113 053	1 987 970
15 - 19	22 040 343	11 303 666	10 736 677	17 946 265	9 149 187	8 797 078	4 094 078	2 154 479	1 939 599
20 - 24	21 585 999	11 014 176	10 571 823	18 653 468	9 450 066	9 203 402	2 932 531	1 564 110	1 368 421
25 - 29	21 101 849	10 635 591	10 466 258	18 163 244	9 110 029	9 053 215	2 938 605	1 525 562	1 413 043
30 - 34	19 962 099	9 996 500	9 965 599	16 857 801	8 409 694	8 448 107	3 104 298	1 586 806	1 517 492
35 - 39	20 179 642	10 042 022	10 137 620	16 629 937	8 249 301	8 380 636	3 549 705	1 792 721	1 756 984
40 - 44	20 890 964	10 393 977	10 496 987	16 837 761	8 347 894	8 489 867	4 053 203	2 046 083	2 007 120
45 - 49	22 708 591	11 209 085	11 499 506	17 847 074	8 760 812	9 086 262	4 861 517	2 448 273	2 413 244
50 - 54	22 298 125	10 933 274	11 364 851	17 279 058	8 401 091	8 877 967	5 019 067	2 532 183	2 486 884
55 - 59	19 664 805	9 523 648	10 141 157	15 060 179	7 204 444	7 855 735	4 604 626	2 319 204	2 285 422
60 - 64	16 817 924	8 077 500	8 740 424	12 750 365	6 020 393	6 729 972	4 067 559	2 057 107	2 010 452
65 - 69	12 435 263	5 852 547	6 582 716	9 299 030	4 275 616	5 023 414	3 136 233	1 576 931	1 559 302
70 - 74	9 278 166	4 243 972	5 034 194	7 011 129	3 115 814	3 895 315	2 267 037	1 128 158	1 138 879
75 - 79	7 317 795	3 182 388	4 135 407	5 693 807	2 409 946	3 283 861	1 623 988	772 442	851 546
80 - 84	5 743 327	2 294 374	3 448 953	4 629 581	1 800 531	2 829 050	1 113 746	493 843	619 903
85 - 89	3 620 459	1 273 867	2 346 592	3 005 285	1 036 583	1 968 702	615 174	237 284	377 890
90 - 94	1 448 366	424 387	1 023 979	1 216 647	351 491	865 156	231 719	72 896	158 823
95 - 99	371 244	82 263	288 981	315 589	69 008	246 581	55 655	13 255	42 400
100 +	53 364	9 162	44 202	45 752	7 713	38 039	7 612	1 449	6 163
United States Virgin Islands - Îles Vierges américaines[28] 1 IV 2010 (CDJC)									
Total	106 405	50 854	55 551	...	...	...	...	...	...
0 - 4	7 500	3 736	3 764	...	...	...	...	...	...
5 - 9	7 150	3 694	3 456	...	...	...	...	...	...
10 - 14	7 484	3 849	3 635	...	...	...	...	...	...
15 - 19	7 560	3 765	3 795	...	...	...	...	...	...
20 - 24	5 894	2 707	3 187	...	...	...	...	...	...
25 - 29	5 969	2 695	3 274	...	...	...	...	...	...
30 - 34	6 137	2 825	3 312	...	...	...	...	...	...
35 - 39	6 675	3 133	3 542	...	...	...	...	...	...
40 - 44	7 450	3 506	3 944	...	...	...	...	...	...
45 - 49	7 743	3 680	4 063	...	...	...	...	...	...
50 - 54	7 900	3 800	4 100	...	...	...	...	...	...
55 - 59	7 192	3 341	3 851	...	...	...	...	...	...
60 - 64	7 367	3 510	3 857	...	...	...	...	...	...
65 - 69	5 853	2 883	2 970	...	...	...	...	...	...
70 - 74	3 717	1 739	1 978	...	...	...	...	...	...
75 - 79	2 328	1 043	1 285	...	...	...	...	...	...
80 - 84	1 332	568	764	...	...	...	...	...	...
85 +	1 154	380	774	...	...	...	...	...	...
AMERICA, SOUTH - AMÉRIQUE DU SUD									
Argentina - Argentine[4] 1 VII 2010 (ESDF)									
Total	40 518 951	19 846 671	20 672 280	36 965 313	18 023 080	18 942 233	3 553 638	1 823 591	1 730 047
0 - 4	3 419 673	1 740 485	1 679 188	3 023 554	1 547 261	1 476 293	396 119	193 224	202 895
5 - 9	3 321 992	1 689 364	1 632 628	2 934 173	1 499 800	1 434 373	387 819	189 564	198 255
10 - 14	3 414 646	1 735 344	1 679 302	3 049 461	1 555 902	1 493 559	365 185	179 442	185 743
15 - 19	3 449 559	1 751 386	1 698 173	3 128 485	1 585 792	1 542 693	321 074	165 594	155 480
20 - 24	3 349 723	1 697 550	1 652 173	3 077 724	1 556 632	1 521 092	271 999	140 918	131 081
25 - 29	3 209 903	1 618 705	1 591 198	2 971 029	1 496 405	1 474 624	238 874	122 300	116 574
30 - 34	3 248 807	1 628 149	1 620 658	3 004 180	1 502 866	1 501 314	244 627	125 283	119 344
35 - 39	2 712 018	1 353 587	1 358 431	2 503 937	1 243 679	1 260 258	208 081	109 908	98 173
40 - 44	2 373 257	1 179 076	1 194 181	2 185 597	1 077 307	1 108 290	187 660	101 769	85 891

Continent, country or area, date, code and age (in years) Continent, pays ou zone, date, code et âge (en annèes)	Total			Urban - Urbaine			Rural - Rurale		
	Both sexes Les deux sexes	Male Masculin	Female Féminin	Both sexes Les deux sexes	Male Masculin	Female Féminin	Both sexes Les deux sexes	Male Masculin	Female Féminin
AMERICA, SOUTH - AMÉRIQUE DU SUD									
Argentina - Argentine[4]									
1 VII 2010 (ESDF)									
45 - 49	2 225 891	1 093 940	1 131 951	2 047 919	997 371	1 050 548	177 972	96 569	81 403
50 - 54	2 068 656	991 757	1 076 899	1 901 341	901 803	999 538	167 315	89 954	77 361
55 - 59	1 903 397	906 470	996 927	1 749 543	821 749	927 794	153 854	84 721	69 133
60 - 64	1 627 136	760 092	867 044	1 493 723	686 872	806 851	133 413	73 220	60 193
65 - 69	1 329 074	602 756	726 318	1 226 914	547 630	679 284	102 160	55 126	47 034
70 - 74	1 071 331	456 960	614 371	993 712	416 654	577 058	77 619	40 306	37 313
75 - 79	845 028	331 313	513 715	787 929	302 437	485 492	57 099	28 876	28 223
80 +	948 860	309 737	639 123	886 092	282 920	603 172	62 768	26 817	35 951
1 VII 2012 (ESDF)									
Total	41 281 631	20 222 859	21 058 772	...	...	...	...	...	...
0 - 4	3 434 364	1 748 173	1 686 191	...	...	...	...	...	...
5 - 9	3 348 495	1 703 248	1 645 247	...	...	...	...	...	...
10 - 14	3 370 938	1 713 399	1 657 539	...	...	...	...	...	...
15 - 19	3 445 105	1 749 391	1 695 714	...	...	...	...	...	...
20 - 24	3 394 040	1 720 628	1 673 412	...	...	...	...	...	...
25 - 29	3 248 452	1 640 412	1 608 040	...	...	...	...	...	...
30 - 34	3 258 684	1 635 349	1 623 335	...	...	...	...	...	...
35 - 39	2 930 370	1 463 224	1 467 146	...	...	...	...	...	...
40 - 44	2 474 125	1 230 119	1 244 006	...	...	...	...	...	...
45 - 49	2 261 083	1 114 888	1 146 195	...	...	...	...	...	...
50 - 54	2 110 391	1 017 583	1 092 808	...	...	...	...	...	...
55 - 59	1 946 918	923 857	1 023 061	...	...	...	...	...	...
60 - 64	1 702 168	794 538	907 630	...	...	...	...	...	...
65 - 69	1 393 127	631 280	761 847	...	...	...	...	...	...
70 - 74	1 105 269	473 807	631 462	...	...	...	...	...	...
75 - 79	857 885	337 342	520 543	...	...	...	...	...	...
80 +	1 000 217	325 621	674 596	...	...	...	...	...	...
Bolivia (Plurinational State of) - Bolivie (État plurinational de)									
1 VII 2009 (ESDF)									
Total	10 227 299	5 101 733	5 125 566	6 748 075	3 283 616	3 464 459	3 479 224	1 818 118	1 661 106
0 - 4	1 300 028	662 908	637 120	805 250	407 537	397 713	494 778	255 371	239 407
5 - 9	1 246 963	635 511	611 452	780 085	392 565	387 520	466 878	242 946	223 932
10 - 14	1 161 669	591 928	569 742	755 554	376 224	379 330	406 115	215 703	190 412
15 - 19	1 089 169	553 645	535 524	767 015	377 488	389 527	322 154	176 157	145 998
20 - 24	945 438	478 021	467 418	686 900	339 263	347 636	258 539	138 757	119 781
25 - 29	824 039	413 804	410 235	586 874	286 594	300 279	237 165	127 210	109 956
30 - 34	724 219	360 533	363 686	508 071	244 738	263 333	216 149	115 796	100 353
35 - 39	635 807	313 829	321 978	434 542	207 023	227 519	201 264	106 806	94 458
40 - 44	516 697	253 484	263 213	349 321	165 762	183 559	167 376	87 722	79 654
45 - 49	429 396	208 765	220 631	278 792	131 250	147 542	150 604	77 515	73 089
50 - 54	361 500	173 823	187 677	228 306	106 119	122 187	133 194	67 704	65 490
55 - 59	294 286	139 345	154 941	176 751	80 749	96 002	117 535	58 597	58 938
60 - 64	235 691	110 601	125 091	135 288	60 434	74 854	100 403	50 167	50 236
65 - 69	177 237	81 857	95 379	98 472	43 452	55 020	78 765	38 405	40 360
70 - 74	134 587	60 381	74 206	73 989	31 617	42 372	60 598	28 764	31 834
75 - 79	88 187	38 187	50 000	49 223	20 098	29 125	38 964	18 089	20 875
80 +	62 385	25 111	37 274	33 644	12 703	20 940	28 742	12 408	16 334
1 VII 2011 (ESDF)									
Total	10 624 495	5 301 942	5 322 553	...	...	...	...	...	...
0 - 4	1 305 603	665 837	639 766	...	...	...	...	...	...
5 - 9	1 267 565	645 949	621 616	...	...	...	...	...	...
10 - 14	1 186 483	604 570	581 913	...	...	...	...	...	...
15 - 19	1 125 398	572 438	552 960	...	...	...	...	...	...
20 - 24	995 794	504 146	491 648	...	...	...	...	...	...
25 - 29	865 916	435 627	430 289	...	...	...	...	...	...
30 - 34	756 561	377 541	379 020	...	...	...	...	...	...
35 - 39	671 903	332 276	339 626	...	...	...	...	...	...
40 - 44	554 806	272 602	282 204	...	...	...	...	...	...
45 - 49	455 176	221 768	233 408	...	...	...	...	...	...
50 - 54	382 142	184 250	197 892	...	...	...	...	...	...

7. Population by age, sex and urban/rural residence: latest available year, 2003 - 2012

Population selon l'âge, le sexe et la résidence, urbaine/rurale : dernière année disponible, 2003 - 2012 (continued - suite)

Continent, country or area, date, code and age (in years) / Continent, pays ou zone, date, code et âge (en annèes)	Total			Urban - Urbaine			Rural - Rurale		
	Both sexes Les deux sexes	Male Masculin	Female Féminin	Both sexes Les deux sexes	Male Masculin	Female Féminin	Both sexes Les deux sexes	Male Masculin	Female Féminin
AMERICA, SOUTH - AMÉRIQUE DU SUD									
Bolivia (Plurinational State of) - Bolivie (État plurinational de)									
1 VII 2011 (ESDF)									
55 - 59	312 411	148 105	164 306	...	...	...	...	...	...
60 - 64	252 284	118 182	134 103	...	...	...	...	...	...
65 - 69	189 105	87 296	101 809	...	...	...	...	...	...
70 - 74	141 389	63 467	77 922	...	...	...	...	...	...
75 - 79	93 054	40 239	52 814	...	...	...	...	...	...
80 +	68 904	27 649	41 256	...	...	...	...	...	...
Brazil - Brésil									
31 VII 2010 (CDJC)									
Total	190 755 799	93 406 990	97 348 809	160 925 804	77 710 179	83 215 625	29 829 995	15 696 811	14 133 184
0	2 713 244	1 378 532	1 334 712	2 246 034	1 141 784	1 104 250	467 210	236 748	230 462
1 - 4	11 082 914	5 638 455	5 444 459	9 055 114	4 603 340	4 451 774	2 027 800	1 035 115	992 685
5 - 9	14 969 375	7 624 144	7 345 231	12 135 285	6 169 531	5 965 754	2 834 090	1 454 613	1 379 477
10 - 14	17 166 761	8 725 413	8 441 348	13 956 987	7 062 057	6 894 930	3 209 774	1 663 356	1 546 418
15 - 19	16 990 872	8 558 868	8 432 004	14 039 001	6 998 102	7 040 899	2 951 871	1 560 766	1 391 105
20 - 24	17 245 192	8 630 229	8 614 963	14 706 068	7 276 963	7 429 105	2 539 124	1 353 266	1 185 858
25 - 29	17 104 414	8 460 995	8 643 419	14 772 957	7 225 732	7 547 225	2 331 457	1 235 263	1 096 194
30 - 34	15 744 512	7 717 658	8 026 854	13 611 921	6 586 877	7 025 044	2 132 591	1 130 781	1 001 810
35 - 39	13 888 579	6 766 664	7 121 915	11 975 407	5 750 498	6 224 909	1 913 172	1 016 166	897 006
40 - 44	13 009 364	6 320 568	6 688 796	11 187 429	5 344 982	5 842 447	1 821 935	975 586	846 349
45 - 49	11 833 352	5 692 014	6 141 338	10 181 394	4 806 322	5 375 072	1 651 958	885 692	766 266
50 - 54	10 140 402	4 834 995	5 305 407	8 708 339	4 074 679	4 633 660	1 432 063	760 316	671 747
55 - 59	8 276 221	3 902 344	4 373 877	7 025 474	3 238 531	3 786 943	1 250 747	663 813	586 934
60 - 64	6 509 120	3 041 035	3 468 085	5 474 944	2 479 882	2 995 062	1 034 176	561 153	473 023
65 - 69	4 840 810	2 224 065	2 616 745	4 040 016	1 792 798	2 247 218	800 794	431 267	369 527
70 - 74	3 741 636	1 667 372	2 074 264	3 142 173	1 349 329	1 792 844	599 463	318 043	281 420
75 - 79	2 563 447	1 090 517	1 472 930	2 174 038	889 908	1 284 130	389 409	200 609	188 800
80 - 84	1 666 972	668 623	998 349	1 423 603	546 865	876 738	243 369	121 758	121 611
85 - 89	819 483	310 759	508 724	695 385	251 112	444 273	124 098	59 647	64 451
90 - 94	326 558	114 964	211 594	273 348	90 960	182 388	53 210	24 004	29 206
95 - 99	98 335	31 529	66 806	81 121	24 365	56 756	17 214	7 164	10 050
100 +	24 236	7 247	16 989	19 766	5 562	14 204	4 470	1 685	2 785
Chile - Chili									
1 VII 2012 (ESDF)									
Total	17 402 630	8 612 483	8 790 147	15 144 277	7 414 026	7 730 251	2 258 353	1 198 457	1 059 896
0 - 4	1 252 797	638 116	614 681	1 092 499	556 240	536 259	160 298	81 876	78 422
5 - 9	1 241 662	632 209	609 453	1 088 719	553 735	534 984	152 943	78 474	74 469
10 - 14	1 292 477	657 727	634 750	1 127 173	572 729	554 444	165 304	84 998	80 306
15 - 19	1 424 361	724 181	700 180	1 232 118	624 688	607 430	192 243	99 493	92 750
20 - 24	1 472 107	746 882	725 225	1 271 444	641 496	629 948	200 663	105 386	95 277
25 - 29	1 376 298	696 167	680 131	1 200 317	600 371	599 946	175 981	95 796	80 185
30 - 34	1 228 806	618 745	610 061	1 084 754	539 537	545 217	144 052	79 208	64 844
35 - 39	1 207 958	604 740	603 218	1 066 453	528 779	537 674	141 505	75 961	65 544
40 - 44	1 230 762	612 990	617 772	1 076 546	530 941	545 605	154 216	82 049	72 167
45 - 49	1 237 498	613 106	624 392	1 075 145	525 291	549 854	162 353	87 815	74 538
50 - 54	1 135 335	558 815	576 520	987 421	477 152	510 269	147 914	81 663	66 251
55 - 59	919 175	447 703	471 472	800 934	382 099	418 835	118 241	65 604	52 637
60 - 64	723 724	346 164	377 560	628 277	293 842	334 435	95 447	52 322	43 125
65 - 69	575 504	267 577	307 927	495 036	224 347	270 689	80 468	43 230	37 238
70 - 74	428 628	191 424	237 204	363 521	157 044	206 477	65 107	34 380	30 727
75 - 79	310 125	129 989	180 136	260 708	104 697	156 011	49 417	25 292	24 125
80 +	345 413	125 948	219 465	293 212	101 038	192 174	52 201	24 910	27 291
Colombia - Colombie[29]									
1 VII 2012 (ESDJ)									
Total	46 581 823	22 997 087	23 584 736	35 377 138	17 073 806	18 303 332	11 204 685	5 923 281	5 281 404
0 - 4	4 291 149	2 195 042	2 096 107	3 038 074	1 551 898	1 486 176	1 253 075	643 144	609 931
0	865 188	442 628	422 560	...	...	...	...	...	...
1 - 4	3 425 961	1 752 414	1 673 547	...	...	...	...	...	...
5 - 9	4 272 011	2 183 050	2 088 961	3 070 080	1 563 985	1 506 095	1 201 931	619 065	582 866
10 - 14	4 359 830	2 225 316	2 134 514	3 184 010	1 610 651	1 573 359	1 175 820	614 665	561 155
15 - 19	4 401 418	2 253 817	2 147 601	3 276 125	1 647 069	1 629 056	1 125 293	606 748	518 545

7. Population by age, sex and urban/rural residence: latest available year, 2003 - 2012
Population selon l'âge, le sexe et la résidence, urbaine/rurale : dernière année disponible, 2003 - 2012 (continued - suite)

Continent, country or area, date, code and age (in years) / Continent, pays ou zone, date, code et âge (en années)	Total			Urban - Urbaine			Rural - Rurale		
	Both sexes Les deux sexes	Male Masculin	Female Féminin	Both sexes Les deux sexes	Male Masculin	Female Féminin	Both sexes Les deux sexes	Male Masculin	Female Féminin
AMERICA, SOUTH - AMÉRIQUE DU SUD									
Colombia - Colombie[29]									
1 VII 2012 (ESDJ)									
20 - 24	4 169 560	2 131 976	2 037 584	3 171 325	1 592 207	1 579 118	998 235	539 769	458 466
25 - 29	3 746 936	1 865 770	1 881 166	2 926 857	1 428 072	1 498 785	820 079	437 698	382 381
30 - 34	3 375 368	1 645 881	1 729 487	2 658 067	1 267 995	1 390 072	717 301	377 886	339 415
35 - 39	3 007 266	1 455 986	1 551 280	2 360 444	1 115 070	1 245 374	646 822	340 916	305 906
40 - 44	2 903 042	1 391 246	1 511 796	2 287 301	1 065 658	1 221 643	615 741	325 588	290 153
45 - 49	2 832 007	1 353 150	1 478 857	2 249 719	1 042 133	1 207 586	582 288	311 017	271 271
50 - 54	2 460 771	1 170 514	1 290 257	1 958 461	899 360	1 059 101	502 310	271 154	231 156
55 - 59	1 969 508	934 289	1 035 219	1 543 530	703 602	839 928	425 978	230 687	195 291
60 - 64	1 533 411	726 244	807 167	1 185 972	536 863	649 109	347 439	189 381	158 058
65 - 69	1 139 440	534 198	605 242	867 438	387 752	479 686	272 002	146 446	125 556
70 - 74	848 094	386 153	461 941	636 616	274 847	361 769	211 478	111 306	100 172
75 - 79	641 029	280 312	360 717	479 845	196 548	283 297	161 184	83 764	77 420
80 +	630 983	264 143	366 840	483 274	190 096	293 178	147 709	74 047	73 662
Ecuador - Équateur									
28 XI 2010 (CDFC)									
Total	14 483 499	7 177 683	7 305 816	9 090 786	4 451 434	4 639 352	5 392 713	2 726 249	2 666 464
0 - 4	1 462 277	744 305	717 972	863 496	439 926	423 570	598 781	304 379	294 402
5 - 9	1 526 806	773 890	752 916	899 684	455 607	444 077	627 122	318 283	308 839
10 - 14	1 539 342	782 977	756 365	915 364	463 344	452 020	623 978	319 633	304 345
15 - 19	1 419 537	713 548	705 989	876 214	436 066	440 148	543 323	277 482	265 841
20 - 24	1 292 126	639 140	652 986	838 504	410 523	427 981	453 622	228 617	225 005
25 - 29	1 200 564	586 950	613 614	795 121	385 870	409 251	405 443	201 080	204 363
30 - 34	1 067 289	520 891	546 398	711 157	343 564	367 593	356 132	177 327	178 805
35 - 39	938 726	456 202	482 524	618 623	296 600	322 023	320 103	159 602	160 501
40 - 44	819 002	399 230	419 772	544 692	260 354	284 338	274 310	138 876	135 434
45 - 49	750 141	366 448	383 693	501 895	240 212	261 683	248 246	126 236	122 010
50 - 54	610 132	298 728	311 404	404 511	195 034	209 477	205 621	103 694	101 927
55 - 59	515 893	253 106	262 787	332 385	159 849	172 536	183 508	93 257	90 251
60 - 64	400 759	196 414	204 345	246 241	117 992	128 249	154 518	78 422	76 096
65 - 69	323 817	156 804	167 013	188 776	88 533	100 243	135 041	68 271	66 770
70 - 74	240 091	116 203	123 888	136 344	63 047	73 297	103 747	53 156	50 591
75 - 79	165 218	78 602	86 616	93 836	42 606	51 230	71 382	35 996	35 386
80 - 84	115 552	53 157	62 395	66 539	29 113	37 426	49 013	24 044	24 969
85 - 89	60 735	26 734	34 001	35 815	14 986	20 829	24 920	11 748	13 172
90 - 94	25 500	10 523	14 977	15 540	6 032	9 508	9 960	4 491	5 469
95 - 99	8 039	3 133	4 906	4 938	1 815	3 123	3 101	1 318	1 783
100 +	1 953	698	1 255	1 111	361	750	842	337	505
1 VII 2012 (ESDF)[30]									
Total	15 495 016	7 678 696	7 816 320	...	...	...	...	...	...
0 - 4	1 673 669	855 702	817 967	...	...	...	...	...	...
5 - 9	1 648 277	843 575	804 702	...	...	...	...	...	...
10 - 14	1 585 826	808 562	777 264	...	...	...	...	...	...
15 - 19	1 476 445	746 298	730 147	...	...	...	...	...	...
20 - 24	1 351 739	674 640	677 099	...	...	...	...	...	...
25 - 29	1 247 955	614 397	633 558	...	...	...	...	...	...
30 - 34	1 134 235	546 942	587 293	...	...	...	...	...	...
35 - 39	1 004 304	481 677	522 627	...	...	...	...	...	...
40 - 44	888 226	426 674	461 552	...	...	...	...	...	...
45 - 49	787 917	379 075	408 842	...	...	...	...	...	...
50 - 54	677 428	327 720	349 708	...	...	...	...	...	...
55 - 59	557 029	270 743	286 286	...	...	...	...	...	...
60 - 64	444 343	215 634	228 709	...	...	...	...	...	...
65 - 69	347 824	167 637	180 187	...	...	...	...	...	...
70 - 74	259 769	123 874	135 895	...	...	...	...	...	...
75 - 79	184 935	88 085	96 850	...	...	...	...	...	...
80 - 84	119 739	57 215	62 524	...	...	...	...	...	...
85 - 89	65 356	31 090	34 266	...	...	...	...	...	...
90 - 94	29 177	13 726	15 451	...	...	...	...	...	...
95 - 99	10 329	5 161	5 168	...	...	...	...	...	...
100 +	494	269	225	...	...	...	...	...	...

7. Population by age, sex and urban/rural residence: latest available year, 2003 - 2012
Population selon l'âge, le sexe et la résidence, urbaine/rurale : dernière année disponible, 2003 - 2012 (continued - suite)

Continent, country or area, date, code and age (in years) Continent, pays ou zone, date, code et âge (en années)	Total			Urban - Urbaine			Rural - Rurale		
	Both sexes Les deux sexes	Male Masculin	Female Féminin	Both sexes Les deux sexes	Male Masculin	Female Féminin	Both sexes Les deux sexes	Male Masculin	Female Féminin
AMERICA, SOUTH - AMÉRIQUE DU SUD									
Falkland Islands (Malvinas) - Îles Falkland (Malvinas)[31] 8 X 2006 (CDFC)									
Total	2 955	1 569	1 386	...	...	...	...	...	...
0 - 4	156	79	77	...	...	...	...	...	...
5 - 9	161	75	86	...	...	...	...	...	...
10 - 14	154	71	83	...	...	...	...	...	...
15 - 19	155	90	65	...	...	...	...	...	...
20 - 24	207	89	118	...	...	...	...	...	...
25 - 29	232	126	106	...	...	...	...	...	...
30 - 34	266	131	135	...	...	...	...	...	...
35 - 39	291	165	126	...	...	...	...	...	...
40 - 44	261	156	105	...	...	...	...	...	...
45 - 49	249	128	121	...	...	...	...	...	...
50 - 54	215	123	92	...	...	...	...	...	...
55 - 59	194	113	81	...	...	...	...	...	...
60 - 64	148	87	61	...	...	...	...	...	...
65 - 69	98	57	41	...	...	...	...	...	...
70 - 74	68	36	32	...	...	...	...	...	...
75 - 79	48	18	30	...	...	...	...	...	...
80 +	52	25	27	...	...	...	...	...	...
French Guiana - Guyane française 1 I 2010* (ESDJ)									
Total	230 441	113 824	116 617	...	...	...	...	...	...
0 - 4	28 440	14 591	13 849	...	...	...	...	...	...
5 - 9	27 708	14 090	13 618	...	...	...	...	...	...
10 - 14	24 867	12 843	12 024	...	...	...	...	...	...
15 - 19	21 401	10 729	10 672	...	...	...	...	...	...
20 - 24	16 206	7 728	8 478	...	...	...	...	...	...
25 - 29	16 390	7 281	9 109	...	...	...	...	...	...
30 - 34	16 368	7 692	8 676	...	...	...	...	...	...
35 - 39	16 742	7 877	8 865	...	...	...	...	...	...
40 - 44	15 065	7 415	7 650	...	...	...	...	...	...
45 - 49	13 280	6 698	6 582	...	...	...	...	...	...
50 - 54	10 545	5 397	5 148	...	...	...	...	...	...
55 - 59	8 314	4 207	4 107	...	...	...	...	...	...
60 - 64	5 615	2 931	2 684	...	...	...	...	...	...
65 - 69	3 433	1 740	1 693	...	...	...	...	...	...
70 - 74	2 343	1 083	1 260	...	...	...	...	...	...
75 - 79	1 726	752	974	...	...	...	...	...	...
80 - 84	1 052	433	619	...	...	...	...	...	...
85 - 89	627	225	402	...	...	...	...	...	...
90 - 94	221	77	144	...	...	...	...	...	...
95 +	98	35	63	...	...	...	...	...	...
Guyana 1 VII 2010 (ESDF)									
Total	784 894	393 059	391 835	...	...	...	...	...	...
0 - 4	67 701	34 029	33 673	...	...	...	...	...	...
5 - 9	65 201	32 778	32 423	...	...	...	...	...	...
10 - 14	77 921	39 978	37 943	...	...	...	...	...	...
15 - 19	85 004	43 487	41 518	...	...	...	...	...	...
20 - 24	69 423	34 877	34 545	...	...	...	...	...	...
25 - 29	55 510	26 816	28 694	...	...	...	...	...	...
30 - 34	54 824	27 189	27 635	...	...	...	...	...	...
35 - 39	53 454	27 764	25 690	...	...	...	...	...	...
40 - 44	52 434	27 112	25 322	...	...	...	...	...	...
45 - 49	50 689	25 775	24 914	...	...	...	...	...	...
50 - 54	45 438	22 163	23 275	...	...	...	...	...	...
55 - 59	35 160	17 672	17 488	...	...	...	...	...	...
60 - 64	27 873	13 995	13 878	...	...	...	...	...	...
65 - 69	17 455	7 988	9 467	...	...	...	...	...	...
70 - 74	12 451	5 440	7 012	...	...	...	...	...	...

7. Population by age, sex and urban/rural residence: latest available year, 2003 - 2012
Population selon l'âge, le sexe et la résidence, urbaine/rurale : dernière année disponible, 2003 - 2012 (continued - suite)

Continent, country or area, date, code and age (in years) / Continent, pays ou zone, date, code et âge (en années)	Total			Urban - Urbaine			Rural - Rurale		
	Both sexes Les deux sexes	Male Masculin	Female Féminin	Both sexes Les deux sexes	Male Masculin	Female Féminin	Both sexes Les deux sexes	Male Masculin	Female Féminin
AMERICA, SOUTH - AMÉRIQUE DU SUD									
Guyana									
1 VII 2010 (ESDF)									
75 - 79	8 114	3 529	4 585	...	...	...	...	...	...
80 +	6 242	2 469	3 773	...	...	...	...	...	...
Paraguay[11]									
1 VII 2008 (ESDF)									
Total	6 230 143	3 149 475	3 080 668	3 597 588	1 758 138	1 839 450	2 632 555	1 391 337	1 241 218
0	148 736	75 881	72 855	80 755	41 202	39 553	67 981	34 679	33 301
1 - 4	586 306	298 652	287 655	319 965	162 577	157 388	266 342	136 075	130 267
5 - 9	717 813	365 319	352 495	391 720	198 122	193 598	326 093	167 196	158 897
10 - 14	695 085	353 531	341 554	372 499	186 968	185 531	322 586	166 563	156 023
15 - 19	664 150	337 205	326 945	356 119	176 802	179 317	308 030	160 402	147 628
20 - 24	615 570	311 726	303 843	343 986	165 459	178 527	271 584	146 268	125 316
25 - 29	526 498	266 188	260 310	324 202	151 981	172 221	202 297	114 207	88 089
30 - 34	413 975	208 623	205 352	274 380	130 593	143 787	139 595	78 030	61 565
35 - 39	353 019	177 236	175 782	229 002	110 770	118 232	124 017	66 466	57 551
40 - 44	324 734	163 671	161 063	203 193	99 103	104 090	121 541	64 568	56 973
45 - 49	286 361	145 212	141 149	174 596	85 410	89 186	111 765	59 802	51 963
50 - 54	246 231	125 645	120 586	148 133	72 624	75 508	98 098	53 021	45 077
55 - 59	199 004	101 836	97 169	117 695	57 920	59 774	81 310	43 915	37 395
60 - 64	147 779	74 741	73 038	86 035	41 621	44 414	61 744	33 120	28 625
65 - 69	111 922	55 483	56 439	64 462	30 273	34 189	47 461	25 211	22 250
70 - 74	81 557	39 265	42 292	46 340	20 701	25 639	35 217	18 564	16 652
75 - 79	56 865	26 066	30 798	32 768	13 820	18 948	24 096	12 246	11 850
80 +	54 537	23 194	31 343	31 740	12 191	19 548	22 798	11 003	11 795
1 VII 2012 (ESDF)									
Total	6 672 631	3 371 117	3 301 514	...	...	...	...	...	...
0 - 4	740 605	377 479	363 126	...	...	...	...	...	...
5 - 9	728 988	371 136	357 852	...	...	...	...	...	...
10 - 14	711 631	362 086	349 545	...	...	...	...	...	...
15 - 19	686 011	348 620	337 391	...	...	...	...	...	...
20 - 24	647 937	328 266	319 671	...	...	...	...	...	...
25 - 29	590 227	298 179	292 048	...	...	...	...	...	...
30 - 34	487 847	246 170	241 676	...	...	...	...	...	...
35 - 39	389 299	195 634	193 665	...	...	...	...	...	...
40 - 44	343 862	172 447	171 415	...	...	...	...	...	...
45 - 49	312 199	157 194	155 005	...	...	...	...	...	...
50 - 54	272 110	137 726	134 384	...	...	...	...	...	...
55 - 59	230 733	117 564	113 169	...	...	...	...	...	...
60 - 64	178 618	90 694	87 924	...	...	...	...	...	...
65 - 69	129 615	64 627	64 988	...	...	...	...	...	...
70 - 74	95 616	46 360	49 257	...	...	...	...	...	...
75 - 79	64 173	29 928	34 245	...	...	...	...	...	...
80 +	63 158	27 006	36 152	...	...	...	...	...	...
Peru - Pérou[18]									
1 VII 2012 (ESDF)									
Total	30 135 875	15 103 003	15 032 872	22 635 742	11 191 332	11 444 410	7 500 133	3 911 671	3 588 462
0 - 4	2 923 685	1 491 938	1 431 747	1 987 612	1 018 153	969 459	936 073	473 785	462 288
5 - 9	2 935 092	1 495 183	1 439 909	2 041 986	1 038 661	1 003 325	893 106	456 522	436 584
10 - 14	2 920 824	1 484 655	1 436 169	2 079 952	1 050 014	1 029 938	840 872	434 641	406 231
15 - 19	2 896 632	1 469 815	1 427 005	2 151 577	1 077 327	1 074 250	745 243	392 488	352 755
20 - 24	2 780 765	1 406 789	1 373 976	2 130 064	1 059 706	1 070 358	650 701	347 083	303 618
25 - 29	2 550 294	1 286 498	1 263 796	1 980 368	979 134	1 001 234	569 926	307 364	262 562
30 - 34	2 363 720	1 190 143	1 173 577	1 852 750	911 417	941 333	510 970	278 726	232 244
35 - 39	2 130 122	1 069 824	1 060 298	1 665 264	816 971	848 293	464 858	252 853	212 005
40 - 44	1 858 204	929 811	928 393	1 461 759	715 916	745 843	396 445	213 895	182 550
45 - 49	1 618 127	805 892	812 235	1 286 900	629 512	657 388	331 227	176 380	154 847
50 - 54	1 349 968	667 687	682 281	1 074 191	523 253	550 938	275 777	144 434	131 343
55 - 59	1 096 482	537 838	558 644	862 890	417 411	445 479	233 592	120 427	113 165
60 - 64	866 009	420 619	445 390	663 767	319 549	344 218	202 242	101 070	101 172
65 - 69	663 104	317 123	345 981	500 875	237 989	262 886	162 229	79 134	83 095
70 - 74	504 827	235 355	269 472	378 427	175 042	203 385	126 400	60 313	66 087
75 - 79	359 863	161 454	198 409	270 548	119 499	151 049	89 315	41 955	47 360
80 +	317 969	132 379	185 590	246 812	101 778	145 034	71 157	30 601	40 556

7. Population by age, sex and urban/rural residence: latest available year, 2003 - 2012

Population selon l'âge, le sexe et la résidence, urbaine/rurale : dernière année disponible, 2003 - 2012 (continued - suite)

Continent, country or area, date, code and age (in years) / Continent, pays ou zone, date, code et âge (en années)	Total			Urban - Urbaine			Rural - Rurale		
	Both sexes Les deux sexes	Male Masculin	Female Féminin	Both sexes Les deux sexes	Male Masculin	Female Féminin	Both sexes Les deux sexes	Male Masculin	Female Féminin
AMERICA, SOUTH - AMÉRIQUE DU SUD									
Suriname									
2 VIII 2004 (CDJC)									
Total	492 829	248 046	244 783	328 932[32]	164 444[32]	164 488[32]	163 897[32]	83 602[32]	80 295[32]
0 - 4	51 837	26 252	25 585	31 603[32]	16 152[32]	15 451[32]	20 234[32]	10 100[32]	10 134[32]
5 - 9	49 409	25 200	24 209	30 886[32]	15 639[32]	15 247[32]	18 523[32]	9 561[32]	8 962[32]
10 - 14	45 143	22 889	22 254	28 942[32]	14 536[32]	14 406[32]	16 201[32]	8 353[32]	7 848[32]
15 - 19	46 508	23 465	23 043	31 775[32]	16 181[32]	15 594[32]	14 733[32]	7 284[32]	7 449[32]
20 - 24	43 843	22 437	21 406	30 989[32]	16 056[32]	14 933[32]	12 854[32]	6 381[32]	6 473[32]
25 - 29	37 901	19 006	18 895	25 895[32]	12 853[32]	13 042[32]	12 006[32]	6 153[32]	5 853[32]
30 - 34	38 994	19 828	19 166	26 462[32]	13 226[32]	13 236[32]	12 532[32]	6 602[32]	5 930[32]
35 - 39	37 279	19 179	18 100	25 388[32]	12 845[32]	12 543[32]	11 891[32]	6 334[32]	5 557[32]
40 - 44	33 985	17 657	16 328	23 386[32]	11 870[32]	11 516[32]	10 599[32]	5 787[32]	4 812[32]
45 - 49	25 635	12 643	12 992	17 893[32]	8 565[32]	9 328[32]	7 742[32]	4 078[32]	3 664[32]
50 - 54	20 420	9 933	10 487	14 421[32]	6 955[32]	7 466[32]	5 999[32]	2 978[32]	3 021[32]
55 - 59	14 982	6 955	8 027	10 487[32]	4 806[32]	5 681[32]	4 495[32]	2 149[32]	2 346[32]
60 - 64	13 259	6 200	7 059	9 309[32]	4 428[32]	4 881[32]	3 950[32]	1 772[32]	2 178[32]
65 - 69	10 602	5 148	5 454	7 101[32]	3 521[32]	3 580[32]	3 501[32]	1 627[32]	1 874[32]
70 - 74	8 659	4 103	4 556	5 745[32]	2 708[32]	3 037[32]	2 914[32]	1 395[32]	1 519[32]
75 - 79	5 152	2 419	2 733	3 410[32]	1 576[32]	1 834[32]	1 742[32]	843[32]	899[32]
80 - 84	2 853	1 235	1 618	1 905[32]	779[32]	1 126[32]	948[32]	456[32]	492[32]
85 - 89	1 075	392	677	770[32]	274[32]	496[32]	299[32]	118[32]	181[32]
90 - 94	490	196	294	371[32]	157[32]	214[32]	119[32]	39[32]	80[32]
95 +	129	34	95	94[32]	24[32]	70[32]	35[32]	10[32]	25[32]
Unknown - Inconnu	4 704	2 885	1 819	2 100[32]	1 293[32]	807[32]	2 604[32]	1 592[32]	1 012[32]
1 VII 2011 (ESDJ)									
Total	539 910	272 690	267 220	...	...	...	...	...	...
0 - 4	49 060	24 910	24 150	...	...	...	...	...	...
5 - 9	51 560	26 400	25 160	...	...	...	...	...	...
10 - 14	50 800	25 950	24 850	...	...	...	...	...	...
15 - 19	48 180	24 510	23 670	...	...	...	...	...	...
20 - 24	45 770	23 270	22 500	...	...	...	...	...	...
25 - 29	43 670	22 310	21 360	...	...	...	...	...	...
30 - 34	41 330	21 180	20 150	...	...	...	...	...	...
35 - 39	39 240	20 130	19 110	...	...	...	...	...	...
40 - 44	36 290	18 570	17 720	...	...	...	...	...	...
45 - 49	32 200	16 370	15 830	...	...	...	...	...	...
50 - 54	27 670	13 940	13 730	...	...	...	...	...	...
55 - 59	22 170	10 970	11 200	...	...	...	...	...	...
60 - 64	17 230	8 340	8 890	...	...	...	...	...	...
65 - 69	13 070	6 200	6 870	...	...	...	...	...	...
70 - 74	9 420	4 360	5 060	...	...	...	...	...	...
75 - 79	6 360	2 860	3 500	...	...	...	...	...	...
80 +	5 890	2 420	3 470	...	...	...	...	...	...
Uruguay									
4 X 2011 (CDJC)									
Total[33]	3 285 877	1 577 416	1 708 461	3 110 264	1 478 658	1 631 606	175 613	98 758	76 855
0 - 4	220 345	112 704	107 641	209 663	107 163	102 500	10 682	5 541	5 141
5 - 9	238 068	121 820	116 248	225 974	115 560	110 414	12 094	6 260	5 834
10 - 14	256 552	131 022	125 530	243 701	124 289	119 412	12 851	6 733	6 118
15 - 19	261 691	133 042	128 649	248 573	125 655	122 918	13 118	7 387	5 731
20 - 24	241 006	119 928	121 078	229 054	112 626	116 428	11 952	7 302	4 650
25 - 29	228 385	112 852	115 533	216 541	105 936	110 605	11 844	6 916	4 928
30 - 34	233 365	113 884	119 481	220 934	106 771	114 163	12 431	7 113	5 318
35 - 39	222 521	108 704	113 817	210 125	101 642	108 483	12 396	7 062	5 334
40 - 44	203 098	98 612	104 486	191 369	92 030	99 339	11 729	6 582	5 147
45 - 49	198 773	95 812	102 961	187 356	89 304	98 052	11 417	6 508	4 909
50 - 54	194 565	93 175	101 390	183 306	86 750	96 556	11 259	6 425	4 834
55 - 59	173 007	81 828	91 179	162 340	75 635	86 705	10 667	6 193	4 474
60 - 64	150 775	69 864	80 911	141 192	64 288	76 904	9 583	5 576	4 007
65 - 69	131 563	58 769	72 794	123 640	54 149	69 491	7 923	4 620	3 303
70 - 74	112 395	47 705	64 690	106 246	44 102	62 144	6 149	3 603	2 546
75 - 79	93 659	36 806	56 853	89 142	34 280	54 862	4 517	2 526	1 991
80 - 84	70 505	24 912	45 593	67 588	23 393	44 195	2 917	1 519	1 398

7. Population by age, sex and urban/rural residence: latest available year, 2003 - 2012
Population selon l'âge, le sexe et la résidence, urbaine/rurale : dernière année disponible, 2003 - 2012 (continued - suite)

Continent, country or area, date, code and age (in years) / Continent, pays ou zone, date, code et âge (en années)	Total			Urban - Urbaine			Rural - Rurale		
	Both sexes Les deux sexes	Male Masculin	Female Féminin	Both sexes Les deux sexes	Male Masculin	Female Féminin	Both sexes Les deux sexes	Male Masculin	Female Féminin
AMERICA, SOUTH - AMÉRIQUE DU SUD									
Uruguay									
4 X 2011 (CDJC)									
85 - 89	37 426	11 535	25 891	35 994	10 888	25 106	1 432	647	785
90 - 94	14 113	3 636	10 477	13 599	3 432	10 167	514	204	310
95 - 99	3 546	733	2 813	3 421	694	2 727	125	39	86
100 +	519	73	446	506	71	435	13	2	11
Venezuela (Bolivarian Republic of) - Venezuela (République bolivarienne du)[4]									
1 VII 2011 (ESDF)									
Total	29 277 736	14 673 402	14 604 334	25 791 535	12 801 370	12 990 165	3 486 201	1 872 032	1 614 169
0 - 4	2 912 647	1 489 651	1 422 996	2 460 039	1 263 404	1 196 635	452 608	226 247	226 361
5 - 9	2 837 261	1 449 771	1 387 490	2 424 010	1 242 045	1 181 965	413 251	207 726	205 525
10 - 14	2 755 888	1 407 049	1 348 839	2 396 701	1 221 895	1 174 806	359 187	185 154	174 033
15 - 19	2 711 858	1 381 341	1 330 517	2 386 279	1 204 434	1 181 845	325 579	176 907	148 672
20 - 24	2 678 629	1 356 690	1 321 939	2 374 151	1 188 517	1 185 634	304 478	168 173	136 305
25 - 29	2 480 862	1 247 545	1 233 317	2 203 958	1 094 325	1 109 633	276 904	153 220	123 684
30 - 34	2 250 300	1 125 519	1 124 781	2 018 543	997 633	1 020 910	231 757	127 886	103 871
35 - 39	1 956 735	975 071	981 664	1 763 046	867 850	895 196	193 689	107 221	86 468
40 - 44	1 814 496	901 661	912 835	1 639 958	805 143	834 815	174 538	96 518	78 020
45 - 49	1 671 604	828 558	843 046	1 509 038	739 325	769 713	162 566	89 233	73 333
50 - 54	1 395 985	689 404	706 581	1 251 776	609 861	641 915	144 209	79 543	64 666
55 - 59	1 164 071	572 058	592 013	1 035 535	499 359	536 176	128 536	72 699	55 837
60 - 64	922 415	450 502	471 913	813 315	387 442	425 873	109 100	63 060	46 040
65 - 69	666 569	319 897	346 672	584 310	272 609	311 701	82 259	47 288	34 971
70 - 74	462 053	215 081	246 972	405 278	183 635	221 643	56 775	31 446	25 329
75 +	596 363	263 604	332 759	525 598	223 893	301 705	70 765	39 711	31 054
1 VII 2012 (ESDF)									
Total	29 718 357	14 888 876	14 829 481	...	...	...	...	...	...
0 - 4	2 914 825	1 490 866	1 423 959	...	...	...	...	...	...
5 - 9	2 851 339	1 457 051	1 394 288	...	...	...	...	...	...
10 - 14	2 772 112	1 415 520	1 356 592	...	...	...	...	...	...
15 - 19	2 716 787	1 384 009	1 332 778	...	...	...	...	...	...
20 - 24	2 681 300	1 358 391	1 322 909	...	...	...	...	...	...
25 - 29	2 524 202	1 269 774	1 254 428	...	...	...	...	...	...
30 - 34	2 292 053	1 146 438	1 145 615	...	...	...	...	...	...
35 - 39	2 014 832	1 003 848	1 010 984	...	...	...	...	...	...
40 - 44	1 830 638	909 425	921 213	...	...	...	...	...	...
45 - 49	1 696 943	840 711	856 232	...	...	...	...	...	...
50 - 54	1 450 247	715 833	734 414	...	...	...	...	...	...
55 - 59	1 198 293	588 318	609 975	...	...	...	...	...	...
60 - 64	961 271	468 771	492 500	...	...	...	...	...	...
65 - 69	705 350	338 635	366 715	...	...	...	...	...	...
70 - 74	487 094	226 978	260 116	...	...	...	...	...	...
75 - 79	337 794	152 162	185 632	...	...	...	...	...	...
80 +	283 277	122 146	161 131	...	...	...	...	...	...
ASIA - ASIE									
Afghanistan[34]									
1 VII 2012 (ESDF)									
Total	25 500 100	13 044 400	12 455 700	6 074 200	3 127 700	2 946 500	19 425 900	9 916 700	9 509 200
0	1 102 469	527 567	574 902	247 708	121 964	125 744	854 761	405 603	449 158
1 - 4	3 876 079	1 894 677	1 981 402	895 537	446 829	448 708	2 980 542	1 447 848	1 532 694
5 - 9	3 821 770	1 941 363	1 880 407	928 937	473 375	455 562	2 892 833	1 467 988	1 424 845
10 - 14	2 957 853	1 556 158	1 401 695	753 967	389 653	364 314	2 203 886	1 166 505	1 037 381
15 - 19	2 417 373	1 276 563	1 140 810	622 489	318 538	303 951	1 794 884	958 025	836 859
20 - 24	2 069 746	1 059 939	1 009 807	516 200	257 574	258 626	1 553 546	802 365	751 181
25 - 29	1 708 705	843 967	864 738	414 922	206 095	208 827	1 293 783	637 872	655 911
30 - 34	1 424 111	678 577	745 534	337 903	169 459	168 444	1 086 208	509 118	577 090
35 - 39	1 250 371	598 045	652 326	285 135	145 571	139 564	965 236	452 474	512 762
40 - 44	1 079 626	546 102	533 524	242 173	127 202	114 971	837 453	418 900	418 553

7. Population by age, sex and urban/rural residence: latest available year, 2003 - 2012
Population selon l'âge, le sexe et la résidence, urbaine/rurale : dernière année disponible, 2003 - 2012 (continued - suite)

Continent, country or area, date, code and age (in years) / Continent, pays ou zone, date, code et âge (en annèes)	Total			Urban - Urbaine			Rural - Rurale		
	Both sexes Les deux sexes	Male Masculin	Female Féminin	Both sexes Les deux sexes	Male Masculin	Female Féminin	Both sexes Les deux sexes	Male Masculin	Female Féminin
ASIA - ASIE									
Afghanistan[34]									
1 VII 2012 (ESDF)									
45 - 49	935 979	495 190	440 789	204 869	111 135	93 734	731 110	384 055	347 055
50 - 54	789 776	435 143	354 633	169 958	94 871	75 087	619 818	340 272	279 546
55 - 59	635 862	360 394	275 468	136 863	78 566	58 297	498 999	281 828	217 171
60 - 64	490 779	281 627	209 152	107 289	62 662	44 627	383 490	218 965	164 525
65 - 69	354 513	204 376	150 137	78 938	46 199	32 739	275 575	158 177	117 398
70 - 74	243 777	141 729	102 048	54 734	32 177	22 557	189 043	109 552	79 491
75 - 79	155 822	91 164	64 658	34 902	20 748	14 154	120 920	70 416	50 504
80 - 84	94 145	55 446	38 699	21 133	12 645	8 488	73 012	42 801	30 211
85 +	91 344	56 373	34 971	20 543	12 437	8 106	70 801	43 936	26 865
Armenia - Arménie									
12 X 2011 (CDJC)									
Total	3 018 854	1 448 052	1 570 802	1 911 287	895 372	1 015 915	1 107 567	552 680	554 887
0 - 4	207 572	110 565	97 007	127 653	67 466	60 187	79 919	43 099	36 820
5 - 9	179 929	96 429	83 500	110 826	58 712	52 114	69 103	37 717	31 386
10 - 14	178 637	95 458	83 179	105 685	56 068	49 617	72 952	39 390	33 562
15 - 19	233 075	117 938	115 137	134 853	67 252	67 601	98 222	50 686	47 536
20 - 24	292 234	143 897	148 337	175 999	83 968	92 031	116 235	59 929	56 306
25 - 29	271 929	132 109	139 820	173 093	81 320	91 773	98 836	50 789	48 047
30 - 34	223 005	108 114	114 891	148 671	71 158	77 513	74 334	36 956	37 378
35 - 39	187 421	89 073	98 348	123 792	58 479	65 313	63 629	30 594	33 035
40 - 44	176 964	82 502	94 462	109 718	49 721	59 997	67 246	32 781	34 465
45 - 49	211 060	98 064	112 996	126 779	55 920	70 859	84 281	42 144	42 137
50 - 54	234 532	109 294	125 238	150 258	66 623	83 635	84 274	42 671	41 603
55 - 59	177 758	80 989	96 769	122 931	54 136	68 795	54 827	26 853	27 974
60 - 64	127 599	56 189	71 410	93 673	40 621	53 052	33 926	15 568	18 358
65 - 69	65 373	28 020	37 353	47 797	20 459	27 338	17 576	7 561	10 015
70 - 74	107 678	44 041	63 637	71 461	29 585	41 876	36 217	14 456	21 761
75 - 79	75 377	30 734	44 643	47 483	19 373	28 110	27 894	11 361	16 533
80 - 84	48 906	18 662	30 244	28 738	10 892	17 846	20 168	7 770	12 398
85 +	19 805	5 974	13 831	11 877	3 619	8 258	7 928	2 355	5 573
Azerbaijan - Azerbaïdjan									
1 VII 2010 (ESDF)									
Total	9 054 300	4 486 300	4 568 000	4 802 200	2 364 400	2 437 800	4 252 100	2 121 900	2 130 200
0	158 800	85 600	73 200	78 300	42 000	36 300	80 500	43 600	36 900
1 - 4	532 300	285 000	247 300	266 000	141 600	124 400	266 300	143 400	122 900
5 - 9	630 400	336 300	294 100	312 900	167 300	145 600	317 500	169 000	148 500
10 - 14	709 600	373 400	336 200	348 300	184 500	163 800	361 300	188 900	172 400
15 - 19	890 300	457 400	432 900	446 700	229 700	217 000	443 600	227 700	215 900
20 - 24	942 600	467 800	474 800	503 000	246 700	256 300	439 600	221 100	218 500
25 - 29	831 500	411 100	420 400	458 100	223 800	234 300	373 400	187 300	186 100
30 - 34	698 600	347 600	351 000	384 600	190 300	194 300	314 000	157 300	156 700
35 - 39	621 600	301 100	320 500	330 000	156 300	173 700	291 600	144 800	146 800
40 - 44	663 900	318 100	345 800	349 000	163 800	185 200	314 900	154 300	160 600
45 - 49	677 100	324 600	352 500	371 600	176 000	195 600	305 500	148 600	156 900
50 - 54	578 400	279 600	298 800	330 400	160 200	170 200	248 000	119 400	128 600
55 - 59	360 500	171 200	189 300	215 500	102 700	112 800	145 000	68 500	76 500
60 - 64	227 100	104 500	122 600	139 100	65 100	74 000	88 000	39 400	48 600
65 - 69	129 700	57 100	72 600	75 200	33 500	41 700	54 500	23 600	30 900
70 - 74	194 500	83 100	111 400	98 800	43 000	55 800	95 700	40 100	55 600
75 - 79	118 100	49 900	68 200	54 400	22 900	31 500	63 700	27 000	36 700
80 - 84	61 300	24 700	36 600	28 200	11 200	17 000	33 100	13 500	19 600
85 - 89	19 400	6 300	13 100	9 100	3 000	6 100	10 300	3 300	7 000
90 - 94	5 500	1 300	4 200	2 100	600	1 500	3 400	700	2 700
95 - 99	1 900	500	1 400	600	200	400	1 300	300	1 000
100 +	1 200	100	1 100	300	-	300	900	100	800
Bahrain - Bahreïn									
1 VII 2011 (ESDJ)									
Total	1 195 020	741 483	453 537	...	...	...	...	...	...
0	17 197	8 676	8 521	...	...	...	...	...	...
1 - 4	74 361	38 005	36 356	...	...	...	...	...	...
5 - 9	83 229	42 537	40 692	...	...	...	...	...	...
10 - 14	75 250	38 672	36 578	...	...	...	...	...	...
15 - 19	72 695	37 759	34 936	...	...	...	...	...	...

Continent, country or area, date, code and age (in years) / Continent, pays ou zone, date, code et âge (en annèes)	Total			Urban - Urbaine			Rural - Rurale		
	Both sexes Les deux sexes	Male Masculin	Female Féminin	Both sexes Les deux sexes	Male Masculin	Female Féminin	Both sexes Les deux sexes	Male Masculin	Female Féminin
ASIA - ASIE									
Bahrain - Bahreïn									
1 VII 2011 (ESDJ)									
20 - 24	104 788	63 936	40 852	...	...	...	...	...	...
25 - 29	167 701	117 047	50 654	...	...	...	...	...	...
30 - 34	151 128	103 644	47 484	...	...	...	...	...	...
35 - 39	123 687	83 978	39 709	...	...	...	...	...	...
40 - 44	102 090	68 838	33 252	...	...	...	...	...	...
45 - 49	80 170	51 082	29 088	...	...	...	...	...	...
50 - 54	60 590	39 057	21 533	...	...	...	...	...	...
55 - 59	37 460	24 174	13 286	...	...	...	...	...	...
60 - 64	17 907	10 797	7 110	...	...	...	...	...	...
65 - 69	9 998	5 176	4 822	...	...	...	...	...	...
70 - 74	7 658	3 736	3 922	...	...	...	...	...	...
75 - 79	4 579	2 180	2 399	...	...	...	...	...	...
80 - 84	2 665	1 269	1 396	...	...	...	...	...	...
85 +	1 867	920	947	...	...	...	...	...	...
Bangladesh[12]									
1 VII 2011 (ESDF)									
Total	150 611 000	77 101 062	73 509 938	39 000 000	20 560 587	18 439 413	111 611 000	56 540 475	55 070 525
0 - 4	14 021 884	7 332 311	6 711 457	3 424 200	1 840 173	1 582 102	10 748 139	5 546 621	5 193 151
5 - 9	16 672 638	8 643 029	8 041 987	4 036 500	2 160 918	1 880 820	12 801 782	6 553 041	6 250 505
10 - 14	17 305 204	9 128 766	8 196 358	4 235 400	2 280 169	1 960 110	13 214 742	6 926 208	6 294 561
15 - 19	14 985 795	8 126 452	6 887 881	3 802 500	2 045 778	1 759 120	11 239 228	6 140 296	5 105 038
20 - 24	14 338 167	6 769 473	7 542 120	3 814 200	1 786 715	2 004 364	10 469 112	4 992 524	5 468 503
25 - 29	12 967 607	6 175 795	6 770 265	3 623 100	1 741 482	1 862 381	9 196 746	4 387 541	4 802 150
30 - 34	11 220 520	5 335 393	5 873 444	3 201 900	1 591 389	1 600 541	7 846 253	3 663 823	4 185 360
35 - 39	10 075 876	4 880 497	5 182 451	2 823 600	1 441 297	1 375 580	7 131 943	3 369 812	3 755 810
40 - 44	9 413 188	4 818 816	4 601 722	2 640 300	1 431 017	1 215 157	6 652 016	3 313 272	3 342 781
45 - 49	7 530 550	4 202 008	3 344 702	2 016 800	1 204 850	829 774	5 480 100	2 951 413	2 527 737
50 - 54	6 717 251	3 500 388	3 212 384	1 758 900	988 964	776 299	4 944 367	2 487 781	2 456 145
55 - 59	4 864 735	2 636 856	2 234 702	1 209 000	709 340	508 928	3 683 163	1 922 376	1 762 257
60 - 64	3 584 542	1 973 787	1 617 219	881 400	514 015	370 632	2 734 470	1 464 398	1 266 622
65 - 69	2 515 204	1 326 138	1 190 861	581 100	316 633	263 684	1 975 515	1 029 037	947 213
70 - 74	1 927 821	1 002 314	918 874	432 900	234 391	199 146	1 529 071	785 913	743 452
75 - 79	1 144 644	601 388	536 623	249 600	131 588	116 168	915 210	486 248	435 057
80 +	1 295 255	655 359	646 887	273 000	139 812	132 764	1 060 305	531 480	528 677
Bhutan - Bhoutan[35]									
1 VII 2011 (ESDF)									
Total	708 268	369 477	338 791	252 041	134 485	117 556	456 227	234 992	221 235
0 - 4	85 918	43 327	42 591	27 291	13 665	13 626	58 627	29 662	28 965
5 - 9	66 979	33 736	33 244	23 603	11 793	11 810	43 376	21 943	21 434
10 - 14	66 365	33 566	32 799	25 269	12 679	12 590	41 096	20 887	20 209
15 - 19	71 544	36 417	35 127	28 617	14 570	14 047	42 927	21 847	21 080
20 - 24	70 170	36 222	33 948	29 907	15 639	14 268	40 263	20 583	19 680
25 - 29	65 819	35 020	30 798	28 238	15 354	12 884	37 581	19 666	17 914
30 - 34	58 918	31 873	27 045	24 709	13 889	10 820	34 209	17 984	16 225
35 - 39	48 903	26 756	22 147	19 383	11 171	8 212	29 520	15 585	13 935
40 - 44	40 678	22 316	18 361	14 011	8 274	5 737	26 667	14 042	12 624
45 - 49	32 815	17 752	15 062	9 986	5 894	4 092	22 829	11 858	10 970
50 - 54	26 710	14 291	12 420	6 864	4 040	2 824	19 846	10 251	9 596
55 - 59	21 632	11 495	10 138	4 850	2 817	2 033	16 782	8 678	8 105
60 - 64	17 230	9 066	8 164	3 355	1 849	1 506	13 875	7 217	6 658
65 - 69	13 277	6 892	6 385	2 341	1 219	1 122	10 936	5 673	5 263
70 - 74	9 622	4 925	4 696	1 570	753	817	8 052	4 172	3 879
75 - 79	6 337	3 190	3 146	1 047	447	600	5 290	2 743	2 546
80 +	5 352	2 632	2 720	1 000	432	568	4 352	2 200	2 152
1 VII 2012 (ESDF)									
Total	720 679	375 554	345 125	...	...	...	...	...	...
0 - 4	82 559	41 610	40 949	...	...	...	...	...	...
5 - 9	67 467	33 872	33 595	...	...	...	...	...	...
10 - 14	66 946	33 974	32 972	...	...	...	...	...	...
15 - 19	74 607	37 645	36 962	...	...	...	...	...	...
20 - 24	75 899	37 422	38 477	...	...	...	...	...	...
25 - 29	72 426	39 398	33 028	...	...	...	...	...	...
30 - 34	62 533	35 205	27 328	...	...	...	...	...	...

7. Population by age, sex and urban/rural residence: latest available year, 2003 - 2012

Population selon l'âge, le sexe et la résidence, urbaine/rurale : dernière année disponible, 2003 - 2012 (continued - suite)

Continent, country or area, date, code and age (in years) / Continent, pays ou zone, date, code et âge (en années)	Total			Urban - Urbaine			Rural - Rurale		
	Both sexes Les deux sexes	Male Masculin	Female Féminin	Both sexes Les deux sexes	Male Masculin	Female Féminin	Both sexes Les deux sexes	Male Masculin	Female Féminin
ASIA - ASIE									
Bhutan - Bhoutan[35]									
1 VII 2012 (ESDF)									
35 - 39	46 873	25 337	21 536	...	...	...	...	...	...
40 - 44	39 237	21 354	17 883	...	...	...	...	...	...
45 - 49	32 072	17 280	14 792	...	...	...	...	...	...
50 - 54	26 931	14 384	12 547	...	...	...	...	...	...
55 - 59	22 705	12 068	10 637	...	...	...	...	...	...
60 - 64	16 167	8 535	7 632	...	...	...	...	...	...
65 - 69	12 560	6 460	6 100	...	...	...	...	...	...
70 - 74	9 570	4 894	4 676	...	...	...	...	...	...
75 - 79	6 397	3 259	3 138	...	...	...	...	...	...
80 +	5 730	2 857	2 873	...	...	...	...	...	...
Brunei Darussalam - Brunéi Darussalam									
20 VI 2011 (CDFC)									
Total	393 372	203 149	190 223	...	...	...	...	...	...
0 - 4	30 331	15 678	14 653	...	...	...	...	...	...
5 - 9	33 634	17 269	16 365	...	...	...	...	...	...
10 - 14	35 463	18 448	17 015	...	...	...	...	...	...
15 - 19	34 961	17 948	17 013	...	...	...	...	...	...
20 - 24	38 207	19 950	18 257	...	...	...	...	...	...
25 - 29	39 194	20 749	18 445	...	...	...	...	...	...
30 - 34	36 941	19 322	17 619	...	...	...	...	...	...
35 - 39	33 752	17 329	16 423	...	...	...	...	...	...
40 - 44	30 081	15 262	14 819	...	...	...	...	...	...
45 - 49	24 590	12 836	11 754	...	...	...	...	...	...
50 - 54	19 776	10 318	9 458	...	...	...	...	...	...
55 - 59	14 042	7 170	6 872	...	...	...	...	...	...
60 - 64	8 514	4 160	4 354	...	...	...	...	...	...
65 - 69	5 084	2 583	2 501	...	...	...	...	...	...
70 - 74	3 912	1 833	2 079	...	...	...	...	...	...
75 - 79	2 593	1 195	1 398	...	...	...	...	...	...
80 - 84	1 404	701	703	...	...	...	...	...	...
85 +	893	398	495	...	...	...	...	...	...
Cambodia - Cambodge[36]									
1 VII 2012 (ESDF)									
Total	14 741 414	7 204 166	7 537 248	3 165 683	1 520 722	1 644 961	11 575 731	5 683 444	5 892 287
0	355 529	180 881	174 648	75 752	38 329	37 423	279 777	142 552	137 225
1 - 4	1 218 716	619 665	599 051	235 102	119 598	115 504	983 614	500 067	483 547
5 - 9	1 396 349	713 683	682 666	216 141	111 356	104 785	1 180 208	602 327	577 881
10 - 14	1 552 671	794 253	758 418	229 759	117 633	112 126	1 322 912	676 620	646 292
15 - 19	1 726 401	889 079	837 322	306 517	149 649	156 868	1 419 884	739 430	680 454
20 - 24	1 609 181	822 414	786 767	426 472	195 489	230 983	1 182 709	626 925	555 784
25 - 29	1 369 725	665 856	703 869	435 031	203 928	231 103	934 694	461 928	472 766
30 - 34	1 156 646	567 183	589 463	319 596	156 041	163 555	837 050	411 142	425 908
35 - 39	689 175	332 111	357 064	157 204	78 437	78 767	531 971	253 674	278 297
40 - 44	859 735	412 995	446 740	188 238	94 023	94 215	671 497	318 972	352 525
45 - 49	724 036	335 983	388 053	150 233	74 290	75 943	573 803	261 693	312 110
50 - 54	624 281	279 684	344 597	131 645	61 463	70 182	492 636	218 221	274 415
55 - 59	459 588	180 895	278 693	102 352	43 087	59 265	357 236	137 808	219 428
60 - 64	355 953	148 290	207 663	73 820	31 648	42 171	282 133	116 642	165 492
65 - 69	243 300	101 701	141 599	46 846	19 348	27 498	196 454	82 353	114 101
70 - 74	179 994	74 089	105 905	31 539	12 432	19 107	148 455	61 657	86 798
75 - 79	118 156	46 609	71 547	20 789	7 662	13 127	97 367	38 947	58 420
80 +	101 978	38 795	63 183	18 648	6 308	12 340	83 330	32 487	50 843
China - Chine[37]									
1 XI 2010 (CDJC)									
Total	1332810869	682 329 104	650 481 765	670 005 546	343 040 783	326 964 763	662 805 323	339 288 321	323 517 002
0 - 4	75 532 610	41 062 566	34 470 044	30 936 470	16 749 729	14 186 741	44 596 140	24 312 837	20 283 303
5 - 9	70 881 549	38 464 665	32 416 884	30 565 659	16 580 910	13 984 749	40 315 890	21 883 755	18 432 135
10 - 14	74 908 462	40 267 277	34 641 185	32 807 526	17 664 790	15 142 736	42 100 936	22 602 487	19 498 449
15 - 19	99 889 114	51 904 830	47 984 284	53 589 992	27 603 777	25 986 215	46 299 122	24 301 053	21 998 069
20 - 24	127 412 518	64 008 573	63 403 945	71 058 518	36 041 784	35 016 734	56 354 000	27 966 789	28 387 211
25 - 29	101 013 852	50 837 038	50 176 814	57 679 956	28 973 516	28 706 440	43 333 896	21 863 522	21 470 374
30 - 34	97 138 203	49 521 822	47 616 381	56 010 957	28 432 073	27 578 884	41 127 246	21 089 749	20 037 497

7. Population by age, sex and urban/rural residence: latest available year, 2003 - 2012

Population selon l'âge, le sexe et la résidence, urbaine/rurale : dernière année disponible, 2003 - 2012 (continued - suite)

Continent, country or area, date, code and age (in years) Continent, pays ou zone, date, code et âge (en annèes)	Total			Urban - Urbaine			Rural - Rurale		
	Both sexes Les deux sexes	Male Masculin	Female Féminin	Both sexes Les deux sexes	Male Masculin	Female Féminin	Both sexes Les deux sexes	Male Masculin	Female Féminin
ASIA - ASIE									
China - Chine[37]									
1 XI 2010 (CDJC)									
35 - 39	118 025 959	60 391 104	57 634 855	65 025 365	33 349 280	31 676 085	53 000 594	27 041 824	25 958 770
40 - 44	124 753 964	63 608 678	61 145 286	63 786 496	32 845 769	30 940 727	60 967 468	30 762 909	30 204 559
45 - 49	105 594 553	53 776 418	51 818 135	53 629 541	27 723 132	25 906 409	51 965 012	26 053 286	25 911 726
50 - 54	78 753 171	40 363 234	38 389 937	39 186 388	20 130 395	19 055 993	39 566 783	20 232 839	19 333 944
55 - 59	81 312 474	41 082 938	40 229 536	37 437 535	18 762 887	18 674 648	43 874 939	22 320 051	21 554 888
60 - 64	58 667 282	29 834 426	28 832 856	26 036 917	13 067 045	12 969 872	32 630 365	16 767 381	15 862 984
65 - 69	41 113 282	20 748 471	20 364 811	17 910 329	8 866 594	9 043 735	23 202 953	11 881 877	11 321 076
70 - 74	32 972 397	16 403 453	16 568 944	14 777 260	7 241 891	7 535 369	18 195 137	9 161 562	9 033 575
75 - 79	23 852 133	11 278 859	12 573 274	10 531 503	5 048 471	5 483 032	13 320 630	6 230 388	7 090 242
80 - 84	13 373 198	5 917 502	7 455 696	5 762 828	2 665 218	3 097 610	7 610 370	3 252 284	4 358 086
85 - 89	5 631 928	2 199 810	3 432 118	2 392 190	982 284	1 409 906	3 239 738	1 217 526	2 022 212
90 - 94	1 578 307	530 872	1 047 435	687 763	246 031	441 732	890 544	284 841	605 703
95 - 99	369 979	117 716	252 263	176 542	60 991	115 551	193 437	56 725	136 712
100 +	35 934	8 852	27 082	15 811	4 216	11 595	20 123	4 636	15 487
31 XII 2011 (ESDF)[38]									
Total	*1347304706*	*690 634 118*	*656 670 588*	...	...	...	...	...	...
0 - 4	*76 270 588*	*41 467 059*	*34 803 529*	...	...	...	...	...	...
5 - 9	*72 092 941*	*39 108 235*	*32 984 706*	...	...	...	...	...	...
10 - 14	*73 507 059*	*39 657 647*	*33 849 412*	...	...	...	...	...	...
15 - 19	*94 574 118*	*49 489 412*	*45 084 706*	...	...	...	...	...	...
20 - 24	*127 725 882*	*64 991 765*	*62 732 941*	...	...	...	...	...	...
25 - 29	*105 010 588*	*52 912 941*	*52 096 471*	...	...	...	...	...	...
30 - 34	*96 644 706*	*49 303 529*	*47 341 176*	...	...	...	...	...	...
35 - 39	*113 994 118*	*58 317 647*	*55 676 471*	...	...	...	...	...	...
40 - 44	*126 342 353*	*64 477 647*	*61 864 706*	...	...	...	...	...	...
45 - 49	*118 650 588*	*60 510 588*	*58 140 000*	...	...	...	...	...	...
50 - 54	*73 181 176*	*37 436 471*	*35 744 706*	...	...	...	...	...	...
55 - 59	*84 314 118*	*42 603 529*	*41 709 412*	...	...	...	...	...	...
60 - 64	*62 009 412*	*31 397 647*	*30 611 765*	...	...	...	...	...	...
65 - 69	*42 416 471*	*21 251 765*	*21 164 706*	...	...	...	...	...	...
70 - 74	*33 912 941*	*16 934 118*	*16 978 824*	...	...	...	...	...	...
75 - 79	*24 910 588*	*11 716 471*	*13 195 294*	...	...	...	...	...	...
80 - 84	*14 075 294*	*6 263 529*	*7 811 765*	...	...	...	...	...	...
85 - 89	*5 642 353*	*2 182 353*	*3 460 000*	...	...	...	...	...	...
90 - 94	*1 690 588*	*524 706*	*1 165 882*	...	...	...	...	...	...
95 +	*341 176*	*85 882*	*254 118*	...	...	...	...	...	...
China, Hong Kong SAR - Chine, Hong Kong RAS									
1 VII 2012 (ESDJ)									
Total	7 154 600	3 327 300	3 827 300	...	...	...	...	...	...
0	51 100	26 600	24 500	...	...	...	...	...	...
1 - 4	211 400	109 800	101 600	...	...	...	...	...	...
5 - 9	244 300	125 800	118 500	...	...	...	...	...	...
10 - 14	306 400	158 200	148 200	...	...	...	...	...	...
15 - 19	419 100	215 000	204 100	...	...	...	...	...	...
20 - 24	458 000	226 300	231 700	...	...	...	...	...	...
25 - 29	529 100	225 900	303 200	...	...	...	...	...	...
30 - 34	562 600	228 400	334 200	...	...	...	...	...	...
35 - 39	567 000	234 400	332 600	...	...	...	...	...	...
40 - 44	576 300	241 400	334 900	...	...	...	...	...	...
45 - 49	638 100	286 400	351 700	...	...	...	...	...	...
50 - 54	641 600	312 000	329 600	...	...	...	...	...	...
55 - 59	540 700	267 500	273 200	...	...	...	...	...	...
60 - 64	428 600	213 600	215 000	...	...	...	...	...	...
65 - 69	264 500	134 900	129 600	...	...	...	...	...	...
70 - 74	221 100	112 800	108 300	...	...	...	...	...	...
75 - 79	209 000	99 100	109 900	...	...	...	...	...	...
80 - 84	151 100	65 400	85 700	...	...	...	...	...	...
85 +	134 600	43 800	90 800	...	...	...	...	...	...

7. Population by age, sex and urban/rural residence: latest available year, 2003 - 2012
Population selon l'âge, le sexe et la résidence, urbaine/rurale : dernière année disponible, 2003 - 2012 (continued - suite)

Continent, country or area, date, code and age (in years) / Continent, pays ou zone, date, code et âge (en années)	Total Both sexes Les deux sexes	Total Male Masculin	Total Female Féminin	Urban - Urbaine Both sexes Les deux sexes	Urban - Urbaine Male Masculin	Urban - Urbaine Female Féminin	Rural - Rurale Both sexes Les deux sexes	Rural - Rurale Male Masculin	Rural - Rurale Female Féminin
ASIA - ASIE									
China, Macao SAR - Chine, Macao RAS									
1 VII 2012 (ESDJ)									
Total	567 900	274 300	293 600	...	...	...	...	...	...
0	5 900	3 100	2 800	...	...	...	...	...	...
1 - 4	18 200	9 600	8 600	...	...	...	...	...	...
5 - 9	18 400	9 600	8 800	...	...	...	...	...	...
10 - 14	23 700	12 300	11 400	...	...	...	...	...	...
15 - 19	36 200	18 300	17 900	...	...	...	...	...	...
20 - 24	53 700	26 100	27 600	...	...	...	...	...	...
25 - 29	60 200	28 700	31 500	...	...	...	...	...	...
30 - 34	47 000	23 100	23 900	...	...	...	...	...	...
35 - 39	44 800	21 200	23 600	...	...	...	...	...	...
40 - 44	47 800	21 000	26 800	...	...	...	...	...	...
45 - 49	50 700	22 300	28 400	...	...	...	...	...	...
50 - 54	49 800	24 300	25 500	...	...	...	...	...	...
55 - 59	41 400	21 000	20 400	...	...	...	...	...	...
60 - 64	27 800	14 400	13 400	...	...	...	...	...	...
65 - 69	15 100	7 900	7 200	...	...	...	...	...	...
70 - 74	8 600	4 300	4 300	...	...	...	...	...	...
75 - 79	7 700	3 300	4 400	...	...	...	...	...	...
80 - 84	5 900	2 300	3 600	...	...	...	...	...	...
85 +	5 000	1 500	3 500	...	...	...	...	...	...
Cyprus - Chypre[39]									
1 X 2011 (CDJC)									
Total	840 407	408 780	431 627	566 191	273 065	293 126	274 216	135 715	138 501
0 - 4	45 015	23 061	21 954	29 726	15 202	14 524	15 289	7 859	7 430
5 - 9	42 635	21 921	20 714	28 050	14 386	13 664	14 585	7 535	7 050
10 - 14	47 298	24 179	23 119	30 926	15 730	15 196	16 372	8 449	7 923
15 - 19	55 818	28 683	27 135	36 345	18 593	17 752	19 473	10 090	9 383
20 - 24	66 073	33 891	32 182	44 948	22 847	22 101	21 125	11 044	10 081
25 - 29	74 114	36 992	37 122	51 855	25 842	26 013	22 259	11 150	11 109
30 - 34	69 834	33 149	36 685	48 938	23 133	25 805	20 896	10 016	10 880
35 - 39	61 862	27 754	34 108	43 232	19 204	24 028	18 630	8 550	10 080
40 - 44	59 728	27 031	32 697	41 295	18 416	22 879	18 433	8 615	9 818
45 - 49	57 240	27 059	30 181	39 233	18 225	21 008	18 007	8 834	9 173
50 - 54	56 128	27 517	28 611	38 287	18 499	19 788	17 841	9 018	8 823
55 - 59	47 762	23 771	23 991	31 716	15 541	16 175	16 046	8 230	7 816
60 - 64	45 034	22 057	22 977	29 704	14 438	15 266	15 330	7 619	7 711
65 - 69	36 328	17 656	18 672	23 459	11 295	12 164	12 869	6 361	6 508
70 - 74	29 433	14 044	15 389	18 991	9 048	9 943	10 442	4 996	5 446
75 - 79	21 058	9 647	11 411	13 545	6 239	7 306	7 513	3 408	4 105
80 +	24 948	10 342	14 606	15 853	6 408	9 445	9 095	3 934	5 161
Unknown - Inconnu	99	26	73	88	19	69	11	7	4
Democratic People's Republic of Korea - République populaire démocratique de Corée									
1 X 2008 (CDJC)									
Total	24 052 231	11 721 838	12 330 393	...	...	...	...	...	...
0 - 4	1 710 039	872 173	837 866	...	...	...	...	...	...
5 - 9	1 846 785	943 048	903 737	...	...	...	...	...	...
10 - 14	2 021 350	1 035 282	986 068	...	...	...	...	...	...
15 - 19	2 052 342	1 050 113	1 002 229	...	...	...	...	...	...
20 - 24	1 841 400	941 017	900 383	...	...	...	...	...	...
25 - 29	1 737 185	887 573	849 612	...	...	...	...	...	...
30 - 34	1 680 272	853 276	826 996	...	...	...	...	...	...
35 - 39	2 214 929	1 118 391	1 096 538	...	...	...	...	...	...
40 - 44	2 015 514	1 005 140	1 010 374	...	...	...	...	...	...
45 - 49	1 559 527	766 054	793 473	...	...	...	...	...	...
50 - 54	1 315 101	637 737	677 364	...	...	...	...	...	...
55 - 59	902 876	423 625	479 251	...	...	...	...	...	...
60 - 64	1 058 263	476 727	581 536	...	...	...	...	...	...
65 - 69	913 304	379 456	533 848	...	...	...	...	...	...
70 - 74	662 627	228 286	434 341	...	...	...	...	...	...

7. Population by age, sex and urban/rural residence: latest available year, 2003 - 2012

Population selon l'âge, le sexe et la résidence, urbaine/rurale : dernière année disponible, 2003 - 2012 (continued - suite)

Continent, country or area, date, code and age (in years) Continent, pays ou zone, date, code et âge (en années)	Total			Urban - Urbaine			Rural - Rurale		
	Both sexes Les deux sexes	Male Masculin	Female Féminin	Both sexes Les deux sexes	Male Masculin	Female Féminin	Both sexes Les deux sexes	Male Masculin	Female Féminin
ASIA - ASIE									
Democratic People's Republic of Korea - République populaire démocratique de Corée									
1 X 2008 (CDJC)									
75 - 79	335 467	79 231	256 236	...	...	...	...	...	...
80 - 84	132 149	18 884	113 265	...	...	...	...	...	...
85 - 89	42 760	4 930	37 830	...	...	...	...	...	...
90 - 94	8 634	809	7 825	...	...	...	...	...	...
95 - 99	1 643	86	1 557	...	...	...	...	...	...
100 +	64	-	64	...	...	...	...	...	...
Georgia - Géorgie									
1 VII 2012 (ESDF)									
Total	4 490 700	2 141 300	2 349 400	...	...	...	...	...	...
0 - 4	289 800	152 650	137 150	...	...	...	...	...	...
5 - 9	233 350	123 200	110 150	...	...	...	...	...	...
10 - 14	238 850	125 850	113 000	...	...	...	...	...	...
15 - 19	293 600	151 600	142 000	...	...	...	...	...	...
20 - 24	368 200	186 250	181 950	...	...	...	...	...	...
25 - 29	359 550	181 250	178 300	...	...	...	...	...	...
30 - 34	330 750	164 650	166 100	...	...	...	...	...	...
35 - 39	313 700	153 900	159 800	...	...	...	...	...	...
40 - 44	302 100	145 300	156 800	...	...	...	...	...	...
45 - 49	312 250	145 550	166 700	...	...	...	...	...	...
50 - 54	327 550	151 550	176 000	...	...	...	...	...	...
55 - 59	272 400	123 800	148 600	...	...	...	...	...	...
60 - 64	230 300	101 950	128 350	...	...	...	...	...	...
65 - 69	129 900	54 950	74 950	...	...	...	...	...	...
70 - 74	191 950	74 350	117 600	...	...	...	...	...	...
75 - 79	139 450	53 750	85 700	...	...	...	...	...	...
80 - 84	93 500	33 600	59 900	...	...	...	...	...	...
85 +	63 500	17 150	46 350	...	...	...	...	...	...
India - Inde[40]									
1 VII 2011* (ESDF)									
Total	*1192503000*	*617 315 000*	*575 188 000*	...	...	...	...	...	...
0 - 4	*114 878 000*	*60 745 000*	*54 133 000*	...	...	...	...	...	...
5 - 9	*113 486 000*	*60 092 000*	*53 394 000*	...	...	...	...	...	...
10 - 14	*118 577 000*	*61 318 000*	*57 259 000*	...	...	...	...	...	...
15 - 19	*121 727 000*	*63 479 000*	*58 248 000*	...	...	...	...	...	...
20 - 24	*118 038 000*	*62 281 000*	*55 757 000*	...	...	...	...	...	...
25 - 29	*101 956 000*	*54 079 000*	*47 877 000*	...	...	...	...	...	...
30 - 34	*88 905 000*	*46 050 000*	*42 855 000*	...	...	...	...	...	...
35 - 39	*80 759 000*	*40 595 000*	*40 164 000*	...	...	...	...	...	...
40 - 44	*73 464 000*	*36 773 000*	*36 691 000*	...	...	...	...	...	...
45 - 49	*65 211 000*	*33 218 000*	*31 993 000*	...	...	...	...	...	...
50 - 54	*54 195 000*	*28 157 000*	*26 038 000*	...	...	...	...	...	...
55 - 59	*42 837 000*	*22 390 000*	*20 447 000*	...	...	...	...	...	...
60 - 64	*32 405 000*	*16 693 000*	*15 712 000*	...	...	...	...	...	...
65 - 69	*24 397 000*	*11 991 000*	*12 406 000*	...	...	...	...	...	...
70 - 74	*18 943 000*	*8 909 000*	*10 034 000*	...	...	...	...	...	...
75 - 79	*13 092 000*	*6 075 000*	*7 017 000*	...	...	...	...	...	...
80 +	*9 633 000*	*4 470 000*	*5 163 000*	...	...	...	...	...	...
Indonesia - Indonésie									
1 V 2010 (CDJC)									
Total	237 641 326	119 630 913	118 010 413	118 320 256	59 559 622	58 760 634	119 321 070	60 071 291	59 249 779
0 - 4	22 678 702	11 662 369	11 016 333	11 025 060	5 679 790	5 345 270	11 653 642	5 982 579	5 671 063
0	4 397 046	2 259 245	2 137 801	...	...	...	...	...	...
1 - 4	18 275 014	9 399 611	8 875 403	11 016 095	5 674 648	5 341 447	12 237 385	6 299 446	5 937 939
5 - 9	23 253 480	11 974 094	11 279 386	11 016 095	5 674 648	5 341 447	12 237 385	6 299 446	5 937 939
10 - 14	22 671 081	11 662 417	11 008 664	10 542 167	5 399 311	5 142 856	12 128 914	6 263 106	5 865 808
15 - 19	20 880 734	10 614 306	10 266 428	10 755 586	5 343 102	5 412 484	10 125 148	5 271 204	4 853 944
20 - 24	19 891 633	9 887 713	10 003 920	10 903 811	5 416 588	5 487 223	8 987 822	4 471 125	4 516 697
25 - 29	21 310 443	10 631 311	10 679 132	11 447 502	5 752 629	5 694 873	9 862 941	4 878 682	4 984 259
30 - 34	19 830 685	9 949 357	9 881 328	10 476 109	5 286 436	5 189 673	9 354 576	4 662 921	4 691 655
35 - 39	18 505 131	9 337 517	9 167 614	9 517 824	4 816 398	4 701 426	8 987 307	4 521 119	4 466 188

194

Continent, country or area, date, code and age (in years) Continent, pays ou zone, date, code et âge (en années)	Total			Urban - Urbaine			Rural - Rurale		
	Both sexes Les deux sexes	Male Masculin	Female Féminin	Both sexes Les deux sexes	Male Masculin	Female Féminin	Both sexes Les deux sexes	Male Masculin	Female Féminin
ASIA - ASIE									
Indonesia - Indonésie									
1 V 2010 (CDJC)									
40 - 44	16 524 852	8 322 712	8 202 140	8 400 678	4 249 643	4 151 035	8 124 174	4 073 069	4 051 105
45 - 49	14 040 982	7 032 740	7 008 242	6 936 515	3 481 077	3 455 438	7 104 467	3 551 663	3 552 804
50 - 54	11 561 321	5 865 997	5 695 324	5 599 670	2 858 242	2 741 428	5 961 651	3 007 755	2 953 896
55 - 59	8 448 570	4 400 316	4 048 254	4 010 840	2 091 487	1 919 353	4 437 730	2 308 829	2 128 901
60 - 64	6 058 761	2 927 191	3 131 570	2 664 404	1 290 725	1 373 679	3 394 357	1 636 466	1 757 891
65 - 69	4 694 031	2 225 133	2 468 898	2 030 370	960 508	1 069 862	2 663 661	1 264 625	1 399 036
70 - 74	3 456 331	1 531 459	1 924 872	1 435 408	630 505	804 903	2 020 923	900 954	1 119 969
75 - 79	1 977 905	842 344	1 135 561	815 975	336 277	479 698	1 161 930	506 067	655 863
80 - 84	1 143 170	481 462	661 708	459 569	186 943	272 626	683 601	294 519	389 082
85 - 89	437 961	182 432	255 529	177 571	69 631	107 940	260 390	112 801	147 589
90 - 94	170 899	63 948	106 951	66 489	23 159	43 330	104 410	40 789	63 621
95 +	104 654	36 095	68 559	38 613	12 523	26 090	66 041	23 572	42 469
Unknown - Inconnu	81 690	45 183	36 507	...	...	...	...	...	...
1 VII 2011 (ESDJ)									
Total	236 954 100	118 591 100	118 363 000	...	...	...	...	...	...
0	4 522 700	2 303 500	2 219 200	...	...	...	...	...	...
1 - 4	17 237 500	8 797 700	8 439 800	...	...	...	...	...	...
5 - 9	20 653 200	10 553 400	10 099 800	...	...	...	...	...	...
10 - 14	20 169 300	10 265 800	9 903 500	...	...	...	...	...	...
15 - 19	20 998 500	10 674 400	10 324 100	...	...	...	...	...	...
20 - 24	21 166 800	10 745 300	10 421 500	...	...	...	...	...	...
25 - 29	20 807 500	10 435 600	10 371 900	...	...	...	...	...	...
30 - 34	20 024 900	9 789 800	10 235 100	...	...	...	...	...	...
35 - 39	18 643 300	9 036 100	9 607 200	...	...	...	...	...	...
40 - 44	16 825 900	8 314 000	8 511 900	...	...	...	...	...	...
45 - 49	14 774 200	7 373 100	7 401 100	...	...	...	...	...	...
50 - 54	12 345 200	6 243 700	6 101 500	...	...	...	...	...	...
55 - 59	9 508 400	4 883 400	4 625 000	...	...	...	...	...	...
60 - 64	6 849 000	3 462 900	3 386 100	...	...	...	...	...	...
65 - 69	4 760 800	2 290 800	2 470 000	...	...	...	...	...	...
70 - 74	3 604 500	1 668 800	1 935 700	...	...	...	...	...	...
75 +	4 062 400	1 752 800	2 309 600	...	...	...	...	...	...
Iran (Islamic Republic of) - Iran (République islamique d')									
24 X 2011 (CDJC)									
Total	75 149 669	37 905 669	37 244 000	53 646 661	27 023 638	26 623 023	21 503 008	10 882 031	10 620 977
0 - 4	6 232 552	3 192 311	3 040 241	4 203 477	2 153 868	2 049 609	2 029 075	1 038 443	990 632
5 - 9	5 657 791	2 898 560	2 759 231	3 832 046	1 963 297	1 868 749	1 825 745	935 263	890 482
10 - 14	5 671 435	2 888 388	2 783 047	3 912 748	1 990 088	1 922 660	1 758 687	898 300	860 387
15 - 19	6 607 043	3 347 436	3 259 607	4 484 448	2 259 770	2 224 678	2 122 595	1 087 666	1 034 929
20 - 24	8 414 497	4 201 575	4 212 922	5 944 593	2 924 622	3 019 971	2 469 904	1 276 953	1 192 951
25 - 29	8 672 654	4 354 634	4 318 020	6 383 685	3 178 858	3 204 827	2 288 969	1 175 776	1 113 193
30 - 34	6 971 924	3 515 828	3 456 096	5 138 203	2 586 546	2 551 657	1 833 721	929 282	904 439
35 - 39	5 571 018	2 850 233	2 720 785	4 079 426	2 085 665	1 993 761	1 491 592	764 568	727 024
40 - 44	4 906 749	2 486 379	2 420 370	3 694 650	1 880 436	1 814 214	1 212 099	605 943	606 156
45 - 49	4 030 481	2 027 338	2 003 143	3 078 142	1 560 170	1 517 972	952 339	467 168	485 171
50 - 54	3 527 408	1 765 113	1 762 295	2 644 028	1 338 591	1 305 437	883 380	426 522	456 858
55 - 59	2 680 119	1 326 634	1 353 485	1 980 283	1 003 799	976 484	699 836	322 835	377 001
60 - 64	1 862 907	880 962	981 945	1 334 489	649 361	685 128	528 418	231 601	296 817
65 - 69	1 343 731	643 342	700 389	948 647	459 597	489 050	395 084	183 745	211 339
70 - 74	1 119 968	561 147	558 821	758 250	378 415	379 835	361 718	182 732	178 986
75 - 79	913 531	477 470	436 061	592 002	301 871	290 131	321 529	175 599	145 930
80 - 84	561 538	280 896	280 642	363 040	172 196	190 844	198 498	108 700	89 798
85 - 89	270 703	137 163	133 540	178 843	86 484	92 359	91 860	50 679	41 181
90 - 94	59 989	28 735	31 254	39 595	18 317	21 278	20 394	10 418	9 976
95 - 99	15 587	7 583	8 004	10 082	4 773	5 309	5 505	2 810	2 695
100 +	11 722	5 424	6 298	6 961	3 082	3 879	4 761	2 342	2 419
Unknown - Inconnu	46 322	28 518	17 804	39 023	23 832	15 191	7 299	4 686	2 613
Iraq									
1 VII 2007 (ESDF)									
Total	29 682 081	14 943 516	14 738 565	19 752 833	9 970 074	9 782 759	9 929 248	4 973 442	4 955 806
0 - 4	4 970 829	2 548 402	2 422 427	3 093 542	1 585 669	1 507 873	1 877 287	962 733	914 554

Continent, country or area, date, code and age (in years) / Continent, pays ou zone, date, code et âge (en annèes)	Total			Urban - Urbaine			Rural - Rurale		
	Both sexes Les deux sexes	Male Masculin	Female Féminin	Both sexes Les deux sexes	Male Masculin	Female Féminin	Both sexes Les deux sexes	Male Masculin	Female Féminin
ASIA - ASIE									
Iraq									
1 VII 2007 (ESDF)									
5 - 9	4 222 028	2 166 818	2 055 210	2 665 680	1 367 692	1 297 988	1 556 348	799 126	757 222
10 - 14	3 605 956	1 833 813	1 772 143	2 313 228	1 174 857	1 138 371	1 292 728	658 956	633 772
15 - 19	3 206 547	1 631 272	1 575 275	2 097 711	1 067 009	1 030 702	1 108 836	564 263	544 573
20 - 24	2 745 916	1 394 941	1 350 975	1 836 580	933 972	902 608	909 336	460 969	448 367
25 - 29	2 342 651	1 184 126	1 158 525	1 595 244	808 530	786 714	747 407	375 596	371 811
30 - 34	1 969 141	987 662	981 479	1 367 432	689 466	677 966	601 709	298 196	303 513
35 - 39	1 623 309	806 089	817 220	1 147 326	574 647	572 679	475 983	231 442	244 541
40 - 44	1 280 968	624 348	656 620	925 668	457 710	467 958	355 300	166 638	188 662
45 - 49	1 024 602	494 742	529 860	748 849	368 114	380 735	275 753	126 628	149 125
50 - 54	790 298	378 954	411 344	581 704	284 864	296 840	208 594	94 090	114 504
55 - 59	611 439	292 240	319 199	451 250	220 282	230 968	160 189	71 958	88 231
60 - 64	453 767	218 171	235 596	333 655	163 325	170 330	120 112	54 846	65 266
65 - 69	325 970	154 180	171 790	238 913	114 733	124 180	87 057	39 447	47 610
70 - 74	214 454	98 274	116 180	156 363	72 358	84 005	58 091	25 916	32 175
75 - 79	133 345	58 821	74 524	94 738	41 841	52 897	38 607	16 980	21 627
80 +	160 861	70 663	90 198	104 950	45 005	59 945	55 911	25 658	30 253
Israel - Israël[41]									
1 VII 2011 (ESDJ)									
Total	7 765 832	3 841 121	3 924 711	7 109 718	3 506 773	3 602 945	656 114	334 348	321 766
0	164 967	84 580	80 386	150 031	76 882	73 150	14 935	7 698	7 237
1 - 4	629 371	322 269	307 102	570 306	291 905	278 401	59 066	30 365	28 701
5 - 9	722 243	370 223	352 021	654 877	335 670	319 206	67 367	34 553	32 814
10 - 14	665 508	342 493	323 015	604 818	311 055	293 763	60 689	31 438	29 251
15 - 19	604 858	312 375	292 482	547 918	281 543	266 376	56 939	30 833	26 107
20 - 24	583 781	293 155	290 626	534 748	267 212	267 536	49 032	25 943	23 089
25 - 29	575 375	289 087	286 288	530 738	266 096	264 642	44 637	22 991	21 646
30 - 34	545 146	271 715	273 431	500 469	249 684	250 785	44 677	22 031	22 646
35 - 39	526 972	261 907	265 065	478 803	238 496	240 307	48 169	23 411	24 758
40 - 44	451 805	223 625	228 180	410 917	202 990	207 927	40 888	20 635	20 253
45 - 49	403 730	198 438	205 292	369 916	181 079	188 837	33 814	17 359	16 455
50 - 54	389 539	188 299	201 240	358 368	172 470	185 898	31 171	15 829	15 342
55 - 59	374 567	179 516	195 051	345 640	164 689	180 951	28 928	14 828	14 100
60 - 64	344 012	163 093	180 919	319 337	150 398	168 939	24 675	12 695	11 980
65 - 69	218 307	102 473	115 833	202 263	94 393	107 871	16 043	8 081	7 962
70 - 74	193 910	86 998	106 912	182 413	81 259	101 155	11 497	5 740	5 758
75 - 79	151 825	65 376	86 449	142 524	61 115	81 409	9 301	4 261	5 040
80 - 84	114 047	45 717	68 330	107 079	42 890	64 189	6 968	2 827	4 141
85 - 89	71 690	26 636	45 054	66 919	24 744	42 175	4 771	1 892	2 879
90 - 94	24 632	9 591	15 041	22 846	8 886	13 960	1 786	705	1 081
95 - 99	7 405	2 633	4 772	6 782	2 444	4 338	624	189	434
100 +	2 143	922	1 221	2 006	875	1 132	137	47	90
Japan - Japon[42]									
1 X 2010 (CDJC)									
Total	128 057 352	62 327 737	65 729 615	116 156 631	56 569 051	59 587 580	11 900 721	5 758 686	6 142 035
0 - 4	5 296 748	2 710 581	2 586 167	4 831 346	2 472 475	2 358 871	465 402	238 106	227 296
5 - 9	5 585 661	2 859 805	2 725 856	5 061 966	2 591 629	2 470 337	523 695	268 176	255 519
10 - 14	5 921 035	3 031 943	2 889 092	5 348 569	2 737 977	2 610 592	572 466	293 966	278 500
15 - 19	6 063 357	3 109 229	2 954 128	5 506 483	2 823 085	2 683 398	556 874	286 144	270 730
20 - 24	6 426 433	3 266 240	3 160 193	5 925 984	3 012 027	2 913 957	500 449	254 213	246 236
25 - 29	7 293 701	3 691 723	3 601 978	6 720 343	3 397 748	3 322 595	573 358	293 975	279 383
30 - 34	8 341 497	4 221 011	4 120 486	7 675 385	3 879 681	3 796 304	666 112	341 330	324 182
35 - 39	9 786 349	4 950 122	4 836 227	9 015 173	4 556 572	4 458 601	771 176	393 550	377 626
40 - 44	8 741 865	4 400 375	4 341 490	8 046 407	4 051 948	3 994 459	695 458	348 427	347 031
45 - 49	8 033 116	4 027 969	4 005 147	7 328 789	3 675 150	3 653 639	704 327	352 819	351 508
50 - 54	7 644 499	3 809 576	3 834 923	6 878 402	3 425 836	3 452 566	766 097	383 740	382 357
55 - 59	8 663 734	4 287 489	4 376 245	7 753 645	3 830 707	3 922 938	910 089	456 782	453 307
60 - 64	10 037 249	4 920 468	5 116 781	9 046 242	4 424 879	4 621 363	991 007	495 589	495 418
65 - 69	8 210 173	3 921 774	4 288 399	7 424 237	3 543 535	3 880 702	785 936	378 239	407 697
70 - 74	6 963 302	3 225 503	3 737 799	6 249 910	2 895 658	3 354 252	713 392	329 845	383 547
75 - 79	5 941 013	2 582 940	3 358 073	5 276 323	2 294 753	2 981 570	664 690	288 187	376 503
80 - 84	4 336 264	1 692 584	2 643 680	3 804 707	1 485 631	2 319 076	531 557	206 953	324 604
85 - 89	2 432 588	744 222	1 688 366	2 121 067	649 324	1 471 743	311 521	94 898	216 623
90 - 94	1 021 707	241 799	779 908	889 810	210 257	679 553	131 897	31 542	100 355

Continent, country or area, date, code and age (in years) Continent, pays ou zone, date, code et âge (en années)	Total			Urban - Urbaine			Rural - Rurale		
	Both sexes Les deux sexes	Male Masculin	Female Féminin	Both sexes Les deux sexes	Male Masculin	Female Féminin	Both sexes Les deux sexes	Male Masculin	Female Féminin
ASIA - ASIE									
Japan - Japon[42]									
1 X 2010 (CDJC)									
95 - 99	296 756	55 739	241 017	258 266	48 545	209 721	38 490	7 194	31 296
100 +	43 882	5 851	38 031	38 068	5 060	33 008	5 814	791	5 023
Unknown - Inconnu	976 423	570 794	405 629	955 509	557 174	398 335	20 914	13 620	7 294
1 VII 2012 (ESDJ)[43]									
Total	127 561 000	62 041 000	65 520 000	...	...	...	...	...	...
0 - 4	5 279 000	2 704 000	2 575 000	...	...	...	...	...	...
5 - 9	5 436 000	2 782 000	2 653 000	...	...	...	...	...	...
10 - 14	5 883 000	3 013 000	2 870 000	...	...	...	...	...	...
15 - 19	6 064 000	3 108 000	2 956 000	...	...	...	...	...	...
20 - 24	6 303 000	3 224 000	3 079 000	...	...	...	...	...	...
25 - 29	7 109 000	3 619 000	3 490 000	...	...	...	...	...	...
30 - 34	7 889 000	4 000 000	3 888 000	...	...	...	...	...	...
35 - 39	9 493 000	4 811 000	4 682 000	...	...	...	...	...	...
40 - 44	9 416 000	4 756 000	4 659 000	...	...	...	...	...	...
45 - 49	8 125 000	4 083 000	4 042 000	...	...	...	...	...	...
50 - 54	7 650 000	3 824 000	3 826 000	...	...	...	...	...	...
55 - 59	8 037 000	3 988 000	4 049 000	...	...	...	...	...	...
60 - 64	10 406 000	5 103 000	5 303 000	...	...	...	...	...	...
65 - 69	8 045 000	3 855 000	4 190 000	...	...	...	...	...	...
70 - 74	7 350 000	3 418 000	3 932 000	...	...	...	...	...	...
75 - 79	6 223 000	2 723 000	3 501 000	...	...	...	...	...	...
80 - 84	4 591 000	1 809 000	2 782 000	...	...	...	...	...	...
85 +	4 263 000	1 218 000	3 046 000	...	...	...	...	...	...
Jordan - Jordanie									
1 X 2004 (CDFC)[44]									
Total	5 103 639	2 626 287	2 477 352	3 997 383	2 055 431	1 941 952	1 106 256	570 856	535 400
0	122 757	62 643	60 114	94 974	48 529	46 445	27 783	14 114	13 669
1 - 4	527 574	270 573	257 001	408 893	209 140	199 753	118 681	61 433	57 248
5 - 9	642 871	329 133	313 738	495 583	253 774	241 809	147 288	75 359	71 929
10 - 14	610 129	313 083	297 046	469 321	240 723	228 598	140 808	72 360	68 448
15 - 19	559 838	287 693	272 145	431 275	221 213	210 062	128 563	66 480	62 083
20 - 24	540 193	279 600	260 593	421 400	217 092	204 308	118 793	62 508	56 285
25 - 29	456 261	239 774	216 487	355 950	186 570	169 380	100 311	53 204	47 107
30 - 34	399 169	207 178	191 991	316 235	164 238	151 997	82 934	42 940	39 994
35 - 39	323 426	167 737	155 689	259 736	134 829	124 907	63 690	32 908	30 782
40 - 44	241 400	123 945	117 455	196 923	101 442	95 481	44 477	22 503	21 974
45 - 49	170 456	87 098	83 358	138 372	70 890	67 482	32 084	16 208	15 876
50 - 54	128 240	64 607	63 633	102 179	51 210	50 969	26 061	13 397	12 664
55 - 59	113 721	55 765	57 956	92 893	45 618	47 275	20 828	10 147	10 681
60 - 64	98 787	52 084	46 703	80 269	42 634	37 635	18 518	9 450	9 068
65 - 69	71 823	37 095	34 728	57 484	29 956	27 528	14 339	7 139	7 200
70 - 74	46 820	23 467	23 353	36 958	18 503	18 455	9 862	4 964	4 898
75 - 79	24 268	12 651	11 617	19 160	9 923	9 237	5 108	2 728	2 380
80 +	22 060	10 137	11 923	16 376	7 369	9 007	5 684	2 768	2 916
80 - 84	13 585	6 144	7 441	...	...	...	...	...	...
85 - 89	5 032	2 444	2 588	...	...	...	...	...	...
90 - 94	2 316	1 012	1 304	...	...	...	...	...	...
95 +	1 127	537	590	...	...	...	...	...	...
Unknown - Inconnu	3 846	2 024	1 822	3 402	1 778	1 624	444	246	198
31 XII 2012 (ESDF)[45]									
Total	6 388 000	3 293 000	3 095 000	...	...	...	...	...	...
0	153 651	78 545	75 106	...	...	...	...	...	...
1 - 4	660 349	339 260	321 089	...	...	...	...	...	...
5 - 9	804 655	412 685	391 970	...	...	...	...	...	...
10 - 14	763 670	392 565	371 105	...	...	...	...	...	...
15 - 19	700 725	360 725	340 000	...	...	...	...	...	...
20 - 24	676 135	350 580	325 555	...	...	...	...	...	...
25 - 29	571 080	300 645	270 435	...	...	...	...	...	...
30 - 34	499 620	259 775	239 845	...	...	...	...	...	...
35 - 39	404 820	210 320	194 500	...	...	...	...	...	...
40 - 44	302 150	155 410	146 740	...	...	...	...	...	...
45 - 49	213 350	109 210	104 140	...	...	...	...	...	...
50 - 54	160 510	81 010	79 500	...	...	...	...	...	...

7. Population by age, sex and urban/rural residence: latest available year, 2003 - 2012
Population selon l'âge, le sexe et la résidence, urbaine/rurale : dernière année disponible, 2003 - 2012 (continued - suite)

Continent, country or area, date, code and age (in years) Continent, pays ou zone, date, code et âge (en annèes)	Total			Urban - Urbaine			Rural - Rurale		
	Both sexes Les deux sexes	Male Masculin	Female Féminin	Both sexes Les deux sexes	Male Masculin	Female Féminin	Both sexes Les deux sexes	Male Masculin	Female Féminin
ASIA - ASIE									
Jordan - Jordanie									
31 XII 2012 (ESDF)[45]									
55 - 59	*142 340*	*69 920*	*72 420*	...	...	...	...	...	...
60 - 64	*123 645*	*65 305*	*58 340*	...	...	...	...	...	...
65 - 69	*91 990*	*47 635*	*44 355*	...	...	...	...	...	...
70 - 74	*59 970*	*30 140*	*29 830*	...	...	...	...	...	...
75 - 79	*31 085*	*16 250*	*14 835*	...	...	...	...	...	...
80 - 84	*17 400*	*7 890*	*9 510*	...	...	...	...	...	...
85 - 89	*6 445*	*3 140*	*3 305*	...	...	...	...	...	...
90 - 94	*2 965*	*1 300*	*1 665*	...	...	...	...	...	...
95 +	*1 445*	*690*	*755*	...	...	...	...	...	...
Kazakhstan									
1 VII 2008 (ESDF)									
Total	15 674 000	7 541 053	8 132 947	8 331 030	3 877 559	4 453 471	7 342 970	3 663 494	3 679 476
0	334 121	171 415	162 706	182 521	93 735	88 786	151 600	77 680	73 920
1 - 4	1 123 822	576 735	547 087	598 929	307 667	291 262	524 893	269 068	255 825
5 - 9	1 102 548	564 701	537 847	524 034	268 924	255 110	578 514	295 777	282 737
10 - 14	1 209 513	617 314	592 199	522 195	266 983	255 212	687 318	350 331	336 987
15 - 19	1 486 438	755 608	730 830	695 164	350 949	344 215	791 274	404 659	386 615
20 - 24	1 550 478	784 675	765 803	800 736	396 991	403 745	749 742	387 684	362 058
25 - 29	1 295 879	651 820	644 059	741 385	357 306	384 079	554 494	294 514	259 980
30 - 34	1 176 482	580 262	596 220	654 261	305 967	348 294	522 221	274 295	247 926
35 - 39	1 092 697	533 348	559 349	613 063	284 686	328 377	479 634	248 662	230 972
40 - 44	1 044 896	501 603	543 293	581 382	267 483	313 899	463 514	234 120	229 394
45 - 49	1 095 437	515 147	580 290	616 824	279 070	337 754	478 613	236 077	242 536
50 - 54	887 374	404 797	482 577	502 890	220 181	282 709	384 484	184 616	199 868
55 - 59	700 438	306 307	394 131	403 592	169 371	234 221	296 846	136 936	159 910
60 - 64	382 873	160 524	222 349	220 385	87 967	132 418	162 488	72 557	89 931
65 - 69	440 247	168 503	271 744	241 208	86 342	154 866	199 039	82 161	116 878
70 - 74	353 774	131 480	222 294	200 160	69 161	130 999	153 614	62 319	91 295
75 - 79	208 952	68 446	140 506	121 852	37 430	84 422	87 100	31 016	56 084
80 - 84	134 530	36 112	98 418	79 726	20 091	59 635	54 804	16 021	38 783
85 - 89	39 793	9 112	30 681	23 445	5 414	18 031	16 348	3 698	12 650
90 - 94	10 304	2 091	8 213	5 713	1 262	4 451	4 591	829	3 762
95 - 99	2 678	731	1 947	1 271	417	854	1 407	314	1 093
100 +	726	322	404	294	162	132	432	160	272
25 II 2009 (CDFC)									
Total	16 009 597	...	...	...	...	...	...	...	...
0 - 9	2 635 355	...	...	...	...	...	...	...	...
10 - 19	2 762 532	...	...	...	...	...	...	...	...
20 - 24	1 605 090	...	...	...	...	...	...	...	...
25 - 29	1 342 309	...	...	...	...	...	...	...	...
30 - 34	1 216 304	...	...	...	...	...	...	...	...
35 - 39	1 138 801	...	...	...	...	...	...	...	...
40 - 44	1 065 799	...	...	...	...	...	...	...	...
45 - 49	1 103 296	...	...	...	...	...	...	...	...
50 - 54	888 729	...	...	...	...	...	...	...	...
55 - 59	693 223	...	...	...	...	...	...	...	...
60 - 64	422 865	...	...	...	...	...	...	...	...
65 - 69	390 760	...	...	...	...	...	...	...	...
70 - 74	370 214	...	...	...	...	...	...	...	...
75 - 79	185 264	...	...	...	...	...	...	...	...
80 +	189 056	...	...	...	...	...	...	...	...
Kuwait - Koweït									
20 IV 2011* (CDFC)									
Total	3 065 850	1 738 372	1 327 478	...	...	...	...	...	...
0 - 4	266 953	138 688	128 265	...	...	...	...	...	...
5 - 9	226 075	116 278	109 797	...	...	...	...	...	...
10 - 14	202 135	104 034	98 101	...	...	...	...	...	...
15 - 19	183 532	96 131	87 401	...	...	...	...	...	...
20 - 24	260 701	132 661	128 040	...	...	...	...	...	...
25 - 29	392 740	219 431	173 309	...	...	...	...	...	...
30 - 34	409 437	249 945	159 492	...	...	...	...	...	...
35 - 39	334 986	201 460	133 526	...	...	...	...	...	...
40 - 44	278 847	170 762	108 085	...	...	...	...	...	...

Continent, country or area, date, code and age (in years) / Continent, pays ou zone, date, code et âge (en années)	Total			Urban - Urbaine			Rural - Rurale		
	Both sexes Les deux sexes	Male Masculin	Female Féminin	Both sexes Les deux sexes	Male Masculin	Female Féminin	Both sexes Les deux sexes	Male Masculin	Female Féminin
ASIA - ASIE									
Kuwait - Koweït									
20 IV 2011* (CDFC)									
45 - 49	198 414	121 610	76 804	...	...	...	...	...	...
50 - 54	131 531	83 022	48 509	...	...	...	...	...	...
55 - 59	80 059	49 821	30 238	...	...	...	...	...	...
60 - 64	43 950	25 262	18 688	...	...	...	...	...	...
65 +	56 490	29 267	27 223	...	...	...	...	...	...
Kyrgyzstan - Kirghizstan[46]									
1 VII 2012 (ESDJ)									
Total	5 607 511	2 770 269	2 837 242	1 878 643	887 727	990 916	3 728 868	1 882 542	1 846 326
0	149 654	76 700	72 954	49 466	25 347	24 119	100 188	51 353	48 835
1 - 4	525 497	268 614	256 883	167 029	85 374	81 655	358 468	183 240	175 228
5 - 9	544 033	277 214	266 819	157 100	79 494	77 606	386 933	197 720	189 213
10 - 14	499 040	254 005	245 035	138 725	70 645	68 080	360 315	183 360	176 955
15 - 19	563 434	286 526	276 908	160 819	80 333	80 486	402 615	206 193	196 422
20 - 24	589 967	296 601	293 366	224 650	105 688	118 962	365 317	190 913	174 404
25 - 29	510 163	256 353	253 810	184 998	88 082	96 916	325 165	168 271	156 894
30 - 34	398 882	200 723	198 159	142 104	67 924	74 180	256 778	132 799	123 979
35 - 39	348 371	172 260	176 111	122 393	56 438	65 955	225 978	115 822	110 156
40 - 44	327 786	160 125	167 661	119 397	54 314	65 083	208 389	105 811	102 578
45 - 49	302 554	145 572	156 982	107 401	48 984	58 417	195 153	96 588	98 565
50 - 54	280 235	132 748	147 487	99 492	44 772	54 720	180 743	87 976	92 767
55 - 59	194 026	89 342	104 684	68 723	29 677	39 046	125 303	59 665	65 638
60 - 64	133 486	58 761	74 725	50 163	20 488	29 675	83 323	38 273	45 050
65 - 69	59 962	25 609	34 353	23 586	9 144	14 442	36 376	16 465	19 911
70 - 74	75 256	30 623	44 633	27 703	10 068	17 635	47 553	20 555	26 998
75 - 79	51 699	19 751	31 948	17 722	5 940	11 782	33 977	13 811	20 166
80 - 84	34 342	12 370	21 972	11 012	3 315	7 697	23 330	9 055	14 275
85 - 89	14 589	5 151	9 438	4 803	1 345	3 458	9 786	3 806	5 980
90 - 94	3 504	1 000	2 504	1 090	302	788	2 414	698	1 716
95 - 99	707	168	539	197	41	156	510	127	383
100 +	324	53	271	70	12	58	254	41	213
Lao People's Democratic Republic - République démocratique populaire lao									
1 III 2005 (CDJC)									
Total	5 621 982	2 800 551	2 821 431	1 522 137[47]	763 043[47]	759 094[47]	4 093 248[47]	2 033 289[47]	2 059 959[47]
0 - 4	700 915	351 559	349 356	135 758[47]	68 543[47]	67 215[47]	565 003[47]	282 939[47]	282 064[47]
5 - 9	749 208	379 137	370 071	155 490[47]	78 713[47]	76 777[47]	593 565[47]	300 341[47]	293 224[47]
10 - 14	767 156	391 785	375 371	188 311[47]	95 769[47]	92 542[47]	578 719[47]	295 944[47]	282 775[47]
15 - 19	647 269	323 729	323 540	202 877[47]	101 383[47]	101 494[47]	443 763[47]	221 962[47]	221 801[47]
20 - 24	515 297	253 926	261 371	180 777[47]	91 079[47]	89 698[47]	332 618[47]	161 532[47]	171 086[47]
25 - 29	429 609	211 279	218 330	132 858[47]	66 079[47]	66 779[47]	295 521[47]	144 368[47]	151 153[47]
30 - 34	359 995	176 515	183 480	110 035[47]	53 414[47]	56 621[47]	249 181[47]	122 647[47]	126 534[47]
35 - 39	329 777	164 415	165 362	99 816[47]	49 495[47]	50 321[47]	229 447[47]	114 592[47]	114 855[47]
40 - 44	265 867	132 335	133 532	80 714[47]	40 532[47]	40 182[47]	184 777[47]	91 575[47]	93 202[47]
45 - 49	227 167	113 869	113 298	65 746[47]	34 044[47]	31 702[47]	161 139[47]	79 640[47]	81 499[47]
50 - 54	177 980	86 770	91 210	47 891[47]	24 815[47]	23 076[47]	129 913[47]	61 854[47]	68 059[47]
55 - 59	128 331	62 691	65 640	34 546[47]	17 693[47]	16 853[47]	93 669[47]	44 925[47]	48 744[47]
60 - 64	105 014	50 006	55 008	26 734[47]	13 110[47]	13 624[47]	78 226[47]	36 864[47]	41 362[47]
65 - 69	79 540	38 289	41 251	21 869[47]	10 664[47]	11 205[47]	57 637[47]	27 609[47]	30 028[47]
70 - 74	59 579	27 652	31 927	16 214[47]	7 614[47]	8 600[47]	43 343[47]	20 020[47]	23 323[47]
75 - 79	37 172	17 964	19 208	10 859[47]	5 142[47]	5 717[47]	26 293[47]	12 813[47]	13 480[47]
80 - 84	22 582	10 402	12 180	6 248[47]	2 842[47]	3 406[47]	16 320[47]	7 553[47]	8 767[47]
85 - 89	10 328	4 631	5 697	3 070[47]	1 256[47]	1 814[47]	7 254[47]	3 371[47]	3 883[47]
90 - 94	4 745	1 964	2 781	1 216[47]	479[47]	737[47]	3 526[47]	1 484[47]	2 042[47]
95 - 99	2 375	982	1 393	665[47]	252[47]	413[47]	1 710[47]	730[47]	980[47]
100 +	1 416	480	936	252[47]	76[47]	176[47]	1 164[47]	404[47]	760[47]
Unknown - Inconnu	660	171	489	191[47]	49[47]	142[47]	460[47]	122[47]	338[47]
1 VII 2012 (ESDF)[48]									
Total	6 548 633	3 271 538	3 277 095	...	...	...	...	...	...
0 - 4	945 502	482 109	463 393	...	...	...	...	...	...
5 - 9	764 366	385 749	378 613	...	...	...	...	...	...
10 - 14	723 497	364 894	358 601	...	...	...	...	...	...

7. Population by age, sex and urban/rural residence: latest available year, 2003 - 2012
Population selon l'âge, le sexe et la résidence, urbaine/rurale : dernière année disponible, 2003 - 2012 (continued - suite)

Continent, country or area, date, code and age (in years) / Continent, pays ou zone, date, code et âge (en années)	Total			Urban - Urbaine			Rural - Rurale		
	Both sexes Les deux sexes	Male Masculin	Female Féminin	Both sexes Les deux sexes	Male Masculin	Female Féminin	Both sexes Les deux sexes	Male Masculin	Female Féminin
ASIA - ASIE									
Lao People's Democratic Republic - République démocratique populaire lao									
1 VII 2012 (ESDF)[48]									
15 - 19	754 658	384 706	369 953	...	...	...	...	...	...
20 - 24	671 864	339 213	332 651	...	...	...	...	...	...
25 - 29	526 351	260 026	266 324	...	...	...	...	...	...
30 - 34	425 878	209 086	216 789	...	...	...	...	...	...
35 - 39	354 609	173 417	181 188	...	...	...	...	...	...
40 - 44	325 002	160 508	164 494	...	...	...	...	...	...
45 - 49	279 368	138 507	140 858	...	...	...	...	...	...
50 - 54	227 336	112 806	114 529	...	...	...	...	...	...
55 - 59	181 483	88 313	93 172	...	...	...	...	...	...
60 - 64	127 141	60 705	66 434	...	...	...	...	...	...
65 - 69	91 582	42 864	48 718	...	...	...	...	...	...
70 - 74	65 161	30 233	34 930	...	...	...	...	...	...
75 - 79	42 001	19 099	22 901	...	...	...	...	...	...
80 +	42 841	19 295	23 547	...	...	...	...	...	...
Lebanon - Liban[49]									
3 III 2007 (SSDF)									
Total	3 759 134	1 857 659	1 901 475	...	...	...	...	...	...
0 - 4	261 021	136 514	124 507	...	...	...	...	...	...
5 - 9	312 902	160 577	152 325	...	...	...	...	...	...
10 - 14	354 049	183 613	170 436	...	...	...	...	...	...
15 - 19	363 626	195 984	167 642	...	...	...	...	...	...
20 - 24	367 778	191 471	176 307	...	...	...	...	...	...
25 - 29	305 933	148 321	157 612	...	...	...	...	...	...
30 - 34	276 775	132 105	144 670	...	...	...	...	...	...
35 - 39	249 550	111 833	137 717	...	...	...	...	...	...
40 - 44	233 003	102 405	130 598	...	...	...	...	...	...
45 - 49	208 752	95 595	113 157	...	...	...	...	...	...
50 - 54	179 899	84 091	95 808	...	...	...	...	...	...
55 - 59	143 376	66 993	76 383	...	...	...	...	...	...
60 - 64	140 030	65 701	74 329	...	...	...	...	...	...
65 - 69	122 014	59 900	62 114	...	...	...	...	...	...
70 - 74	105 259	53 267	51 992	...	...	...	...	...	...
75 - 79	71 315	38 353	32 962	...	...	...	...	...	...
80 - 84	45 481	21 083	24 398	...	...	...	...	...	...
85 +	18 371	9 853	8 518	...	...	...	...	...	...
Malaysia - Malaisie									
1 VII 2011 (ESDJ)[24]									
Total	28 552 712	14 523 912	14 028 800	18 131 157	9 144 410	8 986 747	10 421 555	5 379 502	5 042 053
0	499 945	256 072	243 873	307 272	157 406	149 866	192 673	98 666	94 007
1 - 4	1 955 175	1 001 155	954 020	1 223 525	626 395	597 130	731 650	374 760	356 890
5 - 9	2 459 101	1 258 724	1 200 377	1 558 741	797 527	761 214	900 360	461 197	439 163
10 - 14	2 740 612	1 407 479	1 333 133	1 709 923	877 788	832 135	1 030 689	529 691	500 998
15 - 19	2 681 191	1 382 650	1 298 541	1 601 092	825 926	775 166	1 080 099	556 724	523 375
20 - 24	2 561 192	1 305 753	1 255 439	1 478 208	752 393	725 815	1 082 984	553 360	529 624
25 - 29	2 427 645	1 225 425	1 202 220	1 447 183	722 749	724 434	980 462	502 676	477 786
30 - 34	2 290 823	1 156 987	1 133 836	1 534 984	750 130	784 854	755 839	406 857	348 982
35 - 39	2 140 093	1 084 255	1 055 838	1 493 032	730 576	762 456	647 061	353 679	293 382
40 - 44	2 001 975	1 021 261	980 714	1 369 947	682 865	687 082	632 028	338 396	293 632
45 - 49	1 802 606	923 951	878 655	1 223 054	620 211	602 843	579 552	303 740	275 812
50 - 54	1 522 571	780 930	741 641	1 022 709	523 795	498 914	499 862	257 135	242 727
55 - 59	1 226 382	627 320	599 062	802 655	412 263	390 392	423 727	215 057	208 670
60 - 64	862 383	440 893	421 490	545 523	281 150	264 373	316 860	159 743	157 117
65 - 69	553 009	276 593	276 416	335 456	169 256	166 200	217 553	107 337	110 216
70 - 74	379 512	180 583	198 929	222 447	106 157	116 290	157 065	74 426	82 639
75 - 79	232 774	104 871	127 903	134 143	59 958	74 185	98 631	44 913	53 718
80 - 84	130 023	56 445	73 578	73 213	30 770	42 443	56 810	25 675	31 135
85 - 89	54 539	22 803	31 736	30 442	12 014	18 428	24 097	10 789	13 308
90 +	31 161	9 762	21 399	17 608	5 081	12 527	13 553	4 681	8 872
1 VII 2012 (ESDJ)[50]									
Total	29 336 795	15 093 673	14 243 122	...	...	...	...	...	...
0	509 787	262 049	247 738	...	...	...	...	...	...

Continent, country or area, date, code and age (in years) / Continent, pays ou zone, date, code et âge (en annèes)	Total			Urban - Urbaine			Rural - Rurale		
	Both sexes Les deux sexes	Male Masculin	Female Féminin	Both sexes Les deux sexes	Male Masculin	Female Féminin	Both sexes Les deux sexes	Male Masculin	Female Féminin
ASIA - ASIE									
Malaysia - Malaisie									
1 VII 2012 (ESDJ)[50]									
1 - 4	1 996 762	1 025 830	970 932	...	...	...	...	...	...
5 - 9	2 581 025	1 323 719	1 257 306	...	...	...	...	...	...
10 - 14	2 669 825	1 368 552	1 301 273	...	...	...	...	...	...
15 - 19	2 787 081	1 428 642	1 358 439	...	...	...	...	...	...
20 - 24	2 923 049	1 502 577	1 420 472	...	...	...	...	...	...
25 - 29	2 880 356	1 508 590	1 371 766	...	...	...	...	...	...
30 - 34	2 403 416	1 280 158	1 123 258	...	...	...	...	...	...
35 - 39	2 000 671	1 048 832	951 839	...	...	...	...	...	...
40 - 44	1 843 729	936 821	906 908	...	...	...	...	...	...
45 - 49	1 678 129	862 018	816 111	...	...	...	...	...	...
50 - 54	1 461 394	755 767	705 627	...	...	...	...	...	...
55 - 59	1 162 918	594 854	568 064	...	...	...	...	...	...
60 - 64	893 722	451 637	442 085	...	...	...	...	...	...
65 - 69	605 910	302 463	303 447	...	...	...	...	...	...
70 - 74	421 317	206 477	214 840	...	...	...	...	...	...
75 - 79	265 399	125 557	139 842	...	...	...	...	...	...
80 - 84	144 765	63 825	80 940	...	...	...	...	...	...
85 - 89	72 475	30 494	41 981	...	...	...	...	...	...
90 - 94	35 065	14 811	20 254	...	...	...	...	...	...
Maldives									
21 III 2006 (CDFC)[51]									
Total	298 968	151 459	147 509	103 693	51 992	51 701	195 275	99 467	95 808
0	5 462	2 777	2 685	1 601	832	769	3 861	1 945	1 916
1 - 4	20 709	10 585	10 124	5 743	2 912	2 831	14 966	7 673	7 293
5 - 9	29 867	15 352	14 515	7 538	3 829	3 709	22 329	11 523	10 806
10 - 14	36 999	19 111	17 888	10 082	5 171	4 911	26 917	13 940	12 977
15 - 19	39 904	20 155	19 749	15 656	7 457	8 199	24 248	12 698	11 550
20 - 24	34 809	16 933	17 876	15 535	7 401	8 134	19 274	9 532	9 742
25 - 29	24 581	11 915	12 666	10 176	5 054	5 122	14 405	6 861	7 544
30 - 34	20 635	10 022	10 613	8 137	4 089	4 048	12 498	5 933	6 565
35 - 39	18 174	8 780	9 394	6 616	3 381	3 235	11 558	5 399	6 159
40 - 44	15 871	7 828	8 043	5 529	2 731	2 798	10 342	5 097	5 245
45 - 49	13 569	6 872	6 697	4 394	2 207	2 187	9 175	4 665	4 510
50 - 54	7 936	4 147	3 789	2 601	1 415	1 186	5 335	2 732	2 603
55 - 59	5 859	3 046	2 813	1 863	987	876	3 996	2 059	1 937
60 - 64	5 566	2 852	2 714	1 520	752	768	4 046	2 100	1 946
65 - 69	5 678	3 014	2 664	1 265	619	646	4 413	2 395	2 018
70 - 74	4 186	2 333	1 853	765	363	402	3 421	1 970	1 451
75 - 79	2 377	1 444	933	409	217	192	1 968	1 227	741
80 - 84	1 064	617	447	204	92	112	860	525	335
85 - 89	396	241	155	94	48	46	302	193	109
90 - 94	159	89	70	34	14	20	125	75	50
95 +	84	52	32	19	8	11	65	44	21
Unknown - Inconnu	5 083	3 294	1 789	3 912	2 413	1 499	1 171	881	290
1 VII 2012 (ESDF)									
Total	330 652	167 057	163 595	...	...	...	...	...	...
0	6 990	3 524	3 466	...	...	...	...	...	...
1 - 4	25 029	12 639	12 390	...	...	...	...	...	...
5 - 9	26 644	13 611	13 033	...	...	...	...	...	...
10 - 14	29 233	15 066	14 167	...	...	...	...	...	...
15 - 19	36 442	18 937	17 505	...	...	...	...	...	...
20 - 24	40 715	20 800	19 915	...	...	...	...	...	...
25 - 29	37 135	18 274	18 861	...	...	...	...	...	...
30 - 34	26 764	13 036	13 728	...	...	...	...	...	...
35 - 39	21 515	10 513	11 002	...	...	...	...	...	...
40 - 44	18 878	9 170	9 708	...	...	...	...	...	...
45 - 49	16 423	8 099	8 324	...	...	...	...	...	...
50 - 54	14 295	7 224	7 071	...	...	...	...	...	...
55 - 59	8 761	4 549	4 212	...	...	...	...	...	...
60 - 64	5 813	3 014	2 799	...	...	...	...	...	...
65 - 69	5 090	2 569	2 521	...	...	...	...	...	...
70 - 74	4 882	2 523	2 359	...	...	...	...	...	...

7. Population by age, sex and urban/rural residence: latest available year, 2003 - 2012

Population selon l'âge, le sexe et la résidence, urbaine/rurale : dernière année disponible, 2003 - 2012 (continued - suite)

Continent, country or area, date, code and age (in years) / Continent, pays ou zone, date, code et âge (en années)	Total			Urban - Urbaine			Rural - Rurale		
	Both sexes Les deux sexes	Male Masculin	Female Féminin	Both sexes Les deux sexes	Male Masculin	Female Féminin	Both sexes Les deux sexes	Male Masculin	Female Féminin
ASIA - ASIE									
Maldives									
1 VII 2012 (ESDF)									
75 - 79	3 474	1 912	1 562	...	...	...	...	...	...
80 + ...	2 569	1 598	971	...	...	...	...	...	...
Mongolia - Mongolie									
11 XI 2010 (CDJC)									
Total...................................	2 647 545	1 313 968	1 333 577	1 798 147	872 989	925 158	849 398	440 979	408 419
0 - 4	288 497	146 516	141 981	188 882	95 671	93 211	99 615	50 845	48 770
5 - 9	216 214	110 117	106 097	133 740	68 119	65 621	82 474	41 998	40 476
10 - 14	236 865	120 064	116 801	143 846	72 244	71 602	93 019	47 820	45 199
15 - 19	257 645	130 560	127 085	188 334	92 124	96 210	69 311	38 436	30 875
20 - 24	292 183	147 472	144 711	221 784	107 751	114 033	70 399	39 721	30 678
25 - 29	247 983	124 490	123 493	171 685	83 922	87 763	76 298	40 568	35 730
30 - 34	222 522	111 976	110 546	149 461	73 525	75 936	73 061	38 451	34 610
35 - 39	202 383	100 819	101 564	136 034	66 149	69 885	66 349	34 670	31 679
40 - 44	179 267	88 273	90 994	120 105	57 388	62 717	59 162	30 885	28 277
45 - 49	158 756	77 475	81 281	108 736	51 528	57 208	50 020	25 947	24 073
50 - 54	122 082	58 009	64 073	83 084	38 547	44 537	38 998	19 462	19 536
55 - 59	71 989	33 384	38 605	49 342	22 373	26 969	22 647	11 011	11 636
60 - 64	49 453	22 106	27 347	34 724	15 234	19 490	14 729	6 872	7 857
65 - 69	38 232	17 262	20 970	26 004	11 578	14 426	12 228	5 684	6 544
70 - 74	29 332	13 081	16 251	19 556	8 594	10 962	9 776	4 487	5 289
75 - 79	18 617	7 252	11 365	12 384	4 742	7 642	6 233	2 510	3 723
80 - 84	9 166	3 258	5 908	6 234	2 225	4 009	2 932	1 033	1 899
85 - 89	4 415	1 378	3 037	2 948	945	2 003	1 467	433	1 034
90 - 94	1 459	383	1 076	962	274	688	497	109	388
95 - 99	402	80	322	251	47	204	151	33	118
100 + ...	83	13	70	51	9	42	32	4	28
Myanmar									
1 X 2012 (ESDF)									
Total...................................	60 975 993	30 139 447	30 836 546	...	...	...	...	...	...
0	1 166 843	589 966	576 877	...	...	...	...	...	...
1 - 4	4 569 307	2 302 380	2 266 927	...	...	...	...	...	...
5 - 9	5 953 054	3 019 538	2 933 516	...	...	...	...	...	...
10 - 14	6 001 476	3 061 725	2 939 751	...	...	...	...	...	...
15 - 19	5 770 006	2 939 176	2 830 830	...	...	...	...	...	...
20 - 24	5 533 494	2 804 028	2 729 466	...	...	...	...	...	...
25 - 29	5 186 827	2 608 652	2 578 175	...	...	...	...	...	...
30 - 34	4 792 616	2 378 395	2 414 221	...	...	...	...	...	...
35 - 39	4 347 135	2 134 820	2 212 315	...	...	...	...	...	...
40 - 44	3 853 616	1 868 709	1 984 907	...	...	...	...	...	...
45 - 49	3 342 480	1 604 910	1 737 570	...	...	...	...	...	...
50 - 54	2 785 562	1 325 584	1 459 978	...	...	...	...	...	...
55 - 59	2 295 008	1 081 479	1 213 529	...	...	...	...	...	...
60 - 64	1 801 599	838 871	962 728	...	...	...	...	...	...
65 - 69	1 413 352	647 286	766 066	...	...	...	...	...	...
70 - 74	1 071 614	477 948	593 666	...	...	...	...	...	...
75 - 79	785 379	335 405	449 974	...	...	...	...	...	...
80 + ...	306 625	120 575	186 050	...	...	...	...	...	...
Nepal - Népal									
22 VI 2011 (CDJC)									
Total...................................	26 494 504	12 849 041	13 645 463	4 523 820	2 306 049	2 217 771	21 970 684	10 542 992	11 427 692
0 - 4	2 567 963	1 314 957	1 253 006	327 100	172 598	154 502	2 240 863	1 142 359	1 098 504
5 - 9	3 204 859	1 635 176	1 569 683	431 121	227 618	203 503	2 773 738	1 407 558	1 366 180
10 - 14	3 475 424	1 764 630	1 710 794	507 618	266 722	240 896	2 967 806	1 497 908	1 469 898
15 - 19	2 931 980	1 443 191	1 488 789	520 714	273 601	247 113	2 411 266	1 169 590	1 241 676
20 - 24	2 358 071	1 043 981	1 314 090	520 546	260 529	260 017	1 837 525	783 452	1 054 073
25 - 29	2 079 354	917 243	1 162 111	452 256	220 230	232 026	1 627 098	697 013	930 085
30 - 34	1 735 305	770 577	964 728	372 219	181 542	190 677	1 363 086	589 035	774 051
35 - 39	1 604 319	740 200	864 119	324 965	161 347	163 618	1 279 354	578 853	700 501
40 - 44	1 386 121	660 290	725 831	263 008	136 600	126 408	1 123 113	523 690	599 423
45 - 49	1 172 959	575 101	597 858	205 833	106 627	99 206	967 126	468 474	498 652
50 - 54	1 005 476	505 864	499 612	165 685	86 471	79 214	839 791	419 393	420 398
55 - 59	818 263	412 892	405 371	123 667	63 841	59 826	694 596	349 051	345 545
60 - 64	756 827	368 451	388 376	105 862	52 258	53 604	650 965	316 193	334 772

Continent, country or area, date, code and age (in years) / Continent, pays ou zone, date, code et âge (en annèes)	Total			Urban - Urbaine			Rural - Rurale		
	Both sexes Les deux sexes	Male Masculin	Female Féminin	Both sexes Les deux sexes	Male Masculin	Female Féminin	Both sexes Les deux sexes	Male Masculin	Female Féminin
ASIA - ASIE									
Nepal - Népal									
22 VI 2011 (CDJC)									
65 - 69	554 449	277 782	276 667	76 074	37 256	38 818	478 375	240 526	237 849
70 - 74	395 153	199 610	195 543	55 001	26 400	28 601	340 152	173 210	166 942
75 - 79	235 135	117 358	117 777	35 764	16 538	19 226	199 371	100 820	98 551
80 - 84	128 777	62 787	65 990	21 053	9 435	11 618	107 724	53 352	54 372
85 - 89	52 526	25 810	26 716	9 857	4 350	5 507	42 669	21 460	21 209
90 - 94	20 335	8 940	11 395	3 788	1 474	2 314	16 547	7 466	9 081
95 +	11 208	4 201	7 007	1 689	612	1 077	9 519	3 589	5 930
Oman									
1 VII 2009 (ESDF)									
Total	3 173 917	1 971 115	1 202 802	2 314 865	1 457 197	857 668	859 049	513 917	345 132
0 - 4	272 144	139 614	132 530	184 595	94 803	89 792	87 549	44 811	42 738
5 - 9	245 026	124 776	120 250	162 307	82 954	79 353	82 718	41 821	40 897
10 - 14	254 610	129 964	124 646	168 924	86 326	82 598	85 685	43 638	42 047
15 - 19	284 826	145 215	139 611	194 123	99 854	94 269	90 703	45 361	45 342
20 - 24	387 448	238 483	148 965	285 594	176 341	109 253	101 854	62 142	39 712
25 - 29	475 403	327 686	147 717	362 531	249 782	112 749	112 871	77 904	34 967
30 - 34	367 536	247 107	120 429	288 055	192 969	95 086	79 481	54 138	25 343
35 - 39	272 100	192 483	79 617	212 145	150 865	61 280	59 955	41 618	18 337
40 - 44	207 202	149 090	58 112	161 282	117 670	43 612	45 920	31 420	14 500
45 - 49	145 430	103 908	41 522	111 077	81 065	30 012	34 353	22 843	11 510
50 - 54	113 587	83 057	30 530	84 975	63 752	21 223	28 612	19 305	9 307
55 - 59	59 890	40 488	19 402	42 674	29 489	13 185	17 216	10 999	6 217
60 - 64	39 730	23 538	16 192	26 050	15 494	10 556	13 680	8 044	5 636
65 - 69	20 811	11 811	9 000	13 363	7 537	5 826	7 448	4 274	3 174
70 - 74	14 933	7 721	7 212	9 224	4 703	4 521	5 709	3 018	2 691
75 - 79	6 817	3 303	3 514	4 201	1 981	2 220	2 616	1 322	1 294
80 +	6 424	2 871	3 553	3 745	1 612	2 133	2 679	1 259	1 420
1 VII 2011 (ESDF)									
Total	3 295 298	2 090 883	1 204 415	...	...	...	...	...	...
0 - 4	300 582	153 267	147 315	...	...	...	...	...	...
5 - 9	236 628	120 700	115 928	...	...	...	...	...	...
10 - 14	202 815	104 571	98 244	...	...	...	...	...	...
15 - 19	248 679	128 870	119 809	...	...	...	...	...	...
20 - 24	366 344	228 859	137 485	...	...	...	...	...	...
25 - 29	520 837	375 302	145 535	...	...	...	...	...	...
30 - 34	403 289	281 848	121 441	...	...	...	...	...	...
35 - 39	295 337	208 272	87 065	...	...	...	...	...	...
40 - 44	218 151	159 491	58 660	...	...	...	...	...	...
45 - 49	159 596	113 995	45 601	...	...	...	...	...	...
50 - 54	125 185	87 469	37 716	...	...	...	...	...	...
55 - 59	77 988	51 214	26 774	...	...	...	...	...	...
60 - 64	46 079	26 347	19 732	...	...	...	...	...	...
65 - 69	32 417	17 087	15 330	...	...	...	...	...	...
70 - 74	25 764	13 994	11 770	...	...	...	...	...	...
75 - 79	16 315	9 013	7 302	...	...	...	...	...	...
80 +	19 246	10 575	8 671	...	...	...	...	...	...
Unknown - Inconnu	46	9	37	...	...	...	...	...	...
Pakistan[52]									
1 VII 2007 (ESDJ)									
Total	149 860 388	76 857 737	73 002 651	52 807 585	27 178 203	25 629 382	97 052 803	49 679 534	47 373 269
0 - 4	19 540 467	9 783 859	9 756 608	5 761 626	2 854 601	2 907 026	13 778 841	6 929 259	6 849 582
5 - 9	22 554 631	11 710 324	10 844 307	6 759 356	3 414 295	3 345 061	15 795 276	8 296 029	7 499 246
10 - 14	20 255 889	10 636 015	9 619 874	6 854 564	3 572 029	3 282 536	13 401 325	7 063 987	6 337 339
15 - 19	17 275 679	9 063 876	8 211 804	6 630 532	3 454 683	3 175 849	10 645 147	5 609 193	5 035 954
20 - 24	13 558 584	6 824 723	6 733 861	5 604 996	2 913 936	2 691 060	7 953 588	3 910 786	4 042 801
25 - 29	10 833 092	5 268 436	5 564 656	4 174 036	2 128 117	2 045 919	6 659 055	3 140 318	3 518 737
30 - 34	8 432 325	3 957 414	4 474 911	3 112 553	1 539 219	1 573 334	5 319 772	2 418 195	2 901 576
35 - 39	8 352 417	4 132 910	4 219 507	3 081 885	1 522 176	1 559 709	5 270 532	2 610 734	2 659 798
40 - 44	6 777 652	3 496 263	3 281 389	2 564 848	1 348 144	1 216 704	4 212 804	2 148 119	2 064 685
45 - 49	6 276 492	3 277 150	2 999 342	2 458 241	1 271 498	1 186 743	3 818 252	2 005 652	1 812 599
50 - 54	4 586 117	2 429 295	2 156 822	1 772 219	967 032	805 188	2 813 897	1 462 263	1 351 634
55 - 59	3 544 175	1 864 568	1 679 608	1 325 845	693 075	632 770	2 218 330	1 171 493	1 046 838
60 - 64	2 933 669	1 637 251	1 296 418	1 003 276	574 578	428 698	1 930 393	1 062 673	867 720

7. Population by age, sex and urban/rural residence: latest available year, 2003 - 2012
Population selon l'âge, le sexe et la résidence, urbaine/rurale : dernière année disponible, 2003 - 2012 (continued - suite)

Continent, country or area, date, code and age (in years) / Continent, pays ou zone, date, code et âge (en annèes)	Total			Urban - Urbaine			Rural - Rurale		
	Both sexes Les deux sexes	Male Masculin	Female Féminin	Both sexes Les deux sexes	Male Masculin	Female Féminin	Both sexes Les deux sexes	Male Masculin	Female Féminin
ASIA - ASIE									
Pakistan[52]									
1 VII 2007 (ESDJ)									
65 - 69	2 038 506	1 106 476	932 030	713 604	371 079	342 526	1 324 901	735 397	589 504
70 - 74	1 464 156	857 310	606 846	499 821	282 013	217 808	964 335	575 297	389 039
75 - 79	654 088	358 255	295 833	244 044	125 467	118 577	410 044	232 788	177 256
80 - 84	428 280	250 734	177 547	129 604	84 073	45 531	298 676	166 661	132 015
85 +	354 168	202 880	151 288	116 534	62 189	54 345	237 634	140 691	96 943
Philippines[53]									
1 V 2010 (CDJC)									
Total	92 335 113	46 634 257	45 700 856	...	...	...	...	...	...
0	1 968 131	1 018 386	949 745	...	...	...	...	...	...
1 - 4	8 265 653	4 274 825	3 990 828	...	...	...	...	...	...
5 - 9	10 321 543	5 332 287	4 989 256	...	...	...	...	...	...
10 - 14	10 179 610	5 237 006	4 942 604	...	...	...	...	...	...
15 - 19	9 705 354	4 931 506	4 773 848	...	...	...	...	...	...
20 - 24	8 408 656	4 256 999	4 151 657	...	...	...	...	...	...
25 - 29	7 423 723	3 746 311	3 677 412	...	...	...	...	...	...
30 - 34	6 772 929	3 443 582	3 329 347	...	...	...	...	...	...
35 - 39	6 013 953	3 057 323	2 956 630	...	...	...	...	...	...
40 - 44	5 471 588	2 778 661	2 692 927	...	...	...	...	...	...
45 - 49	4 680 649	2 367 809	2 312 840	...	...	...	...	...	...
50 - 54	3 894 850	1 953 952	1 940 898	...	...	...	...	...	...
55 - 59	2 987 148	1 475 861	1 511 287	...	...	...	...	...	...
60 - 64	2 228 399	1 064 116	1 164 283	...	...	...	...	...	...
65 - 69	1 497 557	680 227	817 330	...	...	...	...	...	...
70 - 74	1 142 562	492 152	650 410	...	...	...	...	...	...
75 - 79	707 115	286 079	421 036	...	...	...	...	...	...
80 - 84	394 188	145 937	248 251	...	...	...	...	...	...
85 - 89	188 511	64 125	124 386	...	...	...	...	...	...
90 - 94	60 102	19 598	40 504	...	...	...	...	...	...
95 - 99	18 099	5 684	12 415	...	...	...	...	...	...
100 +	4 793	1 831	2 962	...	...	...	...	...	...
Qatar									
21 IV 2010 (CDFC)									
Total	1 699 435	1 284 739	414 696	...	...	...	...	...	...
0	19 565	10 042	9 523	...	...	...	...	...	...
1 - 4	69 942	35 796	34 146	...	...	...	...	...	...
5 - 9	78 086	40 007	38 079	...	...	...	...	...	...
10 - 14	64 991	33 295	31 696	...	...	...	...	...	...
15 - 19	60 544	33 868	26 676	...	...	...	...	...	...
20 - 24	191 953	153 931	38 022	...	...	...	...	...	...
25 - 29	279 187	219 575	59 612	...	...	...	...	...	...
30 - 34	270 243	216 278	53 965	...	...	...	...	...	...
35 - 39	234 573	194 313	40 260	...	...	...	...	...	...
40 - 44	178 328	148 899	29 429	...	...	...	...	...	...
45 - 49	116 940	95 688	21 252	...	...	...	...	...	...
50 - 54	68 920	54 751	14 169	...	...	...	...	...	...
55 - 59	37 377	29 327	8 050	...	...	...	...	...	...
60 - 64	14 969	10 820	4 149	...	...	...	...	...	...
65 - 69	6 454	4 075	2 379	...	...	...	...	...	...
70 - 74	3 637	2 108	1 529	...	...	...	...	...	...
75 +	3 726	1 966	1 760	...	...	...	...	...	...
Republic of Korea - République de Corée									
1 XI 2010 (CDJC)[54]									
Total	47 990 761	23 840 896	24 149 865	39 363 373	19 558 869	19 804 504	8 627 388	4 282 027	4 345 361
0 - 4	2 219 084	1 142 220	1 076 864	1 837 552	945 626	891 926	381 532	196 594	184 938
5 - 9	2 394 663	1 243 294	1 151 369	1 993 280	1 034 401	958 879	401 383	208 893	192 490
10 - 14	3 173 226	1 654 964	1 518 262	2 669 649	1 393 007	1 276 642	503 577	261 957	241 620
15 - 19	3 438 414	1 826 179	1 612 235	2 922 281	1 548 832	1 373 449	516 133	277 347	238 786
20 - 24	3 055 420	1 625 371	1 430 049	2 640 489	1 383 435	1 257 054	414 931	241 936	172 995
25 - 29	3 538 949	1 802 805	1 736 144	3 080 113	1 549 579	1 530 534	458 836	253 226	205 610
30 - 34	3 695 348	1 866 397	1 828 951	3 167 638	1 589 121	1 578 517	527 710	277 276	250 434
35 - 39	4 099 147	2 060 233	2 038 914	3 483 148	1 732 781	1 750 367	615 999	327 452	288 547
40 - 44	4 131 423	2 071 431	2 059 992	3 508 366	1 735 872	1 772 494	623 057	335 559	287 498

Continent, country or area, date, code and age (in years) / Continent, pays ou zone, date, code et âge (en annèes)	Total			Urban - Urbaine			Rural - Rurale		
	Both sexes Les deux sexes	Male Masculin	Female Féminin	Both sexes Les deux sexes	Male Masculin	Female Féminin	Both sexes Les deux sexes	Male Masculin	Female Féminin
ASIA - ASIE									
Republic of Korea - République de Corée									
1 XI 2010 (CDJC)[54]									
45 - 49	4 073 358	2 044 641	2 028 717	3 426 557	1 703 858	1 722 699	646 801	340 783	306 018
50 - 54	3 798 131	1 887 973	1 910 158	3 131 150	1 548 965	1 582 185	666 981	339 008	327 973
55 - 59	2 766 695	1 360 747	1 405 948	2 209 244	1 087 271	1 121 973	557 451	273 476	283 975
60 - 64	2 182 236	1 057 035	1 125 201	1 675 619	813 834	861 785	506 617	243 201	263 416
65 - 69	1 812 168	833 242	978 926	1 307 441	612 023	695 418	504 727	221 219	283 508
70 - 74	1 566 014	672 894	893 120	1 035 369	451 635	583 734	530 645	221 259	309 386
75 - 79	1 084 367	410 726	673 641	676 567	257 200	419 367	407 800	153 526	254 274
80 - 84	595 509	186 008	409 501	370 966	113 906	257 060	224 543	72 102	152 441
85 - 89	271 167	74 118	197 049	168 707	44 883	123 824	102 460	29 235	73 225
90 - 94	78 329	17 770	60 559	48 720	10 873	37 847	29 609	6 897	22 712
95 - 99	15 278	2 593	12 685	9 424	1 619	7 805	5 854	974	4 880
100 +	1 835	255	1 580	1 093	148	945	742	107	635
1 VII 2012* (ESDJ)									
Total	50 004 441	25 039 557	24 964 884	...	...	...	...	...	...
0	455 708	235 122	220 586	...	...	...	...	...	...
1 - 4	1 865 191	960 527	904 664	...	...	...	...	...	...
5 - 9	2 284 516	1 182 475	1 102 041	...	...	...	...	...	...
10 - 14	2 953 648	1 543 742	1 409 906	...	...	...	...	...	...
15 - 19	3 423 691	1 811 944	1 611 747	...	...	...	...	...	...
20 - 24	3 345 246	1 777 680	1 567 566	...	...	...	...	...	...
25 - 29	3 473 754	1 810 080	1 663 674	...	...	...	...	...	...
30 - 34	4 003 589	2 052 179	1 951 410	...	...	...	...	...	...
35 - 39	4 006 932	2 048 758	1 958 174	...	...	...	...	...	...
40 - 44	4 365 418	2 216 103	2 149 315	...	...	...	...	...	...
45 - 49	4 166 688	2 124 111	2 042 577	...	...	...	...	...	...
50 - 54	4 179 603	2 098 759	2 080 844	...	...	...	...	...	...
55 - 59	3 237 368	1 609 348	1 628 020	...	...	...	...	...	...
60 - 64	2 353 414	1 140 615	1 212 799	...	...	...	...	...	...
65 - 69	1 873 558	877 461	996 097	...	...	...	...	...	...
70 - 74	1 684 737	736 512	948 225	...	...	...	...	...	...
75 - 79	1 201 931	474 959	726 972	...	...	...	...	...	...
80 - 84	693 903	226 730	467 173	...	...	...	...	...	...
85 - 89	311 458	85 577	225 881	...	...	...	...	...	...
90 - 94	101 701	23 146	78 555	...	...	...	...	...	...
95 - 99	20 001	3 387	16 614	...	...	...	...	...	...
100 +	2 386	342	2 044	...	...	...	...	...	...
Saudi Arabia - Arabie saoudite[55]									
1 VII 2012* (ESDF)									
Total	29 195 895	16 543 836	12 652 059	...	...	...	...	...	...
0 - 4	3 167 691	1 633 572	1 534 119	...	...	...	...	...	...
5 - 9	2 952 321	1 513 790	1 438 531	...	...	...	...	...	...
10 - 14	2 747 749	1 400 265	1 347 484	...	...	...	...	...	...
15 - 19	2 522 817	1 272 690	1 250 127	...	...	...	...	...	...
20 - 24	2 367 651	1 205 747	1 161 904	...	...	...	...	...	...
25 - 29	2 531 191	1 407 320	1 123 871	...	...	...	...	...	...
30 - 34	2 977 277	1 829 598	1 147 679	...	...	...	...	...	...
35 - 39	2 869 678	1 806 034	1 063 644	...	...	...	...	...	...
40 - 44	2 242 581	1 456 742	785 839	...	...	...	...	...	...
45 - 49	1 616 863	1 091 008	525 855	...	...	...	...	...	...
50 - 54	1 142 848	750 777	392 071	...	...	...	...	...	...
55 - 59	774 226	483 991	290 235	...	...	...	...	...	...
60 - 64	486 001	281 396	204 605	...	...	...	...	...	...
65 - 69	314 687	166 489	148 198	...	...	...	...	...	...
70 - 74	206 964	104 259	102 705	...	...	...	...	...	...
75 - 79	130 712	65 183	65 529	...	...	...	...	...	...
80 +	144 638	74 975	69 663	...	...	...	...	...	...
Singapore - Singapour[56]									
30 VI 2012 (ESDJ)									
Total[12]	3 818 200	1 880 000	1 938 200	...	...	...	...	...	...
0 - 4[12]	186 700	94 900	91 700	...	...	...	...	...	...
5 - 9	206 300	105 000	101 300	...	...	...	...	...	...

Continent, country or area, date, code and age (in years) — Continent, pays ou zone, date, code et âge (en annèes)	Total			Urban - Urbaine			Rural - Rurale		
	Both sexes Les deux sexes	Male Masculin	Female Féminin	Both sexes Les deux sexes	Male Masculin	Female Féminin	Both sexes Les deux sexes	Male Masculin	Female Féminin
ASIA - ASIE									
Singapore - Singapour[56]									
30 VI 2012 (ESDJ)									
10 - 14	233 300	119 700	113 600	...	...	...	...	...	...
15 - 19	258 900	132 100	126 800	...	...	...	...	...	...
20 - 24	264 500	132 700	131 800	...	...	...	...	...	...
25 - 29	254 600	123 100	131 500	...	...	...	...	...	...
30 - 34	295 400	140 700	154 700	...	...	...	...	...	...
35 - 39	314 000	152 300	161 700	...	...	...	...	...	...
40 - 44	308 800	151 200	157 600	...	...	...	...	...	...
45 - 49	320 900	161 100	159 800	...	...	...	...	...	...
50 - 54	310 400	156 600	153 800	...	...	...	...	...	...
55 - 59	271 800	136 400	135 400	...	...	...	...	...	...
60 - 64	214 000	105 800	108 200	...	...	...	...	...	...
65 - 69	128 900	62 400	66 500	...	...	...	...	...	...
70 - 74	104 400	47 900	56 500	...	...	...	...	...	...
75 - 79	67 700	29 700	38 000	...	...	...	...	...	...
80 - 84	44 100	17 500	26 600	...	...	...	...	...	...
85 +	33 600	11 100	22 500	...	...	...	...	...	...
Sri Lanka									
1 VII 2010* (ESDF)									
Total	20 653 000	10 249 000	10 404 000	...	...	...	...	...	...
0 - 4	1 755 000	892 000	863 000	...	...	...	...	...	...
5 - 9	1 817 000	922 000	895 000	...	...	...	...	...	...
10 - 14	1 859 000	943 000	916 000	...	...	...	...	...	...
15 - 19	2 003 000	1 015 000	988 000	...	...	...	...	...	...
20 - 24	1 942 000	974 000	968 000	...	...	...	...	...	...
25 - 29	1 631 000	799 000	832 000	...	...	...	...	...	...
30 - 34	1 580 000	779 000	801 000	...	...	...	...	...	...
35 - 39	1 538 000	758 000	780 000	...	...	...	...	...	...
40 - 44	1 425 000	707 000	718 000	...	...	...	...	...	...
45 - 49	1 250 000	615 000	635 000	...	...	...	...	...	...
50 - 54	1 126 000	554 000	572 000	...	...	...	...	...	...
55 - 59	817 000	390 000	427 000	...	...	...	...	...	...
60 - 64	609 000	297 000	312 000	...	...	...	...	...	...
65 - 69	485 000	225 000	260 000	...	...	...	...	...	...
70 - 74	372 000	174 000	198 000	...	...	...	...	...	...
75 +	444 000	205 000	239 000	...	...	...	...	...	...
State of Palestine - État de Palestine									
1 VII 2012 (ESDF)									
Total	4 293 313	2 180 386	2 112 927	...	...	...	...	...	...
0	138 801	70 980	67 821	...	...	...	...	...	...
1 - 4	491 727	250 883	240 844	...	...	...	...	...	...
5 - 9	570 256	291 094	279 162	...	...	...	...	...	...
10 - 14	535 339	273 459	261 880	...	...	...	...	...	...
15 - 19	506 260	258 317	247 943	...	...	...	...	...	...
20 - 24	434 759	221 815	212 944	...	...	...	...	...	...
25 - 29	338 783	173 155	165 628	...	...	...	...	...	...
30 - 34	275 004	140 317	134 687	...	...	...	...	...	...
35 - 39	234 234	118 641	115 593	...	...	...	...	...	...
40 - 44	196 926	100 185	96 741	...	...	...	...	...	...
45 - 49	164 967	85 419	79 548	...	...	...	...	...	...
50 - 54	128 469	66 637	61 832	...	...	...	...	...	...
55 - 59	89 286	45 429	43 857	...	...	...	...	...	...
60 - 64	63 135	30 695	32 440	...	...	...	...	...	...
65 - 69	46 354	20 726	25 628	...	...	...	...	...	...
70 - 74	33 152	13 810	19 342	...	...	...	...	...	...
75 - 79	22 858	9 289	13 569	...	...	...	...	...	...
80 +	23 003	9 535	13 468	...	...	...	...	...	...
Syrian Arab Republic - République arabe syrienne[57]									
1 VII 2011 (ESDF)									
Total	21 124 000	10 794 000	10 330 000	11 297 000	5 795 000	5 502 000	9 827 000	4 999 000	4 828 000
0 - 4	2 775 000	1 428 000	1 347 000	1 384 000	713 000	671 000	1 391 000	715 000	676 000
5 - 9	2 654 000	1 384 000	1 270 000	1 357 000	719 000	638 000	1 297 000	665 000	632 000

Continent, country or area, date, code and age (in years) / Continent, pays ou zone, date, code et âge (en annèes)	Total			Urban - Urbaine			Rural - Rurale		
	Both sexes Les deux sexes	Male Masculin	Female Féminin	Both sexes Les deux sexes	Male Masculin	Female Féminin	Both sexes Les deux sexes	Male Masculin	Female Féminin
ASIA - ASIE									
Syrian Arab Republic - République arabe syrienne[57]									
1 VII 2011 (ESDF)									
10 - 14	2 430 000	1 232 000	1 198 000	1 270 000	637 000	633 000	1 160 000	595 000	565 000
15 - 19	2 279 000	1 191 000	1 088 000	1 193 000	626 000	567 000	1 086 000	565 000	521 000
20 - 24	1 979 000	1 035 000	944 000	1 045 000	545 000	500 000	934 000	490 000	444 000
25 - 29	1 737 000	864 000	873 000	937 000	475 000	462 000	800 000	389 000	411 000
30 - 34	1 371 000	674 000	697 000	733 000	359 000	374 000	638 000	315 000	323 000
35 - 39	1 229 000	601 000	628 000	694 000	336 000	358 000	535 000	265 000	270 000
40 - 44	1 096 000	545 000	551 000	644 000	325 000	319 000	452 000	220 000	232 000
45 - 49	870 000	437 000	433 000	536 000	272 000	264 000	334 000	165 000	169 000
50 - 54	792 000	387 000	405 000	458 000	232 000	226 000	334 000	155 000	179 000
55 - 59	573 000	293 000	280 000	322 000	168 000	154 000	251 000	125 000	126 000
60 - 64	481 000	254 000	227 000	260 000	139 000	121 000	221 000	115 000	106 000
65 +	858 000	469 000	389 000	464 000	249 000	215 000	394 000	220 000	174 000
Tajikistan - Tadjikistan									
1 VII 2011 (ESDF)									
Total	7 714 198	3 893 798	3 820 401	2 042 660	1 032 106	1 010 554	5 671 539	2 861 692	2 809 847
0	230 017	118 849	111 169	53 597	27 636	25 962	176 420	91 213	85 207
1 - 4	809 525	416 596	392 929	189 526	97 476	92 050	619 999	319 120	300 879
5 - 9	835 249	428 980	406 268	205 616	105 865	99 751	629 632	323 114	306 518
10 - 14	866 759	443 864	422 895	221 580	114 016	107 564	645 179	329 848	315 331
15 - 19	860 151	437 196	422 977	232 158	122 990	109 168	628 015	314 206	313 809
20 - 24	849 383	426 706	422 677	238 063	128 611	109 452	611 320	298 095	313 225
25 - 29	678 277	341 825	336 452	170 136	85 036	85 100	508 140	256 789	251 351
30 - 34	516 318	260 595	255 723	138 558	67 409	71 149	377 760	193 186	184 574
35 - 39	444 740	220 668	224 072	127 552	59 988	67 565	317 188	160 680	156 508
40 - 44	402 195	198 234	203 961	120 888	58 174	62 714	281 307	140 060	141 247
45 - 49	365 327	179 316	186 011	107 076	51 510	55 566	258 251	127 806	130 446
50 - 54	299 496	147 771	151 725	86 337	41 802	44 535	213 158	105 968	107 190
55 - 59	190 234	92 892	97 342	54 705	25 969	28 736	135 529	66 923	68 606
60 - 64	120 656	59 156	61 500	35 207	16 746	18 461	85 449	42 411	43 038
65 - 69	68 651	36 213	32 437	19 330	9 551	9 779	49 320	26 662	22 658
70 - 74	78 686	39 185	39 501	20 408	9 772	10 636	58 278	29 413	28 865
75 - 79	51 649	24 289	27 360	11 926	5 374	6 552	39 723	18 914	20 809
80 - 84	30 843	15 057	15 787	6 569	2 919	3 651	24 274	12 138	12 136
85 - 89	11 473	4 924	6 549	2 519	930	1 590	8 954	3 995	4 959
90 - 94	3 374	1 154	2 220	697	251	447	2 677	904	1 773
95 - 99	862	289	573	163	72	91	699	217	482
100 +	316	43	273	50	13	37	267	30	237
Thailand - Thaïlande[2]									
1 VII 2012 (ESDJ)									
Total	67 911 720	33 328 645	34 583 075	23 430 180	11 219 175	12 211 005	44 481 540	22 109 470	22 372 070
0 - 4	3 979 864	2 041 071	1 938 793	1 303 276	660 378	642 898	2 676 588	1 380 693	1 295 895
5 - 9	4 624 088	2 353 198	2 270 890	1 653 192	829 716	823 476	2 970 896	1 523 482	1 447 414
10 - 14	4 766 188	2 438 774	2 327 414	1 567 479	790 354	777 125	3 198 709	1 648 420	1 550 289
15 - 19	5 067 031	2 593 629	2 473 402	1 561 571	784 752	776 819	3 505 460	1 808 877	1 696 583
20 - 24	5 237 205	2 673 846	2 563 359	1 615 627	803 045	812 582	3 621 578	1 870 801	1 750 777
25 - 29	5 262 148	2 673 201	2 588 947	1 709 395	839 146	870 249	3 552 753	1 834 055	1 718 698
30 - 34	5 320 960	2 683 015	2 637 945	1 966 999	953 695	1 013 304	3 353 961	1 729 320	1 624 641
35 - 39	5 432 820	2 673 404	2 759 416	2 079 909	992 437	1 087 472	3 352 911	1 680 967	1 671 944
40 - 44	5 543 422	2 672 891	2 870 531	2 045 686	963 854	1 081 832	3 497 736	1 709 037	1 788 699
45 - 49	5 344 099	2 574 423	2 769 676	1 923 474	905 363	1 018 111	3 420 625	1 669 060	1 751 565
50 - 54	4 818 743	2 315 177	2 503 566	1 713 371	804 718	908 653	3 105 372	1 510 459	1 594 913
55 - 59	3 906 749	1 854 719	2 052 030	1 372 422	637 639	734 783	2 534 327	1 217 080	1 317 247
60 - 64	2 881 942	1 347 251	1 534 691	995 295	456 060	539 235	1 886 647	891 191	995 456
65 - 69	2 118 712	963 728	1 154 984	711 804	317 607	394 197	1 406 908	646 121	760 787
70 - 74	1 603 467	695 434	908 033	533 040	226 340	306 700	1 070 427	469 094	601 333
75 - 79	1 111 421	451 737	659 684	375 550	149 055	226 495	735 871	302 682	433 189
80 +	892 861	323 147	569 714	302 090	105 016	197 074	590 771	218 131	372 640
Timor-Leste[2]									
1 VII 2008 (ESDF)									
Total	1 080 742	...	...	...	...	...	...	...	...
0 - 4	186 543	...	...	...	...	...	...	...	...
5 - 9	167 561	...	...	...	...	...	...	...	...

Continent, country or area, date, code and age (in years) / Continent, pays ou zone, date, code et âge (en années)	Total			Urban - Urbaine			Rural - Rurale		
	Both sexes Les deux sexes	Male Masculin	Female Féminin	Both sexes Les deux sexes	Male Masculin	Female Féminin	Both sexes Les deux sexes	Male Masculin	Female Féminin
ASIA - ASIE									
Timor-Leste[2]									
1 VII 2008 (ESDF)									
10 - 14	132 072	...	...	...	...	...	...	...	...
15 - 19	113 406	...	...	...	...	...	...	...	...
20 - 24	90 086	...	...	...	...	...	...	...	...
25 - 29	70 378	...	...	...	...	...	...	...	...
30 - 34	56 262	...	...	...	...	...	...	...	...
35 - 39	59 945	...	...	...	...	...	...	...	...
40 - 44	46 539	...	...	...	...	...	...	...	...
45 - 49	42 860	...	...	...	...	...	...	...	...
50 - 54	32 303	...	...	...	...	...	...	...	...
55 - 59	29 043	...	...	...	...	...	...	...	...
60 - 64	17 007	...	...	...	...	...	...	...	...
65 - 69	17 018	...	...	...	...	...	...	...	...
70 - 74	8 750	...	...	...	...	...	...	...	...
75 - 79	6 305	...	...	...	...	...	...	...	...
80 +	4 664	...	...	...	...	...	...	...	...
Turkey - Turquie[58]									
1 VII 2012 (ESDJ)									
Total	74 885 000	37 528 000	37 357 000	...	...	...	...	...	...
0 - 4	6 295 000	3 216 000	3 079 000	...	...	...	...	...	...
5 - 9	6 272 000	3 200 000	3 072 000	...	...	...	...	...	...
10 - 14	6 332 000	3 231 000	3 101 000	...	...	...	...	...	...
15 - 19	6 409 000	3 291 000	3 118 000	...	...	...	...	...	...
20 - 24	6 192 000	3 168 000	3 024 000	...	...	...	...	...	...
25 - 29	6 336 000	3 214 000	3 122 000	...	...	...	...	...	...
30 - 34	6 461 000	3 259 000	3 202 000	...	...	...	...	...	...
35 - 39	5 613 000	2 831 000	2 782 000	...	...	...	...	...	...
40 - 44	5 156 000	2 589 000	2 567 000	...	...	...	...	...	...
45 - 49	4 549 000	2 297 000	2 252 000	...	...	...	...	...	...
50 - 54	4 064 000	2 030 000	2 034 000	...	...	...	...	...	...
55 - 59	3 343 000	1 658 000	1 685 000	...	...	...	...	...	...
60 - 64	2 553 000	1 236 000	1 317 000	...	...	...	...	...	...
65 - 69	1 886 000	863 000	1 023 000	...	...	...	...	...	...
70 - 74	1 406 000	630 000	776 000	...	...	...	...	...	...
75 +	2 018 000	815 000	1 203 000	...	...	...	...	...	...
Turkmenistan - Turkménistan[12]									
1 VII 2003 (ESDF)									
Total	5 123 940	2 571 866	2 552 073	...	...	...	...	...	...
0 - 4	571 355	277 748	293 607	...	...	...	...	...	...
5 - 9	613 767	300 841	312 925	...	...	...	...	...	...
10 - 14	645 136	316 247	328 889	...	...	...	...	...	...
15 - 19	579 113	284 926	294 186	...	...	...	...	...	...
20 - 24	479 053	235 762	243 291	...	...	...	...	...	...
25 - 29	423 109	210 578	212 531	...	...	...	...	...	...
30 - 34	380 948	194 438	186 510	...	...	...	...	...	...
35 - 39	341 403	173 922	167 481	...	...	...	...	...	...
40 - 44	316 309	161 800	154 509	...	...	...	...	...	...
45 - 49	233 504	120 701	112 803	...	...	...	...	...	...
50 - 54	161 151	84 220	76 931	...	...	...	...	...	...
55 - 59	85 927	44 454	41 472	...	...	...	...	...	...
60 - 64	92 992	49 068	43 924	...	...	...	...	...	...
65 - 69	76 006	41 263	34 743	...	...	...	...	...	...
70 - 74	61 177	34 393	26 784	...	...	...	...	...	...
75 +	62 987	41 503	21 484	...	...	...	...	...	...
United Arab Emirates - Émirats arabes unis									
5 XII 2005 (CDFC)									
Total	4 106 427	2 806 141	1 300 286	3 384 839[59]	2 328 906[59]	1 055 933[59]	721 588[59]	477 235[59]	244 353[59]
0 - 4	282 139	145 601	136 538	224 169[59]	115 800[59]	108 369[59]	57 970[59]	29 801[59]	28 169[59]
5 - 9	269 382	139 929	129 453	213 815[59]	111 645[59]	102 170[59]	55 567[59]	28 284[59]	27 283[59]
10 - 14	249 057	130 778	118 279	192 350[59]	101 461[59]	90 889[59]	56 707[59]	29 317[59]	27 390[59]
15 - 19	232 226	121 388	110 838	173 192[59]	91 065[59]	82 127[59]	59 034[59]	30 323[59]	28 711[59]
20 - 24	433 566	272 036	161 530	349 079[59]	222 387[59]	126 692[59]	84 487[59]	49 649[59]	34 838[59]

7. Population by age, sex and urban/rural residence: latest available year, 2003 - 2012
Population selon l'âge, le sexe et la résidence, urbaine/rurale : dernière année disponible, 2003 - 2012 (continued - suite)

Continent, country or area, date, code and age (in years) / Continent, pays ou zone, date, code et âge (en années)	Total			Urban - Urbaine			Rural - Rurale		
	Both sexes Les deux sexes	Male Masculin	Female Féminin	Both sexes Les deux sexes	Male Masculin	Female Féminin	Both sexes Les deux sexes	Male Masculin	Female Féminin
ASIA - ASIE									
United Arab Emirates - Émirats arabes unis									
5 XII 2005 (CDFC)									
25 - 29	661 794	483 657	178 137	558 690[59]	410 228[59]	148 462[59]	103 104[59]	73 429[59]	29 675[59]
30 - 34	640 361	489 879	150 482	548 499[59]	417 909[59]	130 590[59]	91 862[59]	71 970[59]	19 892[59]
35 - 39	500 606	386 762	113 844	427 468[59]	329 059[59]	98 409[59]	73 138[59]	57 703[59]	15 435[59]
40 - 44	341 261	262 718	78 543	288 792[59]	220 959[59]	67 833[59]	52 469[59]	41 759[59]	10 710[59]
45 - 49	225 770	174 459	51 311	188 732[59]	145 298[59]	43 434[59]	37 038[59]	29 161[59]	7 877[59]
50 - 54	138 878	107 339	31 539	116 519[59]	89 983[59]	26 536[59]	22 359[59]	17 356[59]	5 003[59]
55 - 59	67 107	51 303	15 804	55 810[59]	42 788[59]	13 022[59]	11 297[59]	8 515[59]	2 782[59]
60 - 64	27 347	18 820	8 527	22 157[59]	15 510[59]	6 647[59]	5 190[59]	3 310[59]	1 880[59]
65 - 69	14 457	9 172	5 285	10 515[59]	6 623[59]	3 892[59]	3 942[59]	2 549[59]	1 393[59]
70 - 74	9 404	5 391	4 013	6 421[59]	3 659[59]	2 762[59]	2 983[59]	1 732[59]	1 251[59]
75 +[59]	...	...	...	8 631	4 532	4 099	4 441	2 377	2 064
75 - 79	4 277	2 440	1 837	...	...	...	...	...	...
80 - 84	2 976	1 537	1 439	...	...	...	...	...	...
85 +	2 415	1 250	1 165	...	...	...	...	...	...
Unknown - Inconnu	3 404	1 682	1 722	...	...	...	...	...	...
Uzbekistan - Ouzbékistan[12]									
1 VII 2003 (ESDF)									
Total	25 567 663	12 809 713	12 757 950	...	...	...	...	...	...
0 - 4	2 584 779	1 257 871	1 326 908	...	...	...	...	...	...
5 - 9	3 057 832	1 492 224	1 565 608	...	...	...	...	...	...
10 - 14	3 247 432	1 593 319	1 654 113	...	...	...	...	...	...
15 - 19	3 036 011	1 502 977	1 533 033	...	...	...	...	...	...
20 - 24	2 440 283	1 210 643	1 229 640	...	...	...	...	...	...
25 - 29	2 077 200	1 032 960	1 044 240	...	...	...	...	...	...
30 - 34	1 852 315	929 765	922 550	...	...	...	...	...	...
35 - 39	1 654 410	848 383	806 026	...	...	...	...	...	...
40 - 44	1 586 930	807 669	779 261	...	...	...	...	...	...
45 - 49	1 170 247	595 727	574 520	...	...	...	...	...	...
50 - 54	821 154	423 337	397 817	...	...	...	...	...	...
55 - 59	426 436	218 173	208 263	...	...	...	...	...	...
60 - 64	499 732	256 051	243 680	...	...	...	...	...	...
65 - 69	416 696	220 394	196 302	...	...	...	...	...	...
70 - 74	324 533	182 720	141 812	...	...	...	...	...	...
75 +	371 669	237 497	134 172	...	...	...	...	...	...
Viet Nam									
1 IV 2009 (CDJC)									
Total	85 846 997	42 413 143	43 433 854	25 436 896	12 349 995	13 086 901	60 410 101	30 063 148	30 346 953
0 - 4	7 034 144	3 662 889	3 371 255	1 949 105	1 019 547	929 558	5 085 039	2 643 342	2 441 697
5 - 9	6 710 737	3 458 159	3 252 578	1 757 679	910 339	847 340	4 953 058	2 547 820	2 405 238
10 - 14	7 248 378	3 725 369	3 523 009	1 761 650	904 731	856 919	5 486 728	2 820 638	2 666 090
15 - 17	5 236 771	2 681 653	2 555 118	1 311 350	662 369	648 981	3 925 421	2 019 284	1 906 137
18 - 19	3 727 131	1 896 261	1 830 870	1 188 578	562 169	626 409	2 538 553	1 334 092	1 204 461
20 - 24	8 432 867	4 253 618	4 179 249	2 759 456	1 305 436	1 454 020	5 673 411	2 948 182	2 725 229
25 - 29	7 790 003	3 904 730	3 885 273	2 519 920	1 205 518	1 314 402	5 270 083	2 699 212	2 570 871
30 - 34	6 868 158	3 462 905	3 405 253	2 164 824	1 062 838	1 101 986	4 703 334	2 400 067	2 303 267
35 - 39	6 531 607	3 298 266	3 233 341	2 059 356	1 027 075	1 032 281	4 472 251	2 271 191	2 201 060
40 - 44	5 966 856	2 967 934	2 998 922	1 818 188	896 290	921 898	4 148 668	2 071 644	2 077 024
45 - 49	5 450 928	2 642 466	2 808 462	1 728 008	840 047	887 961	3 722 920	1 802 419	1 920 501
50 - 54	4 412 051	2 082 098	2 329 953	1 435 970	683 749	752 221	2 976 081	1 398 349	1 577 732
55 - 59	2 984 619	1 364 319	1 620 300	931 382	421 296	510 086	2 053 237	943 023	1 110 214
60 - 64	1 937 948	861 897	1 076 051	590 161	259 193	330 968	1 347 787	602 704	745 083
65 - 69	1 554 678	653 287	901 391	453 756	195 857	257 899	1 100 922	457 430	643 492
70 - 74	1 412 538	568 312	844 226	378 105	155 224	222 881	1 034 433	413 088	621 345
75 - 79	1 198 893	480 088	718 805	306 226	125 948	180 278	892 667	354 140	538 527
80 - 84	725 985	264 997	460 988	182 550	69 573	112 977	543 435	195 424	348 011
85 +	622 705	183 895	438 810	140 632	42 796	97 836	482 073	141 099	340 974
1 VII 2012 (ESDF)									
Total	88 772 884	43 907 154	44 865 730	28 356 363	...	...	60 416 521	...	...
0	1 482 738	787 056	695 682	439 680	...	...	1 043 058	...	...
1 - 4	5 686 701	3 002 821	2 683 880	1 696 249	...	...	3 990 452	...	...
5 - 9	7 060 251	3 673 999	3 386 252	2 140 169	...	...	4 920 082	...	...
10 - 14	6 965 948	3 585 316	3 380 632	2 136 624	...	...	4 829 324	...	...

209

Continent, country or area, date, code and age (in years) / Continent, pays ou zone, date, code et âge (en années)	Total			Urban - Urbaine			Rural - Rurale		
	Both sexes Les deux sexes	Male Masculin	Female Féminin	Both sexes Les deux sexes	Male Masculin	Female Féminin	Both sexes Les deux sexes	Male Masculin	Female Féminin
ASIA - ASIE									
Viet Nam									
1 VII 2012 (ESDF)									
15 - 17	4 669 832	2 415 728	2 254 104	1 424 635	...	...	3 245 197	...	...
18 - 19	2 946 524	1 503 216	1 443 308	912 202	...	...	2 034 322	...	...
20 - 24	7 445 153	3 773 762	3 671 391	2 320 402	...	...	5 124 751	...	...
25 - 29	7 722 537	3 849 246	3 873 291	2 448 020	...	...	5 274 517	...	...
30 - 34	6 989 840	3 466 001	3 523 839	2 227 160	...	...	4 762 680	...	...
35 - 39	6 758 412	3 361 241	3 397 171	2 147 101	...	...	4 611 311	...	...
40 - 44	6 436 678	3 210 198	3 226 480	2 039 219	...	...	4 397 459	...	...
45 - 49	6 045 972	3 051 198	2 994 774	1 892 767	...	...	4 153 205	...	...
50 - 54	5 497 739	2 564 831	2 932 908	1 853 707	...	...	3 644 032	...	...
55 - 59	4 022 901	1 878 962	2 143 939	1 355 050	...	...	2 667 851	...	...
60 - 64	2 720 613	1 224 439	1 496 174	945 646	...	...	1 774 967	...	...
65 - 69	1 707 476	748 724	958 752	605 976	...	...	1 101 500	...	...
70 - 74	1 590 568	663 039	927 529	586 247	...	...	1 004 321	...	...
75 - 79	1 285 283	525 035	760 248	480 519	...	...	804 764	...	...
80 +	1 737 718	622 342	1 115 376	704 990	...	...	1 032 728	...	...
Yemen - Yémen[2]									
1 VII 2010 (ESDJ)									
Total	23 153 982	11 789 814	11 364 168	...	...	...	...	...	...
0	817 680	416 689	400 991	...	...	...	...	...	...
1 - 4	2 996 197	1 531 202	1 464 995	...	...	...	...	...	...
5 - 9	3 000 321	1 529 232	1 471 089	...	...	...	...	...	...
10 - 14	2 993 227	1 542 898	1 450 329	...	...	...	...	...	...
15 - 19	2 882 648	1 501 230	1 381 419	...	...	...	...	...	...
20 - 24	2 484 944	1 289 016	1 195 928	...	...	...	...	...	...
25 - 29	1 886 895	957 595	929 300	...	...	...	...	...	...
30 - 34	1 470 872	736 311	734 560	...	...	...	...	...	...
35 - 39	1 042 186	513 060	529 126	...	...	...	...	...	...
40 - 44	821 193	399 146	422 047	...	...	...	...	...	...
45 - 49	712 596	344 131	368 465	...	...	...	...	...	...
50 - 54	572 054	277 996	294 058	...	...	...	...	...	...
55 - 59	418 294	211 094	207 200	...	...	...	...	...	...
60 - 64	321 946	165 138	156 808	...	...	...	...	...	...
65 - 69	249 056	127 706	121 350	...	...	...	...	...	...
70 - 74	185 783	95 288	90 495	...	...	...	...	...	...
75 - 79	131 164	66 718	64 446	...	...	...	...	...	...
80 +	166 924	85 363	81 561	...	...	...	...	...	...
EUROPE									
Åland Islands - Îles d'Åland[19]									
1 VII 2012 (ESDJ)									
Total	28 429	14 172	14 257	11 305	5 408	5 897	17 124	8 764	8 361
0	294	141	153	106	50	57	188	92	97
1 - 4	1 206	626	580	401	213	188	805	414	392
5 - 9	1 562	810	753	517	261	257	1 045	549	496
10 - 14	1 594	839	755	552	284	268	1 042	555	487
15 - 19	1 695	851	844	679	331	349	1 016	521	495
20 - 24	1 544	848	696	731	397	334	813	451	362
25 - 29	1 542	795	747	763	396	367	780	400	380
30 - 34	1 687	879	808	751	395	356	936	484	452
35 - 39	1 812	932	881	698	354	345	1 114	578	536
40 - 44	1 956	972	984	729	341	388	1 227	631	596
45 - 49	2 086	1 038	1 049	778	358	421	1 308	680	628
50 - 54	1 953	949	1 004	748	338	410	1 205	611	594
55 - 59	2 046	981	1 065	828	378	451	1 218	604	614
60 - 64	2 013	987	1 026	814	364	450	1 200	624	576
65 - 69	1 822	930	893	733	352	382	1 089	578	511
70 - 74	1 231	637	595	486	239	248	745	398	347
75 - 79	940	428	513	386	160	226	554	268	287
80 - 84	686	303	384	269	113	157	417	190	227
85 - 89	512	171	341	221	68	153	291	103	188
90 - 94	197	47	150	94	19	75	103	28	75

7. Population by age, sex and urban/rural residence: latest available year, 2003 - 2012
Population selon l'âge, le sexe et la résidence, urbaine/rurale : dernière année disponible, 2003 - 2012 (continued - suite)

Continent, country or area, date, code and age (in years) / Continent, pays ou zone, date, code et âge (en années)	Total			Urban - Urbaine			Rural - Rurale		
	Both sexes Les deux sexes	Male Masculin	Female Féminin	Both sexes Les deux sexes	Male Masculin	Female Féminin	Both sexes Les deux sexes	Male Masculin	Female Féminin
EUROPE									
Åland Islands - Îles d'Åland[19]									
1 VII 2012 (ESDJ)									
95 - 99	49	11	38	24	5	19	25	7	19
100 +	7	2	5	1	-	1	6	2	5
Albania - Albanie									
1 VII 2012 (ESDF)									
Total	2 801 682	1 404 175	1 397 507	1 514 746	750 821	763 925	1 286 936	653 354	633 582
0 - 4	163 855	85 693	78 162	83 744	43 947	39 796	80 112	41 746	38 366
5 - 9	178 004	93 726	84 278	90 805	48 044	42 761	87 199	45 682	41 517
10 - 14	227 257	117 421	109 836	115 729	59 835	55 894	111 528	57 587	53 942
15 - 19	265 886	134 326	131 559	136 173	67 546	68 627	129 712	66 780	62 932
20 - 24	239 889	126 471	113 418	130 556	65 773	64 783	109 333	60 697	48 636
25 - 29	191 060	99 354	91 706	106 558	53 220	53 338	84 502	46 134	38 369
30 - 34	168 071	81 430	86 641	92 666	44 520	48 146	75 405	36 910	38 495
35 - 39	166 870	78 715	88 155	92 398	43 862	48 536	74 472	34 853	39 619
40 - 44	185 737	88 410	97 327	102 326	48 771	53 555	83 410	39 638	43 772
45 - 49	193 589	94 696	98 893	106 043	51 746	54 297	87 546	42 950	44 596
50 - 54	197 092	98 281	98 811	109 212	54 618	54 594	87 880	43 663	44 217
55 - 59	167 461	83 672	83 789	96 729	47 829	48 899	70 733	35 843	34 890
60 - 64	133 161	67 247	65 914	76 015	38 025	37 989	57 146	29 221	27 924
65 - 69	102 980	51 957	51 024	56 587	27 946	28 640	46 394	24 010	22 383
70 - 74	95 415	46 639	48 776	51 767	25 023	26 743	43 648	21 615	22 033
75 - 79	65 529	32 076	33 453	35 968	17 310	18 657	29 561	14 766	14 795
80 - 84	35 703	15 734	19 970	19 175	8 294	10 882	16 528	7 440	9 088
85 +	24 122	8 328	15 794	12 296	4 511	7 785	11 826	3 817	8 009
Andorra - Andorre[60]									
1 VII 2011 (ESDJ)									
Total	79 280	40 529	38 751	...	...	...	...	...	...
0	279	138	141	...	...	...	...	...	...
1 - 4	3 078	1 545	1 533	...	...	...	...	...	...
5 - 9	4 070	2 134	1 936	...	...	...	...	...	...
10 - 14	4 282	2 223	2 059	...	...	...	...	...	...
15 - 19	3 814	2 043	1 771	...	...	...	...	...	...
20 - 24	3 844	1 953	1 891	...	...	...	...	...	...
25 - 29	5 328	2 623	2 705	...	...	...	...	...	...
30 - 34	6 985	3 511	3 474	...	...	...	...	...	...
35 - 39	7 749	3 907	3 842	...	...	...	...	...	...
40 - 44	7 385	3 776	3 609	...	...	...	...	...	...
45 - 49	7 186	3 694	3 492	...	...	...	...	...	...
50 - 54	5 977	3 132	2 845	...	...	...	...	...	...
55 - 59	4 822	2 569	2 253	...	...	...	...	...	...
60 - 64	3 972	2 142	1 830	...	...	...	...	...	...
65 - 69	3 078	1 631	1 447	...	...	...	...	...	...
70 - 74	2 152	1 062	1 090	...	...	...	...	...	...
75 - 79	1 868	926	942	...	...	...	...	...	...
80 - 84	1 614	753	861	...	...	...	...	...	...
85 - 89	1 013	437	576	...	...	...	...	...	...
90 - 94	479	192	287	...	...	...	...	...	...
95 - 99	196	78	118	...	...	...	...	...	...
100 +	109	60	49	...	...	...	...	...	...
Austria - Autriche									
1 I 2012 (ESDJ)									
Total	8 443 018	4 118 035	4 324 983	...	...	...	...	...	...
0	77 608	40 085	37 523	...	...	...	...	...	...
1 - 4	316 239	162 200	154 039	...	...	...	...	...	...
5 - 9	406 309	207 883	198 426	...	...	...	...	...	...
10 - 14	424 205	217 467	206 738	...	...	...	...	...	...
15 - 19	489 618	251 511	238 107	...	...	...	...	...	...
20 - 24	531 963	269 844	262 119	...	...	...	...	...	...
25 - 29	555 674	279 148	276 526	...	...	...	...	...	...
30 - 34	545 679	274 319	271 360	...	...	...	...	...	...
35 - 39	567 151	281 762	285 389	...	...	...	...	...	...
40 - 44	677 979	340 034	337 945	...	...	...	...	...	...
45 - 49	714 875	360 578	354 297	...	...	...	...	...	...
50 - 54	633 398	317 246	316 152	...	...	...	...	...	...

Continent, country or area, date, code and age (in years) / Continent, pays ou zone, date, code et âge (en annèes)	Total			Urban - Urbaine			Rural - Rurale		
	Both sexes Les deux sexes	Male Masculin	Female Féminin	Both sexes Les deux sexes	Male Masculin	Female Féminin	Both sexes Les deux sexes	Male Masculin	Female Féminin
EUROPE									
Austria - Autriche									
1 I 2012 (ESDJ)									
55 - 59	523 036	255 978	267 058	...	...	...	...	...	...
60 - 64	480 380	231 890	248 490	...	...	...	...	...	...
65 - 69	403 773	189 776	213 997	...	...	...	...	...	...
70 - 74	415 388	190 408	224 980	...	...	...	...	...	...
75 - 79	262 189	111 153	151 036	...	...	...	...	...	...
80 - 84	218 044	83 271	134 773	...	...	...	...	...	...
85 - 89	141 454	40 230	101 224	...	...	...	...	...	...
90 - 94	47 626	11 249	36 377	...	...	...	...	...	...
95 - 99	9 232	1 790	7 442	...	...	...	...	...	...
100 +	1 198	213	985	...	...	...	...	...	...
Belarus - Bélarus[61]									
1 VII 2011 (ESDJ)									
Total	9 473 172	4 403 227	5 069 945	7 148 636	3 303 932	3 844 704	2 324 536	1 099 295	1 225 241
0	108 269	55 732	52 537	83 060	42 702	40 358	25 209	13 030	12 179
1 - 4	417 583	215 070	202 513	323 354	166 613	156 741	94 229	48 457	45 772
5 - 9	442 834	227 317	215 517	337 094	173 258	163 836	105 740	54 059	51 681
10 - 14	452 715	232 517	220 198	329 865	169 490	160 375	122 850	63 027	59 823
15 - 19	566 558	291 416	275 142	461 000	233 092	227 908	105 558	58 324	47 234
20 - 24	749 636	385 381	364 255	620 767	312 785	307 982	128 869	72 596	56 273
25 - 29	768 846	390 486	378 360	632 453	316 586	315 867	136 393	73 900	62 493
30 - 34	691 664	345 761	345 903	562 907	278 743	284 164	128 757	67 018	61 739
35 - 39	663 581	324 426	339 155	515 922	248 384	267 538	147 659	76 042	71 617
40 - 44	649 998	312 880	337 118	485 774	227 347	258 427	164 224	85 533	78 691
45 - 49	723 584	344 207	379 377	541 112	247 577	293 535	182 472	96 630	85 842
50 - 54	775 147	360 662	414 485	582 756	259 670	323 086	192 391	100 992	91 399
55 - 59	638 325	283 790	354 535	485 888	208 003	277 885	152 437	75 787	76 650
60 - 64	522 218	220 818	301 400	392 927	162 176	230 751	129 291	58 642	70 649
65 - 69	299 534	115 147	184 387	203 628	79 149	124 479	95 906	35 998	59 908
70 - 74	399 725	135 855	263 870	255 193	87 711	167 482	144 532	48 144	96 388
75 - 79	284 022	85 115	198 907	156 127	47 078	109 049	127 895	38 037	89 858
80 - 84	208 426	54 870	153 556	113 689	30 236	83 453	94 737	24 634	70 103
85 +	110 507	21 777	88 730	65 120	13 332	51 788	45 387	8 445	36 942
Belgium - Belgique									
1 VII 2009 (ESDJ)									
Total	10 796 493	5 290 436	5 506 057	10 641 089	5 212 557	5 428 532	155 404	77 879	77 525
0	126 739	64 957	61 782	124 924	64 003	60 921	1 815	954	860
1 - 4	496 397	253 965	242 432	489 130	250 206	238 924	7 267	3 759	3 509
5 - 9	593 754	303 278	290 476	584 255	298 464	285 791	9 499	4 814	4 686
10 - 14	606 666	309 906	296 761	596 950	304 933	292 017	9 716	4 973	4 744
15 - 19	652 339	332 874	319 466	641 965	327 569	314 396	10 374	5 305	5 070
20 - 24	655 729	328 943	326 786	646 318	324 129	322 189	9 412	4 815	4 597
25 - 29	691 348	345 642	345 706	682 681	341 256	341 425	8 667	4 387	4 281
30 - 34	693 603	349 074	344 529	684 702	344 543	340 159	8 901	4 531	4 370
35 - 39	752 230	380 458	371 773	741 537	375 028	366 509	10 694	5 430	5 264
40 - 44	795 637	403 721	391 916	781 272	396 282	384 990	14 365	7 439	6 926
45 - 49	815 462	411 301	404 161	806 061	406 393	399 668	9 401	4 908	4 493
50 - 54	760 344	380 695	379 649	749 566	375 081	374 485	10 778	5 614	5 165
55 - 59	684 930	341 607	343 323	675 427	336 660	338 767	9 503	4 948	4 556
60 - 64	622 850	306 371	316 479	614 303	301 982	312 321	8 547	4 390	4 158
65 - 69	463 205	221 118	242 087	456 669	217 893	238 776	6 537	3 226	3 311
70 - 74	452 948	206 729	246 219	446 363	203 640	242 723	6 585	3 089	3 496
75 - 79	407 388	172 000	235 388	401 600	169 449	232 152	5 788	2 552	3 236
80 - 84	296 075	110 773	185 302	291 690	109 037	182 653	4 386	1 736	2 650
85 - 89	171 159	54 035	117 124	168 777	53 215	115 562	2 382	821	1 562
90 - 94	42 880	10 488	32 393	42 262	10 325	31 937	618	163	456
95 - 99	13 296	2 327	10 970	13 139	2 297	10 843	157	30	127
100 +	1 519	179	1 341	1 504	178	1 327	15	1	14
Bosnia and Herzegovina - Bosnie-Herzégovine									
1 VII 2010 (ESDF)									
Total	3 843 126	1 877 587	1 965 539	...	...	...	...	...	...
0 - 4	166 571	85 617	80 954	...	...	...	...	...	...
5 - 9	229 608	117 330	112 278	...	...	...	...	...	...

Continent, country or area, date, code and age (in years) / Continent, pays ou zone, date, code et âge (en années)	Total			Urban - Urbaine			Rural - Rurale		
	Both sexes Les deux sexes	Male Masculin	Female Féminin	Both sexes Les deux sexes	Male Masculin	Female Féminin	Both sexes Les deux sexes	Male Masculin	Female Féminin

EUROPE

Bosnia and Herzegovina - Bosnie-Herzégovine
1 VII 2010 (ESDF)

10 - 14	274 779	139 862	134 917	...	...	...	...	...	...
15 - 19	279 370	146 390	132 980	...	...	...	...	...	...
20 - 24	284 994	144 777	140 217	...	...	...	...	...	...
25 - 29	268 273	131 991	136 282	...	...	...	...	...	...
30 - 34	240 986	120 975	120 011	...	...	...	...	...	...
35 - 39	246 721	121 633	125 088	...	...	...	...	...	...
40 - 44	283 887	141 943	141 944	...	...	...	...	...	...
45 - 49	306 958	150 410	156 548	...	...	...	...	...	...
50 - 54	266 575	135 687	130 888	...	...	...	...	...	...
55 - 59	231 595	105 145	126 450	...	...	...	...	...	...
60 - 64	182 787	86 092	96 695	...	...	...	...	...	...
65 - 69	202 274	90 012	112 262	...	...	...	...	...	...
70 - 74	184 389	82 422	101 967	...	...	...	...	...	...
75 - 79	120 364	50 553	69 811	...	...	...	...	...	...
80 - 84	47 932	19 605	28 327	...	...	...	...	...	...
85 +	25 063	7 143	17 920	...	...	...	...	...	...

Bulgaria - Bulgarie
1 II 2011 (CDJC)

Total	7 364 570	3 586 571	3 777 999	5 338 261	2 580 734	2 757 527	2 026 309	1 005 837	1 020 472
0	66 465	34 235	32 230	49 658	25 518	24 140	16 807	8 717	8 090
1 - 4	276 698	142 248	134 450	203 696	104 800	98 896	73 002	37 448	35 554
5 - 9	316 643	163 076	153 567	228 112	117 347	110 765	88 531	45 729	42 802
10 - 14	315 466	162 159	153 307	227 198	116 532	110 666	88 268	45 627	42 641
15 - 19	377 585	194 099	183 486	274 906	140 192	134 714	102 679	53 907	48 772
20 - 24	488 807	251 720	237 087	380 603	193 264	187 339	108 204	58 456	49 748
25 - 29	491 088	255 616	235 472	381 492	196 083	185 409	109 596	59 533	50 063
30 - 34	533 945	276 726	257 219	418 744	214 733	204 011	115 201	61 993	53 208
35 - 39	545 332	281 170	264 162	425 332	216 578	208 754	120 000	64 592	55 408
40 - 44	513 814	263 969	249 845	390 370	196 935	193 435	123 444	67 034	56 410
45 - 49	495 672	251 056	244 616	369 769	183 121	186 648	125 903	67 935	57 968
50 - 54	516 851	256 509	260 342	383 322	185 706	197 616	133 529	70 803	62 726
55 - 59	523 827	251 297	272 530	383 315	180 295	203 020	140 512	71 002	69 510
60 - 64	540 980	248 710	292 270	377 388	171 509	205 879	163 592	77 201	86 391
65 - 69	415 431	182 565	232 866	267 070	116 661	150 409	148 361	65 904	82 457
70 - 74	345 327	143 726	201 601	211 594	86 511	125 083	133 733	57 215	76 518
75 - 79	301 851	119 774	182 077	181 141	69 275	111 866	120 710	50 499	70 211
80 - 84	191 309	71 526	119 783	118 410	43 485	74 925	72 899	28 041	44 858
85 - 89	86 822	29 824	56 998	53 404	18 145	35 259	33 418	11 679	21 739
90 - 94	17 341	5 581	11 760	10 683	3 417	7 266	6 658	2 164	4 494
95 - 99	3 078	905	2 173	1 904	576	1 328	1 174	329	845
100 +	238	80	158	150	51	99	88	29	59

Croatia - Croatie
1 IV 2011 (CDFC)

Total	4 284 889	2 066 335	2 218 554	...	...	...	...	...	...
0 - 4	212 709	109 251	103 458	...	...	...	...	...	...
5 - 9	204 317	104 841	99 476	...	...	...	...	...	...
10 - 14	235 402	120 633	114 769	...	...	...	...	...	...
15 - 19	244 177	124 918	119 259	...	...	...	...	...	...
20 - 24	261 658	133 455	128 203	...	...	...	...	...	...
25 - 29	289 066	147 416	141 650	...	...	...	...	...	...
30 - 34	294 619	149 998	144 621	...	...	...	...	...	...
35 - 39	284 754	143 984	140 770	...	...	...	...	...	...
40 - 44	286 933	143 603	143 330	...	...	...	...	...	...
45 - 49	307 561	152 446	155 115	...	...	...	...	...	...
50 - 54	320 502	157 981	162 521	...	...	...	...	...	...
55 - 59	311 818	153 750	158 068	...	...	...	...	...	...
60 - 64	272 740	127 851	144 889	...	...	...	...	...	...
65 - 69	202 002	89 364	112 638	...	...	...	...	...	...
70 - 74	212 401	88 912	123 489	...	...	...	...	...	...
75 - 79	175 526	66 456	109 070	...	...	...	...	...	...
80 - 84	108 104	35 999	72 105	...	...	...	...	...	...
85 - 89	47 641	12 415	35 226	...	...	...	...	...	...

7. Population by age, sex and urban/rural residence: latest available year, 2003 - 2012
Population selon l'âge, le sexe et la résidence, urbaine/rurale : dernière année disponible, 2003 - 2012 (continued - suite)

Continent, country or area, date, code and age (in years) / Continent, pays ou zone, date, code et âge (en années)	Total			Urban - Urbaine			Rural - Rurale		
	Both sexes Les deux sexes	Male Masculin	Female Féminin	Both sexes Les deux sexes	Male Masculin	Female Féminin	Both sexes Les deux sexes	Male Masculin	Female Féminin
EUROPE									
Croatia - Croatie									
1 IV 2011 (CDFC)									
90 - 94	10 758	2 580	8 178	...	...	...	...	...	...
95 - 99	2 003	446	1 557	...	...	...	...	...	...
100 +	198	36	162	...	...	...	...	...	...
Czech Republic - République tchèque									
1 I 2012 (ESDJ)									
Total	10 505 445	5 158 210	5 347 235	7 684 940	3 742 560	3 942 380	2 820 505	1 415 650	1 404 855
0	108 753	55 809	52 944	79 377	40 791	38 586	29 376	15 018	14 358
1 - 4	481 937	246 478	235 459	349 738	178 742	170 996	132 199	67 736	64 463
5 - 9	497 702	255 816	241 886	354 390	182 219	172 171	143 312	73 597	69 715
10 - 14	452 849	232 831	220 018	318 514	163 455	155 059	134 335	69 376	64 959
15 - 19	541 105	277 548	263 557	381 320	195 000	186 320	159 785	82 548	77 237
20 - 24	671 462	343 291	328 171	490 644	250 122	240 522	180 818	93 169	87 649
25 - 29	721 200	371 423	349 777	536 389	276 172	260 217	184 811	95 251	89 560
30 - 34	847 314	436 174	411 140	625 004	321 341	303 663	222 310	114 833	107 477
35 - 39	918 039	471 945	446 094	668 049	340 997	327 052	249 990	130 948	119 042
40 - 44	718 925	369 407	349 518	524 435	265 968	258 467	194 490	103 439	91 051
45 - 49	705 709	360 052	345 657	519 776	261 642	258 134	185 933	98 410	87 523
50 - 54	649 679	326 608	323 071	473 995	235 101	238 894	175 684	91 507	84 177
55 - 59	745 595	365 375	380 220	546 209	263 638	282 571	199 386	101 737	97 649
60 - 64	743 740	353 999	389 741	544 642	254 748	289 894	199 098	99 251	99 847
65 - 69	595 116	270 918	324 198	446 112	199 595	246 517	149 004	71 323	77 681
70 - 74	402 749	173 096	229 653	301 119	128 608	172 511	101 630	44 488	57 142
75 - 79	307 188	120 556	186 632	228 005	89 173	138 832	79 183	31 383	47 800
80 - 84	234 820	81 828	152 992	175 118	61 027	114 091	59 702	20 801	38 901
85 - 89	124 404	36 168	88 236	93 835	27 452	66 383	30 569	8 716	21 853
90 - 94	31 495	7 734	23 761	24 009	5 902	18 107	7 486	1 832	5 654
95 - 99	5 050	1 027	4 023	3 799	767	3 032	1 251	260	991
100 +	614	127	487	461	100	361	153	27	126
Denmark - Danemark[62]									
1 VII 2012 (ESDJ)									
Total	5 587 085	2 771 208	2 815 877	...	...	...	...	...	...
0	58 446	29 933	28 513	...	...	...	...	...	...
1 - 4	258 100	132 408	125 692	...	...	...	...	...	...
5 - 9	328 240	168 139	160 101	...	...	...	...	...	...
10 - 14	336 237	171 883	164 354	...	...	...	...	...	...
15 - 19	358 229	183 824	174 405	...	...	...	...	...	...
20 - 24	350 391	178 642	171 749	...	...	...	...	...	...
25 - 29	318 444	160 939	157 505	...	...	...	...	...	...
30 - 34	330 806	165 807	164 999	...	...	...	...	...	...
35 - 39	376 280	188 230	188 050	...	...	...	...	...	...
40 - 44	390 397	197 107	193 290	...	...	...	...	...	...
45 - 49	425 853	215 745	210 108	...	...	...	...	...	...
50 - 54	372 104	187 133	184 971	...	...	...	...	...	...
55 - 59	352 831	176 145	176 686	...	...	...	...	...	...
60 - 64	344 428	170 610	173 818	...	...	...	...	...	...
65 - 69	348 453	171 243	177 210	...	...	...	...	...	...
70 - 74	235 828	112 161	123 667	...	...	...	...	...	...
75 - 79	170 262	76 688	93 574	...	...	...	...	...	...
80 - 84	117 745	48 572	69 173	...	...	...	...	...	...
85 - 89	73 619	25 617	48 002	...	...	...	...	...	...
90 - 94	31 865	8 698	23 167	...	...	...	...	...	...
95 - 99	7 565	1 532	6 033	...	...	...	...	...	...
100 +	962	152	810	...	...	...	...	...	...
Estonia - Estonie									
31 XII 2011 (CDJC)									
Total	1 294 455	600 526	693 929	879 157	396 719	482 438	415 298	203 807	211 491
0 - 4	75 497	38 738	36 759	48 978	25 073	23 905	26 519	13 665	12 854
5 - 9	65 758	33 806	31 952	41 967	21 445	20 522	23 791	12 361	11 430
10 - 14	58 636	30 344	28 292	36 711	18 957	17 754	21 925	11 387	10 538
15 - 19	67 639	34 673	32 966	42 451	21 388	21 063	25 188	13 285	11 903
20 - 24	94 294	48 553	45 741	68 958	34 173	34 785	25 336	14 380	10 956
25 - 29	92 924	47 365	45 559	69 161	34 920	34 241	23 763	12 445	11 318

7. Population by age, sex and urban/rural residence: latest available year, 2003 - 2012
Population selon l'âge, le sexe et la résidence, urbaine/rurale : dernière année disponible, 2003 - 2012 (continued - suite)

Continent, country or area, date, code and age (in years) / Continent, pays ou zone, date, code et âge (en années)	Total			Urban - Urbaine			Rural - Rurale		
	Both sexes Les deux sexes	Male Masculin	Female Féminin	Both sexes Les deux sexes	Male Masculin	Female Féminin	Both sexes Les deux sexes	Male Masculin	Female Féminin
EUROPE									
Estonia - Estonie									
31 XII 2011 (CDJC)									
30 - 34	88 648	45 166	43 482	62 145	31 454	30 691	26 503	13 712	12 791
35 - 39	89 773	45 297	44 476	60 582	29 985	30 597	29 191	15 312	13 879
40 - 44	88 227	43 587	44 640	57 636	27 783	29 853	30 591	15 804	14 787
45 - 49	85 869	41 570	44 299	56 863	26 451	30 412	29 006	15 119	13 887
50 - 54	91 535	42 825	48 710	61 842	27 597	34 245	29 693	15 228	14 465
55 - 59	86 426	38 739	47 687	59 412	25 274	34 138	27 014	13 465	13 549
60 - 64	79 789	33 882	45 907	54 856	22 111	32 745	24 933	11 771	13 162
65 - 69	57 796	23 085	34 711	37 939	14 341	23 598	19 857	8 744	11 113
70 - 74	65 471	23 452	42 019	45 603	15 606	29 997	19 868	7 846	12 022
75 - 79	47 683	15 229	32 454	32 924	10 170	22 754	14 759	5 059	9 700
80 - 84	35 617	9 731	25 886	25 365	6 864	18 501	10 252	2 867	7 385
85 - 89	17 320	3 571	13 749	12 097	2 497	9 600	5 223	1 074	4 149
90 - 94	4 483	756	3 727	3 009	524	2 485	1 474	232	1 242
95 - 99	944	138	806	574	91	483	370	47	323
100 +	126	19	107	84	15	69	42	4	38
Faeroe Islands - Îles Féroé									
1 VII 2008 (ESDJ)									
Total	48 618	25 263	23 355	17 624	8 920	8 704	30 994	16 343	14 651
0	679	331	348	246	122	124	433	209	224
1 - 4	2 805	1 424	1 381	1 014	501	513	1 791	923	868
5 - 9	3 555	1 862	1 693	1 334	695	639	2 221	1 167	1 054
10 - 14	3 656	1 872	1 784	1 388	699	689	2 268	1 173	1 095
15 - 19	3 971	2 055	1 916	1 470	769	701	2 501	1 286	1 215
20 - 24	2 976	1 669	1 307	1 009	549	460	1 967	1 120	847
25 - 29	2 542	1 400	1 142	881	465	416	1 661	935	726
30 - 34	2 994	1 639	1 355	1 093	589	504	1 901	1 050	851
35 - 39	3 205	1 689	1 516	1 172	578	594	2 033	1 111	922
40 - 44	3 594	1 936	1 658	1 510	792	718	2 084	1 144	940
45 - 49	3 278	1 702	1 576	1 258	657	601	2 020	1 045	975
50 - 54	3 033	1 572	1 461	1 140	559	581	1 893	1 013	880
55 - 59	2 973	1 553	1 420	1 091	548	543	1 882	1 005	877
60 - 64	2 535	1 383	1 152	856	448	408	1 679	935	744
65 - 69	2 053	1 076	977	686	337	349	1 367	739	628
70 - 74	1 522	782	740	485	236	249	1 037	546	491
75 - 79	1 358	635	723	420	186	234	938	449	489
80 - 84	1 003	386	617	298	113	185	705	273	432
85 - 89	590	202	388	163	50	113	427	152	275
90 - 94	246	81	165	93	24	69	153	57	96
95 - 99	45	11	34	16	3	13	29	8	21
100 +	5	3	2	1	-	1	4	3	1
Finland - Finlande[63]									
1 VII 2011 (ESDJ)									
Total	5 360 091	2 631 431	2 728 660	3 666 940	1 780 188	1 886 752	1 693 152	851 244	841 908
0	60 313	30 842	29 471	42 903	21 975	20 928	17 411	8 867	8 544
1 - 4	240 488	122 939	117 550	166 963	85 239	81 724	73 525	37 700	35 826
5 - 9	289 721	147 994	141 727	194 344	99 319	95 025	95 377	48 675	46 702
10 - 14	293 195	149 729	143 466	192 377	98 099	94 279	100 818	51 631	49 187
15 - 19	328 203	167 359	160 844	222 323	111 590	110 734	105 880	55 769	50 111
20 - 24	328 859	168 225	160 634	257 622	128 589	129 033	71 238	39 637	31 601
25 - 29	344 203	176 834	167 369	268 734	137 101	131 633	75 470	39 733	35 737
30 - 34	338 097	173 609	164 489	254 623	130 608	124 015	83 475	43 001	40 474
35 - 39	315 604	162 148	153 456	228 201	117 361	110 841	87 403	44 788	42 616
40 - 44	342 412	173 900	168 512	239 511	120 956	118 556	102 901	52 944	49 957
45 - 49	374 317	189 267	185 050	254 694	127 231	127 463	119 624	62 036	57 588
50 - 54	371 287	185 818	185 469	244 474	120 060	124 414	126 813	65 759	61 055
55 - 59	381 892	189 016	192 876	247 184	118 387	128 797	134 708	70 629	64 079
60 - 64	396 414	194 477	201 937	256 422	121 654	134 768	139 992	72 823	67 170
65 - 69	287 628	137 396	150 232	186 965	86 692	100 273	100 663	50 704	49 959
70 - 74	230 194	104 102	126 093	144 594	63 409	81 185	85 600	40 693	44 908
75 - 79	179 146	75 126	104 020	109 835	44 453	65 383	69 311	30 674	38 638
80 - 84	142 237	51 675	90 562	85 643	29 832	55 811	56 594	21 843	34 751
85 - 89	80 689	23 413	57 276	48 028	13 302	34 727	32 661	10 111	22 550
90 - 94	28 433	6 403	22 031	17 277	3 679	13 599	11 156	2 724	8 432

Continent, country or area, date, code and age (in years) — Continent, pays ou zone, date, code et âge (en annèes)	Total			Urban - Urbaine			Rural - Rurale		
	Both sexes Les deux sexes	Male Masculin	Female Féminin	Both sexes Les deux sexes	Male Masculin	Female Féminin	Both sexes Les deux sexes	Male Masculin	Female Féminin
EUROPE									
Finland - Finlande[63]									
1 VII 2011 (ESDJ)									
95 - 99	6 129	1 075	5 054	3 820	604	3 216	2 309	472	1 838
100 +	636	89	547	408	53	355	228	36	192
France[64]									
1 VII 2010* (ESDJ)									
Total	62 959 391	30 495 509	32 463 882	...	...	...	...	...	...
0 - 4	3 879 629	1 982 515	1 897 114	...	...	...	...	...	...
5 - 9	3 860 542	1 975 030	1 885 512	...	...	...	...	...	...
10 - 14	3 823 570	1 960 596	1 862 974	...	...	...	...	...	...
15 - 19	3 825 539	1 954 708	1 870 831	...	...	...	...	...	...
20 - 24	3 962 761	1 998 811	1 963 950	...	...	...	...	...	...
25 - 29	3 907 922	1 937 825	1 970 097	...	...	...	...	...	...
30 - 34	3 847 306	1 909 738	1 937 568	...	...	...	...	...	...
35 - 39	4 315 876	2 147 391	2 168 485	...	...	...	...	...	...
40 - 44	4 354 881	2 157 807	2 197 074	...	...	...	...	...	...
45 - 49	4 371 725	2 150 410	2 221 315	...	...	...	...	...	...
50 - 54	4 189 487	2 043 103	2 146 384	...	...	...	...	...	...
55 - 59	4 087 081	1 985 091	2 101 990	...	...	...	...	...	...
60 - 64	3 916 626	1 900 152	2 016 474	...	...	...	...	...	...
65 - 69	2 589 843	1 232 080	1 357 763	...	...	...	...	...	...
70 - 74	2 395 876	1 082 051	1 313 825	...	...	...	...	...	...
75 - 79	2 242 757	937 363	1 305 394	...	...	...	...	...	...
80 - 84	1 774 359	664 431	1 109 928	...	...	...	...	...	...
85 - 89	1 152 329	367 976	784 353	...	...	...	...	...	...
90 - 94	327 379	84 879	242 500	...	...	...	...	...	...
95 - 99	117 579	21 452	96 127	...	...	...	...	...	...
100 +	16 324	2 100	14 224	...	...	...	...	...	...
Germany - Allemagne									
1 I 2012 (ESDJ)									
Total	81 843 743	40 206 663	41 637 080	...	...	...	...	...	...
0	663 026	339 973	323 053	...	...	...	...	...	...
1 - 4	2 745 736	1 407 684	1 338 052	...	...	...	...	...	...
5 - 9	3 515 789	1 803 899	1 711 890	...	...	...	...	...	...
10 - 14	3 907 537	2 004 013	1 903 524	...	...	...	...	...	...
15 - 19	4 080 462	2 094 790	1 985 672	...	...	...	...	...	...
20 - 24	4 959 920	2 537 958	2 421 962	...	...	...	...	...	...
25 - 29	4 990 602	2 543 493	2 447 109	...	...	...	...	...	...
30 - 34	4 942 914	2 505 090	2 437 824	...	...	...	...	...	...
35 - 39	4 785 171	2 425 249	2 359 922	...	...	...	...	...	...
40 - 44	6 363 154	3 247 053	3 116 101	...	...	...	...	...	...
45 - 49	7 137 634	3 646 794	3 490 840	...	...	...	...	...	...
50 - 54	6 422 953	3 244 803	3 178 150	...	...	...	...	...	...
55 - 59	5 550 054	2 754 763	2 795 291	...	...	...	...	...	...
60 - 64	4 898 241	2 403 404	2 494 837	...	...	...	...	...	...
65 - 69	4 039 543	1 943 797	2 095 746	...	...	...	...	...	...
70 - 74	5 001 255	2 322 171	2 679 084	...	...	...	...	...	...
75 - 79	3 438 528	1 497 504	1 941 024	...	...	...	...	...	...
80 - 84	2 367 684	913 112	1 454 572	...	...	...	...	...	...
85 - 89	1 372 711	398 013	974 698	...	...	...	...	...	...
90 - 94	474 751	113 988	360 763	...	...	...	...	...	...
95 - 99	106 922	28 239	78 683	...	...	...	...	...	...
100 +	79 156	30 873	48 283	...	...	...	...	...	...
Greece - Grèce[65]									
1 VII 2011 (ESDF)									
Total	11 300 025	5 595 107	5 704 918	...	...	...	...	...	...
0	109 988	56 663	53 325	...	...	...	...	...	...
1 - 4	461 313	238 012	223 301	...	...	...	...	...	...
5 - 9	534 417	275 898	258 519	...	...	...	...	...	...
10 - 14	519 165	266 804	252 361	...	...	...	...	...	...
15 - 19	558 425	287 457	270 968	...	...	...	...	...	...
20 - 24	600 041	311 297	288 744	...	...	...	...	...	...
25 - 29	725 937	378 064	347 873	...	...	...	...	...	...
30 - 34	849 983	442 567	407 416	...	...	...	...	...	...
35 - 39	873 500	449 280	424 220	...	...	...	...	...	...

Continent, country or area, date, code and age (in years) Continent, pays ou zone, date, code et âge (en années)	Total			Urban - Urbaine			Rural - Rurale		
	Both sexes Les deux sexes	Male Masculin	Female Féminin	Both sexes Les deux sexes	Male Masculin	Female Féminin	Both sexes Les deux sexes	Male Masculin	Female Féminin
EUROPE									
Greece - Grèce[65]									
1 VII 2011 (ESDF)									
40 - 44	890 858	452 927	437 931	...	...	...	...	...	...
45 - 49	808 389	404 404	403 985	...	...	...	...	...	...
50 - 54	787 839	388 845	398 994	...	...	...	...	...	...
55 - 59	714 373	350 900	363 473	...	...	...	...	...	...
60 - 64	665 490	319 801	345 689	...	...	...	...	...	...
65 - 69	554 206	258 951	295 255	...	...	...	...	...	...
70 - 74	557 761	245 251	312 510	...	...	...	...	...	...
75 - 79	507 739	218 083	289 656	...	...	...	...	...	...
80 - 84	362 280	151 502	210 778	...	...	...	...	...	...
85 - 89	162 096	68 593	93 503	...	...	...	...	...	...
90 - 94	47 738	24 390	23 348	...	...	...	...	...	...
95 - 99	5 116	3 273	1 843	...	...	...	...	...	...
100 +	3 371	2 145	1 226	...	...	...	...	...	...
Guernsey - Guernesey									
31 III 2012 (ESDF)									
Total	63 085	31 155	31 930	...	...	...	...	...	...
0 - 4	3 259	1 709	1 550	...	...	...	...	...	...
5 - 9	3 037	1 581	1 456	...	...	...	...	...	...
10 - 14	3 249	1 663	1 586	...	...	...	...	...	...
15 - 19	3 539	1 801	1 738	...	...	...	...	...	...
20 - 24	4 289	2 160	2 129	...	...	...	...	...	...
25 - 29	4 062	2 086	1 976	...	...	...	...	...	...
30 - 34	3 970	2 031	1 939	...	...	...	...	...	...
35 - 39	4 053	1 975	2 078	...	...	...	...	...	...
40 - 44	4 943	2 419	2 524	...	...	...	...	...	...
45 - 49	5 130	2 555	2 575	...	...	...	...	...	...
50 - 54	4 666	2 282	2 384	...	...	...	...	...	...
55 - 59	4 052	2 065	1 987	...	...	...	...	...	...
60 - 64	3 924	1 938	1 986	...	...	...	...	...	...
65 - 69	3 249	1 613	1 636	...	...	...	...	...	...
70 - 74	2 471	1 215	1 256	...	...	...	...	...	...
75 - 79	2 066	929	1 137	...	...	...	...	...	...
80 - 84	1 554	622	932	...	...	...	...	...	...
85 - 89	1 004	358	646	...	...	...	...	...	...
90 - 94	435	126	309	...	...	...	...	...	...
95 - 99	112	17	95	...	...	...	...	...	...
100 +	21	10	11	...	...	...	...	...	...
Hungary - Hongrie									
1 X 2011 (CDFC)									
Total	9 937 628	4 718 479	5 219 149	6 903 858	3 241 911	3 661 947	3 033 770	1 476 568	1 557 202
0 - 4	475 245	243 333	231 912	326 131	166 896	159 235	149 114	76 437	72 677
5 - 9	482 346	247 960	234 386	319 492	164 190	155 302	162 854	83 770	79 084
10 - 14	490 068	251 952	238 116	318 698	163 446	155 252	171 370	88 506	82 864
15 - 19	593 534	304 075	289 459	409 797	208 575	201 222	183 737	95 500	88 237
20 - 24	618 235	317 039	301 196	437 423	221 824	215 599	180 812	95 215	85 597
25 - 29	611 301	310 238	301 063	438 920	219 655	219 265	172 381	90 583	81 798
30 - 34	765 317	385 903	379 414	556 751	278 203	278 548	208 566	107 700	100 866
35 - 39	815 596	412 285	403 311	580 377	290 555	289 822	235 219	121 730	113 489
40 - 44	714 521	358 261	356 260	493 654	244 494	249 160	220 867	113 767	107 100
45 - 49	601 672	297 246	304 426	404 996	196 257	208 739	196 676	100 989	95 687
50 - 54	657 571	315 132	342 439	439 021	204 403	234 618	218 550	110 729	107 821
55 - 59	781 111	364 059	417 052	544 395	246 571	297 824	236 716	117 488	119 228
60 - 64	653 991	293 440	360 551	458 744	201 534	257 210	195 247	91 906	103 341
65 - 69	522 971	221 918	301 053	373 261	157 577	215 684	149 710	64 341	85 369
70 - 74	423 844	162 896	260 948	293 809	113 541	180 268	130 035	49 355	80 680
75 - 79	331 073	115 657	215 416	227 041	80 618	146 423	104 032	35 039	68 993
80 - 84	234 215	73 546	160 669	163 106	52 281	110 825	71 109	21 265	49 844
85 - 89	122 589	33 035	89 554	86 978	23 526	63 452	35 611	9 509	26 102
90 - 94	35 111	8 709	26 402	25 657	6 388	19 269	9 454	2 321	7 133
95 - 99	6 273	1 409	4 864	4 795	1 093	3 702	1 478	316	1 162
100 +	1 044	386	658	812	284	528	232	102	130

7. Population by age, sex and urban/rural residence: latest available year, 2003 - 2012
Population selon l'âge, le sexe et la résidence, urbaine/rurale : dernière année disponible, 2003 - 2012 (continued - suite)

Continent, country or area, date, code and age (in years) / Continent, pays ou zone, date, code et âge (en années)	Total			Urban - Urbaine			Rural - Rurale		
	Both sexes Les deux sexes	Male Masculin	Female Féminin	Both sexes Les deux sexes	Male Masculin	Female Féminin	Both sexes Les deux sexes	Male Masculin	Female Féminin
EUROPE									
Iceland - Islande[66]									
1 VII 2011 (ESDJ)									
Total	319 014	160 185	158 829	314 413	157 797	156 616	4 601	2 389	2 213
0	4 692	2 422	2 270	4 639	2 395	2 244	53	27	26
1 - 4	18 850	9 680	9 171	18 621	9 557	9 064	229	123	107
5 - 9	21 278	10 833	10 445	20 976	10 672	10 304	302	161	141
10 - 14	21 618	10 995	10 623	21 273	10 813	10 460	346	182	164
15 - 19	23 219	11 910	11 309	22 868	11 748	11 120	351	162	189
20 - 24	23 790	12 173	11 617	23 460	11 997	11 463	330	176	154
25 - 29	22 847	11 584	11 263	22 560	11 436	11 124	287	148	140
30 - 34	22 575	11 501	11 074	22 327	11 372	10 955	248	129	119
35 - 39	21 808	11 118	10 690	21 549	10 986	10 563	259	132	127
40 - 44	20 450	10 286	10 165	20 141	10 139	10 002	310	147	163
45 - 49	21 990	10 923	11 067	21 643	10 742	10 902	347	182	165
50 - 54	21 348	10 794	10 554	21 012	10 624	10 389	336	170	166
55 - 59	18 830	9 491	9 339	18 521	9 320	9 201	309	171	138
60 - 64	15 975	8 141	7 835	15 684	7 989	7 695	292	152	140
65 - 69	12 266	6 114	6 152	12 053	5 996	6 057	214	119	95
70 - 74	8 687	4 190	4 497	8 533	4 101	4 432	154	89	65
75 - 79	7 638	3 534	4 105	7 530	3 477	4 053	108	57	52
80 - 84	6 136	2 673	3 463	6 069	2 635	3 434	68	39	29
85 - 89	3 454	1 337	2 117	3 408	1 322	2 087	46	16	30
90 - 94	1 264	414	850	1 251	408	844	13	7	7
95 - 99	261	69	193	257	65	192	4	4	1
100 +	43	7	36	42	7	36	1	1	-
Ireland - Irlande									
10 IV 2011 (CDFC)[67]									
Total	4 588 252	2 272 699	2 315 553	2 846 882	1 389 160	1 457 722	1 741 370	883 539	857 831
0 - 4	356 329	182 076	174 253	224 004	114 284	109 720	132 325	67 792	64 533
5 - 9	320 770	164 037	156 733	188 818	96 160	92 658	131 952	67 877	64 075
10 - 14	302 491	155 076	147 415	172 930	88 433	84 497	129 561	66 643	62 918
15 - 19	283 019	144 262	138 757	170 523	86 129	84 394	112 496	58 133	54 363
20 - 24	297 231	146 636	150 595	208 146	100 226	107 920	89 085	46 410	42 675
25 - 29	361 122	173 714	187 408	266 457	126 362	140 095	94 665	47 352	47 313
30 - 34	393 945	194 774	199 171	278 935	137 689	141 246	115 010	57 085	57 925
35 - 39	364 261	182 237	182 024	233 417	116 912	116 505	130 844	65 325	65 519
40 - 44	330 812	166 330	164 482	198 432	99 162	99 270	132 380	67 168	65 212
45 - 49	305 185	151 516	153 669	178 630	87 087	91 543	126 555	64 429	62 126
50 - 54	274 386	136 737	137 649	158 031	77 106	80 925	116 355	59 631	56 724
55 - 59	244 522	122 121	122 401	137 973	66 919	71 054	106 549	55 202	51 347
60 - 64	218 786	109 869	108 917	122 606	59 521	63 085	96 180	50 348	45 832
65 - 69	173 638	86 298	87 340	97 999	46 741	51 258	75 639	39 557	36 082
70 - 74	131 190	63 476	67 714	76 683	35 378	41 305	54 507	28 098	26 409
75 - 79	102 036	46 631	55 405	59 519	25 708	33 811	42 517	20 923	21 594
80 - 84	70 113	28 423	41 690	40 585	15 449	25 136	29 528	12 974	16 554
85 - 89	39 887	13 591	26 296	22 742	7 303	15 439	17 145	6 288	10 857
90 - 94	14 877	4 155	10 722	8 363	2 200	6 163	6 514	1 955	4 559
95 - 99	3 263	682	2 581	1 884	360	1 524	1 379	322	1 057
100 +	389	58	331	205	31	174	184	27	157
15 IV 2012 (ESDJ)									
Total	4 585 407	2 269 612	2 315 795	...	...	...	...	...	...
0	74 516	38 137	36 379	...	...	...	...	...	...
1 - 4	290 085	147 892	142 193	...	...	...	...	...	...
5 - 9	324 810	166 119	158 691	...	...	...	...	...	...
10 - 14	305 366	156 359	149 007	...	...	...	...	...	...
15 - 19	275 747	141 324	134 423	...	...	...	...	...	...
20 - 24	277 745	138 558	139 187	...	...	...	...	...	...
25 - 29	341 195	163 466	177 729	...	...	...	...	...	...
30 - 34	392 277	191 274	201 003	...	...	...	...	...	...
35 - 39	364 329	181 465	182 864	...	...	...	...	...	...
40 - 44	335 659	168 528	167 131	...	...	...	...	...	...
45 - 49	308 138	153 131	155 007	...	...	...	...	...	...
50 - 54	278 216	138 195	140 021	...	...	...	...	...	...
55 - 59	247 972	123 640	124 332	...	...	...	...	...	...
60 - 64	219 964	110 031	109 933	...	...	...	...	...	...

7. Population by age, sex and urban/rural residence: latest available year, 2003 - 2012

Population selon l'âge, le sexe et la résidence, urbaine/rurale : dernière année disponible, 2003 - 2012 (continued - suite)

Continent, country or area, date, code and age (in years) / Continent, pays ou zone, date, code et âge (en annèes)	Total			Urban - Urbaine			Rural - Rurale		
	Both sexes Les deux sexes	Male Masculin	Female Féminin	Both sexes Les deux sexes	Male Masculin	Female Féminin	Both sexes Les deux sexes	Male Masculin	Female Féminin
EUROPE									
Ireland - Irlande									
15 IV 2012 (ESDJ)									
65 - 69	181 522	90 603	90 919	...	...	...	...	...	...
70 - 74	132 744	64 431	68 313	...	...	...	...	...	...
75 - 79	103 596	47 649	55 947	...	...	...	...	...	...
80 - 84	71 034	29 419	41 615	...	...	...	...	...	...
85 +	60 492	19 391	41 101	...	...	...	...	...	...
Isle of Man - Île de Man									
27 III 2011* (CDJC)									
Total	84 497	41 971	42 526	...	...	...	...	...	...
0 - 4	4 634	2 386	2 248	...	...	...	...	...	...
5 - 9	4 517	2 373	2 144	...	...	...	...	...	...
10 - 14	4 885	2 543	2 342	...	...	...	...	...	...
15 - 19	5 108	2 627	2 481	...	...	...	...	...	...
20 - 24	4 719	2 441	2 278	...	...	...	...	...	...
25 - 29	4 569	2 228	2 341	...	...	...	...	...	...
30 - 34	4 935	2 423	2 512	...	...	...	...	...	...
35 - 39	5 675	2 754	2 921	...	...	...	...	...	...
40 - 44	6 517	3 297	3 220	...	...	...	...	...	...
45 - 49	6 748	3 430	3 318	...	...	...	...	...	...
50 - 54	6 055	3 017	3 038	...	...	...	...	...	...
55 - 59	5 335	2 707	2 628	...	...	...	...	...	...
60 - 64	5 814	2 953	2 861	...	...	...	...	...	...
65 - 69	4 512	2 239	2 273	...	...	...	...	...	...
70 - 74	3 581	1 748	1 833	...	...	...	...	...	...
75 - 79	2 723	1 280	1 443	...	...	...	...	...	...
80 - 84	2 122	850	1 272	...	...	...	...	...	...
85 +	2 048	675	1 373	...	...	...	...	...	...
Italy - Italie									
1 VII 2010 (ESDJ)									
Total	60 483 385	29 350 339	31 133 047	...	...	...	...	...	...
0	559 179	287 504	271 675	...	...	...	...	...	...
1 - 4	2 286 371	1 174 739	1 111 632	...	...	...	...	...	...
5 - 9	2 838 221	1 458 918	1 379 303	...	...	...	...	...	...
10 - 14	2 811 809	1 447 417	1 364 393	...	...	...	...	...	...
15 - 19	2 950 989	1 519 990	1 431 000	...	...	...	...	...	...
20 - 24	3 126 504	1 596 439	1 530 065	...	...	...	...	...	...
25 - 29	3 487 900	1 757 263	1 730 638	...	...	...	...	...	...
30 - 34	4 132 871	2 082 019	2 050 852	...	...	...	...	...	...
35 - 39	4 799 943	2 411 477	2 388 466	...	...	...	...	...	...
40 - 44	4 949 158	2 477 123	2 472 035	...	...	...	...	...	...
45 - 49	4 717 717	2 340 045	2 377 672	...	...	...	...	...	...
50 - 54	4 095 184	2 010 314	2 084 871	...	...	...	...	...	...
55 - 59	3 716 029	1 807 582	1 908 448	...	...	...	...	...	...
60 - 64	3 757 507	1 814 773	1 942 734	...	...	...	...	...	...
65 - 69	3 107 714	1 468 434	1 639 280	...	...	...	...	...	...
70 - 74	3 068 744	1 400 990	1 667 754	...	...	...	...	...	...
75 - 79	2 531 923	1 078 455	1 453 468	...	...	...	...	...	...
80 - 84	1 912 032	725 761	1 186 271	...	...	...	...	...	...
85 - 89	1 159 477	371 286	788 191	...	...	...	...	...	...
90 - 94	337 840	90 114	247 726	...	...	...	...	...	...
95 - 99	120 716	26 728	93 988	...	...	...	...	...	...
100 +	15 560	2 972	12 588	...	...	...	...	...	...
Jersey									
27 III 2011 (CDFC)									
Total	97 857	48 296	49 561	...	...	...	...	...	...
0 - 4	5 015	2 466	2 549	...	...	...	...	...	...
5 - 9	4 852	2 470	2 382	...	...	...	...	...	...
10 - 14	5 302	2 729	2 573	...	...	...	...	...	...
15 - 19	5 495	2 863	2 632	...	...	...	...	...	...
20 - 24	5 944	3 006	2 938	...	...	...	...	...	...
25 - 29	6 705	3 351	3 354	...	...	...	...	...	...
30 - 34	7 236	3 670	3 566	...	...	...	...	...	...
35 - 39	7 225	3 615	3 610	...	...	...	...	...	...
40 - 44	8 363	4 183	4 180	...	...	...	...	...	...

Continent, country or area, date, code and age (in years) / Continent, pays ou zone, date, code et âge (en annèes)	Total			Urban - Urbaine			Rural - Rurale		
	Both sexes Les deux sexes	Male Masculin	Female Féminin	Both sexes Les deux sexes	Male Masculin	Female Féminin	Both sexes Les deux sexes	Male Masculin	Female Féminin
EUROPE									
Jersey									
27 III 2011 (CDFC)									
45 - 49	8 357	4 187	4 170	...	...	...	...	...	...
50 - 54	7 198	3 536	3 662	...	...	...	...	...	...
55 - 59	6 042	2 955	3 087	...	...	...	...	...	...
60 - 64	5 650	2 832	2 818	...	...	...	...	...	...
65 - 69	4 048	1 938	2 110	...	...	...	...	...	...
70 - 74	3 632	1 732	1 900	...	...	...	...	...	...
75 - 79	2 893	1 343	1 550	...	...	...	...	...	...
80 - 84	2 005	822	1 183	...	...	...	...	...	...
85 - 89	1 225	446	779	...	...	...	...	...	...
90 - 94	483	115	368	...	...	...	...	...	...
95 +	187	37	150	...	...	...	...	...	...
Latvia - Lettonie									
1 VII 2010 (ESDJ)									
Total	2 239 008	1 033 421	1 205 587	1 513 343	679 286	834 057	725 665	354 135	371 530
0	20 648	10 572	10 076	14 185	7 313	6 872	6 463	3 259	3 204
1 - 4	92 213	46 918	45 295	63 608	32 392	31 216	28 605	14 526	14 079
5 - 9	100 721	51 501	49 220	66 676	33 983	32 693	34 045	17 518	16 527
10 - 14	94 258	48 361	45 897	58 775	30 078	28 697	35 483	18 283	17 200
15 - 19	136 908	69 686	67 222	83 416	42 263	41 153	53 492	27 423	26 069
20 - 24	180 995	92 375	88 620	116 278	58 348	57 930	64 717	34 027	30 690
25 - 29	173 672	88 648	85 024	119 518	59 359	60 159	54 154	29 289	24 865
30 - 34	155 484	78 860	76 624	109 055	53 761	55 294	46 429	25 099	21 330
35 - 39	158 204	79 381	78 823	108 874	53 007	55 867	49 330	26 374	22 956
40 - 44	152 833	74 989	77 844	102 463	48 492	53 971	50 370	26 497	23 873
45 - 49	163 593	78 360	85 233	110 040	50 575	59 465	53 553	27 785	25 768
50 - 54	161 808	75 324	86 484	110 819	49 191	61 628	50 989	26 133	24 856
55 - 59	138 705	61 536	77 169	97 234	41 089	56 145	41 471	20 447	21 024
60 - 64	120 298	50 361	69 937	85 433	34 163	51 270	34 865	16 198	18 667
65 - 69	111 402	42 938	68 464	74 524	27 666	46 858	36 878	15 272	21 606
70 - 74	109 653	38 639	71 014	76 211	26 213	49 998	33 442	12 426	21 016
75 - 79	77 923	24 071	53 852	53 037	16 214	36 823	24 886	7 857	17 029
80 - 84	56 203	14 521	41 682	39 880	10 545	29 335	16 323	3 976	12 347
85 - 89	25 352	4 802	20 550	17 640	3 460	14 180	7 712	1 342	6 370
90 - 94	6 067	1 177	4 890	4 216	861	3 355	1 851	316	1 535
95 - 99	1 797	341	1 456	1 259	260	999	538	81	457
100 +	271	60	211	202	53	149	69	7	62
Liechtenstein									
1 VII 2011 (ESDJ)									
Total	36 281	17 950	18 331	...	...	...	...	...	...
0	352	174	178	...	...	...	...	...	...
1 - 4	1 499	804	695	...	...	...	...	...	...
5 - 9	1 848	942	906	...	...	...	...	...	...
10 - 14	2 041	1 013	1 028	...	...	...	...	...	...
15 - 19	2 169	1 074	1 095	...	...	...	...	...	...
20 - 24	2 251	1 157	1 094	...	...	...	...	...	...
25 - 29	2 215	1 135	1 080	...	...	...	...	...	...
30 - 34	2 312	1 189	1 123	...	...	...	...	...	...
35 - 39	2 611	1 264	1 347	...	...	...	...	...	...
40 - 44	3 150	1 582	1 568	...	...	...	...	...	...
45 - 49	3 046	1 508	1 538	...	...	...	...	...	...
50 - 54	2 905	1 412	1 493	...	...	...	...	...	...
55 - 59	2 511	1 254	1 257	...	...	...	...	...	...
60 - 64	2 229	1 159	1 070	...	...	...	...	...	...
65 - 69	1 841	901	940	...	...	...	...	...	...
70 - 74	1 290	618	672	...	...	...	...	...	...
75 - 79	854	357	497	...	...	...	...	...	...
80 - 84	602	240	362	...	...	...	...	...	...
85 - 89	379	105	274	...	...	...	...	...	...
90 - 94	138	48	90	...	...	...	...	...	...
95 - 99	36	14	22	...	...	...	...	...	...
100 +	2	-	2	...	...	...	...	...	...

Continent, country or area, date, code and age (in years) / Continent, pays ou zone, date, code et âge (en annèes)	Total			Urban - Urbaine			Rural - Rurale		
	Both sexes Les deux sexes	Male Masculin	Female Féminin	Both sexes Les deux sexes	Male Masculin	Female Féminin	Both sexes Les deux sexes	Male Masculin	Female Féminin
EUROPE									
Lithuania - Lituanie									
1 III 2011 (CDJC)									
Total	3 483 972	1 629 148	1 854 824	2 332 098	1 071 986	1 260 112	1 151 874	557 162	594 712
0 - 4	179 074	92 217	86 857	115 236	59 354	55 882	63 838	32 863	30 975
5 - 9	228 001	116 630	111 371	145 478	74 438	71 040	82 523	42 192	40 331
10 - 14	272 909	139 593	133 316	175 973	89 636	86 337	96 936	49 957	46 979
15 - 19	265 842	135 379	130 463	180 920	90 777	90 143	84 922	44 602	40 320
20 - 24	234 503	118 772	115 731	169 940	83 158	86 782	64 563	35 614	28 949
25 - 29	240 007	119 588	120 419	172 754	84 097	88 657	67 253	35 491	31 762
30 - 34	255 410	126 012	129 398	178 668	86 026	92 642	76 742	39 986	36 756
35 - 39	271 340	133 606	137 734	190 679	90 642	100 037	80 661	42 964	37 697
40 - 44	266 280	127 830	138 450	187 911	86 416	101 495	78 369	41 414	36 955
45 - 49	217 954	103 192	114 762	154 861	70 122	84 739	63 093	33 070	30 023
50 - 54	195 329	89 110	106 219	136 128	59 469	76 659	59 201	29 641	29 560
55 - 59	184 810	81 285	103 525	122 172	52 277	69 895	62 638	29 008	33 630
60 - 64	182 838	76 694	106 144	116 645	47 808	68 837	66 193	28 886	37 307
65 - 69	167 594	66 243	101 351	100 267	39 211	61 056	67 327	27 032	40 295
70 - 74	143 502	51 762	91 740	84 857	30 858	53 999	58 645	20 904	37 741
75 - 79	97 523	28 930	68 593	55 274	15 999	39 275	42 249	12 931	29 318
80 - 84	43 031	12 149	30 882	23 474	6 434	17 040	19 557	5 715	13 842
85 - 89	24 778	6 120	18 658	13 698	3 259	10 439	11 080	2 861	8 219
90 - 94	10 412	3 143	7 269	5 692	1 557	4 135	4 720	1 586	3 134
95 - 99	2 070	617	1 453	1 063	283	780	1 007	334	673
100 +	438	100	338	198	43	155	240	57	183
Unknown - Inconnu	327	176	151	210	122	88	117	54	63
Luxembourg									
1 I 2012 (ESDJ)									
Total	524 853	261 820	263 033	...	...	...	...	...	...
0	5 842	3 013	2 829	...	...	...	...	...	...
1 - 4	23 719	12 057	11 662	...	...	...	...	...	...
5 - 9	29 397	15 228	14 169	...	...	...	...	...	...
10 - 14	31 017	15 912	15 105	...	...	...	...	...	...
15 - 19	31 557	16 148	15 409	...	...	...	...	...	...
20 - 24	32 160	16 499	15 661	...	...	...	...	...	...
25 - 29	36 618	18 432	18 186	...	...	...	...	...	...
30 - 34	39 697	19 734	19 963	...	...	...	...	...	...
35 - 39	39 897	20 069	19 828	...	...	...	...	...	...
40 - 44	43 190	22 062	21 128	...	...	...	...	...	...
45 - 49	42 825	22 278	20 547	...	...	...	...	...	...
50 - 54	37 597	19 328	18 269	...	...	...	...	...	...
55 - 59	31 757	16 109	15 648	...	...	...	...	...	...
60 - 64	26 319	13 344	12 975	...	...	...	...	...	...
65 - 69	20 633	10 190	10 443	...	...	...	...	...	...
70 - 74	17 625	8 070	9 555	...	...	...	...	...	...
75 - 79	14 497	6 265	8 232	...	...	...	...	...	...
80 - 84	11 841	4 735	7 106	...	...	...	...	...	...
85 - 89	6 071	1 730	4 341	...	...	...	...	...	...
90 - 94	2 054	520	1 534	...	...	...	...	...	...
95 - 99	477	83	394	...	...	...	...	...	...
100 +	63	14	49	...	...	...	...	...	...
Malta - Malte									
27 XI 2005 (CDJC)									
Total	404 962	200 819	204 143	404 544	200 611	203 933	418	208	210
0	3 825	1 947	1 878	3 822	1 946	1 876	3	1	2
1 - 4	15 707	8 027	7 680	15 690	8 014	7 676	17	13	4
5 - 9	23 054	11 837	11 217	23 024	11 820	11 204	30	17	13
10 - 14	26 900	13 828	13 072	26 878	13 817	13 061	22	11	11
15 - 19	28 734	14 781	13 953	28 710	14 769	13 941	24	12	12
20 - 24	29 365	14 980	14 385	29 343	14 962	14 381	22	18	4
25 - 29	29 676	15 346	14 330	29 660	15 337	14 323	16	9	7
30 - 34	27 670	14 192	13 478	27 645	14 181	13 464	25	11	14
35 - 39	24 583	12 514	12 069	24 550	12 496	12 054	33	18	15
40 - 44	27 733	14 144	13 589	27 705	14 130	13 575	28	14	14
45 - 49	30 433	15 233	15 200	30 410	15 225	15 185	23	8	15
50 - 54	28 830	14 411	14 419	28 799	14 394	14 405	31	17	14

7. Population by age, sex and urban/rural residence: latest available year, 2003 - 2012
Population selon l'âge, le sexe et la résidence, urbaine/rurale : dernière année disponible, 2003 - 2012 (continued - suite)

Continent, country or area, date, code and age (in years) / Continent, pays ou zone, date, code et âge (en annèes)	Total			Urban - Urbaine			Rural - Rurale		
	Both sexes Les deux sexes	Male Masculin	Female Féminin	Both sexes Les deux sexes	Male Masculin	Female Féminin	Both sexes Les deux sexes	Male Masculin	Female Féminin
EUROPE									
Malta - Malte									
27 XI 2005 (CDJC)									
55 - 59	31 018	15 423	15 595	30 985	15 410	15 575	33	13	20
60 - 64	21 763	10 538	11 225	21 742	10 532	11 210	21	6	15
65 - 69	17 897	8 368	9 529	17 873	8 357	9 516	24	11	13
70 - 74	14 863	6 366	8 497	14 839	6 358	8 481	24	8	16
75 - 79	10 919	4 429	6 490	10 899	4 419	6 480	20	10	10
80 - 84	7 385	2 899	4 486	7 368	2 891	4 477	17	8	9
85 - 89	3 314	1 190	2 124	3 310	1 188	2 122	4	2	2
90 - 94	1 022	300	722	1 022	300	722	-	-	-
95 - 99	237	59	178	236	58	178	1	1	-
100 +	34	7	27	34	7	27	-	-	-
1 VII 2011 (ESDJ)									
Total	416 725	207 257	209 468	...	...	...	...	...	...
0	4 005	2 045	1 960	...	...	...	...	...	...
1 - 4	15 848	8 239	7 609	...	...	...	...	...	...
5 - 9	19 468	9 990	9 478	...	...	...	...	...	...
10 - 14	22 638	11 560	11 078	...	...	...	...	...	...
15 - 19	26 477	13 633	12 844	...	...	...	...	...	...
20 - 24	29 416	15 109	14 307	...	...	...	...	...	...
25 - 29	30 340	15 677	14 663	...	...	...	...	...	...
30 - 34	30 286	15 677	14 609	...	...	...	...	...	...
35 - 39	28 409	14 570	13 839	...	...	...	...	...	...
40 - 44	25 139	12 791	12 348	...	...	...	...	...	...
45 - 49	27 375	13 841	13 534	...	...	...	...	...	...
50 - 54	30 605	15 266	15 339	...	...	...	...	...	...
55 - 59	29 072	14 553	14 519	...	...	...	...	...	...
60 - 64	30 632	15 137	15 495	...	...	...	...	...	...
65 - 69	22 744	10 934	11 810	...	...	...	...	...	...
70 - 74	16 352	7 463	8 889	...	...	...	...	...	...
75 - 79	13 109	5 436	7 673	...	...	...	...	...	...
80 - 84	8 382	3 159	5 223	...	...	...	...	...	...
85 - 89	4 554	1 612	2 942	...	...	...	...	...	...
90 - 94	1 526	470	1 056	...	...	...	...	...	...
95 - 99	303	80	223	...	...	...	...	...	...
100 +	45	15	30	...	...	...	...	...	...
Monaco									
9 VI 2008 (CDJC)									
Total	31 109[68]	15 076	15 914	...	...	...	...	...	...
0 - 4	1 134	577	557	...	...	...	...	...	...
5 - 9	1 430	706	724	...	...	...	...	...	...
10 - 14	1 401	727	674	...	...	...	...	...	...
15 - 19	1 398	724	674	...	...	...	...	...	...
20 - 24	1 248	647	601	...	...	...	...	...	...
25 - 29	1 305	638	667	...	...	...	...	...	...
30 - 34	1 514	751	766	...	...	...	...	...	...
35 - 39	2 122	1 003	1 119	...	...	...	...	...	...
40 - 44	2 342	1 163	1 179	...	...	...	...	...	...
45 - 64	2 359	1 194	1 165	...	...	...	...	...	...
50 - 54	2 218	1 128	1 090	...	...	...	...	...	...
55 - 59	2 217	1 120	1 097	...	...	...	...	...	...
60 - 64	2 337	1 134	1 203	...	...	...	...	...	...
65 - 69	1 960	945	1 015	...	...	...	...	...	...
70 - 74	1 648	801	847	...	...	...	...	...	...
75 +	3 758	1 530	2 228	...	...	...	...	...	...
Unknown - Inconnu	715[68]	288	308	...	...	...	...	...	...
Montenegro - Monténégro									
1 IV 2011 (CDJC)									
Total	620 029	306 236	313 793	399 264	193 691	205 573	220 765	112 545	108 220
0 - 4	38 950	20 361	18 589	25 277	13 247	12 030	13 673	7 114	6 559
5 - 9	38 430	20 016	18 414	24 781	12 973	11 808	13 649	7 043	6 606
10 - 14	41 371	21 389	19 982	26 526	13 698	12 828	14 845	7 691	7 154
15 - 19	44 093	22 815	21 278	28 376	14 654	13 722	15 717	8 161	7 556
20 - 24	42 816	22 084	20 732	28 218	14 347	13 871	14 598	7 737	6 861
25 - 29	45 793	23 299	22 494	31 083	15 290	15 793	14 710	8 009	6 701

Continent, country or area, date, code and age (in years) / Continent, pays ou zone, date, code et âge (en années)	Total			Urban - Urbaine			Rural - Rurale		
	Both sexes Les deux sexes	Male Masculin	Female Féminin	Both sexes Les deux sexes	Male Masculin	Female Féminin	Both sexes Les deux sexes	Male Masculin	Female Féminin
EUROPE									
Montenegro - Monténégro									
1 IV 2011 (CDJC)									
30 - 34	44 495	22 188	22 307	30 133	14 495	15 638	14 362	7 693	6 669
35 - 39	41 879	20 523	21 356	27 869	13 311	14 558	14 010	7 212	6 798
40 - 44	40 496	20 136	20 360	26 265	12 539	13 726	14 231	7 597	6 634
45 - 49	43 089	21 401	21 688	28 332	13 444	14 888	14 757	7 957	6 800
50 - 54	43 613	21 817	21 796	28 705	13 851	14 854	14 908	7 966	6 942
55 - 59	41 223	20 509	20 714	27 021	13 143	13 878	14 202	7 366	6 836
60 - 64	34 196	15 941	18 255	21 738	9 981	11 757	12 458	5 960	6 498
65 - 69	22 121	9 774	12 347	12 692	5 522	7 170	9 429	4 252	5 177
70 - 74	25 141	10 909	14 232	14 441	6 116	8 325	10 700	4 793	5 907
75 - 79	17 184	7 251	9 933	9 665	4 041	5 624	7 519	3 210	4 309
80 - 84	10 021	4 050	5 971	5 375	2 112	3 263	4 646	1 938	2 708
85 - 89	3 739	1 324	2 415	2 038	699	1 339	1 701	625	1 076
90 - 94	885	283	602	453	130	323	432	153	279
95 - 99	202	61	141	103	30	73	99	31	68
100 +	44	13	31	23	7	16	21	6	15
Unknown - Inconnu	248	92	156	150	61	89	98	31	67
Netherlands - Pays-Bas									
1 I 2011 (ESDJ)									
Total	16 655 799	8 243 482	8 412 317	11 124 721	5 478 213	5 646 508	5 531 078	2 765 269	2 765 809
0 - 4	923 106	472 308	450 798	633 381	323 854	309 527	289 725	148 454	141 271
0	184 007	93 892	90 115	...	...	...	...	...	...
1 - 4	739 099	378 416	360 683	...	...	...	...	...	...
5 - 9	985 229	503 882	481 347	640 541	327 757	312 784	344 688	176 125	168 563
10 - 14	998 740	510 974	487 766	633 115	323 581	309 534	365 625	187 393	178 232
15 - 19	1 006 744	514 830	491 914	658 458	333 676	324 782	348 286	181 154	167 132
20 - 24	1 034 729	522 667	512 062	757 280	373 366	383 914	277 449	149 301	128 148
25 - 29	1 001 538	504 117	497 421	749 880	373 340	376 540	251 658	130 777	120 881
30 - 34	1 004 764	503 323	501 441	736 350	368 630	367 720	268 414	134 693	133 721
35 - 39	1 121 568	560 289	561 279	779 994	391 390	388 604	341 574	168 899	172 675
40 - 44	1 295 925	653 664	642 261	861 292	436 235	425 057	434 633	217 429	217 204
45 - 49	1 298 292	655 302	642 990	850 566	428 796	421 770	447 726	226 506	221 220
50 - 54	1 196 319	601 040	595 279	776 285	388 221	388 064	420 034	212 819	207 215
55 - 59	1 090 247	546 952	543 295	700 036	348 502	351 534	390 211	198 450	191 761
60 - 64	1 103 652	553 446	550 206	700 926	349 188	351 738	402 726	204 258	198 468
65 - 69	790 560	390 725	399 835	488 433	238 792	249 641	302 127	151 933	150 194
70 - 74	637 518	302 542	334 976	401 165	187 850	213 315	236 353	114 692	121 661
75 - 79	499 321	219 108	280 213	316 949	136 949	180 000	182 372	82 159	100 213
80 - 84	360 828	139 348	221 480	234 884	89 412	145 472	125 944	49 936	76 008
85 - 89	212 056	66 949	145 107	141 532	44 184	97 348	70 524	22 765	47 759
90 - 94	76 191	18 812	57 379	51 102	12 438	38 664	25 089	6 374	18 715
95 +	18 472	3 204	15 268	12 552	2 052	10 500	5 920	1 152	4 768
Norway - Norvège[69]									
19 XI 2011 (CDJC)									
Total	4 979 955	...	...	...	...	...	...	...	...
0 - 9	611 148	...	...	...	...	...	...	...	...
10 - 19	637 300	...	...	...	...	...	...	...	...
20 - 29	650 708	...	...	...	...	...	...	...	...
30 - 39	677 249	...	...	...	...	...	...	...	...
40 - 49	723 728	...	...	...	...	...	...	...	...
50 - 59	627 064	...	...	...	...	...	...	...	...
60 - 69	533 770	...	...	...	...	...	...	...	...
70 - 79	296 889	...	...	...	...	...	...	...	...
80 +	222 099	...	...	...	...	...	...	...	...
Poland - Pologne[70]									
1 VII 2011 (ESDJ)									
Total	38 525 670	18 650 105	19 875 565	23 404 926	11 111 443	12 293 483	15 120 744	7 538 662	7 582 082
0	397 660	204 752	192 908	231 052	119 082	111 970	166 608	85 670	80 938
1 - 4	1 668 930	855 557	813 373	964 948	494 364	470 584	703 982	361 193	342 789
5 - 9	1 811 297	929 240	882 057	1 006 251	516 414	489 837	805 046	412 826	392 220
10 - 14	1 956 420	1 003 274	953 146	1 041 311	533 971	507 340	915 109	469 303	445 806
15 - 19	2 369 517	1 210 568	1 158 949	1 280 974	651 930	629 044	1 088 543	558 638	529 905
20 - 24	2 811 950	1 432 391	1 379 559	1 643 681	828 369	815 312	1 168 269	604 022	564 247
25 - 29	3 254 318	1 650 733	1 603 585	2 017 247	1 012 158	1 005 089	1 237 071	638 575	598 496

7. Population by age, sex and urban/rural residence: latest available year, 2003 - 2012
Population selon l'âge, le sexe et la résidence, urbaine/rurale : dernière année disponible, 2003 - 2012 (continued - suite)

Continent, country or area, date, code and age (in years) / Continent, pays ou zone, date, code et âge (en années)	Total			Urban - Urbaine			Rural - Rurale		
	Both sexes Les deux sexes	Male Masculin	Female Féminin	Both sexes Les deux sexes	Male Masculin	Female Féminin	Both sexes Les deux sexes	Male Masculin	Female Féminin
EUROPE									
Poland - Pologne[70]									
1 VII 2011 (ESDJ)									
30 - 34	3 136 511	1 590 376	1 546 135	1 980 470	992 651	987 819	1 156 041	597 725	558 316
35 - 39	2 814 100	1 425 449	1 388 651	1 717 111	859 321	857 790	1 096 989	566 128	530 861
40 - 44	2 392 814	1 206 998	1 185 816	1 408 857	695 947	712 910	983 957	511 051	472 906
45 - 49	2 441 785	1 222 145	1 219 640	1 448 367	699 731	748 636	993 418	522 414	471 004
50 - 54	2 901 241	1 424 839	1 476 402	1 818 604	854 558	964 046	1 082 637	570 281	512 356
55 - 59	2 904 478	1 390 915	1 513 563	1 917 011	880 512	1 036 499	987 467	510 403	477 064
60 - 64	2 411 668	1 115 000	1 296 668	1 614 946	724 913	890 033	796 722	390 087	406 635
65 - 69	1 409 677	615 981	793 696	931 873	400 453	531 420	477 804	215 528	262 276
70 - 74	1 341 122	541 738	799 384	856 637	339 950	516 687	484 485	201 788	282 697
75 - 79	1 145 146	423 429	721 717	713 697	262 713	450 984	431 449	160 716	270 733
80 - 84	820 085	267 352	552 733	492 332	162 017	330 315	327 753	105 335	222 418
85 - 89	408 104	109 424	298 680	242 915	65 060	177 855	165 189	44 364	120 825
90 - 94	103 823	25 030	78 793	60 636	14 326	46 310	43 187	10 704	32 483
95 - 99	23 654	4 706	18 948	14 869	2 825	12 044	8 785	1 881	6 904
100 +	1 370	208	1 162	1 137	178	959	233	30	203
Portugal									
21 III 2011 (CDJC)									
Total	10 562 178	5 046 600	5 515 578	6 438 593	3 047 968	3 390 625	4 123 585	1 998 632	2 124 953
0 - 4	482 647	246 396	236 251	316 068	161 365	154 703	166 579	85 031	81 548
5 - 9	525 087	268 965	256 122	329 692	168 925	160 767	195 395	100 040	95 355
10 - 14	564 595	288 638	275 957	344 809	176 287	168 522	219 786	112 351	107 435
15 - 19	565 250	288 525	276 725	342 328	174 252	168 076	222 922	114 273	108 649
20 - 24	582 065	293 023	289 042	358 412	178 982	179 430	223 653	114 041	109 612
25 - 29	656 076	324 848	331 228	425 629	208 104	217 525	230 447	116 744	113 703
30 - 34	773 567	378 734	394 833	508 225	247 125	261 100	265 342	131 609	133 733
35 - 39	824 683	402 307	422 376	529 287	255 858	273 429	295 396	146 449	148 947
40 - 44	773 098	374 962	398 136	478 840	228 255	250 585	294 258	146 707	147 551
45 - 49	770 294	370 989	399 305	466 564	219 783	246 781	303 730	151 206	152 524
50 - 54	722 360	346 248	376 112	435 982	203 867	232 115	286 378	142 381	143 997
55 - 59	677 651	322 095	355 556	410 020	190 860	219 160	267 631	131 235	136 396
60 - 64	634 741	298 546	336 195	382 547	177 485	205 062	252 194	121 061	131 133
65 - 69	551 701	253 004	298 697	319 398	146 189	173 209	232 303	106 815	125 488
70 - 74	496 438	220 461	275 977	273 513	119 844	153 669	222 925	100 617	122 308
75 - 79	429 706	180 131	249 575	231 208	94 394	136 814	198 498	85 737	112 761
80 - 84	297 888	113 325	184 563	159 578	57 948	101 630	138 310	55 377	82 933
85 - 89	164 356	55 635	108 721	88 444	28 423	60 021	75 912	27 212	48 700
90 - 94	53 847	15 679	38 168	29 038	7 847	21 191	24 809	7 832	16 977
95 - 99	14 602	3 816	10 786	8 158	2 029	6 129	6 444	1 787	4 657
100 +	1 526	273	1 253	853	146	707	673	127	546
Republic of Moldova - République de Moldova[71]									
1 I 2010 (ESDJ)									
Total	3 563 695	1 713 487	1 850 208	1 476 681	694 469	782 212	2 087 014	1 019 018	1 067 996
0	40 118	20 710	19 408	14 606	7 518	7 088	25 512	13 192	12 320
1 - 4	150 479	77 365	73 114	55 046	28 454	26 592	95 433	48 911	46 522
5 - 9	185 434	95 510	89 924	65 706	34 174	31 532	119 728	61 336	58 392
10 - 14	219 465	112 127	107 338	73 842	38 068	35 774	145 623	74 059	71 564
15 - 19	296 521	150 928	145 593	107 544	54 726	52 818	188 977	96 202	92 775
20 - 24	358 005	181 847	176 158	171 031	83 972	87 059	186 974	97 875	89 099
25 - 29	315 855	160 613	155 242	149 348	72 093	77 255	166 507	88 520	77 987
30 - 34	270 624	135 754	134 870	120 151	58 823	61 328	150 473	76 931	73 542
35 - 39	238 750	117 562	121 188	104 074	50 084	53 990	134 676	67 478	67 198
40 - 44	226 562	109 695	116 867	96 212	44 575	51 637	130 350	65 120	65 230
45 - 49	267 820	127 113	140 707	116 796	52 812	63 984	151 024	74 301	76 723
50 - 54	264 730	123 198	141 532	115 371	50 896	64 475	149 359	72 302	77 057
55 - 59	228 954	103 845	125 109	100 088	43 563	56 525	128 866	60 282	68 584
60 - 64	139 577	61 953	77 624	60 359	27 297	33 062	79 218	34 656	44 562
65 - 69	114 976	47 481	67 495	43 306	18 517	24 789	71 670	28 964	42 706
70 - 74	102 431	39 018	63 413	37 282	14 083	23 199	65 149	24 935	40 214
75 - 79	73 385	26 606	46 779	23 192	8 033	15 159	50 193	18 573	31 620
80 - 84	45 414	14 685	30 729	15 087	4 620	10 467	30 327	10 065	20 262
85 - 89	19 565	5 952	13 613	5 938	1 634	4 304	13 627	4 318	9 309
90 - 94	3 648	1 099	2 549	1 238	389	849	2 410	710	1 700

7. Population by age, sex and urban/rural residence: latest available year, 2003 - 2012

Population selon l'âge, le sexe et la résidence, urbaine/rurale : dernière année disponible, 2003 - 2012 (continued - suite)

Continent, country or area, date, code and age (in years) / Continent, pays ou zone, date, code et âge (en années)	Total			Urban - Urbaine			Rural - Rurale		
	Both sexes Les deux sexes	Male Masculin	Female Féminin	Both sexes Les deux sexes	Male Masculin	Female Féminin	Both sexes Les deux sexes	Male Masculin	Female Féminin
EUROPE									
Republic of Moldova - République de Moldova[71]									
1 I 2010 (ESDJ)									
95 - 99	1 141	353	788	363	119	244	778	234	544
100 +	241	73	168	101	19	82	140	54	86
1 VII 2011 (ESDJ)									
Total	3 559 986	1 711 916	1 848 070	...	...	...	...	...	...
0	39 389	20 201	19 188	...	...	...	...	...	...
1 - 4	153 900	79 575	74 325	...	...	...	...	...	...
5 - 9	184 944	95 206	89 738	...	...	...	...	...	...
10 - 14	203 188	104 104	99 084	...	...	...	...	...	...
15 - 19	273 385	139 266	134 119	...	...	...	...	...	...
20 - 24	346 730	176 192	170 538	...	...	...	...	...	...
25 - 29	331 389	168 539	162 850	...	...	...	...	...	...
30 - 34	282 754	142 651	140 103	...	...	...	...	...	...
35 - 39	246 249	121 612	124 637	...	...	...	...	...	...
40 - 44	225 001	109 285	115 716	...	...	...	...	...	...
45 - 49	247 598	117 430	130 168	...	...	...	...	...	...
50 - 54	273 433	127 322	146 111	...	...	...	...	...	...
55 - 59	232 112	105 077	127 036	...	...	...	...	...	...
60 - 64	165 447	72 691	92 756	...	...	...	...	...	...
65 - 69	108 605	45 589	63 017	...	...	...	...	...	...
70 - 74	100 873	38 160	62 714	...	...	...	...	...	...
75 - 79	72 296	25 957	46 339	...	...	...	...	...	...
80 - 84	46 544	15 272	31 272	...	...	...	...	...	...
85 - 89	20 254	5 985	14 269	...	...	...	...	...	...
90 - 94	4 387	1 308	3 079	...	...	...	...	...	...
95 - 99	1 171	382	789	...	...	...	...	...	...
100 +	344	118	227	...	...	...	...	...	...
Romania - Roumanie									
1 VII 2011* (ESDJ)									
Total	21 354 396	10 392 537	10 961 859	11 727 153	5 590 187	6 136 966	9 627 243	4 802 350	4 824 893
0	199 626	102 268	97 358	109 800	56 438	53 362	89 826	45 830	43 996
1 - 4	863 069	443 649	419 420	469 784	241 879	227 905	393 285	201 770	191 515
5 - 9	1 055 229	542 633	512 596	531 650	273 408	258 242	523 579	269 225	254 354
10 - 14	1 095 415	561 371	534 044	502 130	257 097	245 033	593 285	304 274	289 011
15 - 19	1 172 977	600 267	572 710	571 644	290 197	281 447	601 333	310 070	291 263
20 - 24	1 644 400	837 756	806 644	939 900	468 048	471 852	704 500	369 708	334 792
25 - 29	1 590 275	814 169	776 106	957 301	477 465	479 836	632 974	336 704	296 270
30 - 34	1 764 339	904 958	859 381	1 051 660	525 931	525 729	712 679	379 027	333 652
35 - 39	1 672 212	854 430	817 782	933 480	461 763	471 717	738 732	392 667	346 065
40 - 44	1 844 332	929 580	914 752	1 072 233	510 643	561 590	772 099	418 937	353 162
45 - 49	1 168 162	580 336	587 826	699 197	323 344	375 853	468 965	256 992	211 973
50 - 54	1 414 241	686 116	728 125	880 436	404 195	476 241	533 805	281 921	251 884
55 - 59	1 453 901	686 604	767 297	900 136	419 067	481 069	553 765	267 537	286 228
60 - 64	1 221 207	560 775	660 432	676 102	312 157	363 945	545 105	248 618	296 487
65 - 69	882 256	386 399	495 857	428 645	186 992	241 653	453 611	199 407	254 204
70 - 74	893 635	366 556	527 079	403 582	164 387	239 195	490 053	202 169	287 884
75 - 79	717 377	281 185	436 192	302 858	115 642	187 216	414 519	165 543	248 976
80 - 84	451 974	167 793	284 181	189 915	68 005	121 910	262 059	99 788	162 271
85 - 89	196 786	67 747	129 039	83 576	26 652	56 924	113 210	41 095	72 115
90 - 94	39 078	12 810	26 268	18 342	5 346	12 996	20 736	7 464	13 272
95 - 99	9 492	3 491	6 001	3 522	1 073	2 449	5 970	2 418	3 552
100 +	4 413	1 644	2 769	1 260	458	802	3 153	1 186	1 967
Russian Federation - Fédération de Russie									
14 X 2010 (CDJC)									
Total	142 856 536	66 046 579	76 809 957	105 313 773	48 117 546	57 196 227	37 542 763	17 929 033	19 613 730
0 - 4	7 967 526	4 083 535	3 883 991	5 590 695	2 867 296	2 723 399	2 376 831	1 216 239	1 160 592
5 - 9	7 090 952	3 630 042	3 460 910	4 986 063	2 552 384	2 433 679	2 104 889	1 077 658	1 027 231
10 - 14	6 609 822	3 385 168	3 224 654	4 523 301	2 316 235	2 207 066	2 086 521	1 068 933	1 017 588
15 - 19	8 389 394	4 277 893	4 111 501	6 177 938	3 123 981	3 053 957	2 211 456	1 153 912	1 057 544
20 - 24	12 169 457	6 170 174	5 999 283	9 176 216	4 599 234	4 576 982	2 993 241	1 570 940	1 422 301
25 - 29	11 982 085	6 009 771	5 972 314	9 165 129	4 552 985	4 612 144	2 816 956	1 456 786	1 360 170
30 - 34	10 980 070	5 434 071	5 545 999	8 437 604	4 139 186	4 298 418	2 542 466	1 294 885	1 247 581

7. Population by age, sex and urban/rural residence: latest available year, 2003 - 2012
Population selon l'âge, le sexe et la résidence, urbaine/rurale : dernière année disponible, 2003 - 2012 (continued - suite)

Continent, country or area, date, code and age (in years) / Continent, pays ou zone, date, code et âge (en annèes)	Total			Urban - Urbaine			Rural - Rurale		
	Both sexes Les deux sexes	Male Masculin	Female Féminin	Both sexes Les deux sexes	Male Masculin	Female Féminin	Both sexes Les deux sexes	Male Masculin	Female Féminin
EUROPE									
Russian Federation - Fédération de Russie									
14 X 2010 (CDJC)									
35 - 39	10 172 472	4 972 367	5 200 105	7 740 901	3 751 338	3 989 563	2 431 571	1 221 029	1 210 542
40 - 44	9 240 698	4 474 293	4 766 405	6 816 775	3 255 483	3 561 292	2 423 923	1 218 810	1 205 113
45 - 49	10 671 538	5 039 255	5 632 283	7 753 015	3 579 441	4 173 574	2 918 523	1 459 814	1 458 709
50 - 54	11 482 557	5 248 325	6 234 232	8 362 191	3 710 484	4 651 707	3 120 366	1 537 841	1 582 525
55 - 59	10 021 759	4 351 753	5 670 006	7 442 711	3 142 578	4 300 133	2 579 048	1 209 175	1 369 873
60 - 64	7 832 364	3 245 222	4 587 142	5 973 327	2 420 029	3 553 298	1 859 037	825 193	1 033 844
65 - 69	4 001 747	1 491 776	2 509 971	2 991 104	1 106 234	1 884 870	1 010 643	385 542	625 101
70 - 74	6 457 044	2 179 779	4 277 265	4 661 377	1 553 687	3 107 690	1 795 667	626 092	1 169 575
75 - 79	3 552 065	1 068 314	2 483 751	2 486 470	732 112	1 754 358	1 065 595	336 202	729 393
80 - 84	2 870 937	728 763	2 142 174	2 022 172	514 862	1 507 310	848 765	213 901	634 864
85 - 89	1 032 471	189 178	843 293	756 970	144 034	612 936	275 501	45 144	230 357
90 - 94	231 855	39 728	192 127	169 654	31 415	138 239	62 201	8 313	53 888
95 - 99	58 148	9 007	49 141	41 838	7 228	34 610	16 310	1 779	14 531
100 +	7 266	1 379	5 887	5 131	1 186	3 945	2 135	193	1 942
Unknown - Inconnu	34 309	16 786	17 523	33 191	16 134	17 057	1 118	652	466
San Marino - Saint-Marin[19]									
1 VII 2004 (ESDF)									
Total	29 457	14 442	15 015	...	...	...	...	...	...
0	308	160	149	...	...	...	...	...	...
1 - 4	1 274	678	596	...	...	...	...	...	...
5 - 9	1 508	800	708	...	...	...	...	...	...
10 - 14	1 383	707	676	...	...	...	...	...	...
15 - 19	1 292	672	620	...	...	...	...	...	...
20 - 24	1 519	779	740	...	...	...	...	...	...
25 - 29	2 038	983	1 055	...	...	...	...	...	...
30 - 34	2 559	1 256	1 304	...	...	...	...	...	...
35 - 39	2 863	1 385	1 478	...	...	...	...	...	...
40 - 44	2 617	1 297	1 320	...	...	...	...	...	...
45 - 49	2 067	1 054	1 013	...	...	...	...	...	...
50 - 54	1 876	932	944	...	...	...	...	...	...
55 - 59	1 819	892	927	...	...	...	...	...	...
60 - 64	1 526	751	775	...	...	...	...	...	...
65 - 69	1 383	688	696	...	...	...	...	...	...
70 - 74	1 207	553	655	...	...	...	...	...	...
75 - 79	946	413	533	...	...	...	...	...	...
80 - 84	765	290	475	...	...	...	...	...	...
85 - 89	321	102	219	...	...	...	...	...	...
90 - 94	163	47	116	...	...	...	...	...	...
95 - 99	29	9	20	...	...	...	...	...	...
100 +	2	-	2	...	...	...	...	...	...
Serbia - Serbie[72]									
1 X 2011 (CDJC)									
Total	7 186 862	3 499 176	3 687 686	4 271 872	2 039 105	2 232 767	2 914 990	1 460 071	1 454 919
0 - 4	328 255	169 168	159 087	205 228	105 858	99 370	123 027	63 310	59 717
5 - 9	350 154	179 721	170 433	210 455	107 999	102 456	139 699	71 722	67 977
10 - 14	346 869	178 419	168 450	203 937	104 840	99 097	142 932	73 579	69 353
15 - 19	401 994	206 968	195 026	235 903	121 027	114 876	166 091	85 941	80 150
20 - 24	439 741	225 231	214 510	265 548	133 756	131 792	174 193	91 475	82 718
25 - 29	480 286	244 911	235 375	308 162	152 849	155 313	172 124	92 062	80 062
30 - 34	496 362	252 502	243 860	323 991	160 784	163 207	172 371	91 718	80 653
35 - 39	493 934	248 554	245 380	311 081	152 447	158 634	182 853	96 107	86 746
40 - 44	469 928	234 274	235 654	285 240	138 177	147 063	184 688	96 097	88 591
45 - 49	483 986	238 502	245 484	288 789	137 187	151 602	195 197	101 315	93 882
50 - 54	520 344	254 508	265 836	308 230	144 334	163 896	212 114	110 174	101 940
55 - 59	596 279	289 566	306 713	349 498	162 715	186 783	246 781	126 851	119 930
60 - 64	528 414	249 785	278 629	310 804	141 502	169 302	217 610	108 283	109 327
65 - 69	339 444	154 775	184 669	189 052	83 947	105 105	150 392	70 828	79 564
70 - 74	354 142	153 847	200 295	191 716	81 632	110 084	162 426	72 215	90 211
75 - 79	298 612	122 964	175 648	154 304	63 313	90 991	144 308	59 651	84 657
80 - 84	176 568	67 814	108 754	87 202	32 212	54 990	89 366	35 602	53 764
85 - 89	67 233	22 991	44 242	35 133	12 078	23 055	32 100	10 913	21 187
90 - 94	12 689	4 178	8 511	6 676	2 178	4 498	6 013	2 000	4 013

7. Population by age, sex and urban/rural residence: latest available year, 2003 - 2012
Population selon l'âge, le sexe et la résidence, urbaine/rurale : dernière année disponible, 2003 - 2012 (continued - suite)

Continent, country or area, date, code and age (in years) Continent, pays ou zone, date, code et âge (en annèes)	Total			Urban - Urbaine			Rural - Rurale		
	Both sexes Les deux sexes	Male Masculin	Female Féminin	Both sexes Les deux sexes	Male Masculin	Female Féminin	Both sexes Les deux sexes	Male Masculin	Female Féminin
EUROPE									
Serbia - Serbie[72]									
1 X 2011 (CDJC)									
95 - 99	1 461	448	1 013	831	240	591	630	208	422
100 +	167	50	117	92	30	62	75	20	55
Slovakia - Slovaquie									
21 V 2011 (CDJC)									
Total	5 397 036	2 627 772	2 769 264	2 937 735	1 412 818	1 524 917	2 459 301	1 214 954	1 244 347
0 - 4	280 331	143 706	136 625	143 353	73 538	69 815	136 978	70 168	66 810
5 - 9	263 211	135 158	128 053	129 910	66 788	63 122	133 301	68 370	64 931
10 - 14	282 974	145 245	137 729	136 414	70 042	66 372	146 560	75 203	71 357
15 - 19	343 022	175 453	167 569	172 498	88 034	84 464	170 524	87 419	83 105
20 - 24	401 709	204 603	197 106	217 225	110 553	106 672	184 484	94 050	90 434
25 - 29	437 644	223 998	213 646	246 441	125 419	121 022	191 203	98 579	92 624
30 - 34	460 530	236 598	223 932	262 088	133 891	128 197	198 442	102 707	95 735
35 - 39	428 814	218 955	209 859	235 824	118 974	116 850	192 990	99 981	93 009
40 - 44	357 754	180 818	176 936	193 528	94 626	98 902	164 226	86 192	78 034
45 - 49	373 920	186 945	186 975	209 467	100 356	109 111	164 453	86 589	77 864
50 - 54	384 686	189 967	194 719	222 056	105 108	116 948	162 630	84 859	77 771
55 - 59	386 524	185 412	201 112	227 574	106 090	121 484	158 950	79 322	79 628
60 - 64	311 724	143 683	168 041	179 667	81 410	98 257	132 057	62 273	69 784
65 - 69	219 301	93 226	126 075	121 305	51 209	70 096	97 996	42 017	55 979
70 - 74	173 180	68 008	105 172	90 784	35 959	54 825	82 396	32 049	50 347
75 - 79	135 663	48 471	87 192	69 932	25 683	44 249	65 731	22 788	42 943
80 - 84	93 928	29 853	64 075	47 608	15 670	31 938	46 320	14 183	32 137
85 - 89	47 001	13 235	33 766	23 943	6 978	16 965	23 058	6 257	16 801
90 - 94	11 180	3 026	8 154	5 694	1 568	4 126	5 486	1 458	4 028
95 - 99	2 358	627	1 731	1 287	337	950	1 071	290	781
100 +	262	61	201	145	36	109	117	25	92
Unknown - Inconnu	1 320	724	596	992	549	443	328	175	153
Slovenia - Slovénie									
1 I 2011 (CDJC)									
Total	2 050 189	1 014 563	1 035 626	1 024 330	499 283	525 047	1 025 859	515 280	510 579
0 - 4	106 582	54 813	51 769	51 919	26 749	25 170	54 663	28 064	26 599
5 - 9	90 882	46 747	44 135	42 027	21 540	20 487	48 855	25 207	23 648
10 - 14	93 389	48 142	45 247	42 058	21 697	20 361	51 331	26 445	24 886
15 - 19	102 526	52 645	49 881	47 190	24 019	23 171	55 336	28 626	26 710
20 - 24	127 304	66 235	61 069	66 947	34 260	32 687	60 357	31 975	28 382
25 - 29	145 535	76 436	69 099	73 674	38 771	34 903	71 861	37 665	34 196
30 - 34	158 120	83 020	75 100	80 505	42 285	38 220	77 615	40 735	36 880
35 - 39	150 888	78 883	72 005	74 135	38 591	35 544	76 753	40 292	36 461
40 - 44	150 670	77 321	73 349	72 985	37 059	35 926	77 685	40 262	37 423
45 - 49	157 049	80 025	77 024	78 113	39 121	38 992	78 936	40 904	38 032
50 - 54	153 589	78 295	75 294	76 905	38 253	38 652	76 684	40 042	36 642
55 - 59	151 186	76 981	74 205	77 447	38 348	39 099	73 739	38 633	35 106
60 - 64	123 525	60 844	62 681	63 522	30 317	33 205	60 003	30 527	29 476
65 - 69	93 991	43 771	50 220	48 467	21 478	26 989	45 524	22 293	23 231
70 - 74	87 474	38 335	49 139	44 712	19 313	25 399	42 762	19 022	23 740
75 - 79	72 422	27 746	44 676	37 484	14 329	23 155	34 938	13 417	21 521
80 - 84	50 959	16 389	34 570	26 869	8 531	18 338	24 090	7 858	16 232
85 - 89	25 925	6 266	19 659	14 453	3 614	10 839	11 472	2 652	8 820
90 - 94	6 326	1 351	4 975	3 768	809	2 959	2 558	542	2 016
95 - 99	1 625	285	1 340	1 006	179	827	619	106	513
100 +	222	33	189	144	20	124	78	13	65
Spain - Espagne									
1 VII 2012 (ESDJ)									
Total	46 163 114	22 668 768	23 494 346	...	...	...	...	...	...
0	473 298	244 049	229 249	...	...	...	...	...	...
1 - 4	1 992 858	1 026 849	966 009	...	...	...	...	...	...
5 - 9	2 379 157	1 224 056	1 155 101	...	...	...	...	...	...
10 - 14	2 199 247	1 130 113	1 069 134	...	...	...	...	...	...
15 - 19	2 164 280	1 109 754	1 054 526	...	...	...	...	...	...
20 - 24	2 427 108	1 231 892	1 195 216	...	...	...	...	...	...
25 - 29	2 954 866	1 487 434	1 467 432	...	...	...	...	...	...
30 - 34	3 728 745	1 898 405	1 830 340	...	...	...	...	...	...
35 - 39	4 000 091	2 049 944	1 950 147	...	...	...	...	...	...

Continent, country or area, date, code and age (in years) / Continent, pays ou zone, date, code et âge (en annèes)	Total			Urban - Urbaine			Rural - Rurale		
	Both sexes Les deux sexes	Male Masculin	Female Féminin	Both sexes Les deux sexes	Male Masculin	Female Féminin	Both sexes Les deux sexes	Male Masculin	Female Féminin
EUROPE									
Spain - Espagne									
1 VII 2012 (ESDJ)									
40 - 44	3 776 566	1 919 768	1 856 798	...	...	...	...	...	...
45 - 49	3 552 947	1 779 410	1 773 537	...	...	...	...	...	...
50 - 54	3 205 021	1 583 871	1 621 150	...	...	...	...	...	...
55 - 59	2 739 796	1 337 259	1 402 537	...	...	...	...	...	...
60 - 64	2 462 481	1 184 451	1 278 030	...	...	...	...	...	...
65 - 69	2 210 557	1 043 304	1 167 253	...	...	...	...	...	...
70 - 74	1 758 585	802 433	956 152	...	...	...	...	...	...
75 - 79	1 681 210	721 340	959 870	...	...	...	...	...	...
80 - 84	1 317 220	518 374	798 846	...	...	...	...	...	...
85 - 89	763 519	266 745	496 774	...	...	...	...	...	...
90 - 94	296 230	89 374	206 856	...	...	...	...	...	...
95 - 99	70 193	17 485	52 708	...	...	...	...	...	...
100 +	9 139	2 458	6 681	...	...	...	...	...	...
Sweden - Suède[19]									
1 VII 2011 (ESDJ)									
Total	9 449 213	4 708 539	4 740 674	...	...	...	...	...	...
0	114 012	58 428	55 585	...	...	...	...	...	...
1 - 4	450 567	231 851	218 716	...	...	...	...	...	...
5 - 9	523 297	268 348	254 949	...	...	...	...	...	...
10 - 14	486 739	250 119	236 620	...	...	...	...	...	...
15 - 19	605 491	311 471	294 020	...	...	...	...	...	...
20 - 24	641 439	327 945	313 494	...	...	...	...	...	...
25 - 29	588 530	302 573	285 957	...	...	...	...	...	...
30 - 34	583 490	298 216	285 274	...	...	...	...	...	...
35 - 39	629 915	320 049	309 867	...	...	...	...	...	...
40 - 44	648 970	329 590	319 380	...	...	...	...	...	...
45 - 49	652 469	332 124	320 346	...	...	...	...	...	...
50 - 54	584 618	295 442	289 176	...	...	...	...	...	...
55 - 59	572 938	287 739	285 200	...	...	...	...	...	...
60 - 64	605 783	301 743	304 040	...	...	...	...	...	...
65 - 69	563 074	280 104	282 971	...	...	...	...	...	...
70 - 74	395 524	190 272	205 252	...	...	...	...	...	...
75 - 79	304 799	137 622	167 177	...	...	...	...	...	...
80 - 84	245 289	100 617	144 673	...	...	...	...	...	...
85 - 89	164 396	59 447	104 949	...	...	...	...	...	...
90 - 94	70 835	21 214	49 622	...	...	...	...	...	...
95 - 99	15 327	3 369	11 958	...	...	...	...	...	...
100 +	1 715	261	1 454	...	...	...	...	...	...
Switzerland - Suisse									
1 VII 2011 (ESDJ)									
Total	7 912 398	3 899 840	4 012 559	5 831 864	2 857 476	2 974 388	2 080 534	1 042 364	1 038 171
0	39 213	20 212	19 001	29 222	15 123	14 099	9 991	5 089	4 902
1 - 4	316 776	162 714	154 062	233 245	119 805	113 440	83 532	42 909	40 623
5 - 9	384 294	197 193	187 101	277 314	142 405	134 909	106 980	54 788	52 192
10 - 14	409 112	210 028	199 084	289 267	148 312	140 955	119 845	61 716	58 129
15 - 19	445 510	228 269	217 241	311 891	159 706	152 185	133 619	68 563	65 056
20 - 24	486 427	247 265	239 162	351 911	177 283	174 629	134 516	69 983	64 534
25 - 29	520 240	262 926	257 315	399 413	200 151	199 262	120 828	62 775	58 053
30 - 34	541 453	272 672	268 781	421 176	212 040	209 136	120 277	60 632	59 646
35 - 39	550 306	275 833	274 473	418 519	210 255	208 265	131 787	65 579	66 208
40 - 44	622 533	311 754	310 779	459 558	230 288	229 271	162 975	81 466	81 509
45 - 49	661 389	335 230	326 159	483 436	244 446	238 990	177 953	90 785	87 169
50 - 54	582 355	294 257	288 098	421 726	211 982	209 744	160 629	82 275	78 354
55 - 59	500 822	251 496	249 326	363 217	179 998	183 219	137 606	71 499	66 107
60 - 64	459 548	227 118	232 430	335 475	163 052	172 423	124 073	64 066	60 007
65 - 69	413 611	200 717	212 895	305 556	146 036	159 520	108 055	54 681	53 375
70 - 74	314 911	145 578	169 333	235 136	107 241	127 895	79 776	38 338	41 438
75 - 79	262 982	114 598	148 384	195 847	84 538	111 309	67 136	30 061	37 075
80 - 84	202 570	79 323	123 248	151 137	58 420	92 717	51 434	20 903	30 531
85 - 89	129 319	43 732	85 587	96 677	32 281	64 396	32 642	11 451	21 191
90 - 94	53 871	15 516	38 355	40 463	11 495	28 968	13 409	4 022	9 387
95 - 99	13 342	3 110	10 233	10 287	2 399	7 888	3 056	711	2 345
100 +	1 819	303	1 516	1 399	227	1 172	421	77	344

Continent, country or area, date, code and age (in years) / Continent, pays ou zone, date, code et âge (en années)	Total			Urban - Urbaine			Rural - Rurale		
	Both sexes Les deux sexes	Male Masculin	Female Féminin	Both sexes Les deux sexes	Male Masculin	Female Féminin	Both sexes Les deux sexes	Male Masculin	Female Féminin
EUROPE									
TFYR of Macedonia - L'ex-R. y. de Macédoine									
1 VII 2011 (ESDF)									
Total	2 058 539	1 031 403	1 027 136	...	...	...	...	...	...
0	23 364	12 098	11 267	...	...	...	...	...	...
1 - 4	91 632	47 429	44 203	...	...	...	...	...	...
5 - 9	114 402	58 924	55 478	...	...	...	...	...	...
10 - 14	126 951	65 543	61 408	...	...	...	...	...	...
15 - 19	149 164	76 696	72 468	...	...	...	...	...	...
20 - 24	161 507	83 078	78 429	...	...	...	...	...	...
25 - 29	164 584	84 255	80 329	...	...	...	...	...	...
30 - 34	157 817	81 151	76 666	...	...	...	...	...	...
35 - 39	150 835	76 546	74 289	...	...	...	...	...	...
40 - 44	146 504	74 156	72 349	...	...	...	...	...	...
45 - 49	145 866	73 955	71 911	...	...	...	...	...	...
50 - 54	142 164	71 863	70 302	...	...	...	...	...	...
55 - 59	131 841	65 779	66 062	...	...	...	...	...	...
60 - 64	109 480	52 183	57 297	...	...	...	...	...	...
65 - 69	80 630	37 552	43 078	...	...	...	...	...	...
70 - 74	68 536	31 060	37 476	...	...	...	...	...	...
75 - 79	53 282	23 189	30 094	...	...	...	...	...	...
80 - 84	26 854	11 018	15 836	...	...	...	...	...	...
85 - 89	9 756	3 790	5 966	...	...	...	...	...	...
90 - 94	2 147	786	1 361	...	...	...	...	...	...
95 - 99	778	254	525	...	...	...	...	...	...
Unknown - Inconnu	451	105	346	...	...	...	...	...	...
Ukraine									
1 I 2012 (ESDJ)									
Total	45 453 282	20 976 712	24 476 570	31 125 243	14 248 773	16 876 470	14 328 039	6 727 939	7 600 100
0	498 975	257 319	241 656	326 843	168 589	158 254	172 132	88 730	83 402
1 - 4	1 973 342	1 016 849	956 493	1 310 693	676 179	634 514	662 649	340 670	321 979
5 - 9	2 086 091	1 072 035	1 014 056	1 385 484	712 268	673 216	700 607	359 767	340 840
10 - 14	1 973 123	1 011 929	961 194	1 214 108	623 738	590 370	759 015	388 191	370 824
15 - 19	2 538 145	1 299 718	1 238 427	1 669 702	847 769	821 933	868 443	451 949	416 494
20 - 24	3 385 823	1 731 012	1 654 811	2 317 953	1 174 979	1 142 974	1 067 870	556 033	511 837
25 - 29	3 847 761	1 957 830	1 889 931	2 829 353	1 429 368	1 399 985	1 018 408	528 462	489 946
30 - 34	3 407 203	1 707 250	1 699 953	2 474 468	1 224 721	1 249 747	932 735	482 529	450 206
35 - 39	3 284 411	1 613 240	1 671 171	2 321 585	1 127 949	1 193 636	962 826	485 291	477 535
40 - 44	3 064 563	1 481 441	1 583 122	2 106 409	994 040	1 112 369	958 154	487 401	470 753
45 - 49	3 201 777	1 500 407	1 701 370	2 216 738	1 005 857	1 210 881	985 039	494 550	490 489
50 - 54	3 505 998	1 594 074	1 911 924	2 468 929	1 086 235	1 382 694	1 037 069	507 839	529 230
55 - 59	3 068 133	1 331 554	1 736 579	2 198 604	926 804	1 271 800	869 529	404 750	464 779
60 - 64	2 689 497	1 113 768	1 575 729	1 927 280	782 914	1 144 366	762 217	330 854	431 363
65 - 69	1 618 170	609 496	1 008 674	1 077 257	407 484	669 773	540 913	202 012	338 901
70 - 74	2 386 638	830 327	1 556 311	1 547 521	541 060	1 006 461	839 117	289 267	549 850
75 - 79	1 315 395	431 359	884 036	792 630	264 889	527 741	522 765	166 470	356 295
80 - 84	1 024 581	288 631	735 950	598 717	174 013	424 704	425 864	114 618	311 246
85 - 89	460 683	102 126	358 557	266 769	62 418	204 351	193 914	39 708	154 206
90 - 94	102 749	22 194	80 555	61 035	14 500	46 535	41 714	7 694	34 020
95 - 99	18 344	3 671	14 673	11 684	2 646	9 038	6 660	1 025	5 635
100 +	1 880	482	1 398	1 481	353	1 128	399	129	270
United Kingdom of Great Britain and Northern Ireland - Royaume-Uni de Grande-Bretagne et d'Irlande du Nord[73]									
27 III 2011 (CDJC)									
Total	63 182 000	31 028 000	32 154 000	...	...	...	...	...	...
0 - 4	3 914 000	2 002 000	1 912 000	...	...	...	...	...	...
5 - 9	3 517 000	1 800 000	1 717 000	...	...	...	...	...	...
10 - 14	3 670 000	1 879 000	1 790 000	...	...	...	...	...	...
15 - 19	3 997 000	2 041 000	1 956 000	...	...	...	...	...	...
20 - 24	4 297 000	2 164 000	2 133 000	...	...	...	...	...	...
25 - 29	4 307 000	2 145 000	2 162 000	...	...	...	...	...	...
30 - 34	4 126 000	2 060 000	2 066 000	...	...	...	...	...	...

Continent, country or area, date, code and age (in years) / Continent, pays ou zone, date, code et âge (en années)	Total			Urban - Urbaine			Rural - Rurale		
	Both sexes Les deux sexes	Male Masculin	Female Féminin	Both sexes Les deux sexes	Male Masculin	Female Féminin	Both sexes Les deux sexes	Male Masculin	Female Féminin
EUROPE									
United Kingdom of Great Britain and Northern Ireland - Royaume-Uni de Grande-Bretagne et d'Irlande du Nord[73]									
27 III 2011 (CDJC)									
35 - 39	4 194 000	2 082 000	2 112 000	...	...	...	...	...	...
40 - 44	4 626 000	2 283 000	2 341 000	...	...	...	...	...	...
45 - 49	4 643 000	2 293 000	2 350 000	...	...	...	...	...	...
50 - 54	4 095 000	2 029 000	2 066 000	...	...	...	...	...	...
55 - 59	3 614 000	1 785 000	1 829 000	...	...	...	...	...	...
60 - 64	3 807 000	1 869 000	1 939 000	...	...	...	...	...	...
65 - 69	3 017 000	1 464 000	1 555 000	...	...	...	...	...	...
70 - 74	2 463 000	1 163 000	1 300 000	...	...	...	...	...	...
75 - 79	2 006 000	904 000	1 102 000	...	...	...	...	...	...
80 - 84	1 496 000	615 000	883 000	...	...	...	...	...	...
85 - 89	918 000	324 000	594 000	...	...	...	...	...	...
90 +	476 000	127 000	349 000	...	...	...	...	...	...
OCEANIA - OCÉANIE									
American Samoa - Samoas américaines[28]									
1 IV 2010 (CDJC)									
Total	55 519	28 164	27 355	...	...	...	...	...	...
0 - 4	6 611	3 417	3 194	...	...	...	...	...	...
5 - 9	6 535	3 470	3 065	...	...	...	...	...	...
10 - 14	6 279	3 214	3 065	...	...	...	...	...	...
15 - 19	6 296	3 218	3 078	...	...	...	...	...	...
20 - 24	3 891	1 944	1 947	...	...	...	...	...	...
25 - 29	3 324	1 670	1 654	...	...	...	...	...	...
30 - 34	3 510	1 726	1 784	...	...	...	...	...	...
35 - 39	3 609	1 845	1 764	...	...	...	...	...	...
40 - 44	3 600	1 793	1 807	...	...	...	...	...	...
45 - 49	3 389	1 673	1 716	...	...	...	...	...	...
50 - 54	2 679	1 335	1 344	...	...	...	...	...	...
55 - 59	2 049	1 011	1 038	...	...	...	...	...	...
60 - 64	1 480	755	725	...	...	...	...	...	...
65 - 69	960	500	460	...	...	...	...	...	...
70 - 74	654	321	333	...	...	...	...	...	...
75 - 79	337	155	182	...	...	...	...	...	...
80 - 84	206	76	130	...	...	...	...	...	...
85 +	110	41	69	...	...	...	...	...	...
Australia - Australie									
9 VIII 2011 (CDJC)[74]									
Total	21 507 719[75]	10 634 015[75]	10 873 704[75]	19 126 751	9 395 298	9 731 453	2 331 966	1 210 340	1 121 626
0 - 4	1 421 048[75]	729 971[75]	691 077[75]	1 281 987	658 370	623 617	137 033	70 543	66 490
5 - 9	1 351 920[75]	694 561[75]	657 359[75]	1 193 724	613 379	580 345	156 845	80 501	76 344
10 - 14	1 371 054[75]	703 306[75]	667 748[75]	1 197 022	613 614	583 408	172 888	89 088	83 800
15 - 19	1 405 799[75]	722 378[75]	683 421[75]	1 246 896	638 634	608 262	156 533	82 547	73 986
20 - 24	1 460 674[75]	741 119[75]	719 555[75]	1 352 072	681 544	670 528	103 788	57 022	46 766
25 - 29	1 513 238[75]	754 467[75]	758 771[75]	1 409 392	699 987	709 405	98 350	51 392	46 958
30 - 34	1 453 776[75]	719 654[75]	734 122[75]	1 339 303	661 808	677 495	110 058	55 190	54 868
35 - 39	1 520 137[75]	747 118[75]	773 019[75]	1 371 495	673 073	698 422	144 834	71 627	73 207
40 - 44	1 542 877[75]	754 567[75]	788 310[75]	1 364 412	664 736	699 676	174 842	87 474	87 368
45 - 49	1 504 142[75]	740 962[75]	763 180[75]	1 312 154	642 456	669 698	188 614	96 321	92 293
50 - 54	1 447 402[75]	711 742[75]	735 660[75]	1 247 607	608 781	638 826	196 285	100 945	95 340
55 - 59	1 297 245[75]	637 839[75]	659 406[75]	1 109 135	539 734	569 401	184 322	96 008	88 314
60 - 64	1 206 114[75]	597 886[75]	608 228[75]	1 027 206	502 392	524 814	175 026	93 328	81 698
65 - 69	919 321[75]	455 420[75]	463 901[75]	785 985	382 492	403 493	130 659	71 283	59 376
70 - 74	708 089[75]	342 691[75]	365 398[75]	619 017	293 391	325 626	87 641	48 377	39 264
75 - 79	545 263[75]	252 929[75]	292 334[75]	490 311	222 913	267 398	54 335	29 614	24 721
80 - 84	436 936[75]	188 242[75]	248 694[75]	401 232	169 529	231 703	35 373	18 531	16 842

Continent, country or area, date, code and age (in years) Continent, pays ou zone, date, code et âge (en années)	Total			Urban - Urbaine			Rural - Rurale		
	Both sexes Les deux sexes	Male Masculin	Female Féminin	Both sexes Les deux sexes	Male Masculin	Female Féminin	Both sexes Les deux sexes	Male Masculin	Female Féminin
OCEANIA - OCÉANIE									
Australia - Australie									
9 VIII 2011 (CDJC)[74]									
85 - 89	270 798[75]	100 802[75]	169 996[75]	253 314	92 813	160 501	17 272	7 890	9 382
90 - 94	103 772[75]	31 792[75]	71 980[75]	97 936	29 563	68 373	5 747	2 191	3 556
95 - 99	24 836[75]	5 911[75]	18 925[75]	23 460	5 488	17 972	1 347	416	931
100 +	3 278[75]	658[75]	2 620[75]	3 091	601	2 490	174	52	122
1 VII 2012* (ESDJ)[76]									
Total	22 683 573	11 280 804	11 402 769	...	...	...	...	...	...
0	297 297	152 661	144 636	...	...	...	...	...	...
1 - 4	1 184 472	607 610	576 862	...	...	...	...	...	...
5 - 9	1 403 791	721 135	682 656	...	...	...	...	...	...
10 - 14	1 382 636	708 804	673 832	...	...	...	...	...	...
15 - 19	1 460 188	748 674	711 514	...	...	...	...	...	...
20 - 24	1 622 424	827 157	795 267	...	...	...	...	...	...
25 - 29	1 687 846	854 925	832 921	...	...	...	...	...	...
30 - 34	1 584 977	795 158	789 819	...	...	...	...	...	...
35 - 39	1 554 592	774 443	780 149	...	...	...	...	...	...
40 - 44	1 629 940	806 875	823 065	...	...	...	...	...	...
45 - 49	1 538 224	763 031	775 193	...	...	...	...	...	...
50 - 54	1 527 252	755 992	771 260	...	...	...	...	...	...
55 - 59	1 360 720	672 254	688 466	...	...	...	...	...	...
60 - 64	1 238 003	612 489	625 514	...	...	...	...	...	...
65 - 69	1 025 329	509 422	515 907	...	...	...	...	...	...
70 - 74	747 833	364 420	383 413	...	...	...	...	...	...
75 - 79	569 929	264 739	305 190	...	...	...	...	...	...
80 - 84	444 380	192 032	252 348	...	...	...	...	...	...
85 - 89	280 228	105 888	174 340	...	...	...	...	...	...
90 - 94	113 726	35 970	77 756	...	...	...	...	...	...
95 - 99	26 307	6 454	19 853	...	...	...	...	...	...
100 +	3 479	671	2 808	...	...	...	...	...	...
Cook Islands - Îles Cook[77]									
1 XII 2006 (CDJC)									
Total	15 324	7 822	7 502	...	...	...	...	...	...
0 - 4	1 509	782	727	...	...	...	...	...	...
5 - 9	1 513	784	729	...	...	...	...	...	...
10 - 14	1 679	889	790	...	...	...	...	...	...
15 - 19	1 450	820	630	...	...	...	...	...	...
20 - 24	1 058	513	545	...	...	...	...	...	...
25 - 29	913	440	473	...	...	...	...	...	...
30 - 34	1 022	468	554	...	...	...	...	...	...
35 - 39	1 083	532	551	...	...	...	...	...	...
40 - 44	1 096	556	540	...	...	...	...	...	...
45 - 49	931	474	457	...	...	...	...	...	...
50 - 54	725	363	362	...	...	...	...	...	...
55 - 59	634	353	281	...	...	...	...	...	...
60 - 64	549	265	284	...	...	...	...	...	...
65 - 69	451	224	227	...	...	...	...	...	...
70 - 74	352	187	165	...	...	...	...	...	...
75 +	359	172	187	...	...	...	...	...	...
Fiji - Fidji									
16 IX 2007 (CDFC)									
Total	837 271	427 176	410 095	424 846	212 454	212 392	412 425	214 722	197 703
0 - 4	82 718	42 835	39 883	39 209	20 264	18 945	43 509	22 571	20 938
5 - 9	78 019	40 441	37 578	35 981	18 528	17 453	42 038	21 913	20 125
10 - 14	82 384	42 369	40 015	38 916	19 790	19 126	43 468	22 579	20 889
15 - 19	79 518	40 818	38 700	42 458	21 051	21 407	37 060	19 767	17 293
20 - 24	80 352	41 325	39 027	45 837	22 896	22 941	34 515	18 429	16 086
25 - 29	73 487	37 390	36 097	40 669	20 260	20 409	32 818	17 130	15 688
30 - 34	63 535	32 825	30 710	33 612	17 017	16 595	29 923	15 808	14 115
35 - 39	56 552	28 778	27 774	29 288	14 674	14 614	27 264	14 104	13 160
40 - 44	56 274	28 598	27 676	28 147	14 058	14 089	28 127	14 540	13 587
45 - 49	50 322	25 835	24 487	25 556	12 780	12 776	24 766	13 055	11 711
50 - 54	40 009	20 215	19 794	20 581	10 118	10 463	19 428	10 097	9 331
55 - 59	31 161	15 735	15 426	15 667	7 715	7 952	15 494	8 020	7 474
60 - 64	24 120	11 956	12 164	11 655	5 647	6 008	12 465	6 309	6 156

7. Population by age, sex and urban/rural residence: latest available year, 2003 - 2012

Population selon l'âge, le sexe et la résidence, urbaine/rurale : dernière année disponible, 2003 - 2012 (continued - suite)

Continent, country or area, date, code and age (in years) / Continent, pays ou zone, date, code et âge (en années)	Total			Urban - Urbaine			Rural - Rurale		
	Both sexes Les deux sexes	Male Masculin	Female Féminin	Both sexes Les deux sexes	Male Masculin	Female Féminin	Both sexes Les deux sexes	Male Masculin	Female Féminin
OCEANIA - OCÉANIE									
Fiji - Fidji									
16 IX 2007 (CDFC)									
65 - 69	16 808	8 098	8 710	7 597	3 509	4 088	9 211	4 589	4 622
70 - 74	10 110	4 716	5 394	4 360	1 887	2 473	5 750	2 829	2 921
75 +	11 902	5 242	6 660	5 313	2 260	3 053	6 589	2 982	3 607
75 - 79	6 138	2 811	3 327	...	...	...	...	...	...
80 - 84	3 236	1 376	1 860	...	...	...	...	...	...
85 - 89	1 638	702	936	...	...	...	...	...	...
90 - 94	572	212	360	...	...	...	...	...	...
95 +	318	141	177	...	...	...	...	...	...
French Polynesia - Polynésie française									
1 I 2011 (ESDF)									
Total	269 989	138 127	131 862	...	...	...	...	...	...
0 - 4	22 060	11 344	10 716	...	...	...	...	...	...
5 - 9	21 893	11 036	10 857	...	...	...	...	...	...
10 - 14	23 567	12 115	11 452	...	...	...	...	...	...
15 - 19	24 936	12 766	12 170	...	...	...	...	...	...
20 - 24	24 430	12 544	11 886	...	...	...	...	...	...
25 - 29	21 135	10 662	10 473	...	...	...	...	...	...
30 - 34	19 951	10 154	9 797	...	...	...	...	...	...
35 - 39	20 911	10 655	10 256	...	...	...	...	...	...
40 - 44	20 715	10 780	9 935	...	...	...	...	...	...
45 - 49	18 232	9 441	8 791	...	...	...	...	...	...
50 - 54	14 919	7 867	7 052	...	...	...	...	...	...
55 - 59	11 744	6 115	5 629	...	...	...	...	...	...
60 - 64	8 646	4 416	4 230	...	...	...	...	...	...
65 - 69	6 564	3 381	3 183	...	...	...	...	...	...
70 - 74	4 722	2 349	2 373	...	...	...	...	...	...
75 - 79	3 158	1 463	1 695	...	...	...	...	...	...
80 +	2 406	1 039	1 367	...	...	...	...	...	...
Guam[78]									
1 VII 2012 (ESDJ)									
Total	159 914	81 165	78 749	...	...	...	...	...	...
0 - 4	13 907	7 152	6 755	...	...	...	...	...	...
5 - 9	13 936	7 169	6 767	...	...	...	...	...	...
10 - 14	14 944	7 796	7 148	...	...	...	...	...	...
15 - 19	14 046	7 248	6 798	...	...	...	...	...	...
20 - 24	12 900	6 550	6 350	...	...	...	...	...	...
25 - 29	11 290	5 729	5 561	...	...	...	...	...	...
30 - 34	10 091	5 044	5 047	...	...	...	...	...	...
35 - 39	10 392	5 279	5 113	...	...	...	...	...	...
40 - 44	11 101	5 691	5 410	...	...	...	...	...	...
45 - 49	10 908	5 687	5 221	...	...	...	...	...	...
50 - 54	9 541	4 926	4 615	...	...	...	...	...	...
55 - 59	7 754	3 914	3 840	...	...	...	...	...	...
60 - 64	6 532	3 258	3 274	...	...	...	...	...	...
65 - 69	4 426	2 164	2 262	...	...	...	...	...	...
70 - 74	3 384	1 582	1 802	...	...	...	...	...	...
75 - 79	2 478	1 065	1 413	...	...	...	...	...	...
80 - 84	1 370	582	788	...	...	...	...	...	...
85 +	914	329	585	...	...	...	...	...	...
Kiribati									
10 X 2010 (CDFC)									
Total	103 058	50 796	52 262	50 182	24 233	25 949	52 876	26 563	26 313
0 - 4	13 992	7 126	6 866	6 934	3 563	3 371	7 058	3 563	3 495
5 - 9	11 026	5 739	5 287	4 822	2 504	2 318	6 204	3 235	2 969
10 - 14	12 166	6 198	5 968	5 363	2 693	2 670	6 803	3 505	3 298
15 - 19	10 926	5 582	5 344	5 713	2 846	2 867	5 213	2 736	2 477
20 - 24	10 366	5 242	5 124	5 658	2 763	2 895	4 708	2 479	2 229
25 - 29	8 416	4 070	4 346	4 413	2 035	2 378	4 003	2 035	1 968
30 - 34	6 721	3 223	3 498	3 389	1 624	1 765	3 332	1 599	1 733
35 - 39	5 625	2 682	2 943	2 767	1 304	1 463	2 858	1 378	1 480
40 - 44	6 116	2 908	3 208	2 803	1 302	1 501	3 313	1 606	1 707
45 - 49	5 234	2 519	2 715	2 479	1 137	1 342	2 755	1 382	1 373

Continent, country or area, date, code and age (in years) / Continent, pays ou zone, date, code et âge (en annèes)	Total			Urban - Urbaine			Rural - Rurale		
	Both sexes Les deux sexes	Male Masculin	Female Féminin	Both sexes Les deux sexes	Male Masculin	Female Féminin	Both sexes Les deux sexes	Male Masculin	Female Féminin
OCEANIA - OCÉANIE									
Kiribati									
10 X 2010 (CDFC)									
50 - 54	3 892	1 813	2 079	1 897	855	1 042	1 995	958	1 037
55 - 59	2 927	1 349	1 578	1 437	627	810	1 490	722	768
60 - 64	1 985	919	1 066	922	396	526	1 063	523	540
65 - 69	1 520	642	878	700	278	422	820	364	456
70 - 74	1 108	428	680	438	161	277	670	267	403
75 - 79	637	223	414	264	89	175	373	134	239
80 - 84	272	97	175	119	41	78	153	56	97
85 - 89	89	25	64	48	11	37	41	14	27
90 - 94	29	9	20	15	4	11	14	5	9
95 +	11	2	9	1	-	1	10	2	8
Marshall Islands - Îles Marshall[79]									
1 VII 2010 (ESDF)									
Total	54 305	27 843	26 462	...	...	...	...	...	...
0 - 4	7 899	4 053	3 846	...	...	...	...	...	...
5 - 9	7 131	3 660	3 470	...	...	...	...	...	...
10 - 14	7 207	3 732	3 475	...	...	...	...	...	...
15 - 19	6 120	3 126	2 993	...	...	...	...	...	...
20 - 24	6 347	3 310	3 038	...	...	...	...	...	...
25 - 29	4 808	2 478	2 330	...	...	...	...	...	...
30 - 34	2 761	1 389	1 372	...	...	...	...	...	...
35 - 39	2 128	1 071	1 058	...	...	...	...	...	...
40 - 44	2 039	1 043	996	...	...	...	...	...	...
45 - 49	2 023	1 025	998	...	...	...	...	...	...
50 - 54	1 814	878	936	...	...	...	...	...	...
55 - 59	1 592	854	737	...	...	...	...	...	...
60 - 64	1 089	573	516	...	...	...	...	...	...
65 - 69	572	299	273	...	...	...	...	...	...
70 - 74	361	165	196	...	...	...	...	...	...
75 +	412	184	228	...	...	...	...	...	...
Micronesia (Federated States of) - Micronésie (États fédérés de)[2]									
1 VII 2010 (ESDJ)									
Total	107 839	54 158	53 681	...	...	...	...	...	...
0 - 4	13 651	6 992	6 659	...	...	...	...	...	...
5 - 9	13 203	6 753	6 450	...	...	...	...	...	...
10 - 14	12 489	6 387	6 102	...	...	...	...	...	...
15 - 19	11 478	5 878	5 600	...	...	...	...	...	...
20 - 24	9 345	4 862	4 483	...	...	...	...	...	...
25 - 29	7 667	3 782	3 885	...	...	...	...	...	...
30 - 34	6 198	3 118	3 080	...	...	...	...	...	...
35 - 39	6 198	2 920	3 278	...	...	...	...	...	...
40 - 44	5 712	2 673	3 039	...	...	...	...	...	...
45 - 49	5 478	2 694	2 784	...	...	...	...	...	...
50 - 54	5 073	2 546	2 527	...	...	...	...	...	...
55 - 59	4 183	2 149	2 034	...	...	...	...	...	...
60 - 64	2 801	1 428	1 373	...	...	...	...	...	...
65 - 69	1 551	714	837	...	...	...	...	...	...
70 - 74	1 257	580	677	...	...	...	...	...	...
75 +	1 555	682	873	...	...	...	...	...	...
New Caledonia - Nouvelle-Calédonie									
1 VII 2010 (ESDF)									
Total	250 040	126 771	123 269	...	...	...	...	...	...
0 - 4	19 821	10 307	9 514	...	...	...	...	...	...
5 - 9	18 682	9 559	9 123	...	...	...	...	...	...
10 - 14	22 402	11 505	10 897	...	...	...	...	...	...
15 - 19	21 542	11 159	10 383	...	...	...	...	...	...
20 - 24	19 512	9 965	9 547	...	...	...	...	...	...
25 - 29	18 426	9 309	9 117	...	...	...	...	...	...
30 - 34	18 633	9 235	9 398	...	...	...	...	...	...
35 - 39	20 298	10 208	10 090	...	...	...	...	...	...

Continent, country or area, date, code and age (in years) / Continent, pays ou zone, date, code et âge (en annèes)	Total			Urban - Urbaine			Rural - Rurale		
	Both sexes Les deux sexes	Male Masculin	Female Féminin	Both sexes Les deux sexes	Male Masculin	Female Féminin	Both sexes Les deux sexes	Male Masculin	Female Féminin
OCEANIA - OCÉANIE									
New Caledonia - Nouvelle-Calédonie									
1 VII 2010 (ESDF)									
40 - 44	*19 020*	*9 593*	*9 427*	...	...	...	...	...	...
45 - 49	*16 713*	*8 531*	*8 182*	...	...	...	...	...	...
50 - 54	*13 719*	*6 923*	*6 796*	...	...	...	...	...	...
55 - 59	*11 328*	*5 762*	*5 566*	...	...	...	...	...	...
60 - 64	*9 839*	*5 188*	*4 651*	...	...	...	...	...	...
65 - 69	*7 148*	*3 638*	*3 510*	...	...	...	...	...	...
70 - 74	*5 500*	*2 641*	*2 859*	...	...	...	...	...	...
75 - 79	*3 577*	*1 701*	*1 876*	...	...	...	...	...	...
80 +	*3 880*	*1 547*	*2 333*	...	...	...	...	...	...
New Zealand - Nouvelle-Zélande[80]									
1 VII 2012 (ESDJ)									
Total	4 433 000	2 180 100	2 253 000	3 822 700[81]	1 867 400[81]	1 955 300[81]	609 500[81]	312 200[81]	297 300[81]
0 - 4	311 840	160 160	151 680	270 790[81]	139 100[81]	131 690[81]	41 040[81]	21 060[81]	19 990[81]
5 - 9	291 530	149 300	142 230	249 020[81]	127 610[81]	121 410[81]	42 500[81]	21 680[81]	20 820[81]
10 - 14	288 900	147 910	140 980	244 590[81]	125 170[81]	119 410[81]	44 290[81]	22 720[81]	21 560[81]
15 - 19	311 300	160 040	151 260	270 000[81]	137 990[81]	132 010[81]	41 280[81]	22 040[81]	19 250[81]
20 - 24	330 170	171 040	159 130	298 230[81]	153 370[81]	144 850[81]	31 920[81]	17 650[81]	14 270[81]
25 - 29	297 900	149 560	148 340	271 780[81]	135 830[81]	135 950[81]	26 080[81]	13 700[81]	12 370[81]
30 - 34	277 370	134 140	143 220	248 740[81]	120 060[81]	128 680[81]	28 580[81]	14 060[81]	14 520[81]
35 - 39	280 310	133 630	146 680	244 330[81]	115 950[81]	128 380[81]	35 920[81]	17 640[81]	18 280[81]
40 - 44	312 750	148 940	163 810	267 670[81]	127 190[81]	140 480[81]	45 030[81]	21 710[81]	23 320[81]
45 - 49	313 180	151 070	162 100	263 310[81]	126 550[81]	136 760[81]	49 810[81]	24 490[81]	25 320[81]
50 - 54	305 400	148 310	157 090	253 210[81]	122 070[81]	131 140[81]	52 110[81]	26 190[81]	25 920[81]
55 - 59	263 700	128 940	134 760	216 430[81]	104 580[81]	111 850[81]	47 160[81]	24 290[81]	22 870[81]
60 - 64	237 320	116 330	120 980	195 350[81]	94 670[81]	100 680[81]	41 870[81]	21 610[81]	20 260[81]
65 - 69	190 970	93 290	97 670	158 440[81]	76 140[81]	82 310[81]	32 430[81]	17 100[81]	15 330[81]
70 - 74	152 590	73 150	79 440	129 570[81]	60 740[81]	68 830[81]	22 950[81]	12 370[81]	10 590[81]
75 - 79	108 280	50 240	58 040	95 180[81]	43 110[81]	52 060[81]	13 070[81]	7 100[81]	5 970[81]
80 - 84	83 650	36 860	46 790	75 730[81]	32 650[81]	43 070[81]	7 910[81]	4 190[81]	3 720[81]
Niue - Nioué									
1 VII 2010 (ESDJ)									
Total	1 496[82]	754	740	...	...	...	...	...	...
0 - 4	135[82]	69	64	...	...	...	...	...	...
5 - 9	134	58	76	...	...	...	...	...	...
10 - 14	116	60	56	...	...	...	...	...	...
15 - 19	124	79	45	...	...	...	...	...	...
20 - 24	100	50	50	...	...	...	...	...	...
25 - 29	90	38	52	...	...	...	...	...	...
30 - 34	71	39	32	...	...	...	...	...	...
35 - 39	85	45	40	...	...	...	...	...	...
40 - 44	101	55	46	...	...	...	...	...	...
45 - 49	92	42	50	...	...	...	...	...	...
50 - 54	107	58	49	...	...	...	...	...	...
55 - 59	89	42	47	...	...	...	...	...	...
60 - 64	70	34	36	...	...	...	...	...	...
65 - 69	75	37	38	...	...	...	...	...	...
70 - 74	53	23	30	...	...	...	...	...	...
75 +	54	25	29	...	...	...	...	...	...
Norfolk Island - Île Norfolk									
9 VIII 2011 (CDFC)									
Total	2 302	1 082	1 220	...	...	...	...	...	...
0 - 4	106	53	53	...	...	...	...	...	...
5 - 9	123	63	60	...	...	...	...	...	...
10 - 14	132	69	63	...	...	...	...	...	...
15 - 19	73	35	38	...	...	...	...	...	...
20 - 24	41	20	21	...	...	...	...	...	...
25 - 29	60	19	41	...	...	...	...	...	...
30 - 34	100	48	52	...	...	...	...	...	...
35 - 39	127	56	71	...	...	...	...	...	...
40 - 44	146	64	82	...	...	...	...	...	...

Continent, country or area, date, code and age (in years) / Continent, pays ou zone, date, code et âge (en années)	Total			Urban - Urbaine			Rural - Rurale		
	Both sexes Les deux sexes	Male Masculin	Female Féminin	Both sexes Les deux sexes	Male Masculin	Female Féminin	Both sexes Les deux sexes	Male Masculin	Female Féminin
OCEANIA - OCÉANIE									
Norfolk Island - Île Norfolk									
9 VIII 2011 (CDFC)									
45 - 49	167	81	86	...	...	...	...	...	...
50 - 54	180	86	94	...	...	...	...	...	...
55 - 59	232	103	129	...	...	...	...	...	...
60 - 64	262	120	142	...	...	...	...	...	...
65 - 69	205	99	106	...	...	...	...	...	...
70 - 74	142	70	72	...	...	...	...	...	...
75 - 79	96	49	47	...	...	...	...	...	...
80 - 84	58	24	34	...	...	...	...	...	...
85 +	52	23	29	...	...	...	...	...	...
Northern Mariana Islands - Îles Mariannes septentrionales									
1 VII 2003 (ESDF)[83]									
Total	63 419	27 488	35 931	56 941	24 932	32 009	6 478	2 556	3 922
0 - 4	4 555	2 498	2 057	4 230	2 285	1 945	325	213	112
5 - 9	5 534	2 836	2 698	5 212	2 656	2 556	322	180	142
10 - 14	4 586	2 362	2 224	4 322	2 216	2 106	264	145	119
15 - 19	3 825	1 848	1 977	3 538	1 684	1 854	287	165	122
20 - 24	7 253	1 671	5 582	6 101	1 492	4 609	1 152	179	973
25 - 29	8 449	2 405	6 044	7 055	2 026	5 029	1 394	379	1 015
30 - 34	8 085	2 900	5 185	7 168	2 597	4 571	917	303	614
35 - 39	6 330	3 033	3 297	5 928	2 834	3 094	402	199	203
40 - 44	5 117	2 615	2 502	4 547	2 320	2 227	569	294	275
45 - 49	4 105	2 270	1 835	3 815	2 102	1 713	290	168	122
50 - 54	2 263	1 240	1 023	1 995	1 107	888	268	133	135
55 - 59	1 505	729	776	1 339	623	716	166	106	60
60 - 64	886	616	270	804	564	240	82	52	30
65 - 69	370	246	124	333	209	124	38	38	-
70 - 74	329	95	234	327	93	234	2	2	-
75 +	227	124	103	227	124	103	-	-	-
1 VII 2011 (ESDF)									
Total	46 050	22 153	23 897	...	...	...	...	...	...
0 - 4	4 852	2 495	2 357	...	...	...	...	...	...
5 - 9	3 622	1 883	1 739	...	...	...	...	...	...
10 - 14	3 500	1 971	1 529	...	...	...	...	...	...
15 - 19	3 802	2 121	1 681	...	...	...	...	...	...
20 - 24	3 398	1 607	1 791	...	...	...	...	...	...
25 - 29	3 831	1 050	2 781	...	...	...	...	...	...
30 - 34	3 696	1 008	2 688	...	...	...	...	...	...
35 - 39	3 211	1 550	1 661	...	...	...	...	...	...
40 - 44	3 584	1 858	1 726	...	...	...	...	...	...
45 - 49	3 738	1 967	1 771	...	...	...	...	...	...
50 - 54	3 441	1 824	1 617	...	...	...	...	...	...
55 - 59	2 270	1 260	1 010	...	...	...	...	...	...
60 - 64	1 440	769	671	...	...	...	...	...	...
65 - 69	794	366	428	...	...	...	...	...	...
70 - 74	416	248	168	...	...	...	...	...	...
75 - 79	239	101	138	...	...	...	...	...	...
80 - 84	147	54	93	...	...	...	...	...	...
85 - 89	53	17	36	...	...	...	...	...	...
90 - 94	14	3	11	...	...	...	...	...	...
95 - 99	1	1	-	...	...	...	...	...	...
100 +	1	-	1	...	...	...	...	...	...
Palau - Palaos									
1 IV 2005 (CDJC)									
Total	19 907	10 699	9 208	...	...	...	...	...	...
0 - 4	1 363	685	678	...	...	...	...	...	...
5 - 9	1 521	805	716	...	...	...	...	...	...
10 - 14	1 914	964	950	...	...	...	...	...	...
15 - 19	1 462	715	747	...	...	...	...	...	...
20 - 24	1 266	712	554	...	...	...	...	...	...
25 - 29	1 583	942	641	...	...	...	...	...	...
30 - 34	1 856	1 072	784	...	...	...	...	...	...

Continent, country or area, date, code and age (in years) / Continent, pays ou zone, date, code et âge (en années)	Total			Urban - Urbaine			Rural - Rurale		
	Both sexes Les deux sexes	Male Masculin	Female Féminin	Both sexes Les deux sexes	Male Masculin	Female Féminin	Both sexes Les deux sexes	Male Masculin	Female Féminin
OCEANIA - OCÉANIE									
Palau - Palaos									
1 IV 2005 (CDJC)									
35 - 39	1 965	1 132	833	...	...	...	...	...	...
40 - 44	1 887	1 096	791	...	...	...	...	...	...
45 - 49	1 534	842	692	...	...	...	...	...	...
50 - 54	1 182	624	558	...	...	...	...	...	...
55 - 59	732	393	339	...	...	...	...	...	...
60 - 64	506	254	252	...	...	...	...	...	...
65 - 69	373	170	203	...	...	...	...	...	...
70 - 74	257	119	138	...	...	...	...	...	...
75 - 79	214	71	143	...	...	...	...	...	...
80 - 84	151	56	95	...	...	...	...	...	...
85 +	141	47	94	...	...	...	...	...	...
Pitcairn									
10 VIII 2012 (CDFC)									
Total	48	22	26	...	...	...	...	...	...
0 - 4	2	1	1	...	...	...	...	...	...
5 - 14	7	3	4	...	...	...	...	...	...
20 - 29	2	1	1	...	...	...	...	...	...
30 - 39	4	2	2	...	...	...	...	...	...
40 - 49	8	4	4	...	...	...	...	...	...
50 - 64	15	7	8	...	...	...	...	...	...
65 +	10	4	6	...	...	...	...	...	...
Samoa									
7 XI 2011 (CDFC)									
Total	187 820	96 990	90 830	...	...	...	...	...	...
0 - 4	26 829	13 953	12 876	...	...	...	...	...	...
5 - 9	23 044	11 899	11 145	...	...	...	...	...	...
10 - 14	22 017	11 497	10 520	...	...	...	...	...	...
15 - 19	19 814	10 391	9 423	...	...	...	...	...	...
20 - 24	14 833	7 700	7 133	...	...	...	...	...	...
25 - 29	12 767	6 601	6 166	...	...	...	...	...	...
30 - 34	11 543	5 945	5 598	...	...	...	...	...	...
35 - 39	10 877	5 735	5 142	...	...	...	...	...	...
40 - 44	10 436	5 602	4 834	...	...	...	...	...	...
45 - 49	8 887	4 574	4 313	...	...	...	...	...	...
50 - 54	7 576	3 966	3 610	...	...	...	...	...	...
55 - 59	5 904	3 007	2 897	...	...	...	...	...	...
60 - 64	3 978	2 002	1 976	...	...	...	...	...	...
65 - 69	3 374	1 605	1 769	...	...	...	...	...	...
70 - 74	2 557	1 187	1 370	...	...	...	...	...	...
75 +	3 354	1 302	2 052	...	...	...	...	...	...
Unknown - Inconnu	30	24	6	...	...	...	...	...	...
Solomon Islands - Îles Salomon									
22 XI 2009* (CDFC)									
Total	515 870	264 455	251 415	102 030	53 596	48 434	413 840	210 859	202 981
0 - 4	76 227	39 728	36 499	12 500	6 573	5 927	63 727	33 155	30 572
5 - 9	71 126	36 974	34 152	11 328	5 853	5 475	59 798	31 121	28 677
10 - 14	61 931	32 562	29 369	10 354	5 382	4 972	51 577	27 180	24 397
15 - 19	51 212	26 189	25 023	10 995	5 525	5 470	40 217	20 664	19 553
20 - 24	45 419	22 399	23 020	12 344	6 360	5 984	33 075	16 039	17 036
25 - 29	42 674	20 794	21 880	11 160	5 696	5 464	31 514	15 098	16 416
30 - 34	37 592	18 807	18 785	8 817	4 568	4 249	28 775	14 239	14 536
35 - 39	33 151	17 010	16 141	7 447	4 000	3 447	25 704	13 010	12 694
40 - 44	23 638	12 070	11 568	5 161	2 808	2 353	18 477	9 262	9 215
45 - 49	19 713	10 189	9 524	4 064	2 265	1 799	15 649	7 924	7 725
50 - 54	14 339	7 498	6 841	2 818	1 650	1 168	11 521	5 848	5 673
55 - 59	11 787	6 111	5 676	2 011	1 198	813	9 776	4 913	4 863
60 - 64	8 916	4 535	4 381	1 272	726	546	7 644	3 809	3 835
65 - 69	7 021	3 693	3 328	822	466	356	6 199	3 227	2 972
70 - 74	4 698	2 402	2 296	478	259	219	4 220	2 143	2 077
75 - 79	3 374	1 784	1 590	279	160	119	3 095	1 624	1 471
80 - 84	1 525	800	725	102	58	44	1 423	742	681
85 - 89	894	512	382	58	34	24	836	478	358

Continent, country or area, date, code and age (in years) / Continent, pays ou zone, date, code et âge (en années)	Total			Urban - Urbaine			Rural - Rurale		
	Both sexes Les deux sexes	Male Masculin	Female Féminin	Both sexes Les deux sexes	Male Masculin	Female Féminin	Both sexes Les deux sexes	Male Masculin	Female Féminin
OCEANIA - OCÉANIE									
Solomon Islands - Îles Salomon									
22 XI 2009* (CDFC)									
90 - 94	301	170	131	8	4	4	293	166	127
95 - 99	332	228	104	12	11	1	320	217	103
Tokelau - Tokélaou									
18 X 2011 (CDFC)									
Total	1 205	600	605	...	...	...	...	...	...
0 - 4	142	76	66	...	...	...	...	...	...
5 - 9	115	53	62	...	...	...	...	...	...
10 - 14	143	76	67	...	...	...	...	...	...
15 - 19	120	63	57	...	...	...	...	...	...
20 - 24	99	49	50	...	...	...	...	...	...
25 - 29	79	40	39	...	...	...	...	...	...
30 - 34	54	31	23	...	...	...	...	...	...
35 - 39	67	31	36	...	...	...	...	...	...
40 - 44	60	31	29	...	...	...	...	...	...
45 - 49	65	32	33	...	...	...	...	...	...
50 - 54	63	31	32	...	...	...	...	...	...
55 - 59	61	27	34	...	...	...	...	...	...
60 - 64	33	14	19	...	...	...	...	...	...
65 - 69	35	20	15	...	...	...	...	...	...
70 - 74	33	10	23	...	...	...	...	...	...
75 +	34	15	19	...	...	...	...	...	...
Unknown - Inconnu	2	1	1	...	...	...	...	...	...
Tonga									
30 XI 2006 (CDJC)									
Total	101 991	51 772	50 219	23 658	11 860	11 798	78 333	39 912	38 421
0 - 4	13 782	7 174	6 608	3 015	1 514	1 501	10 767	5 660	5 107
5 - 9	12 804	6 745	6 059	2 721	1 447	1 274	10 083	5 298	4 785
10 - 14	12 320	6 412	5 908	2 631	1 357	1 274	9 689	5 055	4 634
15 - 19	10 280	5 383	4 897	2 362	1 196	1 166	7 918	4 187	3 731
20 - 24	9 191	4 648	4 543	2 503	1 276	1 227	6 688	3 372	3 316
25 - 29	7 304	3 639	3 665	1 872	913	959	5 432	2 726	2 706
30 - 34	6 337	3 146	3 191	1 551	787	764	4 786	2 359	2 427
35 - 39	6 229	3 112	3 117	1 448	711	737	4 781	2 401	2 380
40 - 44	5 014	2 578	2 436	1 240	647	593	3 774	1 931	1 843
45 - 49	3 982	1 923	2 059	982	458	524	3 000	1 465	1 535
50 - 54	3 465	1 634	1 831	844	406	438	2 621	1 228	1 393
55 - 59	2 849	1 359	1 490	639	323	316	2 210	1 036	1 174
60 - 64	2 470	1 169	1 301	556	260	296	1 914	909	1 005
65 - 69	2 174	1 092	1 082	466	211	255	1 708	881	827
70 - 74	1 586	777	809	340	152	188	1 246	625	621
75 - 79	1 099	510	589	253	107	146	846	403	443
80 - 84	625	260	365	144	48	96	481	212	269
85 - 89	246	96	150	45	21	24	201	75	126
90 - 94	86	22	64	15	5	10	71	17	54
95 - 99	20	6	14	5	2	3	15	4	11
100 +	6	-	6	-	-	-	6	-	6
Unknown - Inconnu	122	87	35	26	19	7	96	68	28
1 VII 2008 (ESDF)[84]									
Total	103 647	52 972	50 673	...	...	...	...	...	...
0 - 4	11 970	6 164	5 806	...	...	...	...	...	...
5 - 9	11 419	5 910	5 508	...	...	...	...	...	...
10 - 14	11 968	6 212	5 756	...	...	...	...	...	...
15 - 19	11 383	6 060	5 323	...	...	...	...	...	...
20 - 24	10 612	5 573	5 040	...	...	...	...	...	...
25 - 29	8 609	4 406	4 204	...	...	...	...	...	...
30 - 34	5 874	2 955	2 919	...	...	...	...	...	...
35 - 39	5 397	2 718	2 680	...	...	...	...	...	...
40 - 44	5 250	2 661	2 590	...	...	...	...	...	...
45 - 49	4 471	2 186	2 285	...	...	...	...	...	...
50 - 54	3 914	1 867	2 047	...	...	...	...	...	...
55 - 59	3 294	1 556	1 737	...	...	...	...	...	...
60 - 64	2 844	1 355	1 489	...	...	...	...	...	...

Continent, country or area, date, code and age (in years) / Continent, pays ou zone, date, code et âge (en années)	Total			Urban - Urbaine			Rural - Rurale		
	Both sexes Les deux sexes	Male Masculin	Female Féminin	Both sexes Les deux sexes	Male Masculin	Female Féminin	Both sexes Les deux sexes	Male Masculin	Female Féminin
OCEANIA - OCÉANIE									
Tonga									
1 VII 2008 (ESDF)[84]									
65 - 69	*2 482*	*1 243*	*1 239*	...	...	...	...	...	...
70 - 74	*1 896*	*981*	*915*	...	...	...	...	...	...
75 + ...	*2 263*	*1 127*	*1 136*	...	...	...	...	...	...
Vanuatu									
16 XI 2009 (CDJC)									
Total..................................	234 023	119 091	114 932	57 195	29 618	27 577	176 828	89 473	87 355
0 - 4	33 367	17 310	16 057	7 224	3 828	3 396	26 143	13 482	12 661
5 - 9	29 685	15 455	14 230	5 591	2 850	2 741	24 094	12 605	11 489
10 - 14	27 921	14 762	13 159	5 250	2 755	2 495	22 671	12 007	10 664
15 - 19	23 882	12 027	11 855	6 460	3 122	3 338	17 422	8 905	8 517
20 - 24	21 541	10 415	11 126	7 186	3 606	3 580	14 355	6 809	7 546
25 - 29	18 415	9 124	9 291	5 542	2 937	2 605	12 873	6 187	6 686
30 - 34	15 693	7 790	7 903	4 517	2 300	2 217	11 176	5 490	5 686
35 - 39	14 171	7 076	7 095	3 844	1 965	1 879	10 327	5 111	5 216
40 - 44	11 523	5 814	5 709	3 242	1 710	1 532	8 281	4 104	4 177
45 - 49	10 241	5 066	5 175	2 817	1 474	1 343	7 424	3 592	3 832
50 - 54	7 415	3 789	3 626	1 923	1 036	887	5 492	2 753	2 739
55 - 59	6 363	3 261	3 102	1 495	845	650	4 868	2 416	2 452
60 - 64	4 319	2 192	2 127	826	455	371	3 493	1 737	1 756
65 - 69	3 826	2 054	1 772	590	355	235	3 236	1 699	1 537
70 + ...	5 661	2 956	2 705	688	380	308	4 973	2 576	2 397

FOOTNOTES - NOTES

Italics: estimates which are less reliable. - Italiques : estimations moins sûres.

* Provisional. - Données provisoires.

'Code' indicates the source of data, as follows:
CDFC - Census, de facto, complete tabulation
CDFS - Census, de facto, sample tabulation
CDJC - Census, de jure, complete tabulation
CDJS - Census, de jure, sample tabulation
SSDF - Sample survey, de facto
SSDJ - Sample survey, de jure
ESDF - Estimates, de facto
ESDJ - Estimates, de jure

Le 'Code' indique la source des données, comme suit :
CDFC - Recensement, population de fait, tabulation complète
CDFS - Recensement, population de fait, tabulation par sondage
CDJC - Recensement, population de droit, tabulation complète
CDJS - Recensement, population de droit, tabulation par sondage
SSDF - Enquête par sondage, population de fait
SSDJ - Enquête par sondage, population de droit
ESDF - Estimations, population de fait
ESDJ - Estimations, population de droit

[1] Data refer to population in housing units and collective living quarters only. - Correspond aux personnes qui vivent dans des unités d'habitation et dans des logements collectifs seulement.

[2] Data refer to national projections. - Les données se réfèrent aux projections nationales.

[3] Based on the results of 2006 Demographic Survey. - D'après les résultats de l'enquête Démographique par Sondage de 2006.

[4] Data refer to projections based on the 2001 Population Census. - Les données se réfèrent aux projections basées sur le recensement de la population de 2001.

[5] Unrevised data. - Les données n'ont pas été révisées.

[6] Data as reported by national statistical authorities. Figures for urban and rural do not add up to the total. Data refer to national projections. - Les données comme elles ont été déclarées par l'institut national de la statistique. La somme des donées pour la residence urbaine et rurale n'est pas égale au total. Les données se réfèrent aux projections nationales.

[7] As reported by the country. Reasons for discrepancy with other tables not ascertained. - Comme indiqué par le pays. L'on ne connaît pas la raison des écarts avec d'autres tableaux.

[8] Excludes the islands of St. Brandon and Agalega. - Non compris les îles St. Brandon et Agalega.

[9] Based on the results of the 2004 Population Census. - D'après des résultats du recensement de la population de 2004.

[10] Data refer to Saint Helenian resident population. - Pour la population résidante de Sainte-Hélène.

[11] Projections based on the 2002 Population Census. - Projections fondées sur le recensement de la population de 2002.

[12] Because of rounding, totals are not in all cases the sum of the respective components. - Les chiffres étant arrondis, les totaux ne correspondent pas toujours rigoureusement à la somme des composants respectifs.

[13] Because of rounding, totals are not in all cases the sum of the respective components. Data refer to national projections. - Les chiffres étant arrondis, les totaux ne correspondent pas toujours rigoureusement à la somme des composants respectifs. Les données se réfèrent aux projections nationales.

[14] Data as reported by national statistical authorities. Summation of frequencies gives a different total; reason for discrepancy not ascertained. - Les données comme elles ont été déclarées par l'institut national de la statistique. La somme des fréquences un total différent; on ne sait pas comment s'explique la divergence.

[15] Bermuda is 100% urban. - 100 % de la population des Bermudes est urbaine.

[16] Estimates adjusted for census net undercoverage (including adjustment for incompletely enumerated Indian reserves). Preliminary postcensal estimates. - Ajusté pour la sous-estimation du recensement (y compris les réservations en Inde incomplètement énumérées). Estimations post censitaires préliminaires.

[17] As a result of the adjusting method used to calculate midyear population, the totals are not always equal to the sum of the parts. - Du fait de la méthode d'ajustement utilisée pour calculer la population en milieu d'année, les totaux ne correspondent pas nécessairement à la somme des différents éléments.

[18] Estimates based on the 2007 Population Census. - Estimations fondées sur le recensement de la population de 2007.

[19] Population statistics are compiled from registers. - Les statistiques de la population sont compilées à partir des registres.

[20] Excluding data for Saint Barthélémy and Saint Martin. - Non compris les données pour Saint Barthélémy et Saint Martin.

[21] The total in this table is not equal to the 2005 population estimate in table 5 because this dataset of population by age, sex and urban/rural residence has not been revised. - Le total dans ce tableau n'est pas égal à l'estimation de la population pour 2005 dans le tableau 5, parce que cet ensemble de données selon l'âge, le sexe et la résidence, urbaine/rurale n'a pas été révisé.

[22] Projections produced by l'Institut Haïtien de Statistique et d'Informatique (IHSI) and the Latin American and Caribbean Demographic Centre (CELADE) - Population Division of ECLAC. - Les données sont projections produits par l'Institut Haïtien de Statistique et d'Informatique (IHSI) et le centre démographique de l'Amérique latine et les Caraïbes - Division de la population de la CEPALC.

[23] Including an estimation of 1 334 585 persons corresponding to 448 195 housing units without information of the occupants. - Y compris une estimation de 1 334 585 personnes correspondant aux 448 195 unités d'habitation sans information sur les occupants.

[24] Data refer to projections based on the 2000 Population Census. - Les données se réfèrent aux projections basées sur le recensement de la population de 2000.

[25] Including armed forces stationed in the area. Data based on the 2010 Population Census results. - Y compris les militaires en garnison sur le territoire. D'après le résultats du recensement de la population de 2010.

[26] Based on the results of the 2000 Population Census. - Basé sur les résultats du recencement de la population de 2000.

[27] Excluding armed forces overseas and civilian citizens absent from the country for an extended period of time. - Non compris les militaires à l'étranger, et les civils hors du pays pendant une période prolongée.

[28] Including armed forces stationed in the area. - Y compris les militaires en garnison sur le territoire.

[29] Data are revised projections taking into consideration also the results of 2005 census. - Les données sont des projections révisées tenant compte également des résultats du recensement de 2005.

[30] Excludes nomadic Indian tribes. - Non compris les tribus d'Indiens nomades.

[31] A dispute exists between the governments of Argentina and the United Kingdom of Great Britain and Northern Ireland concerning sovereignty over the Falkland Islands (Malvinas). - La souveraineté sur les îles Falkland (Malvinas) fait l'objet d'un différend entre le Gouvernement argentin et le Gouvernement du Royaume-Uni de Grande-Bretagne et d'Irlande du Nord.

[32] The districts of Paramaribo and Wanica are considered urban areas, whereas all other districts are considered more or less rural areas. - Les districts de Paramaribo et de Wanica sont considérés comme des zones urbaines, les autres districts étant considérés comme des zones rurales à divers degrés.

[33] Total excludes 437 homeless persons. - Le chiffre total ne prend pas en compte 437 sans-abri.

[34] Data refer to the settled population based on the 1979 Population Census and the latest household prelisting. The refugees of Afghanistan in Iran, Pakistan, and an estimated 1.5 million nomads, are not included. - Les données se rapportent à la population stationnaire sur la base du recensement de 1979 et du recensement préliminaire des logements le plus récent. Sont exclus les réfugiés d'Afghanistan en Iran et au Pakistan et les nomades estimés à 1,5 million.

[35] Data refer to projections based on the 2005 Population Census. - Les données se réfèrent aux projections basées sur le recensement de la population de 2005.

[36] Excluding foreign diplomatic personnel and their dependants. Data based on 2008 Population Census. - Non compris le personnel diplomatique étranger et les membres de leur famille les accompagnant. Données fondées sur le recensement de population de 2008.

[37] For statistical purposes, the data for China do not include those for the Hong Kong Special Administrative Region (Hong Kong SAR), Macao Special Administrative Region (Macao SAR) and Taiwan province of China. - Pour la présentation des statistiques, les données pour la Chine ne comprennent pas la Région Administrative Spéciale de Hong Kong (Hong Kong RAS), la Région Administrative Spéciale de Macao (Macao RAS) et Taïwan province de Chine.

[38] Because of rounding, totals are not in all cases the sum of the respective components. Data have been adjusted on the basis of the Population Census of 2010. - Les chiffres étant arrondis, les totaux ne correspondent pas toujours rigoureusement à la somme des composants respectifs. Les données ont été ajustées à partir des résultats du recensement de la population de 2010.

[39] Data refer to government controlled areas. - Les données se rapportent aux zones contrôlées par le Gouvernement.

[40] Includes data for the Indian-held part of Jammu and Kashmir, the final status of which has not yet been determined. Data refer to projections based on the 2001 Population Census. - Y compris les données pour la partie du Jammu et du Cachemire occupée par l'Inde dont le statut définitif n'a pas encore été déterminé. Les données se réfèrent aux projections basées sur le recensement de la population de 2001.

[41] Because of rounding, totals are not in all cases the sum of the respective components. Includes data for East Jerusalem and Israeli residents in certain other territories under occupation by Israeli military forces since June 1967. - Les chiffres étant arrondis, les totaux ne correspondent pas toujours rigoureusement à la somme des composants respectifs. Y compris les données pour Jérusalem-Est et les résidents israéliens dans certains autres territoires occupés depuis 1967 par les forces armées israéliennes.

[42] Excluding diplomatic personnel outside the country and foreign military and civilian personnel and their dependants stationed in the area. - Non compris le personnel diplomatique hors du pays ni les militaires et agents civils étrangers en poste sur le territoire et les membres de leur famille les accompagnant.

[43] Because of rounding, totals are not in all cases the sum of the respective components. Estimates based on the complete counts of the 2010 Population Census. - Les chiffres étant arrondis, les totaux ne correspondent pas toujours rigoureusement à la somme des composants respectifs. Estimations basées sur le dénombrement complet du recensement de la population de 2010.

[44] Excluding data for Jordanian territory under occupation since June 1967 by Israeli military forces. Including registered Palestinian refugees and Jordanians abroad. - Non compris les données pour le territoire jordanien occupé depuis juin 1967 par les forces armées israéliennes. Y compris les réfugiés palestiniens enregistrés et les Jordaniens à l'étranger.

[45] Excluding data for Jordanian territory under occupation since June 1967 by Israeli military forces. Excluding foreigners, including registered Palestinian refugees. - Non compris les données pour le territoire jordanien occupé depuis juin 1967 par les forces armées israéliennes. Non compris les étrangers, mais y compris les réfugiés de Palestine enregistrés.

[46] Data are calculated from the results of the Population and Housing Census of 2009. - Les données sont calculées à partir des résultats du recensement de la population et de l'habitat de 2009.

[47] Excluding usual residents not in the country at the time of census. - À l'exclusion des résidents habituels qui ne sont pas dans le pays au moment du recensement.

[48] Based on the results of the 2005 Population and Housing Census. Because of rounding, totals are not in all cases the sum of the respective components. - Données fondées sur les résultats du recensement de la population et de l'habitat de 2005. Les chiffres étant arrondis, les totaux ne correspondent pas toujours rigoureusement à la somme des composants respectifs.

[49] Based on the results of a household survey. - D'après les résultats d'une enquête sur les ménages.

[50] Estimates based on the adjusted Population and Housing Census of 2010. - Les estimations sont fondée sur les résultats ajustées du recensement de la population et de l'habitat de 2010.

[51] Total Population is taken as de facto and de jure together. - Population totale considérée comme de fait et de droit.

[52] Excluding data for the Pakistan-held part of Jammu and Kashmir, the final status of which has not yet been determined. Based on the results of the Pakistan Demographic Survey (PDS 2007). - Non compris les données concernant la partie du Jammu et Cachemire occupée par le Pakistan dont le statut définitif n'a pas été déterminé. D'après les résultats de l'enquête démographique effectuée par le Pakistan en 2007.

[53] Excluding 2739 Filipinos in Philippine Embassies, Consulates and Mission Abroad. - Excepté 2739 Philippins travaillant dans les ambassades, les consulats et les missions des Philippines à l'étranger.

[54] Data refer to Korean population only. - les données ne concernent que la population coréenne.

[55] Data based on the preliminary results of the 2010 Population and Housing Census. - D'après les résultats préliminaires du recensement de la population et des logements de 2010.

[56] Data refer to resident population which comprises Singapore citizens and permanent residents. - Les données se rapportent à la population résidente composé des citoyens de Singapour et des résidents permanents.

[57] Including Palestinian refugees. - Y compris les réfugiés de Palestine.

[58] Data based on Address Based Population Registration System. - Les données sont basées sur le registre national de la population basé sur l'adresse.

[59] As published by the United Nations Economic and Social Commission for Western Asia. - Publié par la Commission économique et sociale des Nations Unies pour l'Asie occidentale.

[60] Population statistics are compiled from registers. Decrease in population due to revision in administrative registers. - Les statistiques de la population sont compilées à partir des registres. Diminution de la population due à la révision des registres administratifs.

[61] Average annual population based on the final data of 2009 Population Census. - La population annuelle moyenne est évaluée à partir des résultats définitifs du recensement de la population de 2009.

[62] Population statistics are compiled from registers. Excluding Faeroe Islands and Greenland shown separately, if available. - Les statistiques de la population sont compilées à partir des registres. Non compris les Îles Féroé et le Groenland, qui font l'objet de rubriques distinctes, si disponible.

[63] Population statistics are compiled from registers. Excluding Åland Islands. - Les statistiques de la population sont compilées à partir des registres. Non compris les Îles d'Åland.

[64] Excluding diplomatic personnel outside the country and including members of alien armed forces not living in military camps and foreign diplomatic personnel not living in embassies or consulates. - Non compris le personnel diplomatique hors du pays et y compris les militaires étrangers ne vivant pas dans des camps militaires et le personnel diplomatique étranger ne vivant pas dans les ambassades ou les consulats.

[65] Excluding armed forces stationed outside the country, but including alien armed forces stationed in the area. - Non compris les militaires en garnison hors du pays, mais y compris les militaires étrangers en garnison sur le territoire.

[66] Population statistics are compiled from registers. Definition of localities was revised from 2011 causing a break with the previous series. - Les statistiques de la population sont compilées à partir des registres. La rupture par rapport aux séries précédentes s'explique par le fait que la définition des localités a été révisée depuis 2011.

[67] The figures refer to usual residents in private households and persons present in communal establishments during the 2011 census. - Données se rapportant aux résidents habituels membres de ménages privés et aux personnes recensées dans des établissements collectifs au recensement de 2011.

[68] Figures for male and female population do not add up to the figure for total population, because they exclude 119 persons of unknown sex. - Les chiffres relatifs à la population masculine et féminine ne correspondent pas au chiffre de la population totale, parce que l'on en a exclu 119 personnes de sexe inconnu.

[69] Population statistics are compiled from registers. Including residents temporarily outside the country. - Les statistiques de la population sont compilées à partir des registres. Y compris les résidents se trouvant temporairement hors du pays.

[70] Excluding civilian aliens within country, but including civilian nationals temporarily outside country. - Non compris les civils étrangers dans le pays, mais y compris les civils nationaux temporairement hors du pays.

[71] Excluding Transnistria and the municipality of Bender. - Les données ne tiennent pas compte de l'information sur la Transnistria et la municipalité de Bender.

[72] Excludes data for Kosovo and Metohia. - Sans les données pour le Kosovo et Metohie.

[73] Excluding Channel Islands (Guernsey and Jersey) and Isle of Man, shown separately, if available. - Non compris les îles Anglo-Normandes (Guernesey et Jersey) et l'île de Man, qui font l'objet de rubriques distinctes, si disponible.

[74] This data has been randomly rounded to protect confidentiality. Individual figures may not add up to totals, and values for the same data may vary in different tables. - Ces données ont été arrondies de façon aléatoire afin d'en préserver la confidentialité. La somme de certains chiffres peut ne pas correspondre aux totaux indiqués et les valeurs des mêmes données peuvent varier d'un tableau à un autre.

[75] Including population in off-shore, migratory and shipping. - Y compris les populations extraterritoriales, les populations nomades et les populations maritimes.

[76] Data are based on Australian Standard Geographical Classification boundaries. - Les données réfèrent au découpage de la nomenclature géographique normalisée d'Australie.

[77] Excluding Niue, shown separately, which is part of Cook Islands, but because of remoteness is administered separately. - Non compris Nioué, qui fait l'objet d'une rubrique distincte et qui fait partie des îles Cook, mais qui, en raison de son éloignement, est administrée séparément.

[78] Including armed forces stationed in the area. Data refer to projections based on the 2010 Population Census. - Y compris les militaires en garnison sur le territoire. Les données se réfèrent aux projections basées sur le recensement de la population de 2010.

[79] Projections are prepared by the Secretariat of the Pacific Community based on 1999 census of population and housing. - Les projections sont préparées par le Secrétariat de la Communauté du Pacifique à partir des résultats du recensement de la population et de l'habitat de 1999.

[80] Based on the census, updated for residents missed or counted more than once by the census (net census undercount); residents temporarily overseas on census night, and births, deaths and net migration between the census night and the date of the estimate. Because of rounding, totals are not in all cases the sum of the respective components. - D'après le recensement, mise à jour pour les résidents omis ou dénombrés plus d'une fois par le recensement (sous-dénombrement net); résidents temporairement à l'étranger la nuit du recensement, et naissances, décès et migration nette entre la nuit du recensement et la date de l'estimation. Les chiffres étant arrondis, les totaux ne correspondent pas toujours rigoureusement à la somme des composants respectifs.

[81] Population estimates by urban/rural residence exclude inland waters and oceanic areas. - Les estimations de la population par lieu de résidence urbaine ou rurale excluent les eaux intérieures et les zones océaniques.

[82] Including unknown sex. - Y compris le sexe inconnu.

[83] Based on the results of a sample survey. Data refer to the island of Saipan only. - D'après les résultats de l'enquête par sondage. Les données se réfèrent uniquement à l'île de Saipan.

[84] Based on the results of the 1996 population census. Data refer to national projections. Because of rounding, totals are not in all cases the sum of the respective components. - À partir des résultats du recensement de la population de 1996. Les données se réfèrent aux projections nationales. Les chiffres étant arrondis, les totaux ne correspondent pas toujours rigoureusement à la somme des composants respectifs.

Table 8 - *Demographic Yearbook 2012*

Table 8 presents population of capital cities and cities of 100 000 or more inhabitants for the latest available year between 1993 and 2012.

Description of variables: Since the way in which cities are delimited differs from one country or area to another, the table not only presents data for the so-called city proper, but also for the urban agglomeration, if available.

City proper is defined as a locality with legally fixed boundaries and an administratively recognized urban status, usually characterized by some form of local government.

Urban agglomeration has been defined as comprising the city or town proper and also the suburban fringe or densely settled territory lying outside of, but adjacent to, the city boundaries.

For some countries or areas, however, the data relate to entire administrative divisions known, for example, as shi or municipalities (municipios) which are composed of a populated centre and adjoining territory, some of which may contain other, often separate urban localities or may be distinctively rural in character. For this group of countries or areas the type of civil division is given in a footnote.

The surface area of the city or urban agglomeration is presented, when available.

City names are presented in the original language of the country or area in which the cities are located. In cases where the original names are not in the Roman alphabet, they have been romanized. Cities are listed in English alphabetical order.

Capital cities are shown in the table regardless of their population size. The names of the capital cities are printed in capital letters. The designation of any specific city as a capital city is as reported by the country or area.

The table also covers cities whose urban agglomeration's population exceeds 100 000; that is, while the urban agglomeration should have a population of 100 000 or more to be included in the table, the city proper may be of a smaller population size.

The reference date of each population figure appears in the left-most column of the table. Estimates based on results of sample surveys and city censuses as well as those derived from other sources are explained by the 'code' also appearing in the left-most column of the table. The codes are explained at the end of the table.

Reliability of data: Specific information is generally not available on the reliability of the estimates of the population of cities or urban agglomerations presented in this table.

In the absence of such quality assessment, data from population censuses, sample surveys and city censuses are considered to be reliable and, therefore, set in Roman type. Other estimates are considered to be reliable if they are based on a complete census (or a sample survey), and have been adjusted by a continuous population register or adjusted on the basis of the calculated balance of births, deaths, and migration.

Limitations: Statistics on the population of capital cities and cities of 100 000 or more inhabitants are subject to the same qualifications as have been set forth for population statistics in general as discussed in section 3 of the Technical Notes.

International comparability of data on city population is limited to a great extent by variations in national concepts and definitions. Although an effort is made to reduce the sources of non-comparability somewhat by presenting the data for both city proper and urban agglomeration, many serious problems of comparability remain.

Data presented in the "city proper" column for some countries represent an urban administrative area legally distinguished from surrounding rural territory, while for other countries these data represent a commune or an equally small administrative unit. In still other countries, the administrative units may be relatively extensive and thereby include considerable territories beyond the urban centre itself.

City data are also especially affected by whether the data refer to *de facto* or *de jure* population, as well as variations among countries in how each of these concepts is applied. With reference to the total population, the difference between the *de facto* and *de jure* population is discussed at length in section 3.1.1 of the Technical Notes.

Data on city populations based on intercensal estimates present additional problems: comparability is impaired by the different methods used in making the estimates and by the loss of precision in applying to selected segments of the population, methods best suited for the whole population. For example, it is far more difficult to apply the component method of estimating population growth to cities than it is to the entire country.

Births and deaths occurring in the cities do not all originate in the population present in or resident of that area. Therefore, the use of natural increase to estimate the probable size of the city population is a potential source of error. Internal migration is another component of population change that cannot be measured with accuracy in many areas. Because of these factors, estimates in this table may be less valuable in general and in particular limited for purposes of international comparison.

City data, even when set in Roman type, are often not as reliable as estimates for the total population of the country or area. Furthermore, because the sources of these data include censuses (national or city), surveys and estimates, the years to which they refer vary widely. In addition, because city boundaries may alter over time, comparisons covering different years should be carried out with caution.

Earlier data: Population of capital cities and cities with a population of 100 000 or more have been shown in previous issues of the *Demographic Yearbook*. For more information on specific topics and years for which data are reported, readers should consult the Historical Index.

Tableau 8 – *Annuaire démographique 2012*

Le tableau 8 présente les données les plus récentes disponibles pour la période 1993 – 2012 sur la population des capitales et des villes de 100 000 habitants ou plus.

Description des variables : étant donné que les villes ne sont pas délimitées de la même manière dans tous les pays ou zones, on s'est efforcé de donner, dans ce tableau, des chiffres correspondant non seulement aux villes proprement dites, mais aussi, le cas échéant, aux agglomérations urbaines.

On entend par villes proprement dites les localités qui ont des limites juridiquement définies et sont administrativement considérées comme villes, ce qui se caractérise généralement par l'existence d'une autorité locale.

L'agglomération urbaine comprend, par définition, la ville proprement dite ainsi que la proche banlieue, c'est-à-dire la zone fortement peuplée qui est extérieure, mais contiguë aux limites de la ville.

En outre, dans certains pays ou zones, les données se rapportent à des divisions administratives entières, connues par exemple sous le nom de shi ou de municipios, qui comportent une agglomération et le territoire avoisinant, lequel peut englober d'autres agglomérations urbaines tout à fait distinctes ou être à caractère essentiellement rural. Pour ce groupe de pays ou zones, le type de division administrative est indiqué en note.

On trouvera à la fin du tableau la superficie de la ville ou agglomération urbaine chaque fois que possible.

Les noms des villes sont indiqués dans la langue du pays ou zone où ces villes sont situées. Les noms de villes qui ne sont pas à l'origine libellés en caractères latins ont été romanisés. Les villes sont énumérées dans l'ordre alphabétique anglais.

Les capitales figurent dans le tableau quel que soit le chiffre de leur population et leur nom a été imprimé en lettres majuscules. Ne sont indiquées comme capitales que les villes ainsi désignées par le pays ou zone intéressé.

En ce qui concerne les autres villes, le tableau indique celles dont la population est égale ou supérieure à 100 000 habitants. Ce chiffre limite s'applique à l'agglomération urbaine et non à la ville proprement dite, dont la population peut être moindre.

La date à laquelle se réfère le chiffre correspondant, figure dans la colonne de gauche du tableau. Le 'code' aussi figurant dans la colonne de gauche du tableau, permet de savoir si les estimations sont fondées sur les résultats d'enquêtes par sondage ou de recensements municipaux ou sont tirées d'autres sources. Les codes utilisés sont expliqués à la fin du tableau.

Fiabilité des données : on ne possède généralement pas de renseignements précis sur la fiabilité des estimations de la population des villes ou agglomérations urbaines présentées dans ce tableau.

Les données provenant de recensements de la population, d'enquêtes par sondage ou de recensements municipaux sont jugées sûres et figurent par conséquent en caractères romains. D'autres estimations sont considérées comme sûres si elles sont fondées sur un recensement complet (ou une enquête par sondage) et ont été ajustées en fonction des données provenant d'un registre permanent de population ou en fonction de la balance, établie par le calcul des naissances, des décès et des migrations.

Insuffisance des données : les statistiques portant sur la population des capitales et des villes de 100 000 habitants ou plus appellent toutes les réserves qui ont été formulées à la section 3 des Notes techniques à propos des statistiques de la population en général.

La comparabilité internationale des données portant sur la population des villes est compromise dans une large mesure par la diversité des définitions nationales. Bien que l'on se soit efforcé de réduire les facteurs de non-comparabilité en présentant à la fois dans le tableau les données relatives aux villes proprement dites et celles concernant les agglomérations urbaines, de graves problèmes de comparabilité n'en subsistent pas moins.

Pour certains pays, les données figurant dans la colonne intitulée « Ville proprement dite » correspondent à une zone administrative urbaine juridiquement distincte du territoire rural environnant, tandis que pour d'autres pays ces données correspondent à une commune ou petite unité administrative analogue. Pour d'autres encore, les unités administratives en cause peuvent être relativement étendues et englober par conséquent un vaste territoire au-delà du centre urbain lui-même.

L'emploi de données se rapportant tantôt à la population de fait, tantôt à la population de droit, ainsi que les différences de traitement de ces deux notions d'un pays à l'autre influent particulièrement sur les statistiques urbaines. En ce qui concerne la population totale, la différence entre population de fait et population de droit est expliquée en détail à la section 3.1.1 des Notes techniques.

Les statistiques relatives à la population urbaine qui sont fondées sur des estimations intercensitaires posent encore plus de problèmes que les données issues de recensement. Leur comparabilité est compromise par la diversité des méthodes employées pour établir les estimations et par l'imprécision qui résulte de l'application de certaines méthodes à telles ou telles composantes de la population alors qu'elles sont conçues pour être appliquées à l'ensemble de la population. La méthode des composantes, par exemple, est beaucoup plus difficile à appliquer en vue de l'estimation de l'accroissement de la population lorsqu'il s'agit de villes que lorsqu'il s'agit d'un pays tout entier.

Les naissances et décès qui surviennent dans les villes ne correspondent pas tous à la population présente ou résidente. En conséquence, des erreurs peuvent se produire si l'on établit pour les villes des estimations fondées sur l'accroissement naturel de la population. Les migrations intérieures constituent un second élément d'estimation que, dans bien des régions, on ne peut pas toujours mesurer avec exactitude. Pour ces raisons, les estimations présentées dans ce tableau risquent dans l'ensemble d'être peu fiables et leur valeur est particulièrement limitée du point de vue des comparaisons internationales.

Même lorsqu'elles figurent en caractères romains, il arrive souvent que les statistiques urbaines ne soient pas aussi fiables que les estimations concernant la population totale de la zone ou du pays considéré. De surcroît, comme ces statistiques proviennent aussi bien de recensements (nationaux ou municipaux) que d'enquêtes ou d'estimations, les années auxquelles elles se rapportent sont extrêmement variables. Enfin, comme les limites urbaines varient parfois d'une époque à une autre, il y a lieu d'être prudent lorsque l'on compare des données se rapportant à des années différentes.

Données publiées antérieurement : des statistiques concernant la population des capitales et des villes de 100 000 habitants ou plus ont été présentées dans des éditions antérieures de l'*Annuaire démographique*. Pour plus de précisions concernant les années et les sujets pour lesquels des données ont été publiées, se reporter à l'index historique.

8. Population of capital cities and cities of 100 000 or more inhabitants: latest available year, 1993 - 2012
Population des capitales et des villes de 100 000 habitants ou plus : dernière année disponible, 1993 - 2012

Continent, country or area, date, code and city / Continent, pays ou zone, date, code et ville	City proper - Ville proprement dite				Urban agglomeration - Agglomération urbaine			
	Population			Surface area - Superficie (km²)	Population			Surface area - Superficie (km²)
	Both sexes - Les deux sexes	Male - Masculin	Female - Féminin		Both sexes - Les deux sexes	Male - Masculin	Female - Féminin	

AFRICA - AFRIQUE

Algeria - Algérie
25 VI 1998 (CDJC)

ALGIERS (EL DJAZAIR)	1 569 897	...	...	...	...	...	...	...
Annaba	352 523	...	...	...	...	...	...	...
Batna	246 800	...	...	...	...	...	...	...
Béchar	134 523	...	...	...	...	...	...	...
Bejaïa	144 405	...	...	...	...	...	...	...
Beskra	177 060	...	...	...	...	...	...	...
Bordj Bou Arreridj	129 004	...	...	...	...	...	...	...
Bordj el Kiffan	103 690	...	...	...	...	...	...	...
Ech Cheliff (El Asnam)	174 314	...	...	...	...	...	...	...
El Boulaïda (Blida)	229 788	...	...	...	...	...	...	...
El Djelfa	158 679	...	...	...	...	...	...	...
El Eulma	104 758	...	...	...	...	...	...	...
El Wad	105 151	...	...	...	...	...	...	...
Ghardaïa	127 959	...	...	...	...	...	...	...
Ghilizane	104 644	...	...	...	...	...	...	...
Guelma	108 682	...	...	...	...	...	...	...
Jijel	106 306	...	...	...	...	...	...	...
Lemdiyya (Medea)	128 427	...	...	...	...	...	...	...
Mestghanem (Mostaganem)	125 911	...	...	...	...	...	...	...
M'Sila	102 151	...	...	...	...	...	...	...
Qacentina (Constantine)	465 021	...	...	...	...	...	...	...
Saïda	113 533	...	...	...	...	...	...	...
Sidi-bel-Abbès	183 931	...	...	...	...	...	...	...
Skikda	153 531	...	...	...	...	...	...	...
Souq Ahras	114 512	...	...	...	...	...	...	...
Stif (Sétif)	214 842	...	...	...	...	...	...	...
Tbessa	154 335	...	...	...	...	...	...	...
Tihert	148 850	...	...	...	...	...	...	...
Tilimsen (Tlemcen)	156 258	...	...	...	...	...	...	...
Touggourt	114 183	...	...	...	...	...	...	...
Wahran (Oran)	705 335	...	...	...	...	...	...	...
Wargla	139 381	...	...	...	...	...	...	...

Angola
1 VII 1993 (ESDF)

Huambo	...	...	...	...	*400 000*	...	...	...
LUANDA	...	...	...	...	*1 822 407*	*855 676*	*936 731*	...

Benin - Bénin
1 VII 2010* (ESDF)

Cotonou	*862 445*[1]	*426 247*[1]	*436 198*[1]	79	...	...	...	...
Parakou	*194 247*[1]	*98 756*[1]	*95 490*[1]	441	...	...	...	...
PORTO-NOVO	*289 880*[1]	*139 960*[1]	*149 920*[1]	50	...	...	...	...

Botswana
9 VIII 2011 (CDFC)

GABORONE	231 592	113 580	118 012	169	...	...	...	...

Burkina Faso
9 XII 2006 (CDFC)

Banfora	75 917	38 399	37 518	...	109 824	54 581	55 243	...
Bobo Dioulasso	489 967	244 136	245 831	...	554 042	275 703	278 339	...
Dori	21 078	10 431	10 647	...	106 808	52 992	53 816	...
Fada N'gourma	41 785	21 220	20 565	...	124 577	62 193	62 384	...
Gorom-Gorom	8 882	4 509	4 373	...	106 346	53 129	53 217	...
Kaya	54 365	26 989	27 376	...	117 122	56 209	60 913	...
Koudougou	88 184	42 803	45 381	...	138 209	64 362	73 847	...
OUAGADOUGOU	1 475 223	745 289	729 934	...	1 475 223	745 289	729 934	...
Ouahigouya	73 153	36 370	36 783	...	125 030	61 002	64 028	...
Solenzo	16 850	8 557	8 293	...	121 819	59 892	61 927	...
Tenkodogo	44 491	21 476	23 015	...	124 985	58 003	66 982	...

Burundi
16 VIII 2008 (CDJC)

BUJUMBURA	497 169	274 979	222 190	...	...	...	...	...

Cabo Verde
1 VII 2011 (ESDF)

PRAIA	...	...	...	...	*133 863*	*65 412*	*68 451*	...

8. Population of capital cities and cities of 100 000 or more inhabitants: latest available year, 1993 - 2012
Population des capitales et des villes de 100 000 habitants ou plus : dernière année disponible, 1993 - 2012 (continued - suite)

Continent, country or area, date, code and city Continent, pays ou zone, date, code et ville	City proper - Ville proprement dite				Urban agglomeration - Agglomération urbaine			
	Population			Surface area - Superficie (km²)	Population			Surface area - Superficie (km²)
	Both sexes - Les deux sexes	Male - Masculin	Female - Féminin		Both sexes - Les deux sexes	Male - Masculin	Female - Féminin	
AFRICA - AFRIQUE								
Cameroon - Cameroun								
11 XI 2005 (CDJC)								
Bafoussam	239 287	...	...	...	...	...	...	...
Bamenda	269 530	...	...	...	...	...	...	...
Douala	1 907 479	...	...	...	...	...	...	...
Garoua	235 996	...	...	...	...	...	...	...
Kumba	144 268	...	...	...	...	...	...	...
Maroua	201 371	...	...	...	...	...	...	...
Ngaoundéré................................	152 698	...	...	...	...	...	...	...
Nkongsamba	104 050	...	...	...	...	...	...	...
YAOUNDE	1 817 524	...	...	...	...	...	...	...
Chad - Tchad								
8 IV 1993 (CDFC)								
N'DJAMENA.................................	530 965	...	...	...	...	...	...	...
Djibouti								
1 VII 1995 (ESDF)								
DJIBOUTI	383 000	...	...	...	...	...	...	...
Egypt - Égypte								
1 VII 2010* (ESDF)								
6th of October City	802 306	420 009	382 297	...	...	...	...	...
Alexandria	4 358 439	2 225 558	2 132 881	...	...	...	...	...
Assyût.......................................	991 929	508 403	483 526	...	...	...	...	...
Aswan	543 396	277 732	265 664	...	...	...	...	...
Behera	985 850	500 999	484 851	...	...	...	...	...
Beni-Suef...................................	582 396	293 887	288 509	...	...	...	...	...
CAIRO	7 248 671	3 682 152	3 566 519	...	...	...	...	...
Dakahlia	1 503 395	758 471	744 924	...	...	...	...	...
Damietta	462 154	236 522	225 632	...	...	...	...	...
Faiyûm.......................................	621 268	318 679	302 589	...	...	...	...	...
Gharbia	1 285 492	645 533	639 959	...	...	...	...	...
Giza	3 122 041	1 592 292	1 529 749	...	...	...	...	...
Helwan	1 295 854	660 776	635 078	...	...	...	...	...
Ismailia	472 655	237 174	235 481	...	...	...	...	...
Kafr-Elsheikh	655 002	327 445	327 557	...	...	...	...	...
Kalyoubia...................................	2 053 859	1 051 232	1 002 627	...	...	...	...	...
Luxer	391 460	200 250	191 210	...	...	...	...	...
Matrouh	258 699	136 995	121 704	...	...	...	...	...
Menia...	859 719	434 498	425 221	...	...	...	...	...
Menoufia	724 352	368 333	356 019	...	...	...	...	...
North Sinai	229 462	120 302	109 160	...	...	...	...	...
Port Said	610 468	310 881	299 587	...	...	...	...	...
Qena..	534 766	270 422	264 344	...	...	...	...	...
Red Sea	295 993	180 622	115 371	...	...	...	...	...
Sharkia	1 340 060	682 941	657 119	...	...	...	...	...
Sohag	870 362	443 082	427 280	...	...	...	...	...
Suez	556 665	283 571	273 094	...	...	...	...	...
Ethiopia - Éthiopie								
1 VII 2002 (ESDF)								
ADDIS ABABA	2 646 000	1 273 000	1 373 000	...	...	...	...	...
Awassa	103 725	52 308	51 417	...	...	...	...	...
Bahir Dar	140 084	72 736	67 348	28	...	...	...	...
Debre Zeit..................................	108 632	53 648	54 984	...	...	...	...	...
Dessie	141 616	72 578	69 038	15	...	...	...	...
Dire Dawa..................................	237 012	118 880	118 132	18	...	...	...	...
Gondar	163 097	82 229	80 868	40	...	...	...	...
Harar	105 000	53 000	52 000	...	...	...	...	...
Jimma	131 708	67 138	64 570	...	...	...	...	...
Mekele	141 433	71 990	69 443	24	...	...	...	...
Nazareth	189 362	94 822	94 540	...	...	...	...	...
Gabon								
31 VII 1993 (CDFC)								
LIBREVILLE	362 386	184 192	178 194	...	418 616	212 383	206 233	...
Gambia - Gambie								
15 IV 1993 (CDFC)								
BANJU..	42 326	22 268	20 058	12	...	...	...	...

8. Population of capital cities and cities of 100 000 or more inhabitants: latest available year, 1993 - 2012
Population des capitales et des villes de 100 000 habitants ou plus : dernière année disponible, 1993 - 2012 (continued - suite)

Continent, country or area, date, code and city / Continent, pays ou zone, date, code et ville	City proper - Ville proprement dite				Urban agglomeration - Agglomération urbaine			
	Population			Surface area - Superficie (km²)	Population			Surface area - Superficie (km²)
	Both sexes - Les deux sexes	Male - Masculin	Female - Féminin		Both sexes - Les deux sexes	Male - Masculin	Female - Féminin	
AFRICA - AFRIQUE								
Ghana								
1 VII 2009 (ESDF)								
ACCRA	...	...	...	...	2 263 785	1 109 255	1 154 530	...
Ashiaman	...	...	...	...	281 283	140 698	140 585	...
Koforidua	...	...	...	...	109 846	52 726	57 120	...
Kumasi	...	...	...	...	1 922 130	964 909	957 221	...
Madina	...	...	...	...	136 415	66 843	69 572	...
Obuasi	...	...	...	...	167 897	82 270	85 627	...
Sekondi	...	...	...	...	151 240	75 166	76 074	...
Takoradi	...	...	...	...	220 718	108 152	112 566	...
Tamale	...	...	...	...	254 669	126 825	127 844	...
Tema	...	...	...	...	172 900	82 992	89 908	...
Guinea - Guinée								
1 XII 1996 (CDFC)								
CONAKRY	1 091 500	...	...	...	...	...	...	...
Kankan	...	...	...	...	261 341	...	...	...
Kindia	...	...	...	...	287 607	...	...	...
Labé	...	...	...	...	249 515	...	...	...
Nzérékoré	...	...	...	...	282 772	...	...	...
Kenya								
24 VIII 2009 (CDFC)								
Eldoret	252 061	127 808	124 253	311	...	...	...	...
Garissa	110 383	56 893	53 490	...	...	...	...	...
Kikuyu	190 208	93 036	97 172	...	...	...	...	...
Kisumu	259 258	131 062	128 196	275	...	...	...	...
Mavoko/AthiRiver	110 396	59 393	51 003	...	...	...	...	...
Mombasa	915 101	473 433	441 668	126	...	...	...	...
NAIROBI	3 133 518	1 602 104	1 531 414	695	...	...	...	...
Nakuru	286 411	145 038	141 373	344	...	...	...	...
Ngong	104 073	52 453	51 620	...	...	...	...	...
Ruiru	236 961	118 143	118 818	...	...	...	...	...
Thika	136 576	68 254	68 322	...	...	...	...	...
Madagascar								
1 VII 2005 (ESDF)								
ANTANANARIVO[2]	1 015 140	495 393	519 747	72	...	...	...	...
Antsirabe	...	...	...	...	180 180	87 691	92 489	...
Fianarantsoa	...	...	...	...	165 220	80 410	84 810	...
Mahajanga	...	...	...	...	152 785	74 359	78 426	...
Toamasina	...	...	...	...	203 469	99 026	104 443	...
Toliara	...	...	...	...	113 993	55 479	58 514	...
Malawi								
8 VI 2008 (CDFC)								
Blantyre City	661 444	...	...	220	...	...	...	...
LILONGWE	669 021	...	...	328	...	...	...	...
Mauritania - Mauritanie[1]								
1 VII 2008 (ESDF)								
NOUAKCHOTT	846 871	471 243	375 628	...	...	...	...	...
Mauritius - Maurice[3]								
1 VII 2011 (ESDJ)								
Beau Bassin - Rose Hill	111 061	53 983	57 078	20	...	...	...	...
PORT LOUIS	148 380	73 248	75 132	46	...	...	...	...
Vacoas - Phoenix	108 613	53 300	55 313	54	...	...	...	...
Morocco - Maroc								
1 VII 2012 (ESDF)								
Agadir	501 000	...	...	...	592 000	...	...	...
Béni-Mellal	497 000	...	...	...	977 000	...	...	...
Casablanca (Dar-el-Beida)	3 083 000	...	...	...	3 083 000	...	...	...
El-Jadida	344 000	...	...	...	1 180 000	...	...	...
Fès	1 090 000	...	...	...	1 111 000	...	...	...
Inezgane ait Melloul	519 000	...	...	...	539 000	...	...	...
Kénitra	684 000	...	...	...	1 295 000	...	...	...
Khemisset	245 000	...	...	...	548 000	...	...	...
Khouribga	357 000	...	...	...	508 000	...	...	...
Laayoune	245 000	...	...	...	255 000	...	...	...
Larache	245 000	...	...	...	490 000	...	...	...

8. Population of capital cities and cities of 100 000 or more inhabitants: latest available year, 1993 - 2012

Population des capitales et des villes de 100 000 habitants ou plus : dernière année disponible, 1993 - 2012 (continued - suite)

Continent, country or area, date, code and city Continent, pays ou zone, date, code et ville	City proper - Ville proprement dite				Urban agglomeration - Agglomération urbaine			
	Population			Surface area - Superficie (km²)	Population			Surface area - Superficie (km²)
	Both sexes - Les deux sexes	Male - Masculin	Female - Féminin		Both sexes - Les deux sexes	Male - Masculin	Female - Féminin	
AFRICA - AFRIQUE								
Morocco - Maroc								
1 VII 2012 (ESDF)								
Marrakech	*1 040 000*	...	...	...	*1 229 000*	...	...	...
Meknès..	*666 000*	...	...	...	*780 000*	...	...	...
Mohammedia	*295 000*	...	...	...	*362 000*	...	...	...
Nador...	*412 000*	...	...	...	*756 000*	...	...	...
Oujda...	*470 000*	...	...	...	*510 000*	...	...	...
RABAT...	*665 000*	...	...	...	*665 000*	...	...	...
Safi	*453 000*	...	...	...	*898 000*	...	...	...
Salé	*947 000*	...	...	...	*981 000*	...	...	...
Settat	*371 000*	...	...	...	*1 017 000*	...	...	...
Skhirate-Témara.......................................	*463 000*	...	...	...	*555 000*	...	...	...
Tanger	*850 000*	...	...	...	*898 000*	...	...	...
Taza...	*264 000*	...	...	...	*764 000*	...	...	...
Tétouan	*460 000*	...	...	...	*589 000*	...	...	...
Mozambique								
1 VIII 1997 (CDFC)								
Beira	397 368	...	...	...	...	...	...	...
Chimoio	171 056	...	...	...	...	...	...	...
MAPUTO..	966 837	...	...	...	1 391 499	...	...	...
Matola..	424 662	...	...	...	...	...	...	...
Mocuba	124 650	...	...	...	...	...	...	...
Nacala	158 248	...	...	...	...	...	...	...
Nampula	303 346	...	...	...	...	...	...	...
Quelimane	150 116	...	...	...	...	...	...	...
Tete	101 984	...	...	...	...	...	...	...
Namibia - Namibie								
27 VIII 2001 (CDFC)								
WINDHOEK...	...	...	...	...	233 529	117 306	116 222	...
Niger								
20 V 2001 (CDJC)								
Maradi	148 017	...	...	...	...	...	...	...
NIAMEY..	707 951	358 500	349 451	...	...	...	...	...
Zinder	170 575	...	...	...	...	...	...	...
Réunion								
1 I 2006 (CDJC)								
SAINT-DENIS..	138 314	64 552	73 762	143	...	...	...	...
Rwanda								
16 VIII 2002 (CDJC)								
Butare..	137 334	...	...	...	...	...	...	...
Gitarama	137 995	...	...	...	...	...	...	...
KIGALI..	603 049	325 778	277 271	...	...	...	...	...
Saint Helena ex. dep. - Sainte-Hélène sans dép.								
10 II 2008 (CDFC)								
JAMESTOWN..	714	354	360	4	...	...	...	...
Sao Tome and Principe - Sao Tomé-et-Principe								
25 VIII 2001 (CDJC)								
SAO TOME...	...	...	...	...	49 957	24 003	25 954	...
Senegal - Sénégal								
31 XII 2011 (ESDJ)								
DAKAR...	1 056 009[4]	526 299[4]	529 710[4]	500	...	...	...	...
Diourbel[4]...	279 667	136 961	142 706	...	...	...	...	...
Guediawaye[4]..	317 464	157 992	159 472	...	...	...	...	...
Kaolack[4]..	410 577	199 057	211 520	...	...	...	...	...
Mbour[4]..	605 346	307 461	297 885	...	...	...	...	...
Pikine[4]...	941 245	472 868	468 377	...	...	...	...	...
Rufisque[4]...	333 032	167 942	165 090	...	...	...	...	...
Saint Louis[4]...	277 245	136 957	140 289	...	...	...	...	...
Thiès[4]..	618 436	304 087	314 349	...	...	...	...	...
Ziguinchor[4]...	337 295	167 048	170 247	...	...	...	...	...
Seychelles								
29 VIII 1997 (CDFC)								
VICTORIA..	...	...	...	...	24 701	...	...	...

Continent, country or area, date, code and city / Continent, pays ou zone, date, code et ville	City proper - Ville proprement dite				Urban agglomeration - Agglomération urbaine			
	Population			Surface area - Superficie (km²)	Population			Surface area - Superficie (km²)
	Both sexes - Les deux sexes	Male - Masculin	Female - Féminin		Both sexes - Les deux sexes	Male - Masculin	Female - Féminin	
AFRICA - AFRIQUE								
Sierra Leone								
1 VII 2010 (ESDF)								
Bo	231 494	111 731	119 763	...	...	...	...	...
FREETOWN	945 423	479 526	465 897	...	...	...	...	...
Kenema	195 498	95 988	99 510	...	...	...	...	...
Makeni	114 960	55 388	59 572	...	...	...	...	...
Somalia - Somalie								
1 VII 2001 (ESDF)								
MOGADISHU	1 212 000	...	...	...				
South Africa - Afrique du Sud								
10 X 1996 (CDFC)								
Alexandra	171 284	...	...	...	...	...	...	...
Benoni	366 343	...	...	...	...	...	...	...
BLOEMFONTEIN[5]	350 504	...	...	...	...	...	...	...
Boksburg	263 179	...	...	...	...	...	...	...
Botshabelo	177 971	...	...	...	...	...	...	...
CAPE TOWN[5]	987 007	...	...	...	...	...	...	...
Durban	669 242	...	...	...	...	...	...	...
Germiston	164 252	...	...	...	...	...	...	...
Johannesburg	752 349	...	...	...	...	...	...	...
Kathlehong	344 803	...	...	...	...	...	...	...
Kempton Park	344 426	...	...	...	...	...	...	...
Khayelitsa	314 239	...	...	...	...	...	...	...
Kimberley	206 070	...	...	...	...	...	...	...
Mangaung	176 525	...	...	...	...	...	...	...
Pietermaritzburg	405 385	...	...	...	...	...	...	...
Port Elizabeth	775 255	...	...	...	...	...	...	...
PRETORIA[5]	692 348	340 363	351 985	...	...	...	...	...
Roodepoort	279 340	...	...	...	...	...	...	...
Soweto	904 165	...	...	...	...	...	...	...
Springs	163 304	...	...	...	...	...	...	...
Tembisa	237 676	...	...	...	...	...	...	...
Umlazi	339 715	...	...	...	...	...	...	...
Vereeniging	379 638	...	...	...	...	...	...	...
Tunisia - Tunisie								
1 VII 1998 (ESDF)								
Bizerte	105 520	...	...	...	...	...	...	...
Gabes	104 950	...	...	...	...	...	...	...
Kairouan	110 280	...	...	...	...	...	...	...
Sfax	248 800	...	...	...	...	...	...	...
TUNIS	702 330	...	...	...	...	...	...	...
Uganda - Ouganda								
1 VII 2009 (ESDF)								
Gulu	...	...	...	...	146 600	72 700	73 900	...
KAMPALA	1 533 600	726 400	807 200	...	...	...	...	...
Kira	...	...	...	...	164 700	77 400	87 300	...
Lira	...	...	...	...	102 200	50 800	51 400	...
Western Sahara - Sahara occidental[6]								
1 VII 1999 (ESDF)								
EL AAIUN	169 000	...	...	...	...	...	...	...
Zambia - Zambie								
1 VII 2000 (ESDF)								
Chingola	164 964	82 643	82 321	1 678	...	...	...	...
Kabwe	170 387	84 041	86 346	1 572	...	...	...	...
Kitwe	362 423	180 865	181 558	777	...	...	...	...
Luanshya	144 009	72 449	71 560	811	...	...	...	...
LUSAKA	1 057 212	528 891	528 321	360	...	...	...	...
Mufulira	137 272	68 253	69 019	1 637	...	...	...	...
Ndola	371 221	185 043	186 178	1 103	...	...	...	...
Zimbabwe								
1 VII 2009 (ESDF)								
Bulawayo	713 532	341 211	372 321	479	...	...	...	...
Chitungwiza	340 724	164 876	175 848	...	...	...	...	...
Gweru	148 488	71 378	77 110	...	...	...	...	...

8. Population of capital cities and cities of 100 000 or more inhabitants: latest available year, 1993 - 2012
Population des capitales et des villes de 100 000 habitants ou plus : dernière année disponible, 1993 - 2012 (continued - suite)

Continent, country or area, date, code and city Continent, pays ou zone, date, code et ville	City proper - Ville proprement dite				Urban agglomeration - Agglomération urbaine			
	Population			Surface area - Superficie (km²)	Population			Surface area - Superficie (km²)
	Both sexes - Les deux sexes	Male - Masculin	Female - Féminin		Both sexes - Les deux sexes	Male - Masculin	Female - Féminin	
AFRICA - AFRIQUE								
Zimbabwe								
1 VII 2009 (ESDF)								
HARARE	*1 513 173*	*758 856*	*754 317*	872	...	...	...	...
Mutare	*179 776*	*89 654*	*90 122*	...	...	...	...	...
AMERICA, NORTH - AMÉRIQUE DU NORD								
Anguilla								
1 VII 2001 (ESDF)								
THE VALLEY	4 904	...	...	...	...	...	...	...
Aruba								
29 IX 2010 (CDJC)								
ORANJESTAD..	28 295	13 139	15 156	...	...	...	...	...
Bahamas								
1 VII 2009 (ESDF)								
NASSAU...	244 400	119 700	124 700	...	...	...	...	...
Belize								
1 VII 2000 (ESDF)								
BELMOPAN..	*8 305*	*4 050*	*4 255*	...	...	...	...	...
Bermuda - Bermudes								
20 V 2000 (CDJC)								
HAMILTON	969[7]	508[7]	461[7]	0[8]	...	...	...	...
Canada								
1 VII 2010 (ESDJ)								
Abbotsford-Mission..................................	...	...	...	...	174 300[9]	87 304[9]	86 996[9]	626[10]
Barrie	...	...	...	...	190 872[9]	95 163[9]	95 709[9]	897[10]
Brantford..	...	...	...	...	139 124[9]	68 432[9]	70 692[9]	1 073[10]
Calgary	...	...	...	...	1 242 624[9]	633 047[9]	609 577[9]	5 107[10]
Edmonton	...	...	...	...	1 176 307[9]	597 335[9]	578 972[9]	9 418[10]
Greater Sudbury / Grand Sudbury	...	...	...	...	164 680[9]	81 066[9]	83 614[9]	3 382[10]
Guelph	...	...	...	...	138 158[9]	68 684[9]	69 474[9]	378[10]
Halifax	...	...	...	...	403 188[9]	195 597[9]	207 591[9]	5 496[10]
Hamilton	...	...	...	...	740 238[9]	364 186[9]	376 052[9]	1 372[10]
Kelowna	...	...	...	...	178 854[9]	88 141[9]	90 713[9]	2 904[10]
Kingston	...	...	...	...	162 543[9]	80 279[9]	82 264[9]	1 907[10]
Kitchener-Cambridge-Waterloo	...	...	...	...	492 390[9]	245 541[9]	246 849[9]	827[10]
London	...	...	...	...	492 249[9]	242 027[9]	250 222[9]	2 665[10]
Moncton...	...	...	...	...	137 346[9]	67 489[9]	69 857[9]	2 406[10]
Montréal	...	...	...	...	3 859 318[9]	1 902 000[9]	1 957 318[9]	4 259[10]
Oshawa	...	...	...	...	364 193[9]	179 822[9]	184 371[9]	903[10]
Ottawa - Gatineau	...	...	...	...	1 239 140[9]	608 662[9]	630 478[9]	5 716[10]
Peterborough...	...	...	...	...	121 054[9]	58 807[9]	62 247[9]	1 506[10]
Québec	...	...	...	...	754 358[9]	369 797[9]	384 561[9]	3 277[10]
Regina	...	...	...	...	215 138[9]	106 222[9]	108 916[9]	3 408[10]
Saguenay	...	...	...	...	152 150[9]	75 590[9]	76 560[9]	1 754[10]
Saint John	...	...	...	...	127 973[9]	61 945[9]	66 028[9]	3 360[10]
Saskatoon	...	...	...	...	265 259[9]	132 073[9]	133 186[9]	5 207[10]
Sherbrooke	...	...	...	...	197 299[9]	96 557[9]	100 742[9]	1 232[10]
St Catharines-Niagara...............................	...	...	...	...	404 357[9]	197 712[9]	206 645[9]	1 397[10]
St. John's	...	...	...	...	192 326[9]	94 159[9]	98 167[9]	805[10]
Thunder Bay	...	...	...	...	126 683[9]	62 866[9]	63 817[9]	2 550[10]
Toronto	...	...	...	...	5 741 419[9]	2 818 996[9]	2 922 423[9]	5 904[10]
Trois-Rivières	...	...	...	...	146 516[9]	71 373[9]	75 143[9]	880[10]
Vancouver..	...	...	...	...	2 391 252[9]	1 182 263[9]	1 208 989[9]	2 877[10]
Victoria	...	...	...	...	358 054[9]	173 360[9]	184 694[9]	695[10]
Windsor	...	...	...	...	330 856[9]	164 246[9]	166 610[9]	1 023[10]
Winnipeg	...	...	...	...	753 555[9]	372 742[9]	380 813[9]	5 303[10]
Cayman Islands - Îles Caïmanes								
1 IV 2007 (SSDJ)								
GEORGE TOWN....................................	28 836	...	...	...	...	...	...	...

8. Population of capital cities and cities of 100 000 or more inhabitants: latest available year, 1993 - 2012
Population des capitales et des villes de 100 000 habitants ou plus : dernière année disponible, 1993 - 2012 (continued - suite)

Continent, country or area, date, code and city / Continent, pays ou zone, date, code et ville	City proper - Ville proprement dite				Urban agglomeration - Agglomération urbaine			
	Population			Surface area - Superficie (km²)	Population			Surface area - Superficie (km²)
	Both sexes - Les deux sexes	Male - Masculin	Female - Féminin		Both sexes - Les deux sexes	Male - Masculin	Female - Féminin	
AMERICA, NORTH - AMÉRIQUE DU NORD								
Costa Rica								
30 V 2011 (CDJC)								
Alajuela	...	...	...	...	254 886	125 773	129 113	...
Cartago	...	...	...	...	147 898	72 491	75 407	...
Desamparados	...	...	...	...	208 411	99 974	108 437	...
Goicoechea	...	...	...	...	115 084	54 269	60 815	...
Heredia	...	...	...	...	123 616	58 667	64 949	...
Perez Zeledon	...	...	...	...	134 534	65 389	69 145	...
Pococi	...	...	...	...	125 962	63 273	62 689	...
Puntarenas	...	...	...	...	115 019	57 246	57 773	...
San Carlos	...	...	...	...	163 745	82 048	81 697	...
SAN JOSE	288 054	136 371	151 683	45	288 054	136 371	151 683	...
Cuba								
31 XII 2011 (ESDJ)								
Bayamo	147 488	...	...	27[11]	...	...	...	
Camagüey	305 989	...	...	82[11]	...	...	...	
Ciego de Avila	109 761	...	...	21[11]	...	...	...	
Cienfuegos	144 521	...	...	46[11]	...	...	...	
Guantánamo	207 739	...	...	34[11]	...	...	...	
Holguín	276 839	...	...	58[11]	...	...	...	
LA HABANA	2 129 013	...	...	721[11]	...	...	...	
Las Tunas	154 837	...	...	31[11]	...	...	...	
Matanzas	132 651	...	...	44[11]	...	...	...	
Pinar del Río	137 726	...	...	32[11]	...	...	...	
Santa Clara	205 245	...	...	44[11]	...	...	...	
Santiago de Cuba	424 862	...	...	70[11]	...	...	...	
Dominican Republic - République dominicaine								
1 VII 2011 (ESDF)								
Azua	102 339[1]	51 620[1]	50 719[1]	155	...	...	...	...
Bajos de Haina	143 807[1]	71 130[1]	72 677[1]	40	...	...	...	...
Baní	177 588[1]	88 818[1]	88 770[1]	740	...	...	...	...
Boca Chica	122 216[1]	61 317[1]	60 899[1]	142	...	...	...	...
Bonao	148 857[1]	73 877[1]	74 980[1]	674	...	...	...	...
Higüey	211 453[1]	106 575[1]	104 878[1]	2 026	...	...	...	...
La Romana	152 454[1]	73 291[1]	79 163[1]	263	...	...	...	...
La Vega	273 547[1]	137 511[1]	136 036[1]	641	...	...	...	...
Los Alcarrizos	249 595[1]	126 001[1]	123 594[1]	46	...	...	...	...
Moca	182 767[1]	91 506[1]	91 261[1]	337	...	...	...	...
Puerto Plata	156 123[1]	76 741[1]	79 382[1]	496	...	...	...	...
San Cristóbal	278 767[1]	138 614[1]	140 153[1]	214	...	...	...	...
San Francisco de Macoris	185 925[1]	92 282[1]	93 643[1]	760	...	...	...	...
San Juan de la Maguana	137 881[1]	70 406[1]	67 475[1]	1 722	...	...	...	...
San Pedro de Macoris	233 255[1]	113 249[1]	120 006[1]	146	...	...	...	...
Santiago de los Caballeros	757 933[1]	372 332[1]	385 601[1]	529	...	...	...	...
SANTO DOMINGO	1 126 306[1]	537 506[1]	588 800[1]	91	1 126 306[1]	537 506[1]	588 800[1]	91
Santo Domingo East - Santo Domingo Este	966 393[1]	468 484[1]	497 909[1]	169	...	...	...	...
Santo Domingo North - Santo Domingo Norte	453 046[1]	228 840[1]	224 206[1]	388	...	...	...	...
Santo Domingo West - Santo Domingo Oeste	349 175[1]	170 849[1]	178 326[1]	54	...	...	...	...
El Salvador								
12 V 2007 (CDJC)								
Ahuachapan	63 981	29 898	34 083	245	110 511	52 808	57 703	...
Apopa	131 286	61 172	70 114	52	...	...	...	...
Ciudad Delgado	112 161	52 381	59 780	33	120 200	56 297	63 903	...
Ilopango	103 862	47 726	56 136	35	...	...	...	...
Mejicanos	140 751	64 509	76 242	22	...	...	...	...
San Miguel	158 136	71 132	87 004	594	218 410	99 672	118 738	...
SAN SALVADOR	316 090	144 217	171 873	886	...	...	...	...
Santa Ana	204 340	97 115	107 225	400	245 421	117 565	127 856	...
Santa Tecla	108 840	49 315	59 525	112	121 908	55 780	66 128	...
Soyapango	241 403	111 234	130 169	30	...	...	...	...
Greenland - Groenland[12]								
1 VII 2012 (ESDJ)								
NUUK (GODTHAB)	16 235	8 528	7 707	...	...	...	...	...

8. Population of capital cities and cities of 100 000 or more inhabitants: latest available year, 1993 - 2012
Population des capitales et des villes de 100 000 habitants ou plus : dernière année disponible, 1993 - 2012 (continued - suite)

Continent, country or area, date, code and city / Continent, pays ou zone, date, code et ville	City proper - Ville proprement dite				Urban agglomeration - Agglomération urbaine			
	Population			Surface area - Superficie (km²)	Population			Surface area - Superficie (km²)
	Both sexes - Les deux sexes	Male - Masculin	Female - Féminin		Both sexes - Les deux sexes	Male - Masculin	Female - Féminin	
AMERICA, NORTH - AMÉRIQUE DU NORD								
Guadeloupe								
8 III 1999 (CDJC)								
BASSE-TERRE	12 377	5 687	6 690	...	44 747	21 252	23 495	...
Pointe-à-Pitre	...	...	...	...	171 773	...	...	...
Guatemala								
1 VII 2001 (ESDF)								
CUIDAD DE GUATEMALA	1 022 001	491 891	530 110	228				
Escuintla	114 626	57 893	56 733	332	...	...	...	...
Mixco	452 134	221 928	230 206	99	...	...	...	...
Quetzaltenango	152 223	76 272	75 951	120	...	...	...	...
Villa Nueva	390 329	192 238	198 091	114	...	...	...	...
Haiti - Haïti								
1 VII 1999 (ESDJ)								
Cap-Haitien	113 555	50 064	63 491	10	...	...	...	...
Carrefour	336 222	146 838	189 384	23	...	...	...	...
Delmas	284 079	124 774	159 305	26	...	...	...	...
PORT-AU-PRINCE	990 558	436 170	554 388	21	...	...	...	...
Honduras								
1 VII 2003 (ESDF)								
La Ceiba	137 815	67 691	70 124	...	...	...	...	...
San Pedro Sula	518 736	251 514	267 222	...	...	...	...	...
TEGUCIGALPA	858 437	411 687	446 749	...	...	...	...	...
Jamaica - Jamaïque								
10 IX 2001 (CDJC)								
KINGSTON	579 137[13]	272 587[13]	306 550[13]	22	...	...	...	...
Portmore[13]	156 467	72 292	84 175	...	...	...	...	...
Spanish Town[13]	131 510	63 791	67 719	...	...	...	...	...
Martinique								
1 I 2006 (CDJC)								
FORT-DE-FRANCE	90 347	40 128	50 219	...	133 281	59 945	73 336	...
Mexico - Mexique								
12 VI 2010 (CDFC)								
Acapulco (de Juárez)	673 479	324 746	348 733	...	863 431	418 236	445 195	...
Acayucan	83 817	40 242	43 575	...	112 996	54 333	58 663	...
Aguascalientes	722 250	348 722	373 528	...	932 369	453 097	479 272	...
Apizaco	76 492	36 269	40 223	...	499 567	240 285	259 282	...
Campeche	...	...	...	...	259 005	125 561	133 444	...
Cancun	628 306	317 990	310 316	...	677 379	343 303	334 076	...
Celaya	...	...	...	...	468 469	225 024	243 445	...
Chalco de Diaz Covarrubias	168 720	81 192	87 528	...	...	...	...	...
Chetumal	...	...	...	...	151 243	74 273	76 970	...
Chicoloapán de Juárez	172 919	84 285	88 634	...	...	...	...	...
Chihuahua	809 232	394 144	415 088	...	852 533	416 866	435 667	...
Chilpacingo (de los Bravo)	...	...	...	...	241 717	115 443	126 274	...
Chimalhuacan	612 383	301 250	311 133	...	...	...	...	...
Ciudad Acuña	...	...	...	...	136 755	68 350	68 405	...
Ciudad Apodaca	467 157	234 492	232 665	...	...	...	...	...
Ciudad de Villa de Alvárez	117 600	57 124	60 476	...	334 240	163 648	170 592	...
Ciudad Del Carmen	...	...	...	...	169 466	83 802	85 664	...
Ciudad General Escobedo	352 444	177 382	175 062	...	...	...	...	...
Ciudad Juárez	151 893	76 140	75 753	...	...	...	...	...
Ciudad López Mateos	489 160	237 729	251 431	...	...	...	...	...
Ciudad Madero	197 216	94 384	102 832	...	859 419	418 362	441 057	...
Ciudad Obregón	...	...	...	...	298 625	146 788	151 837	...
Ciudad Santa Catarina	268 347	134 044	134 303	...	...	...	...	...
Ciudad Valles	...	...	...	...	167 713	81 226	86 487	...
Ciudad Victoria	...	...	...	...	321 953	157 152	164 801	...
Coatzacoalcos	235 983	112 989	122 994	...	347 257	168 301	178 956	...
Colimas	137 383	66 698	70 685	...	334 240	163 648	170 592	...
Córdoba	140 896	65 279	75 617	...	316 032	148 861	167 171	...
Cuauhtemoc	...	...	...	...	154 639	75 936	78 703	...
Cuautitlan Izcalli	484 573	235 136	249 437	...	...	...	...	...
Cuautla	154 358	73 384	80 974	...	434 147	209 752	224 395	...
Cuernavaca	338 650	159 999	178 651	...	876 083	421 781	454 302	...
Culiacán Rosales	...	...	...	...	675 773	329 608	346 165	...

8. Population of capital cities and cities of 100 000 or more inhabitants: latest available year, 1993 - 2012
Population des capitales et des villes de 100 000 habitants ou plus : dernière année disponible, 1993 - 2012 (continued - suite)

Continent, country or area, date, code and city Continent, pays ou zone, date, code et ville	City proper - Ville proprement dite				Urban agglomeration - Agglomération urbaine			
	Population			Surface area - Superficie (km²)	Population			Surface area - Superficie (km²)
	Both sexes - Les deux sexes	Male - Masculin	Female - Féminin		Both sexes - Les deux sexes	Male - Masculin	Female - Féminin	
AMERICA, NORTH - AMÉRIQUE DU NORD								
Mexico - Mexique								
12 VI 2010 (CDFC)								
Delicias	...	...	...	...	137 935	68 013	69 922	...
Durango (Victoria de Durango)	...	...	...	...	518 709	250 073	268 636	...
Ecatepec (de Morelos)	1 655 015	805 890	849 125	...	...	...	...	...
Ensenada	...	...	...	...	466 814	235 130	231 684	...
Fresnillo	...	...	...	...	213 139	104 348	108 791	...
Gómez Palacio	257 352	126 001	131 351	...	1 215 817	596 961	618 856	...
Guadalajara	1 495 182	717 399	777 783	...	4 434 878	2 171 514	2 263 364	...
Guadalupe, Nuevo León	673 616	334 519	339 097	...	4 089 962	2 036 484	2 053 478	...
Guadalupe, Zacatecas	124 623	60 349	64 274	...	298 167	144 140	154 027	...
Guanajuato	...	...	...	...	171 709	82 830	88 879	...
Hermosillo	...	...	...	...	784 342	392 697	391 645	...
Heroica Guaymas	113 082	56 090	56 992	...	203 430	101 736	101 694	...
Heroica Nogales	212 533	106 299	106 234	...	...	...	...	...
Hidalgo del Parral	...	...	...	...	107 061	51 883	55 178	...
Iguala (de la Independencia)	...	...	...	...	140 363	67 611	72 752	...
Irapuato	...	...	...	...	529 440	254 784	274 656	...
Ixtapaluca	322 271	156 847	165 424	...	...	...	...	...
Jiutepec	162 427	78 012	84 415	...	876 083	421 781	454 302	...
Juárez	1 321 004	659 857	661 147	...	1 332 131	665 691	666 440	...
La Paz, Baja California Sur	...	...	...	...	251 871	126 397	125 474	...
La Paz, Distrito Federal	253 845	123 956	129 889	...	...	...	...	...
La Piedad	99 576	47 492	52 084	...	249 512	118 043	131 469	...
Lázaro Cárdenas	...	...	...	...	178 817	89 221	89 596	...
León (de los Aldama)	1 238 962	603 633	635 329	...	1 609 504	785 729	823 775	...
Los Mochis	...	...	...	...	256 613	124 228	132 385	...
Manzanillo	...	...	...	...	161 420	81 007	80 413	...
Matamoros	449 815	221 006	228 809	...	489 193	242 234	246 959	...
Mazatlán	...	...	...	...	438 434	216 266	222 168	...
Mérida	777 615	374 542	403 073	...	973 046	472 213	500 833	...
Mexicali	689 775	346 642	343 133	...	936 826	473 203	463 623	...
MEXICO, CIUDAD DE	8 851 080	4 233 783	4 617 297	...	20 116 842	9 729 967	10 386 875	...
Minatitlán	157 840	76 222	81 618	...	356 137	171 979	184 158	...
Monclova	215 271	106 901	108 370	...	317 313	157 907	159 406	...
Monterrey	1 135 512	561 638	573 874	...	4 089 962	2 036 484	2 053 478	...
Morelia	597 511	284 708	312 803	...	807 902	386 945	420 957	...
Moroleón - Uriangato	...	...	...	...	108 669	51 613	57 056	...
Naucalpan de Juárez	792 211	384 234	407 977	...	...	...	...	...
Navojoa	157 729	78 242	79 487	...	...	...	...	...
Netzahualcóyotl	1 104 585	532 528	572 057	...	...	...	...	...
Nuevo Laredo	373 725	185 747	187 978	...	384 033	191 001	193 032	...
Oaxaca de Juárez	255 029	118 367	136 662	...	593 658	279 311	314 347	...
Ocotlán	92 967	45 453	47 514	...	141 375	69 174	72 201	...
Orizaba	120 844	55 772	65 072	...	410 508	194 618	215 890	...
Pachuca (de Soto)	256 584	121 719	134 865	...	512 196	244 839	267 357	...
Piedras Negras	150 178	74 655	75 523	...	180 734	90 641	90 093	...
Playa del Carmen	149 923	78 169	71 754	...	...	...	...	...
Poza Rica de Hidalgo	185 242	87 456	97 786	...	513 518	247 486	266 032	...
Puebla de Zaragoza	1 434 062	682 505	751 557	...	2 668 437	1 278 555	1 389 882	...
Puerto Vallarta	203 342	101 712	101 630	...	379 886	191 576	188 310	...
Querétaro	626 495	301 972	324 523	...	1 097 025	533 253	563 772	...
Reynosa	589 466	293 880	295 586	...	727 150	363 027	364 123	...
Rioverde - Ciudad Fernández	...	...	...	...	135 452	65 832	69 620	...
Salamanca	...	...	...	...	260 732	126 354	134 378	...
Saltillo	709 671	351 302	358 369	...	823 128	409 208	413 920	...
San Cristobal de las Casas	185 917	88 996	96 921	...	...	...	...	...
San Francisco Coacalco	277 959	134 086	143 873	...	...	...	...	...
San Francisco del Rincón	113 570	55 026	58 544	...	182 365	88 808	93 557	...
San Juan Bautista Tuxtepec	...	...	...	...	155 766	74 788	80 978	...
San Juan del Río	...	...	...	...	241 699	117 628	124 071	...
San Luis Potosí	722 772	347 676	375 096	...	1 040 443	501 897	538 546	...
San Luis Rio Colorado	...	...	...	...	178 380	90 545	87 835	...
San Martín Texmelucan	141 112	67 505	73 607	...	2 668 437	1 278 555	1 389 882	...
San Nicolas de los Garza	443 273	219 337	223 936	...	...	...	...	...

8. Population of capital cities and cities of 100 000 or more inhabitants: latest available year, 1993 - 2012
Population des capitales et des villes de 100 000 habitants ou plus : dernière année disponible, 1993 - 2012 (continued - suite)

Continent, country or area, date, code and city Continent, pays ou zone, date, code et ville	City proper - Ville proprement dite				Urban agglomeration - Agglomération urbaine			
	Population			Surface area - Superficie (km²)	Population			Surface area - Superficie (km²)
	Both sexes - Les deux sexes	Male - Masculin	Female - Féminin		Both sexes - Les deux sexes	Male - Masculin	Female - Féminin	
AMERICA, NORTH - AMÉRIQUE DU NORD								
Mexico - Mexique								
12 VI 2010 (CDFC)								
San Pedro Garza Garcia	122 627	57 608	65 019	...	...	...	...	...
Soledad de Graciano Sanchez	255 015	123 480	131 535	...	1 040 443	501 897	538 546	...
Tampico	297 284	142 189	155 095	...	859 419	418 362	441 057	...
Tapachula (de Cordova y Ordoñez)	...	...	...	...	202 672	95 450	107 222	...
Tecomán	112 726	56 804	55 922	...	141 421	71 260	70 161	...
Tehuacán	248 716	117 127	131 589	...	296 899	140 079	156 820	...
Tepic	332 863	160 708	172 155	...	429 351	209 204	220 147	...
Tijuana	1 300 983	653 241	647 742	...	1 751 430	883 277	868 153	...
Tlalnepantla	653 410	316 348	337 062	...	20 116 842	9 729 967	10 386 875	...
Tlaquepaque	575 942	284 064	291 878	...	4 434 878	2 171 514	2 263 364	...
Tlaxcala	89 795	42 529	47 266	...	499 567	240 285	259 282	...
Toluca (de Lerdo)	489 333	232 774	256 559	...	1 846 116	898 202	947 914	...
Tonala	408 759	202 269	206 490	...	4 434 878	2 171 514	2 263 364	...
Torreón	608 836	296 781	312 055	...	1 215 817	596 961	618 856	...
Tula, Tula de Allende	103 919	50 490	53 429	...	205 812	100 413	105 399	...
Tulancingo, Tulancingo de Bravo	151 584	71 287	80 297	...	239 579	113 118	126 461	...
Tuxpan	...	...	...	...	143 362	69 764	73 598	...
Tuxtla Gutiérrez	537 102	255 879	281 223	...	640 977	307 242	333 735	...
Uruapan	...	...	...	...	315 350	152 442	162 908	...
Veracruz	428 323	201 018	227 305	...	801 295	380 239	421 056	...
Villa Nicolas Romero	281 799	138 181	143 618	...	...	...	...	...
Villahermosa	353 577	169 721	183 856	...	755 425	368 212	387 213	...
Xalapa-Enriquez	424 755	197 560	227 195	...	666 535	314 563	351 972	...
Xico	356 352	175 135	181 217	...	...	...	...	...
Zacatecas	129 011	61 655	67 356	...	298 167	144 140	154 027	...
Zamora de Hidalgo	141 627	67 993	73 634	...	250 113	120 697	129 416	...
Zapopan	1 142 483	557 305	585 178	...	4 434 878	2 171 514	2 263 364	...
Nicaragua								
1 VII 2009 (ESDJ)								
Chinandega	...	...	...	...	*106 635*	...	...	...
León	...	...	...	...	*156 049*	...	...	...
MANAGUA	...	...	...	...	*985 143*	...	...	...
Masaya	...	...	...	...	*110 491*	...	...	...
Tipitapa	...	...	...	...	*105 773*	...	...	...
Panama								
1 VII 2010 (ESDF)								
PANAMA DE PANAMA	*894 565*[14]	*443 516*[14]	*451 049*[14]	107	...	...	...	...
San Miguelito	*373 703*[14]	*182 468*[14]	*191 236*[14]	50	...	...	...	...
Puerto Rico - Porto Rico								
1 VII 2012 (ESDJ)								
Bayamón	202 325[15]	...	...	70	...	...	...	...
Caguas[15]	141 392	...	...	...	...	...	...	...
Carolina	172 728[15]	...	...	53	...	...	...	...
Ponce	160 322[15]	...	...	79	...	...	...	...
SAN JUAN	382 299[15]	...	...	102	...	...	...	...
Saint Lucia - Sainte-Lucie								
22 V 2001 (CDFC)								
CASTRIES	11 092	5 238	5 854	...	...	...	...	...
Saint Pierre and Miquelon - Saint Pierre-et-Miquelon								
8 III 1999 (CDFC)								
SAINT-PIERRE	5 618	2 781	2 837	...	...	...	...	...
Trinidad and Tobago - Trinité-et-Tobago								
1 VII 1996 (ESDF)								
PORT-OF-SPAIN	43 396	20 739	22 657	12	...	...	...	...
Turks and Caicos Islands - Îles Turques et Caïques								
1 VII 2006 (ESDJ)								
GRAND TURK	*5 718*	*2 846*	*2 872*	17	...	...	...	...
United States of America - États-Unis d'Amérique[16]								
1 IV 2010 (CDJC)								
Abilene (TX)	117 063	59 107	57 956	277	...	...	...	...
Akron (OH)	199 110	96 257	102 853	161	...	...	...	...
Albuquerque (NM)	545 852	265 106	280 746	486	...	...	...	...

8. Population of capital cities and cities of 100 000 or more inhabitants: latest available year, 1993 - 2012
Population des capitales et des villes de 100 000 habitants ou plus : dernière année disponible, 1993 - 2012 (continued - suite)

Continent, country or area, date, code and city — Continent, pays ou zone, date, code et ville	City proper - Ville proprement dite				Urban agglomeration - Agglomération urbaine			
	Population			Surface area - Superficie (km²)	Population			Surface area - Superficie (km²)
	Both sexes - Les deux sexes	Male - Masculin	Female - Féminin		Both sexes - Les deux sexes	Male - Masculin	Female - Féminin	

AMERICA, NORTH - AMÉRIQUE DU NORD

United States of America - États-Unis d'Amérique[16]
1 IV 2010 (CDJC)

Alexandria (VA)	139 966	67 262	72 704	39	...	...	...	...
Allentown (PA)	118 032	56 869	61 163	45	...	...	...	...
Amarillo (TX)	190 695	92 465	98 230	258	...	...	...	...
Anaheim (CA)	336 265	167 249	169 016	129	...	...	...	...
Anchorage (AK)	291 826	148 209	143 617	4 415	...	...	...	...
Ann Arbor (MI)	113 934	56 155	57 779	72	...	...	...	...
Antioch (CA)	102 372	49 807	52 565	73	...	...	...	...
Arlington (TX)	365 438	179 279	186 159	248	...	...	...	...
Arlington (VA)	207 627	103 501	104 126	67	...	...	...	...
Arvada (CO)	106 433	51 894	54 539	91	...	...	...	...
Athens (GA)	115 452	54 781	60 671	301	...	...	...	...
Atlanta (GA)	420 003	208 968	211 035	345	...	...	...	...
Augusta (GA)	195 844	94 782	101 062	783	...	...	...	...
Aurora (CO)	325 078	160 099	164 979	401	...	...	...	...
Aurora (IL)	197 899	98 172	99 727	116	...	...	...	...
Austin (TX)	790 390	399 738	390 652	772	...	...	...	...
Bakersfield (CA)	347 483	170 196	177 287	368	...	...	...	...
Baltimore (MD)	620 961	292 249	328 712	210	...	...	...	...
Baton Rouge (LA)	229 493	110 400	119 093	199	...	...	...	...
Beaumont (TX)	118 296	57 603	60 693	214	...	...	...	...
Bellevue (WA)	122 363	61 330	61 033	83	...	...	...	...
Berkeley (CA)	112 580	55 031	57 549	27	...	...	...	...
Billings (MT)	104 170	50 266	53 904	112	...	...	...	...
Birmingham (AL)	212 237	99 337	112 900	378	...	...	...	...
Boise City (ID)	205 671	101 690	103 981	206	...	...	...	...
Boston (MA)	617 594	295 951	321 643	125	...	...	...	...
Brandon (FL)[17]	103 483	50 481	53 002	86	...	...	...	...
Bridgeport (CT)	144 229	69 996	74 233	41	...	...	...	...
Brownsville (TX)	175 023	82 686	92 337	343	...	...	...	...
Buffalo (NY)	261 310	125 208	136 102	105	...	...	...	...
Burbank (CA)	103 340	49 971	53 369	45	...	...	...	...
Cambridge (MA)	105 162	51 109	54 053	17	...	...	...	...
Cape Coral (FL)	154 305	75 364	78 941	274	...	...	...	...
Carlsbad (CA)	105 328	51 485	53 843	98	...	...	...	...
Carrollton (TX)	119 097	58 244	60 853	94	...	...	...	...
Cary (NC)	135 234	65 819	69 415	141	...	...	...	...
Cedar Rapids (IA)	126 326	62 065	64 261	183	...	...	...	...
Centennial (CO)	100 377	49 427	50 950	74	...	...	...	...
Chandler (AZ)	236 123	115 939	120 184	167	...	...	...	...
Charleston (SC)	120 083	56 741	63 342	282	...	...	...	...
Charlotte (NC)	731 424	353 511	377 913	771	...	...	...	...
Chattanooga (TN)	167 674	79 757	87 917	355	...	...	...	...
Chesapeake (VA)	222 209	108 051	114 158	883	...	...	...	...
Chicago (IL)	2 695 598	1 308 072	1 387 526	590	...	...	...	...
Chula Vista (CA)	243 916	118 145	125 771	129	...	...	...	...
Cincinnati (OH)	296 943	142 672	154 271	202	...	...	...	...
Clarksville (TN)	132 929	64 768	68 161	253	...	...	...	...
Clearwater (FL)	107 685	52 044	55 641	66	...	...	...	...
Cleveland (OH)	396 815	190 285	206 530	201	...	...	...	...
Colorado Springs (CO)	416 427	203 944	212 483	504	...	...	...	...
Columbia (MO)	108 500	52 458	56 042	163	...	...	...	...
Columbia (SC)	129 272	66 532	62 740	342	...	...	...	...
Columbus (GA)	189 885	90 870	99 015	560	...	...	...	...
Columbus (OH)	787 033	384 265	402 768	562	...	...	...	...
Concord (CA)	122 067	60 659	61 408	79	...	...	...	...
Coral Springs (FL)	121 096	58 242	62 854	62	...	...	...	...
Corona (CA)	152 374	75 035	77 339	101	...	...	...	...
Corpus Christi (TX)	305 215	149 656	155 559	416	...	...	...	...
Costa Mesa (CA)	109 960	55 968	53 992	41	...	...	...	...
Dallas (TX)	1 197 816	598 962	598 854	882	...	...	...	...
Daly City (CA)	101 123	49 919	51 204	20	...	...	...	...
Dayton (OH)	141 527	68 951	72 576	144	...	...	...	...
Denton (TX)	113 383	55 348	58 035	228	...	...	...	...

8. Population of capital cities and cities of 100 000 or more inhabitants: latest available year, 1993 - 2012
Population des capitales et des villes de 100 000 habitants ou plus : dernière année disponible, 1993 - 2012 (continued - suite)

Continent, country or area, date, code and city / Continent, pays ou zone, date, code et ville	City proper - Ville proprement dite				Urban agglomeration - Agglomération urbaine			
	Population			Surface area - Superficie (km²)	Population			Surface area - Superficie (km²)
	Both sexes - Les deux sexes	Male - Masculin	Female - Féminin		Both sexes - Les deux sexes	Male - Masculin	Female - Féminin	
AMERICA, NORTH - AMÉRIQUE DU NORD								
United States of America - États-Unis d'Amérique[16]								
1 IV 2010 (CDJC)								
Denver (CO)	600 158	300 089	300 069	396	...	...	...	...
Des Moines (IA)	203 433	99 535	103 898	209	...	...	...	...
Detroit (MI)	713 777	337 679	376 098	359	...	...	...	...
Downey (CA)	111 772	54 174	57 598	32	...	...	...	...
Durham (NC)	228 330	108 556	119 774	278	...	...	...	...
East Los Angeles (CA)[17]	126 496	62 901	63 595	19	...	...	...	...
El Monte (CA)	113 475	57 003	56 472	25	...	...	...	...
El Paso (TX)	649 121	311 280	337 841	661	...	...	...	...
Elgin (IL)	108 188	53 888	54 300	96	...	...	...	...
Elizabeth (NJ)	124 969	62 037	62 932	32	...	...	...	...
Elk Grove (CA)	153 015	74 095	78 920	109	...	...	...	...
Enterprise (NV)[17]	108 481	54 786	53 695	120	...	...	...	...
Erie (PA)	101 786	49 126	52 660	49	...	...	...	...
Escondido (CA)	143 911	71 296	72 615	95	...	...	...	...
Eugene (OR)	156 185	76 324	79 861	113	...	...	...	...
Evansville (IN)	117 429	56 493	60 936	114	...	...	...	...
Everett (WA)	103 019	52 392	50 627	87	...	...	...	...
Fairfield (CA)	105 321	51 851	53 470	97	...	...	...	...
Fargo (ND)	105 549	53 248	52 301	126	...	...	...	...
Fayetteville (NC)	200 564	96 976	103 588	378	...	...	...	...
Flint (MI)	102 434	49 140	53 294	87	...	...	...	...
Fontana (CA)	196 069	97 410	98 659	110	...	...	...	...
Fort Collins (CO)	143 986	71 909	72 077	141	...	...	...	...
Fort Lauderdale (FL)	165 521	87 387	78 134	90	...	...	...	...
Fort Wayne (IN)	253 691	122 783	130 908	287	...	...	...	...
Fort Worth (TX)	741 206	363 896	377 310	880	...	...	...	...
Fremont (CA)	214 089	106 441	107 648	201	...	...	...	...
Fresno (CA)	494 665	243 124	251 541	290	...	...	...	...
Frisco (TX)	116 989	57 207	59 782	160	...	...	...	...
Fullerton (CA)	135 161	66 409	68 752	58	...	...	...	...
Gainesville (FL)	124 354	60 212	64 142	159	...	...	...	...
Garden Grove (CA)	170 883	85 289	85 594	46	...	...	...	...
Garland (TX)	226 876	111 193	115 683	148	...	...	...	...
Gilbert (AZ)	208 453	102 634	105 819	176	...	...	...	...
Glendale (AZ)	226 721	111 387	115 334	155	...	...	...	...
Glendale (CA)	191 719	91 387	100 332	79	...	...	...	...
Grand Prairie (TX)	175 396	85 836	89 560	187	...	...	...	...
Grand Rapids (MI)	188 040	91 579	96 461	115	...	...	...	...
Green Bay (WI)	104 057	51 359	52 698	118	...	...	...	...
Greensboro (NC)	269 666	126 793	142 873	328	...	...	...	...
Greshan (OR)	105 594	51 786	53 808	60	...	...	...	...
Hampton (VA)	137 436	65 750	71 686	133	...	...	...	...
Hartford (CT)	124 775	60 260	64 515	45	...	...	...	...
Hayward (CA)	144 186	71 143	73 043	117	...	...	...	...
Henderson (NV)	257 729	126 779	130 950	279	...	...	...	...
Hialeah (FL)	224 669	108 406	116 263	56	...	...	...	...
High Point City (NC)	104 371	49 002	55 369	139	...	...	...	...
Hollywood (FL)	140 768	68 984	71 784	71	...	...	...	...
Honolulu (HI)	337 256	166 500	170 756	157	...	...	...	...
Houston (TX)	2 099 451	1 053 517	1 045 934	1 553	...	...	...	...
Huntington Beach (CA)	189 992	94 260	95 732	69	...	...	...	...
Huntsville (AL)	180 105	87 530	92 575	541	...	...	...	...
Independence (MO)	116 830	56 123	60 707	201	...	...	...	...
Indianapolis (IN)	820 445	396 346	424 099	936	...	...	...	...
Inglewood (CA)	109 673	52 138	57 535	23	...	...	...	...
Irvine (CA)	212 375	103 434	108 941	171	...	...	...	...
Irving (TX)	216 290	108 131	108 159	174	...	...	...	...
Jackson (MS)	173 514	80 615	92 899	288	...	...	...	...
Jacksonville (FL)	821 784	398 294	423 490	1 935	...	...	...	...
Jersey City (NJ)	247 597	122 298	125 299	38	...	...	...	...
Joliet (IL)	147 433	72 892	74 541	161	...	...	...	...
Kansas City (KS)	145 786	72 057	73 729	323	...	...	...	...
Kansas City (MO)	459 787	223 183	236 604	816	...	...	...	...

8. Population of capital cities and cities of 100 000 or more inhabitants: latest available year, 1993 - 2012
Population des capitales et des villes de 100 000 habitants ou plus : dernière année disponible, 1993 - 2012 (continued - suite)

Continent, country or area, date, code and city / Continent, pays ou zone, date, code et ville	City proper - Ville proprement dite				Urban agglomeration - Agglomération urbaine			
	Population			Surface area - Superficie (km²)	Population			Surface area - Superficie (km²)
	Both sexes - Les deux sexes	Male - Masculin	Female - Féminin		Both sexes - Les deux sexes	Male - Masculin	Female - Féminin	
AMERICA, NORTH - AMÉRIQUE DU NORD								
United States of America - États-Unis d'Amérique[16]								
1 IV 2010 (CDJC)								
Killeen (TX)	127 921	62 695	65 226	139	...	...	...	...
Knoxville (TN)	178 874	85 946	92 928	255	...	...	...	...
Lafayette (LA)	120 623	58 564	62 059	128	...	...	...	...
Lakewood (CO)	142 980	69 916	73 064	111	...	...	...	...
Lancaster (CA)	156 633	78 546	78 087	244	...	...	...	...
Lansing (MI)	114 297	55 332	58 965	93	...	...	...	...
Laredo (TX)	236 091	114 287	121 804	230	...	...	...	...
Las Vegas (NV)	583 756	294 100	289 656	352	...	...	...	...
Lexington-Fayette (KY)	295 803	145 591	150 212	735	...	...	...	...
Lincoln (NE)	258 379	129 235	129 144	231	...	...	...	...
Little Rock (AR)	193 524	92 245	101 279	309	...	...	...	...
Long Beach (CA)	462 257	226 520	235 737	130	...	...	...	...
Los Angeles (CA)	3 792 621	1 889 064	1 903 557	1 214	...	...	...	...
Louisville (KY)	597 337	289 236	308 101	842	...	...	...	...
Lowell (MA)	106 519	52 871	53 648	35	...	...	...	...
Lubbock (TX)	229 573	112 743	116 830	317	...	...	...	...
Madison (WI)	233 209	114 832	118 377	199	...	...	...	...
Manchester (NH)	109 565	54 356	55 209	86	...	...	...	...
McAllen (TX)	129 877	62 044	67 833	125	...	...	...	...
McKinney City (TX)	131 117	64 434	66 683	161	...	...	...	...
Memphis (TN)	646 889	307 019	339 870	816	...	...	...	...
Mesa (AZ)	439 041	215 918	223 123	353	...	...	...	...
Mesquite (TX)	139 824	66 728	73 096	119	...	...	...	...
Metairie (LA)[17]	138 481	67 412	71 069	60	...	...	...	...
Miami (FL)	399 457	198 927	200 530	93	...	...	...	...
Miami Gardens (FL)	107 167	50 121	57 046	47	...	...	...	...
Midland City (TX)	111 147	54 129	57 018	187	...	...	...	...
Milwaukee (WI)	594 833	286 949	307 884	249	...	...	...	...
Minneapolis (MN)	382 578	192 421	190 157	140	...	...	...	...
Miramar (FL)	122 041	57 569	64 472	76	...	...	...	...
Mobile (AL)	195 111	91 783	103 328	360	...	...	...	...
Modesto (CA)	201 165	97 989	103 176	95	...	...	...	...
Montgomery (AL)	205 764	96 687	109 077	413	...	...	...	...
Moreno Valley (CA)	193 365	94 273	99 092	133	...	...	...	...
Murfreesboro (TN)	108 755	53 422	55 333	143	...	...	...	...
Murrieta (CA)	103 466	50 460	53 006	87	...	...	...	...
Naperville (IL)	141 853	68 981	72 872	100	...	...	...	...
Nashville-Davidson (TN)	601 222	291 294	309 928	1 231	...	...	...	...
New Haven (CT)	129 779	62 508	67 271	48	...	...	...	...
New Orleans (LA)	343 829	166 248	177 581	439	...	...	...	...
New York (NY)	8 175 133	3 882 544	4 292 589	784	...	...	...	...
Newark (NJ)	277 140	137 116	140 024	63	...	...	...	...
Newport News (VA)	180 719	87 263	93 456	178	...	...	...	...
Norfolk (VA)	242 803	125 797	117 006	140	...	...	...	...
Norman (OK)	110 925	55 172	55 753	463	...	...	...	...
North Las Vegas (NV)	216 961	108 097	108 864	262	...	...	...	...
Norwalk (CA)	105 549	52 364	53 185	25	...	...	...	...
Oakland (CA)	390 724	189 519	201 205	144	...	...	...	...
Oceanside (CA)	167 086	82 424	84 662	107	...	...	...	...
Oklahoma City (OK)	579 999	285 556	294 443	1 571	...	...	...	...
Olathe (KS)	125 872	62 358	63 514	155	...	...	...	...
Omaha (NE)	408 958	201 063	207 895	329	...	...	...	...
Ontario (CA)	163 924	81 563	82 361	129	...	...	...	...
Orange (CA)	136 416	68 723	67 693	64	...	...	...	...
Orlando (FL)	238 300	115 883	122 417	265	...	...	...	...
Overland Park (KS)	173 372	83 735	89 637	194	...	...	...	...
Oxnard (CA)	197 899	100 389	97 510	70	...	...	...	...
Palm Bay City (FL)	103 190	49 807	53 383	170	...	...	...	...
Palmdale (CA)	152 750	74 553	78 197	274	...	...	...	...
Paradise (NV)[17]	223 167	115 508	107 659	121	...	...	...	...
Pasadena (CA)	137 122	66 854	70 268	59	...	...	...	...
Pasadena (TX)	149 043	74 143	74 900	111	...	...	...	...
Paterson (NJ)	146 199	70 669	75 530	22	...	...	...	...

8. Population of capital cities and cities of 100 000 or more inhabitants: latest available year, 1993 - 2012
Population des capitales et des villes de 100 000 habitants ou plus : dernière année disponible, 1993 - 2012 (continued - suite)

Continent, country or area, date, code and city Continent, pays ou zone, date, code et ville	City proper - Ville proprement dite				Urban agglomeration - Agglomération urbaine			
	Population			Surface area - Superficie (km²)	Population			Surface area - Superficie (km²)
	Both sexes - Les deux sexes	Male - Masculin	Female - Féminin		Both sexes - Les deux sexes	Male - Masculin	Female - Féminin	
AMERICA, NORTH - AMÉRIQUE DU NORD								
United States of America - États-Unis d'Amérique[16]								
1 IV 2010 (CDJC)								
Pembroke Pines (FL)	154 750	71 515	83 235	86	...	...	...	...
Peoria (AZ)	154 065	73 916	80 149	452	...	...	...	...
Peoria (IL)	115 007	54 763	60 244	124	...	...	...	...
Philadelphia (PA)	1 526 006	719 813	806 193	347	...	...	...	...
Phoenix (AZ)	1 445 632	725 020	720 612	1 338	...	...	...	...
Pittsburgh (PA)	305 704	148 101	157 603	143	...	...	...	...
Plano (TX)	259 841	127 078	132 763	185	...	...	...	...
Pomona (CA)	149 058	74 543	74 515	59	...	...	...	...
Port St. Lucie (FL)	164 603	80 003	84 600	295	...	...	...	...
Portland (OR)	583 776	289 211	294 565	346	...	...	...	...
Providence (RI)	178 042	85 802	92 240	48	...	...	...	...
Provo (UT)	112 488	55 737	56 751	108	...	...	...	...
Pueblo (CO)	106 595	52 050	54 545	139	...	...	...	...
Raleigh (NC)	403 892	195 143	208 749	370	...	...	...	...
Rancho Cucamonga (CA)	165 269	81 615	83 654	103	...	...	...	...
Reno (NV)	225 221	114 494	110 727	267	...	...	...	...
Richmond (CA)	103 701	50 476	53 225	78	...	...	...	...
Richmond (VA)	204 214	97 331	106 883	155	...	...	...	...
Riverside (CA)	303 871	150 112	153 759	210	...	...	...	...
Rochester (MN)	106 769	51 700	55 069	141	...	...	...	...
Rochester (NY)	210 565	101 707	108 858	93	...	...	...	...
Rockford (IL)	152 871	73 867	79 004	158	...	...	...	...
Roseville (CA)	118 788	56 894	61 894	94	...	...	...	...
Sacramento (CA)	466 488	227 101	239 387	254	...	...	...	...
Salem (OR)	154 637	77 115	77 522	124	...	...	...	...
Salinas (CA)	150 441	76 007	74 434	60	...	...	...	...
Salt Lake City (UT)	186 440	95 627	90 813	288	...	...	...	...
San Antonio (TX)	1 327 407	647 690	679 717	1 194	...	...	...	...
San Bernardino (CA)	209 924	103 491	106 433	153	...	...	...	...
San Buenaventura (CA)	106 433	52 592	53 841	56	...	...	...	...
San Diego (CA)	1 307 402	660 626	646 776	842	...	...	...	...
San Francisco (CA)	805 235	408 462	396 773	121	...	...	...	...
San Jose (CA)	945 942	475 668	470 274	457	...	...	...	...
Santa Ana (CA)	324 528	165 752	158 776	71	...	...	...	...
Santa Clara (CA)	116 468	58 810	57 658	48	...	...	...	...
Santa Clarita (CA)	176 320	86 884	89 436	137	...	...	...	...
Santa Rosa (CA)	167 815	81 846	85 969	107	...	...	...	...
Savannah (GA)	136 286	65 301	70 985	267	...	...	...	...
Scottsdale (AZ)	217 385	104 930	112 455	476	...	...	...	...
Seattle (WA)	608 660	304 030	304 630	217	...	...	...	...
Shreveport (LA)	199 311	93 354	105 957	273	...	...	...	...
Simi Valley (CA)	124 237	61 043	63 194	107	...	...	...	...
Sioux Falls (SD)	153 888	76 268	77 620	189	...	...	...	...
South Bend (IN)	101 168	48 982	52 186	107	...	...	...	...
Spokane (WA)	208 916	101 853	107 063	153	...	...	...	...
Spring Valley (NV)[17]	178 395	88 819	89 576	86	...	...	...	...
Springfield (IL)	116 250	54 825	61 425	154	...	...	...	...
Springfield (MA)	153 060	72 573	80 487	83	...	...	...	...
Springfield (MO)	159 498	77 326	82 172	212	...	...	...	...
St. Louis (MO)	319 294	154 171	165 123	160	...	...	...	...
St. Paul (MN)	285 068	139 355	145 713	135	...	...	...	...
St. Petersburg (FL)	244 769	117 704	127 065	160	...	...	...	...
Stamford (CT)	122 643	60 402	62 241	97	...	...	...	...
Sterling Heights (MI)	129 699	62 862	66 837	95	...	...	...	...
Stockton (CA)	291 707	142 925	148 782	160	...	...	...	...
Sunnyvale (CA)	140 081	70 560	69 521	57	...	...	...	...
Sunrise Manor (NV)[17]	189 372	94 399	94 973	86	...	...	...	...
Surprise (AZ)	117 517	56 751	60 766	274	...	...	...	...
Syracuse (NY)	145 170	69 180	75 990	65	...	...	...	...
Tacoma (WA)	198 397	97 958	100 439	129	...	...	...	...
Tallahassee (FL)	181 376	85 358	96 018	260	...	...	...	...
Tampa (FL)	335 709	164 061	171 648	294	...	...	...	...
Temecula (CA)	100 097	49 002	51 095	78	...	...	...	...

8. Population of capital cities and cities of 100 000 or more inhabitants: latest available year, 1993 - 2012
Population des capitales et des villes de 100 000 habitants ou plus : dernière année disponible, 1993 - 2012 (continued - suite)

Continent, country or area, date, code and city / Continent, pays ou zone, date, code et ville	City proper - Ville proprement dite				Urban agglomeration - Agglomération urbaine			
	Population			Surface area - Superficie (km²)	Population			Surface area - Superficie (km²)
	Both sexes - Les deux sexes	Male - Masculin	Female - Féminin		Both sexes - Les deux sexes	Male - Masculin	Female - Féminin	
AMERICA, NORTH - AMÉRIQUE DU NORD								
United States of America - États-Unis d'Amérique[16]								
1 IV 2010 (CDJC)								
Tempe (AZ)	161 719	84 200	77 519	103	...	...	...	...
Thornton (CO)	118 772	58 745	60 027	90	...	...	...	...
Thousand Oaks (CA)	126 683	61 989	64 694	143	...	...	...	...
Toledo (OH)	287 208	138 973	148 235	209	...	...	...	...
Topeka (KS)	127 473	60 941	66 532	156	...	...	...	...
Torrance (CA)	145 438	70 732	74 706	53	...	...	...	...
Tucson (AZ)	520 116	257 312	262 804	587	...	...	...	...
Tulsa (OK)	391 906	190 944	200 962	510	...	...	...	...
Vallejo (CA)	115 942	56 277	59 665	79	...	...	...	...
Vancouver (WA)	161 791	78 884	82 907	120	...	...	...	...
Victorville City (CA)	115 903	58 073	57 830	190	...	...	...	...
Virginia Beach (VA)	437 994	214 441	223 553	645	...	...	...	...
Visalia (CA)	124 442	60 696	63 746	94	...	...	...	...
Waco (TX)	124 805	59 740	65 065	230	...	...	...	...
Warren (MI)	134 056	64 884	69 172	89	...	...	...	...
WASHINGTON (DC)	601 723	284 222	317 501	158	...	...	...	...
Waterbury (CT)	110 366	52 517	57 849	74	...	...	...	...
West Covina (CA)	106 098	51 159	54 939	42	...	...	...	...
West Jordan (UT)	103 712	51 569	52 143	84	...	...	...	...
West Valley City (UT)	129 480	65 285	64 195	92	...	...	...	...
Westminster (CO)	106 114	52 585	53 529	82	...	...	...	...
Wichita (KS)	382 368	188 523	193 845	413	...	...	...	...
Wichita Falls (TX)	104 553	54 172	50 381	187	...	...	...	...
Wilmington (NC)	106 476	50 857	55 619	133	...	...	...	...
Winston-Salem (NC)	229 617	107 878	121 739	343	...	...	...	...
Worcester (MA)	181 045	88 150	92 895	97	...	...	...	...
Yonkers (NY)	195 976	92 855	103 121	47	...	...	...	...
United States Virgin Islands - Îles Vierges américaines[15]								
1 IV 2010 (CDJC)								
CHARLOTTE AMALIE	10 354	...	...	...	...	...	...	...
AMERICA, SOUTH - AMÉRIQUE DU SUD								
Argentina - Argentine[18]								
1 VII 2012 (ESDF)								
Bahía Blanca-Cerri	...	...	...	...	314 948	...	...	...
BUENOS AIRES[19]	...	...	...	...	13 242 375	...	...	...
Catamarca	...	...	...	...	212 174	...	...	...
Comodoro Rivadavia-Rada Tilly	...	...	...	...	145 475	...	...	...
Concordia	...	...	...	...	155 905	...	...	...
Córdoba	...	...	...	...	1 429 922	...	...	...
Corrientes	...	...	...	...	368 778	...	...	...
Formosa	...	...	...	...	249 062	...	...	...
La Plata	...	...	...	...	757 980	...	...	...
La Rioja	...	...	...	...	189 845	...	...	...
Mar del Plata-Batán	...	...	...	...	628 672	...	...	...
Mendoza	...	...	...	...	916 220	...	...	...
Neuquén-Plottier	...	...	...	...	273 503	...	...	...
Paraná	...	...	...	...	283 328	...	...	...
Posadas	...	...	...	...	307 619	...	...	...
Rawson-Trelew-Playa Unión	...	...	...	...	132 097	...	...	...
Resistencia	...	...	...	...	400 869	...	...	...
Río Cuarto	...	...	...	...	167 057	...	...	...
Rosario	...	...	...	...	1 277 149	...	...	...
Salta	...	...	...	...	554 291	...	...	...
San Juan	...	...	...	...	480 354	...	...	...
San Luis - El Chorrillo	...	...	...	...	212 154	...	...	...
San Nicolás-Villa Constitución	...	...	...	...	181 730	...	...	...
San Salvador de Jujuy-Palpalá	...	...	...	...	318 287	...	...	...
Santa Fé	...	...	...	...	516 203	...	...	...
Santa Rosa-Toay	...	...	...	...	125 354	...	...	...

8. Population of capital cities and cities of 100 000 or more inhabitants: latest available year, 1993 - 2012
Population des capitales et des villes de 100 000 habitants ou plus : dernière année disponible, 1993 - 2012 (continued - suite)

Continent, country or area, date, code and city Continent, pays ou zone, date, code et ville	City proper - Ville proprement dite				Urban agglomeration - Agglomération urbaine			
	Population			Surface area - Superficie (km²)	Population			Surface area - Superficie (km²)
	Both sexes - Les deux sexes	Male - Masculin	Female - Féminin		Both sexes - Les deux sexes	Male - Masculin	Female - Féminin	
AMERICA, SOUTH - AMÉRIQUE DU SUD								
Argentina - Argentine[18]								
1 VII 2012 (ESDF)								
Santiago del Estero-La Banda	...	...	...	...	381 767	...	...	...
Tucumán-Tafí Viejo[20]	...	...	...	...	828 258	...	...	...
Ushuaia-Río Grande	...	...	...	...	127 797	...	...	...
Bolivia (Plurinational State of) - Bolivie (État plurinational de)								
1 VII 2010 (ESDF)								
Cochabamba	618 376	294 711	323 666	...	...	...	...	...
El Alto	953 253	463 069	490 184	...	...	...	...	...
LA PAZ	835 361	397 608	437 753	...	...	...	...	...
Oruro	216 724	104 294	112 430	...	...	...	...	...
Potosí	154 693	74 591	80 103	...	...	...	...	...
Sacaba	155 668	75 113	80 555	...	...	...	...	...
Santa Cruz	1 616 063	785 941	830 122	...	...	...	...	...
SUCRE	284 032	137 943	146 090	...	...	...	...	...
Tarija	194 313	94 231	100 082	...	...	...	...	...
Yacuiba	112 096	55 346	56 750	...	...	...	...	...
Brazil - Brésil								
31 VII 2010 (CDJC)								
Aguas Lindas de Goiás	159 138	79 587	79 551	...	159 138	79 587	79 551	154
Alagoinhas	122 324	57 341	64 983	...	124 042	58 132	65 910	55
Alvorada	175 575	85 010	90 565	...	195 673	95 080	100 593	71
Americana	209 654	102 644	107 010	...	209 654	102 644	107 010	99
Ananindeua	470 819	226 022	244 797	...	470 819	226 022	244 797	81
Anápolis	325 163	158 366	166 798	...	328 755	160 123	168 632	191
Angra dos Reis	65 364	32 348	33 016	...	163 199	81 424	81 775	220
Aparecida de Goiania	157 296	79 581	77 715	...	455 193	224 602	230 591	227
Apucarana	108 887	52 548	56 339	...	114 104	55 070	59 034	121
Aracaju	571 149	265 484	305 665	...	571 149	265 484	305 665	182
Araçatuba	178 077	85 466	92 611	...	178 077	85 466	92 611	69
Araguaina	142 925	69 468	73 457	...	142 925	69 468	73 457	133
Araguario	100 753	49 272	51 480	...	102 583	50 186	52 397	75
Arapiraca	181 481	85 682	95 799	...	181 481	85 682	95 799	68
Arapongas	101 851	49 820	52 031	...	101 851	49 820	52 031	123
Araraquara	143 071	68 476	74 594	...	202 739	97 512	105 227	81
Araras	112 444	55 341	57 103	...	112 444	55 341	57 103	33
Araruama	76 872	36 937	39 935	...	106 486	51 488	54 998	219
Araucária	109 484	54 663	54 820	...	110 205	55 026	55 179	91
Atibaia	115 229	56 235	58 994	...	115 229	56 235	58 994	170
Balneário Camboriú	108 089	51 393	56 696	...	108 089	51 393	56 696	46
Barbacena	107 207	50 395	56 812	...	115 568	54 566	61 002	48
Barra Mansa	171 125	82 488	88 637	...	176 230	84 915	91 315	96
Barreiras	123 741	60 645	63 096	...	123 741	60 645	63 096	112
Barretos	108 306	52 145	56 161	...	108 686	52 342	56 344	58
Barueri	112 726	54 658	58 068	...	240 749	117 051	123 698	66
Bauru	337 094	161 473	175 621	...	338 186	162 058	176 128	188
Belém	143 474	63 156	80 318	...	1 381 475	652 860	728 615	285
Belford Roxo	469 332	226 757	242 575	...	469 332	226 757	242 575	78
Belo Horizonte	1 433 244	663 016	770 227	...	2 375 151	1 113 513	1 261 638	331
Betim	375 331	184 905	190 426	...	375 331	184 905	190 426	225
Birigui	105 487	51 249	54 238	...	105 487	51 249	54 238	51
Blumenou	248 655	122 039	126 616	...	294 821	144 384	150 437	207
Boa Vista	277 799	136 877	140 922	...	277 799	136 877	140 922	508
Botucatu	115 606	55 535	60 071	...	122 744	59 384	63 360	141
Bragança Paulista	142 255	69 700	72 555	...	142 255	69 700	72 555	311
BRASILIA	2 481 272	1 180 060	1 301 212	...	2 481 272	1 180 060	1 301 212	1 190
Brusque	102 025	50 586	51 439	...	102 025	50 586	51 439	139
Cabo de Santo Agostinho	95 979	46 752	49 227	...	167 783	81 917	85 866	108
Cabo Frio	140 269	67 889	72 380	...	140 486	68 010	72 476	113
Cachoeirinha	118 278	57 173	61 105	...	118 278	57 173	61 105	44
Cachoeiro de Itapemirim	162 947	78 891	84 056	...	173 589	84 201	89 388	146
Camacari	161 226	79 499	81 726	...	231 973	114 874	117 099	299
Camaragibe	144 466	69 212	75 254	...	144 466	69 212	75 254	51
Campina Grande	355 014	167 240	187 774	...	367 209	173 191	194 018	99

Continent, country or area, date, code and city / Continent, pays ou zone, date, code et ville	City proper - Ville proprement dite				Urban agglomeration - Agglomération urbaine			
	Population			Surface area - Superficie (km²)	Population			Surface area - Superficie (km²)
	Both sexes - Les deux sexes	Male - Masculin	Female - Féminin		Both sexes - Les deux sexes	Male - Masculin	Female - Féminin	
AMERICA, SOUTH - AMÉRIQUE DU SUD								
Brazil - Brésil								
31 VII 2010 (CDJC)								
Campinas	952 659	458 571	494 087	...	1 061 540	511 483	550 057	384
Campo Grande	774 202	374 202	400 000	...	776 242	375 248	400 994	359
Campos dos Goytacazes	356 608	169 535	187 073	...	418 725	200 256	218 469	364
Canoas	323 827	155 936	167 891	...	323 827	155 936	167 891	131
Carapicuíba	230 355	110 869	119 486	...	369 584	179 284	190 300	34
Cariacica	115 513	56 889	58 625	...	337 643	164 374	173 269	106
Caruaru	277 982	130 512	147 470	...	279 589	131 317	148 272	113
Cascavel	266 835	129 171	137 664	...	270 049	130 813	139 236	112
Castanhal	149 918	72 577	77 341	...	153 378	74 176	79 202	75
Catanduva	111 914	54 307	57 607	...	111 914	54 307	57 607	96
Caucaia	149 896	73 475	76 421	...	290 220	141 210	149 010	221
Caxias	118 534	55 811	62 723	...	118 534	55 811	62 723	124
Caxias do Sul	415 822	203 357	212 466	...	419 406	205 081	214 325	255
Chapecó	166 040	81 182	84 858	...	168 113	82 179	85 934	55
Colombo	203 203	100 016	103 187	...	203 203	100 016	103 187	77
Conselheiro Lafaiete	110 588	53 478	57 110	...	111 266	53 751	57 515	88
Contagem	379 044	185 545	193 499	...	601 400	291 709	309 691	148
Coronel Fabriciano	47 625	22 800	24 825	...	102 395	49 378	53 017	73
Cotia	170 507	83 280	87 227	...	201 150	98 455	102 695	323
Crato	93 469	43 665	49 804	...	100 916	47 285	53 631	76
Criciúma	133 031	65 077	67 954	...	189 630	93 047	96 583	168
Cubatao	118 720	59 229	59 491	...	118 720	59 229	59 491	142
Cuiabá	220 859	105 753	115 106	...	540 814	263 510	277 304	270
Curitiba	1 751 907	835 115	916 792	...	1 751 907	835 115	916 792	435
Diadema	386 089	186 803	199 286	...	386 089	186 803	199 286	31
Divinópolis	202 220	98 046	104 174	...	207 516	100 880	106 636	212
Dourados	173 647	84 344	89 303	...	181 005	88 555	92 450	118
Duque de Caxias	341 304	161 359	179 945	...	852 138	409 537	442 601	267
Embu	240 230	116 728	123 502	...	240 230	116 728	123 502	70
Feira de Santana	495 516	234 015	261 501	...	510 635	241 310	269 325	172
Ferraz de Vasconcelos	111 727	54 485	57 242	...	160 754	78 255	82 499	17
Florianópolis	249 477	118 470	131 007	...	405 189	194 916	210 273	258
Fortaleza	862 750	394 154	468 596	...	2 452 185	1 147 918	1 304 267	314
Foz do Iguaçu	253 962	123 104	130 858	...	253 962	123 104	130 858	161
Franca	313 046	152 402	160 644	...	313 046	152 402	160 644	80
Francisco Morato	154 207	76 459	77 748	...	154 207	76 459	77 748	43
Franco da Rocha	121 244	59 594	61 650	...	121 244	59 594	61 650	53
Garanhuns	112 462	52 448	60 014	...	115 356	53 825	61 531	62
Goiânia	1 296 324	617 923	678 401	...	1 297 154	618 292	678 862	424
Governador Valadares	245 125	115 658	129 467	...	253 300	119 609	133 691	172
Gravatai	228 093	110 712	117 381	...	243 497	118 532	124 965	158
Guarapari	100 528	48 985	51 543	...	100 528	48 985	51 543	259
Guarapuava	142 163	68 934	73 230	...	152 993	74 273	78 720	92
Guaratinguetá	106 762	51 197	55 565	...	106 762	51 197	55 565	69
Guarujá	138 753	67 812	70 941	...	290 696	141 682	149 014	132
Guarulhos	784 971	380 278	404 693	...	1 221 979	595 043	626 936	317
Hortolandia	192 692	97 439	95 253	...	192 692	97 439	95 253	61
Ibirité	83 765	41 054	42 712	...	158 590	77 644	80 946	50
Ilhéus	148 437	70 579	77 858	...	155 281	74 049	81 232	113
Imperatriz	234 547	112 566	121 981	...	234 547	112 566	121 981	90
Indaiatuba	199 592	99 101	100 491	...	199 592	99 101	100 491	203
Ipatinga	148 687	72 081	76 606	...	236 968	114 954	122 014	75
Itabiraí	100 300	47 822	52 478	...	102 316	48 931	53 385	64
Itaboraí	107 527	52 098	55 429	...	215 327	104 856	110 471	216
Itabuna	199 749	94 271	105 478	...	199 749	94 271	105 478	47
Itaguaí	104 195	51 776	52 419	...	104 209	51 783	52 426	81
Itajaí	173 452	85 030	88 422	...	173 452	85 030	88 422	100
Itapecerica da Serra	151 349	75 626	75 723	...	151 349	75 626	75 723	134
Itapetininga	123 439	59 980	63 460	...	131 050	63 919	67 131	87
Itapevi	200 769	98 746	102 023	...	200 769	98 746	102 023	83
Itaquaquecetuba	321 770	158 542	163 228	...	321 770	158 542	163 228	83
Itu	144 269	71 002	73 267	...	144 269	71 002	73 267	115
Jaboatao dos Guarapes	335 371	157 757	177 614	...	630 595	297 903	332 692	154

8. Population of capital cities and cities of 100 000 or more inhabitants: latest available year, 1993 - 2012
Population des capitales et des villes de 100 000 habitants ou plus : dernière année disponible, 1993 - 2012 (continued - suite)

Continent, country or area, date, code and city / Continent, pays ou zone, date, code et ville	City proper - Ville proprement dite				Urban agglomeration - Agglomération urbaine			
	Population			Surface area - Superficie (km²)	Population			Surface area - Superficie (km²)
	Both sexes - Les deux sexes	Male - Masculin	Female - Féminin		Both sexes - Les deux sexes	Male - Masculin	Female - Féminin	
AMERICA, SOUTH - AMÉRIQUE DU SUD								
Brazil - Brésil								
31 VII 2010 (CDJC)								
Jacareí	187 144	91 007	96 138	...	208 297	101 489	106 808	196
Jandira	108 344	53 063	55 281	...	108 344	53 063	55 281	18
Jaraguá do Sul	132 800	66 511	66 289	...	132 800	66 511	66 289	123
Jaú	118 895	57 902	60 993	...	126 943	62 004	64 939	65
Jequié	136 518	65 445	71 074	...	139 426	66 855	72 571	71
Ji-Paraná	103 256	50 786	52 470	...	104 858	51 589	53 269	116
Joao Pessoa	720 954	336 616	384 338	...	720 954	336 616	384 338	165
Joinville	486 803	241 130	245 673	...	497 850	246 707	251 143	218
Juazeiro	151 336	73 035	78 301	...	160 775	77 799	82 976	73
Juàzeiro do Norte	238 889	112 789	126 099	...	240 128	113 404	126 724	79
Juiz de Fora	489 801	230 511	259 290	...	510 378	240 877	269 501	412
Jundiaí	354 204	171 931	182 273	...	354 204	171 931	182 273	176
Lages	153 676	74 329	79 347	...	153 937	74 458	79 479	213
Lauro de Freitas	163 449	79 276	84 173	...	163 449	79 276	84 173	58
Limeira	267 804	131 372	136 432	...	267 804	131 372	136 432	168
Linhares	109 653	53 923	55 729	...	121 567	59 882	61 685	101
Londrina	485 822	231 869	253 953	...	493 520	235 638	257 882	249
Luziânia	98 752	48 951	49 801	...	162 807	80 684	82 123	127
Macae	194 652	96 205	98 447	...	202 859	100 337	102 522	228
Macapá	369 287	180 649	188 638	...	381 091	186 588	194 503	319
Maceió	932 078	436 139	495 938	...	932 078	436 139	495 938	221
Magé	54 633	26 750	27 883	...	215 236	104 479	110 757	160
Manaus	1 792 881	874 749	918 132	...	1 792 881	874 749	918 132	860
Maraba	186 270	92 780	93 490	...	186 270	92 780	93 490	111
Maracanau	163 853	79 680	84 173	...	207 635	101 359	106 276	81
Maricá	40 074	18 993	21 082	...	125 401	61 585	63 816	244
Marília	197 342	93 820	103 523	...	207 021	99 682	107 339	101
Maringá	342 310	164 162	178 148	...	350 653	168 417	182 236	135
Marituba	107 123	53 327	53 796	...	107 123	53 327	53 796	42
Mauá	417 064	204 093	212 971	...	417 064	204 093	212 971	61
Mesquita	168 376	79 790	88 586	...	168 376	79 790	88 586	39
Moji das Cruzes	163 259	78 240	85 019	...	357 313	173 193	184 120	233
Moji-Guaçu	127 452	63 013	64 439	...	130 295	64 407	65 888	43
Montes Claros	338 381	161 936	176 445	...	344 427	164 985	179 442	108
Mossoró	237 241	113 580	123 661	...	237 241	113 580	123 661	114
Natal	803 739	377 947	425 792	...	803 739	377 947	425 792	166
Nilópolis	102 161	47 772	54 389	...	157 425	73 674	83 751	19
Niterói	487 562	225 838	261 724	...	487 562	225 838	261 724	134
Nossa Senhora do Socorro	155 823	75 707	80 116	...	155 823	75 707	80 116	71
Nova Friburgo	113 217	53 310	59 906	...	159 372	75 599	83 773	152
Nova Iguaçu	787 563	377 336	410 227	...	787 563	377 336	410 227	399
Nôvo Hamburgo	234 798	113 628	121 170	...	234 798	113 628	121 170	103
Olinda	370 332	171 066	199 266	...	370 332	171 066	199 266	35
Osasco	666 740	320 436	346 304	...	666 740	320 436	346 304	64
Ourinhos	100 374	48 586	51 788	...	100 374	48 586	51 788	63
Palhoça	119 360	59 293	60 067	...	135 311	67 385	67 926	194
Palmas	217 056	106 742	110 314	...	221 742	109 092	112 650	290
Paranaguá	133 761	65 667	68 094	...	135 421	66 562	68 859	91
Parauapebas	138 690	70 054	68 636	...	138 690	70 054	68 636	49
Parnaíba	137 485	65 418	72 067	...	137 485	65 418	72 067	96
Parnamirim	202 456	96 995	105 461	...	202 456	96 995	105 461	124
Passo Fundo	179 630	85 396	94 235	...	180 120	85 646	94 474	73
Passos	100 859	49 518	51 341	...	100 859	49 518	51 341	40
Patos de Minas	124 349	60 210	64 139	...	127 724	61 949	65 775	58
Paulista	300 466	141 630	158 836	...	300 466	141 630	158 836	97
Pelotas	306 193	142 848	163 345	...	306 193	142 848	163 345	197
Petrolina	217 093	103 808	113 285	...	219 172	104 817	114 355	132
Petrópolis	185 876	87 599	98 277	...	281 286	133 694	147 592	371
Pindamonhangaba	103 395	50 374	53 021	...	141 708	69 505	72 203	150
Pinhais	117 008	56 809	60 199	...	117 008	56 809	60 199	61
Piracicaba	297 767	144 689	153 079	...	356 743	174 190	182 553	206
Poà	99 116	47 857	51 259	...	104 338	50 443	53 895	16
Poços de Caldas	148 722	71 676	77 046	...	148 722	71 676	77 046	87

Continent, country or area, date, code and city / Continent, pays ou zone, date, code et ville	City proper - Ville proprement dite				Urban agglomeration - Agglomération urbaine			
	Population			Surface area - Superficie (km²)	Population			Surface area - Superficie (km²)
	Both sexes - Les deux sexes	Male - Masculin	Female - Féminin		Both sexes - Les deux sexes	Male - Masculin	Female - Féminin	

AMERICA, SOUTH - AMÉRIQUE DU SUD

Brazil - Brésil
31 VII 2010 (CDJC)

Ponta Grossa	303 399	147 034	156 366	...	304 717	147 714	157 003	204
Porto Alegre	1 409 351	653 787	755 564	...	1 409 351	653 787	755 564	497
Porto Seguro	80 240	39 610	40 630	...	104 078	51 512	52 566	132
Porto Velho	369 259	182 618	186 641	...	392 475	195 229	197 246	180
Pouso Alegre	118 847	58 159	60 687	...	119 590	58 566	61 024	41
Praia Grande	201 259	96 557	104 702	...	262 051	125 926	136 125	148
Presidente Prudente	200 042	95 432	104 609	...	203 382	97 105	106 277	124
Queimados	137 962	66 585	71 377	...	137 962	66 585	71 377	76
Recife	1 537 704	709 819	827 885	...	1 537 704	709 819	827 885	218
Resende	77 848	37 498	40 350	...	112 331	54 405	57 926	60
Ribeirao das Neves	134 449	67 974	66 475	...	294 158	145 902	148 256	140
Ribeirao Pires	77 660	37 507	40 153	...	113 068	55 318	57 750	99
Ribeirao Prêto	590 593	283 287	307 306	...	603 186	289 446	313 741	352
Rio Branco	308 545	148 437	160 108	...	308 545	148 437	160 108	145
Rio Claro	178 613	86 652	91 961	...	181 720	88 224	93 496	81
Rio de Janeiro	6 320 446	2 959 817	3 360 629	...	6 320 446	2 959 817	3 360 629	1 198
Rio Grande	178 454	84 991	93 463	...	189 429	90 514	98 915	160
Rio Verde	160 661	81 404	79 257	...	163 540	82 870	80 670	61
Rondonópolis	144 049	71 561	72 488	...	188 028	93 785	94 243	313
Sabára	44 206	21 375	22 830	...	123 084	59 080	64 004	45
Salto	104 688	51 738	52 950	...	104 688	51 738	52 950	90
Salvador	2 674 923	1 248 513	1 426 410	...	2 674 923	1 248 513	1 426 410	348
Santa Bárbara D'Oeste	178 596	88 478	90 118	...	178 596	88 478	90 118	82
Santa Cruz do Sul	102 891	48 988	53 903	...	105 190	50 142	55 048	154
Santa Luzia (Minas Gerais)	72 187	35 327	36 860	...	202 378	98 202	104 176	194
Santa Maria	246 544	116 243	130 300	...	248 347	117 104	131 243	136
Santa Rita	101 319	48 482	52 838	...	103 717	49 703	54 014	24
Santana de Parnaíba	108 813	53 671	55 142	...	108 813	53 671	55 142	179
Santarém	205 711	98 921	106 790	...	215 790	104 001	111 789	99
Santo André	568 538	271 994	296 544	...	676 407	324 458	351 949	175
Santos	419 086	191 754	227 332	...	419 086	191 754	227 332	80
Sao Bernardo do Campo	736 466	355 313	381 154	...	752 658	363 148	389 510	148
Sao Caetano do Sul	149 263	68 853	80 410	...	149 263	68 853	80 410	15
Sao Carlo	116 765	56 422	60 342	...	213 061	104 241	108 820	80
Sao Gonçalo	337 273	159 766	177 507	...	998 999	474 894	524 105	210
Sao Joao de Meriti	234 340	111 799	122 540	...	458 673	218 104	240 569	35
Sao José	25 993	11 699	14 294	...	207 312	100 118	107 194	94
Sao José do Rio Prêto	372 492	177 603	194 889	...	383 490	182 947	200 543	115
Sao José dos Campos	533 501	260 627	272 874	...	617 119	301 893	315 226	362
Sao José dos Pinhais	200 521	98 276	102 244	...	236 895	116 457	120 438	101
Sao Leopoldo	213 238	103 790	109 448	...	213 238	103 790	109 448	72
Sao Luís	958 545	447 020	511 525	...	958 545	447 020	511 525	322
Sao Paulo	105 269	49 119	56 150	...	11 152 968	5 278 434	5 874 534	991
Sao Vicente	331 817	159 303	172 514	...	331 817	159 303	172 514	71
Sapucaia do Sul	130 469	63 500	66 969	...	130 469	63 500	66 969	46
Serra	112 555	55 292	57 263	...	406 411	199 645	206 766	227
Sertaozinho	101 784	50 254	51 530	...	108 772	54 013	54 759	71
Sete Lagoas	208 847	101 205	107 642	...	208 956	101 263	107 693	92
Simoes Filho	105 811	51 624	54 187	...	105 811	51 624	54 187	57
Sobral	147 353	70 898	76 455	...	166 310	80 213	86 097	80
Sorocaba	580 621	283 854	296 767	...	580 621	283 854	296 767	229
Sumaré	97 696	48 435	49 261	...	238 470	118 381	120 089	73
Susano	152 003	74 026	77 977	...	253 240	123 883	129 357	103
Taboao da Serra	244 528	116 895	127 633	...	244 528	116 895	127 633	20
Tatuí	102 256	50 323	51 933	...	102 256	50 323	51 933	137
Taubaté	232 049	113 563	118 486	...	272 673	133 530	139 143	138
Teixeira de Freitas	128 407	62 801	65 605	...	129 263	63 334	65 929	45
Teófilo Otoni	105 621	49 404	56 217	...	110 076	51 536	58 540	29
Teresina	767 559	356 608	410 951	...	767 559	356 608	410 951	251
Teresópolis	134 156	63 517	70 640	...	146 231	69 454	76 777	223
Timon	134 827	64 855	69 972	...	135 133	65 025	70 108	100
Toledo	103 644	50 409	53 235	...	108 259	52 625	55 634	71
Trindade	100 106	49 070	51 036	...	100 106	49 070	51 036	47

8. Population of capital cities and cities of 100 000 or more inhabitants: latest available year, 1993 - 2012
Population des capitales et des villes de 100 000 habitants ou plus : dernière année disponible, 1993 - 2012 (continued - suite)

Continent, country or area, date, code and city / Continent, pays ou zone, date, code et ville	City proper - Ville proprement dite				Urban agglomeration - Agglomération urbaine			
	Population			Surface area - Superficie (km²)	Population			Surface area - Superficie (km²)
	Both sexes - Les deux sexes	Male - Masculin	Female - Féminin		Both sexes - Les deux sexes	Male - Masculin	Female - Féminin	
AMERICA, SOUTH - AMÉRIQUE DU SUD								
Brazil - Brésil								
31 VII 2010 (CDJC)								
Uberaba	289 376	140 640	148 736	...	289 376	140 640	148 736	411
Uberlândia	584 102	283 948	300 154	...	587 266	285 611	301 655	224
Uruguaiana	116 276	55 938	60 339	...	117 415	56 486	60 929	52
Valinhos	101 626	49 974	51 652	...	101 626	49 974	51 652	62
Valparaíso de Goiás	132 982	64 624	68 358	...	132 982	64 624	68 358	61
Varginha	119 061	57 831	61 230	...	119 061	57 831	61 230	61
Varzea Grande	184 069	91 183	92 886	...	248 704	123 112	125 592	167
Varzea Paulista	107 089	53 415	53 674	...	107 089	53 415	53 674	34
Vespasiano	104 527	51 006	53 521	...	104 527	51 006	53 521	71
Viamao	87 753	42 460	45 293	...	224 943	109 013	115 930	175
Vila Velha	171 772	81 290	90 482	...	412 575	197 926	214 649	120
Vitória	211 529	100 014	111 515	...	327 801	153 948	173 853	88
Vitória da Conquista	260 260	123 976	136 284	...	274 739	131 262	143 477	286
Vitória de Santo Antao	111 541	52 913	58 629	...	113 429	53 820	59 609	31
Volta Redonda	257 686	122 859	134 827	...	257 686	122 859	134 827	140
Votorantim	104 659	51 858	52 801	...	104 659	51 858	52 801	28
Chile - Chili								
1 VII 2012 (ESDF)								
Antofagasta	380 695	197 970	182 725	44[21]	...	...	...	...
Arica	161 972	75 979	85 993	42[21]	...	...	...	...
Calama	147 886	75 165	72 721	18[21]	...	...	...	...
Chiguallante	128 277	59 946	68 331	34[21]	...	...	...	...
Chillán	162 764	77 386	85 378	33[21]	...	...	...	...
Concepción	224 288	108 555	115 733	56[21]	...	...	...	...
Copiapó	162 183	81 352	80 831	48[21]	...	...	...	...
Coquimbo	196 838	96 875	99 963	42[21]	...	...	...	...
Coronel	105 065	51 011	54 054	25[21]	...	...	...	...
Iquique	182 049	87 465	94 584	22[21]	...	...	...	...
La Serena	201 681	97 772	103 909	66[21]	...	...	...	...
Los Angeles	143 251	69 801	73 450	27[21]	...	...	...	...
Osorno	147 753	72 628	75 125	32[21]	...	...	...	...
Puente Alto	757 692	371 446	386 246	64[21]	...	...	...	...
Puerto Montt	211 751	105 984	105 767	40[21]	...	...	...	...
Punta Arenas	122 850	61 531	61 319	39[21]	...	...	...	...
Quilpué	162 320	79 126	83 194	38[21]	...	...	...	...
Rancagua	241 364	120 295	121 069	50[21]	...	...	...	...
San Bernardo	307 185	150 791	156 394	52[21]	...	...	...	...
SANTIAGO	6 148 754[22]	2 987 044[22]	3 161 710[22]	843[21]	...	...	...	...
Talca	220 425	107 167	113 258	46[21]	...	...	...	...
Talcahuano	132 365	60 374	71 991	51[21]	...	...	...	...
Temuco	267 619	128 807	138 812	46[21]	...	...	...	...
Valdivia	140 934	69 178	71 756	42[21]	...	...	...	...
Valparaíso	253 580	126 486	127 094	47[21]	...	...	...	...
Villa Alemana	133 706	65 410	68 296	31[21]	...	...	...	...
Viña del Mar	289 970	139 162	150 808	87[21]	...	...	...	...
Colombia - Colombie[23]								
1 VII 2012 (ESDJ)								
Apartadó	...	...	...	...	162 914	82 438	80 476	607[11]
Armenia	...	...	...	...	292 045	140 849	151 196	115[11]
Barrancabermeja	...	...	...	...	191 718	94 449	97 269	1 274[11]
Barranquilla	...	...	...	...	1 200 513	581 745	618 768	166[11]
Bello	...	...	...	...	430 034	207 821	222 213	151[11]
BOGOTA, D.C.	...	...	...	...	7 571 345	3 653 868	3 917 477	1 605[11]
Bucaramanga	...	...	...	...	526 056	252 130	273 926	154[11]
Buenaventura	...	...	...	...	377 105	183 430	193 675	6 785[11]
Cali	...	...	...	...	2 294 653	1 097 219	1 197 434	552[11]
Cartagena	...	...	...	...	967 103	466 529	500 574	559[11]
Cartago	...	...	...	...	130 076	62 458	67 618	260[11]
Caucasia	...	...	...	...	104 318	50 458	53 860	1 058[11]
Chía	...	...	...	...	117 786	56 573	61 213	76[11]

8. Population of capital cities and cities of 100 000 or more inhabitants: latest available year, 1993 - 2012
Population des capitales et des villes de 100 000 habitants ou plus : dernière année disponible, 1993 - 2012 (continued - suite)

Continent, country or area, date, code and city / Continent, pays ou zone, date, code et ville	City proper - Ville proprement dite				Urban agglomeration - Agglomération urbaine			
	Population			Surface area - Superficie (km²)	Population			Surface area - Superficie (km²)
	Both sexes - Les deux sexes	Male - Masculin	Female - Féminin		Both sexes - Les deux sexes	Male - Masculin	Female - Féminin	
AMERICA, SOUTH - AMÉRIQUE DU SUD								
Colombia - Colombie[23]								
1 VII 2012 (ESDJ)								
Ciénaga	...	...	...	...	103 546	51 639	51 907	1 366[11]
Colombia: Jamundí	...	...	...	...	112 346	54 730	57 616	603[11]
Colombia: Yumbo	...	...	...	...	116 215	57 072	59 143	194[11]
Cúcuta	...	...	...	...	630 971	305 235	325 736	1 098[11]
Dosquebradas	...	...	...	...	193 024	93 270	99 754	80[11]
Duitama	...	...	...	...	111 367	52 040	59 327	229[11]
Envigado	...	...	...	...	207 290	99 853	107 437	51[11]
Facatativá	...	...	...	...	124 779	62 169	62 610	160[11]
Florencia	...	...	...	...	163 354	80 222	83 132	2 292[11]
Floridablanca	...	...	...	...	263 041	124 745	138 296	101[11]
Fusagasugá	...	...	...	...	126 691	62 422	64 269	206[11]
Girardot	...	...	...	...	103 175	48 820	54 355	130[11]
Girón	...	...	...	...	166 115	82 565	83 550	681[11]
Gudalajara de Buga	...	...	...	...	115 772	56 725	59 047	873[11]
Ibagué	...	...	...	...	537 467	261 191	276 276	1 439[11]
Ipiales	...	...	...	...	129 362	63 550	65 812	1 707[11]
Itagüi	...	...	...	...	258 520	125 652	132 868	17[11]
Lorica	...	...	...	...	115 808	58 069	57 739	890[11]
Magangué	...	...	...	...	123 312	62 322	60 990	1 102[11]
Maicao	...	...	...	...	148 427	72 921	75 506	1 789[11]
Malambo	...	...	...	...	115 274	58 461	56 813	108[11]
Manizales	...	...	...	...	391 640	186 423	205 217	477[11]
Medellín	...	...	...	...	2 393 011	1 126 595	1 266 416	387[11]
Montería	...	...	...	...	422 198	204 845	217 353	3 043[11]
Neiva	...	...	...	...	335 490	160 524	174 966	1 468[11]
Palmira	...	...	...	...	298 671	144 598	154 073	1 044[11]
Pasto	...	...	...	...	423 217	203 756	219 461	1 131[11]
Pereira	...	...	...	...	462 209	220 078	242 131	702[11]
Piedecuesta	...	...	...	...	139 178	67 750	71 428	481[11]
Pitalito	...	...	...	...	118 677	58 940	59 737	653[11]
Popayán	...	...	...	...	270 340	130 760	139 580	464[11]
Quibdo	...	...	...	...	115 052	57 199	57 853	3 075[11]
Riohacha	...	...	...	...	231 653	113 809	117 844	3 171[11]
Rionegro	...	...	...	...	114 299	56 809	57 490	198[11]
San Andres de Tumaco	...	...	...	...	187 084	93 782	93 302	3 778[11]
Santa Marta	...	...	...	...	461 900	224 789	237 111	2 369[11]
Sincelejo	...	...	...	...	263 776	129 153	134 623	292[11]
Soacha	...	...	...	...	477 918	235 749	242 169	187[11]
Sogamoso	...	...	...	...	114 676	54 495	60 181	214[11]
Soledad	...	...	...	...	566 784	280 307	286 477	67[11]
Tuluá	...	...	...	...	204 138	98 216	105 922	818[11]
Tunja	...	...	...	...	177 971	84 875	93 096	118[11]
Turbo	...	...	...	...	147 243	74 565	72 678	3 090[11]
Uribia	...	...	...	...	156 496	76 754	79 742	7 904[11]
Valledupar	...	...	...	...	423 278	205 944	217 334	4 225[11]
Villavicencio	...	...	...	...	452 522	219 377	233 145	1 328[11]
Yopal	...	...	...	...	129 943	65 110	64 833	2 532[11]
Zipaquirá	...	...	...	...	109 131	54 725	54 406	243[11]
Ecuador - Équateur								
28 XI 2010 (CDFC)								
Ambato	165 185	79 764	85 421	31	178 538	86 299	92 239	...
Calderon (Carapungo)	...	...	...	...	152 242	74 682	77 560	...
Cuenca	329 928	157 426	172 502	56	331 888	158 365	173 523	...
Durán	230 839	113 746	117 093	40	235 769	116 401	119 368	...
Esmeraldas	154 035	73 735	80 300	8	161 868	77 505	84 363	...
Guayaquil	2 278 691	1 120 331	1 158 360	369	2 291 158	1 127 137	1 164 021	...
Ibarra	131 856	63 349	68 507	36	139 721	67 165	72 556	...
Loja	170 280	81 475	88 805	25	180 617	86 631	93 986	...
Machala	231 260	115 221	116 039	34	241 606	120 643	120 963	...
Manta	217 553	106 871	110 682	45	221 122	108 677	112 445	...

8. Population of capital cities and cities of 100 000 or more inhabitants: latest available year, 1993 - 2012
Population des capitales et des villes de 100 000 habitants ou plus : dernière année disponible, 1993 - 2012 (continued - suite)

Continent, country or area, date, code and city Continent, pays ou zone, date, code et ville	City proper - Ville proprement dite				Urban agglomeration - Agglomération urbaine			
	Population			Surface area - Superficie (km²)	Population			Surface area - Superficie (km²)
	Both sexes - Les deux sexes	Male - Masculin	Female - Féminin		Both sexes - Les deux sexes	Male - Masculin	Female - Féminin	
AMERICA, SOUTH - AMÉRIQUE DU SUD								
Ecuador - Équateur								
28 XI 2010 (CDFC)								
Milagro	133 508	66 062	67 446	19	145 025	72 031	72 994	...
Portoviejo	206 682	100 506	106 176	50	223 086	108 878	114 208	...
Quevedo	150 827	75 065	75 762	20	158 694	79 218	79 476	...
QUITO	1 607 734	777 939	829 795	181	1 619 146	783 616	835 530	...
Riobamba	146 324	69 641	76 683	29	156 723	74 634	82 089	...
Santa Elena	270 875	132 501	138 374	36	305 632	150 428	155 204	...
Falkland Islands (Malvinas) - Îles Falkland (Malvinas)								
8 X 2006 (CDFC)								
STANLEY	2 115	...	...	...	...	...	...	...
French Guiana - Guyane française								
1 I 2006 (CDJC)								
CAYENNE	58 004	27 412	30 591	24	75 740	36 484	39 256	70
Guyana								
15 IX 2002 (CDFC)								
GEORGETOWN	134 497	63 973	70 524	...	...	...	...	...
Paraguay								
1 VII 2008 (ESDF)								
ASUNCION[24]	518 792	240 940	277 852	117	2 448 710	1 191 827	1 256 883	2 582
Capiatá	209 012	104 112	104 900	82	...	...	...	...
Ciudad del Este	279 655	140 381	139 274	149	...	...	...	...
Fernando de la Mora	162 652	77 609	85 042	21	...	...	...	...
Lambaré	171 282	82 375	88 907	27	...	...	...	...
Luque	291 225	143 243	147 982	152	...	...	...	...
San Lorenzo	287 977	139 637	148 339	57	...	...	...	...
Peru - Pérou[25]								
1 VII 2012 (ESDF)								
Arequipa	844 407	407 634	436 773	...	...	...	...	...
Ayacucho	170 750	84 551	86 199	...	...	...	...	...
Cajamarca	204 543	100 329	104 214	...	...	...	...	...
Chiclayo	583 159	278 102	305 057	...	...	...	...	...
Chimbote	361 291	181 399	179 892	...	...	...	...	...
Chincha Alta	169 237	84 257	84 980	...	...	...	...	...
Cuzco	405 842	198 231	207 611	...	...	...	...	...
Huancayo	353 535	169 268	184 267	...	...	...	...	...
Huánuco	168 548	80 919	87 629	...	...	...	...	...
Huaraz	117 774	57 927	59 847	...	...	...	...	...
Ica	236 772	116 226	120 546	...	...	...	...	...
Iquitos	422 055	212 337	209 718	...	...	...	...	...
Juliaca	254 175	124 490	129 685	...	...	...	...	...
LIMA[26]	9 437 493	4 597 427	4 840 066	...	...	...	...	...
Pisco	103 638	52 772	50 866	...	...	...	...	...
Piura	417 892	202 580	215 312	...	...	...	...	...
Pucallpa	211 591	108 902	102 689	...	...	...	...	...
Puno	134 573	65 699	68 874	...	...	...	...	...
Sullana	196 102	95 827	100 275	...	...	...	...	...
Tacna	279 750	142 519	137 231	...	...	...	...	...
Tarapoto	134 804	69 859	64 945	...	...	...	...	...
Trujillo	765 495	371 037	394 458	...	...	...	...	...
Suriname								
2 VIII 2004 (CDJC)								
PARAMARIBO	...	...	...	...	242 946	120 292	122 405	182
Uruguay								
1 VII 2009 (ESDF)								
MONTEVIDEO	1 338 408[1]	624 746[1]	713 662[1]	530	...	...	...	...
Venezuela (Bolivarian Republic of) - Venezuela (République bolivarienne du)								
1 VII 2011 (ESDF)								
Acarigua-Araure	290 146[18]	142 812[18]	147 334[18]	1 065	...	...	...	...
Anaco(F) (Capital)[18]	149 380	81 172	68 208	...	...	...	...	...
Barcelona	326 460[18]	163 915[18]	162 545[18]	463	...	...	...	...
Barcelona-Puerto La Cruz	435 940[18]	221 667[18]	214 273[18]	707	...	...	...	...
Barinas	307 364[18]	150 145[18]	157 219[18]	848	...	...	...	...

8. Population of capital cities and cities of 100 000 or more inhabitants: latest available year, 1993 - 2012
Population des capitales et des villes de 100 000 habitants ou plus : dernière année disponible, 1993 - 2012 (continued - suite)

Continent, country or area, date, code and city / Continent, pays ou zone, date, code et ville	City proper - Ville proprement dite				Urban agglomeration - Agglomération urbaine			
	Population			Surface area - Superficie (km²)	Population			Surface area - Superficie (km²)
	Both sexes - Les deux sexes	Male - Masculin	Female - Féminin		Both sexes - Les deux sexes	Male - Masculin	Female - Féminin	
AMERICA, SOUTH - AMÉRIQUE DU SUD								
Venezuela (Bolivarian Republic of) - Venezuela (République bolivarienne du)								
1 VII 2011 (ESDF)								
Barquisimeto	1 000 632[18]	489 530[18]	511 102[18]	2 645	...	...	...	...
Baruta[18]	266 261	124 876	141 385	...	...	...	...	...
Cabimas	240 765[18]	119 731[18]	121 034[18]	175	...	...	...	...
Cagua[18]	130 763	64 202	66 561	...	...	...	...	...
CARACAS	2 104 423[18]	1 019 207[18]	1 085 216[18]	433	...	...	...	...
Carora[18]	112 626	55 773	56 853	...	...	...	...	...
Carúpano	135 969[18]	66 660[18]	69 309[18]	203	...	...	...	...
Ciudad Bolívar	371 566[18]	182 183[18]	189 383[18]	5 851	...	...	...	...
Ciudad Guayana	850 262[18]	426 168[18]	424 094[18]	1 612	...	...	...	...
Ciudad Ojeda[18]	146 509	73 463	73 046	...	...	...	...	...
Coro	199 603[18]	97 900[18]	101 703[18]	438	...	...	...	...
Cua[18]	138 784	67 821	70 963	...	...	...	...	...
Cumaná	341 441[18]	168 253[18]	173 188[18]	405	...	...	...	...
El Silencio[18]	125 014	73 463	51 551	...	...	...	...	...
El Tigre[18]	224 887	122 795	102 092	...	...	...	...	...
Guacara[18]	147 733	74 070	73 663	...	...	...	...	...
Guanare[18]	151 170	73 851	77 319	...	...	...	...	...
Guarenas	285 561[18]	139 992[18]	145 569[18]	180	...	...	...	...
Guatire[18]	184 375	88 570	95 805	...	...	...	...	...
Los Guayos[18]	166 116	83 614	82 502	...	...	...	...	...
Los Teques	272 301[18]	132 277[18]	140 024[18]	98	...	...	...	...
Maracaibo	1 339 019[18]	660 297[18]	678 722[18]	604	...	...	...	...
Maracay	446 271[18]	218 426[18]	227 845[18]	169	...	...	...	...
Maturín[18]	445 444	241 844	203 600	...	...	...	...	...
Mérida	231 861[18]	107 125[18]	124 736[18]	482	...	...	...	...
Naguanagua[18]	162 281	77 380	84 901	...	...	...	...	...
Ocumare Del Tuy[18]	134 451	66 675	67 776	...	...	...	...	...
Petare[18]	116 159	57 865	58 294	...	...	...	...	...
Pozuelos (F) (Capital)[18]	165 563	91 154	74 409	...	...	...	...	...
Puerto Cabello	203 859[18]	103 228[18]	100 631[18]	309	...	...	...	...
Puerto La Cruz[18]	109 480	57 752	51 728	...	...	...	...	...
Punto Fijo	150 496[18]	74 119[18]	76 377[18]	31	...	...	...	...
San Cristóbal	271 424[18]	130 059[18]	141 365[18]	248	...	...	...	...
San Fernando de Apure[18]	133 487	60 585	72 902	...	...	...	...	...
San Francisco[18]	128 509	63 495	65 014	...	...	...	...	...
Santa Lucia[18]	112 227	57 961	54 266	...	...	...	...	...
Táriba[18]	102 009	51 718	50 291	...	...	...	...	...
Tocuyito[18]	186 743	94 425	92 318	...	...	...	...	...
Valencia	917 999[18]	451 421[18]	466 578[18]	1 212	...	...	...	...
Valera	125 590[18]	60 672[18]	64 918[18]	55	...	...	...	...
ASIA - ASIE								
Afghanistan								
1 VII 2012 (ESDF)								
Baghalan Center (Puli Khumry)	101 100	51 800	49 300	...	203 600	104 500	99 100	...
Balkh Center (Mazar- Sharif)	368 100	188 800	179 300	...	368 100	188 800	179 300	...
Herat Center	436 300	221 600	214 700	...	436 300	221 600	214 700	...
KABUL CENTER	3 289 000	1 702 300	1 586 700	...	3 289 000	1 702 300	1 586 700	...
Kandhar Center (Kndhar)	397 500	204 600	192 900	...	491 500	252 900	238 600	...
Kunduz Center	143 800	73 900	69 900	...	304 600	155 500	149 100	...
Nngarhar Center (Jlal Abad)	206 500	106 300	100 200	...	206 500	106 300	100 200	...
Armenia - Arménie								
12 X 2011 (CDJC)								
Gyumri (Leninakan)	121 976	57 132	64 844	44	...	...	...	...
YEREVAN	1 060 138	490 362	569 776	223	...	...	...	...

8. Population of capital cities and cities of 100 000 or more inhabitants: latest available year, 1993 - 2012
Population des capitales et des villes de 100 000 habitants ou plus : dernière année disponible, 1993 - 2012 (continued - suite)

Continent, country or area, date, code and city Continent, pays ou zone, date, code et ville	City proper - Ville proprement dite				Urban agglomeration - Agglomération urbaine			
	Population			Surface area - Superficie (km²)	Population			Surface area - Superficie (km²)
	Both sexes - Les deux sexes	Male - Masculin	Female - Féminin		Both sexes - Les deux sexes	Male - Masculin	Female - Féminin	
ASIA - ASIE								
Azerbaijan - Azerbaïdjan								
1 VII 2010 (ESDF)								
BAKU	2 078 485	1 029 007	1 049 478	2 130	...	...	...	...
Ganja	315 454	152 536	162 918	110	...	...	...	...
Sumgayit	313 290	153 700	159 590	80	...	...	...	...
Bahrain - Bahreïn								
1 VII 2006 (ESDF)								
MANAMA	*176 909*	*113 503*	*63 406*	30	...	...	...	...
Bangladesh								
22 I 2001 (CDFC)								
Barisal	...	...	...	...	192 810	103 785	89 025	20
Bogra	...	...	...	...	154 807	82 368	72 439	11
Brahmanbaria	...	...	...	...	129 278	66 890	62 388	18
Chittagong	...	...	...	...	2 023 489	1 127 516	895 973	168
Comilla	...	...	...	...	166 519	88 927	77 592	11
DHAKA	...	...	...	...	5 333 571	3 025 395	2 308 176	154
Dinajpur	...	...	...	...	157 914	82 068	75 846	19
Gazipur	...	...	...	...	122 801	65 522	57 279	49
Jamalpur	...	...	...	...	120 955	62 059	58 896	53
Jessore	...	...	...	...	176 655	94 203	82 452	15
Kadamrasul	...	...	...	...	128 561	66 799	61 762	6
Khulna	...	...	...	...	770 498	412 661	357 837	60
Mymensingh	...	...	...	...	227 204	119 172	108 032	22
Naogaon	...	...	...	...	124 046	65 406	58 640	37
Narayanganj	...	...	...	...	241 393	131 168	110 225	13
Narsingdi	...	...	...	...	124 204	67 575	56 629	9
Nawabganj	...	...	...	...	152 223	75 375	76 848	34
Pabna	...	...	...	...	116 305	60 666	55 639	27
Rajshahi	...	...	...	...	388 811	208 525	180 286	97
Rangpur	...	...	...	...	241 310	124 296	117 014	51
Saidpur	...	...	...	...	112 609	58 289	54 320	34
Sirajganj	...	...	...	...	128 144	66 673	61 471	28
Tangail	...	...	...	...	128 785	66 856	61 929	29
Tongi	...	...	...	...	283 099	156 335	126 764	30
Bhutan - Bhoutan								
30 V 2005 (CDFC)								
THIMPHU	...	...	...	...	79 185	42 465	36 720	...
Brunei Darussalam - Brunéi Darussalam								
21 VIII 2001 (CDFC)								
BANDAR SERI BEGAWAN	27 285	13 639	13 646	100	...	...	...	...
Cambodia - Cambodge								
1 VII 2011 (ESDF)								
Bat Dambang	*1 126 345*[27]	*558 945*[27]	*567 400*[27]	114	...	...	...	...
PHNOM PENH	*1 570 791*[27]	*738 159*[27]	*832 631*[27]	21	...	...	...	...
Seam Reab	*999 703*[27]	*493 184*[27]	*506 519*[27]	292	...	...	...	...
China - Chine								
1 VII 2010 (ESDF)								
BEIJING (PEKING)	*19 610 000*[28]	*10 130 000*[28]	*9 490 000*[28]	16 410	...	...	...	...
China, Hong Kong SAR - Chine, Hong Kong RAS								
1 VII 2012 (ESDJ)								
HONG KONG SAR	7 154 600	3 327 300	3 827 300	1 104	...	...	...	...
China, Macao SAR - Chine, Macao RAS								
1 VII 2012 (ESDJ)								
MACAO	567 900	274 300	293 600	30	...	...	...	...
Cyprus - Chypre								
1 I 2006 (ESDJ)								
LEFKOSIA[29]	...	...	...	...	*224 500*	...	...	...
Lemesos[30]	...	...	...	...	*176 900*	...	...	...
Democratic People's Republic of Korea - République populaire démocratique de Corée								
1 X 2008 (CDJC)								
Anju	167 646	79 187	88 459	...	...	...	...	...
Chongjin	614 892	292 741	322 151	...	...	...	...	...
Haeju	241 599	116 594	125 005	...	...	...	...	...
Hamhung	614 198	292 058	322 140	...	...	...	...	...

8. Population of capital cities and cities of 100 000 or more inhabitants: latest available year, 1993 - 2012
Population des capitales et des villes de 100 000 habitants ou plus : dernière année disponible, 1993 - 2012 (continued - suite)

Continent, country or area, date, code and city — Continent, pays ou zone, date, code et ville	City proper - Ville proprement dite				Urban agglomeration - Agglomération urbaine			
	Population			Surface area - Superficie (km²)	Population			Surface area - Superficie (km²)
	Both sexes - Les deux sexes	Male - Masculin	Female - Féminin		Both sexes - Les deux sexes	Male - Masculin	Female - Féminin	
ASIA - ASIE								
Democratic People's Republic of Korea - République populaire démocratique de Corée								
1 X 2008 (CDJC)								
Huichon	136 093	64 547	71 546	...	...	...	...	...
Hyesan	174 015	82 604	91 411	...	...	...	...	...
Jongju	102 659	48 423	54 236	...	...	...	...	...
Kaechon	262 389	124 222	138 167	...	...	...	...	...
Kaesong	192 578	90 653	101 925	...	...	...	...	...
Kanggye	251 971	120 305	131 666	...	...	...	...	...
Kim Chaek	155 284	73 133	82 151	...	...	...	...	...
Kusong	155 181	73 677	81 504	...	...	...	...	...
Nampho	310 864	150 091	160 773	...	...	...	...	...
Phyongsong	236 583	115 817	120 766	...	...	...	...	...
PYONGYANG	2 581 076	1 233 765	1 347 311	...	...	...	...	...
Rason	158 337	74 777	83 560	...	...	...	...	...
Sariwon	271 434	130 181	141 253	...	...	...	...	...
Sinpho	130 951	63 207	67 744	...	...	...	...	...
Sinuiju	334 031	158 139	175 892	...	...	...	...	...
Sunchon	250 738	119 727	131 011	...	...	...	...	...
Tanchon	240 873	113 221	127 652	...	...	...	...	...
Tokchon	210 571	99 655	110 916	...	...	...	...	...
Wonsan	328 467	155 903	172 564	...	...	...	...	...
Georgia - Géorgie								
1 VII 2011 (ESDF)								
Batumi	125 800	...	...	...	...	...	...	...
Kutaisi	196 800	...	...	...	...	...	...	...
Rustavi	122 500	...	...	...	...	...	...	...
TBILISI	1 172 700	...	...	...	...	...	...	...
India - Inde[31]								
1 III 2001 (CDFC)								
Abohar	124 339	66 445	57 894	23	...	...	...	...
Achalpur	107 316	55 687	51 629	17	...	...	...	...
Adilabad	109 529	55 641	53 888	16	129 403	65 501	63 902	21
Adityapur	119 233	63 837	55 396	50	...	...	...	...
Adoni	157 305	79 639	77 666	30	162 458	82 345	80 113	...
Agartala	189 998	94 742	95 256	16	...	...	...	...
Agra	1 275 134	690 599	584 535	121	1 331 339	720 707	610 632	141
Ahmedabad	3 520 085	1 867 249	1 652 836	191	4 525 013	2 401 422	2 123 591	438
Ahmednagar	307 615	159 564	148 051	18	347 549	184 765	162 784	30
Aizawl	228 280	115 986	112 294	110	...	...	...	...
Ajmer	485 575	254 164	231 411	218	490 520	256 695	233 825	223
Akola	400 520	206 649	193 871	23	...	...	...	...
Alandur	146 287	74 836	71 451	20	...	...	...	...
Alappuzha	177 029	85 725	91 304	70	282 675	137 244	145 431	84
Aligarh	669 087	356 725	312 362	40	...	...	...	...
Alipurduar	...	...	...	...	114 035	58 503	55 532	26
Allahabad	975 393	539 772	435 621	63	1 042 229	576 122	466 107	86
Alwar	260 593	139 585	121 008	...	266 203	143 699	122 504	58
Ambala	139 279	74 016	65 263	17	168 316	92 977	75 339	38
Ambala Sadar	106 568	55 750	50 818	...	...	...	...	...
Ambarnath	203 804	107 325	96 479	36	...	...	...	...
Ambattur	310 967	160 282	150 685	40	...	...	...	...
Amravati	549 510	284 247	265 263	122	...	...	...	...
Amritsar	966 862	518 388	448 474	136	1 003 917	538 744	465 173	...
Amroha	165 129	86 943	78 186	6	...	...	...	...
Anand	130 685	68 074	62 611	21	218 486	115 295	103 191	60
Anantapur	218 808	110 979	107 829	...	243 143	123 713	119 430	...
Anklesvar	...	...	...	...	112 643	60 249	52 394	...
Arcot	...	...	...	...	126 671	62 787	63 884	19
Arrah	203 380	109 867	93 513	31	...	...	...	...
Asansol	475 439	250 886	224 553	128	1 067 369	564 837	502 532	352
Ashoknagar Kalyangarh	111 607	56 490	55 117	...	...	...	...	...
Aurangabad	873 311	459 295	414 016	139	892 483	469 237	423 246	148
Avadi	229 403	117 991	111 412	65	...	...	...	...
Bahadurgarh	119 846	65 859	53 987	21	131 925	72 873	59 052	30

Continent, country or area, date, code and city / Continent, pays ou zone, date, code et ville	City proper - Ville proprement dite				Urban agglomeration - Agglomération urbaine			
	Population			Surface area - Superficie (km²)	Population			Surface area - Superficie (km²)
	Both sexes - Les deux sexes	Male - Masculin	Female - Féminin		Both sexes - Les deux sexes	Male - Masculin	Female - Féminin	
ASIA - ASIE								
India - Inde[31]								
1 III 2001 (CDFC)								
Baharampur	160 143	81 737	78 406	17	170 322	86 969	83 353	19
Bahraich	168 323	89 581	78 742	13	...	...	...	...
Baidyabati	108 229	56 394	51 835	8	...	...	...	...
Baleshwar	106 082	55 691	50 391	...	156 430	82 106	74 324	42
Ballia	101 465	54 496	46 969	16	...	...	...	...
Bally	260 906	149 603	111 303	12	...	...	...	...
Balurghat	135 737	68 871	66 866	10	143 321	72 764	70 557	12
Banda	134 839	72 632	62 207	16	139 436	75 174	64 262	28
Bangalore	4 301 326	2 242 835	2 058 491	...	5 701 446	2 988 561	2 712 885	540
Bangaon	102 163	52 537	49 626	25	...	...	...	...
Bankura	128 781	66 429	62 352	19	...	...	...	...
Bansberia	104 412	55 389	49 023	9	...	...	...	...
Baranagar	250 768	132 559	118 209	7	...	...	...	...
Barasat	231 521	118 374	113 147	31	...	...	...	...
Barddhaman	285 602	148 562	137 040	23	...	...	...	...
Bareilly	718 395	378 848	339 547	106	748 353	397 304	351 049	125
Baripada	...	...	...	...	100 651	53 606	47 045	38
Barrackpur	144 391	76 299	68 092	11	...	...	...	...
Barshi	104 785	53 848	50 937	36	...	...	...	...
Basirhat	113 159	57 965	55 194	22	...	...	...	...
Basti	107 601	57 053	50 548	19	...	...	...	...
Batala	125 677	66 508	59 169	9	147 872	78 393	69 479	...
Bathinda	217 256	116 946	100 310	110	...	...	...	...
Beawar	123 759	64 417	59 342	18	125 981	65 586	60 395	24
Begusarai	...	...	...	...	107 623	57 541	50 082	12
Belgaum	399 653	204 598	195 055	100	506 480	261 639	244 841	173
Bellary	316 766	162 699	154 067	66	...	...	...	...
Bettiah	116 670	61 753	54 917	8	...	...	...	...
Bhadravati	160 662	81 351	79 311	...	...	...	...	...
Bhadreswar	106 071	58 040	48 031	6	...	...	...	...
Bhagalpur	340 767	182 806	157 961	30	350 133	187 723	162 410	31
Bhalswa Jahangir Pur	152 339	83 802	68 537	7	...	...	...	...
Bharatpur	204 587	110 057	94 530	41	205 235	110 397	94 838	51
Bharuch	148 140	76 506	71 634	18	176 364	91 281	85 083	20
Bhatpara	442 385	243 157	199 228	30	...	...	...	...
Bhavani	...	...	...	...	104 646	52 998	51 648	10
Bhavnagar	511 085	266 838	244 247	90	517 708	270 278	247 430	91
Bheemavaram	137 409	69 473	67 936	26	142 064	71 929	70 135	26
Bhilai Nagar	556 366	291 070	265 296	141	...	...	...	...
Bhilwara	280 128	148 794	131 334	118	...	...	...	...
Bhind	153 752	82 945	70 807	17	...	...	...	...
Bhiwandi	598 741	367 565	231 176	26	621 427	382 184	239 243	28
Bhiwani	169 531	91 697	77 834	28	...	...	...	...
Bhopal	1 437 354	757 408	679 946	285	1 458 416	768 391	690 025	298
Bhubaneswar	648 032	360 739	287 293	135	658 220	366 134	292 086	148
Bhuj	...	...	...	...	136 429	71 056	65 373	...
Bhusawal	172 372	89 208	83 164	13	187 564	97 243	90 321	25
Bid	138 196	71 827	66 369	8	...	...	...	...
Bidar	172 877	89 934	82 943	...	174 257	90 662	83 595	47
Bidhan Nagar	164 221	83 220	81 001	34	...	...	...	...
Bihar	232 071	122 019	110 052	24	...	...	...	...
Bijapur	228 175	117 375	110 800	...	253 891	130 416	123 475	75
Bikaner	529 690	283 067	246 623	166	...	...	...	...
Bilaspur	275 694	143 518	132 176	36	335 293	174 351	160 942	46
Birnagar	...	...	...	...	115 127	59 232	55 895	40
Bokaro Steel City	393 805	213 231	180 574	163	497 780	268 969	228 811	188
Bommanahalli	201 652	108 108	93 544	36	...	...	...	...
Botad	100 194	52 752	47 442	10	...	...	...	...
Brahmapur	307 792	160 354	147 438	80	...	...	...	...
Budaun	148 029	78 141	69 888	4	...	...	...	...
Bulandshahr	176 425	93 531	82 894	12	...	...	...	...
Burhanpur	193 725	99 751	93 974	13	...	...	...	...
Byatarayanapura	181 744	95 508	86 236	45	...	...	...	...

Continent, country or area, date, code and city / Continent, pays ou zone, date, code et ville	City proper - Ville proprement dite				Urban agglomeration - Agglomération urbaine			
	Population			Surface area - Superficie (km²)	Population			Surface area - Superficie (km²)
	Both sexes - Les deux sexes	Male - Masculin	Female - Féminin		Both sexes - Les deux sexes	Male - Masculin	Female - Féminin	
ASIA - ASIE								
India - Inde[31]								
1 III 2001 (CDFC)								
Chakdaha	...	...	...	...	101 320	51 485	49 835	...
Champdani	103 246	57 842	45 404	6	...	...	...	...
Chandan Nagar	162 187	84 181	78 006	22	...	...	...	...
Chandausi	103 749	55 127	48 622	9	...	...	...	...
Chandigarh	808 515	450 122	358 393	79	...	...	...	...
Chandrapur	289 450	151 202	138 248	56	...	...	...	...
Chapra	179 190	95 494	83 696	17	...	...	...	...
Chennai (Madras)	4 343 645	2 219 539	2 124 106	174	6 560 242	3 355 524	3 204 718	702
Cherthala	...	...	...	...	141 558	68 756	72 802	92
Chhatarpur	...	...	...	...	109 078	58 421	50 657	17
Chhindwara	122 247	63 584	58 663	11	153 552	79 889	73 663	22
Chikmagalur	101 251	51 694	49 557	33	...	...	...	...
Chirala	...	...	...	...	166 294	82 954	83 340	48
Chirkunda	...	...	...	...	106 227	56 536	49 691	26
Chitradurga	122 702	62 845	59 857	24	125 170	64 112	61 058	26
Chittoor	152 654	76 879	75 775	33	...	...	...	...
Churu	...	...	...	...	101 874	53 079	48 795	30
Coimbatore	930 882	477 937	452 945	106	1 461 139	748 376	712 763	379
Coonoor	...	...	...	...	101 490	51 208	50 282	44
Cuddalore	158 634	80 012	78 622	28	...	...	...	...
Cuddapah	126 505	63 669	62 836	42	262 506	133 224	129 282	78
Cuttack	534 654	285 838	248 816	149	587 182	314 101	273 081	195
Dallo Pura	132 621	71 362	61 259	2	...	...	...	...
Damoh	112 185	58 962	53 223	16	127 967	67 321	60 646	36
Darbhanga	267 348	142 377	124 971	19	...	...	...	...
Darjiling	107 197	55 963	51 234	11	108 830	56 769	52 061	13
Dasarahalli	264 940	143 909	121 031	23	...	...	...	...
Davangere	364 523	187 987	176 536	...	...	...	...	...
Dehradun	426 674	224 546	202 128	52	530 263	283 064	247 199	103
Dehri	119 057	63 540	55 517	21	...	...	...	...
Delhi	9 879 172	5 412 497	4 466 675	554	12 877 470[32]	7 069 371[32]	5 808 099[32]	889[32]
Delhi Cantonment	124 917	75 827	49 090	43	...	...	...	...
Deoghar	...	...	...	...	112 525	61 442	51 083	22
Deoli	119 468	66 594	52 874	10	...	...	...	...
Deoria	104 227	54 681	49 546	16	...	...	...	...
Dewas	231 672	121 075	110 597	100	...	...	...	...
Dhanbad	199 258	108 512	90 746	23	1 065 327	579 150	486 177	223
Dharmavaram	103 357	52 785	50 572	40	...	...	...	...
Dhule	341 755	177 772	163 983	46	...	...	...	...
Dibrugarh	121 893	65 118	56 775	25	137 661	73 307	64 354	26
Dinapur Nizamat	131 176	69 419	61 757	12	...	...	...	...
Dindigul	196 955	99 124	97 831	14	...	...	...	...
Dohad	...	...	...	...	112 026	57 642	54 384	26
Dumdum	101 296	52 890	48 406	9	...	...	...	...
Durg	232 517	119 315	113 202	66	...	...	...	...
Durgapur	493 405	263 721	229 684	154	...	...	...	...
Durg-Bhilai Nagar	...	...	...	...	927 864	482 304	445 560	341
Eluru	190 062	92 790	97 272	15	215 804	105 476	110 328	...
English Bazar	161 456	82 845	78 611	...	224 415	115 356	109 059	19
Erode	150 541	76 462	74 079	8	389 906	198 842	191 064	132
Etah	107 110	56 763	50 347	13	...	...	...	...
Etawah	210 453	111 749	98 704	9	...	...	...	...
Faizabad	144 705	75 935	68 770	33	208 162	114 330	93 832	63
Faridabad	1 055 938	581 069	474 869	199	...	...	...	...
Farrukhabad-cum-Fategarh	228 333	120 829	107 504	17	242 997	129 643	113 354	21
Fatehpur	152 078	80 011	72 067	57	...	...	...	...
Firozabad	279 102	148 263	130 839	9	432 866	230 802	202 064	12
Gadag-Betgeri	154 982	78 713	76 269	35	...	...	...	...
Gajuwaka	259 180	133 469	125 711	128	...	...	...	...
Gandhidham	151 693	79 379	72 314	30	...	...	...	...
Gandhinagar	195 985	103 876	92 109	57	...	...	...	...
Ganganagar	210 713	115 321	95 392	21	222 858	121 865	100 993	...
Gangapur City	...	...	...	...	105 396	56 009	49 387	12

8. Population of capital cities and cities of 100 000 or more inhabitants: latest available year, 1993 - 2012
Population des capitales et des villes de 100 000 habitants ou plus : dernière année disponible, 1993 - 2012 (continued - suite)

Continent, country or area, date, code and city Continent, pays ou zone, date, code et ville	City proper - Ville proprement dite				Urban agglomeration - Agglomération urbaine			
	Population			Surface area - Superficie (km²)	Population			Surface area - Superficie (km²)
	Both sexes - Les deux sexes	Male - Masculin	Female - Féminin		Both sexes - Les deux sexes	Male - Masculin	Female - Féminin	
ASIA - ASIE								
India - Inde[31]								
1 III 2001 (CDFC)								
Gangawati	...	...	...	...	101 392	51 211	50 181	16
Gaya	385 432	204 483	180 949	29	394 945	210 410	184 535	32
Ghatlodiya	106 684	56 219	50 465	4	...	...	...	...
Ghaziabad	968 256	521 026	447 230	145	...	...	...	...
Ghazipur	...	...	...	...	103 298	54 371	48 927	20
Giridih	...	...	...	...	105 634	55 490	50 144	11
Godhra	121 879	63 176	58 703	20	131 172	67 969	63 203	23
Gonda	120 301	66 207	54 094	15	...	...	...	...
Gondiya	120 902	61 418	59 484	18	...	...	...	...
Gorakhpur	622 701	329 807	292 894	141	...	...	...	...
Gudivada	113 054	55 867	57 187	13	...	...	...	...
Gudiyatham	...	...	...	...	100 115	49 794	50 321	14
Gulbarga	422 569	219 409	203 160	...	430 265	223 594	206 671	43
Guna	137 175	72 538	64 637	46	...	...	...	...
Guntakul	117 103	59 211	57 892	41	...	...	...	...
Guntur	514 461	257 775	256 686	46	...	...	...	...
Gurgaon	172 955	92 934	80 021	15	228 820	123 377	105 443	24
Guruvayur	...	...	...	...	138 681	64 554	74 127	57
Guwahati	809 895	440 288	369 607	217	818 809	446 311	372 498	217
Gwalior	827 026	442 343	384 683	167	865 548	465 057	400 491	180
Habra	127 602	65 141	62 461	18	239 209	121 631	117 578	37
Hajipur	119 412	63 838	55 574	20	...	...	...	...
Haldia	170 673	89 893	80 780	69	...	...	...	...
Haldwani-cum-Kathgodam	129 015	68 755	60 260	11	158 896	84 541	74 355	...
Halisahar	124 510	67 151	57 359	8	...	...	...	...
Hanumangarh	129 556	69 532	60 024	13	...	...	...	...
Haora (Howrah)	1 007 532	547 068	460 464	52	...	...	...	...
Hapur	211 983	113 175	98 808	14	...	...	...	...
Hardoi	112 486	59 876	52 610	6	...	...	...	...
Hardwar	175 340	94 736	80 604	15	220 767	119 234	101 533	42
Hassan	116 574	59 743	56 831	27	133 262	68 242	65 020	30
Hathras	123 244	65 778	57 466	8	126 355	67 436	58 919	8
Hazaribag	127 269	67 900	59 369	26	135 473	72 288	63 185	27
Hindupur	125 074	64 132	60 942	38	...	...	...	...
Hisar	256 689	140 083	116 606	45	263 186	143 795	119 391	49
Hoshiarpur	149 668	79 454	70 214	35	...	...	...	...
Hospet	164 240	83 767	80 473	28	...	...	...	...
Hubli-Dharwad	786 195	403 085	383 110	213	...	...	...	...
Hugli-Chinsurah	170 206	86 788	83 418	17	...	...	...	...
Hyderabad	3 637 483	1 883 064	1 754 419	173	5 742 036	2 973 472	2 768 564	822
Ichalakaranji	257 610	136 063	121 547	30	285 860	150 977	134 883	38
Imphal	221 492	109 815	111 677	33	250 234	123 859	126 375	37
Indore	1 474 968	774 540	700 428	130	1 516 918	796 673	720 245	165
Itarsi	...	...	...	...	107 831	56 347	51 484	24
Jabalpur	932 484	488 479	444 005	119	1 098 000	580 038	517 962	205
Jagadhri	101 290	55 844	45 446	...	...	...	...	...
Jagdalpur	...	...	...	...	103 123	52 909	50 214	26
Jaipur	2 322 575	1 237 765	1 084 810	485	...	...	...	...
Jalandhar	706 043	379 439	326 604	102	714 077	383 624	330 453	...
Jalgaon	368 618	193 496	175 122	62	...	...	...	...
Jalna	235 795	121 922	113 873	82	...	...	...	...
Jalpaiguri	100 348	50 629	49 719	13	...	...	...	...
Jammu	369 959	198 956	171 003	40	612 163	334 452	277 711	202
Jamnagar	443 518	232 845	210 673	26	556 956	292 168	264 788	...
Jamshedpur	573 096	301 433	271 663	60	1 104 713	581 829	522 884	160
Jamuria	129 484	68 695	60 789	73	...	...	...	...
Jaunpur	160 055	84 203	75 852	25	...	...	...	...
Jetpur Navagadh	104 312	54 768	49 544	36	...	...	...	...
Jhansi	383 644	202 745	180 899	58	460 278	244 169	216 109	84
Jhunjhunun	100 485	52 781	47 704	37	...	...	...	...
Jind	135 855	73 407	62 448	15	...	...	...	...
Jodhpur	851 051	454 075	396 976	79	860 818	459 198	401 620	90
Jorhat	...	...	...	...	137 814	73 213	64 601	69

8. Population of capital cities and cities of 100 000 or more inhabitants: latest available year, 1993 - 2012
Population des capitales et des villes de 100 000 habitants ou plus : dernière année disponible, 1993 - 2012 (continued - suite)

Continent, country or area, date, code and city / Continent, pays ou zone, date, code et ville	City proper - Ville proprement dite				Urban agglomeration - Agglomération urbaine			
	Population			Surface area - Superficie (km²)	Population			Surface area - Superficie (km²)
	Both sexes - Les deux sexes	Male - Masculin	Female - Féminin		Both sexes - Les deux sexes	Male - Masculin	Female - Féminin	
ASIA - ASIE								
India - Inde[31]								
1 III 2001 (CDFC)								
Junagadh	168 515	86 980	81 535	13	252 108	130 461	121 647	...
Kaithal	117 285	63 098	54 187	44	...	...	...	...
Kakinada	296 329	146 476	149 853	39	376 861	187 064	189 797	58
Kalol	100 008	53 110	46 898	17	112 013	59 539	52 474	30
Kalyan	1 193 512	633 508	560 004	105	...	...	...	...
Kamarhati	314 507	168 555	145 952	11	...	...	...	...
Kamptee	...	...	...	...	136 491	71 270	65 221	37
Kancheepuram	153 140	77 069	76 071	12	188 733	95 068	93 665	40
Kanchrapara	126 191	65 264	60 927	9	...	...	...	...
Kanhangad	65 503	31 627	33 876	40	129 367	62 002	67 365	84
Kannur	...	...	...	...	498 207	237 108	261 099	154
Kanpur	2 551 337	1 374 121	1 177 216	267	2 715 555	1 465 142	1 250 413	301
Kapra	159 002	82 579	76 423	65	...	...	...	...
Karaikkudi	...	...	...	...	125 717	62 479	63 238	43
Karawal Nagar	148 624	80 495	68 129	5	...	...	...	...
Karimnagar	205 653	105 336	100 317	24	218 302	111 875	106 427	...
Karnal	207 640	110 595	97 045	22	221 236	117 875	103 361	24
Karur	...	...	...	...	153 365	77 207	76 158	33
Katihar	175 199	93 617	81 582	25	190 873	102 161	88 712	...
Khammam	159 544	80 574	78 970	...	198 620	100 930	97 690	26
Khandwa	172 242	88 950	83 292	36	...	...	...	...
Khanna	103 099	55 276	47 823	25	...	...	...	...
Kharagpur	188 761	97 721	91 040	91	272 865	140 730	132 135	125
Khardaha	116 470	61 214	55 256	7	...	...	...	...
Khargone	...	...	...	...	103 448	53 921	49 527	33
Kirari Suleman Nagar	154 633	85 362	69 271	5	...	...	...	...
Kishangarh	116 222	61 075	55 147	25	...	...	...	...
Koch Bihar	...	...	...	...	103 008	52 275	50 733	17
Kochi	595 575	294 756	300 819	95	1 355 972	670 340	685 632	453
Kolar	113 907	58 060	55 847	18	...	...	...	...
Kolhapur	493 167	255 778	237 389	67	505 541	262 258	243 283	67
Kolkata (Calcutta)	4 572 876	2 500 040	2 072 836	185	13 205 697[33]	7 064 138[33]	6 141 559[33]	1 034[33]
Kollam	361 560	177 677	183 883	41	380 091	186 924	193 167	68
Korba	315 690	164 768	150 922	35	...	...	...	...
Kota	694 316	368 451	325 865	221	703 150	373 094	330 056	226
Kothagudem	...	...	...	...	105 266	52 318	52 948	25
Kottayam	...	...	...	...	172 878	84 960	87 918	64
Kozhikode	436 556	211 888	224 668	84	880 247	429 163	451 084	235
Krishnanagar	139 110	70 576	68 534	16	148 709	75 495	73 214	18
Krishnarajapura	186 210	97 412	88 798	25	...	...	...	...
Kukatpalle	292 289	153 331	138 958	72	...	...	...	...
Kulti	289 903	152 821	137 082	100	...	...	...	...
Kumbakonam	139 954	69 785	70 169	13	160 767	80 188	80 579	15
Kurnool	269 122	136 619	132 503	15	342 973	174 190	168 783	46
Lakhimpur	121 486	65 236	56 250	7	...	...	...	...
Lal Bahadur Nagar	268 689	138 667	130 022	85	...	...	...	...
Lalitpur	111 892	58 993	52 899	...	...	...	...	...
Latur	299 985	156 547	143 438	21	...	...	...	...
Loni	120 945	65 278	55 667	7	...	...	...	...
Lucknow	2 185 927	1 156 151	1 029 776	310	2 245 509	1 189 466	1 056 043	338
Ludhiana	1 398 467	793 142	605 325	159	...	...	...	...
Machilipatnam	179 353	89 100	90 253	27	...	...	...	...
Madanapalle	...	...	...	...	107 449	54 497	52 952	13
Madhyamgram	155 451	79 728	75 723	21	...	...	...	...
Madurai	928 869	469 396	459 473	52	1 203 095	608 531	594 564	141
Mahadevapura	135 794	72 882	62 912	53	...	...	...	...
Mahbubnagar	130 986	67 007	63 979	14	139 662	71 516	68 146	14
Mahesana	...	...	...	...	141 453	74 866	66 587	...
Maheshtala	385 266	202 304	182 962	44	...	...	...	...
Mainpuri	...	...	...	...	104 851	55 462	49 389	17
Malappuram	...	...	...	...	170 409	83 709	86 700	111
Malegaon	409 403	208 864	200 539	13	...	...	...	...
Malerkotla	107 009	56 767	50 242	21	...	...	...	...

8. Population of capital cities and cities of 100 000 or more inhabitants: latest available year, 1993 - 2012
Population des capitales et des villes de 100 000 habitants ou plus : dernière année disponible, 1993 - 2012 (continued - suite)

Continent, country or area, date, code and city / Continent, pays ou zone, date, code et ville	City proper - Ville proprement dite				Urban agglomeration - Agglomération urbaine			
	Population			Surface area - Superficie (km²)	Population			Surface area - Superficie (km²)
	Both sexes - Les deux sexes	Male - Masculin	Female - Féminin		Both sexes - Les deux sexes	Male - Masculin	Female - Féminin	

ASIA - ASIE

India - Inde[31]
1 III 2001 (CDFC)

Malkajgiri	193 863	98 972	94 891	18	...	...	...	...
Mancherial	...	...	...	...	118 195	60 371	57 824	62
Mandsaur	116 505	60 269	56 236	...	117 555	60 859	56 696	...
Mandya	131 179	66 551	64 628	17	...	...	...	...
Mangalore	399 565	200 630	198 935	118	539 387	269 562	269 825	201
Mango	166 125	87 375	78 750	19	...	...	...	...
Mathura	302 770	162 021	140 749	9	323 315	174 335	148 980	22
Maunath Bhanjan	212 657	109 958	102 699	9	...	...	...	...
Medinipur	149 769	76 503	73 266	15	...	...	...	...
Meerut	1 068 772	568 081	500 691	142	1 161 716	621 481	540 235	178
Mira-Bhayandar	520 388	286 391	233 997	79	...	...	...	...
Mirzapur-cum-Vindhyachal	205 053	109 647	95 406	39	...	...	...	...
Modinagar	113 218	60 468	52 750	16	139 929	74 788	65 141	23
Moga	125 573	66 888	58 685	16	135 279	72 043	63 236	...
Moradabad	641 583	340 314	301 269	89	...	...	...	...
Morena	150 959	82 305	68 654	12	...	...	...	...
Mormugoa	...	...	...	...	104 758	55 954	48 804	40
Morvi	145 719	75 745	69 974	25	178 055	92 639	85 416	...
Motihari	100 683	54 261	46 422	14	108 428	59 148	49 280	16
Mughalsarai	...	...	...	...	116 308	61 579	54 729	29
Mumbai (Bombay)	11 978 450	6 619 966	5 358 484	603	16 434 386	9 021 789	7 412 597	1 133
Munger	188 050	101 264	86 786	18	...	...	...	...
Murwara (Katni)	187 029	97 843	89 186	107	...	...	...	...
Muzaffarnagar	316 729	167 397	149 332	...	331 668	175 283	156 385	12
Muzaffarpur	305 525	164 000	141 525	26	...	...	...	...
Mysore	755 379	383 480	371 899	89	799 228	406 363	392 865	132
Nabadwip	115 016	58 287	56 729	12	125 341	63 574	61 767	13
Nadiad	192 913	100 322	92 591	28	196 793	102 336	94 457	30
Nagaon	107 667	56 815	50 852	...	123 265	64 895	58 370	16
Nagercoil	208 179	102 907	105 272	24	...	...	...	...
Nagpur	2 052 066	1 059 765	992 301	218	2 129 500	1 102 009	1 027 491	229
Naihati	215 303	113 777	101 526	12	...	...	...	...
Nala Sopara	184 538	98 870	85 668	...	...	...	...	...
Nalgonda	110 286	56 299	53 987	12	111 380	56 848	54 532	51
Nanded	430 733	224 843	205 890	21	...	...	...	...
Nandyal	152 676	77 273	75 403	15	157 120	79 500	77 620	...
Nangloi Jat	150 948	82 687	68 261	7	...	...	...	...
Nashik	1 077 236	575 737	501 499	259	1 152 326	616 088	536 238	322
Navghar-Manikpur	116 723	61 757	54 966	...	...	...	...	...
Navi Mumbai (New Bombay)	704 002	395 705	308 297	133	...	...	...	...
Navsari	134 017	69 794	64 223	...	232 411	122 282	110 129	...
Neemuch	107 663	56 588	51 075	13	112 852	59 320	53 532	13
Nellore	378 428	190 522	187 906	48	404 775	203 823	200 952	...
NEW DELHI[34]	302 363	165 723	136 640	43	...	...	...	...
Neyveli	127 552	65 348	62 204	97	138 035	70 746	67 289	116
Nizamabad	288 722	146 198	142 524	37	...	...	...	...
Noida	305 058	168 958	136 100	90	...	...	...	...
North Barrackpur	123 668	63 796	59 872	9	...	...	...	...
North Dumdum	220 042	113 034	107 008	26	...	...	...	...
Ongole	150 471	76 511	73 960	27	153 829	78 242	75 587	27
Orai	139 318	74 703	64 615	20	...	...	...	...
Ozhukarai	217 707	110 042	107 665	35	...	...	...	...
Palakkad	130 767	64 379	66 388	30	197 369	96 928	100 441	59
Palanpur	110 419	58 055	52 364	20	122 300	64 365	57 935	40
Pali	187 641	99 267	88 374	84	...	...	...	...
Pallavaram	144 623	73 385	71 238	18	...	...	...	...
Palwal	100 722	53 648	47 074	8	...	...	...	...
Panchkula Urban Estate	140 925	75 897	65 028	26	...	...	...	...
Panihati	348 438	180 307	168 131	19	...	...	...	...
Panipat	261 740	143 644	118 096	21	354 148	194 850	159 298	...
Panvel	104 058	54 963	49 095	12	...	...	...	...
Parbhani	259 329	133 959	125 370	58	...	...	...	...
Patan	112 219	59 097	53 122	14	113 749	59 955	53 794	...

8. Population of capital cities and cities of 100 000 or more inhabitants: latest available year, 1993 - 2012
Population des capitales et des villes de 100 000 habitants ou plus : dernière année disponible, 1993 - 2012 (continued - suite)

Continent, country or area, date, code and city / Continent, pays ou zone, date, code et ville	City proper - Ville proprement dite				Urban agglomeration - Agglomération urbaine			
	Population			Surface area - Superficie (km²)	Population			Surface area - Superficie (km²)
	Both sexes - Les deux sexes	Male - Masculin	Female - Féminin		Both sexes - Les deux sexes	Male - Masculin	Female - Féminin	
ASIA - ASIE								
India - Inde[31]								
1 III 2001 (CDFC)								
Pathankot	157 925	86 520	71 405	22	168 485	92 003	76 482	...
Patiala	303 151	162 573	140 578	65	323 884	173 682	150 202	...
Patna	1 366 444	746 344	620 100	99	1 697 976	922 971	775 005	135
Phagwara	...	...	...	...	102 253	55 335	46 918	...
Phusro	...	...	...	...	174 402	93 700	80 702	84
Pilibhit	124 245	65 853	58 392	10	...	...	...	...
Pimpri Chinchwad	1 012 472	547 050	465 422	171	...	...	...	...
Pollachi	...	...	...	...	128 458	64 657	63 801	29
Pondicherry	220 865	109 389	111 476	20	505 959	253 375	252 584	72
Porbandar	133 051	68 201	64 850	12	197 382	101 824	95 558	...
Proddatur	150 309	75 372	74 937	7	...	...	...	...
Pudukkottai	109 217	54 614	54 603	13	...	...	...	...
Pune	2 538 473	1 321 338	1 217 135	430	3 760 636	1 980 621	1 780 015	669
Puri	157 837	82 269	75 568	17	...	...	...	...
Purnia	171 687	92 826	78 861	45	197 211	106 313	90 898	60
Puruliya	113 806	59 092	54 714	14	...	...	...	...
Quthbullapur	231 108	120 690	110 418	47	...	...	...	...
Rae Bareli	169 333	88 911	80 422	50	...	...	...	...
Raichur	207 421	105 763	101 658	...	...	...	...	...
Raiganj	165 212	87 458	77 754	11	175 047	92 703	82 344	15
Raigarh	111 154	57 650	53 504	18	115 908	60 101	55 807	21
Raipur	605 747	314 584	291 163	56	700 113	364 436	335 677	116
Rajahmundry	315 251	158 454	156 797	52	413 616	207 869	205 747	64
Rajapalayam	122 307	61 221	61 086	10	...	...	...	...
Rajarhat Gopalpur	271 811	140 218	131 593	35	...	...	...	...
Rajendranagar	143 240	74 889	68 351	52	...	...	...	...
Rajkot	967 476	506 993	460 483	105	1 003 015	525 898	477 117	163
Rajnandgaon	143 770	72 949	70 821	78	...	...	...	...
Rajpur Sonarpur	336 707	174 140	162 567	55	...	...	...	...
Ramagundam	236 600	120 687	115 913	28	237 686	121 250	116 436	...
Ramgarh	...	...	...	...	110 496	61 591	48 905	50
Rampur	281 494	146 652	134 842	20	...	...	...	...
Ranaghat	...	...	...	...	145 285	73 933	71 352	25
Ranchi	847 093	450 727	396 366	177	863 495	459 462	404 033	182
Raniganj	111 116	59 270	51 846	23	...	...	...	...
Ratlam	222 202	114 370	107 832	39	234 419	120 874	113 545	41
Raurkela	224 987	121 240	103 747	133	484 874	258 731	226 143	157
Raurkela Industrialship	206 693	109 394	97 299	122	...	...	...	...
Rewa	183 274	98 793	84 481	55	...	...	...	...
Rewari	100 684	53 935	46 749	12	...	...	...	...
Rishra	113 305	62 585	50 720	6	...	...	...	...
Robertson Pet	141 424	70 619	70 805	...	157 084	78 578	78 506	...
Rohtak	286 807	154 148	132 659	28	294 577	158 287	136 290	...
Roorkee	...	...	...	...	115 278	64 240	51 038	17
S.A.S. Nagar (Mohali)	123 484	65 642	57 842	24	...	...	...	...
Sagar	232 133	122 385	109 748	36	308 922	162 919	146 003	52
Saharanpur	455 754	241 508	214 246	26	...	...	...	...
Saharasa	125 167	67 718	57 449	21	...	...	...	...
Salem	696 760	353 933	342 827	91	751 438	382 211	369 227	108
Sambalpur	153 643	79 683	73 960	50	226 469	117 745	108 724	90
Sambhal	182 478	97 011	85 467	16	...	...	...	...
Sangli-Miraj-Kupwad	436 781	224 300	212 481	118	447 774	229 958	217 816	121
Santipur	138 235	70 089	68 146	25	...	...	...	...
Sasaram	131 172	69 682	61 490	11	...	...	...	...
Satara	108 048	55 938	52 110	...	...	...	...	...
Satna	225 464	120 277	105 187	...	229 307	122 401	106 906	...
Sawai Madhopur	...	...	...	...	101 997	53 903	48 094	60
Secunderabad	206 102	104 335	101 767	40	...	...	...	...
Serampore	197 857	105 415	92 442	15	...	...	...	...
Serilingampalle	153 364	79 225	74 139	98	...	...	...	...
Shahjahanpur	296 662	160 178	136 484	13	321 885	174 276	147 609	23
Shillong	132 867	66 106	66 761	10	267 662	134 497	133 165	25
Shimla	142 555	81 186	61 369	29	144 975	82 840	62 135	30

8. Population of capital cities and cities of 100 000 or more inhabitants: latest available year, 1993 - 2012
Population des capitales et des villes de 100 000 habitants ou plus : dernière année disponible, 1993 - 2012 (continued - suite)

Continent, country or area, date, code and city / Continent, pays ou zone, date, code et ville	City proper - Ville proprement dite				Urban agglomeration - Agglomération urbaine			
	Population			Surface area - Superficie (km²)	Population			Surface area - Superficie (km²)
	Both sexes - Les deux sexes	Male - Masculin	Female - Féminin		Both sexes - Les deux sexes	Male - Masculin	Female - Féminin	

ASIA - ASIE

India - Inde[31]
1 III 2001 (CDFC)

Shimoga	274 352	140 224	134 128	...	...	...	...	...
Shivapuri	146 892	78 433	68 459	81	...	...	...	...
Sikar	185 323	96 379	88 944	23	185 925	96 697	89 228	...
Silchar	142 199	72 679	69 520	16	184 105	94 306	89 799	...
Siliguri	472 374	250 645	221 729	42	...	...	...	...
Singrauli	185 190	100 149	85 041	...	...	...	...	...
Sirsa	160 735	85 993	74 742	19	...	...	...	...
Sitapur	151 908	79 767	72 141	26	...	...	...	...
Sivakasi	...	...	...	...	121 358	60 841	60 517	27
Siwan	109 919	58 262	51 657	13	...	...	...	...
Solapur	872 478	444 734	427 744	179	...	...	...	...
Sonipat	214 974	117 020	97 954	28	225 074	122 480	102 594	...
South Dum Dum	392 444	200 298	192 146	14	...	...	...	...
Srikakulam	109 905	54 926	54 979	12	117 320	58 753	58 567	14
Srinagar	898 440	484 627	413 813	184	988 210	537 512	450 698	243
Sultan Pur Majra	164 426	88 729	75 697	3	...	...	...	...
Sultanpur	100 065	53 189	46 876	12	...	...	...	...
Surat	2 433 835	1 372 415	1 061 420	112	2 811 614	1 597 156	1 214 458	237
Surendranagar Dudhrej	156 161	81 377	74 784	39	...	...	...	...
Tadepalligudem	102 622	50 925	51 697	21	...	...	...	...
Tambaram	137 933	70 419	67 514	21	...	...	...	...
Tenali	153 756	77 404	76 352	15	...	...	...	...
Tezpur	...	...	...	...	105 377	59 869	45 508	23
Thane	1 262 551	675 147	587 404	128	...	...	...	...
Thanesar	119 687	65 525	54 162	33	122 319	66 978	55 341	36
Thanjavur	215 314	106 625	108 689	15	...	...	...	...
Thiruvananthapuram	744 983	366 235	378 748	142	889 635	437 407	452 228	178
Thoothukkudi (Tuticorin)	216 054	107 758	108 296	13	243 415	121 428	121 987	140
Thrissur	317 526	154 248	163 278	...	330 122	160 443	169 679	88
Tinsukia	...	...	...	...	108 123	59 561	48 562	26
Tiruchchirappalli	752 066	376 125	375 941	147	866 354	434 321	432 033	196
Tirunelveli	411 831	203 232	208 599	109	433 352	214 133	219 219	135
Tirupati	228 202	118 187	110 015	16	303 521	155 468	148 053	20
Tiruppur	344 543	179 930	164 613	27	550 826	286 862	263 964	147
Tiruvannamalai	130 567	66 125	64 442	14	...	...	...	...
Tiruvottiyur	212 281	108 720	103 561	21	...	...	...	...
Titagarh	124 213	70 705	53 508	3	...	...	...	...
Tonk	135 689	70 255	65 434	61	...	...	...	...
Tumkur	248 929	129 273	119 656	...	...	...	...	...
Udaipur	389 438	205 335	184 103	64	...	...	...	...
Udupi	113 112	55 893	57 219	64	127 124	62 596	64 528	73
Ujjain	430 427	223 998	206 429	...	431 162	224 475	206 687	92
Ulhasnagar	473 731	251 888	221 843	13	...	...	...	...
Uluberia	202 135	105 843	96 292	34	...	...	...	...
Unnao	144 662	76 254	68 408	21	...	...	...	...
Uppal Kalan	117 217	60 857	56 360	20	...	...	...	...
Uttarpara Kotrung	150 363	78 808	71 555	16	...	...	...	...
Vadakara	...	...	...	...	124 083	59 803	64 280	51
Vadodara	1 306 227	684 013	622 214	108	1 491 045	782 251	708 794	214
Valsad	...	...	...	...	145 592	75 216	70 376	...
Vaniyambadi	...	...	...	...	103 950	51 886	52 064	16
Varanasi	1 091 918	582 096	509 822	92	1 203 961	643 043	560 918	111
Vasai	...	...	...	...	174 396	91 030	83 366	...
Vejalpur	113 445	58 878	54 567	7	...	...	...	...
Vellore	177 230	87 977	89 253	12	386 746	193 176	193 570	62
Veraval	141 357	72 148	69 209	38	158 032	80 889	77 143	41
Vidisha	125 453	66 572	58 881	6	...	...	...	...
Vijayawada	851 282	431 243	420 039	60	1 039 518	527 307	512 211	101
Virar	118 928	63 704	55 224	20	...	...	...	...
Visakhapatnam	982 904	501 406	481 498	112	1 345 938	687 985	657 953	326
Vizianagarm	174 651	86 375	88 276	21	195 801	97 032	98 769	30
Wadhwan	...	...	...	...	219 585	114 175	105 410	59
Warangal	530 636	268 954	261 682	68	579 216	293 709	285 507	97

8. Population of capital cities and cities of 100 000 or more inhabitants: latest available year, 1993 - 2012
Population des capitales et des villes de 100 000 habitants ou plus : dernière année disponible, 1993 - 2012 (continued - suite)

Continent, country or area, date, code and city / Continent, pays ou zone, date, code et ville	City proper - Ville proprement dite				Urban agglomeration - Agglomération urbaine			
	Population			Surface area - Superficie (km²)	Population			Surface area - Superficie (km²)
	Both sexes - Les deux sexes	Male - Masculin	Female - Féminin		Both sexes - Les deux sexes	Male - Masculin	Female - Féminin	
ASIA - ASIE								
India - Inde[31]								
1 III 2001 (CDFC)								
Wardha	111 118	57 499	53 619	8	...	...	...	...
Yamunanagar	189 696	101 782	87 914	16	306 740	166 137	140 603	42
Yavatmal	120 676	61 780	58 896	10	139 835	71 908	67 927	13
Indonesia - Indonésie								
1 V 2010 (CDJC)								
Ambon	331 254	165 926	165 328	359	...	...	...	...
Balikpapan	557 579	288 847	268 732	503	...	...	...	...
Banda Aceh	223 446	115 097	108 349	61	...	...	...	...
Bandar Lampung	881 801	445 959	435 842	193	...	...	...	...
Bandjarmasin	625 481	312 740	312 741	72	...	...	...	...
Bandung	2 394 873	1 215 348	1 179 525	1 670	...	...	...	...
Batam	944 285	484 867	459 418	969	...	...	...	...
Bengkulu	308 544	155 288	153 256	145	...	...	...	...
Binjai	246 154	122 997	123 157	9	...	...	...	...
Bitung	187 652	96 001	91 651	304	...	...	...	...
Blitar	131 968	65 441	66 527	33	...	...	...	...
Bogor	950 334	484 791	465 543	119	...	...	...	...
Cirebon (Tjirebon)	296 389	148 600	147 789	37	...	...	...	...
Denpasar	788 589	403 293	385 296	124	...	...	...	...
Gorontalo	180 127	88 283	91 844	65	...	...	...	...
JAKARTA	9 607 787	4 870 938	4 736 849	740	...	...	...	...
Jambi	531 857	268 102	263 755	205	...	...	...	...
Jayapura	256 705	136 587	120 118	740	...	...	...	...
Kediri	268 507	133 884	134 623	63	...	...	...	...
Madiun	170 964	82 738	88 226	34	...	...	...	...
Magelang	118 227	58 311	59 916	18	...	...	...	...
Makasar (Ujung Pandang)	1 338 663	662 009	676 654	199	...	...	...	...
Malang	820 243	404 553	415 690	145	...	...	...	...
Manado	410 481	206 292	204 189	157	...	...	...	...
Mataram	402 843	199 332	203 511	61	...	...	...	...
Medan	2 097 610	1 036 926	1 060 684	265	...	...	...	...
Mojokerto	120 196	59 127	61 069	16	...	...	...	...
Padang	833 562	415 315	418 247	694	...	...	...	...
Pakalongan	281 434	140 983	140 451	45	...	...	...	...
Pakanbaru	897 767	456 385	441 382	632	...	...	...	...
Palangkaraya	220 962	113 005	107 957	2 400	...	...	...	...
Palembang	1 455 284	728 296	726 988	369	...	...	...	...
Pangkal Pinang	174 758	89 500	85 258	89	...	...	...	...
Pare Pare	129 262	63 481	65 781	99	...	...	...	...
Pasuruan	186 262	92 370	93 892	35	...	...	...	...
Pematang Siantar	234 698	114 561	120 137	80	...	...	...	...
Pontianak	234 021	118 980	115 041	108	...	...	...	...
Probolinggo	217 062	106 915	110 147	57	...	...	...	...
Salatiga	170 332	83 479	86 853	57	...	...	...	...
Samarinda	727 500	377 283	350 217	781	...	...	...	...
Semarang	1 555 984	764 487	791 497	374	...	...	...	...
Sukabumi	298 681	152 080	146 601	48	...	...	...	...
Surabaya	2 765 487	1 367 841	1 397 646	351	...	...	...	...
Surakarta	499 337	243 296	256 041	44	...	...	...	...
Tangerang	1 798 601	921 043	877 558	187	...	...	...	...
Tanjung Balai	154 445	77 933	76 512	68	...	...	...	...
Tebing Tinggi	145 248	71 892	73 356	32	...	...	...	...
Tegal	239 599	118 872	120 727	35	...	...	...	...
Yogyakarta	388 627	189 137	199 490	33	...	...	...	...
Iran (Islamic Republic of) - Iran (République islamique d')								
24 X 2011 (CDJC)								
Abadan	...	...	...	...	212 744	106 181	106 563	...
Ahwaz	...	...	...	...	1 112 021	558 346	553 675	...
Andimeshk	...	...	...	...	126 811	63 990	62 821	...
Arak	...	...	...	...	484 212	244 614	239 598	...
Ardabil	...	...	...	...	482 632	245 335	237 297	...
Babol	...	...	...	...	219 467	109 407	110 060	...

8. Population of capital cities and cities of 100 000 or more inhabitants: latest available year, 1993 - 2012
Population des capitales et des villes de 100 000 habitants ou plus : dernière année disponible, 1993 - 2012 (continued - suite)

Continent, country or area, date, code and city Continent, pays ou zone, date, code et ville	City proper - Ville proprement dite				Urban agglomeration - Agglomération urbaine			
	Population			Surface area - Superficie (km²)	Population			Surface area - Superficie (km²)
	Both sexes - Les deux sexes	Male - Masculin	Female - Féminin		Both sexes - Les deux sexes	Male - Masculin	Female - Féminin	
ASIA - ASIE								
Iran (Islamic Republic of) - Iran (République islamique d')								
24 X 2011 (CDJC)								
Bandar Anzali	...	...	...	...	116 664	57 675	58 989	...
Bandar-e-Abbas	...	...	...	...	435 751	222 798	212 953	...
Bandar-e-Mahshahr	...	...	...	...	153 778	77 487	76 291	...
Behbahan	...	...	...	...	107 412	54 163	53 249	...
Birjand	...	...	...	...	178 020	90 092	87 928	...
Bojnurd	...	...	...	...	199 791	100 605	99 186	...
Borujerd	...	...	...	...	240 654	118 508	122 146	...
Bukand	...	...	...	...	170 600	85 835	84 765	...
Bushehr	...	...	...	...	704 393	383 488	320 905	...
Dezful	...	...	...	...	248 380	128 430	119 950	...
Esfahan	...	...	...	...	4 168 219	2 109 775	2 058 444	...
Golestan (Soltanabad)	...	...	...	...	259 480	133 531	125 949	...
Gonbad-e-Kavus	...	...	...	...	144 546	71 986	72 560	...
Gorgan	...	...	...	...	329 536	165 001	164 535	...
Hamadan	...	...	...	...	525 794	261 577	264 217	...
Ilam	...	...	...	...	172 213	87 221	84 992	...
Islam Shahr (Qasemabad)	...	...	...	...	389 102	198 080	191 022	...
Izeh	...	...	...	...	117 093	58 080	59 013	...
Jahrom	...	...	...	...	114 108	57 865	56 243	...
Karaj	...	...	...	...	1 614 626	813 551	801 075	...
Kashan	...	...	...	...	275 325	139 866	135 459	...
Kerman	...	...	...	...	534 441	269 661	264 780	...
Kermanshah	...	...	...	...	851 405	426 129	425 276	...
Khomeini shahr	...	...	...	...	244 696	126 326	118 370	...
Khoramabad	...	...	...	...	348 216	173 264	174 952	...
Khoramshahr	...	...	...	...	129 418	63 804	65 614	...
Khoy	...	...	...	...	200 958	100 593	100 365	...
Malard	...	...	...	...	290 817	147 954	142 863	...
Malayer	...	...	...	...	159 848	79 477	80 371	...
Marand	...	...	...	...	124 323	62 848	61 475	...
Maraqeh	...	...	...	...	162 275	81 229	81 046	...
Marvadsht	...	...	...	...	138 649	70 221	68 428	...
Mashhad	...	...	...	...	2 766 258	1 384 599	1 381 659	...
Masjed Soleyman	...	...	...	...	103 369	51 852	51 517	...
Miandoab	...	...	...	...	123 081	62 883	60 198	...
Najafabad	...	...	...	...	221 814	111 915	109 899	...
Nasim Shahr	...	...	...	...	157 474	80 947	76 527	...
Neyshabur	...	...	...	...	239 185	119 845	119 340	...
Orumiyeh	...	...	...	...	667 499	334 136	333 363	...
Pakdasht	...	...	...	...	206 490	105 814	100 676	...
Qaem shahr	...	...	...	...	196 050	97 358	98 692	...
Qarchak	...	...	...	...	191 588	97 678	93 910	...
Qazvin	...	...	...	...	381 598	192 960	188 638	...
Qods	...	...	...	...	283 517	144 911	138 606	...
Qom	...	...	...	...	1 095 871	557 132	538 739	...
Quchan	...	...	...	...	103 760	52 240	51 520	...
Rafsanjan	...	...	...	...	151 420	75 643	75 777	...
Rasht	...	...	...	...	639 951	316 833	323 118	...
Sabzewar	...	...	...	...	231 557	115 158	116 399	...
Sanandaj	...	...	...	...	373 987	189 047	184 940	...
Saqez	...	...	...	...	139 738	69 856	69 882	...
Sari	...	...	...	...	296 417	147 875	148 542	...
Saveh	...	...	...	...	200 481	102 578	97 903	...
Semnan	...	...	...	...	486 345	244 424	241 921	...
Shahinshahr	...	...	...	...	143 308	71 357	71 951	...
Shahr-e-Kord	...	...	...	...	159 775	79 681	80 094	...
Shahreza	...	...	...	...	123 767	62 314	61 453	...
Shahriar	...	...	...	...	249 473	126 246	123 227	...
Shahrud	...	...	...	...	140 474	70 616	69 858	...
Shiraz	...	...	...	...	1 460 665	732 380	728 285	...
Sirjan	...	...	...	...	185 623	94 943	90 680	...
Tabriz	...	...	...	...	1 494 998	755 553	739 445	...

8. Population of capital cities and cities of 100 000 or more inhabitants: latest available year, 1993 - 2012
Population des capitales et des villes de 100 000 habitants ou plus : dernière année disponible, 1993 - 2012 (continued - suite)

Continent, country or area, date, code and city / Continent, pays ou zone, date, code et ville	City proper - Ville proprement dite				Urban agglomeration - Agglomération urbaine			
	Population			Surface area - Superficie (km²)	Population			Surface area - Superficie (km²)
	Both sexes - Les deux sexes	Male - Masculin	Female - Féminin		Both sexes - Les deux sexes	Male - Masculin	Female - Féminin	
ASIA - ASIE								
Iran (Islamic Republic of) - Iran (République islamique d')								
24 X 2011 (CDJC)								
TEHRAN	...	...	...	...	8 154 051	4 059 301	4 094 750	...
Torbat-e-heydariyeh	...	...	...	...	131 150	66 310	64 840	...
Varamin	...	...	...	...	218 991	111 074	107 917	...
Yasooj	...	...	...	...	108 505	54 825	53 680	...
Yazd	...	...	...	...	486 152	246 985	239 167	...
Zabol	...	...	...	...	137 722	69 726	67 996	...
Zahedan	...	...	...	...	560 725	283 680	277 045	...
Zanjan	...	...	...	...	386 851	195 382	191 469	...
Israel - Israël								
1 VII 2011 (ESDJ)								
Ashdod	211 418	103 364	108 054	47	...	...	...	...
Ashqelon	115 942	56 357	59 585	48	...	...	...	...
Bat Yam	129 267	61 370	67 897	8	...	...	...	...
Be'er Sheva	195 849	95 196	100 653	53	...	...	...	...
Bene Beraq	161 095	81 702	79 393	7	...	...	...	...
Haifa	269 281[28]	128 889[28]	140 393[28]	64	...	...	...	...
Holon	182 039	88 075	93 964	19	...	...	...	...
JERUSALEM[35]	796 204[28]	395 040[28]	401 163[28]	125	...	...	...	...
Netanya	188 230	91 306	96 924	29	...	...	...	...
Petah Tiqwa	210 753[28]	102 596[28]	108 156[28]	36	...	...	...	...
Ramat Gan	146 955	69 926	77 029	13	...	...	...	...
Rehovot	116 871[28]	57 104[28]	59 766[28]	23	...	...	...	...
Rishon Leziyyon	231 727[28]	113 491[28]	118 237[28]	59	...	...	...	...
Tel Aviv-Yafo	404 543	198 033	206 510	52	...	...	...	...
Japan - Japon								
1 X 2010 (CDJC)								
Abiko	134 017[36]	65 732[36]	68 285[36]	43[37]	...	...	...	...
Ageo	223 926[36]	111 784[36]	112 142[36]	46[37]	...	...	...	...
Aizuwakamatsu	126 220[36]	59 854[36]	66 366[36]	383[37]	...	...	...	...
Akashi	290 959[36]	141 344[36]	149 615[36]	49[37]	...	...	...	...
Akishima	112 297[36]	56 320[36]	55 977[36]	17[37]	...	...	...	...
Akita	323 600[36]	152 456[36]	171 144[36]	906[37]	...	...	...	...
Amagasaki	453 748[36]	221 216[36]	232 532[36]	50[37]	...	...	...	...
Anjo	178 691[36]	91 424[36]	87 267[36]	86[37]	...	...	...	...
Aomori	299 520[36]	139 084[36]	160 436[36]	825[37]	...	...	...	...
Asahikawa	347 095[36]	160 094[36]	187 001[36]	748[37]	...	...	...	...
Asaka	129 691[36]	65 503[36]	64 188[36]	18[37]	...	...	...	...
Ashikaga	154 530[36]	75 382[36]	79 148[36]	178[37]	...	...	...	...
Atsugi	224 420[36]	116 927[36]	107 493[36]	94[37]	...	...	...	...
Beppu	125 385[36]	56 868[36]	68 517[36]	125[37]	...	...	...	...
Chiba	961 749[36]	480 194[36]	481 555[36]	272[37]	...	...	...	...
Chigasaki	235 081[36]	115 245[36]	119 836[36]	36[37]	...	...	...	...
Chikusei	108 527[36]	53 680[36]	54 847[36]	205[37]	...	...	...	...
Chikushino	100 172[36]	47 750[36]	52 422[36]	88[37]	...	...	...	...
Chofu	223 593[36]	110 805[36]	112 788[36]	22[37]	...	...	...	...
Daito	127 534[36]	63 810[36]	63 724[36]	18[37]	...	...	...	...
Ebetsu	123 722[36]	59 320[36]	64 402[36]	188[37]	...	...	...	...
Ebina	127 707[36]	64 483[36]	63 224[36]	26[37]	...	...	...	...
Fuchu	255 506[36]	131 558[36]	123 948[36]	29[37]	...	...	...	...
Fuji	254 027[36]	125 240[36]	128 787[36]	245[37]	...	...	...	...
Fujieda	142 151[36]	69 484[36]	72 667[36]	194[37]	...	...	...	...
Fujimi	106 736[36]	53 134[36]	53 602[36]	20[37]	...	...	...	...
Fujimino	105 695[36]	52 640[36]	53 055[36]	15[37]	...	...	...	...
Fujinomiya	132 001[36]	64 909[36]	67 092[36]	389[37]	...	...	...	...
Fujisawa	409 657[36]	203 778[36]	205 879[36]	70[37]	...	...	...	...
Fukaya	144 618[36]	72 146[36]	72 472[36]	138[37]	...	...	...	...
Fukui	266 796[36]	128 692[36]	138 104[36]	536[37]	...	...	...	...
Fukuoka	1 463 743[36]	692 648[36]	771 095[36]	341[37]	...	...	...	...
Fukushima	292 590[36]	140 723[36]	151 867[36]	768[37]	...	...	...	...
Fukuyama	461 357[36]	222 729[36]	238 628[36]	518[37]	...	...	...	...

8. Population of capital cities and cities of 100 000 or more inhabitants: latest available year, 1993 - 2012
Population des capitales et des villes de 100 000 habitants ou plus : dernière année disponible, 1993 - 2012 (continued - suite)

Continent, country or area, date, code and city / Continent, pays ou zone, date, code et ville	City proper - Ville proprement dite				Urban agglomeration - Agglomération urbaine			
	Population			Surface area - Superficie (km²)	Population			Surface area - Superficie (km²)
	Both sexes - Les deux sexes	Male - Masculin	Female - Féminin		Both sexes - Les deux sexes	Male - Masculin	Female - Féminin	
ASIA - ASIE								
Japan - Japon								
1 X 2010 (CDJC)								
Funabashi	609 040[36]	306 399[36]	302 641[36]	86[37]	...	...	...	...
Gifu	413 136[36]	196 525[36]	216 611[36]	203[37]	...	...	...	...
Habikino	117 681[36]	55 737[36]	61 944[36]	26[37]	...	...	...	...
Hachinohe	237 615[36]	113 340[36]	124 275[36]	305[37]	...	...	...	...
Hachioji	580 053[36]	293 462[36]	286 591[36]	186[37]	...	...	...	...
Hadano	170 145[36]	87 291[36]	82 854[36]	104[37]	...	...	...	...
Hakodate	279 127[36]	127 046[36]	152 081[36]	678[37]	...	...	...	...
Hakusan	110 459[36]	53 563[36]	56 896[36]	755[37]	...	...	...	...
Hamamatsu	800 866[36]	397 146[36]	403 720[36]	1 558[37]	...	...	...	...
Hanamaki	101 438[36]	48 076[36]	53 362[36]	908[37]	...	...	...	...
Handa	118 828[36]	59 291[36]	59 537[36]	47[37]	...	...	...	...
Hatsukaichi	114 038[36]	54 101[36]	59 937[36]	489[37]	...	...	...	...
Higashihiroshima	190 135[36]	96 952[36]	93 183[36]	635[37]	...	...	...	...
Higashikurume	116 546[36]	57 613[36]	58 933[36]	13[37]	...	...	...	...
Higashimurayama	153 557[36]	75 461[36]	78 096[36]	17[37]	...	...	...	...
Higashiomi	115 479[36]	56 872[36]	58 607[36]	389[37]	...	...	...	...
Higashiosaka	509 533[36]	249 964[36]	259 569[36]	62[37]	...	...	...	...
Hikone	112 156[36]	55 173[36]	56 983[36]	197[37]	...	...	...	...
Himeji	536 270[36]	259 320[36]	276 950[36]	534[37]	...	...	...	...
Hino	180 052[36]	91 236[36]	88 816[36]	28[37]	...	...	...	...
Hirakata	407 978[36]	195 570[36]	212 408[36]	65[37]	...	...	...	...
Hiratsuka	260 780[36]	132 048[36]	128 732[36]	68[37]	...	...	...	...
Hirosaki	183 473[36]	84 064[36]	99 409[36]	524[37]	...	...	...	...
Hiroshima	1 173 843[36]	565 482[36]	608 361[36]	905[37]	...	...	...	...
Hitachi	193 129[36]	96 747[36]	96 382[36]	226[37]	...	...	...	...
Hitachinaka	157 060[36]	79 046[36]	78 014[36]	99[37]	...	...	...	...
Hofu	116 611[36]	56 191[36]	60 420[36]	189[37]	...	...	...	...
Ibaraki	274 822[36]	133 621[36]	141 201[36]	77[37]	...	...	...	...
Ichihara	280 416[36]	143 338[36]	137 078[36]	368[37]	...	...	...	...
Ichikawa	473 919[36]	239 222[36]	234 697[36]	57[37]	...	...	...	...
Ichinomiya	378 566[36]	184 221[36]	194 345[36]	114[37]	...	...	...	...
Ichinoseki	118 578[36]	56 885[36]	61 693[36]	1 133[37]	...	...	...	...
Iida	105 335[36]	50 105[36]	55 230[36]	659[37]	...	...	...	...
Iizuka	131 492[36]	62 166[36]	69 326[36]	214[37]	...	...	...	...
Ikeda	104 229[36]	50 721[36]	53 508[36]	22[37]	...	...	...	...
Ikoma	118 113[36]	56 311[36]	61 802[36]	53[37]	...	...	...	...
Imabari	166 532[36]	77 893[36]	88 639[36]	420[37]	...	...	...	...
Inazawa	136 442[36]	67 394[36]	69 048[36]	79[37]	...	...	...	...
Iruma	149 872[36]	74 107[36]	75 765[36]	45[37]	...	...	...	...
Isahaya	140 752[36]	66 192[36]	74 560[36]	321[37]	...	...	...	...
Ise	130 271[36]	61 482[36]	68 789[36]	209[37]	...	...	...	...
Isehara	101 039[36]	51 601[36]	49 438[36]	56[37]	...	...	...	...
Isesaki	207 221[36]	103 210[36]	104 011[36]	139[37]	...	...	...	...
Ishinomaki	160 826[36]	77 143[36]	83 683[36]	556[37]	...	...	...	...
Itami	196 127[36]	95 665[36]	100 462[36]	25[37]	...	...	...	...
Iwaki	342 249[36]	165 339[36]	176 910[36]	1 231[37]	...	...	...	...
Iwakuni	143 857[36]	67 597[36]	76 260[36]	874[37]	...	...	...	...
Iwata	168 625[36]	84 716[36]	83 909[36]	164[37]	...	...	...	...
Izumi (Osaka)	184 988[36]	89 613[36]	95 375[36]	85[37]	...	...	...	...
Izumisano	100 801[36]	48 161[36]	52 640[36]	55[37]	...	...	...	...
Izumo	143 796[36]	68 563[36]	75 233[36]	543[37]	...	...	...	...
Joetsu	203 899[36]	99 115[36]	104 784[36]	974[37]	...	...	...	...
Kadoma	130 282[36]	64 423[36]	65 859[36]	12[37]	...	...	...	...
Kagoshima	605 846[36]	281 133[36]	324 713[36]	547[37]	...	...	...	...
Kakamigahara	145 604[36]	71 516[36]	74 088[36]	88[37]	...	...	...	...
Kakegawa	116 363[36]	57 921[36]	58 442[36]	266[37]	...	...	...	...
Kakogawa	266 937[36]	130 931[36]	136 006[36]	139[37]	...	...	...	...
Kamagaya	107 853[36]	53 178[36]	54 675[36]	21[37]	...	...	...	...
Kamakura	174 314[36]	82 235[36]	92 079[36]	40[37]	...	...	...	...

8. Population of capital cities and cities of 100 000 or more inhabitants: latest available year, 1993 - 2012
Population des capitales et des villes de 100 000 habitants ou plus : dernière année disponible, 1993 - 2012 (continued - suite)

Continent, country or area, date, code and city / Continent, pays ou zone, date, code et ville	City proper - Ville proprement dite				Urban agglomeration - Agglomération urbaine			
	Population			Surface area - Superficie (km²)	Population			Surface area - Superficie (km²)
	Both sexes - Les deux sexes	Male - Masculin	Female - Féminin		Both sexes - Les deux sexes	Male - Masculin	Female - Féminin	

ASIA - ASIE

Japan - Japon
1 X 2010 (CDJC)

Kanazawa	462 361[36]	224 087[36]	238 274[36]	468[37]	...	...	...	...
Kanoya	105 070[36]	49 808[36]	55 262[36]	448[37]	...	...	...	...
Kanuma	102 348[36]	50 452[36]	51 896[36]	491[37]	...	...	...	...
Karatsu	126 926[36]	59 221[36]	67 705[36]	487[37]	...	...	...	...
Kariya	145 781[36]	76 598[36]	69 183[36]	50[37]	...	...	...	...
Kashihara	125 605[36]	59 879[36]	65 726[36]	40[37]	...	...	...	...
Kashiwa	404 012[36]	201 045[36]	202 967[36]	115[37]	...	...	...	...
Kasuga	106 780[36]	51 445[36]	55 335[36]	14[37]	...	...	...	...
Kasugai	305 569[36]	152 765[36]	152 804[36]	93[37]	...	...	...	...
Kasukabe	237 171[36]	117 798[36]	119 373[36]	66[37]	...	...	...	...
Kawachinagano	112 490[36]	52 964[36]	59 526[36]	110[37]	...	...	...	...
Kawagoe	342 670[36]	171 590[36]	171 080[36]	109[37]	...	...	...	...
Kawaguchi	500 598[36]	255 780[36]	244 818[36]	56[37]	...	...	...	...
Kawanishi	156 423[36]	73 930[36]	82 493[36]	53[37]	...	...	...	...
Kawasaki	1 425 512[36]	728 525[36]	696 987[36]	143[37]	...	...	...	...
Kazo	115 002[36]	57 241[36]	57 761[36]	133[37]	...	...	...	...
Kirishima	127 487[36]	61 135[36]	66 352[36]	604[37]	...	...	...	...
Kiryu	121 704[36]	58 765[36]	62 939[36]	275[37]	...	...	...	...
Kisarazu	129 312[36]	65 242[36]	64 070[36]	139[37]	...	...	...	...
Kishiwada	199 234[36]	95 730[36]	103 504[36]	72[37]	...	...	...	...
Kitakyushu	976 846[36]	459 305[36]	517 541[36]	488[37]	...	...	...	...
Kitami	125 689[36]	60 171[36]	65 518[36]	1 428[37]	...	...	...	...
Kobe	1 544 200[36]	731 114[36]	813 086[36]	553[37]	...	...	...	...
Kochi	343 393[36]	159 644[36]	183 749[36]	309[37]	...	...	...	...
Kodaira	187 035[36]	92 886[36]	94 149[36]	20[37]	...	...	...	...
Kofu	198 992[36]	97 754[36]	101 238[36]	212[37]	...	...	...	...
Koga	142 995[36]	71 450[36]	71 545[36]	124[37]	...	...	...	...
Koganei	118 852[36]	59 515[36]	59 337[36]	11[37]	...	...	...	...
Kokubunji	120 650[36]	59 967[36]	60 683[36]	11[37]	...	...	...	...
Komaki	147 132[36]	74 161[36]	72 971[36]	63[37]	...	...	...	...
Komatsu	108 433[36]	52 465[36]	55 968[36]	371[37]	...	...	...	...
Konosu	119 639[36]	59 152[36]	60 487[36]	67[37]	...	...	...	...
Koriyama	338 712[36]	166 336[36]	172 376[36]	757[37]	...	...	...	...
Koshigaya	326 313[36]	162 374[36]	163 939[36]	60[37]	...	...	...	...
Kuki	154 310[36]	77 175[36]	77 135[36]	82[37]	...	...	...	...
Kumagaya	203 180[36]	101 430[36]	101 750[36]	160[37]	...	...	...	...
Kumamoto	734 474[36]	344 291[36]	390 183[36]	390[37]	...	...	...	...
Kurashiki	475 513[36]	230 061[36]	245 452[36]	355[37]	...	...	...	...
Kure	239 973[36]	115 432[36]	124 541[36]	354[37]	...	...	...	...
Kurume	302 402[36]	143 885[36]	158 517[36]	230[37]	...	...	...	...
Kusatsu	130 874[36]	67 819[36]	63 055[36]	68[37]	...	...	...	...
Kushiro	181 169[36]	85 474[36]	95 695[36]	1 363[37]	...	...	...	...
Kuwana	140 290[36]	68 914[36]	71 376[36]	137[37]	...	...	...	...
Kyoto	1 474 015[36]	701 088[36]	772 927[36]	828[37]	...	...	...	...
Machida	426 987[36]	209 580[36]	217 407[36]	72[37]	...	...	...	...
Maebashi	340 291[36]	166 043[36]	174 248[36]	312[37]	...	...	...	...
Marugame	110 473[36]	53 633[36]	56 840[36]	112[37]	...	...	...	...
Matsubara	124 594[36]	60 017[36]	64 577[36]	17[37]	...	...	...	...
Matsudo	484 457[36]	240 674[36]	243 783[36]	61[37]	...	...	...	...
Matsue	194 258[36]	93 736[36]	100 522[36]	530[37]	...	...	...	...
Matsumoto	243 037[36]	119 271[36]	123 766[36]	979[37]	...	...	...	...
Matsusaka	168 017[36]	80 960[36]	87 057[36]	624[37]	...	...	...	...
Matsuyama	517 231[36]	241 586[36]	275 645[36]	429[37]	...	...	...	...
Mihara	100 509[36]	47 865[36]	52 644[36]	471[37]	...	...	...	...
Minoh	129 895[36]	62 468[36]	67 427[36]	48[37]	...	...	...	...
Misato	131 415[36]	66 747[36]	64 668[36]	30[37]	...	...	...	...
Mishima	111 838[36]	54 911[36]	56 927[36]	62[37]	...	...	...	...
Mitaka	186 083[36]	91 997[36]	94 086[36]	17[37]	...	...	...	...
Mito	268 750[36]	130 918[36]	137 832[36]	217[37]	...	...	...	...

8. Population of capital cities and cities of 100 000 or more inhabitants: latest available year, 1993 - 2012
Population des capitales et des villes de 100 000 habitants ou plus : dernière année disponible, 1993 - 2012 (continued - suite)

Continent, country or area, date, code and city / Continent, pays ou zone, date, code et ville	City proper - Ville proprement dite				Urban agglomeration - Agglomération urbaine			
	Population			Surface area - Superficie (km²)	Population			Surface area - Superficie (km²)
	Both sexes - Les deux sexes	Male - Masculin	Female - Féminin		Both sexes - Les deux sexes	Male - Masculin	Female - Féminin	
ASIA - ASIE								
Japan - Japon								
1 X 2010 (CDJC)								
Miyakonojo	169 602[36]	79 553[36]	90 049[36]	653[37]	...	...	...	...
Miyazaki	400 583[36]	187 619[36]	212 964[36]	645[37]	...	...	...	...
Moriguchi	146 697[36]	71 272[36]	75 425[36]	13[37]	...	...	...	...
Morioka	298 348[36]	141 566[36]	156 782[36]	886[37]	...	...	...	...
Musashino	138 734[36]	66 406[36]	72 328[36]	11[37]	...	...	...	...
Nagahama	124 131[36]	60 973[36]	63 158[36]	681[37]	...	...	...	...
Nagano	381 511[36]	184 128[36]	197 383[36]	835[37]	...	...	...	...
Nagaoka	282 674[36]	137 780[36]	144 894[36]	891[37]	...	...	...	...
Nagareyama	163 984[36]	81 721[36]	82 263[36]	35[37]	...	...	...	...
Nagasaki	443 766[36]	203 574[36]	240 192[36]	406[37]	...	...	...	...
Nagoya	2 263 894[36]	1 116 211[36]	1 147 683[36]	326[37]	...	...	...	...
Naha	315 954[36]	151 848[36]	164 106[36]	39[37]	...	...	...	...
Nara	366 591[36]	171 410[36]	195 181[36]	277[37]	...	...	...	...
Narashino	164 530[36]	83 184[36]	81 346[36]	21[37]	...	...	...	...
Narita	128 933[36]	64 852[36]	64 081[36]	214[37]	...	...	...	...
Nasushiobara	117 812[36]	58 402[36]	59 410[36]	593[37]	...	...	...	...
Neyagawa	238 204[36]	116 132[36]	122 072[36]	25[37]	...	...	...	...
Niigata	811 901[36]	390 406[36]	421 495[36]	726[37]	...	...	...	...
Niihama	121 735[36]	58 219[36]	63 516[36]	234[37]	...	...	...	...
Niiza	158 777[36]	79 416[36]	79 361[36]	23[37]	...	...	...	...
Nishinomiya	482 640[36]	227 660[36]	254 980[36]	99[37]	...	...	...	...
Nishio	106 823[36]	54 066[36]	52 757[36]	76[37]	...	...	...	...
Nishitokyo	196 511[36]	96 437[36]	100 074[36]	16[37]	...	...	...	...
Nobeoka	131 182[36]	61 457[36]	69 725[36]	868[37]	...	...	...	...
Noda	155 491[36]	77 963[36]	77 528[36]	104[37]	...	...	...	...
Numazu	202 304[36]	99 184[36]	103 120[36]	187[37]	...	...	...	...
Obihiro	168 057[36]	80 584[36]	87 473[36]	619[37]	...	...	...	...
Odawara	198 327[36]	96 839[36]	101 488[36]	114[37]	...	...	...	...
Ogaki	161 160[36]	78 282[36]	82 878[36]	207[37]	...	...	...	...
Oita	474 094[36]	227 608[36]	246 486[36]	501[37]	...	...	...	...
Okayama	709 584[36]	341 158[36]	368 426[36]	790[37]	...	...	...	...
Okazaki	372 357[36]	187 649[36]	184 708[36]	387[37]	...	...	...	...
Okinawa	130 249[36]	63 195[36]	67 054[36]	49[37]	...	...	...	...
Ome	139 339[36]	69 742[36]	69 597[36]	103[37]	...	...	...	...
Omuta	123 638[36]	56 215[36]	67 423[36]	82[37]	...	...	...	...
Onomichi	145 202[36]	69 283[36]	75 919[36]	285[37]	...	...	...	...
Osaka	2 665 314[36]	1 293 798[36]	1 371 516[36]	222[37]	...	...	...	...
Osaki	135 147[36]	65 624[36]	69 523[36]	797[37]	...	...	...	...
Oshu	124 746[36]	59 935[36]	64 811[36]	993[37]	...	...	...	...
Ota	216 465[36]	109 204[36]	107 261[36]	176[37]	...	...	...	...
Otaru	131 928[36]	59 514[36]	72 414[36]	243[37]	...	...	...	...
Otsu	337 634[36]	163 250[36]	174 384[36]	464[37]	...	...	...	...
Oyama	164 454[36]	82 825[36]	81 629[36]	172[37]	...	...	...	...
Saga	237 506[36]	112 173[36]	125 333[36]	431[37]	...	...	...	...
Sagamihara	717 544[36]	361 394[36]	356 150[36]	329[37]	...	...	...	...
Saijo	112 091[36]	53 757[36]	58 334[36]	509[37]	...	...	...	...
Saitama	1 222 434[36]	611 236[36]	611 198[36]	217[37]	...	...	...	...
Sakado	101 700[36]	51 155[36]	50 545[36]	41[37]	...	...	...	...
Sakai	841 966[36]	404 756[36]	437 210[36]	150[37]	...	...	...	...
Sakata	111 151[36]	52 610[36]	58 541[36]	603[37]	...	...	...	...
Saku	100 552[36]	49 090[36]	51 462[36]	424[37]	...	...	...	...
Sakura	172 183[36]	84 246[36]	87 937[36]	104[37]	...	...	...	...
Sanda	114 216[36]	55 175[36]	59 041[36]	210[37]	...	...	...	...
Sanjo	102 292[36]	49 368[36]	52 924[36]	432[37]	...	...	...	...
Sano	121 249[36]	59 499[36]	61 750[36]	356[37]	...	...	...	...
Sapporo	1 913 545[36]	896 850[36]	1 016 695[36]	1 121[37]	...	...	...	...
Sasebo	261 101[36]	122 430[36]	138 671[36]	426[37]	...	...	...	...
Sayama	155 727[36]	78 637[36]	77 090[36]	49[37]	...	...	...	...
Sendai	1 045 986[36]	507 833[36]	538 153[36]	784[37]	...	...	...	...

8. Population of capital cities and cities of 100 000 or more inhabitants: latest available year, 1993 - 2012
Population des capitales et des villes de 100 000 habitants ou plus : dernière année disponible, 1993 - 2012 (continued - suite)

Continent, country or area, date, code and city / Continent, pays ou zone, date, code et ville	City proper - Ville proprement dite				Urban agglomeration - Agglomération urbaine			
	Population			Surface area - Superficie (km²)	Population			Surface area - Superficie (km²)
	Both sexes - Les deux sexes	Male - Masculin	Female - Féminin		Both sexes - Les deux sexes	Male - Masculin	Female - Féminin	
ASIA - ASIE								
Japan - Japon								
1 X 2010 (CDJC)								
Seto	132 224[36]	65 123[36]	67 101[36]	112[37]	...	...	...	...
Shibata	101 202[36]	48 606[36]	52 596[36]	533[37]	...	...	...	...
Shimada	100 276[36]	48 876[36]	51 400[36]	316[37]	...	...	...	...
Shimonoseki	280 947[36]	130 105[36]	150 842[36]	716[37]	...	...	...	...
Shizuoka	716 197[36]	348 609[36]	367 588[36]	1 412[37]	...	...	...	...
Shunan	149 487[36]	72 150[36]	77 337[36]	656[37]	...	...	...	...
Soka	243 855[36]	124 553[36]	119 302[36]	27[37]	...	...	...	...
Suita	355 798[36]	171 769[36]	184 029[36]	36[37]	...	...	...	...
Suzuka	199 293[36]	99 925[36]	99 368[36]	195[37]	...	...	...	...
Tachikawa	179 668[36]	89 470[36]	90 198[36]	24[37]	...	...	...	...
Tajimi	112 595[36]	54 342[36]	58 253[36]	91[37]	...	...	...	...
Takamatsu	419 429[36]	203 312[36]	216 117[36]	375[37]	...	...	...	...
Takaoka	176 061[36]	84 292[36]	91 769[36]	209[37]	...	...	...	...
Takarazuka	225 700[36]	105 289[36]	120 411[36]	102[37]	...	...	...	...
Takasaki	371 302[36]	181 667[36]	189 635[36]	459[37]	...	...	...	...
Takatsuki	357 359[36]	171 927[36]	185 432[36]	105[37]	...	...	...	...
Tama	147 648[36]	73 083[36]	74 565[36]	21[37]	...	...	...	...
Tochigi	139 262[36]	67 859[36]	71 403[36]	253[37]	...	...	...	...
Toda	123 079[36]	64 080[36]	58 999[36]	18[37]	...	...	...	...
Tokai	107 690[36]	56 305[36]	51 385[36]	43[37]	...	...	...	...
Tokorozawa	341 924[36]	170 598[36]	171 326[36]	72[37]	...	...	...	...
Tokushima	264 548[36]	125 619[36]	138 929[36]	192[37]	...	...	...	...
TOKYO	8 945 695[38]	4 412 050[38]	4 533 645[38]	622[37]	...	...	...	...
Tomakomai	173 320[36]	84 687[36]	88 633[36]	561[37]	...	...	...	...
Tondabayashi	119 576[36]	56 778[36]	62 798[36]	40[37]	...	...	...	...
Toride	109 651[36]	54 054[36]	55 597[36]	70[37]	...	...	...	...
Tottori	197 449[36]	95 959[36]	101 490[36]	766[37]	...	...	...	...
Toyama	421 953[36]	204 515[36]	217 438[36]	1 242[37]	...	...	...	...
Toyohashi	376 665[36]	188 200[36]	188 465[36]	261[37]	...	...	...	...
Toyokawa	181 928[36]	90 328[36]	91 600[36]	161[37]	...	...	...	...
Toyonaka	389 341[36]	185 103[36]	204 238[36]	36[37]	...	...	...	...
Toyota	421 487[36]	221 198[36]	200 289[36]	918[37]	...	...	...	...
Tsu	285 746[36]	138 643[36]	147 103[36]	711[37]	...	...	...	...
Tsuchiura	143 839[36]	71 600[36]	72 239[36]	123[37]	...	...	...	...
Tsukuba	214 590[36]	110 230[36]	104 360[36]	284[37]	...	...	...	...
Tsuruoka	136 623[36]	64 846[36]	71 777[36]	1 312[37]	...	...	...	...
Tsuyama	106 788[36]	50 787[36]	56 001[36]	506[37]	...	...	...	...
Ube	173 772[36]	83 000[36]	90 772[36]	288[37]	...	...	...	...
Ueda	159 597[36]	77 589[36]	82 008[36]	552[37]	...	...	...	...
Uji	189 609[36]	91 971[36]	97 638[36]	68[37]	...	...	...	...
Urasoe	110 351[36]	53 948[36]	56 403[36]	19[37]	...	...	...	...
Urayasu	164 877[36]	82 177[36]	82 700[36]	17[37]	...	...	...	...
Uruma	116 979[36]	58 198[36]	58 781[36]	86[37]	...	...	...	...
Utsunomiya	511 739[36]	254 605[36]	257 134[36]	417[37]	...	...	...	...
Wakayama	370 364[36]	174 104[36]	196 260[36]	209[37]	...	...	...	...
Yachiyo	189 781[36]	93 688[36]	96 093[36]	51[37]	...	...	...	...
Yaizu	143 249[36]	69 901[36]	73 348[36]	71[37]	...	...	...	...
Yamagata	254 244[36]	121 433[36]	132 811[36]	381[37]	...	...	...	...
Yamaguchi	196 628[36]	92 997[36]	103 631[36]	1 023[37]	...	...	...	...
Yamato	228 186[36]	114 700[36]	113 486[36]	27[37]	...	...	...	...
Yao	271 460[36]	131 121[36]	140 339[36]	42[37]	...	...	...	...
Yatsushiro	132 266[36]	61 446[36]	70 820[36]	681[37]	...	...	...	...
Yokkaichi	307 766[36]	152 580[36]	155 186[36]	206[37]	...	...	...	...
Yokohama	3 688 773[36]	1 849 767[36]	1 839 006[36]	437[37]	...	...	...	...
Yokosuka	418 325[36]	208 966[36]	209 359[36]	101[37]	...	...	...	...
Yonago	148 271[36]	70 133[36]	78 138[36]	132[37]	...	...	...	...
Zama	129 436[36]	65 448[36]	63 988[36]	18[37]	...	...	...	...

8. Population of capital cities and cities of 100 000 or more inhabitants: latest available year, 1993 - 2012
Population des capitales et des villes de 100 000 habitants ou plus : dernière année disponible, 1993 - 2012 (continued - suite)

Continent, country or area, date, code and city / Continent, pays ou zone, date, code et ville	City proper - Ville proprement dite				Urban agglomeration - Agglomération urbaine			
	Population			Surface area - Superficie (km²)	Population			Surface area - Superficie (km²)
	Both sexes - Les deux sexes	Male - Masculin	Female - Féminin		Both sexes - Les deux sexes	Male - Masculin	Female - Féminin	
ASIA - ASIE								
Jordan - Jordanie								
31 XII 2012 (ESDF)								
AMMAN	2 248 799	1 155 840	1 092 959	...	...	...	...	...
Aqaba	109 150	61 245	47 905	...	...	...	...	...
Irbid	307 033	157 596	149 437	...	...	...	...	...
Russiefa	283 475	147 435	136 040	...	...	...	...	...
Zarqa	491 951	254 195	237 756	...	...	...	...	...
Kazakhstan								
1 I 2009 (ESDF)								
Aktau	152 227	74 261	77 966	29	154 353	75 319	79 034	...
Aktobe	273 599	126 591	147 008	234	312 942	145 877	167 065	...
Almaty	1 365 105	620 876	744 229	319	...	...	...	...
ASTANA	639 311	311 810	327 501	710	...	...	...	...
Atirau	167 902	79 027	88 875	347	222 516	105 581	116 935	...
Ekibastuz	121 814	56 700	65 114	31	143 933	67 458	76 475	...
Karaganda	465 634	211 149	254 485	50	465 698	211 169	254 529	...
Koktshetau	132 426	60 201	72 225	43	145 676	66 402	79 274	...
Kustanai	212 378	95 648	116 730	21	...	...	...	...
Kyzylorda	169 914	80 921	88 993	236	211 943	102 266	109 677	...
Pavlodar	307 880	139 518	168 362	56	328 100	149 232	178 868	...
Petropavlovsk (Severo- Kazakhstanskaya oblast)	193 268	86 739	106 529	22	194 094	87 176	106 918	...
Rudni	110 900	50 877	60 023	19	124 098	57 285	66 813	...
Semipalatinsk	285 473	128 584	156 889	9	313 503	142 416	171 087	...
Shimkent	566 996	269 600	297 396	36	...	...	...	...
Taldykorgan	116 558	52 183	64 375	39	141 143	64 361	76 782	...
Taraz	347 486	159 035	188 451	13	...	...	...	...
Temirtau	164 969	75 390	89 579	30	174 402	79 954	94 448	...
Uralsk	211 116	94 992	116 124	71	243 544	110 575	132 969	...
Ust-Kamenogorsk	287 308	128 518	158 790	54	298 866	134 162	164 704	...
Kuwait - Koweït								
1 VII 2010 (ESDF)								
Farwanyiah -	101 867	68 326	33 541	...	...	...	...	...
Hawalli	127 982	84 506	43 477	...	...	...	...	...
Jaleeb Al-Shuykh	219 629	180 786	38 843	...	...	...	...	...
Salmiya	177 009	103 119	73 890	...	...	...	...	...
South Kheetan	113 426	104 655	8 770	...	...	...	...	...
Kyrgyzstan - Kirghizstan								
1 VII 2012 (ESDJ)								
BISHKEK	870 663[39]	404 348[39]	466 315[39]	...	884 456[39]	411 175[39]	473 281[39]	127
Osh	232 258[39]	110 460[39]	121 798[39]	...	258 150[39]	123 775[39]	134 375[39]	182
Lao People's Democratic Republic - République démocratique populaire lao[40]								
1 VII 2011 (ESDF)								
VIENTIANE CAPITAL	...	...	...	...	783 032	...	...	...
Lebanon - Liban[41]								
3 III 2007 (SSDF)								
BEIRUT	361 366	166 282	195 084	...	...	...	...	...
Malaysia - Malaisie[14]								
1 VII 2011 (ESDJ)								
Alor Setar	155 439	...	...	...	...	...	...	...
Ampang/Ulu Kelang	120 936	...	...	...	...	...	...	...
Bintulu	136 412	...	...	...	...	...	...	...
Georgetown	191 619	...	...	...	...	...	...	...
Kajang dan Sungai Chua	118 652	...	...	...	...	...	...	...
Klang	375 566	...	...	...	...	...	...	...
Kota Kinabalu	303 428	...	...	...	...	...	...	...
KUALA LUMPUR	1 644 783	...	...	...	...	...	...	...
Kuala Terengganu	203 813	...	...	...	...	...	...	...
Kuantan	352 565	...	...	...	...	...	...	...
Kuching	215 745	...	...	...	...	...	...	...
MB Ipoh	505 434	...	...	...	...	...	...	...
MB Johor Bahru	557 333	...	...	...	...	...	...	...
Miri	174 619	...	...	...	...	...	...	...
MP Kota Bharu	245 779	...	...	...	...	...	...	...

8. Population of capital cities and cities of 100 000 or more inhabitants: latest available year, 1993 - 2012
Population des capitales et des villes de 100 000 habitants ou plus : dernière année disponible, 1993 - 2012 (continued - suite)

Continent, country or area, date, code and city Continent, pays ou zone, date, code et ville	City proper - Ville proprement dite				Urban agglomeration - Agglomération urbaine			
	Population			Surface area - Superficie (km²)	Population			Surface area - Superficie (km²)
	Both sexes - Les deux sexes	Male - Masculin	Female - Féminin		Both sexes - Les deux sexes	Male - Masculin	Female - Féminin	
ASIA - ASIE								
Malaysia - Malaisie[14]								
1 VII 2011 (ESDJ)								
Petaling Jaya	245 419	...	...	...	...	...	...	...
Sandakan	222 330	...	...	...	...	...	...	...
Seleyang Baru	188 295	...	...	...	...	...	...	...
Seremban	290 139	...	...	...	...	...	...	...
Shah Alam	190 420	...	...	...	...	...	...	...
Sibu	199 057	...	...	...	...	...	...	...
Subang Jaya	197 165	...	...	...	...	...	...	...
Sungai Petani	215 050	...	...	...	...	...	...	...
Taiping	205 567	...	...	...	...	...	...	...
Tawau	136 799	...	...	...	...	...	...	...
Maldives								
1 VII 2012 (ESDF)								
MALÉ	116 618	58 288	58 330	2	...	...	...	...
Mongolia - Mongolie								
11 XI 2010 (CDJC)								
Hovsgol	114 331	56 899	57 432	...	...	...	...	...
Ovorhangay	100 444	50 333	50 111	...	...	...	...	...
ULAANBAATAR	...	...	...	...	1 154 290	558 247	596 043	...
Nepal - Népal								
22 VI 2011 (CDJC)								
Bharatpur	147 777	74 205	73 572	...	...	...	...	...
Bhimdutta	106 666	53 098	53 568	...	...	...	...	...
Biratnagar	204 949	104 935	100 014	58	...	...	...	...
Birgunj	139 068	75 382	63 686	21	...	...	...	...
Butwal	120 982	60 870	60 112	...	...	...	...	...
Dhangadhi	104 047	53 237	50 810	...	...	...	...	...
Dharan	119 915	57 562	62 353	...	...	...	...	...
KATHMANDU	1 003 285	533 127	470 158	49	...	...	...	...
Lalitpur	226 728	117 932	108 796	15	...	...	...	...
Pokhara	264 991	133 318	131 673	55	...	...	...	...
Oman								
7 XII 2003 (CDFC)								
As Seeb	223 449	128 068	95 381	...	...	...	...	...
As Suwayq	101 122	54 997	46 125	...	...	...	...	...
Bawshar	150 420	91 687	58 733	...	...	...	...	...
MUSCAT	24 893	13 695	11 198	...	...	...	...	...
Mutrah	153 526	96 878	56 648	...	...	...	...	...
Salalah	156 530	92 489	64 041	...	...	...	...	...
Sohar	104 312	57 695	46 617	...	...	...	...	...
Pakistan[42]								
2 III 1998 (CDFC)								
Abbotabad	106 101	61 698	44 403	...	...	...	...	...
Bahawalnagar	111 313	57 779	53 534	...	...	...	...	...
Bahawalpur	408 395	222 228	186 167	...	...	...	...	...
Burewala	152 097	78 726	73 371	...	...	...	...	...
Chiniot	172 522	90 474	82 048	...	...	...	...	...
Chishtian	102 287	52 427	49 860	...	...	...	...	...
Dadu	102 550	53 508	49 042	...	...	...	...	...
Daska	102 883	52 359	50 524	...	...	...	...	...
Dera Ghazi Khan	190 542	98 738	91 804	...	...	...	...	...
Faisalabad (Lyallpur)	2 008 861	1 053 085	955 776	...	...	...	...	...
Gojra	117 872	60 598	57 274	...	...	...	...	...
Gujranwala	1 132 509	588 512	543 997	...	...	...	...	...
Gujrat	251 792	128 524	123 268	...	...	...	...	...
Hafizabad	133 678	69 231	64 447	...	...	...	...	...
Hyderabad	1 166 894	612 283	554 611	...	...	...	...	...
ISLAMABAD	529 180	290 717	238 463	...	...	...	...	...
Jacobabad	138 780	71 854	66 926	...	...	...	...	...
Jaranwala	106 785	55 619	51 166	...	...	...	...	...
Jhang	293 366	153 123	140 243	...	...	...	...	...
Jhelum	147 392	79 169	68 223	...	...	...	...	...
Kamoke	152 288	78 848	73 440	...	...	...	...	...
Karachi	9 339 023	5 029 900	4 309 123	...	...	...	...	...

8. Population of capital cities and cities of 100 000 or more inhabitants: latest available year, 1993 - 2012
Population des capitales et des villes de 100 000 habitants ou plus : dernière année disponible, 1993 - 2012 (continued - suite)

Continent, country or area, date, code and city / Continent, pays ou zone, date, code et ville	City proper - Ville proprement dite				Urban agglomeration - Agglomération urbaine			
	Population			Surface area - Superficie (km²)	Population			Surface area - Superficie (km²)
	Both sexes - Les deux sexes	Male - Masculin	Female - Féminin		Both sexes - Les deux sexes	Male - Masculin	Female - Féminin	
ASIA - ASIE								
Pakistan[42]								
2 III 1998 (CDFC)								
Kasur	245 321	129 553	115 768	...	...	...	...	...
Khairpur	105 637	55 358	50 279	...	...	...	...	...
Khanewal	133 986	69 145	64 841	...	...	...	...	...
Khanpur	120 382	62 371	58 011	...	...	...	...	...
Kohat	126 627	71 505	55 122	...	...	...	...	...
Lahore	5 143 495	2 707 220	2 436 275	...	...	...	...	...
Larkana	270 283	140 622	129 661	...	...	...	...	...
Mangora	173 868	91 742	82 126	...	...	...	...	...
Mardan	245 926	129 247	116 679	...	...	...	...	...
Mirpur Khas	189 671	97 940	91 731	...	...	...	...	...
Multan	1 197 384	637 911	559 473	...	...	...	...	...
Muridke	111 951	58 210	53 741	...	...	...	...	...
Muzaffargharh	123 404	66 556	56 848	...	...	...	...	...
Nawabshah	189 244	98 116	91 128	...	...	...	...	...
Okara	201 815	104 245	97 570	...	...	...	...	...
Pakpattan	109 033	56 676	52 357	...	...	...	...	...
Peshawar	982 816	521 901	460 915	...	...	...	...	...
Quetta	565 137	307 759	257 378	...	...	...	...	...
Rahimyar Khan	233 537	121 446	112 091	...	...	...	...	...
Rawalpindi	1 409 768	750 530	659 238	...	...	...	...	...
Sadiqabad	144 391	75 217	69 174	...	...	...	...	...
Sahiwal	208 778	108 992	99 786	...	...	...	...	...
Sargodha	458 440	239 837	218 603	...	...	...	...	...
Shakkarpur	134 883	69 713	65 170	...	...	...	...	...
Sheikhu Pura	280 263	146 739	133 524	...	...	...	...	...
Sialkote	421 502	227 398	194 104	...	...	...	...	...
Sukkur	335 551	175 679	159 872	...	...	...	...	...
Tandoadam	104 907	54 670	50 237	...	...	...	...	...
Wah Cantonment	198 891	104 230	94 661	...	...	...	...	...
Philippines								
1 V 2010 (CDJC)								
Angeles	326 336	161 791	164 545	60	...	...	...	...
Angono	102 407	50 859	51 548	26	...	...	...	...
Antipolo	677 741	338 392	339 349	306	...	...	...	...
Apalit	101 537	51 788	49 749	61	...	...	...	...
Arayat	121 348	61 593	59 755	134	...	...	...	...
Bacolod	511 820	251 910	259 910	163	...	...	...	...
Bacoor City	520 216	255 375	264 841	46	...	...	...	...
Bago	163 045	84 114	78 931	401	...	...	...	...
Baguio	318 676	156 259	162 417	58	...	...	...	...
Baliuag	143 565	71 947	71 618	45	...	...	...	...
Batangas	305 607	152 499	153 108	283	...	...	...	...
Bayambang	111 521	56 423	55 098	144	...	...	...	...
Bayawan (Tulong)	114 074	59 336	54 738	699	...	...	...	...
Baybay	102 841	52 935	49 906	459	...	...	...	...
Biñan	283 396	140 351	143 045	44	...	...	...	...
Binangonan	249 872	125 027	124 845	66	...	...	...	...
Bocaue	106 407	53 248	53 159	32	...	...	...	...
Butuan	309 709	157 204	152 505	817	...	...	...	...
Cabanatuan	272 676	136 432	136 244	283	...	...	...	...
Cabuyao	248 436	123 110	125 326	43	...	...	...	...
Cadiz	151 500	78 049	73 451	525	...	...	...	...
Cagayan de Oro	602 088	300 853	301 235	413	...	...	...	...
Cainta	311 845	152 400	159 445	43	...	...	...	...
Calamba	389 377	191 773	197 604	150	...	...	...	...
Calapan	124 173	62 588	61 585	250	...	...	...	...
Calbayog	172 778	88 540	84 238	881	...	...	...	...
Calumpit	101 068	50 840	50 228	56	...	...	...	...
Candaba	102 399	51 815	50 584	176	...	...	...	...
Candelaria	110 570	55 137	55 433	129	...	...	...	...
Capas	125 852	64 479	61 373	376	...	...	...	...
Carcar	107 323	54 718	52 605	117	...	...	...	...
Cauayan	122 335	62 362	59 973	336	...	...	...	...

8. Population of capital cities and cities of 100 000 or more inhabitants: latest available year, 1993 - 2012
Population des capitales et des villes de 100 000 habitants ou plus : dernière année disponible, 1993 - 2012 (continued - suite)

Continent, country or area, date, code and city Continent, pays ou zone, date, code et ville	City proper - Ville proprement dite				Urban agglomeration - Agglomération urbaine			
	Population			Surface area - Superficie (km²)	Population			Surface area - Superficie (km²)
	Both sexes - Les deux sexes	Male - Masculin	Female - Féminin		Both sexes - Les deux sexes	Male - Masculin	Female - Féminin	
ASIA - ASIE								
Philippines								
1 V 2010 (CDJC)								
Cavite City	101 120	49 710	51 410	11	...	...	...	...
Cebu	866 171	426 738	439 433	315	...	...	...	...
Concepcion	139 832	71 709	68 123	243	...	...	...	...
Consolacion	106 649	53 204	53 445	147	...	...	...	...
Cotabato	271 786	133 457	138 329	176	...	...	...	...
Dagupan	163 676	81 788	81 888	37	...	...	...	...
Danao City	119 252	60 251	59 001	107	...	...	...	...
Daraga (Locsin)	115 804	58 060	57 744	119	...	...	...	...
Dasmariñas	575 817	283 823	291 994	90	...	...	...	...
Davao	1 449 296	724 565	724 731	2 444	...	...	...	...
Digos	149 891	75 664	74 227	287	...	...	...	...
Dipolog	120 460	60 243	60 217	241	...	...	...	...
Dumaguete	120 883	58 711	62 172	34	...	...	...	...
Floridablanca	110 846	56 249	54 597	175	...	...	...	...
Gapan	101 488	51 331	50 157	164	...	...	...	...
Gen. Mariano Alvarez	138 540	69 226	69 314	9	...	...	...	...
General Santos	538 086	272 216	265 870	493	...	...	...	...
General Trias	243 322	118 771	124 551	90	...	...	...	...
Gingoog	117 908	60 628	57 280	568	...	...	...	...
Glan	106 518	54 919	51 599	534	...	...	...	...
Guagua	111 199	56 191	55 008	49	...	...	...	...
Guimba	104 894	53 633	51 261	245	...	...	...	...
Hagonoy	125 689	63 231	62 458	103	...	...	...	...
Himamaylan	103 006	53 254	49 752	367	...	...	...	...
Ilagan	135 174	69 256	65 918	1 166	...	...	...	...
Iligan	322 821	161 924	160 897	813	...	...	...	...
Iloilo	424 619	207 301	217 318	78	...	...	...	...
Imus City	301 624	145 358	156 266	172	...	...	...	...
Iriga	105 919	53 452	52 467	137	...	...	...	...
Jolo	118 307	58 271	60 036	126	...	...	...	...
Kabankalan	167 666	86 721	80 945	697	...	...	...	...
Kalookan (Caloocan)	1 489 040	742 113	746 927	56	...	...	...	...
Kidapawan	125 447	63 842	61 605	358	...	...	...	...
Koronadal	158 273	79 987	78 286	277	...	...	...	...
La Trinidad	107 188	52 999	54 189	70	...	...	...	...
Laoag	104 904	51 581	53 323	116	...	...	...	...
Lapu-Lapu	350 467	172 839	177 628	58	...	...	...	...
Las Piñas	552 573	268 114	284 459	33	...	...	...	...
Legazpi	182 201	91 174	91 027	154	...	...	...	...
Libmanan	100 002	51 549	48 453	343	...	...	...	...
Liloan	100 500	50 317	50 183	46	...	...	...	...
Lipa	283 468	141 822	141 646	209	...	...	...	...
Los Baños	101 884	50 245	51 639	54	...	...	...	...
Lubao	150 843	76 467	74 376	156	...	...	...	...
Lucena City	246 392	122 774	123 618	80	...	...	...	...
Mabalacat	215 610	107 996	107 614	83	...	...	...	...
Magalang	103 597	52 858	50 739	97	...	...	...	...
Makati	529 039	249 509	279 530	22	...	...	...	...
Malabalay	153 085	79 366	73 719	969	...	...	...	...
Malabon	353 337	176 450	176 887	16	...	...	...	...
Malasiqui	123 566	62 599	60 967	131	...	...	...	...
Malita	109 568	56 155	53 413	883	...	...	...	...
Malolos	234 945	117 260	117 685	67	...	...	...	...
Mandaluyong	328 699	162 235	166 464	9	...	...	...	...
Mandaue	331 320	164 513	166 807	25	...	...	...	...
MANILA	1 652 171	811 788	840 383	25	...	...	...	...
Marawi	187 106	91 003	96 103	88	...	...	...	...
Marikina	424 150	206 821	217 329	22	...	...	...	...
Marilao	185 624	92 323	93 301	34	...	...	...	...
Mariveles	112 707	56 448	56 259	154	...	...	...	...
Mati	126 143	64 742	61 401	589	...	...	...	...
Mexico	146 851	74 426	72 425	117	...	...	...	...
Meycauayan	199 154	99 517	99 637	32	...	...	...	...

8. Population of capital cities and cities of 100 000 or more inhabitants: latest available year, 1993 - 2012
Population des capitales et des villes de 100 000 habitants ou plus : dernière année disponible, 1993 - 2012 (continued - suite)

Continent, country or area, date, code and city / Continent, pays ou zone, date, code et ville	City proper - Ville proprement dite				Urban agglomeration - Agglomération urbaine			
	Population			Surface area - Superficie (km²)	Population			Surface area - Superficie (km²)
	Both sexes - Les deux sexes	Male - Masculin	Female - Féminin		Both sexes - Les deux sexes	Male - Masculin	Female - Féminin	
ASIA - ASIE								
Philippines								
1 V 2010 (CDJC)								
Midsayap	134 170	68 475	65 695	290	...	...	...	...
Minglanilla	113 178	57 598	55 580	66	...	...	...	...
Muntinlupa	459 941	233 606	226 335	40	...	...	...	...
Naga (Camarines Sur)	174 931	86 055	88 876	84	...	...	...	...
Naga (Cebu)	101 571	51 551	50 020	102	...	...	...	...
Nasugbu	122 483	61 972	60 511	279	...	...	...	...
Navotas	249 131	125 924	123 207	9	...	...	...	...
Norzagaray	103 095	52 419	50 676	310	...	...	...	...
Olongapo	221 178	109 316	111 862	185	...	...	...	...
Ormoc	191 200	97 722	93 478	614	...	...	...	...
Ozamis	131 527	65 963	65 564	170	...	...	...	...
Pagadian	186 852	93 264	93 588	379	...	...	...	...
Panabo	174 364	88 643	85 721	251	...	...	...	...
Paranaque	588 126	286 371	301 755	47	...	...	...	...
Pasay	392 869	192 097	200 772	14	...	...	...	...
Pasig	669 773	326 875	342 898	48	...	...	...	...
Philippines: Ligao	104 914	53 510	51 404	247	...	...	...	...
Pikit	113 014	56 762	56 252	605	...	...	...	...
Plaridel	101 441	50 554	50 887	32	...	...	...	...
Polomolok	138 273	70 501	67 772	340	...	...	...	...
Porac	111 441	56 693	54 748	314	...	...	...	...
Puerto Princesa	222 673	114 837	107 836	2 381	...	...	...	...
Quezon City	2 761 720	1 349 016	1 412 704	172	...	...	...	...
Rodriguez (Montalban)	280 904	141 127	139 777	173	...	...	...	...
Rosario	105 561	53 192	52 369	227	...	...	...	...
Roxas	156 197	77 693	78 504	95	...	...	...	...
Sagay City	140 740	72 410	68 330	330	...	...	...	...
San Carlos (Negros Occidental)	129 981	66 600	63 381	452	...	...	...	...
San Carlos (Pangasinan)	175 103	88 715	86 388	169	...	...	...	...
San Fernando (La Union)	114 963	57 002	57 961	103	...	...	...	...
San Fernando (Pampanga)	285 912	143 738	142 174	68	...	...	...	...
San Jose (Occidental Mindoro)	131 188	66 824	64 364	447	...	...	...	...
San Jose City (Nueva Ecija)	129 424	65 867	63 557	186	...	...	...	...
San Jose Del Monte	454 553	227 047	227 506	106	...	...	...	...
San Juan	121 430	54 796	66 634	6	...	...	...	...
San Mateo	205 255	101 991	103 264	55	...	...	...	...
San Miguel	142 854	72 199	70 655	231	...	...	...	...
San Pablo	248 890	123 210	125 680	198	...	...	...	...
San Pedro	294 310	144 967	149 343	24	...	...	...	...
Santa Cruz	110 943	55 794	55 149	39	...	...	...	...
Santa Maria	218 351	109 718	108 633	91	...	...	...	...
Santa Rosa	284 670	137 821	146 849	55	...	...	...	...
Santiago	132 804	67 134	65 670	256	...	...	...	...
Santo Tomas (Davao Del Norte)	109 269	56 703	52 566	222	...	...	...	...
Santo Tomas (Batangas)	124 740	61 500	63 240	95	...	...	...	...
Sariaya	138 894	70 418	68 476	212	...	...	...	...
Silang	213 490	105 117	108 373	209	...	...	...	...
Silay	120 999	61 335	59 664	215	...	...	...	...
Sorsogon	155 144	78 175	76 969	276	...	...	...	...
Surigao	140 540	70 424	70 116	245	...	...	...	...
Tabaco	125 083	63 437	61 646	117	...	...	...	...
Tabuk	103 912	52 894	51 018	700	...	...	...	...
Tacloban	221 174	110 568	110 606	202	...	...	...	...
Taguig	644 473	319 916	324 557	45	...	...	...	...
Tagum	242 801	121 863	120 938	196	...	...	...	...
Talavera	112 515	56 975	55 540	141	...	...	...	...
Talisay	200 772	99 951	100 821	40	...	...	...	...
Tanauan	152 393	75 642	76 751	107	...	...	...	...
Tanza	188 755	93 634	95 121	96	...	...	...	...
Tarlac	318 332	161 365	156 967	275	...	...	...	...
Taytay	288 956	144 538	144 418	39	...	...	...	...
Toledo	157 078	80 619	76 459	216	...	...	...	...
Trece Martires	104 559	52 291	52 268	39	...	...	...	...

8. Population of capital cities and cities of 100 000 or more inhabitants: latest available year, 1993 - 2012
Population des capitales et des villes de 100 000 habitants ou plus : dernière année disponible, 1993 - 2012 (continued - suite)

Continent, country or area, date, code and city / Continent, pays ou zone, date, code et ville	City proper - Ville proprement dite				Urban agglomeration - Agglomération urbaine			
	Population			Surface area - Superficie (km²)	Population			Surface area - Superficie (km²)
	Both sexes - Les deux sexes	Male - Masculin	Female - Féminin		Both sexes - Les deux sexes	Male - Masculin	Female - Féminin	
ASIA - ASIE								
Philippines								
1 V 2010 (CDJC)								
Tuguegarao	138 865	68 807	70 058	145	...	...	...	...
Urdaneta	125 451	63 025	62 426	100	...	...	...	...
Valencia	181 556	93 417	88 139	587	...	...	...	...
Valenzuela	575 356	288 659	286 697	47	...	...	...	...
Zamboanga	807 129	405 435	401 694	1 415	...	...	...	...
Qatar								
21 IV 2010 (CDFC)								
Al-Khoor	193 983	181 005	12 978	...	...	...	...	...
Al-Rayyan	455 623	301 842	153 781	...	...	...	...	...
Al-Wakrah	141 222	114 698	26 524	...	...	...	...	...
DOHA	796 947	610 817	186 130	...	...	...	...	...
Republic of Korea - République de Corée								
1 VII 2011* (ESDJ)								
Busan (Pusan)	3 420 679	1 694 784	1 725 895	767	...	...	...	...
Daegu (Taegu)	2 417 943	1 210 715	1 207 228	884	...	...	...	...
Daejeon (Taejon)	1 523 840	766 034	757 806	540	...	...	...	...
Gwangju (Kwangchu)	1 451 394	722 562	728 832	501	...	...	...	...
Incheon	2 675 476	1 351 896	1 323 580	1 029	...	...	...	...
SEOUL	10 038 905	4 966 717	5 072 188	605	...	...	...	...
Ulsan	1 097 354	567 988	529 366	1 059	...	...	...	...
Saudi Arabia - Arabie saoudite								
15 IX 2004 (CDFC)								
Abha	201 912	113 102	88 810	...	...	...	...	...
Ad-Dammam	744 321	450 494	293 827	...	...	...	...	...
Al-Hawiyah	132 078	69 481	62 597	...	...	...	...	...
Al-Hufuf	287 841	155 924	131 917	...	...	...	...	...
Al-Jubayl	222 544	135 659	86 885	...	...	...	...	...
Al-Kharj	200 958	109 112	91 846	...	...	...	...	...
Al-Khubar	165 799	101 818	63 981	...	...	...	...	...
Al-Madinah	918 889	493 929	424 960	...	...	...	...	...
Al-Mubarraz	285 067	150 449	134 618	...	...	...	...	...
Al-Qurrayyat	100 436	52 869	47 567	...	...	...	...	...
Ar'ar	145 237	77 744	67 493	...	...	...	...	...
Ath-Thuqbah	191 826	117 165	74 661	...	...	...	...	...
At-Ta'if	521 273	274 531	246 742	...	...	...	...	...
Buraydah	378 422	211 317	167 105	...	...	...	...	...
Hafar al-Batin	231 978	122 781	109 197	...	...	...	...	...
Ha'il	267 005	142 015	124 990	...	...	...	...	...
Jiddah	2 801 481	1 619 932	1 181 549	...	...	...	...	...
Jizan	100 694	57 988	42 706	...	...	...	...	...
Khamis Mushayt	372 695	208 397	164 298	...	...	...	...	...
Makkah	1 294 168	704 672	589 496	...	...	...	...	...
Najran (Aba as-Suud)	246 880	133 405	113 475	...	...	...	...	...
RIYADH	4 087 152	2 354 246	1 732 906	...	...	...	...	...
Sekaka	122 686	66 672	56 014	...	...	...	...	...
Tabuk	441 351	241 913	199 438	...	...	...	...	...
Unayzah	128 930	71 841	57 089	...	...	...	...	...
Yanbu al-Bahr	188 430	105 966	82 464	...	...	...	...	...
Singapore - Singapour								
30 VI 2012 (ESDJ)								
SINGAPORE	5 312 400[43]	...	...	716	...	...	...	...
Sri Lanka[44]								
17 VII 2001 (CDFC)								
COLOMBO	647 100	346 366	300 734	...	...	...	...	...
Dehiwala-Mount Lavinia	210 546	105 522	105 024	...	...	...	...	...
Kandy	109 343	54 288	55 055	...	...	...	...	...
Moratuwa	177 563	87 313	90 250	...	...	...	...	...
Negombo	121 701	60 947	60 754	...	...	...	...	...
Sri Jayawardanapura Kotte	116 366	59 993	56 373	...	...	...	...	...
State of Palestine - État de Palestine								
1 VII 2012 (ESDF)								
Gaza	515 556	...	...	38	...	...	...	...
Hebron	189 444	...	...	49	...	...	...	...

8. Population of capital cities and cities of 100 000 or more inhabitants: latest available year, 1993 - 2012
Population des capitales et des villes de 100 000 habitants ou plus : dernière année disponible, 1993 - 2012 (continued - suite)

Continent, country or area, date, code and city Continent, pays ou zone, date, code et ville	City proper - Ville proprement dite				Urban agglomeration - Agglomération urbaine			
	Population			Surface area - Superficie (km²)	Population			Surface area - Superficie (km²)
	Both sexes - Les deux sexes	Male - Masculin	Female - Féminin		Both sexes - Les deux sexes	Male - Masculin	Female - Féminin	
ASIA - ASIE								
State of Palestine - État de Palestine								
1 VII 2012 (ESDF)								
Jabalya	146 609	...	...	...	...	...	...	...
Khan Yunis	163 634	...	...	...	...	...	...	...
Nablus	140 009	...	...	26	...	...	...	...
Rafah	142 427	...	...	...	...	...	...	...
Syrian Arab Republic - République arabe syrienne								
1 VII 2008 (ESDF)								
Aleppo	4 450 000	2 292 000	2 158 000	...	...	...	...	...
Al-Hasakeh	1 392 000	701 000	691 000	...	...	...	...	...
Al-Raqqah	865 000	456 000	409 000	...	...	...	...	...
Al-Sweida	349 000	171 000	178 000	...	...	...	...	...
DAMASCUS	1 680 000	857 000	823 000	...	...	...	...	...
Damasus rural	2 529 000	1 302 000	1 227 000	...	...	...	...	...
Deir El-Zor	1 111 000	563 000	548 000	...	...	...	...	...
Dra'a	930 000	472 000	458 000	...	...	...	...	...
Hama	1 508 000	768 000	740 000	...	...	...	...	...
Homs	1 667 000	852 000	815 000	...	...	...	...	...
Idleb	1 376 000	704 000	672 000	...	...	...	...	...
Lattakia	951 000	480 000	471 000	...	...	...	...	...
Tartous	756 000	383 000	373 000	...	...	...	...	...
Tajikistan - Tadjikistan								
1 VII 2011 (ESDF)								
DUSHANBE	739 556	382 520	357 036	...	...	...	...	...
Thailand - Thaïlande								
1 IX 2010 (CDJC)								
Ang Thong	...	...	...	...	109 207	51 540	57 667	...
BANGKOK	...	...	...	...	8 305 218	4 032 586	4 272 632	1 569
Buri Ram	...	...	...	...	375 999	181 546	194 453	...
Chachoengsao	...	...	...	...	206 250	101 475	104 775	...
Chai Nat	...	...	...	...	205 456	97 373	108 083	...
Chaiyaphum	...	...	...	...	205 112	99 280	105 832	...
Chanthaburi	...	...	...	...	243 126	118 221	124 905	...
Chiang Mai	...	...	...	...	967 020	466 145	500 875	...
Chiang Rai	...	...	...	...	455 732	220 391	235 341	...
Chon Buri	...	...	...	...	1 158 989	575 208	583 781	...
Chumphon	...	...	...	...	147 912	75 339	72 573	...
Kalasin	...	...	...	...	428 940	208 863	220 077	...
Kamphaeng Phet	...	...	...	...	211 774	101 456	110 318	...
Kanchanaburi	...	...	...	...	292 521	143 986	148 535	...
Khon Kaen	...	...	...	...	703 123	339 011	364 112	...
Lampang	...	...	...	...	372 463	180 360	192 103	...
Lamphun	...	...	...	...	262 832	126 662	136 170	...
Loei	...	...	...	...	164 180	81 302	82 878	...
Lop Buri	...	...	...	...	235 827	118 964	116 863	...
Maha Sarakham	...	...	...	...	153 740	72 143	81 597	...
Mukdahan	...	...	...	...	180 600	89 190	91 410	...
Nakhon Pathom	...	...	...	...	339 736	166 150	173 586	...
Nakhon Phanom	...	...	...	...	123 720	59 683	64 037	...
Nakhon Ratchasima	...	...	...	...	653 075	316 329	336 746	...
Nakhon Sawan	...	...	...	...	225 903	107 298	118 605	...
Nakhon Si Thammarat	...	...	...	...	265 606	127 460	138 146	...
Narathiwat	...	...	...	...	133 718	64 616	69 102	...
Nong Bua Lam Phu	...	...	...	...	203 142	98 164	104 978	...
Nong Khai	...	...	...	...	232 798	113 989	118 809	...
Nonthaburi	...	...	...	...	797 739	383 826	413 913	...
Pathum Thani	...	...	...	...	757 175	358 679	398 496	...
Pattani	...	...	...	...	104 617	51 305	53 312	...
Phatthalung	...	...	...	...	244 783	117 039	127 744	...
Phayao	...	...	...	...	221 062	106 657	114 405	...
Phetchabun	...	...	...	...	172 275	82 257	90 018	...
Phetchaburi	...	...	...	...	175 675	83 735	91 940	...
Phichit	...	...	...	...	131 283	62 446	68 837	...
Phitsanulok	...	...	...	...	201 466	93 098	108 368	...
Phra Nakhon Si Ayutthaya	...	...	...	...	365 736	173 280	192 456	...

Continent, country or area, date, code and city Continent, pays ou zone, date, code et ville	City proper - Ville proprement dite				Urban agglomeration - Agglomération urbaine			
	Population			Surface area - Superficie (km²)	Population			Surface area - Superficie (km²)
	Both sexes - Les deux sexes	Male - Masculin	Female - Féminin		Both sexes - Les deux sexes	Male - Masculin	Female - Féminin	
ASIA - ASIE								
Thailand - Thaïlande								
1 IX 2010 (CDJC)								
Phrae	...	...	...	...	156 099	75 175	80 924	...
Phuket	...	...	...	...	358 159	175 144	183 015	...
Prachuap Khiri Khan	...	...	...	...	177 011	87 525	89 486	...
Ranong	...	...	...	...	123 596	62 090	61 506	...
Ratchaburi	...	...	...	...	317 886	149 460	168 426	...
Rayong	...	...	...	...	445 939	224 068	221 871	...
Roi Et	...	...	...	...	365 113	176 648	188 465	...
Sa Kaeo	...	...	...	...	135 536	66 447	69 089	...
Sakon Nakhon	...	...	...	...	315 788	153 785	162 003	...
Samut Prakan	...	...	...	...	1 082 993	527 487	555 506	...
Samut Sakhon	...	...	...	...	479 186	237 778	241 408	...
Saraburi	...	...	...	...	239 281	114 885	124 396	...
Si Sa Ket	...	...	...	...	160 508	77 363	83 145	...
Songkhla	...	...	...	...	800 970	382 828	418 142	...
Sukhothai	...	...	...	...	166 782	79 139	87 643	...
Suphan Buri	...	...	...	...	228 496	108 666	119 830	...
Surat Thani	...	...	...	...	410 984	198 909	212 075	...
Surin	...	...	...	...	153 159	73 082	80 077	...
Tak	...	...	...	...	146 769	70 754	76 015	...
Trat	...	...	...	...	110 398	52 309	58 089	...
Ubon Ratchathani	...	...	...	...	411 954	198 655	213 299	...
Udon Thani	...	...	...	...	483 057	232 326	250 731	...
Uttaradit	...	...	...	...	151 047	72 244	78 803	...
Yala	...	...	...	...	119 744	58 041	61 703	...
Yasothon	...	...	...	...	127 173	63 885	63 288	...
Timor-Leste								
11 VII 2010* (CDFC)								
DILI	193 563	103 096	90 467	...	...	...	...	...
Turkey - Turquie								
1 VII 2007 (ESDF)								
Adana[45]	...	...	...	...	1 251 863	...	...	...
Adiyaman	241 260	...	...	...	...	...	...	...
Afyon	1 488 350	...	...	...	...	...	...	...
Aksaray	157 232	...	...	...	...	...	...	...
Alanya (Antalya)	115 927	...	...	...	...	...	...	...
ANKARA[46]	...	...	...	...	3 953 344	...	...	...
Antalya	763 205	...	...	...	...	...	...	...
Aydin	164 525	...	...	...	...	...	...	...
Balikesir	241 682	...	...	...	...	...	...	...
Bandirma	109 000	...	...	...	...	...	...	...
Batman	321 222	...	...	...	...	...	...	...
Bursa[47]	...	...	...	...	1 597 162	...	...	...
Ceyhan	122 699	...	...	...	...	...	...	...
Corlu	199 714	...	...	...	...	...	...	...
Corum	190 430	...	...	...	...	...	...	...
Denizli	320 460	...	...	...	...	...	...	...
Derince[48]	111 659	...	...	...	...	...	...	...
Diyarbakir	662 954	...	...	...	...	...	...	...
Edirne	125 753	...	...	...	...	...	...	...
Elazig	297 703	...	...	...	...	...	...	...
Erzincan	112 069	...	...	...	...	...	...	...
Erzurum	443 423	...	...	...	...	...	...	...
Eskisehir	512 972	...	...	...	...	...	...	...
Gaziantep[49]	...	...	...	...	1 024 411	...	...	...
Gebze	325 021	...	...	...	...	...	...	...
Hatay	153 581	...	...	...	...	...	...	...
Içel	604 236	...	...	...	...	...	...	...
Inegol	125 507	...	...	...	...	...	...	...
Iskenderun	154 706	...	...	...	...	...	...	...
Isparta	168 872	...	...	...	...	...	...	...
Istanbul[50]	...	...	...	...	10 822 846	...	...	...
Izmir[51]	...	...	...	...	2 583 670	...	...	...
Kahramanmaras	393 583	...	...	...	...	...	...	...

8. Population of capital cities and cities of 100 000 or more inhabitants: latest available year, 1993 - 2012

Population des capitales et des villes de 100 000 habitants ou plus : dernière année disponible, 1993 - 2012 (continued - suite)

Continent, country or area, date, code and city / Continent, pays ou zone, date, code et ville	City proper - Ville proprement dite				Urban agglomeration - Agglomération urbaine			
	Population			Surface area - Superficie (km²)	Population			Surface area - Superficie (km²)
	Both sexes - Les deux sexes	Male - Masculin	Female - Féminin		Both sexes - Les deux sexes	Male - Masculin	Female - Féminin	
ASIA - ASIE								
Turkey - Turquie								
1 VII 2007 (ESDF)								
Karaman	124 603	...	...	...	...	...	...	...
Kayseri[52]	...	...	...	...	710 735	...	...	...
Kirikkale	207 613	...	...	...	...	...	...	...
Kiziltepe	157 834	...	...	...	...	...	...	...
Kocaeli	186 951	...	...	...	...	...	...	...
Konya	...	...	...	...	994 883	...	...	...
Kütahya	186 516	...	...	...	...	...	...	...
Malatya	454 249	...	...	...	...	...	...	...
Manavgat (Antalya)	100 588	...	...	...	...	...	...	...
Manisa	250 943	...	...	...	...	...	...	...
Nazilli	119 972	...	...	...	...	...	...	...
Ordu	112 746	...	...	...	...	...	...	...
Osmaniye	209 907	...	...	...	...	...	...	...
Patnos (Agri)	108 507	...	...	...	...	...	...	...
Sakarya	276 713	...	...	...	...	...	...	...
Samsun	393 334	...	...	...	...	...	...	...
Sanliurfa	438 134	...	...	...	...	...	...	...
Siirt	118 567	...	...	...	...	...	...	...
Sivas	258 746	...	...	...	...	...	...	...
Siverek	184 121	...	...	...	...	...	...	...
Tarsus	227 595	...	...	...	...	...	...	...
Tekirdag	119 518	...	...	...	...	...	...	...
Tokat	132 929	...	...	...	...	...	...	...
Trabzon	242 445	...	...	...	...	...	...	...
Turgutlu (Manisa)	105 565	...	...	...	...	...	...	...
Turhal	113 457	...	...	...	...	...	...	...
Usak	156 672	...	...	...	...	...	...	...
Van	381 653	...	...	...	...	...	...	...
Viransehir	182 095	...	...	...	...	...	...	...
United Arab Emirates - Émirats arabes unis								
1 VII 2002 (ESDF)								
ABU DHABI	527 000	359 000	168 000	...	...	...	...	...
Ajman	205 000	122 000	83 000	...	...	...	...	...
Al-Ayn	328 000	215 000	113 000	...	...	...	...	...
Al-Sharjah	488 000	317 000	171 000	...	...	...	...	...
Dubai	1 089 000	759 000	330 000	...	...	...	...	...
Uzbekistan - Ouzbékistan								
1 VII 2001 (ESDF)								
Almalyk	113 114	56 317	56 797	...	...	...	...	...
Andizhan	338 366	165 159	173 207	...	...	...	...	...
Angren	128 757	64 060	64 697	...	...	...	...	...
Banjzak	131 512	68 441	63 071	...	...	...	...	...
Bukhara	237 361	118 613	118 748	...	...	...	...	...
Chirchik	141 742	70 203	71 539	...	...	...	...	...
Fergana	183 037	87 142	95 895	...	...	...	...	...
Karshi	204 690	104 159	100 531	...	...	...	...	...
Kokand	197 450	95 872	101 578	...	...	...	...	...
Margilan	149 646	73 899	75 747	...	...	...	...	...
Namangan	391 297	197 962	193 335	...	...	...	...	...
Navoi	138 082	70 577	67 505	...	...	...	...	...
Nukus	212 012	103 918	108 094	...	...	...	...	...
Samarkand	361 339	178 608	182 731	...	...	...	...	...
TASHKENT	2 137 218	1 043 213	1 094 005	...	...	...	...	...
Termez	116 467	60 031	56 436	...	...	...	...	...
Urgentch	138 609	67 667	70 942	...	...	...	...	...
Yemen - Yémen								
1 VII 2009* (ESDF)								
Adan	684 322	...	...	...	684 322	...	...	...
SANA'A	1 976 286	...	...	...	2 022 867	...	...	...

8. Population of capital cities and cities of 100 000 or more inhabitants: latest available year, 1993 - 2012
Population des capitales et des villes de 100 000 habitants ou plus : dernière année disponible, 1993 - 2012 (continued - suite)

Continent, country or area, date, code and city / Continent, pays ou zone, date, code et ville	City proper - Ville proprement dite				Urban agglomeration - Agglomération urbaine			
	Population			Surface area - Superficie (km²)	Population			Surface area - Superficie (km²)
	Both sexes - Les deux sexes	Male - Masculin	Female - Féminin		Both sexes - Les deux sexes	Male - Masculin	Female - Féminin	

EUROPE

Åland Islands - Îles d'Åland								
1 VII 2012 (ESDJ)								
MARIEHAMN	11 305[12]	5 408[12]	5 897[12]	12	...	...	...	...
Albania - Albanie								
1 X 2011* (CDJC)								
Durrës	115 550	57 643	57 907	...	...	...	...	...
TIRANA	421 286	207 391	213 895	31	...	...	...	...
Andorra - Andorre[12]								
1 VII 2011 (ESDJ)								
ANDORRA LA VELLA	...	...	...	...	22 205	11 056	11 149	...
Austria - Autriche								
1 I 2012 (ESDJ)								
Graz	265 318	128 268	137 050	128	...	...	...	...
Innsbruck	121 329	57 934	63 395	105	...	...	...	...
Linz	191 107	91 151	99 956	96	...	...	...	...
Salzburg	148 521	70 264	78 257	66	...	...	...	...
WIEN	1 731 236	830 937	900 299	415	...	...	...	...
Belarus - Bélarus								
1 VII 2011 (ESDJ)								
Baranovichi	169 468[53]	76 766[53]	92 702[53]	50	...	...	...	...
Bobruisk	216 093[53]	100 988[53]	115 105[53]	90	...	...	...	...
Borisov	146 159[53]	68 753[53]	77 406[53]	53	...	...	...	...
Brest	318 372[53]	146 370[53]	172 002[53]	145	...	...	...	...
Gomel	...	...	...	...	504 500[53]	229 370[53]	275 130[53]	135
Grodno	342 444[53]	156 224[53]	186 220[53]	144	...	...	...	...
MINSK	1 874 579[53]	857 387[53]	1 017 192[53]	307	...	...	...	...
Mogilev	362 140[53]	166 719[53]	195 421[53]	119	...	...	...	...
Mozir	110 307[53]	52 473[53]	57 834[53]	38	...	...	...	...
Novopolotsk	...	...	...	...	105 604[53]	50 090[53]	55 514[53]	49
Orsha	...	...	...	...	132 477[53]	61 223[53]	71 254[53]	39
Pinsk	133 298[53]	61 839[53]	71 459[53]	47	...	...	...	...
Soligorsk	103 525[53]	48 693[53]	54 832[53]	11	...	...	...	...
Vitebsk	...	...	...	...	364 391[53]	161 795[53]	202 596[53]	125
Belgium - Belgique								
1 VII 2009 (ESDJ)								
Anderlecht	103 009	50 406	52 603	17	...	...	...	...
Antwerpen (Anvers)	480 721	237 285	243 436	205	699 039	343 611	355 428	394
Brugge	116 855	56 649	60 206	138	116 855	56 649	60 206	138
BRUXELLES (BRUSSEL)	155 526	78 208	77 318	33	1 486 414	718 128	768 286	573
Charleroi	202 416	98 140	104 276	102	289 664	139 795	149 869	199
Gent (Gand)	241 708	118 803	122 905	156	273 000	134 047	138 953	207
Liège (Luik)	191 624	93 988	97 636	69	483 777	233 524	250 253	367
Namur	108 733	52 239	56 494	176	108 733	52 239	56 494	176
Schaerbeek	119 754	58 949	60 805	8	...	...	...	...
Bulgaria - Bulgarie								
1 II 2011 (CDJC)								
Burgas	200 271	97 150	103 121	...	...	...	...	...
Pleven	106 954	51 746	55 208	...	...	...	...	...
Plovdiv	338 153	161 376	176 777	...	...	...	...	...
Ruse	149 642	72 217	77 425	...	...	...	...	...
SOFIA	1 202 761	571 635	631 126	...	...	...	...	...
Stara Zagora	138 272	67 174	71 098	...	...	...	...	...
Varna	334 870	162 668	172 202	...	...	...	...	...
Croatia - Croatie[54]								
31 III 2001 (CDJC)								
Osijek	114 616	53 497	61 119	...	...	...	...	...
Rijeka	144 043	68 511	75 532	...	...	...	...	...
Split	188 694	90 484	98 210	...	...	...	...	...
ZAGREB	779 145	363 992	415 153	...	...	...	...	...
Czech Republic - République tchèque								
1 I 2012 (ESDJ)								
Brno	378 965	182 733	196 232	230	...	...	...	...
Liberec	102 005	49 265	52 740	106	...	...	...	...
Ostrava	299 622	145 067	154 555	214	...	...	...	...

8. Population of capital cities and cities of 100 000 or more inhabitants: latest available year, 1993 - 2012
Population des capitales et des villes de 100 000 habitants ou plus : dernière année disponible, 1993 - 2012 (continued - suite)

Continent, country or area, date, code and city / Continent, pays ou zone, date, code et ville	City proper - Ville proprement dite				Urban agglomeration - Agglomération urbaine			
	Population			Surface area - Superficie (km²)	Population			Surface area - Superficie (km²)
	Both sexes - Les deux sexes	Male - Masculin	Female - Féminin		Both sexes - Les deux sexes	Male - Masculin	Female - Féminin	
EUROPE								
Czech Republic - République tchèque								
1 I 2012 (ESDJ)								
Plzen	167 302	81 252	86 050	138	...	...	...	...
PRAHA	1 241 664	602 987	638 677	496	...	...	...	...
Denmark - Danemark[55]								
1 VII 2012 (ESDJ)								
Ålborg	200 884[12]	100 540[12]	100 344[12]	1 137	...	...	...	...
Århus	314 887[12]	154 774[12]	160 113[12]	468	...	...	...	...
Esbjerg	115 105[12]	57 509[12]	57 596[12]	795	...	...	...	...
Frederiksberg	100 637	47 448	53 189	8	...	...	...	...
KOBENHAVN	551 900[12]	272 917[12]	278 983[12]	75	...	...	...	...
Odense	191 692[12]	94 127[12]	97 565[12]	306	...	...	...	...
Vejle	108 471[12]	54 003[12]	54 468[12]	1 059	...	...	...	...
Estonia - Estonie								
1 VII 2011 (ESDJ)								
TALLINN	400 682	181 545	219 137	158	...	...	...	...
Tartu	103 924	46 737	57 187	39	...	...	...	...
Faeroe Islands - Îles Féroé								
1 VII 2008 (ESDJ)								
THORSHAVN	17 624	8 920	8 704	63	19 540	9 945	9 595	110
Finland - Finlande								
1 VII 2011 (ESDJ)								
Espoo	250 205	123 415	126 790	312	...	...	...	...
HELSINKI	591 967	278 213	313 754	214	...	...	...	...
Jyvaskyla	131 439	64 012	67 428	1 171	...	...	...	...
Lahti	101 948	48 381	53 568	135	...	...	...	...
Oulu	142 790	70 343	72 448	1 410	...	...	...	...
Tampere	214 193	103 446	110 747	525	...	...	...	...
Turku	177 978	84 154	93 824	246	...	...	...	...
Vantaa	201 528	98 727	102 801	238	...	...	...	...
France								
1 I 2009 (ESDJ)								
Aix-en-Provence	141 895	...	...	186[56]	...	...	...	...
Amiens	133 998	...	...	49[56]	...	...	...	...
Angers	147 305	...	...	43[56]	...	...	...	...
Argenteuil	102 844	...	...	...	...	...	...	...
Besançon	117 392	...	...	65[56]	...	...	...	...
Bordeaux	236 725	...	...	49[56]	...	...	...	...
Boulogne-Billancourt	113 085	...	...	6[56]	...	...	...	...
Brest	141 315	...	...	50[56]	...	...	...	...
Caen	109 312	...	...	26[56]	...	...	...	...
Clermont-Ferrand	138 588	...	...	43[56]	...	...	...	...
Dijon	152 110	...	...	40[56]	...	...	...	...
Grenoble	155 632	...	...	18[56]	...	...	...	...
Le Havre	177 259	...	...	47[56]	...	...	...	...
Le Mans	142 281	...	...	53[56]	...	...	...	...
Lille	226 827	...	...	30[57]	...	...	...	...
Limoges	139 216	...	...	77[56]	...	...	...	...
Lyon	479 803	...	...	48[56]	...	...	...	...
Marseille	850 602	...	...	241[56]	...	...	...	...
Metz	121 841	...	...	42[56]	...	...	...	...
Montpellier	255 080	...	...	57[56]	...	...	...	...
Montreuil	103 192	...	...	...	...	...	...	...
Mulhouse	111 156	...	...	22[56]	...	...	...	...
Nancy	106 318	...	...	15[56]	...	...	...	...
Nantes	282 047	...	...	65[56]	...	...	...	...
Nice	340 735	...	...	72[56]	...	...	...	...
Nîmes	140 747	...	...	162[56]	...	...	...	...
Orléans	113 224	...	...	27[56]	...	...	...	...
PARIS	2 234 105	...	...	105[56]	...	...	...	...
Perpignan	117 905	...	...	68[56]	...	...	...	...
Reims	180 842	...	...	47[56]	...	...	...	...
Rennes	206 604	...	...	50[56]	...	...	...	...

8. Population of capital cities and cities of 100 000 or more inhabitants: latest available year, 1993 - 2012
Population des capitales et des villes de 100 000 habitants ou plus : dernière année disponible, 1993 - 2012 (continued - suite)

Continent, country or area, date, code and city / Continent, pays ou zone, date, code et ville	City proper - Ville proprement dite				Urban agglomeration - Agglomération urbaine			
	Population			Surface area - Superficie (km²)	Population			Surface area - Superficie (km²)
	Both sexes - Les deux sexes	Male - Masculin	Female - Féminin		Both sexes - Les deux sexes	Male - Masculin	Female - Féminin	
EUROPE								
France								
1 I 2009 (ESDJ)								
Rouen	110 688	...	...	21[56]	...	...	...	...
Saint-Denis	105 749	...	...	...	...	...	...	...
Saint-Denis (La Réunion)	145 209	...	...	...	...	...	...	...
Saint-Étienne	171 961	...	...	80[56]	...	...	...	...
Saint-Paul (La Réunion)	103 498	...	...	...	...	...	...	...
Strasbourg	271 708	...	...	78[57]	...	...	...	...
Toulon	165 514	...	...	43[56]	...	...	...	...
Toulouse	440 204	...	...	118[56]	...	...	...	...
Tours	135 218	...	...	34[56]	...	...	...	...
Villeurbanne	144 751	...	...	15[56]	...	...	...	...
Germany - Allemagne								
1 I 2012 (ESDJ)								
Aachen	260 454	134 998	125 456	161	...	...	...	...
Augsburg	266 647	129 743	136 904	147	...	...	...	...
Bergisch Gladbach	105 836	50 958	54 878	83	...	...	...	...
BERLIN	3 501 872	1 717 645	1 784 227	892	...	...	...	...
Bielefeld	323 395	154 922	168 473	258	...	...	...	...
Bochum	373 976	182 585	191 391	146	...	...	...	...
Bonn	327 913	157 518	170 395	141	...	...	...	...
Bottrop	116 361	56 170	60 191	101	...	...	...	...
Braunschweig	250 556	123 934	126 622	192	...	...	...	...
Bremen	548 319	266 554	281 765	325	...	...	...	...
Bremerhaven	112 982	56 223	56 759	94	...	...	...	...
Chemnitz	243 173	117 404	125 769	221	...	...	...	...
Cottbus	102 129	50 338	51 791	164	...	...	...	...
Darmstadt	149 052	75 293	73 759	122	...	...	...	...
Dortmund	580 956	285 444	295 512	281	...	...	...	...
Dresden	529 781	260 936	268 845	328	...	...	...	...
Duisburg	488 005	239 730	248 275	233	...	...	...	...
Düsseldorf	592 393	282 408	309 985	217	...	...	...	...
Erfurt	206 384	100 028	106 356	269	...	...	...	...
Erlangen	106 326	52 243	54 083	77	...	...	...	...
Essen	573 468	276 029	297 439	210	...	...	...	...
Frankfurt am Main	691 518	339 541	351 977	248	...	...	...	...
Freiburg im Breisgau	229 144	109 357	119 787	153	...	...	...	...
Fürth	116 317	56 583	59 734	63	...	...	...	...
Gelsenkirchen	256 652	125 063	131 589	105	...	...	...	...
Göttingen	121 364	58 864	62 500	117	...	...	...	...
Hagen	187 447	90 456	96 991	160	...	...	...	...
Halle	233 705	111 343	122 362	135	...	...	...	...
Hamburg	1 798 836	880 972	917 864	755	...	...	...	...
Hamm	182 112	90 817	91 295	226	...	...	...	...
Hannover	525 875	254 872	271 003	204	...	...	...	...
Heidelberg	149 633	70 991	78 642	109	...	...	...	...
Heilbronn	124 257	61 698	62 559	100	...	...	...	...
Herne	164 244	80 903	83 341	51	...	...	...	...
Hildesheim	102 584	48 476	54 108	92	...	...	...	...
Ingolstadt	126 732	63 519	63 213	133	...	...	...	...
Jena	105 463	52 240	53 223	114	...	...	...	...
Karlsruhe	297 488	149 559	147 929	173	...	...	...	...
Kassel	196 496	94 760	101 736	107	...	...	...	...
Kiel	242 041	118 724	123 317	119	...	...	...	...
Koblenz	106 677	51 312	55 365	105	...	...	...	...
Köln	1 017 155	492 416	524 739	405	...	...	...	...
Krefeld	234 396	114 084	120 312	138	...	...	...	...
Leipzig	531 809	258 599	273 210	297	...	...	...	...
Leverkusen	161 195	78 161	83 034	79	...	...	...	...
Lübeck	210 577	100 356	110 221	214	...	...	...	...
Ludwigshafen am Rhein	165 560	82 734	82 826	78	...	...	...	...
Magdeburg	232 364	113 076	119 288	201	...	...	...	...
Mainz	200 957	96 929	104 028	98	...	...	...	...
Mannheim	314 931	156 890	158 041	145	...	...	...	...
Moers	105 102	50 675	54 427	68	...	...	...	...

8. Population of capital cities and cities of 100 000 or more inhabitants: latest available year, 1993 - 2012
Population des capitales et des villes de 100 000 habitants ou plus : dernière année disponible, 1993 - 2012 (continued - suite)

Continent, country or area, date, code and city / Continent, pays ou zone, date, code et ville	City proper - Ville proprement dite				Urban agglomeration - Agglomération urbaine			
	Population			Surface area - Superficie (km²)	Population			Surface area - Superficie (km²)
	Both sexes - Les deux sexes	Male - Masculin	Female - Féminin		Both sexes - Les deux sexes	Male - Masculin	Female - Féminin	
EUROPE								
Germany - Allemagne								
1 I 2012 (ESDJ)								
Mönchengladbach	257 208	124 957	132 251	170	...	...	...	...
Mülheim an der Ruhr	167 156	80 226	86 930	91	...	...	...	...
München	1 378 176	670 940	707 236	311	...	...	...	...
Münster (Westf.)	291 754	136 802	154 952	303	...	...	...	...
Neuss	152 010	73 572	78 438	100	...	...	...	...
Nürnberg	510 602	247 939	262 663	186	...	...	...	...
Oberhausen	212 568	103 548	109 020	77	...	...	...	...
Offenbach am Main	122 705	61 820	60 885	45	...	...	...	...
Oldenburg	162 481	78 432	84 049	103	...	...	...	...
Osnabrück	165 021	79 147	85 874	120	...	...	...	...
Paderborn	147 688	72 756	74 932	180	...	...	...	...
Pforzheim	120 709	58 646	62 063	98	...	...	...	...
Potsdam	158 902	77 074	81 828	188	...	...	...	...
Recklinghausen	117 672	56 896	60 776	66	...	...	...	...
Regensburg	136 577	65 760	70 817	81	...	...	...	...
Remscheid	109 596	53 346	56 250	75	...	...	...	...
Reutlingen	112 735	55 071	57 664	87	...	...	...	...
Rostock	204 260	100 478	103 782	181	...	...	...	...
Saarbrücken	176 135	85 020	91 115	167	...	...	...	...
Salzgitter	101 750	49 935	51 815	224	...	...	...	...
Siegen	103 370	51 036	52 334	115	...	...	...	...
Solingen	159 699	77 409	82 290	90	...	...	...	...
Stuttgart	613 392	305 347	308 045	207	...	...	...	...
Trier	105 675	50 255	55 420	117	...	...	...	...
Ulm	123 672	60 965	62 707	119	...	...	...	...
Wiesbaden	278 919	134 566	144 353	204	...	...	...	...
Wolfsburg	122 583	60 370	62 213	204	...	...	...	...
Wuppertal	349 470	168 999	180 471	168	...	...	...	...
Würzburg	133 808	62 513	71 295	88	...	...	...	...
Gibraltar[58]								
1 VII 2010 (ESDF)								
GIBRALTAR	29 436	14 746	14 690	...	...	...	...	...
Greece - Grèce								
18 III 2001 (CDJC)								
ATHINAI	789 166[59]	374 900[59]	414 266[59]	39	...	...	...	...
Calithèa	115 150[59]	54 137[59]	61 013[59]	5	...	...	...	...
Iraclion	135 761[59]	66 956[59]	68 805[59]	52	...	...	...	...
Larissa	131 095[59]	64 000[59]	67 095[59]	88	...	...	...	...
Patrai	168 530[59]	82 981[59]	85 549[59]	57	...	...	...	...
Pésterion	146 743[59]	72 391[59]	74 352[59]	10	...	...	...	...
Pireas[59]	181 933	87 362	94 571	...	...	...	...	...
Thessaloniki[59]	385 406	180 122	205 284	...	...	...	...	...
Guernsey - Guernesey								
29 IV 2001 (CDJC)								
ST. PETER PORT	16 488	...	...	...	...	...	...	...
Holy See - Saint-Siège[60]								
1 VII 2000* (CDFC)								
VATICAN CITY	798[12]	529[12]	269[12]	0[61]	...	...	...	...
Hungary - Hongrie								
1 VII 2011 (ESDJ)								
BUDAPEST	1 736 863	794 463	942 401	525	2 558 672	1 190 897	1 367 775	2 538
Debrecen	207 805	96 163	111 643	462	243 225	113 697	129 528	805
Györ	131 416	61 550	69 866	175	190 023	90 347	99 676	783
Kecskemét	113 751	52 865	60 886	323	146 224	68 861	77 363	840
Miskolc	167 449	77 176	90 274	237	206 629	96 215	110 414	460
Nyiregyhaza	117 755	54 235	63 520	275	134 452	62 367	72 086	405
Pécs	157 261	71 915	85 347	163	182 322	84 306	98 016	430
Szeged	170 169	77 794	92 375	281	208 889	96 975	111 915	713
Székesfehérvar	101 833	47 436	54 397	171	127 001	60 022	66 979	543
Iceland - Islande[62]								
1 VII 2012 (ESDJ)								
REYKJAVIK	118 856[63]	58 964[63]	59 892[63]	274[64]	202 968[65]	100 815[65]	102 153[65]	1 044[64]

8. Population of capital cities and cities of 100 000 or more inhabitants: latest available year, 1993 - 2012
Population des capitales et des villes de 100 000 habitants ou plus : dernière année disponible, 1993 - 2012 (continued - suite)

Continent, country or area, date, code and city / Continent, pays ou zone, date, code et ville	City proper - Ville proprement dite				Urban agglomeration - Agglomération urbaine			
	Population			Surface area - Superficie (km²)	Population			Surface area - Superficie (km²)
	Both sexes - Les deux sexes	Male - Masculin	Female - Féminin		Both sexes - Les deux sexes	Male - Masculin	Female - Féminin	
EUROPE								
Ireland - Irlande								
10 IV 2011 (CDFC)								
Cork	119 230	58 812	60 418	40	198 582	97 463	101 119	...
DUBLIN	527 612	257 303	270 309	118	1 110 627	539 742	570 885	...
Isle of Man - Île de Man								
23 IV 2006 (CDJC)								
DOUGLAS	26 218	13 000	13 218	...	...	...	...	...
Italy - Italie								
1 VII 2011* (ESDJ)								
Ancona	103 017	49 000	54 017	123	...	...	...	...
Bari	319 915	153 402	166 513	116	...	...	...	...
Bergamo	119 943	56 009	63 934	40	...	...	...	...
Bologna	381 483	178 697	202 786	141	...	...	...	...
Bolzano	104 435	49 946	54 489	52	...	...	...	...
Brescia	194 094	91 320	102 774	91	...	...	...	...
Cagliari	156 188	72 241	83 947	86	...	...	...	...
Catania	292 366	137 478	154 888	181	...	...	...	...
Ferrara	135 407	63 206	72 201	404	...	...	...	...
Firenze	372 076	173 622	198 454	102	...	...	...	...
Foggia	152 522	73 322	79 201	508	...	...	...	...
Forli	118 568	57 146	61 422	228	...	...	...	...
Genova	607 442	285 487	321 956	244	...	...	...	...
Giugliano in Campania	118 536	58 336	60 200	94	...	...	...	...
Latina	119 948	57 735	62 213	278	...	...	...	...
Livorno	161 169	76 920	84 249	104	...	...	...	...
Messina	241 907	115 196	126 711	211	...	...	...	...
Milano	1 333 670	633 853	699 818	182	...	...	...	...
Modena	185 179	88 596	96 583	183	...	...	...	...
Monza	122 894	58 855	64 039	33	...	...	...	...
Napoli	958 157	454 744	503 413	117	...	...	...	...
Novara	105 095	50 443	54 652	103	...	...	...	...
Padova	214 149	100 535	113 614	93	...	...	...	...
Palermo	654 998	310 775	344 224	159	...	...	...	...
Parma	187 693	89 233	98 460	261	...	...	...	...
Perugia	168 740	80 407	88 333	450	...	...	...	...
Pescara	122 990	57 473	65 517	34	...	...	...	...
Piacenza	103 522	49 386	54 137	119	...	...	...	...
Prato	188 295	91 349	96 946	98	...	...	...	...
Ravenna	159 216	77 307	81 909	653	...	...	...	...
Reggio di Calabria	186 497	89 461	97 036	236	...	...	...	...
Reggio nell'Emilia	170 887	83 189	87 699	232	...	...	...	...
Rimini	143 938	68 884	75 054	135	...	...	...	...
ROMA	2 771 585	1 307 015	1 464 570	1 308	...	...	...	...
Salerno	138 869	64 071	74 799	59	...	...	...	...
Sassari	130 637	62 758	67 879	546	...	...	...	...
Siracusa	123 613	60 265	63 349	204	...	...	...	...
Taranto	191 113	90 582	100 532	210	...	...	...	...
Terni	113 369	53 420	59 949	212	...	...	...	...
Torino	906 672	430 944	475 728	130	...	...	...	...
Trento	116 682	55 831	60 851	158	...	...	...	...
Trieste	205 365	96 332	109 033	85	...	...	...	...
Venezia	270 737	127 848	142 889	416	...	...	...	...
Verona	264 063	125 346	138 717	207	...	...	...	...
Vicenza	115 791	55 052	60 740	81	...	...	...	...
Jersey								
11 III 2001 (CDJC)								
ST. HELIER	28 310	13 669	14 641	9	...	...	...	...
Latvia - Lettonie								
1 VII 2010 (ESDJ)								
Daugavpils	103 396	46 227	57 169	72	...	...	...	...
RIGA	703 260	312 393	390 867	304	...	...	...	...
Liechtenstein								
1 VII 2011 (ESDJ)								
VADUZ	5 229	2 528	2 701	17	...	...	...	...

Continent, country or area, date, code and city / Continent, pays ou zone, date, code et ville	City proper - Ville proprement dite				Urban agglomeration - Agglomération urbaine			
	Population			Surface area - Superficie (km²)	Population			Surface area - Superficie (km²)
	Both sexes - Les deux sexes	Male - Masculin	Female - Féminin		Both sexes - Les deux sexes	Male - Masculin	Female - Féminin	
EUROPE								
Lithuania - Lituanie								
1 III 2011 (CDJC)								
Kaunas	378 943	171 050	207 893	157	...	...	...	...
Klaipeda	192 954	89 521	103 433	98	...	...	...	...
Panevezhis	119 749	54 564	65 185	50	...	...	...	...
Shauliai	133 883	61 205	72 678	81	...	...	...	...
VILNIUS	542 287	247 097	295 190	401	...	...	...	...
Luxembourg								
1 I 2012* (ESDJ)								
LUXEMBOURG-VILLE	99 852	...	...	51	...	...	...	...
Malta - Malte								
1 I 2011 (ESDJ)								
VALLETTA	5 770	2 804	2 966	1	...	...	...	...
Monaco								
1 VII 2000 (ESDJ)								
MONACO	*32 020*	*15 544*	*16 476*	...	...	...	...	...
Montenegro - Monténégro								
1 VII 2009 (ESDJ)								
PODGORICA	180 810	88 381	92 429	1 441	...	...	...	...
Netherlands - Pays-Bas								
1 I 2011 (ESDJ)								
Almere	190 655	94 639	96 016	130	...	...	...	...
Amersfoort	146 592	71 979	74 613	63	175 201	85 980	89 221	122
AMSTERDAM	779 808	383 802	396 006	166	1 068 724	524 640	544 084	337
Apeldoorn	...	...	...	...	156 199	77 088	79 111	340
Arnhem	148 070	73 507	74 563	98	149 582	74 260	75 322	126
Breda	174 599	85 006	89 593	127	...	...	...	...
Dordrecht	118 810	58 526	60 284	79	236 734	116 326	120 408	139
Ede	108 285	53 146	55 139	318	...	...	...	...
Eindhoven	216 036	109 977	106 059	88	330 152	166 592	163 560	199
Emmen	109 259	54 040	55 219	337	...	...	...	...
Enschede	157 838	80 122	77 716	141	...	...	...	...
Geleen-Sittard	...	...	...	...	137 071	67 445	69 626	121
Groningen	189 991	94 064	95 927	78	208 506	102 801	105 705	124
Haarlem	150 670	73 260	77 410	29	199 006	96 039	102 967	94
Haarlemmermeer	143 374	71 310	72 064	179	...	...	...	...
Heerlen-Kerkrade	...	...	...	...	204 182	100 807	103 375	109
Leiden	117 915	57 527	60 388	22	253 200	123 679	129 521	77
Maastricht	119 664	57 538	62 126	57	...	...	...	...
Nijmegen	164 223	78 582	85 641	54	...	...	...	...
Rotterdam	610 386	300 319	310 067	206	1 003 088	492 492	510 596	329
s-Gravenhage	...	...	...	...	639 652	312 813	326 839	180
s-Hertogenbosch	140 786	69 200	71 586	84	166 440	81 951	84 489	118
The Hague	495 083	244 040	251 043	82	...	...	...	...
Tilburg	206 240	102 366	103 874	117	229 047	113 670	115 377	159
Utrecht	311 367	150 571	160 796	95	469 712	228 404	241 308	167
Zaanstad	190 655	94 639	96 016	74	...	...	...	...
Zoetermeer	146 592	71 979	74 613	35	...	...	...	...
Zwolle	120 355	58 697	61 658	112	...	...	...	...
Norway - Norvège								
1 VII 2011 (ESDJ)								
Bergen	262 077	131 098	130 980	445	...	...	...	...
OSLO	606 258	300 639	305 619	426	...	...	...	...
Stavanger	126 764	63 763	63 001	68	...	...	...	...
Trondheim	174 917	87 817	87 101	322	...	...	...	...
Poland - Pologne[66]								
1 VII 2011 (ESDJ)								
Bialystok	294 197	138 249	155 948	102[11]	...	...	...	...
Bielsko-Biala	174 541	82 269	92 272	125[11]	...	...	...	...
Bydgoszcz	363 607	171 119	192 488	176[11]	...	...	...	...
Bytom	176 705	84 878	91 827	69[11]	...	...	...	...
Chorzów	111 662	53 196	58 466	33[11]	...	...	...	...
Czestochowa	236 581	111 261	125 320	160[11]	...	...	...	...
Dabrowa Górnicza	125 751	60 576	65 175	189[11]	...	...	...	...
Elblag	124 488	59 676	64 812	80[11]	...	...	...	...

8. Population of capital cities and cities of 100 000 or more inhabitants: latest available year, 1993 - 2012
Population des capitales et des villes de 100 000 habitants ou plus : dernière année disponible, 1993 - 2012 (continued - suite)

Continent, country or area, date, code and city / Continent, pays ou zone, date, code et ville	City proper - Ville proprement dite				Urban agglomeration - Agglomération urbaine			
	Population			Surface area - Superficie (km²)	Population			Surface area - Superficie (km²)
	Both sexes - Les deux sexes	Male - Masculin	Female - Féminin		Both sexes - Les deux sexes	Male - Masculin	Female - Féminin	
EUROPE								
Poland - Pologne[66]								
1 VII 2011 (ESDJ)								
Gdansk	460 435	218 356	242 079	262[11]	...	...	...	...
Gdynia	249 081	118 472	130 609	135[11]	...	...	...	...
Gliwice	187 366	90 351	97 015	134[11]	...	...	...	...
Gorzów Wielkopolski	124 605	59 414	65 191	86[11]	...	...	...	...
Kalisz	105 278	49 019	56 259	69[11]	...	...	...	...
Katowice	310 434	147 693	162 741	165[11]	...	...	...	...
Kielce	202 166	95 465	106 701	110[11]	...	...	...	...
Koszalin	109 319	51 655	57 664	98[11]	...	...	...	...
Kraków	758 241	353 821	404 420	327[11]	...	...	...	...
Legnica	103 174	48 861	54 313	56[11]	...	...	...	...
Lódz	727 884	331 106	396 778	293[11]	...	...	...	...
Lublin	349 060	160 835	188 225	147[11]	...	...	...	...
Olsztyn	175 317	81 777	93 540	88[11]	...	...	...	...
Opole	122 563	57 341	65 222	97[11]	...	...	...	...
Plock	124 516	59 033	65 483	88[11]	...	...	...	...
Poznan	554 290	258 278	296 012	262[11]	...	...	...	...
Radom	221 066	105 223	115 843	112[11]	...	...	...	...
Ruda Slaska	143 255	69 608	73 647	78[11]	...	...	...	...
Rybnik	140 988	68 870	72 118	148[11]	...	...	...	...
Rzeszów	179 634	84 849	94 785	117[11]	...	...	...	...
Sosnowiec	216 061	102 613	113 448	91[11]	...	...	...	...
Szczecin	409 906	195 158	214 748	301[11]	...	...	...	...
Tarnów	113 838	53 832	60 006	72[11]	...	...	...	...
Torun	205 041	95 370	109 671	116[11]	...	...	...	...
Tychy	129 364	62 597	66 767	82[11]	...	...	...	...
Walbrzych	120 504	56 904	63 600	85[11]	...	...	...	...
WARSZAWA	1 703 163	781 541	921 622	517[11]	...	...	...	...
Wloclawek	116 685	55 107	61 578	84[11]	...	...	...	...
Wroclaw	630 583	294 469	336 114	293[11]	...	...	...	...
Zabrze	180 860	87 497	93 363	80[11]	...	...	...	...
Zielona Góra	119 119	56 033	63 086	58[11]	...	...	...	...
Portugal								
1 VII 2011* (ESDJ)								
Amadora	175 220	82 348	92 873	24	...	...	...	...
LISBOA	547 696	250 942	296 754	85	...	...	...	...
Porto	237 461	108 038	129 423	41	...	...	...	...
Republic of Moldova - République de Moldova								
1 I 2011 (ESDJ)								
Balti (Beltsy)	143 645	65 919	77 726	41	148 551	68 262	80 289	78
CHIŞINĂU (KISHINEV)	664 686	309 660	355 026	123	787 900	370 264	417 636	572
Romania - Roumanie								
1 VII 2011* (ESDJ)								
Arad	164 208	76 628	87 580	253	...	...	...	...
Bacau	174 182	82 802	91 380	43	...	...	...	...
Baia Mare	137 455	65 522	71 933	233	...	...	...	...
Botosani	114 799	54 734	60 065	41	...	...	...	...
Braila	208 464	98 988	109 476	44	...	...	...	...
Brasov	275 901	130 672	145 229	267	...	...	...	...
BUCURESTI	1 919 352	894 482	1 024 870	238	...	...	...	...
Buzau	130 320	61 878	68 442	81	...	...	...	...
Cluj-Napoca	301 913	141 498	160 415	180	...	...	...	...
Constanta	299 824	140 369	159 455	125	...	...	...	...
Craiova	297 510	141 315	156 195	81	...	...	...	...
Drobeta Turnu-Severin	105 232	50 611	54 621	55	...	...	...	...
Galati	287 046	138 065	148 981	246	...	...	...	...
Iasi	302 971	142 073	160 898	94	...	...	...	...
Oradea	204 358	95 811	108 547	116	...	...	...	...
Piatra Neamt	105 892	49 925	55 967	77	...	...	...	...
Pitesti	165 733	78 361	87 372	41	...	...	...	...
Ploiesti	225 636	105 731	119 905	58	...	...	...	...
Rimnicu Vilcea	110 697	52 708	57 989	90	...	...	...	...

8. Population of capital cities and cities of 100 000 or more inhabitants: latest available year, 1993 - 2012
Population des capitales et des villes de 100 000 habitants ou plus : dernière année disponible, 1993 - 2012 (continued - suite)

Continent, country or area, date, code and city Continent, pays ou zone, date, code et ville	City proper - Ville proprement dite				Urban agglomeration - Agglomération urbaine			
	Population			Surface area - Superficie (km²)	Population			Surface area - Superficie (km²)
	Both sexes - Les deux sexes	Male - Masculin	Female - Féminin		Both sexes - Les deux sexes	Male - Masculin	Female - Féminin	
EUROPE								
Romania - Roumanie								
1 VII 2011* (ESDJ)								
Satu-Mare	110 930	52 234	58 696	150	...	...	...	...
Sibiu	154 224	72 217	82 007	122	...	...	...	...
Suceava	106 682	50 947	55 735	52	...	...	...	...
Timisoara	307 561	143 145	164 416	122	...	...	...	...
Tirgu-Mures	143 221	67 475	75 746	49	...	...	...	...
Russian Federation - Fédération de Russie								
1 VII 2011 (ESDJ)								
Abakan	166 666	76 301	90 365	...	...	...	...	...
Achinsk	108 705	48 448	60 257	...	...	...	...	...
Almetievsk	147 095	68 909	78 186	...	...	...	...	...
Anapa	...	...	...	...	150 843	...	...	...
Angarsk	232 958	105 955	127 003	...	...	...	...	...
Arkhangelsk	349 088	155 990	193 098	...	356 073	...	...	...
Armavir	189 576	86 916	102 660	...	208 698	...	...	...
Artem (Primorskiy Krai)	102 635	49 050	53 585	...	112 144	...	...	...
Arzamas	105 958	47 484	58 474	...	...	...	...	...
Astrakhan	522 893	239 389	283 504	...	...	...	...	...
Balakovo	198 446	88 808	109 638	...	...	...	...	...
Balashikha	219 241	107 546	111 695	...	228 914	...	...	...
Barnaul	617 337	275 337	342 000	...	...	...	...	...
Bataisk	113 368	53 567	59 801	...	...	...	...	...
Belgorod	361 883	163 632	198 251	...	...	...	...	...
Belovo	...	...	...	...	133 446	...	...	...
Berezniki	155 468	69 100	86 368	...	...	...	...	...
Biisk	208 710	93 050	115 660	...	...	...	...	...
Blagoveshchensk (Amurskaya oblast)	215 057	96 793	118 264	...	220 477	...	...	...
Bor	...	...	...	...	121 378	...	...	...
Bratsk	245 136	110 840	134 296	...	...	...	...	...
Bryansk	413 914	184 456	229 458	...	433 297	...	...	...
Cheboksary	457 820	204 687	253 133	...	468 327	...	...	...
Chelyabinsk	1 137 283	508 783	628 500	...	...	...	...	...
Cherepovets	313 775	142 392	171 383	...	...	...	...	...
Cherkessk	128 139	56 275	71 864	...	...	...	...	...
Chita	326 328	150 875	175 453	...	326 814	...	...	...
Derbent	119 396	57 452	61 944	...	...	...	...	...
Dimitrovgrad	121 875	56 412	65 463	...	...	...	...	...
Domodedovo	...	...	...	...	138 181	...	...	...
Dzerzhinsk (Nizhegorodskaya oblast)	239 822	105 975	133 847	...	250 090	...	...	...
Ekaterinburg	1 365 266	610 874	754 392	...	1 398 690	...	...	...
Elektrostal	155 477	70 716	84 761	...	...	...	...	...
Elets	107 989	49 042	58 947	...	...	...	...	...
Elista	103 815	47 255	56 560	...	108 349	...	...	...
Engels	205 159	93 744	111 415	...	...	...	...	...
Esentuky	101 289	45 111	56 178	...	...	...	...	...
Groznyi	273 906	135 137	138 769	...	...	...	...	...
Gubkin	...	...	...	...	121 852	...	...	...
Hasaviurt	131 902	63 330	68 572	...	...	...	...	...
Irkutsk	593 898	265 632	328 266	...	...	...	...	...
Ivanovo	408 614	179 898	228 716	...	...	...	...	...
Izhevsk	628 495	280 602	347 893	...	...	...	...	...
Kaliningrad (Kaliningradskaya oblast)	432 536	198 757	233 779	...	...	...	...	...
Kaluga	325 436	144 305	181 131	...	340 855	...	...	...
Kamensk-Uralsky	173 876	77 949	95 927	...	175 743	...	...	...
Kamyshin	118 629	54 450	64 179	...	...	...	...	...
Kaspiysk	100 970	48 724	52 246	...	...	...	...	...
Kazan	1 153 366	513 105	640 261	...	...	...	...	...
Kemerovo	534 494	238 990	295 504	...	...	...	...	...
Khabarovsk	581 665	269 749	311 906	...	...	...	...	...
Khimki	212 173	96 376	115 797	...	...	...	...	...
Kirov	476 046	209 201	266 845	...	500 694	...	...	...
Kiselevsk	...	...	...	...	102 261	...	...	...
Kislovodsk	128 883	58 568	70 315	...	135 693	...	...	...
Kolomna	144 848	66 375	78 473	...	...	...	...	...

Continent, country or area, date, code and city / Continent, pays ou zone, date, code et ville	City proper - Ville proprement dite				Urban agglomeration - Agglomération urbaine			
	Population			Surface area - Superficie (km²)	Population			Surface area - Superficie (km²)
	Both sexes - Les deux sexes	Male - Masculin	Female - Féminin		Both sexes - Les deux sexes	Male - Masculin	Female - Féminin	
EUROPE								
Russian Federation - Fédération de Russie								
1 VII 2011 (ESDJ)								
Komsomolsk-na-Amure	261 797	121 615	140 182	...	...	...	...	...
Kopeysk	138 043	65 672	72 370	...	140 178	...	...	...
Korolev (Moskovskaya oblast)	184 496	83 233	101 263	...	...	...	...	...
Kostroma	268 964	119 893	149 071	...	...	...	...	...
Kovrov	144 219	65 444	78 775	...	...	...	...	...
Krasnodar	755 210	341 970	413 240	...	842 611	...	...	...
Krasnogorsk	120 428	54 057	66 371	...	...	...	...	...
Krasnoyarsk	988 061	446 959	541 102	...	...	...	...	...
Kurgan	330 351	147 907	182 444	...	...	...	...	...
Kursk	420 022	186 444	233 578	...	...	...	...	...
Kyzyl	111 119	51 596	59 523	...	...	...	...	...
Leninsk-Kuznetsky	100 975	46 139	54 836	...	103 224	...	...	...
Lipetsk	508 478	230 392	278 086	...	...	...	...	...
Lyubertsy	174 763	78 645	96 118	...	...	...	...	...
Magadan	...	...	...	...	102 351	...	...	...
Magnitogorsk	408 744	185 825	222 919	...	...	...	...	...
Maikop	144 271	64 327	79 944	...	166 685	...	...	...
Makhachkala	573 673	271 286	302 387	...	699 259	...	...	...
Mezhdurechensk	101 150	46 940	54 210	...	103 389	...	...	...
Miass	151 268	68 045	83 223	...	166 274	...	...	...
MOSKVA	11 577 022	5 337 790	6 239 232	...	...	...	...	...
Murmansk	305 969	140 731	165 238	...	...	...	...	...
Murom	114 955	50 986	63 969	...	124 142	...	...	...
Mytishchi	174 174	79 114	95 060	...	...	...	...	...
Naberezhnye Tchelny	515 205	236 632	278 573	...	...	...	...	...
Nakhodka	159 224	75 257	83 967	...	160 242	...	...	...
Naltchik	239 614	106 877	132 737	...	265 521	...	...	...
Neftekamsk	122 572	56 958	65 614	...	134 419	...	...	...
Nefteyugansk	124 229	61 103	63 126	...	...	...	...	...
Nevinnomyssk	118 219	53 735	64 484	...	...	...	...	...
Nizhnekamsk	234 508	110 907	123 601	...	...	...	...	...
Nizhnevartovsk	255 634	123 529	132 105	...	...	...	...	...
Nizhny Novgorod	1 253 524	550 487	703 037	...	1 262 589	...	...	...
Nizhny Tagil	360 123	163 536	196 587	...	363 718	...	...	...
Noginsk	100 929	45 297	55 632	...	...	...	...	...
Norilsk	176 242	88 220	88 022	...	...	...	...	...
Novocheboksarsk	124 071	57 209	66 862	...	124 366	...	...	...
Novocherkassk	169 008	80 324	88 684	...	...	...	...	...
Novokuybishevsk	107 947	48 719	59 228	...	110 229	...	...	...
Novokuznetsk	548 858	247 290	301 568	...	...	...	...	...
Novomoskovsk (Tulskaya oblast)	130 672	58 511	72 161	...	143 097	...	...	...
Novorossiysk	244 649	129 066	115 583	...	300 982	...	...	...
Novoshakhtinsk	110 636	50 535	60 101	...	...	...	...	...
Novosibirsk	1 487 029	682 948	804 081	...	...	...	...	...
Novotroitsk	...	...	...	...	104 477	...	...	...
Novy Urengoy	108 811	55 189	53 622	...	...	...	...	...
Noyabrsk	109 912	54 048	55 864	...	...	...	...	...
Obninsk	105 052	48 043	57 009	...	...	...	...	...
Odintsovo	138 118	63 637	74 481	...	...	...	...	...
Oktyabrsky	110 162	51 476	58 686	...	...	...	...	...
Omsk	1 155 352	525 235	630 117	...	...	...	...	...
Orekhovo-Zuevo	120 977	53 048	67 929	...	...	...	...	...
Orel	318 114	139 629	178 485	...	...	...	...	...
Orenburg	551 747	251 413	300 334	...	567 321	...	...	...
Orsk	238 804	106 775	132 029	...	242 987	...	...	...
Penza	518 785	234 016	284 769	...	...	...	...	...
Perm	996 092	439 296	556 798	...	996 102	...	...	...
Pervouralsk	124 995	55 909	69 086	...	...	...	...	...
Petropavlovsk-Kamchatsky	179 748	87 633	92 115	...	...	...	...	...
Petrozavodsk	263 679	117 097	146 582	...	...	...	...	...
Podolsk	191 009	85 300	105 709	...	...	...	...	...
Prokopyevsk	208 419	93 015	115 404	...	...	...	...	...
Pskov	203 428	91 671	111 757	...	...	...	...	...

8. Population of capital cities and cities of 100 000 or more inhabitants: latest available year, 1993 - 2012
Population des capitales et des villes de 100 000 habitants ou plus : dernière année disponible, 1993 - 2012 (continued - suite)

Continent, country or area, date, code and city / Continent, pays ou zone, date, code et ville	City proper - Ville proprement dite				Urban agglomeration - Agglomération urbaine			
	Population			Surface area - Superficie (km²)	Population			Surface area - Superficie (km²)
	Both sexes - Les deux sexes	Male - Masculin	Female - Féminin		Both sexes - Les deux sexes	Male - Masculin	Female - Féminin	
EUROPE								
Russian Federation - Fédération de Russie								
1 VII 2011 (ESDJ)								
Pushkino	103 076	46 263	56 813	...	...	...	...	...
Pyatigorsk	143 224	64 140	79 084	...	211 718	...	...	...
Rostov-na-Donu	1 093 701	497 510	596 191	...	...	...	...	...
Rubtsovsk	146 629	69 273	77 356	...	...	...	...	...
Ryazan	525 108	236 834	288 274	...	...	...	...	...
Rybinsk	199 229	88 672	110 557	...	...	...	...	...
Salavat	155 786	72 908	82 878	...	...	...	...	...
Samara (Samarskaya oblast)	1 167 842	522 025	645 817	...	1 167 948	...	...	...
Saransk	298 014	132 434	165 580	...	326 000	...	...	...
Sarapyul	100 931	44 942	55 989	...	...	...	...	...
Saratov	837 199	373 096	464 103	...	...	...	...	...
Sergiev Posad	110 276	49 458	60 818	...	...	...	...	...
Serov	...	...	...	...	108 192	...	...	...
Serpukhov	126 775	57 473	69 302	...	...	...	...	...
Severodvinsk	190 983	88 223	102 760	...	192 221	...	...	...
Seversk	109 089	50 441	58 648	...	115 824	...	...	...
Shakhty	239 208	108 045	131 163	...	...	...	...	...
Shchelkovo	110 159	50 265	59 894	...	...	...	...	...
Smolensk	328 295	145 873	182 422	...	...	...	...	...
Sochi	352 293	159 191	193 102	...	429 560	...	...	...
St. Petersburg	4 926 282	2 212 121	2 714 161	...	...	...	...	...
Stary Oskol	220 768	101 057	119 711	...	256 465	...	...	...
Stavropol	401 894	184 801	217 093	...	402 101	...	...	...
Sterlitamak	274 019	125 103	148 916	...	...	...	...	...
Surgut	312 566	150 098	162 468	...	...	...	...	...
Syktivkar	237 166	107 157	130 009	...	253 044	...	...	...
Syzran	178 294	80 207	98 087	...	179 091	...	...	...
Taganrog	256 888	114 998	141 890	...	...	...	...	...
Tambov	280 485	125 530	154 955	...	...	...	...	...
Tobolsk	...	...	...	...	102 754	...	...	...
Tolyatti	719 599	331 520	388 079	...	...	...	...	...
Tomsk	532 624	247 197	285 427	...	554 010	...	...	...
Tula	499 933	221 011	278 922	...	...	...	...	...
Tver	405 474	179 124	226 350	...	...	...	...	...
Tyumen	597 283	275 279	322 004	...	620 207	...	...	...
Ufa	1 068 956	482 805	586 151	...	1 078 309	...	...	...
Uhta	99 874	47 543	52 331	...	121 850	...	...	...
Ulan-Ude	408 757	189 535	219 222	...	...	...	...	...
Ulyanovsk	614 324	277 882	336 442	...	637 091	...	...	...
Ussuriisk	159 898	77 740	82 158	...	185 945	...	...	...
Velikiy Novgorod	219 311	95 415	123 896	...	...	...	...	...
Vladikavkaz (Osetinskaya ASSR)	310 817	140 825	169 992	...	329 203	...	...	...
Vladimir	345 928	153 888	192 040	...	348 553	...	...	...
Vladivostok	594 351	279 432	314 919	...	619 351	...	...	...
Volgodonsk	170 484	78 289	92 195	...	...	...	...	...
Volgograd	1 019 778	460 738	559 040	...	...	...	...	...
Vologda	303 357	134 381	168 976	...	311 226	...	...	...
Volzhsky	314 183	145 205	168 978	...	327 562	...	...	...
Voronezh	985 390	441 524	543 866	...	...	...	...	...
Yakutsk	274 429	129 205	145 224	...	290 911	...	...	...
Yaroslavl	593 265	260 353	332 912	...	...	...	...	...
Yoshkar-Ola	250 867	112 555	138 312	...	261 377	...	...	...
Yuzhno-Sakhalinsk	183 959	87 086	96 873	...	191 072	...	...	...
Zheleznodorozhny	133 865	60 542	73 323	...	...	...	...	...
Zhukovsky	105 524	48 518	57 006	...	...	...	...	...
Zlatoust	174 214	78 649	95 565	...	176 411	...	...	...
San Marino - Saint-Marin								
1 VII 2004 (ESDF)								
SAN MARINO	4 464	2 168	2 296	...	...	...	...	...
Serbia - Serbie[67]								
1 VII 2011 (ESDJ)								
BEOGRAD (BELGRADE)	1 346 930	626 293	720 637	389	1 647 490[68]	776 229[68]	871 261[68]	3 215[68]
Kragujevac	147 081	71 023	76 058	83	174 100[68]	84 451[68]	89 649[68]	847[68]

8. Population of capital cities and cities of 100 000 or more inhabitants: latest available year, 1993 - 2012
Population des capitales et des villes de 100 000 habitants ou plus : dernière année disponible, 1993 - 2012 (continued - suite)

Continent, country or area, date, code and city / Continent, pays ou zone, date, code et ville	City proper - Ville proprement dite				Urban agglomeration - Agglomération urbaine			
	Population			Surface area - Superficie (km²)	Population			Surface area - Superficie (km²)
	Both sexes - Les deux sexes	Male - Masculin	Female - Féminin		Both sexes - Les deux sexes	Male - Masculin	Female - Féminin	
EUROPE								
Serbia - Serbie[67] 1 VII 2011 (ESDJ)								
Kraljevo	64 315	30 957	33 358	22	117 701[68]	57 674[68]	60 027[68]	1 529[68]
Kruševac	57 252	27 207	30 045	11	126 012[68]	61 346[68]	64 666[68]	854[68]
Leskovac	67 097	32 668	34 429	24	146 640[68]	73 077[68]	73 563[68]	1 025[68]
Niš	182 801	87 773	95 028	43	255 612[68]	124 639[68]	130 973[68]	597[68]
Novi Sad	265 387	123 765	141 622	103	333 268[68]	157 371[68]	175 897[68]	699[68]
Pancevo	90 027	43 196	46 831	162	123 021[68]	59 797[68]	63 224[68]	756[68]
Šabac	54 063	25 523	28 540	31	117 388[68]	57 444[68]	59 944[68]	795[68]
Smederevo	63 068	30 605	32 463	40	107 170[68]	52 803[68]	54 367[68]	481[68]
Subotica	106 468	50 758	55 710	164	143 179[68]	68 949[68]	74 230[68]	1 007[68]
Zrenjanin	76 336	36 543	39 793	50	123 536[68]	60 175[68]	63 361[68]	1 327[68]
Slovakia - Slovaquie 21 V 2011 (CDJC)								
BRATISLAVA	411 228	192 256	218 972	368[11]	...	...	...	...
Kosice	240 433	115 449	124 984	244[11]	...	...	...	...
Slovenia - Slovénie 1 I 2011 (CDJC)								
LJUBLJANA	272 220	130 862	141 358	164	274 319	131 927	142 392	171
Maribor	95 171	46 153	49 018	41	109 118	53 049	56 069	99
Spain - Espagne 1 XI 2011 (CDJC)								
A Coruña	245 053	113 916	131 137	38	...	...	...	...
Albacete	171 999	84 557	87 442	1 126	...	...	...	...
Alcalá de Henares	200 505	99 931	100 574	88	...	...	...	...
Alcobendas	110 351	53 489	56 861	45	...	...	...	...
Alcorcón	167 217	81 956	85 261	34	...	...	...	...
Algeciras	117 695	61 123	56 572	86	...	...	...	...
Alicante	329 325	159 958	169 367	201	...	...	...	...
Almería	189 680	92 329	97 351	296	...	...	...	...
Badajoz	151 214	73 485	77 729	1 470	...	...	...	...
Badalona	219 241	109 177	110 064	21	...	...	...	...
Baracaldo	100 064	48 562	51 502	...	...	...	...	...
Barcelona	1 611 013	763 066	847 947	98	...	...	...	...
Bilbao	351 356	166 117	185 239	41	...	...	...	...
Burgos	178 864	85 879	92 985	107	...	...	...	...
Cádiz	124 014	58 819	65 195	12	...	...	...	...
Cartagena	215 757	108 806	106 951	558	...	...	...	...
Castellón de la Plana	176 298	86 605	89 692	109	...	...	...	...
Córdoba	328 326	157 957	170 369	1 255	...	...	...	...
Donostia - San Sebastián	185 512	87 060	98 452	61	...	...	...	...
Dos Hermanas	128 433	63 413	65 020	161	...	...	...	...
Elche	227 417	113 242	114 176	326	...	...	...	...
Fuenlabrada	196 986	98 989	97 997	39	...	...	...	...
Getafe	168 642	83 333	85 310	78	...	...	...	...
Gijón	276 969	131 256	145 714	182	...	...	...	...
Granada	241 003	112 343	128 660	88	...	...	...	...
Hospitalet de Llobregat	256 509	125 017	131 493	14	...	...	...	...
Huelva	147 808	71 287	76 522	151	...	...	...	...
Jaén	116 469	56 343	60 126	424	...	...	...	...
Jérez de la Frontera	211 784	103 803	107 981	1 188	...	...	...	...
Leganés	185 758	91 314	94 444	43	...	...	...	...
León	131 411	60 283	71 128	39	...	...	...	...
Lleida	137 283	67 934	69 349	212	...	...	...	...
Logroño	152 698	73 445	79 253	80	...	...	...	...
MADRID	3 198 645	1 495 337	1 703 308	606	...	...	...	...
Málaga	561 435	270 275	291 160	395	...	...	...	...
Marbella	135 124	65 778	69 346	117	...	...	...	...
Mataró	123 367	61 511	61 856	22	...	...	...	...
Móstoles	203 493	100 562	102 931	45	...	...	...	...
Murcia	437 667	215 625	222 042	886	...	...	...	...
Ourense	107 314	49 523	57 791	85	...	...	...	...
Oviedo	225 005	105 004	120 001	187	...	...	...	...
Palma	402 044	196 784	205 259	...	...	...	...	...

8. Population of capital cities and cities of 100 000 or more inhabitants: latest available year, 1993 - 2012
Population des capitales et des villes de 100 000 habitants ou plus : dernière année disponible, 1993 - 2012 (continued - suite)

Continent, country or area, date, code and city / Continent, pays ou zone, date, code et ville	City proper - Ville proprement dite				Urban agglomeration - Agglomération urbaine			
	Population			Surface area - Superficie (km²)	Population			Surface area - Superficie (km²)
	Both sexes - Les deux sexes	Male - Masculin	Female - Féminin		Both sexes - Les deux sexes	Male - Masculin	Female - Féminin	
EUROPE								
Spain - Espagne								
1 XI 2011 (CDJC)								
Palmas de Gran Canaria	381 271	185 254	196 018	101	...	...	...	...
Pamplona	195 943	93 561	102 383	25	...	...	...	...
Parla	122 045	61 834	60 210	25	...	...	...	...
Reus	106 849	52 502	54 347	53	...	...	...	...
Sabadell	206 949	101 041	105 908	38	...	...	...	...
Salamanca	151 658	69 841	81 817	39	...	...	...	...
San Cristóbal de La Laguna	152 025	74 362	77 663	102	...	...	...	...
Santa Coloma de Gramanet	119 391	60 352	59 039	7	...	...	...	...
Santa Cruz de Tenerife	204 476	98 071	106 405	43	...	...	...	...
Santander	178 095	82 373	95 722	35	...	...	...	...
Sevilla	698 042	332 204	365 838	141	...	...	...	...
Tarragona	133 223	65 524	67 700	62	...	...	...	...
Telde	101 080	50 293	50 787	...	...	...	...	...
Terrassa	214 406	106 179	108 227	70	...	...	...	...
Torrejón de Ardoz	123 213	61 277	61 937	33	...	...	...	...
Valencia	792 054	379 286	412 768	135	...	...	...	...
Valladolid	311 682	147 714	163 968	197	...	...	...	...
Vigo	295 623	140 919	154 704	109	...	...	...	...
Vitoria-Gasteiz	240 753	118 645	122 109	277	...	...	...	...
Zaragoza	678 115	328 320	349 795	973	...	...	...	...
Sweden - Suède								
1 VII 2007 (ESDJ)								
Göteborg	491 630	242 916	248 714	449	...	...	...	...
Helsingborg	124 188	60 672	63 516	346	...	...	...	...
Jönköping	122 952	60 462	62 490	1 485	...	...	...	...
Linköping	139 474	70 239	69 235	1 431	...	...	...	...
Malmö	278 523	135 997	142 526	154	...	...	...	...
Norrköping	126 072	62 323	63 749	1 491	...	...	...	...
Orebro	129 703	63 123	66 581	1 371	...	...	...	...
STOCKHOLM	789 024	384 243	404 781	187	...	...	...	...
Umeå	111 503	55 549	55 955	2 316	...	...	...	...
Uppsala	186 364	91 149	95 215	2 465	...	...	...	...
Västerås	133 324	66 056	67 269	956	...	...	...	...
Switzerland - Suisse								
1 VII 2011 (ESDJ)								
Baden-Brugg	28 522	14 393	14 130	19	118 268	59 001	59 268	124
Bâle	163 866	78 689	85 177	24	499 144	242 267	256 877	481
BERNE	125 031	59 532	65 500	52	354 428	170 895	183 533	481
Fribourg	35 289	17 283	18 006	9	106 086	52 673	53 413	212
Genève	187 852	89 798	98 054	16	528 585	255 766	272 820	457
Lausanne	128 602	61 429	67 173	41	339 487	164 685	174 802	312
Lugano	54 909	26 124	28 785	32	133 880	64 369	69 511	228
Luzern	77 792	37 089	40 703	16	210 809	103 057	107 752	198
Olten-Zofingen	27 882	13 629	14 253	23	111 291	55 334	55 957	183
St. Gallen	73 232	35 561	37 671	39	150 794	73 907	76 888	175
Winterthur	102 192	49 810	52 382	68	141 135	69 209	71 926	151
Zug	26 614	13 408	13 206	22	109 713	55 311	54 403	180
Zürich	374 924	184 986	189 938	88	1 196 282	593 017	603 265	1 086
TFYR of Macedonia - L'ex-R. y. de Macédoine								
1 VII 2010 (ESDF)								
SKOPJE	531 444	260 462	270 982	...	...	...	...	...
Ukraine								
1 I 2012 (ESDJ)								
Alchevsk	111 589	51 076	60 513	49	...	...	...	...
Belaya Tserkov (Bila Crkva)	206 622	95 187	111 435	34	...	...	...	...
Berdyansk	116 778	51 782	64 996	83	119 909	53 270	66 639	90
Cherkassy	283 688	129 730	153 958	67	284 445	130 122	154 323	78
Chernigov	290 903	133 869	157 034	78	...	...	...	...
Chernovtsy	252 171	115 470	136 701	153	...	...	...	...
Dneprodzerzhinsk	242 096	108 790	133 306	118	248 992	111 893	137 099	138
Dnepropetrovsk	989 452	448 304	541 148	387	991 830	449 461	542 369	405
Donetsk (Donestskaya oblast)	946 376	418 136	528 240	363	962 445	425 450	536 995	571
Enakievo (Yenakievo)	84 499	37 423	47 076	67	133 428	59 872	73 556	425

8. Population of capital cities and cities of 100 000 or more inhabitants: latest available year, 1993 - 2012
Population des capitales et des villes de 100 000 habitants ou plus : dernière année disponible, 1993 - 2012 (continued - suite)

Continent, country or area, date, code and city / Continent, pays ou zone, date, code et ville	City proper - Ville proprement dite				Urban agglomeration - Agglomération urbaine			
	Population			Surface area - Superficie (km²)	Population			Surface area - Superficie (km²)
	Both sexes - Les deux sexes	Male - Masculin	Female - Féminin		Both sexes - Les deux sexes	Male - Masculin	Female - Féminin	

EUROPE

Ukraine
1 I 2012 (ESDJ)

Evpatoriya (Yevpatoriya)	104 252	46 494	57 758	43	120 352	53 856	66 496	66
Gorlovka	256 691	114 981	141 710	186	277 325	124 306	153 019	422
Ivano-Frankovsk	221 807	104 053	117 754	37	238 972	112 004	126 968	84
Kamyanetsk Podilsky	102 265	47 741	54 524	29	...	...	...	...
Kertch	147 139	66 307	80 832	108	...	...	...	...
Kharkov	1 421 795	650 982	770 813	306	...	...	...	...
Kherson	297 064	133 112	163 952	65	334 141	150 416	183 725	423
Khmelnitsky (Hmilnyk)	260 869	120 612	140 257	86	...	...	...	...
KIEV	2 772 951	1 279 505	1 493 446	836	...	...	...	...
Kirovograd	231 778	104 569	127 209	96	239 891	108 265	131 626	103
Kramatorsk	165 017	73 440	91 577	77	198 660	89 013	109 647	356
Krasny Lutch	83 414	38 478	44 936	58	125 310	58 101	67 209	154
Krementchug	225 454	102 407	123 047	96	...	...	...	...
Kryvy Rig	658 689	296 589	362 100	430	661 501	298 015	363 486	431
Lugansk	423 712	187 679	236 033	257	462 955	206 192	256 763	286
Lutsk	209 980	94 671	115 309	42	...	...	...	...
Lvov	723 175	338 011	385 164	149	750 291	350 885	399 406	171
Lysychansk	104 828	47 313	57 515	76	120 700	54 537	66 163	96
Makeyevka	354 427	159 754	194 673	185	393 083	177 693	215 390	426
Mariupol	461 062	209 473	251 589	150	482 904	219 742	263 162	244
Melitopol	156 732	70 819	85 913	43	...	...	...	...
Mykolaiv (Nikolaevskaya oblast)	492 537	222 865	269 672	260	...	...	...	...
Nikopol	122 054	54 388	67 666	50	...	...	...	...
Odessa	990 499	460 825	529 674	162	...	...	...	...
Pavlograd	111 413	51 247	60 166	59	...	...	...	...
Poltava	290 568	132 999	157 569	104	...	...	...	...
Rivne	246 752	112 941	133 811	58	...	...	...	...
Sevastopol	338 714	154 022	184 692	...	379 271	172 764	206 507	864
Severodonetsk	110 216	49 149	61 067	32	120 615	54 094	66 521	58
Simferopol	330 233	145 414	184 819	107	354 792	156 665	198 127	107
Slavyansk	115 882	50 398	65 484	61	134 885	59 109	75 776	74
Sumy	268 861	121 257	147 604	111	271 747	122 630	149 117	146
Ternopol	215 818	99 890	115 928	59	...	...	...	...
Uzhgorod	114 996	53 360	61 636	32	...	...	...	...
Vinnutsya	368 976	168 758	200 218	69	...	...	...	...
Yevpatoriya	104 252	46 494	57 758	43	120 352	53 856	66 496	66
Zaporozhye	768 691	347 037	421 654	278	...	...	...	...
Zhitomir	270 638	124 670	145 968	61	...	...	...	...

United Kingdom of Great Britain and Northern Ireland - Royaume-Uni de Grande-Bretagne et d'Irlande du Nord[69]
29 IV 2001 (CDFC)

Aberdeen	...	...	...	...	212 125	103 818	108 307	...
Aberdeenshire	...	...	...	...	226 871	112 470	114 401	...
Aldershot	...	...	...	...	243 344	121 127	122 217	...
Angus	...	...	...	...	108 400	52 458	55 942	...
Basildon/North Benfleet	...	...	...	...	101 492	48 649	52 843	...
Bedford/Kempston	...	...	...	...	101 928	50 341	51 587	...
Belfast[70]	...	...	...	...	276 459	129 321	147 138	...
Birkenhead	...	...	...	...	319 675	152 133	167 542	...
Blackburn/Darwen	...	...	...	...	136 655	66 834	69 821	...
Blackpool	...	...	...	...	261 088	124 698	136 390	...
Bournemouth	...	...	...	...	383 713	182 875	200 838	...
Brighton/Worthing/Littlehampton	...	...	...	...	461 181	220 275	240 906	...
Bristol	...	...	...	...	551 066	269 689	281 377	...
Burnley/Nelson	...	...	...	...	149 796	72 657	77 139	...
Cambridge	...	...	...	...	131 465	65 343	66 122	...
Cardiff[71]	...	...	...	...	327 706	156 272	171 434	...
Cheltenham/Charlton Kings	...	...	...	...	110 320	53 526	56 794	...
Chesterfield/Staveley	...	...	...	...	100 879	49 204	51 675	...
Colchester	...	...	...	...	104 390	51 652	52 738	...
Coventry/Bedworth	...	...	...	...	336 452	166 666	169 786	...
Crawley	...	...	...	...	180 177	88 404	91 773	...

8. Population of capital cities and cities of 100 000 or more inhabitants: latest available year, 1993 - 2012
Population des capitales et des villes de 100 000 habitants ou plus : dernière année disponible, 1993 - 2012 (continued - suite)

Continent, country or area, date, code and city / Continent, pays ou zone, date, code et ville	City proper - Ville proprement dite				Urban agglomeration - Agglomération urbaine			
	Population			Surface area - Superficie (km²)	Population			Surface area - Superficie (km²)
	Both sexes - Les deux sexes	Male - Masculin	Female - Féminin		Both sexes - Les deux sexes	Male - Masculin	Female - Féminin	

EUROPE

United Kingdom of Great Britain and Northern Ireland - Royaume-Uni de Grande-Bretagne et d'Irlande du Nord[69]
  29 IV 2001 (CDFC)

Dearne Valley	...	...	...	...	207 726	100 992	106 734	...
Derby	...	...	...	...	236 738	115 644	121 094	...
Doncaster	...	...	...	...	127 851	62 127	65 724	...
Dumfries & Galloway	...	...	...	...	147 765	71 303	76 462	...
Dundee	...	...	...	...	145 663	69 140	76 523	...
East Ayrshire	...	...	...	...	120 235	57 842	62 393	...
East Dunbartonshire	...	...	...	...	108 243	52 014	56 229	...
Eastbourne	...	...	...	...	106 562	49 369	57 193	...
Edinburgh[72]	...	...	...	...	448 624	214 711	233 913	...
Exeter	...	...	...	...	106 772	52 045	54 727	...
Falkirk	...	...	...	...	145 191	70 016	75 175	...
Fife	...	...	...	...	349 429	167 628	181 801	...
Glasgow	...	...	...	...	577 869	272 309	305 560	...
Gloucester	...	...	...	...	136 203	66 669	69 534	...
Grimsby/Cleethorpes	...	...	...	...	138 842	67 360	71 482	...
Hastings/Bexhill	...	...	...	...	126 386	59 247	67 139	...
High Wycombe	...	...	...	...	118 229	57 857	60 372	...
Highland	...	...	...	...	208 914	102 297	106 617	...
Ipswich	...	...	...	...	141 658	69 468	72 190	...
Kingston-upon-Hull	...	...	...	...	301 416	146 926	154 490	...
Leicester	...	...	...	...	441 213	214 060	227 153	...
Lincoln	...	...	...	...	104 221	50 794	53 427	...
Liverpool	...	...	...	...	816 216	389 119	427 097	...
LONDON[73]	...	...	...	...	8 278 251	4 007 297	4 270 954	...
Luton/Dunstable	...	...	...	...	236 318	117 707	118 611	...
Manchester	...	...	...	...	2 244 931	1 090 898	1 154 033	...
Mansfield	...	...	...	...	158 114	76 884	81 230	...
Milton Keynes	...	...	...	...	184 506	91 441	93 065	...
Newport	...	...	...	...	139 298	66 884	72 414	...
North Ayrshire	...	...	...	...	135 817	64 238	71 579	...
North Lanarkshire	...	...	...	...	321 067	153 966	167 101	...
Northampton	...	...	...	...	197 199	96 670	100 529	...
Norwich	...	...	...	...	194 839	94 523	100 316	...
Nottingham	...	...	...	...	666 358	327 851	338 507	...
Nuneaton	...	...	...	...	132 236	64 837	67 399	...
Oxford	...	...	...	...	143 016	70 462	72 554	...
Perth & Kinross	...	...	...	...	134 949	65 172	69 777	...
Peterborough	...	...	...	...	136 292	66 139	70 153	...
Plymouth	...	...	...	...	243 795	119 076	124 719	...
Portsmouth	...	...	...	...	442 252	216 341	225 911	...
Preston	...	...	...	...	264 601	129 665	134 936	...
Reading/Wokingham	...	...	...	...	369 804	185 475	184 329	...
Renfrewshire	...	...	...	...	172 867	82 525	90 342	...
Scottish Borders	...	...	...	...	106 764	51 361	55 403	...
Sheffield	...	...	...	...	640 720	312 619	328 101	...
Slough	...	...	...	...	141 848	70 286	71 562	...
South Ayrshire	...	...	...	...	112 097	53 406	58 691	...
South Lanarkshire	...	...	...	...	302 216	144 206	158 010	...
Southampton	...	...	...	...	304 400	151 534	152 866	...
Southend	...	...	...	...	269 415	129 650	139 765	...
Southport/Formby	...	...	...	...	115 882	54 337	61 545	...
St. Albans/Hatfield	...	...	...	...	114 710	56 585	58 125	...
Sunderland	...	...	...	...	182 974	88 892	94 082	...
Swansea	...	...	...	...	270 506	130 648	139 858	...
Swindon	...	...	...	...	155 432	77 551	77 881	...
Teesside	...	...	...	...	365 323	176 475	188 848	...
Telford	...	...	...	...	138 241	67 770	70 471	...
Thanet	...	...	...	...	119 144	56 266	62 878	...
The Medway Towns	...	...	...	...	231 659	114 069	117 590	...
The Potteries	...	...	...	...	362 403	176 467	185 936	...
Torbay	...	...	...	...	110 366	52 551	57 815	...

Continent, country or area, date, code and city / Continent, pays ou zone, date, code et ville	City proper - Ville proprement dite				Urban agglomeration - Agglomération urbaine			
	Population			Surface area - Superficie (km²)	Population			Surface area - Superficie (km²)
	Both sexes - Les deux sexes	Male - Masculin	Female - Féminin		Both sexes - Les deux sexes	Male - Masculin	Female - Féminin	
EUROPE								
United Kingdom of Great Britain and Northern Ireland - Royaume-Uni de Grande-Bretagne et d'Irlande du Nord[69]								
29 IV 2001 (CDFC)								
Tyneside	...	...	...	...	879 996	425 119	454 877	...
Warrington	...	...	...	...	158 195	77 334	80 861	...
West Lothian	...	...	...	...	158 714	76 701	82 013	...
West Midlands	...	...	...	...	2 284 093	1 109 397	1 174 696	...
West Yorkshire	...	...	...	...	1 499 465	724 818	774 647	...
Wigan	...	...	...	...	166 840	81 254	85 586	...
York	...	...	...	...	137 505	66 142	71 363	...
OCEANIA - OCÉANIE								
American Samoa - Samoas américaines[15]								
1 IV 2000 (CDJC)								
PAGO PAGO	4 278	2 086	2 192	...	...	...	...	...
Australia - Australie[74]								
9 VIII 2011 (CDJC)								
Adelaide	1 198 468	586 502	611 966	...	1 225 235	600 011	625 224	...
Brisbane	1 977 315	974 866	1 002 449	...	2 065 996	1 019 557	1 046 439	...
Cairns	...	...	...	...	133 911	66 187	67 724	...
CANBERRA	356 585	176 414	180 171	...	391 645	193 942	197 703	...
Central Coast	...	...	...	...	304 753	146 926	157 827	...
Darwin	106 255	55 424	50 831	...	120 584	62 896	57 688	...
Geelong	...	...	...	...	173 454	84 414	89 040	...
Gold Coast-Tweed Heads	...	...	...	...	557 822	271 876	285 946	...
Greater Wollongong	...	...	...	...	268 944	132 771	136 173	...
Hobart	200 501	97 250	103 251	...	211 656	102 880	108 776	...
Melbourne	3 847 570	1 890 871	1 956 699	...	3 999 982	1 966 503	2 033 479	...
Newcastle	...	...	...	...	398 770	195 429	203 341	...
Perth	1 670 953	828 733	842 220	...	1 728 866	858 306	870 560	...
Sunshine Coast	...	...	...	...	270 770	130 928	139 842	...
Sydney	4 028 524	1 985 922	2 042 602	...	4 391 673	2 162 220	2 229 453	...
Toowoomba	...	...	...	...	105 984	50 863	55 121	...
Townsville	...	...	...	...	162 292	80 736	81 556	...
Cook Islands - Îles Cook[75]								
1 XII 2001 (CDFC)								
RAROTONGA	12 188	...	...	...	...	...	...	...
Fiji - Fidji								
25 VIII 1996 (CDFC)								
SUVA	77 366	38 518	38 848	...	167 975	83 910	84 065	...
French Polynesia - Polynésie française								
7 XI 2002 (CDFC)								
PAPEETE	26 181	...	...	...	124 864	...	...	...
Guam								
1 IV 2000 (CDJC)								
AGANA	1 100[15]	672[15]	428[15]	3	...	...	...	...
Kiribati								
7 XII 2005 (CDFC)								
TARAWA	...	...	...	...	40 311	...	...	...
Marshall Islands - Îles Marshall								
1 VI 1999 (CDFC)								
MAJURO	23 676	12 075	11 601	...	...	...	...	...
Micronesia (Federated States of) - Micronésie (États fédérés de)								
1 IV 2000 (CDJC)								
PALIKIR	6 227	...	...	...	...	...	...	...
New Caledonia - Nouvelle-Calédonie								
16 IV 1996 (CDFC)								
NOUMEA	76 293	38 443	37 850	46	118 823	60 327	58 496	1 643

8. Population of capital cities and cities of 100 000 or more inhabitants: latest available year, 1993 - 2012
Population des capitales et des villes de 100 000 habitants ou plus : dernière année disponible, 1993 - 2012 (continued - suite)

Continent, country or area, date, code and city — Continent, pays ou zone, date, code et ville	City proper - Ville proprement dite				Urban agglomeration - Agglomération urbaine			
	Population			Surface area - Superficie (km²)	Population			Surface area - Superficie (km²)
	Both sexes - Les deux sexes	Male - Masculin	Female - Féminin		Both sexes - Les deux sexes	Male - Masculin	Female - Féminin	
OCEANIA - OCÉANIE								
New Zealand - Nouvelle-Zélande								
1 VII 2012 (ESDJ)								
Auckland	1 507 600	740 900	766 700	4 938	...	...	...	...
Christchurch	375 900	185 100	190 900	1 415	...	...	...	...
Dunedin	126 900	61 500	65 400	3 287	...	...	...	...
Hamilton	148 200	72 000	76 200	110	209 300	102 000	107 300	1 100
Lower Hutt	102 700	50 400	52 300	376	...	...	...	...
Napier-Hastings	...	...	...	...	125 000	60 200	64 800	390
Tauranga	116 400	56 000	60 500	135	122 200	58 800	63 400	185
WELLINGTON	202 200	99 000	103 200	290	395 600	194 000	201 600	448
Niue - Nioué								
7 IX 2001 (CDFC)								
ALOFI	615	...	...	...	...	...	...	...
Norfolk Island - Île Norfolk								
1 VII 1997 (ESDF)								
KINGSTON	*800*	...	...	...	...	...	...	...
Northern Mariana Islands - Îles Mariannes septentrionales								
1 IV 2000 (CDFC)								
GARAPAN	3 588	...	...	...	...	...	...	...
Palau - Palaos								
15 IV 2000 (CDFC)								
KOROR	10 600	...	...	...	...	...	...	...
Papua New Guinea - Papouasie-Nouvelle-Guinée								
9 VII 2000 (CDFC)								
PORT MORESBY	254 158	138 974	115 184	...	...	...	...	...
Pitcairn								
10 VIII 2012 (CDFC)								
ADAMSTOWN	48	22	26	0[76]	...	...	...	...
Samoa								
5 XI 2001 (CDFC)								
APIA	38 836	...	...	...	...	...	...	...
Solomon Islands - Îles Salomon								
21 XI 1999 (CDFC)								
HONIARA	49 107	...	...	...	...	...	...	...
Tonga								
1 VII 2000 (ESDF)								
NUKU'ALOFA	*21 538*	*10 625*	*10 913*	...	*30 336*	*15 115*	*15 221*	...
Tuvalu								
1 XI 2002 (CDFC)								
FUNAFUTI	4 492	2 281	2 211	...	...	...	...	...
Vanuatu								
16 XI 1999 (CDJC)								
PORT VILA	29 356	...	...	...	...	...	...	...
Wallis and Futuna Islands - Îles Wallis et Futuna								
3 X 1996 (CDFC)								
META-UTU	1 137	...	...	...	...	...	...	...

FOOTNOTES - NOTES

The capital city of each country is shown in capital letters. Figures in italics are estimates of questionnable reliability. For definition of city proper and urban agglomeration, method of evaluation and limitations of data see Technical Notes for this table. - Le nom de la capitale de chaque pays est imprimé en majuscules. Les chiffres en italique sont des estimations dont la fiabilité n'est pas assurée. Pour la définition de la ville proprement dite et de l'agglomération urbaine, et pour les méthodes d'évaluation et les insuffisances de données, voir les notes techniques pour ce tableau.

Italics: estimates which are less reliable. - Italiques : estimations moins sûres.

* Provisional. - Données provisoires.

'Code' indicates the source of data, as follows:
CDFC - Census, de facto, complete tabulation
CDFS - Census, de facto, sample tabulation
CDJC - Census, de jure, complete tabulation
CDJS - Census, de jure, sample tabulation
SSDF - Sample survey, de facto
SSDJ - Sample survey, de jure
ESDF - Estimates, de facto
ESDJ - Estimates, de jure

Le 'Code' indique la source des données, comme suit :
CDFC - Recensement, population de fait, tabulation complète
CDFS - Recensement, population de fait, tabulation par sondage
CDJC - Recensement, population de droit, tabulation complète
CDJS - Recensement, population de droit, tabulation par sondage
SSDF - Enquête par sondage, population de fait

SSDJ - Enquête par sondage, population de droit
ESDF - Estimations, population de fait
ESDJ - Estimations, population de droit

[1] Data refer to national projections. - Les données se réfèrent aux projections nationales.

[2] Data refer to the urban commune of Antananarivo. - Pour la commune urbaine de Antananarivo.

[3] Excludes the islands of St. Brandon and Agalega. - Non compris les îles St. Brandon et Agalega.

[4] Projections based on the 2002 Population Census. - Projections fondées sur le recensement de la population de 2002.

[5] Bloemfontein is the judicial capital, Cape Town is the legislative capital and Pretoria is the administrative capital. - Bloemfontein est la capitale judiciaire, Le Cap est la capitale législative et Pretoria est la capitale administrative.

[6] Comprising the Northern Region (former Saguia el Hamra) and Southern Region (former Rio de Oro). - Comprend la région septentrionale (ancien Saguia-el-Hamra) et la région méridionale (ancien Rio de Oro).

[7] Excludes the institutional population. - Non compris la population dans les institutions.

[8] Surface area is 0.28 Km2. - Superficie: 0,28 Km2.

[9] Updated postcensal estimates. Estimates adjusted for census net undercoverage (including adjustment for incompletely enumerated Indian reserves). - Estimations post censitaires mises à jour. Ajusté pour la sous-estimation du recensement (y compris les réservations en Inde incomplètement énumérées).

[10] Area (Sq.Km) are based on the 2006 Census boundaries. - La superficie (kilomètres carrés) est fondée sur les limites du recensement de 2006.

[11] Surface area includes interior waters. - La superficie comprend les eaux intérieures.

[12] Population statistics are compiled from registers. - Les statistiques de la population sont compilées à partir des registres.

[13] Total represents population in private dwellings, the non-institutional population and persons found on the streets between the hours of 5am and 7am on September 26, 2001; the figures represent the census counts adjusted for under-coverage. - Le total représente la population vivant dans des logements privés et les personnes trouvées dans la rue entre 5 et 7 heures du matin le 26 septembre 2001, mais ne tient pas compte des personnes vivant dans des établissements; les chiffres sont ceux du recensement corrigés pour tenir compte du sous-dénombrement.

[14] Data refer to projections based on the 2000 Population Census. - Les données se réfèrent aux projections basées sur le recensement de la population de 2000.

[15] Including armed forces stationed in the area. - Y compris les militaires en garnison sur le territoire.

[16] Excluding armed forces overseas and civilian citizens absent from the country for an extended period of time. City refers to a type of incorporated place in 49 states and the District of Columbia, that has an elected government and provides a range of government functions and services. Also included are Honolulu, Hawaii Census Designated Place (CDP), for which the Census Bureau reports data under agreement with the State of Hawaii (instead of the combined city and county of Honolulu), and Arlington, VA CDP (which is coextensive with Arlington County - an entirely urban county that provides the same levels of services and functions as a municipality). - Non compris les militaires à l'étranger, et les civils hors du pays pendant une période prolongée. Par ville, on entend un lieu doté de la personnalité morale dans 49 États et dans le district de Columbia, qui a un gouvernement élu et fournit tout un ensemble de fonctions et de services publics. Sont également inclus Honolulu, lieu chargé du recensement pour Hawaii, pour lequel le Census Bureau établit les données en accord avec l'État de Hawaii (au lieu de la ville et du comté d'Honolulu), et Arlington, lieu chargé du recensement pour la Virginie, qui est de même étendue que le comté d'Arlington, lequel est un comté entièrement urbain qui offre les mêmes niveaux de services et de fonctions qu'une municipalité.

[17] Census Designated Place. - Endroit classé au cours du recensement.

[18] Data refer to projections based on the 2001 Population Census. - Les données se réfèrent aux projections basées sur le recensement de la population de 2001.

[19] The urban agglomeration of Buenos Aires includes the city of Buenos Aires, and the 24 parts of the Buenos Aires province; among them, General San Martín, La Matanza, Lanús, Lomas de Zamora, Morón, Quilmes, San Fernando, San Isidro y Vicente López. - L'agglomération urbaine de Buenos Aires englobe la ville de Buenos Aires et les 24 circonscriptions de la province de Buenos Aires, dont General San Martín, La Matanza, Lanús, Lomas de Zamora, Morón, Quilmes, San Fernando, San Isidro et Vicente López.

[20] The urban agglomeration of Tucumán-Tafí Viejo includes San Miguel de Tucumán. - L'agglomération urbaine de Tucumán-Tafí Viejo englobe San Miguel de Tucumán.

[21] Excluding interior waters. - Eaux intérieures non comprises.

[22] Data include the population of the cities of Puente Alto and San Bernardo. - Y compris les villes de Puente Alto et de San Bernardo.

[23] Data are revised projections taking into consideration also the results of 2005 census. - Les données sont des projections révisées tenant compte également des résultats du recensement de 2005.

[24] The Metropolitan Area of Asunción is made up of Asunción and the 19 Central Department districts. - La zone métropolitaine d'Asunción est composée d'Asunción et de 19 districts du Département central.

[25] Estimates based on the 2007 Population Census. - Estimations fondées sur le recensement de la population de 2007.

[26] Data refer to the Province of Lima and the Constitutional Province of Callao. - Les données concernent la province de Lima et la province constitutionnelle de Callao.

[27] Excluding foreign diplomatic personnel and their dependants. Data based on 2008 Population Census. - Non compris le personnel diplomatique étranger et les membres de leur famille les accompagnant. Données fondées sur le recensement de population de 2008.

[28] Because of rounding, totals are not in all cases the sum of the respective components. - Les chiffres étant arrondis, les totaux ne correspondent pas toujours rigoureusement à la somme des composants respectifs.

[29] Lefkosia urban agglomeration is composed of Lefkosia municipality, Agios Dometios, Egkomi, Strovolos, Aglangia, Lakatameia, Anthoupoli, Latsia and Geri. - L'agglomération urbaine de Lefkosia se comprend de la municipalité de Lefkosia et Agios Dometios, Egkomi, Strovolos, Aglangia, Lakatameia, Anthoupoli, Latsia et Geri.

[30] Lemesos urban agglomeration is composed of Lemesos municipality, Mesa Geitonia, Agios Athanasios, Germasogeia, Pano Polemidia, Ypsonas, Kato Polemidia, and parts of Mouttagiaka, Agios Tychon, Parekklisia, Monagrouli, Moni, Pyrgos and Tserkezoi. - L'agglomération urbaine de Lemesos se comprend de la municipalité de Lemesos et Mesa Geitonia, Agios Athanasios, Germasogeia, Pano Polemidia, Ypsonas, Kato Polemidia, et certaines parties des Mouttagiaka, Agios Tychon, Parekklisia, Monagrouli, Moni, Pyrgos et Tserkezoi.

[31] Includes data for the Indian-held part of Jammu and Kashmir, the final status of which has not yet been determined. - Y compris les données pour la partie du Jammu et du Cachemire occupée par l'Inde dont le statut définitif n'a pas encore été déterminé.

[32] Data for urban agglomeration include New Delhi. - Les données pour l'agglomération urbaine y compris New Delhi.

[33] Data for urban agglomeration include Bally, Baranagar, Barrackpur, Bhatpara, Calcutta Municipal Corporation, Chandan Nagar, Garden Reach, Houghly-Chinsura, Howrah, Jadarpur, Kamarhati, Naihati, Panihati, Serampore, South Dum Dum, South Suburban, and Titagarh. - Les données pour l'agglomération urbaine y compris Bally, Baranagar, Barrackpur, Bhatpara, Calcutta Municipal Corporation, Chandan Nagar, Garden Reach, Houghly Chinsura, Howrah, Jadarpur, Kamarhati, Naihati, Panihati, Serampopre, South Dum Dum, South Suburban et Titagarh.

[34] Included in urban agglomeration of Delhi. Data refer to the New Delhi Municipal Council. - Comprise dans l'agglomération urbaine de Delhi. Les données se rapportent au New Delhi Municipal Council.

[35] Designation and data provided by Israel. The position of the United Nations on the question of Jerusalem is contained in General Assembly resolution 181 (II) and subsequent resolutions of the General Assembly and the Security Council concerning this question. Including East Jerusalem. - Appelation de données fournies par Israel. La position des Nations Unies concernant la question de Jérusalem est décrite dans la resolution 181 (II) de l'Assemblée générale et résolutions ultérieures de l'Assemblée générale et du Conseil de sécurité sur cette question. Y compris Jérusalem-Est.

[36] Excluding diplomatic personnel outside the country and foreign military and civilian personnel and their dependants stationed in the area. - Non compris le personnel diplomatique hors du pays ni les militaires et agents civils étrangers en poste sur le territoire et les membres de leur famille les accompagnant.

[37] Land areas are based on the "Municipalities Area Statistics of Japan, 2010" published by the Geospatial Information Authority of Japan, Ministry of Land, Infrastructure, Transport and Tourism. The areas with indefinable boundaries are estimated by the Statistics Bureau, Ministry of Internal Affairs and Communications. - Les zones terrestres sont déterminées selon les statistiques relatives aux municipalités du Japon en 2010, publiées par l'Autorité japonaise d'information géospatiale du Ministère de l'aménagement foncier, des infrastructures, des transports et du tourisme. Les zones sans délimitations définissables font l'objet d'une estimation réalisée par le Bureau de la statistique du Ministère des affaires intérieures et des communications.

[38] Excluding diplomatic personnel outside the country and foreign military and civilian personnel and their dependants stationed in the area. Data for Tokyo refer to 23 ku (wards) of Tokyo. - Non compris le personnel diplomatique hors du pays ni les militaires et agents civils étrangers en poste sur le territoire et les

membres de leur famille les accompagnant. Données relatives à Tokyo concernant 23 ku (arrondissements de la ville).

[39] Data refer to annual average population. - Les données correspondent à la population annuelle moyenne.

[40] Based on the results of the 2005 Population and Housing Census. - Données fondées sur les résultats du recensement de la population et de l'habitat de 2005.

[41] Based on the results of a household survey. - D'après les résultats d'une enquête des ménages.

[42] Excluding data for the Pakistan-held part of Jammu and Kashmir, the final status of which has not yet been determined, and for Junagardh, Manavadar, Gilgit and Baltistan. - Non compris les données pour la partie de Jammu-Cachemire occupée par le Pakistan dont le status definitif n'a pas encore été déterminé, et le Junagardh, le Manavadar, le Gilgit et le Baltistan.

[43] Data refer to total population, which comprises Singapore residents and non-residents. - Les données se rapportent à la population totale composé des résidents de Singapour et les non résidents.

[44] The Population and Housing Census 2001 did not cover the whole area of the country due to the security problems; data refer to the 18 districts for which the census was completed only (in three districts it was not possible to conduct the census at all and in four districts it was partially conducted). - Le recensement de la population et du logement de 2001 n'a pas été réalisé sur la superficie totale du pays à cause de problèmes de sécurité; les données ne concernent que les 18 districts entièrement recensés (3 districts n'ont pas été recensés du tout, et 4 ont été recensés en partie).

[45] Covering Seyhan and Yuregir districts in Adana. - Y compris la population des districts de Seyhan et de Yuregir.

[46] Covering Altindag, Cankaya, Etimesgut, Golbasi, Kecioren, Mamak, Sincan, and Yenimahalle districts in Ankara. - Y compris la population des districts de Altindag, de Cankaya, de Etimesgut, de Golbasi, de Kecioren, de Mamak, de Sincan, et de Yenimahalle.

[47] Covering Nilufer, Osmangazi and Yildirim districts in Bursa. - Y compris la population des districts de Nilufer, de Osmangazi et de Yildirim.

[48] District centre. - Le centre du district.

[49] Covering Sahinbey and Sehitkamil districts in Gaziantep. - Y compris la population des districts de Sahinbey et de Sehitkamil.

[50] Covering Adalar, Avcilar, Bagcilar, Bahcelievler, Bakirkoy, Bayrampasa, Besiktas, Beykoz, Beyoglu, Eminonu, Esenler, Eyup, Fatih, Gaziosmanpasa, Gungoren, Kadikoy, Kagithane, Kartal, Kucukcekmece, Maltepe, Pendik, Sariyer, Sisli, Sultanbeyli, Tuzla, Umraniye, Uskudar, Zentinburnu districts in Istanbul. - Y compris la population des districts de Adalar, de Avcilar, de Bagcilar, de Bahcelievler, de Bakirkoy, de Bayrampasa, de Besiktas, de Beykoz, de Beyoglu, de Eminonu, de Esenler, de Eyup, de Fatih, de Gaziosmanpasa, de Gungoren, de Kadikoy, de Kagithane, de Kartal, de Kucukcekmece, de Maltepe, de Pendik, de Sariyer, de Sisli, de Sultanbeyli, de Tuzla, de Umraniye, de Uskudar, et de Zentinburnu.

[51] Covering Bolcova, Bornova, Buca, Cigli, Gaziemir, Guzelbahce, Karsiyaka, Konak and Narlidere districts in Izmir. - Y compris la population des districts de Bolcova, de Bornova, de Buca, de Cigli, de Gaziemir, de Guzelbahce, de Karsiyaka, de Konak et de Narlidere.

[52] Covering Kocasinan and Melikgazi districts in Kayseri. - Y compris la population des districts de Kocasinan et de Melikgazi.

[53] Average annual population based on the final data of 2009 Population Census. - La population annuelle moyenne est évaluée à partir des résultats définitifs du recensement de la population de 2009.

[54] City proper refers to the 'town' which is a local self-government unit at the same level as a municipality, and represents a natural, urban, economic and social unity. - La ville proprement dite correspond à la commune qui est une unité locale auto-administrée au meme titre qu'une municipalité, et représente une entité naturelle, urbaine, économique et sociale.

[55] Excluding Faeroe Islands and Greenland shown separately, if available. - Non compris les Iles Féroé et le Groenland, qui font l'objet de rubriques distinctes, si disponible.

[56] Data for cities proper refer to communes which are centres for urban agglomeration. - Les données concernant les villes proprement dites se rapportent à des communes qui sont des centres d'agglomérations urbaines.

[57] Data for cities proper refer to communes which are centres for urban agglomeration. Data refer to French territory of this international agglomeration. - Les données concernant les villes proprement dites se rapportent à des communes qui sont des centres d'agglomérations urbaines. Les données se rapportent aux habitants de cette agglomération internationale qui vivent en territoire francais.

[58] Excluding military personnel, visitors and transients. - Non compris les militaires, ni les visiteurs et transients.

[59] Including armed forces stationed outside the country and alien armed forces in the area. - Y compris les militaires nationaux hors du pays et les militaires étrangers en garnison sur le territoire.

[60] Data refer to the Vatican City State. - Les données se rapportent à l'Etat de la Cité du Vatican.

[61] Surface area is 0.44 Km2. - Superficie: 0,44 Km2.

[62] The boundaries of the city are related to the boundaries of the respective commune. - Les limites de la ville correspondent aux limites de la commune respective.

[63] Definition of localities was revised from 2011 causing a break with the previous series. - La rupture par rapport aux séries précédentes s'explique par le fait que la définition des localités a été révisée depuis 2011.

[64] Land area includes inland water. - La zone terrestre comprend les eaux intérieures.

[65] The urban agglomeration of the capital area includes the following communes: Bessastaðahreppur, Garðabær, Hafnarfjörður, Kjósarhreppur, Kópavogur, Mosfellsbær ,Reykjavík, Seltjarnarnes. Definition of localities was revised from 2011 causing a break with the previous series. - L'agglomération urbaine de la capitale comprend les communes suivantes : Bessastaðahreppur, Garðabær, Hafnarfjörður, Kjósarhreppur, Kópavogur, Mosfellsbær ,Reykjavík, Seltjarnarnes. La rupture par rapport aux séries précédentes s'explique par le fait que la définition des localités a été révisée depuis 2011.

[66] City is defined as an administratively separated area entitled to civil (municipal) rights. - Une ville est définie comme une zone administrativement distincte dotée de droits municipaux.

[67] Excludes data for Kosovo and Metohia. - Sans les données pour le Kosovo et Metohie.

[68] Data for urban agglomeration refer to communes which are administrative divisions. - Les données pour l'agglomération urbaine se rapportent aux communes qui sont des divisions administrative.

[69] Excluding Channel Islands (Guernsey and Jersey) and Isle of Man, shown separately, if available. Data refer to urban areas with more than 100 000 residents. - Non compris les îles Anglo-Normandes (Guernesey et Jersey) et l'île de Man, qui font l'objet de rubriques distinctes, si disponible. Les données se rapportent aux zones urbaines avec plus de 100 000 résidents.

[70] Capital of Northern Ireland. - Capitale de l'Irlande du Nord.

[71] Capital of Wales for certain purposes. - Considérée à certains égards comme la capitale du pays de Galles.

[72] Capital of Scotland. - Capitale de l'Ecosse.

[73] 'Greater London' conurbation as reconstituted in 1965 and comprising 32 new Greater London Boroughs. - Ensemble urbain du 'Grand Londres', tel qu'il a été reconstitué en 1965, comprenant 32 nouveaux Greater London Boroughs.

[74] This data has been randomly rounded to protect confidentiality. Individual figures may not add up to totals, and values for the same data may vary in different tables. Data refer to geographic areas of statistical divisions in the Australian Standard Geographical Classification hierarchy. - Ces données ont été arrondies de façon aléatoire afin d'en préserver la confidentialité. La somme de certains chiffres peut ne pas correspondre aux totaux indiqués et les valeurs des mêmes données peuvent varier d'un tableau à un autre. Données relatives aux zones géographiques figurant dans les divisions statistiques de la classification géographique australienne normalisée (Australian Standard Geographical Classification).

[75] Excluding Niue, shown separately, which is part of Cook Islands, but because of remoteness is administered separately. - Non compris Nioué, qui fait l'objet d'une rubrique distincte et qui fait partie des îles Cook, mais qui, en raison de son éloignement, est administrée séparément.

[76] Surface area is 0.24 Km2. - Superficie: 0,24 Km2.

Table 9 - *Demographic Yearbook 2012*

Table 9 presents live births and crude birth rates by urban/rural residence for as many years as possible between 2008 and 2012.

Description of variables: Live birth is defined as the complete expulsion or extraction from its mother of a product of conception, irrespective of the duration of pregnancy, which after such separation, breathes or shows any other evidence of life such as beating of the heart, pulsation of the umbilical cord, or definite movements of voluntary muscles, whether or not the umbilical cord has been cut or the placenta is attached; each product of such a birth is considered live-born[1].

Statistics on the number of live births are obtained from civil registers unless otherwise noted. For those countries or areas where civil registration statistics on live births are considered reliable the birth rates shown have been calculated on the basis of registered live births.

For certain countries, there is a discrepancy between the total number of live births shown in this table and those shown in subsequent tables for the same year. Usually this discrepancy arises because the total number of live births occurring in a given year is revised but not the remaining tabulations.

Rate computation: Crude birth rates are the annual number of live births per 1 000 mid-year population.

Rates by urban/rural residence are the annual number of live births, in the appropriate urban or rural category, per 1 000 corresponding mid-year population. Rates are calculated only for data considered complete, that is, coded with a "C" and for estimates and live births statistics for the 12 month period prior to the census date, coded with a "|". These rates are calculated by the Statistics Division of the United Nations based on the appropriate reference population (for example: total population, nationals only, etc.) if known and available. If the reference population is not known or unavailable, the total population is used to calculate the rates. Therefore, if the population that is used to calculate the rates is different from the correct reference population, the rates presented might under- or overstate the true situation in a country or area.

Rates presented in this table are limited to those countries or areas having a minimum number of 30 live births in a given year.

Reliability of data: Each country or area has been asked to indicate the estimated completeness of the live births recorded in its civil register. These national assessments are indicated by the quality codes "C" and "U" that appear in the first column of this table.

"C" indicates that the data are estimated to be virtually complete, that is, representing at least 90 per cent of the live births occurring each year, whereas "U" indicates that data are estimated to be incomplete, that is, representing less than 90 per cent of the live births occurring each year. A third code "..." indicates that no information was provided regarding completeness.

Data from civil registers that are reported as incomplete or of unknown completeness (coded "U" or "...") are considered unreliable. They appear in italics in this table and rates are not calculated for these data.

These quality codes apply only to data from civil registers. If data from other sources are presented, the symbol "|" is shown instead of the quality code. For more information about the quality of vital statistics data in general, and the information available on the basis of the completeness estimates in particular, see section 4.2 of the Technical Notes.

Limitations: Statistics on live births are subject to the same qualifications as have been set forth for vital statistics in general and birth statistics in particular as discussed in section 4 of the Technical Notes.

The reliability of data, an indication of which is described above, is an important factor in considering the limitations. In addition, some live births are tabulated by date of registration and not by date of occurrence; these have been indicated by a plus sign "+". Whenever the lag between the date of occurrence and date of registration is prolonged and, therefore, a large proportion of the live birth registrations are delayed, birth statistics for any given year may be seriously affected.

Another factor that limits international comparability is the practice of some countries or areas not to include in live birth statistics infants who were born alive but died before the registration of the birth or within the first 24 hours of life, thus underestimating the total number of life births. Statistics of this type are footnoted.

In addition, it should be noted that rates are affected also by the quality and limitations of the population estimates that are used in their computation. The problems of under-enumeration or over-enumeration and, to some extent, the differences in definition of total population have been discussed in section 3 of the Technical Notes dealing with population data in general, and specific information pertaining to individual countries or areas is given in the footnotes to table 3.

The rates estimated from the results of sample surveys are subject to possibilities of considerable error as a result of omissions in reporting of births, or as a result of erroneous reporting of births that occurred outside the reference period. However, rates estimated from sample surveys have the advantage of the availability of a built-in and strictly corresponding population base.

It should be emphasized that crude birth rates - like crude death, marriage and divorce rates - may be seriously affected by the age-sex structure of the populations to which they relate. Nevertheless, they do provide a simple measure of the level of and changes in natality.

The urban/rural classification of birth may refer to the residence of mother or the place of delivery, as the national practices vary and is provided by each country or area. In addition, the comparability of data by urban/rural residence is affected by the national definition of urban and rural used in tabulating these data. It is assumed, in the absence of specific information to the contrary, that the definitions of urban and rural used in connection with the national population census were also used in the compilation of the vital statistics for each country or area. However, it cannot be ruled out that, for a given country or area, different definitions of urban and rural are used for the vital statistics data and the population census data respectively. When known, the definitions of urban used in national population census are presented at the end of the technical notes to table 6. As discussed in detail in the technical notes to table 6, these definitions vary considerably from one area or country to another. Urban/rural differentials in vital rates may also be affected by whether the vital events have been tabulated in terms of place of occurrence or place of usual residence. This problem is discussed in more detail in section 4.1.4.1 of the Technical notes.

Earlier data: Live births have been shown in each issue of the *Demographic Yearbook*. Information on the years and specific topics covered is presented in the Historical Index.

NOTES

[1] *Principles and Recommendations for a Vital Statistics System Revision 2,* Sales No. E. 01.XVII.10, United Nations, New York, 2001.

Tableau 9 – *Annuaire démographique 2012*

Le tableau 9 présente des données sur les naissances vivantes et les taux bruts de natalité selon le lieu de résidence (zone urbaine ou rurale) pour le plus grand nombre d'années possible entre 2008 et 2012.

Description des variables : La naissance vivante est l'expulsion ou l'extraction complète du corps de la mère, indépendamment de la durée de gestation, d'un produit de la conception qui, après cette séparation, respire ou manifeste tout autre signe de vie, tel que battement de cœur, pulsation du cordon ombilical ou contraction effective d'un muscle soumis à l'action de la volonté, que le cordon ombilical ait été coupé ou non et que le placenta soit ou non demeuré attaché ; tout produit d'une telle naissance est considéré comme « enfant né vivant »[1].

Sauf indication contraire, les statistiques relatives au nombre de naissances vivantes sont établies sur la base des registres de l'état civil. Pour les pays ou zones où les statistiques obtenues auprès des services de l'état civil sont jugées sûres, les taux de natalité indiqués ont été calculés par la Division de statistique de l'ONU d'après les naissances vivantes enregistrées.

Pour quelques pays il y a une discordance entre le nombre total des décès présenté dans ce tableau et ceux présentés après pour la même année. Habituellement ces différences apparaissent lorsque le nombre total des décès pour une certaine année a été révisé alors que les autres tabulations ne l'ont pas été.

Calcul des taux : Les taux bruts de natalité représentent le nombre annuel de naissances vivantes pour 1 000 habitants au milieu de l'année.

Les taux selon le lieu de résidence (zone urbaine ou rurale) représentent le nombre annuel de naissances vivantes, classées selon la catégorie urbaine ou rurale appropriée pour 1 000 habitants au milieu de l'année. Les taux ont été calculés seulement pour les données considérées complètes, c'est-à-dire celles associées au code « C », ainsi que pour les estimations et les statistiques des naissances vivantes dans la periode des douze mois précédante la date de recensement associées au code « | ». Ces taux sont calculés par la division de statistique des Nations Unies sur la base de la population de référence adéquate (par exemple : population totale, nationaux seulement, etc.) si connue et disponible. Si la population de référence n'est pas connue ou n'est pas disponible, la population totale est utilisée pour calculer les taux. Par conséquent, si la population utilisée pour calculer les taux est différente de la population de référence adéquate, les taux présentés sont susceptibles de sous ou sur estimer la situation réelle d'un pays ou d'un territoire.

Les taux présentés dans ce tableau se rapportent seulement aux pays ou zones où l'on a enregistré un nombre minimal de 30 naissances vivantes au cours d'une année donnée.

Fiabilité des données : Il a été demandé à chaque pays ou zone d'indiquer le degré estimatif de complétude des données sur les naissances vivantes figurant dans ses registres d'état civil. Ces évaluations nationales sont signalées par les codes de qualité "C" et "U" qui apparaissent dans la deuxième colonne du tableau.

La lettre "C" indique que les données sont jugées à peu près complètes, c'est-à-dire qu'elles représentent au moins 90 p. 100 des naissances vivantes survenues chaque année ; la lettre "U" signifie que les données sont jugées incomplètes, c'est-à-dire qu'elles représentent moins de 90 p. 100 des naissances vivantes survenues chaque année. Un troisième code, "...", indique qu'aucun renseignement n'a été communiqué quant à la complétude des données.

Les données provenant des registres de l'état civil qui sont déclarées incomplètes ou dont le degré de complétude n'est pas connu (code "U" ou "...") sont jugées douteuses. Elles apparaissent en italique dans le tableau. Les taux pour ces données ne sont pas calculés.

Les codes de qualité ne s'appliquent qu'aux données provenant des registres de l'état civil. Si l'on présente des données autres que celles de l'état civil, le signe "|" est utilisé à la place du code de qualité. Pour plus de précisions sur la qualité des données reposant sur les statistiques de l'état civil en général et les estimations de complétude en particulier, voir la section 4.2 des Notes techniques.

Insuffisance des données : Les statistiques concernant les naissances vivantes appellent toutes les réserves qui ont été formulées à propos des statistiques de l'état civil en général et des statistiques des naissances en particulier (voir la section 4 des Notes techniques).

La fiabilité des données, au sujet de laquelle des indications ont été fournies plus haut, est un facteur important. Il faut également tenir compte du fait que, dans certains cas, les données relatives aux naissances vivantes sont exploitées selon la date de l'enregistrement et non selon la date de l'événement ; ces cas ont été signalés par le signe '+'. Chaque fois que le décalage entre l'événement et son enregistrement est grand et qu'une forte proportion des naissances vivantes fait l'objet d'un enregistrement tardif, les statistiques des naissances vivantes pour une année donnée peuvent être considérablement faussées.

Un autre facteur qui nuit à la comparabilité internationale est la pratique de certains pays ou zones qui consiste à ne pas inclure dans les statistiques des naissances vivantes les enfants nés vivants mais décédés avant l'enregistrement de leur naissance ou dans les 24 heures qui ont suivi la naissance, pratique qui conduit à sous-estimer le nombre total de naissances vivantes. Lorsque ce facteur a joué, cela a été signalé en note à la fin du tableau.

La qualité et les limitations des estimations concernant la population ont également une incidence sur le calcul des taux. Les problèmes liés au sur-dénombrement ou au sous-dénombrement et, dans une certaine mesure, aux différences dans la définition de la population totale ont été abordés à la section 3 des Notes techniques relative aux données sur la population en général et des précisions sur certains pays ou zones sont données dans les notes se rapportant au tableau 3.

Les taux estimatifs fondés sur les résultats d'enquêtes par sondage comportent des possibilités d'erreurs considérables dues soit à des omissions dans les déclarations, soit au fait que l'on a déclaré à tort des naissances survenues en réalité hors de la période considérée. Toutefois, les taux estimatifs fondés sur les résultats d'enquêtes par sondage présentent un gros avantage : le chiffre de population utilisé comme base est, par définition, rigoureusement correspondant.

Il faut souligner que les taux bruts de natalité, de même que les taux bruts de mortalité, de nuptialité et de divortialité, peuvent varier très sensiblement selon la structure par âge et par sexe de la population à laquelle ils se rapportent. Ils offrent néanmoins un moyen simple de mesurer le niveau et l'évolution de la natalité.

La classification des naissances selon le lieu de résidence (zone urbaine ou rurale) peut se rapporter au lieu de résidence de la mère ou au lieu d'occurrence et correspond à celle indiquée par chaque pays ou zone. En outre, la comparabilité des données selon le lieu de résidence (zone urbaine ou rurale) peut être limitée par les définitions nationales des termes « urbain » et « rural » utilisées pour la mise en tableaux de ces données. En l'absence d'indications contraires, on a supposé que les mêmes définitions avaient servi pour le recensement national de la population et pour l'établissement des statistiques de l'état civil pour chaque pays ou zone. Toutefois, il n'est pas exclu que, pour une zone ou un pays donné, des définitions différentes aient été retenues. Les définitions du terme « urbain » utilisées pour les recensements nationaux de population ont été présentées à la fin des notes techniques du tableau 6 lorsqu'elles étaient connues. Comme on l'a précisé dans les notes techniques relatives au tableau 6, ces définitions varient considérablement d'un pays ou d'une zone à l'autre. La différence entre ces taux pour les zones urbaines et rurales pourra aussi être faussée selon que les faits d'état civil auront été classés d'après le lieu de l'événement ou le lieu de résidence habituel. Ce problème est examiné plus en détail à la section 4.1.4.1 des Notes techniques.

Données publiées antérieurement : Les différentes éditions de l'*Annuaire démographique* contiennent des données sur les naissances vivantes. Pour plus de précisions concernant les années et les sujets pour lesquels des données ont été publiées, se reporter à l'index historique.

NOTES

[1] *Principes et recommandations pour un système de statistique de l'état civil, deuxième révision,* numéro de vente : F.01.XVII.10, publication des Nations Unies, New York, 2003.

9. Live births and crude birth rates, by urban/rural residence: 2008 - 2012
Naissances vivantes et taux bruts de natalité selon la résidence, urbaine/rurale : 2008 - 2012

Continent, country or area, and urban/rural residence / Continent, pays ou zone et résidence, urbaine/rurale	Co-de[a]	Number - Nombre					Rate - Taux				
		2008	2009	2010	2011	2012	2008	2009	2010	2011	2012
AFRICA - AFRIQUE											
Algeria - Algérie[1]											
Total	C	817 000	849 000	887 810	910 000	977 992	23.6	24.1	24.7	24.8	26.1
Burkina Faso[2]											
Total	I	679 200	...	...	...	...	46.1	...	...	...	...
Cabo Verde											
Total	C	12 697	13 044	13 415	...	...	25.4	25.6	25.9	...	...
Egypt - Égypte											
Total	+C	2 050 704	2 217 409	2 261 409	2 442 094	...	27.3	28.8	28.7	30.4	...
Urban - Urbaine	+C	799 571	913 141	900 085	942 639	...	24.8	27.6	26.6	27.3	...
Rural - Rurale	+C	1 251 134	1 304 268	1 361 324	1 499 455	...	29.1	29.7	30.3	32.7	...
Ghana[3]											
Total	+U	553 119	...	...	...	...	...	...	...	...	...
Kenya											
Total	U	660 383	698 447	747 576	746 643	754 429	...	...	...	...	...
Urban - Urbaine	U	436 480	462 476	...	...	...	...	...	...	...	...
Rural - Rurale	U	223 903	228 836	...	...	...	...	...	...	...	...
Liberia - Libéria[4]											
Total	I	63 171	...	...	...	...	18.2	...	...	...	...
Libya - Libye[5]											
Total	+U	132 826	134 682	...	...	...	...	...	...	...	...
Malawi[6]											
Total	I	516 629	...	...	...	...	37.9	...	...	...	...
Mauritius - Maurice[7]											
Total	+C	16 372	15 344	15 005	14 701	*14 494	12.9	12.0	11.7	11.4	*11.2
Urban - Urbaine	+C	6 284	5 895	5 731	5 586	...	11.8	11.1	10.7	10.4	...
Rural - Rurale	+C	10 088	9 449	9 274	9 115	...	13.7	12.7	12.4	12.1	...
Réunion[8]											
Total	C	14 927	14 299	14 146	...	...	18.5	17.5	17.1	...	...
Rwanda											
Total	U	407 157	408 353	408 267	406 838	404 067	...	...	...	...	...
Saint Helena ex. dep. - Sainte-Hélène sans dép.											
Total	C	36	35	34	34	32	9.0	8.5	8.0	8.0	7.9
Senegal - Sénégal[9]											
Total	I	488 754	498 714	509 230	...	...	41.3	41.0	40.7	...	...
Urban - Urbaine	I	194 084	198 984	204 137	...	...	40.3	40.2	40.1	...	...
Rural - Rurale	I	294 670	299 730	305 093	...	...	41.9	41.5	41.1	...	...
Seychelles											
Total	+C	1 546	1 580	1 504	1 625	...	17.8	18.1	16.8	18.6	...
Sierra Leone											
Total	+...	114 823	107 947	101 185	117 207	147 958	...	...	...	...	...
Urban - Urbaine	+...	14 279	12 467	15 421	16 270	18 392	...	...	...	...	...
Rural - Rurale	+...	100 544	95 480	85 764	100 937	129 566	...	...	...	...	...
South Africa - Afrique du Sud											
Total	U	1 062 689	1 000 741	939 646	1 059 417	...	...	...	...	...	...
Tunisia - Tunisie											
Total	C	182 990	184 282	196 039	201 120	...	17.7	17.7	18.6	18.8	...
United Republic of Tanzania - République Unie de Tanzanie											
Total	...	1 656 216	1 667 889	1 678 325	1 687 203	1 694 943	...	...	...	...	...
AMERICA, NORTH - AMÉRIQUE DU NORD											
Anguilla											
Total	+C	154	181	182	185	...	9.9	11.3	11.1	11.1	...
Antigua and Barbuda - Antigua-et-Barbuda											
Total	+C	1 452	1 418	1 255	...	...	16.6	15.9	13.8	...	...
Aruba											
Total	C	1 218	1 213	1 141	...	...	11.6	11.3	11.2	...	...
Bahamas											
Total	+U	5 124	5 027	4 915	4 747	...	...	...	...	...	...
Bermuda - Bermudes[10]											
Total	C	821	819	769	670	...	12.8	12.7	11.9	10.4	...

9. Live births and crude birth rates, by urban/rural residence: 2008 - 2012
Naissances vivantes et taux bruts de natalité selon la résidence, urbaine/rurale : 2008 - 2012 (continued - suite)

Continent, country or area, and urban/rural residence / Continent, pays ou zone et résidence, urbaine/rurale	Co-dea	Number - Nombre					Rate - Taux				
		2008	2009	2010	2011	2012	2008	2009	2010	2011	2012
AMERICA, NORTH - AMÉRIQUE DU NORD											
Canada[11]											
Total	C	377 886	380 863	377 213	377 636	...	11.3	11.3	11.1	11.0	...
Cayman Islands - Îles Caïmanes[12]											
Total	C	793	824	821	800	*759	14.2	15.6	15.0	14.5	*13.4
Costa Rica											
Total	C	75 187	75 000	*70 922	*73 459	*73 326	16.9	16.6	*15.5	*15.9	*15.7
Urban - Urbaine	C	28 828	28 308	*26 047	...	...	...	...	...	...	...
Rural - Rurale	C	46 359	46 692	*44 875	...	...	...	...	...	...	...
Cuba											
Total	C	122 569	130 036	127 746	133 067	...	10.9	11.6	11.4	11.8	...
Urban - Urbaine	C	93 735	99 754	99 099	102 342	...	11.1	11.8	11.7	12.1	...
Rural - Rurale	C	28 834	30 282	28 647	30 725	...	10.4	10.9	10.3	11.1	...
Curaçao											
Total	C	2 001	1 898	2 032	1 974	...	13.8	13.0	13.6	13.1	...
Dominica - Dominique											
Total	+C	964	943	933	...	...	13.5	13.2	...	...	...
Dominican Republic - République dominicaine											
Total	U	141 702	141 184	138 753	128 836		...	...	...	...	...
Urban - Urbaine[13]	U	113 166	117 158	114 222	105 724		...	...	...	...	...
Rural - Rurale[13]	U	28 447	23 918	24 242	21 727		...	...	...	...	...
El Salvador[14]											
Total	C	111 278	107 880	104 939	109 384	...	18.2	17.5	17.0	17.6	...
Urban - Urbaine	C	69 427	68 529	66 619	75 495	...	18.1	17.6	16.8	18.8	...
Rural - Rurale	C	41 851	39 351	38 320	33 889	...	18.2	17.4	17.2	15.4	...
Greenland - Groenland											
Total	C	834	895	869	821	786	14.8	15.9	15.4	14.5	13.8
Urban - Urbaine	C	677	736	737	705	654	14.4	15.6	15.5	14.7	13.6
Rural - Rurale	C	157	159	132	116	132	17.0	17.5	14.9	13.4	15.3
Guadeloupe[8]											
Total	C	5 758	5 487	5 341	...	...	14.3	13.7	13.3	...	...
Guatemala											
Total	C	369 769	351 628	361 906	373 692	...	27.0	25.1	25.2	...	...
Urban - Urbaine[13]	C	178 831	188 763	201 656	221 638	...	...	...	...	...	...
Rural - Rurale[13]	C	189 436	156 068	154 536	146 505	...	...	...	...	...	...
Honduras											
Total	+U	223 390	223 483	223 345	224 409	...	...	...	...	...	...
Jamaica - Jamaïque[15]											
Total	C	43 112	42 782	40 508	39 673	39 348	16.0	15.9	15.0	14.7	14.5
Martinique[8]											
Total	C	5 333	5 174	4 889	...	...	13.4	13.1	12.3	...	...
Mexico - Mexique[16]											
Total	+U	2 243 145	2 252 786	2 643 908	2 586 287	...	...	...	...	...	...
Urban - Urbaine[13]	+U	1 607 242	510 900	...	...	...	...	...	...	...	...
Rural - Rurale[13]	+U	508 590	1 509 344	...	...	...	...	...	...	...	...
Montserrat											
Total	+C	72	50	62	46	...	14.8	9.9	12.4	9.3	...
Nicaragua											
Total	+U	125 028	...	...	...	...	...	...	...	...	...
Urban - Urbaine	+U	65 690	...	...	...	...	...	...	...	...	...
Rural - Rurale	+U	59 338	...	...	...	...	...	...	...	...	...
Panama											
Total	C	68 759	68 364	67 955	*73 292	...	20.3	19.8	19.4	*20.1	...
Urban - Urbaine	C	42 326	42 483	42 225	...	...	19.4	19.1	18.7	...	...
Rural - Rurale	C	26 433	25 881	25 730	...	...	21.7	21.1	20.7	...	...
Puerto Rico - Porto Rico											
Total	C	45 675	...	42 153	...	...	11.6	...	11.3	...	...
Urban - Urbaine[13]	C	23 899	...	...	...	...	...	...	...	...	...
Rural - Rurale[13]	C	21 750	...	...	...	...	...	...	...	...	...
Saint Vincent and the Grenadines - Saint-Vincent-et-les Grenadines											
Total	+C	1 901	1 905	...	...	...	19.2	18.9	...	...	...

9. Live births and crude birth rates, by urban/rural residence: 2008 - 2012
Naissances vivantes et taux bruts de natalité selon la résidence, urbaine/rurale : 2008 - 2012 (continued - suite)

Continent, country or area, and urban/rural residence / Continent, pays ou zone et résidence, urbaine/rurale	Code[a]	Number - Nombre					Rate - Taux				
		2008	2009	2010	2011	2012	2008	2009	2010	2011	2012
AMERICA, NORTH - AMÉRIQUE DU NORD											
Sint Maarten (Dutch part) - Saint-Martin (partie néerlandaise)											
Total	+C	526	...	...	...	...	13.1	...	...	...	...
Turks and Caicos Islands - Îles Turques et Caïques[17]											
Total	C	453	...	...	...	...	12.4	...	...	...	...
United States of America - États-Unis d'Amérique											
Total	C	4 247 694	4 130 665	3 999 386	3 953 590	...	14.0	13.5	12.9	12.7	...
United States Virgin Islands - Îles Vierges américaines											
Total	C	...	...	1 600	...	...	...	...	14.5	...	...
AMERICA, SOUTH - AMÉRIQUE DU SUD											
Argentina - Argentine											
Total	C	746 066	745 336	756 176	758 042	...	18.8	18.6	18.7	18.5	...
Brazil - Brésil											
Total	U	2 789 820	2 752 401	2 760 961[18]	2 824 776[18]	...	...	...	...	...	...
Chile - Chili											
Total	C	246 581	252 240	250 643	...	...	14.7	14.9	14.7	...	...
Urban - Urbaine	C	226 170	226 650	225 225	...	...	15.5	15.4	15.1	...	...
Rural - Rurale	C	20 411	25 590	25 418	...	...	9.3	11.6	11.4	...	...
Colombia - Colombie											
Total	U	715 453	699 775	654 627	*621 901	*662 554	...	...	...	...	...
Urban - Urbaine[13]	U	558 545	545 640	512 468	...	...	...	...	...	...	...
Rural - Rurale[13]	U	143 892	140 822	133 019	...	...	...	...	...	...	...
Ecuador - Équateur											
Total	+U	291 055	215 906	219 162	...	...	...	...	...	...	...
Urban - Urbaine	+U	228 647	171 489[19]	176 364[19]	...	...	...	...	...	...	...
Rural - Rurale	+U	62 408	38 221[19]	36 599[19]	...	...	...	...	...	...	...
French Guiana - Guyane française[8]											
Total	C	6 247	6 171	6 083	...	...	28.5	27.5	26.4	...	...
Paraguay											
Total	+U	99 674	...	...	...	...	...	...	...	...	...
Urban - Urbaine	+U	71 747	...	...	...	...	...	...	...	...	...
Rural - Rurale	+U	27 927	...	...	...	...	...	...	...	...	...
Peru - Pérou[20]											
Total	+U	359 140	396 616	402 493	396 839	...	...	...	...	...	...
Suriname[21]											
Total	C	10 097	9 792	...	...	...	19.5	18.7	...	...	...
Uruguay											
Total	C	53 199	47 152	47 420	46 699	48 200	16.0	14.1	14.1	13.9	14.3
Venezuela (Bolivarian Republic of) - Venezuela (République bolivarienne du)											
Total	C	581 480	593 845	591 303	615 132	...	20.8	20.9	20.5	21.0	...
ASIA - ASIE											
Armenia - Arménie											
Total	C	41 185	44 413	44 825	43 340	*42 333	12.7	13.7	13.8	13.3	*12.9
Urban - Urbaine	C	26 176	28 260	...	...	...	12.6	13.6	...	...	...
Rural - Rurale	C	15 009	16 153	...	...	...	12.9	13.8	...	...	...
Azerbaijan - Azerbaïdjan[22]											
Total	+C	152 086	152 139	165 643	176 072	174 469	17.2	17.0	18.3	19.2	18.8
Urban - Urbaine	+C	73 923	74 700	81 752	...	...	15.8	15.7	17.0	...	...
Rural - Rurale	+C	78 163	77 439	83 891	...	...	18.8	18.5	19.7	...	...
Bahrain - Bahreïn											
Total	C	17 022	17 841	17 791	17 213	*18 725	15.4	15.1	14.5	14.4	*15.2

9. Live births and crude birth rates, by urban/rural residence: 2008 - 2012
Naissances vivantes et taux bruts de natalité selon la résidence, urbaine/rurale : 2008 - 2012 (continued - suite)

Continent, country or area, and urban/rural residence / Continent, pays ou zone et résidence, urbaine/rurale	Co-de[a]	Number - Nombre					Rate - Taux				
		2008	2009	2010	2011	2012	2008	2009	2010	2011	2012
ASIA - ASIE											
Bangladesh											
Total	U	...	...	2 868 494	2 891 000	...	...	...	...	...	...
Urban - Urbaine	U	...	...	658 570	631 000	...	...	...	...	...	...
Rural - Rurale	U	...	...	2 209 924	2 260 000	...	...	...	...	...	...
Brunei Darussalam - Brunéi Darussalam											
Total	+C	6 424	...	...	...	...	16.1	...	...	...	...
China - Chine[23]											
Total	I	16 080 000	16 190 396	15 920 000	16 040 000	16 350 000	12.1	12.2	11.9	11.9	12.1
China, Hong Kong SAR - Chine, Hong Kong RAS											
Total	C	78 822	82 095	88 584	95 451	*91 600	11.3	11.8	12.6	13.5	*12.8
China, Macao SAR - Chine, Macao RAS											
Total	C	4 717	4 764	5 114	5 852	7 315	8.7	8.9	9.5	10.6	12.9
Cyprus - Chypre[24]											
Total	C	9 205	9 608	9 801	9 622	...	11.7	11.9	11.8	11.3	...
Urban - Urbaine[13]	C	5 467	5 774	6 563	6 461	...	...	...	...	...	...
Rural - Rurale[13]	C	2 967	3 015	3 119	3 074	...	...	...	...	...	...
Democratic People's Republic of Korea - République populaire démocratique de Corée[25]											
Total	I	345 630	...	...	...	...	14.4	...	...	...	...
Urban - Urbaine	I	200 910	...	...	...	...	...	...	...	...	...
Rural - Rurale	I	144 720	...	...	...	...	...	...	...	...	...
Georgia - Géorgie											
Total	C	56 565	63 377	62 585	58 014	57 031	12.9	14.4	14.1	12.9	12.7
Urban - Urbaine	C	39 206	43 663	34 129	33 452	...	17.0	18.7	14.5	14.0	...
Rural - Rurale	C	17 359	19 714	28 456	24 562	...	8.4	9.5	13.6	11.7	...
India - Inde[26]											
Total	I	...	...	...	...	...	22.8	22.5	22.1	...	...
Urban - Urbaine	I	...	...	...	...	...	18.5	18.3	18.0	...	...
Rural - Rurale	I	...	...	...	...	...	24.4	24.1	23.7	...	...
Iran (Islamic Republic of) - Iran (République islamique d')[27]											
Total	+C	1 300 166	...	...	...	...	18.0	...	...	...	...
Urban - Urbaine	+C	895 117	...	...	...	...	18.1	...	...	...	...
Rural - Rurale	+C	405 049	...	...	...	...	17.9	...	...	...	...
Total	C	...	1 348 546	1 363 542	1 382 229	...	...	18.4	18.3	18.3	...
Urban - Urbaine	C	...	937 639	...	...	...	...	18.6	...	...	...
Rural - Rurale	C	...	410 907	...	...	...	...	18.0	...	...	...
Israel - Israël[28]											
Total	C	156 923	161 042	166 255	166 296	*168 654	21.5	21.5	21.8	21.4	*21.3
Urban - Urbaine	C	142 664[13]	146 305	150 839	150 895	...	21.3	21.3	21.6	21.2	...
Rural - Rurale	C	14 239[13]	14 737	15 416	15 401	...	23.5	23.7	24.2	23.5	...
Japan - Japon[29]											
Total	C	1 091 156	1 070 035	1 071 304	1 050 806	...	8.7	8.4	8.4	8.2	...
Urban - Urbaine[30]	C	991 477	973 701	980 669	963 922	...	...	...	...	...	...
Rural - Rurale[30]	C	99 506	96 235	90 510	86 762	...	...	...	...	...	...
Jordan - Jordanie[31]											
Total	C	181 328	179 872	183 948	178 435	...	31.0	30.1	30.1	28.6	...
Kazakhstan[22]											
Total	C	356 575	357 552	367 752	372 544	...	22.7	22.2	22.5	22.5	...
Urban - Urbaine	C	196 839	...	...	...	...	23.6	...	...	...	...
Rural - Rurale	C	159 736	...	...	...	...	21.8	...	...	...	...
Kuwait - Koweït											
Total	C	54 571	56 503	57 533	58 198	...	21.9	20.3	19.6	18.8	...
Kyrgyzstan - Kirghizstan											
Total	C	127 332	135 494	146 123	149 612	...	25.1	26.4	28.1	28.4	...
Urban - Urbaine	C	43 974	46 924	49 905	48 906	...	24.5	25.9	27.3	26.5	...
Rural - Rurale	C	83 358	88 570	96 218	100 706	...	25.4	26.7	28.6	29.5	...
Lebanon - Liban											
Total	C	84 823	90 388	95 218	98 569	94 842	...	...	...	...	...

9. Live births and crude birth rates, by urban/rural residence: 2008 - 2012
Naissances vivantes et taux bruts de natalité selon la résidence, urbaine/rurale : 2008 - 2012 (continued - suite)

Continent, country or area, and urban/rural residence / Continent, pays ou zone et résidence, urbaine/rurale	Code[a]	Number - Nombre					Rate - Taux				
		2008	2009	2010	2011	2012	2008	2009	2010	2011	2012
ASIA - ASIE											
Malaysia - Malaisie											
Total	C	487 346	496 313	*475 816	*494 600	...	17.7	17.7	*16.6	*17.1	...
Urban - Urbaine	C	307 793	314 264	...	...	...	...	...	...	...	...
Rural - Rurale	C	179 553	182 049	...	...	...	...	...	...	...	...
Maldives											
Total	C	6 989	7 423	7 115	7 180	...	22.6	23.6	22.3	22.1	...
Urban - Urbaine	C	3 349	3 685	3 811[32]	3 987[32]	...	...	...	...	...	...
Rural - Rurale	C	3 640	3 738	3 249[32]	3 155[32]	...	...	...	...	...	...
Mongolia - Mongolie											
Total	+C	63 768	69 167	63 270	...	...	24.0	25.5	22.9	...	...
Urban - Urbaine	+C	40 590	44 897	41 907	...	...	24.9	26.6	24.1	...	...
Rural - Rurale	+C	23 178	24 270	21 363	...	...	22.5	23.7	20.9	...	...
Myanmar											
Total	+U	890 034	948 106	965 937	*1 007 039	...	...	...	...	...	...
Urban - Urbaine	+U	248 600	275 932	282 176	...	...	...	...	...	...	...
Rural - Rurale	+U	641 434	672 174	683 761	...	...	...	...	...	...	...
Oman[33]											
Total	U	58 280	64 735	65 528	67 922	...	...	...	...	...	...
Philippines											
Total	C	1 784 316	1 745 585	*1 782 981	...	...	19.7	18.9	*19.0	...	...
Qatar											
Total	C	17 210	18 351	19 504	*14 879	...	11.9	11.2	11.4	*8.6	...
Republic of Korea - République de Corée[34]											
Total	C	465 892	444 849	470 171	471 265	...	9.4	9.0	9.4	9.4	...
Urban - Urbaine[13]	C	384 901	366 022	386 271	389 640	...	9.6	9.1	9.6	9.6	...
Rural - Rurale[13]	C	80 728	78 524	83 519	81 503	...	8.7	8.4	8.8	8.6	...
Saudi Arabia - Arabie saoudite[35]											
Total	...	598 126	601 949	...	...	...	...	...	...	...	...
Singapore - Singapour											
Total	C	39 826	39 570	37 967	39 654	42 663	10.9	10.6	10.1	10.5	11.2
Sri Lanka											
Total	+C	373 575[36]	*376 843	*364 565	*363 415	...	18.5	*18.4	*17.7	*17.4	...
Urban - Urbaine[36]	+C	260 136	...	...	...	...	...	...	...	...	...
Rural - Rurale[36]	+C	113 439	...	...	...	...	...	...	...	...	...
Syrian Arab Republic - République arabe syrienne[37]											
Total	+U	750 321	721 587	870 100	...	...	...	...	...	...	...
Tajikistan - Tadjikistan[38]											
Total	U	203 332	199 826	239 805	224 178	...	...	...	...	...	...
Urban - Urbaine	U	51 582	45 193	54 563	55 081	...	...	...	...	...	...
Rural - Rurale	U	151 750	154 633	185 242	169 097	...	...	...	...	...	...
Thailand - Thaïlande											
Total	+U	784 256	765 047	761 689	795 031	...	...	...	...	...	...
Turkey - Turquie											
Total	C	1 292 839	1 261 299	1 253 309	1 237 172	1 279 864	18.2	17.5	17.1	16.7	17.0
United Arab Emirates - Émirats arabes unis[39]											
Total	...	68 779	76 366	79 625	83 950	...	...	...	...	...	...
Uzbekistan - Ouzbékistan											
Total	C	646 096	651 320	634 810	622 835	625 106	23.9	23.7	22.7	21.4	21.2
Yemen - Yémen											
Total	U	309 373	271 269	318 936	239 980	279 719	...	...	...	...	...
EUROPE											
Åland Islands - Îles d'Åland											
Total	C	294	267	286	285	*293	10.8	9.7	10.3	10.1	*10.3
Urban - Urbaine	C	121	95	108	110	*96	11.0	8.6	9.7	9.8	*8.5
Rural - Rurale	C	173	172	178	175	*197	10.6	10.4	10.6	10.3	*11.5
Albania - Albanie											
Total	C	36 251	...	...	32 628	...	12.4	...	...	11.5	...
Andorra - Andorre											
Total	C	875	838	828	793	737	10.4	9.8	9.8	10.0	9.5

9. Live births and crude birth rates, by urban/rural residence: 2008 - 2012
Naissances vivantes et taux bruts de natalité selon la résidence, urbaine/rurale : 2008 - 2012 (continued - suite)

Continent, country or area, and urban/rural residence — Continent, pays ou zone et résidence, urbaine/rurale	Co-de[a]	Number - Nombre					Rate - Taux				
		2008	2009	2010	2011	2012	2008	2009	2010	2011	2012
EUROPE											
Austria - Autriche											
Total	C	77 752	76 344	78 742	78 109	78 952	9.3	9.1	9.4	9.3	9.3
Belarus - Bélarus											
Total	C	107 876	109 263	108 050	109 147	115 893	11.1	11.4	11.4	11.5	12.2
Urban - Urbaine	C	81 643	82 780	82 306	83 445	...	...	...	...	11.7	...
Rural - Rurale	C	26 233	26 483	25 744	25 702	...	...	...	...	11.1	...
Belgium - Belgique[40]											
Total	C	127 205	127 297	129 909	128 678	*127 000	11.9	11.8	11.9	11.7	*11.4
Urban - Urbaine	C	125 474	125 507	...	...	...	11.9	11.8	...	...	...
Rural - Rurale	C	1 731	1 790	...	...	...	11.2	11.5	...	...	...
Bosnia and Herzegovina - Bosnie-Herzégovine											
Total	C	34 176	34 550	33 528	31 875	*32 072	8.9	9.0	8.7	8.3	*8.4
Bulgaria - Bulgarie											
Total	C	77 712	80 956	75 513	70 846	69 121	10.2	10.7	10.0	9.6	9.5
Urban - Urbaine	C	58 367	60 664	57 077	53 396	...	10.8	11.2	10.6	10.0	...
Rural - Rurale	C	19 345	20 292	18 436	17 450	...	8.7	9.3	8.6	8.7	...
Croatia - Croatie											
Total	C	43 753	44 577	43 361	41 197	...	9.9	10.1	9.8	9.4	...
Urban - Urbaine	C	24 316	24 927	24 583	...	...	...	...	...	...	...
Rural - Rurale	C	19 437	19 650	18 778	...	...	...	...	...	...	...
Czech Republic - République tchèque[41]											
Total	C	119 570	118 348	117 153	108 673	108 576	11.5	11.3	11.1	10.4	10.3
Urban - Urbaine	C	88 648	87 245	86 078	79 742	...	11.5	11.3	11.1	10.4	...
Rural - Rurale	C	30 922	31 103	31 075	28 931	...	11.3	11.3	11.2	10.3	...
Denmark - Danemark[42]											
Total	C	65 038	62 818	63 411	58 998	57 916	11.8	11.4	11.4	10.6	10.4
Estonia - Estonie											
Total	C	16 028	15 763	15 825	14 679	14 056	12.0	11.8	11.8	11.0	10.5
Urban - Urbaine	C	11 078	10 807	10 645	10 057	...	11.9	11.6	11.4	10.8	...
Rural - Rurale	C	4 950	4 956	5 180	4 622	...	12.1	12.1	12.7	11.3	...
Faeroe Islands - Îles Féroé											
Total	C	665	614	639	576	617	13.7	12.6	13.2	11.9	12.8
Finland - Finlande											
Total	C	59 530	60 163[43]	60 694[43]	59 676[43]	59 493	11.2	11.3	11.4	11.1	11.1
Urban - Urbaine	C	42 534	42 919[43]	43 543[43]	42 637[43]	...	11.8	11.9	12.0	11.6	...
Rural - Rurale	C	16 996	17 244[43]	17 151[43]	17 039[43]	...	9.9	10.2	10.1	10.1	...
France[44]											
Total	C	796 044	793 420	802 224	792 996	*792 000	12.8	12.7	12.7	12.5	*12.5
Urban - Urbaine[45]	C	593 785	593 291	635 898	...	...	...	...	...	...	...
Rural - Rurale[45]	C	200 753	198 595	164 776	...	...	...	...	...	...	...
Germany - Allemagne											
Total	C	682 514	665 126	677 947	662 685	*671 000	8.3	8.1	8.3	8.1	*8.2
Gibraltar[46]											
Total	+C	400	417	493	442	...	13.7	14.2	16.7	14.9	...
Greece - Grèce											
Total	C	118 302	117 933	114 766	106 428	...	10.5	10.5	10.1	9.4	...
Urban - Urbaine	C	80 476	80 678	78 756	75 224	...	...	...	...	...	...
Rural - Rurale	C	37 826	37 255	36 010	31 204	...	...	...	...	...	...
Guernsey - Guernesey											
Total	C	603	646	613	650	674	9.8	10.4	9.8	10.3	10.7
Hungary - Hongrie											
Total	C	99 149	96 442	90 335	88 049	*90 300	9.9	9.6	9.0	8.8	*9.1
Urban - Urbaine[47]	C	66 877	65 684	62 454	60 698	...	9.8	9.6	9.0	8.7	...
Rural - Rurale[47]	C	31 475	29 747	26 938	26 349	...	9.8	9.4	8.8	8.7	...
Iceland - Islande											
Total	C	4 835	5 026	4 907	4 492[48]	*4 533	15.1	15.7	15.4	14.1	*14.1
Urban - Urbaine	C	4 605	4 792	4 705	4 441[48]	...	15.5	16.0	15.8	14.1	...
Rural - Rurale	C	230	234	202	51[48]	...	10.8	11.5	9.8	11.1	...
Ireland - Irlande											
Total[49]	C	75 173	75 554	...	...	...	17.0	16.9	...	...	...
Total	+C	...	...	74 976	74 650	*72 291	...	...	16.8	16.6	*15.8
Italy - Italie											
Total	+C	576 659	568 857	561 944	*546 607	...	9.6	9.5	9.3	*9.0	...
Jersey[16]											
Total	+C	973	...	...	...	...	10.3	...	...	...	...

9. Live births and crude birth rates, by urban/rural residence: 2008 - 2012
Naissances vivantes et taux bruts de natalité selon la résidence, urbaine/rurale : 2008 - 2012 (continued - suite)

Continent, country or area, and urban/rural residence — Continent, pays ou zone et résidence, urbaine/rurale	Code[a]	Number - Nombre					Rate - Taux				
		2008	2009	2010	2011	2012	2008	2009	2010	2011	2012
EUROPE											
Latvia - Lettonie											
Total	C	23 948	21 677	19 219	18 825	19 897	10.6	9.6	8.6	9.1	9.8
Urban - Urbaine	C	16 574	14 849	13 164	...	...	10.8	9.7	8.7	...	...
Rural - Rurale	C	7 374	6 828	6 055	...	...	10.1	9.4	8.3	...	...
Liechtenstein											
Total	C	350	406	329	395	356	9.9	11.3	9.1	10.9	9.8
Lithuania - Lituanie											
Total	C	35 065	36 682	35 626	34 385	30 459	10.4	11.0	10.8	11.3	9.6
Urban - Urbaine	C	23 824	25 043	24 614	23 817	...	10.6	11.2	11.2	11.8	...
Rural - Rurale	C	11 241	11 639	11 012	10 568	...	10.1	10.5	10.1	10.5	...
Luxembourg											
Total	C	5 596	5 638	5 874	5 639	6 026	11.5	11.3	11.6	10.9	11.3
Malta - Malte											
Total	C	4 126	4 143	4 008	4 283	...	10.1	10.0	9.7	10.3	...
Montenegro - Monténégro											
Total	C	8 258	8 642	7 418	7 215	7 459	13.1	13.7	12.0	11.6	12.0
Urban - Urbaine	C	6 431	6 579	...	...	...	16.2	16.4	...	...	...
Rural - Rurale	C	1 827	2 063	...	...	...	7.9	8.9	...	...	...
Netherlands - Pays-Bas[50]											
Total	C	184 634	184 915	184 397	180 060	175 959	11.2	11.2	11.1	10.8	10.5
Urban - Urbaine	C	127 683	128 524	129 450	...	...	11.7	11.7	11.7	...	...
Rural - Rurale	C	56 951	56 391	54 947	...	...	10.2	10.1	10.0	...	...
Norway - Norvège											
Total	C	60 497	61 807	61 442	60 220	60 255	12.7	12.8	12.6	12.2	12.0
Poland - Pologne											
Total	C	414 499	417 589	413 300	388 416	386 257	10.9	10.9	10.7	10.1	10.0
Urban - Urbaine	C	241 288	246 429	241 920	225 701	...	10.4	10.6	10.3	9.6	...
Rural - Rurale	C	173 211	171 160	171 380	162 715	...	11.7	11.5	11.4	10.8	...
Portugal[16]											
Total	C	104 594	99 491	101 381	96 856	89 841	9.8	9.4	9.5	9.2	8.5
Republic of Moldova - République de Moldova[51]											
Total	C	39 018	40 803	40 474	39 182	39 435	10.9	11.4	11.4	11.0	11.1
Urban - Urbaine	C	14 288	14 906	15 142	...	...	9.7	10.1	10.2	...	...
Rural - Rurale	C	24 730	25 897	25 332	...	...	11.8	12.4	12.2	...	...
Romania - Roumanie											
Total	C	221 900	222 388	212 199	196 242	201 104	10.3	10.4	9.9	9.2	9.4
Urban - Urbaine	C	121 518	121 864	117 851	106 667	...	10.3	10.3	10.0	9.1	...
Rural - Rurale	C	100 382	100 524	94 348	89 575	...	10.4	10.4	9.8	9.3	...
Russian Federation - Fédération de Russie[22]											
Total	C	1 713 947	1 761 687	1 788 948	1 796 629	*1 896 263	12.0	12.3	12.5	12.6	*13.3
Urban - Urbaine	C	1 194 820	1 237 615	1 263 893	1 270 047	...	11.4	11.8	12.0	12.0	...
Rural - Rurale	C	519 127	524 072	525 055	526 582	...	13.7	13.9	14.0	14.1	...
San Marino - Saint-Marin											
Total	+C	349	306	334	325	292	11.0	9.3	10.5	9.7	8.7
Serbia - Serbie[52]											
Total	+C	69 083	70 299	68 304	65 598	67 257	9.4	9.6	9.4	9.0	9.3
Urban - Urbaine	+C	45 389	46 896	46 684	45 430	...	10.6	11.0	10.9	10.6	...
Rural - Rurale	+C	23 694	23 403	21 620	20 168	...	7.7	7.7	7.2	6.8	...
Slovakia - Slovaquie											
Total	C	57 360	61 217	60 410	60 813	55 535	10.6	11.3	11.1	11.3	10.3
Urban - Urbaine	C	30 663	32 636	32 119	32 238	...	10.3	11.0	10.8	11.0	...
Rural - Rurale	C	26 697	28 581	28 291	28 575	...	11.0	11.7	11.5	11.6	...
Slovenia - Slovénie											
Total	C	21 817	21 856	22 343	21 947	*21 711	10.8	10.7	10.9	10.7	*10.6
Urban - Urbaine	C	10 612	10 761	10 893	10 651	...	10.5	10.5	10.6	10.4	...
Rural - Rurale	C	11 205	11 095	11 450	11 296	...	11.1	10.9	11.2	11.0	...
Spain - Espagne											
Total	C	518 503	493 717	485 252	470 553	*456 778	11.4	10.7	10.5	10.2	*9.9
Sweden - Suède											
Total	C	109 301	111 801	115 641	111 770	113 177	11.9	12.0	12.3	11.8	11.9
Switzerland - Suisse											
Total	C	76 691	78 286	80 290	80 808	*82 164	10.0	10.1	10.3	10.2	*10.3
Urban - Urbaine	C	57 114	58 542	60 131	60 544	...	10.2	10.3	...	10.4	...
Rural - Rurale	C	19 577	19 744	20 159	20 264	...	9.7	9.7	...	9.7	...

Continent, country or area, and urban/rural residence / Continent, pays ou zone et résidence, urbaine/rurale	Co-de[a]	Number - Nombre					Rate - Taux				
		2008	2009	2010	2011	2012	2008	2009	2010	2011	2012
EUROPE											
TFYR of Macedonia - L'ex-R. y. de Macédoine											
Total	C	22 945	23 684	24 296	22 770	23 568	11.2	11.5	11.8	11.1	11.4
Urban - Urbaine	C	13 200	13 621	13 904	...	...	...	...	...	...	...
Rural - Rurale	C	9 745	10 063	10 392	...	...	...	...	...	...	...
Ukraine[53]											
Total	+C	510 589	512 525	497 689	502 595	520 705	11.0	11.1	10.9	11.0	11.4
Urban - Urbaine	+C	340 594	339 497	326 587	328 934	...	10.8	10.8	...	...	...
Rural - Rurale	+C	169 995	173 028	171 102	173 661	...	11.6	11.9	...	...	...
United Kingdom of Great Britain and Northern Ireland - Royaume-Uni de Grande-Bretagne et d'Irlande du Nord[54]											
Total	C	794 383	790 204	*807 272	807 776	...	12.9	12.8	*13.0	12.9	...
OCEANIA - OCÉANIE											
American Samoa - Samoas américaines											
Total	C	...	...	1 234	...	...	...	...	18.7	...	...
Australia - Australie											
Total	+C	296 621	295 738	297 903	301 617	...	13.9	13.6	13.5	13.5	...
Urban - Urbaine[55]	+C	253 900	253 471	256 055	261 069	...	14.5	14.2	14.1	14.2	...
Rural - Rurale[55]	+C	41 924	41 681	41 150	39 847	...	10.9	10.7	10.5	10.1	...
Cook Islands - Îles Cook[56]											
Total	+C	261	255	279	*262	*259	11.9	11.3	11.8	*12.6	...
Fiji - Fidji											
Total	+C	18 944	18 166	...	...	...	...	21.5	...	...	...
French Polynesia - Polynésie française											
Total	C	4 627	4 544	4 579	...	...	17.6	17.1	17.1	...	...
Guam[57]											
Total	C	3 466	3 423	3 419	3 298	...	21.8	21.5	21.5	20.7	...
New Caledonia - Nouvelle-Calédonie											
Total	C	4 015	4 103	4 178	...	...	16.6	16.7	16.7	...	...
New Zealand - Nouvelle-Zélande											
Total	+C	64 343	62 543	63 897	61 403	61 178	15.1	14.5	14.6	13.9	13.8
Urban - Urbaine[13]	+C	56 220	54 650	55 879	53 967	53 917	15.3	14.7	14.8	14.2	14.1
Rural - Rurale[13]	+C	8 066	7 809	7 945	7 419	7 253	13.7	13.2	13.2	12.2	11.9
Niue - Nioué[58]											
Total	C	20	31	...	...	...	...	20.0	...	...	...
Norfolk Island - Île Norfolk[59]											
Total	+C	22	...	...	...	...	...	...	...	...	...
Northern Mariana Islands - Îles Mariannes septentrionales											
Total	U	*1 260*[60]	*1 110*[61]	*1 072*[61]	...	...	...	...	...	...	...
Pitcairn											
Total	C	1	...	...	...	...	...	...	...	...	...
Samoa											
Total	C	2 371	1 602	...	...	...	13.0	8.7	...	...	...
Total[62]		...	...	...	5 703	...	...	...	...	30.8	...
Urban - Urbaine[62]		...	...	...	1 057	...	...	...	...	27.4	...
Rural - Rurale[62]		...	...	...	4 646	...	...	...	...	31.8	...
Wallis and Futuna Islands - Îles Wallis et Futuna											
Total	C	185	...	...	...	...	13.8	...	...	...	...

FOOTNOTES - NOTES

Italics: data from civil registers which are incomplete or of unknown completeness. - Italiques : données incomplètes ou dont le degré d'exactitude

n'est pas connu, provenant des registres de l'état civil.

* Provisional. - Données provisoires.

1 Excluding live-born infants who died before their birth was registered. Data refer to Algerian population only. - Non compris les enfants nés vivants décédés avant l'enregistrement de leur naissance. Les données ne concernent que la population algérienne.

2 Data refer to national projections. - Les données se réfèrent aux projections nationales.

3 Excluding data for November and December. Coverage of live births is below 60 per cent. - Ne comprend pas les données pour novembre et décembre. La couverture des naissances vivantes est inférieure à 60 pour cent.

4 Data refer to the 12 months preceding the census in March. - Les données se rapportent aux 12 mois précédant le recensement de mars.

5 Data refer to Libyan nationals only. - Les données se raportent aux nationaux libyens seulement.

6 Data refer to the 12 months preceding the census in June. - Les données se raportent aux 12 mois précédant le recensement de juin.

7 Excludes the islands of St. Brandon and Agalega. - Non compris les îles St. Brandon et Agalega.

8 Excluding live-born infants who died before their birth was registered. - Non compris les enfants nés vivants décédés avant l'enregistrement de leur naissance.

9 Based on estimates and projections from 'Agence Nationale de la Statistique et de la Démographie'. - Données fondées sur des estimations et des projections provenant de l'Agence Nationale de la Statistique et de la Démographie.

10 Excluding non-residents and foreign service personnel and their dependants. - À l'exclusion des non-résidents et du personnel diplomatique et de leurs charges de famille.

11 Including Canadian residents temporarily in the United States, but excluding United States residents temporarily in Canada. - Y compris les résidents canadiens se trouvant temporairement aux Etats-Unis, mais ne comprenant pas les résidents des Etats-Unis se trouvant temporairement au Canada.

12 Resident births outside the islands are excluded. - Non compris les naissances de résidents hors des îles.

13 The total number includes 'Unknown residence', but the categories urban and rural do not. - Le nombre total englobe les personnes dont la résidence n'est pas connue, à l'inverse des catégories de population urbaine et rurale.

14 Excluding children born in the country of non-resident mothers. - Exceptés les enfants nés dans le pays des mères non-résidentes.

15 Data have been adjusted for underenumeration. - Les données ont été ajustées pour compenser les lacunes du dénombrement.

16 Data refer to births to resident mothers. - Ces données concernent les enfants de mères résidentes.

17 Excluding births of nationals outside the country. - Non compris les naissances de nationaux hors du pays.

18 Including births abroad and births of unknown residence. - Y compris les naissances survenues à l'étranger et les naissances d'enfants dont la résidence n'était pas connue.

19 Total is not equal to the sum of Urban and Rural because it includes "zona periférica". - Le total ne correspond pas à la somme des données urbaines et rurales car il englobe la « zona periférica ».

20 Source: Reports of the Ministry of Health. - Source: Rapports du Ministère de la Santé.

21 Including births to non-resident mothers. - Y compris les naissances de femmes non résidentes.

22 Excluding infants born alive of less than 28 weeks' gestation, of less than 1 000 grams in weight and 35 centimeters in length, who die within seven days of birth. - Non compris les enfants nés vivants après moins de 28 semaines de gestations, pesant moins de 1 000 grammes, mesurant moins de 35 centimètres et décédés dans les sept jours qui ont suivi leur naissance.

23 Data have been estimated on the basis of the annual National Sample Survey on Population Changes. For statistical purposes, the data for China do not include those for the Hong Kong Special Administrative Region (Hong Kong SAR), Macao Special Administrative Region (Macao SAR) and Taiwan province of China. - Les données ont été estimées sur la base de l'enquête annuelle "National Sample Survey on Population Changes". Pour la présentation des statistiques, les données pour la Chine ne comprennent pas la Région Administrative Spéciale de Hong Kong (Hong Kong RAS), la Région Administrative Spéciale de Macao (Macao RAS) et Taïwan province de Chine.

24 Data refer to government controlled areas. - Les données se rapportent aux zones contrôlées par le Gouvernement.

25 Data refer to the 12 months preceding the census in October. - Les données se rapportent aux 12 mois précédant le recensement de octobre.

26 Rates were obtained by the Sample Registration System of India, which is a large demographic survey. Includes data for the Indian-held part of Jammu and Kashmir, the final status of which has not yet been determined. - Les taux ont été obtenus par le Système de l'enregistrement par échantillon de l'Inde qui est une large enquête démographique. Y compris les données pour la partie du Jammu et du Cachemire occupée par l'Inde dont le statut définitif n'a pas encore été déterminé.

27 Data refer to the Iranian Year which begins on 21 March and ends on 20 March of the following year. - Les données concernent l'année iranienne, qui commence le 21 mars et se termine le 20 mars de l'année suivante.

28 Includes data for East Jerusalem and Israeli residents in certain other territories under occupation by Israeli military forces since June 1967. - Y compris les données pour Jérusalem-Est et les résidents israéliens dans certains autres territoires occupés depuis 1967 par les forces armées israéliennes.

29 Data refer to Japanese nationals in Japan only. - Les données se raportent aux nationaux japonais au Japon seulement.

30 The total number includes 'Unknown residence', but the categories urban and rural do not. Urban and rural distribution refers to the residence of the child. - Le nombre total englobe les personnes dont la résidence n'est pas connue, à l'inverse des catégories de population urbaine et rurale. La répartition urbain/rural se réfère au domicile de l'enfant.

31 Excluding data for Jordanian territory under occupation since June 1967 by Israeli military forces. Excluding foreigners, including registered Palestinian refugees. - Non compris les données pour le territoire jordanien occupé depuis juin 1967 par les forces armées israéliennes. Non compris les étrangers, mais y compris les réfugiés de Palestine enregistrés.

32 Excluding births occurred abroad. - Hormis les naissances intervenues à l'étranger.

33 Data from Births and Deaths Notification System (Ministry of Health and all health care providers). - Les données proviennent du système de notification des naissances et des décès (Ministère de la santé et tous prestataires de soins de santé).

34 Data refer to residence of child. Excluding alien armed forces, civilian aliens employed by armed forces, and foreign diplomatic personnel and their dependants. - Les données correspondent à la résidence de l'enfant. Non compris les militaires étrangers, les civils étrangers employés par les forces armées ni le personnel diplomatique étranger et les membres de leur famille les accompagnant.

35 Projections based on the final results of the 2004 Population and Housing Census. - Projections basées sur les résultats définitifs du recensement de la population et de l'habitat de 2004.

36 Excluding data from Mulative and Killnochchi districts. - À l'exclusion des données des districts de Mulative et Killnochchi.

37 Excluding nomad population and Palestinian refugees. Excluding live-born infants who died before their birth was registered. - Non compris la population nomade et les réfugiés de Palestine. Non compris les enfants nés vivants décédés avant l'enregistrement de leur naissance.

38 Excluding infants born alive of less than 28 weeks' gestation, of less than 1 000 grams in weight and 35 centimeters in length, who die within seven days of birth. Data have been adjusted for under-registration. - Non compris les enfants nés vivants après moins de 28 semaines de gestations, pesant moins de 1 000 grammes, mesurant moins de 35 centimètres et décédés dans les sept jours qui ont suivi leur naissance. Y compris un ajustement pour sous-enregistrement.

39 The registration of births and deaths is conducted by the Ministry of Health. An estimate of completeness is not provided. - L'enregistrement des naissances et des décès est mené par le Ministère de la Santé. Le degré estimatif de complétude n'est pas fourni.

40 Including armed forces stationed outside the country, but excluding alien armed forces stationed in the area. - Y compris les militaires nationaux hors du pays, mais non compris les militaires étrangers en garnison sur le territoire.

41 A live-born child is a child fully expelled or removed out of the mother's body, who gives a sign of life and whose birth weight is (a) 500 g or more, or (b) lower than 500 g, if it survives 24 hours after delivery. - Un enfant né vivant est un enfant qui a été entièrement expulsé ou retiré du corps de la mère, qui présente des signes de vie et dont le poids à la naissance est : a) soit égal ou supérieur à 500 grammes; b) soit inférieur à 500 grammes s'il survit plus de 24 heures après l'accouchement.

[42] Excluding Faeroe Islands and Greenland shown separately, if available. - Non compris les Îles Féroé et le Groenland, qui font l'objet de rubriques distinctes, si disponible.

[43] Excluding Åland Islands. - Non compris les Îles d'Åland.

[44] Including armed forces stationed outside the country. - Y compris les militaires nationaux hors du pays.

[45] The data for urban and rural exclude the nationals outside the country. - Les données relatives à la population urbaine et rurale n'englobent pas les nationaux se trouvant à l'étranger.

[46] Including live births by military personnel and their dependants. - Y compris les naissances vivantes parmi les membres du personnel militaire et leurs personnes à charge.

[47] Total includes the data of foreigners, persons of unknown residence and homeless, but the categories urban and rural do not. - Le total englobe les données relatives aux étrangers, aux personnes dont la résidence n'est pas connue et aux personnes sans domicile fixe, à l'inverse des chiffres portant sur la population urbaine et rurale.

[48] Definition of localities was revised from 2011 causing a break with the previous series. - La rupture par rapport aux séries précédentes s'explique par le fait que la définition des localités a été révisée depuis 2011.

[49] Data refer to events registered within one year of occurrence. - Les données portent sur des événements enregistrés dans l'année pendant laquelle ils sont survenus.

[50] Including residents outside the country if listed in a Netherlands population register. - Englobe les résidents se trouvant à l'étranger à condition qu'ils soient inscrits sur le registre de population des Pays-Bas.

[51] Excluding Transnistria and the municipality of Bender. - Les données ne tiennent pas compte de l'information sur la Transnistria et la municipalité de Bender.

[52] Excludes data for Kosovo and Metohia. - Sans les données pour le Kosovo et Metohie.

[53] Data refer to births with weight 500g and more (if weight is unknown - with length 25 centimeters and more, or with gestation during 22 weeks or more). - Données concernant les nouveau-nés de 500 grammes ou plus (si le poids est inconnu – de 25 centimètres de long ou plus, ou après une grossesse de 22 semaines ou plus).

[54] Excluding Channel Islands (Guernsey and Jersey) and Isle of Man, shown separately, if available. Data tabulated by date of occurrence for England and Wales, and by date of registration for Northern Ireland and Scotland. - Non compris les îles Anglo-Normandes (Guernesey et Jersey) et l'île de Man, qui font l'objet de rubriques distinctes, si disponible. Données exploitées selon la date de l'événement pour l'Angleterre et le pays de Galles, et selon la date de l'enregistrement pour l'Irlande du Nord et l'Ecosse.

[55] Excluding data where place of usual residence of mother was overseas, undefined, no fixed place of abode, offshore, migratory or unknown. - Les données n'ont pas été prises en compte lorsque le domicile habituel de la mère était à l'étranger ou dans une zone extraterritoriale, était indéfini ou inconnu ou que la mère n'avait pas de domicile fixe ou était une migrante.

[56] Excluding Niue, shown separately, which is part of Cook Islands, but because of remoteness is administered separately. - Non compris Nioué, qui fait l'objet d'une rubrique distincte et qui fait partie des îles Cook, mais qui, en raison de son éloignement, est administrée séparément.

[57] Including United States military personnel, their dependants and contract employees. - Y compris les militaires des Etats-Unis, les membres de leur famille les accompagnant et les agents contractuels des Etats-Unis.

[58] Includes children born in New Zealand to women resident in Niue who chose to travel to New Zealand to give birth. - Y compris les enfants nés en Nouvelle-Zélande de femmes résidant à Nioué qui ont choisi de se rendre en Nouvelle-Zélande pour accoucher.

[59] Data cover the period from 1 July of the previous year to 30 June of the present year. - Pour la période allant du 1er juillet de l'année précédente au 30 juin de l'année en cours.

[60] Source: Commonwealth Health Center - Vital Statistics Office - Source : Centre de Santé du Commonwealth - Bureau des statistiques d'État civil

[61] Source: U.S. National Center for Health Statistics, National Vital Statistics Reports (NVSR). - Source : US National Center for Health Statistics, National Vital Statistics Reports (NVSR).

[62] Data refer to the 12 months preceding the census in November. - Données se rapportant aux 12 mois précédant le recensement de novembre.

Table 10 - *Demographic Yearbook 2012*

Table 10 presents live births by age of mother and sex of the child, general fertility rate, and age-specific fertility rates for the latest available year between 2003 and 2012.

Description of variables: Age is defined as age at last birthday, that is, the difference between the date of birth and the date of the occurrence of the event, expressed in completed solar years. The age classification used in this table is the following: under 15 years, 5-year age groups through 45-49 years, and 50 years and over. A different classification may appear as provided by reporting country or area.

Rate computation: Age-specific fertility rates are the annual number of births to women in each age group per 1 000 female population in the same age group. These rates are calculated by the Statistics Division of the United Nations.

Since relatively few births occur to women below 15 or above 50 years of age, age-specific fertility rates for women under 20 years of age and for those 45 years of age or over are computed on the female population aged 15-19 and 45-49, respectively. Similarly, the rate for women of "All ages" is based on all live births irrespective of age of mother, and is computed on the female population aged 15-49 years. This rate for "All ages" is known as the general fertility rate. The age-specific fertility rates for age groups of women below 15 or 50 and above years of age are not calculated.

Births to mothers of unknown age are distributed proportionately across the age groups, by the Statistics Division of the United Nations, in accordance with the distribution of births by age of mother prior to the calculation of the rates.

The population used in computing the rates is the estimated or enumerated distribution of females by age. First priority was given to the estimated population and second priority to the enumerated population, i.e. to census returns of the year to which the births referred.

Rates presented in this table are limited to those for countries or areas having at least a total of 100 live births in a given year.

Reliability of data: Data from civil registers of live births which are reported as incomplete (less than 90 per cent completeness) or of unknown completeness are considered unreliable and are set in *italics* rather than in roman type. Rates are not computed if the data on live births from civil registers are reported as incomplete (less than 90 per cent completeness) or of unknown completeness. Table 9 and the technical notes for that table provide more detailed information on the completeness of live-birth registration. For more information about the quality of vital statistics data in general, see section 4.2 of the Technical Notes.

Limitations: Statistics on live births by age of mother are subject to the same qualifications as have been set forth for vital statistics in general and birth statistics in particular as discussed in section 4 of the Technical Notes. These include differences in the completeness of registration, the method used to determine age of mother and the quality of the reported information relating to age of mother.

The reliability of the data described above, is an important factor in considering the limitations. In addition, some live births are tabulated by date of registration and not by date of occurrence; these are indicated in the table by a plus sign "+". Whenever the lag between the date of occurrence and date of registration is prolonged and, therefore, a large proportion of the live birth registrations are delayed, birth statistics for any given year may be seriously affected. For example, the age of the mother will almost always refer to the date of registration rather than to the date of birth of the child. Hence, in those countries or areas where registration of births is delayed, possibly for years, statistics on births by age of mother should be used with caution.

Another factor which limits international comparability is the practice of some countries or areas of not including in live birth statistics infants who were born alive but died before the registration of the birth or within the first 24 hours of life, thus underestimating the total number of live births. Statistics of this type are footnoted.

Because these statistics are classified according to age, they are subject to the limitations with respect to accuracy of age reporting similar to those already discussed in connection with section 3.1.3 of the Technical Notes. The factors influencing the accuracy of reporting may be somewhat dissimilar in vital statistics (because of the differences in the method of taking a census and registering a birth) but, in general, the same errors can be observed. The absence of frequencies in the unknown age group does not necessarily indicate completely accurate reporting and tabulation of the age item. It is often an indication that the unknowns have been eliminated by assigning ages to them before tabulation, or by proportionate distribution after tabulation.

On the other hand, large frequencies in the unknown age category may indicate that a large proportion of the births are born outside of wedlock, the records for which tend to be incomplete so far as characteristics of the parents are concerned.

Another limitation of age reporting may result from calculating age of mother at birth of child (or at time of registration) from year of birth rather than from day, month and year of birth. Information on this factor is given in footnotes when known.

In few countries, data by age refer to deliveries rather than to live births causing under-enumeration in the event of a multiple birth. This practice leads to lack of strict comparability, both among countries or areas relying on this practice and between data shown in this table and table 9.

Rates shown in this table are subject to the same limitations that affect the corresponding statistics on live births. In cases of rates based on births tabulated by date of registration and not by date of occurrence; the effect of including delayed registration on the distribution of births by age of mother may be noted in the age-specific fertility rates for women at older ages. In some cases, high age-specific rates for women aged 45 years and over may reflect age of mother at registration of birth and not fertility at these older ages.

Earlier data: Live births and live-birth rates by age of mother (i.e. age-specific fertility rates), have been shown for the latest available year in each issue of the Yearbook. Information on the years and specific topics covered is presented in the Historical Index.

Tableau 10 – *Annuaire démographique 2012*

Le tableau 10 présente les données les plus récentes disponibles pour la période 2003 -2012 sur les naissances vivantes selon l'âge de la mère et le sexe de l'enfant, le taux de fécondité et les taux de fécondité par âge.

Description des variables : l'âge désigne l'âge au dernier anniversaire, c'est-à-dire la différence entre la date de naissance et la date de l'événement exprimée en années solaires révolues. La classification par âge utilisée dans ce tableau comprend les catégories suivantes : moins de 15 ans, groupes quinquennaux jusqu'à 45-49 ans, 50 ans et plus, et âge inconnu. Des groupes d'âge différents sont parfois utilisés lorsque les pays ou territoires ont fourni les données dans une autre classification.

Les taux de fécondité par âge représentent le nombre annuel de naissances vivantes intervenues dans un groupe d'âge donné pour 1 000 femmes du groupe d'âge. Ces taux ont été calculés par la Division de statistique de l'ONU.

Étant donné que le nombre de naissances parmi les femmes de moins de 15 ans ou de plus de 50 ans est relativement peu élevé, les taux de fécondité par âge parmi les femmes âgées de moins de 20 ans et celles de 45 ans et plus ont été calculés sur la base des populations féminines âgées de 15 à 19 ans et de 45 à 49 ans, respectivement. De même, le taux pour les femmes de « tous âges » est fondé sur la totalité des naissances vivantes, indépendamment de l'âge de la mère et ce chiffre est rapporté à l'effectif de la population féminine âgée de 15 à 49 ans. Ce taux « tous âges » est le taux global de fécondité ou simplement taux de fécondité. Les taux de fécondité parmi les femmes âgées de moins de 15 ans ou celles de 50 ans et plus n'ont pas été calculés.

Les naissances pour lesquelles l'âge de la mère était inconnu ont été réparties par la Division de statistique de l'ONU, avant le calcul des taux, suivant les proportions observées pour celles où l'âge de la mère était connu.

Les chiffres de population utilisés pour le calcul des taux proviennent de dénombrements ou de répartitions estimatives de la population féminine selon l'âge. On a utilisé de préférence les estimations de la population; à défaut, on s'est contenté des données censitaires se rapportant à l'année des naissances.

Les taux présentés dans ce tableau ne concernent que les pays ou zones où l'on a enregistré un total d'au moins 100 naissances vivantes dans une année donnée.

Fiabilité des données : les données sur les naissances vivantes provenant des registres de l'état civil qui sont déclarées incomplètes (degré de complétude inférieur à 90 p. 100) ou dont le degré de complétude n'est pas connu sont jugées douteuses et apparaissent en italique et non en caractères romains. On a choisi de ne pas faire figurer des taux calculés à partir de données sur les naissances vivantes issues de registres de l'état civil qui sont déclarées incomplètes (degré de complétude inférieur à 90 p. 100) ou dont le degré de complétude n'est pas connu. Le tableau 9 et les notes techniques qui s'y rapportent présentent des renseignements plus détaillés sur le degré de complétude de l'enregistrement des naissances vivantes. Pour plus de précisions sur la qualité des statistiques de l'état civil en général, voir la section 4.2 des Notes techniques.

Insuffisance des données : les statistiques relatives aux naissances vivantes selon l'âge de la mère appellent toutes les réserves qui ont été formulées à propos des statistiques de l'état civil en général et des statistiques de naissances en particulier (voir la section 4 des Notes techniques). Ceci inclut les différences de complétude d'enregistrement des faits d'état civil, de méthode pour déterminer l'âge de la mère et de qualité d'information concernant l'âge de la mère.

La fiabilité des données, au sujet de laquelle des indications ont été données plus haut, est un facteur important. Il faut également tenir compte du fait que, dans certains cas, les données relatives aux naissances vivantes sont exploitées selon la date de l'enregistrement et non la date de l'événement ; ces cas ont été signalés dans le tableau par le signe '+'. Chaque fois que le décalage entre l'événement et son enregistrement est grand et qu'une forte proportion des naissances vivantes fait l'objet d'un enregistrement tardif, les statistiques des naissances vivantes pour une année donnée peuvent être considérablement faussées. Par exemple, l'âge de la mère représente presque toujours son âge à la date de l'enregistrement et non à la date de la naissance de l'enfant. Ainsi, dans les pays ou zones où l'enregistrement des naissances est tardif, le retard atteignant parfois plusieurs années, il faut utiliser avec prudence les statistiques concernant les naissances selon l'âge de la mère.

Un autre facteur qui nuit à la comparabilité internationale est la pratique de certains pays ou zones qui consiste à ne pas inclure dans les statistiques des naissances vivantes les enfants nés vivants mais décédés avant l'enregistrement de leur naissance ou dans les 24 heures qui ont suivi la naissance, pratique qui conduit à sous-estimer le nombre total de naissances vivantes. Quand pareil facteur a joué, cela a été signalé en note à la fin du tableau.

Étant donné que les statistiques du tableau 10 sont classées selon l'âge, elles appellent les mêmes réserves concernant l'exactitude des déclarations d'âge que celles formulées à la section 3.1.3 des Notes techniques. Dans le cas des statistiques de l'état civil, les facteurs qui interviennent à cet égard sont parfois différents, étant donné que le recensement de la population et l'enregistrement des naissances se font par des méthodes différentes, mais, d'une manière générale, les erreurs observées seront les mêmes. Si aucun nombre ne figure dans la rangée réservée aux âges inconnus, cela ne signifie pas nécessairement que les déclarations d'âge et l'exploitation des données par âge ont été tout à fait exactes. C'est souvent une indication que l'on a attribué un âge aux personnes d'âge inconnu avant l'exploitation des données ou qu'elles ont été réparties proportionnellement entre les différents groupes après cette opération.

À l'inverse, lorsque le nombre des personnes d'âge inconnu est important, cela peut signifier que la proportion de naissances parmi les mères célibataires est élevée, étant donné qu'en pareil cas l'acte de naissance ne contient pas tous les renseignements concernant les parents.

Les déclarations par âge peuvent comporter des distorsions, du fait que l'âge de la mère au moment de la naissance d'un enfant (ou de la déclaration de naissance) est donné par année de naissance et non par date exacte (jour, mois et année).

Dans quelques pays, la classification par âges se réfère aux accouchements, et non aux naissances vivantes, ce qui conduit à un sous-dénombrement en cas de naissances gémellaires. Cette pratique nuit à la comparabilité des données, à la fois entre pays ou zones qui recourent à cette méthode et entre les données présentées dans le tableau 10 et celles du tableau 9.

Les taux présentés dans ce tableau sont sujets aux mêmes limitations qui affectent les statistiques correspondantes de naissances vivantes. Dans le cas des taux basés sur des naissances par date d'enregistrement et non par date d'occurrence, l'effet peut être visible sur les taux de fécondité par âge des femmes aux âges plus élevés. Dans certains cas, les taux de fécondité des femmes de plus de 45 ans peuvent refléter l'âge de la mère à l'enregistrement plus que la fécondité à ces âges.

Données publiées antérieurement : les différentes éditions de l'*Annuaire démographique* regroupent les dernières statistiques dont on disposait à l'époque sur les naissances vivantes selon l'âge de la mère et les taux des naissances vivantes selon l'âge de la mère (taux de fécondité par âge). Pour plus de précisions concernant les années pour lesquels des données ont été publiées, se reporter à l'index historique.

10. Live births by age of mother and sex of child, general and age-specific fertility rates: latest available year, 2003 - 2012
Naissances vivantes selon l'âge de la mère et le sexe de l'enfant, taux de fécondité et taux de fécondité par âge : dernière année disponible, 2003 - 2012

Continent, country or area, year, code and age of mother (in years) / Continent, pays ou zone, année, code et âge de la mère (en années)	Total	Male Masculin	Female Féminin	Rate Taux
AFRICA - AFRIQUE				
Botswana[1]				
2006 (+U)				
Total	44 709	23 534	21 175	...
15 - 19	5 493	2 916	2 577	...
20 - 24	15 118	7 883	7 235	...
25 - 29	11 383	6 023	5 360	...
30 - 34	7 115	3 760	3 355	...
35 - 39	3 813	1 989	1 824	...
40 - 44	1 556	838	718	...
45 +	231	125	106	...
Egypt - Égypte				
2011 (+C)				
Total	2 442 094	1 252 319	1 189 775	112.1
0 - 19	79 996	41 281	38 715	31.8
20 - 24	646 670	331 858	314 812	278.0
25 - 29	321 935	165 157	156 778	164.4
30 - 34	195 618	100 567	95 051	139.6
35 - 39	69 475	35 799	33 676	48.9
40 - 44	19 546	10 134	9 412	16.0
45 +	4 881	2 311	2 570	4.5
Unknown - Inconnu	1 103 973	565 212	538 761	..
Kenya				
2009 (U)				
Total	691 312	354 154	337 158	...
0 - 14	3 877	2 019	1 858	..
15 - 19	89 664	45 562	44 102	...
20 - 24	221 828	113 572	108 256	...
25 - 29	174 571	89 674	84 897	...
30 - 34	103 940	53 395	50 545	...
35 - 39	49 527	25 424	24 103	...
40 - 44	13 231	6 713	6 518	...
45 - 49	2 165	1 097	1 068	...
50 +	823	423	400	...
Unknown - Inconnu	31 686	16 275	15 411	..
2012 (U)				
Total	754 429	...	...	...
0 - 14	3 047	...	...	..
15 - 19	90 928	...	...	...
20 - 24	234 290	...	...	...
25 - 29	204 221	...	...	...
30 - 34	122 883	...	...	...
35 - 39	64 386	...	...	...
40 - 44	16 674	...	...	...
45 - 49	2 975	...	...	...
50 +	560	...	...	..
Unknown - Inconnu	14 462	...	...	..
Liberia - Libéria[2]				
2008 (|)				
Total	63 171	33 511	29 660	73.1
12 - 14	304	157	147	..
15 - 19	6 973	3 668	3 305	37.4
20 - 24	16 181	8 486	7 695	89.4
25 - 29	14 915	8 017	6 898	98.9
30 - 34	10 277	5 433	4 844	91.5
35 - 39	8 336	4 374	3 962	79.8
40 - 44	3 961	2 138	1 823	53.5
45 - 49	2 224	1 238	986	40.5
Libya - Libye[3]				
2009 (+U)				
Total	134 682	...	...	...
0 - 19	733	...	...	...
20 - 24	7 067	...	...	...
25 - 29	17 792	...	...	...
30 - 34	18 491	...	...	...
35 - 39	9 801	...	...	...
AFRICA - AFRIQUE				
Libya - Libye[3]				
2009 (+U)				
40 - 44	3 334	...	...	...
45 +	409	...	...	...
Unknown - Inconnu	77 055	...	...	...
Malawi[4]				
2008 (|)				
Total	516 629	247 753	268 876	160.1
12 - 14	1 621	751	870	..
15 - 19	70 737	34 137	36 600	101.2
20 - 24	169 406	81 379	88 027	284.1
25 - 29	130 331	62 810	67 521	241.6
30 - 34	79 232	37 758	41 474	153.2
35 - 39	43 747	20 776	22 971	116.8
40 - 44	15 956	7 553	8 403	57.8
45 - 49	5 599	2 589	3 010	25.0
Mauritius - Maurice[5]				
2011 (C)				
Total	14 626	7 385	7 241	41.5
0 - 14	25	11	14	..
15 - 19	1 530	748	782	29.3
20 - 24	3 704	1 875	1 829	75.3
25 - 29	4 250	2 161	2 089	90.1
30 - 34	3 350	1 728	1 622	60.2
35 - 39	1 264	602	662	27.0
40 - 44	299	156	143	6.4
45 - 49	25	12	13	♦0.5
50 +	3	1	2	..
Unknown - Inconnu	176	91	85	...
Nigeria - Nigéria				
2007 (...)				
Total	1 807 025	...	...	...
0 - 14	2 528	...	...	...
15 - 19	129 716	...	...	...
20 - 24	471 036	...	...	...
25 - 29	588 454	...	...	...
30 - 34	377 593	...	...	...
35 - 39	172 081	...	...	...
40 - 44	49 519	...	...	...
45 - 49	13 411	...	...	...
50 +	2 687	...	...	...
Réunion[6]				
2007 (C)				
Total	14 808	7 711	7 097	69.2
0 - 14	23	11	12	..
15 - 19	1 517	769	748	44.1
20 - 24	3 348	1 752	1 596	117.2
25 - 29	3 968	2 075	1 893	144.2
30 - 34	3 429	1 779	1 650	116.2
35 - 39	1 931	1 009	922	58.6
40 - 44	572	307	265	16.8
45 +	20	9	11	♦0.7
Seychelles				
2011 (+C)				
Total	1 625	807	818	66.8
0 - 14	4	3	1	..
15 - 19	244	122	122	70.3
20 - 24	404	204	200	133.7
25 - 29	392	192	200	114.3
30 - 34	318	153	165	86.5
35 - 39	203	95	108	55.3
40 - 44	58	37	21	16.3
45 +	2	1	1	♦0.6

10. Live births by age of mother and sex of child, general and age-specific fertility rates: latest available year, 2003 - 2012
Naissances vivantes selon l'âge de la mère et le sexe de l'enfant, taux de fécondité et taux de fécondité par âge : dernière année disponible, 2003 - 2012 (continued - suite)

Continent, country or area, year, code and age of mother (in years) / Continent, pays ou zone, année, code et âge de la mère (en années)	Number - Nombre			Rate Taux
	Total	Male Masculin	Female Féminin	
AFRICA - AFRIQUE				
South Africa - Afrique du Sud				
2007 (U)[7]				
Total	858 866	432 282	426 584	...
0 - 14	804	381	423	..
15 - 19	93 451	47 102	46 349	...
20 - 24	246 545	124 213	122 332	...
25 - 29	222 601	112 241	110 360	...
30 - 34	165 240	83 254	81 986	...
35 - 39	95 875	47 952	47 923	...
40 - 44	29 099	14 544	14 555	...
45 - 49	4 196	2 093	2 103	...
50 +	659	310	349	..
Unknown - Inconnu	396	192	204	..
2010 (U)[8]				
Total	890 586	...	...	...
0 - 14	895	...	...	..
15 - 19	110 342	...	...	...
20 - 24	246 018	...	...	...
25 - 29	236 995	...	...	...
30 - 34	166 055	...	...	...
35 - 39	95 571	...	...	...
40 - 44	30 399	...	...	...
45 - 49	3 088	...	...	...
50 - 54	266	...	...	..
55 +	957	...	...	..
Swaziland[9]				
2007 (I)				
Total	33 084	18 905	14 179	152.2
0 - 14	67	33	34	..
15 - 19	3 581	1 775	1 806	71.0
20 - 24	8 303	4 449	3 854	184.4
25 - 29	6 839	3 830	3 009	187.1
30 - 34	5 039	2 969	2 070	188.5
35 - 39	3 839	2 324	1 515	166.8
40 - 44	2 008	1 340	668	104.7
45 - 49	1 246	892	354	75.8
50 +	2 155	1 288	867	..
Unknown - Inconnu	7	5	2	..
Tunisia - Tunisie				
2011 (C)				
Total	201 120	...	...	...
15 - 19	2 550	...	...	...
20 - 24	23 594	...	...	...
25 - 29	52 266	...	...	...
30 - 34	51 003	...	...	...
35 - 39	28 565	...	...	...
40 - 44	7 282	...	...	...
45 - 49	596	...	...	..
Unknown - Inconnu	35 265	...	...	..
AMERICA, NORTH - AMÉRIQUE DU NORD				
Anguilla				
2006 (+C)				
Total	183	...	...	...
0 - 14	2	...	...	..
15 - 19	26	...	...	...
20 - 24	56	...	...	...
25 - 29	42	...	...	...
30 - 34	26	...	...	...
35 - 39	27	...	...	...
40 +	4	...	...	...

Continent, country or area, year, code and age of mother (in years) / Continent, pays ou zone, année, code et âge de la mère (en années)	Number - Nombre			Rate Taux
	Total	Male Masculin	Female Féminin	
AMERICA, NORTH - AMÉRIQUE DU NORD				
Aruba				
2007 (C)				
Total	1 239	642	597	43.2
0 - 14	3	2	1	..
15 - 19	149	78	71	41.0
20 - 24	305	157	148	101.2
25 - 29	314	149	165	94.7
30 - 34	280	159	121	71.7
35 - 39	149	79	70	31.6
40 - 44	36	17	19	7.1
45 - 49	2	1	1	♦0.4
50 +	-	-	-	..
Unknown - Inconnu	1	-	1	..
2010 (C)				
Total	1 141	...	...	44.3
0 - 14	-	...	...	..
15 - 19	149	...	...	42.3
20 - 24	282	...	...	110.5
25 - 29	280	...	...	95.8
30 - 34	264	...	...	75.4
35 - 39	128	...	...	32.3
40 - 44	37	...	...	8.4
45 - 49	1	...	...	♦0.2
50 +	-	...	...	..
Bahamas				
2010 (+U)				
Total	4 915	2 514	2 401	...
0 - 14	13	8	5	..
15 - 19	560	302	258	...
20 - 24	1 135	580	555	...
25 - 29	1 251	639	612	...
30 - 34	1 085	530	555	...
35 - 39	660	344	316	...
40 - 44	198	101	97	...
45 - 49	13	10	3	...
50 +	-	-	-	..
Barbados - Barbade				
2007 (+C)				
Total	3 537	1 850	1 687	..
0 - 14	10	7	3	..
15 - 19	462	226	236	...
20 - 24	894	487	407	...
25 - 29	805	420	385	...
30 - 34	730	387	343	...
35 - 39	463	235	228	...
40 - 44	164	84	80	...
45 - 49	7	3	4	...
Unknown - Inconnu	2	1	1	..
Bermuda - Bermudes[10]				
2011 (C)				
Total	670	330	340	41.6
0 - 14	-	-	-	..
15 - 19	12	3	9	♦6.5
20 - 24	84	46	38	44.9
25 - 29	169	86	83	73.9
30 - 34	212	100	112	92.5
35 - 39	146	72	74	61.7
40 - 44	44	22	22	17.0
45 - 49	3	1	2	♦1.0
50 +	-	-	-	..
Canada[11]				
2009 (C)				
Total	380 863	195 445	185 418	46.0
0 - 14	104	52	52	..
15 - 19	15 534	7 997	7 537	14.1

10. Live births by age of mother and sex of child, general and age-specific fertility rates: latest available year, 2003 - 2012
Naissances vivantes selon l'âge de la mère et le sexe de l'enfant, taux de fécondité et taux de fécondité par âge : dernière année disponible, 2003 - 2012 (continued - suite)

Continent, country or area, year, code and age of mother (in years) / Continent, pays ou zone, année, code et âge de la mère (en années)	Total	Male Masculin	Female Féminin	Rate Taux	Continent, country or area, year, code and age of mother (in years) / Continent, pays ou zone, année, code et âge de la mère (en années)	Total	Male Masculin	Female Féminin	Rate Taux
AMERICA, NORTH - AMÉRIQUE DU NORD					**AMERICA, NORTH - AMÉRIQUE DU NORD**				
Canada[11]					Curaçao				
2009 (C)					2011 (C)				
20 - 24	57 778	29 564	28 214	51.2	40 - 44	78	38	40	12.6
25 - 29	116 878	60 099	56 779	100.7	45 - 49	3	1	2	♦0.4
30 - 34	120 734	62 132	58 602	107.0	50 +	-	-	-	..
35 - 39	57 733	29 493	28 240	50.6	Unknown - Inconnu	28	15	13	..
40 - 44	11 364	5 720	5 644	9.2	Dominica - Dominique				
45 - 49	605	316	289	0.4	2006 (+C)				
Unknown - Inconnu[12]	133	72	61	..	Total	1 056	505	551	62.4
Cayman Islands - Îles Caïmanes[13]					0 - 14	3	-	3	..
2010 (C)					15 - 19	154	80	74	45.8
Total	821	...	...	48.0	20 - 24	250	115	135	116.8
0 - 14	1	...	...	..	25 - 29	197	91	106	78.2
15 - 19	50	...	...	35.9	30 - 34	207	99	108	74.5
20 - 24	138	...	...	89.4	35 - 39	179	86	93	72.9
25 - 29	167	...	...	65.0	40 - 44	59	29	30	28.7
30 - 34	237	...	...	80.8	45 - 49	5	3	2	♦3.1
35 - 39	184	...	...	57.7	Dominican Republic - République dominicaine				
40 +	44	...	...	8.1	2011 (U)				
Costa Rica					Total	128 837	65 863	62 974	...
2010* (C)					0 - 14	282	140	142	..
Total	70 922	36 382	34 540	56.8	15 - 19	18 114	9 216	8 898	...
0 - 14	428	234	194	..	20 - 24	39 505	20 181	19 324	...
15 - 19	12 828	6 598	6 230	62.0	25 - 29	32 827	16 786	16 041	...
20 - 24	21 353	10 945	10 408	99.5	30 - 34	21 346	10 909	10 437	...
25 - 29	18 001	9 303	8 698	91.2	35 - 39	8 412	4 299	4 113	...
30 - 34	11 648	5 907	5 741	66.5	40 - 44	1 930	960	970	...
35 - 39	5 098	2 577	2 521	33.5	45 - 49	153	88	65	...
40 - 44	1 265	666	599	8.3	50 +	23	10	13	..
45 +	95	52	43	0.6	Unknown - Inconnu	6 245	3 274	2 971	..
Unknown - Inconnu	206	100	106	..	El Salvador[14]				
2011* (C)					2011 (C)				
Total	73 459	...	...	58.2	Total	109 384	56 963	52 421	63.0
0 - 14	476	...	...	..	0 - 14	1 022	524	498	..
15 - 19	13 391	...	...	65.3	15 - 19	22 723	11 674	11 049	65.0
20 - 24	21 375	...	...	100.3	20 - 24	31 937	16 650	15 287	104.9
25 - 29	18 750	...	...	92.5	25 - 29	24 463	12 805	11 658	94.0
30 - 34	12 312	...	...	68.0	30 - 34	17 861	9 313	8 548	76.2
35 - 39	5 547	...	...	35.9	35 - 39	8 511	4 479	4 032	39.0
40 - 44	1 250	...	...	8.3	40 - 44	2 300	1 215	1 085	11.8
45 +	84	...	...	0.6	45 - 49	145	79	66	0.9
Unknown - Inconnu	274	...	...	..	50 +	14	8	6	..
Cuba					Unknown - Inconnu	408	216	192	..
2011 (C)					Greenland - Groenland				
Total	133 067	68 464	64 603	45.3	2011* (C)				
0 - 14	408	211	197	..	Total	821	436	385	57.2
15 - 19	19 895	10 238	9 657	56.1	0 - 14	1	-	1	..
20 - 24	44 987	23 208	21 779	111.6	15 - 19	92	46	46	40.7
25 - 29	34 925	17 947	16 978	98.2	20 - 24	238	122	116	103.8
30 - 34	18 526	9 450	9 076	57.1	25 - 29	247	128	119	122.8
35 - 39	11 533	5 971	5 562	24.8	30 - 34	169	92	77	98.9
40 - 44	2 581	1 333	1 248	5.0	35 - 39	63	39	24	43.3
45 - 49	107	50	57	0.2	40 - 44	11	9	2	♦5.1
50 +	43	24	19	..	45 - 49	-	-	-	..
Unknown - Inconnu	62	32	30	..	Guadeloupe[6]				
Curaçao					2003 (C)				
2011 (C)					Total	7 047	3 543	3 504	60.4
Total	1 974	992	982	52.3	0 - 14	7	2	5	..
0 - 14	6	3	3	..	15 - 19	431	215	216	25.5
15 - 19	193	104	89	35.0	20 - 24	1 148	588	560	81.3
20 - 24	425	203	222	103.6	25 - 29	1 815	912	903	132.3
25 - 29	504	266	238	119.2	30 - 34	2 001	1 005	996	108.6
30 - 34	453	217	236	98.7	35 - 39	1 280	637	643	64.6
35 - 39	284	145	139	51.7					

10. Live births by age of mother and sex of child, general and age-specific fertility rates: latest available year, 2003 - 2012

Naissances vivantes selon l'âge de la mère et le sexe de l'enfant, taux de fécondité et taux de fécondité par âge : dernière année disponible, 2003 - 2012 (continued - suite)

Continent, country or area, year, code and age of mother (in years) / Continent, pays ou zone, année, code et âge de la mère (en années)	Number - Nombre			Rate Taux
	Total	Male Masculin	Female Féminin	

AMERICA, NORTH - AMÉRIQUE DU NORD

Guadeloupe[6]				
2003 (C)				
40 - 44	352	177	175	19.3
45 +	13	7	6	♦0.8
Guatemala				
2011 (C)				
Total	373 692	189 724	183 968	...
0 - 14	2 841	1 426	1 415	..
15 - 19	75 175	38 415	36 760	...
20 - 24	108 949	55 558	53 391	...
25 - 29	85 914	43 599	42 315	...
30 - 34	58 050	29 264	28 786	...
35 - 39	30 892	15 540	15 352	...
40 - 44	10 220	5 136	5 084	...
45 - 49	1 176	573	603	...
50 +	290	127	163	..
Unknown - Inconnu	185	86	99	..
Jamaica - Jamaïque[15]				
2006 (C)				
Total	42 387	21 671	20 716	...
0 - 14	211	111	100	..
15 - 19	7 809	4 029	3 780	...
20 - 24	11 699	5 972	5 727	...
25 - 29	9 283	4 722	4 561	...
30 - 34	7 339	3 781	3 558	...
35 - 39	4 455	2 280	2 175	...
40 - 44	1 496	732	764	...
45 +	79	35	44	...
Unknown - Inconnu	16	9	7	..
Martinique[6]				
2007 (C)				
Total	5 317	2 676	2 641	51.0
0 - 14	2	1	1	..
15 - 19	305	165	140	19.8
20 - 24	911	447	464	77.6
25 - 29	1 202	617	585	117.2
30 - 34	1 376	678	698	98.2
35 - 39	1 105	560	545	64.1
40 - 44	393	194	199	20.9
45 +	23	14	9	♦1.4
Mexico - Mexique				
2009 (+U)[16]				
Total	2 252 786	1 147 390[17]	1 105 092[17]	...
0 - 14	8 105	4 184[17]	3 920[17]	..
15 - 19	409 097	208 885[17]	200 176[17]	...
20 - 24	661 928	338 003[17]	323 858[17]	...
25 - 29	556 810	283 370[17]	273 407[17]	...
30 - 34	377 652	191 772[17]	185 843[17]	...
35 - 39	180 761	91 480[17]	89 261[17]	...
40 - 44	41 018	20 598[17]	20 411[17]	...
45 - 49	3 515	1 725[17]	1 790[17]	...
50 +	671	345[17]	325[17]	..
Unknown - Inconnu	13 229	7 028[17]	6 101[17]	..
2010 (I)[18]				
Total	2 031 806	...	...	66.2
12 - 14	4 451	...	...	..
15 - 19	312 007	...	...	56.7
20 - 24	604 533	...	...	119.0
25 - 29	506 678	...	...	110.6
30 - 34	362 970	...	...	81.7
35 - 39	184 971	...	...	42.7
40 - 44	48 527	...	...	13.3
45 - 49	6 351	...	...	2.0
50 +	1 318	...	...	

Continent, country or area, year, code and age of mother (in years) / Continent, pays ou zone, année, code et âge de la mère (en années)	Number - Nombre			Rate Taux
	Total	Male Masculin	Female Féminin	

AMERICA, NORTH - AMÉRIQUE DU NORD

Montserrat				
2011 (+C)				
Total	46	24	22	...
0 - 14	1	1	-	..
15 - 19	7	4	3	..
20 - 24	9	2	7	...
25 - 29	13	7	6	...
30 - 34	7	4	3	...
35 - 39	6	4	2	...
40 - 44	2	2	-	...
45 - 49	1	-	1	...
50 +	-	-	-	...
Nicaragua				
2008 (+U)				
Total	125 028	64 802	60 226	...
0 - 14	1 448	706	742	..
15 - 19	32 390	16 748	15 642	...
20 - 24	37 567	19 505	18 062	...
25 - 29	28 795	14 966	13 829	...
30 - 34	15 493	8 104	7 389	...
35 - 39	7 357	3 728	3 629	...
40 - 44	1 796	948	848	...
45 - 49	170	89	81	...
50 +	12	8	4	..
Panama				
2010 (C)				
Total	67 955	34 651	33 304	74.3
0 - 14	608	303	305	..
15 - 19	12 945	6 660	6 285	86.0
20 - 24	19 605	9 976	9 629	133.7
25 - 29	16 130	8 349	7 781	118.0
30 - 34	11 136	5 542	5 594	85.5
35 - 39	5 881	2 988	2 893	45.5
40 - 44	1 414	714	700	12.0
45 - 49	105	54	51	1.0
50 +	18	9	9	..
Unknown - Inconnu	113	56	57	..
Puerto Rico - Porto Rico				
2008 (C)				
Total	45 675	23 443	22 232	46.5
0 - 14	147	72	75	..
15 - 19	7 989	4 036	3 953	54.6
20 - 24	14 580	7 399	7 181	106.0
25 - 29	11 828	6 135	5 693	81.9
30 - 34	7 297	3 785	3 512	52.4
35 - 39	3 124	1 652	1 472	23.0
40 - 44	657	339	318	4.7
45 - 49	35	17	18	0.3
50 +	2	1	1	..
Unknown - Inconnu	16	7	9	..
Saint Lucia - Sainte-Lucie				
2005* (C)				
Total	2 215	...	...	47.6
0 - 14	6	...	...	..
15 - 19	374	...	...	42.1
20 - 24	624	...	...	77.6
25 - 29	526	...	...	75.7
30 - 34	378	...	...	58.4
35 - 39	236	...	...	38.7
40 - 44	62	...	...	10.9
45 +	10	...	...	♦2.3

10. Live births by age of mother and sex of child, general and age-specific fertility rates: latest available year, 2003 - 2012
Naissances vivantes selon l'âge de la mère et le sexe de l'enfant, taux de fécondité et taux de fécondité par âge : dernière année disponible, 2003 - 2012 (continued - suite)

AMERICA, NORTH - AMÉRIQUE DU NORD

Continent, pays ou zone, année, code et âge de la mère (en années)	Total	Male Masculin	Female Féminin	Rate Taux
Saint Vincent and the Grenadines - Saint-Vincent-et-les Grenadines				
2009 (+C)				
Total	1 905	949	956	...
0 - 14	9	3	6	..
15 - 19	365	164	201	..
20 - 24	511	269	242	..
25 - 29	446	226	220	..
30 - 34	332	162	170	..
35 - 39	172	95	77	..
40 - 44	64	28	36	..
45 +	5	2	3	...
Unknown - Inconnu	1	-	1	..
Trinidad and Tobago - Trinité-et-Tobago				
2006 (C)				
Total	18 090	9 330	8 760	...
0 - 14	27	7	20	..
15 - 19	2 115	1 114	1 001	..
20 - 24	5 640	2 912	2 728	...
25 - 29	4 938	2 523	2 415	...
30 - 34	3 268	1 710	1 558	...
35 - 39	1 578	805	773	...
40 - 44	462	228	234	...
45 - 49	28	16	12	...
50 +	1	-	1	..
Unknown - Inconnu	33	15	18	..
Turks and Caicos Islands - Îles Turques et Caïques				
2005 (C)				
Total	318	158	160	...
0 - 14	1	-	1	..
15 - 19	28	13	15	..
20 - 24	65	29	36	...
25 - 29	83	40	43	...
30 - 34	76	47	29	...
35 - 39	52	23	29	...
40 - 44	11	5	6	...
45 +	2	1	1	...
United States of America - États-Unis d'Amérique				
2008 (C)				
Total	4 247 694	...	...	57.8
0 - 14	5 764	...	...	..
15 - 19	434 758	...	...	41.5
20 - 24	1 052 184	...	...	103.0
25 - 29	1 195 774	...	...	115.1
30 - 34	956 716	...	...	99.3
35 - 39	488 875	...	...	46.9
40 - 44	105 973	...	...	9.8
45 - 49	7 109	...	...	0.6
50 +	541	...	...	..
United States Virgin Islands - Îles Vierges américaines				
2007 (C)				
Total	1 771	...	...	65.9
0 - 14	2	...	...	..
15 - 19	226	...	...	53.1
20 - 24	550	...	...	146.6
25 - 29	424	...	...	146.1
30 - 34	319	...	...	93.9
35 - 39	196	...	...	48.6
40 +	46	...	...	5.5
Unknown - Inconnu	8	...	...	...

AMERICA, SOUTH - AMÉRIQUE DU SUD

Continent, pays ou zone, année, code et âge de la mère (en années)	Total	Male Masculin	Female Féminin	Rate Taux
Argentina - Argentine				
2011 (C)				
Total	758 042	...	...	...
0 - 14	3 156	...	...	..
15 - 19	115 856	...	...	..
20 - 24	186 004	...	...	..
25 - 29	173 015	...	...	..
30 - 34	161 321	...	...	..
35 - 39	87 141	...	...	..
40 - 44	22 665	...	...	..
45 - 49	1 537	...	...	..
50 +	129	...	...	..
Unknown - Inconnu	7 218	...	...	..
Brazil - Brésil				
2011 (U)				
Total[19]	2 824 776	1 446 926[17]	1 377 588[17]	...
0 - 14	21 859	11 186[17]	10 671[17]	..
15 - 19	498 365	255 554[17]	242 774[17]	...
20 - 24	753 774	386 622[17]	367 113[17]	...
25 - 29	707 369	362 637[17]	344 690[17]	...
30 - 34	515 553	263 358[17]	252 161[17]	...
35 - 39	244 665	124 932[17]	119 715[17]	...
40 - 44	60 388	30 906[17]	29 477[17]	...
45 - 49	4 052	2 052[17]	2 000[17]	...
50 +	287	144[17]	143[17]	..
Chile - Chili				
2010 (C)				
Total	250 643	127 682	122 961	55.0
0 - 14	963	496	467	..
15 - 19	38 047	19 432	18 615	52.0
20 - 24	59 884	30 545	29 339	83.1
25 - 29	59 623	30 260	29 363	91.3
30 - 34	50 841	25 932	24 909	87.5
35 - 39	32 300	16 388	15 912	52.3
40 - 44	8 478	4 390	4 088	13.7
45 - 49	449	213	236	0.7
50 +	5	3	2	..
Unknown - Inconnu	53	23	30	..
Colombia - Colombie				
2011* (U)				
Total	621 901	319 091	302 810	...
10 - 14	5 849	3 032	2 817	..
15 - 19	139 871	72 236	67 635	..
20 - 24	179 044	91 890	87 154	..
25 - 29	139 846	71 715	68 131	..
30 - 34	95 750	49 091	46 681	..
35 - 39	46 714	23 701	23 013	..
40 - 44	13 238	6 644	6 594	..
45 - 49	1 046	523	523	..
50 +	144	81	63	..
Unknown - Inconnu	377	178	199	..
Ecuador - Équateur[20]				
2009 (+U)				
Total	215 906	110 413	105 493	..
0 - 14	1 358	683	675	..
15 - 19	42 554	21 716	20 838	..
20 - 24	62 732	32 294	30 438	..
25 - 29	49 771	25 380	24 391	..
30 - 34	33 006	16 869	16 137	..
35 - 39	16 832	8 523	8 309	..
40 - 44	5 110	2 607	2 503	..
45 - 49	567	304	263	..
50 +	-	-	-	..
Unknown - Inconnu	3 976	2 037	1 939	..

10. Live births by age of mother and sex of child, general and age-specific fertility rates: latest available year, 2003 - 2012
Naissances vivantes selon l'âge de la mère et le sexe de l'enfant, taux de fécondité et taux de fécondité par âge : dernière année disponible, 2003 - 2012 (continued - suite)

Continent, country or area, year, code and age of mother (in years) / Continent, pays ou zone, année, code et âge de la mère (en années)	Total	Male Masculin	Female Féminin	Rate Taux
AMERICA, SOUTH - AMÉRIQUE DU SUD				
French Guiana - Guyane française[6]				
2007 (C)				
Total	6 386	3 269	3 117	114.5
0 - 14	23	12	11	..
15 - 19	828	428	400	83.3
20 - 24	1 477	726	751	182.2
25 - 29	1 590	821	769	195.5
30 - 34	1 312	707	605	154.0
35 - 39	844	414	430	102.2
40 - 44	289	152	137	40.9
45 - 49	22	8	14	♦3.8
50 +	1	1	-	..
Paraguay				
2008 (+U)				
Total	99 674	51 066	48 608	...
0 - 14	538	269	269	..
15 - 19	20 188	10 404	9 784	...
20 - 24	28 246	14 396	13 850	...
25 - 29	23 863	12 261	11 602	...
30 - 34	14 721	7 480	7 241	...
35 - 39	8 899	4 600	4 299	...
40 - 44	2 819	1 440	1 379	...
45 - 49	250	134	116	..
50 +	2	2	-	..
Unknown - Inconnu	148	80	68	..
Peru - Pérou[21]				
2011 (+U)				
Total	396 839	203 259	193 580	...
0 - 14	1 678	881	797	..
15 - 19	59 961	30 865	29 096	...
20 - 24	101 131	52 099	49 032	...
25 - 29	95 322	48 725	46 597	...
30 - 34	76 115	38 859	37 256	...
35 - 39	46 900	23 796	23 104	...
40 - 44	14 563	7 447	7 116	...
45 - 49	1 039	522	517	...
50 +	116	55	61	..
Unknown - Inconnu	14	10	4	..
Suriname[22]				
2007 (C)				
Total	9 769	...	...	73.6
0 - 14	65	...	...	..
15 - 19	1 485	...	...	65.5
20 - 24	2 818	...	...	130.8
25 - 29	2 487	...	...	121.9
30 - 34	1 716	...	...	88.8
35 - 39	943	...	...	52.0
40 - 44	243	...	...	14.9
45 +	12	...	...	♦0.8
Uruguay[23]				
2011 (|)				
Total	41 305	...	...	51.2
12 - 14	64	...	...	..
15 - 19	5 253	...	...	40.8
20 - 24	9 411	...	...	77.7
25 - 29	9 384	...	...	81.2
30 - 34	9 512	...	...	79.6
35 - 39	5 925	...	...	52.1
40 - 44	1 623	...	...	15.5
45 - 49	128	...	...	1.2
50 +	5	...	...	..

Continent, country or area, year, code and age of mother (in years) / Continent, pays ou zone, année, code et âge de la mère (en années)	Total	Male Masculin	Female Féminin	Rate Taux
AMERICA, SOUTH - AMÉRIQUE DU SUD				
Venezuela (Bolivarian Republic of) - Venezuela (République bolivarienne du)				
2011 (C)				
Total	615 132	316 884	298 248	79.4
0 - 14	7 599	3 899	3 700	..
15 - 19	133 900	69 341	64 559	101.9
20 - 24	176 311	90 892	85 419	135.0
25 - 29	141 059	72 575	68 484	115.8
30 - 34	92 483	47 490	44 993	83.2
35 - 39	43 049	22 098	20 951	44.4
40 - 44	11 654	5 943	5 711	12.9
45 - 49	1 255	622	633	1.5
50 +	438	204	234	..
Unknown - Inconnu	7 384	3 820	3 564	..
ASIA - ASIE				
Armenia - Arménie				
2009 (C)				
Total	44 413	23 652	20 761	48.4
15 - 19	4 035	2 055	1 980	27.6
20 - 24	19 686	10 292	9 394	125.8
25 - 29	13 628	7 422	6 206	95.4
30 - 34	5 156	2 859	2 297	43.1
35 - 39	1 590	866	724	15.3
40 - 44	287	141	146	2.6
45 - 49	27	14	13	♦0.2
50 +	4	3	1	..
Azerbaijan - Azerbaïdjan[24]				
2010 (+C)				
Total	165 643	89 134	76 509	61.4
12 - 14	7	6	1	..
15 - 19	21 028	10 903	10 125	48.6
20 - 24	70 530	37 285	33 245	148.5
25 - 29	46 351	25 446	20 905	110.3
30 - 34	18 775	10 396	8 379	53.5
35 - 39	6 958	3 977	2 981	21.7
40 - 44	1 760	1 001	759	5.1
45 - 49	202	101	101	0.6
50 +	32	19	13	..
Bahrain - Bahreïn				
2012* (C)				
Total	18 725	9 571	9 154	..
0 - 14	1	-	1	..
15 - 19	492	258	234	...
20 - 24	3 925	2 013	1 912	...
25 - 29	6 172	3 185	2 987	...
30 - 34	4 844	2 494	2 350	...
35 - 39	2 513	1 218	1 295	...
40 - 44	694	361	333	...
45 - 49	72	37	35	...
50 +	9	4	5	..
Unknown - Inconnu	3	1	2	..
Bangladesh				
2010 (U)				
Total	2 868 494	1 451 664	1 416 831	...
15 - 19	404 570	209 615	194 955	...
20 - 24	1 055 194	527 993	527 201	...
25 - 29	762 338	383 627	378 710	...
30 - 34	389 547	199 767	189 780	...
35 - 39	192 438	97 826	94 613	...
40 - 44	49 380	25 206	24 174	...
45 +	15 027	7 630	7 397	...

Continent, country or area, year, code and age of mother (in years) — Continent, pays ou zone, année, code et âge de la mère (en années)	Number - Nombre			Rate Taux	Continent, country or area, year, code and age of mother (in years) — Continent, pays ou zone, année, code et âge de la mère (en années)	Number - Nombre			Rate Taux
	Total	Male Masculin	Female Féminin			Total	Male Masculin	Female Féminin	
ASIA - ASIE					**ASIA - ASIE**				
Bhutan - Bhoutan[9]					**Cyprus - Chypre[25]**				
2005 (|)					2011 (C)				
Total	12 538	6 306	6 232	79.4	30 - 34	3 325	1 696	1 629	92.1
15 - 19	1 376	711	665	36.5	35 - 39	1 333	690	643	39.9
20 - 24	4 211	2 156	2 055	138.9	40 - 44	287	144	143	9.3
25 - 29	3 677	1 814	1 863	141.6	45 - 49	29	11	18	♦1.0
30 - 34	1 753	880	873	89.4	Unknown - Inconnu	9	5	4	..
35 - 39	960	463	497	54.5	**Democratic People's Republic of Korea - République populaire démocratique de Corée[23]**				
40 - 44	434	207	227	31.3	2008 (|)				
45 - 49	127	75	52	9.9	Total	345 630	176 399	169 231	53.3
Brunei Darussalam - Brunéi Darussalam					15 - 19	633	330	303	0.6
2008 (+C)					20 - 24	52 214	26 657	25 557	58.0
Total	6 424	3 332	3 092	...	25 - 29	178 032	90 850	87 182	209.5
0 - 14	4	-	4	..	30 - 34	90 973	46 224	44 749	110.0
15 - 19	279	159	120	...	35 - 39	20 275	10 505	9 770	18.5
20 - 24	1 206	654	552	...	40 - 44	3 202	1 673	1 529	3.2
25 - 29	2 113	1 092	1 021	...	45 - 49	301	160	141	0.4
30 - 34	1 697	866	831	...	**Georgia - Géorgie**				
35 - 39	913	453	460	...	2012 (C)				
40 - 44	198	99	99	...	Total	57 031	29 801	27 230	49.5
45 - 49	12	7	5	...	0 - 14	26	15	11	..
50 +	-	-	-	..	15 - 19	5 636	2 956	2 680	39.7
Unknown - Inconnu	2	2	-	..	20 - 24	19 571	10 238	9 333	107.6
Cambodia - Cambodge					25 - 29	16 833	8 851	7 982	94.4
2004 (U)					30 - 34	9 734	5 070	4 664	58.6
Total	320 594	...	...	...	35 - 39	4 131	2 116	2 015	25.9
15 - 19	23 238	...	...	...	40 - 44	980	500	480	6.3
20 - 24	106 787	...	...	...	45 - 49	91	38	53	0.5
25 - 29	66 573	...	...	...	50 +	16	8	8	..
30 - 34	57 861	...	...	...	Unknown - Inconnu	13	9	4	..
35 - 39	43 391	...	...	...	**Iran (Islamic Republic of) - Iran (République islamique d')[23]**				
40 - 44	19 386	...	...	...	2006 (|)				
45 - 49	3 358	...	...	...	Total	950 660	489 902	460 758	44.8
China, Hong Kong SAR - Chine, Hong Kong RAS					0 - 14	1 706	901	805	..
2011 (C)					15 - 19	77 246	39 549	37 697	18.0
Total	95 451	51 286	44 165	45.9	20 - 24	28 966	146 585	142 681	6.4
0 - 14	9	5	4	..	25 - 29	290 575	150 174	140 401	81.5
15 - 19	774	434	340	3.8	30 - 34	180 284	92 809	87 475	66.4.
20 - 24	9 089	4 861	4 228	39.6	35 - 39	84 634	45 024	39 610	35.1
25 - 29	25 327	13 554	11 773	83.2	40 - 44	21 436	12 006	9 430	10.7
30 - 34	33 356	17 950	15 406	102.9	45 - 49	4 185	2 062	2 123	2.4
35 - 39	22 245	11 948	10 297	67.8	50 +	1 331	794	537	..
40 - 44	4 364	2 369	1 995	13.2	**Israel - Israël[26]**				
45 - 49	207	119	88	0.6	2011 (C)				
50 +	24	16	8	..	Total	166 296	85 162	81 134	90.3
Unknown - Inconnu	56	30	26	..	0 - 14	3	1	2	..
China, Macao SAR - Chine, Macao RAS					15 - 19	3 659	1 894	1 765	12.5
2012 (C)					20 - 24	30 897	15 914	14 983	106.5
Total	7 315	3 894	3 421	40.7	25 - 29	49 259	25 196	24 063	172.4
0 - 24	1 030	536	494	22.6	30 - 34	47 913	24 568	23 345	175.5
25 - 29	2 927	1 568	1 359	92.9	35 - 39	27 406	13 950	13 456	103.6
30 - 34	2 116	1 112	1 004	88.5	40 - 44	6 252	3 194	3 058	27.4
35 - 39	1 021	558	463	43.3	45 - 49	542	268	274	2.6
40 +	220	119	101	4.0	50 +	83	40	43	..
Unknown - Inconnu	1	1	-	..	Unknown - Inconnu	282	137	145	..
Cyprus - Chypre[25]					**Japan - Japon[27]**				
2011 (C)					2011 (C)				
Total	9 622	4 891	4 731	41.4	Total	1 050 806	538 271	512 535	38.9
12 - 14	2	-	2	..	0 - 14	44	24	20	..
15 - 19	171	87	84	5.7	15 - 19	13 274	6 879	6 395	4.5
20 - 24	1 187	598	589	34.1					
25 - 29	3 277	1 660	1 617	87.0					

10. Live births by age of mother and sex of child, general and age-specific fertility rates: latest available year, 2003 - 2012
Naissances vivantes selon l'âge de la mère et le sexe de l'enfant, taux de fécondité et taux de fécondité par âge : dernière année disponible, 2003 - 2012 (continued - suite)

Continent, country or area, year, code and age of mother (in years) / Continent, pays ou zone, année, code et âge de la mère (en années)	Number - Nombre			Rate Taux
	Total	Male Masculin	Female Féminin	

ASIA - ASIE

	Total	Male Masculin	Female Féminin	Rate Taux
Japan - Japon[27]				
2011 (C)				
20 - 24	104 059	53 157	50 902	33.2
25 - 29	300 384	153 788	146 596	84.2
30 - 34	373 490	191 778	181 712	92.9
35 - 39	221 272	112 914	108 358	46.0
40 - 44	37 437	19 330	18 107	8.3
45 - 49	802	385	417	0.2
50 +	41	15	26	..
Unknown - Inconnu	3	1	2	..
Kazakhstan[24]				
2008 (C)				
Total	356 575	183 263	173 312	80.7
0 - 14	35	19	16	..
15 - 19	22 689	11 697	10 992	31.1
20 - 24	121 095	62 340	58 755	158.2
25 - 29	103 323	53 053	50 270	160.5
30 - 34	66 732	34 153	32 579	112.0
35 - 39	33 931	17 534	16 397	60.7
40 - 44	8 105	4 125	3 980	14.9
45 - 49	396	203	193	0.7
50 +	17	12	5	..
Unknown - Inconnu	252	127	125	..
Kuwait - Koweït				
2011 (C)				
Total	58 198	29 656	28 542	67.2
15 - 19	869	465	404	10.6
20 - 24	10 660	5 471	5 189	89.1
25 - 29	17 997	9 109	8 888	111.1
30 - 34	14 820	7 591	7 229	99.4
35 - 39	7 638	3 960	3 678	61.2
40 - 44	2 224	1 098	1 126	22.0
45 +	189	95	94	2.6
Unknown - Inconnu	3 801	1 867	1 934	..
Kyrgyzstan - Kirghizstan				
2011 (C)				
Total	149 612	76 753	72 859	98.7
0 - 14	1	1	-	..
15 - 19	11 756	6 221	5 535	41.5
20 - 24	55 178	28 362	26 816	186.2
25 - 29	42 522	21 840	20 682	176.3
30 - 34	23 701	12 017	11 684	122.9
35 - 39	12 140	6 135	6 005	69.2
40 - 44	3 554	1 795	1 759	21.5
45 - 49	510	242	268	3.2
50 +	17	8	9	..
Unknown - Inconnu	233	132	101	..
Malaysia - Malaisie				
2009 (C)				
Total	496 313	256 060	240 253	64.9
0 - 14	214	103	111	..
15 - 19	18 911	9 854	9 057	14.8
20 - 24	85 650	44 195	41 455	69.1
25 - 29	166 783	86 130	80 653	141.7
30 - 34	132 826	68 479	64 347	119.6
35 - 39	69 546	35 785	33 761	67.3
40 - 44	19 374	9 944	9 430	20.4
45 - 49	1 660	856	804	2.0
50 +	102	62	40	..
Unknown - Inconnu	1 247	652	595	..
Maldives				
2011 (C)				
Total	7 180	3 796	3 384	73.7
0 - 14	-	-	-	..
15 - 19	277	139	138	15.3

ASIA - ASIE

	Total	Male Masculin	Female Féminin	Rate Taux
Maldives				
2011 (C)				
20 - 24	2 304	1 205	1 099	115.1
25 - 29	2 415	1 273	1 142	133.3
30 - 34	1 366	730	636	106.5
35 - 39	679	374	305	63.3
40 - 44	124	66	58	13.1
45 - 49	8	2	6	♦1.0
50 +	3	3	-	..
Unknown - Inconnu	4	4	-	..
Mongolia - Mongolie				
2010 (+C)				
Total	63 270	32 299	30 971	75.0
15 - 19	2 638	1 339	1 299	18.6
20 - 24	19 864	10 325	9 539	127.7
25 - 29	19 286	9 850	9 436	145.1
30 - 34	12 522	6 407	6 115	104.1
35 - 39	6 908	3 412	3 496	63.1
40 - 44	1 828	859	969	18.7
45 +	224	107	117	2.6
Myanmar[28]				
2010 (+U)				
Total	282 176	...	...	...
15 - 19	9 830	...	...	...
20 - 24	61 041	...	...	...
25 - 29	90 958	...	...	...
30 - 34	69 455	...	...	...
35 - 39	39 250	...	...	...
40 - 44	10 627	...	...	...
45 +	1 015	...	...	...
Oman[29]				
2011 (U)				
Total	67 922	34 549[30]	33 357[30]	...
0 - 14	10	4[30]	6[30]	...
15 - 19	1 419	737[30]	682[30]	...
20 - 24	13 200	6 819[30]	6 379[30]	...
25 - 29	23 081	11 793[30]	11 285[30]	...
30 - 34	17 629	8 925[30]	8 700[30]	...
35 - 39	8 665	4 333[30]	4 331[30]	...
40 - 44	2 452	1 239[30]	1 213[30]	...
45 - 49	417	195[30]	222[30]	...
50 +	48	28[30]	20[30]	...
Unknown - Inconnu	1 001	476[30]	519[30]	...
Pakistan[31]				
2005 (|)				
Total	3 772 494	1 993 492	1 779 002	110.6
15 - 19	161 490	90 049	71 441	20.3
20 - 24	1 050 830	556 310	494 520	157.6
25 - 29	1 166 365	611 186	555 179	225.5
30 - 34	754 513	395 425	359 088	179.9
35 - 39	425 352	222 186	203 166	106.6
40 - 44	161 914	86 273	75 641	50.1
45 +	52 030	32 063	19 967	18.1
Philippines				
2009 (C)				
Total	1 745 585	907 221	838 364	...
0 - 14	1 113	568	545	..
15 - 19	194 549	101 139	93 410	..
20 - 24	495 958	258 047	237 911	..
25 - 29	461 020	240 170	220 850	..
30 - 34	328 063	170 311	157 752	..
35 - 39	187 578	97 061	90 517	..
40 - 44	66 064	34 216	31 848	..
45 - 49	7 712	3 885	3 827	..

10. Live births by age of mother and sex of child, general and age-specific fertility rates: latest available year, 2003 - 2012
Naissances vivantes selon l'âge de la mère et le sexe de l'enfant, taux de fécondité et taux de fécondité par âge : dernière année disponible, 2003 - 2012 (continued - suite)

Continent, country or area, year, code and age of mother (in years) / Continent, pays ou zone, année, code et âge de la mère (en années)	Number - Nombre			Rate Taux
	Total	Male Masculin	Female Féminin	
ASIA - ASIE				
Philippines				
2009 (C)				
50 +	528	282	246	..
Unknown - Inconnu	3 000	1 542	1 458	..
Qatar				
2010 (C)				
Total	19 504	9 926	9 578	71.8
15 - 19	409	207	202	15.2
20 - 24	3 450	1 789	1 661	89.8
25 - 29	6 279	3 252	3 027	104.4
30 - 34	5 464	2 759	2 705	100.3
35 - 39	2 908	1 419	1 489	71.6
40 - 44	900	461	439	30.3
45 - 49	79	32	47	3.7
50 +	13	7	6	..
Unknown - Inconnu	2	-	2	..
Republic of Korea - République de Corée[32]				
2011 (C)				
Total	471 265	242 121	229 144	36.1
0 - 14	19	14	5	..
15 - 19	2 979	1 541	1 438	1.8
20 - 24	24 648	12 729	11 919	16.0
25 - 29	137 008	70 418	66 590	78.3
30 - 34	221 434	113 510	107 924	115.1
35 - 39	74 245	38 326	35 919	36.7
40 - 44	10 126	5 189	4 937	4.8
45 - 49	443	204	239	0.2
50 +	66	27	39	..
Unknown - Inconnu	297	163	134	..
Saudi Arabia - Arabie saoudite[33]				
2005 (...)				
Total	582 582	298 396	284 186	...
15 - 19	25 652	13 139	12 513	...
20 - 24	153 901	78 827	75 074	...
25 - 29	194 252	99 495	94 757	...
30 - 34	135 325	69 313	66 012	...
35 - 39	57 941	29 677	28 264	...
40 - 44	14 373	7 362	7 011	...
45 - 49	1 137	583	555	...
Singapore - Singapour				
2012 (C)				
Total	42 663	22 102	20 561	41.7
0 - 14	7	4	3	..
15 - 19	568	281	287	4.5
20 - 24	3 100	1 590	1 510	23.5
25 - 29	11 399	5 859	5 540	86.7
30 - 34	17 556	9 225	8 331	113.5
35 - 39	8 546	4 395	4 151	52.9
40 - 44	1 441	720	721	9.1
45 - 49	44	26	18	0.3
50 +	2	2	-	..
Unknown - Inconnu	-	-	-	..
Sri Lanka				
2006 (+C)				
Total	373 538	191 263	182 275	67.9
0 - 14	113	57	56	..
15 - 19	20 040	10 335	9 705	21.2
20 - 24	81 003	41 508	39 495	87.5
25 - 29	121 968	62 480	59 488	151.5
30 - 34	90 483	46 346	44 137	118.4
35 - 39	46 534	23 759	22 775	61.6
40 - 44	12 104	6 149	5 955	17.4

Continent, country or area, year, code and age of mother (in years) / Continent, pays ou zone, année, code et âge de la mère (en années)	Number - Nombre			Rate Taux
	Total	Male Masculin	Female Féminin	
ASIA - ASIE				
Sri Lanka				
2006 (+C)				
45 - 49	1 275	622	653	2.1
50 +	18	7	11	..
Thailand - Thaïlande				
2011 (+U)				
Total	795 031	409 699	385 332	...
0 - 14	3 415	1 793	1 622	...
15 - 19	129 321	66 645	62 676	...
20 - 24	186 942	96 371	90 571	...
25 - 29	204 684	105 355	99 329	...
30 - 34	167 671	86 515	81 156	...
35 - 39	80 348	41 311	39 037	...
40 - 44	20 089	10 251	9 838	...
45 - 49	1 293	653	640	...
50 +	73	30	43	..
Unknown - Inconnu	1 195	775	420	..
Timor-Leste				
2004 (C)				
Total	39 168	...	...	187.3
15 - 19	1 999	...	...	42.2
20 - 24	9 387	...	...	246.6
25 - 29	9 335	...	...	324.4
30 - 34	9 214	...	...	305.3
35 - 39	5 403	...	...	226.0
40 - 44	2 814	...	...	120.1
45 - 49	787	...	...	45.2
50 +	229	...	...	..
Turkey - Turquie[34]				
2010 (C)				
Total	1 238 970	636 722	602 248	63.6
12 - 14	347	203	144	..
15 - 19	97 010	49 756	47 254	32.1
20 - 24	339 002	174 657	164 345	110.9
25 - 29	392 497	201 402	191 095	123.3
30 - 34	258 667	133 167	125 500	89.3
35 - 39	115 789	59 294	56 495	42.5
40 - 44	24 110	12 324	11 786	10.6
45 - 49	4 002	2 017	1 985	1.8
50 +	594	284	310	..
Unknown - Inconnu	6 952	3 618	3 334	..
United Arab Emirates - Émirats arabes unis[33]				
2003 (...)				
Total	61 165	31 241	29 924	...
15 - 19	2 647	1 415	1 232	...
20 - 24	12 551	6 386	6 165	...
25 - 29	18 710	9 605	9 105	...
30 - 34	14 699	7 484	7 215	...
35 - 39	7 670	3 876	3 794	...
40 - 44	2 796	1 409	1 387	...
45 - 49	620	316	304	...
50 +	101	51	50	..
Unknown - Inconnu	1 371	699	672	..
EUROPE				
Åland Islands - Îles d'Åland				
2011 (C)				
Total	285	136	149	47.7
0 - 14	-	-	-	..
15 - 19	4	2	2	♦4.7
20 - 24	28	14	14	♦42.4
25 - 29	80	36	44	105.8

10. Live births by age of mother and sex of child, general and age-specific fertility rates: latest available year, 2003 - 2012
Naissances vivantes selon l'âge de la mère et le sexe de l'enfant, taux de fécondité et taux de fécondité par âge : dernière année disponible, 2003 - 2012 (continued - suite)

Continent, country or area, year, code and age of mother (in years) / Continent, pays ou zone, année, code et âge de la mère (en années)	Number - Nombre			Rate Taux
	Total	Male Masculin	Female Féminin	
EUROPE				
Åland Islands - Îles d'Åland				
2011 (C)				
30 - 34	107	49	58	132.4
35 - 39	53	29	24	60.5
40 - 44	13	6	7	♦12.8
45 - 49	-	-	-	-
50 +	-	-	-	..
Albania - Albanie				
2004 (C)				
Total	43 022	22 859	20 163	54.8
15 - 19	2 249	1 213	1 036	14.6
20 - 24	13 516	7 006	6 510	106.7
25 - 29	14 476	7 669	6 807	149.8
30 - 34	8 491	4 597	3 894	87.6
35 - 39	3 239	1 800	1 439	31.8
40 - 44	736	419	317	6.8
45 - 49	64	38	26	0.7
50 +	12	7	5	..
Unknown - Inconnu	239	110	129	..
2007 (C)				
Total	33 163	...	...	43.3
0 - 19	1 705	...	...	11.3
20 - 24	10 330	...	...	80.4
25 - 29	11 053	...	...	119.8
30 - 34	6 504	...	...	74.0
35 - 39	2 683	...	...	27.4
40 - 44	554	...	...	5.5
45 - 49	76	...	...	0.7
50 +	22	...	...	..
Unknown - Inconnu	236	...	...	..
Andorra - Andorre				
2010 (C)				
Total	828	427	401	37.7
12 - 14	-	-	-	..
15 - 19	8	6	2	♦4.4
20 - 24	69	36	33	34.0
25 - 29	223	112	111	74.5
30 - 34	305	161	144	80.9
35 - 39	181	88	93	45.3
40 - 44	39	22	17	10.3
45 - 49	3	2	1	♦0.8
50 +	-	-	-	..
2011 (C)				
Total	793	...	...	38.2
15 - 19	9	...	...	♦5.1
20 - 24	51	...	...	27.0
25 - 29	176	...	...	65.1
30 - 34	317	...	...	91.2
35 - 39	202	...	...	52.6
40 - 44	38	...	...	10.5
45 +	-	...	...	-
Austria - Autriche				
2011 (C)				
Total	78 109	40 395	37 714	38.5
12 - 14	11	6	5	..
15 - 19	2 178	1 121	1 057	9.1
20 - 24	11 957	6 235	5 722	45.9
25 - 29	23 975	12 464	11 511	86.5
30 - 34	24 235	12 485	11 750	90.4
35 - 39	12 689	6 547	6 142	43.8
40 - 44	2 908	1 456	1 452	8.5
45 - 49	142	75	67	0.4
50 +	14	6	8	..

Continent, country or area, year, code and age of mother (in years) / Continent, pays ou zone, année, code et âge de la mère (en années)	Number - Nombre			Rate Taux
	Total	Male Masculin	Female Féminin	
EUROPE				
Belarus - Bélarus				
2006 (C)				
Total	96 721	49 849	46 872	36.6
0 - 14	10	5	5	..
15 - 19	8 238	4 234	4 004	21.9
20 - 24	36 120	18 613	17 507	88.9
25 - 29	29 846	15 372	14 474	83.0
30 - 34	15 950	8 229	7 721	46.3
35 - 39	5 488	2 846	2 642	16.1
40 - 44	935	488	447	2.4
45 - 49	47	23	24	0.1
50 +	-	-	-	..
Unknown - Inconnu	87	39	48	..
2008 (C)				
Total	107 876	...	...	41.6
12 - 14	14	...	...	..
15 - 19	7 399	...	...	22.1
20 - 24	37 635	...	...	91.9
25 - 29	35 122	...	...	93.2
30 - 34	19 355	...	...	56.0
35 - 39	7 055	...	...	20.7
40 - 44	1 151	...	...	3.2
45 - 49	38	...	...	0.1
Unknown - Inconnu	105	...	...	..
Belgium - Belgique[35]				
2011 (C)				
Total	128 678	65 884	62 794	50.9
12 - 14	19	12	7	..
15 - 19	2 887	1 480	1 407	9.1
20 - 24	18 062	9 355	8 707	53.2
25 - 29	44 493	22 936	21 557	127.4
30 - 34	42 021	21 225	20 796	117.3
35 - 39	17 445	8 952	8 493	47.7
40 - 44	3 560	1 833	1 727	9.2
45 - 49	175	80	95	0.4
50 +	13	8	5	..
Unknown - Inconnu	3	3	-	..
Bosnia and Herzegovina - Bosnie-Herzégovine				
2010 (C)				
Total	33 528	17 277	16 251	35.2
12 - 14	8	6	2	..
15 - 19	1 792	950	842	13.5
20 - 24	8 293	4 282	4 011	59.4
25 - 29	11 690	5 949	5 741	86.2
30 - 34	7 985	4 144	3 841	66.8
35 - 39	3 027	1 560	1 467	24.3
40 - 44	557	287	270	3.9
45 - 49	30	14	16	0.2
50 +	1	-	1	..
Unknown - Inconnu	145	85	60	..
Bulgaria - Bulgarie				
2011 (C)				
Total	70 846	36 533	34 313	42.6
12 - 14	335	168	167	..
15 - 19	7 464	3 828	3 636	41.7
20 - 24	16 504	8 584	7 920	70.4
25 - 29	21 226	11 023	10 203	90.1
30 - 34	16 983	8 660	8 323	66.8
35 - 39	7 137	3 660	3 477	26.9
40 - 44	1 128	572	556	4.5
45 - 49	58	30	28	0.2
50 +	4	2	2	..
Unknown - Inconnu	7	6	1	..

10. Live births by age of mother and sex of child, general and age-specific fertility rates: latest available year, 2003 - 2012
Naissances vivantes selon l'âge de la mère et le sexe de l'enfant, taux de fécondité et taux de fécondité par âge : dernière année disponible, 2003 - 2012 (continued - suite)

Continent, country or area, year, code and age of mother (in years) / Continent, pays ou zone, année, code et âge de la mère (en années)	Number - Nombre			Rate Taux
	Total	Male Masculin	Female Féminin	

EUROPE

Croatia - Croatie				
2011 (C)				
Total.................................	41 197	21 177	20 020	40.4
12 - 14	8	4	4	..
15 - 19	1 412	704	708	11.4
20 - 24	6 902	3 523	3 379	51.2
25 - 29	13 934	7 135	6 799	92.3
30 - 34	12 678	6 589	6 089	82.8
35 - 39	5 291	2 754	2 537	36.0
40 - 44	922	444	478	6.2
45 - 49	41	18	23	0.3
50 + ...	1	1	-	..
Unknown - Inconnu	8	5	3	..
Czech Republic - République tchèque				
2011 (C)				
Total.................................	108 673	55 789	52 884	43.3
12 - 14	19	13	6	..
15 - 19	3 054	1 585	1 469	10.8
20 - 24	13 947	7 242	6 705	42.2
25 - 29	32 894	16 797	16 097	93.1
30 - 34	40 247	20 726	19 521	93.7
35 - 39	16 292	8 301	7 991	37.9
40 - 44	2 121	1 078	1 043	6.2
45 - 49	91	45	46	0.3
50 + ...	8	2	6	..
Denmark - Danemark[36]				
2011 (C)				
Total.................................	58 998	30 014	28 984	46.8
15 - 19	795	402	393	4.6
20 - 24	6 435	3 279	3 156	38.6
25 - 29	17 700	8 971	8 729	113.7
30 - 34	21 282	10 795	10 487	126.7
35 - 39	10 756	5 537	5 219	55.6
40 - 44	1 923	984	939	9.8
45 - 49	99	43	56	0.5
50 + ...	6	2	4	..
Estonia - Estonie				
2011 (C)				
Total.................................	14 679	7 555	7 124	45.4
12 - 14	1	1	-	..
15 - 19	560	288	272	15.9
20 - 24	2 785	1 439	1 346	54.9
25 - 29	4 707	2 373	2 334	91.8
30 - 34	4 054	2 101	1 953	86.5
35 - 39	2 096	1 095	1 001	45.3
40 - 44	460	250	210	10.0
45 - 49	16	8	8	♦0.3
50 + ...	-	-	-	..
Faeroe Islands - Îles Féroé				
2007 (C)				
Total.................................	674	318	356	64.7
15 - 19	20	11	9	♦10.5
20 - 24	104	47	57	83.5
25 - 29	187	93	94	160.9
30 - 34	211	102	109	154.4
35 - 39	129	56	73	83.0
40 - 44	23	9	14	♦13.9
45 + ...	-	-	-	-
Finland - Finlande				
2011 (C)				
Total.................................	59 961	30 546	29 415	51.7
12 - 14	2	1	1	..
15 - 19	1 245	661	584	7.7
20 - 24	8 843	4 438	4 405	55.1
25 - 29	19 017	9 691	9 326	113.6

Continent, country or area, year, code and age of mother (in years) / Continent, pays ou zone, année, code et âge de la mère (en années)	Number - Nombre			Rate Taux
	Total	Male Masculin	Female Féminin	

EUROPE

Finland - Finlande				
2011 (C)				
30 - 34	19 563	9 968	9 595	118.9
35 - 39	9 112	4 627	4 485	59.4
40 - 44	2 051	1 096	955	12.2
45 - 49	125	62	63	0.7
50 + ...	3	2	1	..
France[37]				
2011 (C)				
Total.................................	792 996	405 206	387 790	55.5
12 - 14	110	50	60	..
15 - 19	17 718	9 019	8 699	9.4
20 - 24	114 375	58 622	55 753	59.0
25 - 29	258 165	132 164	126 001	131.9
30 - 34	250 435	127 487	122 948	128.0
35 - 39	122 440	62 727	59 713	57.0
40 - 44	28 162	14 330	13 832	12.8
45 - 49	1 480	760	720	0.7
50 + ...	111	47	64	..
Germany - Allemagne				
2011 (C)				
Total.................................	662 685	339 899	322 786	36.1
15 - 19	16 436	8 383	8 053	8.2
20 - 24	88 708	45 575	43 133	36.5
25 - 29	190 893	98 164	92 729	78.2
30 - 34	222 109	113 808	108 301	92.0
35 - 39	115 555	59 061	56 494	48.1
40 - 44	27 097	13 928	13 169	8.5
45 - 49	1 251	663	588	0.4
50 + ...	81	38	43	..
Unknown - Inconnu	438	214	224	..
Greece - Grèce				
2011 (C)				
Total.................................	106 428	54 862	51 566	41.2
12 - 14	106	55	51	..
15 - 19	2 644	1 401	1 243	9.8
20 - 24	11 690	6 071	5 619	40.5
25 - 29	28 102	14 467	13 635	80.8
30 - 34	38 600	19 953	18 647	94.7
35 - 39	20 328	10 407	9 921	47.9
40 - 44	4 312	2 189	2 123	9.8
45 - 49	574	286	288	1.4
50 + ...	72	33	39	..
Unknown - Inconnu	-	-	-	..
Hungary - Hongrie				
2011 (C)				
Total.................................	88 049	45 390	42 659	37.1
13 - 14	80	41	39	..
15 - 19	5 070	2 615	2 455	18.0
20 - 24	12 224	6 355	5 869	39.0
25 - 29	23 290	11 878	11 412	69.9
30 - 34	30 114	15 680	14 434	76.3
35 - 39	14 698	7 517	7 181	37.1
40 - 44	2 502	1 268	1 234	7.2
45 - 49	68	34	34	0.2
50 + ...	3	2	1	..
Unknown - Inconnu	-	-	-	..
Iceland - Islande[38]				
2011 (C)				
Total.................................	4 492	2 326	2 166	58.2
12 - 14	-	-	-	..
15 - 19	124	71	53	11.0
20 - 24	732	395	337	63.0
25 - 29	1 446	732	714	128.4
30 - 34	1 354	705	649	122.3

10. Live births by age of mother and sex of child, general and age-specific fertility rates: latest available year, 2003 - 2012
Naissances vivantes selon l'âge de la mère et le sexe de l'enfant, taux de fécondité et taux de fécondité par âge : dernière année disponible, 2003 - 2012 (continued - suite)

Continent, country or area, year, code and age of mother (in years) / Continent, pays ou zone, année, code et âge de la mère (en années)	Number - Nombre			Rate Taux
	Total	Male Masculin	Female Féminin	
EUROPE				
Iceland - Islande[38]				
2011 (C)				
35 - 39	677	349	328	63.3
40 - 44	149	68	81	14.7
45 - 49	10	6	4	♦0.9
Unknown - Inconnu	-	-	-	..
Ireland - Irlande[39]				
2011 (|)				
Total	74 845	38 206	36 639	63.7
0 - 14	8	4	4	..
15 - 19	1 943	982	961	14.0
20 - 24	7 825	4 030	3 795	51.4
25 - 29	17 535	8 965	8 570	92.5
30 - 34	26 350	13 398	12 952	133.5
35 - 39	17 504	8 959	8 545	96.9
40 - 44	3 491	1 778	1 713	21.5
45 - 49	171	85	86	1.1
50 +	18	5	13	..
Italy - Italie				
2011* (+C)				
Total	546 607	281 087	265 520	39.2
12 - 14	26	8	18	..
15 - 19	8 975	4 645	4 330	6.3
20 - 24	50 822	26 306	24 516	33.1
25 - 29	121 658	62 583	59 075	70.6
30 - 34	185 076	95 048	90 028	91.8
35 - 39	142 223	73 107	69 116	59.7
40 - 44	35 267	18 101	17 166	14.3
45 - 49	2 349	1 184	1 165	1.0
50 +	211	105	106	..
Jersey[16]				
2007 (+C)				
Total	1 031	515	516	...
0 - 14	-	-	-	...
15 - 19	29	14	15	...
20 - 24	114	56	58	...
25 - 29	228	114	114	...
30 - 34	325	170	155	...
35 - 39	273	134	139	...
40 - 44	61	27	34	...
45 - 49	1	-	1	...
50 +	-	-	-	...
Latvia - Lettonie				
2011 (C)				
Total	18 825	9 649	9 176	37.7
12 - 14	3	3	-	..
15 - 19	1 118	588	530	18.7
20 - 24	4 156	2 147	2 009	54.5
25 - 29	6 150	3 155	2 995	84.9
30 - 34	4 518	2 277	2 241	67.3
35 - 39	2 317	1 204	1 113	32.2
40 - 44	522	253	269	7.2
45 - 49	18	7	11	♦0.2
Unknown - Inconnu	23	15	8	..
Liechtenstein				
2011* (C)				
Total	395	203	192	44.7
12 - 14	-	-	-	..
15 - 19	2	2	-	♦1.8
20 - 24	33	17	16	30.2
25 - 29	102	55	47	94.4
30 - 34	145	76	69	129.1
35 - 39	99	46	53	73.5
40 - 44	11	7	4	♦7.0

Continent, country or area, year, code and age of mother (in years) / Continent, pays ou zone, année, code et âge de la mère (en années)	Number - Nombre			Rate Taux
	Total	Male Masculin	Female Féminin	
EUROPE				
Liechtenstein				
2011* (C)				
45 - 49	3	-	3	♦2.0
50 +	-	-	-	..
Lithuania - Lituanie				
2011 (C)				
Total	34 385	17 816	16 569	47.1
12 - 14	10	7	3	..
15 - 19	1 507	791	716	14.8
20 - 24	6 786	3 553	3 233	64.2
25 - 29	12 851	6 702	6 149	135.0
30 - 34	8 696	4 429	4 267	94.4
35 - 39	3 768	1 931	1 837	36.5
40 - 44	739	390	349	6.6
45 - 49	25	12	13	♦0.2
50 +	-	-	-	..
Unknown - Inconnu	3	1	2	..
Luxembourg				
2011 (C)				
Total	5 639	2 913	2 726	44.4
12 - 14	-	-	-	..
15 - 19	109	64	45	7.4
20 - 24	632	338	294	42.0
25 - 29	1 469	746	723	84.4
30 - 34	2 064	1 061	1 003	109.4
35 - 39	1 098	577	521	55.3
40 - 44	241	112	129	11.5
45 - 49	20	12	8	♦1.0
Unknown - Inconnu	6	3	3	..
Malta - Malte				
2011 (C)				
Total	4 283	2 182	2 101	44.5
12 - 14	-	-	-	..
15 - 19	220	109	111	17.1
20 - 24	602	319	283	42.1
25 - 29	1 322	704	618	90.2
30 - 34	1 430	705	725	97.9
35 - 39	616	295	321	44.5
40 - 44	84	44	40	6.8
45 - 49	5	4	1	♦0.4
50 +	3	2	1	..
Unknown - Inconnu	1	-	1	..
Montenegro - Monténégro				
2011 (C)				
Total	7 215	3 754	3 461	48.0
12 - 14	5	4	1	..
15 - 19	303	147	156	14.3
20 - 24	1 567	807	760	75.3
25 - 29	2 485	1 303	1 182	110.3
30 - 34	1 865	993	872	83.4
35 - 39	823	427	396	38.5
40 - 44	155	69	86	7.6
45 - 49	10	3	7	♦0.5
50 +	2	1	1	..
Netherlands - Pays-Bas[40]				
2011 (C)				
Total	180 060	92 353	87 707	46.8
15 - 19	2 365	1 220	1 145	4.8
20 - 24	18 272	9 384	8 888	35.7
25 - 29	54 389	27 939	26 450	109.3
30 - 34	67 191	34 401	32 790	134.0
35 - 39	31 733	16 251	15 482	56.5
40 - 44	5 841	3 021	2 820	9.1
45 - 49	246	128	118	0.4
50 +	23	9	14	..

340

10. Live births by age of mother and sex of child, general and age-specific fertility rates: latest available year, 2003 - 2012
Naissances vivantes selon l'âge de la mère et le sexe de l'enfant, taux de fécondité et taux de fécondité par âge : dernière année disponible, 2003 - 2012 (continued - suite)

Continent, country or area, year, code and age of mother (in years) / Continent, pays ou zone, année, code et âge de la mère (en années)	Number - Nombre			Rate Taux
	Total	Male Masculin	Female Féminin	

EUROPE

Norway - Norvège				
2011 (C)				
Total	60 220	31 006	29 214	52.3
12 - 14	2	1	1	..
15 - 19	1 114	579	535	7.1
20 - 24	8 662	4 448	4 214	54.3
25 - 29	18 840	9 656	9 184	120.7
30 - 34	19 570	10 086	9 484	123.9
35 - 39	9 964	5 195	4 769	57.8
40 - 44	1 969	983	986	10.9
45 - 49	93	55	38	0.6
50 +	3	1	2	..
Unknown - Inconnu	3	2	1	..
Poland - Pologne				
2011 (C)				
Total	388 416	199 921	188 495	41.0
12 - 14	44	20	24	..
15 - 19	16 098	8 245	7 853	13.9
20 - 24	70 754	36 503	34 251	51.3
25 - 29	142 865	73 589	69 276	89.1
30 - 34	109 558	56 410	53 148	70.9
35 - 39	41 587	21 392	20 195	29.9
40 - 44	7 176	3 585	3 591	6.1
45 - 49	330	175	155	0.3
50 +	4	2	2	..
Unknown - Inconnu	-	-	-	..
Portugal[16]				
2011 (C)				
Total	96 855	49 688	47 167	38.7
12 - 14	59	33	26	..
15 - 19	3 604	1 877	1 727	13.1
20 - 24	11 704	5 977	5 727	40.7
25 - 29	24 612	12 609	12 003	75.4
30 - 34	33 760	17 237	16 523	86.6
35 - 39	19 247	9 947	9 300	45.5
40 - 44	3 702	1 932	1 770	9.3
45 - 49	166	76	90	0.4
50 +	1	-	1	..
Unknown - Inconnu	-	-	-	..
Republic of Moldova - République de Moldova[41]				
2011 (C)				
Total	39 182	20 176	19 006	40.1
10 - 14	7	3	4	..
15 - 19	3 441	1 783	1 658	25.7
20 - 24	13 684	7 136	6 548	80.3
25 - 29	12 907	6 605	6 302	79.3
30 - 34	6 308	3 218	3 090	45.0
35 - 39	2 398	1 210	1 188	19.2
40 - 44	413	212	201	3.6
45 - 49	17	7	10	♦0.1
50 +	2	1	1	..
Unknown - Inconnu	5	1	4	..
Romania - Roumanie				
2011 (C)				
Total	196 242	100 985	95 257	36.8
12 - 14	748	369	379	..
15 - 19	20 150	10 408	9 742	35.2
20 - 24	48 171	24 794	23 377	59.7
25 - 29	56 343	29 032	27 311	72.6
30 - 34	47 715	24 482	23 233	55.5
35 - 39	19 171	9 831	9 340	23.4
40 - 44	3 803	1 990	1 813	4.2
45 - 49	134	76	58	0.2
50 +	7	3	4	..

EUROPE

Russian Federation - Fédération de Russie[24]				
2011 (C)				
Total	1 796 629	923 804	872 825	48.3
12 - 14	351	174	177	..
15 - 19	103 533	53 162	50 371	25.2
20 - 24	510 184	262 085	248 099	85.1
25 - 29	603 791	311 250	292 541	101.2
30 - 34	379 884	195 518	184 366	68.6
35 - 39	165 364	84 832	80 532	31.8
40 - 44	30 221	15 168	15 053	6.3
45 - 49	1 481	680	801	0.3
50 +	138	65	73	..
Unknown - Inconnu	1 682	870	812	..
San Marino - Saint-Marin				
2003 (+C)				
Total	300	161	139	40.1
0 - 14	1	-	1	..
15 - 19	4	1	3	♦6.4
20 - 24	17	10	7	♦22.2
25 - 29	72	40	32	66.4
30 - 34	121	66	55	91.5
35 - 39	73	36	37	50.0
40 - 44	11	8	3	♦9.0
45 +	1	-	1	♦1.0
2012 (+C)				
Total	292	...	...	...
0 - 14	-	...	...	..
15 - 19	1	...	...	...
20 - 24	11	...	...	...
25 - 29	51	...	...	...
30 - 34	96	...	...	...
35 - 39	88	...	...	...
40 - 44	20	...	...	...
45 - 49	1	...	...	...
50 +	-	...	...	...
Unknown - Inconnu	24	...	...	...
Serbia - Serbie[42]				
2011 (+C)				
Total	65 598	33 933	31 665	39.5
12 - 14	48	25	23	..
15 - 19	3 748	1 992	1 756	18.6
20 - 24	13 631	6 972	6 659	61.3
25 - 29	21 295	10 982	10 313	86.3
30 - 34	17 826	9 281	8 545	70.7
35 - 39	7 330	3 788	3 542	29.5
40 - 44	1 293	676	617	5.4
45 - 49	88	48	40	0.4
50 +	13	6	7	..
Unknown - Inconnu	326	163	163	..
Slovakia - Slovaquie				
2011 (C)				
Total	60 813	31 114	29 699	44.3
12 - 14	41	17	24	..
15 - 19	3 653	1 945	1 708	22.0
20 - 24	10 265	5 188	5 077	52.3
25 - 29	19 067	9 751	9 316	89.4
30 - 34	19 153	9 830	9 323	85.7
35 - 39	7 445	3 791	3 654	35.4
40 - 44	1 116	546	570	6.3
45 - 49	68	43	25	0.4
50 +	5	3	2	..

10. Live births by age of mother and sex of child, general and age-specific fertility rates: latest available year, 2003 - 2012
Naissances vivantes selon l'âge de la mère et le sexe de l'enfant, taux de fécondité et taux de fécondité par âge : dernière année disponible, 2003 - 2012 (continued - suite)

Continent, country or area, year, code and age of mother (in years) / Continent, pays ou zone, année, code et âge de la mère (en années)	Total	Male Masculin	Female Féminin	Rate Taux
EUROPE				
Slovenia - Slovénie				
2011 (C)				
Total	21 947	11 248	10 699	46.2
12 - 14	1	1		..
15 - 19	254	135	119	5.2
20 - 24	2 529	1 301	1 228	41.8
25 - 29	7 534	3 911	3 623	110.6
30 - 34	7 975	4 027	3 948	106.5
35 - 39	3 182	1 636	1 546	43.7
40 - 44	456	231	225	6.3
45 - 49	15	6	9	♦0.2
Unknown - Inconnu	-	-	-	..
Spain - Espagne				
2011 (C)				
Total	470 553	242 556	227 997	41.8
12 - 14	145	70	75	..
15 - 19	10 202	5 360	4 842	9.6
20 - 24	38 374	19 624	18 750	31.3
25 - 29	92 347	48 030	44 317	60.0
30 - 34	179 276	92 537	86 739	94.8
35 - 39	124 160	63 709	60 451	64.0
40 - 44	24 485	12 462	12 023	13.3
45 - 49	1 462	714	748	0.8
50 +	102	50	52	..
Unknown - Inconnu	-	-	-	..
Sweden - Suède				
2011 (C)				
Total	111 770	57 205	54 565	52.5
12 - 14	5	2	3	..
15 - 19	1 725	917	808	5.9
20 - 24	15 016	7 720	7 296	47.9
25 - 29	32 003	16 398	15 605	111.9
30 - 34	37 596	19 243	18 353	131.8
35 - 39	20 852	10 576	10 276	67.3
40 - 44	4 330	2 243	2 087	13.6
45 - 49	225	99	126	0.7
50 +	18	7	11	..
Unknown - Inconnu	-	-	-	..
Switzerland - Suisse				
2011 (C)				
Total	80 808	41 626	39 182	42.7
12 - 14	3	1	2	..
15 - 19	733	378	355	3.4
20 - 24	7 661	3 943	3 718	32.0
25 - 29	21 279	10 989	10 290	82.7
30 - 34	29 735	15 335	14 400	110.6
35 - 39	17 498	8 960	8 538	63.8
40 - 44	3 675	1 895	1 780	11.8
45 - 49	210	119	91	0.6
50 +	14	6	8	..
Unknown - Inconnu	-	-	-	..
TFYR of Macedonia - L'ex-R. y. de Macédoine				
2011 (C)				
Total	22 770	11 752	11 018	43.3
12 - 14	23	12	11	..
15 - 19	1 310	687	623	18.1
20 - 24	5 594	2 933	2 661	71.3
25 - 29	8 027	4 163	3 864	100.0
30 - 34	5 530	2 798	2 732	72.2
35 - 39	1 979	993	986	26.6
40 - 44	285	153	132	3.9
45 - 49	15	9	6	♦0.2
50 +	-	-	-	..
Unknown - Inconnu	7	4	3	..
EUROPE				
Ukraine[43]				
2011 (+C)				
Total	502 595	...	...	43.6
12 - 14	141	...	...	..
15 - 19	35 559	...	...	27.9
20 - 24	152 369	...	...	89.8
25 - 29	166 675	...	...	89.2
30 - 34	98 457	...	...	58.0
35 - 39	40 918	...	...	24.6
40 - 44	7 294	...	...	4.6
45 - 49	350	...	...	0.2
50 +	40	...	...	..
Unknown - Inconnu	792	...	...	..
United Kingdom of Great Britain and Northern Ireland - Royaume-Uni de Grande-Bretagne et d'Irlande du Nord[44]				
2011 (C)				
Total	807 776	413 910	393 866	54.6
12 - 14	178	101	77	..
15 - 19	40 813	21 108	19 705	21.8
20 - 24	149 667	76 709	72 958	70.7
25 - 29	223 613	114 930	108 683	105.5
30 - 34	231 658	118 372	113 286	117.2
35 - 39	129 139	65 974	63 165	63.3
40 - 44	30 601	15 654	14 947	13.2
45 - 49	1 869	934	935	0.8
50 +	128	67	61	..
Unknown - Inconnu	110	61	49	..
OCEANIA - OCÉANIE				
American Samoa - Samoas américaines				
2006 (C)				
Total	1 442	...	...	...
0 - 14	1	...	...	..
15 - 19	110	...	...	..
20 - 24	342	...	...	..
25 - 29	410	...	...	..
30 - 34	303	...	...	..
35 - 39	218	...	...	..
40 - 44	55	...	...	..
45 - 49	3	...	...	..
Australia - Australie				
2011 (+C)				
Total	301 617	154 996	146 621	55.3
0 - 14	99	51	48	..
15 - 19	11 245	5 719	5 526	15.9
20 - 24	41 769	21 397	20 372	53.1
25 - 29	84 160	43 200	40 960	103.1
30 - 34	95 688	49 273	46 415	124.9
35 - 39	55 628	28 695	26 933	70.3
40 - 44	12 144	6 197	5 947	15.2
45 - 49	608	332	276	0.8
50 +	53	22	31	..
Unknown - Inconnu	223	110	113	..
Cook Islands - Îles Cook[45]				
2006 (I)				
Total	306	...	...	...
15 - 19	37	...	...	...
20 - 24	73	...	...	...
25 - 29	62	...	...	...

10. Live births by age of mother and sex of child, general and age-specific fertility rates: latest available year, 2003 - 2012
Naissances vivantes selon l'âge de la mère et le sexe de l'enfant, taux de fécondité et taux de fécondité par âge : dernière année disponible, 2003 - 2012 (continued - suite)

Continent, country or area, year, code and age of mother (in years) / Continent, pays ou zone, année, code et âge de la mère (en années)	Number - Nombre			Rate Taux
	Total	Male Masculin	Female Féminin	

OCEANIA - OCÉANIE

Cook Islands - Îles Cook[45]				
2006 (|)				
30 - 34	70	...	...	...
35 - 39	45	...	...	...
40 - 44	16	...	...	...
45 - 49	3	...	...	...
Fiji - Fidji				
2004 (+C)				
Total	17 189	8 944	8 245	79.4
0 - 14	7	1	6	..
15 - 19	1 194	622	572	29.7
20 - 24	5 684	2 961	2 723	154.7
25 - 29	5 126	2 665	2 461	155.8
30 - 34	3 033	1 526	1 507	100.4
35 - 39	1 592	868	724	57.0
40 - 44	464	254	210	18.2
45 - 49	43	23	20	1.9
50 +	-	-	-	..
Unknown - Inconnu	46	24	22	..
Guam[46]				
2004 (C)				
Total	3 427	1 783	1 644	85.9
10 - 14	2	1	1	..
15 - 19	352	168	184	53.8
20 - 24	887	486	401	154.4
25 - 29	939	483	456	171.2
30 - 34	738	393	345	121.3
35 - 39	395	196	199	68.1
40 - 44	102	50	52	18.2
45 - 49	10	5	5	♦2.2
50 +	-	-	-	..
Unknown - Inconnu	2	1	1	..
Marshall Islands - Îles Marshall[47]				
2006 (+U)				
Total	1 576	...	...	...
0 - 14	2	...	...	...
15 - 19	268	...	...	...
20 - 24	551	...	...	...
25 - 29	431	...	...	...
30 - 34	211	...	...	...
35 - 39	91	...	...	...
40 - 44	19	...	...	...
45 - 49	3	...	...	...
Micronesia (Federated States of) - Micronésie (États fédérés de)				
2006 (+U)				
Total	2 148	...	...	...
10 - 14	8	...	...	..
15 - 17	89	...	...	...
18 - 19	155	...	...	...
20 - 24	619	...	...	...
25 - 29	514	...	...	...
30 - 34	379	...	...	...
35 - 39	259	...	...	...
40 - 44	43	...	...	...
45 +	9	...	...	...
Unknown - Inconnu	73	...	...	..
New Caledonia - Nouvelle-Calédonie				
2010 (C)				
Total	4 178	...	...	63.2
15 - 19	236	...	...	22.7
20 - 24	949	...	...	99.4

OCEANIA - OCÉANIE

New Caledonia - Nouvelle-Calédonie				
2010 (C)				
25 - 29	1 142	...	...	125.3
30 - 34	1 046	...	...	111.3
35 - 39	641	...	...	63.5
40 - 44	159	...	...	16.9
45 - 49	5	...	...	♦0.6
New Zealand - Nouvelle-Zélande				
2012 (+C)				
Total	61 178	31 243	29 935	56.9
0 - 14	18	12	6	..
15 - 19	3 768	1 999	1 769	24.9
20 - 24	11 301	5 809	5 492	71.0
25 - 29	15 614	7 893	7 721	105.3
30 - 34	17 472	8 929	8 543	122.0
35 - 39	10 369	5 267	5 102	70.7
40 - 44	2 523	1 268	1 255	15.4
45 - 49	111	64	47	0.7
50 +	2	2	-	..
Niue - Nioué[48]				
2009 (C)				
Total	31	...	...	...
0 - 14	-	...	...	...
15 - 19	1	...	...	...
20 - 24	9	...	...	...
25 - 29	12	...	...	...
30 - 34	6	...	...	...
35 - 39	1	...	...	...
40 - 44	1	...	...	...
45 +	1	...	...	...
Palau - Palaos				
2003 (C)				
Total	312	163	149	...
15 - 19	21	13	8	...
20 - 24	71	34	37	...
25 - 29	81	40	41	...
30 - 34	63	35	28	...
35 - 39	56	29	27	...
40 - 44	16	11	5	...
45 - 49	4	1	3	...
2005 (C)				
Total	279	...	...	55.3
0 - 14	-	...	...	...
15 - 19	23	...	...	♦30.8
20 - 24	65	...	...	117.3
25 - 29	56	...	...	87.4
30 - 34	73	...	...	93.1
35 - 39	40	...	...	48.0
40 - 44	20	...	...	♦25.3
45 - 49	2	...	...	♦2.9
Samoa[49]				
2011 (|)				
Total	5 703	3 055	2 648	133.8
15 - 19	369	209	160	39.2
20 - 24	1 557	831	726	218.3
25 - 29	1 471	793	678	238.6
30 - 34	1 154	603	551	206.1
35 - 39	741	398	343	144.1
40 - 44	338	180	158	69.9
45 - 49	73	41	32	16.9

10. Live births by age of mother and sex of child, general and age-specific fertility rates: latest available year, 2003 - 2012
Naissances vivantes selon l'âge de la mère et le sexe de l'enfant, taux de fécondité et taux de fécondité par âge : dernière année disponible, 2003 - 2012 (continued - suite)

Continent, country or area, year, code and age of mother (in years) / Continent, pays ou zone, année, code et âge de la mère (en années)	Number - Nombre			Rate Taux
	Total	Male Masculin	Female Féminin	

OCEANIA - OCÉANIE

Tonga
2003 (+C)

Total	2 781	...	...	114.1
0 - 14	-	...	...	
15 - 19	94	...	...	17.5
20 - 24	619	...	...	129.9
25 - 29	787	...	...	230.6
30 - 34	643	...	...	222.6
35 - 39	405	...	...	155.0
40 - 44	110	...	...	48.2
45 - 49	10	...	...	♦4.8
50 +	-	...	...	
Unknown - Inconnu	113	...	...	..

Tuvalu
2003 (U)

Total	239	...	...	...
15 - 19	17	...	...	...
20 - 24	76	...	...	...
25 - 29	53	...	...	...

Continent, country or area, year, code and age of mother (in years) / Continent, pays ou zone, année, code et âge de la mère (en années)	Number - Nombre			Rate Taux
	Total	Male Masculin	Female Féminin	

OCEANIA - OCÉANIE

Tuvalu
2003 (U)

30 - 34	35	...	...	...
35 - 39	37	...	...	...
40 - 44	20	...	...	...
45 - 49	-	...	...	...

Wallis and Futuna Islands - Îles Wallis et Futuna
2008 (C)

Total	185	...	...	...
0 - 14	-	...	...	...
15 - 19	9	...	...	...
20 - 24	38	...	...	...
25 - 29	53	...	...	...
30 - 34	51	...	...	...
35 - 39	29	...	...	...
40 - 44	5	...	...	...
45 +	-	...	...	...

FOOTNOTES - NOTES

♦ Rates based on 30 or fewer births. - Taux basés sur 30 naissances ou moins.

* Provisional. - Données provisoires.

'Code' indicates the source of data, as follows:
C - Civil registration, estimated over 90% complete
U - Civil registration, estimated less than 90% complete
| - Other source, estimated reliable
+ - Data tabulated by date of registration rather than occurrence
... Information not available

Le 'Code' indique la source des données, comme suit :
C - Registres de l'état civil considérés complets à 90 p. 100 au moins
U - Registres de l'état civil qui ne sont pas considérés complets à 90 p. 100 au moins
| - Autre source, considérée fiable
+ - Données exploitées selon la date de l'enregistrement et non la date de l'événement
... Information non disponible

[1] Data from Health Statistics Reports since 1998, due to incompleteness of civil registration. - Données provenant des "Health Statistics Reports" (bulletins statistiques de santé) depuis 1998, en raison des déficiences de l'état civil.
[2] Data refer to the 12 months preceding the census in March. - Les données se rapportent aux 12 mois précédant le recensement de mars.
[3] Data refer to Libyan nationals only. - Les données se raportent aux nationaux libyens seulement.
[4] Data refer to the 12 months preceding the census in June. - Les données se raportent aux 12 mois précédant le recensement de juin.
[5] Excludes the islands of St. Brandon and Agalega. - Non compris les îles St. Brandon et Agalega.
[6] Excluding live-born infants who died before their birth was registered. - Non compris les enfants nés vivants décédés avant l'enregistrement de leur naissance.
[7] Excluding late registration (after 28/29 February of the following year). - En excluant les enregistrements tardifs (après les 28/29 février de l'année suivante).
[8] Data as reported by national statistical authorities; they may differ from data presented in other tables. - Les données comme elles ont été déclarées par l'institut national de la statistique; elles peuvent être différentes de celles présentées dans d'autres tableaux.
[9] Data refer to the 12 months preceding the census in May. - Les données se rapportent aux 12 mois précédant le recensement de mai.

[10] Excluding non-residents and foreign service personnel and their dependants. - À l'exclusion des non-résidents et du personnel diplomatique et de leurs charges de famille.
[11] Including Canadian residents temporarily in the United States, but excluding United States residents temporarily in Canada. - Y compris les résidents canadiens se trouvant temporairement aux Etats-Unis, mais ne comprenant pas les résidents des Etats-Unis se trouvant temporairement au Canada.
[12] For confidentiality reasons, live births to mothers aged 50 and over and the adopted children with no information on their birth mother are included in 'age of mother Unknown'. - Pour des raisons de confidentialité, on a classé dans la catégorie « âge de la mère Inconnu» les naissances vivantes concernant des femmes âgées de plus de 50 ans et les enfants adoptés nés de mères sur lesquelles on ne dispose pas d'information.
[13] Resident births outside the islands are excluded. - Non compris les naissances de résidents hors des îles.
[14] Excluding children born in the country of non-resident mothers. - Exceptés les enfants nés dans le pays des mères non-résidentes.
[15] Data have not been adjusted for underenumeration. - Les données n'ont pas été ajustées pour compenser les lacunes du dénombrement.
[16] Data refer to births to resident mothers. - Ces données concernent les enfants nés de mères résidentes.
[17] Figures for male and female do not add up to the total, since they do not include the category "Unknown". - La somme des chiffres indiqués pour les sexes masculin et féminin n'est pas égale au total parce qu'elle n'inclut pas la catégorie " inconnue ".
[18] Data refer to births from June 2009 to May 2010 compiled from the Population and Housing Census. - Données concernant les naissances enregistrées entre juin 2009 et mai 2010 d'après le recensement de la population et de l'habitat.
[19] Including births abroad and births of unknown residence. - Y compris les naissances survenues à l'étranger et les naissances d'enfants dont la résidence n'était pas connue.
[20] Excluding events registered late. - Non compris les enregistrements tardifs.
[21] Source: Reports of the Ministry of Health. - Source: Rapports du Ministère de la Santé.
[22] Including births to non-resident mothers. - Y compris les naissances de femmes non résidentes.
[23] Data refer to the 12 months preceding the census in October. - Les données se rapportent aux 12 mois précédant le recensement d'octobre.
[24] Excluding infants born alive of less than 28 weeks' gestation, of less than 1 000 grams in weight and 35 centimeters in length, who die within seven days of birth. - Non compris les enfants nés vivants après moins de 28 semaines de gestation, pesant moins de 1 000 grammes, mesurant moins de 35 centimètres et décédés dans les sept jours qui ont suivi leur naissance.

25 Data refer to government controlled areas. - Les données se rapportent aux zones contrôlées par le Gouvernement.

26 Includes data for East Jerusalem and Israeli residents in certain other territories under occupation by Israeli military forces since June 1967. - Y compris les données pour Jérusalem-Est et les résidents israéliens dans certains autres territoires occupés depuis 1967 par les forces armées israéliennes.

27 Data refer to Japanese nationals in Japan only. - Les données se raportent aux nationaux japonais au Japon seulement.

28 Data refer to urban areas only. - Données ne concernant que les zones urbaines.

29 Data from Births and Deaths Notification System (Ministry of Health and all health care providers). - Les données proviennent du système de notification des naissances et des décès (Ministère de la santé et tous prestataires de soins de santé).

30 Excluding unknown sex. - Non compris le sexe inconnu.

31 Excluding data for the Pakistan-held part of Jammu and Kashmir, the final statu · of which has not yet been determined. Based on the results of the Pakistan Demographic Survey. - Non compris les données concernant la partie du Jammu et Cachemire occupée par le Pakistan dont le statut définitif n'a pas été déterminé. Données extraites de l'enquête démographique effectuée par le Pakistan.

32 Excluding alien armed forces, civilian aliens employed by armed forces, and foreign diplomatic personnel and their dependants. - Non compris les militaires étrangers, les civils étrangers employés par les forces armées ni le personnel diplomatique étranger et les membres de leur famille les accompagnant.

33 The registration of births and deaths is conducted by the Ministry of Health. An estimate of completeness is not provided. - L'enregistrement des naissances et des décès est mené par le Ministère de la Santé. Le degré estimatif de complétude n'est pas fourni.

34 Unrevised data. - Les données n'ont pas été révisées.

35 Including armed forces stationed outside the country, but excluding alien armed forces stationed in the area. - Y compris les militaires nationaux hors du pays, mais non compris les militaires étrangers en garnison sur le territoire.

36 Excluding Faeroe Islands and Greenland shown separately, if available. - Non compris les Iles Féroé et le Groenland, qui font l'objet de rubriques distinctes, si disponible.

37 Including armed forces stationed outside the country. - Y compris les militaires nationaux hors du pays.

38 Definition of localities was revised from 2011 causing a break with the previous series. - La rupture par rapport aux séries précédentes s'explique par le fait que la définition des localités a été révisée depuis 2011.

39 Data refer to the 12 months preceding the census in April. - Les données se rapportent aux douze mois précédant le recensement d'avril.

40 Including residents outside the country if listed in a Netherlands population register. - Englobe les résidents se trouvant à l'étranger à condition qu'ils soient inscrits sur le registre de population des Pays-Bas.

41 Excluding Transnistria and the municipality of Bender. - Les données ne tiennent pas compte de l'information sur la Transnistria et la municipalité de Bender.

42 Excludes data for Kosovo and Metohia. - Sans les données pour le Kosovo et Metohie.

43 Data refer to births with weight 500g and more (if weight is unknown - with length 25 centimeters and more, or with gestation during 22 weeks or more). - Données concernant les nouveau-nés de 500 grammes ou plus (si le poids est inconnu – de 25 centimètres de long ou plus, ou après une grossesse de 22 semaines ou plus).

44 Excluding Channel Islands (Guernsey and Jersey) and Isle of Man, shown separately, if available. Data tabulated by date of occurrence for England and Wales, and by date of registration for Northern Ireland and Scotland. - Non compris les îles Anglo-Normandes (Guernesey et Jersey) et l'île de Man, qui font l'objet de rubriques distinctes, si disponible. Données exploitées selon la date de l'événement pour l'Angleterre et le pays de Galles, et selon la date de l'enregistrement pour l'Irlande du Nord et l'Ecosse.

45 Excluding Niue, shown separately, which is part of Cook Islands, but because of remoteness is administered separately. Data refer to the 12 months preceding the census in December. - Non compris Nioué, qui fait l'objet d'une rubrique distincte et qui fait partie des îles Cook, mais qui, en raison de son éloignement, est administrée séparément. Les données se rapportent aux 12 mois précédant le recensement de décembre.

46 Including United States military personnel, their dependants and contract employees. - Y compris les militaires des Etats-Unis, les membres de leur famille les accompagnant et les agents contractuels des Etats-Unis.

47 Excluding United States military personnel, their dependants and contract employees. - Non compris les militaires des Etats-Unis, les membres de leur famille les accompagnant et les agents contractuels des Etats-Unis.

48 Includes children born in New Zealand to women resident in Niue who chose to travel to New Zealand to give birth. - Y compris les enfants nés en Nouvelle-Zélande de femmes résidant à Nioué qui ont choisi de se rendre en Nouvelle-Zélande pour accoucher.

49 Data refer to the 12 months preceding the census in November. - Données se rapportant aux 12 mois précédant le recensement de novembre.

Table 11 - *Demographic Yearbook 2012*

Table 11 presents live births by age of father and live birth rates by age of father for the latest available year between 2003 and 2012.

Description of variables: Age is defined as age at last birthday, that is, the difference between the date of birth and the date of the occurrence of the event, expressed in completed solar years. The age classification used in this table is the following: under 20 years, 5-year age groups through 60-64 years, 65 years and over, and age unknown. A different classification may appear as provided by reporting country or area.

Rate computation: Live-birth rates specific to age of father are the annual number of births to a man in each age group per 1 000 male population in the same age group. These rates are calculated by the Statistics Division of the United Nations.

Since relatively few births occur to men below 15 or above 59 years of age, birth rates for men under 20 years of age and for those 55 years of age or over are computed on the male population aged 15-19 and 55-59, respectively. Similarly, the rate for men of "All ages" is based on all live births irrespective of age of father, and is computed on the male population aged 15-59 years.

Births to fathers of unknown age are distributed proportionately across the age groups, by the Statistics Division of the United Nations, in accordance with the distribution of births by age of father prior to the calculation of the rates.

The population used in computing the rates is the estimated or enumerated distribution of males by age. First priority is given to the estimated population and second priority to the enumerated population, i.e. to census returns of the year to which the births refer.

Rates presented in this table are limited to those for countries or areas having at least a total of 100 live births in a given year.

Reliability of data: Data from civil registers of live births which are reported as incomplete (less than 90 per cent completeness) or of unknown completeness are considered unreliable and are set in *italics* rather than in roman type. Rates are not computed if the data on live births from civil registers are reported as incomplete (less than 90 per cent completeness) or of unknown completeness. Table 9 and the technical notes for that table provide more detailed information on the completeness of birth registration. For more information about the quality of vital statistics data in general, see section 4.2 of the Technical Notes.

Limitations: Statistics on live births by age of father are subject to the same qualifications as have been set forth for vital statistics in general and birth statistics in particular as discussed in section 4 of the Technical Notes. These include differences in the completeness of registration, the method used to determine age of father and the quality of the reported information relating to age of father.

The reliability of the data described above, is an important factor in considering the limitations. In addition, some live births are tabulated by date of registration and not by date of occurrence; these are indicated in the table by a plus sign "+". Whenever the lag between the date of occurrence and date of registration is prolonged and, therefore, a large proportion of the live-birth registrations are delayed, birth statistics for any given year may be seriously affected. For example, the age of the father will almost always refer to the date of registration rather than to the date of birth of the child. Hence, in those countries or areas where registration of births is delayed, possibly for years, statistics on births by age of father should be used with caution.

Another factor which limits international comparability is the practice of some countries or areas of not including in live birth statistics infants who were born alive but died before the registration of the birth or within the first 24 hours of life, thus underestimating the total number of live births. Statistics of this type are footnoted.

Because these statistics are classified according to age, they are subject to the limitations with respect to accuracy of age reporting similar to those already discussed in connection with section 3.1.3 of the Technical Notes. The factors influencing the accuracy of reporting may be somewhat dissimilar in vital statistics (because of the differences in the method of taking a census and registering a birth) but, in general, the same errors can be observed. The absence of frequencies in the unknown age group does not necessarily indicate completely accurate reporting and tabulation of the age item. It is often an indication that the unknowns have been eliminated by assigning ages to them before tabulation, or by proportionate distribution after tabulation.

On the other hand, large frequencies in the unknown age category may indicate that a large proportion of the births are born outside of wedlock, the records for which tend to be incomplete so far as characteristics of the parents are concerned.

Another limitation of age reporting may result from calculating age of father at birth of child (or at time of registration) from year of birth rather than from day, month and year of birth. Information on this factor is given in footnotes when known.

In few countries, data by age refer to deliveries rather than to live births causing under-enumeration in the event of a multiple birth. This practice leads to lack of strict comparability, both among countries or areas relying on this practice and between data shown in this table and table 9.

Rates shown in this table are subject to the same limitations that affect the corresponding statistics on live births. In cases of rates based on births tabulated by date of registration and not by date of occurrence; the effect of including delayed registration on the distribution of births by age of father may be noted in the age-specific fertility rates for men at older ages. In some cases, high age-specific rates for men aged 55 years and over may reflect age of father at registration of birth and not fertility at these older ages.

Earlier data: Live births and live birth rates by age of father have been shown in previous issues of the *Demographic Yearbook*. Information on the specific years is presented in the Historical Index.

Tableau 11 – *Annuaire démographique 2012*

Le tableau 11 présente les données les plus récentes disponibles pour la période 2003 - 2012 sur les naissances vivantes selon l'âge du père et les taux des naissances vivantes selon l'âge du père.

Description des variables : l'âge désigne l'âge au dernier anniversaire, c'est-à-dire la différence entre la date de naissance et la date de l'événement exprimée en années solaires révolues. La classification par âge utilisée dans ce tableau comprend les catégories suivantes : moins de 20 ans, groupes quinquennaux jusqu'à 60-64 ans, 65 ans et plus, et âge inconnu. Des groupes d'âge différents sont parfois utilisés lorsque les pays ou territoires ont fourni les données dans une autre classification.

Les taux de natalité selon l'âge du père représentent le nombre annuel de naissances vivantes intervenues dans un groupe d'âge donné pour 1 000 hommes du groupe d'âge. Ces taux ont été calculés par la Division de statistique de l'ONU.

Étant donné que le nombre de naissances parmi les hommes de moins de 15 ans ou de plus de 59 ans est relativement peu élevé, les taux de natalité parmi les hommes âgées de moins de 20 ans et celles de 55 ans et plus ont été calculés sur la base des populations masculines âgées de 15 à 19 ans et de 55 à 59 ans, respectivement. De même, le taux pour les hommes de « tous âges » est fondé sur la totalité des naissances vivantes, indépendamment de l'âge du père et ce chiffre est rapporté à l'effectif de la population masculine âgée de 15 à 59 ans.

Les naissances pour lesquelles l'âge du père était inconnu ont été réparties par la Division de statistique de l'ONU, avant le calcul des taux, suivant les proportions observées pour celles où l'âge du père était connu.

Les chiffres de population utilisés pour le calcul des taux proviennent de dénombrements ou de répartitions estimatives de la population masculine selon l'âge. On a utilisé de préférence les estimations de la population; à défaut, on s'est contenté des données censitaires se rapportant à l'année des naissances.

Les taux présentés dans ce tableau ne concernent que les pays ou zones où l'on a enregistré un total d'au moins 100 naissances vivantes dans une année donnée.

Fiabilité des données : les données sur les naissances vivantes provenant des registres de l'état civil qui sont déclarées incomplètes (degré de complétude inférieur à 90 p. 100) ou dont le degré de complétude n'est pas connu sont jugées douteuses et apparaissent en italique et non en caractères romains. On a choisi de ne pas faire figurer dans le tableau 11 des taux calculés à partir de données sur les naissances vivantes issues de registres de l'état civil qui sont déclarées incomplètes (degré de complétude inférieur à 90 p. 100) ou dont le degré de complétude n'est pas connu. Le tableau 9 et les notes techniques qui s'y rapportent présentent des renseignements plus détaillés sur le degré de complétude de l'enregistrement des naissances vivantes. Pour plus de précisions sur la qualité des statistiques de l'état civil en général, voir la section 4.2 des Notes techniques.

Insuffisance des données : les statistiques relatives aux naissances vivantes selon l'âge du père appellent toutes les réserves qui ont été formulées à propos des statistiques de l'état civil en général et des statistiques de naissances en particulier (voir la section 4 des Notes techniques). Ceci inclut les différences de complétude d'enregistrement des faits d'état civil, de méthode pour déterminer l'âge du père et de qualité d'information concernant l'âge du père.

La fiabilité des données, au sujet de laquelle des indications ont été données plus haut, est un facteur important. Il faut également tenir compte du fait que, dans certains cas, les données relatives aux naissances vivantes sont exploitées selon la date de l'enregistrement et non la date de l'événement ; ces cas ont été signalés dans le tableau par le signe '+'. Chaque fois que le décalage entre l'événement et son enregistrement est grand et qu'une forte proportion des naissances vivantes fait l'objet d'un enregistrement tardif, les statistiques des naissances vivantes pour une année donnée peuvent être considérablement faussées. Par exemple, l'âge du père représente presque toujours son âge à la date de l'enregistrement et non à la date de la naissance de l'enfant. Ainsi, dans les pays ou zones où l'enregistrement des naissances est tardif, le retard atteignant parfois plusieurs années, il faut utiliser avec prudence les statistiques concernant les naissances selon l'âge du père.

Un autre facteur qui nuit à la comparabilité internationale est la pratique de certains pays ou zones qui consiste à ne pas inclure dans les statistiques des naissances vivantes les enfants nés vivants mais décédés avant l'enregistrement de leur naissance ou dans les 24 heures qui ont suivi la naissance, pratique qui conduit à sous-estimer le nombre total de naissances vivantes. Quand pareil facteur a joué, cela a été signalé en note à la fin du tableau.

Étant donné que les statistiques du tableau 11 sont classées selon l'âge, elles appellent les mêmes réserves concernant l'exactitude des déclarations d'âge que celles formulées à la section 3.1.3 des Notes techniques. Dans le cas des statistiques de l'état civil, les facteurs qui interviennent à cet égard sont parfois différents, étant donné que le recensement de la population et l'enregistrement des naissances se font par des méthodes différentes, mais, d'une manière générale, les erreurs observées seront les mêmes. Si aucun nombre ne figure dans la rangée réservée aux âges inconnus, cela ne signifie pas nécessairement que les déclarations d'âge et l'exploitation des données par âge ont été tout à fait exactes. C'est souvent une indication que l'on a attribué un âge aux personnes d'âge inconnu avant l'exploitation des données ou qu'elles ont été réparties proportionnellement entre les différents groupes après cette opération.

À l'inverse, lorsque le nombre des personnes d'âge inconnu est important, cela peut signifier que la proportion de naissances parmi les parents célibataires est élevée, étant donné qu'en pareil cas l'acte de naissance ne contient pas tous les renseignements concernant les parents.

Les déclarations par âge peuvent comporter des distorsions, du fait que l'âge du père au moment de la naissance d'un enfant (ou de la déclaration de naissance) est donné par année de naissance et non par date exacte (jour, mois et année).

Dans quelques pays, la classification par âges se réfère aux accouchements, et non aux naissances vivantes, ce qui conduit à un sous-dénombrement en cas de naissances gémellaires. Cette pratique nuit à la comparabilité des données, à la fois entre pays ou zones qui recourent à cette méthode et entre les données présentées dans le tableau 11 et celles du tableau 9.

Les taux présentés dans ce tableau, sont sujets aux mêmes limitations qui affectent les statistiques correspondantes de naissances vivantes. Dans le cas des taux basés sur des naissances par date d'enregistrement et non par date d'occurrence, l'effet peut être visible sur les taux de fécondité par âge des hommes aux âges plus élevés. Dans certains cas, les taux de fécondité des hommes de plus de 55 ans peuvent refléter l'âge du père à l'enregistrement plus que la fécondité à ces âges.

Données publiées antérieurement : Les données sur les naissances vivantes selon l'âge du père et les taux des naissances vivantes selon l'âge du père ont été publié antérieurement dans l'*Annuaire démographique*. Pour plus de précisions concernant les années pour lesquels des données ont été publiées, se reporter à l'index historique.

11. Live births and live birth rates by age of father: latest available year, 2003 - 2012
Naissances vivantes et taux de natalité selon l'âge du père : dernière année disponible, 2003 - 2012

Continent, country or area, year, code and age of father (in years) / Continent, pays ou zone, année, code et âge du père (en années)	Number - Nombre — Both sexes / Les deux sexes	Rate Taux
AFRICA - AFRIQUE		
Egypt - Égypte		
2011 (+C)		
Total	2 442 094	96.1
0 - 19	3 862	0.8
20 - 24	247 013	55.5
25 - 29	732 629	210.1
30 - 34	789 689	295.6
35 - 39	455 442	178.3
40 - 44	128 383	56.2
45 - 49	55 419	26.7
50 - 54	17 526	10.3
55 - 59	6 297	4.7
60 +	5 834	..
Mauritius - Maurice[1]		
2011 (C)		
Total	14 626	34.0
0 - 19	223	4.3
20 - 24	1 582	32.5
25 - 29	3 166	68.2
30 - 34	4 594	86.4
35 - 39	2 640	59.9
40 - 44	1 115	25.1
45 - 49	463	9.7
50 - 54	130	3.2
55 - 59	38	1.1
60 - 64	13	..
65 +	7	..
Unknown - Inconnu	655	..
Réunion[2]		
2007 (C)		
Total	14 808	61.9
0 - 19	352	10.0
20 - 24	2 409	88.2
25 - 29	3 283	139.4
30 - 34	3 693	141.6
35 - 39	2 860	96.2
40 - 44	1 488	46.6
45 - 49	491	19.2
50 - 54	151	6.8
55 - 59	53	3.0
60 - 64	28	..
AMERICA, NORTH - AMÉRIQUE DU NORD		
Bahamas[3]		
2011 (+U)		
Total	4 747	...
0 - 19	84	...
20 - 24	504	...
25 - 29	980	...
30 - 34	706	...
35 - 39	993	...
40 - 44	342	...
45 - 49	334	...
50 - 54	62	...
55 - 59	52	...
60 - 64	8	..
65 +	8	..
Unknown - Inconnu	674	..
Barbados - Barbade		
2007 (+C)		
Total	3 537	...
0 - 19	95	...
20 - 24	564	...
25 - 29	745	...
30 - 34	784	...
AMERICA, NORTH - AMÉRIQUE DU NORD		
Barbados - Barbade		
2007 (+C)		
35 - 39	605	...
40 - 44	381	...
45 - 49	163	...
50 - 54	53	...
55 - 59	17	...
60 - 64	8	...
65 +	3	..
Unknown - Inconnu	119	..
Canada[4]		
2009 (C)		
Total	380 863	35.1
0 - 19	4 918	4.5
20 - 24	29 959	26.5
25 - 29	84 206	75.0
30 - 34	117 201	109.5
35 - 39	79 126	72.1
40 - 44	31 813	26.9
45 - 49	9 913	7.5
50 - 54	2 642	2.2
55 - 59	683	0.7
60 - 64	200	..
65 +	77	..
Unknown - Inconnu	20 125	..
Costa Rica		
2010* (C)		
Total	70 922	46.4
0 - 19	1 593	10.5
20 - 24	9 156	58.3
25 - 29	11 340	78.6
30 - 34	10 082	78.6
35 - 39	5 970	54.1
40 - 44	3 149	28.6
45 - 49	1 393	13.3
50 - 54	550	6.3
55 - 59	177	2.7
60 - 64	67	..
65 +	5 769	..
Unknown - Inconnu	21 676	..
Cuba		
2011 (C)		
Total	133 067	36.2
0 - 19	3 394	10.4
20 - 24	24 504	65.0
25 - 29	31 018	92.3
30 - 34	22 408	73.4
35 - 39	18 725	44.2
40 - 44	10 873	24.0
45 - 49	4 294	9.6
50 - 54	1 134	3.8
55 - 59	405	1.5
60 - 64	154	..
65 +	90	..
Unknown - Inconnu	16 068	..
Dominican Republic - République dominicaine		
2011 (U)		
Total	128 837	...
0 - 19	1 994	...
20 - 24	18 424	...
25 - 29	26 799	...
30 - 34	24 102	...
35 - 39	14 800	...
40 - 44	8 058	...
45 - 49	3 835	...
50 - 54	1 722	...
55 - 59	853	...

Continent, country or area, year, code and age of father (in years) Continent, pays ou zone, année, code et âge du père (en années)	Number - Nombre Both sexes Les deux sexes	Rate Taux
AMERICA, NORTH - AMÉRIQUE DU NORD		
Dominican Republic - République dominicaine		
2011 (U)		
60 - 64	*346*	..
65 +	*191*	..
Unknown - Inconnu	*27 713*	..
El Salvador		
2011 (C)		
Total	109 384	65.6
0 - 19	6 580	21.5
20 - 24	22 778	94.9
25 - 29	22 364	122.7
30 - 34	19 678	125.6
35 - 39	11 744	80.1
40 - 44	6 226	47.8
45 - 49	3 029	27.3
50 - 54	1 396	14.8
55 - 59	693	8.5
60 - 64	347	..
65 +	266	..
Unknown - Inconnu	14 283	..
Greenland - Groenland		
2008 (C)		
Total	834	...
0 - 19	25	...
20 - 24	109	...
25 - 29	169	...
30 - 34	150	...
35 - 39	112	...
40 - 44	91	...
45 - 49	35	...
50 - 54	9	...
55 - 59	1	...
60 +	-	..
Unknown - Inconnu	133	..
Guadeloupe[2]		
2003 (C)		
Total	7 047	55.0
0 - 19	112	6.4
20 - 24	809	55.5
25 - 29	1 303	103.0
30 - 34	1 950	125.6
35 - 39	1 698	102.0
40 - 44	877	53.1
45 - 49	211	15.9
50 - 54	59	5.1
55 - 59	20	♦2.1
60 +	8	..
Guatemala		
2011 (C)		
Total	373 692	...
0 - 19	23 425	...
20 - 24	82 898	...
25 - 29	83 786	...
30 - 34	64 952	...
35 - 39	39 412	...
40 - 44	20 601	...
45 - 49	9 366	...
50 - 54	3 893	...
55 - 59	1 723	...
60 - 64	769	..
65 +	556	..
Unknown - Inconnu	42 311	..
Jamaica - Jamaïque[5]		
2006 (C)		
Total	42 399	...
0 - 19	496	...
20 - 24	3 756	

Continent, country or area, year, code and age of father (in years) Continent, pays ou zone, année, code et âge du père (en années)	Number - Nombre Both sexes Les deux sexes	Rate Taux
AMERICA, NORTH - AMÉRIQUE DU NORD		
Jamaica - Jamaïque[5]		
2006 (C)		
25 - 29	5 341	...
30 - 34	5 069	...
35 - 39	3 635	...
40 - 44	2 166	...
45 - 49	986	...
50 - 54	373	...
55 - 59	131	...
60 - 64	53	...
65 +	37	...
Unknown - Inconnu	20 356	...
Martinique[2]		
2007 (C)		
Total	5 317	47.3
0 - 19	98	6.2
20 - 24	710	60.7
25 - 29	1 043	119.9
30 - 34	1 173	111.7
35 - 39	1 293	95.6
40 - 44	702	46.1
45 - 49	235	16.2
50 - 54	42	3.5
55 - 59	16	♦1.5
60 +	3	..
Mexico - Mexique[6]		
2009 (+U)		
Total	*2 252 786*	...
0 - 19	*149 066*	...
20 - 24	*496 403*	...
25 - 29	*537 328*	...
30 - 34	*429 165*	...
35 - 39	*257 373*	...
40 - 44	*109 838*	...
45 - 49	*43 537*	...
50 - 54	*16 979*	...
55 - 59	*6 812*	...
60 - 64	*2 745*	...
65 +	*2 006*	...
Unknown - Inconnu	*201 534*	...
Panama		
2010 (C)		
Total	67 955	62.9
0 - 19	3 057	19.5
20 - 24	13 588	89.5
25 - 29	15 334	109.1
30 - 34	12 772	96.1
35 - 39	8 775	67.3
40 - 44	4 644	39.1
45 - 49	2 107	20.9
50 - 54	867	10.6
55 - 59	396	6.0
60 - 64	337	..
65 +	6 078	..
Puerto Rico - Porto Rico		
2008 (C)		
Total	45 675	39.5
0 - 19	3 200	21.8
20 - 24	11 615	86.9
25 - 29	12 284	90.2
30 - 34	8 969	70.4
35 - 39	4 753	38.3
40 - 44	2 060	16.9
45 - 49	752	6.4
50 - 54	284	2.6
55 - 59	142	1.4
60 - 64	63	..

11. Live births and live birth rates by age of father: latest available year, 2003 - 2012
Naissances vivantes et taux de natalité selon l'âge du père : dernière année disponible, 2003 - 2012 (continued - suite)

Continent, country or area, year, code and age of father (in years) / Continent, pays ou zone, année, code et âge du père (en années)	Number - Nombre — Both sexes Les deux sexes	Rate Taux
AMERICA, NORTH - AMÉRIQUE DU NORD		
Puerto Rico - Porto Rico		
2008 (C)		
65 +	27	..
Unknown - Inconnu	1 526	..
Trinidad and Tobago - Trinité-et-Tobago		
2006 (C)		
Total	18 090	...
0 - 19	400	...
20 - 24	3 291	...
25 - 29	4 889	...
30 - 34	4 079	...
35 - 39	2 713	...
40 - 44	1 491	...
45 - 49	616	...
50 - 54	248	...
55 - 59	87	..
60 +	45	..
Unknown - Inconnu	231	..
United States of America - États-Unis d'Amérique		
2009 (C)		
Total	4 130 665	43.3
0 - 19	414 831	37.5
20 - 24	1 005 982	90.7
25 - 29	1 166 787	105.0
30 - 34	955 246	94.5
35 - 39	474 103	45.8
40 - 44	105 827	10.1
45 - 49	7 320	0.6
50 - 54	569	0.1
Unknown - Inconnu	-	..
AMERICA, SOUTH - AMÉRIQUE DU SUD		
Chile - Chili		
2010 (C)		
Total	250 643	45.3
0 - 19	15 358	22.8
20 - 24	42 149	64.0
25 - 29	50 964	85.9
30 - 34	49 414	94.6
35 - 39	36 578	66.6
40 - 44	17 740	32.6
45 - 49	7 038	12.8
50 +	3 470	4.2
Unknown - Inconnu	27 932	..
Colombia - Colombie		
2010 (U)		
Total	*654 627*	...
0 - 19	*40 842*	...
20 - 24	*152 100*	...
25 - 29	*165 232*	...
30 - 34	*126 916*	...
35 - 39	*76 083*	...
40 - 44	*40 809*	...
45 - 49	*17 448*	...
50 - 54	*7 278*	...
55 - 59	*2 473*	...
60 - 64	*1 038*	...
65 +	*538*	..
Unknown - Inconnu	*23 870*	..
French Guiana - Guyane française[2]		
2007 (C)		
Total	6 386	104.6
0 - 19	323	32.6
20 - 24	1 263	164.2
25 - 29	1 401	203.5

Continent, country or area, year, code and age of father (in years) / Continent, pays ou zone, année, code et âge du père (en années)	Number - Nombre — Both sexes Les deux sexes	Rate Taux
AMERICA, SOUTH - AMÉRIQUE DU SUD		
French Guiana - Guyane française[2]		
2007 (C)		
30 - 34	1 334	175.5
35 - 39	1 043	138.4
40 - 44	622	90.0
45 - 49	230	38.8
50 - 54	94	19.2
55 - 59	59	16.1
60 - 64	17	..
65 +	-	..
Uruguay		
2004 (C)		
Total	50 052	52.8
0 - 19	805	10.3
20 - 24	4 203	57.8
25 - 29	7 179	100.3
30 - 34	7 629	118.5
35 - 39	5 142	87.4
40 - 44	2 622	43.3
45 - 49	978	17.9
50 - 54	420	8.5
55 - 59	117	2.8
60 - 64	43	..
65 +	32	..
Unknown - Inconnu	20 882	..
Venezuela (Bolivarian Republic of) - Venezuela (République bolivarienne du)		
2007 (C)		
Total	615 371	72.6
0 - 19	37 015	32.7
20 - 24	124 442	117.3
25 - 29	130 575	136.4
30 - 34	96 162	114.7
35 - 39	60 376	79.4
40 - 44	32 010	45.3
45 - 49	14 774	24.4
50 - 54	6 837	13.5
55 - 59	2 888	7.0
60 - 64	977	..
65 +	525	..
Unknown - Inconnu	108 790	..
ASIA - ASIE		
Azerbaijan - Azerbaïdjan[7]		
2010 (+C)		
Total	147 603	47.9
0 - 19	611	1.3
20 - 24	26 551	56.8
25 - 29	56 773	138.1
30 - 34	37 950	109.2
35 - 39	16 722	55.5
40 - 44	6 383	20.1
45 - 49	1 903	5.9
50 - 54	471	1.7
55 +	239	1.4
Bahrain - Bahreïn		
2007 (C)		
Total	16 062	32.1
0 - 14	-	..
15 - 19	19	♦0.5
20 - 24	930	16.1
25 - 29	3 652	39.9
30 - 34	4 486	52.6
35 - 39	3 447	46.4
40 - 44	2 200	37.8

Continent, country or area, year, code and age of father (in years) / Continent, pays ou zone, année, code et âge du père (en années)	Number - Nombre — Both sexes Les deux sexes	Rate Taux
ASIA - ASIE		
Bahrain - Bahreïn		
2007 (C)		
45 - 49	911	19.5
50 - 54	255	7.8
55 - 59	89	5.0
60 - 64	35	..
65 +	30	..
Unknown - Inconnu	8	..
Brunei Darussalam - Brunéi Darussalam		
2008 (+C)		
Total	6 424	...
0 - 19	23	...
20 - 24	466	...
25 - 29	1 612	...
30 - 34	1 733	...
35 - 39	1 125	...
40 - 44	555	...
45 - 49	212	...
50 - 54	57	...
55 +	23	...
Unknown - Inconnu	618	..
China, Hong Kong SAR - Chine, Hong Kong RAS		
2011 (C)		
Total	95 451	42.7
0 - 19	164	0.8
20 - 24	3 511	16.4
25 - 29	14 185	64.2
30 - 34	26 571	122.2
35 - 39	26 870	119.0
40 - 44	12 802	54.8
45 - 49	5 056	17.8
50 - 54	1 700	5.6
55 - 59	723	3.0
60 - 64	242	..
65 +	98	..
Unknown - Inconnu	3 529	..
China, Macao SAR - Chine, Macao RAS		
2012 (C)		
Total	7 315	35.5
0 - 24	488	11.1
25 - 29	2 051	72.3
30 - 34	2 115	92.6
35 - 39	1 415	67.5
40 - 44	687	33.1
45 +	477	7.1
Unknown - Inconnu	82	..
Cyprus - Chypre[8]		
2011 (C)		
Total	9 622	35.8
0 - 19	29	♦0.9
20 - 24	537	15.2
25 - 29	2 280	63.7
30 - 34	3 329	104.2
35 - 39	1 999	72.9
40 - 44	857	33.1
45 - 49	292	10.9
50 +	155	3.1
Unknown - Inconnu	144	..
Israel - Israël[9]		
2011 (C)		
Total	166 296	75.0
0 - 19	375	1.3
20 - 24	13 369	48.2
25 - 29	36 651	133.9
30 - 34	50 077	194.6
35 - 39	36 660	147.8
40 - 44	14 892	70.3

Continent, country or area, year, code and age of father (in years) / Continent, pays ou zone, année, code et âge du père (en années)	Number - Nombre — Both sexes Les deux sexes	Rate Taux
ASIA - ASIE		
Israel - Israël[9]		
2011 (C)		
45 - 49	3 985	21.2
50 - 54	1 045	5.9
55 - 59	274	1.6
60 - 64	93	..
65 +	58	..
Unknown - Inconnu	8 817	..
Japan - Japon[10]		
2011 (C)		
Total	1 027 452	28.7
0 - 19	4 106	1.3
20 - 24	64 599	19.7
25 - 29	235 150	63.6
30 - 34	346 253	83.6
35 - 39	257 295	52.0
40 - 44	91 554	19.8
45 - 49	21 398	5.3
50 - 54	5 042	1.3
55 - 59	1 392	0.3
60 - 64	539	..
65 +	120	..
Unknown - Inconnu	4	..
Kazakhstan[11]		
2006 (C)		
Total	301 756	61.4
0 - 19	2 897	4.2
20 - 24	46 772	73.1
25 - 29	82 596	152.2
30 - 34	66 344	134.3
35 - 39	41 180	90.8
40 - 44	17 594	38.6
45 - 49	4 336	10.0
50 - 54	873	2.7
55 - 59	296	1.2
60 - 64	74	..
65 +	74	..
Unknown - Inconnu	38 720	..
Kyrgyzstan - Kirghizstan		
2011 (C)		
Total	149 612	87.0
0 - 19	661	2.6
20 - 24	21 565	83.3
25 - 29	44 486	209.1
30 - 34	31 746	186.7
35 - 39	18 888	127.5
40 - 44	8 803	63.8
45 - 49	2 865	22.5
50 - 54	690	6.2
55 - 59	199	2.7
60 - 64	81	..
65 +	49	..
Unknown - Inconnu	19 579	..
Malaysia - Malaisie		
2009 (C)		
Total	496 313	53.7
0 - 19	2 353	1.8
20 - 24	33 080	27.2
25 - 29	121 520	106.7
30 - 34	137 676	127.0
35 - 39	97 218	95.7
40 - 44	50 924	53.6
45 - 49	19 553	23.3
50 - 54	5 889	8.5
55 - 59	1 764	3.2
60 - 64	481	..

Continent, country or area, year, code and age of father (in years) Continent, pays ou zone, année, code et âge du père (en années)	Number - Nombre Both sexes Les deux sexes	Rate Taux	Continent, country or area, year, code and age of father (in years) Continent, pays ou zone, année, code et âge du père (en années)	Number - Nombre Both sexes Les deux sexes	Rate Taux
ASIA - ASIE			**ASIA - ASIE**		
Malaysia - Malaisie			Republic of Korea - République de Corée[13]		
2009 (C)			2011 (C)		
65 +	267	..	30 - 34	205 090	102.6
Unknown - Inconnu	25 588	..	35 - 39	138 749	66.1
Maldives			40 - 44	37 866	17.5
2011 (C)			45 - 49	6 506	3.0
Total	7 180	66.5	50 - 54	1 375	0.7
0 - 19	3	♦0.2	55 - 59	249	0.2
20 - 24	961	48.6	60 - 64	50	..
25 - 29	2 260	136.0	65 +	6	..
30 - 34	1 652	141.4	Unknown - Inconnu	4 760	..
35 - 39	1 073	109.3	Singapore - Singapour		
40 - 44	587	68.4	2012 (C)		
45 - 49	230	30.2	Total	42 663	33.2
50 - 54	74	11.2	0 - 19	141	1.1
55 - 59	24	♦6.1	20 - 24	1 161	8.9
60 - 64	5	..	25 - 29	6 341	52.2
65 +	4	..	30 - 34	15 252	109.8
Unknown - Inconnu	307	..	35 - 39	12 267	81.6
Oman[12]			40 - 44	4 795	32.1
2011 (U)			45 - 49	1 475	9.3
Total	*67 922*	...	50 - 54	485	3.1
0 - 19	*46*	...	55 - 59	135	1.0
20 - 24	*3 572*	...	60 - 64	36	..
25 - 29	*17 681*	...	65 +	17	..
30 - 34	*19 930*	...	Unknown - Inconnu	558	..
35 - 39	*12 744*	...	Turkey - Turquie		
40 - 44	*6 637*	...	2010* (C)		
45 - 49	*3 190*	...	Total	1 238 970	52.9
50 - 54	*1 343*	...	0 - 19	9 494	3.0
55 - 59	*573*	...	20 - 24	127 978	40.2
60 - 64	*328*	..	25 - 29	407 523	124.2
65 +	*368*	..	30 - 34	368 143	123.7
Unknown - Inconnu	*1 510*	..	35 - 39	204 896	74.7
Philippines			40 - 44	76 458	32.4
2009 (C)			45 - 49	25 157	11.3
Total	1 745 585	...	50 - 54	6 197	3.3
0 - 19	195 662	...	55 - 59	2 220	1.5
20 - 24	495 958	...	60 - 64	911	..
25 - 29	461 020	...	65 +	657	..
30 - 34	328 063	...	Unknown - Inconnu	9 336	..
35 - 39	187 578	...			
40 - 44	66 064	...			
45 - 49	7 712	...	**EUROPE**		
50 - 54	494	...			
55 - 59	34	...	Åland Islands - Îles d'Åland		
60 - 64	-	..	2011 (C)		
65 +	-	..	Total	285	34.8
Unknown - Inconnu	3 000	..	0 - 19	-	-
Qatar			20 - 24	20	♦26.1
2010 (C)			25 - 29	47	62.9
Total	19 504	16.9	30 - 34	76	94.0
0 - 19	17	♦0.5	35 - 39	76	86.0
20 - 24	1 050	6.8	40 - 44	36	38.4
25 - 29	3 770	17.0	45 - 49	13	♦13.5
30 - 34	5 727	26.3	50 - 54	1	♦1.1
35 - 39	4 537	23.2	55 - 59	-	-
40 - 44	2 584	17.2	60 - 64	-	..
45 - 49	1 179	12.2	65 +	-	..
50 +	637	7.5	Unknown - Inconnu	16	..
Unknown - Inconnu	3	..	Albania - Albanie		
Republic of Korea - République de Corée[13]			2004 (C)		
2011 (C)			Total	43 022	47.6
Total	471 265	27.0	0 - 19	293	1.9
0 - 19	750	0.4	20 - 24	2 812	23.7
20 - 24	6 315	3.7	25 - 29	11 631	130.9
25 - 29	69 549	37.2	30 - 34	14 648	164.2

11. Live births and live birth rates by age of father: latest available year, 2003 - 2012
Naissances vivantes et taux de natalité selon l'âge du père : dernière année disponible, 2003 - 2012 (continued - suite)

Continent, country or area, year, code and age of father (in years) / Continent, pays ou zone, année, code et âge du père (en années)	Number - Nombre, Both sexes Les deux sexes	Rate Taux
EUROPE		
Albania - Albanie		
2004 (C)		
35 - 39	8 622	90.8
40 - 44	3 353	31.4
45 - 49	835	8.5
50 - 54	180	2.3
55 - 59	68	1.1
60 - 64	36	..
Unknown - Inconnu	544	..
Austria - Autriche[14]		
2011 (C)		
Total	46 587	17.8
0 - 19	89	0.4
20 - 24	2 420	9.0
25 - 29	9 330	33.4
30 - 34	14 895	54.9
35 - 39	11 593	40.5
40 - 44	5 578	16.2
45 - 49	1 932	5.4
50 - 54	545	1.7
55 - 59	135	0.5
60 - 64	51	..
65 +	19	..
Belarus - Bélarus[14]		
2011 (C)		
Total	88 413	29.0
0 - 19	702	2.3
20 - 24	16 327	41.7
25 - 29	33 256	86.1
30 - 34	22 911	66.7
35 - 39	10 549	32.5
40 - 44	3 413	10.9
45 - 49	946	2.7
50 - 54	229	0.6
55 +	80	0.3
Belgium - Belgique[15]		
2008 (C)		
Total	127 205	39.1
0 - 19	630	2.0
20 - 24	7 857	25.8
25 - 29	30 846	94.8
30 - 34	40 588	123.9
35 - 39	25 177	69.1
40 - 44	10 190	26.2
45 - 49	3 529	9.2
50 - 54	1 073	3.1
55 - 59	316	1.0
60 - 64	97	..
65 +	66	..
Unknown - Inconnu	6 836	..
Bosnia and Herzegovina - Bosnie-Herzégovine		
2010 (C)		
Total	33 528	28.0
0 - 19	99	0.7
20 - 24	3 174	23.3
25 - 29	9 300	75.0
30 - 34	10 238	90.1
35 - 39	5 624	49.2
40 - 44	2 203	16.5
45 - 49	672	4.8
50 - 54	150	1.2
55 - 59	29	0.3
60 - 64	9	..
65 +	4	..
Unknown - Inconnu	2 026	..
EUROPE		
Bulgaria - Bulgarie		
2011 (C)		
Total	70 846	31.2
0 - 19	862	5.5
20 - 24	6 264	30.5
25 - 29	15 161	71.9
30 - 34	18 902	83.6
35 - 39	11 543	49.5
40 - 44	4 059	18.5
45 - 49	1 184	5.8
50 - 54	379	1.8
55 - 59	120	0.6
60 - 64	36	..
65 +	9	..
Unknown - Inconnu	12 327	..
Croatia - Croatie		
2010 (C)		
Total	43 361	31.7
0 - 19	228	1.8
20 - 24	3 243	23.4
25 - 29	11 311	73.0
30 - 34	14 458	94.3
35 - 39	8 479	58.3
40 - 44	3 265	22.0
45 - 49	984	6.4
50 - 54	198	1.2
55 - 59	71	0.5
60 - 64	11	..
65 +	5	..
Unknown - Inconnu	1 108	..
Czech Republic - République tchèque[16]		
2011 (C)		
Total	108 673	32.4
0 - 19	452	1.7
20 - 24	4 944	15.7
25 - 29	19 176	56.3
30 - 34	38 296	92.6
35 - 39	24 622	59.6
40 - 44	7 418	22.6
45 - 49	2 611	8.1
50 - 54	785	2.6
55 - 59	319	0.9
60 - 64	83	..
65 +	22	..
Unknown - Inconnu	9 945	..
Denmark - Danemark[17]		
2011 (C)		
Total	58 998	35.8
0 - 19	11	♦0.1
20 - 24	821	8.6
25 - 29	5 540	63.8
30 - 34	12 191	131.3
35 - 39	9 206	86.3
40 - 44	3 307	29.9
45 - 49	1 004	8.7
50 - 54	242	2.4
55 - 59	84	0.9
60 - 64	31	..
65 +	12	..
Unknown - Inconnu	26 549	..
Estonia - Estonie		
2011 (C)		
Total	14 679	36.4
0 - 19	114	3.3
20 - 24	1 392	28.0
25 - 29	3 620	74.0
30 - 34	3 967	89.1

Continent, country or area, year, code and age of father (in years) / Continent, pays ou zone, année, code et âge du père (en années)	Number - Nombre — Both sexes Les deux sexes	Rate Taux	Continent, country or area, year, code and age of father (in years) / Continent, pays ou zone, année, code et âge du père (en années)	Number - Nombre — Both sexes Les deux sexes	Rate Taux
EUROPE			EUROPE		
Estonia - Estonie			Greece - Grèce		
2011 (C)			2011 (C)		
35 - 39	2 788	65.4	65 +	9	..
40 - 44	1 244	30.8	Unknown - Inconnu	7 546	..
45 - 49	387	9.8	Hungary - Hongrie		
50 - 54	138	3.4	2011 (C)		
55 - 59	31	0.9	Total	88 049	28.4
60 - 64	12	..	0 - 19	903	3.4
65 +	4	..	20 - 24	5 018	17.1
Unknown - Inconnu	982	..	25 - 29	13 502	43.7
Finland - Finlande[18]			30 - 34	28 315	76.8
2011 (C)			35 - 39	20 656	56.4
Total	59 676	37.6	40 - 44	7 278	22.9
0 - 19	382	2.4	45 - 49	1 953	7.4
20 - 24	4 906	30.1	50 - 54	657	2.4
25 - 29	14 628	85.5	55 - 59	276	0.9
30 - 34	19 114	113.8	60 - 64	69	..
35 - 39	11 732	74.8	65 +	26	..
40 - 44	4 834	28.7	Unknown - Inconnu	9 396	..
45 - 49	1 567	8.6	Iceland - Islande[20]		
50 - 54	436	2.4	2011 (C)		
55 - 59	107	0.6	Total	4 492	45.0
60 - 64	41	..	0 - 19	42	3.6
65 +	13	..	20 - 24	427	35.6
Unknown - Inconnu	1 916	..	25 - 29	1 139	99.9
France[19]			30 - 34	1 353	119.5
2010 (C)			35 - 39	913	83.4
Total	802 224	43.9	40 - 44	378	37.3
0 - 19	3 235	1.7	45 - 49	117	10.9
20 - 24	52 892	26.5	50 - 54	40	3.8
25 - 29	183 322	94.6	55 - 59	12	♦1.3
30 - 34	260 153	136.2	60 - 64	-	..
35 - 39	183 348	85.4	65 +	-	..
40 - 44	78 729	36.5	Unknown - Inconnu	71	..
45 - 49	27 067	12.6	Ireland - Irlande		
50 - 54	8 978	4.4	2006 (+C)		
55 - 59	3 130	1.6	Total	64 237	46.8
60 - 64	1 261	..	0 - 19	714	5.1
65 +	109	..	20 - 24	4 382	26.9
Germany - Allemagne			25 - 29	10 351	57.1
2011 (C)			30 - 34	19 695	121.1
Total	662 685	26.5	35 - 39	16 702	111.2
0 - 19	2 543	1.3	40 - 44	6 268	45.2
20 - 24	36 505	15.4	45 - 49	1 585	12.4
25 - 29	117 313	50.0	50 - 54	374	3.2
30 - 34	191 733	83.3	55 - 59	119	1.1
35 - 39	151 290	65.9	60 - 64	27	..
40 - 44	80 830	26.3	65 +	6	..
45 - 49	25 727	7.6	Unknown - Inconnu	4 014	..
50 - 54	6 651	2.2	Italy - Italie		
55 - 59	1 829	0.7	2010 (+C)		
60 - 64	597	..	Total	561 944	31.2
65 +	273	..	0 - 19	1 792	1.3
Unknown - Inconnu	47 394	..	20 - 24	16 945	11.5
Greece - Grèce			25 - 29	65 671	40.6
2011 (C)			30 - 34	154 329	80.5
Total	106 428	30.7	35 - 39	166 658	75.1
0 - 19	180	0.7	40 - 44	81 055	35.5
20 - 24	2 259	7.8	45 - 49	23 794	11.0
25 - 29	14 009	39.9	50 - 54	5 621	3.0
30 - 34	33 994	82.7	55 - 59	1 414	0.8
35 - 39	29 712	71.2	60 - 64	64	..
40 - 44	13 318	31.6	65 +	-	..
45 - 49	4 022	10.7	Unknown - Inconnu	44 601	..
50 - 54	1 062	2.9			
55 - 59	261	0.8			
60 - 64	56	..			

11. Live births and live birth rates by age of father: latest available year, 2003 - 2012
Naissances vivantes et taux de natalité selon l'âge du père : dernière année disponible, 2003 - 2012 (continued - suite)

Continent, country or area, year, code and age of father (in years) / Continent, pays ou zone, année, code et âge du père (en années)	Number - Nombre — Both sexes Les deux sexes	Rate Taux	Continent, country or area, year, code and age of father (in years) / Continent, pays ou zone, année, code et âge du père (en années)	Number - Nombre — Both sexes Les deux sexes	Rate Taux
EUROPE			EUROPE		
Latvia - Lettonie			Montenegro - Monténégro		
2010 (C)			2009 (C)		
Total	19 219	27.5	35 - 39	1 574	85.9
0 - 19	144	2.2	40 - 44	800	43.7
20 - 24	2 212	25.8	45 - 49	287	14.9
25 - 29	5 180	62.9	50 - 54	89	4.6
30 - 34	4 932	67.3	55 - 59	23	♦1.3
35 - 39	3 153	42.7	60 - 64	1	..
40 - 44	1 433	20.6	65 +	6	..
45 - 49	550	7.5	Unknown - Inconnu	935	..
50 - 54	174	2.5	Netherlands - Pays-Bas[21]		
55 - 59	59	1.0	2010 (C)		
60 - 64	24	..	Total	184 397	36.4
65 +	7	..	0 - 19	284	0.6
Unknown - Inconnu	1 351	..	20 - 24	5 721	11.6
Lithuania - Lituanie			25 - 29	29 787	62.2
2011 (C)			30 - 34	60 664	127.1
Total	34 385	37.7	35 - 39	49 829	91.0
0 - 19	252	2.5	40 - 44	21 179	34.0
20 - 24	3 414	32.8	45 - 49	5 812	9.4
25 - 29	10 148	110.3	50 - 54	1 479	2.6
30 - 34	10 339	120.0	55 - 59	379	0.7
35 - 39	5 194	56.8	60 - 64	116	..
40 - 44	1 986	20.3	65 +	37	..
45 - 49	654	6.4	Unknown - Inconnu	9 110	..
50 - 54	182	1.8	Norway - Norvège		
55 - 59	55	0.7	2011 (C)		
60 - 64	18	..	Total	60 220	39.4
65 +	5	..	0 - 19	290	1.8
Unknown - Inconnu	2 138	..	20 - 24	4 144	26.0
Luxembourg			25 - 29	13 030	83.7
2011 (C)			30 - 34	18 539	116.4
Total	5 639	34.2	35 - 39	13 594	77.8
0 - 19	22	♦1.5	40 - 44	5 802	31.6
20 - 24	301	19.9	45 - 49	1 877	10.9
25 - 29	967	55.8	50 - 54	504	3.2
30 - 34	1 826	99.2	55 - 59	188	1.3
35 - 39	1 426	73.7	60 - 64	56	..
40 - 44	626	29.9	65 +	11	..
45 - 49	205	9.9	Unknown - Inconnu	2 185	..
50 - 54	69	3.9	Poland - Pologne		
55 - 59	22	♦1.5	2011 (C)		
60 - 64	4	..	Total	388 416	30.9
65 +	4	..	0 - 19	2 103	1.8
Unknown - Inconnu	167	..	20 - 24	34 939	25.4
Malta - Malte			25 - 29	117 782	74.2
2011 (C)			30 - 34	126 400	82.6
Total	4 283	32.7	35 - 39	63 343	46.2
0 - 19	45	3.5	40 - 44	20 257	17.4
20 - 24	315	22.2	45 - 49	6 086	5.2
25 - 29	887	60.3	50 - 54	1 917	1.4
30 - 34	1 522	103.5	55 - 59	554	0.4
35 - 39	827	60.5	60 +	208	..
40 - 44	293	24.4	Unknown - Inconnu	14 827	..
45 - 49	89	6.9	Portugal[6]		
50 - 54	26	♦1.8	2011 (C)		
55 - 59	10	♦0.7	Total	96 856	31.4
60 - 64	-	..	0 - 19	1 195	4.2
65 +	2	..	20 - 24	7 052	24.5
Unknown - Inconnu	267	..	25 - 29	18 810	59.7
Montenegro - Monténégro			30 - 34	32 011	87.3
2009 (C)			35 - 39	23 655	59.9
Total	8 642	43.2	40 - 44	8 767	23.8
0 - 19	32	1.5	45 - 49	2 579	7.1
20 - 24	616	27.3	50 - 54	777	2.3
25 - 29	2 011	90.0	55 - 59	256	0.8
30 - 34	2 268	113.7	60 - 64	63	..

11. Live births and live birth rates by age of father: latest available year, 2003 - 2012
Naissances vivantes et taux de natalité selon l'âge du père : dernière année disponible, 2003 - 2012 (continued - suite)

Continent, country or area, year, code and age of father (in years) Continent, pays ou zone, année, code et âge du père (en années)	Number - Nombre Both sexes Les deux sexes	Rate Taux	Continent, country or area, year, code and age of father (in years) Continent, pays ou zone, année, code et âge du père (en années)	Number - Nombre Both sexes Les deux sexes	Rate Taux
EUROPE			**EUROPE**		
Portugal[6]			Serbia - Serbie[23]		
2011 (C)			2011 (+C)		
65 +	29	..	35 - 39	11 389	51.3
Unknown - Inconnu	1 662	..	40 - 44	4 081	19.6
Republic of Moldova - République de Moldova[22]			45 - 49	1 142	5.4
2010 (C)			50 - 54	316	1.4
Total	40 474	33.5	55 - 59	93	0.4
0 - 19	359	2.7	60 - 64	33	..
20 - 24	7 778	47.9	65 +	10	..
25 - 29	13 137	89.5	Unknown - Inconnu	7 519	..
30 - 34	8 649	69.6	Slovakia - Slovaquie[14]		
35 - 39	4 395	41.1	2011 (C)		
40 - 44	1 481	15.0	Total	40 110	22.3
45 - 49	445	4.0	0 - 19	230	1.3
50 - 54	111	1.0	20 - 24	2 402	11.8
55 - 59	59	0.6	25 - 29	9 023	40.3
60 - 64	11	..	30 - 34	15 622	66.2
65 +	4	..	35 - 39	9 075	41.3
Unknown - Inconnu	4 045	..	40 - 44	2 725	15.1
Romania - Roumanie			45 - 49	774	4.1
2011 (C)			50 - 54	165	0.9
Total	196 242	28.5	55 - 59	67	0.4
0 - 19	3 065	5.5	60 - 64	17	..
20 - 24	22 763	29.2	65 +	10	..
25 - 29	47 079	62.2	Slovenia - Slovénie		
30 - 34	60 405	71.8	2011 (C)		
35 - 39	32 259	40.6	Total	21 947	32.9
40 - 44	12 566	14.5	0 - 19	64	1.3
45 - 49	2 837	5.3	20 - 24	1 084	16.9
50 - 54	1 056	1.7	25 - 29	4 977	67.4
55 - 59	355	0.6	30 - 34	8 413	103.0
60 - 64	92	..	35 - 39	4 894	62.4
65 +	21	..	40 - 44	1 574	20.9
Unknown - Inconnu	13 744	..	45 - 49	452	5.7
Russian Federation - Fédération de Russie[11]			50 - 54	119	1.6
2011 (C)			55 - 59	41	0.5
Total	1 796 629	39.1	60 - 64	11	..
0 - 19	13 699	3.7	65 +	4	..
20 - 24	263 262	49.1	Unknown - Inconnu	314	..
25 - 29	520 811	99.7	Spain - Espagne		
30 - 34	399 070	84.5	2011 (C)		
35 - 39	225 463	52.2	Total	470 553	32.4
40 - 44	92 522	23.8	0 - 19	2 533	2.3
45 - 49	31 887	7.3	20 - 24	18 171	14.6
50 - 54	10 693	2.3	25 - 29	59 619	38.5
55 - 59	2 954	0.8	30 - 34	155 441	79.8
60 +	1 044	..	35 - 39	150 000	74.5
Unknown - Inconnu	235 224	..	40 - 44	60 958	32.6
San Marino - Saint-Marin			45 - 49	9 784	5.7
2012 (+C)			50 - 54	3 819	2.5
Total	292	...	55 - 59	1 083	0.8
0 - 19	-	...	60 - 64	313	..
20 - 24	8	...	65 +	84	..
25 - 29	32	...	Unknown - Inconnu	8 748	..
30 - 34	74	...	Sweden - Suède		
35 - 39	93	...	2011 (C)		
40 - 44	41	...	Total	111 770	39.8
45 - 49	14	...	0 - 19	537	1.7
50 - 54	5	...	20 - 24	6 975	21.6
Unknown - Inconnu	25	..	25 - 29	23 304	78.1
Serbia - Serbie[23]			30 - 34	35 529	120.8
2011 (+C)			35 - 39	26 926	85.3
Total	65 598	29.5	40 - 44	11 262	34.6
0 - 19	366	1.9	45 - 49	3 952	12.1
20 - 24	4 872	23.5	50 - 54	1 192	4.1
25 - 29	15 818	69.5	55 - 59	390	1.4
30 - 34	19 959	86.3	60 - 64	135	

Continent, country or area, year, code and age of father (in years) / Continent, pays ou zone, année, code et âge du père (en années)	Number - Nombre	Rate Taux
	Both sexes Les deux sexes	

Continent, country or area, year, code and age of father (in years) / Continent, pays ou zone, année, code et âge du père (en années)	Number - Nombre	Rate Taux
	Both sexes Les deux sexes	

EUROPE

Sweden - Suède		
2011 (C)		
65 +	45	..
Unknown - Inconnu	1 523	..
Switzerland - Suisse[14]		
2011 (C)		
Total	65 205	26.3
0 - 19	21	♦0.1
20 - 24	1 611	6.5
25 - 29	9 961	37.9
30 - 34	21 089	77.3
35 - 39	19 314	70.0
40 - 44	10 000	32.1
45 - 49	2 046	6.1
50 - 54	791	2.7
55 - 59	225	0.9
60 - 64	95	..
65 +	52	..
Unknown - Inconnu	-	..
TFYR of Macedonia - L'ex-R. y. de Macédoine		
2010 (C)		
Total	24 296	35.4
0 - 19	206	2.8
20 - 24	2 424	30.8
25 - 29	7 329	92.1
30 - 34	7 526	99.2
35 - 39	3 795	53.3
40 - 44	1 248	17.7
45 - 49	292	4.2
50 - 54	77	1.1
55 - 59	16	♦0.3
60 - 64	5	..
65 +	4	..
Unknown - Inconnu	1 374	..
Ukraine[24]		
2011 (+C)		
Total	502 595	35.2
0 - 19	4 639	4.0
20 - 24	77 621	50.5
25 - 29	148 106	88.4
30 - 34	111 213	75.5
35 - 39	60 664	43.6
40 - 44	22 708	17.8
45 - 49	7 072	5.3
50 - 54	2 199	1.6
55 +	798	0.7
Unknown - Inconnu	67 575	..
United Kingdom of Great Britain and Northern Ireland - Royaume-Uni de Grande-Bretagne et d'Irlande du Nord[25]		
2009 (C)		
Total	790 204	42.5
0 - 19	16 030	8.4
20 - 24	87 703	43.0
25 - 29	163 634	83.4
30 - 34	207 503	114.9
35 - 39	161 952	79.6
40 - 44	72 397	33.1
45 - 49	23 214	11.4
50 - 54	6 250	3.5
55 - 59	1 781	1.1
60 - 64	606	..
65 +	269	..
Unknown - Inconnu	48 865	..

OCEANIA - OCÉANIE

Australia - Australie		
2011 (+C)		
Total	301 617	43.6
0 - 19	4 230	5.9
20 - 24	24 285	30.5
25 - 29	61 570	75.9
30 - 34	91 446	123.1
35 - 39	68 542	90.7
40 - 44	28 532	37.7
45 - 49	8 816	11.9
50 - 54	2 667	3.7
55 - 59	807	1.3
60 - 64	311	..
65 +	107	..
Unknown - Inconnu[26]	10 304	..
Fiji - Fidji		
2004 (+C)		
Total	17 189	65.6
0 - 19	45	1.3
20 - 24	1 677	52.6
25 - 29	4 265	151.0
30 - 34	3 706	144.1
35 - 39	2 382	99.7
40 - 44	1 242	57.2
45 - 49	403	21.6
50 - 54	106	6.9
55 - 59	44	3.7
60 +	19	..
Unknown - Inconnu	3 300	..
Guam[27]		
2004 (C)		
Total	3 425	69.4
0 - 19	113	21.7
20 - 24	511	112.7
25 - 29	654	145.0
30 - 34	651	133.9
35 - 39	412	82.9
40 - 44	222	46.3
45 +	107	11.2
Unknown - Inconnu	757	..
New Caledonia - Nouvelle-Calédonie		
2010 (C)		
Total	4 178	51.8
0 - 19	37	4.0
20 - 24	425	51.4
25 - 29	761	98.5
30 - 34	892	116.3
35 - 39	775	91.4
40 - 44	362	45.4
45 - 49	136	19.2
50 - 54	56	9.7
55 - 59	15	♦3.1
60 - 64	10	..
Unknown - Inconnu	709	..
New Zealand - Nouvelle-Zélande		
2012 (+C)		
Total	61 178	46.1
0 - 19	1 913	12.6
20 - 24	7 530	46.3
25 - 29	12 308	86.6
30 - 34	16 136	126.6
35 - 39	12 125	95.5
40 - 44	5 566	39.3
45 - 49	1 769	12.3
50 - 54	558	4.0
55 - 59	159	1.3
60 - 64	52	..

Continent, country or area, year, code and age of father (in years) / Continent, pays ou zone, année, code et âge du père (en années)	Number - Nombre		Rate Taux
	Both sexes Les deux sexes		

OCEANIA - OCÉANIE

New Zealand - Nouvelle-Zélande		
2012 (+C)		
65 + ...	20	..
Unknown - Inconnu	3 042	..
Palau - Palaos		
2003 (C)		
Total..	312	...
0 - 19	6	...
20 - 24	50	...

Continent, country or area, year, code and age of father (in years) / Continent, pays ou zone, année, code et âge du père (en années)	Number - Nombre		Rate Taux
	Both sexes Les deux sexes		

OCEANIA - OCÉANIE

Palau - Palaos		
2003 (C)		
25 - 29	56	...
30 - 34	76	...
35 - 39	59	...
40 - 44	29	...
45 - 49	17	...
50 - 54	9	...
Unknown - Inconnu	10	..

FOOTNOTES - NOTES

♦ Rates based on 30 or fewer births. - Taux basés sur 30 naissances ou moins.

* Provisional. - Données provisoires.

'Code' indicates the source of data, as follows:
C - Civil registration, estimated over 90% complete
U - Civil registration, estimated less than 90% complete
| - Other source, estimated reliable
+ - Data tabulated by date of registration rather than occurrence
... Information not available

Le 'Code' indique la source des données, comme suit :
C - Registres de l'état civil considérés complets à 90 p. 100 au moins
U - Registres de l'état civil qui ne sont pas considérés complets à 90 p. 100 au moins
| - Autre source, considérée fiable
+ - Données exploitées selon la date de l'enregistrement et non la date de l'événement
... Information non disponible

[1] Excludes the islands of St. Brandon and Agalega. - Non compris les îles St. Brandon et Agalega.
[2] Excluding live-born infants who died before their birth was registered. - Non compris les enfants nés vivants décédés avant l'enregistrement de leur naissance.
[3] Data refer to registered events only. - Les données ne concernent que les événements enregistrés.
[4] Including Canadian residents temporarily in the United States, but excluding United States residents temporarily in Canada. - Y compris les résidents canadiens se trouvant temporairement aux Etats-Unis, mais ne comprenant pas les résidents des Etats-Unis se trouvant temporairement au Canada.
[5] Data have not been adjusted for underenumeration. - Les données n'ont pas été ajustées pour compenser les lacunes du dénombrement.
[6] Data refer to births to resident mothers. - Ces données concernent les enfants nés de mères résidentes.
[7] Excluding newborns registered by application of mothers. Excluding infants born alive of less than 28 weeks' gestation, of less than 1 000 grams in weight and 35 centimeters in length, who die within seven days of birth. - Exception faite des nouveau-nés qui ont été enregistrés à la demande des mères. Non compris les enfants nés vivants après moins de 28 semaines de gestations, pesant moins de 1 000 grammes, mesurant moins de 35 centimètres et décédés dans les sept jours qui ont suivi leur naissance.
[8] Data refer to government controlled areas. - Les données se rapportent aux zones contrôlées par le Gouvernement.
[9] Includes data for East Jerusalem and Israeli residents in certain other territories under occupation by Israeli military forces since June 1967. - Y compris les données pour Jérusalem-Est et les résidents israéliens dans certains autres territoires occupés depuis 1967 par les forces armées israéliennes.
[10] Data refer to Japanese nationals in Japan only. Data refer to live births in wedlock only. - Les données se raportent aux nationaux japonais au Japon seulement. Les données ne concernent que les naissances vivantes de parents mariés.
[11] Excluding infants born alive of less than 28 weeks' gestation, of less than 1 000 grams in weight and 35 centimeters in length, who die within seven days of

birth. - Non compris les enfants nés vivants après moins de 28 semaines de gestations, pesant moins de 1 000 grammes, mesurant moins de 35 centimètres et décédés dans les sept jours qui ont suivi leur naissance.
[12] Data from Births and Deaths Notification System (Ministry of Health and all health care providers). - Les données proviennent du système de notification des naissances et des décès (Ministère de la santé et tous prestataires de soins de santé).
[13] Excluding alien armed forces, civilian aliens employed by armed forces, and foreign diplomatic personnel and their dependants. - Non compris les militaires étrangers, les civils étrangers employés par les forces armées ni le personnel diplomatique étranger et les membres de leur famille les accompagnant.
[14] Data refer to live births in wedlock only. - Les données ne concernent que les naissances vivantes de parents mariés.
[15] Including armed forces stationed outside the country, but excluding alien armed forces stationed in the area. - Y compris les militaires nationaux hors du pays, mais non compris les militaires étrangers en garnison sur le territoire.
[16] A live-born child is a child fully expelled or removed out of the mother's body, who gives a sign of life and whose birth weight is (a) 500 g or more, or (b) lower than 500 g, if it survives 24 hours after delivery. - Un enfant né vivant est un enfant qui a été entièrement expulsé ou retiré du corps de la mère, qui présente des signes de vie et dont le poids à la naissance est : a) soit égal ou supérieur à 500 grammes; b) soit inférieur à 500 grammes s'il survit plus de 24 heures après l'accouchement.
[17] Excluding Faeroe Islands and Greenland shown separately, if available. - Non compris les Iles Féroé et le Groenland, qui font l'objet de rubriques distinctes, si disponible.
[18] Excluding Åland Islands. - Non compris les Îles d'Åland.
[19] Including armed forces stationed outside the country. - Y compris les militaires nationaux hors du pays.
[20] Definition of localities was revised from 2011 causing a break with the previous series. - La rupture par rapport aux séries précédentes s'explique par le fait que la définition des localités a été révisée depuis 2011.
[21] Including residents outside the country if listed in a Netherlands population register. - Englobe les résidents se trouvant à l'étranger à condition qu'ils soient inscrits sur le registre de population des Pays-Bas.
[22] Excluding Transnistria and the municipality of Bender. - Les données ne tiennent pas compte de l'information sur la Transnistria et la municipalité de Bender.
[23] Excludes data for Kosovo and Metohia. - Sans les données pour le Kosovo et Metohie.
[24] Data refer to births with weight 500g and more (if weight is unknown - with length 25 centimeters and more, or with gestation during 22 weeks or more). - Données concernant les nouveau-nés de 500 grammes ou plus (si le poids est inconnu – de 25 centimètres de long ou plus, ou après une grossesse de 22 semaines ou plus).
[25] Excluding Channel Islands (Guernsey and Jersey) and Isle of Man, shown separately, if available. Data tabulated by date of occurrence for England and Wales, and by date of registration for Northern Ireland and Scotland. - Non compris les îles Anglo-Normandes (Guernesey et Jersey) et l'île de Man, qui font l'objet de rubriques distinctes, si disponible. Données exploitées selon la date de l'événement pour l'Angleterre et le pays de Galles, et selon la date de l'enregistrement pour l'Irlande du Nord et l'Ecosse.

²⁶ Data includes births born in wedlock for which age of father is unknown and births born out of wedlock not acknowledged by the father for which therefore age of father is unknown. - Les données se rapportent aux enfants légitimes pour lesquels l'âge du père n'est pas connu et aux naissances hors mariage non reconnues par le père et pour lesquelles l'âge du père n'est par conséquent pas connu.

²⁷ Including United States military personnel, their dependants and contract employees. - Y compris les militaires des Etats-Unis, les membres de leur famille les accompagnant et les agents contractuels des Etats-Unis.

Table 12 - Demographic Yearbook 2012

Table 12 presents late foetal deaths and late foetal-death ratios by urban/rural residence for as many years as possible between 2008 and 2012.

Description of variables: Late foetal deaths are foetal deaths[1] of 28 or more completed weeks of gestation. Foetal deaths of unknown gestational age are included with those 28 or more weeks.

Statistics on the number of late foetal deaths are obtained from civil registers unless otherwise noted.

The urban/rural classification of late foetal deaths is as provided by each country or area; it is presumed to be based on the national census definitions of urban population that have been set forth at the end of the technical notes for table 6.

Ratio computation: Late foetal-death ratios are the annual number of late foetal deaths per 1 000 live births (as shown in table 9) in the same year. The live-birth base was adopted because it is assumed to be more comparable from one country or area to another than the sum of live births and foetal deaths.

Ratios by urban/rural residence are the annual number of late foetal deaths, in the appropriate urban or rural category, per 1 000 corresponding live births (as shown in table 9). These ratios are calculated by the Statistics Division of the United Nations.

Ratios presented in this table are limited to those for countries or areas and urban/rural areas having at least a total of 30 late foetal deaths in a given year.

Reliability of data: Each country or area is asked to indicate the estimated completeness of the late foetal deaths recorded in its civil register. These national assessments are indicated by the quality codes "C", "U" and "..." that appear in the first column of this table.

"C" indicates that the data are estimated to be virtually complete, that is, representing at least 90 per cent of the late foetal deaths occurring each year, while "U" indicates that data are estimated to be incomplete, that is, representing less than 90 per cent of the late foetal deaths occurring each year. The code "..." indicates that no information was provided regarding completeness.

Data from civil registers which are reported as incomplete or of unknown completeness (coded "U" or "...") are considered unreliable. They appear in italics in this table. Ratios are not computed for data so coded.

For more information about the quality of vital statistics data in general, see section 4.2 of the Technical Notes.

Limitations: Statistics on late foetal deaths are subject to the same qualifications as have been set forth for vital statistics in general and foetal-death statistics in particular as discussed in section 4 of the Technical Notes.

The reliability of the data is a very important factor. Of all vital statistics, the registration of foetal deaths is probably the most incomplete.

Variation in the definition of foetal deaths, and in particular late foetal deaths, also limits international comparability. The criterion of 28 or more completed weeks of gestation to distinguish late foetal deaths is not universally used; some countries or areas use different durations of gestation or other criteria such as size of the foetus. In addition, the difficulty of accurately determining gestational age further reduces comparability. However, to promote comparability, late foetal deaths shown in this table are restricted to those of at least 28 or more completed weeks of gestation. Wherever this is not possible, a footnote is provided.

Late foetal-death ratios are subject to the limitations of the data on live births with which they have been calculated. These have been set forth in the technical notes for table 9.

It must be pointed out that when late foetal deaths and live births are both under registered, the resulting ratios may be of reasonable magnitude. For the countries or areas where live-birth registration is poorest, the late foetal-death ratios may be the largest, effectively masking the completeness of the base

362

data. For this reason, possible variations in birth-registration completeness as well as the reported completeness of late foetal deaths must always be borne in mind in evaluating late foetal-death ratios.

In addition to the indirect effect of live-birth under-registration, late foetal-death ratios may be seriously affected by date-of-registration tabulation of live births. When the annual number of live births registered and reported fluctuates over a wide range due to changes in legislation or to special needs for proof of birth on the part of large segments of the population, then the late foetal-death ratios will also fluctuate, but inversely. Because of these effects, data for countries or areas known to tabulate live births by date of registration should be used with caution.

Finally, it may be noted that the counting of live-born infants as late foetal deaths, because they died before the registration of the birth or within the first 24 hours of life, has the effect of inflating the late foetal-death ratios unduly by decreasing the birth denominator and increasing the foetal-death numerator. This factor should not be overlooked in using data from this table.

The comparability of data by urban/rural residence is affected by the national definitions of urban and rural used in tabulating these data. It is assumed, in the absence of specific information to the contrary, that the definitions of urban and rural used in connection with the national population census were also used in the compilation of the vital statistics for each country or area. However, it cannot be excluded that, for a given country or area, different definitions of urban and rural are used for the vital statistics data and the population census data respectively. When known, the definitions of urban used in national population censuses are presented at the end of the technical notes for table 6. As discussed in detail in the technical notes for table 6, these definitions vary considerably from one country or area to another.

Urban/rural differentials in late foetal death ratios may also be affected by whether the late foetal deaths and live births have been tabulated in terms of place of occurrence or place of usual residence. This problem is discussed in more detail in section 4.1.4.1 of the Introduction.

Earlier data: Late foetal deaths and late foetal-death ratios have been shown in each issue of the Demographic Yearbook beginning with the 1951 issue. A special topic CD on natality published in 2001 presents the data for all available years from 1990 to 1998. For more information on specific topics, and years for which data are reported, readers should consult the Historical Index.

NOTES

[1] For definition, see section 4.1.1 of the Introduction.

Tableau 12 – *Annuaire démographique 2012*

Le tableau 12 présente des données sur les morts fœtales tardives et les rapports de mortinatalité selon le lieu de résidence (zone urbaine ou rurale) pour le plus grand nombre d'années possible entre 2008 et 2012.

Description des variables : Par mort fœtale tardive, on entend le décès d'un fœtus[1] survenu après 28 semaines complètes de gestation au moins. Les morts fœtales pour lesquelles la durée de la période de gestation n'est pas connue sont comprises dans cette catégorie.

Sauf indication contraire, les statistiques du nombre de morts fœtales tardives sont établies sur la base des registres de l'état civil.

La classification des morts fœtales tardives selon le lieu de résidence (zone urbaine ou rurale) est celle qui a été communiquée par chaque pays ou zone ; on part du principe qu'elle repose sur les définitions de la population urbaine utilisées pour les recensements nationaux, telles qu'elles sont reproduites à la fin des notes techniques du tableau 6.

Calcul des rapports : les rapports de mortinatalité représentent le nombre annuel de morts fœtales tardives pour 1 000 naissances vivantes (telles qu'elles sont présentées au tableau 9) survenues pendant la même année. On a pris pour base de calcul les naissances vivantes parce que l'on pense qu'elle sont plus facilement comparables d'un pays ou d'une zone à l'autre que la somme des naissances vivantes et des morts fœtales.

Les rapports selon le lieu de résidence (zone urbaine ou rurale) représentent le nombre annuel de morts fœtales tardives, classées selon la catégorie urbaine ou rurale appropriée pour 1 000 naissances vivantes (telles qu'elles sont présentées au tableau 9) survenues parmi la population correspondante. Ces rapports ont été calculés par la Division de statistique de l'ONU.

Les rapports présentés dans le tableau 12 ne concernent que les pays ou zones où l'on a enregistré un total d'au moins 30 morts fœtales tardives pendant une année donnée.

Fiabilité des données : il a été demandé à chaque pays ou zone d'indiquer le degré estimatif de complétude des données sur les morts fœtales tardives figurant dans ses registres d'état civil. Ces évaluations nationales sont signalées par les codes de qualité "C", "U" et "..." qui apparaissent dans la deuxième colonne du tableau.

La lettre "C" indique que les données sont jugées à peu près complètes, c'est-à-dire qu'elles représentent au moins 90 p. 100 des morts fœtales tardives survenues chaque année ; la lettre "U" signifie que les données sont jugées incomplètes, c'est-à-dire qu'elles représentent moins de 90 p.100 des morts fœtales tardives survenues chaque année. Le code "..." indique qu'aucun renseignement n'a été communiqué quant à la complétude des données.

Les données provenant des registres de l'état civil qui sont déclarées incomplètes ou dont le degré de complétude n'est pas connu (code "U" ou "...") sont jugées douteuses. Elles apparaissent en italique dans le tableau ; les rapports, dans ces cas, n'ont pas été calculés.

Pour plus de précisions sur la qualité des données reposant sur les statistiques de l'état civil en général, voir la section 4.2 des Notes techniques.

Insuffisance des données : les statistiques des morts fœtales tardives appellent toutes les réserves qui ont été formulées à propos des statistiques de l'état civil en général et des statistiques concernant les morts fœtales en particulier (voir la section 4 des Notes techniques).

La fiabilité des données est un facteur très important. Les statistiques concernant les morts fœtales sont probablement les moins complètes de toutes les statistiques de l'état civil.

L'hétérogénéité des définitions de la mort fœtale et, en particulier, de la mort fœtale tardive nuit aussi à la comparabilité internationale des données. Le critère des 28 semaines complètes de gestation au moins n'est pas universellement utilisé ; certains pays ou zones retiennent des critères différents pour la durée de la période de gestation ou d'autres critères tels que la taille du fœtus. De surcroît, la comparabilité est rendue malaisée par le fait qu'il est difficile d'établir avec précision l'âge gestationnel. Pour faciliter les comparaisons, les morts fœtales tardives considérées ici sont exclusivement celles qui sont survenues au terme de 28 semaines de gestation au moins. Les exceptions sont signalées en note.

Les rapports de mortinatalité appellent en outre toutes les réserves qui ont été formulées à propos des statistiques des naissances vivantes qui ont servi à leur calcul (voir à ce sujet les notes techniques relatives au tableau 9).

En ce qui concerne le calcul des rapports, il convient de noter que, si l'enregistrement des morts fœtales tardives et celui des naissances vivantes sont loin d'être exhaustifs, les rapports de mortinatalité peuvent être raisonnables. C'est parfois pour les pays ou zones où l'enregistrement des naissances vivantes laisse le plus à désirer que les rapports de mortinatalité sont les plus élevés, ce qui masque le caractère incomplet des données de base. Aussi, pour porter un jugement sur la qualité des rapports de mortinatalité, il ne faut jamais oublier que la complétude de l'enregistrement des naissances comme celle de l'enregistrement des morts fœtales tardives peuvent varier sensiblement.

Hormis les effets indirects des lacunes de l'enregistrement des naissances vivantes, il arrive que les rapports de mortinatalité soient considérablement faussés lorsque l'exploitation des données relatives aux naissances se fait d'après la date de l'enregistrement. Si le nombre des naissances vivantes enregistrées vient à varier notablement d'une année à l'autre par suite de modifications de la législation ou parce que de très nombreuses personnes ont besoin de se procurer une attestation de naissance, les rapports de mortinatalité varient également, mais en sens inverse. Il convient donc d'utiliser avec prudence le données des pays ou zones où les statistiques sont établies d'après la date de l'enregistrement.

Enfin, on notera que l'inclusion parmi les morts fœtales tardives des décès d'enfants nés vivants qui sont décédés avant l'enregistrement de leur naissance ou dans les 24 heures qui ont suivi la naissance conduit à des rapports de mortinatalité exagérés parce que le dénominateur (nombre de naissances) se trouve alors diminué et le numérateur (morts fœtales) augmenté. Il importe de ne pas négliger ce facteur lorsque l'on utilise les données du tableau 12.

La comparabilité des données selon le lieu de résidence (zone urbaine ou rurale) peut être limitée par les définitions nationales des termes « urbain » et « rural » utilisées pour la mise en tableaux de ces données. En l'absence d'indications contraires, on a supposé que les mêmes définitions avaient servi pour le recensement national de la population et pour l'établissement des statistiques de l'état civil pour chaque pays ou zone. Toutefois, il n'est pas exclu que, pour une zone ou un pays donné, des définitions différentes aient été retenues. Les définitions du terme « urbain » utilisées pour les recensements nationaux de population ont été présentées à la fin des notes techniques du tableau 6 lorsqu'elles étaient connues. Comme on l'a précisé dans les notes techniques relatives au tableau 6, ces définitions varient considérablement d'un pays ou d'une zone à l'autre.

La différence entre les rapports de mortinatalité pour les zones urbaines et rurales pourra aussi être faussée selon que les morts fœtales tardives et les naissances vivantes auront été classées d'après le lieu de l'événement ou le lieu de résidence habituel. Ce problème est examiné plus en détail à la section 4.1.4.1 des Notes techniques.

Données publiées antérieurement : les éditions de l'*Annuaire démographique* parues à partir de 1951 contiennent des statistiques concernant les morts fœtales tardives et les rapports de mortinatalité. Un CD-ROM sur la natalité paru en 2001 présente les données pour toutes les années disponibles de 1990 à 1998. Pour plus de précisions concernant les années et les sujets pour lesquels des données ont été publiées, se reporter à l'index.

NOTE

[1] Pour la définition, voir la section 4.1.1 de l'Introduction.

12. Late foetal deaths and late foetal death ratios, by urban/rural residence: 2008 - 2012
Morts foetales tardives et rapports de mortinatalité, selon la résidence, urbaine/rurale : 2008 - 2012

Continent, country or area, and urban/rural residence / Continent, pays ou zone et résidence, urbaine/rurale	Co-de	Number - Nombre					Ratio - Rapport				
		2008	2009	2010	2011	2012	2008	2009	2010	2011	2012
AFRICA - AFRIQUE											
Algeria - Algérie											
Total	+U	16 588	15 937	16 444	15 480	15 795	...	...	...	...	...
Egypt - Égypte											
Total	+U	4 105	4 039	...	...	...	...	...	...	...	...
Urban - Urbaine	+U	3 495	3 314	...	...	...	...	...	...	...	...
Rural - Rurale	+U	610	725	...	...	...	...	...	...	...	...
Total	C	...	...	4 031	4 067		...	...	1.8	1.7	...
Urban - Urbaine	C	...	...	3 295	3 247		...	...	3.7	3.4	...
Rural - Rurale	C	...	...	736	820		...	...	0.5	0.5	...
Mauritius - Maurice[1]											
Total	+C	165	138	103	139	...	10.1	9.0	6.9	9.5	...
Urban - Urbaine	+C	65	51	43	57	...	10.3	8.7	7.5	10.2	...
Rural - Rurale	+C	100	87	60	82	...	9.9	9.2	6.5	9.0	...
Sierra Leone											
Total	+...	1 682	1 630	1 834	1 663	1 638	...	...	...	...	...
Urban - Urbaine	+...	438	579	586	230	1 066	...	...	...	...	...
Rural - Rurale	+...	1 244	1 051	1 248	1 433	572	...	...	...	...	...
South Africa - Afrique du Sud											
Total	...	14 626	...	...	...	...	...	...	...	...	...
Tunisia - Tunisie											
Total	U	1 582	1 757	1 995	2 074	...	...	...	...	...	...
AMERICA, NORTH - AMÉRIQUE DU NORD											
Bahamas											
Total	+C	82	74	*61	...	...	16.0	14.7	*12.4	...	...
Bermuda - Bermudes											
Total	C	...	...	6	2	4	...	...	...	...	...
Canada[2]											
Total	C	1 170	...	...	...	...	3.1	...	...	...	...
Costa Rica											
Total	C	400	409	*389	*471[3]	...	5.3	5.5	*5.5	*6.4	...
Urban - Urbaine	C	180	181	*169	...	...	6.2	6.4	*6.5	...	...
Rural - Rurale	C	220	228	*220	...	...	4.7	4.9	*4.9	...	...
Cuba[4]											
Total	C	1 513	1 460	1 344	1 365	...	12.3	11.2	10.5	10.3	...
El Salvador											
Total	C	412	...	...	...	...	3.7	...	...	...	...
Greenland - Groenland											
Total	C	5	...	...	...	...	...	...	...	...	...
Mexico - Mexique[5]											
Total	+U	11 929	11 459	11 188	11 096	...	...	...	...	...	...
Urban - Urbaine[6]	+U	8 822	8 451	8 344	8 299	...	...	...	...	...	...
Rural - Rurale[6]	+U	2 911	2 830	2 701	2 631	...	...	...	...	...	...
Montserrat											
Total	+C	2	1	-	-	...	...	...	...	...	...
Panama											
Total	U	449	369	396	...	...	...	...	...	...	...
Puerto Rico - Porto Rico											
Total	C	460	...	...	...	...	10.1	...	...	...	...
Urban - Urbaine[6]	C	273	...	...	...	...	11.4	...	...	...	...
Rural - Rurale[6]	C	179	...	...	...	...	8.2	...	...	...	...
Turks and Caicos Islands - Îles Turques et Caïques											
Total	C	7	...	...	...	...	...	...	...	...	...
AMERICA, SOUTH - AMÉRIQUE DU SUD											
Argentina - Argentine											
Total	C	5 167	5 100	4 692	4 712	...	6.9	6.8	6.2	6.2	...
Brazil - Brésil											
Total	U	23 868	23 580	22 874	24 083	...	...	...	...	...	...

12. Late foetal deaths and late foetal death ratios, by urban/rural residence: 2008 - 2012
Morts foetales tardives et rapports de mortinatalité, selon la résidence, urbaine/rurale : 2008 - 2012 (continued - suite)

Continent, country or area, and urban/rural residence / Continent, pays ou zone et résidence, urbaine/rurale	Co-de	Number - Nombre					Ratio - Rapport				
		2008	2009	2010	2011	2012	2008	2009	2010	2011	2012
AMERICA, SOUTH - AMÉRIQUE DU SUD											
Chile - Chili											
Total	C	2 167[7]	2 252[7]	1 380[8]	...	...	8.8	8.9	5.5	...	...
Urban - Urbaine	C	1 951[7]	2 050[7]	1 210[8]	...	...	8.6	9.0	5.4	...	...
Rural - Rurale	C	216[7]	202[7]	170[8]	...	...	10.6	7.9	6.7	...	...
Colombia - Colombie[9]											
Total	...	11 669	11 415	12 660	...	...	...	...	...	...	...
Urban - Urbaine[6]	...	9 149	8 755	10 295	...	...	...	...	...	...	...
Rural - Rurale[6]	...	1 990	2 250	2 067	...	...	...	...	...	...	...
Ecuador - Équateur[10]											
Total	...	1 310	1 295	1 815[7]	...	...	...	...	...	...	...
Paraguay											
Total	+U	679	...	...	...	...	...	...	...	...	...
Urban - Urbaine	+U	503	...	...	...	...	...	...	...	...	...
Rural - Rurale	+U	176	...	...	...	...	...	...	...	...	...
ASIA - ASIE											
Armenia - Arménie											
Total	C	601	802	...	...	...	14.6	18.1	...	...	...
Urban - Urbaine	C	370	473	...	...	...	14.1	16.7	...	...	...
Rural - Rurale	C	231	329	...	...	...	15.4	20.4	...	...	...
Azerbaijan - Azerbaïdjan											
Total	+C	677	672	728	...	...	4.5	4.4	4.4	...	...
Bahrain - Bahreïn											
Total	...	112	95	104	140	...	...	...	...	...	...
China, Hong Kong SAR - Chine, Hong Kong RAS											
Total	...	169	158	152	184	...	...	...	...	...	...
China, Macao SAR - Chine, Macao RAS											
Total	C	8	8	9	12	14	...	...	...	...	...
Georgia - Géorgie											
Total	C	660	484	653	563	...	11.7	7.6	10.4	9.7	...
Urban - Urbaine	C	495	350	345	323	...	12.6	8.0	10.1	9.7	...
Rural - Rurale	C	165	134	308	240	...	9.5	6.8	10.8	9.8	...
Israel - Israël[11]											
Total	C	544	535	518	...	...	3.5	3.3	3.1	...	...
Urban - Urbaine[6]	C	494	485	463	...	...	3.5	3.3	3.1	...	...
Rural - Rurale[6]	C	44	42	52	...	...	3.1	2.8	3.4	...	...
Japan - Japon[12]											
Total	C	2 209	2 222	2 187	2 137	...	2.0	2.1	2.0	2.0	...
Urban - Urbaine	C	1 971[6]	2 030[6]	2 009[6]	1 946	...	2.0	2.1	2.0	2.0	...
Rural - Rurale	C	234[6]	191[6]	175[6]	191	...	2.4	2.0	1.9	2.2	...
Kazakhstan											
Total	C	3 798	...	...	...	...	10.7	...	...	...	...
Urban - Urbaine	C	2 509	...	...	...	...	12.7	...	...	...	...
Rural - Rurale	C	1 289	...	...	...	...	8.1	...	...	...	...
Kuwait - Koweït											
Total	C	367	335	346	313	...	6.7	5.9	6.0	5.4	...
Kyrgyzstan - Kirghizstan											
Total	C	1 664	1 703	1 624	1 675	...	13.1	12.6	11.1	11.2	...
Urban - Urbaine	C	1 127	1 161	1 124	1 176	...	25.6	24.7	22.5	24.0	...
Rural - Rurale	C	537	542	500	499	...	6.4	6.1	5.2	5.0	...
Malaysia - Malaisie											
Total	C	2 128	2 216	*2 175	...	...	4.4	4.5	*4.6	...	...
Urban - Urbaine	C	1 262	1 314	...	...	...	4.1	4.2	...	...	...
Rural - Rurale	C	866	902	...	...	...	4.8	5.0	...	...	...
Maldives[7]											
Total	...	49	54	48	43	...	...	...	...	...	...
Urban - Urbaine	...	26	23	23	25	...	...	...	...	...	...
Rural - Rurale	...	23	31	25	18	...	...	...	...	...	...
Myanmar											
Total	+U	10 783	11 642	12 234	...	...	...	...	...	...	...
Urban - Urbaine	+U	2 610	2 950	3 131	...	...	...	...	...	...	...
Rural - Rurale	+U	8 173	8 692	9 103	...	...	...	...	...	...	...

12. Late foetal deaths and late foetal death ratios, by urban/rural residence: 2008 - 2012
Morts foetales tardives et rapports de mortinatalité, selon la résidence, urbaine/rurale : 2008 - 2012 (continued - suite)

Continent, country or area, and urban/rural residence / Continent, pays ou zone et résidence, urbaine/rurale	Co-de	Number - Nombre					Ratio - Rapport				
		2008	2009	2010	2011	2012	2008	2009	2010	2011	2012
ASIA - ASIE											
Oman[13]											
Total	U	454	495	392	333	...	...	...	...	...	...
Philippines											
Total	...	4 178	4 180	...	...	...	...	...	...	...	...
Qatar											
Total	C	133	123	130	...	...	7.7	6.7	6.7	...	...
Republic of Korea - République de Corée[14]											
Total	C	1 055	869	882	853	...	2.3	2.0	1.9	1.8	...
Urban - Urbaine[6]	C	...	725	703	697	...	...	2.0	1.8	1.8	...
Rural - Rurale[6]	C	...	138	177	153	...	...	1.8	2.1	1.9	...
Singapore - Singapour											
Total	+C	86	79	99	106	111	2.2	2.0	2.6	2.7	2.6
Tajikistan - Tadjikistan											
Total	U	1 578	2 010	2 122	1 966	...	...	...	...	...	...
Urban - Urbaine	U	1 281	1 517	1 349	1 283	...	...	...	...	...	...
Rural - Rurale	U	297	493	773	683	...	...	...	...	...	...
EUROPE											
Åland Islands - Îles d'Åland											
Total	C	-	-	-	1	...	...	...	...	...	...
Urban - Urbaine	C	-	-	-	...	...	...	...	...	...	...
Rural - Rurale	C	-	-	-	...	...	...	...	...	...	...
Andorra - Andorre											
Total	C	2	3	...	...	...	...	...	...	...	...
Austria - Autriche											
Total	C	175	188	192	294	...	2.3	2.5	2.4	3.8	...
Belarus - Bélarus											
Total	C	318	304	265	249	...	2.9	2.8	2.5	2.3	...
Urban - Urbaine	C	230	223	187	174	...	2.8	2.7	2.3	2.1	...
Rural - Rurale	C	88	81	78	75	...	3.4	3.1	3.0	2.9	...
Belgium - Belgique											
Total	C	574	...	...	...	...	4.5	...	...	...	...
Urban - Urbaine	C	566	...	...	...	...	4.5	...	...	...	...
Rural - Rurale	C	8	...	...	...	...	...	...	...	...	...
Bosnia and Herzegovina - Bosnie-Herzégovine											
Total	C	171	...	...	...	...	5.0	...	...	...	...
Bulgaria - Bulgarie											
Total	C	571	616	592	556	...	7.3	7.6	7.8	7.8	...
Urban - Urbaine	C	383	424	409	401	...	6.6	7.0	7.2	7.5	...
Rural - Rurale	C	188	192	183	155	...	9.7	9.5	9.9	8.9	...
Croatia - Croatie[15]											
Total	C	176	177	185	145	...	4.0	4.0	4.3	3.5	...
Urban - Urbaine	C	108	98	95	...	...	4.4	3.9	3.9	...	...
Rural - Rurale	C	68	79	90	...	...	3.5	4.0	4.8	...	...
Czech Republic - République tchèque[16]											
Total	C	261	309	283	303	...	2.2	2.6	2.4	2.8	...
Urban - Urbaine	C	187	234	202	228	...	2.1	2.7	2.3	2.9	...
Rural - Rurale	C	74	75	81	75	...	2.4	2.4	2.6	2.6	...
Denmark - Danemark[17]											
Total	C	314	272	269	...	...	4.8	4.3	4.2	...	...
Estonia - Estonie											
Total	C	52	61	41	42	...	3.2	3.9	2.6	2.9	...
Urban - Urbaine	C	34	44	28	33	...	3.1	4.1	...	3.3	...
Rural - Rurale	C	18	17	13	9	...	...	...	...	...	...
Finland - Finlande											
Total	C	122	129	128[18]	...	...	2.0	2.1	2.1	...	...
Urban - Urbaine	C	83	87	81[18]	...	...	2.0	2.0	1.9	...	...
Rural - Rurale	C	39	42	47[18]	...	...	2.3	2.4	2.7	...	...

12. Late foetal deaths and late foetal death ratios, by urban/rural residence: 2008 - 2012
Morts foetales tardives et rapports de mortinatalité, selon la résidence, urbaine/rurale : 2008 - 2012 (continued - suite)

Continent, country or area, and urban/rural residence / Continent, pays ou zone et résidence, urbaine/rurale	Co-de	Number - Nombre					Ratio - Rapport				
		2008	2009	2010	2011	2012	2008	2009	2010	2011	2012
EUROPE											
France[19]											
Total	C	8 356	9 377	8 206	...	...	10.5	11.8	10.2	...	...
Urban - Urbaine[20]	C	6 317	7 092	...	...	...	10.6	12.0	...	...	...
Rural - Rurale[20]	C	1 936	2 190	...	...	...	9.6	11.0	...	...	...
Germany - Allemagne											
Total	C	2 412	2 338	2 466	2 387	...	3.5	3.5	3.6	3.6	...
Greece - Grèce											
Total	C	317	394	500[7]	431[7]	...	2.7	3.3	4.4	4.0	...
Urban - Urbaine[7]	C	...	...	358	308	...	...	...	4.5	4.1	...
Rural - Rurale[7]	C	...	...	142	123	...	...	...	3.9	3.9	...
Hungary - Hongrie[21]											
Total	C	431	519	387	392	...	4.3	5.4	4.3	4.5	...
Urban - Urbaine[22]	C	254	313	231	237	...	3.8	4.8	3.7	3.9	...
Rural - Rurale[22]	C	174	202	150	153	...	5.5	6.8	5.6	5.8	...
Iceland - Islande											
Total	C	11	12	9	4[23]	...	...	...	...	...	...
Urban - Urbaine	C	11	11	8	4[23]	...	...	...	...	...	...
Rural - Rurale	C	-	1	1	-[23]	...	...	...	...	...	...
Ireland - Irlande[24]											
Total	C	221	224	...	...	...	2.9	3.0	...	...	...
Italy - Italie											
Total	C	1 568	1 564	1 532	*1 422	...	2.7	2.7	2.7	*2.6	...
Latvia - Lettonie[25]											
Total	C	150	130	109	124	...	6.3	6.0	5.7	6.6	...
Urban - Urbaine	C	100	85	65	...	...	6.0	5.7	4.9	...	...
Rural - Rurale	C	50	45	44	...	...	6.8	6.6	7.3	...	...
Lithuania - Lituanie[15]											
Total	C	164	151	147	148	...	4.7	4.1	4.1	4.3	...
Urban - Urbaine	C	109	90	97	89	...	4.6	3.6	3.9	3.7	...
Rural - Rurale	C	55	61	50	59	...	4.9	5.2	4.5	5.6	...
Luxembourg											
Total	C	21	31	18	22	...	...	5.5	...	...	...
Malta - Malte[15]											
Total	C	29	28	14	18	...	...	...	...	...	...
Montenegro - Monténégro[7]											
Total	C	34	43	...	...	...	4.1	5.0	...	...	...
Urban - Urbaine	C	24	37	...	...	...	...	5.6	...	...	...
Rural - Rurale	C	10	6	...	...	...	...	...	...	...	...
Netherlands - Pays-Bas[26]											
Total	C	774	648	648	620	...	4.2	3.5	3.5	3.4	...
Urban - Urbaine	C	...	453	...	...	...	...	3.5	...	...	...
Rural - Rurale	C	...	195	...	...	...	...	3.5	...	...	...
Norway - Norvège											
Total	C	221	215	190	198	...	3.7	3.5	3.1	3.3	...
Poland - Pologne											
Total	C	1 422	1 157	1 226	1 182	...	3.4	2.8	3.0	3.0	...
Urban - Urbaine	C	767	634	682	644	...	3.2	2.6	2.8	2.9	...
Rural - Rurale	C	655	523	544	538	...	3.8	3.1	3.2	3.3	...
Portugal[5]											
Total	C	265	291	241	227	...	2.5	2.9	2.4	2.3	...
Romania - Roumanie											
Total	C	993	969	856	811	...	4.5	4.4	4.0	4.1	...
Urban - Urbaine	C	468	474	420	363	...	3.9	3.9	3.6	3.4	...
Rural - Rurale	C	525	495	436	448	...	5.2	4.9	4.6	5.0	...
Russian Federation - Fédération de Russie											
Total	C	8 594	8 380	8 300	8 109	...	5.0	4.8	4.6	4.5	...
Urban - Urbaine	C	6 112	5 815	5 795	5 590	...	5.1	4.7	4.6	4.4	...
Rural - Rurale	C	2 482	2 565	2 505	2 519	...	4.8	4.9	4.8	4.8	...
Serbia - Serbie[27]											
Total	+C	345	366	388	328	...	5.0	5.2	5.7	5.0	...
Urban - Urbaine	+C	240	243	257	224	...	5.3	5.2	5.5	4.9	...
Rural - Rurale	+C	105	123	131	104	...	4.4	5.3	6.1	5.2	...
Slovakia - Slovaquie[28]											
Total	C	226	228	189	190	...	3.9	3.7	3.1	3.1	...
Urban - Urbaine	C	101	99	86	78	...	3.3	3.0	2.7	2.4	...
Rural - Rurale	C	125	129	103	112	...	4.7	4.5	3.6	3.9	...

12. Late foetal deaths and late foetal death ratios, by urban/rural residence: 2008 - 2012
Morts foetales tardives et rapports de mortinatalité, selon la résidence, urbaine/rurale : 2008 - 2012 (continued - suite)

Continent, country or area, and urban/rural residence / Continent, pays ou zone et résidence, urbaine/rurale	Co-de	Number - Nombre					Ratio - Rapport				
		2008	2009	2010	2011	2012	2008	2009	2010	2011	2012
EUROPE											
Slovenia - Slovénie											
Total	C	69	64	60	59	...	3.2	2.9	2.7	2.7	...
Spain - Espagne											
Total	C	1 136	1 071	1 046	1 296	...	2.2	2.2	2.2	2.8	...
Sweden - Suède											
Total	C	396	451	426	429	...	3.6	4.0	3.7	3.8	...
Switzerland - Suisse[7]											
Total	C	341	345	346	349	...	4.4	4.4	4.3	4.3	...
Urban - Urbaine	C	270	255	266	246	...	4.7	4.4	4.4	4.1	...
Rural - Rurale	C	71	90	80	103	...	3.6	4.6	4.0	5.1	...
TFYR of Macedonia - L'ex-R. y. de Macédoine											
Total	C	222	226	211	202		9.7	9.5	8.7	8.9	...
Urban - Urbaine	C	117	125	101	...	...	8.9	9.2	7.3	...	...
Rural - Rurale	C	105	101	110	...	...	10.8	10.0	10.6	...	...
Ukraine											
Total	+C	3 416	3 351	3 300	3 158	...	6.7	6.5	6.6	6.3	...
Urban - Urbaine	+C	2 304	2 247	2 075	2 006	...	6.8	6.6	6.4	6.1	...
Rural - Rurale	+C	1 112	1 104	1 225	1 152	...	6.5	6.4	7.2	6.6	...
United Kingdom of Great Britain and Northern Ireland - Royaume-Uni de Grande-Bretagne et d'Irlande du Nord[29]											
Total	C	4 057	4 124	4 110	4 201	...	5.1	5.2	5.1	5.2	...
OCEANIA - OCÉANIE											
Australia - Australie[9]											
Total	+C	1 323	...	...	...	...	4.5	...	...	...	...
Guam[7]											
Total	C	...	42	49	...	...	...	12.3	14.3	...	...
New Zealand - Nouvelle-Zélande[5]											
Total	+C	234	175	185	184	158	3.6	2.8	2.9	3.0	2.6
Urban - Urbaine	+C	210	159	165	160	141	3.7	2.9	3.0	3.0	2.6
Rural - Rurale	+C	24	16	19	24	17	...	...	...	...	...

FOOTNOTES - NOTES

Italics: data from civil registers which are incomplete or of unknown completeness. - Italiques : données incomplètes ou dont le degré d'exactitude n'est pas connu, provenant des registres de l'état civil.

* Provisional. - Données provisoires.

[1] Excludes the islands of St. Brandon and Agalega. - Non compris les îles St. Brandon et Agalega.

[2] Including Canadian residents temporarily in the United States, but excluding United States residents temporarily in Canada. - Y compris les résidents canadiens se trouvant temporairement aux Etats-Unis, mais ne comprenant pas les résidents des Etats-Unis se trouvant temporairement au Canada.

[3] Including unknown sex. - Y compris le sexe inconnu.

[4] Late foetal death is indicated by the fact that the foetus is at least 500 grams or more in weight. - Les décès foetaux tardifs sont caractérisés par le fait que le foetus pèse au moins 500 grammes.

[5] Data refer to resident population only. - Pour la population résidante seulement.

[6] The total number includes 'Unknown residence', but the categories urban and rural do not. - Le nombre total englobe les personnes dont la résidence n'est pas connue, à l'inverse des catégories de population urbaine et rurale.

[7] Data refer to total foetal deaths. - Y compris toutes les morts foetales.

[8] Late foetal death is indicated by the fact that the foetus is at least 22 completed weeks of gestational age. - Les décès intra-utérins tardifs sont définis comme survenant après 22 semaines au moins de gestation.

[9] Data include foetal deaths of unknown gestational weeks. - Les données comprennent les morts foetales où le nombre de semaines de gestation n'est pas connu.

[10] Excludes nomadic Indian tribes. - Non compris les tribus d'Indiens nomades.

[11] Includes data for East Jerusalem and Israeli residents in certain other territories under occupation by Israeli military forces since June 1967. - Y compris les données pour Jérusalem-Est et les résidents israéliens dans certains autres territoires occupés depuis 1967 par les forces armées israéliennes.

[12] Data refer to Japanese nationals in Japan only. Data exclude unknown duration of pregnancy. - Les données se raportent aux nationaux japonais au Japon seulement. Exception faite des grossesses dont la durée n'est pas connue.

[13] Data from Births and Deaths Notification System (Ministry of Health and all health care providers). - Les données proviennent du système de notification des naissances et des décès (Ministère de la santé et tous prestataires de soins de santé).

[14] Excluding alien armed forces, civilian aliens employed by armed forces, and foreign diplomatic personnel and their dependants. - Non compris les militaires étrangers, les civils étrangers employés par les forces armées ni le personnel diplomatique étranger et les membres de leur famille les accompagnant.

[15] Late foetal death is defined as an infant born without any signs of life, weighing at least 500 grams, after duration of pregnancy of at least 22 weeks. - On dit qu'il y a mort intra-utérine tardive lorsqu'un enfant pesant au minimum 500 grammes naît sans donner aucun signe de vie au terme d'une grossesse qui a duré au moins 22 semaines.

[16] Late foetal death is defined as an infant born without any signs of life, weighing at least 1000 grams. - La mortalité fœtale en fin de période de gestation s'entend de nourrissons mort-nés et pesant au moins 1 kilo.

[17] Excluding Faeroe Islands and Greenland shown separately, if available. - Non compris les Iles Féroé et le Groenland, qui font l'objet de rubriques distinctes, si disponible.

[18] Excluding Åland Islands. - Non compris les Îles d'Åland.

[19] Foetal deaths after at least 180 days (6 calendar months or 26 weeks) of gestation. - Morts fœtales survenues après 180 jours (6 mois civils ou 26 semaines) au moins de gestation.

[20] The data for urban and rural exclude the nationals outside the country. - Les données relatives à la population urbaine et rurale n'englobent pas les nationaux se trouvant à l'étranger.

[21] Late foetal death is indicated by the fact that the foetus is at least 24 (it has been 28 weeks until 1996) completed weeks of gestation and does not show any sign of life after the separation from its mother; the foetus has to be 30 cm or more in length or 500 grams or more in weight if its gestational age cannot be determined. - Pour qu'il y ait mort fœtale tardive, il faut que le décès d'un fœtus survienne après 24 semaines complètes de gestation au moins (28 semaines jusqu'en 1996), que le fœtus n'ait pas donné signe de vie après avoir été séparé de la mère, qu'il mesure 30 centimètres au moins ou pèse 500 grammes si la durée de la période de gestation n'est pas connue.

[22] Total includes the data of foreigners, persons of unknown residence and homeless, but the categories urban and rural do not. - Le total englobe les données relatives aux étrangers, aux personnes dont la résidence n'est pas connue et aux personnes sans domicile fixe, à l'inverse des chiffres portant sur la population urbaine et rurale.

[23] Definition of localities was revised from 2011 causing a break with the previous series. - La rupture par rapport aux séries précédentes s'explique par le fait que la définition des localités a été révisée depuis 2011.

[24] Data refer to events registered within one year of occurrence. - Les données portent sur des événements enregistrés dans l'année pendant laquelle ils sont survenus.

[25] Data refer to the death of a foetus at least 22 completed weeks of gestation. - Les données concernent le décès d'un fœtus après 22 semaines de gestation au moins.

[26] Including residents outside the country if listed in a Netherlands population register. - Englobe les résidents se trouvant à l'étranger à condition qu'ils soient inscrits sur le registre de population des Pays-Bas.

[27] Data refer to total foetal deaths. Excludes data for Kosovo and Metohia. - Y compris toutes les morts fœtales. Sans les données pour le Kosovo et Metohie.

[28] Including foetal deaths of at least 1 000 grams in weight or 28 weeks of gestation. - Y compris les morts de fœtus pesant au moins 1 000 grammes ou après 28 semaines de gestation.

[29] Excluding Channel Islands (Guernsey and Jersey) and Isle of Man, shown separately, if available. - Non compris les îles Anglo-Normandes (Guernesey et Jersey) et l'île de Man, qui font l'objet de rubriques distinctes, si disponible.

Table 13 - *Demographic Yearbook 2012*

Table 13 presents legally induced abortions for as many years as available between 2003 and 2012.

Description of variables: There are two major categories of abortion: spontaneous and induced. Induced abortions are those initiated by deliberate action undertaken with the intention of terminating pregnancy; all other abortions are considered spontaneous.

The induction of abortion is subject to governmental regulation in most, if not all, countries or areas. This regulation varies from complete prohibition in some countries or areas to abortion on request, with services provided by governmental health authorities, in others. More generally, governments have attempted to define the conditions under which a pregnancy may lawfully be terminated and have established procedures for authorizing abortion in individual cases.

Information on abortion policies is collected by the United Nations Population Division and published in the World Population Policies[1]. An overview of abortion policies is also published as a wall chart[2].

Reliability of data: Unlike data on live births and foetal deaths, which are generally collected through systems of vital registration, data on abortion are collected from a variety of sources. Because of this, the quality specification on the completeness of civil registers, which is presented for other tables, does not appear here.

Limitations: With regard to the collection of information on abortions, a variety of sources are used, but hospital records are the most common source of information. This implies that most cases that have no contact with hospitals are missed. Data from other sources are probably also incomplete. The data in the present table are limited to legally induced abortions, which, by their nature, might be assumed to be more complete than data on all induced abortions.

Earlier data: Legally induced abortions have been shown previously in all issues of the *Demographic Yearbook* since the 1971 issue. For more information on specific topics and years for which data are reported, readers should consult the Historical Index.

NOTES

[1] World Population Policies 2011 (United Nations Publication, Sales No. E.13.XIII.2), New York 2013. See also:
http://www.un.org/en/development/desa/population/publications/policy/world-population-policies-2011.shtml

[2] World Abortion Policies 2011 (United Nations Publication, Sales No. E.11.XIII.4), New York, 2011. See also:
http://www.un.org/en/development/desa/population/publications/pdf/abortion/worldAbortionPoliciesWallChart2011.pdf

Tableau 13 – *Annuaire démographique 2012*

Le tableau 13 présente des données disponible, relatives aux avortements provoqués légalement, entre 2003 et 2012.

Description des variables : l'avortement peut être spontané ou provoqué. L'avortement provoqué est celui qui résulte de manœuvres délibérées, entreprises afin d'interrompre la grossesse ; tous les autres avortements sont considérés comme spontanés.

L'interruption délibérée de la grossesse fait l'objet d'une réglementation officielle dans la plupart des pays ou zones, sinon dans tous. Cette réglementation va de l'interdiction totale à l'autorisation de l'avortement sur demande, pratiqué par des services de santé publique. Le plus souvent, les gouvernements se sont efforcés de définir les circonstances dans lesquelles la grossesse peut être interrompue licitement et de fixer une procédure d'autorisation.

La Division de la population des Nations Unies collecte des informations sur les politiques en matière d'avortement et les publient dans "World Population Policies"[1]. Une vue d'ensemble sur les politiques en matière d'avortement est également publiée sous forme de poster[2].

Fiabilité des données : à la différence des données sur les naissances vivantes et les morts fœtales, qui proviennent généralement des registres d'état civil, les données sur l'avortement sont tirées de sources diverses. Aussi ne trouve-t-on pas ici une évaluation de la qualité des données semblable à celle qui indique, pour les autres tableaux, le degré d'exhaustivité des données de l'état civil.

Insuffisance des données : en ce qui concerne les renseignements sur l'avortement, un grand nombre de sources sont utilisées, les relevés hospitaliers restant cependant la source la plus commune. Il s'ensuit que la plupart des cas qui ne passent pas par les hôpitaux sont ignorés. Il faut aussi tenir compte du fait que les données provenant d'autres sources sont probablement incomplètes. Les données du tableau 13 se limitent aux avortements provoqués pour raisons légales dont on peut supposer, en raison de leur nature même, que les statistiques sont plus complètes que les données concernant l'ensemble des avortements provoqués.

Données publiées antérieurement : des statistiques concernant les avortements provoqués pour raisons légales sont publiées dans *l'Annuaire démographique* depuis 1971. Pour plus de précisions concernant les années et les sujets pour lesquels des données ont été publiées, se reporter à l'index historique.

NOTES

[1] World Population Policies 2011 (publication des Nations Unies, Numéro de vente E.13.XIII.2), New York 2013. Voir aussi : http://www.un.org/en/development/desa/population/publications/policy/world-population-policies-2011.shtml

[2] World Abortion Policies 2011 (publication des Nations Unies, Numéro de vente E.11.XIII.4), New York, 2011. Voir aussi : http://www.un.org/en/development/desa/population/publications/pdf/abortion/worldAbortionPoliciesWallChart2011.pdf

13. Legally induced abortions: 2003 - 2012
Avortements provoqués légalement : 2003 - 2012

Continent and country or area Continent et pays ou zone	Number - Nombre									
	2003	2004	2005	2006	2007	2008	2009	2010	2011	2012
AFRICA - AFRIQUE										
Réunion	4 129	4 155	4 421	4 523	...	...	...	...	...	...
Seychelles	440	435	413	443	446	453	471	556	...	...
AMERICA, NORTH - AMÉRIQUE DU NORD										
Anguilla	24	26	21	...	...	...	...	...	...	...
Bermuda - Bermudes	63	215	237	222	90	283	294	271	269	272
Canada[1]	103 768	100 039	96 815	91 310[2]	...	...	...	...	...	...
Costa Rica[3]	8 446	8 801	8 411	8 367	8 504	8 733	7 848[4]	7 697[4]	...	...
Cuba	65 628	67 277	62 530	67 903	66 008	74 905	84 724	71 398	83 943	...
Dominican Republic - République dominicaine	24 899	26 438	29 167	...	...	...	...	...	...	...
Greenland - Groenland	869	905	899	904	887	899	799	858	...	...
Martinique	2 394	2 426	2 304	2 392	...	...	...	...	...	...
Mexico - Mexique[5]	675	748	729	793	833	764	867	*986	1 041	...
Puerto Rico - Porto Rico[6]	7 781	9 215	6 904	5 538[7]	...	...	...	...	...	...
Turks and Caicos Islands - Îles Turques et Caïques[8]	32	43	32	...	...	...	...	...	...	...
United States of America - États-Unis d'Amérique[9]	848 163	839 226	820 151	852 385	827 609	825 564	...	...	...	...
AMERICA, SOUTH - AMÉRIQUE DU SUD										
Chile - Chili	1 404	1 510	1 841	...	...	...	...	...	...	...
French Guiana - Guyane française ...	1 783	1 639	1 612	1 661	...	...	...	...	...	...
ASIA - ASIE										
Armenia - Arménie	10 290	10 487	10 925	11 132	11 501	12 469	13 797	...	...	...
Azerbaijan - Azerbaïdjan	16 903	19 798	19 577	20 864	22 323	25 247	24 554	26 799	...	...
Bahrain - Bahreïn[10]	1 630	1 505	2 078	2 297	2 014	2 575	2 394	2 525	2 452	...
China, Hong Kong SAR - Chine, Hong Kong RAS	17 420	15 882	14 192	13 510	13 515	13 199	12 028	11 231	11 863	...
Georgia - Géorgie	13 834	17 210	19 681	21 204	20 644	22 062	24 311	25 585	30 590	...
Israel - Israël[11]	19 671	19 712	19 090	19 452	19 470	19 638	19 849	19 575	...	...
Japan - Japon	319 831	301 673	289 127	276 352	256 672	242 326	226 878	212 694[12]	202 106	...
Kyrgyzstan - Kirghizstan[13]	19 225	19 984	20 035	19 762	21 884	20 800	22 088	21 675	...	...
Mongolia - Mongolie	10 472	8 919	9 064	12 594	15 817	10 688	12 602	12 492	...	...
Qatar	131	172	169	...	...	...	...	...	...	...
Singapore - Singapour	12 272	12 070	11 482	12 032	11 933	12 222	12 318	12 082	11 940	10 624
Tajikistan - Tadjikistan	18 822	20 495	19 418	17 489	18 986	18 481	19 470	19 510	17 503	...
EUROPE										
Åland Islands - Îles d'Åland	70	59	68	53	73	67	68	70	73	...
Albania - Albanie	12 087	10 517	9 403	9 552	9 030	8 335	...	...	...	...
Belarus - Bélarus	80 174	71 700	64 655	58 516	46 285	42 197	35 967	33 262	32 031	...
Belgium - Belgique	15 595	16 024	16 696	17 640	18 033	18 595	18 870	19 095	19 578	...
Bulgaria - Bulgarie	48 035	47 223	41 795	37 272	37 594	36 593	33 733	31 548	31 716	...
Croatia - Croatie	5 923	5 232	4 563	4 733	4 573	4 497	4 450	3 774	4 347	...
Czech Republic - République tchèque	29 298	27 574	26 453	25 352	25 414	25 760	24 636	23 998	24 055	...
Denmark - Danemark[14]	15 622	15 231	15 183	15 197	16 071	16 776	16 657	16 362	...	...
Estonia - Estonie[1]	10 619	10 074	9 610	9 378	8 883	8 409	7 542	7 068	6 668	...
Faeroe Islands - Îles Féroé	37	44	29	41	46	...	...	...	...	...
Finland - Finlande	10 767	11 162	10 969	10 645	10 533	10 423	10 359[15]	10 172[15]	10 491[15]	...
France	202 591	209 907	205 392	214 360	212 285	208 242	208 290	...	...	...
Germany - Allemagne	128 030	129 650	124 023	119 710	116 871	114 484	110 694	110 431	108 867	...
Greece - Grèce	15 782	16 135	16 495	...	...	...	...	...	...	...
Hungary - Hongrie	53 789	52 539	48 689	46 324	43 870	44 089	43 181	40 449	38 443	...
Iceland - Islande	951	889	868	904	905	957	971	977	969[16]	...

Continent and country or area / Continent et pays ou zone	Number - Nombre									
	2003	2004	2005	2006	2007	2008	2009	2010	2011	2012

EUROPE

Italy - Italie	124 118[17]	137 140[18]	129 272[19]	125 782[20]	125 116[21]	118 891[22]	114 793[23]	...	...	...
Latvia - Lettonie	14 508	13 723	12 785	11 825	11 814	10 425	8 881	7 443	7 089	...
Lithuania - Lituanie	11 513	10 644	9 972	9 536	9 596	9 031	8 024	6 989	6 205	...
Montenegro - Monténégro	...	...	1 952	...	...	...	...	...	...	...
Norway - Norvège	13 888	14 071	13 989	14 417	15 165	16 054	15 774	15 735	15 343	...
Poland - Pologne[24]	174	199	225	339	328	506	538	644	669	...
Portugal	563	710	798	1 215	4 325[25]	13 541[25]	17 932[25]	...	...	...
Republic of Moldova - République de Moldova	17 551	17 965	16 642	15 742	15 843	15 900	14 634	14 785	...	...
Romania - Roumanie	224 803	191 038	163 359	150 246	137 226	127 907	116 060	101 915	103 386	...
Russian Federation - Fédération de Russie	1 864 647	1 797 567	1 675 693	1 582 398	1 479 010	1 385 600	1 292 389	1 186 108	1 124 880	...
Serbia - Serbie[26]	29 856	29 650	26 645	25 665	24 273	22 867	...	...	...	...
Slovakia - Slovaquie	16 222	15 307	14 427	14 243	13 424	13 394	13 240	12 582	11 789	...
Slovenia - Slovénie	6 873	6 403	5 851	5 632	5 176	4 946	4 653	4 328		...
Spain - Espagne	79 788	84 985	91 664	101 592	112 138	115 812	111 482	113 031	118 359	...
Sweden - Suède	34 473	34 454	34 978	36 045	37 205	38 049	37 524	37 693	37 696	...
Switzerland - Suisse	10 820	10 959	10 818	10 594	10 035[27]	10 310[27]	10 187[27]	10 650[27]	10 694[27]	...
Ukraine[28]	315 835	289 065	263 590	229 618	225 336	217 413	194 845	176 774	169 131	...
United Kingdom of Great Britain and Northern Ireland - Royaume-Uni de Grande-Bretagne et d'Irlande du Nord[29]	193 890	198 175	199 081	206 900	212 277	209 199	202 211	202 506	202 402	...

OCEANIA - OCÉANIE

New Zealand - Nouvelle-Zélande	18 511	18 211	17 531	17 934	18 382	17 940	17 550	16 630	15 863	...

FOOTNOTES - NOTES

* Provisional. - Données provisoires.

[1] Data refer to resident population only. - Pour la population résidante seulement.

[2] Significant undercoverage of medically induced abortions in clinics in 2006 due to non response in some provinces. - Sous-dénombrement notable des interruptions volontaires de grossesse pratiquées dans les centres médicaux en 2006 faute de réponse dans certaines provinces.

[3] Number of abortions the woman had before the birth of the registered child. - Nombre d'avortements de la femme avant la naissance de l'enfant enregistré.

[4] Excluding abortions performed in private hospitals. - Non comprises les interruptions volontaires de grossesse effectuées dans des hôpitaux privés.

[5] Data refer to 'Therapeutic Abortions'. According to the Mexican law, only the induced abortions, prescribed by medical reasons and induced because of pregnancy coming from sexual agression, are considered as legal. Data refer to abortions prescribed by a physician. Refers to residence of the mother. To calculate the total number of abortions, foetal deaths of less than 20 weeks of gestation were considered. - Les données se rapportent aux « interruptions volontaires de grossesse pour des motifs thérapeutiques ». D'après la loi mexicaine, seuls sont considérés légaux les avortements déclenchés pour des raisons médicales ou parce que la grossesse est le résultat d'une agression sexuelle. Les données se réfèrent aux avortements prescrits par un médecin. Correspond à la résidence de la mère. Les morts fœtales survenues à moins de 20 semaines de gestation ont été prises en compte aux fins du calcul du nombre total d'avortements.

[6] Data refer to the fiscal year from 1 July to 30 June. - Les données se réfèrent à l'année budgétaire de 1 juillet à 30 juin.

[7] Excluding abortions performed in a clinic which closed operations without reporting the data. - Non comprises les avortements effectuées dans une clinique qui a fermé sans envoyer les données.

[8] Data refer to abortions performed in hospitals at Grand Turk and Providenciales. - Pour des avortements exécutés dans les hôpitaux dans Grand Turk et Providenciales.

[9] Includes areas that reported abortion counts every year during the period of analysis. Excludes states that did not report abortion numbers to CDC: Alaska(1998-2002), California (1997-2008), Louisiana (2005), Maryland (2006-2008), New Hampshire (1998-2008), Oklahoma (1998-1999), and West Virginia (2003-2004). - Sont couvertes les régions qui ont indiqué le nombre annuel d'avortements pour la période analysée. Ne sont pas couverts les États qui n'ont pas fourni de chiffres : l'Alaska (1998-2002), la Californie (1997-2008), la Louisiane (2005), le Maryland (2006-2008), le New Hampshire (1998-2008), l'Oklahoma (1998-1999) et la Virginie occidentale (2003-2004).

[10] Data refer to spontaneous abortions and miscarriages. - Données se rapportant aux avortements spontanés et fausses couches.

[11] Includes data for East Jerusalem and Israeli residents in certain other territories under occupation by Israeli military forces since June 1967. Data refer to applications to commissions for termination of pregnancy and not to authorizations. - Y compris les données pour Jérusalem-Est et les résidents israéliens dans certains autres territoires occupés depuis 1967 par les forces armées israéliennes. Les données relatives aux avortements provoqués légalement se rapportent aux demandes d'autorisation et non aux autorisations elles-mêmes.

[12] Excluding data of cities and towns in the jurisdiction of Sousou Public Health and Welfare Office of Fukushima Prefecture due to the impact of the Great East Japan Earthquake. - Ne sont pas incluses les données relatives aux agglomérations relevant du bureau de la santé publique et des services sociaux de Sousou dans la préfecture de Fukushima, en raison des conséquences du grand séisme dans l'est du Japon.

[13] Based on administrative reporting of the Ministry of Health. - Les données reposent sur les rapports administratifs du Ministère de la santé.

[14] Excluding Faeroe Islands and Greenland shown separately, if available. - Non compris les Iles Féroé et le Groenland, qui font l'objet de rubriques distinctes, si disponible.

[15] Excluding Åland Islands. - Non compris les Îles d'Åland.

[16] Definition of localities was revised from 2011 causing a break with the previous series. - La rupture par rapport aux séries précédentes s'explique par le fait que la définition des localités a été révisée depuis 2011.

[17] Data are incomplete for Campania region. - Les données sont incomplètes pour la région de la Campanie.

[18] Data are incomplete for Sicilia region. - Les données sont incomplètes pour la région de la Sicile.

[19] Data are incomplete for Friuli-Venezia Giulia, Campania, Molise and Sicilia regions. - Les données sont incomplètes pour le Frioul-Vénétie julienne, la Campanie, la Molise et la Sicile.

[20] Data are incomplete for Friuli-Venezia Giulia, Campania and Sicilia regions. - Les données sont incomplètes pour les régions Frioul-Vénétie julienne, la Campanie et la Sicile.

[21] Data are incomplete for Campania and Sicilia regions. - Les données sont incomplètes pour les régions de la Campanie et de la Sicile.

[22] Data are incomplete for Campania, Calabria, Sicilia and Sardegna regions. - Les données sont incomplètes pour les régions de Campanie, de Calabrie, de Sicile et de Sardaigne.

[23] Data are incomplete for Abruzzo, Campania, Basilicata, Sicilia and Sardegna regions. - Données incomplètes pour les régions des Abruzzes, de Campanie, de Basilicate, de Sicile et de Sardaigne.

[24] Based on hospital and polyclinic records. - D'après les registres des hôpitaux et des polycliniques.

[25] From July 2007, includes legally induced abortions up to the first 10 weeks of pregnancy due to the change in abortion related laws and regulations of the country. - Depuis juillet 2007, comprend les interruptions volontaires de grossesse pratiquées jusqu'à la dixième semaine de grossesse, par suite des modifications apportées aux lois régissant les avortements dans le pays.

[26] Excludes data for Kosovo and Metohia. Data refer to institutions included in the Health Institutions Network Plan in the Republic of Serbia. - Sans les données pour le Kosovo et Metohie. Les données se rapportent aux institutions membres du "Health Institutions Network Plan" de la République de Serbie.

[27] Data refer to termination of pregnancy for women who are Switzerland residents. - Les données portent sur les interruptions de grossesse pratiquées sur des femmes qui résident en Suisse.

[28] Data refer to the recorded events in Ministry of Health institutions only. - Données ne concernant que les faits enregistrés dans les institutions du Ministère de la santé.

[29] Excluding Northern Ireland. Data refer to resident population only. Excluding Channel Islands (Guernsey and Jersey) and Isle of Man, shown separately, if available. - Non compris l'Irlande du Nord. Pour la population résidante seulement. Non compris les îles Anglo-Normandes (Guernesey et Jersey) et l'île de Man, qui font l'objet de rubriques distinctes, si disponible.

Table 14 - *Demographic Yearbook 2012*

Table 14 presents legally induced abortions by age and number of previous live births of women for the latest available year between 2003 and 2012.

Description of variables: Age is defined as age at last birthday, that is, the difference between the date of birth and the date of the occurrence of the event, expressed in complete solar years. The age classification used in this table is the following: under 15 years, 5-year age groups through 45-49 years and 50 years and over.

Except where otherwise indicated, eight categories are used in classifying the number of previous live births: 0 through 5, 6 or more live births, and, if required, number of live births unknown.

Information on abortion policies is collected by the United Nations Population Division and published in the World Population Policies[1]. An overview of abortion policies is also available in a wall chart[2].

Reliability of data: Unlike data on live births and foetal deaths, which are generally collected through systems of vital registration, data on abortion are collected from a variety of sources. Because of this, the quality specification on the completeness of civil registers, which is presented for other tables, does not appear here.

Limitations: With regard to the collection of information on abortions, a variety of sources are used, but hospital records are the most common source of information. This implies that most cases that have no contact with hospitals are missed. Data from other sources are probably also incomplete. The data in the present table are limited to legally induced abortions, which, by their nature, might be assumed to be more complete than data on all induced abortions.

In addition, deficiencies in the reporting of age and number of previous live births of the woman, differences in the method used for obtaining the age of the woman, and the proportion of abortions for which age or previous live births of the woman are unknown must all be taken into account in using these data.

Earlier data: Legally induced abortions by age and previous live births of women have been shown previously in most issues of the *Demographic Yearbook* since the 1971 issue. For more information on specific topics and years for which data are reported, readers should consult the Historical Index.

NOTES

[1] World Population Policies 2011 (United Nations Publication, Sales No. E.13.XIII.2), New York 2013. See also:
http://www.un.org/en/development/desa/population/publications/policy/world-population-policies-2011.shtml

[2] World Abortion Policies 2011 (United Nations Publication, Sales No. E. 11.XIII.4), New York, 2011. See also:
http://www.un.org/en/development/desa/population/publications/pdf/abortion/worldAbortionPoliciesWallChart2011.pdf

Tableau 14 – *Annuaire démographique 2012*

Le tableau 14 présente les données les plus récentes disponible entre 2003 et 2012 sur les avortements provoqués pour des raisons légales, selon l'âge de la mère et le nombre de naissances vivantes précédentes.

Description des variables : L'âge considéré est l'âge au dernier anniversaire, c'est-à-dire la différence entre la date de naissance et la date de l'avortement, exprimée en années solaires révolues. La classification par âge utilisée dans le tableau 14 est la suivante : moins de 15 ans, groupes quinquennaux jusqu'à 45-49 ans, 50 ans et plus, et âge inconnu.

Sauf indication contraire, les naissances vivantes antérieures sont classées dans les huit catégories suivantes: 0 à 5 naissances vivantes, 6 naissances vivantes ou plus et, le cas échéant, nombre de naissances vivantes inconnu.

La Division de la population des Nations Unies collecte des informations sur les politiques en matière d'avortement et les publient dans "World Population Policies"[1]. Une vue d'ensemble sur les politiques en matière d'avortement est également publiée sous forme de poster[2].

Fiabilité des données : à la différence des données sur les naissances vivantes et les morts fœtales, qui proviennent généralement des registres d'état civil, les données sur l'avortement sont tirées de sources diverses. Aussi ne trouve-t-on pas ici une évaluation de la qualité des données semblable à celle qui indique, pour les autres tableaux, le degré d'exhaustivité des données de l'état civil.

Insuffisance des données : en ce qui concerne les renseignements sur l'avortement, un grand nombre de sources sont utilisées, les relevés hospitaliers restant cependant la source la plus commune. Il s'ensuit que la plupart des cas qui ne passent pas par les hôpitaux sont ignorés. Il faut aussi tenir compte du fait que les données provenant d'autres sources sont probablement incomplètes. Les données du tableau 14 se limitent aux avortements provoqués pour raisons légales dont on peut supposer, en raison de leur nature même, que les statistiques sont plus complètes que les données concernant l'ensemble des avortements provoqués.

En outre, on doit tenir compte, lorsque l'on utilise ces données, des erreurs de déclaration de l'âge de la mère et du nombre des naissances vivantes précédentes, de l'hétérogénéité des méthodes de calcul de l'âge de la mère et de la proportion d'avortements pour lesquels l'âge de la mère ou le nombre des naissances vivantes ne sont pas connus.

Données publiées antérieurement : Depuis 1971, la plupart des éditions de l'*Annuaire démographique* contiennent des statistiques concernant les avortements provoqués pour raisons légales, selon l'âge de la mère et le nombre de naissances vivantes antérieures. Pour plus de précisions concernant les années et les sujets pour lesquels des données ont été publiées, se reporter à l'index historique.

NOTES

[1] World Population Policies 2011 (publication des Nations Unies, Numéro de vente E.13.XIII.2), New York 2013. Voir aussi : http://www.un.org/en/development/desa/population/publications/policy/world-population-policies-2011.shtml.

[2] World Abortion Policies 2011 (publication des Nations Unies, Numéro de vente E. 11.XIII.4), New York, 2011. Voir aussi : http://www.un.org/en/development/desa/population/publications/pdf/abortion/worldAbortionPoliciesWallChart2011.pdf

14. Legally induced abortions by age and number of previous live births of women: latest available year, 2003 - 2012
Avortments provoqués légalement selon l'âge de la femme et selon le nombre des naissances vivantes précédentes : dernière année disponible, 2003 - 2012

Continent, country or area, year and age / Continent, pays ou zone, année et âge	Number of previous live births / Nombre des naissances vivantes précédentes								
	Total	0	1	2	3	4	5	6+	Unknown - Inconnu

AMERICA, NORTH - AMÉRIQUE DU NORD

Bermuda - Bermudes
2012

Total	272	...	...	...	...	...	...	...	...
0 - 14	1	...	...	...	...	...	...	...	...
15 - 19	28	...	...	...	...	...	...	...	...
20 - 24	63	...	...	...	...	...	...	...	...
25 - 29	78	...	...	...	...	...	...	...	...
30 - 34	63	...	...	...	...	...	...	...	...
35 - 39	30	...	...	...	...	...	...	...	...
40 - 44	9	...	...	...	...	...	...	...	...
45 - 49	-	...	...	...	...	...	...	...	...
50 +	-	...	...	...	...	...	...	...	...

Canada[1]
2006

Total	91 310	...	...	...	...	...	...	...	...
0 - 14	267	...	...	...	...	...	...	...	...
15 - 19	15 217	...	...	...	...	...	...	...	...
20 - 24	28 358	...	...	...	...	...	...	...	...
25 - 29	20 315	...	...	...	...	...	...	...	...
30 - 34	13 615	...	...	...	...	...	...	...	...
35 - 39	9 444	...	...	...	...	...	...	...	...
40 +	3 938	...	...	...	...	...	...	...	...
Unknown - Inconnu	156	...	...	...	...	...	...	...	...

Costa Rica[2]
2009

Total	7 848	...	...	...	...	...	...	...	...
10 - 14	68	...	...	...	...	...	...	...	...
15 - 19	1 275	...	...	...	...	...	...	...	...
20 - 44	6 437	...	...	...	...	...	...	...	...
45 +	68	...	...	...	...	...	...	...	...

Cuba
2011

Total	83 943	...	...	...	...	...	...	...	...
0 - 14	1 295	...	...	...	...	...	...	...	...
15 - 19	20 878	...	...	...	...	...	...	...	...
20 - 34	50 951	...	...	...	...	...	...	...	...
35 - 39	10 819	...	...	...	...	...	...	...	...

Mexico - Mexique[3]
2011

Total	1 041	238	288	221	77	23	11	11	172
0 - 14	6	2	-	-	-	-	-	-	4
15 - 19	149	69	35	3	1	-	-	-	41
20 - 24	232	69	59	48	6	2	-	-	48
25 - 29	191	40	63	50	13	5	1	-	19
30 - 34	175	23	59	53	18	4	3	1	14
35 - 39	123	11	26	33	23	6	4	5	15
40 - 44	30	1	9	5	7	2	3	2	1
45 - 49	1	-	1	-	-	-	-	-	-
50 +	-	-	-	-	-	-	-	-	-
Unknown - Inconnu	134	23	36	29	9	4	-	3	30

Puerto Rico - Porto Rico[4]
2006

Total	5 538	1 991	1 639	1 013	588	229	46	32	-
0 - 14	21	...	...	...	...	...	...	...	...
15 - 19	968	...	...	...	...	...	...	...	...
20 - 24	1 868	...	...	...	...	...	...	...	...
25 - 29	1 413	...	...	...	...	...	...	...	...
30 - 34	767	...	...	...	...	...	...	...	...
35 - 39	351	...	...	...	...	...	...	...	...
40 - 44	129	...	...	...	...	...	...	...	...
45 +	21	...	...	...	...	...	...	...	...

Turks and Caicos Islands - Îles Turques et Caïques[5]
2005

Total	32	...	...	...	...	...	...	...	...
15 - 19	4	...	...	...	...	...	...	...	...
20 - 24	7	...	...	...	...	...	...	...	...
25 - 29	9	...	...	...	...	...	...	...	...

14. Legally induced abortions by age and number of previous live births of women: latest available year, 2003 - 2012
Avortments provoqués légalement selon l'âge de la femme et selon le nombre des naissances vivantes précédentes : dernière année disponible, 2003 - 2012 (continued - suite)

Continent, country or area, year and age Continent, pays ou zone, année et âge	Total	Number of previous live births Nombre des naissances vivantes précédentes							
		0	1	2	3	4	5	6+	Unknown - Inconnu

AMERICA, NORTH - AMÉRIQUE DU NORD

Turks and Caicos Islands - Îles Turques et Caïques[5]
2005

30 - 34	6	...	...	...	...	...	...	...	...
35 - 39	4	...	...	...	...	...	...	...	...
40 - 44	1	...	...	...	...	...	...	...	...
45 +	1	...	...	...	...	...	...	...	...

ASIA - ASIE

Armenia - Arménie
2008

Total	12 469	...	...	...	...	...	...	...	...
0 - 14	1	...	...	...	...	...	...	...	...
15 - 19	610	...	...	...	...	...	...	...	...
20 - 24	9 459	...	...	...	...	...	...	...	...
25 +	2 399	...	...	...	...	...	...	...	...

Azerbaijan - Azerbaïdjan
2010

Total	26 799	...	...	...	...	...	...	...	...
0 - 14	-	...	...	...	...	...	...	...	...
15 - 19	1 165	...	...	...	...	...	...	...	...
20 - 24	6 058	...	...	...	...	...	...	...	...
25 - 29	8 545	...	...	...	...	...	...	...	...
30 - 34	6 632	...	...	...	...	...	...	...	...
35 +	4 399	...	...	...	...	...	...	...	...
Unknown - Inconnu	-	...	...	...	...	...	...	...	...

China, Hong Kong SAR - Chine, Hong Kong RAS
2011

Total	11 863	6 802	2 351	2 209	416	^85	...	...	...
0 - 14	32	32	-	-	-	^_	...	...	...
15 - 19	1 011	975	29	7	-	^_	...	...	...
20 - 24	2 504	2 264	180	58	2	^_	...	...	...
25 - 29	2 548	1 800	474	230	37	^7	...	...	...
30 - 34	2 320	1 022	613	576	88	^21	...	...	...
35 - 39	2 208	510	684	822	170	^22	...	...	...
40 - 44	1 126	181	344	473	102	^26	...	...	...
45 +	114	18	27	43	17	^9	...	...	...

Georgia - Géorgie
2011

Total	30 590	...	...	...	...	...	...	...	...
0 - 14	15	...	...	...	...	...	...	...	...
15 - 19	1 681	...	...	...	...	...	...	...	...
20 - 29	15 055	...	...	...	...	...	...	...	...
30 - 34	8 562	...	...	...	...	...	...	...	...
35 - 39	3 923	...	...	...	...	...	...	...	...
40 - 49	1 220	...	...	...	...	...	...	...	...
50 +	134	...	...	...	...	...	...	...	...

Israel - Israël[6]
2010

Total	19 575	8 923	2 673	3 704	2 548	1 033	386	308	...
0 - 14	62	58	2	1	-	-	-	1	...
15 - 19	2 522	2 456	53	8	4	-	1	-	...
20 - 24	3 978	3 202	502	222	44	5	3	-	...
25 - 29	3 971	1 987	794	732	288	109	44	17	...
30 - 34	3 853	775	761	1 183	711	274	108	41	...
35 - 39	3 460	323	413	1 112	970	376	128	138	...
40 - 44	1 548	98	136	407	478	242	95	92	...
45 - 49	168	19	11	37	49	26	7	19	...
50 +	13	5	1	2	4	1	-	-	...

Japan - Japon
2011

Total	202 106	...	...	...	...	...	...	...	...
0 - 14	406	...	...	...	...	...	...	...	...
15 - 19	20 497	...	...	...	...	...	...	...	...
20 - 24	44 087	...	...	...	...	...	...	...	...

14. Legally induced abortions by age and number of previous live births of women: latest available year, 2003 - 2012
Avortments provoqués légalement selon l'âge de la femme et selon le nombre des naissances vivantes précédentes : dernière année disponible, 2003 - 2012 (continued - suite)

Continent, country or area, year and age / Continent, pays ou zone, année et âge	Number of previous live births / Nombre des naissances vivantes précédentes								
	Total	0	1	2	3	4	5	6+	Unknown - Inconnu
ASIA - ASIE									
Japan - Japon									
2011									
25 - 29	42 708	...	...	...	...	...	...	...	...
30 - 34	39 917	...	...	...	...	...	...	...	...
35 - 39	37 648	...	...	...	...	...	...	...	...
40 - 44	15 697	...	...	...	...	...	...	...	...
45 - 49	1 108	...	...	...	...	...	...	...	...
50 +	21	...	...	...	...	...	...	...	...
Unknown - Inconnu	17	...	...	...	...	...	...	...	...
Kyrgyzstan - Kirghizstan[7]									
2008									
Total	20 800	...	...	...	...	...	...	...	...
0 - 14	1	...	...	...	...	...	...	...	...
15 - 19	1 814	...	...	...	...	...	...	...	...
20 - 24	5 018	...	...	...	...	...	...	...	...
25 - 29	5 462	...	...	...	...	...	...	...	...
30 - 34	4 598	...	...	...	...	...	...	...	...
35 - 39	2 776	...	...	...	...	...	...	...	...
40 - 44	1 019	...	...	...	...	...	...	...	...
45 +	112	...	...	...	...	...	...	...	...
Singapore - Singapour									
2012									
Total	10 624	7 152	2 287	791	246	148	...	...	...
0 - 14	14	12	2	-	-	-	...	...	...
15 - 19	713	593	102	15	3	-	...	...	...
20 - 24	2 386	1 743	470	131	32	10	...	...	...
25 - 29	2 718	1 847	564	195	71	41	...	...	...
30 - 34	2 404	1 512	579	202	69	42	...	...	...
35 - 39	1 700	1 038	406	170	48	38	...	...	...
40 - 44	659	385	162	75	20	17	...	...	...
45 +	30	22	2	3	3	-	...	...	...
Tajikistan - Tadjikistan									
2011									
Total	17 503	...	...	...	...	...	...	...	...
0 - 14	-	...	...	...	...	...	...	...	...
15 - 17	28	...	...	...	...	...	...	...	...
18 - 19	1 323	...	...	...	...	...	...	...	...
20 - 34	11 948	...	...	...	...	...	...	...	...
35 +	4 204	...	...	...	...	...	...	...	...
EUROPE									
Åland Islands - Îles d'Åland									
2011									
Total	73	40	14	15	2	-	1	1	...
0 - 14	-	-	-	-	-	-	-	-	...
15 - 19	12	12	-	-	-	-	-	-	...
20 - 24	21	16	3	2	-	-	-	-	...
25 - 29	18	10	5	3	-	-	-	-	...
30 - 34	14	2	4	5	2	-	1	-	...
35 - 39	7	-	2	4	-	-	-	1	...
40 - 44	1	-	-	1	-	-	-	-	...
45 - 49	-	-	-	-	-	-	-	-	...
50 +	-	-	-	-	-	-	-	-	...
Belarus - Bélarus									
2011									
Total	32 031	...	...	...	...	...	...	...	...
0 - 14	23	...	...	...	...	...	...	...	...
15 - 19	2 227	...	...	...	...	...	...	...	...
20 - 24	7 010	...	...	...	...	...	...	...	...
25 - 29	8 343	...	...	...	...	...	...	...	...
30 - 34	7 740	...	...	...	...	...	...	...	...
35 - 39	4 623	...	...	...	...	...	...	...	...
40 - 44	1 856	...	...	...	...	...	...	...	...
45 - 49	209	...	...	...	...	...	...	...	...
50 +	-	...	...	...	...	...	...	...	...

14. Legally induced abortions by age and number of previous live births of women: latest available year, 2003 - 2012
Avortments provoqués légalement selon l'âge de la femme et selon le nombre des naissances vivantes précédentes : dernière année disponible, 2003 - 2012 (continued - suite)

Continent, country or area, year and age / Continent, pays ou zone, année et âge	Number of previous live births / Nombre des naissances vivantes précédentes								
	Total	0	1	2	3	4	5	6+	Unknown - Inconnu
EUROPE									
Belgium - Belgique									
2011									
Total	19 578	9 145	4 266	3 698	1 636	581	174	78	...
0 - 14	87	86	1	-	-	-	-	-	...
15 - 19	2 575	2 339	207	28	1	-	-	-	...
20 - 24	5 027	3 430	1 070	425	87	12	3	-	...
25 - 29	4 688	1 992	1 249	983	332	104	20	8	...
30 - 34	3 745	863	997	1 131	512	176	46	20	...
35 - 39	2 454	349	538	796	483	184	70	34	...
40 - 44	923	78	188	308	207	99	30	13	...
45 - 49	78	7	16	27	14	6	5	3	...
50 +	1	1	-	-	-	-	-	-	...
Bulgaria - Bulgarie									
2011									
Total	31 716	...	...	...	...	...	...	...	...
0 - 14	182	...	...	...	...	...	...	...	...
15 - 19	3 087	...	...	...	...	...	...	...	...
20 - 24	6 635	...	...	...	...	...	...	...	...
25 - 29	7 782	...	...	...	...	...	...	...	...
30 - 34	7 410	...	...	...	...	...	...	...	...
35 - 39	5 112	...	...	...	...	...	...	...	...
40 - 44	1 388	...	...	...	...	...	...	...	...
45 - 49	118	...	...	...	...	...	...	...	...
50 +	2	...	...	...	...	...	...	...	...
Croatia - Croatie									
2011									
Total	4 347	1 559	823	1 190	515	118	57	29	56
0 - 14	4	3	1	-	-	-	-	-	-
15 - 19	342	300	32	6	2	-	-	-	2
20 - 24	724	437	161	78	25	8	5	-	10
25 - 29	855	302	195	237	85	16	7	1	12
30 - 34	1 018	259	206	326	157	32	14	8	16
35 - 39	940	158	168	363	171	38	14	16	12
40 - 44	408	84	48	163	67	22	17	4	3
45 - 49	29	4	9	10	4	2	-	-	-
50 +	3	1	-	-	2	-	-	-	-
Unknown - Inconnu	24	11	3	7	2	-	-	-	1
Czech Republic - République tchèque									
2011									
Total	24 055	6 742	6 255	7 959	2 274	568	154	103	...
0 - 14	28	28	-	-	-	-	-	-	...
15 - 19	1 913	1 662	225	22	4	-	-	-	...
20 - 24	4 388	2 519	1 284	483	83	17	1	1	...
25 - 29	4 750	1 488	1 576	1 267	304	77	24	14	...
30 - 34	5 733	731	1 678	2 445	635	162	52	30	...
35 - 39	5 153	259	1 132	2 593	864	215	55	35	...
40 - 44	1 909	54	332	1 040	355	85	22	21	...
45 - 49	179	1	28	107	29	12	-	2	...
50 +	2	-	-	2	-	-	-	-	...
Denmark - Danemark[8]									
2006									
Total	15 053	...	...	...	...	...	...	...	...
15 - 19	2 518	...	...	...	...	...	...	...	...
20 - 24	3 138	...	...	...	...	...	...	...	...
25 - 29	2 861	...	...	...	...	...	...	...	...
30 - 34	2 973	...	...	...	...	...	...	...	...
35 - 39	2 373	...	...	...	...	...	...	...	...
40 - 44	1 107	...	...	...	...	...	...	...	...
45 - 49	83	...	...	...	...	...	...	...	...
50 +	-	...	...	...	...	...	...	...	...
Estonia - Estonie[9]									
2011									
Total	6 668	1 664	2 298	1 899	585	140	54	25	3
0 - 14	9	9	-	-	-	-	-	-	-
15 - 19	642	530	100	11	-	-	-	-	1
20 - 24	1 633	721	686	188	33	4	1	-	-
25 - 29	1 506	273	695	418	96	18	4	2	-
30 - 34	1 317	93	419	562	178	43	16	5	1
35 - 39	1 051	30	293	478	177	40	19	13	1

14. Legally induced abortions by age and number of previous live births of women: latest available year, 2003 - 2012
Avortments provoqués légalement selon l'âge de la femme et selon le nombre des naissances vivantes précédentes : dernière année disponible, 2003 - 2012 (continued - suite)

Continent, country or area, year and age / Continent, pays ou zone, année et âge	Number of previous live births / Nombre des naissances vivantes précédentes								
	Total	0	1	2	3	4	5	6+	Unknown - Inconnu
EUROPE									
Estonia - Estonie[9]									
2011									
40 - 44	475	6	98	227	94	32	13	5	-
45 - 49	34	2	7	14	7	3	1	-	-
50 +	1	-	-	1	-	-	-	-	-
Faeroe Islands - Îles Féroé									
2005									
Total	29	...	...	...	...	...	...	...	...
0 - 14	-	...	...	...	...	...	...	...	...
15 - 19	6	...	...	...	...	...	...	...	...
20 - 24	2	...	...	...	...	...	...	...	...
25 - 29	5	...	...	...	...	...	...	...	...
30 - 34	8	...	...	...	...	...	...	...	...
35 - 39	5	...	...	...	...	...	...	...	...
40 - 44	3	...	...	...	...	...	...	...	...
45 - 49	-	...	...	...	...	...	...	...	...
50 +	-	...	...	...	...	...	...	...	...
Finland - Finlande[10]									
2011									
Total	10 491	5 332	1 935	1 788	829	287	66	35	219
0 - 14	56	54	-	-	-	-	-	-	2
15 - 19	1 951	1 817	95	10	1	-	-	-	28
20 - 24	2 929	1 978	611	222	37	9	1	-	71
25 - 29	2 151	899	524	462	161	44	12	4	45
30 - 34	1 709	382	378	524	251	102	22	10	40
35 - 39	1 154	149	222	376	251	101	17	14	24
40 - 44	506	51	102	180	119	28	12	7	7
45 - 49	34	1	3	14	9	3	2	-	2
50 +	1	1	-	-	-	-	-	-	2
France									
2009									
Total	208 290	...	...	...	...	...	...	...	...
0 - 14	29 004	...	...	...	...	...	...	...	...
15 - 19	52 360	...	...	...	...	...	...	...	...
20 - 24	46 237	...	...	...	...	...	...	...	...
25 - 29	36 351	...	...	...	...	...	...	...	...
30 - 34	30 125	...	...	...	...	...	...	...	...
35 - 39	12 805	...	...	...	...	...	...	...	...
40 - 44	1 408	...	...	...	...	...	...	...	...
Germany - Allemagne									
2011									
Total	108 867	43 937	28 126	24 724	8 508	2 437	735	400	-
0 - 14	374	374	-	-	-	-	-	-	-
15 - 19	10 539	9 594	850	92	3	-	-	-	-
20 - 24	27 054	16 880	7 149	2 417	506	73	18	11	-
25 - 29	25 152	9 239	7 931	5 779	1 635	419	98	51	-
30 - 34	21 886	4 722	6 215	7 240	2 583	787	216	123	-
35 - 39	15 655	2 142	3 961	5 989	2 432	737	263	131	-
40 - 44	7 511	900	1 866	2 916	1 247	382	123	77	-
45 - 49	674	82	147	287	98	37	17	6	-
50 +	22	4	7	4	4	2	-	1	-
Greece - Grèce									
2003									
Total	15 782	...	...	...	...	...	...	...	...
0 - 14	8	...	...	...	...	...	...	...	...
15 - 19	569	...	...	...	...	...	...	...	...
20 - 29	5 934	...	...	...	...	...	...	...	...
30 - 39	7 557	...	...	...	...	...	...	...	...
40 - 49	1 345	...	...	...	...	...	...	...	...
50 +	48	...	...	...	...	...	...	...	...
Unknown - Inconnu	321	...	...	...	...	...	...	...	...
Hungary - Hongrie									
2011									
Total	38 443	10 525	9 608	9 584	5 224	2 021	800	681	-
0 - 14	170	166	3	1	-	-	-	-	-
15 - 19	4 539	3 502	867	139	28	3	-	-	-
20 - 24	7 841	3 386	2 317	1 380	568	153	32	5	-
25 - 29	7 596	1 860	2 013	1 834	1 137	483	170	99	-
30 - 34	8 390	1 075	2 177	2 528	1 423	617	307	263	-

14. Legally induced abortions by age and number of previous live births of women: latest available year, 2003 - 2012
Avortments provoqués légalement selon l'âge de la femme et selon le nombre des naissances vivantes précédentes : dernière année disponible, 2003 - 2012 (continued - suite)

Continent, country or area, year and age / Continent, pays ou zone, année et âge	Number of previous live births / Nombre des naissances vivantes précédentes								
	Total	0	1	2	3	4	5	6+	Unknown - Inconnu
EUROPE									
Hungary - Hongrie									
2011									
35 - 39	7 231	440	1 678	2 596	1 491	560	227	239	-
40 - 44	2 563	87	531	1 054	558	198	62	73	-
45 - 49	110	9	21	50	19	7	2	2	-
50 +	3	-	1	2	-	-	-	-	-
Unknown - Inconnu	-	-	-	-	-	-	-	-	-
Iceland - Islande[11]									
2011									
Total	969	415	249	186	83	29	5	2	-
0 - 14	2	2	-	-	-	-	-	-	-
15 - 19	174	155	16	3	-	-	-	-	-
20 - 24	289	182	84	21	2	-	-	-	-
25 - 29	187	46	73	52	10	6	-	-	-
30 - 34	169	25	40	56	36	11	1	-	-
35 - 39	109	5	29	45	20	9	1	-	-
40 - 44	35	-	7	8	12	3	3	2	-
45 - 49	4	-	-	1	3	-	-	-	-
50 +	-	-	-	-	-	-	-	-	-
Unknown - Inconnu	-	-	-	-	-	-	-	-	-
Italy - Italie[12]									
2009									
Total	114 793	45 152	26 909	29 348	8 647	1 918	494	192	2 133
0 - 14	236	222	1	-	-	-	-	-	13
15 - 19	9 603	8 227	753	108	7	2	-	-	506
20 - 24	20 950	13 921	4 461	1 589	242	46	14	6	671
25 - 29	23 302	10 106	6 503	4 865	1 113	206	37	21	451
30 - 34	25 699	6 750	6 895	8 555	2 543	523	109	41	283
35 - 39	22 916	4 038	5 541	9 189	2 994	716	205	74	159
40 - 44	10 228	1 390	2 341	4 405	1 530	369	108	42	43
45 - 49	955	131	192	409	155	40	17	8	3
50 +	25	8	1	13	1	2	-	-	-
Unknown - Inconnu	879	359	221	215	62	14	4	-	4
Latvia - Lettonie									
2011									
Total	7 089	...	...	...	...	...	...	...	...
0 - 14	7	...	...	...	...	...	...	...	...
15 - 19	511	...	...	...	...	...	...	...	...
20 - 24	1 693	...	...	...	...	...	...	...	...
25 - 29	1 732	...	...	...	...	...	...	...	...
30 - 34	1 384	...	...	...	...	...	...	...	...
35 - 39	1 238	...	...	...	...	...	...	...	...
40 - 44	485	...	...	...	...	...	...	...	...
45 - 49	38	...	...	...	...	...	...	...	...
50 +	1	...	...	...	...	...	...	...	...
Unknown - Inconnu	-	...	...	...	...	...	...	...	...
Lithuania - Lituanie									
2011									
Total	6 205	...	...	...	...	...	...	...	...
0 - 14	4	...	...	...	...	...	...	...	...
15 - 19	489	...	...	...	...	...	...	...	...
20 - 24	1 226	...	...	...	...	...	...	...	...
25 - 29	1 311	...	...	...	...	...	...	...	...
30 - 34	1 379	...	...	...	...	...	...	...	...
35 - 39	1 153	...	...	...	...	...	...	...	...
40 - 44	580	...	...	...	...	...	...	...	...
45 - 49	63	...	...	...	...	...	...	...	...
50 +	-	...	...	...	...	...	...	...	...
Unknown - Inconnu	-	...	...	...	...	...	...	...	...
Montenegro - Monténégro									
2005									
Total	1 952	307	283	677	473	139	45	26	2
0 - 14	3	-	2	1	-	-	-	-	-
15 - 16	5	5	-	-	-	-	-	-	1
17 - 19	46	31	7	4	2	1	-	-	1
20 - 29	685	179	155	219	98	21	10	3	-
30 - 39	982	80	108	365	286	91	33	18	1
40 - 49	223	11	11	86	82	26	2	5	-

14. Legally induced abortions by age and number of previous live births of women: latest available year, 2003 - 2012
Avortments provoqués légalement selon l'âge de la femme et selon le nombre des naissances vivantes précédentes : dernière année disponible, 2003 - 2012 (continued - suite)

Continent, country or area, year and age / Continent, pays ou zone, année et âge	Number of previous live births / Nombre des naissances vivantes précédentes								
	Total	0	1	2	3	4	5	6+	Unknown - Inconnu

EUROPE

Montenegro - Monténégro
2005
50 +	4	1	-	1	2	-	-	-	-
Unknown - Inconnu	4	-	-	1	3	-	-	-	-

Norway - Norvège[13]
2006
Total	14 132	...	...	...	...	...	...	...	...
0 - 14	37	...	...	...	...	...	...	...	...
15 - 19	2 307	...	...	...	...	...	...	...	...
20 - 24	3 740	...	...	...	...	...	...	...	...
25 - 29	2 904	...	...	...	...	...	...	...	...
30 - 34	2 495	...	...	...	...	...	...	...	...
35 - 39	1 877	...	...	...	...	...	...	...	...
40 - 44	694	...	...	...	...	...	...	...	...
45 - 49	55	...	...	...	...	...	...	...	...
50 +	-	...	...	...	...	...	...	...	...
Unknown - Inconnu	23	...	...	...	...	...	...	...	...

Poland - Pologne[14]
2011
Total	669	...	...	...	...	...	...	...	...
15 - 19	23	...	...	...	...	...	...	...	...
20 - 24	136	...	...	...	...	...	...	...	...
25 - 29	172	...	...	...	...	...	...	...	...
30 - 34	179	...	...	...	...	...	...	...	...
35 - 39	159	...	...	...	...	...	...	...	...

Republic of Moldova - République de Moldova
2010
Total	14 785	...	...	...	...	...	...	...	...
0 - 14	11	...	...	...	...	...	...	...	...
15 - 19	1 350	...	...	...	...	...	...	...	...
20 - 24	10 770	...	...	...	...	...	...	...	...
25 +	2 654	...	...	...	...	...	...	...	...

Romania - Roumanie
2011
Total	103 386	...	...	...	...	...	...	...	...
0 - 14	466	...	...	...	...	...	...	...	...
15 - 19	9 589	...	...	...	...	...	...	...	...
20 - 24	22 812	...	...	...	...	...	...	...	...
25 - 29	23 005	...	...	...	...	...	...	...	...
30 - 34	23 241	...	...	...	...	...	...	...	...
35 - 39	16 893	...	...	...	...	...	...	...	...
40 - 44	6 875	...	...	...	...	...	...	...	...
45 - 49	481	...	...	...	...	...	...	...	...
50 +	24	...	...	...	...	...	...	...	...
Unknown - Inconnu	-	...	...	...	...	...	...	...	...

Russian Federation - Fédération de Russie
2011
Total	1 124 880	...	...	...	...	...	...	...	...
0 - 14	585	...	...	...	...	...	...	...	...
15 - 19	66 275	...	...	...	...	...	...	...	...
20 - 24	264 346	...	...	...	...	...	...	...	...
25 - 29	309 875	...	...	...	...	...	...	...	...
30 - 34	248 494	...	...	...	...	...	...	...	...
35 - 39	168 461	...	...	...	...	...	...	...	...
40 - 44	60 768	...	...	...	...	...	...	...	...
45 - 49	5 904	...	...	...	...	...	...	...	...
50 +	172	...	...	...	...	...	...	...	...
Unknown - Inconnu	-	...	...	...	...	...	...	...	...

Serbia - Serbie[15]
2008
Total	22 867	6 601	4 346	8 509	2 437	663	198	113	-
0 - 14	9	6	1	2	-	-	-	-	-
15 - 19	975	808	124	35	7	1	-	-	-
20 - 24	3 427	1 823	848	570	122	52	9	3	-
25 - 29	5 117	1 510	1 173	1 757	479	141	47	10	-
30 - 34	5 953	1 240	1 114	2 569	719	212	62	37	-
35 - 39	4 929	806	768	2 354	730	170	59	42	-
40 - 44	2 174	363	279	1 072	347	76	17	20	-

14. Legally induced abortions by age and number of previous live births of women: latest available year, 2003 - 2012
Avortments provoqués légalement selon l'âge de la femme et selon le nombre des naissances vivantes précédentes :
dernière année disponible, 2003 - 2012 (continued - suite)

Continent, country or area, year and age / Continent, pays ou zone, année et âge	Total	0	1	2	3	4	5	6+	Unknown - Inconnu
EUROPE									
Serbia - Serbie[15]									
2008									
45 - 49	266	40	34	146	31	10	4	1	-
50 +	16	5	4	4	2	1	-	-	-
Unknown - Inconnu	1	-	1	-	-	-	-	-	-
Slovakia - Slovaquie									
2011									
Total	11 789	3 616	3 315	3 129	1 073	333	167	156	-
0 - 14	18	18	-	-	-	-	-	-	-
15 - 19	950	781	148	21	-	-	-	-	-
20 - 24	1 968	1 047	597	238	63	16	5	2	-
25 - 29	2 664	961	870	544	171	74	30	14	-
30 - 34	2 896	544	970	909	298	83	47	45	-
35 - 39	2 328	207	556	991	364	102	53	55	-
40 - 44	899	55	170	389	161	54	30	40	-
45 - 49	65	3	4	37	15	4	2	-	-
50 +	1	-	-	-	1	-	-	-	-
Unknown - Inconnu	-	-	-	-	-	-	-	-	-
Slovenia - Slovénie									
2009									
Total	4 653	1 679	1 070	1 408	401	62	19	10	4
0 - 14	4	4	-	-	-	-	-	-	-
15 - 19	342	319	17	6	-	-	-	-	-
20 - 24	847	639	151	47	6	-	1	-	3
25 - 29	1 058	429	304	270	47	5	3	-	-
30 - 34	1 127	210	309	439	145	14	5	5	-
35 - 39	838	56	203	413	130	27	7	2	-
40 - 44	392	19	79	210	62	15	3	3	1
45 - 49	44	3	7	23	10	1	-	-	-
50 +	1	-	-	-	1	-	-	-	-
Spain - Espagne									
2004									
Total	84 985	42 757	19 962	15 023	4 772	1 400	^741	...	330
0 - 14	369	365	1	-	-	-	^-	...	3
15 - 19	11 677	10 415	1 057	145	16	4	^-	...	40
20 - 24	22 461	15 193	5 127	1 680	353	33	^13	...	62
25 - 29	20 309	9 931	5 541	3 457	981	239	^77	...	83
30 - 34	15 212	4 630	4 381	4 186	1 329	424	^195	...	67
35 - 39	10 572	1 777	2 846	3 757	1 373	476	^288	...	55
40 - 44	4 072	414	949	1 665	661	211	^153	...	19
45 - 49	313	32	60	133	59	13	^15	...	1
50 +	-	-	-	-	-	-	^-	...	-
Unknown - Inconnu	-	...	...	...	...	...	...	...	...
2011									
Total	118 359	...	...	...	...	...	...	...	...
0 - 14	455	...	...	...	...	...	...	...	...
15 - 19	14 131	...	...	...	...	...	...	...	...
20 - 24	26 195	...	...	...	...	...	...	...	...
25 - 29	27 273	...	...	...	...	...	...	...	...
30 - 34	25 266	...	...	...	...	...	...	...	...
35 - 39	17 918	...	...	...	...	...	...	...	...
40 - 44	6 523	...	...	...	...	...	...	...	...
45 - 49	598	...	...	...	...	...	...	...	...
Sweden - Suède[16]									
2010									
Total	37 693	19 435	6 240	7 203	2 993	814	264	137	607
0 - 14	191	178	4	1	-	-	-	-	8
15 - 19	6 199	5 826	214	14	2	-	-	-	143
20 - 24	10 068	7 708	1 587	480	76	5	2	2	208
25 - 29	7 495	3 558	1 838	1 476	385	79	28	10	121
30 - 34	6 124	1 424	1 336	2 113	884	208	77	18	64
35 - 39	5 073	572	862	2 073	1 053	318	88	62	45
40 - 44	2 248	137	353	948	524	174	58	39	15
45 - 49	238	11	33	85	66	27	10	4	2
50 +	56	20	13	13	3	3	1	2	1
Unknown - Inconnu	1	1	-	-	-	-	-	-	-

14. Legally induced abortions by age and number of previous live births of women: latest available year, 2003 - 2012
Avortments provoqués légalement selon l'âge de la femme et selon le nombre des naissances vivantes précédentes : dernière année disponible, 2003 - 2012 (continued - suite)

Continent, country or area, year and age / Continent, pays ou zone, année et âge	Number of previous live births / Nombre des naissances vivantes précédentes								
	Total	0	1	2	3	4	5	6+	Unknown - Inconnu

EUROPE

Switzerland - Suisse[17]
2011
Total	10 694	2 073	904	846	284	79	...	...	6 508
0 - 14	14	8	-	-	-	-	...	...	6
15 - 19	1 011	385	18	2	1	-	...	...	605
20 - 24	2 387	728	151	46	4	1	...	...	1 457
25 - 29	2 384	463	244	166	40	11	...	...	1 460
30 - 34	2 242	300	219	239	64	24	...	...	1 396
35 - 39	1 727	139	182	251	113	25	...	...	1 017
40 - 44	800	36	81	126	53	14	...	...	490
45 - 49	115	7	7	15	8	4	...	...	74
50 +	6	2	1	-	1	-	...	...	2
Unknown - Inconnu	8	5	1	1	-	-	...	...	1

Ukraine[18]
2010
Total	176 774	...	...	...	...	...	...	...	...
0 - 14	84	...	...	...	...	...	...	...	...
15 - 19	12 919	...	...	...	...	...	...	...	...
20 - 24	131 823	...	...	...	...	...	...	...	...
25 - 39	31 948	...	...	...	...	...	...	...	...

United Kingdom of Great Britain and Northern Ireland - Royaume-Uni de Grande-Bretagne et d'Irlande du Nord[19]
2011
Total	202 402	...	...	...	...	...	...	...	...
0 - 14	1 086	...	...	...	...	...	...	...	...
15 - 19	36 540	...	...	...	...	...	...	...	...
20 - 24	59 756	...	...	...	...	...	...	...	...
25 - 29	45 017	...	...	...	...	...	...	...	...
30 - 34	31 271	...	...	...	...	...	...	...	...
35 - 39	19 944	...	...	...	...	...	...	...	...
40 - 44	8 064	...	...	...	...	...	...	...	...
45 - 49	700	...	...	...	...	...	...	...	...
50 +	24	...	...	...	...	...	...	...	...

OCEANIA - OCÉANIE

New Zealand - Nouvelle-Zélande
2011
Total	15 863	7 147	3 352	3 039	1 429	535	206	155	-
0 - 14	68	68	-	-	-	-	-	-	-
15 - 19	2 822	2 347	420	52	3	-	-	-	-
20 - 24	5 160	2 823	1 367	696	229	37	7	1	-
25 - 29	3 340	1 221	718	793	409	131	56	12	-
30 - 34	2 220	456	445	664	348	189	61	57	-
35 - 39	1 593	180	292	583	288	127	62	61	-
40 - 44	605	44	104	231	141	49	16	20	-
45 - 49	55	8	6	20	11	2	4	4	-
50 +	-	-	-	-	-	-	-	-	-

FOOTNOTES - NOTES

* Provisional. - Données provisoires.

^ Indicates an open-ended group, for example 4+. - indique un groupe d'âge ouvert, par exemple 4 ou plus.

[1] Data refer to resident population only. Significant undercoverage of medically induced abortions in clinics in 2006 due to non response in some provinces. - Pour la population résidante seulement. Sous-dénombrement notable des interruptions volontaires de grossesse pratiquées dans les centres médicaux en 2006 faute de réponse dans certaines provinces.

[2] Excluding abortions performed in private hospitals. Number of abortions the woman had before the birth of the registered child. - Non comprises les interruptions volontaires de grossesse effectuées dans des hôpitaux privés. Nombre d'avortements de la femme avant la naissance de l'enfant enregistré.

[3] Data refer to abortions prescribed by a physician. Data refer to 'Therapeutic Abortions'. According to the Mexican law, only the induced abortions, prescribed by medical reasons and induced because of pregnancy coming from sexual agression, are considered as legal. Refers to residence of the mother. To calculate the total number of abortions, foetal deaths of less than 20 weeks of gestation were considered. - Les données se réfèrent aux avortements prescrits par un médecin. Les données se rapportent aux « interruptions volontaires de grossesse pour des motifs thérapeutiques ». D'après la loi mexicaine, seuls sont considérés légaux les avortements déclenchés pour des raisons médicales ou parce que la grossesse est le résultat d'une agression sexuelle. Correspond à la résidence de la mère. Les morts fœtales survenues à moins de 20 semaines de gestation ont été prises en compte aux fins du calcul du nombre total d'avortements.

[4] Excluding abortions performed in a clinic which closed operations without reporting the data. Data refer to the fiscal year from 1 July to 30 June. - Non comprises les avortements effectuées dans une clinique qui a fermé sans

envoyer les données. Les données se réfèrent à l'année budgétaire de 1 juillet à 30 juin.

[5] Data refer to abortions performed in hospitals at Grand Turk and Providenciales. - Pour des avortements exécutés dans les hôpitaux dans Grand Turk et Providenciales.

[6] Data refer to applications to commissions for termination of pregnancy and not to authorizations. Includes data for East Jerusalem and Israeli residents in certain other territories under occupation by Israeli military forces since June 1967. - Les données relatives aux avortements provoqués légalement se rapportent aux demandes d'autorisation et non aux autorisations elles-mêmes. Y compris les données pour Jérusalem-Est et les résidents israéliens dans certains autres territoires occupés depuis 1967 par les forces armées israéliennes.

[7] Based on administrative reporting of the Ministry of Health. - Les données reposent sur les rapports administratifs du Ministère de la santé.

[8] Excluding Faeroe Islands and Greenland shown separately, if available. Unrevised data. - Non compris les Iles Féroé et le Groenland, qui font l'objet de rubriques distinctes, si disponible. Les données n'ont pas été révisées.

[9] Data refer to resident population only. - Pour la population résidante seulement.

[10] Excluding Åland Islands. - Non compris les Îles d'Åland.

[11] Definition of localities was revised from 2011 causing a break with the previous series. - La rupture par rapport aux séries précédentes s'explique par le fait que la définition des localités a été révisée depuis 2011.

[12] Data are incomplete for Abruzzo, Campania, Basilicata, Sicilia and Sardegna regions. - Données incomplètes pour les régions des Abruzzes, de Campanie, de Basilicate, de Sicile et de Sardaigne.

[13] Unrevised data. - Les données n'ont pas été révisées.

[14] Based on hospital and polyclinic records. - D'après les registres des hôpitaux et des polycliniques.

[15] Data refer to institutions included in the Health Institutions Network Plan in the Republic of Serbia. Excludes data for Kosovo and Metohia. - Les données se rapportent aux institutions membres du "Health Institutions Network Plan" de la République de Serbie. Sans les données pour le Kosovo et Metohie.

[16] Data refer to abortions by previous deliveries of mother rather than previous live births of mother. - Avortements selon les accouchements précédents de la mère plutôt que selon les naissances vivantes de la mère.

[17] Data refer to termination of pregnancy for women who are Switzerland residents. - Les données portent sur les interruptions de grossesse pratiquées sur des femmes qui résident en Suisse.

[18] Data refer to the recorded events in Ministry of Health institutions only. - Données ne concernant que les faits enregistrés dans les institutions du Ministère de la santé.

[19] Excluding Channel Islands (Guernsey and Jersey) and Isle of Man, shown separately, if available. Data refer to resident population only. Excluding Northern Ireland. - Non compris les îles Anglo-Normandes (Guernesey et Jersey) et l'île de Man, qui font l'objet de rubriques distinctes, si disponible. Pour la population résidante seulement. Non compris l'Irlande du Nord.

Table 15 - *Demographic Yearbook 2012*

Table 15 presents infant deaths and infant mortality rates by urban/rural residence for as many years as possible between 2008 and 2012.

Description of variables: Infant deaths are deaths of live-born infants under one year of age.

Statistics on the number of infant deaths are obtained from civil registers unless otherwise noted. Infant mortality rates are, in most instances, calculated from data on registered infant deaths and registered live births for a country or area where civil registration is considered reliable (that is, with an estimated completeness of 90 per cent or more).

The urban/rural classification of infant deaths is that provided by each reporting country or area; it is presumed to be based on the national census definitions of urban population that have been set forth at the end of the technical notes of table 6.

Rate computation: Infant mortality rates are the annual number of deaths of infants under one year of age per 1 000 live births (as shown in table 9) in the same year.

Rates by urban/rural residence are the annual number of infant deaths, in the appropriate urban or rural category, per 1 000 corresponding live births (as shown in table 9). These rates have been calculated by the Statistics Division of the United Nations Department of Economic and Social Affairs.

Rates presented in this table have been limited to those countries or areas having at least a total of 30 infant deaths in a given year and for which the quality code is represented by a "C" or a symbol "|".

Reliability of data: Each country or area has been asked to indicate the estimated completeness of the infant deaths recorded in its civil register. These national assessments are indicated by the quality codes "C", "U" and "|" that appear in the first column of this table.

"C" indicates that the data are estimated to be virtually complete, that is, representing at least 90 per cent of the infant deaths occurring each year, while "U" indicates that data are estimated to be incomplete that is, representing less than 90 per cent of the infant deaths occurring each year. The code "|" indicates that the source of data is not civil registration, but is still considered reliable. The code "..." indicates that no information was provided regarding completeness.

Data from civil registers that are reported as incomplete or of unknown completeness (coded "U" or "...") are considered unreliable. They appear in italics in this table; rates are not computed for data so coded.

Limitations: Statistics on infant deaths are subject to the same qualifications as have been set forth for vital statistics in general and death statistics in particular as discussed in section 4 of the Technical Notes.

The reliability of the data, an indication of which is described above, is an important factor in considering the limitations. In addition, some infant deaths are tabulated by date of registration and not by date of occurrence; these have been indicated by a plus sign "+". Whenever the lag between the date of occurrence and date of registration is prolonged and, therefore, a large proportion of the infant-death registrations are delayed, infant-death statistics for any given year may be seriously affected.

Another factor that limits international comparability is the practice of some countries or areas not to include in infant-death statistics infants who were born alive but died before the registration of the birth or within the first 24 hours of life, thus underestimating the total number of infant deaths. Statistics of this type are footnoted.

The method of reckoning age at death for infants may also introduce non-comparability. If year alone, rather than completed minutes, hours, days and months elapsed since birth, is used to calculate age at time of death, many of the infants who died during the eleventh month of life and some of those who died at younger ages will be classified as having completed one year of age and thus be excluded. The effect would be to underestimate the number of infant deaths. Information on this factor is given in footnotes when known. Reckoning of infant age is further discussed in the technical notes for table 16.

In addition, infant mortality rates are subject to the limitations of the data on live births that have been used as denominators for these rates. These have been set forth in the technical notes for table 9.

Because the two components of the infant mortality rate, infant deaths in the numerator and live births in the denominator, are both obtained from systems of civil registration, the limitations which affect live birth statistics are very similar to those which have been mentioned above in connection with the infant death statistics. It is important to consider the reliability of the data (the completeness of registration) and the method of tabulation (by date of occurrence or by date of registration) of live birth statistics as well as infant death statistics, both of which are used to calculate infant mortality rates. The quality code and use of italics to indicate unreliable data presented in this table refer only to infant deaths. Similarly, the indication of the basis of tabulation (the use of the symbol "+" to indicate data tabulated by date of registration) presented in this table also refers only to infant deaths. Table 9 provides the corresponding information for live births.

If the registration of infant deaths is more complete than the registration of live births, then infant mortality rates would be biased upwards. If, however, the registration of live births is more complete than registration of infant deaths, infant mortality rates would be biased downwards. If both infant deaths and live births are tabulated by registration, it should be noted that deaths tend to be more promptly reported than births.

Infant mortality rates may be seriously affected by the practice of some countries or areas of not considering infants that were born alive but died before the registration of the birth or within the first 24 hours of life as live birth and subsequently infant death. Although this practice results in both the number of infant deaths in the numerator and the number of live births in the denominator being underestimated, its impact is greater on the numerator of the infant mortality rate. As a result this practice causes infant mortality rates to be biased downwards.

Infant mortality rates will also be underestimated if the method of reckoning age at death results in an underestimation of the number of infant deaths. This point has been discussed above.

Because of all these factors care should be taken in comparing infant mortality rates.

With respect to the method of calculating infant mortality rates used in this table, it should be noted that no adjustment was made to take account of the fact that a proportion of the infant deaths that occur during a given year are deaths of infants that were born during the preceding year and hence are not taken from the universe of births used to compute the rates. However, unless the number of live births or infant deaths is changing rapidly, the error involved is insignificant.

The comparability of data by urban/rural residence is affected by the national definitions of urban and rural used in tabulating these data. It is assumed, in the absence of specific information to the contrary, that the definitions of urban and rural used in connection with the national population census were also used in the compilation of the vital statistics for each country or area. However, it cannot be denied that, for some countries or areas, different definitions of urban and rural may be used for the vital statistics data and the population census data respectively. When known, the definitions of urban used in national population censuses are presented at the end of the technical notes for table 6. As discussed in detail in the technical notes for table 6, these definitions vary considerably from one country or area to another.

Urban/rural differentials in infant mortality rates may also be affected by whether the infant deaths and live births have been tabulated in terms of place of occurrence or place of usual residence. This problem is discussed in more detail in section 4.1.4.1 of the Technical Notes.

Earlier data: Infant deaths and infant mortality rates have been shown in previous issues of the *Demographic Yearbook*. For more information on specific topics and years for which data are reported, readers should consult the Historical Index.

Tableau 15 – *Annuaire démographique 2012*

Le tableau 15 présente des données sur les décès d'enfants de moins d'un an et les taux de mortalité infantile selon le lieu de résidence (zone urbaine ou rurale) pour le plus grand nombre d'années possible entre 2008 et 2012.

Description des variables : les chiffres se rapportent aux décès d'enfants de moins d'un an.

Sauf indication contraire, les statistiques concernant le nombre de décès d'enfants de moins d'un an sont établies à partir des registres de l'état civil. Dans la plupart des cas, les taux de mortalité infantile sont calculés à partir des données relatives aux décès enregistrés d'enfants de moins d'un an et aux naissances vivantes enregistrées dans un pays ou une zone lorsque les registres de l'état civil sont jugés fiables (exhaustivité estimée à 90 p. 100 ou plus).

La classification des décès d'enfants de moins d'un an selon le lieu de résidence (zone urbaine ou rurale) est celle qui a été communiquée par chaque pays ou zone ; on part du principe qu'elle repose sur les définitions de la population urbaine utilisées pour les recensements nationaux, telles qu'elles sont reproduites à la fin des notes techniques du tableau 6.

Calcul des taux : Les taux de mortalité infantile représentent le nombre annuel de décès d'enfants de moins d'un an pour 1 000 naissances vivantes (présentées dans le tableau 9) survenues pendant la même année.

Les taux selon le lieu de résidence (zone urbaine ou rurale) représentent le nombre annuel de décès d'enfants de moins d'un an, classés selon la catégorie urbaine ou rurale appropriée pour 1 000 naissances vivantes survenues parmi la population correspondante (présentées dans le tableau 9). Ces taux ont été calculés par la Division de statistique du Département des affaires économiques et sociales de l'Organisation des Nations Unies.

Les taux présentés dans ce tableau se rapportent seulement aux pays ou zones où l'on a enregistré au moins un total de 30 décès d'enfants de moins d'un an au cours d'une année donnée et pour lesquels le code de qualité est soit "C" ou "|".

Fiabilité des données : il a été demandé à chaque pays ou zone d'indiquer le degré estimatif de complétude des données sur les décès d'enfants de moins d'un an figurant dans ses registres d'état civil. Ces évaluations nationales sont signalées par les codes de qualité "C", "U" et "|" qui apparaissent dans la deuxième colonne du tableau.

La lettre "C" indique que les données sont jugées à peu près complètes, c'est-à-dire qu'elles représentent au moins 90 p. 100 des décès d'enfants de moins d'un an survenus chaque année ; la lettre "U" signifie que les données sont jugées incomplètes, c'est-à-dire qu'elles représentent moins de 90 p.100 des décès d'enfants de moins d'un an survenus chaque année. Le symbole 'I' indique que la source des données n'est pas un registre de l'état civil, mais est quand même considérée fiable. Le code "..." dénote qu'aucun renseignement n'a été communiqué quant à la complétude des données.

Les données provenant des registres de l'état civil qui sont déclarées incomplètes ou dont le degré de complétude n'est pas connu (code "U" ou "...") sont jugées douteuses. Elles apparaissent en italique dans le tableau ; les taux, dans ces cas là, n'ont pas été calculés.

Insuffisance des données : les statistiques des décès d'enfants de moins d'un an appellent toutes les réserves qui ont été formulées à propos des statistiques de l'état civil en général et des statistiques concernant les décès en particulier (voir la section 4 des notes techniques).

La fiabilité des données, au sujet de laquelle des indications ont été fournies plus haut, est un facteur important. Il faut également tenir compte du fait que, dans certains cas, les données relatives aux décès d'enfants de moins d'un an sont exploitées selon la date de l'enregistrement et non la date de l'événement ; ces cas ont été signalés par le signe "+". Chaque fois que le décalage entre l'événement et son enregistrement est grand et qu'une forte proportion des décès d'enfants de moins d'un an fait l'objet d'un enregistrement tardif, les statistiques des décès d'enfants de moins d'un an pour une année donnée peuvent être considérablement faussées.

Un autre facteur qui nuit à la comparabilité internationale est la pratique de certains pays ou zones qui consiste à ne pas inclure dans les statistiques des décès d'enfants de moins d'un an les enfants nés vivants mais décédés avant l'enregistrement de leur naissance ou dans les 24 heures qui ont suivi la naissance, pratique qui conduit à sous-estimer le nombre total de décès d'enfants de moins d'un an. Quand pareil facteur a joué, cela a été signalé en note.

Les méthodes appliquées pour calculer l'âge au moment du décès peuvent également nuire à la comparabilité des données. Si l'on utilise à cet effet l'année seulement, et non pas les minutes, heures, jours et mois qui se sont écoulés depuis la naissance, de nombreux enfants décédés au cours du onzième mois qui a suivi leur naissance et certains enfants décédés encore plus jeunes seront classés comme décédés à un an révolu et donc exclus des données. Cette pratique conduit à sous-estimer le nombre de décès d'enfants de moins d'un an. Les renseignements dont on dispose sur ce facteur apparaissent en note à la fin du tableau. La question du calcul de l'âge au moment du décès est examinée plus en détail dans les notes techniques se rapportant au tableau 16.

Les taux de mortalité infantile appellent en outre toutes les réserves qui ont été formulées à propos des statistiques des naissances vivantes qui ont servi à leur calcul (voir à ce sujet les notes techniques relatives au tableau 9).

Les deux composantes du taux de mortalité infantile - décès d'enfants de moins d'un an au numérateur et naissances vivantes au dénominateur - étant obtenues à partir des registres de l'état civil, les statistiques des naissances vivantes appellent des réserves presque identiques à celles qui ont été formulées plus haut à propos des statistiques des décès d'enfants de moins d'un an. Il importe de prendre en considération la fiabilité des données (complétude de l'enregistrement) et le mode d'exploitation (selon la date de l'événement ou selon la date de l'enregistrement) dans le cas des statistiques des naissances vivantes tout comme dans le cas de celles des décès d'enfants de moins d'un an, puisque les unes et les autres servent au calcul des taux de mortalité infantile. Dans le tableau 15, le code de qualité et l'emploi de caractères italiques pour signaler les données moins sûres ne concernent que les décès d'enfants de moins d'un an. L'indication du mode d'exploitation des données (emploi du signe "+" pour signaler les données exploitées selon la date de l'enregistrement) ne porte là aussi que sur les décès d'enfants de moins d'un an. Le tableau 9 contient les renseignements correspondants pour les naissances vivantes.

Si l'enregistrement des décès d'enfants de moins d'un an est plus complet que l'enregistrement des naissances vivantes, les taux de mortalité infantile seront entachés d'une erreur par excès. En revanche, si l'enregistrement des naissances vivantes est plus complet que l'enregistrement des décès d'enfants de moins d'un an, les taux de mortalité infantile seront entachés d'une erreur par défaut. Si les décès d'enfants de moins d'un an et les naissances vivantes sont exploitées selon la date de l'enregistrement, il convient de ne pas perdre de vue que les décès sont, en règle générale, déclarés plus rapidement que les naissances.

Les taux de mortalité infantile peuvent être gravement faussés par la pratique de certains pays ou zones qui consiste à ne pas classer dans les naissances vivantes et ensuite dans les décès d'enfants de moins d'un an les enfants nés vivants mais décédés soit avant l'enregistrement de leur naissance, soit dans les 24 heures qui ont suivi la naissance. Cette pratique conduit à sous-estimer aussi bien le nombre des décès d'enfants de moins d'un an, qui constitue le numérateur, que le nombre des naissances vivantes, qui constitue le dénominateur, mais c'est pour le numérateur du taux de mortalité infantile que la distorsion est la plus marquée. Ce système a pour effet d'introduire une erreur par défaut dans les taux de mortalité infantile.

Les taux de mortalité infantile seront également sous-estimés si la méthode utilisée pour calculer l'âge au moment du décès conduit à sous-estimer le nombre de décès d'enfants de moins d'un an. Cette question a été examinée plus haut.

Tous ces facteurs sont importants et il faut donc en tenir compte lorsque l'on compare les taux de mortalité infantile.

En ce qui concerne la méthode de calcul des taux de mortalité infantile utilisée dans le tableau, il convient de noter qu'il n'a pas été tenu compte du fait qu'une partie des décès survenus pendant une année donnée sont des décès d'enfants nés l'année précédente et ne correspondent donc pas à l'ensemble des naissances utilisé pour le calcul des taux. Toutefois, l'erreur n'est pas grave, à moins que le nombre des naissances vivantes ou des décès d'enfants de moins d'un an ne varie rapidement.

La comparabilité des données selon le lieu de résidence (zone urbaine ou rurale) peut être limitée par les définitions nationales des termes « urbain » et « rural » utilisées pour la mise en tableaux de ces données. En l'absence d'indications contraires, on a supposé que les mêmes définitions avaient servi pour le recensement national de la population et pour l'établissement des statistiques de l'état civil pour chaque pays ou zone. Toutefois, il n'est pas exclu que, pour une zone ou un pays donné, des définitions différentes aient été retenues. Les définitions du terme « urbain » utilisées pour les recensements nationaux de population ont été présentées à la fin des notes techniques du tableau 6 lorsqu'elles étaient connues. Comme on l'a précisé dans les notes techniques relatives au tableau 6, ces définitions varient considérablement d'un pays ou d'une zone à l'autre.

La différence entre les taux de mortalité infantile pour les zones urbaines et rurales pourra aussi être faussée selon que les décès d'enfants de moins d'un an et les naissances vivantes auront été classés d'après le lieu de l'événement ou le lieu de résidence habituel. Ce problème est examiné plus en détail à la section 4.1.4.1 des Notes techniques.

Données publiées antérieurement : des statistiques concernant les décès d'enfants de moins d'un an et les taux de mortalité infantile ont déjà été présentées dans des éditions antérieures de l'*Annuaire démographique*. Pour plus de précisions concernant les années et les sujets pour lesquels des données ont été publiées, se reporter à l'index historique.

15. Infant deaths and infant mortality rates, by urban/rural residence: 2008 - 2012
Décès d'enfants de moins d'un an et taux de mortalité infantile, selon la résidence, urbaine/rurale : 2008 - 2012

Continent, country or area, and urban/rural residence / Continent, pays ou zone et résidence, urbaine/rurale	Co-de[a]	Number - Nombre					Rate - Taux				
		2008	2009	2010	2011	2012	2008	2009	2010	2011	2012
AFRICA - AFRIQUE											
Algeria - Algérie[1]											
Total	U	20 793	21 076	21 046	21 055	22 088	...	...	...	...	...
Cabo Verde											
Total	C	316	...	...	...	...	24.9	...	...	...	...
Egypt - Égypte											
Total	C	32 174	25 760	31 698	35 997	...	15.7	11.6	14.0	14.7	...
Urban - Urbaine	C	15 916	12 728	15 001	17 601	...	19.9	13.9	16.7	18.7	...
Rural - Rurale	C	16 258	13 032	16 697	18 396	...	13.0	10.0	12.3	12.3	...
Ghana											
Total	+U	52 038	...	...	...	...	...	...	...	...	...
Kenya											
Total	U	46 565	40 190	...	23 167	...	...	...	...	...	...
Mauritius - Maurice[2]											
Total	+C	236	205	187	189	...	14.4	13.4	12.5	12.9	...
Urban - Urbaine	+C	92	75	67	64	...	14.6	12.7	11.7	11.5	...
Rural - Rurale	+C	144	130	120	125	...	14.3	13.8	12.9	13.7	...
Rwanda											
Total	U	...	...	27	...	...	...	...	...	...	...
Saint Helena ex. dep. - Sainte-Hélène sans dép.											
Total	C	-	-	-	-	1	...	...	...	...	...
Senegal - Sénégal[3]											
Total	I	31 889	32 094	32 314	...	...	65.2	64.4	63.5	...	...
Seychelles											
Total	+C	20	17	21	16	...	...	...	...	...	...
Sierra Leone											
Total	+...	2 895	3 137	1 935	1 289	2 135	...	...	...	...	...
Urban - Urbaine	+...	887	796	749	547	1 508	...	...	...	...	...
Rural - Rurale	+...	2 008	2 341	1 186	742	627	...	...	...	...	...
South Africa - Afrique du Sud											
Total	...	45 316	...	...	...	...	...	...	...	...	...
AMERICA, NORTH - AMÉRIQUE DU NORD											
Anguilla											
Total	+C	-	...	...	...	...	...	...	...	...	...
Antigua and Barbuda - Antigua-et-Barbuda											
Total	+C	14	7	11	...	...	...	...	...	...	...
Bahamas											
Total	+C	71	71	*67	*48	...	13.9	14.1	*13.6	*10.1	...
Bermuda - Bermudes											
Total	C	4	1	1	-	...	...	...	...	...	...
Canada[4]											
Total	C	1 911	...	...	...	...	5.1	...	...	...	...
Cayman Islands - Îles Caïmanes											
Total	C	...	3	2	...	...	...	...	...	...	...
Costa Rica											
Total	C	673	663	*671	*666	*624	9.0	8.8	*9.5	*9.1	*8.5
Urban - Urbaine	C	321	293	*323	...	...	11.1	10.4	*12.4	...	...
Rural - Rurale	C	352	370	*348	...	...	7.6	7.9	*7.8	...	...
Cuba											
Total	C	579	626	*581	*653	...	4.7	4.8	*4.5	*4.9	...
Urban - Urbaine	C	423	470	*417	*485	...	4.5	4.7	*4.2	*4.7	...
Rural - Rurale	C	156	156	*164	*168	...	5.4	5.2	*5.7	*5.5	...
Curaçao											
Total	C	13	20	26	15	...	...	...	...	...	...
Dominican Republic - République dominicaine											
Total	U	491	473	491	672	...	...	...	...	...	...
Urban - Urbaine[5]	U	309	245	324	586	...	...	...	...	...	...
Rural - Rurale[5]	U	65	58	49	77	...	...	...	...	...	...

15. Infant deaths and infant mortality rates, by urban/rural residence: 2008 - 2012
Décès d'enfants de moins d'un an et taux de mortalité infantile, selon la résidence, urbaine/rurale : 2008 - 2012 (continued - suite)

Continent, country or area, and urban/rural residence / Continent, pays ou zone et résidence, urbaine/rurale	Code[a]	Number - Nombre					Rate - Taux				
		2008	2009	2010	2011	2012	2008	2009	2010	2011	2012
AMERICA, NORTH - AMÉRIQUE DU NORD											
El Salvador[6]											
Total	C	947	888	749	826	...	8.5	8.2	7.1	7.6	...
Urban - Urbaine	C	...	747	554	563	...	...	10.9	8.3	7.5	...
Rural - Rurale	C	...	141	195	263	...	...	3.6	5.1	7.8	...
Greenland - Groenland											
Total	C	8	4	6	9	7	...	...	...	...	...
Urban - Urbaine	C	5	2	-	7	4	...	...	...	...	...
Rural - Rurale	C	3	2	6	2	3	...	...	...	...	...
Guatemala											
Total	C	...	...	7 562	7 413	...	...	...	20.9	19.8	...
Mexico - Mexique[7]											
Total	+U	29 519	28 983	28 861	29 037	...	...	...	...	...	...
Urban - Urbaine[5]	+U	22 141	22 061	21 930	21 980	...	...	...	...	...	...
Rural - Rurale[5]	+U	6 894	6 453	6 415	6 574	...	...	...	...	...	...
Montserrat											
Total	+C	-	-	1	-	...	...	...	...	...	...
Nicaragua											
Total	+U	1 932	...	...	...	...	...	...	...	...	...
Urban - Urbaine	+U	977	...	...	...	...	...	...	...	...	...
Rural - Rurale	+U	955	...	...	...	...	...	...	...	...	...
Panama											
Total	U	877	837	910	...	...	...	...	...	...	...
Urban - Urbaine	U	473	428	474	...	...	...	...	...	...	...
Rural - Rurale	U	404	409	436	...	...	...	...	...	...	...
Puerto Rico - Porto Rico											
Total	C	400	...	...	...	...	8.8	...	...	...	...
Urban - Urbaine[5]	C	206	...	...	...	...	8.6	...	...	...	...
Rural - Rurale[5]	C	136	...	...	...	...	6.3	...	...	...	...
Saint Vincent and the Grenadines - Saint-Vincent-et-les Grenadines											
Total	+C	34	32	...	...	...	17.9	16.8	...	...	...
Turks and Caicos Islands - Îles Turques et Caïques											
Total	C	3	...	...	...	...	...	...	...	...	...
United States of America - États-Unis d'Amérique											
Total	C	28 059	26 412	*24 548	...	...	6.6	6.4	*6.1	...	...
AMERICA, SOUTH - AMÉRIQUE DU SUD											
Argentina - Argentine											
Total	C	9 326	9 013	8 961	8 878	...	12.5	12.1	11.9	11.7	...
Brazil - Brésil[8]											
Total	U	34 375	33 713	31 733	32 184	...	...	...	...	...	...
Chile - Chili											
Total	C	1 948	1 997	1 862	...	...	7.9	7.9	7.4	...	...
Urban - Urbaine	C	1 766	1 730	1 602	...	...	7.8	7.6	7.1	...	...
Rural - Rurale	C	182	267	260	...	...	8.9	10.4	10.2	...	...
Colombia - Colombie											
Total	U	10 560	9 580	8 355	*7 060	...	...	...	...	...	...
Urban - Urbaine[5]	U	7 759	6 810	6 108	...	...	...	...	...	...	...
Rural - Rurale[5]	U	2 312	2 354	1 983	...	...	...	...	...	...	...
Ecuador - Équateur[9]											
Total	U	3 380	3 279	3 204	...	...	...	...	...	...	...
Urban - Urbaine	U	2 669	2 657	2 573	...	...	...	...	...	...	...
Rural - Rurale	U	711	622	631	...	...	...	...	...	...	...
Paraguay											
Total	+U	1 674	...	...	...	...	...	...	...	...	...
Urban - Urbaine	+U	1 162	...	...	...	...	...	...	...	...	...
Rural - Rurale	+U	512	...	...	...	...	...	...	...	...	...
Peru - Pérou[10]											
Total	+U	5 581	5 993	5 287	4 569	...	...	...	...	...	...
Uruguay											
Total	C	504	451	364	*417	...	9.5	9.6	7.7	*8.9	...

15. Infant deaths and infant mortality rates, by urban/rural residence: 2008 - 2012
Décès d'enfants de moins d'un an et taux de mortalité infantile, selon la résidence, urbaine/rurale : 2008 - 2012 (continued - suite)

Continent, country or area, and urban/rural residence / Continent, pays ou zone et résidence, urbaine/rurale	Code[a]	Number - Nombre					Rate - Taux				
		2008	2009	2010	2011	2012	2008	2009	2010	2011	2012
ASIA - ASIE											
Armenia - Arménie[11]											
Total	C	442	454	512	507	...	10.7	10.2	11.4	11.7	...
Urban - Urbaine	C	312	269	...	...	...	11.9	9.5	...	...	...
Rural - Rurale	C	130	185	...	...	...	8.7	11.5	...	...	...
Azerbaijan - Azerbaïdjan[11]											
Total	+C	1 715	1 731	1 843	1 903	1 884	11.3	11.4	11.1	10.8	10.8
Urban - Urbaine	+C	1 047	1 094	1 173	...	...	14.2	14.6	14.3	...	...
Rural - Rurale	+C	668	637	670	...	...	8.5	8.2	8.0	...	...
Bahrain - Bahreïn											
Total	C	127	128	...	...	...	7.5	7.2	...	...	...
Bangladesh											
Total	U	...	...	*104 591*	*100 751*	...	...	...	...	...	...
Urban - Urbaine	U	...	...	*23 094*	*20 484*	...	...	...	...	...	...
Rural - Rurale	U	...	...	*81 497*	*80 267*	...	...	...	...	...	...
Brunei Darussalam - Brunéi Darussalam											
Total	+C	45	...	...	...	...	7.0	...	...	...	...
China, Hong Kong SAR - Chine, Hong Kong RAS											
Total	C	145	136	149	127	*127	1.8	1.7	1.7	1.3	*1.4
China, Macao SAR - Chine, Macao RAS											
Total	C	15	10	15	17	18	...	...	...	...	...
Cyprus - Chypre[12]											
Total	C	32	32	31	30	...	3.5	3.3	3.2	3.1	...
Democratic People's Republic of Korea - République populaire démocratique de Corée[13]											
Total	|	6 686	...	...	...	...	19.3	...	...	...	...
Urban - Urbaine	|	3 540	...	...	...	...	17.6	...	...	...	...
Rural - Rurale	|	3 146	...	...	...	...	21.7	...	...	...	...
Georgia - Géorgie[11]											
Total	C	959	945	701	703	715	17.0	14.9	11.2	12.1	12.5
Urban - Urbaine	C	724	708	379	342	...	18.5	16.2	11.1	10.2	...
Rural - Rurale	C	235	237	322	361	...	13.5	12.0	11.3	14.7	...
India - Inde[14]											
Total	|	...	...	...	...	...	53.0	50.0	47.0	...	...
Urban - Urbaine	|	...	...	...	...	...	36.0	34.0	31.0	...	...
Rural - Rurale	|	...	...	...	...	...	58.0	55.0	51.0	...	...
Israel - Israël[15]											
Total	C	602	619	618	585	563	3.8	3.8	3.7	3.5	3.3
Urban - Urbaine	C	537	570	545[5]	519[5]	501[5]	3.8	3.9	3.6	3.4	...
Rural - Rurale	C	65	49	72[5]	65[5]	61[5]	4.6	3.3	4.7	4.2	...
Japan - Japon[16]											
Total	C	2 798	2 556	2 450	2 463	...	2.6	2.4	2.3	2.3	...
Urban - Urbaine[5]	C	2 526	2 324	2 247	2 244	...	2.5	2.4	2.3	2.3	...
Rural - Rurale[5]	C	267	227	200	214	...	2.7	2.4	2.2	2.5	...
Kazakhstan[11]											
Total	C	7 322	...	...	...	...	20.5	...	...	...	...
Urban - Urbaine	C	4 419	...	...	...	...	22.4	...	...	...	...
Rural - Rurale	C	2 903	...	...	...	...	18.2	...	...	...	...
Kuwait - Koweït											
Total	C	494	596	496	484	...	9.1	10.5	8.6	8.3	...
Kyrgyzstan - Kirghizstan											
Total	C	3 453	3 393	3 337	3 150	...	27.1	25.0	22.8	21.1	...
Urban - Urbaine	C	1 852	1 893	1 888	1 767	...	42.1	40.3	37.8	36.1	...
Rural - Rurale	C	1 601	1 500	1 449	1 383	...	19.2	16.9	15.1	13.7	...
Malaysia - Malaisie											
Total	C	3 045	3 404	*3 251	...	...	6.2	6.9	*6.8	...	...
Urban - Urbaine	C	1 841	2 064	...	...	...	6.0	6.6	...	...	...
Rural - Rurale	C	1 204	1 340	...	...	...	6.7	7.4	...	...	...
Maldives											
Total	C	76	81	78	65	...	10.9	10.9	11.0	9.1	...
Urban - Urbaine	C	39	52	43[17]	41[17]	...	11.6	14.1	11.3	10.3	...
Rural - Rurale	C	37	29	33[17]	20[17]	...	10.2	...	10.2	...	...

15. Infant deaths and infant mortality rates, by urban/rural residence: 2008 - 2012
Décès d'enfants de moins d'un an et taux de mortalité infantile, selon la résidence, urbaine/rurale : 2008 - 2012 (continued - suite)

Continent, country or area, and urban/rural residence / Continent, pays ou zone et résidence, urbaine/rurale	Code[a]	Number - Nombre					Rate - Taux				
		2008	2009	2010	2011	2012	2008	2009	2010	2011	2012
ASIA - ASIE											
Mongolia - Mongolie											
Total	+C	1 240	1 386	1 275	...	...	19.4	20.0	20.2	...	...
Myanmar											
Total	+U	26 265	25 782	26 206	...	...	...	...	...	...	...
Urban - Urbaine	+U	7 004	7 097	7 223	...	...	...	...	...	...	...
Rural - Rurale	+U	19 261	18 685	18 983	...	...	...	...	...	...	...
Oman[18]											
Total	U	534	676	600	598	...	...	...	...	...	...
Philippines											
Total	C	22 351	21 659	...	...	...	12.5	12.4	...	...	...
Qatar											
Total	C	132	130	132	156	...	7.7	7.1	6.8	10.5	...
Republic of Korea - République de Corée[19]											
Total	C	1 580	1 415	1 508	1 435	...	3.4	3.2	3.2	3.0	...
Urban - Urbaine[5]	C	1 282	1 139	1 187	1 158	...	3.3	3.1	3.1	3.0	...
Rural - Rurale[5]	C	285	265	296	265	...	3.5	3.4	3.5	3.3	...
Saudi Arabia - Arabie saoudite[20]											
Total	...	10 576	10 409	10 219	10 023	9 843	...	...	...	...	...
Singapore - Singapour											
Total	+C	104	102	100	97	98	2.6	2.6	2.6	2.4	2.3
Sri Lanka[21]											
Total	+C	3 362	...	...	...	...	9.0	...	...	...	...
Urban - Urbaine	+C	2 908	...	...	...	...	11.2	...	...	...	...
Rural - Rurale	+C	454	...	...	...	...	4.0	...	...	...	...
Tajikistan - Tadjikistan[11]											
Total	U	2 480	2 814	3 092	3 131	...	...	...	...	...	...
Urban - Urbaine	U	1 123	1 521	1 350	1 281	...	...	...	...	...	...
Rural - Rurale	U	1 357	1 293	1 742	1 850	...	...	...	...	...	...
Thailand - Thaïlande											
Total	+U	5 721	5 416	5 357	5 275	...	...	...	...	...	...
Turkey - Turquie											
Total	U	18 968	17 388	15 049	16 103	14 845	...	...	...	...	...
EUROPE											
Åland Islands - Îles d'Åland											
Total	C	1	-	1	-	...	...	...	...	...	...
Urban - Urbaine	C	1	-	-	-	...	...	...	...	...	...
Rural - Rurale	C	-	-	1	-	...	...	...	...	...	...
Albania - Albanie											
Total	C	217	...	...	...	...	6.0	...	...	...	...
Andorra - Andorre											
Total	C	3	1	-	...	4	...	...	...	...	...
Austria - Autriche											
Total	C	287	289	307	281	252	3.7	3.8	3.9	3.6	3.2
Belarus - Bélarus											
Total	C	483	511	429	420	386	4.5	4.7	4.0	3.8	3.3
Urban - Urbaine	C	317	345	278	286	...	3.9	4.2	3.4	3.4	...
Rural - Rurale	C	166	166	151	134	...	6.3	6.3	5.9	5.2	...
Belgium - Belgique[22]											
Total	C	478	439	463	*426	*415	3.8	3.4	3.6	*3.3	*3.3
Urban - Urbaine	C	472	433	...	...	...	3.8	3.5	...	...	...
Rural - Rurale	C	6	6	...	...	...	...	...	...	...	...
Bosnia and Herzegovina - Bosnie-Herzégovine											
Total	C	235	224	216	...	*161	6.9	6.5	6.4	...	*5.0
Bulgaria - Bulgarie											
Total	C	668	729	708	601	536	8.6	9.0	9.4	8.5	7.8
Urban - Urbaine	C	444	468	461	412	...	7.6	7.7	8.1	7.7	...
Rural - Rurale	C	224	261	247	189	...	11.6	12.9	13.4	10.8	...
Croatia - Croatie											
Total	C	195	235	192	192	...	4.5	5.3	4.4	4.7	...
Urban - Urbaine	C	107	141	109	...	...	4.4	5.7	4.4	...	...
Rural - Rurale	C	88	94	83	...	...	4.5	4.8	4.4	...	...

15. Infant deaths and infant mortality rates, by urban/rural residence: 2008 - 2012
Décès d'enfants de moins d'un an et taux de mortalité infantile, selon la résidence, urbaine/rurale : 2008 - 2012 (continued - suite)

Continent, country or area, and urban/rural residence / Continent, pays ou zone et résidence, urbaine/rurale	Code[a]	Number - Nombre					Rate - Taux				
		2008	2009	2010	2011	2012	2008	2009	2010	2011	2012
EUROPE											
Czech Republic - République tchèque											
Total	C	338	341	313	298	285	2.8	2.9	2.7	2.7	2.6
Urban - Urbaine	C	241	254	235	231	...	2.7	2.9	2.7	2.9	...
Rural - Rurale	C	97	87	78	67	...	3.1	2.8	2.5	2.3	...
Denmark - Danemark[23]											
Total	C	262	193	216	208	197	4.0	3.1	3.4	3.5	3.4
Estonia - Estonie											
Total	C	80	57	53	36	50	5.0	3.6	3.3	2.5	3.6
Urban - Urbaine	C	52	35	37	25	...	4.7	3.2	3.5	...	...
Rural - Rurale	C	28	22	16	11	...	...	...	...	...	...
Finland - Finlande											
Total	C	157	158[24]	139[24]	143	141	2.6	2.6	2.3	2.4	2.4
Urban - Urbaine	C	99	100[24]	96[24]	...	...	2.3	2.3	2.2	...	...
Rural - Rurale	C	58	58[24]	43[24]	...	...	3.4	3.4	2.5	...	...
France[25]											
Total	C	2 856	2 903	2 785	2 604	*2 626	3.6	3.7	3.5	3.3	*3.3
Urban - Urbaine[26]	C	2 251	2 242	2 252	...	...	3.8	3.8	3.5	...	...
Rural - Rurale[26]	C	582	636	492	...	...	2.9	3.2	3.0	...	...
Germany - Allemagne											
Total	C	2 414	2 334	2 322	2 408	*2 300	3.5	3.5	3.4	3.6	*3.4
Greece - Grèce											
Total	C	314	371	436	357	...	2.7	3.1	3.8	3.4	...
Urban - Urbaine	C	223	261	312	250	...	2.8	3.2	4.0	3.3	...
Rural - Rurale	C	91	110	124	107	...	2.4	3.0	3.4	3.4	...
Hungary - Hongrie											
Total	C	553	495	481	433	*440	5.6	5.1	5.3	4.9	*4.9
Urban - Urbaine[27]	C	328	301	316	268	...	4.9	4.6	5.1	4.4	...
Rural - Rurale[27]	C	218	187	156	160	...	6.9	6.3	5.8	6.1	...
Iceland - Islande											
Total	C	12	9	11	4[28]	...	...	...	...	...	...
Urban - Urbaine	C	12	8	10	4[28]	...	...	...	...	...	...
Rural - Rurale	C	-	1	1	-[28]	...	...	...	...	...	...
Ireland - Irlande											
Total[29]	C	284	247	...	...	...	3.8	3.3	...	...	...
Total	+C	...	...	282	258	...	...	...	3.8	3.5	...
Italy - Italie											
Total	C	1 896	1 947	1 887	1 762	*1 786	3.3	3.4	3.4	3.2	...
Latvia - Lettonie											
Total	C	161	168	110	124	125	6.7	7.8	5.7	6.6	6.3
Urban - Urbaine	C	90	99	68	...	...	5.4	6.7	5.2	...	...
Rural - Rurale	C	71	69	42	...	...	9.6	10.1	6.9	...	...
Liechtenstein											
Total	C	-	1	1	*1	*3	...	...	...	...	...
Lithuania - Lituanie											
Total	C	172	181	153	144	118	4.9	4.9	4.3	4.2	3.9
Urban - Urbaine	C	130	136	114	87	...	5.5	5.4	4.6	3.7	...
Rural - Rurale	C	42	45	39	57	...	3.7	3.9	3.5	5.4	...
Luxembourg											
Total	C	10	14	20	24	15	...	...	...	...	...
Malta - Malte											
Total	C	34	22	22	27	...	8.2	...	...	...	...
Montenegro - Monténégro											
Total	C	62	49	50	32	*33	7.5	5.7	6.7	4.4	*4.4
Urban - Urbaine	C	58	45	...	...	...	9.0	6.8	...	...	...
Rural - Rurale	C	4	4	...	...	...	...	...	...	...	...
Netherlands - Pays-Bas[30]											
Total	C	698	711	695	654	...	3.8	3.8	3.8	3.6	...
Urban - Urbaine	C	500	514	503	...	...	3.9	4.0	3.9	...	...
Rural - Rurale	C	198	197	192	...	...	3.5	3.5	3.5	...	...
Norway - Norvège[31]											
Total	C	163	192	171	142	150	2.7	3.1	2.8	2.4	2.5
Poland - Pologne											
Total	C	2 338	2 327	2 057	1 836	1 791	5.6	5.6	5.0	4.7	4.6
Urban - Urbaine	C	1 363	1 385	1 198	1 059	...	5.6	5.6	5.0	4.7	...
Rural - Rurale	C	975	942	859	777	...	5.6	5.5	5.0	4.8	...

15. Infant deaths and infant mortality rates, by urban/rural residence: 2008 - 2012
Décès d'enfants de moins d'un an et taux de mortalité infantile, selon la résidence, urbaine/rurale : 2008 - 2012 (continued - suite)

Continent, country or area, and urban/rural residence — Continent, pays ou zone et résidence, urbaine/rurale	Code[a]	Number - Nombre					Rate - Taux				
		2008	2009	2010	2011	2012	2008	2009	2010	2011	2012
EUROPE											
Portugal[7]											
Total	C	340	362	256	301	303	3.3	3.6	2.5	3.1	3.4
Republic of Moldova - République de Moldova[32]											
Total	C	473	492	476	431	387	12.1	12.1	11.8	11.0	9.8
Urban - Urbaine	C	159	168	153	...	...	11.1	11.3	10.1	...	...
Rural - Rurale	C	314	324	323	...	...	12.7	12.5	12.8	...	...
Romania - Roumanie											
Total	C	2 434	2 250	2 078	1 850	1 812	11.0	10.1	9.8	9.4	9.0
Urban - Urbaine	C	1 030	982	913	797	...	8.5	8.1	7.7	7.5	...
Rural - Rurale	C	1 404	1 268	1 165	1 053	...	14.0	12.6	12.3	11.8	...
Russian Federation - Fédération de Russie[11]											
Total	C	14 436	14 271	13 405	13 168	...	8.4	8.1	7.5	7.3	...
Urban - Urbaine	C	9 273	9 189	8 641	8 398	...	7.8	7.4	6.8	6.6	...
Rural - Rurale	C	5 163	5 082	4 764	4 770	...	9.9	9.7	9.1	9.1	...
San Marino - Saint-Marin											
Total	+C	...	...	...	1	-	...	...	...	...	...
Serbia - Serbie[33]											
Total	+C	460	492	460	414	415	6.7	7.0	6.7	6.3	6.2
Urban - Urbaine	+C	331	346	310	283	...	7.3	7.4	6.6	6.2	...
Rural - Rurale	+C	129	146	150	131	...	5.4	6.2	6.9	6.5	...
Slovakia - Slovaquie											
Total	C	336	346	344	300	321	5.9	5.7	5.7	4.9	5.8
Urban - Urbaine	C	158	159	172	130	...	5.2	4.9	5.4	4.0	...
Rural - Rurale	C	178	187	172	170	...	6.7	6.5	6.1	5.9	...
Slovenia - Slovénie											
Total	C	52	52	56	64	*35	2.4	2.4	2.5	2.9	*1.6
Urban - Urbaine	C	26	21	34	28	...	...	...	3.1	...	...
Rural - Rurale	C	26	31	22	36	...	...	2.8	...	3.2	...
Spain - Espagne											
Total	C	1 741	1 578	1 531	1 477	*1 620	3.4	3.2	3.2	3.1	*3.5
Sweden - Suède											
Total	C	272	278	294	235	293	2.5	2.5	2.5	2.1	2.6
Switzerland - Suisse											
Total	C	308	337	307	305	*296	4.0	4.3	3.8	3.8	*3.6
Urban - Urbaine	C	245	258	230	218	...	4.3	4.4	3.8	3.6	...
Rural - Rurale	C	63	79	77	87	...	3.2	4.0	3.8	4.3	...
TFYR of Macedonia - L'ex-R. y. de Macédoine											
Total	C	223	278	185	*174	230	9.7	11.7	7.6	*7.6	9.8
Urban - Urbaine	C	120	150	89	...	...	9.1	11.0	6.4	...	...
Rural - Rurale	C	103	128	96	...	...	10.6	12.7	9.2	...	...
Ukraine[34]											
Total	+C	5 049	4 801	4 564	4 511	4 371	9.9	9.4	9.2	9.0	8.4
Urban - Urbaine	+C	3 220	3 050	2 792	2 811	...	9.5	9.0	8.5	8.5	...
Rural - Rurale	+C	1 829	1 751	1 772	1 700	...	10.8	10.1	10.4	9.8	...
United Kingdom of Great Britain and Northern Ireland - Royaume-Uni de Grande-Bretagne et d'Irlande du Nord[35]											
Total	+C	3 745	3 677	3 416	3 386	...	4.7	4.7	4.2	4.2	...
OCEANIA - OCÉANIE											
Australia - Australie											
Total	+C	1 226	1 261	1 229	1 140	...	4.1	4.3	4.1	3.8	...
Urban - Urbaine[36]	+C	1 012	1 010	1 008	888	...	4.0	4.0	3.9	3.4	...
Rural - Rurale[36]	+C	184	222	187	212	...	4.4	5.3	4.5	5.3	...
Cook Islands - Îles Cook[37]											
Total	+C	1	2	2	*2	*1	...	...	...	...	...
French Polynesia - Polynésie française											
Total	C	23	26	25	...	...	...	...	...	...	...

399

15. Infant deaths and infant mortality rates, by urban/rural residence: 2008 - 2012

Décès d'enfants de moins d'un an et taux de mortalité infantile, selon la résidence, urbaine/rurale : 2008 - 2012 (continued - suite)

Continent, country or area, and urban/rural residence / Continent, pays ou zone et résidence, urbaine/rurale	Co-de[a]	Number - Nombre					Rate - Taux				
		2008	2009	2010	2011	2012	2008	2009	2010	2011	2012
OCEANIA - OCÉANIE											
Guam[38]											
Total	C	31	...	...	...	...	8.9	...	...	...	...
New Caledonia - Nouvelle-Calédonie											
Total	C	20	23	19	...	...	...	...	...	...	...
New Zealand - Nouvelle-Zélande[7]											
Total	+C	322	308	325	290	256	5.0	4.9	5.1	4.7	4.2
Urban - Urbaine[5]	+C	271	273	282	255	229	4.8	5.0	5.0	4.7	4.2
Rural - Rurale[5]	+C	38	17	35	31	24	4.7	...	4.4	4.2	...
Northern Mariana Islands - Îles Mariannes septentrionales[39]											
Total	U	*4*	...	...	...	...	...	...	...	...	...

FOOTNOTES - NOTES

Italics: data from civil registers which are incomplete or of unknown completeness. - Italiques : données incomplètes ou dont le degré d'exactitude n'est pas connu, provenant des registres de l'état civil.

* Provisional. - Données provisoires.

[a] 'Code' indicates the source of data, as follows:
C - Civil registration, estimated over 90% complete
U - Civil registration, estimated less than 90% complete
| - Other source, estimated reliable
+ - Data tabulated by date of registration rather than occurence
... - Information not available

Le 'Code' indique la source des données, comme suit :
C - Registres de l'état civil considérés complets à 90 p. 100 au moins
U - Registres de l'état civil qui ne sont pas considérés complets à 90 p. 100 au moins
| - Autre source, considérée pas douteuses
+ - Données exploitées selon la date de l'enregistrement et non la date de l'événement
... - Information pas disponible

[1] Excluding live-born infants who died before their birth was registered. Data refer to Algerian population only. - Non compris les enfants nés vivants décédés avant l'enregistrement de leur naissance. Les données ne concernent que la population algérienne.
[2] Excludes the islands of St. Brandon and Agalega. - Non compris les îles St. Brandon et Agalega.
[3] Based on estimates and projections from 'Agence Nationale de la Statistique et de la Démographie'. - Données fondées sur des estimations et des projections provenant de l'Agence Nationale de la Statistique et de la Démographie.
[4] Including Canadian residents temporarily in the United States, but excluding United States residents temporarily in Canada. - Y compris les résidents canadiens se trouvant temporairement aux Etats-Unis, mais ne comprenant pas les résidents des Etats-Unis se trouvant temporairement au Canada.
[5] The total number includes 'Unknown residence', but the categories urban and rural do not. - Le nombre total englobe les personnes dont la résidence n'est pas connue, à l'inverse des catégories de population urbaine et rurale.
[6] Excluding infant deaths to mothers living abroad. - Exception faite des décès d'enfants en bas âge survenus lorsque la mère résidait à l'étranger.
[7] Data refer to resident population only. - Pour la population résidante seulement.
[8] Including deaths abroad and deaths of unknown residence. - Y compris les décès à l'étranger et les décès dont on ignore la résidence.
[9] Excludes nomadic Indian tribes. - Non compris les tribus d'Indiens nomades.
[10] Source: Reports of the Ministry of Health. Completeness of coverage estimated at 40 per cent. - Source: Rapports du Ministère de la Santé. Degré de complétude évalué à 40 pour cent.

[11] Excluding infants born alive of less than 28 weeks' gestation, of less than 1 000 grams in weight and 35 centimeters in length, who die within seven days of birth. - Non compris les enfants nés vivants après moins de 28 semaines de gestations, pesant moins de 1 000 grammes, mesurant moins de 35 centimètres et décédés dans les sept jours qui ont suivi leur naissance.
[12] Data refer to government controlled areas. - Les données se rapportent aux zones contrôlées par le Gouvernement.
[13] Data refer to the 12 months preceding the census in October. - Les données se rapportent aux 12 mois précédant le recensement de octobre.
[14] Includes data for the Indian-held part of Jammu and Kashmir, the final status of which has not yet been determined. Rates were obtained by the Sample Registration System of India, which is a large demographic survey. - Y compris les données pour la partie du Jammu et du Cachemire occupée par l'Inde dont le statut définitif n'a pas encore été déterminé. Les taux ont été obtenus par le Système de l'enregistrement par échantillon de l'Inde qui est une large enquête démographique.
[15] Includes data for East Jerusalem and Israeli residents in certain other territories under occupation by Israeli military forces since June 1967. Including deaths abroad of Israeli residents who were out of the country for less than a year. - Y compris les données pour Jérusalem-Est et les résidents israéliens dans certains autres territoires occupés depuis 1967 par les forces armées israéliennes. Y compris les décès à l'étranger de résidents israéliens qui ont quitté le pays depuis moins d'un an.
[16] Data refer to Japanese nationals in Japan only. - Les données se raportent aux nationaux japonais au Japon seulement.
[17] Excluding deaths occurred abroad. - Hormis les décès à l'étranger.
[18] Data from Births and Deaths Notification System (Ministry of Health and all health care providers). - Les données proviennent du système de notification des naissances et des décès (Ministère de la santé et tous prestataires de soins de santé).
[19] Excluding alien armed forces, civilian aliens employed by armed forces, and foreign diplomatic personnel and their dependants. - Non compris les militaires étrangers, les civils étrangers employés par les forces armées ni le personnel diplomatique étranger et les membres de leur famille les accompagnant.
[20] Projections based on the final results of the 2004 Population and Housing Census. - Projections basées sur les résultats définitifs du recensement de la population et de l'habitat de 2004.
[21] Excluding data from Mulative and Killnochchi districts. - À l'exclusion des données des districts de Mulative et Killnochchi.
[22] Including armed forces stationed outside the country, but excluding alien armed forces stationed in the area. - Y compris les militaires nationaux hors du pays, mais non compris les militaires étrangers en garnison sur le territoire.
[23] Excluding Faeroe Islands and Greenland shown separately, if available. - Non compris les Iles Féroé et le Groenland, qui font l'objet de rubriques distinctes, si disponible.
[24] Excluding Åland Islands. - Non compris les Îles d'Åland.
[25] Including armed forces stationed outside the country. - Y compris les militaires nationaux hors du pays.
[26] The data for urban and rural exclude the nationals outside the country. - Les données relatives à la population urbaine et rurale n'englobent pas les nationaux se trouvant à l'étranger.

²⁷ Total includes the data of foreigners, persons of unknown residence and homeless, but the categories urban and rural do not. - Le total englobe les données relatives aux étrangers, aux personnes dont la résidence n'est pas connue et aux personnes sans domicile fixe, à l'inverse des chiffres portant sur la population urbaine et rurale.

²⁸ Definition of localities was revised from 2011 causing a break with the previous series. - La rupture par rapport aux séries précédentes s'explique par le fait que la définition des localités a été révisée depuis 2011.

²⁹ Data refer to events registered within one year of occurrence. - Les données portent sur des événements enregistrés dans l'année pendant laquelle ils sont survenus.

³⁰ Including residents outside the country if listed in a Netherlands population register. - Englobe les résidents se trouvant à l'étranger à condition qu'ils soient inscrits sur le registre de population des Pays-Bas.

³¹ Including residents temporarily outside the country. - Y compris les résidents se trouvant temporairement hors du pays.

³² Excluding Transnistria and the municipality of Bender. - Les données ne tiennent pas compte de l'information sur la Transnistria et la municipalité de Bender.

³³ Excludes data for Kosovo and Metohia. - Sans les données pour le Kosovo et Metohie.

³⁴ Data includes deaths resulting from births with weight 500g and more (if weight is unknown - with length 25 centimeters and more, or with gestation during 22 weeks or more). - Y compris les décès de nouveau-nés de 500 grammes ou plus (si le poids est inconnu – de 25 centimètres de long ou plus, ou après une grossesse de 22 semaines ou plus).

³⁵ Excluding Channel Islands (Guernsey and Jersey) and Isle of Man, shown separately, if available. - Non compris les îles Anglo-Normandes (Guernesey et Jersey) et l'île de Man, qui font l'objet de rubriques distinctes, si disponible.

³⁶ Excluding data where place of usual residence was overseas, undefined, no fixed place of abode or offshore or migratory and unknown. - Les données n'ont pas été prises en compte lorsque le domicile habituel était à l'étranger ou dans une zone extraterritoriale, était indéfini ou inconnu ou que la personne n'avait pas de domicile fixe ou était une migrante.

³⁷ Excluding Niue, shown separately, which is part of Cook Islands, but because of remoteness is administered separately. - Non compris Nioué, qui fait l'objet d'une rubrique distincte et qui fait partie des îles Cook, mais qui, en raison de son éloignement, est administrée séparément.

³⁸ Including United States military personnel, their dependants and contract employees. - Y compris les militaires des Etats-Unis, les membres de leur famille les accompagnant et les agents contractuels des Etats-Unis.

³⁹ Source: Commonwealth Health Center - Vital Statistics Office - Source : Centre de Santé du Commonwealth - Bureau des statistiques d'État civil

Table 16 - *Demographic Yearbook 2012*

Table 16 presents infant deaths and infant mortality rates by age and sex for latest available year between 2003 and 2012.

Description of variables: Age is defined as hours, days and months of life completed, based on the difference between the hour, day, month and year of birth and the hour, day, month and year of death. The age classification used in this table is as follows: Main categories are "under 1 day", "1-6 days", "7-27 days" and "28 days – 11 months". Additional subcategories are shown within "7-27 days" and "28 days to 11 months" wherever available.

Rate computation: Infant mortality rates by age and sex are the annual number of infant deaths that occurred in a specific age-sex group per 1 000 live births of the corresponding sex. These rates have been calculated by the Statistics Division of the United Nations Department of Economic and Social Affairs. The denominator for all these rates, regardless of age of infant at death, is the total number of live births by sex.

Infant deaths of unknown age are included only in the rate for under one year of age. Infant deaths of unknown sex are included in the rate for the total and, hence, these rates, should agree with the infant mortality rates shown in table 15. Discrepancies are explained in footnotes.

Rates presented in this table have been limited to those for countries or areas having at least a total of 100 deaths in a given year. Moreover, rates specific for individual sub-categories based on 30 or fewer infant deaths are identified by the symbol "♦".

Reliability of data: Data from civil registers of infant deaths which are reported as incomplete (less than 90 percent completeness) or of unknown completeness are considered unreliable and are set in italics rather than in roman type. Rates on these data are not computed. Table 15 and its technical notes provide more detailed information on the completeness of infant death registration. For more information about the quality of vital statistics, and the information available on the basis of the completeness of estimates in particular, see section 4.2 of the Technical Notes.

Limitations: Statistics on infant deaths by age and sex are subject to the same qualifications as have been set forth for vital statistics in general and death statistics in particular as discussed in section 4 of the Technical Notes.

The reliability of the data, an indication of which is described above, is an important factor in considering the limitations. In addition, some infant deaths are tabulated by date of registration and not by date of occurrence; these have been indicated by a plus sign "+". Whenever the lag between the date of occurrence and date of registration is prolonged and, therefore, a large proportion of the infant-death registrations are delayed, infant-death statistics for any given year may be seriously affected.

Another factor that limits international comparability is the practice of some countries or areas of not including in infant-death statistics infants who were born alive but died before the registration of the birth or within the first 24 hours of life, thus underestimating the total number of infant deaths. Statistics of this type are footnoted. In this table in particular, this practice may contribute to the lack of comparability among deaths under one year, under 28 days, under one week and under one day.

Variation in the method of reckoning age at the time of death may also introduce non-comparability. Although it is to some degree a limiting factor throughout the age span, it is an especially important consideration with respect to deaths at ages under one day and under one week (early neonatal deaths) and under 28 days (neonatal deaths). As noted above, the recommended method of reckoning infant age at death is to calculate duration of life in minutes, hours and days, as appropriate. This gives age in completed units of time. In some countries or areas, however, infant age is calculated to the nearest day only, that is, age at death for an infant is the difference between the day, month and year of birth and the day, month and year of death. The result of this procedure is to classify as deaths at age one day, many deaths of infants that occurred before the infants had completed 24 hours of life. The under-one-day class is thus understated while the frequency in the 1-6-day age group is inflated.

A special limitation on comparability of neonatal (under 28 days) deaths is the variation in the classification of infant age used. It is evident from the footnotes that some countries or areas continue to report infant age in calendar, rather than lunar month (4-week or 28-day) periods. This failure to tabulate infant deaths under 4 weeks of age in terms of completed days introduces another source of variation between countries or areas. Deaths classified as occurring under one month usually connote deaths within any one calendar month; these frequencies are not strictly comparable with those referring to deaths within 4 weeks or 27 completed days.

In addition, infant mortality rates by age and sex are subject to the limitations of the data on live births with which they have been calculated. These have been set forth in the technical notes for table 9. These limitations have also been discussed in the technical notes for table 15.

In addition, it should be noted that infant mortality rates by age are affected by the problems related to the practice of excluding infants who were born alive but died before the registration of the birth or within the first 24 hours of life from both infant-death and live-birth statistics and the problems related to the reckoning of infant age at death. These factors, which have been described above, may affect certain age groups more than others. In so far as the numbers of infant deaths for the various age groups are underestimated or overestimated, the corresponding rates for the various age groups will also be underestimated or overestimated. The youngest age groups are more likely to be underestimated than other age groups; the youngest age group (under one day) is likely to be the most seriously affected.

Earlier data: Infant deaths and infant mortality rates by age and sex have been shown in previous issues of the *Demographic Yearbook*. For information on specific years covered, readers should consult the Historical Index.

Tableau 16 – *Annuaire démographique 2012*

Le tableau 16 présente les données les plus récentes disponible, entre 2003 et 2012, sur les décès d'enfants de moins d'un an et les taux de mortalité infantile selon l'âge et le sexe.

Description des variables : l'âge est exprimé en heures, jours et mois révolus et est calculé en retranchant la date de la naissance (heure, jour, mois et année) de celle du décès (heure, jour, mois et année). Les tranches d'âge utilisées dans ce tableau se présentent comme suit : les catégories principales sont « moins d'un jour », « 1-6 jours », « 7-27 jours » et « 28 jours à 11 mois ». Des sous-catégories additionnelles pour « 7-27 jours » et « 28 jours à 11 mois » sont présentées lorsque disponibles.

Calcul des taux : les taux de mortalité infantile selon l'âge et le sexe représentent le nombre annuel de décès d'enfants de moins d'un an intervenu dans un groupe d'âge donné parmi la population de sexe masculin ou féminin pour 1 000 naissances vivantes survenues parmi la population du même sexe. Ces taux ont été calculés par la Division de statistique du Département des affaires économiques et sociales de l'Organisation des Nations Unies. Le dénominateur de tous ces taux, quel que soit l'âge de l'enfant au moment du décès, est le nombre total de naissances vivantes selon le sexe.

Il n'est tenu compte des décès d'enfants d'âge « inconnu » que pour le calcul du taux relatif à l'ensemble des décès de moins d'un an. Étant donné que les décès d'enfants de sexe inconnu sont compris dans le numérateur des taux concernant le total, les chiffres obtenus devraient concorder avec les taux de mortalité infantile du tableau 15. Les divergences sont expliquées en note.

Les taux présentés dans le tableau 16 ne concernent que les pays ou zones où l'on a enregistré un total d'au moins 100 décès au cours d'une année donnée. Les taux relatifs à des sous-catégories qui sont fondées sur un nombre égal ou inférieur à 30 décès d'enfants âgés de moins d'un an sont signalés par le signe "♦".

Fiabilité des données : les données relatives aux décès d'enfants de moins d'un an provenant de registres de l'état civil qui sont déclarées incomplètes (degré de complétude inférieur à 90 p.100) ou dont le degré de complétude n'est pas connu sont jugées douteuses et apparaissent en italique et non en caractères romains. Les taux à partir de ces données n'ont pas été calculés. Le tableau 15 et les notes techniques se rapportant à ce tableau comportent des renseignements plus détaillés sur le degré de complétude de l'enregistrement des décès d'enfants de moins d'un an. Pour plus de précisions sur la qualité des données reposant sur les statistiques de l'état civil en général et les estimations de complétude en particulier, voir la section 4.2 des Notes techniques.

Insuffisance des données : les statistiques des décès d'enfants de moins d'un an selon l'âge et le sexe appellent toutes les réserves qui ont été formulées à propos des statistiques de l'état civil en général et des statistiques concernant les décès en particulier (voir la section 4 des Notes techniques).

La fiabilité des données, au sujet de laquelle des indications ont été fournies plus haut, est un facteur important. Il faut également tenir compte du fait que, dans certains cas, les données relatives aux décès d'enfants de moins d'un an sont exploitées selon la date de l'enregistrement et non la date de l'événement ; ces cas ont été signalés par le signe "+". Chaque fois que le décalage entre l'événement et son enregistrement est grand et qu'une forte proportion des décès d'enfants de moins d'un an fait l'objet d'un enregistrement tardif, les statistiques des décès d'enfants de moins d'un an pour une année donnée peuvent être considérablement faussées.

Un autre facteur qui nuit à la comparabilité internationale est la pratique de certains pays ou zones qui consiste à ne pas inclure dans les statistiques des décès d'enfants de moins d'un an les enfants nés vivants mais décédés soit avant l'enregistrement de leur naissance, soit dans les 24 heures qui ont suivi la naissance, pratique qui conduit à sous-estimer le nombre total de décès d'enfants de moins d'un an. Quand pareil facteur a joué, cela a été signalé en note. Dans le tableau 16 en particulier, ce système peut limiter la comparabilité des données concernant les décès d'enfants de moins d'un an, de moins de 28 jours, de moins d'une semaine et de moins d'un jour.

Le manque d'uniformité des méthodes suivies pour calculer l'âge au moment du décès nuit également à la comparabilité des données. Ce facteur influe dans une certaine mesure sur les données relatives à la mortalité à tous les âges, mais il a des répercussions particulièrement marquées sur les statistiques des décès de moins d'un jour et de moins d'une semaine (mortalité néo-natale précoce) et de moins de 28 jours (mortalité néo-natale). Comme on l'a dit, l'âge d'un enfant de moins d'un an à son décès est calculé, selon la méthode recommandée, en évaluant la durée de vie en minutes, heures et jours, selon le cas. L'âge est ainsi exprimé en unités de temps révolues. Toutefois, dans certains pays ou zones, l'âge de ces enfants est ramené au jour le plus proche en retranchant la date de la naissance (jour, mois et année) de celle du décès (jour, mois et année). Il s'ensuit que de nombreux décès survenus dans les vingt-quatre heures qui suivent la naissance sont classés comme décès d'un jour. Dans ces conditions, les données concernant les décès de moins d'un jour sont entachées d'une erreur par défaut et celles qui se rapportent aux décès de 1 à 6 jours d'une erreur par excès.

La comparabilité des données relatives à la mortalité néo-natale (moins de 28 jours) est influencée par un facteur spécial : l'hétérogénéité de la classification par âge utilisée pour les enfants de moins d'un an. Les notes figurant à la fin des tableaux montrent que, dans un certain nombre de pays ou zones, on continue d'utiliser le mois civil au lieu du mois lunaire (4 semaines ou 28 jours).

Lorsque les données relatives aux décès de moins de 4 semaines ne sont pas exploitées sur la base de l'âge en jours révolus, il existe une nouvelle cause de non-comparabilité internationale. Les décès de moins d'un mois sont généralement ceux qui se produisent au cours d'un mois civil ; les taux calculés sur la base de ces données ne sont pas strictement comparables à ceux qui sont établis à partir des données concernant les décès survenus dans les 4 semaines ou 27 jours révolus qui suivent la naissance.

Les taux de mortalité infantile selon l'âge et le sexe appellent en outre toutes les réserves qui ont été formulées à propos des statistiques des naissances vivantes qui ont servi à leur calcul (voir à ce sujet les notes techniques relatives au tableau 9). Ces insuffisances ont également été examinées dans les notes techniques relatives au tableau 15.

Il convient de signaler aussi que les taux de mortalité infantile selon l'âge peuvent être gravement faussés par la pratique qui consiste à ne pas classer dans les naissances vivantes et ensuite dans les décès d'enfants de moins d'un an les enfants nés vivants mais décédés soit avant l'enregistrement de leur naissance, soit dans les 24 heures qui ont suivi la naissance, et par les problèmes que pose le calcul de l'âge de l'enfant au moment du décès. Ces facteurs, qui ont été décrits plus haut, peuvent fausser les statistiques concernant certains groupes d'âge plus que d'autres. Si le nombre des décès d'enfants de moins d'un an pour chaque groupe d'âge est sous-estimé ou surestimé, les taux correspondants pour chacun de ces groupes d'âge seront eux aussi sous-estimés ou surestimés. Les risques de sous-estimation sont plus grands pour les groupes les plus jeunes ; c'est pour le groupe d'âge le plus jeune de tous (moins d'un jour) que les données risquent de comporter les plus grosses erreurs.

Données publiées antérieurement : des statistiques des décès d'enfants de moins d'un an et des taux de mortalité infantile selon l'âge et le sexe ont déjà été présentées dans des éditions antérieures de l'*Annuaire démographique*. Pour plus de précisions concernant les années pour lesquelles ces données ont été publiées, se reporter à l'index historique.

16. Infant deaths and infant mortality rates by age and sex: latest available year, 2003 - 2012
Décès d'enfants de moins d'un an et taux de mortalité infantile selon l'âge et le sexe : dernière année disponible, 2003 - 2012

Continent, country or area, year and age / Continent, pays ou zone, année et âge	Number - Nombre			Rate - Taux		
	Both sexes Les deux sexes	Male Masculin	Female Féminin	Both sexes Les deux sexes	Male Masculin	Female Féminin
AFRICA - AFRIQUE						
Cabo Verde						
2008 (C)						
Total...	316	...	...	24.9	...	...
Less than 7 days - Moins de 7 jours.................................	160	...	...	12.6	...	...
7 - 27 days - 7 - 27 jours.................................	52	...	...	4.1	...	...
28 days - 11 months - 28 jours - 11 mois.................................	104	...	...	8.2	...	...
Egypt - Égypte						
2011 (C)						
Total...	35 997	19 385	16 612	14.7	15.5	14.0
Less than 1 day - Moins de 1 jour	-	-	-	-	-	-
1 - 6 days - 1 - 6 jours	7 246	4 177	3 069	3.0	3.3	2.6
7 - 27 days - 7 - 27 jours	8 539	4 845	3 694	3.5	3.9	3.1
7 - 13 days - 7 - 13 jours	4 163	2 373	1 790	1.7	1.9	1.5
14 - 20 days - 14 - 20 jours	2 725	1 541	1 184	1.1	1.2	1.0
21 - 27 days - 21 - 27 jours	1 651	931	720	0.7	0.7	0.6
28 days - 11 months - 28 jours - 11 mois.................................	20 212	10 363	9 849	8.3	8.3	8.3
28 days - less than 2 months - 28 jours - moins de 2 mois	4 735	2 522	2 213	1.9	2.0	1.9
2 months - 2 mois.................................	3 400	1 668	1 732	1.4	1.3	1.5
3 months - 3 mois.................................	2 637	1 340	1 297	1.1	1.1	1.1
4 months - 4 mois.................................	2 067	1 084	983	0.8	0.9	0.8
5 months - 5 mois.................................	1 584	746	838	0.6	0.6	0.7
6 months - 6 mois.................................	1 500	715	785	0.6	0.6	0.7
7 months - 7 mois.................................	1 367	821	546	0.6	0.7	0.5
8 months - 8 mois.................................	924	446	478	0.4	0.4	0.4
9 months - 9 mois.................................	858	417	441	0.4	0.3	0.4
10 months - 10 mois.................................	688	343	345	0.3	0.3	0.3
11 months - 11 mois.................................	452	261	191	0.2	0.2	0.2
Mauritius - Maurice[1]						
2011 (+C)						
Total...	189	102	87	12.9	13.7	12.0
Less than 1 day - Moins de 1 jour	25	9	16	♦1.7	♦1.2	♦2.2
1 - 6 days - 1 - 6 jours	70	40	30	4.8	5.4	4.1
7 - 27 days - 7 - 27 jours	48	30	18	3.3	4.0	♦2.5
7 - 13 days - 7 - 13 jours	19	13	6	♦1.3	♦1.7	♦0.8
14 - 20 days - 14 - 20 jours	14	6	8	♦1.0	♦0.8	♦1.1
21 - 27 days - 21 - 27 jours	15	11	4	♦1.0	♦1.5	♦0.6
28 days - 11 months - 28 jours - 11 mois.................................	46	23	23	3.1	♦3.1	♦3.2
28 days - less than 2 months - 28 jours - moins de 2 mois	21	12	9	♦1.4	♦1.6	♦1.2
2 months - 2 mois.................................	9	3	6	♦0.6	♦0.4	♦0.8
3 months - 3 mois.................................	4	2	2	♦0.3	♦0.3	♦0.3
4 months - 4 mois.................................	1	1	-	♦0.1	♦0.1	-
5 months - 5 mois.................................	-	-	-	-	-	-
6 months - 6 mois.................................	3	1	2	♦0.2	♦0.1	♦0.3
7 months - 7 mois.................................	2	-	2	♦0.1	-	♦0.3
8 months - 8 mois.................................	1	1	-	♦0.1	♦0.1	-
9 months - 9 mois.................................	2	1	1	♦0.1	♦0.1	♦0.1
10 months - 10 mois.................................	2	2	-	♦0.1	♦0.3	-
11 months - 11 mois.................................	1	-	1	♦0.1	-	♦0.1
Unknown - Inconnu	-	-	-	-	-	-
Réunion[2]						
2007 (C)						
Total...	91	48	43	...	...	...
Less than 1 day - Moins de 1 jour	24	14	10	...	...	...
1 - 6 days - 1 - 6 jours	20	9	11	...	...	...
7 - 27 days - 7 - 27 jours	18	7	11	...	...	...
7 - 13 days - 7 - 13 jours	7	3	4	...	...	...
14 - 20 days - 14 - 20 jours	9	2	7	...	...	...
21 - 27 days - 21 - 27 jours	7	2	5	...	...	...
28 days - 11 months - 28 jours - 11 mois.................................	30	18	12	...	...	...
Saint Helena ex. dep. - Sainte-Hélène sans dép.						
2012 (C)						
Total...	1	-	1	...	...	...
Less than 1 day - Moins de 1 jour	-	-	-	...	...	...
1 - 6 days - 1 - 6 jours	1	-	1	...	...	...
7 - 27 days - 7 - 27 jours	-	-	-	...	...	...
7 - 13 days - 7 - 13 jours	-	-	-	...	...	...
14 - 20 days - 14 - 20 jours	-	-	-	...	...	...
21 - 27 days - 21 - 27 jours	-	-	-	...	...	...

Continent, country or area, year and age / Continent, pays ou zone, année et âge	Number - Nombre			Rate - Taux		
	Both sexes Les deux sexes	Male Masculin	Female Féminin	Both sexes Les deux sexes	Male Masculin	Female Féminin
AFRICA - AFRIQUE						
Saint Helena ex. dep. - Sainte-Hélène sans dép.						
2012 (C)						
28 days - 11 months - 28 jours - 11 mois	-	-	-	...	...	...
28 days - less than 2 months - 28 jours - moins de 2 mois	-	-	-	...	...	...
2 months - 2 mois	-	-	-	...	...	...
3 months - 3 mois	-	-	-	...	...	...
4 months - 4 mois	-	-	-	...	...	...
5 months - 5 mois	-	-	-	...	...	...
6 months - 6 mois	-	-	-	...	...	...
7 months - 7 mois	-	-	-	...	...	...
8 months - 8 mois	-	-	-	...	...	...
9 months - 9 mois	-	-	-	...	...	...
10 months - 10 mois	-	-	-	...	...	...
11 months - 11 mois	-	-	-	...	...	...
Seychelles						
2006 (+C)						
Total	14	5	9	...	...	...
Less than 1 day - Moins de 1 jour	5	1	4	...	...	...
1 - 6 days - 1 - 6 jours	2	1	1	...	...	...
7 - 27 days - 7 - 27 jours	2	-	2	...	...	...
7 - 13 days - 7 - 13 jours	1	-	1	...	...	...
14 - 20 days - 14 - 20 jours	-	-	-	...	...	...
21 - 27 days - 21 - 27 jours	1	-	1	...	...	...
28 days - 11 months - 28 jours - 11 mois	5	3	2	...	...	...
28 days - less than 2 months - 28 jours - moins de 2 mois	1	1	-	...	...	...
2 months - 2 mois	-	-	-	...	...	...
3 months - 3 mois	-	-	-	...	...	...
4 months - 4 mois	1	-	1	...	...	...
5 months - 5 mois	2	2	-	...	...	...
6 months - 6 mois	1	-	1	...	...	...
7 months - 7 mois	-	-	-	...	...	...
8 months - 8 mois	-	-	-	...	...	...
9 months - 9 mois	-	-	-	...	...	...
10 months - 10 mois	-	-	-	...	...	...
11 months - 11 mois	-	-	-	...	...	...
South Africa - Afrique du Sud[3]						
2006 (...)						
Total	47 703	25 178[4]	21 810[4]	...	...	...
Less than 1 day - Moins de 1 jour	2 422	1 387[4]	969[4]	...	...	...
1 - 6 days - 1 - 6 jours	7 217	4 146[4]	2 892[4]	...	...	...
7 - 27 days - 7 - 27 jours	3 640	1 991[4]	1 568[4]	...	...	...
7 - 13 days - 7 - 13 jours	1 613	912[4]	667[4]	...	...	...
14 - 20 days - 14 - 20 jours	1 074	589[4]	460[4]	...	...	...
21 - 27 days - 21 - 27 jours	953	490[4]	441[4]	...	...	...
28 days - 11 months - 28 jours - 11 mois	34 424	17 654	16 381	...	...	...
28 days - less than 2 months - 28 jours - moins de 2 mois	4 770	2 509[4]	2 175[4]	...	...	...
2 months - 2 mois	5 786	2 784[4]	2 934[4]	...	...	...
3 months - 3 mois	5 472	2 783[4]	2 621[4]	...	...	...
4 months - 4 mois	3 711	1 958[4]	1 714[4]	...	...	...
5 months - 5 mois	3 041	1 548[4]	1 465[4]	...	...	...
6 months - 6 mois	2 704	1 393[4]	1 281[4]	...	...	...
7 months - 7 mois	2 258	1 181[4]	1 059[4]	...	...	...
8 months - 8 mois	1 948	1 020[4]	910[4]	...	...	...
9 months - 9 mois	1 811	954[4]	841[4]	...	...	...
10 months - 10 mois	1 544	803[4]	730[4]	...	...	...
11 months - 11 mois	1 379	721[4]	651[4]	...	...	...
AMERICA, NORTH - AMÉRIQUE DU NORD						
Aruba						
2007 (+U)						
Total	4	2	2	...	...	...
Less than 1 day - Moins de 1 jour	-	-	-	...	...	...
1 - 6 days - 1 - 6 jours	2	1	1	...	...	...
7 - 27 days - 7 - 27 jours	1	1	-	...	...	...
7 - 13 days - 7 - 13 jours	1	1	-	...	...	...

16. Infant deaths and infant mortality rates by age and sex: latest available year, 2003 - 2012
Décès d'enfants de moins d'un an et taux de mortalité infantile selon l'âge et le sexe : dernière année disponible, 2003 - 2012 (continued - suite)

Continent, country or area, year and age Continent, pays ou zone, année et âge	Number - Nombre			Rate - Taux		
	Both sexes Les deux sexes	Male Masculin	Female Féminin	Both sexes Les deux sexes	Male Masculin	Female Féminin
AMERICA, NORTH - AMÉRIQUE DU NORD						
Aruba						
2007 (+U)						
14 - 27 days - 14 - 27 jours	-	-	-	...	...	...
28 days - 11 months - 28 jours - 11 mois	1	-	1	...	...	...
28 days - less than 2 months - 28 jours - moins de 2 mois	-	-	-	...	...	...
2 - 9 months - 2 - 9 mois	-	-	-	...	...	...
10 months - 10 mois	1	-	1	...	...	...
11 months - 11 mois	-	-	-	...	...	...
Bahamas						
2011* (+C)						
Total	48	26	22	...	...	...
Less than 1 day - Moins de 1 jour	-	-	-	...	...	...
1 - 6 days - 1 - 6 jours	18	9	9	...	...	...
7 - 27 days - 7 - 27 jours	11	8	3	...	...	...
7 - 13 days - 7 - 13 jours	6	5	1	...	...	...
14 - 20 days - 14 - 20 jours	3	2	1	...	...	...
21 - 27 days - 21 - 27 jours	2	1	1	...	...	...
28 days - 11 months - 28 jours - 11 mois	19	9	10	...	...	...
28 days - less than 2 months - 28 jours - moins de 2 mois	7	2	5	...	...	...
2 months - 2 mois	-	-	-	...	...	...
3 months - 3 mois	3	2	1	...	...	...
4 months - 4 mois	3	2	1	...	...	...
5 months - 5 mois	1	-	1	...	...	...
6 months - 6 mois	-	-	-	...	...	...
7 months - 7 mois	-	-	-	...	...	...
8 months - 8 mois	1	1	-	...	...	...
9 months - 9 mois	1	1	-	...	...	...
10 months - 10 mois	1	-	1	...	...	...
11 months - 11 mois	2	1	1	...	...	...
Unknown - Inconnu	-	-	-	...	...	...
Barbados - Barbade						
2007 (+C)						
Total	31	18	13	...	...	...
Less than 1 day - Moins de 1 jour	-	1	1	...	...	...
1 - 6 days - 1 - 6 jours	10	8	18	...	...	...
7 - 27 days - 7 - 27 jours	6	4	2	...	...	...
7 - 20 days - 7 - 20 jours	6	4	2	...	...	...
21 - 27 days - 21 - 27 jours	-	-	-	...	...	...
28 days - 11 months - 28 jours - 11 mois	4	2	2	...	...	...
28 days - 2 months - 28 jours - 2 mois	3	2	1	...	...	...
3 - 4 months - 3 - 4 mois	1	-	1	...	...	...
5 - 11 months - 5 - 11 mois	-	-	-	...	...	...
Unknown - Inconnu	2	2	-	...	...	...
Bermuda - Bermudes						
2011 (C)						
Total	-	-	-	...	...	...
Canada[5]						
2006 (C)						
Total	1 771	983	788	5.0	5.4	4.6
Less than 1 day - Moins de 1 jour	888	481	407	2.5	2.6	2.4
1 - 6 days - 1 - 6 jours	194	110	84	0.5	0.6	0.5
7 - 27 days - 7 - 27 jours	214	123	91	0.6	0.7	0.5
7 - 13 days - 7 - 13 jours	110	62	48	0.3	0.3	0.3
14 - 20 days - 14 - 20 jours	60	34	26	0.2	0.2	♦0.2
21 - 27 days - 21 - 27 jours	44	27	17	0.1	♦0.1	♦0.1
28 days - 11 months - 28 jours - 11 mois	475	269	206	1.3	1.5	1.2
28 days - less than 2 months - 28 jours - moins de 2 mois	141	80	61	0.4	0.4	0.4
2 months - 2 mois	78	42	36	0.2	0.2	0.2
3 months - 3 mois	60	37	23	0.2	0.2	♦0.1
4 months - 4 mois	55	33	22	0.2	0.2	♦0.1
5 months - 5 mois	42	21	21	0.1	♦0.1	♦0.1
6 months - 6 mois	24	16	8	♦0.1	♦0.1	-
7 months - 7 mois	19	9	10	♦0.1	-	♦0.1
8 months - 8 mois	19	14	5	♦0.1	♦0.1	-
9 months - 9 mois	18	8	10	♦0.1	-	♦0.1
10 months - 10 mois	9	4	5	-	-	-
11 months - 11 mois	10	5	5	-	-	-

16. Infant deaths and infant mortality rates by age and sex: latest available year, 2003 - 2012
Décès d'enfants de moins d'un an et taux de mortalité infantile selon l'âge et le sexe : dernière année disponible, 2003 - 2012 (continued - suite)

Continent, country or area, year and age / Continent, pays ou zone, année et âge	Number - Nombre			Rate - Taux		
	Both sexes Les deux sexes	Male Masculin	Female Féminin	Both sexes Les deux sexes	Male Masculin	Female Féminin
AMERICA, NORTH - AMÉRIQUE DU NORD						
Cayman Islands - Îles Caïmanes						
2007 (C)						
Total	5	4	1	...	...	...
Less than 1 day - Moins de 1 jour	3	2	1	...	...	...
1 - 6 days - 1 - 6 jours	2	2	-	...	...	...
7 - 27 days - 7 - 27 jours	-	-	-	...	...	...
28 days - 11 months - 28 jours - 11 mois	-	-	-	...	...	...
Cost.. Rica						
2011* (C)						
Total	666	374	292	9.1	9.9	8.2
Less than 1 day - Moins de 1 jour	217	120	97	3.0	3.2	2.7
1 - 6 days - 1 - 6 jours	161	91	70	2.2	2.4	2.0
7 - 27 days - 7 - 27 jours	102	68	34	1.4	1.8	0.9
7 - 13 days - 7 - 13 jours	47	32	15	0.6	0.8	♦0.4
14 - 20 days - 14 - 20 jours	31	21	10	0.4	♦0.6	♦0.3
21 - 27 days - 21 - 27 jours	24	15	9	♦0.3	♦0.4	♦0.3
28 days - 11 months - 28 jours - 11 mois	171	90	81	2.3	2.4	2.3
28 days - less than 2 months - 28 jours - moins de 2 mois	47	25	22	0.6	♦0.7	♦0.6
2 months - 2 mois	25	15	10	♦0.3	♦0.4	♦0.3
3 months - 3 mois	20	8	12	♦0.3	♦0.2	♦0.3
4 months - 4 mois	18	10	8	♦0.2	♦0.3	♦0.2
5 months - 5 mois	15	8	7	♦0.2	♦0.2	♦0.2
6 months - 6 mois	15	7	8	♦0.2	♦0.2	♦0.2
7 months - 7 mois	6	2	4	♦0.1	♦0.1	♦0.1
8 months - 8 mois	5	3	2	♦0.1	♦0.1	♦0.1
9 months - 9 mois	7	5	2	♦0.1	♦0.1	♦0.1
10 months - 10 mois	8	4	4	♦0.1	♦0.1	♦0.1
11 months - 11 mois	5	3	2	♦0.1	♦0.1	♦0.1
Unknown - Inconnu	15	5	10	♦0.2	♦0.1	♦0.3
Cuba						
2011* (C)						
Total	653	375	278	4.9	5.5	4.3
Less than 1 day - Moins de 1 jour	74	45	29	0.6	0.7	♦0.4
1 - 6 days - 1 - 6 jours	174	109	65	1.3	1.6	1.0
7 - 27 days - 7 - 27 jours	145	80	65	1.1	1.2	1.0
7 - 13 days - 7 - 13 jours	78	44	34	0.6	0.6	0.5
14 - 20 days - 14 - 20 jours	49	27	22	0.4	♦0.4	♦0.3
21 - 27 days - 21 - 27 jours	18	9	9	♦0.1	♦0.1	♦0.1
28 days - 11 months - 28 jours - 11 mois	260	141	119	2.0	2.1	1.8
28 days - less than 2 months - 28 jours - moins de 2 mois	88	51	37	0.7	0.7	0.6
2 months - 2 mois	46	23	23	0.3	♦0.3	♦0.4
3 months - 3 mois	28	15	13	♦0.2	♦0.2	♦0.2
4 months - 4 mois	26	13	13	♦0.2	♦0.2	♦0.2
5 months - 5 mois	13	6	7	♦0.1	♦0.1	♦0.1
6 months - 6 mois	13	7	6	♦0.1	♦0.1	♦0.1
7 months - 7 mois	9	7	2	♦0.1	♦0.1	-
8 months - 8 mois	12	6	6	♦0.1	♦0.1	♦0.1
9 months - 9 mois	9	5	4	♦0.1	♦0.1	♦0.1
10 months - 10 mois	10	5	5	♦0.1	♦0.1	♦0.1
11 months - 11 mois	6	3	3	-	-	-
Curaçao						
2011 (C)						
Total	15	6	9	...	...	...
Less than 1 day - Moins de 1 jour	3	2	1	...	...	...
1 - 6 days - 1 - 6 jours	5	1	4	...	...	...
7 - 27 days - 7 - 27 jours	2	2	-	...	...	...
7 - 13 days - 7 - 13 jours	1	1	-	...	...	...
14 - 20 days - 14 - 20 jours	1	1	-	...	...	...
21 - 27 days - 21 - 27 jours	-	-	-	...	...	...
28 days - 11 months - 28 jours - 11 mois	5	1	4	...	...	...
28 days - less than 2 months - 28 jours - moins de 2 mois	2	-	2	...	...	...
2 months - 2 mois	-	-	-	...	...	...
3 months - 3 mois	1	-	1	...	...	...
4 months - 4 mois	2	1	1	...	...	...
5 months - 5 mois	-	-	-	...	...	...
6 months - 6 mois	-	-	-	...	...	...
7 months - 7 mois	-	-	-	...	...	...
8 months - 8 mois	-	-	-	...	...	...

16. Infant deaths and infant mortality rates by age and sex: latest available year, 2003 - 2012
Décès d'enfants de moins d'un an et taux de mortalité infantile selon l'âge et le sexe : dernière année disponible, 2003 - 2012 (continued - suite)

Continent, country or area, year and age / Continent, pays ou zone, année et âge	Number - Nombre			Rate - Taux		
	Both sexes Les deux sexes	Male Masculin	Female Féminin	Both sexes Les deux sexes	Male Masculin	Female Féminin
AMERICA, NORTH - AMÉRIQUE DU NORD						
Curaçao						
2011 (C)						
9 months - 9 mois	-	-	-	...	...	...
10 months - 10 mois	-	-	-	...	...	...
11 months - 11 mois	-	-	-	...	...	...
Unknown - Inconnu	-	-	-	...	...	...
Dominican Republic - République dominicaine						
2011 (U)						
Total	672	435	237	...	...	...
Less than 1 day - Moins de 1 jour	98	65	33	...	...	...
1 - 6 days - 1 - 6 jours	80	62	18	...	...	...
7 - 27 days - 7 - 27 jours	67	38	29	...	...	...
7 - 13 days - 7 - 13 jours	33	18	15	...	...	...
14 - 20 days - 14 - 20 jours	13	7	6	...	...	...
21 - 27 days - 21 - 27 jours	21	14	7	...	...	...
28 days - 11 months - 28 jours - 11 mois	132	68	64	...	...	...
28 days - less than 2 months - 28 jours - moins de 2 mois	31	15	16	...	...	...
2 months - 2 mois	22	10	12	...	...	...
3 months - 3 mois	13	7	6	...	...	...
4 months - 4 mois	9	7	2	...	...	...
5 months - 5 mois	10	4	6	...	...	...
6 months - 6 mois	9	6	3	...	...	...
7 months - 7 mois	8	6	2	...	...	...
8 months - 8 mois	6	3	3	...	...	...
9 months - 9 mois	9	5	4	...	...	...
10 months - 10 mois	8	2	6	...	...	...
11 months - 11 mois	7	3	4	...	...	...
Unknown - Inconnu	295	201	94	...	...	...
El Salvador[6]						
2011 (C)						
Total	826	461	365	7.6	8.1	7.0
Less than 1 day - Moins de 1 jour	120	67	53	1.1	1.2	1.0
1 - 6 days - 1 - 6 jours	145	83	62	1.3	1.5	1.2
7 - 27 days - 7 - 27 jours	132	72	60	1.2	1.3	1.1
7 - 13 days - 7 - 13 jours	64	35	29	0.6	0.6	♦0.6
14 - 20 days - 14 - 20 jours	35	17	18	0.3	♦0.3	♦0.3
21 - 27 days - 21 - 27 jours	33	20	13	0.3	♦0.4	♦0.2
28 days - 11 months - 28 jours - 11 mois	429	239	190	3.9	4.2	3.6
28 days - less than 2 months - 28 jours - moins de 2 mois	118	68	50	1.1	1.2	1.0
2 months - 2 mois	69	37	32	0.6	0.6	0.6
3 months - 3 mois	53	30	23	0.5	0.5	♦0.4
4 months - 4 mois	40	25	15	0.4	♦0.4	♦0.3
5 months - 5 mois	31	18	13	0.3	♦0.3	♦0.2
6 months - 6 mois	25	10	15	♦0.2	♦0.2	♦0.3
7 months - 7 mois	20	12	8	♦0.2	♦0.2	♦0.2
8 months - 8 mois	19	10	9	♦0.2	♦0.2	♦0.2
9 months - 9 mois	17	10	7	♦0.2	♦0.2	♦0.1
10 months - 10 mois	16	8	8	♦0.1	♦0.1	♦0.2
11 months - 11 mois	21	11	10	♦0.2	♦0.2	♦0.2
Greenland - Groenland[3]						
2006 (C)						
Total	13	7	6	...	...	...
Less than 1 day - Moins de 1 jour	8	5	3	...	...	...
1 - 6 days - 1 - 6 jours	-	-	-	...	...	...
7 - 27 days - 7 - 27 jours	-	-	-	...	...	...
28 days - 11 months - 28 jours - 11 mois	5	2	3	...	...	...
28 days - less than 2 months - 28 jours - moins de 2 mois	5	2	3	...	...	...
2 - 11 months - 2 - 11 mois	-	-	-	...	...	...
Guadeloupe[2]						
2003 (C)						
Total	56	34	22	...	...	...
Less than 1 day - Moins de 1 jour	13	5	8	...	...	...
1 - 6 days - 1 - 6 jours	8	4	4	...	...	...
7 - 27 days - 7 - 27 jours	19	12	7	...	...	...
7 - 13 days - 7 - 13 jours	5	3	2	...	...	...
14 - 20 days - 14 - 20 jours	10	5	5	...	...	...
21 - 27 days - 21 - 27 jours	4	4	-	...	...	...

16. Infant deaths and infant mortality rates by age and sex: latest available year, 2003 - 2012
Décès d'enfants de moins d'un an et taux de mortalité infantile selon l'âge et le sexe : dernière année disponible, 2003 - 2012 (continued - suite)

Continent, country or area, year and age Continent, pays ou zone, année et âge	Number - Nombre			Rate - Taux		
	Both sexes Les deux sexes	Male Masculin	Female Féminin	Both sexes Les deux sexes	Male Masculin	Female Féminin
AMERICA, NORTH - AMÉRIQUE DU NORD						
Guadeloupe[2]						
2003 (C)						
28 days - 11 months - 28 jours - 11 mois	16	13	3	...	...	...
28 days - less than 2 months - 28 jours - moins de 2 mois	7	6	1	...	...	...
2 months - 2 mois	4	2	2	...	...	...
3 months - 3 mois	3	3	-	...	...	...
4 months - 4 mois	1	1	-	...	...	...
5 months - 5 mois	-	-	-	...	...	...
6 months - 6 mois	1	1	-	...	...	...
7 months - 7 mois	-	-	-	...	...	...
8 months - 8 mois	-	-	-	...	...	...
9 months - 9 mois	-	-	-	...	...	...
10 months - 10 mois	-	-	-	...	...	...
11 months - 11 mois	-	-	-	...	...	...
Guatemala						
2011 (C)						
Total	7 413	4 202	3 211	19.8	22.1	17.5
Less than 1 day - Moins de 1 jour	123	76	47	0.3	0.4	0.3
1 - 6 days - 1 - 6 jours	1 481	860	621	4.0	4.5	3.4
7 - 27 days - 7 - 27 jours	1 684	938	746	4.5	4.9	4.1
7 - 13 days - 7 - 13 jours	813	451	362	2.2	2.4	2.0
14 - 20 days - 14 - 20 jours	521	288	233	1.4	1.5	1.3
21 - 27 days - 21 - 27 jours	350	199	151	0.9	1.0	0.8
28 days - 11 months - 28 jours - 11 mois	4 125	2 328	1 797	11.0	12.3	9.8
28 days - less than 2 months - 28 jours - moins de 2 mois	1 198	694	504	3.2	3.7	2.7
2 months - 2 mois	685	396	289	1.8	2.1	1.6
3 months - 3 mois	475	283	192	1.3	1.5	1.0
4 months - 4 mois	345	196	149	0.9	1.0	0.8
5 months - 5 mois	290	159	131	0.8	0.8	0.7
6 months - 6 mois	265	146	119	0.7	0.8	0.6
7 months - 7 mois	245	129	116	0.7	0.7	0.6
8 months - 8 mois	200	102	98	0.5	0.5	0.5
9 months - 9 mois	207	115	92	0.6	0.6	0.5
10 months - 10 mois	209	107	102	0.6	0.6	0.6
11 months - 11 mois	6	1	5	-	-	-
Unknown - Inconnu	-	-	-			
Martinique[7]						
2007 (C)						
Total	43	26	17	...	...	...
Less than 1 day - Moins de 1 jour	18	10	8	...	...	...
1 - 6 days - 1 - 6 jours	8	7	1	...	...	...
7 - 27 days - 7 - 27 jours	9	3	6	...	...	...
7 - 13 days - 7 - 13 jours	5	1	4	...	...	...
14 - 20 days - 14 - 20 jours	3	2	1	...	...	...
21 - 27 days - 21 - 27 jours	1	-	1	...	...	...
28 days - 11 months - 28 jours - 11 mois	8	6	2	...	...	...
28 days - less than 2 months - 28 jours - moins de 2 mois	-	-	-	...	...	...
2 months - 2 mois	5	3	2	...	...	...
3 months - 3 mois	-	-	-	...	...	...
4 months - 4 mois	1	1	-	...	...	...
5 months - 5 mois	-	-	-	...	...	...
6 months - 6 mois	-	-	-	...	...	...
7 months - 7 mois	1	1	-	...	...	...
8 months - 8 mois	-	-	-	...	...	...
9 - 11 months - 9 - 11 mois	1	1	-	...	...	...
Mexico - Mexique[8]						
2011 (+U)						
Total	29 037	16 148[4]	12 754[4]	...	...	...
Less than 1 day - Moins de 1 jour	5 773	3 219[4]	2 481[4]	...	...	...
1 - 6 days - 1 - 6 jours	6 980	3 966[4]	2 996[4]	...	...	...
7 - 27 days - 7 - 27 jours	5 474	3 067[4]	2 401[4]	...	...	...
7 - 13 days - 7 - 13 jours	2 879	1 649[4]	1 226[4]	...	...	...
14 - 20 days - 14 - 20 jours	1 565	871	694	...	...	...
21 - 27 days - 21 - 27 jours	1 030	547[4]	481[4]	...	...	...
28 days - 11 months - 28 jours - 11 mois	10 778	5 894	4 876	...	...	...
28 days - less than 2 months - 28 jours - moins de 2 mois	3 302	1 793[4]	1 505[4]	...	...	...
2 months - 2 mois	1 922	1 104[4]	817[4]	...	...	...

16. Infant deaths and infant mortality rates by age and sex: latest available year, 2003 - 2012
Décès d'enfants de moins d'un an et taux de mortalité infantile selon l'âge et le sexe : dernière année disponible, 2003 - 2012 (continued - suite)

Continent, country or area, year and age / Continent, pays ou zone, année et âge	Number - Nombre			Rate - Taux		
	Both sexes Les deux sexes	Male Masculin	Female Féminin	Both sexes Les deux sexes	Male Masculin	Female Féminin
AMERICA, NORTH - AMÉRIQUE DU NORD						
Mexico - Mexique[8]						
2011 (+U)						
3 months - 3 mois	1 362	747[4]	612[4]	...	...	...
4 months - 4 mois	950	523	427	...	...	...
5 months - 5 mois	732	383	349	...	...	...
6 months - 6 mois	602	324	278	...	...	...
7 months - 7 mois	485	259	226	...	...	...
8 months - 8 mois	420	225	195	...	...	...
9 months - 9 mois	361	201	160	...	...	...
10 months - 10 mois	323	161	162	...	...	...
11 months - 11 mois	319	174	145	...	...	...
Unknown - Inconnu	2	2	-	...	...	...
Montserrat						
2011 (+C)						
Total	-	-	-	...	...	...
Less than 1 day - Moins de 1 jour	-	-	-	...	...	...
1 - 6 days - 1 - 6 jours	-	-	-	...	...	...
7 - 27 days - 7 - 27 jours	-	-	-	...	...	...
7 - 13 days - 7 - 13 jours	-	-	-	...	...	...
14 - 20 days - 14 - 20 jours	-	-	-	...	...	...
21 - 27 days - 21 - 27 jours	-	-	-	...	...	...
28 days - 11 months - 28 jours - 11 mois	-	-	-	...	...	...
28 days - less than 2 months - 28 jours - moins de 2 mois	-	-	-	...	...	...
2 months - 2 mois	-	-	-	...	...	...
3 months - 3 mois	-	-	-	...	...	...
4 months - 4 mois	-	-	-	...	...	...
5 months - 5 mois	-	-	-	...	...	...
6 months - 6 mois	-	-	-	...	...	...
7 months - 7 mois	-	-	-	...	...	...
8 months - 8 mois	-	-	-	...	...	...
9 months - 9 mois	-	-	-	...	...	...
10 months - 10 mois	-	-	-	...	...	...
11 months - 11 mois	-	-	-	...	...	...
Nicaragua						
2008 (+U)						
Total	1 932	1 123	809	...	...	...
Less than 1 day - Moins de 1 jour	386	219	167	...	...	...
1 - 6 days - 1 - 6 jours	664	418	246	...	...	...
7 - 27 days - 7 - 27 jours	277	151	126	...	...	...
7 - 13 days - 7 - 13 jours	156	89	67	...	...	...
14 - 20 days - 14 - 20 jours	74	41	33	...	...	...
21 - 27 days - 21 - 27 jours	47	21	26	...	...	...
28 days - 11 months - 28 jours - 11 mois	591	326	265	...	...	...
28 days - less than 2 months - 28 jours - moins de 2 mois	169	86	83	...	...	...
2 months - 2 mois	116	74	42	...	...	...
3 months - 3 mois	66	38	28	...	...	...
4 months - 4 mois	49	29	20	...	...	...
5 months - 5 mois	45	22	23	...	...	...
6 months - 6 mois	27	13	14	...	...	...
7 months - 7 mois	36	18	18	...	...	...
8 months - 8 mois	27	17	10	...	...	...
9 months - 9 mois	18	8	10	...	...	...
10 months - 10 mois	21	9	12	...	...	...
11 months - 11 mois	17	12	5	...	...	...
Panama						
2010 (U)						
Total	910	510	400	...	...	...
Less than 1 day - Moins de 1 jour	101	51	50	...	...	...
1 - 6 days - 1 - 6 jours	215	124	91	...	...	...
7 - 27 days - 7 - 27 jours	144	78	66	...	...	...
7 - 13 days - 7 - 13 jours	62	42	20	...	...	...
14 - 20 days - 14 - 20 jours	41	17	24	...	...	...
21 - 27 days - 21 - 27 jours	41	19	22	...	...	...
28 days - 11 months - 28 jours - 11 mois	450	257	193	...	...	...
28 days - less than 2 months - 28 jours - moins de 2 mois	112	67	45	...	...	...
2 months - 2 mois	72	46	26	...	...	...
3 months - 3 mois	51	25	26	...	...	...
4 months - 4 mois	38	26	12	...	...	...

16. Infant deaths and infant mortality rates by age and sex: latest available year, 2003 - 2012
Décès d'enfants de moins d'un an et taux de mortalité infantile selon l'âge et le sexe : dernière année disponible, 2003 - 2012 (continued - suite)

Continent, country or area, year and age Continent, pays ou zone, année et âge	Number - Nombre			Rate - Taux		
	Both sexes Les deux sexes	Male Masculin	Female Féminin	Both sexes Les deux sexes	Male Masculin	Female Féminin
AMERICA, NORTH - AMÉRIQUE DU NORD						
Panama						
2010 (U)						
5 months - 5 mois	38	18	20	...	...	...
6 months - 6 mois	29	16	13	...	...	...
7 months - 7 mois	21	12	9	...	...	...
8 months - 8 mois	31	17	14	...	...	...
9 months - 9 mois	23	11	12	...	...	...
10 months - 10 mois	14	9	5	...	...	...
11 months - 11 mois	21	10	11	...	...	...
Puerto Rico - Porto Rico						
2008 (C)						
Total	400	225	175	8.8	9.6	7.9
Less than 1 day - Moins de 1 jour	75	38	37	1.6	1.6	1.7
1 - 6 days - 1 - 6 jours	110	72	38	2.4	3.1	1.7
7 - 27 days - 7 - 27 jours	61	36	25	1.3	1.5	♦1.1
7 - 13 days - 7 - 13 jours	30	19	11	0.7	♦0.8	♦0.5
14 - 20 days - 14 - 20 jours	18	9	9	♦0.4	♦0.4	♦0.4
21 - 27 days - 21 - 27 jours	13	8	5	♦0.3	♦0.3	♦0.2
28 days - 11 months - 28 jours - 11 mois	96	44	52	2.1	1.9	2.3
28 days - less than 2 months - 28 jours - moins de 2 mois	5	3	2	♦0.1	♦0.1	♦0.1
2 - 11 months - 2 - 11 mois	91	41	50	2.0	1.7	2.2
Unknown - Inconnu	58	35	23	1.3	1.5	♦1.0
Saint Vincent and the Grenadines - Saint-Vincent-et-les Grenadines						
2005 (+C)						
Total	29	17	12	...	...	...
Less than 1 day - Moins de 1 jour	6	3	3	...	...	...
1 - 6 days - 1 - 6 jours	11	6	5	...	...	...
7 - 27 days - 7 - 27 jours	3	2	1	...	...	...
28 days - 11 months - 28 jours - 11 mois	9	6	3	...	...	...
28 days - less than 2 months - 28 jours - moins de 2 mois	-	-	-	...	...	...
2 - 11 months - 2 - 11 mois	9	6	3	...	...	...
United States of America - États-Unis d'Amérique						
2009 (C)						
Total	26 412	14 823	11 589	6.4	7.0	5.7
Less than 1 day - Moins de 1 jour	10 538	5 888	4 650	2.6	2.8	2.3
1 - 6 days - 1 - 6 jours	3 224	1 788	1 436	0.8	0.8	0.7
7 - 27 days - 7 - 27 jours	3 493	1 902	1 591	0.8	0.9	0.8
7 - 13 days - 7 - 13 jours	1 618	869	749	0.4	0.4	0.4
14 - 20 days - 14 - 20 jours	1 007	552	455	0.2	0.3	0.2
21 - 27 days - 21 - 27 jours	868	481	387	0.2	0.2	0.2
28 days - 11 months - 28 jours - 11 mois	9 157	5 245	3 912	2.2	2.5	1.9
28 days - less than 2 months - 28 jours - moins de 2 mois	2 499	1 449	1 050	0.6	0.7	0.5
2 months - 2 mois	1 731	1 003	728	0.4	0.5	0.4
3 months - 3 mois	1 252	724	528	0.3	0.3	0.3
4 months - 4 mois	930	521	409	0.2	0.2	0.2
5 months - 5 mois	713	416	297	0.2	0.2	0.1
6 months - 6 mois	540	319	221	0.1	0.2	0.1
7 months - 7 mois	462	270	192	0.1	0.1	0.1
8 months - 8 mois	330	168	162	0.1	0.1	0.1
9 months - 9 mois	274	151	123	0.1	0.1	0.1
10 months - 10 mois	205	116	89	-	0.1	-
11 months - 11 mois	221	108	113	0.1	0.1	0.1
AMERICA, SOUTH - AMÉRIQUE DU SUD						
Argentina - Argentine						
2006 (C)						
Total	8 986	5 063[4]	3 911[4]	12.9	14.1	11.7
Less than 7 days - Moins de 7 jours	4 312	2 465[4]	1 838[4]	6.2	6.8	5.5
7 - 27 days - 7 - 27 jours	1 591	898[4]	691[4]	2.3	2.5	2.1
28 days - 11 months - 28 jours - 11 mois	3 083	1 700[4]	1 382[4]	4.4	4.7	4.1
Brazil - Brésil[9]						
2011 (U)						
Total	32 184	17 995	14 189	...	...	...
Less than 1 day - Moins de 1 jour	7 521	4 269	3 252	...	...	...
1 - 6 days - 1 - 6 jours	8 949	5 176	3 773	...	...	...

16. Infant deaths and infant mortality rates by age and sex: latest available year, 2003 - 2012
Décès d'enfants de moins d'un an et taux de mortalité infantile selon l'âge et le sexe : dernière année disponible, 2003 - 2012 (continued - suite)

Continent, country or area, year and age / Continent, pays ou zone, année et âge	Number - Nombre			Rate - Taux		
	Both sexes Les deux sexes	Male Masculin	Female Féminin	Both sexes Les deux sexes	Male Masculin	Female Féminin
AMERICA, SOUTH - AMÉRIQUE DU SUD						
Brazil - Brésil[9]						
2011 (U)						
7 - 27 days - 7 - 27 jours	5 518	3 047	2 471	...	...	...
7 - 13 days - 7 - 13 jours	2 869	1 596	1 273	...	...	...
14 - 20 days - 14 - 20 jours	1 587	859	728	...	...	...
21 - 27 days - 21 - 27 jours	1 062	592	470	...	...	...
28 days - 11 months - 28 jours - 11 mois	10 196	5 503	4 693	...	...	...
28 days - less than 2 months - 28 jours - moins de 2 mois	3 200	1 765	1 435	...	...	...
2 months - 2 mois	1 719	943	776	...	...	...
3 months - 3 mois	1 235	672	563	...	...	...
4 months - 4 mois	845	459	386	...	...	...
5 months - 5 mois	733	388	345	...	...	...
6 months - 6 mois	581	300	281	...	...	...
7 months - 7 mois	475	253	222	...	...	...
8 months - 8 mois	405	195	210	...	...	...
9 months - 9 mois	378	207	171	...	...	...
10 months - 10 mois	323	163	160	...	...	...
11 months - 11 mois	302	158	144	...	...	...
Chile - Chili						
2010 (C)						
Total	1 862	1 038	824	7.4	8.1	6.7
Less than 1 day - Moins de 1 jour	678	387	291	2.7	3.0	2.4
1 - 6 days - 1 - 6 jours	310	185	125	1.2	1.4	1.0
7 - 27 days - 7 - 27 jours	295	165	130	1.2	1.3	1.1
7 - 13 days - 7 - 13 jours	160	91	69	0.6	0.7	0.6
14 - 20 days - 14 - 20 jours	88	50	38	0.4	0.4	0.3
21 - 27 days - 21 - 27 jours	47	24	23	0.2	◆0.2	◆0.2
28 days - 11 months - 28 jours - 11 mois	579	301	278	2.3	2.4	2.3
28 days - less than 2 months - 28 jours - moins de 2 mois	170	91	79	0.7	0.7	0.6
2 months - 2 mois	91	42	49	0.4	0.3	0.4
3 months - 3 mois	66	30	36	0.3	0.2	0.3
4 months - 4 mois	54	30	24	0.2	0.2	◆0.2
5 months - 5 mois	61	38	23	0.2	0.3	◆0.2
6 months - 6 mois	33	16	17	0.1	◆0.1	◆0.1
7 months - 7 mois	28	13	15	◆0.1	◆0.1	◆0.1
8 months - 8 mois	28	16	12	◆0.1	◆0.1	◆0.1
9 months - 9 mois	21	11	10	◆0.1	◆0.1	◆0.1
10 months - 10 mois	9	4	5	-	-	-
11 months - 11 mois	18	10	8	◆0.1	◆0.1	◆0.1
Unknown - Inconnu	-	-	-	-	-	-
Colombia - Colombie						
2011* (U)						
Total	7 060	3 944[4]	3 115[4]	...	...	...
Less than 1 day - Moins de 1 jour	1 473	823	650	...	...	...
1 - 6 days - 1 - 6 jours	1 587	914	673	...	...	...
7 - 27 days - 7 - 27 jours	1 531	827	704	...	...	...
28 days - 11 months - 28 jours - 11 mois	2 469	1 380	1 088	...	...	...
28 days - less than 2 months - 28 jours - moins de 2 mois	1 812	1 021	791	...	...	...
2 - 11 months - 2 - 11 mois	657	359[4]	297[4]	...	...	...
Ecuador - Équateur[10]						
2010 (U)						
Total	3 204	1 735	1 469	...	...	...
Less than 1 day - Moins de 1 jour	634	342	292	...	...	...
1 - 6 days - 1 - 6 jours	670	379	291	...	...	...
7 - 27 days - 7 - 27 jours	505	288	217	...	...	...
7 - 13 days - 7 - 13 jours	252	146	106	...	...	...
14 - 20 days - 14 - 20 jours	157	85	72	...	...	...
21 - 27 days - 21 - 27 jours	96	57	39	...	...	...
28 days - 11 months - 28 jours - 11 mois	1 395	726	669	...	...	...
28 days - less than 2 months - 28 jours - moins de 2 mois	225	121	104	...	...	...
2 months - 2 mois	243	134	109	...	...	...
3 months - 3 mois	160	92	68	...	...	...
4 months - 4 mois	148	73	75	...	...	...
5 months - 5 mois	114	58	56	...	...	...
6 months - 6 mois	118	62	56	...	...	...
7 months - 7 mois	96	43	53	...	...	...
8 months - 8 mois	87	37	50	...	...	...
9 months - 9 mois	82	43	39	...	...	...

16. Infant deaths and infant mortality rates by age and sex: latest available year, 2003 - 2012

Décès d'enfants de moins d'un an et taux de mortalité infantile selon l'âge et le sexe : dernière année disponible, 2003 - 2012 (continued - suite)

Continent, country or area, year and age / Continent, pays ou zone, année et âge	Number - Nombre			Rate - Taux		
	Both sexes Les deux sexes	Male Masculin	Female Féminin	Both sexes Les deux sexes	Male Masculin	Female Féminin
AMERICA, SOUTH - AMÉRIQUE DU SUD						
Ecuador - Équateur[10]						
2010 (U)						
10 months - 10 mois	64	33	31	...	...	...
11 months - 11 mois	58	30	28	...	...	...
French Guiana - Guyane française						
2007 (C)						
Total	73	39	34	...	...	...
Less than 1 day - Moins de 1 jour	18	10	8	...	...	...
1 - 6 days - 1 - 6 jours	15	5	10	...	...	...
7 - 27 days - 7 - 27 jours	17	12	5	...	...	...
7 - 13 days - 7 - 13 jours	9	5	4	...	...	...
14 - 20 days - 14 - 20 jours	3	3	-	...	...	...
21 - 27 days - 21 - 27 jours	5	4	1	...	...	...
28 days - 11 months - 28 jours - 11 mois	23	12	11	...	...	...
28 days - less than 2 months - 28 jours - moins de 2 mois	1	-	1	...	...	...
2 months - 2 mois	7	4	3	...	...	...
3 months - 3 mois	4	1	3	...	...	...
4 months - 4 mois	2	1	1	...	...	...
5 months - 5 mois	2	2	-	...	...	...
6 months - 6 mois	2	1	1	...	...	...
7 months - 7 mois	1	1	-	...	...	...
8 months - 8 mois	1	1	-	...	...	...
9 months - 9 mois	2	1	1	...	...	...
10 months - 10 mois	-	-	-	...	...	...
11 months - 11 mois	1	-	1	...	...	...
Paraguay						
2006 (U)						
Total	549	...	...	...	...	...
Less than 28 days - Moins de 28 jours	270	...	...	...	...	...
28 days - 11 months - 28 jours - 11 mois[11]	279	...	...	...	...	...
Peru - Pérou[12]						
2010 (+U)						
Total	5 287	2 911	2 376	...	...	...
Less than 1 day - Moins de 1 jour	892	515	377	...	...	...
1 - 6 days - 1 - 6 jours	1 238	712	526	...	...	...
7 - 27 days - 7 - 27 jours	823	436	387	...	...	...
7 - 13 days - 7 - 13 jours	402	212	190	...	...	...
14 - 20 days - 14 - 20 jours	246	132	114	...	...	...
21 - 27 days - 21 - 27 jours	175	92	83	...	...	...
28 days - 11 months - 28 jours - 11 mois	2 333	1 247	1 086	...	...	...
28 days - less than 2 months - 28 jours - moins de 2 mois	590	315	275	...	...	...
2 months - 2 mois	455	247	208	...	...	...
3 months - 3 mois	251	132	119	...	...	...
4 months - 4 mois	206	111	95	...	...	...
5 months - 5 mois	167	89	78	...	...	...
6 months - 6 mois	160	81	79	...	...	...
7 months - 7 mois	118	61	57	...	...	...
8 months - 8 mois	109	53	56	...	...	...
9 months - 9 mois	97	56	41	...	...	...
10 months - 10 mois	90	51	39	...	...	...
11 months - 11 mois	90	51	39	...	...	...
Unknown - Inconnu	1	1	-	...	...	...
Venezuela (Bolivarian Republic of) - Venezuela (République bolivarienne du)						
2007 (C)						
Total	6 340	3 715	2 625	10.3	11.7	8.8
Less than 28 days - Moins de 28 jours	4 379	2 599	1 780	7.1	8.2	6.0
28 days - 11 months - 28 jours - 11 mois	1 961	1 116	845	3.2	3.5	2.8
28 days - less than 2 months - 28 jours - moins de 2 mois	455	258	197	0.7	0.8	0.7
2 months - 2 mois	325	182	143	0.5	0.6	0.5
3 months - 3 mois	231	136	95	0.4	0.4	0.3
4 months - 4 mois	190	119	71	0.3	0.4	0.2
5 months - 5 mois	157	87	70	0.3	0.3	0.2
6 months - 6 mois	153	89	64	0.2	0.3	0.2
7 months - 7 mois	104	57	47	0.2	0.2	0.2
8 months - 8 mois	122	63	59	0.2	0.2	0.2
9 months - 9 mois	77	39	38	0.1	0.1	0.1

16. Infant deaths and infant mortality rates by age and sex: latest available year, 2003 - 2012
Décès d'enfants de moins d'un an et taux de mortalité infantile selon l'âge et le sexe : dernière année disponible, 2003 - 2012 (continued - suite)

Continent, country or area, year and age / Continent, pays ou zone, année et âge	Number - Nombre			Rate - Taux		
	Both sexes Les deux sexes	Male Masculin	Female Féminin	Both sexes Les deux sexes	Male Masculin	Female Féminin
AMERICA, SOUTH - AMÉRIQUE DU SUD						
Venezuela (Bolivarian Republic of) - Venezuela (République bolivarienne du)						
2007 (C)						
10 months - 10 mois	81	50	31	0.1	0.2	0.1
11 months - 11 mois	66	36	30	0.1	0.1	0.1
ASIA - ASIE						
Armenia - Arménie[13]						
2009 (C)						
Total	454	258	196	10.2	10.9	9.4
Less than 1 day - Moins de 1 jour	82	47	35	1.8	2.0	1.7
1 - 6 days - 1 - 6 jours	165	93	72	3.7	3.9	3.5
7 - 27 days - 7 - 27 jours	72	37	35	1.6	1.6	1.7
7 - 13 days - 7 - 13 jours	28	16	12	♦0.6	♦0.7	♦0.6
14 - 20 days - 14 - 20 jours	24	12	12	♦0.5	♦0.5	♦0.6
21 - 27 days - 21 - 27 jours	20	9	11	♦0.5	♦0.4	♦0.5
28 days - 11 months - 28 jours - 11 mois	135	81	54	3.0	3.4	2.6
28 days - less than 2 months - 28 jours - moins de 2 mois	37	23	14	0.8	♦1.0	♦0.7
2 months - 2 mois	24	14	10	♦0.5	♦0.6	♦0.5
3 months - 3 mois	20	10	10	♦0.5	♦0.4	♦0.5
4 months - 4 mois	15	12	3	♦0.3	♦0.5	♦0.1
5 months - 5 mois	13	7	6	♦0.3	♦0.3	♦0.3
6 months - 6 mois	4	2	2	♦0.1	♦0.1	♦0.1
7 months - 7 mois	1	1	-	-	-	-
8 months - 8 mois	4	3	1	♦0.1	♦0.1	-
9 months - 9 mois	9	6	3	♦0.2	♦0.3	♦0.1
10 months - 10 mois	6	3	3	♦0.1	♦0.1	♦0.1
11 months - 11 mois	2	-	2	-	-	♦0.1
Azerbaijan - Azerbaïdjan[13]						
2010 (+C)						
Total	1 843	1 018	825	11.1	11.4	10.8
Less than 1 day - Moins de 1 jour	268	176	92	1.6	2.0	1.2
1 - 6 days - 1 - 6 jours	704	424	280	4.3	4.8	3.7
7 - 27 days - 7 - 27 jours	87	36	51	0.5	0.4	0.7
7 - 13 days - 7 - 13 jours	49	14	35	0.3	♦0.2	0.5
14 - 20 days - 14 - 20 jours	22	9	13	♦0.1	♦0.1	♦0.2
21 - 27 days - 21 - 27 jours	16	13	3	♦0.1	♦0.1	-
28 days - 11 months - 28 jours - 11 mois	784	382	402	4.7	4.3	5.3
28 days - less than 2 months - 28 jours - moins de 2 mois	74	29	45	0.4	♦0.3	0.6
2 months - 2 mois	90	40	50	0.5	0.4	0.7
3 months - 3 mois	85	51	34	0.5	0.6	0.4
4 months - 4 mois	78	42	36	0.5	0.5	0.5
5 months - 5 mois	101	42	59	0.6	0.5	0.8
6 months - 6 mois	64	25	39	0.4	♦0.3	0.5
7 months - 7 mois	76	30	46	0.5	0.3	0.6
8 months - 8 mois	80	55	25	0.5	0.6	♦0.3
9 months - 9 mois	42	23	19	0.3	♦0.3	♦0.2
10 months - 10 mois	42	13	29	0.3	♦0.1	♦0.4
11 months - 11 mois	52	32	20	0.3	0.4	♦0.3
Bahrain - Bahreïn						
2008 (C)						
Total	127	69	58	7.5	8.0	7.0
Less than 1 day - Moins de 1 jour	18	11	7	♦1.1	♦1.3	♦0.8
1 - 6 days - 1 - 6 jours	20	7	13	♦1.2	♦0.8	♦1.6
7 - 27 days - 7 - 27 jours	15	8	7	♦0.9	♦0.9	♦0.8
7 - 13 days - 7 - 13 jours	4	3	1	♦0.2	♦0.3	♦0.1
14 - 20 days - 14 - 20 jours	7	4	3	♦0.4	♦0.5	♦0.4
21 - 27 days - 21 - 27 jours	4	1	3	♦0.2	♦0.1	♦0.4
28 days - 11 months - 28 jours - 11 mois	74	43	31	4.3	5.0	3.7
28 days - less than 2 months - 28 jours - moins de 2 mois	28	14	14	♦1.6	♦1.6	♦1.7
2 months - 2 mois	11	9	2	♦0.6	♦1.0	♦0.2
3 months - 3 mois	10	7	3	♦0.6	♦0.8	♦0.4
4 months - 4 mois	5	2	3	♦0.3	♦0.2	♦0.4
5 months - 5 mois	5	3	2	♦0.3	♦0.3	♦0.2
6 months - 6 mois	6	5	1	♦0.4	♦0.6	♦0.1
7 months - 7 mois	1	-	1	♦0.1	-	♦0.1

16. Infant deaths and infant mortality rates by age and sex: latest available year, 2003 - 2012
Décès d'enfants de moins d'un an et taux de mortalité infantile selon l'âge et le sexe : dernière année disponible, 2003 - 2012 (continued - suite)

Continent, country or area, year and age / Continent, pays ou zone, année et âge	Number - Nombre			Rate - Taux		
	Both sexes Les deux sexes	Male Masculin	Female Féminin	Both sexes Les deux sexes	Male Masculin	Female Féminin

ASIA - ASIE

Bahrain - Bahreïn
2008 (C)

8 months - 8 mois	4	1	3	◆0.2	◆0.1	◆0.4
9 months - 9 mois	2	1	1	◆0.1	◆0.1	◆0.1
10 months - 10 mois	1	1	-	◆0.1	◆0.1	-
11 months - 11 mois	1	-	1	◆0.1	-	◆0.1

Bangladesh
2010 (U)

Total	104 591	55 178	49 413	...	...	...
1 - 6 days - 1 - 6 jours	56 108	30 276	25 832	...	...	...
7 - 27 days - 7 - 27 jours	17 576	9 234	8 342	...	...	...
7 - 13 days - 7 - 13 jours	8 488	4 491	3 997	...	...	...
14 - 20 days - 14 - 20 jours	4 845	2 546	2 299	...	...	...
21 - 27 days - 21 - 27 jours	4 243	2 197	2 046	...	...	...
28 days - 11 months - 28 jours - 11 mois	30 907	15 668	15 239	...	...	...
28 days - less than 2 months - 28 jours - moins de 2 mois	7 377	3 906	3 471	...	...	...
2 months - 2 mois	5 234	2 674	2 560	...	...	...
3 months - 3 mois	4 381	2 248	2 133	...	...	...
4 months - 4 mois	2 628	1 333	1 295	...	...	...
5 months - 5 mois	1 188	606	582	...	...	...
6 months - 6 mois	2 123	1 050	1 073	...	...	...
7 months - 7 mois	1 361	669	692	...	...	...
8 months - 8 mois	1 905	918	987	...	...	...
9 months - 9 mois	1 420	696	724	...	...	...
10 months - 10 mois	1 188	566	622	...	...	...
11 months - 11 mois	2 102	1 002	1 100	...	...	...

China, Hong Kong SAR - Chine, Hong Kong RAS
2011 (C)

Total	127	82	45	1.3	1.6	1.0
Less than 1 day - Moins de 1 jour	16	9	7	◆0.2	◆0.2	◆0.2
1 - 6 days - 1 - 6 jours	38	30	8	0.4	0.6	◆0.2
7 - 27 days - 7 - 27 jours	17	10	7	◆0.2	◆0.2	◆0.2
7 - 13 days - 7 - 13 jours	8	4	4	◆0.1	◆0.1	◆0.1
14 - 20 days - 14 - 20 jours	2	2	-	-	-	-
21 - 27 days - 21 - 27 jours	7	4	3	◆0.1	◆0.1	◆0.1
28 days - 11 months - 28 jours - 11 mois	56	33	23	0.6	0.6	◆0.5
28 days - less than 2 months - 28 jours - moins de 2 mois	13	8	5	◆0.1	◆0.2	◆0.1
2 months - 2 mois	16	9	7	◆0.2	◆0.2	◆0.2
3 months - 3 mois	5	2	3	◆0.1	-	◆0.1
4 months - 4 mois	4	3	1	-	◆0.1	-
5 months - 5 mois	3	1	2	-	-	-
6 months - 6 mois	1	1	-	-	-	-
7 months - 7 mois	3	1	2	-	-	-
8 months - 8 mois	5	5	-	◆0.1	◆0.1	-
9 months - 9 mois	3	2	1	-	-	-
10 months - 10 mois	2	-	2	-	-	-
11 months - 11 mois	1	1	-	-	-	-

China, Macao SAR - Chine, Macao RAS
2010 (C)

Total	15	7	8	...	...	...
Less than 1 day - Moins de 1 jour	7	3	4	...	...	...
1 - 6 days - 1 - 6 jours	4	2	2	...	...	...
7 - 27 days - 7 - 27 jours	2	1	1	...	...	...
7 - 13 days - 7 - 13 jours	-	-	-	...	...	...
14 - 20 days - 14 - 20 jours	1	-	1	...	...	...
21 - 27 days - 21 - 27 jours	1	1	-	...	...	...
28 days - 11 months - 28 jours - 11 mois	2	1	1	...	...	...
28 days - less than 2 months - 28 jours - moins de 2 mois	1	-	1	...	...	...
2 months - 2 mois	-	-	-	...	...	...
3 months - 3 mois	-	-	-	...	...	...
4 months - 4 mois	1	1	-	...	...	...
5 months - 5 mois	-	-	-	...	...	...
6 months - 6 mois	-	-	-	...	...	...
7 months - 7 mois	-	-	-	...	...	...
8 months - 8 mois	-	-	-	...	...	...
9 months - 9 mois	-	-	-	...	...	...
10 months - 10 mois	-	-	-	...	...	...
11 months - 11 mois	-	-	-	...	...	...

16. Infant deaths and infant mortality rates by age and sex: latest available year, 2003 - 2012
Décès d'enfants de moins d'un an et taux de mortalité infantile selon l'âge et le sexe : dernière année disponible, 2003 - 2012 (continued - suite)

Continent, country or area, year and age Continent, pays ou zone, année et âge	Number - Nombre			Rate - Taux		
	Both sexes Les deux sexes	Male Masculin	Female Féminin	Both sexes Les deux sexes	Male Masculin	Female Féminin
ASIA - ASIE						
Cyprus - Chypre[14]						
2011 (C)						
Total..	30	18	12	...	...	...
Less than 1 day - Moins de 1 jour	10	6	4	...	...	...
1 - 6 days - 1 - 6 jours	8	4	4	...	...	...
7 - 27 days - 7 - 27 jours	3	2	1	...	...	...
28 days - 11 months - 28 jours - 11 mois...................................	9	6	3	...	...	...
Georgia - Géorgie[13]						
2012 (C)						
Total..	715	419	296	12.5	14.1	10.9
Less than 1 day - Moins de 1 jour	130	72	58	2.3	2.4	2.1
1 - 6 days - 1 - 6 jours	247	155	92	4.3	5.2	3.4
7 - 27 days - 7 - 27 jours	158	94	64	2.8	3.2	2.4
7 - 13 days - 7 - 13 jours	74	45	29	1.3	1.5	♦1.1
14 - 20 days - 14 - 20 jours	55	33	22	1.0	1.1	♦0.8
21 - 27 days - 21 - 27 jours	29	16	13	♦0.5	♦0.5	♦0.5
28 days - 11 months - 28 jours - 11 mois...................................	180	98	82	3.2	3.3	3.0
28 days - less than 2 months - 28 jours - moins de 2 mois	9	3	6	♦0.2	♦0.1	♦0.2
2 months - 2 mois...	53	25	28	0.9	♦0.8	♦1.0
3 months - 3 mois...	15	10	5	♦0.3	♦0.3	♦0.2
4 months - 4 mois...	20	10	10	♦0.4	♦0.3	♦0.4
5 months - 5 mois...	13	5	8	♦0.2	♦0.2	♦0.3
6 months - 6 mois...	7	5	2	♦0.1	♦0.2	♦0.1
7 months - 7 mois...	10	6	4	♦0.2	♦0.2	♦0.1
8 months - 8 mois...	11	9	2	♦0.2	♦0.3	♦0.1
9 months - 9 mois...	11	9	2	♦0.2	♦0.3	♦0.1
10 months - 10 mois...	8	5	3	♦0.1	♦0.2	♦0.1
11 months - 11 mois...	23	11	12	♦0.4	♦0.4	♦0.4
Israel - Israël[15]						
2012 (C)						
Total..	563	313[4]	249[4]	3.3	...	...
Less than 1 day - Moins de 1 jour	114	58[4]	55[4]	0.7	...	...
1 - 6 days - 1 - 6 jours	158	97	61	0.9	...	...
7 - 27 days - 7 - 27 jours	105	63	42	0.6	...	...
7 - 13 days - 7 - 13 jours	47	34	13	0.3	...	...
14 - 20 days - 14 - 20 jours	43	21	22	0.3	...	...
21 - 27 days - 21 - 27 jours	15	8	7	♦0.1	...	...
28 days - 11 months - 28 jours - 11 mois...................................	186	95	91	1.1	...	...
28 days - less than 2 months - 28 jours - moins de 2 mois	49	24	25	0.3	...	...
2 months - 2 mois...	32	15	17	0.2	...	...
3 months - 3 mois...	23	12	11	♦0.1	...	...
4 months - 4 mois...	18	8	10	♦0.1	...	...
5 months - 5 mois...	13	8	5	♦0.1	...	...
6 months - 6 mois...	13	8	5	♦0.1	...	...
7 months - 7 mois...	9	6	3	♦0.1	...	...
8 months - 8 mois...	10	5	5	♦0.1	...	...
9 months - 9 mois...	7	2	5	-	...	...
10 months - 10 mois...	8	6	2	-	...	...
11 months - 11 mois...	4	1	3	-	...	...
Japan - Japon[16]						
2011 (C)						
Total..	2 463	1 269	1 194	2.3	2.4	2.3
Less than 1 day - Moins de 1 jour	549	279	270	0.5	0.5	0.5
1 - 6 days - 1 - 6 jours	275	139	136	0.3	0.3	0.3
7 - 27 days - 7 - 27 jours	323	163	160	0.3	0.3	0.3
7 - 13 days - 7 - 13 jours	152	78	74	0.1	0.1	0.1
14 - 20 days - 14 - 20 jours	103	48	55	0.1	0.1	0.1
21 - 27 days - 21 - 27 jours	68	37	31	0.1	0.1	0.1
28 days - 11 months - 28 jours - 11 mois...................................	1 316	688	628	1.3	1.3	1.2
28 days - less than 2 months - 28 jours - moins de 2 mois	262	132	130	0.2	0.2	0.3
2 months - 2 mois...	179	94	85	0.2	0.2	0.2
3 months - 3 mois...	160	79	81	0.2	0.1	0.2
4 months - 4 mois...	122	69	53	0.1	0.1	0.1
5 months - 5 mois...	128	71	57	0.1	0.1	0.1
6 months - 6 mois...	127	59	68	0.1	0.1	0.1
7 months - 7 mois...	95	52	43	0.1	0.1	0.1
8 months - 8 mois...	77	46	31	0.1	0.1	0.1
9 months - 9 mois...	71	40	31	0.1	0.1	0.1

16. Infant deaths and infant mortality rates by age and sex: latest available year, 2003 - 2012
Décès d'enfants de moins d'un an et taux de mortalité infantile selon l'âge et le sexe : dernière année disponible, 2003 - 2012 (continued - suite)

Continent, country or area, year and age	Number - Nombre			Rate - Taux		
Continent, pays ou zone, année et âge	Both sexes Les deux sexes	Male Masculin	Female Féminin	Both sexes Les deux sexes	Male Masculin	Female Féminin
ASIA - ASIE						
Japan - Japon[16]						
2011 (C)						
10 months - 10 mois.........................	48	21	27	-	-	♦0.1
11 months - 11 mois.........................	47	25	22	-	-	-
Unknown - Inconnu	-	-	-	-	-	-
Kazakhstan[13]						
2008 (C)						
Total...	7 322	4 154	3 168	20.5	22.7	18.3
Less than 1 day - Moins de 1 jour	1 445	789	656	4.1	4.3	3.8
1 - 6 days - 1 - 6 jours	2 944	1 696	1 248	8.3	9.3	7.2
7 - 27 days - 7 - 27 jours	962	536	426	2.7	2.9	2.5
7 - 13 days - 7 - 13 jours	579	321	258	1.6	1.8	1.5
14 - 20 days - 14 - 20 jours	241	135	106	0.7	0.7	0.6
21 - 27 days - 21 - 27 jours	142	80	62	0.4	0.4	0.4
28 days - 11 months - 28 jours - 11 mois........	1 969	1 133	836	5.5	6.2	4.8
28 days - less than 2 months - 28 jours - moins de 2 mois	560	338	222	1.6	1.8	1.3
2 months - 2 mois............................	280	167	113	0.8	0.9	0.7
3 months - 3 mois............................	237	122	115	0.7	0.7	0.7
4 months - 4 mois............................	206	111	95	0.6	0.6	0.5
5 months - 5 mois............................	168	93	75	0.5	0.5	0.4
6 months - 6 mois............................	131	71	60	0.4	0.4	0.3
7 months - 7 mois............................	93	60	33	0.3	0.3	0.2
8 months - 8 mois............................	96	56	40	0.3	0.3	0.2
9 months - 9 mois............................	97	57	40	0.3	0.3	0.2
10 months - 10 mois.........................	58	32	26	0.2	0.2	♦0.2
11 months - 11 mois.........................	43	26	17	0.1	♦0.1	♦0.1
Unknown - Inconnu	2	-	2	-	-	-
Kuwait - Koweït						
2011 (C)						
Total...	484	276	208	8.3	9.3	7.3
Less than 1 day - Moins de 1 jour	124	66	58	2.1	2.2	2.0
1 - 6 days - 1 - 6 jours	81	51	30	1.4	1.7	1.1
7 - 27 days - 7 - 27 jours	113	64	49	1.9	2.2	1.7
7 - 13 days - 7 - 13 jours	51	32	19	0.9	1.1	♦0.7
14 - 20 days - 14 - 20 jours	35	18	17	0.6	♦0.6	♦0.6
21 - 27 days - 21 - 27 jours	27	14	13	♦0.5	♦0.5	♦0.5
28 days - 11 months - 28 jours - 11 mois........	166	95	71	2.9	3.2	2.5
28 days - less than 2 months - 28 jours - moins de 2 mois	51	23	28	0.9	♦0.8	♦1.0
2 months - 2 mois............................	32	20	12	0.5	♦0.7	♦0.4
3 months - 3 mois............................	21	15	6	♦0.4	♦0.5	♦0.2
4 months - 4 mois............................	13	9	4	♦0.2	♦0.3	♦0.1
5 months - 5 mois............................	15	10	5	♦0.3	♦0.3	♦0.2
6 months - 6 mois............................	5	4	1	♦0.1	♦0.1	-
7 months - 7 mois............................	4	1	3	♦0.1	-	♦0.1
8 months - 8 mois............................	13	8	5	♦0.2	♦0.3	♦0.2
9 months - 9 mois............................	5	3	2	♦0.1	♦0.1	♦0.1
10 months - 10 mois.........................	3	1	2	♦0.1	-	♦0.1
11 months - 11 mois.........................	4	1	3	♦0.1	-	♦0.1
Kyrgyzstan - Kirghizstan						
2011 (C)						
Total...	3 150	1 779	1 371	21.1	23.2	18.8
Less than 1 day - Moins de 1 jour	988	558	430	6.6	7.3	5.9
1 - 6 days - 1 - 6 jours	1 096	617	479	7.3	8.0	6.6
7 - 27 days - 7 - 27 jours	212	112	100	1.4	1.5	1.4
7 - 13 days - 7 - 13 jours	127	65	62	0.8	0.8	0.9
14 - 20 days - 14 - 20 jours	41	24	17	0.3	♦0.3	♦0.2
21 - 27 days - 21 - 27 jours	44	23	21	0.3	♦0.3	♦0.3
28 days - 11 months - 28 jours - 11 mois........	854	492	362	5.7	6.4	5.0
28 days - less than 2 months - 28 jours - moins de 2 mois	180	104	76	1.2	1.4	1.0
2 months - 2 mois............................	106	59	47	0.7	0.8	0.6
3 months - 3 mois............................	102	58	44	0.7	0.8	0.6
4 months - 4 mois............................	105	66	39	0.7	0.9	0.5
5 months - 5 mois............................	79	48	31	0.5	0.6	0.4
6 months - 6 mois............................	63	44	19	0.4	0.6	♦0.3
7 months - 7 mois............................	64	34	30	0.4	0.4	0.4
8 months - 8 mois............................	44	24	20	0.3	♦0.3	♦0.3
9 months - 9 mois............................	30	18	12	0.2	♦0.2	♦0.2
10 months - 10 mois.........................	39	19	20	0.3	♦0.2	♦0.3

16. Infant deaths and infant mortality rates by age and sex: latest available year, 2003 - 2012
Décès d'enfants de moins d'un an et taux de mortalité infantile selon l'âge et le sexe : dernière année disponible, 2003 - 2012 (continued - suite)

Continent, country or area, year and age / Continent, pays ou zone, année et âge	Number - Nombre			Rate - Taux		
	Both sexes Les deux sexes	Male Masculin	Female Féminin	Both sexes Les deux sexes	Male Masculin	Female Féminin
ASIA - ASIE						
Kyrgyzstan - Kirghizstan						
2011 (C)						
11 months - 11 mois	42	18	24	0.3	♦0.2	♦0.3
Unknown - Inconnu	-	-	-	-	-	-
Malaysia - Malaisie						
2004 (C)						
Total......	3 105	1 784	1 321	6.5	7.2	5.7
Less than 1 day - Moins de 1 jour	443	262	181	0.9	1.1	0.8
1 - 6 days - 1 - 6 jours	834	500	334	1.7	2.0	1.4
7 - 27 days - 7 - 27 jours	492	268	224	1.0	1.1	1.0
28 days - 11 months - 28 jours - 11 mois......	1 336	754	582	2.8	3.1	2.5
28 days - 2 months - 28 jours - 2 mois	568	335	233	1.2	1.4	1.0
3 - 5 months - 3 - 5 mois	393	216	177	0.8	0.9	0.8
6 - 8 months - 6 - 8 mois	220	122	98	0.5	0.5	0.4
9 - 11 months - 9 - 11 mois	155	81	74	0.3	0.3	0.3
Maldives						
2011 (C)						
Total......	65	37	28	...	...	...
Less than 1 day - Moins de 1 jour	27	15	12	...	...	...
1 - 6 days - 1 - 6 jours	14	8	6	...	...	...
7 - 27 days - 7 - 27 jours	8	3	5	...	...	...
7 - 13 days - 7 - 13 jours	2	1	1	...	...	...
14 - 20 days - 14 - 20 jours	3	-	3	...	...	...
21 - 27 days - 21 - 27 jours	3	2	1	...	...	...
28 days - 11 months - 28 jours - 11 mois......	16	11	5	...	...	...
28 days - less than 2 months - 28 jours - moins de 2 mois	3	1	2	...	...	...
2 months - 2 mois......	2	-	2	...	...	...
3 months - 3 mois	3	3	-	...	...	...
4 months - 4 mois	3	3	-	...	...	...
5 months - 5 mois	-	-	-	...	...	...
6 months - 6 mois	2	2	-	...	...	...
7 months - 7 mois	1	-	1	...	...	...
8 months - 8 mois	-	-	-	...	...	...
9 months - 9 mois	1	1	-	...	...	...
10 months - 10 mois	-	-	-	...	...	...
11 months - 11 mois	1	1	-	...	...	...
Unknown - Inconnu	-	-	-	...	...	...
Oman[17]						
2011 (U)						
Total......	598	316[18]	269[18]	...	...	...
Less than 1 day - Moins de 1 jour	100	50[18]	47[18]	...	...	...
1 - 6 days - 1 - 6 jours	118	57[18]	61[18]	...	...	...
7 - 27 days - 7 - 27 jours	75	34[18]	41[18]	...	...	...
7 - 13 days - 7 - 13 jours	36	16[18]	20[18]	...	...	...
14 - 20 days - 14 - 20 jours	23	10[18]	13[18]	...	...	...
21 - 27 days - 21 - 27 jours	16	8[18]	8[18]	...	...	...
28 days - 11 months - 28 jours - 11 mois......	174	95	79			
28 days - less than 2 months - 28 jours - moins de 2 mois	54	26[18]	28[18]	...	...	...
2 months - 2 mois......	24	16[18]	8[18]	...	...	...
3 months - 3 mois......	22	10[18]	12[18]	...	...	...
4 months - 4 mois	12	10[18]	2[18]	...	...	...
5 months - 5 mois	16	10[18]	6[18]	...	...	...
6 months - 6 mois	13	6[18]	7[18]	...	...	...
7 months - 7 mois	3	2[18]	1[18]	...	...	...
8 months - 8 mois	10	4[18]	6[18]	...	...	...
9 months - 9 mois	3	1[18]	2[18]	...	...	...
10 months - 10 mois	9	4[18]	5[18]	...	...	...
11 months - 11 mois	8	6[18]	2[18]	...	...	...
Unknown - Inconnu	131	81[18]	40[18]	...	...	...
Pakistan[19]						
2007 (|)						
Total......	288 191	167 402	120 789	75.2	83.5	66.2
Less than 1 day - Moins de 1 jour	11 990	8 027	3 963	3.1	4.0	2.2
1 - 6 days - 1 - 6 jours	115 664	74 312	41 352	30.2	37.0	22.7
7 - 27 days - 7 - 27 jours	39 726	23 382	16 344	10.4	11.7	9.0
7 - 13 days - 7 - 13 jours	21 846	13 191	8 655	5.7	6.6	4.7
14 - 20 days - 14 - 20 jours	16 376	9 475	6 901	4.3	4.7	3.8

Continent, country or area, year and age	Number - Nombre			Rate - Taux		
Continent, pays ou zone, année et âge	Both sexes Les deux sexes	Male Masculin	Female Féminin	Both sexes Les deux sexes	Male Masculin	Female Féminin

ASIA - ASIE

Pakistan[19]
2007 (I)

21 - 27 days - 21 - 27 jours	1 504	716	788	0.4	0.4	0.4
28 days - 11 months - 28 jours - 11 mois	120 811	61 681	59 130	31.5	30.8	32.4
28 days - less than 2 months - 28 jours - moins de 2 mois	23 563	9 553	14 010	6.2	4.8	7.7
2 months - 2 mois	10 666	7 662	3 004	2.8	3.8	1.6
3 months - 3 mois	16 938	9 692	7 246	4.4	4.8	4.0
4 months - 4 mois	10 577	4 135	6 442	2.8	2.1	3.5
5 months - 5 mois	14 148	8 863	5 285	3.7	4.4	2.9
6 months - 6 mois	17 012	6 641	10 371	4.4	3.3	5.7
7 months - 7 mois	8 480	4 209	4 271	2.2	2.1	2.3
8 months - 8 mois	6 221	5 116	1 105	1.6	2.6	0.6
9 months - 9 mois	7 602	3 819	3 783	2.0	1.9	2.1
10 months - 10 mois	3 546	1 291	2 255	0.9	0.6	1.2
11 months - 11 mois	2 058	700	1 358	0.5	0.3	0.7

Philippines
2009 (C)

Total	21 659	12 503	9 156	12.4	13.8	10.9
Less than 1 day - Moins de 1 jour	3 843	2 236	1 607	2.2	2.5	1.9
1 - 6 days - 1 - 6 jours	5 538	3 343	2 195	3.2	3.7	2.6
7 - 27 days - 7 - 27 jours	2 709	1 568	1 141	1.6	1.7	1.4
7 - 13 days - 7 - 13 jours	1 461	857	604	0.8	0.9	0.7
14 - 20 days - 14 - 20 jours	714	404	310	0.4	0.4	0.4
21 - 27 days - 21 - 27 jours	534	307	227	0.3	0.3	0.3
28 days - 11 months - 28 jours - 11 mois	9 569	5 356	4 213	5.5	5.9	5.0
28 days - less than 2 months - 28 jours - moins de 2 mois	2 173	1 293	880	1.2	1.4	1.0
2 months - 2 mois	1 322	750	572	0.8	0.8	0.7
3 months - 3 mois	941	527	414	0.5	0.6	0.5
4 months - 4 mois	773	444	329	0.4	0.5	0.4
5 months - 5 mois	714	387	327	0.4	0.4	0.4
6 months - 6 mois	773	391	382	0.4	0.4	0.5
7 months - 7 mois	708	384	324	0.4	0.4	0.4
8 months - 8 mois	649	369	280	0.4	0.4	0.3
9 months - 9 mois	556	296	260	0.3	0.3	0.3
10 months - 10 mois	473	240	233	0.3	0.3	0.3
11 months - 11 mois	487	275	212	0.3	0.3	0.3

Qatar
2011 (C)

Total	156	93	63	10.5	12.2	8.7
Less than 1 day - Moins de 1 jour	-	-	-	-	-	-
1 - 6 days - 1 - 6 jours	58	33	25	3.9	4.3	♦3.4
7 - 27 days - 7 - 27 jours	33	16	17	2.2	♦2.1	♦2.3
7 - 13 days - 7 - 13 jours	17	11	6	♦1.1	♦1.4	♦0.8
14 - 20 days - 14 - 20 jours	14	5	9	♦0.9	♦0.7	♦1.2
21 - 27 days - 21 - 27 jours	2	-	2	♦0.1	-	♦0.3
28 days - 11 months - 28 jours - 11 mois	65	44	21	4.4	5.8	♦2.9
28 days - less than 2 months - 28 jours - moins de 2 mois	18	12	6	♦1.2	♦1.6	♦0.8
2 months - 2 mois	19	15	4	♦1.3	♦2.0	♦0.6
3 months - 3 mois	14	10	4	♦0.9	♦1.3	♦0.6
4 months - 4 mois	5	2	3	♦0.3	♦0.3	♦0.4
5 months - 5 mois	2	1	1	♦0.1	♦0.1	♦0.1
6 months - 6 mois	3	3	-	♦0.2	♦0.4	-
7 months - 7 mois	-	-	-	-	-	-
8 months - 8 mois	-	-	-	-	-	-
9 months - 9 mois	2	-	2	♦0.1	-	♦0.3
10 months - 10 mois	1	-	1	♦0.1	-	♦0.1
11 months - 11 mois	1	1	-	♦0.1	♦0.1	-

Republic of Korea - République de Corée[20]
2011 (C)

Total	1 435	818	617	3.0	3.4	2.7
Less than 1 day - Moins de 1 jour	216	114	102	0.5	0.5	0.4
1 - 6 days - 1 - 6 jours	321	193	128	0.7	0.8	0.6
7 - 27 days - 7 - 27 jours	269	157	112	0.6	0.6	0.5
7 - 13 days - 7 - 13 jours	125	76	49	0.3	0.3	0.2
14 - 20 days - 14 - 20 jours	70	38	32	0.1	0.2	0.1
21 - 27 days - 21 - 27 jours	74	43	31	0.2	0.2	0.1
28 days - 11 months - 28 jours - 11 mois	629	354	275	1.3	1.5	1.2
28 days - less than 2 months - 28 jours - moins de 2 mois	185	110	75	0.4	0.5	0.3

16. Infant deaths and infant mortality rates by age and sex: latest available year, 2003 - 2012
Décès d'enfants de moins d'un an et taux de mortalité infantile selon l'âge et le sexe : dernière année disponible, 2003 - 2012 (continued - suite)

Continent, country or area, year and age / Continent, pays ou zone, année et âge	Number - Nombre			Rate - Taux		
	Both sexes Les deux sexes	Male Masculin	Female Féminin	Both sexes Les deux sexes	Male Masculin	Female Féminin
ASIA - ASIE						
Republic of Korea - République de Corée[20]						
2011 (C)						
2 months - 2 mois	89	53	36	0.2	0.2	0.2
3 months - 3 mois	82	48	34	0.2	0.2	0.1
4 months - 4 mois	72	42	30	0.2	0.2	0.1
5 months - 5 mois	43	24	19	0.1	♦0.1	♦0.1
6 months - 6 mois	36	19	17	0.1	♦0.1	♦0.1
7 months - 7 mois	32	13	19	0.1	♦0.1	♦0.1
8 months - 8 mois	29	14	15	♦0.1	♦0.1	♦0.1
9 months - 9 mois	16	9	7	-	-	-
10 months - 10 mois	21	9	12	-	-	♦0.1
11 months - 11 mois	24	13	11	♦0.1	♦0.1	-
Singapore - Singapour						
2012 (+C)						
Total	98	52	46	...	...	...
Less than 1 day - Moins de 1 jour	17	11	6	...	...	...
1 - 6 days - 1 - 6 jours	28	19	9	...	...	...
7 - 27 days - 7 - 27 jours	13	5	8	...	...	...
7 - 13 days - 7 - 13 jours	6	2	4	...	...	...
14 - 20 days - 14 - 20 jours	2	1	1	...	...	...
21 - 27 days - 21 - 27 jours	5	2	3	...	...	...
28 days - 11 months - 28 jours - 11 mois	40	17	23	...	...	...
28 days - less than 2 months - 28 jours - moins de 2 mois	11	5	6	...	...	...
2 months - 2 mois	4	2	2	...	...	...
3 months - 3 mois	6	3	3	...	...	...
4 months - 4 mois	2	1	1	...	...	...
5 months - 5 mois	6	2	4	...	...	...
6 months - 6 mois	1	-	1	...	...	...
7 months - 7 mois	2	-	2	...	...	...
8 months - 8 mois	3	2	1	...	...	...
9 months - 9 mois	1	-	1	...	...	...
10 months - 10 mois	2	2	-	...	...	...
11 months - 11 mois	2	-	2	...	...	...
Unknown - Inconnu	-	-	-	...	...	...
State of Palestine - État de Palestine						
2007 (U)						
Total	794	420	374	...	...	...
Less than 1 day - Moins de 1 jour	42	24	18	...	...	...
1 - 6 days - 1 - 6 jours	183	113	70	...	...	...
7 - 27 days - 7 - 27 jours	156	79	77	...	...	...
7 - 13 days - 7 - 13 jours	79	44	35	...	...	...
14 - 20 days - 14 - 20 jours	47	19	28	...	...	...
21 - 27 days - 21 - 27 jours	30	16	14	...	...	...
28 days - 11 months - 28 jours - 11 mois	413	204	209	...	...	...
28 days - less than 2 months - 28 jours - moins de 2 mois	111	64	47	...	...	...
2 months - 2 mois	56	25	31	...	...	...
3 months - 3 mois	50	28	22	...	...	...
4 months - 4 mois	32	14	18	...	...	...
5 months - 5 mois	40	20	20	...	...	...
6 months - 6 mois	28	17	11	...	...	...
7 months - 7 mois	19	8	11	...	...	...
8 months - 8 mois	19	10	9	...	...	...
9 months - 9 mois	22	8	14	...	...	...
10 months - 10 mois	21	5	16	...	...	...
11 months - 11 mois	15	5	10	...	...	...
Tajikistan - Tadjikistan[13]						
2008 (U)						
Total	2 480	1 478	1 002	...	...	...
Less than 1 day - Moins de 1 jour	420	255	165	...	...	...
1 - 6 days - 1 - 6 jours	699	443	256	...	...	...
7 - 27 days - 7 - 27 jours	248	140	108	...	...	...
7 - 13 days - 7 - 13 jours	145	87	58	...	...	...
14 - 20 days - 14 - 20 jours	63	33	30	...	...	...
21 - 27 days - 21 - 27 jours	40	20	20	...	...	...
28 days - 11 months - 28 jours - 11 mois	1 113	640	473	...	...	...
28 days - less than 2 months - 28 jours - moins de 2 mois	180	103	77	...	...	...
2 months - 2 mois	155	92	63	...	...	...
3 months - 3 mois	138	77	61	...	...	...

Continent, country or area, year and age Continent, pays ou zone, année et âge	Number - Nombre			Rate - Taux		
	Both sexes Les deux sexes	Male Masculin	Female Féminin	Both sexes Les deux sexes	Male Masculin	Female Féminin
ASIA - ASIE						
Tajikistan - Tadjikistan[13]						
2008 (U)						
4 months - 4 mois	111	71	40	...	...	...
5 months - 5 mois	106	56	50	...	...	...
6 months - 6 mois	106	62	44	...	...	...
7 months - 7 mois	75	43	32	...	...	...
8 months - 8 mois	79	49	30	...	...	...
9 months - 9 mois	56	23	33	...	...	...
10 months - 10 mois	56	39	17	...	...	...
11 months - 11 mois	51	25	26	...	...	...
Thailand - Thaïlande						
2011 (+U)						
Total	5 275	2 964	2 311	...	...	...
Less than 1 day - Moins de 1 jour	587	326	261	...	...	...
1 - 6 days - 1 - 6 jours	1 612	931	681	...	...	...
7 - 27 days - 7 - 27 jours	987	534	453	...	...	...
7 - 13 days - 7 - 13 jours	527	285	242	...	...	...
14 - 20 days - 14 - 20 jours	276	149	127	...	...	...
21 - 27 days - 21 - 27 jours	184	100	84	...	...	...
28 days - 11 months - 28 jours - 11 mois	2 089	1 173	916	...	...	...
28 days - less than 2 months - 28 jours - moins de 2 mois	556	329	227	...	...	...
2 months - 2 mois	360	203	157	...	...	...
3 months - 3 mois	249	152	97	...	...	...
4 months - 4 mois	193	98	95	...	...	...
5 months - 5 mois	160	91	69	...	...	...
6 months - 6 mois	141	74	67	...	...	...
7 months - 7 mois	103	55	48	...	...	...
8 months - 8 mois	106	51	55	...	...	...
9 months - 9 mois	87	41	46	...	...	...
10 months - 10 mois	77	45	32	...	...	...
11 months - 11 mois	57	34	23	...	...	...
Turkey - Turquie						
2010 (C)						
Total	15 049	8 184	6 865	12.0	12.7	11.3
Less than 1 day - Moins de 1 jour	2 172	1 116	1 056	1.7	1.7	1.7
1 - 6 days - 1 - 6 jours	4 796	2 754	2 042	3.8	4.3	3.4
7 - 27 days - 7 - 27 jours	2 523	1 400	1 123	2.0	2.2	1.8
7 - 13 days - 7 - 13 jours	1 317	719	598	1.1	1.1	1.0
14 - 20 days - 14 - 20 jours	694	379	315	0.6	0.6	0.5
21 - 27 days - 21 - 27 jours	512	302	210	0.4	0.5	0.3
28 days - 11 months - 28 jours - 11 mois	5 558	2 914	2 644	4.4	4.5	4.3
28 days - less than 2 months - 28 jours - moins de 2 mois	1 402	798	604	1.1	1.2	1.0
2 months - 2 mois	871	463	408	0.7	0.7	0.7
3 months - 3 mois	720	378	342	0.6	0.6	0.6
4 months - 4 mois	573	287	286	0.5	0.4	0.5
5 months - 5 mois	413	222	191	0.3	0.3	0.3
6 months - 6 mois	358	183	175	0.3	0.3	0.3
7 months - 7 mois	316	153	163	0.3	0.2	0.3
8 months - 8 mois	262	118	144	0.2	0.2	0.2
9 months - 9 mois	224	117	107	0.2	0.2	0.2
10 months - 10 mois	215	101	114	0.2	0.2	0.2
11 months - 11 mois	204	94	110	0.2	0.1	0.2
Unknown - Inconnu	-	-	-	-	-	-
EUROPE						
Åland Islands - Îles d'Åland						
2010 (C)						
Total	1	-	1	...	...	...
Less than 1 day - Moins de 1 jour	1	-	1	...	...	...
1 - 6 days - 1 - 6 jours	-	-	-	...	...	...
7 - 27 days - 7 - 27 jours	-	-	-	...	...	...
7 - 13 days - 7 - 13 jours	-	-	-	...	...	...
14 - 20 days - 14 - 20 jours	-	-	-	...	...	...
21 - 27 days - 21 - 27 jours	-	-	-	...	...	...
28 days - 11 months - 28 jours - 11 mois	-	-	-	...	...	...
28 days - less than 2 months - 28 jours - moins de 2 mois	-	-	-	...	...	...

16. Infant deaths and infant mortality rates by age and sex: latest available year, 2003 - 2012
Décès d'enfants de moins d'un an et taux de mortalité infantile selon l'âge et le sexe : dernière année disponible, 2003 - 2012 (continued - suite)

Continent, country or area, year and age / Continent, pays ou zone, année et âge	Number - Nombre			Rate - Taux		
	Both sexes Les deux sexes	Male Masculin	Female Féminin	Both sexes Les deux sexes	Male Masculin	Female Féminin
EUROPE						
Åland Islands - Îles d'Åland						
2010 (C)						
2 months - 2 mois	-	-	-	...	...	...
3 months - 3 mois	-	-	-	...	...	...
4 months - 4 mois	-	-	-	...	...	...
5 months - 5 mois	-	-	-	...	...	...
6 months - 6 mois	-	-	-	...	...	...
7 months - 7 mois	-	-	-	...	...	...
8 months - 8 mois	-	-	-	...	...	...
9 months - 9 mois	-	-	-	...	...	...
10 months - 10 mois	-	-	-	...	...	...
11 months - 11 mois	-	-	-	...	...	...
Albania - Albanie						
2006 (C)						
Total	253	...	...	7.4	...	...
Less than 1 day - Moins de 1 jour	10	...	...	♦0.3	...	...
1 - 6 days - 1 - 6 jours	40	...	...	1.2	...	...
7 - 27 days - 7 - 27 jours	21	...	...	♦0.6	...	...
28 days - 11 months - 28 jours - 11 mois	182	...	...	5.3	...	...
28 days - less than 2 months - 28 jours - moins de 2 mois	35	...	...	1.0	...	...
2 - 11 months - 2 - 11 mois	147	...	...	4.3	...	...
Andorra - Andorre						
2009 (C)						
Total	1	-	1	...	...	...
Less than 1 day - Moins de 1 jour	-	-	-	...	...	...
1 - 6 days - 1 - 6 jours	1	-	1	...	...	...
7 - 27 days - 7 - 27 jours	-	-	-	...	...	...
28 days - 11 months - 28 jours - 11 mois	-	-	-	...	...	...
Austria - Autriche						
2011 (C)						
Total	281	176	105	3.6	4.4	2.8
Less than 1 day - Moins de 1 jour	109	62	47	1.4	1.5	1.2
1 - 6 days - 1 - 6 jours	45	32	13	0.6	0.8	♦0.3
7 - 27 days - 7 - 27 jours	37	25	12	0.5	♦0.6	♦0.3
7 - 13 days - 7 - 13 jours	18	13	5	♦0.2	♦0.3	♦0.1
14 - 20 days - 14 - 20 jours	9	7	2	♦0.1	♦0.2	♦0.1
21 - 27 days - 21 - 27 jours	10	5	5	♦0.1	♦0.1	♦0.1
28 days - 11 months - 28 jours - 11 mois	90	57	33	1.2	1.4	0.9
28 days - less than 2 months - 28 jours - moins de 2 mois	28	17	11	♦0.4	♦0.4	♦0.3
2 months - 2 mois	15	12	3	♦0.2	♦0.3	♦0.1
3 months - 3 mois	4	3	1	♦0.1	♦0.1	-
4 months - 4 mois	11	7	4	♦0.1	♦0.2	♦0.1
5 months - 5 mois	6	5	1	♦0.1	♦0.1	-
6 months - 6 mois	7	5	2	♦0.1	♦0.1	♦0.1
7 months - 7 mois	8	3	5	♦0.1	♦0.1	♦0.1
8 months - 8 mois	3	-	3	-	-	♦0.1
9 months - 9 mois	5	4	1	♦0.1	♦0.1	-
10 months - 10 mois	1	1	-	-	-	-
11 months - 11 mois	2	-	2	-	-	♦0.1
Belarus - Bélarus						
2011 (C)						
Total	420	240	180	3.8	4.3	3.4
Less than 1 day - Moins de 1 jour	34	14	20	0.3	♦0.2	♦0.4
1 - 6 days - 1 - 6 jours	85	52	33	0.8	0.9	0.6
7 - 27 days - 7 - 27 jours	73	39	34	0.7	0.7	0.6
7 - 13 days - 7 - 13 jours	28	13	15	♦0.3	♦0.2	♦0.3
14 - 20 days - 14 - 20 jours	27	17	10	♦0.2	♦0.3	♦0.2
21 - 27 days - 21 - 27 jours	18	9	9	♦0.2	♦0.2	♦0.2
28 days - 11 months - 28 jours - 11 mois	228	135	93	2.1	2.4	1.8
28 days - less than 2 months - 28 jours - moins de 2 mois	67	43	24	0.6	0.8	♦0.5
2 months - 2 mois	46	28	18	0.4	♦0.5	♦0.3
3 months - 3 mois	32	17	15	0.3	♦0.3	♦0.3
4 months - 4 mois	20	12	8	♦0.2	♦0.2	♦0.2
5 months - 5 mois	14	8	6	♦0.1	♦0.1	♦0.1
6 months - 6 mois	17	10	7	♦0.2	♦0.2	♦0.1
7 months - 7 mois	9	4	5	♦0.1	♦0.1	♦0.1
8 months - 8 mois	9	6	3	♦0.1	♦0.1	♦0.1
9 months - 9 mois	7	2	5	♦0.1	-	♦0.1

16. Infant deaths and infant mortality rates by age and sex: latest available year, 2003 - 2012

Décès d'enfants de moins d'un an et taux de mortalité infantile selon l'âge et le sexe : dernière année disponible, 2003 - 2012 (continued - suite)

Continent, country or area, year and age Continent, pays ou zone, année et âge	Number - Nombre			Rate - Taux		
	Both sexes Les deux sexes	Male Masculin	Female Féminin	Both sexes Les deux sexes	Male Masculin	Female Féminin
EUROPE						
Belarus - Bélarus						
2011 (C)						
10 months - 10 mois..	3	3	-	-	♦0.1	-
11 months - 11 mois	4	2	2	-	-	-
Belgium - Belgique[21]						
2009 (C)						
Total...	439	248	191	3.4	3.8	3.1
Less than 1 day - Moins de 1 jour	90	48	42	0.7	0.7	0.7
1 - 6 days - 1 - 6 jours	114	64	50	0.9	1.0	0.8
7 - 27 days - 7 - 27 jours	81	42	39	0.6	0.6	0.6
7 - 13 days - 7 - 13 jours	47	24	23	0.4	♦0.4	♦0.4
14 - 20 days - 14 - 20 jours	18	10	8	♦0.1	♦0.2	♦0.1
21 - 27 days - 21 - 27 jours	16	8	8	♦0.1	♦0.1	♦0.1
28 days - 11 months - 28 jours - 11 mois...........................	154	94	60	1.2	1.4	1.0
28 days - less than 2 months - 28 jours - moins de 2 mois	32	20	12	0.3	♦0.3	♦0.2
2 months - 2 mois..	21	13	8	♦0.2	♦0.2	♦0.1
3 months - 3 mois..	15	6	9	♦0.1	♦0.1	♦0.1
4 months - 4 mois..	18	14	4	♦0.1	♦0.2	♦0.1
5 months - 5 mois..	13	7	6	♦0.1	♦0.1	♦0.1
6 months - 6 mois..	14	10	4	♦0.1	♦0.2	♦0.1
7 months - 7 mois..	11	7	4	♦0.1	♦0.1	♦0.1
8 months - 8 mois..	7	3	4	♦0.1	-	♦0.1
9 months - 9 mois..	6	3	3	-	-	-
10 months - 10 mois...	4	2	2	-	-	-
11 months - 11 mois	13	9	4	♦0.1	♦0.1	♦0.1
Bosnia and Herzegovina - Bosnie-Herzégovine						
2010 (C)						
Total...	216	125	91	6.4	7.2	5.6
Less than 1 day - Moins de 1 jour	74	43	31	2.2	2.5	1.9
1 - 6 days - 1 - 6 jours	89	56	33	2.7	3.2	2.0
7 - 27 days - 7 - 27 jours	19	13	6	♦0.6	♦0.8	♦0.4
7 - 13 days - 7 - 13 jours	10	6	4	♦0.3	♦0.3	♦0.2
14 - 20 days - 14 - 20 jours	6	6	-	♦0.2	♦0.3	-
21 - 27 days - 21 - 27 jours	3	1	2	♦0.1	♦0.1	♦0.1
28 days - 11 months - 28 jours - 11 mois...........................	34	13	21	1.0	♦0.8	♦1.3
28 days - less than 2 months - 28 jours - moins de 2 mois	5	2	3	♦0.1	♦0.1	♦0.2
2 months - 2 mois..	10	6	4	♦0.3	♦0.3	♦0.2
3 months - 3 mois..	1	-	1	-	-	♦0.1
4 months - 4 mois..	5	2	3	♦0.1	♦0.1	♦0.2
5 months - 5 mois..	3	1	2	♦0.1	♦0.1	♦0.1
6 months - 6 mois..	3	1	2	♦0.1	♦0.1	♦0.1
7 months - 7 mois..	-	-	-	-	-	-
8 months - 8 mois..	1	-	1	-	-	♦0.1
9 months - 9 mois..	4	-	4	♦0.1	-	♦0.2
10 months - 10 mois...	1	1	-	-	♦0.1	-
11 months - 11 mois	1	-	1	-	-	♦0.1
Bulgaria - Bulgarie						
2011 (C)						
Total...	601	349	252	8.5	9.6	7.3
Less than 1 day - Moins de 1 jour	129	71	58	1.8	1.9	1.7
1 - 6 days - 1 - 6 jours	150	93	57	2.1	2.5	1.7
7 - 27 days - 7 - 27 jours	100	59	41	1.4	1.6	1.2
7 - 13 days - 7 - 13 jours	51	31	20	0.7	0.8	♦0.6
14 - 20 days - 14 - 20 jours	30	19	11	0.4	♦0.5	♦0.3
21 - 27 days - 21 - 27 jours	19	9	10	♦0.3	♦0.2	♦0.3
28 days - 11 months - 28 jours - 11 mois...........................	222	126	96	3.1	3.4	2.8
28 days - less than 2 months - 28 jours - moins de 2 mois	81	50	31	1.1	1.4	0.9
2 months - 2 mois..	39	23	16	0.6	♦0.6	♦0.5
3 months - 3 mois..	20	12	8	♦0.3	♦0.3	♦0.2
4 months - 4 mois..	18	10	8	♦0.3	♦0.3	♦0.2
5 months - 5 mois..	20	7	13	♦0.3	♦0.2	♦0.4
6 months - 6 mois..	9	4	5	♦0.1	♦0.1	♦0.1
7 months - 7 mois..	11	7	4	♦0.2	♦0.2	♦0.1
8 months - 8 mois..	8	5	3	♦0.1	♦0.1	♦0.1
9 months - 9 mois..	3	-	3	-	-	♦0.1
10 months - 10 mois...	8	4	4	♦0.1	♦0.1	♦0.1
11 months - 11 mois	5	4	1	♦0.1	♦0.1	-

16. Infant deaths and infant mortality rates by age and sex: latest available year, 2003 - 2012
Décès d'enfants de moins d'un an et taux de mortalité infantile selon l'âge et le sexe : dernière année disponible, 2003 - 2012 (continued - suite)

Continent, country or area, year and age / Continent, pays ou zone, année et âge	Number - Nombre			Rate - Taux		
	Both sexes Les deux sexes	Male Masculin	Female Féminin	Both sexes Les deux sexes	Male Masculin	Female Féminin
EUROPE						
Croatia - Croatie						
2010 (C)						
Total	192	111	81	4.4	5.0	3.9
Less than 1 day - Moins de 1 jour	70	43	27	1.6	1.9	♦1.3
1 - 6 days - 1 - 6 jours	42	26	16	1.0	♦1.2	♦0.8
7 - 27 days - 7 - 27 jours	33	18	15	0.8	♦0.8	♦0.7
7 - 13 days - 7 - 13 jours	22	11	11	♦0.5	♦0.5	♦0.5
14 - 20 days - 14 - 20 jours	6	3	3	♦0.1	♦0.1	♦0.1
21 - 27 days - 21 - 27 jours	5	4	1	♦0.1	♦0.2	-
28 days - 11 months - 28 jours - 11 mois	47	24	23	1.1	♦1.1	♦1.1
28 days - less than 2 months - 28 jours - moins de 2 mois	13	7	6	♦0.3	♦0.3	♦0.3
2 months - 2 mois	8	3	5	♦0.2	♦0.1	♦0.2
3 months - 3 mois	8	4	4	♦0.2	♦0.2	♦0.2
4 months - 4 mois	5	3	2	♦0.1	♦0.1	♦0.1
5 months - 5 mois	2	2	-	-	♦0.1	-
6 months - 6 mois	-	-	-	-	-	-
7 months - 7 mois	4	2	2	♦0.1	♦0.1	♦0.1
8 months - 8 mois	1	-	1	-	-	-
9 months - 9 mois	2	1	1	-	-	-
10 months - 10 mois	2	1	1	-	-	-
11 months - 11 mois	2	1	1	-	-	-
Czech Republic - République tchèque						
2011 (C)						
Total	298	174	124	2.7	3.1	2.3
Less than 1 day - Moins de 1 jour	41	24	17	0.4	♦0.4	♦0.3
1 - 6 days - 1 - 6 jours	79	51	28	0.7	0.9	♦0.5
7 - 27 days - 7 - 27 jours	66	34	32	0.6	0.6	0.6
7 - 13 days - 7 - 13 jours	36	17	19	0.3	♦0.3	♦0.4
14 - 20 days - 14 - 20 jours	18	11	7	♦0.2	♦0.2	♦0.1
21 - 27 days - 21 - 27 jours	12	6	6	♦0.1	♦0.1	♦0.1
28 days - 11 months - 28 jours - 11 mois	112	65	47	1.0	1.2	0.9
28 days - less than 2 months - 28 jours - moins de 2 mois	32	18	14	0.3	♦0.3	♦0.3
2 months - 2 mois	18	11	7	♦0.2	♦0.2	♦0.1
3 months - 3 mois	14	9	5	♦0.1	♦0.2	♦0.1
4 months - 4 mois	12	8	4	♦0.1	♦0.1	♦0.1
5 months - 5 mois	7	3	4	♦0.1	♦0.1	♦0.1
6 months - 6 mois	5	4	1	-	♦0.1	-
7 months - 7 mois	4	3	1	-	♦0.1	-
8 months - 8 mois	5	3	2	-	♦0.1	-
9 months - 9 mois	6	2	4	♦0.1	-	♦0.1
10 months - 10 mois	5	1	4	-	-	♦0.1
11 months - 11 mois	4	3	1	-	♦0.1	-
Denmark - Danemark[22]						
2011 (C)						
Total	208	107	101	3.5	3.6	3.5
Less than 1 day - Moins de 1 jour	89	48	41	1.5	1.6	1.4
1 - 6 days - 1 - 6 jours	48	24	24	0.8	♦0.8	♦0.8
7 - 27 days - 7 - 27 jours	28	15	13	♦0.5	♦0.5	♦0.4
7 - 13 days - 7 - 13 jours	22	11	11	♦0.4	♦0.4	♦0.4
14 - 20 days - 14 - 20 jours	3	1	2	♦0.1	-	♦0.1
21 - 27 days - 21 - 27 jours	3	3	-	♦0.1	♦0.1	-
28 days - 11 months - 28 jours - 11 mois	43	20	23	0.7	♦0.7	♦0.8
28 days - less than 2 months - 28 jours - moins de 2 mois	15	4	11	♦0.3	♦0.1	♦0.4
2 months - 2 mois	8	4	4	♦0.1	♦0.1	♦0.1
3 months - 3 mois	1	1	-	-	-	-
4 months - 4 mois	3	1	2	♦0.1	-	♦0.1
5 months - 5 mois	3	-	3	♦0.1	-	♦0.1
6 months - 6 mois	3	2	1	♦0.1	♦0.1	-
7 months - 7 mois	-	-	-	-	-	-
8 months - 8 mois	2	2	-	-	♦0.1	-
9 months - 9 mois	3	2	1	♦0.1	♦0.1	-
10 months - 10 mois	1	1	-	-	-	-
11 months - 11 mois	4	3	1	♦0.1	♦0.1	-
Estonia - Estonie						
2011 (C)						
Total	36	18	18	...	...	...
Less than 1 day - Moins de 1 jour	9	4	5	...	...	...
1 - 6 days - 1 - 6 jours	6	3	3	...	...	...

16. Infant deaths and infant mortality rates by age and sex: latest available year, 2003 - 2012

Décès d'enfants de moins d'un an et taux de mortalité infantile selon l'âge et le sexe : dernière année disponible, 2003 - 2012 (continued - suite)

Continent, country or area, year and age / Continent, pays ou zone, année et âge	Number - Nombre			Rate - Taux		
	Both sexes Les deux sexes	Male Masculin	Female Féminin	Both sexes Les deux sexes	Male Masculin	Female Féminin
EUROPE						
Estonia - Estonie						
2011 (C)						
7 - 27 days - 7 - 27 jours	9	4	5	...	...	...
7 - 13 days - 7 - 13 jours	4	2	2	...	...	...
14 - 20 days - 14 - 20 jours	4	1	3	...	...	...
21 - 27 days - 21 - 27 jours	1	1	-	...	...	...
28 days - 11 months - 28 jours - 11 mois	12	7	5	...	...	...
28 days - less than 2 months - 28 jours - moins de 2 mois	3	3	-	...	...	...
2 months - 2 mois	1	1	-	...	...	...
3 months - 3 mois	1	-	1	...	...	...
4 months - 4 mois	4	2	2	...	...	...
5 months - 5 mois	-	-	-	...	...	...
6 months - 6 mois	1	-	1	...	...	...
7 months - 7 mois	-	-	-	...	...	...
8 months - 8 mois	-	-	-	...	...	...
9 months - 9 mois	1	1	-	...	...	...
10 months - 10 mois	-	-	-	...	...	...
11 months - 11 mois	1	-	1	...	...	...
Finland - Finlande[23]						
2010 (C)						
Total	139	80	59	2.3	2.6	2.0
Less than 1 day - Moins de 1 jour	36	23	13	0.6	♦0.7	♦0.4
1 - 6 days - 1 - 6 jours	32	17	15	0.5	♦0.5	♦0.5
7 - 27 days - 7 - 27 jours	23	15	8	♦0.4	♦0.5	♦0.3
7 - 13 days - 7 - 13 jours	6	4	2	♦0.1	♦0.1	♦0.1
14 - 20 days - 14 - 20 jours	9	7	2	♦0.1	♦0.2	♦0.1
21 - 27 days - 21 - 27 jours	8	4	4	♦0.1	♦0.1	♦0.1
28 days - 11 months - 28 jours - 11 mois	48	25	23	0.8	♦0.8	♦0.8
28 days - less than 2 months - 28 jours - moins de 2 mois	17	11	6	♦0.3	♦0.4	♦0.2
2 months - 2 mois	3	2	1	-	♦0.1	-
3 months - 3 mois	3	-	3	-	-	♦0.1
4 months - 4 mois	4	1	3	♦0.1	-	♦0.1
5 months - 5 mois	6	2	4	♦0.1	♦0.1	♦0.1
6 months - 6 mois	4	3	1	♦0.1	♦0.1	-
7 months - 7 mois	2	1	1	-	-	-
8 months - 8 mois	3	2	1	-	♦0.1	-
9 months - 9 mois	2	1	1	-	-	-
10 months - 10 mois	2	1	1	-	-	-
11 months - 11 mois	2	1	1	-	-	-
France[24]						
2010 (C)						
Total	2 785	1 558	1 227	3.5	3.8	3.1
Less than 1 day - Moins de 1 jour	589	326	263	0.7	0.8	0.7
1 - 6 days - 1 - 6 jours	680	409	271	0.8	1.0	0.7
7 - 27 days - 7 - 27 jours	612	316	296	0.8	0.8	0.8
7 - 13 days - 7 - 13 jours	325	167	158	0.4	0.4	0.4
14 - 20 days - 14 - 20 jours	165	88	77	0.2	0.2	0.2
21 - 27 days - 21 - 27 jours	122	61	61	0.2	0.1	0.2
28 days - 11 months - 28 jours - 11 mois	904	507	397	1.1	1.2	1.0
28 days - less than 2 months - 28 jours - moins de 2 mois	288	152	136	0.4	0.4	0.3
2 months - 2 mois	122	68	54	0.2	0.2	0.1
3 months - 3 mois	115	72	43	0.1	0.2	0.1
4 months - 4 mois	98	59	39	0.1	0.1	0.1
5 months - 5 mois	58	34	24	0.1	0.1	♦0.1
6 months - 6 mois	51	27	24	0.1	♦0.1	♦0.1
7 months - 7 mois	45	28	17	0.1	♦0.1	-
8 months - 8 mois	46	25	21	0.1	♦0.1	♦0.1
9 months - 9 mois	27	14	13	-	-	-
10 months - 10 mois	28	17	11	-	-	-
11 months - 11 mois	26	11	15	-	-	-
Germany - Allemagne						
2011 (C)						
Total	2 408	1 347	1 061	3.6	4.0	3.3
Less than 1 day - Moins de 1 jour	754	404	350	1.1	1.2	1.1
1 - 6 days - 1 - 6 jours	496	298	198	0.7	0.9	0.6
7 - 27 days - 7 - 27 jours	354	194	160	0.5	0.6	0.5
7 - 13 days - 7 - 13 jours	185	104	81	0.3	0.3	0.3
14 - 20 days - 14 - 20 jours	105	60	45	0.2	0.2	0.1

16. Infant deaths and infant mortality rates by age and sex: latest available year, 2003 - 2012
Décès d'enfants de moins d'un an et taux de mortalité infantile selon l'âge et le sexe : dernière année disponible, 2003 - 2012 (continued - suite)

Continent, country or area, year and age / Continent, pays ou zone, année et âge	Number - Nombre			Rate - Taux		
	Both sexes Les deux sexes	Male Masculin	Female Féminin	Both sexes Les deux sexes	Male Masculin	Female Féminin
EUROPE						
Germany - Allemagne						
2011 (C)						
21 - 27 days - 21 - 27 jours	64	30	34	0.1	0.1	0.1
28 days - 11 months - 28 jours - 11 mois.....	804	451	353	1.2	1.3	1.1
28 days - less than 2 months - 28 jours - moins de 2 mois	181	102	79	0.3	0.3	0.2
2 months - 2 mois.....	134	69	65	0.2	0.2	0.2
3 months - 3 mois.....	107	54	53	0.2	0.2	0.2
4 months - 4 mois.....	85	47	38	0.1	0.1	0.1
5 months - 5 mois.....	62	39	23	0.1	0.1	♦0.1
6 months - 6 mois.....	62	37	25	0.1	0.1	♦0.1
7 months - 7 mois.....	56	33	23	0.1	0.1	♦0.1
8 months - 8 mois.....	33	17	16	-	♦0.1	-
9 months - 9 mois.....	30	16	14	-	-	-
10 months - 10 mois.....	23	19	4	-	♦0.1	-
11 months - 11 mois.....	31	18	13	-	♦0.1	-
Gibraltar						
2006 (+C)						
Total.....	1	1	-	...	...	...
Less than 7 days - Moins de 7 jours.....	-	-	-	...	...	...
7 - 27 days - 7 - 27 jours	-	-	-	...	...	...
28 days - 11 months - 28 jours - 11 mois.....	1	1	-	...	...	...
28 days - 2 months - 28 jours - 2 mois.....	-	-	-	...	...	...
3 months - 3 mois.....	1	1	-	...	...	...
4 - 11 months - 4 - 11 mois	-	-	-	...	...	...
Greece - Grèce						
2011 (C)						
Total.....	357	197	160	3.4	3.6	3.1
Less than 1 day - Moins de 1 jour	46	28	18	0.4	♦0.5	♦0.3
1 - 6 days - 1 - 6 jours	97	53	44	0.9	1.0	0.9
7 - 27 days - 7 - 27 jours	91	53	38	0.9	1.0	0.7
7 - 13 days - 7 - 13 jours	46	26	20	0.4	♦0.5	♦0.4
14 - 20 days - 14 - 20 jours	30	18	12	0.3	♦0.3	♦0.2
21 - 27 days - 21 - 27 jours	15	9	6	♦0.1	♦0.2	♦0.1
28 days - 11 months - 28 jours - 11 mois.....	123	63	60	1.2	1.1	1.2
28 days - less than 2 months - 28 jours - moins de 2 mois	45	27	18	0.4	♦0.5	♦0.3
2 months - 2 mois.....	13	7	6	♦0.1	♦0.1	♦0.1
3 months - 3 mois.....	9	3	6	♦0.1	♦0.1	♦0.1
4 months - 4 mois.....	11	6	5	♦0.1	♦0.1	♦0.1
5 months - 5 mois.....	9	5	4	♦0.1	♦0.1	♦0.1
6 months - 6 mois.....	9	2	7	♦0.1	-	♦0.1
7 months - 7 mois.....	8	4	4	♦0.1	♦0.1	♦0.1
8 months - 8 mois.....	9	4	5	♦0.1	♦0.1	♦0.1
9 months - 9 mois.....	4	3	1	-	♦0.1	-
10 months - 10 mois.....	2	-	2	-	-	-
11 months - 11 mois.....	4	2	2	-	-	-
Unknown - Inconnu	-	-	-	-	-	-
Hungary - Hongrie						
2011 (C)						
Total.....	433	240	193	4.9	5.3	4.5
Less than 1 day - Moins de 1 jour	92	54	38	1.0	1.2	0.9
1 - 6 days - 1 - 6 jours	98	54	44	1.1	1.2	1.0
7 - 27 days - 7 - 27 jours	83	54	29	0.9	1.2	♦0.7
7 - 13 days - 7 - 13 jours	40	26	14	0.5	♦0.6	♦0.3
14 - 20 days - 14 - 20 jours	27	16	11	♦0.3	♦0.4	♦0.3
21 - 27 days - 21 - 27 jours	16	12	4	♦0.2	♦0.3	♦0.1
28 days - 11 months - 28 jours - 11 mois.....	160	78	82	1.8	1.7	1.9
28 days - less than 2 months - 28 jours - moins de 2 mois	50	26	24	0.6	♦0.6	♦0.6
2 months - 2 mois.....	28	11	17	♦0.3	♦0.2	♦0.4
3 months - 3 mois.....	15	9	6	♦0.2	♦0.2	♦0.1
4 months - 4 mois.....	14	7	7	♦0.2	♦0.2	♦0.2
5 months - 5 mois.....	9	4	5	♦0.1	♦0.1	♦0.1
6 months - 6 mois.....	10	7	3	♦0.1	♦0.2	♦0.1
7 months - 7 mois.....	9	2	7	♦0.1	-	♦0.2
8 months - 8 mois.....	5	4	1	♦0.1	♦0.1	-
9 months - 9 mois.....	9	4	5	♦0.1	♦0.1	♦0.1
10 months - 10 mois.....	9	3	6	♦0.1	♦0.1	♦0.1
11 months - 11 mois.....	2	1	1	-	-	-

16. Infant deaths and infant mortality rates by age and sex: latest available year, 2003 - 2012
Décès d'enfants de moins d'un an et taux de mortalité infantile selon l'âge et le sexe : dernière année disponible, 2003 - 2012 (continued - suite)

Continent, country or area, year and age / Continent, pays ou zone, année et âge	Number - Nombre			Rate - Taux		
	Both sexes Les deux sexes	Male Masculin	Female Féminin	Both sexes Les deux sexes	Male Masculin	Female Féminin
EUROPE						
Iceland - Islande[25]						
2011 (C)						
Total	4	3	1	...	...	...
Less than 1 day - Moins de 1 jour	1	1	-	...	...	...
1 - 6 days - 1 - 6 jours	-	-	-	...	...	...
7 - 27 days - 7 - 27 jours	2	1	1	...	...	...
7 - 13 days - 7 - 13 jours	2	1	1	...	...	...
14 - 20 days - 14 - 20 jours	-	-	-	...	...	...
21 - 27 days - 21 - 27 jours	-	-	-	...	...	...
28 days - 11 months - 28 jours - 11 mois	1	1	-	...	...	...
28 days - less than 2 months - 28 jours - moins de 2 mois	-	-	-	...	...	...
2 months - 2 mois	-	-	-	...	...	...
3 months - 3 mois	-	-	-	...	...	...
4 months - 4 mois	-	-	-	...	...	...
5 months - 5 mois	-	-	-	...	...	...
6 months - 6 mois	-	-	-	...	...	...
7 months - 7 mois	-	-	-	...	...	...
8 months - 8 mois	-	-	-	...	...	...
9 months - 9 mois	1	1	-	...	...	...
10 months - 10 mois	-	-	-	...	...	...
11 months - 11 mois	-	-	-	...	...	...
Unknown - Inconnu	-	-	-	...	...	...
Ireland - Irlande						
2011* (+C)						
Total	271	151	120	3.6	4.0	3.3
Less than 1 day - Moins de 1 jour	89	47	42	1.2	1.2	1.2
1 - 6 days - 1 - 6 jours	56	34	22	0.8	0.9	♦0.6
7 - 27 days - 7 - 27 jours	45	30	15	0.6	0.8	♦0.4
7 - 13 days - 7 - 13 jours	20	14	6	♦0.3	♦0.4	♦0.2
14 - 20 days - 14 - 20 jours	18	12	6	♦0.2	♦0.3	♦0.2
21 - 27 days - 21 - 27 jours	7	4	3	♦0.1	♦0.1	♦0.1
28 days - 11 months - 28 jours - 11 mois	68	34	34	0.9	0.9	0.9
28 days - less than 2 months - 28 jours - moins de 2 mois	13	6	7	♦0.2	♦0.2	♦0.2
2 months - 2 mois	15	7	8	♦0.2	♦0.2	♦0.2
3 months - 3 mois	11	2	9	♦0.1	♦0.1	♦0.2
4 months - 4 mois	7	6	1	♦0.1	♦0.2	-
5 months - 5 mois	8	5	3	♦0.1	♦0.1	♦0.1
6 months - 6 mois	3	1	2	-	-	♦0.1
7 months - 7 mois	2	1	1	-	-	-
8 months - 8 mois	-	-	-	-	-	-
9 months - 9 mois	4	3	1	♦0.1	♦0.1	-
10 months - 10 mois	2	1	1	-	-	-
11 months - 11 mois	3	2	1	-	♦0.1	-
Unknown - Inconnu	-	-	-	-	-	-
Isle of Man - Île de Man						
2004 (+C)						
Total	2	1	1	...	...	...
Less than 7 days - Moins de 7 jours	-	-	-	...	...	...
7 - 27 days - 7 - 27 jours	1	-	1	...	...	...
7 - 13 days - 7 - 13 jours	1	-	1	...	...	...
14 - 27 days - 14 - 27 jours	-	-	-	...	...	...
28 days - 11 months - 28 jours - 11 mois	1	1	-	...	...	...
28 days - 4 months - 28 jours - 4 mois	-	-	-	...	...	...
5 months - 5 mois	1	1	-	...	...	...
6 - 11 months - 6 - 11 mois	-	-	-	...	...	...
Italy - Italie						
2009 (C)						
Total	1 947	1 078	869	3.4	3.7	3.1
Less than 1 day - Moins de 1 jour	486	274	212	0.9	0.9	0.8
1 - 6 days - 1 - 6 jours	499	270	229	0.9	0.9	0.8
7 - 27 days - 7 - 27 jours	426	230	196	0.7	0.8	0.7
7 - 13 days - 7 - 13 jours	212	112	100	0.4	0.4	0.4
14 - 20 days - 14 - 20 jours	130	67	63	0.2	0.2	0.2
21 - 27 days - 21 - 27 jours	84	51	33	0.1	0.2	0.1
28 days - 11 months - 28 jours - 11 mois	536	304	232	0.9	1.0	0.8
28 days - less than 2 months - 28 jours - moins de 2 mois	179	103	76	0.3	0.4	0.3
2 months - 2 mois	71	48	23	0.1	0.2	♦0.1
3 months - 3 mois	57	30	27	0.1	0.1	♦0.1

16. Infant deaths and infant mortality rates by age and sex: latest available year, 2003 - 2012
Décès d'enfants de moins d'un an et taux de mortalité infantile selon l'âge et le sexe : dernière année disponible, 2003 - 2012 (continued - suite)

Continent, country or area, year and age Continent, pays ou zone, année et âge	Number - Nombre			Rate - Taux		
	Both sexes Les deux sexes	Male Masculin	Female Féminin	Both sexes Les deux sexes	Male Masculin	Female Féminin
EUROPE						
Italy - Italie						
2009 (C)						
4 months - 4 mois	45	25	20	0.1	◆0.1	◆0.1
5 months - 5 mois	37	22	15	0.1	◆0.1	◆0.1
6 months - 6 mois	41	13	28	0.1	-	◆0.1
7 months - 7 mois	24	13	11	-	-	-
8 months - 8 mois	26	19	7	-	◆0.1	-
9 months - 9 mois	16	9	7	-	-	-
10 months - 10 mois	23	17	6	-	◆0.1	-
11 months - 11 mois	17	5	12	-	-	-
Latvia - Lettonie						
2010 (C)						
Total	110	58	52	5.7	5.8	5.6
Less than 1 day - Moins de 1 jour	19	10	9	◆1.0	◆1.0	◆1.0
1 - 6 days - 1 - 6 jours	29	13	16	◆1.5	◆1.3	◆1.7
7 - 27 days - 7 - 27 jours	20	10	10	◆1.0	◆1.0	◆1.1
7 - 13 days - 7 - 13 jours	11	6	5	◆0.6	◆0.6	◆0.5
14 - 20 days - 14 - 20 jours	7	4	3	◆0.4	◆0.4	◆0.3
21 - 27 days - 21 - 27 jours	2	-	2	◆0.1	-	◆0.2
28 days - 11 months - 28 jours - 11 mois	42	25	17	2.2	◆2.5	◆1.8
28 days - less than 2 months - 28 jours - moins de 2 mois	12	7	5	◆0.6	◆0.7	◆0.5
2 - 11 months - 2 - 11 mois	30	18	12	1.6	◆1.8	◆1.3
Liechtenstein						
2011* (C)						
Total	1	-	1	...	...	...
Lithuania - Lituanie						
2011 (C)						
Total	144	80	64	4.2	4.5	3.9
Less than 1 day - Moins de 1 jour	34	18	16	1.0	◆1.0	◆1.0
1 - 6 days - 1 - 6 jours	30	19	11	0.9	◆1.1	◆0.7
7 - 27 days - 7 - 27 jours	26	14	12	◆0.8	◆0.8	◆0.7
7 - 13 days - 7 - 13 jours	10	6	4	◆0.3	◆0.3	◆0.2
14 - 20 days - 14 - 20 jours	10	4	6	◆0.3	◆0.2	◆0.4
21 - 27 days - 21 - 27 jours	6	4	2	◆0.2	◆0.2	◆0.1
28 days - 11 months - 28 jours - 11 mois	54	29	25	1.6	◆1.6	◆1.5
28 days - less than 2 months - 28 jours - moins de 2 mois	19	16	3	◆0.6	◆0.9	◆0.2
2 months - 2 mois	9	5	4	◆0.3	◆0.3	◆0.2
3 months - 3 mois	4	3	1	◆0.1	◆0.2	◆0.1
4 months - 4 mois	7	2	5	◆0.2	◆0.1	◆0.3
5 months - 5 mois	5	-	5	◆0.1	-	◆0.3
6 months - 6 mois	4	2	2	◆0.1	◆0.1	◆0.1
7 months - 7 mois	2	-	2	◆0.1	-	◆0.1
8 months - 8 mois	1	-	1	-	-	◆0.1
9 months - 9 mois	1	-	1	-	-	◆0.1
10 months - 10 mois	-	-	-	-	-	-
11 months - 11 mois	2	1	1	◆0.1	◆0.1	◆0.1
Unknown - Inconnu	-	-	-	-	-	-
Luxembourg						
2011 (C)						
Total	24	16	8	...	...	...
Less than 1 day - Moins de 1 jour	8	5	3	...	...	...
1 - 6 days - 1 - 6 jours	5	3	2	...	...	...
7 - 27 days - 7 - 27 jours	3	2	1	...	...	...
7 - 13 days - 7 - 13 jours	1	-	1	...	...	...
14 - 20 days - 14 - 20 jours	2	2	-	...	...	...
21 - 27 days - 21 - 27 jours	-	-	-	...	...	...
28 days - 11 months - 28 jours - 11 mois	8	6	2	...	...	...
28 days - less than 2 months - 28 jours - moins de 2 mois	-	-	-	...	...	...
2 months - 2 mois	3	3	-	...	...	...
3 months - 3 mois	-	-	-	...	...	...
4 months - 4 mois	2	1	1	...	...	...
5 months - 5 mois	-	-	-	...	...	...
6 months - 6 mois	1	-	1	...	...	...
7 months - 7 mois	-	-	-	...	...	...
8 months - 8 mois	1	1	-	...	...	...
9 months - 9 mois	-	-	-	...	...	...
10 months - 10 mois	-	-	-	...	...	...

Continent, country or area, year and age / Continent, pays ou zone, année et âge	Number - Nombre			Rate - Taux		
	Both sexes Les deux sexes	Male Masculin	Female Féminin	Both sexes Les deux sexes	Male Masculin	Female Féminin
EUROPE						
Luxembourg						
2011 (C)						
11 months - 11 mois	1	1	-	...	...	...
Unknown - Inconnu	-	-	-	...	...	...
Malta - Malte						
2011 (C)						
Total	27	13	14	...	...	...
Less than 1 day - Moins de 1 jour	12	6	6	...	...	...
1 - 6 days - 1 - 6 jours	6	3	3	...	...	...
7 - 27 days - 7 - 27 jours	5	2	3	...	...	...
7 - 13 days - 7 - 13 jours	3	2	1	...	...	...
14 - 20 days - 14 - 20 jours	2	-	2	...	...	...
21 - 27 days - 21 - 27 jours	-	-	-	...	...	...
28 days - 11 months - 28 jours - 11 mois	4	2	2	...	...	...
28 days - less than 2 months - 28 jours - moins de 2 mois	1	1	-	...	...	...
2 months - 2 mois	-	-	-	...	...	...
3 months - 3 mois	2	1	1	...	...	...
4 months - 4 mois	1	-	1	...	...	...
5 months - 5 mois	-	-	-	...	...	...
6 months - 6 mois	-	-	-	...	...	...
7 months - 7 mois	-	-	-	...	...	...
8 months - 8 mois	-	-	-	...	...	...
9 months - 9 mois	-	-	-	...	...	...
10 months - 10 mois	-	-	-	...	...	...
11 months - 11 mois	-	-	-	...	...	...
Unknown - Inconnu	-	-	-	...	...	...
Montenegro - Monténégro						
2009 (C)						
Total	49	28	21	...	...	...
Less than 1 day - Moins de 1 jour	7	4	3	...	...	...
1 - 6 days - 1 - 6 jours	20	11	9	...	...	...
7 - 27 days - 7 - 27 jours	7	4	3	...	...	...
7 - 13 days - 7 - 13 jours	2	1	1	...	...	...
14 - 20 days - 14 - 20 jours	3	2	1	...	...	...
21 - 27 days - 21 - 27 jours	2	1	1	...	...	...
28 days - 11 months - 28 jours - 11 mois	15	9	6	...	...	...
28 days - less than 2 months - 28 jours - moins de 2 mois	10	7	3	...	...	...
2 months - 2 mois	1	1	-	...	...	...
3 months - 3 mois	3	1	2	...	...	...
4 months - 4 mois	1	-	1	...	...	...
5 - 11 months - 5 - 11 mois	-	-	-	...	...	...
Netherlands - Pays-Bas[26]						
2009 (C)						
Total	711	...	...	3.8	...	...
Less than 1 day - Moins de 1 jour	240	...	...	1.3	...	...
1 - 6 days - 1 - 6 jours	166	...	...	0.9	...	...
7 - 27 days - 7 - 27 jours	122	...	...	0.7	...	...
7 - 13 days - 7 - 13 jours	73	...	...	0.4	...	...
14 - 20 days - 14 - 20 jours	41	...	...	0.2	...	...
21 - 27 days - 21 - 27 jours	8	...	...	-	...	...
28 days - 11 months - 28 jours - 11 mois	183	...	...	1.0	...	...
28 days - less than 2 months - 28 jours - moins de 2 mois	59	...	...	0.3	...	...
2 months - 2 mois	25	...	...	♦0.1	...	...
3 months - 3 mois	20	...	...	♦0.1	...	...
4 months - 4 mois	15	...	...	♦0.1	...	...
5 months - 5 mois	13	...	...	♦0.1	...	...
6 months - 6 mois	15	...	...	♦0.1	...	...
7 months - 7 mois	12	...	...	♦0.1	...	...
8 months - 8 mois	9	...	...	-	...	...
9 months - 9 mois	4	...	...	-	...	...
10 months - 10 mois	8	...	...	-	...	...
11 months - 11 mois	3	...	...	-	...	...
Norway - Norvège[27]						
2011 (C)						
Total	142	92	50	2.4	3.0	1.7
Less than 1 day - Moins de 1 jour	35	19	16	0.6	♦0.6	♦0.5
1 - 6 days - 1 - 6 jours	42	30	12	0.7	1.0	♦0.4

16. Infant deaths and infant mortality rates by age and sex: latest available year, 2003 - 2012
Décès d'enfants de moins d'un an et taux de mortalité infantile selon l'âge et le sexe : dernière année disponible, 2003 - 2012 (continued - suite)

Continent, country or area, year and age / Continent, pays ou zone, année et âge	Number - Nombre			Rate - Taux		
	Both sexes Les deux sexes	Male Masculin	Female Féminin	Both sexes Les deux sexes	Male Masculin	Female Féminin
EUROPE						
Norway - Norvège[27]						
2011 (C)						
7 - 27 days - 7 - 27 jours	26	19	7	♦0.4	♦0.6	♦0.2
7 - 13 days - 7 - 13 jours	13	11	2	♦0.2	♦0.4	♦0.1
14 - 20 days - 14 - 20 jours	12	7	5	♦0.2	♦0.2	♦0.2
21 - 27 days - 21 - 27 jours	1	1	-	-	-	-
28 days - 11 months - 28 jours - 11 mois	39	24	15	0.6	♦0.8	♦0.5
28 days - less than 2 months - 28 jours - moins de 2 mois	14	10	4	♦0.2	♦0.3	♦0.1
2 months - 2 mois	3	1	2	-	-	♦0.1
3 months - 3 mois	3	2	1	-	♦0.1	-
4 months - 4 mois	2	-	2	-	-	♦0.1
5 months - 5 mois	3	3	-	-	♦0.1	-
6 months - 6 mois	4	2	2	♦0.1	♦0.1	♦0.1
7 months - 7 mois	4	3	1	♦0.1	♦0.1	-
8 months - 8 mois	4	3	1	♦0.1	♦0.1	-
9 months - 9 mois	1	-	1	-	-	-
10 months - 10 mois	1	-	1	-	-	-
11 months - 11 mois	-	-	-	-	-	-
Unknown - Inconnu	-	-	-	-	-	-
Poland - Pologne						
2011 (C)						
Total	1 836	1 027	809	4.7	5.1	4.3
Less than 1 day - Moins de 1 jour	569	326	243	1.5	1.6	1.3
1 - 6 days - 1 - 6 jours	374	218	156	1.0	1.1	0.8
7 - 27 days - 7 - 27 jours	315	163	152	0.8	0.8	0.8
7 - 13 days - 7 - 13 jours	165	93	72	0.4	0.5	0.4
14 - 20 days - 14 - 20 jours	88	38	50	0.2	0.2	0.3
21 - 27 days - 21 - 27 jours	62	32	30	0.2	0.2	0.2
28 days - 11 months - 28 jours - 11 mois	578	320	258	1.5	1.6	1.4
28 days - less than 2 months - 28 jours - moins de 2 mois	164	84	80	0.4	0.4	0.4
2 months - 2 mois	86	51	35	0.2	0.3	0.2
3 months - 3 mois	78	48	30	0.2	0.2	0.2
4 months - 4 mois	50	33	17	0.1	0.2	♦0.1
5 months - 5 mois	44	25	19	0.1	♦0.1	♦0.1
6 months - 6 mois	46	19	27	0.1	♦0.1	♦0.1
7 months - 7 mois	31	19	12	0.1	♦0.1	♦0.1
8 months - 8 mois	34	21	13	0.1	♦0.1	♦0.1
9 months - 9 mois	14	7	7	-	-	-
10 months - 10 mois	14	6	8	-	-	-
11 months - 11 mois	17	7	10	-	-	♦0.1
Unknown - Inconnu	-	-	-	-	-	-
Portugal						
2011 (C)						
Total	302	175[28]	126[28]	3.1	3.5	2.7
Less than 1 day - Moins de 1 jour	76	46[28]	29[28]	0.8	0.9	♦0.6
1 - 6 days - 1 - 6 jours	71	40	31	0.7	0.8	0.7
7 - 27 days - 7 - 27 jours	83	48	35	0.9	1.0	0.7
7 - 13 days - 7 - 13 jours	43	21	22	0.4	♦0.4	♦0.5
14 - 20 days - 14 - 20 jours	27	19	8	♦0.3	♦0.4	♦0.2
21 - 27 days - 21 - 27 jours	13	8	5	♦0.1	♦0.2	♦0.1
28 days - 11 months - 28 jours - 11 mois	72	...	31	0.7	...	0.7
28 days - less than 2 months - 28 jours - moins de 2 mois	21	12	9	♦0.2	♦0.2	♦0.2
2 months - 2 mois	10	7	3	♦0.1	♦0.1	♦0.1
3 months - 3 mois	9	3	6	♦0.1	♦0.1	♦0.1
4 months - 4 mois	8	5	3	♦0.1	♦0.1	♦0.1
5 months - 5 mois	4	3	1	-	♦0.1	-
6 months - 6 mois	6	2	4	♦0.1	-	♦0.1
7 months - 7 mois	4	1	3	-	-	♦0.1
8 months - 8 mois	3	3	-	-	♦0.1	-
9 months - 9 mois	1	...	1	-	...	-
10 months - 10 mois	3	...	1	-	...	-
11 months - 11 mois	3	...		-	...	-
Unknown - Inconnu	-	-	-	-	-	-
Republic of Moldova - République de Moldova[29]						
2010 (C)						
Total	476	288	188	11.8	13.9	9.5
Less than 1 day - Moins de 1 jour	87	51	36	2.1	2.5	1.8
1 - 6 days - 1 - 6 jours	147	89	58	3.6	4.3	2.9

16. Infant deaths and infant mortality rates by age and sex: latest available year, 2003 - 2012
Décès d'enfants de moins d'un an et taux de mortalité infantile selon l'âge et le sexe : dernière année disponible, 2003 - 2012 (continued - suite)

Continent, country or area, year and age / Continent, pays ou zone, année et âge	Number - Nombre			Rate - Taux		
	Both sexes Les deux sexes	Male Masculin	Female Féminin	Both sexes Les deux sexes	Male Masculin	Female Féminin
EUROPE						
Republic of Moldova - République de Moldova[29]						
2010 (C)						
7 - 27 days - 7 - 27 jours	69	48	21	1.7	2.3	♦1.1
7 - 13 days - 7 - 13 jours	37	29	8	0.9	♦1.4	♦0.4
14 - 20 days - 14 - 20 jours	16	9	7	♦0.4	♦0.4	♦0.4
21 - 27 days - 21 - 27 jours	16	10	6	♦0.4	♦0.5	♦0.3
28 days - 11 months - 28 jours - 11 mois	173	100	73	4.3	4.8	3.7
28 days - less than 2 months - 28 jours - moins de 2 mois	54	31	23	1.3	1.5	♦1.2
2 months - 2 mois	34	19	15	0.8	♦0.9	♦0.8
3 months - 3 mois	26	16	10	♦0.6	♦0.8	♦0.5
4 months - 4 mois	12	5	7	♦0.3	♦0.2	♦0.4
5 months - 5 mois	13	4	9	♦0.3	♦0.2	♦0.5
6 months - 6 mois	9	7	2	♦0.2	♦0.3	♦0.1
7 months - 7 mois	6	3	3	♦0.1	♦0.1	♦0.2
8 months - 8 mois	4	4	-	♦0.1	♦0.2	-
9 months - 9 mois	7	4	3	♦0.2	♦0.2	♦0.2
10 months - 10 mois	7	6	1	♦0.2	♦0.3	♦0.1
11 months - 11 mois	1	1	-	-	-	-
Romania - Roumanie						
2011 (C)						
Total	1 850	1 067	783	9.4	10.6	8.2
Less than 1 day - Moins de 1 jour	185	110	75	0.9	1.1	0.8
1 - 6 days - 1 - 6 jours	510	310	200	2.6	3.1	2.1
7 - 27 days - 7 - 27 jours	348	186	162	1.8	1.8	1.7
7 - 13 days - 7 - 13 jours	173	90	83	0.9	0.9	0.9
14 - 20 days - 14 - 20 jours	95	47	48	0.5	0.5	0.5
21 - 27 days - 21 - 27 jours	80	49	31	0.4	0.5	0.3
28 days - 11 months - 28 jours - 11 mois	807	461	346	4.1	4.6	3.6
28 days - less than 2 months - 28 jours - moins de 2 mois	265	149	116	1.4	1.5	1.2
2 months - 2 mois	138	75	63	0.7	0.7	0.7
3 months - 3 mois	101	57	44	0.5	0.6	0.5
4 months - 4 mois	62	34	28	0.3	0.3	♦0.3
5 months - 5 mois	59	36	23	0.3	0.4	♦0.2
6 months - 6 mois	43	25	18	0.2	♦0.2	♦0.2
7 months - 7 mois	35	19	16	0.2	♦0.2	♦0.2
8 months - 8 mois	33	21	12	0.2	♦0.2	♦0.1
9 months - 9 mois	19	10	9	♦0.1	♦0.1	♦0.1
10 months - 10 mois	29	17	12	♦0.1	♦0.2	♦0.1
11 months - 11 mois	23	18	5	♦0.1	♦0.2	♦0.1
Unknown - Inconnu	-	-	-	-	-	-
Russian Federation - Fédération de Russie[13]						
2011 (C)						
Total	13 168	7 572	5 596	7.3	8.2	6.4
Less than 1 day - Moins de 1 jour	1 231	684	547	0.7	0.7	0.6
1 - 6 days - 1 - 6 jours	3 580	2 162	1 418	2.0	2.3	1.6
7 - 27 days - 7 - 27 jours	2 722	1 563	1 159	1.5	1.7	1.3
7 - 13 days - 7 - 13 jours	1 366	779	587	0.8	0.8	0.7
14 - 20 days - 14 - 20 jours	765	443	322	0.4	0.5	0.4
21 - 27 days - 21 - 27 jours	591	341	250	0.3	0.4	0.3
28 days - 11 months - 28 jours - 11 mois	5 626	3 158	2 468	3.1	3.4	2.8
28 days - less than 2 months - 28 jours - moins de 2 mois	1 793	1 024	769	1.0	1.1	0.9
2 months - 2 mois	935	548	387	0.5	0.6	0.4
3 months - 3 mois	675	388	287	0.4	0.4	0.3
4 months - 4 mois	512	292	220	0.3	0.3	0.3
5 months - 5 mois	425	230	195	0.2	0.2	0.2
6 months - 6 mois	330	171	159	0.2	0.2	0.2
7 months - 7 mois	264	145	119	0.1	0.2	0.1
8 months - 8 mois	227	125	102	0.1	0.1	0.1
9 months - 9 mois	156	77	79	0.1	0.1	0.1
10 months - 10 mois	163	86	77	0.1	0.1	0.1
11 months - 11 mois	146	72	74	0.1	0.1	0.1
Unknown - Inconnu	9	5	4	-	-	-
San Marino - Saint-Marin						
2003 (+C)						
Total	2	1	1	...	...	...
Less than 1 day - Moins de 1 jour	1	-	1	...	...	...
1 - 6 days - 1 - 6 jours	-	-	-	...	...	...

16. Infant deaths and infant mortality rates by age and sex: latest available year, 2003 - 2012
Décès d'enfants de moins d'un an et taux de mortalité infantile selon l'âge et le sexe : dernière année disponible, 2003 - 2012 (continued - suite)

Continent, country or area, year and age / Continent, pays ou zone, année et âge	Number - Nombre			Rate - Taux		
	Both sexes Les deux sexes	Male Masculin	Female Féminin	Both sexes Les deux sexes	Male Masculin	Female Féminin
EUROPE						
San Marino - Saint-Marin						
2003 (+C)						
7 - 27 days - 7 - 27 jours	1	1	-	...	...	...
28 days - 11 months - 28 jours - 11 mois	-	-	-	...	...	...
Serbia - Serbie[30]						
2011 (+C)						
Total	414	231	183	6.3	6.8	5.8
Less than 1 day - Moins de 1 jour	127	73	54	1.9	2.2	1.7
1 - 6 days - 1 - 6 jours	122	70	52	1.9	2.1	1.6
7 - 27 days - 7 - 27 jours	61	30	31	0.9	0.9	1.0
7 - 13 days - 7 - 13 jours	28	11	17	♦0.4	♦0.3	♦0.5
14 - 20 days - 14 - 20 jours	18	13	5	♦0.3	♦0.4	♦0.2
21 - 27 days - 21 - 27 jours	15	6	9	♦0.2	♦0.2	♦0.3
28 days - 11 months - 28 jours - 11 mois	104	58	46	1.6	1.7	1.5
28 days - less than 2 months - 28 jours - moins de 2 mois	26	11	15	♦0.4	♦0.3	♦0.5
2 months - 2 mois	18	14	4	♦0.3	♦0.4	♦0.1
3 months - 3 mois	11	9	2	♦0.2	♦0.3	♦0.1
4 months - 4 mois	13	9	4	♦0.2	♦0.3	♦0.1
5 months - 5 mois	6	3	3	♦0.1	♦0.1	♦0.1
6 months - 6 mois	4	2	2	♦0.1	♦0.1	♦0.1
7 months - 7 mois	6	2	4	♦0.1	♦0.1	♦0.1
8 months - 8 mois	7	3	4	♦0.1	♦0.1	♦0.1
9 months - 9 mois	4	2	2	♦0.1	♦0.1	♦0.1
10 months - 10 mois	5	2	3	♦0.1	♦0.1	♦0.1
11 months - 11 mois	4	1	3	♦0.1	-	♦0.1
Unknown - Inconnu	-	-	-	-	-	-
Slovakia - Slovaquie						
2011 (C)						
Total	300	172	128	4.9	5.5	4.3
Less than 1 day - Moins de 1 jour	47	26	21	0.8	♦0.8	♦0.7
1 - 6 days - 1 - 6 jours	68	40	28	1.1	1.3	♦0.9
7 - 27 days - 7 - 27 jours	62	37	25	1.0	1.2	♦0.8
7 - 13 days - 7 - 13 jours	40	22	18	0.7	♦0.7	♦0.6
14 - 20 days - 14 - 20 jours	12	9	3	♦0.2	♦0.3	♦0.1
21 - 27 days - 21 - 27 jours	10	6	4	♦0.2	♦0.2	♦0.1
28 days - 11 months - 28 jours - 11 mois	123	69	54	2.0	2.2	1.8
28 days - less than 2 months - 28 jours - moins de 2 mois	37	26	11	0.6	♦0.8	♦0.4
2 months - 2 mois	25	12	13	♦0.4	♦0.4	♦0.4
3 months - 3 mois	11	4	7	♦0.2	♦0.1	♦0.2
4 months - 4 mois	13	6	7	♦0.2	♦0.2	♦0.2
5 months - 5 mois	10	7	3	♦0.2	♦0.2	♦0.1
6 months - 6 mois	8	5	3	♦0.1	♦0.2	♦0.1
7 months - 7 mois	3	1	2	-	-	♦0.1
8 months - 8 mois	7	5	2	♦0.1	♦0.2	♦0.1
9 months - 9 mois	4	1	3	♦0.1	-	♦0.1
10 months - 10 mois	2	-	2	-	-	♦0.1
11 months - 11 mois	3	2	1	-	♦0.1	-
Slovenia - Slovénie						
2011 (C)						
Total	64	41	23	...	...	...
Less than 1 day - Moins de 1 jour	22	15	7	...	...	...
1 - 6 days - 1 - 6 jours	13	9	4	...	...	...
7 - 27 days - 7 - 27 jours	8	5	3	...	...	...
7 - 13 days - 7 - 13 jours	2	1	1	...	...	...
14 - 20 days - 14 - 20 jours	4	2	2	...	...	...
21 - 27 days - 21 - 27 jours	2	2	-	...	...	...
28 days - 11 months - 28 jours - 11 mois	21	12	9	...	...	...
28 days - less than 2 months - 28 jours - moins de 2 mois	7	6	1	...	...	...
2 months - 2 mois	2	1	1	...	...	...
3 months - 3 mois	2	-	2	...	...	...
4 months - 4 mois	4	1	3	...	...	...
5 months - 5 mois	1	1	-	...	...	...
6 months - 6 mois	-	-	-	...	...	...
7 months - 7 mois	3	1	2	...	...	...
8 months - 8 mois	-	-	-	...	...	...
9 months - 9 mois	1	1	-	...	...	...
10 months - 10 mois	-	-	-	...	...	...

16. Infant deaths and infant mortality rates by age and sex: latest available year, 2003 - 2012
Décès d'enfants de moins d'un an et taux de mortalité infantile selon l'âge et le sexe : dernière année disponible, 2003 - 2012 (continued - suite)

Continent, country or area, year and age / Continent, pays ou zone, année et âge	Number - Nombre			Rate - Taux		
	Both sexes Les deux sexes	Male Masculin	Female Féminin	Both sexes Les deux sexes	Male Masculin	Female Féminin
EUROPE						
Slovenia - Slovénie						
2011 (C)						
11 months - 11 mois	1	1	-	...	...	...
Unknown - Inconnu	-	-	-	...	...	...
Spain - Espagne						
2011 (C)						
Total	1 477	804	673	3.1	3.3	3.0
Less than 1 day - Moins de 1 jour	262	139	123	0.6	0.6	0.5
1 - 6 days - 1 - 6 jours	375	207	168	0.8	0.9	0.7
7 - 27 days - 7 - 27 jours	349	193	156	0.7	0.8	0.7
7 - 13 days - 7 - 13 jours	184	103	81	0.4	0.4	0.4
14 - 20 days - 14 - 20 jours	104	59	45	0.2	0.2	0.2
21 - 27 days - 21 - 27 jours	61	31	30	0.1	0.1	0.1
28 days - 11 months - 28 jours - 11 mois	491	265	226	1.0	1.1	1.0
28 days - less than 2 months - 28 jours - moins de 2 mois	165	87	78	0.4	0.4	0.3
2 months - 2 mois	66	29	37	0.1	♦0.1	0.2
3 months - 3 mois	54	34	20	0.1	0.1	♦0.1
4 months - 4 mois	43	26	17	0.1	♦0.1	♦0.1
5 months - 5 mois	48	22	26	0.1	♦0.1	♦0.1
6 months - 6 mois	33	21	12	0.1	♦0.1	♦0.1
7 months - 7 mois	23	10	13	-	-	♦0.1
8 months - 8 mois	19	12	7	-	-	-
9 months - 9 mois	14	7	7	-	-	-
10 months - 10 mois	14	10	4	-	-	-
11 months - 11 mois	12	7	5	-	-	-
Unknown - Inconnu	-	-	-	-	-	-
Sweden - Suède						
2011 (C)						
Total	235	128	107	2.1	2.2	2.0
Less than 1 day - Moins de 1 jour	57	31	26	0.5	0.5	♦0.5
1 - 6 days - 1 - 6 jours	41	19	22	0.4	♦0.3	♦0.4
7 - 27 days - 7 - 27 jours	56	27	29	0.5	♦0.5	♦0.5
7 - 13 days - 7 - 13 jours	29	14	15	♦0.3	♦0.2	♦0.3
14 - 20 days - 14 - 20 jours	18	9	9	♦0.2	♦0.2	♦0.2
21 - 27 days - 21 - 27 jours	9	4	5	♦0.1	♦0.1	♦0.1
28 days - 11 months - 28 jours - 11 mois	81	...	30	0.7	...	0.5
28 days - less than 2 months - 28 jours - moins de 2 mois	17	10	7	♦0.2	♦0.2	♦0.1
2 months - 2 mois	13	10	3	♦0.1	♦0.2	♦0.1
3 months - 3 mois	15	10	5	♦0.1	♦0.2	♦0.1
4 months - 4 mois	7	5	2	♦0.1	♦0.1	-
5 months - 5 mois	7	4	3	♦0.1	♦0.1	♦0.1
6 months - 6 mois	6	3	3	♦0.1	♦0.1	♦0.1
7 months - 7 mois	5	4	1	-	♦0.1	-
8 months - 8 mois	1	...	1	-	...	-
9 months - 9 mois	5	...	2	-	...	-
10 months - 10 mois	1	...	1	-	...	-
11 months - 11 mois	4	...	2	-	...	-
Switzerland - Suisse						
2011 (C)						
Total	305	168	137	3.8	4.0	3.5
Less than 1 day - Moins de 1 jour	153	82	71	1.9	2.0	1.8
1 - 6 days - 1 - 6 jours	51	27	24	0.6	♦0.6	♦0.6
7 - 27 days - 7 - 27 jours	28	18	10	♦0.3	♦0.4	♦0.3
7 - 13 days - 7 - 13 jours	17	10	7	♦0.2	♦0.2	♦0.2
14 - 20 days - 14 - 20 jours	7	5	2	♦0.1	♦0.1	♦0.1
21 - 27 days - 21 - 27 jours	4	3	1	-	♦0.1	-
28 days - 11 months - 28 jours - 11 mois	73	41	32	0.9	1.0	0.8
28 days - less than 2 months - 28 jours - moins de 2 mois	21	11	10	♦0.3	♦0.3	♦0.3
2 months - 2 mois	12	8	4	♦0.1	♦0.2	♦0.1
3 months - 3 mois	6	2	4	♦0.1	-	♦0.1
4 months - 4 mois	7	4	3	♦0.1	♦0.1	♦0.1
5 months - 5 mois	5	2	3	♦0.1	-	♦0.1
6 months - 6 mois	4	1	3	-	-	♦0.1
7 months - 7 mois	9	8	1	♦0.1	♦0.2	-
8 months - 8 mois	4	2	2	-	-	♦0.1
9 months - 9 mois	4	3	1	-	♦0.1	-
10 months - 10 mois	-	-	-	-	-	-

16. Infant deaths and infant mortality rates by age and sex: latest available year, 2003 - 2012
Décès d'enfants de moins d'un an et taux de mortalité infantile selon l'âge et le sexe : dernière année disponible, 2003 - 2012 (continued - suite)

Continent, country or area, year and age / Continent, pays ou zone, année et âge	Number - Nombre			Rate - Taux		
	Both sexes Les deux sexes	Male Masculin	Female Féminin	Both sexes Les deux sexes	Male Masculin	Female Féminin
EUROPE						
Switzerland - Suisse						
2011 (C)						
11 months - 11 mois	1	-	1	-	-	-
Unknown - Inconnu	-	-	-	-	-	-
TFYR of Macedonia - L'ex-R. y. de Macédoine						
2010 (C)						
Total	185	104	81	7.6	8.2	6.9
Less than 1 day - Moins de 1 jour	34	16	18	1.4	♦1.3	♦1.5
1 - 6 days - 1 - 6 jours	64	38	26	2.6	3.0	♦2.2
7 - 27 days - 7 - 27 jours	36	21	15	1.5	♦1.7	♦1.3
7 - 13 days - 7 - 13 jours	17	9	8	♦0.7	♦0.7	♦0.7
14 - 20 days - 14 - 20 jours	11	6	5	♦0.5	♦0.5	♦0.4
21 - 27 days - 21 - 27 jours	8	6	2	♦0.3	♦0.5	♦0.2
28 days - 11 months - 28 jours - 11 mois	51	29	22	2.1	♦2.3	♦1.9
28 days - less than 2 months - 28 jours - moins de 2 mois	17	7	10	♦0.7	♦0.6	♦0.9
2 months - 2 mois	10	8	2	♦0.4	♦0.6	♦0.2
3 months - 3 mois	3	1	2	♦0.1	♦0.1	♦0.2
4 months - 4 mois	3	1	2	♦0.1	♦0.1	♦0.2
5 months - 5 mois	3	1	2	♦0.1	♦0.1	♦0.2
6 months - 6 mois	3	2	1	♦0.1	♦0.2	♦0.1
7 months - 7 mois	5	4	1	♦0.2	♦0.3	♦0.1
8 months - 8 mois	4	3	1	♦0.2	♦0.2	♦0.1
9 months - 9 mois	-	-	-	-	-	-
10 months - 10 mois	-	-	-	-	-	-
11 months - 11 mois	3	2	1	♦0.1	♦0.2	♦0.1
Ukraine[31]						
2011 (+C)						
Total	4 511	2 603	1 908	9.0	10.0	7.8
Less than 1 day - Moins de 1 jour	683	383	300	1.4	1.5	1.2
1 - 6 days - 1 - 6 jours	1 271	727	544	2.5	2.8	2.2
7 - 27 days - 7 - 27 jours	835	510	325	1.7	2.0	1.3
7 - 13 days - 7 - 13 jours	431	264	167	0.9	1.0	0.7
14 - 20 days - 14 - 20 jours	242	143	99	0.5	0.6	0.4
21 - 27 days - 21 - 27 jours	162	103	59	0.3	0.4	0.2
28 days - 11 months - 28 jours - 11 mois	1 722	983	739	3.4	3.8	3.0
28 days - less than 2 months - 28 jours - moins de 2 mois	536	304	232	1.1	1.2	1.0
2 months - 2 mois	321	182	139	0.6	0.7	0.6
3 months - 3 mois	215	131	84	0.4	0.5	0.3
4 months - 4 mois	165	85	80	0.3	0.3	0.3
5 months - 5 mois	121	76	45	0.2	0.3	0.2
6 months - 6 mois	88	51	37	0.2	0.2	0.2
7 months - 7 mois	93	46	47	0.2	0.2	0.2
8 months - 8 mois	62	31	31	0.1	0.1	0.1
9 months - 9 mois	53	34	19	0.1	0.1	♦0.1
10 months - 10 mois	39	27	12	0.1	♦0.1	-
11 months - 11 mois	29	16	13	♦0.1	♦0.1	♦0.1
Unknown - Inconnu	-	-	-	-	-	-
United Kingdom of Great Britain and Northern Ireland - Royaume-Uni de Grande-Bretagne et d'Irlande du Nord[32]						
2009 (+C)						
Total	3 677	2 067	1 610	4.7	5.1	4.2
Less than 1 day - Moins de 1 jour	1 096	605	491	1.4	1.5	1.3
1 - 6 days - 1 - 6 jours	819	463	356	1.0	1.1	0.9
7 - 27 days - 7 - 27 jours	598	335	263	0.8	0.8	0.7
7 - 13 days - 7 - 13 jours	317	179	138	0.4	0.4	0.4
14 - 20 days - 14 - 20 jours	165	95	70	0.2	0.2	0.2
21 - 27 days - 21 - 27 jours	116	61	55	0.1	0.2	0.1
28 days - 11 months - 28 jours - 11 mois	1 164	664	500	1.5	1.6	1.3
28 days - less than 2 months - 28 jours - moins de 2 mois	375	222	153	0.5	0.5	0.4
2 months - 2 mois	189	98	91	0.2	0.2	0.2
3 months - 3 mois	134	83	51	0.2	0.2	0.1
4 months - 4 mois	96	50	46	0.1	0.1	0.1
5 months - 5 mois	78	51	27	0.1	0.1	♦0.1
6 months - 6 mois	72	37	35	0.1	0.1	0.1
7 months - 7 mois	54	29	25	0.1	♦0.1	♦0.1
8 months - 8 mois	49	22	27	0.1	♦0.1	♦0.1
9 months - 9 mois	47	33	14	0.1	0.1	-

Continent, country or area, year and age / Continent, pays ou zone, année et âge	Number - Nombre			Rate - Taux		
	Both sexes Les deux sexes	Male Masculin	Female Féminin	Both sexes Les deux sexes	Male Masculin	Female Féminin
EUROPE						
United Kingdom of Great Britain and Northern Ireland - Royaume-Uni de Grande-Bretagne et d'Irlande du Nord[32]						
2009 (+C)						
10 months - 10 mois	35	21	14	-	♦0.1	-
11 months - 11 mois	35	18	17	-	-	-
OCEANIA - OCÉANIE						
Australia - Australie						
2011 (+C)						
Total	1 140	638	502	3.8	4.1	3.4
Less than 1 day - Moins de 1 jour	428	233	195	1.4	1.5	1.3
1 - 6 days - 1 - 6 jours	236	141	95	0.8	0.9	0.6
7 - 27 days - 7 - 27 jours	141	76	65	0.5	0.5	0.4
7 - 13 days - 7 - 13 jours	65	35	30	0.2	0.2	0.2
14 - 20 days - 14 - 20 jours	39	24	15	0.1	♦0.2	♦0.1
21 - 27 days - 21 - 27 jours	37	17	20	0.1	♦0.1	♦0.1
28 days - 11 months - 28 jours - 11 mois	335	188	147	1.1	1.2	1.0
28 days - less than 2 months - 28 jours - moins de 2 mois	101	55	46	0.3	0.4	0.3
2 months - 2 mois	55	35	20	0.2	0.2	♦0.1
3 months - 3 mois	50	28	22	0.2	♦0.2	♦0.2
4 months - 4 mois	21	14	7	♦0.1	♦0.1	-
5 months - 5 mois	30	16	14	0.1	♦0.1	♦0.1
6 months - 6 mois	17	8	9	♦0.1	♦0.1	♦0.1
7 months - 7 mois	12	8	4	-	♦0.1	-
8 months - 8 mois	13	8	5	-	♦0.1	-
9 months - 9 mois	9	4	5	-	-	-
10 months - 10 mois	16	8	8	♦0.1	♦0.1	♦0.1
11 months - 11 mois	11	4	7	-	-	-
Unknown - Inconnu	-	-	-	-	-	-
French Polynesia - Polynésie française						
2008 (C)						
Total	23	...	...	...	...	...
Less than 7 days - Moins de 7 jours	14	...	...	...	...	...
7 - 27 days - 7 - 27 jours	-	...	...	...	...	...
28 days - 11 months - 28 jours - 11 mois	9	...	...	...	...	...
New Caledonia - Nouvelle-Calédonie						
2007 (C)						
Total	25	15	10	...	...	...
Less than 1 day - Moins de 1 jour	-	-	-	...	...	...
1 - 6 days - 1 - 6 jours	11	9	2	...	...	...
7 - 27 days - 7 - 27 jours	6	2	4	...	...	...
7 - 13 days - 7 - 13 jours	6	2	4	...	...	...
14 - 20 days - 14 - 20 jours	-	-	-	...	...	...
21 - 27 days - 21 - 27 jours	-	-	-	...	...	...
28 days - 11 months - 28 jours - 11 mois	8	4	4	...	...	...
28 days - less than 2 months - 28 jours - moins de 2 mois	-	-	-	...	...	...
2 months - 2 mois	-	-	-	...	...	...
3 months - 3 mois	-	2	-	...	...	...
4 months - 4 mois	-	-	-	...	...	...
5 months - 5 mois	-	-	-	...	...	...
6 months - 6 mois	2	2	-	...	...	...
7 months - 7 mois	-	-	-	...	...	...
8 months - 8 mois	-	-	-	...	...	...
9 months - 9 mois	-	-	-	...	...	...
10 months - 10 mois	-	-	-	...	...	...
11 months - 11 mois	4	-	4	...	...	...
New Zealand - Nouvelle-Zélande[8]						
2012 (+C)						
Total	256	142	114	4.2	4.5	3.8
Less than 1 day - Moins de 1 jour	90	47	43	1.5	1.5	1.4
1 - 6 days - 1 - 6 jours	38	22	16	0.6	♦0.7	♦0.5
7 - 27 days - 7 - 27 jours	30	14	16	0.5	♦0.4	♦0.5
7 - 13 days - 7 - 13 jours	18	9	9	♦0.3	♦0.3	♦0.3
14 - 20 days - 14 - 20 jours	6	3	3	♦0.1	♦0.1	♦0.1
21 - 27 days - 21 - 27 jours	6	2	4	♦0.1	♦0.1	♦0.1

16. Infant deaths and infant mortality rates by age and sex: latest available year, 2003 - 2012

Décès d'enfants de moins d'un an et taux de mortalité infantile selon l'âge et le sexe : dernière année disponible, 2003 - 2012 (continued - suite)

Continent, country or area, year and age Continent, pays ou zone, année et âge	Number - Nombre			Rate - Taux		
	Both sexes Les deux sexes	Male Masculin	Female Féminin	Both sexes Les deux sexes	Male Masculin	Female Féminin
OCEANIA - OCÉANIE						
New Zealand - Nouvelle-Zélande[8]						
2012 (+C)						
28 days - 11 months - 28 jours - 11 mois....................................	98	59	39	1.6	1.9	1.3
28 days - less than 2 months - 28 jours - moins de 2 mois	28	15	13	♦0.5	♦0.5	♦0.4
2 months - 2 mois..	20	13	7	♦0.3	♦0.4	♦0.2
3 months - 3 mois..	10	7	3	♦0.2	♦0.2	♦0.1
4 months - 4 mois..	7	5	2	♦0.1	♦0.2	♦0.1
5 months - 5 mois..	7	2	5	♦0.1	♦0.1	♦0.2
6 months - 6 mois..	5	3	2	♦0.1	♦0.1	♦0.1
7 months - 7 mois..	5	4	1	♦0.1	♦0.1	-
8 months - 8 mois..	7	3	4	♦0.1	♦0.1	♦0.1
9 months - 9 mois..	3	1	2	-	-	♦0.1
10 months - 10 mois...	6	6	-	♦0.1	♦0.2	-
11 months - 11 mois	-	-	-	-	-	-

FOOTNOTES - NOTES

Italics: data from civil registers which are incomplete or of unknown completeness. - Italiques : données incomplètes ou dont le degré d'exactitude n'est pas connu, provenant des registres de l'état civil.

♦ Rates based on 30 or fewer infant deaths. - Taux basés sur 30 décès d'enfants ou moins.

* Provisional. - Données provisoires.

'Code' indicates the source of data, as follows:
C - Civil registration, estimated over 90% complete
U - Civil registration, estimated less than 90% complete
| - Other source, estimated reliable
+ - Data tabulated by date of registration rather than occurence
... - Information not available

Le 'Code' indique la source des données, comme suit :
C - Registres de l'état civil considérés complets à 90 p. 100 au moins
U - Registres de l'état civil qui ne sont pas considérés complets à 90 p. 100 au moins
| - Autre source, considérée pas douteuses
+ - Données exploitées selon la date de l'enregistrement et non la date de l'événement
... - Information pas disponible

[1] Excludes the islands of St. Brandon and Agalega. - Non compris les îles St. Brandon et Agalega.
[2] Excluding live-born infants who died before their birth was registered. - Non compris les enfants nés vivants décédés avant l'enregistrement de leur naissance.
[3] Unrevised data. - Les données n'ont pas été révisées.
[4] Data for male and female categories exclude infant deaths of unknown sex. - Il n'est pas tenu compte dans les données classées par sexe des décès d'enfant de moins d'un an de sexe inconnu.
[5] Including Canadian residents temporarily in the United States, but excluding United States residents temporarily in Canada. - Y compris les résidents canadiens se trouvant temporairement aux Etats-Unis, mais ne comprenant pas les résidents des Etats-Unis se trouvant temporairement au Canada.
[6] Excluding infant deaths to mothers living abroad. - Exception faite des décès d'enfants en bas âge survenus lorsque la mère résidait à l'étranger.
[7] Data refer to urban areas only. - Données ne concernant que les zones urbaines.
[8] Data refer to resident population only. - Pour la population résidante seulement.
[9] Including deaths abroad and deaths of unknown residence. - Y compris les décès à l'étranger et les décès dont on ignore la résidence.
[10] Excludes nomadic Indian tribes. - Non compris les tribus d'Indiens nomades.
[11] Data refer to infants 30 days - 12 months old. - Les données se réfèrent aux nouveaux-nés âgées de 30 jours à 12 mois.

[12] Completeness of coverage estimated at 40 per cent. Source: Reports of the Ministry of Health. - Degré de complétude évalué à 40 pour cent. Source: Rapports du Ministère de la Santé.
[13] Excluding infants born alive of less than 28 weeks' gestation, of less than 1 000 grams in weight and 35 centimeters in length, who die within seven days of birth. - Non compris les enfants nés vivants après moins de 28 semaines de gestation, pesant moins de 1 000 grammes, mesurant moins de 35 centimètres et décédés dans les sept jours qui ont suivi leur naissance.
[14] Data refer to government controlled areas. - Les données se rapportent aux zones contrôlées par le Gouvernement.
[15] Includes data for East Jerusalem and Israeli residents in certain other territories under occupation by Israeli military forces since June 1967. Including deaths abroad of Israeli residents who were out of the country for less than a year. - Y compris les données pour Jérusalem-Est et les résidents israéliens dans certains autres territoires occupés depuis 1967 par les forces armées israéliennes. Y compris les décès à l'étranger de résidents israéliens qui ont quitté le pays depuis moins d'un an.
[16] Data refer to Japanese nationals in Japan only. - Les données se raportent aux nationaux japonais au Japon seulement.
[17] Data from Births and Deaths Notification System (Ministry of Health and all health care providers). - Les données proviennent du système de notification des naissances et des décès (Ministère de la santé et tous prestataires de soins de santé).
[18] Excluding unknown sex. - Non compris le sexe inconnu.
[19] Excluding data for the Pakistan-held part of Jammu and Kashmir, the final status of which has not yet been determined. Based on the results of the Pakistan Demographic Survey. - Non compris les données concernant la partie du Jammu et Cachemire occupée par le Pakistan dont le statut définitif n'a pas été déterminé. Données extraites de l'enquête démographique effectuée par le Pakistan.
[20] Excluding alien armed forces, civilian aliens employed by armed forces, and foreign diplomatic personnel and their dependants. - Non compris les militaires étrangers, les civils étrangers employés par les forces armées ni le personnel diplomatique étranger et les membres de leur famille les accompagnant.
[21] Including armed forces stationed outside the country, but excluding alien armed forces stationed in the area. - Y compris les militaires nationaux hors du pays, mais non compris les militaires étrangers en garnison sur le territoire.
[22] Excluding Faeroe Islands and Greenland shown separately, if available. - Non compris les Iles Féroé et le Groenland, qui font l'objet de rubriques distinctes, si disponible.
[23] Excluding Åland Islands. - Non compris les Îles d'Åland.
[24] Including armed forces stationed outside the country. - Y compris les militaires nationaux hors du pays.
[25] Definition of localities was revised from 2011 causing a break with the previous series. - La rupture par rapport aux séries précédentes s'explique par le fait que la définition des localités a été révisée depuis 2011.
[26] Including residents outside the country if listed in a Netherlands population register. - Englobe les résidents se trouvant à l'étranger à condition qu'ils soient inscrits sur le registre de population des Pays-Bas.
[27] Including residents temporarily outside the country. - Y compris les résidents se trouvant temporairement hors du pays.

[28] Figures for male and female do not add up to the total, since they do not include the category "Unknown". - La somme des chiffres indiqués pour les sexes masculin et féminin n'est pas égale au total parce qu'elle n'inclut pas la catégorie " inconnue ".

[29] Excluding Transnistria and the municipality of Bender. - Les données ne tiennent pas compte de l'information sur la Transnistria et la municipalité de Bender.

[30] Excludes data for Kosovo and Metohia. - Sans les données pour le Kosovo et Metohie.

[31] Data includes deaths resulting from births with weight 500g and more (if weight is unknown - with length 25 centimeters and more, or with gestation during 22 weeks or more). - Y compris les décès de nouveau-nés de 500 grammes ou plus (si le poids est inconnu – de 25 centimètres de long ou plus, ou après une grossesse de 22 semaines ou plus).

[32] Excluding Channel Islands (Guernsey and Jersey) and Isle of Man, shown separately, if available. - Non compris les îles Anglo-Normandes (Guernesey et Jersey) et l'île de Man, qui font l'objet de rubriques distinctes, si disponible.

Table 17 - *Demographic Yearbook 2012*

Table 17 presents maternal deaths and maternal mortality ratios for as many years available between 2001 and 2010.

Description of variables: Maternal deaths are defined for the purposes of the Demographic Yearbook as those caused by deliveries and complications of pregnancy, childbirth and the puerperium, within 42 days of termination of pregnancy. They are usually defined as deaths coded "38-41" for ICD-9 Basic Tabulation List or as deaths coded "A34", "O00-O95", "O98-O99" for ICD-10, respectively. However, data for ICD-10 shown in this table include deaths due to "O96" and "O97" which refer to deaths from any obstetric cause occurring more than 42 days but less than one year after delivery and death from sequelae of direct obstetric causes occurring one year or more after delivery.

For further information on the definition of maternal mortality from the tenth revisions of the *International Statistical Classification of Diseases and Related Health Problems*[1], see also section 4.3 of the Technical Notes.

Statistics on maternal death presented in this table are provided by the World Health Organisation. They are limited to countries or areas that meet the criterion that cause-of-death statistics are either classified by or convertible to the ninth or tenth revisions mentioned above. Data that are classified by the tenth revision are set in bold in the table.

Ratios computation: Maternal mortality ratios are the annual number of maternal deaths per 100 000 live births (table 9) in the same year. These ratios have been calculated by the Statistics Division of the United Nations Department of Economic and Social Affairs. If maternal mortality data are considered incomplete, or if live birth data for the year are not available, no ratio has been calculated. Ratios based on 30 or fewer maternal deaths are identified by the symbol "♦".

Reliability of data: Countries and areas that have incomplete (less than 90 per cent completeness) or of unknown completeness of cause of deaths data coverage are considered to provide unreliable data, which are set in *italics* rather than in roman type. Ratios on these data are not computed. Information on completeness is normally provided by the World Health Organisation. When this is not the case, information on completeness is set to coincide with that of table 18. The reliability of data for the completeness of cause of death provided by the World Health Organisation[2] may differ from the reliability of data for the total number of reported deaths. Therefore, there are cases when the quality code in table 18 does not correspond with the typeface used in this table.

Territorial composition as set in Section 2.2 of "Technical Notes on the Statistical Tables", including or excluding certain population of a country refers only to the denominator.

Limitations: Statistics on maternal deaths are subject to the same qualifications that have been set forth for vital statistics in general and death statistics in particular as discussed in section 4 of the Technical Notes. The reliability of the data, an indication of which is described above, is an important factor in considering the limitations. In addition, maternal-death statistics are subject to all the qualifications relating to cause-of-death statistics. These have been set forth in section 4 of the Technical Notes.

Maternal mortality ratios are subject to the limitations of the data on live births with which they have been calculated. These have been set forth in the technical notes for table 9. Specific information pertaining to individual countries or areas is given in the footnotes to table 9.

The calculation of the maternal mortality ratios based on the total number of live births approximates the risk of dying from complications of pregnancy, childbirth or puerperium. Ideally this rate should be based on the number of women exposed to the risk of pregnancy, in other words, the number of women conceiving. Since it is impossible to know how many women have conceived, the total number of live births is used in calculating this rate.

Earlier data: Maternal deaths and maternal mortality ratios have been shown in previous issues of the *Demographic Yearbook*. For information on specific years covered, the reader should consult the Index.

It should however be noted that in issues prior to 1975, maternal mortality rates were calculated using the female population rather than live births. Therefore, maternal mortality ratios published since 1975 are not comparable to the earlier maternal death rates.

NOTES

[1] *International Statistical Classification of Diseases and Related Health Problems*, Tenth Revision, Volume 2, World Health Organization, Geneva, 1992.

[2] For more information on specific method used for countries, see "Mathers CD, Bernard C, Iburg KM, Inoue M, Ma Fat D, Shibuya K et al. *Global burden of disease in 2002: data sources, methods and results*. Geneva, World Health Organization, 2003 (GPE Discussion Paper No. 54).

Tableau 17 – *Annuaire démographique 2012*

Le tableau 17 présente des statistiques et des taux de mortalité liée à la maternité pour les années disponibles entre 2001 et 2010.

Description des variables : aux fins de *l'Annuaire démographique*, les décès liés à la maternité sont ceux entraînés par l'accouchement ou les complications de la grossesse, de l'accouchement et des suites de couches dans un délai de 42 jours après la terminaison de la grossesse. Ils sont généralement associés aux codes 38 à 41 dans le cas de la liste de base pour la mise en tableaux de la CIM-9 et aux codes A34, O00 à O95 et O98 et O99 dans le cas de la CIM-10. Les statistiques associées à des codes correspondant à la CIM-10 englobent des décès de type O96 et O97, qui désignent les décès liés à des causes obstétriques se produisant après 42 jours mais moins d'un an après l'accouchement et les décès entraînés par les séquelles de complications obstétriques directes qui se produisent un an ou plus après l'accouchement.

Pour plus de précisions concernant les définitions de la mortalité liée à la maternité dans la dixième révision de la *Classification statistique internationale des maladies et des problèmes de santé connexes*[1], se reporter également à la section 4.3 des Notes techniques.

Les statistiques de mortalité liée à la maternité présentées dans le tableau 17 émanent de l'Organisation mondiale de la santé. Elles ne se rapportent qu'aux pays ou zones qui répondent aux critères selon lesquels les statistiques relatives à la cause des décès sont conformes à la liste de la neuvième ou de la dixième révision de la CIM ou peuvent être aisément comparées aux catégories de cette liste. Les données conformes à la dixième révision sont indiquées en gras dans le tableau.

Calcul des taux : les taux de mortalité maternelle représentent le nombre annuel de décès dus à la maternité pour 100 000 naissances vivantes (données du tableau 9) de la même année. Ces taux ont été calculés par la Division de statistique du Département des affaires économiques et sociales de l'Organisation des Nations Unies. Si les données des décès dus à la maternité sont incomplètes ou si les naissances vivantes pour l'année ne sont pas disponibles, les taux ne sont pas calculés. Les taux fondés sur 30 décès liés à la maternité ou moins sont signalés par le signe "♦".

Fiabilité des données : les statistiques relatives aux pays et aux zones pour lesquels la couverture des données concernant les causes de décès est incomplète (mois de 90 pour cent) ou dont le degré de complétude n'est pas connue sont jugés douteuses et apparaissent en *italique* et non en caractères romains. Les taux correspondant ne sont pas calculés. L'information sur la complétude est normalement fournie par l'Organisation Mondiale de la Santé. Si ce n'est pas le cas, l'information sur la complétude est reprise de tableau 18. La fiabilité des données relatives aux causes de décès fournie par l'Organisation Mondiale de la Santé[2] peut différer de la fiabilité des données relatives au nombre de décès enregistrés. En conséquence, il peut apparaitre de différences entre les codes de fiabilité du tableau 18 et du présent tableau.

La composition territoriale est définie dans la Section 2.2 des "Notes Techniques sur les tableaux statistiques". L'inclusion ou l'exclusion de certaines populations d'un pays ne concerne que le dénominateur.

Insuffisance des données : les statistiques de la mortalité liée à la maternité appellent toutes les réserves qui ont été formulées à propos des statistiques de l'état civil en général et des statistiques relatives à la mortalité en particulier (voir la section 4 des Notes techniques). La fiabilité des données, au sujet de laquelle des indications ont été fournies plus haut, est un facteur important. En outre, les statistiques de la mortalité liée à la maternité appellent les mêmes réserves que celles exposées à la section 4 des Notes techniques en ce qui concerne les statistiques des causes de décès.

Les taux de mortalité maternelle appellent également toutes les réserves formulées à propos des statistiques des naissances vivantes qui ont servi à leur calcul (voir à ce sujet les notes techniques relatives au tableau 9). Des précisions sur certains pays ou zones sont données dans les notes se rapportant au tableau 9.

En prenant le nombre total des naissances vivantes comme base pour le calcul des taux de mortalité maternelle, on obtient une mesure approximative de la probabilité de décès dus aux complications de la grossesse, de l'accouchement et des suites de couches. Idéalement, ces taux devraient être calculés sur la base du nombre de femmes exposées aux risques liés à la grossesse, c'est-à-dire sur la base du nombre de femmes qui conçoivent. Étant donné qu'il est impossible de connaître le nombre de femmes ayant conçu, c'est le nombre total de naissances vivantes que l'on utilise pour calculer ces taux.

Données publiées antérieurement : des statistiques concernant les décès liés à la maternité (nombre de décès et taux) ont déjà été présentées dans des éditions antérieures de l'*Annuaire démographique*. Pour plus de précisions concernant les années pour lesquelles ces données ont été publiées, se reporter à l'index.

Il faut souligner que, avant 1975, les taux de mortalité maternelle étaient calculés sur la base de la population féminine et non sur celle du nombre de naissances vivantes. Ils ne sont donc pas comparables à ceux qui figurent dans les éditions de l'*Annuaire démographique* parues après 1975.

NOTES

[1] *Classification statistique internationale des maladies et des problèmes de santé connexes*, dixième révision, volume 2. Genève, Organisation mondiale de la santé, 1992.
[2] Pour plus d'information sur les méthodes spécifiques utilisées pour les pays, voir "Mathers CD, Bernard C, Iburg KM, Inoue M, Ma Fat D, Shibuya K et al. *Global burden of disease in 2002: data sources, methods and results*. Geneva, World Health Organization, 2003 (GPE Discussion Paper No. 54).

17. Maternal deaths and maternal mortality ratios: 2001 - 2010
Mortalité liée à la maternité, nombre de décès et taux : 2001 - 2010

Continent and country or area / Continent et pays ou zone	Code[a]	2001	2002	2003	2004	2005	2006	2007	2008	2009	2010
AFRICA - AFRIQUE											
Egypt - Égypte											
Number - Nombre	...	...	...	...	...	...	604[1]	567[1]	449[2]	579[1]	519[1]
Rate - Taux	...	...	...	...	...	...	32.6	29.1	...	26.1	23.0
Mauritius - Maurice											
Number - Nombre	+C	4	1	4	3	4	3	6	6	10	4
Rate - Taux	+C	♦20.3	♦5.0	♦20.7	♦15.6	♦21.3	♦17.0	♦35.2	♦36.6	♦65.2	♦26.7
Morocco - Maroc											
Number - Nombre	U	...	...	...	...	...	...	...	74	...	...
Réunion											
Number - Nombre	...	-	3	3	4	4	5	...	2	...	...
Seychelles											
Number - Nombre	+C	-	1	1	-	1	-	-	1	1	...
Rate - Taux	+C	-	♦67.5	♦66.8	-	♦65.1	-	-	♦64.7	♦63.3	...
South Africa - Afrique du Sud											
Number - Nombre	...	854[2]	794[2]	898[2]	1 158[2]	1 249[2]	1 388[2]	1 762[2]	1 808[1]	1 880[1]	...
Rate - Taux	...	...	...	...	...	...	...	...	170.1	187.9	...
AMERICA, NORTH - AMÉRIQUE DU NORD											
Anguilla											
Number - Nombre	+...	-	...	-	-	-	-	...	...	...	...
Antigua and Barbuda - Antigua-et-Barbuda											
Number - Nombre	+U	-	-	-	-	-	-	1	-	...	...
Aruba											
Number - Nombre	...	...	...	...	1	...	-	-	...	...	...
Bahamas											
Number - Nombre	...	...	...	...	2[2]	4[1]	...	...	...	...	...
Rate - Taux	...	...	...	...	...	♦72.1	...	...	...	...	...
Barbados - Barbade											
Number - Nombre	C	-	...	...	...	...	1	...	...	...	...
Rate - Taux	C	-	...	...	...	...	♦29.3	...	...	...	...
Belize											
Number - Nombre	...	3[2]	...	...	3[2]	10[1]	3[1]	2[1]	2[1]	...	...
Rate - Taux	...	...	...	...	...	♦119.1	...	...	...	...	...
Bermuda - Bermudes											
Number - Nombre	...	-	-	...	-	-	1	-	...	...	...
British Virgin Islands - Îles Vierges britanniques											
Number - Nombre	...	-	-	-	...	...	...	...	...	...	...
Canada											
Number - Nombre	C	26	15	23	20	...	28	24	34	29	...
Rate - Taux	C	♦7.8	♦4.6	♦6.9	♦5.9	...	♦7.9	♦6.5	9.0	♦7.6	...
Cayman Islands - Îles Caïmanes											
Number - Nombre	...	...	...	...	-	...	...	...	...	...	...
Costa Rica											
Number - Nombre	+U	24	27	24	25	24	24	10	20	10	...
Cuba											
Number - Nombre	C	57	65	62	56	66	62	42	57	...	...
Rate - Taux	C	41.1	46.0	45.3	44.0	54.7	55.7	37.3	46.5	...	...
Dominica - Dominique											
Number - Nombre	+C	1	1	-	-	-	-	-	1	-	...
Rate - Taux	+C	♦82.2	♦92.5	-	-	-	-	-	♦103.7	-	...
Dominican Republic - République dominicaine											
Number - Nombre	U	64	...	58	85	...	...	...	...	...	...
El Salvador											
Number - Nombre	+U	28	32	27	22	23	21	17	18	...	...
Grenada - Grenade											
Number - Nombre	U	-	1	...	-	-	-	-	-	...	...
Guadeloupe											
Number - Nombre	...	2	6	4	3	1	2	...	2	...	...
Guatemala											
Number - Nombre	U	278	280	293	296	354	298	310	328	...	...
Haiti - Haïti											
Number - Nombre	...	180	135	124	...	...	...	...	...	...	...

17. Maternal deaths and maternal mortality ratios: 2001 - 2010
Mortalité liée à la maternité, nombre de décès et taux : 2001 - 2010 (continued - suite)

Continent and country or area Continent et pays ou zone	Co- de[a]	2001	2002	2003	2004	2005	2006	2007	2008	2009	2010
AMERICA, NORTH - AMÉRIQUE DU NORD											
Martinique											
Number - Nombre................	...	1	2	2	1	-	1	...	1	...	...
Mexico - Mexique											
Number - Nombre................	+C	1 268	1 324	1 332	1 266	1 269	1 188	1 122	1 135	1 230	1 000
Rate - Taux..........................	+C	56.9	59.9	61.5	58.7	59.3	55.2	51.3	50.6	54.6	37.8
Montserrat											
Number - Nombre................	+...	-	-	-	-	-	-	...	...	...	...
Nicaragua											
Number - Nombre................	+U	124	114	88	108	93	93	...	...	...	...
Panama											
Number - Nombre................	...	37[3]	38[3]	34[3]	23[3]	...	36[3]	40[4]	41[4]	...	...
Rate - Taux..........................	...	...	...	...	...	...	...	59.4	59.6	...	...
Puerto Rico - Porto Rico											
Number - Nombre................	+...	6	5	8	...	5	...	...	...	...	...
Saint Kitts and Nevis - Saint-Kitts-et-Nevis											
Number - Nombre................	+U	2	-	2	-	-	1	-	1	...	...
Saint Lucia - Sainte-Lucie											
Number - Nombre................	C	1	1	...	...	...	...	...	...	...	...
Rate - Taux..........................	C	♦35.9	♦38.5	...	...	...	...	...	...	...	...
Saint Pierre and Miquelon - Saint Pierre-et-Miquelon											
Number - Nombre................	...	...	...	...	...	...	...	...	-	...	...
Saint Vincent and the Grenadines - Saint-Vincent-et-les Grenadines											
Number - Nombre................	...	-	-	-	1	...	-	-	2	...	...
Rate - Taux..........................	...	-	-	-	♦55.4	...	...	...	...	...	...
Trinidad and Tobago - Trinité-et-Tobago											
Number - Nombre................	C	7	5	...	...	...	12	...	...	...	...
Rate - Taux..........................	C	♦38.7	♦29.4	...	...	...	♦66.3	...	...	...	...
Turks and Caicos Islands - Îles Turques et Caïques											
Number - Nombre................	...	1	-	1	1	-	...	...	...	...	...
United States of America - États-Unis d'Amérique											
Number - Nombre................	C	416	379	545	697	760	756	766	795	...	...
Rate - Taux..........................	C	10.3	9.4	13.3	17.0	18.4	17.7	17.7	18.7	...	...
United States Virgin Islands - Îles Vierges américaines											
Number - Nombre................	...	2	-	-	...	-	...	...	...	...	...
AMERICA, SOUTH - AMÉRIQUE DU SUD											
Argentina - Argentine											
Number - Nombre................	+C	309	356	321	313	290	341	332	319	...	...
Rate - Taux..........................	+C	45.2	51.2	46.0	42.5	40.7	49.0	47.4	42.8	...	...
Brazil - Brésil											
Number - Nombre................	U	1 587	1 648	1 597	1 672	1 661	1 634	1 613	1 641	1 884	1 665
Chile - Chili											
Number - Nombre................	C	45	42	33	42	48	47	42	36	43	...
Rate - Taux..........................	C	18.3	17.6	14.1	18.2	20.8	20.3	17.5	14.6	17.0	...
Colombia - Colombie											
Number - Nombre................	...	689[2]	577[2]	...	546[2]	504[2]	519[1]	503[1]	433[1]	496[1]	...
Rate - Taux..........................	...	...	...	...	...	...	72.6	70.9	60.5	70.9	...
Ecuador - Équateur											
Number - Nombre................	U	187	149	139	129	143	135	176	162	208	...
French Guiana - Guyane française											
Number - Nombre................	...	2	2	1	1	1	1	...	4	...	...
Guyana											
Number - Nombre................	U	17	20	21	19	24	20	...	...	...	...
Paraguay											
Number - Nombre................	+U	132	163	150	154	135	123	...	117	...	...

17. Maternal deaths and maternal mortality ratios: 2001 - 2010
Mortalité liée à la maternité, nombre de décès et taux : 2001 - 2010 (continued - suite)

Continent and country or area Continent et pays ou zone	Co-de[a]	2001	2002	2003	2004	2005	2006	2007	2008	2009	2010
AMERICA, SOUTH - **AMÉRIQUE DU SUD**											
Peru - Pérou											
Number - Nombre................	+U	...	...	...	...	...	...	*155*	...	...	...
Suriname											
Number - Nombre................	U	...	...	...	*7*	*4*	...	...	...	...	...
Uruguay											
Number - Nombre................	C	**19**	...	...	**9**	...	...	...	...	...	...
Rate - Taux...........................	C	♦**36.6**	...	...	♦**18.0**	...	...	...	...	...	...
Venezuela (Bolivarian Republic of) - Venezuela (République bolivarienne du)											
Number - Nombre................	C	**356**	**335**	**321**	**318**	**351**	**356**	**332**	...	...	...
Rate - Taux...........................	C	**67.2**	**68.0**	**57.8**	**49.9**	**52.7**	**55.1**	**54.0**	...	...	...
ASIA - ASIE											
Armenia - Arménie											
Number - Nombre................	U	*7*	*3*	*8*	...	...	*10*	...	*16*	*12*	...
Azerbaijan - Azerbaïdjan											
Number - Nombre................	U	*27*	*22*	*21*	*34*	...	...	*30*	...	...	...
Bahrain - Bahreïn											
Number - Nombre................	C	**3**	...	...	...	...	-	**3**	**3**	**3**	...
Rate - Taux...........................	C	♦**22.3**	...	...	...	...	-	♦**18.7**	♦**17.6**	♦**16.8**	...
Brunei Darussalam - Brunéi Darussalam											
Number - Nombre................	+C	...	...	...	...	...	...	**1**	-	**1**	...
Rate - Taux...........................	+C	...	...	...	...	...	...	♦**15.8**	-	...	...
China, Hong Kong SAR - Chine, Hong Kong RAS											
Number - Nombre................	...	*1*	*1*	*2*	*2*	*2*	*1*	*1*	*2*	*2*	...
Cyprus - Chypre											
Number - Nombre................	U	...	...	...	-	*2*	*1*	-	*1*	-	*1*
Georgia - Géorgie											
Number - Nombre................	...	*4[2]*	...	...	...	...	*11[1]*	*2[1]*	...	*32[1]*	...
Rate - Taux...........................	...	...	...	...	...	...	♦**23.0**	♦**4.1**	...	**50.5**	...
Iraq											
Number - Nombre................	U	...	...	...	...	...	...	...	*62*	...	...
Israel - Israël											
Number - Nombre................	C	**9**	**6**	**3**	**6**	**4**	**11**	**7**	**8**	**5**	...
Rate - Taux...........................	C	♦**6.6**	♦**4.3**	♦**2.1**	♦**4.1**	♦**2.8**	♦**7.4**	♦**4.6**	♦**5.1**	♦**3.1**	...
Japan - Japon											
Number - Nombre................	C	**79**	**90**	**74**	**56**	**66**	**63**	**39**	**41**	**61**	**49**
Rate - Taux...........................	C	**6.7**	**7.8**	**6.6**	**5.0**	**6.2**	**5.8**	**3.6**	**3.8**	**5.7**	**4.6**
Jordan - Jordanie											
Number - Nombre................	U	...	...	...	...	...	...	...	*25*	...	...
Kazakhstan											
Number - Nombre................	U	*87*	*80*	*67*	*63*	*81*	*100*	*107*	*86*	*94*	...
Kuwait - Koweït											
Number - Nombre................	C	**1**	**3**	...	...	...	**1**	-	**5**	**7**	...
Rate - Taux...........................	C	♦**2.4**	♦**6.9**	...	...	...	♦**1.9**	-	♦**9.2**	♦**12.4**	...
Kyrgyzstan - Kirghizstan											
Number - Nombre................	U	*43*	*54*	*52*	*56*	*66*	*67*	*64*	*70*	*86*	...
Malaysia - Malaisie											
Number - Nombre................	U	...	...	...	...	...	*128*	...	...	...	...
Maldives											
Number - Nombre................	...	*3[3]*	*7[3]*	*-[3]*	*2[3]*	*1[3]*	...	*2[4]*	*4[4]*	...	...
Rate - Taux...........................	...	...	...	...	...	...	...	♦**30.4**	♦**57.2**	...	...
Oman											
Number - Nombre................	U	...	...	...	...	...	...	...	...	**3**	...
Philippines											
Number - Nombre................	C	...	...	...	...	...	...	...	**1 731**	...	...
Rate - Taux...........................	C	...	...	...	...	...	...	...	**97.0**	...	...
Qatar											
Number - Nombre................	C	...	...	...	...	...	**1**	**5**	**2**	**4**	...
Rate - Taux...........................	C	...	...	...	...	...	♦**7.1**	♦**31.9**	♦**11.6**	♦**21.8**	...

Continent and country or area / Continent et pays ou zone	Code[a]	2001	2002	2003	2004	2005	2006	2007	2008	2009	2010
ASIA - ASIE											
Republic of Korea - République de Corée											
Number - Nombre	C	70	71	58	59	53	54	...	...	48	...
Rate - Taux	C	12.6	14.4	11.8	12.5	12.2	12.0	...	...	10.8	...
Saudi Arabia - Arabie saoudite											
Number - Nombre	U	...	...	...	...	...	...	...	...	54	...
Singapore - Singapour											
Number - Nombre	+U	4	4	2	1	4	3	...	...	...	...
Sri Lanka											
Number - Nombre	+U	...	...	...	...	...	53	...	...	...	...
Tajikistan - Tadjikistan											
Number - Nombre	U	40	57	36	37	28	...	...	...	...	...
Thailand - Thaïlande											
Number - Nombre	+U	...	114	...	...	...	92	...	...	...	...
Uzbekistan - Ouzbékistan											
Number - Nombre	U	...	143	151	156	145	...	...	...	...	...
EUROPE											
Albania - Albanie											
Number - Nombre	U	2	5	1	1	...	...	...	...	...	...
Austria - Autriche											
Number - Nombre	C	5	2	2	3	3	2	3	2	2	1
Rate - Taux	C	♦6.6	♦2.6	♦2.6	♦3.8	♦3.8	♦2.6	♦3.9	♦2.6	♦2.6	♦1.3
Belarus - Bélarus											
Number - Nombre	C	13	17	18	...	...	...	7	3	1	...
Rate - Taux	C	♦14.2	♦19.2	♦20.3	...	...	...	♦6.8	♦2.8	♦0.9	...
Belgium - Belgique											
Number - Nombre	C	...	...	...	1	...	9	...	...	...	...
Rate - Taux	C	...	...	...	♦0.9	...	♦7.3	...	...	...	...
Bulgaria - Bulgarie											
Number - Nombre	C	13	11	4	7	8	5	8	5	4	6
Rate - Taux	C	♦19.1	♦16.5	♦5.9	♦10.0	♦11.3	♦6.8	♦10.6	♦6.4	♦4.9	♦7.9
Croatia - Croatie											
Number - Nombre	C	1	4	3	3	3	4	6	3	6	4
Rate - Taux	C	♦2.4	♦10.0	♦7.6	♦7.4	♦7.1	♦9.7	♦14.3	♦6.9	♦13.5	♦9.2
Czech Republic - République tchèque											
Number - Nombre	C	3	3	4	5	3	9	3	7	3	3
Rate - Taux	C	♦3.3	♦3.1	♦4.3	♦5.1	♦2.9	♦8.5	♦2.6	♦5.9	♦2.5	♦2.6
Denmark - Danemark											
Number - Nombre	C	2	...	...	-	-	5	...	...	...	...
Rate - Taux	C	♦3.1	...	...	-	-	♦7.7	...	...	...	...
Estonia - Estonie											
Number - Nombre	C	1	1	4	4	2	1	-	-	-	1
Rate - Taux	C	♦7.9	♦7.7	♦30.7	♦28.6	♦13.9	♦6.7	-	-	-	♦6.3
Finland - Finlande											
Number - Nombre	C	3	3	2	7	3	4	1	5	1	3
Rate - Taux	C	♦5.3	♦5.4	♦3.5	♦12.1	♦5.2	♦6.8	♦1.7	♦8.4	♦1.7	♦4.9
France											
Number - Nombre	C	56	67	56	53	41	59	60	52	...	...
Rate - Taux	C	7.3	8.8	7.4	6.9	5.3	7.4	7.6	6.5	...	...
Germany - Allemagne											
Number - Nombre	C	27	21	30	37	28	41	28	36	35	35
Rate - Taux	C	♦3.7	♦2.9	♦4.2	5.2	♦4.1	6.1	♦4.1	5.3	5.3	5.2
Greece - Grèce											
Number - Nombre	C	4	1	2	3	-	3	2	-	...	...
Rate - Taux	C	♦3.9	♦1.0	♦1.9	♦2.8	-	♦2.7	♦1.8	-	...	...
Hungary - Hongrie											
Number - Nombre	C	5	8	7	4	5	8	8	17	18	...
Rate - Taux	C	♦5.2	♦8.3	♦7.4	♦4.2	♦5.1	♦8.0	♦8.2	♦17.1	♦18.7	...
Iceland - Islande											
Number - Nombre	C	1	-	-	-	-	-	-	-	-	...
Rate - Taux	C	♦24.4	-	-	-	-	-	-	-	-	...
Ireland - Irlande											
Number - Nombre	...	3	5	-	1	2	-	1	2	3	3
Rate - Taux	...	♦5.2	♦8.3	-	♦1.6	♦3.3	-	♦1.4	♦2.7	♦4.0	♦4.0

17. Maternal deaths and maternal mortality ratios: 2001 - 2010
Mortalité liée à la maternité, nombre de décès et taux : 2001 - 2010 (continued - suite)

Continent and country or area Continent et pays ou zone	Co-de[a]	2001	2002	2003	2004	2005	2006	2007	2008	2009	2010
EUROPE											
Italy - Italie											
Number - Nombre	C	11	17	28	...	...	11	13	13	19	...
Rate - Taux	C	♦2.1	♦3.2	♦5.1	...	...	♦2.0	♦2.3	♦2.3	♦3.3	...
Latvia - Lettonie											
Number - Nombre	+C	5	1	3	2	1	2	6	2	7	4
Rate - Taux	+C	♦25.4	♦5.0	♦14.3	♦9.8	♦4.7	♦9.0	♦25.8	♦8.4	♦32.3	♦20.8
Lithuania - Lituanie											
Number - Nombre	+C	4	6	1	5	4	-	2	3	-	2
Rate - Taux	+C	♦12.7	♦20.0	♦3.3	♦16.4	♦13.1	-	♦6.2	♦8.6	-	♦5.6
Luxembourg											
Number - Nombre	+C	-	-	-	1	1	-	1	1	-	...
Rate - Taux	+C	-	-	-	♦18.3	♦18.6	-	♦18.3	♦17.9	-	...
Malta - Malte											
Number - Nombre	+C	2	-	-	-	-	-	-	1	-	-
Rate - Taux	+C	♦50.5	-	-	-	-	-	-	♦24.2	-	-
Montenegro - Monténégro											
Number - Nombre	C	...	...	...	...	...	-	1	-	-	...
Rate - Taux	C	...	...	...	...	...	-	♦12.8	-	-	...
Netherlands - Pays-Bas											
Number - Nombre	+C	14	20	8	10	16	15	9	8	9	4
Rate - Taux	+C	♦6.9	♦9.9	♦4.0	♦5.2	♦8.5	♦8.1	♦5.0	♦4.3	♦4.9	♦2.2
Norway - Norvège											
Number - Nombre	+C	3	2	7	-	2	5	4	3	1	3
Rate - Taux	+C	♦5.3	♦3.6	♦12.4	-	♦3.5	♦8.5	♦6.8	♦5.0	♦1.6	♦4.9
Poland - Pologne											
Number - Nombre	C	13	19	14	17	11	11	11	19	8	9
Rate - Taux	C	♦3.5	♦5.4	♦4.0	♦4.8	♦3.0	♦2.9	♦2.8	♦4.6	♦1.9	♦2.2
Portugal											
Number - Nombre	+C	6	8	8	...	...	...	5	4	7	8
Rate - Taux	+C	♦5.3	♦7.0	♦7.1	...	...	...	♦4.9	♦3.8	♦7.0	♦7.9
Republic of Moldova - République de Moldova											
Number - Nombre	...	16[3]	11[3]	8[3]	9[3]	8[3]	6[4]	7[4]	17[4]	7[4]	18[4]
Rate - Taux	...	...	...	...	...	...	♦16.0	♦18.4	♦43.6	♦17.2	♦44.5
Romania - Roumanie											
Number - Nombre	+C	75	47	65	52	37	34	33	30	47	51
Rate - Taux	+C	34.0	22.3	30.6	24.0	16.7	15.5	15.4	♦13.5	21.1	24.0
Russian Federation - Fédération de Russie											
Number - Nombre	+C	479[5]	469[5]	463[5]	352	370	352	356	359	388	298
Rate - Taux	+C	36.5	33.6	31.3	23.4	25.4	23.8	22.1	20.9	22.0	16.7
San Marino - Saint-Marin											
Number - Nombre	+U	...	-	...	...	-	...	...	...	...	...
Serbia - Serbie											
Number - Nombre	+U	...	...	...	2	10	9	-	4	6	12
Slovakia - Slovaquie											
Number - Nombre	C	7	4	2	3	2	3	-	2	6	-
Rate - Taux	C	♦13.7	♦7.9	♦3.9	♦5.6	♦3.7	♦5.6	-	♦3.5	♦9.8	-
Slovenia - Slovénie											
Number - Nombre	C	3	-	-	2	1	3	3	2	1	-
Rate - Taux	C	♦17.2	-	-	♦11.1	♦5.5	♦15.8	♦15.1	♦9.2	♦4.6	-
Spain - Espagne											
Number - Nombre	C	17	14	20	21	18	14	13	24	17	...
Rate - Taux	C	♦4.2	♦3.4	♦4.5	♦4.6	♦3.9	♦2.9	♦2.6	♦4.6	♦3.4	...
Sweden - Suède											
Number - Nombre	C	3	4	2	2	6	5	2	6	6	3
Rate - Taux	C	♦3.3	♦4.2	♦2.0	♦2.0	♦5.9	♦4.7	♦1.9	♦5.5	♦5.4	♦2.6
Switzerland - Suisse											
Number - Nombre	C	1	3	4	4	4	6	1	...	...	...
Rate - Taux	C	♦1.4	♦4.1	♦5.6	♦5.5	♦5.5	♦8.2	♦1.3	...	...	...
TFYR of Macedonia - L'ex-R. y. de Macédoine											
Number - Nombre	...	4	3	1	...	...	1	-	-	1	2
Rate - Taux	...	♦14.8	♦10.8	♦3.7	...	...	...	...	...	...	...
Ukraine											
Number - Nombre	+C	90	85	71	56	75	70	...	79	129	116
Rate - Taux	+C	23.9	21.8	17.4	13.1	17.6	15.2	...	15.5	25.2	23.3

Continent and country or area Continent et pays ou zone	Co-de[a]	2001	2002	2003	2004	2005	2006	2007	2008	2009	2010
EUROPE											
United Kingdom of Great Britain and Northern Ireland - Royaume-Uni de Grande-Bretagne et d'Irlande du Nord											
Number - Nombre	+C	50	40	53	55	51	50	56	49	74	40
Rate - Taux	+C	7.5	6.0	7.6	7.7	7.1	6.7	7.3	6.2	9.4	5.0
OCEANIA - OCÉANIE											
Australia - Australie											
Number - Nombre	C	12	13	8	12	...	9	...	...	...	...
Rate - Taux	C	♦4.9	♦5.2	♦3.2	♦4.7	...	♦3.4	...	...	...	...
Fiji - Fidji											
Number - Nombre	+C	...	...	...	...	...	...	...	...	5	...
Rate - Taux	+C	...	...	...	...	...	...	...	...	♦27.5	...
Kiribati											
Number - Nombre	U	1	...	...	...	...	...	...	...	...	...
New Zealand - Nouvelle-Zélande											
Number - Nombre	+C	3	8	4	4	6	9	13	7	...	...
Rate - Taux	+C	♦5.4	♦14.8	♦7.1	♦6.9	♦10.4	♦15.2	♦20.3	♦10.9	...	...

FOOTNOTES - NOTES

Data in bold refer to maternal deaths based on ICD-10 Classification, otherwise data refer to maternal deaths based on ICD-9 Classification. - Les données en typographie gras se rapportent aux décès maternelles basées sur la classification CIM-10, autrement les données se rapportent aux décès maternelles basées sur la classification CIM-9.

Italics: data from civil registers which are incomplete or of unknown completeness. - Italiques : données incomplètes ou dont le degré d'exactitude n'est pas connu, provenant des registres de l'état civil.

* Provisional. - Données provisoires.

♦ Rates based on 30 or fewer deaths. - Taux basés sur 30 décès ou moins.

a 'Code' indicates the source of data, as follows:
   C - Civil registration, estimated over 90% complete
   U - Civil registration, estimated less than 90% complete
   | - Other source, estimated reliable
   + - Data tabulated by date of registration rather than occurence
   ... - Information not available

Le 'Code' indique la source des données, comme suit :
   C - Registres de l'état civil considérés complèts à 90 p. 100 au moins
   U - Registres de l'état civil qui ne sont pas considérés complèts à 90 p. 100 au moins
   | - Autre source, considérée pas douteuses
   + - Données exploitées selon la date de l'enregistrement et non la date de l'événement
   ... - Information pas disponible

1 The code is C. - Le code est C.
2 The code is U. - Le code est U.
3 The code is +U. - Le code est +U.
4 The code is +C. - Le code est +C.
5 For 2003 and before, data on cause of death do not include the Chechnya region. Therefore, rates must be used with caution as they are based on the total population, which is assumed to include all regions. - Pour 2003 et avant, les données sur les causes de décès ne comprennent par la région de Chechnya. Par conséquent, les taux doivent être utilisés avec précaution car ils sont basés sur la population totale, qui est supposée inclure toutes les régions.

Table 18 - *Demographic Yearbook 2012*

Table 18 presents deaths and crude death rates by urban/rural residence for as many years as possible between 2008 and 2012.

Description of variables: Death is defined as the permanent disappearance of all evidence of life at any time after live birth has taken place (post-natal cessation of vital functions without capability of resuscitation).

Statistics on the number of deaths are obtained from civil registers unless otherwise noted. For those countries or areas where civil registration statistics on deaths are considered reliable (estimated completeness of 90 per cent or more), the death rates shown have been calculated on the basis of registered deaths.

The urban/rural classification of deaths is that provided by each country or area; it is presumed to be based on the national census definitions of urban population that have been set forth at the end of the technical notes for table 6.

For certain countries, there is a discrepancy between the total number of deaths shown in this table and those shown in subsequent tables for the same year. Usually this discrepancy arises because the total number of deaths occurring in a given year is revised although the remaining tabulations are not.

Rate computation: Crude death rates are the annual number of deaths per 1 000 mid-year population.

Rates by urban/rural residence are the annual number of deaths, in the appropriate urban or rural category, per 1 000 corresponding mid-year population. These rates are calculated by the Statistics Division of the United Nations based on the appropriate reference population (for example: total population, nationals only etc.) if known and available. If the reference population is not known or unavailable the total population is used to calculate the rates. Therefore, if the population that is used to calculate the rates is different from the correct reference population, the rates presented might under- or overstate the true situation in a country or area.

Rates presented in this table are limited to those countries or areas with a minimum number of 30 deaths in a given year.

Reliability of data: Each country or area has been asked to indicate the estimated completeness of the deaths recorded in its civil register. These national assessments are indicated by the quality codes "C", "U" and "|" that appear in the first column of this table. "C" indicates that the data are estimated to be virtually complete, that is, representing at least 90 per cent of the deaths occurring each year, while "U" indicates that data are estimated to be incomplete that is, representing less than 90 per cent of the deaths occurring each year. The code "|" indicates that the source of data is different than civil registration and is explained by a footnote. The code "..." indicates that no information was provided regarding completeness or no assessment has been done in the country.

Data from civil registers that are reported as incomplete or of unknown completeness (code "U" or "...") are considered unreliable. They appear in italics in this table; rates based on these data are not computed.

Limitations: Statistics on deaths are subject to the same qualifications as have been set forth for vital statistics in general and death statistics in particular as discussed in section 4 of the Introduction.

The reliability of the data, an indication of which is described above, is an important factor in considering the limitations. In addition, some deaths are tabulated by date of registration and not by date of occurrence; these have been indicated with a plus sign "+". Whenever the lag between the date of occurrence and date of registration is prolonged and, therefore, a large proportion of the death registrations are delayed, death statistics for any given year may be seriously affected. However, delays in the registration of deaths are less common and shorter than in the registration of live births.

International comparability in mortality statistics may also be affected by the exclusion of deaths of infants who were born alive but died before the registration of the birth or within the first 24 hours of life. Statistics of this type are footnoted.

In addition, it should be noted that rates are affected also by the quality and limitations of the population estimates that are used in their computation. The problems of under-enumeration or over-enumeration and, to some extent, the differences in definition of total population have been discussed in section 3 of the Introduction dealing with population data in general, and specific information pertaining to individual countries or areas is given in the footnotes to table 3.

Estimated rates based directly on the results of sample surveys are subject to considerable error as a result of omissions in reporting deaths or as a result of erroneous reporting of those that occurred outside the period of reference. However, such rates do have the advantage of having a "built-in" and corresponding base.

It should be emphasized that crude death rates -- like other crude rates, such as of birth, marriage and divorce -- may be seriously affected by the age-sex structure of the populations to which they relate. Nevertheless, they do provide a simple measure of the level and changes in mortality.

The comparability of data by urban/rural residence is affected by the national definitions of urban and rural used in tabulating these data. It is assumed, in the absence of specific information to the contrary, that the definitions of urban and rural used in connection with the national population census were also used in the compilation of the vital statistics for each country or area. However, it cannot be excluded that, for a given country or area, different definitions of urban and rural are used for the vital statistics data and the population census data respectively. When known, the definitions of urban used in national population censuses are presented at the end of the technical notes for table 6. As discussed in detail in the technical notes for table 6, these definitions vary considerably from one country or area to another.

In addition to problems of comparability, vital rates classified by urban/rural residence are also subject to certain types of bias. If, when calculating vital rates, different definitions of urban are used in connection with the vital events and the population data and if this results in a net difference between the numerator and denominator of the rate in the population at risk, then the vital rates would be biased. Urban/rural differentials in vital rates may also be affected by whether the vital events have been tabulated in terms of place of occurrence or place of usual residence. This problem is discussed in more detail in section 4.1.4.1 of the Introduction.

Earlier data: Deaths and crude death rates have been shown in each issue of the Demographic Yearbook. For information on specific years covered, the reader should consult the Index.

Tableau 18 – *Annuaire démographique 2012*

Le tableau 18 présente le nombre des décès et les taux bruts de mortalité selon le lieu de résidence (zone urbaine ou rurale) pour le plus grand nombre d'années possible entre 2008 et 2012.

Description des variables : Le décès est défini comme la disparition permanente de tout signe de vie à un moment quelconque postérieur à la naissance vivante (cessation des fonctions vitales après la naissance sans possibilité de réanimation).

Sauf indication contraire, les statistiques relatives au nombre de décès sont établies sur la base des registres d'état civil. Pour les pays ou zones où les données concernant l'enregistrement des décès par les services de l'état civil sont jugées sûres (complétude estimée à 90 p. 100 ou plus), les taux de mortalité ont été calculés d'après les décès enregistrés.

La répartition des décès entre zones urbaines et zones rurales est celle qui a été communiquée par chaque pays ou zone ; on part du principe qu'elle repose sur les définitions de la population urbaine utilisées pour les recensements nationaux, qui sont reproduites à la fin des notes techniques du tableau 6.

Pour quelques pays il y a une discordance entre le nombre total des décès présenté dans ce tableau et ceux présentés après pour la même année. Habituellement ces différences apparaissent lorsque le nombre total des décès pour une certaine année a été révisé alors que les autres tabulations ne l'ont pas été.

Calcul des taux : Les taux bruts de mortalité représentent le nombre annuel de décès pour 1 000 habitants en milieu d'année.

Les taux selon le lieu de résidence (zone urbaine ou rurale) représentent le nombre annuel de décès, classés selon la catégorie urbaine ou rurale appropriée, pour 1 000 habitants en milieu d'année. Ces taux sont calculés par la division de statistique des Nations Unies sur la base de la population de référence adéquate (par exemple : population totale, nationaux seulement, etc.) si connue et disponible. Si la population de référence n'est pas connue ou n'est pas disponible, la population totale est utilisée pour calculer les taux. Par conséquent, si la population utilisée pour calculer les taux est différente de la population de référence adéquate, les taux présentés sont susceptibles de sous ou sur estimer la situation réelle d'un pays ou d'un territoire.

Les taux présentés dans ce tableau se rapportent seulement aux pays ou zones où l'on a enregistré un nombre minimal de 30 décès au cours d'une année donnée.

Fiabilité des données : Il a été demandé à chaque pays ou zone d'indiquer le degré estimatif de complétude des données sur les décès d'enfants de moins d'un an figurant dans ses registres d'état civil. Ces évaluations nationales sont signalées par les codes de qualité "C", "U" et "|" qui apparaissent dans la deuxième colonne du tableau.

La lettre "C" indique que les données sont jugées à peu près complètes, c'est-à-dire qu'elles représentent au moins 90 p. 100 des décès d'enfants de moins d'un an survenus chaque année ; la lettre "U" signifie que les données sont jugées incomplètes, c'est-à-dire qu'elles représentent moins de 90 p.100 des décès d'enfants de moins d'un an survenus chaque année. Le symbole "|" indique que la source des données n'est pas un registre de l'état civil ; le symbole, dans ce cas, est accompagné par une note explicative. Le code "..." dénote qu'aucun renseignement n'a été communiqué quant à la complétude des données.

Les données provenant des registres de l'état civil qui sont déclarées incomplètes ou dont le degré de complétude n'est pas connu (code "U" ou "...") sont jugées douteuses. Elles apparaissent en italique dans le présent tableau et les taux correspondants n'ont pas été calculés.

Insuffisance des données : Les statistiques relatives à la mortalité appellent les mêmes réserves que celles qui ont été formulées à propos des statistiques de l'état civil en général et des statistiques relatives aux décès en particulier (voir la section 4 des Notes techniques).

La fiabilité des données, au sujet de laquelle des indications ont été fournies plus haut, est un facteur important. Il faut également tenir compte du fait que, dans certains cas, les décès sont classés par date d'enregistrement et non par date d'occurrence ; ces cas ont été signalés par le signe "+". Chaque fois que le décalage entre le décès et son enregistrement est grand et qu'une forte proportion des décès fait l'objet d'un enregistrement tardif, les statistiques relatives aux décès survenus pendant l'année peuvent être considérablement faussées.

En règle générale, toutefois, les décès sont enregistrés beaucoup plus rapidement que les naissances vivantes, et les retards prolongés sont rares.

Un autre facteur qui nuit à la comparabilité internationale est la pratique qui consiste à ne pas inclure dans les statistiques de la mortalité les enfants nés vivants mais décédés avant l'enregistrement de leur naissance ou dans les 24 heures qui ont suivi la naissance. Quand pareil facteur a joué, cela a été signalé en note à la fin du tableau.

Il convient de noter par ailleurs que l'exactitude des taux dépend également de la qualité et des limitations des estimations de la population qui sont utilisées pour leur calcul. Le problème des erreurs par excès ou par défaut commises lors du dénombrement et, dans une certaine mesure, le problème de l'hétérogénéité des définitions de la population totale ont été examinés à la section 3 de l'Introduction, relative à la population en général ; des indications concernant certains pays ou zones sont données en note à la fin du tableau 3.

Les taux estimatifs fondés directement sur les résultats d'enquêtes par sondage comportent des possibilités d'erreurs considérables dues soit à des omissions dans les déclarations des décès, soit au fait que l'on a déclaré à tort des décès survenus en réalité hors de la période considérée. Toutefois, ces taux présentent un avantage : le chiffre de population utilisé comme base est connu par définition et rigoureusement correspondant.

Il faut souligner que les taux bruts de mortalité, de même que les taux bruts de natalité, de nuptialité et de divortialité, peuvent varier très sensiblement selon la composition par âge et par sexe de la population à laquelle ils se rapportent. Ils offrent néanmoins un moyen simple de mesurer le niveau et l'évolution de la mortalité.

La comparabilité des données selon le lieu de résidence (zone urbaine ou rurale) peut être limitée par les définitions nationales des termes « urbain » et « rural » utilisées pour le classement de ces données. En l'absence d'indications contraires, on a supposé que les mêmes définitions avaient servi pour le recensement national de la population et pour l'établissement des statistiques de l'état civil pour chaque pays ou zone. Toutefois, il n'est pas exclu que, pour une zone ou un pays donné, des définitions différentes aient été retenues. Les définitions du terme « urbain » utilisées pour les recensements nationaux de population ont été présentées à la fin du tableau 6 lorsqu'elles étaient connues. Comme on l'a précisé dans les notes techniques relatives au tableau 6, ces définitions varient considérablement d'un pays ou d'une zone à l'autre.

Outre les problèmes de comparabilité, les taux démographiques classés selon le lieu de résidence « urbaine » ou « rurale » sont également sujets à des distorsions particulières. Si l'on utilise des définitions différentes du terme « urbain » pour classer les faits d'état civil et les données relatives à la population lors du calcul des taux et qu'il en résulte une différence nette entre le numérateur et le dénominateur pour le taux de la population exposée au risque, les taux démographiques s'en trouveront faussés. La différence entre ces taux pour les zones urbaines et rurales pourra aussi être faussée selon que les faits d'état civil auront été classés d'après le lieu où ils se sont produits ou d'après le lieu de résidence habituel. Ce problème est examiné plus en détail à la section 4.1.4.1 de l'Introduction.

Données publiées antérieurement : les différentes éditions de l'*Annuaire démographique* contiennent des statistiques des décès et des taux bruts de mortalité. Pour plus de précisions concernant les années pour lesquelles ces données ont été publiées, se reporter à l'index.

18. Deaths and crude death rates, by urban/rural residence: 2008 - 2012
Décès et taux bruts de mortalité, selon la résidence, urbaine/rurale : 2008 - 2012

Continent, country or area, and urban/rural residence — Continent, pays ou zone et résidence, urbaine/rurale	Code[a]	Number - Nombre					Rate - Taux				
		2008	2009	2010	2011	2012	2008	2009	2010	2011	2012
AFRICA - AFRIQUE											
Algeria - Algérie[1]											
Total	U	*153 000*	*159 000*	*157 000*	*162 000*	*170 000*	...	...	...	...	...
Burkina Faso[2]											
Total	|	174 800	...	...	...	...	11.9	...	...	...	...
Cabo Verde											
Total	C	2 873	2 897	2 917	...	...	5.7	5.7	5.6	...	...
Egypt - Égypte											
Total	C	461 934	476 592	483 385	493 086	...	6.1	6.2	6.1	6.1	...
Urban - Urbaine	C	216 023	217 897	226 304	228 368	...	6.7	6.6	6.7	6.6	...
Rural - Rurale	C	245 911	258 695	257 081	264 718	...	5.7	5.9	5.7	5.8	...
Kenya											
Total	U	*219 477*	*178 352*	*175 760*	*174 487*	*173 912*	...	...	...	...	...
Libya - Libye[3]											
Total	+U	*21 481*	*22 859*	...	...	...	...	...	...	...	...
Malawi[4]											
Total	|	135 865	...	...	...	...	10.0	...	...	...	...
Mauritius - Maurice[5]											
Total	+C	9 004	9 224	9 131	9 170	*9 343	7.1	7.2	7.1	7.1	*7.2
Urban - Urbaine	+C	4 159	4 324	4 251	4 182	...	7.8	8.1	8.0	7.8	...
Rural - Rurale	+C	4 845	4 900	4 880	4 988	...	6.6	6.6	6.5	6.6	...
Republic of South Sudan - République de Soudan du Sud[6]											
Total	|	165 897	...	...	...	...	20.1	...	...	...	...
Réunion											
Total	C	4 115	4 109	4 221	...	...	5.1	5.0	5.1	...	...
Rwanda											
Total	U	*141 640*	*141 648*	*141 256*	*140 519*	*139 499*	...	...	...	...	...
Saint Helena ex. dep. - Sainte-Hélène sans dép.											
Total	C	44	41	53	49	62	11.1	9.9	12.5	11.5	15.3
Senegal - Sénégal[7]											
Total	|	136 839	138 182	139 651	...	...	11.6	11.4	11.2	...	...
Urban - Urbaine	|	50 477	50 975	51 518	...	...	10.5	10.3	10.1	...	...
Rural - Rurale	|	86 362	87 207	88 133	...	...	12.3	12.1	11.9	...	...
Seychelles											
Total	+C	662	684	664	691	...	7.6	7.8	7.4	7.9	...
Sierra Leone											
Total	+...	*14 045*	*11 819*	*10 847*	*13 674*	*12 767*	...	...	...	...	...
Urban - Urbaine	+...	*4 546*	*796*	*5 441*	*2 967*	*4 948*	...	...	...	...	...
Rural - Rurale	+...	*9 499*	*11 023*	*5 406*	*10 707*	*7 819*	...	...	...	...	...
South Africa - Afrique du Sud											
Total	U	*592 073*	*572 673*	...	...	...	...	...	...	...	...
Total[8]	|	...	...	...	604 545	...	...	...	...	12.0	...
Tunisia - Tunisie											
Total	U	*59 975*	*59 499*	*60 438*	*63 258*	...	...	...	...	...	...
United Republic of Tanzania - République Unie de Tanzanie											
Total	...	*576 705*	*577 393*	*573 213*	*565 099*	*555 975*	...	...	...	...	...
AMERICA, NORTH - AMÉRIQUE DU NORD											
Anguilla[9]											
Total	+C	52	59	66	57	...	3.3	3.7	4.0	3.4	...
Antigua and Barbuda - Antigua-et-Barbuda											
Total	+C	531	507	491	...	...	6.1	5.7	5.4	...	...
Aruba											
Total	C	523	623	610	...	...	5.0	5.8	6.0	...	...
Bahamas											
Total	+C	1 863	2 021	*2 023	*2 117	...	5.5	5.9	*5.8	*6.0	...
Bermuda - Bermudes[10]											
Total	C	443	471	475	429	...	6.9	7.3	7.4	6.6	...

18. Deaths and crude death rates, by urban/rural residence: 2008 - 2012
Décès et taux bruts de mortalité, selon la résidence, urbaine/rurale : 2008 - 2012 (continued - suite)

Continent, country or area, and urban/rural residence — Continent, pays ou zone et résidence, urbaine/rurale	Code[a]	Number - Nombre					Rate - Taux				
		2008	2009	2010	2011	2012	2008	2009	2010	2011	2012
AMERICA, NORTH - AMÉRIQUE DU NORD											
Canada[11]											
Total	C	238 617	238 418	240 075	242 074	...	7.2	7.1	7.0	7.0	...
Cayman Islands - Îles Caïmanes											
Total	C	166	152	152	176	*172	3.0	2.9	2.8	3.2	*3.0
Costa Rica											
Total	C	18 021	18 560	*19 077	*18 801	*19 200	4.0	4.1	*4.2	*4.1	*4.1
Urban - Urbaine	C	9 170	9 561	*9 887	...	...	...	...	...	...	...
Rural - Rurale	C	8 851	8 999	*9 190	...	...	...	...	...	...	...
Cuba											
Total	C	86 423	86 940	91 065	*87 040	...	7.7	7.7	8.1	*7.7	...
Urban - Urbaine	C	71 444	72 233	76 091	...	...	8.4	8.5	9.0	...	...
Rural - Rurale	C	14 979	14 707	14 974	...	...	5.4	5.3	5.4	...	...
Curaçao											
Total	C	1 209	1 114	1 246	1 276	...	8.3	7.6	8.3	8.5	...
Dominica - Dominique											
Total	+C	545	559	588	...	...	7.6	7.8		...	...
Dominican Republic - République dominicaine											
Total	U	33 017	32 856	35 269	34 006	...	...	...	...	...	...
Urban - Urbaine[12]	U	23 226	23 934	26 699	25 858	...	...	...	...	...	...
Rural - Rurale[12]	U	7 888	6 837	7 296	7 418	...	...	...	...	...	...
El Salvador											
Total	C	31 594	32 872	32 586	33 211	...	5.2	5.3	5.3	5.3	...
Urban - Urbaine	C	24 052	25 517	23 684	23 621	...	6.3	6.6	6.0	5.9	...
Rural - Rurale	C	7 542	7 355	8 902	9 590	...	3.3	3.3	4.0	4.4	...
Greenland - Groenland											
Total	C	428	437	504	476	453	7.6	7.8	8.9	8.4	8.0
Urban - Urbaine	C	354	366	415	407	384	7.5	7.7	8.7	8.5	8.0
Rural - Rurale	C	74	71	89	69	69	8.0	7.8	10.0	8.0	8.0
Guadeloupe[13]											
Total	C	2 786	2 857	2 963	...	...	6.9	7.1	7.4	...	...
Guatemala											
Total	C	70 233	71 707	72 748	72 354	...	5.1	5.1	5.1	...	...
Urban - Urbaine[12]	C	38 866	38 610	39 331	37 781	...	...	...	...	...	...
Rural - Rurale[12]	C	31 009	30 859	32 219	33 137	...	...	...	...	...	...
Honduras											
Total	+U	36 260	36 536	36 812	37 211	...	...	...	...	...	...
Jamaica - Jamaïque[14]											
Total	U	19 966	18 855	21 503	16 926	16 998	...	...	...	...	...
Martinique[13]											
Total	C	2 793	2 771	2 844	...	...	7.0	7.0	7.2	...	...
Mexico - Mexique[15]											
Total	+C	538 288	563 516	590 886	589 646	...	5.0	5.2	5.3	...	...
Urban - Urbaine[12]	+C	403 798	424 362	446 324	444 372	...	4.9	5.1	...	...	...
Rural - Rurale[12]	+C	128 004	131 946	134 637	133 517	...	5.2	5.4	...	...	...
Montserrat											
Total	+C	45	44	40	55	...	9.2	8.7	8.0	11.2	...
Nicaragua											
Total	+U	18 079	...	...	...	...	...	...	...	...	...
Urban - Urbaine	+U	11 982	...	...	...	...	...	...	...	...	...
Rural - Rurale	+U	6 097	...	...	...	...	...	...	...	...	...
Panama											
Total	U	15 115	15 498	16 542	16 367	...	...	...	...	...	...
Urban - Urbaine	U	10 238	9 201	10 864	...	...	...	...	...	...	...
Rural - Rurale	U	4 877	6 297	5 678	...	...	...	...	...	...	...
Puerto Rico - Porto Rico											
Total	C	29 100	...	...	...	...	7.4	...	...	...	...
Urban - Urbaine[12]	C	15 477	...	...	...	...	...	...	...	...	...
Rural - Rurale[12]	C	13 440	...	...	...	...	...	...	...	...	...
Saint Vincent and the Grenadines - Saint-Vincent-et-les Grenadines											
Total	+C	848	765	...	...	...	8.6	7.6	...	...	...

455

Continent, country or area, and urban/rural residence / Continent, pays ou zone et résidence, urbaine/rurale	Code[a]	Number - Nombre					Rate - Taux				
		2008	2009	2010	2011	2012	2008	2009	2010	2011	2012
AMERICA, NORTH - AMÉRIQUE DU NORD											
Sint Maarten (Dutch part) - Saint-Martin (partie néerlandaise)											
Total	+C	152	...	...	...	...	3.8	...	...	...	...
Turks and Caicos Islands - Îles Turques et Caïques											
Total	C	65	...	...	...	...	1.8	...	...	...	...
United States of America - États-Unis d'Amérique											
Total	C	2 471 984	2 437 163	2 465 936	*2 513 171	...	8.1	7.9	8.0	*8.1	...
AMERICA, SOUTH - AMÉRIQUE DU SUD											
Argentina - Argentine											
Total	C	301 801	304 525	318 602	319 059	...	7.6	7.6	7.9	7.8	...
Brazil - Brésil											
Total	U	1 060 365	1 079 228	1 117 675[16]	1 148 165[16]	...	...	...	...	...	...
Chile - Chili											
Total	C	90 168	91 965	97 930	...	...	5.4	5.4	5.7	...	...
Urban - Urbaine	C	78 790	77 360	82 966	...	...	5.4	5.3	5.6	...	...
Rural - Rurale	C	11 378	14 605	14 964	...	...	5.2	6.6	6.7	...	...
Colombia - Colombie											
Total	U	196 943	196 933	200 524	*162 706	*179 646	...	...	...	...	...
Urban - Urbaine[12]	U	153 016	153 055	157 143	...	...	...	...	...	...	...
Rural - Rurale[12]	U	36 715	36 427	36 577	...	...	...	...	...	...	...
Ecuador - Équateur[17]											
Total	U	60 023	59 714	61 681	...	...	...	...	...	...	...
Urban - Urbaine	U	44 700	45 419	46 324	...	...	...	...	...	...	...
Rural - Rurale	U	15 323	14 295	15 357	...	...	...	...	...	...	...
French Guiana - Guyane française[13]											
Total	C	762	699	773	...	...	3.5	3.1	3.4	...	...
Guyana											
Total	+C	5 003	3 849	4 649	...	...	6.5	5.0	5.9	...	...
Paraguay											
Total	+U	24 417	...	...	...	...	...	...	...	...	...
Urban - Urbaine	+U	16 722	...	...	...	...	...	...	...	...	...
Rural - Rurale	+U	7 695	...	...	...	...	...	...	...	...	...
Peru - Pérou[18]											
Total	+U	91 277	95 722	99 334	96 852	...	...	...	...	...	...
Suriname[19]											
Total	C	3 357	3 293	...	...	...	6.5	6.3	...	...	...
Uruguay											
Total	C	31 363	32 179	33 474	*32 807	*33 002	9.4	9.6	10.0	*9.7	*9.8
Venezuela (Bolivarian Republic of) - Venezuela (République bolivarienne du)											
Total	C	124 062	123 530	130 597	136 803	...	4.4	4.4	4.5	4.7	...
ASIA - ASIE											
Armenia - Arménie[20]											
Total	C	27 412	27 560	27 921	27 963	*27 514	8.5	8.5	8.6	8.6	*8.4
Urban - Urbaine	C	17 451	17 433	...	...	...	8.4	8.4	...	...	...
Rural - Rurale	C	9 961	10 127	...	...	...	8.6	8.7	...	...	...
Azerbaijan - Azerbaïdjan[20]											
Total	+C	52 710	52 514	53 580	53 762	55 017	6.0	5.9	5.9	5.9	5.9
Urban - Urbaine	+C	27 817	27 690	28 369	...	...	5.9	5.8	5.9	...	...
Rural - Rurale	+C	24 893	24 824	25 211	...	...	6.0	5.9	5.9	...	...
Bahrain - Bahreïn											
Total	C	2 390	2 387	2 388	2 513	*2 299	2.2	2.0	1.9	2.1	*1.9

Continent, country or area, and urban/rural residence / Continent, pays ou zone et résidence, urbaine/rurale	Code[a]	Number - Nombre					Rate - Taux				
		2008	2009	2010	2011	2012	2008	2009	2010	2011	2012
ASIA - ASIE											
Bangladesh											
Total	U	...	...	842 095	828 000	...	...	...	...	...	...
Urban - Urbaine	U	...	...	187 470	176 000	...	...	...	...	...	...
Rural - Rurale	U	...	...	654 625	652 000	...	...	...	...	...	...
Brunei Darussalam - Brunéi Darussalam											
Total	+C	1 091	...	...	...	...	2.7	...	...	...	...
China - Chine[21]											
Total	I	9 350 000	9 449 959	9 510 000	9 600 000	9 660 000	7.1	7.1	7.1	7.1	7.2
China, Hong Kong SAR - Chine, Hong Kong RAS											
Total	C	41 796	41 175	42 194	42 346	*43 200	6.0	5.9	6.0	6.0	*6.0
China, Macao SAR - Chine, Macao RAS											
Total	C	1 756	1 664	1 774	1 845	1 841	3.2	3.1	3.3	3.4	3.2
Cyprus - Chypre[22]											
Total	C	5 194	5 182	5 103	5 504	...	6.6	6.4	6.2	6.5	...
Democratic People's Republic of Korea - République populaire démocratique de Corée[8]											
Total	I	216 616	...	...	...	...	9.0	...	...	...	...
Urban - Urbaine	I	119 805	...	...	...	...	...	...	...	...	...
Rural - Rurale	I	96 811	...	...	...	...	...	...	...	...	...
Georgia - Géorgie[20]											
Total	C	43 011	46 625	47 864	49 818	49 348	9.8	10.6	10.7	11.1	11.0
Urban - Urbaine	C	27 321	29 522	24 866	25 771	...	11.8	12.7	10.5	10.8	...
Rural - Rurale	C	15 690	17 103	22 998	24 047	...	7.6	8.2	11.0	11.4	...
India - Inde[23]											
Total	I	...	...	...	...	...	7.4	7.3	7.2	...	...
Urban - Urbaine	I	...	...	...	...	...	5.9	5.8	5.8	...	...
Rural - Rurale	I	...	...	...	...	...	8.0	7.8	7.7	...	...
Iran (Islamic Republic of) - Iran (République islamique d')[24]											
Total	+U	417 798	...	...	...	...	...	...	...	...	...
Urban - Urbaine	+U	270 877	...	...	...	...	...	...	...	...	...
Rural - Rurale	+U	146 921	...	...	...	...	...	...	...	...	...
Total	C	...	393 514	441 042	422 133	...	...	5.4	5.9	5.6	...
Urban - Urbaine	C	...	261 137	...	...	...	...	5.2	...	...	...
Rural - Rurale	C	...	132 377	...	...	...	...	5.8	...	...	...
Israel - Israël[25]											
Total	C	39 484	38 812	39 613	40 835	40 736	5.4	5.2	5.2	5.3	5.2
Urban - Urbaine	C	37 178	36 603[12]	37 190[12]	38 388[12]	38 297[12]	5.5	5.3	5.3	5.4	...
Rural - Rurale	C	2 306	2 208[12]	2 417[12]	2 443[12]	2 433[12]	3.8	3.6	3.8	3.7	...
Japan - Japon[26]											
Total	C	1 142 407	1 141 865	1 197 012	1 253 066	...	9.1	8.9	9.3	9.8	...
Urban - Urbaine[12]	C	997 547	998 621	1 054 725	1 103 338	...	...	...	...	...	...
Rural - Rurale[12]	C	142 989	141 387	140 473	147 235	...	...	...	...	...	...
Jordan - Jordanie[27]											
Total	U	19 403	20 251	21 550	21 730	...	...	...	...	...	...
Kazakhstan[20]											
Total	C	152 706	142 780	145 875	144 213	...	9.7	8.9	8.9	8.7	...
Urban - Urbaine	C	88 767	...	...	...	...	10.7	...	...	...	...
Rural - Rurale	C	63 939	...	...	...	...	8.7	...	...	...	...
Kuwait - Koweït											
Total	C	5 701	6 266	5 448	5 339	...	2.3	2.3	1.9	1.7	...
Kyrgyzstan - Kirghizstan											
Total	C	37 710	35 898	36 174	35 941	...	7.4	7.0	7.0	6.8	...
Urban - Urbaine	C	14 096	13 351	13 328	13 098	...	7.9	7.4	7.3	7.1	...
Rural - Rurale	C	23 614	22 547	22 846	22 843	...	7.2	6.8	6.8	6.7	...
Lebanon - Liban											
Total	C	21 048	22 260	22 926	26 070	23 452	...	...	...	...	...
Malaysia - Malaisie											
Total	C	124 857	130 135	*129 327	*133 400	...	4.5	4.6	*4.5	*4.6	...
Urban - Urbaine	C	73 427	76 539	...	...	...	...	...	...	...	...
Rural - Rurale	C	51 430	53 596	...	...	...	...	...	...	...	...

18. Deaths and crude death rates, by urban/rural residence: 2008 - 2012
Décès et taux bruts de mortalité, selon la résidence, urbaine/rurale : 2008 - 2012 (continued - suite)

Continent, country or area, and urban/rural residence / Continent, pays ou zone et résidence, urbaine/rurale	Co-de[a]	Number - Nombre					Rate - Taux				
		2008	2009	2010	2011	2012	2008	2009	2010	2011	2012
ASIA - ASIE											
Maldives											
Total	C	1 083	1 163	1 105	1 137	...	3.5	3.7	3.5	3.5	...
Urban - Urbaine	C	390	450	458[28]	468[28]	...	...	...	...	...	...
Rural - Rurale	C	693	713	611[28]	615[28]	...	...	...	...	...	...
Mongolia - Mongolie											
Total	+C	15 413	16 911	18 293	...	...	5.8	6.2	6.6	...	...
Urban - Urbaine	+C	9 968	10 627	11 580	...	...	6.1	6.3	6.7	...	...
Rural - Rurale	+C	5 445	6 284	6 713	...	...	5.3	6.1	6.6	...	...
Myanmar											
Total	+U	483 373	325 343	346 205	*342 420	...	...	...	...	...	...
Urban - Urbaine	+U	135 114	92 795	95 672	...	...	...	...	...	...	...
Rural - Rurale	+U	348 259	232 548	250 533	...	...	...	...	...	...	...
Oman[29]											
Total	U	7 298	7 098	6 974	7 667	...	...	...	...	...	...
Philippines											
Total	C	461 581	480 820	*488 265	...	...	5.1	5.2	*5.2	...	...
Qatar											
Total	C	1 942	2 008	1 970	1 949	...	1.3	1.2	1.1	1.1	...
Republic of Korea - République de Corée[30]											
Total	C	246 113	246 942	255 405	257 396	...	5.0	5.0	5.1	5.1	...
Urban - Urbaine[12]	C	164 439	166 356	172 779	174 968	...	4.1	4.1	4.3	4.3	...
Rural - Rurale[12]	C	81 664	80 575	82 590	82 416	...	8.8	8.6	8.7	8.7	...
Saudi Arabia - Arabie saoudite[31]											
Total	...	96 641	98 289	100 073	102 066	104 195	...	...	...	...	...
Singapore - Singapour											
Total	+C	17 222	17 101	17 610	18 027	18 481	4.7	4.6	4.7	4.8	4.8
Sri Lanka											
Total	+C	123 814[32]	*120 085	*128 603	*123 261	...	6.1	*5.9	*6.2	*5.9	...
Urban - Urbaine[32]	+C	53 616	...	...	...	...	...	...	...	...	...
Rural - Rurale[32]	+C	70 198	...	...	...	...	...	...	...	...	...
Syrian Arab Republic - République arabe syrienne[33]											
Total	+U	85 811	86 642	91 981	...	...	...	...	...	...	...
Tajikistan - Tadjikistan[20]											
Total	U	30 743	30 895	31 937	32 909	...	...	...	...	...	...
Urban - Urbaine	U	9 276	9 561	9 723	9 876	...	...	...	...	...	...
Rural - Rurale	U	21 467	21 334	22 214	23 033	...	...	...	...	...	...
Thailand - Thaïlande											
Total	+U	397 327	393 916	411 331	414 670	...	...	...	...	...	...
Turkey - Turquie											
Total	U	454 000	368 390	365 190	465 000	374 855	...	...	...	...	...
United Arab Emirates - Émirats arabes unis[34]											
Total	...	7 755	7 789	7 414	7 350	...	...	...	...	...	...
Uzbekistan - Ouzbékistan[20]											
Total	C	138 792	133 610	138 411	143 253	145 988	5.1	4.9	4.9	4.9	4.9
Yemen - Yémen											
Total	U	30 463	31 914	28 494	23 662	28 596	...	...	...	...	...
EUROPE											
Åland Islands - Îles d'Åland											
Total	C	250	247	233	277	*313	9.2	9.0	8.4	9.8	*11.0
Urban - Urbaine	C	114	101	92	120	*120	10.4	9.1	8.2	10.7	*10.6
Rural - Rurale	C	136	146	141	157	*193	8.3	8.8	8.4	9.3	*11.3
Albania - Albanie											
Total	C	16 143	...	...	19 636	...	5.5	...	...	6.9	...
Andorra - Andorre											
Total	C	237	272	239	275	303	2.8	3.2	2.8	3.5	3.9
Austria - Autriche											
Total	C	75 083	77 381[35]	77 199[35]	76 479[35]	79 436[35]	9.0	9.3	9.2	9.1	9.4

Continent, country or area, and urban/rural residence / Continent, pays ou zone et résidence, urbaine/rurale	Code[a]	Number - Nombre					Rate - Taux				
		2008	2009	2010	2011	2012	2008	2009	2010	2011	2012
EUROPE											
Belarus - Bélarus											
Total	C	133 879	135 097	137 132	135 090	126 531	13.8	14.1	14.5	14.3	13.4
Urban - Urbaine	C	75 536	76 629	78 840	78 947	...	...	...	...	11.0	...
Rural - Rurale	C	58 343	58 468	58 292	56 143	...	...	...	...	24.2	...
Belgium - Belgique[36]											
Total	C	104 587	104 509	105 094	*106 000	*103 500	9.8	9.7	9.6	*9.6	*9.3
Urban - Urbaine	C	102 962	102 981	...	...	...	9.8	9.7	...	...	...
Rural - Rurale	C	1 625	1 528	...	...	...	10.5	9.8	...	...	...
Bosnia and Herzegovina - Bosnie-Herzégovine											
Total	C	34 026	34 904	35 118	35 522	*35 692	8.9	9.1	9.1	9.2	*9.3
Bulgaria - Bulgarie											
Total	C	110 523	108 068	110 165	108 258	109 281	14.5	14.2	14.6	14.7	15.0
Urban - Urbaine	C	65 168	64 335	65 759	65 182	...	12.1	11.9	12.2	12.2	...
Rural - Rurale	C	45 355	43 733	44 406	43 076	...	20.4	20.1	20.7	21.4	...
Croatia - Croatie											
Total	C	52 151	52 414	52 096	51 019	...	11.8	11.8	11.8	11.6	...
Urban - Urbaine	C	26 172	26 275	26 508	...	...	...	...	...	...	...
Rural - Rurale	C	25 979	26 139	25 588	...	...	...	...	...	...	...
Czech Republic - République tchèque											
Total	C	104 948	107 421	106 844	106 848	108 189	10.1	10.2	10.2	10.2	10.3
Urban - Urbaine	C	76 664	78 590	78 001	78 209	...	10.0	10.2	10.1	10.2	...
Rural - Rurale	C	28 284	28 831	28 843	28 639	...	10.4	10.4	10.4	10.2	...
Denmark - Danemark[37]											
Total	C	54 591	54 872	54 368	52 516	52 325	9.9	9.9	9.8	9.4	9.4
Estonia - Estonie											
Total	C	16 675	16 081	15 790	15 244	15 450	12.4	12.0	11.8	11.4	11.5
Urban - Urbaine	C	11 227[12]	10 805	10 784[12]	10 428	...	12.1	11.6	11.6	11.2	...
Rural - Rurale	C	5 445[12]	5 276	5 004[12]	4 816	...	13.3	12.9	12.2	11.8	...
Faeroe Islands - Îles Féroé											
Total	C	378	387	348	364	407	7.8	8.0	7.2	7.5	8.4
Finland - Finlande											
Total	C	49 094	49 636[38]	50 654[38]	50 308[38]	51 707	9.2	9.3	9.5	9.4	9.6
Urban - Urbaine	C	29 624	30 346[38]	30 844[38]	30 835[38]	...	8.2	8.4	8.5	8.4	...
Rural - Rurale	C	19 470	19 290[38]	19 810[38]	19 473[38]	...	11.4	11.4	11.7	11.5	...
France[39]											
Total	C	532 131	538 116	540 469	534 795	*560 000	8.5	8.6	8.6	8.4	*8.8
Urban - Urbaine[40]	C	377 265	381 865	408 348	...	...	...	...	...	...	...
Rural - Rurale[40]	C	153 136	154 512	130 094	...	...	...	...	...	...	...
Germany - Allemagne											
Total	C	844 439	854 544	858 768	852 328	*863 000	10.3	10.4	10.5	10.4	*10.5
Gibraltar[41]											
Total	+C	227	234	231	241	...	7.8	8.0	7.8	8.1	...
Greece - Grèce											
Total	C	107 979	108 316	109 084	111 099	...	9.6	9.6	9.6	9.8	...
Urban - Urbaine	C	59 738	60 342	60 992	62 095	...	...	...	...	...	...
Rural - Rurale	C	48 241	47 974	48 092	49 004	...	...	...	...	...	...
Guernsey - Guernesey											
Total	C	495	535	497	535	547	8.0	8.6	8.0	8.5	8.7
Hungary - Hongrie											
Total	C	130 027	130 414	130 456	128 795	*129 500	13.0	13.0	13.0	12.9	*13.1
Urban - Urbaine[42]	C	84 390	85 507	86 304	85 721	...	12.4	12.5	12.4	12.3	...
Rural - Rurale[42]	C	44 968	44 304	43 570	42 498	...	13.9	14.0	14.3	14.0	...
Iceland - Islande											
Total	C	1 987	2 002	2 020	1 986[43]	*1 952	6.2	6.3	6.4	6.2	*6.1
Urban - Urbaine	C	1 851	1 861	1 869	1 958[43]	...	6.2	6.2	6.3	6.2	...
Rural - Rurale	C	136	141	151	28[43]	...	6.4	6.9	7.3	...	...
Ireland - Irlande											
Total[44]	C	28 274	28 380	...	...	...	6.4	6.4	...	...	...
Total	+C	...	...	27 565	28 995	*29 365	...	...	6.2	6.5	*6.4
Italy - Italie											
Total	C	578 192	585 182	581 307	*593 404	...	9.7	9.7	9.6	*9.8	...
Jersey											
Total	+C	743	...	...	...	...	7.8	...	...	...	...

18. Deaths and crude death rates, by urban/rural residence: 2008 - 2012
Décès et taux bruts de mortalité, selon la résidence, urbaine/rurale : 2008 - 2012 (continued - suite)

Continent, country or area, and urban/rural residence Continent, pays ou zone et résidence, urbaine/rurale	Co-de[a]	Number - Nombre					Rate - Taux				
		2008	2009	2010	2011	2012	2008	2009	2010	2011	2012
EUROPE											
Latvia - Lettonie											
Total	C	31 006	29 897	30 040	28 540	29 025	13.7	13.3	13.4	13.8	14.3
Urban - Urbaine	C	20 323	19 326	19 557	...	...	13.2	12.7	12.9	...	...
Rural - Rurale	C	10 683	10 571	10 483	...	...	14.6	14.5	14.4	...	...
Liechtenstein											
Total	C	205	229	238	248	224	5.8	6.4	6.6	6.8	6.1
Lithuania - Lituanie											
Total	C	43 832	42 032	42 120	41 037	40 938	13.1	12.6	12.8	13.5	12.9
Urban - Urbaine	C	25 863	24 972	25 114	24 822	...	11.5	11.2	11.4	12.3	...
Rural - Rurale	C	17 969	17 060	17 006	16 215	...	16.2	15.4	15.7	16.1	...
Luxembourg											
Total	C	3 595	3 655	3 760	3 819	3 876	7.4	7.3	7.4	7.4	7.3
Malta - Malte											
Total	C	3 243	3 221	3 010	3 290	...	7.9	7.8	7.2	7.9	...
Montenegro - Monténégro											
Total	C	5 708	5 862	5 633	5 847	5 922	9.1	9.3	9.1	9.4	9.5
Urban - Urbaine	C	3 602	3 809	...	...	...	9.1	9.5	...	...	...
Rural - Rurale	C	2 106	2 053	...	...	...	9.1	8.9	...	...	...
Netherlands - Pays-Bas[45]											
Total	C	135 136	134 235	136 058	135 741	...	8.2	8.1	8.2	8.1	...
Urban - Urbaine	C	90 365	89 495	90 257	...	...	8.3	8.2	8.1	...	...
Rural - Rurale	C	44 771	44 740	45 801	...	...	8.0	8.0	8.3	...	...
Norway - Norvège[46]											
Total	C	41 712	41 449	41 499	41 393	41 992	8.7	8.6	8.5	8.4	8.4
Poland - Pologne											
Total	C	379 399	384 940	378 478	375 501	384 788	10.0	10.1	9.8	9.7	10.0
Urban - Urbaine	C	228 650	231 772	227 452	225 524	...	9.8	9.9	9.7	9.6	...
Rural - Rurale	C	150 749	153 168	151 026	149 977	...	10.2	10.3	10.0	9.9	...
Portugal[15]											
Total	C	104 280	104 434	105 954	102 848[47]	107 598	9.8	9.8	10.0	9.7	10.2
Republic of Moldova - République de Moldova[48]											
Total	C	41 948	42 139	43 631	39 249	39 560	11.7	11.8	12.2	11.0	11.1
Urban - Urbaine	C	13 463	13 296	13 413	...	...	9.1	9.0	9.1	...	...
Rural - Rurale	C	28 485	28 843	30 218	...	...	13.6	13.8	14.5	...	...
Romania - Roumanie											
Total	C	253 202	257 213	259 723	251 439	255 539	11.8	12.0	12.1	11.8	12.0
Urban - Urbaine	C	114 352	116 168	117 632	114 648	...	9.7	9.8	10.0	9.8	...
Rural - Rurale	C	138 850	141 045	142 091	136 791	...	14.4	14.6	14.8	14.2	...
Russian Federation - Fédération de Russie[20]											
Total	C	2 075 954	2 010 543	2 028 516	1 925 720	*1 898 836	14.5	14.1	14.2	13.5	*13.3
Urban - Urbaine	C	1 443 529	1 397 591	1 421 734	1 356 696	...	13.8	13.3	13.5	12.8	...
Rural - Rurale	C	632 425	612 952	606 782	569 024	...	16.7	16.2	16.1	15.2	...
San Marino - Saint-Marin											
Total	+C	190	233	222	222	237	6.0	7.1	7.0	6.7	7.1
Serbia - Serbie[49]											
Total	+C	102 711	104 000	103 211	102 935	102 400	14.0	14.2	14.2	14.2	14.1
Urban - Urbaine	+C	52 783	54 234	53 822	54 128	...	12.3	12.7	12.6	12.6	...
Rural - Rurale	+C	49 928	49 766	49 389	48 807	...	16.2	16.4	16.4	16.4	...
Slovakia - Slovaquie											
Total	C	53 164	52 913	53 445	51 903	52 437	9.8	9.8	9.8	9.6	9.7
Urban - Urbaine	C	26 189	26 197	26 549	25 991	...	8.8	8.8	8.9	8.8	...
Rural - Rurale	C	26 975	26 716	26 896	25 912	...	11.1	10.9	11.0	10.5	...
Slovenia - Slovénie											
Total	C	18 308	18 750	18 609	18 699	*19 189	9.1	9.2	9.1	9.1	*9.3
Urban - Urbaine	C	9 294	9 666	9 675	9 717	...	9.2	9.4	9.4	9.5	...
Rural - Rurale	C	9 014	9 084	8 934	8 982	...	8.9	8.9	8.7	8.7	...
Spain - Espagne											
Total	C	384 198	383 209	381 409	386 017	*410 966	8.4	8.3	8.3	8.4	*8.9
Sweden - Suède											
Total	C	91 449	90 080	90 487	89 938	91 938	9.9	9.7	9.6	9.5	9.7
Switzerland - Suisse											
Total	C	61 233	62 476	62 649	62 091	*64 174	8.0	8.1	8.0	7.8	*8.0
Urban - Urbaine	C	44 777	45 798	45 923	45 451	...	8.0	8.0	...	7.8	...
Rural - Rurale	C	16 456	16 678	16 726	16 640	...	8.1	8.2	...	8.0	...

18. Deaths and crude death rates, by urban/rural residence: 2008 - 2012
Décès et taux bruts de mortalité, selon la résidence, urbaine/rurale : 2008 - 2012 (continued - suite)

Continent, country or area, and urban/rural residence — Continent, pays ou zone et résidence, urbaine/rurale	Code[a]	Number - Nombre					Rate - Taux				
		2008	2009	2010	2011	2012	2008	2009	2010	2011	2012
EUROPE											
TFYR of Macedonia - L'ex-R. y. de Macédoine											
Total	C	18 982	19 060	19 113	19 465	20 134	9.3	9.3	9.3	9.5	9.8
Urban - Urbaine	C	11 099	11 201	11 442	...	...	...	...	...	...	...
Rural - Rurale	C	7 883	7 859	7 671	...	...	...	...	...	...	...
Ukraine[50]											
Total	+C	754 460	706 739	698 235	664 588	663 139	16.3	15.3	15.3	14.6	14.6
Urban - Urbaine	+C	462 897	432 294	431 130	411 025	...	14.6	13.7	...	...	...
Rural - Rurale	+C	291 563	274 445	267 105	253 563	...	19.9	18.9	...	...	...
United Kingdom of Great Britain and Northern Ireland - Royaume-Uni de Grande-Bretagne et d'Irlande du Nord[51]											
Total	+C	579 697	559 617	561 666	552 232	...	9.4	9.1	9.0	8.8	...
OCEANIA - OCÉANIE											
Australia - Australie											
Total	+C	143 946	140 760	143 473	146 932	...	6.7	6.5	6.5	6.6	...
Urban - Urbaine[52]	+C	118 922	115 812	117 629	121 610	...	6.8	6.5	6.5	6.6	...
Rural - Rurale[52]	+C	24 540	24 504	25 076	24 791	...	6.4	6.3	6.4	6.3	...
Cook Islands - Îles Cook[53]											
Total	+C	56	67	95	*72	*104	2.6	3.0	4.0	*3.5	...
French Polynesia - Polynésie française											
Total	C	1 166	1 261	1 261	...	...	4.4	4.8	4.7	...	...
Guam											
Total	C	787	850[54]	872[54]	842[54]	...	4.9	5.3	5.5	5.3	...
New Caledonia - Nouvelle-Calédonie											
Total	C	1 169	1 261	1 191	...	...	4.8	5.1	4.8	...	...
New Zealand - Nouvelle-Zélande[15]											
Total	+C	29 188	28 964	28 438	30 082	30 099	6.8	6.7	6.5	6.8	6.8
Urban - Urbaine[12]	+C	26 238	26 036	25 475	27 138	27 050	7.1	7.0	6.8	7.1	7.1
Rural - Rurale[12]	+C	2 850	2 867	2 915	2 920	3 029	4.9	4.8	4.9	4.8	5.0
Niue - Nioué[55]											
Total	C	13	12	...	...	...	...	...	...	...	...
Norfolk Island - Île Norfolk[56]											
Total	+C	20	...	...	...	...	...	...	...	...	...
Northern Mariana Islands - Îles Mariannes septentrionales[57]											
Total	U	*176*	...	...	...	...	...	...	...	...	...
Samoa											
Total	U	*409*	*561*	...	...	...	...	...	...	...	...
Total[58]	|	...	...	...	812	...	...	...	...	4.4	...
Wallis and Futuna Islands - Îles Wallis et Futuna											
Total	C	90	...	...	...	...	6.7	...	...	...	...

FOOTNOTES - NOTES

Italics: data from civil registers which are incomplete or of unknown completeness. - Italiques : données incomplètes ou dont le degré d'exactitude n'est pas connu, provenant des registres de l'état civil.

* Provisional. - Données provisoires.

[a] 'Code' indicates the source of data, as follows:
C - Civil registration, estimated over 90% complete
U - Civil registration, estimated less than 90% complete
| - Other source, estimated reliable
+ - Data tabulated by date of registration rather than occurence

... - Information not available

Le 'Code' indique la source des données, comme suit :
C - Registres de l'état civil considérés complets à 90 p. 100 au moins
U - Registres de l'état civil qui ne sont pas considérés complets à 90 p. 100 au moins
| - Autre source, considérée pas douteuses
+ - Données exploitées selon la date de l'enregistrement et non la date de l'événement
... - Information pas disponible

[1] Excluding live-born infants who died before their birth was registered. Data refer to Algerian population only. - Non compris les enfants nés vivants décédés avant l'enregistrement de leur naissance. Les données ne concernent que la population algérienne.

[2] Data refer to national projections. - Les données se réfèrent aux projections nationales.

[3] Data refer to Libyan nationals only. - Les données se raportent aux nationaux libyens seulement.

[4] Data refer to the 12 months preceding the census in June. - Les données se raportent aux 12 mois précédant le recensement de juin.

[5] Excludes the islands of St. Brandon and Agalega. - Non compris les îles St. Brandon et Agalega.

[6] The figures in this table are derived from survey data. They are representative only of private households, internally displaced persons, refugees and nomads, and do not include cattle camps, institutional households, homeless people or overnight travelers. Data refer to the 12 months preceding the census in April. - Les chiffres de ce tableau proviennent de données d'enquête. Ils représentent exclusivement les ménages privés et les déplacés, réfugiés et nomades; ils ne comprennent ni les personnes se trouvant dans des camps pastoraux et des établissements collectifs, ni les sans-abri, ni les voyageurs. Les données se rapportent aux douze mois précédant le recensement d'avril.

[7] Based on estimates and projections from 'Agence Nationale de la Statistique et de la Démographie'. - Données fondées sur des estimations et des projections provenant de l'Agence Nationale de la Statistique et de la Démographie.

[8] Data refer to the 12 months preceding the census in October. - Les données se rapportent aux 12 mois précédant le recensement de octobre.

[9] Excluding visitors. - Ne comprend pas les visiteurs.

[10] Excluding non-residents and foreign service personnel and their dependants. - À l'exclusion des non-résidents et du personnel diplomatique et de leurs charges de famille.

[11] Including Canadian residents temporarily in the United States, but excluding United States residents temporarily in Canada. - Y compris les résidents canadiens se trouvant temporairement aux Etats-Unis, mais ne comprenant pas les résidents des Etats-Unis se trouvant temporairement au Canada.

[12] The total number includes 'Unknown residence', but the categories urban and rural do not. - Le nombre total englobe les personnes dont la résidence n'est pas connue, à l'inverse des catégories de population urbaine et rurale.

[13] Excluding live-born infants who died before their birth was registered. - Non compris les enfants nés vivants décédés avant l'enregistrement de leur naissance.

[14] Data have been adjusted for undercoverage of infant deaths and sudden and violent deaths. - Ajusté pour la sous-estimation de la mortalité infantile, du nombre de morts soudaines et de morts violentes.

[15] Data refer to resident population only. - Pour la population résidante seulement.

[16] Including deaths abroad and deaths of unknown residence. - Y compris les décès à l'étranger et les décès dont on ignore la résidence.

[17] Excludes nomadic Indian tribes. - Non compris les tribus d'Indiens nomades.

[18] Source: Reports of the Ministry of Health. - Source: Rapports du Ministère de la Santé.

[19] Including non-residents. - Y compris les non-résidents.

[20] Excluding infants born alive of less than 28 weeks' gestation, of less than 1 000 grams in weight and 35 centimeters in length, who die within seven days of birth. - Non compris les enfants nés vivants après moins de 28 semaines de gestations, pesant moins de 1 000 grammes, mesurant moins de 35 centimètres et décédés dans les sept jours qui ont suivi leur naissance.

[21] For statistical purposes, the data for China do not include those for the Hong Kong Special Administrative Region (Hong Kong SAR), Macao Special Administrative Region (Macao SAR) and Taiwan province of China. Data have been estimated on the basis of the annual National Sample Survey on Population Changes. - Pour la présentation des statistiques, les données pour la Chine ne comprennent pas la Région Administrative Spéciale de Hong Kong (Hong Kong RAS), la Région Administrative Spéciale de Macao (Macao RAS) et Taïwan province de Chine. Les données ont été estimées sur la base de l'enquête annuelle "National Sample Survey on Population Changes".

[22] Data refer to government controlled areas. - Les données se rapportent aux zones contrôlées par le Gouvernement.

[23] Rates were obtained by the Sample Registration System of India, which is a large demographic survey. Includes data for the Indian-held part of Jammu and Kashmir, the final status of which has not yet been determined. - Les taux ont été obtenus par le Système de l'enregistrement par échantillon de l'Inde qui est une large enquête démographique. Y compris les données pour la partie du Jammu et du Cachemire occupée par l'Inde dont le statut définitif n'a pas encore été déterminé.

[24] Data refer to the Iranian Year which begins on 21 March and ends on 20 March of the following year. - Les données concernent l'année iranienne, qui commence le 21 mars et se termine le 20 mars de l'année suivante.

[25] Including deaths abroad of Israeli residents who were out of the country for less than a year. Includes data for East Jerusalem and Israeli residents in certain other territories under occupation by Israeli military forces since June 1967. - Y compris les décès à l'étranger de résidents israéliens qui ont quitté le pays depuis moins d'un an. Y compris les données pour Jérusalem-Est et les résidents israéliens dans certains autres territoires occupés depuis 1967 par les forces armées israéliennes.

[26] Data refer to Japanese nationals in Japan only. - Les données se raportent aux nationaux japonais au Japon seulement.

[27] Excluding data for Jordanian territory under occupation since June 1967 by Israeli military forces. Excluding foreigners, including registered Palestinian refugees. - Non compris les données pour le territoire jordanien occupé depuis juin 1967 par les forces armées israéliennes. Non compris les étrangers, mais y compris les réfugiés de Palestine enregistrés.

[28] Excluding deaths occurred abroad. - Hormis les décès à l'étranger.

[29] Data from Births and Deaths Notification System (Ministry of Health and all health care providers). - Les données proviennent du système de notification des naissances et des décès (Ministère de la santé et tous prestataires de soins de santé).

[30] Excluding alien armed forces, civilian aliens employed by armed forces, and foreign diplomatic personnel and their dependants. - Non compris les militaires étrangers, les civils étrangers employés par les forces armées ni le personnel diplomatique étranger et les membres de leur famille les accompagnant.

[31] Projections based on the final results of the 2004 Population and Housing Census. - Projections basées sur les résultats définitifs du recensement de la population et de l'habitat de 2004.

[32] Excluding data from Mulative and Killnochchi districts. - À l'exclusion des données des districts de Mulative et Killnochchi.

[33] Excluding live-born infants who died before their birth was registered. Excluding nomad population and Palestinian refugees. - Non compris les enfants nés vivants décédés avant l'enregistrement de leur naissance. Non compris la population nomade et les réfugiés de Palestine.

[34] The registration of births and deaths is conducted by the Ministry of Health. An estimate of completeness is not provided. - L'enregistrement des naissances et des décès est mené par le Ministère de la Santé. Le degré estimatif de complétude n'est pas fourni.

[35] Including deaths of nationals abroad. - Y compris les décès des nationaux survenus à l'étranger.

[36] Including armed forces stationed outside the country, but excluding alien armed forces stationed in the area. - Y compris les militaires nationaux hors du pays, mais non compris les militaires étrangers en garnison sur le territoire.

[37] Excluding Faeroe Islands and Greenland shown separately, if available. - Non compris les Iles Féroé et le Groenland, qui font l'objet de rubriques distinctes, si disponible.

[38] Excluding Åland Islands. - Non compris les Îles d'Åland.

[39] Including armed forces stationed outside the country. - Y compris les militaires nationaux hors du pays.

[40] The data for urban and rural exclude the nationals outside the country. - Les données relatives à la population urbaine et rurale n'englobent pas les nationaux se trouvant à l'étranger.

[41] Excluding armed forces. - Non compris les militaires en garnison.

[42] Total includes the data of foreigners, persons of unknown residence and homeless, but the categories urban and rural do not. - Le total englobe les données relatives aux étrangers, aux personnes dont la résidence n'est pas connue et aux personnes sans domicile fixe, à l'inverse des chiffres portant sur la population urbaine et rurale.

[43] Definition of localities was revised from 2011 causing a break with the previous series. - La rupture par rapport aux séries précédentes s'explique par le fait que la définition des localités a été révisée depuis 2011.

[44] Data refer to events registered within one year of occurrence. - Les données portent sur des événements enregistrés dans l'année pendant laquelle ils sont survenus.

[45] Including residents outside the country if listed in a Netherlands population register. - Englobe les résidents se trouvant à l'étranger à condition qu'ils soient inscrits sur le registre de population des Pays-Bas.

[46] Including residents temporarily outside the country. - Y compris les résidents se trouvant temporairement hors du pays.

[47] Including unknown sex. - Y compris le sexe inconnu.

[48] Excluding Transnistria and the municipality of Bender. - Les données ne tiennent pas compte de l'information sur la Transnistria et la municipalité de Bender.

[49] Excludes data for Kosovo and Metohia. - Sans les données pour le Kosovo et Metohie.

[50] Data includes deaths resulting from births with weight 500g and more (if weight is unknown - with length 25 centimeters and more, or with gestation during 22 weeks or more). - Y compris les décès de nouveau-nés de 500 grammes ou

plus (si le poids est inconnu – de 25 centimètres de long ou plus, ou après une grossesse de 22 semaines ou plus).

[51] Excluding Channel Islands (Guernsey and Jersey) and Isle of Man, shown separately, if available. - Non compris les îles Anglo-Normandes (Guernesey et Jersey) et l'île de Man, qui font l'objet de rubriques distinctes, si disponible.

[52] Excluding data where place of usual residence was overseas, undefined, no fixed place of abode or offshore or migratory and unknown. - Les données n'ont pas été prises en compte lorsque le domicile habituel était à l'étranger ou dans une zone extraterritoriale, était indéfini ou inconnu ou que la personne n'avait pas de domicile fixe ou était une migrante.

[53] Excluding Niue, shown separately, which is part of Cook Islands, but because of remoteness is administered separately. - Non compris Nioué, qui fait l'objet d'une rubrique distincte et qui fait partie des îles Cook, mais qui, en raison de son éloignement, est administrée séparément.

[54] Including United States military personnel, their dependants and contract employees. - Y compris les militaires des Etats-Unis, les membres de leur famille les accompagnant et les agents contractuels des Etats-Unis.

[55] Includes deaths occurred in New Zealand but buried in Niue and deaths occurred in Niue but buried elsewhere. - Y compris les personnes décédées en Nouvelle-Zélande qui sont enterrées à Nioué et les personnes décédées à Nioué qui sont enterrées ailleurs.

[56] Data cover the period from 1 July of the previous year to 30 June of the present year. - Pour la période allant du 1er juillet de l'année précédente au 30 juin de l'année en cours.

[57] Source: Commonwealth Health Center - Vital Statistics Office - Source : Centre de Santé du Commonwealth - Bureau des statistiques d'État civil

[58] Data refer to the 12 months preceding the census in November. - Données se rapportant aux 12 mois précédant le recensement de novembre.

Table 19 - *Demographic Yearbook 2012*

Table 19 presents deaths by age and sex and age-specific death rates by sex for the latest available year between 2003 and 2012.

Description of variables: Age is defined as age at last birthday, that is, the difference between the date of birth and the date of the occurrence of the event, expressed in completed solar years. The age classification used in this table is the following: under 1 year, 1-4 years, 5-year age groups through 95-99 years, and 100 years or over.

Rate computation: Age-specific death rates by sex are the annual number of deaths in each age-sex group per 1 000 population in the same age-sex group. These rates are calculated by the Statistics Division of the United Nations.

Deaths at unknown age and the population of unknown age are excluded from age-specific rate calculations but are part of the death rate for all ages combined.

Death rates for infants under one year of age in this table differ from the infant mortality rates shown elsewhere, because the latter are computed per 1 000 live births rather than per 1 000 population.

The population used in computing the rates is the estimated or the enumerated population by age and sex reported to United Nations Statistics Division. First priority is given to an estimate and second priority to census returns of the year to which the deaths refer.

Rates presented in this table have been limited to those for countries or areas having at least a total of 100 deaths in a given year. Moreover, rates specific for individual sub-categories that are based on 30 or fewer deaths are identified by the symbol "♦".

Reliability of data: Data from civil registers of deaths that are reported as incomplete (less than 90 per cent completeness) or of unknown completeness are considered unreliable and are set in italics rather than in roman type. Table 18 and the technical notes for that table provide more detailed information on the completeness of death registration. For more information about the quality of vital statistics data in general and the information available on the basis of the completeness estimates in particular, see section 4.2 of the Introduction.

Rates are not computed if data from civil registers of deaths are reported as incomplete (less than 90 per cent completeness) or of unknown completeness, and therefore deemed unreliable.

Limitations: Statistics on deaths by age and sex are subject to the same qualifications as are set forth for vital statistics in general and death statistics in particular as discussed in section 4 of the Introduction.

The reliability of the data is an important factor in considering the limitations. In addition, some deaths are tabulated by date of registration and not by date of occurrence; these have been indicated by a plus sign "+". Whenever the lag between the date of occurrence and date of registration is prolonged and, therefore, a large proportion of the death registrations are delayed, death statistics for any given year may be seriously affected. However, delays in the registration of deaths are less common and shorter than in the registration of live births.

International comparability in mortality statistics may also be affected by the exclusion of deaths of infants who were born alive but died before the registration of the birth or within the first 24 hours of life. Statistics of this type are footnoted.

Because these statistics are classified according to age, they are subject to the limitations with respect to accuracy of age reporting similar to those already discussed in connection with section 3.1.3 of the Introduction. The factors influencing the accuracy of reporting may be somewhat dissimilar in vital statistics (because of the differences in the method of taking a census and registering a death) but, in general, the same errors can be observed.

The absence of data in the unknown age group does not necessarily indicate completely accurate reporting and tabulation of the age item. It is often an indication that the unknowns have been eliminated by assigning ages to them before tabulation, or by proportionate distribution after tabulation.

International comparability of statistics on deaths by age is also affected by the use of different methods to determine age at death. If age is obtained from an item that simply requests age at death in completed years or is derived from information on year of birth and death rather than from information on complete date (day, month and year) of birth and death, the number of deaths classified in the under-one-year age group will tend to be reduced and the number of deaths in the next age group will tend to be somewhat increased. A similar bias may affect other age groups but its impact is usually negligible. Information on this factor is given in the footnotes when known.

Limitations of rates: Rates shown in this table are subject to the same limitations that affect the corresponding data and are set forth in the technical notes for table 18. These include differences in the completeness of registration, the treatment of infants who were born alive but died before the registration of their birth or within the first 24 hours of life, the method used to determine age at death and the quality of the reported information relating to age at death. In addition, some rates are based on deaths tabulated by date of registration and not by date of occurrence; these have been indicated with a plus sign "+".

The problem of obtaining precise correspondence between deaths (numerator) and population (denominator) as regards the inclusion or exclusion of armed forces, refugees, displaced persons and other special groups is particularly difficult where age-specific death rates are concerned. Even when deaths and population do correspond conceptually, comparability of the rates may be affected by abnormal conditions such as absence from the country or area of large numbers of young men in the military forces or working abroad as temporary workers. Death rates may appear high in the younger ages, simply because a large section of the able-bodied members of the age group, whose death rates under normal conditions might be less than the average for persons of their age, is not included. Therefore, care should be exercised in using these rates for comparative purposes.

Also, in a number of cases the rates shown here for all ages combined differ from crude death rates shown elsewhere, because in this table they are computed on the population for which an appropriate age-sex distribution was available, while the crude death rates shown elsewhere may utilize a different total population. The population by age and sex might refer to a census date within the year rather than to the mid-point, or it might be more or less inclusive as regards ethnic groups, armed forces and so forth. In a few instances, the difference is attributable to the fact that the rates in this table were computed on the mean population whereas the corresponding rates in other tables were computed on an estimate for 1 July.

Earlier data: Age-specific deaths and death rates by sex have been shown for the latest available year in each issue of the Yearbook since the 1955 issue. For information on specific years covered, the reader should consult the Historical Index.

Tableau 19 – *Annuaire démographique 2012*

Le tableau 19 présente les données disponibles les plus récentes, entre 2003 et 2012, sur les décès et les taux de mortalité selon l'âge et le sexe.

Description des variables : L'âge considéré est l'âge au dernier anniversaire, c'est-à-dire la différence entre la date de naissance et la date du décès, exprimée en années solaires révolues. La classification par âge est la suivante : moins d'un an, 1 à 4 ans, groupes quinquennaux jusqu'à 95-99 ans et 100 ans et plus.

Calcul des taux : les taux de mortalité selon l'âge et le sexe représentent le nombre annuel de décès survenus pour chaque sexe et chaque groupe d'âge pour 1 000 personnes du même groupe. Ces taux ont été calculés par la Division de statistique de l'ONU.

On n'a pas tenu compte des décès à un âge inconnu ni de la population d'âge inconnu, sauf dans les taux de mortalité pour tous les âges combinés.

Il convient de noter que, dans ce tableau, les taux de mortalité des groupes de moins d'un an sont différents des taux de mortalité infantile qui figurent dans d'autres tableaux, ces derniers ayant été établis pour 1 000 naissances vivantes et non pour 1 000 habitants.

Les chiffres de population utilisés pour le calcul des taux proviennent de dénombrements ou de répartitions estimatives de la population selon l'âge et le sexe. On a utilisé de préférence les estimations de la population; à défaut, on s'est contenté des données censitaires se rapportant à l'année des décès.

Les taux présentés dans ce tableau ne se rapportent qu'aux pays ou zones où l'on a enregistré un total d'au moins 100 décès pendant l'année. Les taux relatifs à des sous-catégories, qui sont fondés sur 30 décès ou moins, sont signalés par le signe "♦".

Fiabilité des données : Les données sur les décès issues des registres d'état civil qui sont déclarées incomplètes (degré d'exhaustivité inférieur à 90 p.100) ou dont le degré d'exhaustivité n'est pas connu sont jugées douteuses et apparaissent en italique et non en caractères romains. Le tableau 18 et les notes techniques s'y rapportant présentent des renseignements plus détaillés sur le degré d'exhaustivité de l'enregistrement des décès. Pour plus de précisions sur la qualité des statistiques de l'état civil en général et le degré de complétude en particulier, voir la section 4.2 de l'Introduction.

On a choisi de ne pas faire figurer dans le tableau 19 des taux calculés à partir de données sur les décès issues de registres d'état civil qui sont déclarées incomplètes (degré d'exhaustivité inférieur à 90 p. 100) ou dont le degré d'exhaustivité n'est pas connu.

Insuffisance des données : Les statistiques des décès selon l'âge et le sexe appellent les mêmes réserves que les statistiques de l'état civil en général et les statistiques relatives à la mortalité en particulier (voir la section 4 de l'Introduction).

La fiabilité des données est un facteur important. Il faut également tenir compte du fait que, dans certains cas, les données relatives aux décès sont classées par date d'enregistrement et non par date d'occurrence ; ces cas ont été signalés par le signe "+". Chaque fois que le décalage entre le décès et son enregistrement est grand et qu'une forte proportion des décès fait l'objet d'un enregistrement tardif, les statistiques des décès de l'année peuvent être considérablement faussées. En règle générale, toutefois, les décès sont enregistrés beaucoup plus rapidement que les naissances vivantes, et les retards prolongés sont rares.

Un autre facteur qui nuit à la comparabilité internationale est la pratique de certains pays ou zones qui consiste à ne pas inclure dans les statistiques des décès les enfants nés vivants mais décédés avant l'enregistrement de leur naissance ou dans les 24 heures qui ont suivi la naissance, pratique qui conduit à sous-évaluer le nombre de décès à moins d'un an. Quand pareil facteur a joué, cela a été signalé en note à la fin du tableau.

Étant donné que les statistiques relatives à la mortalité sont classées selon l'âge, elles appellent les mêmes réserves concernant l'exactitude des déclarations d'âge que celles qui ont été formulées à la section 3.1.3 des Introduction. Dans le cas des données d'état civil, les facteurs qui interviennent à cet égard sont parfois un peu différents, du fait que le recensement et l'enregistrement des décès se font par des méthodes différentes, mais, d'une manière générale, les erreurs observées sont les mêmes.

Si aucun nombre ne figure dans la rangée réservée aux âges inconnus, cela ne signifie pas nécessairement que les déclarations d'âge et le classement par âge sont tout à fait exacts. C'est souvent une indication que l'on a attribué un âge aux personnes d'âge inconnu avant l'exploitation des données ou qu'elles ont été réparties proportionnellement entre les différents groupes après cette opération.

Le manque d'uniformité des méthodes suivies pour obtenir l'âge au moment du décès nuit également à la comparabilité internationale des données. Si l'âge est connu, soit d'après la réponse à une simple question sur l'âge du décès en années révolues, soit d'après l'année de la naissance et l'année du décès, et non d'après des renseignements concernant la date exacte (jour, mois et année) de la naissance et du décès, le nombre de décès classés dans la catégorie « moins d'un an » sera entaché d'une erreur par défaut et le chiffre figurant dans la catégorie suivante d'une erreur par excès.

Les données pour les autres groupes d'âge pourront être entachées d'une distorsion analogue, mais les répercussions seront généralement négligeables. Les imperfections, lorsqu'elles étaient connues, ont été signalées en note à la fin du tableau.

Insuffisance des taux : les taux présentés dans le tableau 19 appellent les mêmes réserves que celles formulées à propos des fréquences correspondantes (voir à ce sujet les notes techniques se rapportant au tableau 18). Leurs imperfections tiennent notamment aux différences d'exhaustivité de l'enregistrement, au classement des enfants nés vivants mais décédés avant l'enregistrement de leur naissance ou dans les 24 heures qui ont suivi la naissance, à la méthode utilisée pour obtenir l'âge au moment du décès, et à la qualité des déclarations concernant l'âge au moment du décès. En outre, dans certains cas, les données relatives aux décès sont classées par date d'enregistrement et non par date de l'événement ; ces cas ont été signalés par le signe "+".

S'agissant des taux de mortalité par âge, il est particulièrement difficile d'établir une correspondance exacte entre les décès (numérateur) et la population (dénominateur) du fait de l'inclusion ou de l'exclusion des militaires, des réfugiés, des personnes déplacées et d'autres groupes spéciaux. Il convient d'ajouter que, même lorsque population et décès correspondent, la comparabilité des taux peut être compromise par des conditions anormales telles que l'absence du pays ou de la zone d'un grand nombre de jeunes gens qui sont sous les drapeaux ou qui travaillent à l'étranger comme travailleurs temporaires. Il arrive ainsi que les taux de mortalité paraissent élevés parmi les groupes les plus jeunes simplement parce que l'on en a exclu un grand nombre d'individus en bonne santé pour lesquels le taux de mortalité pourrait être, dans des conditions normales, inférieur à la moyenne observée pour les personnes du même âge. Par conséquent, il importe d'être prudent quand on les utilise ces taux de mortalité dans des comparaisons.

De même, les taux indiqués pour tous les âges combinés diffèrent dans plusieurs cas des taux bruts de mortalité qui figurent dans d'autres tableaux, parce qu'ils se rapportent à une population pour laquelle on disposait d'une répartition par âge et par sexe appropriée, tandis que les taux bruts de mortalité indiqués ailleurs peuvent avoir été calculés sur la base d'un chiffre de population totale différent. Ainsi, il est possible que les chiffres de population par âge et par sexe proviennent d'un recensement effectué dans le courant de l'année et non au milieu de l'année, et qu'ils se différencient des autres chiffres de population en excluant ou en incluant certains groupes ethniques, les militaires, etc. Quelquefois, la différence tient à ce que les taux du tableau 19 ont été calculés sur la base de la population moyenne, alors que les taux correspondants des autres tableaux reposent sur une estimation au 1er juillet.

Données publiées antérieurement : Les éditions de l'*Annuaire démographique* parues depuis 1955 présentent les statistiques les plus récentes dont on disposait à l'époque sur les décès selon l'âge et le sexe et sur les taux de mortalité selon l'âge et le sexe. Pour plus de précisions concernant les années pour lesquelles ces données ont été publiées, se reporter à l'index historique.

19. Deaths by age and sex, age-specific death rates by sex: latest available year, 2003 - 2012
Décès et taux de mortalité selon l'âge et le sexe : dernière année disponible, 2003 - 2012

Continent, country or area, date, code and age (in years) / Continent, pays ou zone, date, code et âge (en années)	Number - Nombre			Rate - Taux		
	Both sexes Les deux sexes	Male Masculin	Female Féminin	Both sexes Les deux sexes	Male Masculin	Female Féminin
AFRICA - AFRIQUE						
Botswana[1]						
2007 (+U)						
Total	11 074	5 971	5 103	...	...	...
0	658	353	305	...	...	...
1 - 4	643	338	305	...	...	...
5 - 14	192	100	92	...	...	...
15 - 24	438	132	306	...	...	...
25 - 34	2 330	1 047	1 283	...	...	...
35 - 44	2 202	1 293	909	...	...	...
45 - 54	1 509	937	572	...	...	...
55 - 64	1 045	659	386	...	...	...
65 +	2 039	1 106	933	...	...	...
Unknown - Inconnu	18	6	12	..	..	..
Egypt - Égypte						
2011 (C)						
Total	493 086	275 537	217 549	6.1	6.7	5.5
0	35 997	19 385	16 612	...	...	...
1 - 4	10 749	6 155	4 594	...	...	...
5 - 9	4 006	2 398	1 608	0.5	0.6	0.4
10 - 14	3 702	2 398	1 304	0.4	0.5	0.3
15 - 19	6 340	4 601	1 739	0.7	1.0	0.4
20 - 24	8 324	5 885	2 439	1.0	1.3	0.6
25 - 29	8 515	5 649	2 866	1.2	1.6	0.8
30 - 34	8 848	5 637	3 211	1.7	2.1	1.3
35 - 39	8 946	5 373	3 573	1.7	2.1	1.4
40 - 44	12 107	7 551	4 556	2.7	3.3	2.0
45 - 49	20 974	13 587	7 387	5.2	6.5	3.7
50 - 54	20 974	13 587	7 387	6.2	8.0	4.4
55 - 59	32 562	20 995	11 567	13.0	15.7	10.0
60 - 64	43 703	28 390	15 313	23.2	28.6	17.2
65 - 69	51 151	30 726	20 425	38.8	43.4	33.5
70 - 74	46 285	25 518	20 767	53.0	57.4	48.5
75 +	134 947	63 471	71 476	165.0	152.1	178.5
75 - 79	52 489	27 344	25 145	...	...	...
80 - 84	43 221	20 296	22 925	...	...	...
85 +	39 237	15 831	23 406	...	...	...
Unknown - Inconnu	34 956	14 231	20 725	..	..	..
Kenya						
2011 (U)						
Total	174 487	96 026	78 461	...	...	...
0	23 167	12 119	11 048	...	...	...
1 - 4	12 129	6 530	5 599	...	...	...
5 - 14	9 145	4 949	4 196	...	...	...
15 - 24	11 961	5 931	6 030	...	...	...
25 - 34	21 054	11 329	9 725	...	...	...
35 - 44	21 605	12 382	9 223	...	...	...
45 - 54	18 606	11 124	7 482	...	...	...
55 - 74	29 686	17 525	12 161	...	...	...
75 +	27 134	14 137	12 997	...	...	...
Malawi[2]						
2008 (|)						
Total	135 865	70 991	64 874	10.0	10.6	9.4
0	30 508	16 606	13 902	...	...	...
1 - 4	26 213	13 226	12 987	12.4	12.5	12.4
5 - 9	6 413	3 350	3 063	2.8	2.9	2.7
10 - 14	5 333	3 071	2 262	3.5	4.1	2.9
15 - 19	4 266	1 863	2 403	3.1	2.7	3.4
20 - 24	7 188	3 038	4 150	6.1	5.1	7.0
25 - 29	7 903	3 405	4 498	7.6	6.8	8.3
30 - 34	9 042	4 280	4 762	9.7	10.4	9.2
35 - 39	7 200	3 813	3 387	9.7	10.3	9.0
40 - 44	6 004	3 410	2 594	10.8	12.2	9.4
45 - 49	4 275	2 436	1 839	9.7	11.3	8.2
50 - 54	3 414	2 092	1 322	10.7	13.3	8.2
55 +	18 106	10 401	7 705	34.1	40.9	27.9
55 - 59	2 447	1 523	924	...	...	...
60 - 64	2 978	1 827	1 151	...	...	...

19. Deaths by age and sex, age-specific death rates by sex: latest available year, 2003 - 2012
Décès et taux de mortalité selon l'âge et le sexe : dernière année disponible, 2003 - 2012 (continued - suite)

Continent, country or area, date, code and age (in years) / Continent, pays ou zone, date, code et âge (en années)	Number - Nombre			Rate - Taux		
	Both sexes Les deux sexes	Male Masculin	Female Féminin	Both sexes Les deux sexes	Male Masculin	Female Féminin
AFRICA - AFRIQUE						
Malawi[2]						
2008 (|)						
65 - 69	2 314	1 372	942	...	...	...
70 - 74	2 871	1 665	1 206	...	...	...
75 - 79	2 149	1 254	895	...	...	...
80 - 84	2 151	1 138	1 013	...	...	...
85 +	3 196	1 622	1 574	...	...	...
Mauritius - Maurice[3]						
2011 (+C)						
Total	9 170	5 236	3 934	7.1	8.3	6.0
0	189	102	87	13.1	14.0	12.2
1 - 4	45	20	25	0.7	◆0.6	◆0.8
5 - 9	17	9	8	◆0.2	◆0.2	◆0.2
10 - 14	20	10	10	◆0.2	◆0.2	◆0.2
15 - 19	53	38	15	0.5	0.7	◆0.3
20 - 24	88	64	24	0.9	1.3	◆0.5
25 - 29	121	97	24	1.3	2.0	◆0.5
30 - 34	162	127	35	1.4	2.3	0.6
35 - 39	215	151	64	2.3	3.3	1.3
40 - 44	310	226	84	3.3	4.9	1.8
45 - 49	503	355	148	5.0	7.1	2.9
50 - 54	669	470	199	7.7	10.9	4.5
55 - 59	756	484	272	10.4	13.7	7.3
60 - 64	968	620	348	17.2	23.3	11.7
65 - 69	859	503	356	24.9	32.8	18.5
70 - 74	923	522	401	37.2	49.2	28.2
75 - 79	935	472	463	53.4	67.4	44.1
80 - 84	935	427	508	87.0	110.6	73.7
85 +	1 402	539	863	182.7	228.6	162.3
Morocco - Maroc						
2007 (U)						
Total	105 222	66 522	38 700	...	...	...
0	5 140	2 823	2 317	...	...	...
1 - 4	2 320	1 266	1 054	...	...	...
5 - 9	1 075	591	484	...	...	...
10 - 14	859	533	326	...	...	...
15 - 19	1 575	1 024	551	...	...	...
20 - 24	2 204	1 442	762	...	...	...
25 - 29	2 503	1 570	933	...	...	...
30 - 34	2 705	1 660	1 045	...	...	...
35 - 39	2 948	1 767	1 181	...	...	...
40 - 44	3 400	2 052	1 348	...	...	...
45 - 49	4 547	2 766	1 781	...	...	...
50 - 54	5 616	3 672	1 944	...	...	...
55 - 59	6 132	4 046	2 086	...	...	...
60 - 64	7 193	4 626	2 567	...	...	...
65 - 69	10 331	6 494	3 837	...	...	...
70 - 74	12 441	7 990	4 451	...	...	...
75 - 79	13 183	8 491	4 692	...	...	...
80 +	20 051	13 159	6 892	...	...	...
Unknown - Inconnu	999	550	449	..	..	...
Republic of South Sudan - République de Soudan du Sud[4]						
2008 (|)						
Total	165 897	88 797	77 100	20.1	20.7	19.4
0	29 218	12 384	16 833	...	...	...
1 - 4	55 675	29 144	26 530	...	...	...
5 - 9	22 572	12 351	10 220	17.4	17.9	16.8
10 - 14	12 486	6 785	5 702	11.8	11.9	11.7
15 - 19	11 665	6 297	5 368	13.1	13.6	12.6
20 - 24	9 257	5 556	3 700	12.5	15.4	9.8
25 - 29	6 022	4 063	1 959	8.6	12.1	5.4
30 - 34	4 496	2 634	1 862	8.4	10.2	6.7
35 - 39	3 045	2 237	809	6.4	9.4	3.4
40 - 44	2 627	1 605	1 022	7.7	9.3	6.1
45 - 49	1 656	993	663	6.0	6.6	5.3
50 - 54	1 513	977	536	7.7	9.3	5.8

469

19. Deaths by age and sex, age-specific death rates by sex: latest available year, 2003 - 2012
Décès et taux de mortalité selon l'âge et le sexe : dernière année disponible, 2003 - 2012 (continued - suite)

Continent, country or area, date, code and age (in years) / Continent, pays ou zone, date, code et âge (en années)	Number - Nombre			Rate - Taux		
	Both sexes Les deux sexes	Male Masculin	Female Féminin	Both sexes Les deux sexes	Male Masculin	Female Féminin
AFRICA - AFRIQUE						
Republic of South Sudan - République de Soudan du Sud[4]						
2008 (|)						
55 - 59	945	618	328	7.8	9.1	6.1
60 - 64	1 094	668	426	9.5	10.4	8.3
65 +	3 626	2 483	1 142	17.2	20.2	13.0
Réunion						
2007 (C)						
Total	4 045	2 247	1 798	5.1	5.9	4.4
0 - 4	114	58	56	1.7	1.7	1.7
0	99	49	50	...	...	...
1 - 4	15	9	6	...	...	...
5 - 9	6	6	-	♦0.1	♦0.2	-
10 - 14	10	7	3	♦0.1	♦0.2	♦0.1
15 - 19	32	25	7	0.5	♦0.7	♦0.2
20 - 24	44	35	9	0.8	1.3	♦0.3
25 - 29	39	27	12	0.8	♦1.1	♦0.4
30 - 34	55	37	18	1.0	1.4	♦0.6
35 - 39	97	68	29	1.5	2.3	♦0.9
40 - 44	158	106	52	2.4	3.3	1.5
45 - 49	211	150	61	4.0	5.9	2.3
50 - 54	236	183	53	5.1	8.2	2.2
55 - 59	266	188	78	7.5	10.7	4.4
60 - 64	287	176	111	10.8	14.1	7.9
65 - 69	375	246	129	17.4	24.8	11.1
70 - 74	427	250	177	25.9	34.7	19.1
75 - 79	448	231	217	39.5	50.3	32.2
80 - 84	496	222	274	65.3	78.9	57.3
85 - 89	393	149	244	106.6	140.6	92.9
90 - 94	233	66	167	166.1	182.8	160.3
95 +	118	17	101	308.9	♦369.6	300.6
95 - 99	96	15	81	...	...	...
100 +	22	2	20	...	...	...
Saint Helena ex. dep. - Sainte-Hélène sans dép.						
2012 (C)						
Total	62	36	26	...	...	...
0	1	-	1	...	...	...
1 - 4	-	-	-	...	...	...
5 - 9	-	-	-	...	...	...
10 - 14	-	-	-	...	...	...
15 - 19	-	-	-	...	...	...
20 - 24	1	1	-	...	...	...
25 - 29	-	-	-	...	...	...
30 - 34	-	-	-	...	...	...
35 - 39	-	-	-	...	...	...
40 - 44	2	2	-	...	...	...
45 - 49	2	2	-	...	...	...
50 - 54	1	-	1	...	...	...
55 - 59	5	4	1	...	...	...
60 - 64	10	7	3	...	...	...
65 - 69	3	2	1	...	...	...
70 - 74	6	3	3	...	...	...
75 - 79	10	8	2	...	...	...
80 - 84	10	3	7	...	...	...
85 - 89	4	3	1	...	...	...
90 - 94	5	1	4	...	...	...
95 - 99	1	-	1	...	...	...
100 +	1	-	1	...	...	...
Seychelles						
2011 (+C)						
Total	691	392	299	7.9	9.1	6.7
0	16	10	6	♦10.4	♦12.9	♦7.9
1 - 4	8	6	2	♦1.5	♦2.3	♦0.8
5 - 9	1	1	-	♦0.2	♦0.3	-
10 - 14	1	1	-	♦0.2	♦0.3	-
15 - 19	3	3	-	♦0.4	♦0.8	-
20 - 24	9	7	2	♦1.4	♦2.0	♦0.7

19. Deaths by age and sex, age-specific death rates by sex: latest available year, 2003 - 2012
Décès et taux de mortalité selon l'âge et le sexe : dernière année disponible, 2003 - 2012 (continued - suite)

Continent, country or area, date, code and age (in years) / Continent, pays ou zone, date, code et âge (en années)	Number - Nombre			Rate - Taux		
	Both sexes Les deux sexes	Male Masculin	Female Féminin	Both sexes Les deux sexes	Male Masculin	Female Féminin

AFRICA - AFRIQUE

Seychelles
2011 (+C)

25 - 29	16	10	6	♦2.4	♦3.2	♦1.7
30 - 34	15	11	4	♦2.1	♦3.2	♦1.1
35 - 39	18	13	5	♦2.4	♦3.5	♦1.4
40 - 44	29	23	6	♦4.2	♦6.8	♦1.7
45 - 49	39	27	12	5.7	♦8.1	♦3.4
50 - 54	49	36	13	8.5	11.9	♦4.8
55 - 59	36	28	8	9.0	♦14.1	♦4.0
60 - 64	54	35	19	20.2	26.4	♦14.1
65 - 69	44	32	12	20.6	31.8	♦10.7
70 - 74	70	41	29	39.3	57.6	♦27.2
75 - 79	78	42	36	57.9	86.1	41.9
80 - 84	85	33	52	97.4	117.4	87.8
85 - 89	72	25	47	146.9	♦176.1	135.1
90 - 94	33	8	25	186.4	♦222.2	♦177.3
95 - 99	13	1	12	♦240.7	♦125.0	♦260.9
100 +	3	-	3	♦375.0	-	♦428.6

Sierra Leone[5]
2004 (|)

Total	99 020	...	...	20.1	...	...
0	16 637	...	...	106.6	...	...
1 - 4	20 362	...	...	34.1	...	...
5 - 9	6 806	...	...	9.2	...	...
10 - 14	3 087	...	...	5.5	...	...
15 - 19	3 679	...	...	6.9	...	...
20 - 24	5 278	...	...	12.7	...	...
25 - 29	3 809	...	...	9.4	...	...
30 - 34	3 707	...	...	11.9	...	...
35 - 39	3 387	...	...	11.3	...	...
40 - 44	3 689	...	...	17.3	...	...
45 - 49	3 045	...	...	17.2	...	...
50 - 54	3 491	...	...	27.2	...	...
55 - 59	2 022	...	...	23.8	...	...
60 - 64	3 885	...	...	44.3	...	...
65 - 69	2 446	...	...	40.0	...	...
70 - 74	3 423	...	...	62.9	...	...
75 - 79	2 390	...	...	65.1	...	...
80 - 84	2 780	...	...	102.6	...	...
85 +	5 097	...	...	142.3	...	...

South Africa - Afrique du Sud[6]
2011 (|)

Total	604 545	252 390	231 230	12.0	10.3	8.9
0	41 635	22 144	19 004	...	...	...
1 - 4	13 839	7 195	6 217	...	...	...
5 - 9	6 152	3 204	2 816	1.2	1.2	1.1
10 - 14	4 294	2 280	1 922	0.8	0.9	0.7
15 - 19	8 187	4 390	3 757	1.6	1.7	1.5
20 - 24	19 172	9 446	9 649	3.9	3.8	4.0
25 - 29	31 546	15 190	16 202	6.9	6.8	6.9
30 - 34	37 024	18 936	17 954	9.2	9.4	8.9
35 - 39	37 700	20 526	17 034	10.5	11.8	9.2
40 - 44	32 415	18 052	14 262	12.4	14.9	10.2
45 - 49	31 135	17 748	13 275	13.9	17.6	10.8
50 - 54	29 502	16 764	12 608	14.5	18.5	11.1
55 - 59	28 383	16 459	11 830	17.0	22.1	12.7
60 - 64	28 373	16 103	12 150	21.0	27.6	15.8
65 - 69	23 703	13 109	10 506	24.0	31.3	18.4
70 - 74	24 686	12 580	12 010	34.5	43.5	28.2
75 - 79	20 343	9 441	10 814	44.1	54.6	37.5
80 - 84	18 203	7 603	10 523	...	...	...
85 - 89	11 462	4 428	6 992	...	...	...
90 - 120	13 037	4 049	8 912	...	...	...
Unknown - Inconnu	143 755	12 741	12 794	..	..	..

19. Deaths by age and sex, age-specific death rates by sex: latest available year, 2003 - 2012
Décès et taux de mortalité selon l'âge et le sexe : dernière année disponible, 2003 - 2012 (continued - suite)

Continent, country or area, date, code and age (in years) / Continent, pays ou zone, date, code et âge (en années)	Number - Nombre			Rate - Taux		
	Both sexes Les deux sexes	Male Masculin	Female Féminin	Both sexes Les deux sexes	Male Masculin	Female Féminin
AFRICA - AFRIQUE						
Swaziland[7]						
2007 (|)						
Total	18 367	8 738	9 629	21.8	21.5	22.0
0	3 613	1 555	2 058	...	...	...
1 - 4	1 230	576	654	...	...	...
5 - 9	408	198	210	3.6	3.5	3.8
10 - 14	302	165	137	2.7	3.0	2.4
15 - 19	431	174	257	4.3	3.5	5.1
20 - 24	1 145	353	792	13.0	8.3	17.6
25 - 29	1 773	707	1 066	25.2	20.9	29.2
30 - 34	1 792	839	953	34.3	32.8	35.7
35 - 39	1 586	828	758	36.3	40.0	32.9
40 - 44	1 145	652	493	33.7	44.0	25.7
45 - 49	865	502	363	29.6	39.3	22.1
50 - 54	752	453	299	32.9	43.5	24.0
55 - 59	557	364	193	30.8	43.7	19.8
60 - 64	618	342	276	37.0	51.0	27.6
65 - 69	436	238	198	32.9	43.1	25.6
70 - 74	392	214	178	48.0	66.7	35.9
75 - 79	283	158	125	45.4	68.0	31.9
80 +	612	261	351	95.3	122.1	82.0
Unknown - Inconnu	427	159	268	..	..	..
AMERICA, NORTH - AMÉRIQUE DU NORD						
Anguilla[8]						
2011 (+C)						
Total	57	25	32	...	...	...
0 - 4	2	-	2	...	...	...
5 - 14	-	-	-	...	...	...
15 - 29	3	3	-	...	...	...
30 - 44	6	5	1	...	...	...
45 - 59	6	4	2	...	...	...
60 - 64	4	3	1	...	...	...
65 - 69	7	3	4	...	...	...
70 - 74	2	1	1	...	...	...
75 - 79	6	2	4	...	...	...
80 - 84	5	1	4	...	...	...
85 +	16	3	13	...	...	...
Aruba						
2007 (C)						
Total	521	279	242	5.0	5.6	4.4
0	4	2	2	♦3.2	♦3.2	♦3.3
1 - 4	-	-	-	-	-	-
5 - 9	-	-	-	-	-	-
10 - 14	-	-	-	-	-	-
15 - 19	7	6	1	♦1.0	♦1.6	♦0.3
20 - 24	3	2	1	♦0.5	♦0.7	♦0.3
25 - 29	6	3	3	♦1.0	♦1.0	♦0.9
30 - 34	5	3	2	♦0.7	♦0.9	♦0.5
35 - 39	9	4	5	♦1.0	♦1.0	♦1.1
40 - 44	16	11	5	♦1.7	♦2.4	♦1.0
45 - 49	22	13	9	♦2.3	♦2.9	♦1.8
50 - 54	23	14	9	♦3.0	♦3.9	♦2.2
55 - 59	47	28	19	7.8	♦9.9	♦5.9
60 - 64	45	28	17	10.0	♦13.4	♦7.0
65 - 69	55	31	24	16.1	20.0	♦12.8
70 - 74	60	37	23	22.9	34.0	♦15.0
75 - 79	60	39	21	35.5	55.3	♦21.4
80 - 84	62	30	32	74.2	♦89.6	63.8
85 - 89	32	8	24	74.6	♦52.0	♦87.3
90 - 94	44	13	31	228.4	♦255.6	218.6
95 - 99	18	7	11	...	...	...
100 +	3	-	3	♦176.5	-	♦187.5

19. Deaths by age and sex, age-specific death rates by sex: latest available year, 2003 - 2012
Décès et taux de mortalité selon l'âge et le sexe : dernière année disponible, 2003 - 2012 (continued - suite)

Continent, country or area, date, code and age (in years) / Continent, pays ou zone, date, code et âge (en annèes)	Number - Nombre			Rate - Taux		
	Both sexes Les deux sexes	Male Masculin	Female Féminin	Both sexes Les deux sexes	Male Masculin	Female Féminin
AMERICA, NORTH - AMÉRIQUE DU NORD						
Aruba						
2010 (C)						
Total	610	...	...	6.0	...	...
0	4	...	...	♦3.6	...	...
1 - 49	59	...	...	0.9	...	...
50 - 59	76	...	...	5.0	...	...
60 - 69	114	...	...	12.9	...	...
70 - 79	165	...	...	33.6	...	...
80 - 89	140	...	...	87.9	...	...
90 +	52	...	...	179.3	...	...
Bahamas						
2011* (+C)						
Total	2 117	1 180	937	6.0	6.9	5.2
0	48	26	22	7.8	♦8.0	♦7.6
1 - 4	15	9	6	♦0.6	♦0.7	♦0.5
5 - 9	9	2	7	♦0.3	♦0.1	♦0.5
10 - 14	14	5	9	♦0.5	♦0.4	♦0.6
15 - 19	29	12	17	♦0.9	♦0.8	♦1.1
20 - 24	55	41	14	1.9	3.0	♦1.0
25 - 29	80	55	25	3.1	4.2	♦1.9
30 - 34	81	58	23	3.2	4.6	♦1.8
35 - 39	82	57	25	2.9	4.2	♦1.7
40 - 44	113	68	45	4.2	5.2	3.2
45 - 49	141	87	54	5.3	6.7	3.9
50 - 54	165	95	70	7.5	9.0	6.1
55 - 59	143	86	57	8.8	11.2	6.7
60 - 64	163	92	71	14.2	17.0	11.6
65 - 69	180	102	78	20.5	25.5	16.3
70 - 74	169	101	68	26.8	36.1	19.4
75 - 79	193	100	93	51.1	62.5	42.7
80 +	437	182	255	150.7	260.0	115.9
80 - 84	172	71	101	...	...	...
85 - 89	142	61	81	...	...	...
90 - 94	74	30	44	...	...	...
95 - 99	40	17	23	...	...	...
100 +	9	3	6	...	...	...
Unknown - Inconnu	-	-	-	..	..	..
Barbados - Barbade[9]						
2007 (+C)						
Total	2 195	1 143	1 052	...	...	...
0	31	18	13	...	...	...
1 - 4	8	5	3	...	...	...
5 - 9	5	3	2	...	...	...
10 - 14	8	6	2	...	...	...
15 - 19	17	13	4	...	...	...
20 - 24	10	4	6	...	...	...
25 - 29	15	14	1	...	...	...
30 - 34	30	16	14	...	...	...
35 - 39	38	23	15	...	...	...
40 - 44	45	26	19	...	...	...
45 - 49	58	28	30	...	...	...
50 - 54	76	46	30	...	...	...
55 - 59	90	54	36	...	...	...
60 - 64	113	63	50	...	...	...
65 - 69	142	83	59	...	...	...
70 - 74	182	105	77	...	...	...
75 - 79	309	160	149	...	...	...
80 - 84	281	152	129	...	...	...
85 - 89	339	139	200	...	...	...
90 - 94	199	59	140	...	...	...
95 +	97	30	67	...	...	...
Unknown - Inconnu	102	96	6	..	..	...
Bermuda - Bermudes[10]						
2011 (C)						
Total	429	211	218	6.6	6.9	6.4
0	-	-	-	-	-	-
1 - 4	1	1	-	♦0.3	♦0.7	-

19. Deaths by age and sex, age-specific death rates by sex: latest available year, 2003 - 2012
Décès et taux de mortalité selon l'âge et le sexe : dernière année disponible, 2003 - 2012 (continued - suite)

Continent, country or area, date, code and age (in years) / Continent, pays ou zone, date, code et âge (en années)	Number - Nombre			Rate - Taux		
	Both sexes Les deux sexes	Male Masculin	Female Féminin	Both sexes Les deux sexes	Male Masculin	Female Féminin
AMERICA, NORTH - AMÉRIQUE DU NORD						
Bermuda - Bermudes[10]						
2011 (C)						
5 - 9	-	-	-	-	-	-
10 - 14	-	-	-	-	-	-
15 - 19	3	3	-	♦0.8	♦1.6	-
20 - 24	6	6	-	♦1.7	♦3.4	-
25 - 29	4	4	-	♦0.9	♦1.9	-
30 - 34	5	4	1	♦1.2	♦2.0	♦0.4
35 - 39	1	1	-	♦0.2	♦0.5	-
40 - 44	7	5	2	♦1.4	♦2.0	♦0.8
45 - 49	8	2	6	♦1.4	♦0.7	♦2.1
50 - 54	15	12	3	♦2.7	♦4.6	♦1.0
55 - 59	19	11	8	♦4.2	♦5.1	♦3.3
60 - 64	25	13	12	♦6.7	♦7.4	♦6.0
65 - 69	39	21	18	13.6	♦16.4	♦11.3
70 - 74	42	26	16	20.6	♦30.3	♦13.5
75 - 79	58	27	31	34.2	♦38.8	30.9
80 - 84	59	29	30	50.3	♦63.0	♦42.0
85 +	137	46	91	161.6	181.1	153.2
85 - 89	64	22	42	...	...	...
90 - 94	46	20	26	...	...	...
95 - 99	19	3	16	...	...	...
100 +	8	1	7	...	...	...
Canada[11]						
2008 (C)						
Total	238 617	120 426	118 191	7.2	7.3	7.0
0	1 911	1 057	854	5.3	5.7	4.8
1 - 4	265	153	112	0.2	0.2	0.2
5 - 9	201	117	84	0.1	0.1	0.1
10 - 14	246	160	86	0.1	0.2	0.1
15 - 19	894	607	287	0.4	0.5	0.3
20 - 24	1 264	935	329	0.6	0.8	0.3
25 - 29	1 282	878	404	0.6	0.8	0.4
30 - 34	1 376	911	465	0.6	0.8	0.4
35 - 39	2 064	1 290	774	0.9	1.1	0.7
40 - 44	3 392	2 063	1 329	1.3	1.6	1.0
45 - 49	5 803	3 453	2 350	2.1	2.5	1.7
50 - 54	8 635	5 300	3 335	3.4	4.2	2.6
55 - 59	11 334	6 904	4 430	5.3	6.5	4.1
60 - 64	14 606	8 946	5 660	8.1	10.1	6.2
65 - 69	17 282	10 349	6 933	12.8	15.9	10.0
70 - 74	22 194	13 006	9 188	20.9	26.1	16.3
75 - 79	30 733	17 061	13 672	34.0	42.2	27.4
80 - 84	38 476	19 414	19 062	57.7	72.4	47.8
85 - 89	38 943	16 289	22 654	99.3	120.8	88.0
90 - 94	25 509	8 717	16 792	170.3	207.4	155.8
95 - 99	10 191	2 465	7 726	262.3	284.7	255.5
100 +	2 011	347	1 664	364.8	326.4	373.9
Unknown - Inconnu	5	4	1	..	..	..
Cayman Islands - Îles Caïmanes						
2010 (C)						
Total	152	85	67	2.8	3.1	2.4
0	2	1	1	♦2.6	♦2.6	♦2.5
1 - 4	2	2	-	♦0.7	♦1.3	-
5 - 9	-	-	-	-	-	-
10 - 14	-	-	-	-	-	-
15 - 19	2	2	-	♦0.7	♦1.4	-
20 - 24	4	2	2	♦1.4	♦1.4	♦1.3
25 - 29	6	5	1	♦1.2	♦2.1	♦0.4
30 - 34	3	1	2	♦0.5	♦0.3	♦0.7
35 - 39	2	2	-	♦0.3	♦0.6	-
40 - 44	3	2	1	♦0.5	♦0.7	♦0.3
45 - 49	6	6	-	♦1.2	♦2.4	-
50 - 54	10	8	2	♦2.6	♦4.4	♦1.0
55 - 59	7	6	1	♦2.6	♦4.8	♦0.7
60 - 64	13	7	6	♦7.5	♦7.9	♦7.2

19. Deaths by age and sex, age-specific death rates by sex: latest available year, 2003 - 2012
Décès et taux de mortalité selon l'âge et le sexe : dernière année disponible, 2003 - 2012 (continued - suite)

Continent, country or area, date, code and age (in years) / Continent, pays ou zone, date, code et âge (en années)	Number - Nombre			Rate - Taux		
	Both sexes Les deux sexes	Male Masculin	Female Féminin	Both sexes Les deux sexes	Male Masculin	Female Féminin

AMERICA, NORTH - AMÉRIQUE DU NORD

Cayman Islands - Îles Caïmanes
2010 (C)

65 +	88	38	50	29.5	27.7	31.0
Unknown - Inconnu	4	3	1	..	..	..

Costa Rica
2011* (C)

Total	18 801	10 666	8 135	4.1	4.6	3.6
0	666	374	292	...	...	...
1 - 4	100	54	46	...	...	...
5 - 9	63	32	31	0.2	0.2	0.2
10 - 14	107	65	42	0.3	0.3	0.2
15 - 19	236	164	72	0.6	0.8	0.3
20 - 24	311	225	86	0.7	1.0	0.4
25 - 29	384	293	91	0.9	1.4	0.4
30 - 34	392	273	119	1.1	1.4	0.7
35 - 39	410	266	144	1.3	1.6	0.9
40 - 44	541	366	175	1.7	2.3	1.2
45 - 49	686	457	229	2.3	3.0	1.5
50 - 54	981	630	351	3.8	4.8	2.7
55 - 59	1 090	669	421	5.4	6.6	4.2
60 - 64	1 273	761	512	8.6	10.4	6.9
65 - 69	1 442	859	583	13.6	16.7	10.7
70 - 74	1 705	995	710	21.5	26.3	17.1
75 - 79	2 008	1 148	860	35.0	43.9	27.6
80 - 84	2 365	1 239	1 126	60.5	72.1	51.4
85 +	4 034	1 790	2 244	130.8	140.8	123.8
Unknown - Inconnu	7	6	1	..	..	..

Cuba
2010 (C)

Total	91 065	49 080	41 985	8.1	8.7	7.5
0	581	349	232	4.5	5.3	3.7
1 - 4	152	93	59	0.3	0.4	0.3
5 - 9	127	70	57	0.2	0.2	0.2
10 - 14	162	95	67	0.2	0.3	0.2
15 - 19	266	181	85	0.3	0.5	0.2
20 - 24	450	306	144	0.5	0.7	0.4
25 - 29	493	332	161	0.7	0.9	0.5
30 - 34	624	430	194	0.9	1.2	0.6
35 - 39	1 098	704	394	1.1	1.4	0.8
40 - 44	1 884	1 166	718	1.8	2.2	1.4
45 - 49	2 975	1 756	1 219	3.0	3.6	2.5
50 - 54	3 350	2 076	1 274	5.1	6.4	3.8
55 - 59	4 771	2 832	1 939	7.7	9.4	6.1
60 - 64	6 709	3 968	2 741	12.1	14.9	9.5
65 - 69	8 533	4 968	3 565	18.3	22.0	14.8
70 - 74	10 353	5 941	4 412	28.6	34.1	23.6
75 - 79	11 464	6 214	5 250	46.3	54.0	39.6
80 - 84	12 840	6 644	6 196	72.9	84.0	63.9
85 +	24 228	10 950	13 278	145.0	154.1	138.3
85 - 89	11 602	5 609	5 993	...	...	...
90 - 94	8 058	3 504	4 554	...	...	...
95 - 99	3 648	1 462	2 186	...	...	...
100 +	920	375	545	...	...	...
Unknown - Inconnu	5	5	-	..	..	..

Curaçao
2011 (C)

Total	1 276	669	607	8.5	9.7	7.4
0	15	6	9	♦8.1	♦6.5	♦9.7
1 - 4	4	4	-	♦0.6	♦1.1	-
5 - 9	-	-	-	-	-	-
10 - 14	2	2	-	♦0.2	♦0.4	-
15 - 19	3	-	3	♦0.3	-	♦0.5
20 - 24	10	7	3	♦1.2	♦1.8	♦0.7
25 - 29	13	9	4	♦1.7	♦2.6	♦0.9
30 - 34	13	10	3	♦1.6	♦3.0	♦0.6
35 - 39	14	10	4	♦1.4	♦2.4	♦0.7
40 - 44	16	7	9	♦1.4	♦1.4	♦1.4

475

19. Deaths by age and sex, age-specific death rates by sex: latest available year, 2003 - 2012
Décès et taux de mortalité selon l'âge et le sexe : dernière année disponible, 2003 - 2012 (continued - suite)

Continent, country or area, date, code and age (in years) / Continent, pays ou zone, date, code et âge (en années)	Number - Nombre			Rate - Taux		
	Both sexes Les deux sexes	Male Masculin	Female Féminin	Both sexes Les deux sexes	Male Masculin	Female Féminin

AMERICA, NORTH - AMÉRIQUE DU NORD

Curaçao
2011 (C)

45 - 49	23	14	9	♦1.8	♦2.5	♦1.3
50 - 54	56	42	14	4.6	8.0	♦2.1
55 - 59	75	48	27	7.2	10.5	♦4.6
60 - 64	117	72	45	12.8	17.4	8.9
65 - 69	121	70	51	16.8	22.3	12.5
70 - 74	148	82	66	27.6	35.5	21.7
75 - 79	181	97	84	46.2	57.8	37.5
80 - 84	160	81	79	65.5	82.6	54.1
85 - 89	146	56	90	108.7	124.2	100.9
90 - 94	100	42	58	197.6	315.8	155.5
95 - 99	41	9	32	292.9	♦236.8	313.7
100 +	18	1	17	♦450.0	♦142.9	♦515.2
Unknown - Inconnu	-	-	-	..	..	..

Dominica - Dominique
2006 (+C)

Total	536	285	251	7.5	7.9	7.2
0 - 4	14	12	2	♦2.2	♦3.7	♦0.7
0	13	11	2	...	...	...
1 - 4	1	1	-	...	...	...
5 - 9	1	1	-	♦0.1	♦0.3	-
10 - 14	2	2	-	♦0.3	♦0.6	-
15 - 19	8	7	1	♦1.2	♦2.0	♦0.3
20 - 24	9	6	3	♦2.0	♦2.5	♦1.4
25 - 29	5	3	2	♦1.0	♦1.2	♦0.8
30 - 34	9	5	4	♦1.6	♦1.7	♦1.4
35 - 39	8	6	2	♦1.5	♦2.1	♦0.8
40 - 44	8	5	3	♦1.8	♦2.1	♦1.5
45 - 49	23	7	16	♦6.5	♦3.6	♦9.9
50 - 54	17	9	8	♦6.0	♦6.1	♦5.9
55 - 59	19	11	8	♦7.9	♦9.1	♦6.8
60 - 64	19	13	6	♦8.4	♦12.7	♦4.9
65 - 69	34	16	18	14.6	♦14.7	♦14.6
70 - 74	57	26	31	30.9	♦29.9	31.9
75 - 79	76	39	37	57.1	65.4	50.3
80 - 84	68	38	30	75.5	107.3	♦54.8
85 +	152	73	79	184.2	253.5	147.1
Unknown - Inconnu	7	6	1	..	..	..

Dominican Republic - République dominicaine
2011 (U)

Total	34 006	21 681	12 325	...	...	...
0	672	434	238	...	...	...
1 - 4	234	154	80	...	...	...
5 - 9	136	91	45	...	...	...
10 - 14	204	142	62	...	...	...
15 - 19	569	435	134	...	...	...
20 - 24	950	739	211	...	...	...
25 - 29	955	711	244	...	...	...
30 - 34	1 024	757	267	...	...	...
35 - 39	1 039	722	317	...	...	...
40 - 44	1 206	833	373	...	...	...
45 - 49	1 411	979	432	...	...	...
50 - 54	1 791	1 202	589	...	...	...
55 - 59	2 148	1 404	744	...	...	...
60 - 64	2 524	1 637	887	...	...	...
65 - 69	2 589	1 680	909	...	...	...
70 - 74	3 176	1 997	1 179	...	...	...
75 - 79	3 515	2 074	1 441	...	...	...
80 - 84	3 595	2 120	1 475	...	...	...
85 - 89	2 437	1 390	1 047	...	...	...
90 - 94	1 647	883	764	...	...	...
95 - 99	970	495	475	...	...	...
Unknown - Inconnu	1 214	802	412	..	..	..

19. Deaths by age and sex, age-specific death rates by sex: latest available year, 2003 - 2012
Décès et taux de mortalité selon l'âge et le sexe : dernière année disponible, 2003 - 2012 (continued - suite)

Continent, country or area, date, code and age (in years) Continent, pays ou zone, date, code et âge (en années)	Number - Nombre			Rate - Taux		
	Both sexes Les deux sexes	Male Masculin	Female Féminin	Both sexes Les deux sexes	Male Masculin	Female Féminin
AMERICA, NORTH - AMÉRIQUE DU NORD						
El Salvador						
2011 (C)						
Total...........................	33 211	18 972	14 239	5.3	6.5	4.3
0	826	461	365	6.7	7.3	6.0
1 - 4	275	146	129	0.6	0.6	0.5
5 - 9	157	87	70	0.3	0.3	0.2
10 - 14	272	166	106	0.4	0.5	0.3
15 - 19	1 095	828	267	1.6	2.3	0.8
20 - 24	1 171	952	219	2.0	3.4	0.7
25 - 29	1 078	847	231	2.3	4.0	0.9
30 - 34	1 358	1 058	300	3.3	5.9	1.3
35 - 39	1 211	866	345	3.1	5.1	1.6
40 - 44	1 235	883	352	3.6	5.9	1.8
45 - 49	1 404	907	497	4.8	7.1	3.0
50 - 54	1 479	882	597	5.9	8.1	4.2
55 - 59	1 775	990	785	8.3	10.6	6.5
60 - 64	2 011	1 087	924	11.2	13.8	9.2
65 - 69	2 277	1 242	1 035	15.4	18.9	12.6
70 - 74	2 611	1 393	1 218	21.8	26.3	18.2
75 - 79	3 114	1 566	1 548	35.3	40.5	31.2
80 - 84	3 602	1 778	1 824	...	...	...
85 - 89	6 151	2 750	3 401	...	...	...
Unknown - Inconnu	109	83	26	..	..	..
Greenland - Groenland						
2012 (C)						
Total...........................	453	266	187	8.0	8.8	7.0
0	7	4	3	♦8.8	♦10.2	♦7.6
1 - 4	1	1	-	♦0.3	♦0.6	-
5 - 9	1	-	1	♦0.2	-	♦0.5
10 - 14	1	1	-	♦0.2	♦0.5	-
15 - 19	7	5	2	♦1.6	♦2.3	♦0.9
20 - 24	12	9	3	♦2.5	♦3.7	♦1.3
25 - 29	7	7	-	♦1.7	♦3.3	-
30 - 34	6	3	3	♦1.6	♦1.5	♦1.7
35 - 39	5	4	1	♦1.6	♦2.3	♦0.7
40 - 44	15	12	3	♦3.6	♦5.3	♦1.6
45 - 49	15	10	5	♦2.7	♦3.4	♦2.0
50 - 54	25	15	10	♦5.3	♦5.7	♦4.9
55 - 59	31	16	15	9.0	♦8.2	♦10.0
60 - 64	45	29	16	19.0	♦20.7	♦16.6
65 - 69	58	42	16	31.6	40.1	♦20.3
70 - 74	75	44	31	67.0	75.3	57.9
75 - 79	62	36	26	90.6	112.9	♦71.2
80 - 84	50	20	30	139.7	♦149.3	♦133.9
85 - 89	23	8	15	♦230.0	♦250.0	♦220.6
90 - 94	5	-	5	♦312.5	-	♦384.6
95 - 99	2	-	2	♦666.7	...	♦666.7
Guadeloupe[12]						
2003 (C)						
Total...........................	2 636	1 405	1 231	6.0	6.7	5.4
0	56	34	22	8.1	9.7	♦6.5
1 - 4	9	5	4	♦0.3	♦0.3	♦0.3
5 - 9	5	4	1	♦0.1	♦0.2	♦0.1
10 - 14	5	3	2	♦0.1	♦0.2	♦0.1
15 - 19	21	18	3	♦0.6	♦1.0	♦0.2
20 - 24	23	19	4	♦0.8	♦1.3	♦0.3
25 - 29	23	17	6	♦0.9	♦1.3	♦0.4
30 - 34	39	31	8	1.1	2.0	♦0.4
35 - 39	60	40	20	1.6	2.4	♦1.0
40 - 44	76	47	29	2.2	2.8	♦1.6
45 - 49	102	71	31	3.5	5.3	2.0
50 - 54	112	87	25	4.5	7.5	♦1.9
55 - 59	128	85	43	6.3	8.7	4.1
60 - 64	177	96	81	10.9	12.7	9.3
65 - 69	213	126	87	14.9	19.1	11.2
70 - 74	257	141	116	22.7	28.5	18.2
75 - 79	316	180	136	34.1	45.4	25.6

Continent, country or area, date, code and age (in years) / Continent, pays ou zone, date, code et âge (en années)	Number - Nombre			Rate - Taux		
	Both sexes Les deux sexes	Male Masculin	Female Féminin	Both sexes Les deux sexes	Male Masculin	Female Féminin
AMERICA, NORTH - AMÉRIQUE DU NORD						
Guadeloupe[12]						
2003 (C)						
80 - 84	356	185	171	53.8	68.2	43.8
85 - 89	329	124	205	96.8	98.9	95.6
90 +	329	92	237	148.6	142.2	151.2
90 - 94	205	65	140	...	...	...
95 - 99	96	19	77	...	...	...
100 +	28	8	20	...	...	...
Guatemala						
2011 (C)						
Total	72 354	41 295	31 059	...	...	...
0	7 413	4 202	3 211	...	...	...
1 - 4	2 552	1 313	1 239	...	...	...
5 - 9	705	387	318	...	...	...
10 - 14	907	502	405	...	...	...
15 - 19	2 281	1 581	700	...	...	...
20 - 24	2 738	2 111	627	...	...	...
25 - 29	2 864	2 167	697	...	...	...
30 - 34	2 819	2 051	768	...	...	...
35 - 39	2 680	1 855	825	...	...	...
40 - 44	2 659	1 778	881	...	...	...
45 - 49	2 920	1 832	1 088	...	...	...
50 - 54	3 400	1 928	1 472	...	...	...
55 - 59	3 786	1 999	1 787	...	...	...
60 - 64	4 096	2 157	1 939	...	...	...
65 - 69	4 250	2 199	2 051	...	...	...
70 - 74	4 824	2 499	2 325	...	...	...
75 - 79	5 709	2 944	2 765	...	...	...
80 - 84	6 215	3 110	3 105	...	...	...
85 - 89	4 931	2 418	2 513	...	...	...
90 - 94	2 716	1 267	1 449	...	...	...
95 - 99	793	315	478	...	...	...
100 +	148	49	99	...	...	...
Unknown - Inconnu	948	631	317	..	..	..
Haiti - Haïti[13]						
2003 (U)						
Total	8 011	4 135	3 876	...	...	...
0	724	388	336	...	...	...
1 - 4	501	270	231	...	...	...
5 - 9	161	85	76	...	...	...
10 - 14	135	66	69	...	...	...
15 - 19	216	114	102	...	...	...
20 - 24	324	158	166	...	...	...
25 - 29	371	179	192	...	...	...
30 - 34	442	229	213	...	...	...
35 - 39	392	215	177	...	...	...
40 - 44	434	234	200	...	...	...
45 - 49	363	190	173	...	...	...
50 - 54	346	177	169	...	...	...
55 - 59	316	176	140	...	...	...
60 - 64	397	205	192	...	...	...
65 - 69	378	196	182	...	...	...
70 - 74	460	245	215	...	...	...
75 - 79	416	223	193	...	...	...
80 - 84	417	208	209	...	...	...
85 - 89	266	110	156	...	...	...
90 - 94	162	57	105	...	...	...
95 +	132	48	84	...	...	...
Unknown - Inconnu	658	362	296	..	..	..
Jamaica - Jamaïque[14]						
2005 (U)						
Total	17 552	9 473	8 079	...	...	...
0	1 007	517	490	...	...	...
1 - 4	197	98	99	...	...	...
5 - 9	75	45	30	...	...	...
10 - 14	73	32	41	...	...	...
15 - 19	248	195	53	...	...	...

Continent, country or area, date, code and age (in years) Continent, pays ou zone, date, code et âge (en années)	Number - Nombre			Rate - Taux		
	Both sexes Les deux sexes	Male Masculin	Female Féminin	Both sexes Les deux sexes	Male Masculin	Female Féminin
AMERICA, NORTH - AMÉRIQUE DU NORD						
Jamaica - Jamaïque[14]						
2005 (U)						
20 - 24	505	404	101	...	...	...
25 - 29	550	398	152	...	...	...
30 - 34	555	386	169	...	...	...
35 - 39	568	350	218	...	...	...
40 - 44	597	370	227	...	...	...
45 - 49	597	329	268	...	...	...
50 - 54	636	382	254	...	...	...
55 - 59	670	397	273	...	...	...
60 - 64	981	566	415	...	...	...
65 - 69	1 159	658	501	...	...	...
70 - 74	1 701	974	727	...	...	...
75 +	7 433	3 372	4 061	...	...	...
Martinique[12]						
2007 (C)						
Total	2 830	1 439	1 391	7.1	7.7	6.5
0 - 4	51	31	20	2.0	2.4	♦1.6
0	47	28	19	...	...	...
1 - 4	4	3	1	...	...	...
5 - 9	4	3	1	♦0.1	♦0.2	♦0.1
10 - 14	7	5	2	♦0.2	♦0.3	♦0.1
15 - 19	16	12	4	♦0.5	♦0.8	♦0.3
20 - 24	26	22	4	♦1.1	♦1.9	♦0.3
25 - 29	19	13	6	♦1.0	♦1.5	♦0.6
30 - 34	35	22	13	1.4	♦2.1	♦0.9
35 - 39	36	22	14	1.2	♦1.6	♦0.8
40 - 44	53	31	22	1.6	2.0	♦1.2
45 - 49	64	46	18	2.0	3.2	♦1.1
50 - 54	107	68	39	4.1	5.6	2.8
55 - 59	97	57	40	4.3	5.5	3.2
60 - 64	146	91	55	7.8	10.3	5.5
65 - 69	226	135	91	14.2	18.7	10.4
70 - 74	305	173	132	21.3	27.2	16.6
75 - 79	382	200	182	35.8	44.2	29.6
80 - 84	443	217	226	59.2	76.6	48.6
85 - 89	388	168	220	92.5	122.1	78.1
90 - 94	269	91	178	137.9	159.6	128.9
95 +	156	32	124	212.8	196.3	217.5
Mexico - Mexique[15]						
2011 (+C)						
Total	589 646	331 919	257 148	...	...	...
0	29 037	16 164	12 767	...	...	...
1 - 4	5 673	3 119	2 551	...	...	...
5 - 9	2 833	1 583	1 250	...	...	...
10 - 14	3 445	2 013	1 432	...	...	...
15 - 19	9 953	7 192	2 760	...	...	...
20 - 24	13 325	10 364	2 958	...	...	...
25 - 29	14 306	11 117	3 182	...	...	...
30 - 34	15 401	11 739	3 652	...	...	...
35 - 39	18 151	13 327	4 820	...	...	...
40 - 44	20 078	13 942	6 130	...	...	...
45 - 49	24 371	15 741	8 623	...	...	...
50 - 54	30 528	18 590	11 934	...	...	...
55 - 59	35 947	21 057	14 890	...	...	...
60 - 64	41 691	23 551	18 139	...	...	...
65 - 69	47 196	25 957	21 238	...	...	...
70 - 74	54 210	29 239	24 968	...	...	...
75 - 79	59 429	30 860	28 568	...	...	...
80 - 84	60 308	29 521	30 787	...	...	...
85 - 89	52 079	24 198	27 879	...	...	...
90 - 94	30 417	12 920	17 497	...	...	...
95 - 99	12 833	4 983	7 844	...	...	...
100 +	4 371	1 598	2 773	...	...	...
Unknown - Inconnu	4 064	3 144	506	..	..	..

19. Deaths by age and sex, age-specific death rates by sex: latest available year, 2003 - 2012
Décès et taux de mortalité selon l'âge et le sexe : dernière année disponible, 2003 - 2012 (continued - suite)

Continent, country or area, date, code and age (in years) / Continent, pays ou zone, date, code et âge (en années)	Number - Nombre			Rate - Taux		
	Both sexes Les deux sexes	Male Masculin	Female Féminin	Both sexes Les deux sexes	Male Masculin	Female Féminin

AMERICA, NORTH - AMÉRIQUE DU NORD

Montserrat						
2011 (+C)						
Total	55	36	19	...	...	...
0	-	-	-	...	...	...
1 - 4	-	-	-	...	...	...
5 - 9	1	1	-	...	...	...
10 - 14	-	-	-	...	...	...
15 - 19	-	-	-	...	...	...
20 - 24	1	1	-	...	...	...
25 - 29	-	-	-	...	...	...
30 - 34	-	-	-	...	...	...
35 - 39	-	-	-	...	...	...
40 - 44	-	-	-	...	...	...
45 - 49	-	-	-	...	...	...
50 - 54	2	1	1	...	...	...
55 - 59	6	4	2	...	...	...
60 - 64	9	8	1	...	...	...
65 - 69	2	2	-	...	...	...
70 - 74	2	2	-	...	...	...
75 - 79	3	2	1	...	...	...
80 - 84	10	5	5	...	...	...
85 - 89	12	7	5	...	...	...
90 +	7	3	4	...	...	...
Nicaragua						
2008 (+U)						
Total	18 079	10 385	7 694	...	...	...
0	1 932	1 123	809	...	...	...
1 - 4	287	155	132	...	...	...
5 - 9	164	95	69	...	...	...
10 - 14	198	118	80	...	...	...
15 - 19	448	289	159	...	...	...
20 - 24	577	431	146	...	...	...
25 - 29	595	463	132	...	...	...
30 - 34	619	442	177	...	...	...
35 - 39	530	398	132	...	...	...
40 - 44	663	449	214	...	...	...
45 - 49	793	525	268	...	...	...
50 - 54	955	578	377	...	...	...
55 - 59	1 001	548	453	...	...	...
60 - 64	1 120	632	488	...	...	...
65 - 69	1 143	638	505	...	...	...
70 - 74	1 446	763	683	...	...	...
75 - 79	1 529	812	717	...	...	...
80 - 84	1 490	778	712	...	...	...
85 - 89	1 271	588	683	...	...	...
90 - 94	780	328	452	...	...	...
95 +	538	232	306	...	...	...
Panama						
2010 (U)						
Total	16 542	9 740	6 802	...	...	...
0	910	510	400	...	...	...
1 - 4	297	152	145	...	...	...
5 - 9	101	68	33	...	...	...
10 - 14	130	77	53	...	...	...
15 - 19	311	234	77	...	...	...
20 - 24	419	329	90	...	...	...
25 - 29	438	335	103	...	...	...
30 - 34	460	337	123	...	...	...
35 - 39	458	305	153	...	...	...
40 - 44	474	325	149	...	...	...
45 - 49	544	344	200	...	...	...
50 - 54	676	412	264	...	...	...
55 - 59	749	473	276	...	...	...
60 - 64	1 012	628	384	...	...	...
65 - 69	1 141	720	421	...	...	...
70 - 74	1 362	813	549	...	...	...
75 - 79	1 639	980	659	...	...	...

Continent, country or area, date, code and age (in years) / Continent, pays ou zone, date, code et âge (en années)	Number - Nombre			Rate - Taux		
	Both sexes Les deux sexes	Male Masculin	Female Féminin	Both sexes Les deux sexes	Male Masculin	Female Féminin
AMERICA, NORTH - AMÉRIQUE DU NORD						
Panama						
2010 (U)						
80 - 84	1 774	996	778	...	...	...
85 - 89	1 663	841	822	...	...	...
90 - 94	1 248	567	681	...	...	...
95 - 99	544	210	334	...	...	...
100 +	131	39	92	...	...	...
Unknown - Inconnu	61	45	16	..	..	..
Puerto Rico - Porto Rico						
2008 (C)						
Total	29 100	15 906	13 194	7.4	8.4	6.4
0 - 4	442	250	192	1.8	2.0	1.6
0	400	225	175	...	...	...
1 - 4	42	25	17	...	...	...
5 - 9	22	15	7	♦0.1	♦0.1	♦0.1
10 - 14	33	23	10	0.1	♦0.2	♦0.1
15 - 19	201	160	41	0.7	1.1	0.3
20 - 24	345	293	52	1.3	2.1	0.4
25 - 29	429	353	76	1.5	2.5	0.5
30 - 34	389	305	84	1.4	2.3	0.6
35 - 39	466	326	140	1.8	2.5	1.0
40 - 44	635	426	209	2.4	3.4	1.5
45 - 49	902	599	303	3.5	4.9	2.2
50 - 54	1 206	780	426	4.9	6.9	3.2
55 - 59	1 497	967	530	6.5	9.3	4.3
60 - 64	2 151	1 346	805	10.0	13.8	6.9
65 - 69	2 504	1 500	1 004	14.8	19.7	10.8
70 - 74	2 883	1 637	1 246	21.4	27.1	16.7
75 - 79	3 264	1 726	1 538	32.8	40.5	27.1
80 - 84	4 023	1 907	2 116	57.1	66.8	50.5
85 +	7 658	3 250	4 408	115.4	130.2	106.5
85 - 89	3 684	1 704	1 980	...	...	...
90 - 94	2 565	1 009	1 556	...	...	...
95 - 99	1 146	449	697	...	...	...
100 +	263	88	175	...	...	...
Unknown - Inconnu	50	43	7	..	..	..
Saint Lucia - Sainte-Lucie						
2005* (C)						
Total	1 107	625	482	6.7	7.8	5.7
0 - 4	53	30	23	3.9	♦4.4	♦3.3
0	46	28	18	...	...	...
1 - 4	7	2	5	...	...	...
5 - 9	2	1	1	♦0.1	♦0.1	♦0.1
10 - 14	7	4	3	♦0.4	♦0.5	♦0.3
15 - 19	14	12	2	♦0.8	♦1.4	♦0.2
20 - 24	19	15	4	♦1.2	♦1.9	♦0.5
25 - 29	24	18	6	♦1.8	♦2.7	♦0.9
30 - 34	33	21	12	2.6	♦3.5	♦1.9
35 - 39	25	19	6	♦2.1	♦3.3	♦1.0
40 - 44	40	30	10	3.6	♦5.6	♦1.8
45 - 49	38	28	10	4.4	♦6.5	♦2.3
50 - 54	49	25	24	7.6	♦7.6	♦7.5
55 - 59	42	23	19	8.4	♦9.6	♦7.3
60 - 64	82	52	30	20.1	27.5	♦13.7
65 - 69	103	63	40	28.8	37.5	21.1
70 - 74	88	52	36	29.2	36.6	22.6
75 - 79	114	72	42	58.7	79.4	40.5
80 +	361	154	207	127.0	129.4	125.3
80 - 84	154	70	84	...	...	...
85 +	207	84	123	...	...	...
Unknown - Inconnu	13	6	7	..	..	..
Saint Vincent and the Grenadines - Saint-Vincent-et-les Grenadines						
2009 (+C)						
Total	765	395	370	...	...	...
0	32	19	13	...	...	...
1 - 4	4	2	2	...	...	...

19. Deaths by age and sex, age-specific death rates by sex: latest available year, 2003 - 2012
Décès et taux de mortalité selon l'âge et le sexe : dernière année disponible, 2003 - 2012 (continued - suite)

Continent, country or area, date, code and age (in years) / Continent, pays ou zone, date, code et âge (en années)	Number - Nombre			Rate - Taux		
	Both sexes Les deux sexes	Male Masculin	Female Féminin	Both sexes Les deux sexes	Male Masculin	Female Féminin

AMERICA, NORTH - AMÉRIQUE DU NORD

Saint Vincent and the Grenadines - Saint-Vincent-et-les Grenadines
2009 (+C)

5 - 9	2	2	-	...	...	...
10 - 14	7	3	4	...	...	...
15 - 19	8	5	3	...	...	...
20 - 24	13	9	4	...	...	...
25 - 29	21	13	8	...	...	...
30 - 34	18	10	8	...	...	...
35 - 39	17	13	4	...	...	...
40 - 44	27	17	10	...	...	...
45 - 49	36	27	9	...	...	...
50 - 54	26	13	13	...	...	...
55 - 59	24	13	11	...	...	...
60 - 64	35	23	12	...	...	...
65 - 69	56	30	26	...	...	...
70 - 74	69	38	31	...	...	...
75 - 79	102	53	49	...	...	...
80 - 84	106	45	61	...	...	...
85 +	159	58	101	...	...	...
Unknown - Inconnu	3	2	1	..	..	..
Trinidad and Tobago - Trinité-et-Tobago 2005 (C)						
Total	9 885	5 702	4 183	...	...	...
0	266	149	117	...	...	...
1 - 4	39	23	16	...	...	...
5 - 9	20	13	7	...	...	...
10 - 14	31	14	17	...	...	...
15 - 19	136	94	42	...	...	...
20 - 24	234	185	49	...	...	...
25 - 29	246	182	64	...	...	...
30 - 34	252	170	82	...	...	...
35 - 39	258	161	97	...	...	...
40 - 44	434	284	150	...	...	...
45 - 49	479	306	173	...	...	...
50 - 54	540	345	195	...	...	...
55 - 59	712	452	260	...	...	...
60 - 64	812	482	330	...	...	...
65 - 69	949	568	381	...	...	...
70 - 74	927	515	412	...	...	...
75 - 79	1 057	572	485	...	...	...
80 - 84	1 043	552	491	...	...	...
85 +	1 445	631	814	...	...	...
Unknown - Inconnu	5	4	1	..	..	..
Turks and Caicos Islands - Îles Turques et Caïques 2005 (C)						
Total	53	32	21	...	...	...
0	1	1	-	...	...	...
1 - 4	-	-	-	...	...	...
5 - 9	-	-	-	...	...	...
10 - 14	1	1	-	...	...	...
15 - 19	1	1	-	...	...	...
20 - 24	-	-	-	...	...	...
25 - 29	2	2	-	...	...	...
30 - 34	8	5	3	...	...	...
35 - 39	3	2	1	...	...	...
40 - 44	3	1	2	...	...	...
45 - 49	1	1	-	...	...	...
50 - 54	2	-	2	...	...	...
55 - 59	2	2	-	...	...	...
60 - 64	2	2	-	...	...	...
65 - 69	-	-	-	...	...	...
70 - 74	3	3	-	...	...	...
75 - 79	6	1	5	...	...	...
80 - 84	5	3	2	...	...	...
85 +	11	5	6	...	...	...
Unknown - Inconnu	2	2	-	..	..	..

19. Deaths by age and sex, age-specific death rates by sex: latest available year, 2003 - 2012
Décès et taux de mortalité selon l'âge et le sexe : dernière année disponible, 2003 - 2012 (continued - suite)

Continent, country or area, date, code and age (in years) / Continent, pays ou zone, date, code et âge (en années)	Number - Nombre			Rate - Taux		
	Both sexes Les deux sexes	Male Masculin	Female Féminin	Both sexes Les deux sexes	Male Masculin	Female Féminin
AMERICA, NORTH - AMÉRIQUE DU NORD						
United States of America - États-Unis d'Amérique						
2009 (C)						
Total	2 437 163	1 217 379	1 219 784	7.9	8.0	7.8
0	26 412	14 823	11 589	6.2	6.8	5.6
1 - 4	4 450	2 495	1 955	0.3	0.3	0.2
5 - 9	2 523	1 398	1 125	0.1	0.1	0.1
10 - 14	3 128	1 850	1 278	0.2	0.2	0.1
15 - 19	11 520	8 176	3 344	0.5	0.7	0.3
20 - 24	18 896	14 136	4 760	0.9	1.3	0.5
25 - 29	20 612	14 571	6 041	1.0	1.3	0.6
30 - 34	21 890	14 628	7 262	1.1	1.4	0.7
35 - 39	29 510	18 781	10 729	1.4	1.8	1.1
40 - 44	45 155	27 774	17 381	2.2	2.6	1.7
45 - 49	76 407	46 373	30 034	3.3	4.1	2.6
50 - 54	111 161	68 447	42 714	5.1	6.4	3.9
55 - 59	137 706	85 207	52 499	7.3	9.3	5.4
60 - 64	165 601	98 935	66 666	10.5	13.1	8.1
65 - 69	185 771	107 198	78 573	15.8	19.5	12.5
70 - 74	215 261	118 596	96 665	23.9	29.1	19.6
75 - 79	274 987	143 233	131 754	37.5	45.5	31.5
80 - 84	352 740	167 799	184 941	60.6	73.0	52.5
85 +	733 178	262 782	470 396	130.2	147.4	122.2
Unknown - Inconnu	255	177	78	..	..	..
United States Virgin Islands - Îles Vierges américaines						
2007 (C)						
Total	727	424	303	6.6	8.1	5.2
0 - 4	14	8	6	♦1.9	♦2.1	♦1.6
0	12	6	6	...	...	...
1 - 4	2	2	-	...	...	...
5 - 9	-	-	-	-	-	-
10 - 14	2	1	1	♦0.2	♦0.2	♦0.2
15 - 19	9	8	1	♦1.1	♦2.0	♦0.2
20 - 24	16	15	1	♦2.3	♦4.7	♦0.3
25 - 29	20	14	6	♦3.7	♦5.7	♦2.1
30 - 34	16	10	6	♦2.6	♦3.7	♦1.8
35 - 39	16	13	3	♦2.2	♦3.9	♦0.7
40 - 44	33	21	12	4.1	♦5.6	♦2.8
45 - 49	26	13	13	♦3.2	♦3.3	♦3.1
50 - 54	50	34	16	6.6	9.6	♦3.9
55 - 59	51	29	22	6.8	♦8.1	♦5.6
60 - 64	79	55	24	10.7	15.3	♦6.3
65 - 69	50	36	14	10.1	14.8	♦5.5
70 - 74	68	43	25	18.8	26.6	♦12.5
75 +	273	120	153	59.0	63.7	55.7
Unknown - Inconnu	4	4	-	..	..	..
AMERICA, SOUTH - AMÉRIQUE DU SUD						
Argentina - Argentine						
2011 (C)						
Total	319 059	164 866[16]	153 922[16]	...	...	...
0	8 878	4 952[16]	3 912[16]	...	...	...
1 - 4	1 347	755[16]	590[16]	...	...	...
5 - 9	762	433[16]	329[16]	...	...	...
10 - 14	1 002	603[16]	396[16]	...	...	...
15 - 19	2 832	2 054[16]	778[16]	...	...	...
20 - 24	3 406	2 585[16]	814[16]	...	...	...
25 - 29	3 365	2 426[16]	936[16]	...	...	...
30 - 34	3 696	2 457[16]	1 237[16]	...	...	...
35 - 39	4 161	2 617[16]	1 542[16]	...	...	...
40 - 44	5 374	3 301[16]	2 067[16]	...	...	...
45 - 49	7 707	4 778[16]	2 922[16]	...	...	...
50 - 54	11 526	7 219[16]	4 302[16]	...	...	...
55 - 59	16 533	10 532[16]	5 992[16]	...	...	...

19. Deaths by age and sex, age-specific death rates by sex: latest available year, 2003 - 2012
Décès et taux de mortalité selon l'âge et le sexe : dernière année disponible, 2003 - 2012 (continued - suite)

Continent, country or area, date, code and age (in years) Continent, pays ou zone, date, code et âge (en années)	Number - Nombre			Rate - Taux		
	Both sexes Les deux sexes	Male Masculin	Female Féminin	Both sexes Les deux sexes	Male Masculin	Female Féminin
AMERICA, SOUTH - AMÉRIQUE DU SUD						
Argentina - Argentine						
2011 (C)						
60 - 64	22 319	13 970[16]	8 335[16]	...	...	...
65 - 69	27 474	17 192[16]	10 259[16]	...	...	...
70 - 74	32 456	19 322[16]	13 116[16]	...	...	...
75 - 79	39 544	21 375[16]	18 152[16]	...	...	...
80 - 84	46 777	21 649[16]	25 107[16]	...	...	...
85 +	79 126	26 203[16]	52 885[16]	...	...	...
Unknown - Inconnu	774	443[16]	251[16]	..	..	..
Brazil - Brésil						
2011 (U)						
Total	1 148 165	655 068[16]	492 887[16]	...	...	...
0	32 184	17 995	14 189	...	...	...
1 - 4	6 193	3 458	2 735	...	...	...
5 - 9	3 941	2 246	1 695	...	...	...
10 - 14	5 236	3 230	2 006	...	...	...
15 - 19	18 843	14 894	3 949	...	...	...
20 - 24	26 340	21 524	4 816	...	...	...
25 - 29	27 857	21 689	6 168	...	...	...
30 - 34	29 659	21 996	7 663	...	...	...
35 - 39	31 628	22 226	9 402	...	...	...
40 - 44	40 244	26 988	13 256	...	...	...
45 - 49	52 750	34 240	18 510	...	...	...
50 - 54	66 107	42 190	23 917	...	...	...
55 - 59	77 783	48 685	29 098	...	...	...
60 - 64	88 518	53 983	34 535	...	...	...
65 - 69	96 668	56 559	40 109	...	...	...
70 - 74	112 339	63 383	48 956	...	...	...
75 - 79	120 543	63 377	57 166	...	...	...
80 - 84	123 458	59 079	64 379	...	...	...
85 - 89	96 886	42 148	54 738	...	...	...
90 - 94	56 024	21 342	34 682	...	...	...
95 - 99	24 553	8 813	15 740	...	...	...
100 +	6 212	1 871	4 341	...	...	...
Unknown - Inconnu	4 199	3 152[16]	837[16]	..	..	..
Chile - Chili						
2010 (C)						
Total	97 930	52 237	45 693	5.7	6.2	5.3
0	1 862	1 038	824	7.4	8.1	6.7
1 - 4	312	171	141	0.3	0.3	0.3
5 - 9	188	111	77	0.2	0.2	0.1
10 - 14	234	138	96	0.2	0.2	0.1
15 - 19	733	523	210	0.5	0.7	0.3
20 - 24	1 065	806	259	0.7	1.1	0.4
25 - 29	1 085	820	265	0.8	1.2	0.4
30 - 34	1 146	822	324	1.0	1.4	0.6
35 - 39	1 545	1 091	454	1.2	1.8	0.7
40 - 44	2 273	1 508	765	1.8	2.5	1.2
45 - 49	3 318	2 193	1 125	2.7	3.5	1.8
50 - 54	4 219	2 677	1 542	3.9	5.1	2.8
55 - 59	5 087	3 192	1 895	6.1	7.9	4.4
60 - 64	6 838	4 193	2 645	10.2	13.1	7.5
65 - 69	8 472	5 087	3 385	15.7	20.4	11.7
70 - 74	10 024	5 792	4 232	25.7	33.5	19.6
75 - 79	12 491	6 843	5 648	42.3	55.8	32.7
80 +	37 038	15 232	21 806	116.5	132.1	107.6
80 - 84	14 152	6 872	7 280	...	...	...
85 +	22 886	8 360	14 526	...	...	...
Colombia - Colombie						
2011* (U)						
Total	162 706	89 856[16]	72 843[16]	...	...	...
0	7 060	3 944[16]	3 115[16]	...	...	...
1 - 4	1 363	729	634	...	...	...
5 - 9	723	420	303	...	...	...
10 - 14	981	580	401	...	...	...
15 - 19	3 037	2 311	726	...	...	...
20 - 24	4 075	3 320	755	...	...	...

19. Deaths by age and sex, age-specific death rates by sex: latest available year, 2003 - 2012
Décès et taux de mortalité selon l'âge et le sexe : dernière année disponible, 2003 - 2012 (continued - suite)

Continent, country or area, date, code and age (in years) Continent, pays ou zone, date, code et âge (en années)	Number - Nombre			Rate - Taux		
	Both sexes Les deux sexes	Male Masculin	Female Féminin	Both sexes Les deux sexes	Male Masculin	Female Féminin
AMERICA, SOUTH - AMÉRIQUE DU SUD						
Colombia - Colombie						
2011* (U)						
25 - 29	4 385	3 397	988	...	...	...
30 - 34	4 072	3 031	1 041	...	...	...
35 - 39	4 006	2 741[16]	1 263[16]	...	...	...
40 - 44	4 430	2 830	1 600	...	...	...
45 - 49	5 718	3 392[16]	2 325[16]	...	...	...
50 - 54	7 275	4 150	3 125	...	...	...
55 - 59	8 623	4 969	3 654	...	...	...
60 - 64	10 554	6 058	4 496	...	...	...
65 - 69	12 212	6 893	5 319	...	...	...
70 - 74	15 647	8 533	7 114	...	...	...
75 - 79	18 604	9 643	8 961	...	...	...
80 - 84	20 588	10 252	10 336	...	...	...
85 - 89	15 670	7 146	8 524	...	...	...
90 - 94	9 375	3 893	5 482	...	...	...
95 - 99	3 355	1 239	2 116	...	...	...
100 +	755	229	526	...	...	...
Unknown - Inconnu	198	156[16]	39[16]	..	..	..
Ecuador - Équateur[17]						
2010 (U)						
Total	61 681	34 895	26 786	...	...	...
0	3 204	1 735	1 469	...	...	...
1 - 4	1 129	623	506	...	...	...
5 - 9	540	302	238	...	...	...
10 - 14	609	381	228	...	...	...
15 - 19	1 353	939	414	...	...	...
20 - 24	1 945	1 466	479	...	...	...
25 - 29	1 996	1 528	468	...	...	...
30 - 34	1 929	1 437	492	...	...	...
35 - 39	1 740	1 173	567	...	...	...
40 - 44	2 018	1 314	704	...	...	...
45 - 49	2 252	1 424	828	...	...	...
50 - 54	2 662	1 605	1 057	...	...	...
55 - 59	3 152	1 888	1 264	...	...	...
60 - 64	3 587	1 991	1 596	...	...	...
65 - 69	4 026	2 315	1 711	...	...	...
70 - 74	4 942	2 753	2 189	...	...	...
75 - 79	5 885	3 161	2 724	...	...	...
80 - 84	6 344	3 285	3 059	...	...	...
85 - 89	5 838	2 839	2 999	...	...	...
90 - 94	4 075	1 718	2 357	...	...	...
95 +	2 366	957	1 409	...	...	...
Unknown - Inconnu	89	61	28	..	..	..
French Guiana - Guyane française[12]						
2007 (C)						
Total	690	405	285	3.2	3.8	2.6
0 - 4	95	50	45	3.5	3.6	3.3
0	77	39	38	...	...	...
1 - 4	18	11	7	...	...	...
5 - 9	9	4	5	◆0.3	◆0.3	◆0.4
10 - 14	8	5	3	◆0.3	◆0.4	◆0.3
15 - 19	13	10	3	◆0.7	◆1.0	◆0.3
20 - 24	14	12	2	◆0.9	◆1.6	◆0.2
25 - 29	16	11	5	◆1.1	◆1.6	◆0.6
30 - 34	23	15	8	◆1.4	◆2.0	◆0.9
35 - 39	28	21	7	◆1.8	◆2.8	◆0.8
40 - 44	41	24	17	2.9	◆3.5	◆2.4
45 - 49	48	35	13	4.1	5.9	◆2.3
50 - 54	26	16	10	◆2.7	◆3.3	◆2.1
55 - 59	32	24	8	4.6	◆6.5	◆2.4
60 - 64	33	25	8	7.4	◆10.5	◆3.8
65 - 69	48	24	24	17.0	◆16.5	◆17.5
70 - 74	46	29	17	21.8	◆28.3	◆15.7
75 - 79	62	32	30	46.6	53.9	◆40.8
80 - 84	57	26	31	60.7	◆66.5	56.6
85 - 89	50	27	23	84.0	◆112.0	◆65.0

19. Deaths by age and sex, age-specific death rates by sex: latest available year, 2003 - 2012
Décès et taux de mortalité selon l'âge et le sexe : dernière année disponible, 2003 - 2012 (continued - suite)

Continent, country or area, date, code and age (in years) / Continent, pays ou zone, date, code et âge (en années)	Number - Nombre			Rate - Taux		
	Both sexes Les deux sexes	Male Masculin	Female Féminin	Both sexes Les deux sexes	Male Masculin	Female Féminin
AMERICA, SOUTH - AMÉRIQUE DU SUD						
French Guiana - Guyane française[12]						
2007 (C)						
90 - 94	28	12	16	♦129.0	♦176.5	♦107.4
95 +	13	3	10	♦123.8	♦111.1	♦128.2
95 - 99	10	3	7	...	...	...
100 +	3	-	3	...	...	...
Guyana[13]						
2003 (+C)						
Total	4 986	2 898	2 088	...	...	...
0	290	157	133	...	...	...
1 - 4	72	40	32	...	...	...
5 - 9	33	21	12	...	...	...
10 - 14	43	24	19	...	...	...
15 - 19	64	39	25	...	...	...
20 - 24	148	97	51	...	...	...
25 - 29	175	120	55	...	...	...
30 - 34	263	169	94	...	...	...
35 - 39	274	188	86	...	...	...
40 - 44	277	195	82	...	...	...
45 - 49	305	197	108	...	...	...
50 - 54	338	207	131	...	...	...
55 - 59	339	212	127	...	...	...
60 - 64	377	228	149	...	...	...
65 - 69	401	226	175	...	...	...
70 - 74	418	214	204	...	...	...
75 - 79	441	224	217	...	...	...
80 - 84	291	145	146	...	...	...
85 - 89	220	97	123	...	...	...
90 - 94	104	39	65	...	...	...
95 - 99	36	12	24	...	...	...
100 +	77	47	30	...	...	...
Paraguay						
2006 (U)						
Total	19 298	10 544[16]	8 709[16]	...	...	...
0	549	318[16]	229[16]	...	...	...
1 - 4	235	123	112	...	...	...
5 - 9	154	89	65	...	...	...
10 - 14	161	93[16]	67[16]	...	...	...
15 - 19	403	275	128	...	...	...
20 - 24	493	380[16]	112[16]	...	...	...
25 - 29	472	336[16]	135[16]	...	...	...
30 - 34	438	292[16]	145[16]	...	...	...
35 - 39	519	328	191	...	...	...
40 - 44	678	403	275	...	...	...
45 - 49	829	489[16]	336[16]	...	...	...
50 - 54	976	583	393	...	...	...
55 - 59	1 190	689[16]	499[16]	...	...	...
60 - 64	1 283	739[16]	542[16]	...	...	...
65 - 69	1 479	821[16]	655[16]	...	...	...
70 - 74	1 737	957[16]	775[16]	...	...	...
75 - 79	2 187	1 188[16]	994[16]	...	...	...
80 - 84	2 040	993[16]	1 040[16]	...	...	...
85 +	3 256	1 330[16]	1 921[16]	...	...	...
Unknown - Inconnu	219	118[16]	95[16]	..	..	...
Peru - Pérou[18]						
2011 (+U)						
Total	96 852	52 183	44 669	...	...	...
0	4 569	2 528	2 041	...	...	...
1 - 4	1 403	768	635	...	...	...
5 - 9	752	429	323	...	...	...
10 - 14	752	388	364	...	...	...
15 - 19	1 398	854	544	...	...	...
20 - 24	1 846	1 273	573	...	...	...
25 - 29	2 060	1 433	627	...	...	...
30 - 34	2 240	1 418	822	...	...	...
35 - 39	2 484	1 546	938	...	...	...

Continent, country or area, date, code and age (in years) / Continent, pays ou zone, date, code et âge (en annèes)	Number - Nombre			Rate - Taux		
	Both sexes Les deux sexes	Male Masculin	Female Féminin	Both sexes Les deux sexes	Male Masculin	Female Féminin

AMERICA, SOUTH - AMÉRIQUE DU SUD

Peru - Pérou[18]
2011 (+U)

40 - 44	2 867	1 661	1 206	...	...	...
45 - 49	3 394	1 914	1 480	...	...	...
50 - 54	4 198	2 305	1 893	...	...	...
55 - 59	5 016	2 823	2 193	...	...	...
60 - 64	6 003	3 273	2 730	...	...	...
65 - 69	7 147	4 021	3 126	...	...	...
70 - 74	8 670	4 783	3 887	...	...	...
75 - 79	10 683	5 894	4 789	...	...	...
80 - 84	11 832	6 070	5 762	...	...	...
85 - 89	10 079	4 936	5 143	...	...	...
90 - 94	6 206	2 709	3 497	...	...	...
95 - 99	2 557	928	1 629	...	...	...
100 +	696	229	467	...	...	...

Suriname[19]
2007 (C)

Total	3 374	1 864	1 510	6.6	7.2	6.0
0	134	72	62	13.7	14.7	12.7
1 - 4	42	21	21	1.0	♦1.0	♦1.1
5 - 9	16	9	7	♦0.3	♦0.3	♦0.3
10 - 14	19	10	9	♦0.4	♦0.4	♦0.4
15 - 19	48	26	22	1.0	♦1.1	♦1.0
20 - 24	71	45	26	1.6	2.0	♦1.2
25 - 29	96	51	45	2.3	2.4	2.2
30 - 34	107	62	45	2.7	3.1	2.3
35 - 39	127	89	38	3.4	4.7	2.1
40 - 44	148	96	52	4.4	5.7	3.2
45 - 49	192	116	76	6.6	7.9	5.3
50 - 54	178	111	67	7.4	9.3	5.6
55 - 59	204	122	82	10.7	13.2	8.4
60 - 64	242	142	100	16.1	19.6	12.8
65 - 69	289	165	124	25.2	30.4	20.5
70 - 74	407	226	181	47.7	56.8	39.8
75 - 79	373	204	169	63.0	74.8	52.9
80 +	681	297	384	130.2	135.9	126.1
80 - 84	333	162	171	...	...	...
85 - 89	200	85	115	...	...	...
90 - 94	103	36	67	...	...	...
95 - 99	36	13	23	...	...	...
100 +	9	1	8	...	...	...

Uruguay
2007 (C)

Total	33 706	...	...	10.1	...	...
0	572	...	...	11.9	...	...
1 - 4	83	...	...	0.4	...	...
5 - 9	50	...	...	0.2	...	...
10 - 14	76	...	...	0.3	...	...
15 - 19	185	...	...	0.7	...	...
20 - 24	224	...	...	0.9	...	...
25 - 29	267	...	...	1.1	...	...
30 - 34	301	...	...	1.3	...	...
35 - 39	358	...	...	1.7	...	...
40 - 44	454	...	...	2.2	...	...
45 - 49	679	...	...	3.3	...	...
50 - 54	1 080	...	...	5.9	...	...
55 - 59	1 468	...	...	9.0	...	...
60 - 64	2 058	...	...	14.6	...	...
65 - 69	2 689	...	...	21.1	...	...
70 - 74	3 656	...	...	32.6	...	...
75 - 79	4 953	...	...	51.6	...	...
80 - 84	5 324	...	...	86.1	...	...
85 - 89	4 690	...	...	141.7	...	...
90 +	4 122	...	...	255.6	...	...

19. Deaths by age and sex, age-specific death rates by sex: latest available year, 2003 - 2012
Décès et taux de mortalité selon l'âge et le sexe : dernière année disponible, 2003 - 2012 (continued - suite)

Continent, country or area, date, code and age (in years) Continent, pays ou zone, date, code et âge (en années)	Number - Nombre			Rate - Taux		
	Both sexes Les deux sexes	Male Masculin	Female Féminin	Both sexes Les deux sexes	Male Masculin	Female Féminin

AMERICA, SOUTH - AMÉRIQUE DU SUD

Venezuela (Bolivarian Republic of) - Venezuela (République bolivarienne du)

2007 (C)

Total	118 594	73 756	44 838	4.3	5.3	3.3
0 - 4	7 678	4 456	3 222	2.7	3.0	2.3
0	6 340	3 715	2 625	...	...	...
1 - 4	1 338	741	597	...	...	...
5 - 9	740	461	279	0.3	0.3	0.2
10 - 14	940	597	343	0.3	0.4	0.3
15 - 19	4 010	3 393	617	1.5	2.5	0.5
20 - 24	5 900	5 166	734	2.3	4.0	0.6
25 - 29	5 436	4 633	803	2.4	4.0	0.7
30 - 34	4 327	3 403	924	2.1	3.3	0.9
35 - 39	4 074	2 995	1 079	2.2	3.2	1.2
40 - 44	4 495	3 115	1 380	2.6	3.6	1.6
45 - 49	5 391	3 511	1 880	3.6	4.8	2.5
50 - 54	6 398	4 121	2 277	5.2	6.7	3.6
55 - 59	7 386	4 739	2 647	7.3	9.5	5.2
60 - 64	7 726	4 824	2 902	10.2	13.0	7.5
65 - 69	8 761	5 357	3 404	16.1	20.5	12.0
70 - 74	9 915	5 779	4 136	24.8	31.1	19.4
75 - 79	10 992	5 992	5 000	38.0	45.9	31.5
80 +	24 422	11 213	13 209	112.2	120.0	106.2
80 - 84	10 121	5 148	4 973	...	...	...
85 - 89	7 745	3 504	4 241	...	...	...
90 - 94	4 364	1 757	2 607	...	...	...
95 - 99	1 682	608	1 074	...	...	...
100 +	510	196	314	...	...	...
Unknown - Inconnu	3	1	2	..	..	..

2011 (C)

Total	136 803	...	...	4.7	...	...
0	7 121	...	...	12.1	...	...
1 - 4	1 240	...	...	0.5	...	...
5 - 9	626	...	...	0.2	...	...
10 - 14	896	...	...	0.3	...	...
15 - 19	4 270	...	...	1.6	...	...
20 - 24	6 144	...	...	2.3	...	...
25 - 29	5 410	...	...	2.2	...	...
30 - 34	4 763	...	...	2.1	...	...
35 - 39	4 440	...	...	2.3	...	...
40 - 44	4 528	...	...	2.5	...	...
45 - 49	5 625	...	...	3.4	...	...
50 - 54	7 431	...	...	5.3	...	...
55 - 59	8 940	...	...	7.7	...	...
60 - 64	10 059	...	...	10.9	...	...
65 - 69	10 169	...	...	15.3	...	...
70 - 74	11 245	...	...	24.3	...	...
75 +	43 896	...	...	73.6	...	...
75 - 79	12 278	...	...	...	...	...
80 - 84	12 959	...	...	...	...	...
85 - 89	9 851	...	...	...	...	...
90 - 94	5 958	...	...	...	...	...
95 - 99	2 216	...	...	...	...	...
100 +	634	...	...	...	...	...

ASIA - ASIE

Armenia - Arménie[20]

2009 (C)

Total	27 560	14 253	13 307	8.5	9.1	8.0
0 - 4	528	299	229	2.7	2.9	2.5
0	454	258	196	10.7	11.4	9.9
1 - 4	74	41	33	0.5	0.5	0.5
5 - 9	40	18	22	0.2	◆0.2	◆0.3
10 - 14	40	31	9	0.2	0.3	◆0.1
15 - 19	145	106	39	0.5	0.7	0.3

19. Deaths by age and sex, age-specific death rates by sex: latest available year, 2003 - 2012
Décès et taux de mortalité selon l'âge et le sexe : dernière année disponible, 2003 - 2012 (continued - suite)

Continent, country or area, date, code and age (in years) Continent, pays ou zone, date, code et âge (en années)	Number - Nombre			Rate - Taux		
	Both sexes Les deux sexes	Male Masculin	Female Féminin	Both sexes Les deux sexes	Male Masculin	Female Féminin
ASIA - ASIE						
Armenia - Arménie[20]						
2009 (C)						
20 - 24	152	107	45	0.5	0.7	0.3
25 - 29	211	155	56	0.7	1.1	0.4
30 - 34	243	183	60	1.0	1.6	0.5
35 - 39	320	223	97	1.6	2.3	0.9
40 - 44	547	404	143	2.6	4.1	1.3
45 - 49	1 044	728	316	4.0	5.8	2.3
50 - 54	1 431	980	451	6.2	9.0	3.7
55 - 59	1 715	1 142	573	10.1	14.8	6.2
60 - 64	1 539	962	577	15.5	22.1	10.3
65 - 69	2 522	1 477	1 045	27.0	37.7	19.3
70 - 74	4 463	2 419	2 044	40.9	54.4	31.5
75 - 79	5 211	2 484	2 727	68.1	81.3	59.3
80 - 84	4 781	1 854	2 927	110.6	129.6	101.2
85 +	2 628	681	1 947	262.4	271.6	259.3
85 - 89	1 702	454	1 248	...	...	...
90 - 94	637	141	496	...	...	...
95 - 99	212	52	160	...	...	...
100 +	77	34	43	...	...	...
Azerbaijan - Azerbaïdjan[20]						
2010 (+C)						
Total	53 580	28 248	25 332	5.9	6.3	5.5
0 - 4	2 307	1 271	1 036	3.3	3.4	3.2
0	1 843	1 018	825	11.6	11.9	11.3
1 - 4	464	253	211	0.9	0.9	0.9
5 - 9	222	132	90	0.4	0.4	0.3
10 - 14	200	118	82	0.3	0.3	0.2
15 - 19	466	321	145	0.5	0.7	0.3
20 - 24	615	398	217	0.7	0.9	0.5
25 - 29	668	453	215	0.8	1.1	0.5
30 - 34	796	540	256	1.1	1.6	0.7
35 - 39	964	651	313	1.6	2.2	1.0
40 - 44	1 500	1 006	494	2.3	3.2	1.4
45 - 49	2 488	1 642	846	3.7	5.1	2.4
50 - 54	3 503	2 319	1 184	6.1	8.3	4.0
55 - 59	3 794	2 489	1 305	10.5	14.5	6.9
60 - 64	3 623	2 175	1 448	16.0	20.8	11.8
65 - 69	3 632	2 085	1 547	28.0	36.5	21.3
70 - 74	8 822	4 473	4 349	45.4	53.8	39.0
75 - 79	8 676	4 021	4 655	73.5	80.6	68.3
80 - 84	6 725	2 908	3 817	109.7	117.7	104.3
85 - 89	2 799	886	1 913	144.3	140.6	146.0
90 - 94	1 025	227	798	186.4	174.6	190.0
95 - 99	430	89	341	226.3	178.0	243.6
100 +	325	44	281	270.8	440.0	255.5
Bahrain - Bahreïn						
2012* (C)						
Total	2 299	1 375	924	...	...	...
0	111	64	47	...	...	...
1 - 4	22	10	12	...	...	...
5 - 9	11	6	5	...	...	...
10 - 14	14	12	2	...	...	...
15 - 19	42	27	15	...	...	...
20 - 24	53	40	13	...	...	...
25 - 29	85	67	18	...	...	...
30 - 34	76	55	21	...	...	...
35 - 39	89	57	32	...	...	...
40 - 44	96	68	28	...	...	...
45 - 49	114	77	37	...	...	...
50 - 54	161	110	51	...	...	...
55 - 59	200	131	69	...	...	...
60 - 64	170	104	66	...	...	...
65 - 69	160	85	75	...	...	...
70 - 74	237	122	115	...	...	...
75 +	658	340	318	...	...	...

19. Deaths by age and sex, age-specific death rates by sex: latest available year, 2003 - 2012
Décès et taux de mortalité selon l'âge et le sexe : dernière année disponible, 2003 - 2012 (continued - suite)

Continent, country or area, date, code and age (in years) / Continent, pays ou zone, date, code et âge (en années)	Number - Nombre			Rate - Taux		
	Both sexes Les deux sexes	Male Masculin	Female Féminin	Both sexes Les deux sexes	Male Masculin	Female Féminin
ASIA - ASIE						
Bhutan - Bhoutan[7]						
2005 (|)						
Total	4 498	2 390	2 108	7.1	7.2	7.0
0	503	270	233	40.8	44.3	37.5
1 - 4	269	143	126	5.4	5.6	5.1
5 - 9	139	85	54	2.0	2.4	1.5
10 - 14	88	46	42	1.1	1.2	1.1
15 - 19	126	65	61	1.7	1.7	1.6
20 - 24	123	65	58	1.7	1.6	1.9
25 - 29	133	74	59	2.3	2.4	2.3
30 - 34	145	79	66	3.4	3.4	3.4
35 - 39	182	107	75	4.7	5.1	4.3
40 - 44	174	95	79	5.8	5.9	5.7
45 - 49	250	129	121	9.0	8.7	9.5
50 - 54	204	113	91	9.3	9.6	8.9
55 - 59	239	126	113	14.6	14.4	14.8
60 - 64	291	145	146	20.0	19.2	20.8
65 - 69	331	163	168	29.1	27.2	31.3
70 - 74	368	188	180	42.1	41.8	42.4
75 +	933	497	436	96.8	102.7	90.8
Brunei Darussalam - Brunéi Darussalam						
2008 (+C)						
Total	1 091	636	455	...	...	...
0	45	24	21	...	...	...
1 - 4	16	11	5	...	...	...
5 - 9	6	2	4	...	...	...
10 - 14	5	1	4	...	...	...
15 - 19	13	7	6	...	...	...
20 - 24	20	13	7	...	...	...
25 - 29	25	22	3	...	...	...
30 - 34	29	19	10	...	...	...
35 - 39	38	23	15	...	...	...
40 - 44	45	32	13	...	...	...
45 - 49	73	43	30	...	...	...
50 - 54	69	47	22	...	...	...
55 - 59	73	38	35	...	...	...
60 - 64	63	36	27	...	...	...
65 - 69	105	59	46	...	...	...
70 - 74	103	51	52	...	...	...
75 - 79	131	76	55	...	...	...
80 - 84	105	52	53	...	...	...
85 - 89	65	45	20	...	...	...
90 - 94	33	16	17	...	...	...
95 - 99	24	14	10	...	...	...
100 +	5	5	-	...	...	...
China - Chine[21]						
2010 (|)						
Total	7 421 990	4 293 783	3 128 207	5.6	6.3	4.8
0	60 217	32 026	28 191	4.4	4.3	4.5
1 - 4	39 591	23 119	16 472	0.6	0.7	0.6
5 - 9	21 183	13 621	7 562	0.3	0.4	0.2
10 - 14	23 088	15 243	7 845	0.3	0.4	0.2
15 - 19	40 469	28 088	12 381	0.4	0.5	0.3
20 - 24	62 552	43 738	18 814	0.5	0.7	0.3
25 - 29	60 661	42 497	18 164	0.6	0.8	0.4
30 - 34	79 960	55 804	24 156	0.8	1.1	0.5
35 - 39	140 531	98 382	42 149	1.2	1.6	0.7
40 - 44	216 353	149 111	67 242	1.7	2.3	1.1
45 - 49	262 531	179 446	83 085	2.5	3.3	1.6
50 - 54	337 397	226 888	110 509	4.3	5.6	2.9
55 - 59	494 339	324 817	169 522	6.1	7.9	4.2
60 - 64	586 160	377 069	209 091	10.0	12.6	7.3
65 - 69	695 662	435 007	260 655	16.9	21.0	12.8
70 - 74	999 653	599 394	400 259	30.3	36.5	24.2
75 - 79	1 162 694	657 140	505 554	48.7	58.3	40.2
80 - 84	1 081 704	553 704	528 000	80.9	93.6	70.8
85 - 89	686 462	306 678	379 784	121.9	139.4	110.7

Continent, country or area, date, code and age (in years) Continent, pays ou zone, date, code et âge (en annèes)	Number - Nombre			Rate - Taux		
	Both sexes Les deux sexes	Male Masculin	Female Féminin	Both sexes Les deux sexes	Male Masculin	Female Féminin
ASIA - ASIE						
China - Chine[21]						
2010 (|)						
90 - 94	279 569	104 048	175 521	177.1	196.0	167.6
95 - 99	74 729	23 292	51 437	202.0	197.9	203.9
100 +	16 485	4 671	11 814	458.8	527.7	436.2
China, Hong Kong SAR - Chine, Hong Kong RAS						
2011 (C)						
Total	42 346	23 705[16]	18 636[16]	6.0	7.2	4.9
0	127	82	45	2.4	3.0	1.8
1 - 4	45	21	24	0.2	♦0.2	♦0.3
5 - 9	18	9	9	♦0.1	♦0.1	♦0.1
10 - 14	33	21	12	0.1	♦0.1	♦0.1
15 - 19	67	42	25	0.2	0.2	♦0.1
20 - 24	125	79	46	0.3	0.4	0.2
25 - 29	165	101	64	0.3	0.4	0.2
30 - 34	225	143	82	0.4	0.6	0.3
35 - 39	400	230	170	0.7	1.0	0.5
40 - 44	533	307	226	0.9	1.3	0.7
45 - 49	1 028	626	402	1.6	2.1	1.1
50 - 54	1 708	1 098	610	2.7	3.5	1.9
55 - 59	2 052	1 373	679	4.0	5.4	2.6
60 - 64	2 597	1 767	830	6.3	8.6	4.1
65 - 69	2 494	1 826	668	10.6	15.0	5.9
70 - 74	3 829	2 615	1 214	16.6	22.4	10.7
75 - 79	5 993	3 775	2 218	29.2	38.9	20.5
80 - 84	7 500	4 305	3 195	51.3	69.1	38.1
85 +	13 382	5 270	8 112	106.7	129.5	95.8
Unknown - Inconnu	25	15[16]	5[16]	..	..	..
China, Macao SAR - Chine, Macao RAS						
2012 (C)						
Total	1 841	1 036	805	3.2	3.8	2.7
0	18	14	4	♦3.1	♦4.5	♦1.4
1 - 14	6	3	3	♦0.1	♦0.1	♦0.1
15 - 39	90	61	29	0.4	0.5	♦0.2
40 - 64	523	354	169	2.4	3.4	1.5
65 - 79	460	291	169	14.6	18.8	10.6
80 +	743	312	431	68.2	82.1	60.7
Unknown - Inconnu	1	1	-	..	..	..
Cyprus - Chypre[22]						
2011 (C)						
Total	5 504	2 828	2 676	6.5	6.8	6.1
0 - 4	38	22	16	0.8	♦0.9	♦0.7
0	30	18	12	...	...	...
1 - 4	8	4	4	...	...	...
5 - 9	3	1	2	♦0.1	-	♦0.1
10 - 14	3	2	1	♦0.1	♦0.1	-
15 - 19	13	12	1	♦0.2	♦0.4	-
20 - 24	27	21	6	♦0.4	♦0.6	♦0.2
25 - 29	39	25	14	0.5	♦0.7	♦0.4
30 - 34	46	34	12	0.7	1.0	♦0.3
35 - 39	40	22	18	0.7	♦0.8	♦0.5
40 - 44	56	33	23	1.0	1.3	♦0.7
45 - 49	105	68	37	1.8	2.5	1.2
50 - 54	143	88	55	2.6	3.2	1.9
55 - 59	179	117	62	3.7	4.9	2.6
60 - 64	268	175	93	5.8	7.7	4.0
65 - 69	327	215	112	9.4	12.8	6.3
70 - 74	546	327	219	18.9	23.7	14.5
75 - 79	723	390	333	34.7	41.9	28.8
80 +	2 847	1 221	1 626	116.8	122.1	113.0
80 - 84	1 005	451	554	...	...	...
85 - 89	1 021	455	566	...	...	...
90 - 94	596	239	357	...	...	...
95 - 99	192	68	124	...	...	...
100 +	33	8	25	...	...	...
Unknown - Inconnu	101	55	46	..	..	..

Continent, country or area, date, code and age (in years) Continent, pays ou zone, date, code et âge (en annèes)	Number - Nombre			Rate - Taux		
	Both sexes Les deux sexes	Male Masculin	Female Féminin	Both sexes Les deux sexes	Male Masculin	Female Féminin
ASIA - ASIE						
Democratic People's Republic of Korea - République populaire démocratique de Corée[6]						
2008 (|)						
Total...	216 616	112 827	103 789	9.0	9.6	8.4
0	6 686	3 593	3 093	19.6	20.6	18.5
1 - 4	2 552	1 372	1 180	1.9	2.0	1.8
5 - 9	1 680	960	720	0.9	1.0	0.8
10 - 14	1 614	869	745	0.8	0.8	0.8
15 - 19	2 426	1 348	1 078	1.2	1.3	1.1
20 - 24	3 171	1 922	1 249	1.7	2.0	1.4
25 - 29	3 528	2 160	1 368	2.0	2.4	1.6
30 - 34	3 907	2 424	1 483	2.3	2.8	1.8
35 - 39	5 792	3 655	2 137	2.6	3.3	1.9
40 - 44	6 312	3 907	2 405	3.1	3.9	2.4
45 - 49	6 468	3 915	2 553	4.1	5.1	3.2
50 - 54	7 630	4 715	2 915	5.8	7.4	4.3
55 - 59	11 295	7 113	4 182	12.5	16.8	8.7
60 - 64	26 360	16 815	9 545	24.9	35.3	16.4
65 - 69	34 068	22 281	11 787	37.3	58.7	22.1
70 - 74	34 093	18 886	15 207	51.5	82.7	35.0
75 - 79	28 690	10 991	17 699	85.5	138.7	69.1
80 + ...	30 344	5 901	24 443	163.8	238.8	152.3
Georgia - Géorgie[20]						
2012 (C)						
Total...	49 348	25 453	23 895	11.0	11.9	10.2
0	715	419	296	...	...	...
1 - 4	109	68	41	0.5	0.6	0.4
5 - 9	46	28	18	0.2	♦0.2	♦0.2
10 - 14	68	46	22	0.3	0.4	♦0.2
15 - 19	122	90	32	0.4	0.6	0.2
20 - 24	273	218	55	0.7	1.2	0.3
25 - 29	337	269	68	0.9	1.5	0.4
30 - 34	411	324	87	1.2	2.0	0.5
35 - 39	593	459	134	1.9	3.0	0.8
40 - 44	809	609	200	2.7	4.2	1.3
45 - 49	1 447	1 086	361	4.6	7.5	2.2
50 - 54	2 244	1 596	648	6.9	10.5	3.7
55 - 59	2 764	1 950	814	10.1	15.8	5.5
60 - 64	3 460	2 287	1 173	15.0	22.4	9.1
65 - 69	2 991	1 887	1 104	23.0	34.3	14.7
70 - 74	7 190	3 906	3 284	37.5	52.5	27.9
75 - 79	8 306	4 017	4 289	59.6	74.7	50.0
80 - 84	9 015	3 651	5 364	96.4	108.7	89.5
85 + ...	8 209	2 370	5 839	129.3	138.2	126.0
Unknown - Inconnu	239	173	66	..	..	..
Iran (Islamic Republic of) - Iran (République islamique d')[23]						
2011 (+C)						
Total...	340 990	193 648	147 342	4.5	5.1	4.0
0	11 021	6 115	4 906	8.9	9.7	8.2
1 - 4	3 773	2 089	1 684	0.8	0.8	0.7
5 - 9	2 251	1 279	972	0.4	0.4	0.4
10 - 14	2 169	1 244	925	0.4	0.4	0.3
15 - 19	5 499	3 860	1 639	0.8	1.2	0.5
20 - 24	9 659	6 454	3 205	1.1	1.5	0.8
25 - 29	10 772	6 760	4 012	1.2	1.6	0.9
30 - 34	9 179	6 268	2 911	1.3	1.8	0.8
35 - 39	7 796	5 546	2 250	1.4	1.9	0.8
40 - 44	8 811	6 051	2 760	1.8	2.4	1.1
45 - 49	10 611	7 103	3 508	2.6	3.5	1.8
50 - 54	14 662	9 649	5 013	4.2	5.5	2.8
55 - 59	17 625	10 978	6 647	6.6	8.3	4.9
60 - 64	18 901	10 893	8 008	10.1	12.4	8.2
65 - 69	21 563	11 949	9 614	16.0	18.6	13.7
70 - 74	30 520	16 997	13 523	27.3	30.3	24.2
75 - 79	43 896	24 050	19 846	48.1	50.4	45.5
80 - 84	45 705	23 397	22 308	81.4	83.3	79.5

19. Deaths by age and sex, age-specific death rates by sex: latest available year, 2003 - 2012
Décès et taux de mortalité selon l'âge et le sexe : dernière année disponible, 2003 - 2012 (continued - suite)

Continent, country or area, date, code and age (in years) / Continent, pays ou zone, date, code et âge (en années)	Number - Nombre			Rate - Taux		
	Both sexes Les deux sexes	Male Masculin	Female Féminin	Both sexes Les deux sexes	Male Masculin	Female Féminin
ASIA - ASIE						
Iran (Islamic Republic of) - Iran (République islamique d')[23]						
2011 (+C)						
85 - 89	48 900	24 175	24 725	180.6	176.3	185.2
Unknown - Inconnu	17 677	8 791	8 886	..	..	..
Israel - Israël[24]						
2012 (C)						
Total...	40 736	20 092[16]	20 643[16]	...	...	...
0	563	313[16]	249[16]	...	...	...
1 - 4	122	67	55	...	...	...
5 - 9	71	40	31	...	...	...
10 - 14	58	40	18	...	...	...
15 - 19	141	94	47	...	...	...
20 - 24	193	138	55	...	...	...
25 - 29	202	153	49	...	...	...
30 - 34	232	140	92	...	...	...
35 - 39	329	202	127	...	...	...
40 - 44	435	272	163	...	...	...
45 - 49	650	418	232	...	...	...
50 - 54	1 039	686	353	...	...	...
55 - 59	1 573	981	592	...	...	...
60 - 64	2 278	1 380	898	...	...	...
65 - 69	2 632	1 567	1 065	...	...	...
70 - 74	3 638	2 068	1 570	...	...	...
75 - 79	5 045	2 640	2 405	...	...	...
80 - 84	6 870	3 166	3 704	...	...	...
85 - 89	7 766	3 092	4 674	...	...	...
90 - 94	4 684	1 866	2 818	...	...	...
95 - 99	1 811	608	1 203	...	...	...
100 + ...	404	161	243	...	...	...
Japan - Japon[25]						
2011 (C)						
Total...	1 253 066	656 540	596 526	9.8	10.6	9.1
0	2 463	1 269	1 194	...	...	...
1 - 4	1 159	605	554	...	...	...
5 - 9	749	404	345	0.1	0.1	0.1
10 - 14	728	442	286	0.1	0.1	0.1
15 - 19	1 740	1 131	609	0.3	0.4	0.2
20 - 24	2 964	1 988	976	0.5	0.6	0.3
25 - 29	3 683	2 391	1 292	0.5	0.6	0.4
30 - 34	4 916	3 141	1 775	0.6	0.8	0.4
35 - 39	7 964	4 979	2 985	0.8	1.0	0.6
40 - 44	11 190	7 106	4 084	1.2	1.5	0.9
45 - 49	14 979	9 477	5 502	1.9	2.4	1.4
50 - 54	22 437	14 791	7 646	2.9	3.9	2.0
55 - 59	37 455	25 206	12 249	4.5	6.1	2.9
60 - 64	72 120	49 819	22 301	6.8	9.5	4.1
65 - 69	82 062	56 561	25 501	10.4	15.1	6.2
70 - 74	113 113	75 161	37 952	15.9	22.8	10.0
75 - 79	167 707	105 186	62 521	27.4	39.5	18.1
80 - 84	220 110	124 245	95 865	49.3	71.1	35.3
85 + ...	484 151	171 855	312 296	120.2	152.1	107.8
85 - 89	222 793	98 638	124 155	...	...	...
90 - 94	162 024	51 432	110 592	...	...	...
95 - 99	79 763	18 749	61 014	...	...	...
100 + ...	19 571	3 036	16 535	...	...	...
Unknown - Inconnu	1 376	783	593	..	..	..
Kazakhstan[20]						
2008 (C)						
Total...	152 706	85 174	67 532	9.7	11.3	8.3
0	7 322	4 154	3 168	21.9	24.2	19.5
1 - 4	1 066	614	452	0.9	1.1	0.8
5 - 9	477	292	185	0.4	0.5	0.3
10 - 14	500	310	190	0.4	0.5	0.3
15 - 19	1 574	1 055	519	1.1	1.4	0.7
20 - 24	2 971	2 203	768	1.9	2.8	1.0
25 - 29	3 858	2 905	953	3.0	4.5	1.5

19. Deaths by age and sex, age-specific death rates by sex: latest available year, 2003 - 2012
Décès et taux de mortalité selon l'âge et le sexe : dernière année disponible, 2003 - 2012 (continued - suite)

Continent, country or area, date, code and age (in years) / Continent, pays ou zone, date, code et âge (en années)	Number - Nombre			Rate - Taux		
	Both sexes Les deux sexes	Male Masculin	Female Féminin	Both sexes Les deux sexes	Male Masculin	Female Féminin
ASIA - ASIE						
Kazakhstan[20]						
2008 (C)						
30 - 34	4 882	3 722	1 160	4.1	6.4	1.9
35 - 39	5 282	3 928	1 354	4.8	7.4	2.4
40 - 44	6 449	4 711	1 738	6.2	9.4	3.2
45 - 49	9 230	6 696	2 534	8.4	13.0	4.4
50 - 54	10 390	7 374	3 016	11.7	18.2	6.2
55 - 59	11 726	7 738	3 988	16.7	25.3	10.1
60 - 64	9 003	5 653	3 350	23.5	35.2	15.1
65 - 69	15 730	9 038	6 692	35.7	53.6	24.6
70 - 74	17 675	9 321	8 354	50.0	70.9	37.6
75 - 79	16 379	7 276	9 103	78.4	106.3	64.8
80 - 84	15 793	5 141	10 652	117.4	142.4	108.2
85 - 89	7 333	1 783	5 550	184.3	195.7	180.9
90 - 94	3 173	651	2 522	307.9	311.3	307.1
95 - 99	1 084	181	903	404.8	247.6	463.8
100 +	369	52	317	508.3	161.5	784.7
Unknown - Inconnu	440	376	64	..	..	..
Kuwait - Koweït						
2011 (C)						
Total	5 339	3 308	2 031	1.7	1.9	1.5
0	484	276	208	...	...	...
1 - 4	71	36	35	...	...	...
5 - 9	56	29	27	0.2	♦0.2	♦0.2
10 - 14	53	31	22	0.3	0.3	♦0.2
15 - 19	109	93	16	0.6	1.0	♦0.2
20 - 24	108	81	27	0.4	0.6	♦0.2
25 - 29	181	133	48	0.5	0.6	0.3
30 - 34	212	161	51	0.5	0.6	0.3
35 - 39	234	170	64	0.7	0.8	0.5
40 - 44	305	219	86	1.1	1.3	0.8
45 - 49	317	243	74	1.6	2.0	1.0
50 - 54	326	228	98	2.5	2.7	2.0
55 - 59	397	288	109	5.0	5.8	3.6
60 - 64	386	239	147	8.8	9.5	7.9
65 +	1 995	1 021	974	35.3	34.9	35.8
65 - 69	435	229	206	...	...	...
70 - 74	467	256	211	...	...	...
75 - 79	433	223	210	...	...	...
80 - 84	341	169	172	...	...	...
85 - 89	176	83	93	...	...	...
90 - 94	84	39	45	...	...	...
95 +	59	22	37	...	...	...
Unknown - Inconnu	105	60	45	..	..	..
Kyrgyzstan - Kirghizstan						
2011 (C)						
Total	35 941	20 126	15 815	6.5	7.4	5.7
0	3 150	1 779	1 371	21.7	23.9	19.3
1 - 4	483	279	204	1.0	1.1	0.8
5 - 9	162	99	63	0.3	0.4	0.2
10 - 14	169	103	66	0.3	0.4	0.3
15 - 19	396	238	158	0.7	0.8	0.6
20 - 24	562	346	216	0.9	1.2	0.7
25 - 29	713	494	219	1.5	2.0	0.9
30 - 34	1 008	713	295	2.6	3.6	1.5
35 - 39	1 198	882	316	3.5	5.2	1.8
40 - 44	1 547	1 108	439	4.8	7.0	2.6
45 - 49	1 964	1 368	596	6.4	9.3	3.8
50 - 54	2 581	1 764	817	9.6	13.8	5.8
55 - 59	2 558	1 716	842	13.9	20.3	8.5
60 - 64	2 586	1 601	985	20.7	29.1	14.1
65 - 69	1 862	1 111	751	33.0	45.5	23.5
70 - 74	3 807	2 069	1 738	47.6	63.8	36.6
75 - 79	3 892	1 836	2 056	77.2	95.1	66.2
80 - 84	4 061	1 730	2 331	115.6	134.5	104.7
85 - 89	2 030	622	1 408	155.1	141.3	162.0
90 - 94	799	191	608	246.2	222.1	254.9

19. Deaths by age and sex, age-specific death rates by sex: latest available year, 2003 - 2012
Décès et taux de mortalité selon l'âge et le sexe : dernière année disponible, 2003 - 2012 (continued - suite)

Continent, country or area, date, code and age (in years) Continent, pays ou zone, date, code et âge (en annèes)	Number - Nombre			Rate - Taux		
	Both sexes Les deux sexes	Male Masculin	Female Féminin	Both sexes Les deux sexes	Male Masculin	Female Féminin
ASIA - ASIE						
Kyrgyzstan - Kirghizstan						
2011 (C)						
95 - 99	218	44	174	309.7	307.7	310.2
100 +	175	17	158	456.9	♦320.8	478.8
Unknown - Inconnu	20	16	4	..	..	..
Malaysia - Malaisie						
2009 (C)						
Total	130 135	75 277	54 858	4.7	5.3	4.0
0	3 404	1 925	1 479	6.9	7.6	6.2
1 - 4	818	441	377	0.4	0.4	0.4
5 - 9	660	387	273	0.3	0.3	0.2
10 - 14	814	526	288	0.3	0.4	0.2
15 - 19	1 918	1 447	471	0.7	1.1	0.4
20 - 24	2 348	1 759	589	0.9	1.4	0.5
25 - 29	2 355	1 721	634	1.0	1.4	0.5
30 - 34	2 798	2 103	695	1.2	1.8	0.6
35 - 39	3 515	2 543	972	1.7	2.4	0.9
40 - 44	4 393	3 018	1 375	2.2	3.0	1.4
45 - 49	6 410	4 287	2 123	3.7	4.8	2.5
50 - 54	8 494	5 538	2 956	5.9	7.5	4.3
55 - 59	10 096	6 489	3 607	9.0	11.3	6.6
60 - 64	11 871	7 549	4 322	15.5	19.2	11.6
65 - 69	12 913	7 790	5 123	25.3	30.6	20.0
70 - 74	16 450	9 263	7 187	46.3	55.4	38.2
75 - 79	14 468	7 209	7 259	66.7	73.8	61.0
80 - 84	12 212	5 747	6 465	102.1	109.5	96.3
85 - 89	8 624	3 476	5 148	176.2	171.0	179.8
90 +	5 569	2 059	3 510	188.3	221.0	173.3
90 - 94	3 829	1 449	2 380	...	...	...
95 +	1 740	610	1 130	...	...	...
Unknown - Inconnu	5	-	5	..	..	..
Maldives						
2011 (C)						
Total	1 137	686	451	3.5	4.2	2.8
0	65	37	28	9.3	10.6	♦8.1
1 - 4	16	9	7	♦0.7	♦0.8	♦0.6
5 - 9	9	5	4	♦0.3	♦0.4	♦0.3
10 - 14	10	5	5	♦0.3	♦0.3	♦0.3
15 - 19	11	5	6	♦0.3	♦0.3	♦0.3
20 - 24	22	17	5	♦0.5	♦0.8	♦0.2
25 - 29	14	10	4	♦0.4	♦0.6	♦0.2
30 - 34	12	9	3	♦0.5	♦0.7	♦0.2
35 - 39	12	4	8	♦0.6	♦0.4	♦0.7
40 - 44	17	11	6	♦0.9	♦1.2	♦0.6
45 - 49	26	16	10	♦1.6	♦2.0	♦1.2
50 - 54	47	31	16	3.5	4.5	♦2.4
55 - 59	39	27	12	5.0	♦6.6	♦3.2
60 - 64	45	25	20	7.9	♦8.5	♦7.3
65 - 69	110	61	49	21.2	23.2	19.1
70 - 74	203	121	82	40.6	46.3	34.4
75 - 79	212	130	82	63.6	70.3	55.3
80 +	267	163	104	111.1	108.1	116.2
80 - 84	146	84	62	...	...	...
85 - 89	85	56	29	...	...	...
90 - 94	24	14	10	...	...	...
95 - 99	10	8	2	...	...	...
100 +	2	1	1	...	...	...
Unknown - Inconnu	-	-	-	..	..	..
Mongolia - Mongolie						
2010 (+C)						
Total	18 293	10 781	7 512	6.6	8.0	5.3
0	1 275	721	554	21.0	23.5	18.5
1 - 4	446	233	213	2.1	2.2	2.1
5 - 9	124	74	50	0.5	0.6	0.4
10 - 14	122	71	51	0.5	0.6	0.4
15 - 19	219	152	67	0.8	1.1	0.5
20 - 24	424	294	130	1.4	2.0	0.8

19. Deaths by age and sex, age-specific death rates by sex: latest available year, 2003 - 2012
Décès et taux de mortalité selon l'âge et le sexe : dernière année disponible, 2003 - 2012 (continued - suite)

Continent, country or area, date, code and age (in years) / Continent, pays ou zone, date, code et âge (en années)	Number - Nombre			Rate - Taux		
	Both sexes Les deux sexes	Male Masculin	Female Féminin	Both sexes Les deux sexes	Male Masculin	Female Féminin
ASIA - ASIE						
Mongolia - Mongolie						
2010 (+C)						
25 - 29	493	335	158	1.9	2.7	1.2
30 - 34	703	505	198	3.0	4.5	1.6
35 - 39	843	635	208	4.0	6.2	1.9
40 - 44	1 073	740	333	5.8	8.3	3.4
45 - 49	1 455	997	458	8.9	12.8	5.3
50 - 54	1 623	1 089	534	13.2	18.8	8.3
55 - 59	1 364	865	499	17.7	23.9	12.1
60 - 64	1 361	840	521	26.2	35.7	18.4
65 - 69	1 437	827	610	33.4	41.9	26.3
70 +	5 331	2 403	2 928	79.1	86.9	73.7
Myanmar[26]						
2010 (+U)						
Total	95 672	...	...	...	...	...
0	7 223	...	...	...	...	...
1 - 4	2 492	...	...	...	...	...
5 - 9	556	...	...	...	...	...
10 - 14	485	...	...	...	...	...
15 - 19	1 138	...	...	...	...	...
20 - 24	2 024	...	...	...	...	...
25 - 29	3 714	...	...	...	...	...
30 - 34	5 370	...	...	...	...	...
35 - 39	6 720	...	...	...	...	...
40 - 44	6 297	...	...	...	...	...
45 - 49	6 182	...	...	...	...	...
50 - 54	6 509	...	...	...	...	...
55 - 59	6 724	...	...	...	...	...
60 - 64	6 669	...	...	...	...	...
65 - 69	6 478	...	...	...	...	...
70 - 74	7 207	...	...	...	...	...
75 - 79	7 429	...	...	...	...	...
80 - 84	6 422	...	...	...	...	...
85 +	6 033	...	...	...	...	...
Oman[27]						
2011 (U)						
Total	7 667	4 967[28]	2 678[28]	...	...	...
0	598	316[28]	269[28]	...	...	...
1 - 4	150	87	63	...	...	...
5 - 9	67	39	28	...	...	...
10 - 14	83	59	24	...	...	...
15 - 19	174	144	30	...	...	...
20 - 24	319	270	49	...	...	...
25 - 29	319	269	50	...	...	...
30 - 34	269	216	53	...	...	...
35 - 39	230	181	49	...	...	...
40 - 44	248	195[28]	52[28]	...	...	...
45 - 49	284	232	52	...	...	...
50 - 54	393	291	102	...	...	...
55 - 59	453	306	146	...	...	...
60 - 64	535	350	185	...	...	...
65 - 69	639	376	263	...	...	...
70 - 74	819	477	342	...	...	...
75 - 79	620	395	225	...	...	...
80 - 84	509	299	210	...	...	...
85 - 89	251	150	101	...	...	...
90 - 94	186	94	92[28]	...	...	...
95 - 99	56	31[28]	24	...	...	...
100 +	25	13	12	...	...	...
Unknown - Inconnu	440	177[28]	257[28]	..	..	..
Pakistan[29]						
2007 (|)						
Total	1 019 533	598 820	420 713	6.8	7.8	5.8
0 - 4	365 729	205 840	159 889	18.7	21.0	16.4
5 - 9	33 029	16 652	16 376	1.5	1.4	1.5
10 - 14	20 510	6 871	13 640	1.0	0.6	1.4
15 - 19	27 417	16 500	10 917	1.6	1.8	1.3

Continent, country or area, date, code and age (in years) Continent, pays ou zone, date, code et âge (en annèes)	Number - Nombre			Rate - Taux		
	Both sexes Les deux sexes	Male Masculin	Female Féminin	Both sexes Les deux sexes	Male Masculin	Female Féminin
ASIA - ASIE						
Pakistan[29]						
2007 (I)						
20 - 24	20 192	11 195	8 997	1.5	1.6	1.3
25 - 29	23 990	13 101	10 888	2.2	2.5	2.0
30 - 34	11 624	8 007	3 617	1.4	2.0	0.8
35 - 39	24 880	11 482	13 398	3.0	2.8	3.2
40 - 44	30 926	18 802	12 124	4.6	5.4	3.7
45 - 49	27 537	17 884	9 652	4.4	5.5	3.2
50 - 54	43 405	30 870	12 535	9.5	12.7	5.8
55 - 59	51 031	35 120	15 911	14.4	18.8	9.5
60 - 64	68 531	41 470	27 061	23.4	25.3	20.9
65 - 69	58 286	35 664	22 621	28.6	32.2	24.3
70 - 74	82 325	49 296	33 029	56.2	57.5	54.4
75 - 79	37 357	24 072	13 285	57.1	67.2	44.9
80 - 84	34 079	21 720	12 359	79.6	86.6	69.6
85 +	58 685	34 274	24 411	165.7	168.9	161.4
Philippines						
2009 (C)						
Total	480 820	279 513	201 307	...	...	...
0	21 659	12 503	9 156	...	...	...
1 - 4	9 837	5 401	4 436	...	...	...
5 - 9	5 393	3 100	2 293	...	...	...
10 - 14	4 892	2 889	2 003	...	...	...
15 - 19	8 194	5 348	2 846	...	...	...
20 - 24	11 049	7 602	3 447	...	...	...
25 - 29	12 459	8 471	3 988	...	...	...
30 - 34	13 568	9 203	4 365	...	...	...
35 - 39	16 543	11 049	5 494	...	...	...
40 - 44	20 499	13 481	7 018	...	...	...
45 - 49	25 805	17 110	8 695	...	...	...
50 - 54	31 766	21 083	10 683	...	...	...
55 - 59	36 956	24 396	12 560	...	...	...
60 - 64	40 524	26 186	14 338	...	...	...
65 - 69	42 795	26 546	16 249	...	...	...
70 - 74	47 439	26 912	20 527	...	...	...
75 - 79	45 007	23 245	21 762	...	...	...
80 - 84	37 889	17 145	20 744	...	...	...
85 - 89	28 660	11 159	17 501	...	...	...
90 - 94	13 177	4 455	8 722	...	...	...
95 +	5 979	1 872	4 107	...	...	...
Unknown - Inconnu	730	357	373	..	..	...
Qatar						
2011 (C)						
Total	1 949	1 402	547	...	...	...
0	156	93	63	...	...	...
1 - 4	29	8	21	...	...	...
5 - 9	23	13	10	...	...	...
10 - 14	17	8	9	...	...	...
15 - 19	35	32	3	...	...	...
20 - 24	92	83	9	...	...	...
25 - 29	124	111	13	...	...	...
30 - 34	119	105	14	...	...	...
35 - 39	106	92	14	...	...	...
40 - 44	143	123	20	...	...	...
45 - 49	141	121	20	...	...	...
50 - 54	147	117	30	...	...	...
55 - 59	168	129	39	...	...	...
60 - 64	126	82	44	...	...	...
65 - 69	103	58	45	...	...	...
70 - 74	118	59	59	...	...	...
75 - 79	122	65	57	...	...	...
80 - 84	87	49	38	...	...	...
85 - 89	58	30	28	...	...	...
90 - 94	19	12	7	...	...	...
95 +	16	12	4	...	...	...

19. Deaths by age and sex, age-specific death rates by sex: latest available year, 2003 - 2012
Décès et taux de mortalité selon l'âge et le sexe : dernière année disponible, 2003 - 2012 (continued - suite)

Continent, country or area, date, code and age (in years) / Continent, pays ou zone, date, code et âge (en années)	Number - Nombre			Rate - Taux		
	Both sexes Les deux sexes	Male Masculin	Female Féminin	Both sexes Les deux sexes	Male Masculin	Female Féminin
ASIA - ASIE						
Republic of Korea - République de Corée[30]						
2011 (C)						
Total	257 396	143 250	114 146	5.2	5.7	4.6
0	1 435	818	617	3.0	3.3	2.6
1 - 4	389	213	176	0.2	0.2	0.2
5 - 9	239	142	97	0.1	0.1	0.1
10 - 14	402	240	162	0.1	0.1	0.1
15 - 19	1 003	699	304	0.3	0.4	0.2
20 - 24	1 318	860	458	0.4	0.5	0.3
25 - 29	2 158	1 400	758	0.6	0.7	0.4
30 - 34	2 779	1 720	1 059	0.7	0.9	0.6
35 - 39	4 062	2 692	1 370	1.0	1.3	0.7
40 - 44	6 576	4 559	2 017	1.5	2.1	1.0
45 - 49	9 770	7 159	2 611	2.3	3.3	1.3
50 - 54	14 436	10 851	3 585	3.6	5.3	1.8
55 - 59	14 853	11 083	3 770	4.9	7.4	2.5
60 - 64	16 557	12 026	4 531	7.3	10.9	3.9
65 - 69	21 751	14 905	6 846	11.8	17.4	6.9
70 - 74	32 028	20 649	11 379	19.7	29.3	12.4
75 - 79	38 060	20 849	17 211	33.2	46.7	24.6
80 - 84	37 670	16 155	21 515	59.0	78.1	49.8
85 - 89	30 833	10 741	20 092	105.9	134.6	95.1
90 - 94	15 642	4 390	11 252	172.7	212.4	160.9
95 - 99	4 565	930	3 635	252.7	303.8	242.3
100 +	852	169	683	398.3	528.1	375.5
Unknown - Inconnu	18	-	18	..	..	..
Saudi Arabia - Arabie saoudite[31]						
2005 (...)						
Total	92 486	54 253	38 233	...	...	...
0 - 4	12 889	6 692	6 197	...	...	...
5 - 9	977	524	453	...	...	...
10 - 14	977	566	411	...	...	...
15 - 19	1 350	791	559	...	...	...
20 - 24	1 695	998	697	...	...	...
25 - 29	2 248	1 371	877	...	...	...
30 - 34	2 750	1 681	1 069	...	...	...
35 - 39	3 309	2 131	1 178	...	...	...
40 - 44	3 997	2 698	1 299	...	...	...
45 - 49	4 754	3 266	1 488	...	...	...
50 - 54	5 285	3 629	1 656	...	...	...
55 - 59	5 538	3 658	1 880	...	...	...
60 - 64	6 116	3 756	2 360	...	...	...
65 - 69	6 924	3 985	2 939	...	...	...
70 - 74	8 082	4 448	3 634	...	...	...
75 - 79	8 176	4 484	3 692	...	...	...
80 +	17 419	9 575	7 844	...	...	...
Singapore - Singapour						
2012 (+C)						
Total	18 481	10 075	8 406	4.8	5.4	4.3
0	98	52	46	...	...	...
1 - 4	36	20	16	...	...	...
5 - 9	20	13	7	◆0.1	◆0.1	◆0.1
10 - 14	36	22	14	0.2	◆0.2	◆0.1
15 - 19	66	40	26	0.3	0.3	◆0.2
20 - 24	157	112	45	0.6	0.8	0.3
25 - 29	157	114	43	0.6	0.9	0.3
30 - 34	200	127	73	0.7	0.9	0.5
35 - 39	228	136	92	0.7	0.9	0.6
40 - 44	359	238	121	1.2	1.6	0.8
45 - 49	583	345	238	1.8	2.1	1.5
50 - 54	853	527	326	2.7	3.4	2.1
55 - 59	1 316	842	474	4.8	6.2	3.5
60 - 64	1 666	1 078	588	7.8	10.2	5.4
65 - 69	1 616	1 004	612	12.5	16.1	9.2
70 - 74	2 209	1 339	870	21.2	28.0	15.4
75 - 79	2 350	1 303	1 047	34.7	43.9	27.6
80 - 84	2 520	1 255	1 265	57.1	71.7	47.6

19. Deaths by age and sex, age-specific death rates by sex: latest available year, 2003 - 2012
Décès et taux de mortalité selon l'âge et le sexe : dernière année disponible, 2003 - 2012 (continued - suite)

Continent, country or area, date, code and age (in years) Continent, pays ou zone, date, code et âge (en annèes)	Number - Nombre			Rate - Taux		
	Both sexes Les deux sexes	Male Masculin	Female Féminin	Both sexes Les deux sexes	Male Masculin	Female Féminin
ASIA - ASIE						
Singapore - Singapour						
2012 (+C)						
85 +	4 010	1 507	2 503	119.3	135.8	111.2
85 - 89	2 058	888	1 170	...	...	...
90 - 94	1 276	443	833	...	...	...
95 - 99	533	145	388	...	...	...
100 +	143	31	112	...	...	...
Unknown - Inconnu	1	1	-	..	..	..
Sri Lanka[32]						
2008 (+C)						
Total	123 814	73 690	50 124	6.1	7.4	4.9
0	3 362	1 888	1 474	...	...	...
1 - 4	770	415	355	...	...	...
5 - 9	473	257	216	0.3	0.3	0.2
10 - 14	527	303	224	0.3	0.3	0.2
15 - 19	1 312	879	433	0.7	0.9	0.4
20 - 24	2 043	1 569	474	1.1	1.7	0.5
25 - 29	2 199	1 666	533	1.4	2.1	0.7
30 - 34	2 112	1 560	552	1.4	2.1	0.7
35 - 39	2 515	1 859	656	1.7	2.5	0.9
40 - 44	3 540	2 670	870	2.5	3.9	1.2
45 - 49	5 149	3 809	1 340	4.2	6.4	2.1
50 - 54	6 879	4 999	1 880	6.2	9.3	3.3
55 - 59	8 597	6 052	2 545	10.8	16.0	6.1
60 - 64	10 087	6 740	3 347	16.9	23.3	10.9
65 - 69	11 431	7 044	4 387	24.0	32.0	17.1
70 - 74	14 912	8 437	6 475	41.0	49.6	33.4
75 - 79	14 766	7 803	6 963	63.4	70.9	56.6
80 +	33 101	15 707	17 394	163.1	174.5	153.9
80 - 84	15 413	7 616	7 797	...	...	...
85 - 89	10 467	4 915	5 552	...	...	...
90 - 94	4 842	2 216	2 626	...	...	...
95 - 99	1 842	773	1 069	...	...	...
100 +	537	187	350	...	...	...
Unknown - Inconnu	39	33	6	..	..	..
State of Palestine - État de Palestine						
2007 (U)						
Total	9 887	5 697	4 190	...	...	...
0	794	420	374	...	...	...
1 - 4	299	165	134	...	...	...
5 - 9	143	71	72	...	...	...
10 - 14	134	101	33	...	...	...
15 - 19	263	223	40	...	...	...
20 - 24	410	361	49	...	...	...
25 - 29	254	207	47	...	...	...
30 - 34	229	178	51	...	...	...
35 - 39	193	129	64	...	...	...
40 - 44	264	173	91	...	...	...
45 - 49	293	204	89	...	...	...
50 - 54	397	253	144	...	...	...
55 - 59	534	341	193	...	...	...
60 - 64	728	410	318	...	...	...
65 - 69	751	377	374	...	...	...
70 - 74	1 031	534	497	...	...	...
75 - 79	1 069	509	560	...	...	...
80 - 84	937	464	473	...	...	...
85 - 89	617	290	327	...	...	...
90 - 94	317	154	163	...	...	...
95 - 99	117	69	48	...	...	...
100 +	113	64	49	...	...	...
Tajikistan - Tadjikistan[20]						
2011 (U)						
Total	32 909	18 069	14 840	...	...	...
0	3 131	1 775	1 356	...	...	...
1 - 4	848	468	380	...	...	...
5 - 9	247	148	99	...	...	...
10 - 14	231	135	96	...	...	...

19. Deaths by age and sex, age-specific death rates by sex: latest available year, 2003 - 2012
Décès et taux de mortalité selon l'âge et le sexe : dernière année disponible, 2003 - 2012 (continued - suite)

Continent, country or area, date, code and age (in years) / Continent, pays ou zone, date, code et âge (en années)	Number - Nombre			Rate - Taux		
	Both sexes Les deux sexes	Male Masculin	Female Féminin	Both sexes Les deux sexes	Male Masculin	Female Féminin

ASIA - ASIE

Tajikistan - Tadjikistan[20]
2011 (U)

15 - 19	433	256	177	...	...	...
20 - 24	580	356	224	...	...	...
25 - 29	668	410	258	...	...	...
30 - 34	694	438	256	...	...	...
35 - 39	818	533	285	...	...	...
40 - 44	891	541	350	...	...	...
45 - 49	1 274	752	522	...	...	...
50 - 54	1 779	1 109	670	...	...	...
55 - 59	2 021	1 189	832	...	...	...
60 - 64	2 095	1 180	915	...	...	...
65 - 69	2 031	1 228	803	...	...	...
70 - 74	4 078	2 230	1 848	...	...	...
75 - 79	4 289	2 211	2 078	...	...	...
80 - 84	3 824	1 975	1 849	...	...	...
85 - 89	1 857	803	1 054	...	...	...
90 - 94	777	241	536	...	...	...
95 - 99	200	51	149	...	...	...
100 +	132	34	98	...	...	...
Unknown - Inconnu	11	6	5	..	..	..

Thailand - Thaïlande
2011 (+U)

Total	414 670	235 189	179 481	...	...	...
0	5 275	2 964	2 311	...	...	...
1 - 4	7 182	4 102	3 080	...	...	...
5 - 9	1 616	978	638	...	...	...
10 - 14	2 060	1 317	743	...	...	...
15 - 19	5 140	3 896	1 244	...	...	...
20 - 24	5 659	4 383	1 276	...	...	...
25 - 29	7 307	5 531	1 776	...	...	...
30 - 34	10 659	7 862	2 797	...	...	...
35 - 39	13 981	10 135	3 846	...	...	...
40 - 44	18 346	12 894	5 452	...	...	...
45 - 49	23 390	16 016	7 374	...	...	...
50 - 54	27 255	18 201	9 054	...	...	...
55 - 59	29 801	19 075	10 726	...	...	...
60 - 64	33 121	20 047	13 074	...	...	...
65 - 69	34 744	20 202	14 542	...	...	...
70 +	189 134	87 586	101 548	...	...	...

Turkey - Turquie
2009 (U)

Total	367 971	203 096	164 875	...	...	...
0 - 4	21 918	11 839	10 079	...	...	...
0	17 354	9 417	7 937	...	...	...
1 - 4	4 564	2 422	2 142	...	...	...
5 - 9	3 433	1 804	1 629	...	...	...
10 - 14	2 541	1 452	1 089	...	...	...
15 - 19	3 412	2 250	1 162	...	...	...
20 - 24	3 585	2 424	1 161	...	...	...
25 - 29	4 166	2 789	1 377	...	...	...
30 - 34	4 269	2 756	1 513	...	...	...
35 - 39	5 554	3 514	2 040	...	...	...
40 - 44	7 777	5 075	2 702	...	...	...
45 - 49	11 929	7 944	3 985	...	...	...
50 - 54	16 711	11 618	5 093	...	...	...
55 - 59	21 603	14 932	6 671	...	...	...
60 - 64	26 201	17 153	9 048	...	...	...
65 - 69	33 378	20 622	12 756	...	...	...
70 - 74	41 469	23 611	17 858	...	...	...
75 - 79	61 705	33 198	28 507	...	...	...
80 - 84	53 694	23 719	29 975	...	...	...
85 - 89	28 151	10 990	17 161	...	...	...
90 - 94	10 286	3 336	6 950	...	...	...
Unknown - Inconnu	961	728	233	..	..	..

19. Deaths by age and sex, age-specific death rates by sex: latest available year, 2003 - 2012
Décès et taux de mortalité selon l'âge et le sexe : dernière année disponible, 2003 - 2012 (continued - suite)

Continent, country or area, date, code and age (in years) / Continent, pays ou zone, date, code et âge (en années)	Number - Nombre			Rate - Taux		
	Both sexes Les deux sexes	Male Masculin	Female Féminin	Both sexes Les deux sexes	Male Masculin	Female Féminin
ASIA - ASIE						
United Arab Emirates - Émirats arabes unis[31]						
2003 (...)						
Total	6 002	4 305	1 697	...	...	...
0	477	272	205	...	...	...
1 - 4	132	74	58	...	...	...
5 - 9	94	59	35	...	...	...
10 - 14	79	57	22	...	...	...
15 - 19	174	134	40	...	...	...
20 - 24	253	221	32	...	...	...
25 - 29	302	249	53	...	...	...
30 - 34	297	256	41	...	...	...
35 - 39	308	269	39	...	...	...
40 - 44	405	347	58	...	...	...
45 - 49	515	437	78	...	...	...
50 - 54	502	411	91	...	...	...
55 - 59	357	284	73	...	...	...
60 - 64	565	348	217	...	...	...
65 - 69	418	225	193	...	...	...
70 - 74	386	204	182	...	...	...
75 - 79	244	147	97	...	...	...
80 +	378	209	169	...	...	...
Unknown - Inconnu	116	102	14	..	..	..
EUROPE						
Åland Islands - Îles d'Åland						
2011 (C)						
Total	277	132	145	9.8	9.4	10.3
0	-	-	-	-	-	-
1 - 4	-	-	-	-	-	-
5 - 9	-	-	-	-	-	-
10 - 14	-	-	-	-	-	-
15 - 19	1	1	-	♦0.6	♦1.2	-
20 - 24	-	-	-	-	-	-
25 - 29	-	-	-	-	-	-
30 - 34	1	1	-	♦0.6	♦1.2	-
35 - 39	2	2	-	♦1.1	♦2.1	-
40 - 44	-	-	-	-	-	-
45 - 49	1	1	-	♦0.5	♦1.0	-
50 - 54	5	4	1	♦2.6	♦4.3	♦1.0
55 - 59	11	6	5	♦5.3	♦6.0	♦4.7
60 - 64	13	6	7	♦6.3	♦5.9	♦6.8
65 - 69	21	12	9	♦12.4	♦13.6	♦11.0
70 - 74	22	16	6	♦18.7	♦26.9	♦10.3
75 - 79	33	21	12	35.6	♦49.6	♦23.8
80 - 84	40	23	17	57.2	♦77.2	♦42.3
85 - 89	62	26	36	126.8	♦159.0	110.6
90 - 94	35	6	29	184.7	♦146.3	♦195.3
95 - 99	21	7	14	♦350.0	♦583.3	♦291.7
100 +	9	-	9	♦1200.0	-	♦1384.6
Albania - Albanie						
2004 (C)						
Total	17 749	9 950	7 799	5.9	6.6	5.2
0	336	181	155	...	...	...
1 - 4	237	132	105	...	...	...
5 - 9	164	108	56	0.6	0.8	0.4
10 - 14	140	86	54	0.5	0.6	0.4
15 - 19	157	106	51	0.5	0.7	0.3
20 - 24	219	147	72	0.9	1.2	0.6
25 - 29	181	140	41	1.0	1.6	0.4
30 - 34	225	159	66	1.2	1.8	0.7
35 - 39	244	160	84	1.2	1.7	0.8
40 - 44	365	249	116	1.7	2.3	1.1
45 - 49	469	313	156	2.4	3.1	1.6
50 - 54	586	397	189	3.8	5.1	2.5
55 - 59	676	451	225	5.6	7.2	3.8

19. Deaths by age and sex, age-specific death rates by sex: latest available year, 2003 - 2012
Décès et taux de mortalité selon l'âge et le sexe : dernière année disponible, 2003 - 2012 (continued - suite)

Continent, country or aréa, date, code and age (in years) / Continent, pays ou zone, date, code et âge (en années)	Number - Nombre			Rate - Taux		
	Both sexes Les deux sexes	Male Masculin	Female Féminin	Both sexes Les deux sexes	Male Masculin	Female Féminin
EUROPE						
Albania - Albanie						
2004 (C)						
60 - 64	1 248	820	428	10.6	13.8	7.2
65 - 69	1 720	1 158	562	17.2	22.7	11.5
70 - 74	2 428	1 478	950	33.7	41.8	25.9
75 - 79	2 608	1 462	1 146	56.2	69.9	45.0
80 - 84	2 768	1 256	1 512	106.8	121.5	97.1
85 +	2 978	1 147	1 831	208.5	247.2	189.9
85 - 89	1 652	719	933	...	...	...
90 - 94	936	298	638	...	...	...
95 - 99	300	103	197	...	...	...
100 +	90	27	63	...	...	...
2007 (C)						
Total	14 528	...	...	4.9	...	...
0 - 4	289	...	...	1.5	...	...
0	205	...	...	...	...	...
1 - 4	84	...	...	...	...	...
5 - 9	87	...	...	0.4	...	...
10 - 14	99	...	...	0.4	...	...
15 - 19	137	...	...	0.4	...	...
20 - 24	159	...	...	0.6	...	...
25 - 29	161	...	...	0.9	...	...
30 - 34	165	...	...	1.0	...	...
35 - 39	198	...	...	1.0	...	...
40 - 44	238	...	...	1.2	...	...
45 - 49	398	...	...	1.9	...	...
50 - 54	539	...	...	3.2	...	...
55 - 59	626	...	...	4.5	...	...
60 - 64	741	...	...	6.8	...	...
65 - 69	1 348	...	...	12.5	...	...
70 - 74	1 884	...	...	23.2	...	...
75 - 79	2 371	...	...	45.1	...	...
80 - 84	2 121	...	...	78.2	...	...
85 +	2 954	...	...	162.6	...	...
Unknown - Inconnu	13	...	...	..	..	..
Andorra - Andorre						
2010 (C)						
Total	239	138	101	2.8	3.1	2.5
0 - 4	1	-	1	♦0.3	-	♦0.6
0	-	-	-	-	-	-
1 - 4	1	-	1	♦0.3	-	♦0.7
5 - 9	-	-	-	-	-	-
10 - 14	2	1	1	♦0.5	♦0.5	♦0.5
15 - 19	1	1	-	♦0.3	♦0.5	-
20 - 24	1	1	-	♦0.2	♦0.5	-
25 - 29	2	2	-	♦0.3	♦0.7	-
30 - 34	1	1	-	♦0.1	♦0.3	-
35 - 39	-	-	-	-	-	-
40 - 44	8	4	4	♦1.0	♦1.0	♦1.1
45 - 49	9	5	4	♦1.2	♦1.2	♦1.1
50 - 54	6	4	2	♦0.9	♦1.2	♦0.7
55 - 59	15	11	4	♦2.9	♦4.0	♦1.7
60 - 64	19	15	4	♦4.4	♦6.3	♦2.1
65 - 69	22	18	4	♦6.9	♦10.5	♦2.7
70 - 74	14	8	6	♦5.8	♦6.6	♦5.1
75 - 79	17	11	6	♦8.4	♦10.6	♦6.1
80 - 84	41	24	17	23.6	♦30.1	♦18.1
85 - 89	33	17	16	29.9	♦33.4	♦26.9
90 - 94	27	9	18	♦52.8	♦41.1	♦61.6
95 - 99	17	5	12	♦67.5	♦42.4	♦89.6
100 +	3	1	2	♦14.0	♦9.5	♦18.3
Austria - Autriche[33]						
2011 (C)						
Total	76 479	36 539	39 940	9.1	8.9	9.3
0 - 4	337	213	124	0.9	1.1	0.6
0	281	176	105	3.6	4.4	2.8
1 - 4	56	37	19	0.2	0.2	♦0.1

19. Deaths by age and sex, age-specific death rates by sex: latest available year, 2003 - 2012
Décès et taux de mortalité selon l'âge et le sexe : dernière année disponible, 2003 - 2012 (continued - suite)

Continent, country or area, date, code and age (in years) / Continent, pays ou zone, date, code et âge (en années)	Number - Nombre			Rate - Taux		
	Both sexes / Les deux sexes	Male / Masculin	Female / Féminin	Both sexes / Les deux sexes	Male / Masculin	Female / Féminin

EUROPE

Austria - Autriche[33]
2011 (C)

5 - 9	36	17	19	0.1	♦0.1	♦0.1
10 - 14	35	19	16	0.1	♦0.1	♦0.1
15 - 19	173	121	52	0.4	0.5	0.2
20 - 24	271	200	71	0.5	0.7	0.3
25 - 29	268	179	89	0.5	0.6	0.3
30 - 34	296	208	88	0.5	0.8	0.3
35 - 39	406	274	132	0.7	1.0	0.5
40 - 44	787	523	264	1.1	1.5	0.8
45 - 49	1 466	934	532	2.1	2.6	1.5
50 - 54	2 172	1 427	745	3.5	4.6	2.4
55 - 59	2 838	1 845	993	5.5	7.3	3.8
60 - 64	4 341	2 875	1 466	9.1	12.5	5.9
65 - 69	5 454	3 465	1 989	13.2	17.9	9.1
70 - 74	7 288	4 471	2 817	18.3	24.5	13.0
75 - 79	8 679	4 903	3 776	32.9	44.1	24.8
80 - 84	13 404	6 421	6 983	61.5	77.9	51.5
85 - 89	15 900	5 339	10 561	112.9	135.8	104.1
90 - 94	8 597	2 359	6 238	195.9	226.9	186.2
95 - 99	3 204	660	2 544	330.9	353.8	325.4
100 +	527	86	441	465.5	439.9	470.9

Belarus - Bélarus
2011 (C)

Total	135 090	71 349	63 741	14.2	16.2	12.6
0 - 4	549	319	230	1.1	1.2	0.9
0	420	240	180	3.9	4.3	3.4
1 - 4	129	79	50	0.3	0.4	0.3
5 - 9	81	50	31	0.2	0.2	0.1
10 - 14	99	66	33	0.2	0.3	0.1
15 - 19	328	230	98	0.6	0.8	0.3
20 - 24	804	653	151	1.1	1.7	0.4
25 - 29	1 363	1 096	267	1.8	2.8	0.7
30 - 34	2 007	1 564	443	2.9	4.6	1.3
35 - 39	2 639	2 080	559	4.0	6.4	1.6
40 - 44	3 650	2 801	849	5.6	8.9	2.5
45 - 49	5 477	4 201	1 276	7.4	11.9	3.3
50 - 54	8 770	6 595	2 175	11.4	18.4	5.3
55 - 59	10 515	7 423	3 092	16.7	26.5	8.8
60 - 64	12 582	8 783	3 799	24.8	40.9	13.0
65 - 69	9 028	5 776	3 252	29.6	49.6	17.3
70 - 74	16 985	9 212	7 773	41.7	66.6	28.9
75 - 79	18 694	8 278	10 416	66.9	98.5	53.3
80 - 84	21 515	7 551	13 964	102.4	137.2	90.0
85 +	19 931	4 614	15 317	188.2	221.0	180.2
85 - 89	13 921	3 406	10 515	...	...	...
90 - 94	4 408	939	3 469	...	...	...
95 - 99	1 318	219	1 099	...	...	...
100 +	284	50	234	...	...	...
Unknown - Inconnu	73	57	16	..	..	..

Belgium - Belgique[34]
2010 (C)

Total	105 094	52 023	53 071	9.7	9.8	9.6
0 - 4	566	339	227	0.9	1.1	0.7
0	463	275	188	3.7	4.2	3.0
1 - 4	103	64	39	0.2	0.2	0.2
5 - 9	49	31	18	0.1	0.1	♦0.1
10 - 14	69	43	26	0.1	0.1	♦0.1
15 - 19	190	132	58	0.3	0.4	0.2
20 - 24	353	256	97	0.5	0.8	0.3
25 - 29	438	305	133	0.6	0.9	0.4
30 - 34	470	321	149	0.7	0.9	0.4
35 - 39	722	468	254	1.0	1.2	0.7
40 - 44	1 114	687	427	1.4	1.7	1.1
45 - 49	1 950	1 211	739	2.4	2.9	1.8
50 - 54	3 042	1 880	1 162	4.0	4.9	3.0
55 - 59	4 202	2 701	1 501	6.1	7.9	4.3

19. Deaths by age and sex, age-specific death rates by sex: latest available year, 2003 - 2012
Décès et taux de mortalité selon l'âge et le sexe : dernière année disponible, 2003 - 2012 (continued - suite)

Continent, country or area, date, code and age (in years) / Continent, pays ou zone, date, code et âge (en années)	Number - Nombre			Rate - Taux		
	Both sexes Les deux sexes	Male Masculin	Female Féminin	Both sexes Les deux sexes	Male Masculin	Female Féminin
EUROPE						
Belgium - Belgique[34]						
2010 (C)						
60 - 64	6 020	3 864	2 156	9.5	12.4	6.7
65 - 69	6 505	4 078	2 427	14.0	18.3	10.0
70 - 74	9 372	5 762	3 610	20.7	27.8	14.7
75 - 79	14 487	8 187	6 300	35.5	47.4	26.8
80 - 84	19 597	9 498	10 099	65.8	84.9	54.3
85 - 89	21 065	8 345	12 720	119.6	149.5	105.8
90 - 94	9 661	2 889	6 772	218.9	262.1	204.5
95 - 99	4 448	923	3 525	326.7	384.1	314.4
100 +	774	103	671	496.5	553.8	488.7
Bosnia and Herzegovina - Bosnie-Herzégovine						
2010 (C)						
Total	35 118	17 900	17 218	9.1	9.5	8.8
0 - 4	252	143	109	1.5	1.7	1.3
0	216	125	91	...	...	...
1 - 4	36	18	18	0.3	♦0.3	♦0.3
5 - 9	28	19	9	♦0.1	♦0.2	♦0.1
10 - 14	27	14	13	♦0.1	♦0.1	♦0.1
15 - 19	84	58	26	0.3	0.4	♦0.2
20 - 24	120	92	28	0.4	0.6	♦0.2
25 - 29	165	130	35	0.6	1.0	0.3
30 - 34	160	109	51	0.7	0.9	0.4
35 - 39	254	180	74	1.0	1.5	0.6
40 - 44	432	265	167	1.5	1.9	1.2
45 - 49	844	553	291	2.7	3.7	1.9
50 - 54	1 465	980	485	5.5	7.2	3.7
55 - 59	2 141	1 429	712	9.2	13.6	5.6
60 - 64	2 610	1 647	963	14.3	19.1	10.0
65 - 69	3 390	2 032	1 358	16.8	22.6	12.1
70 - 74	6 045	3 199	2 846	32.8	38.8	27.9
75 - 79	6 948	3 344	3 604	57.7	66.1	51.6
80 - 84	6 006	2 440	3 566	125.3	124.5	125.9
85 +	4 119	1 254	2 865	164.3	175.6	159.9
85 - 89	3 105	966	2 139	...	...	...
90 - 94	737	210	527	...	...	...
95 - 99	245	69	176	...	...	...
100 +	32	9	23	...	...	...
Unknown - Inconnu	28	12	16	..	..	..
Bulgaria - Bulgarie						
2011 (C)						
Total	108 258	56 634	51 624	14.7	15.8	13.7
0 - 4	723	420	303	2.1	2.4	1.8
0	601	349	252	9.0	10.2	7.8
1 - 4	122	71	51	0.4	0.5	0.4
5 - 9	65	30	35	0.2	♦0.2	0.2
10 - 14	66	41	25	0.2	0.3	♦0.2
15 - 19	180	116	64	0.5	0.6	0.4
20 - 24	319	236	83	0.7	0.9	0.4
25 - 29	387	282	105	0.8	1.1	0.4
30 - 34	568	420	148	1.1	1.5	0.6
35 - 39	863	553	310	1.6	2.0	1.2
40 - 44	1 355	889	466	2.6	3.3	1.9
45 - 49	2 236	1 572	664	4.6	6.3	2.7
50 - 54	3 783	2 705	1 078	7.4	10.6	4.2
55 - 59	5 917	4 199	1 718	11.3	16.6	6.3
60 - 64	8 731	5 953	2 778	16.3	24.2	9.6
65 - 69	9 788	6 262	3 526	23.1	33.6	14.8
70 - 74	12 461	7 201	5 260	36.3	50.5	26.3
75 - 79	18 388	9 149	9 239	60.6	76.3	50.4
80 - 84	20 333	8 726	11 607	106.7	122.6	97.3
85 - 89	15 746	5 813	9 933	177.8	190.6	171.1
90 - 94	5 088	1 694	3 394	271.4	279.4	267.5
95 - 99	1 127	334	793	398.1	400.5	397.1
100 +	134	39	95	489.1	398.0	539.8

Continent, country or area, date, code and age (in years) Continent, pays ou zone, date, code et âge (en annèes)	Number - Nombre			Rate - Taux		
	Both sexes Les deux sexes	Male Masculin	Female Féminin	Both sexes Les deux sexes	Male Masculin	Female Féminin
EUROPE						
Croatia - Croatie						
2011 (C)						
Total	51 019	25 184	25 835	11.6	11.8	11.3
0 - 4	217	121	96	1.0	1.1	0.9
0	192	107	85	4.4	4.8	4.1
1 - 4	25	14	11	◊0.1	◊0.2	◊0.1
5 - 9	23	12	11	◊0.1	◊0.1	◊0.1
10 - 14	25	18	7	◊0.1	◊0.1	◊0.1
15 - 19	94	72	22	0.4	0.6	◊0.2
20 - 24	137	111	26	0.5	0.8	◊0.2
25 - 29	171	129	42	0.6	0.8	0.3
30 - 34	217	153	64	0.7	1.0	0.4
35 - 39	275	197	78	0.9	1.3	0.5
40 - 44	473	332	141	1.6	2.2	0.9
45 - 49	945	625	320	3.0	4.0	2.0
50 - 54	1 701	1 190	511	5.2	7.4	3.1
55 - 59	2 657	1 878	779	8.4	12.1	4.8
60 - 64	3 415	2 405	1 010	12.6	18.8	7.1
65 - 69	3 836	2 436	1 400	18.8	27.0	12.3
70 - 74	6 273	3 622	2 651	29.6	40.9	21.5
75 - 79	9 188	4 654	4 534	52.9	71.2	41.8
80 - 84	10 097	4 041	6 056	95.0	114.3	85.3
85 +	11 268	3 184	8 084	194.2	216.7	186.6
85 - 89	7 654	2 301	5 353	...	...	...
90 - 94	2 748	702	2 046	...	...	...
95 - 99	762	163	599	...	...	...
100 +	104	18	86	...	...	...
Unknown - Inconnu	7	4	3	..	..	..
Czech Republic - République tchèque						
2011 (C)						
Total	106 848	54 141	52 707	10.2	10.5	9.9
0 - 4	375	224	151	0.6	0.7	0.5
0	298	174	124	2.5	2.8	2.1
1 - 4	77	50	27	0.2	0.2	◊0.1
5 - 9	41	23	18	0.1	◊0.1	◊0.1
10 - 14	54	25	29	0.1	◊0.1	◊0.1
15 - 19	210	144	66	0.4	0.5	0.2
20 - 24	381	287	94	0.6	0.8	0.3
25 - 29	376	291	85	0.5	0.8	0.2
30 - 34	590	424	166	0.7	0.9	0.4
35 - 39	886	617	269	1.0	1.4	0.6
40 - 44	1 173	788	385	1.7	2.2	1.1
45 - 49	1 881	1 299	582	2.7	3.7	1.7
50 - 54	3 215	2 274	941	4.8	6.7	2.8
55 - 59	5 993	4 134	1 859	7.9	11.2	4.8
60 - 64	9 327	6 340	2 987	12.5	17.9	7.6
65 - 69	10 848	6 940	3 908	19.6	27.6	12.9
70 - 74	10 933	6 373	4 560	28.4	38.8	20.7
75 - 79	14 423	7 427	6 996	46.0	60.7	36.7
80 - 84	19 271	8 121	11 150	83.2	101.8	73.4
85 - 89	17 900	6 039	11 861	147.3	173.6	136.7
90 - 94	6 770	1 888	4 882	264.0	298.1	252.8
95 - 99	1 948	439	1 509	342.7	372.0	335.0
100 +	253	44	209	475.6	403.7	494.1
Denmark - Danemark[35]						
2011 (C)						
Total	52 516	25 939	26 577	9.4	9.4	9.5
0 - 4	248	130	118	0.8	0.8	0.8
0	208	107	101	3.4	3.4	3.3
1 - 4	40	23	17	0.2	◊0.2	◊0.1
5 - 9	30	11	19	◊0.1	◊0.1	◊0.1
10 - 14	30	17	13	◊0.1	◊0.1	◊0.1
15 - 19	82	55	27	0.2	0.3	◊0.2
20 - 24	129	90	39	0.4	0.5	0.2
25 - 29	105	80	25	0.3	0.5	◊0.2
30 - 34	191	134	57	0.6	0.8	0.3
35 - 39	307	220	87	0.8	1.1	0.4

19. Deaths by age and sex, age-specific death rates by sex: latest available year, 2003 - 2012
Décès et taux de mortalité selon l'âge et le sexe : dernière année disponible, 2003 - 2012 (continued - suite)

Continent, country or area, date, code and age (in years) / Continent, pays ou zone, date, code et âge (en annèes)	Number - Nombre			Rate - Taux		
	Both sexes Les deux sexes	Male Masculin	Female Féminin	Both sexes Les deux sexes	Male Masculin	Female Féminin
EUROPE						
Denmark - Danemark[35]						
2011 (C)						
40 - 44	518	329	189	1.3	1.6	1.0
45 - 49	977	590	387	2.3	2.8	1.9
50 - 54	1 449	889	560	3.9	4.8	3.1
55 - 59	2 251	1 387	864	6.4	7.9	4.9
60 - 64	3 397	2 050	1 347	9.5	11.6	7.5
65 - 69	4 773	2 907	1 866	14.4	17.8	11.1
70 - 74	5 393	3 092	2 301	23.8	28.8	19.3
75 - 79	6 918	3 747	3 171	41.9	50.6	34.8
80 - 84	8 146	3 978	4 168	69.5	83.0	60.2
85 - 89	8 610	3 624	4 986	117.6	145.5	103.2
90 - 94	6 163	2 022	4 141	200.3	242.5	184.6
95 - 99	2 328	518	1 810	313.6	346.5	305.3
100 +	471	69	402	523.3	492.9	528.9
Estonia - Estonie						
2011 (C)						
Total	15 244	7 483	7 761	11.4	12.1	10.7
0 - 4	47	24	23	0.6	♦0.6	♦0.6
0	36	18	18	2.4	♦2.3	♦2.4
1 - 4	11	6	5	♦0.2	♦0.2	♦0.2
5 - 9	7	5	2	♦0.1	♦0.1	♦0.1
10 - 14	19	12	7	♦0.3	♦0.4	♦0.2
15 - 19	30	18	12	♦0.4	♦0.5	♦0.3
20 - 24	79	65	14	0.8	1.2	♦0.3
25 - 29	138	114	24	1.3	2.2	♦0.5
30 - 34	162	136	26	1.7	2.8	♦0.6
35 - 39	159	110	49	1.7	2.4	1.1
40 - 44	262	192	70	2.9	4.4	1.5
45 - 49	392	285	107	4.4	6.7	2.3
50 - 54	586	423	163	6.3	9.8	3.2
55 - 59	843	616	227	9.7	16.0	4.7
60 - 64	1 109	772	337	14.1	23.4	7.4
65 - 69	1 227	809	418	21.0	35.2	11.8
70 - 74	1 853	1 048	805	28.6	45.7	19.3
75 - 79	2 124	997	1 127	44.6	66.0	34.6
80 - 84	2 668	1 032	1 636	75.2	106.8	63.3
85 - 89	2 192	543	1 649	129.0	154.4	122.3
90 - 94	938	182	756	217.3	233.9	213.6
95 - 99	331	70	261	269.1	300.4	261.8
100 +	55	11	44	132.5	♦139.2	131.0
Unknown - Inconnu	23	19	4	..	..	..
Faeroe Islands - Îles Féroé						
2008 (C)						
Total	378	201	177	7.8	8.0	7.6
0	2	1	1	♦2.9	♦3.0	♦2.9
1 - 4	1	1	-	♦0.4	♦0.7	-
5 - 9	-	-	-	-	-	-
10 - 14	-	-	-	-	-	-
15 - 19	1	-	1	♦0.3	-	♦0.5
20 - 24	-	-	-	-	-	-
25 - 29	1	1	-	♦0.4	♦0.7	-
30 - 34	2	1	1	♦0.7	♦0.6	♦0.7
35 - 39	2	1	1	♦0.6	♦0.6	♦0.7
40 - 44	2	2	-	♦0.6	♦1.0	-
45 - 49	7	5	2	♦2.1	♦2.9	♦1.3
50 - 54	7	4	3	♦2.3	♦2.5	♦2.1
55 - 59	20	16	4	♦6.7	♦10.3	♦2.8
60 - 64	24	17	7	♦9.5	♦12.3	♦6.1
65 - 69	26	17	9	♦12.7	♦15.8	♦9.2
70 - 74	34	19	15	22.3	♦24.3	♦20.3
75 - 79	46	32	14	33.9	50.4	♦19.4
80 - 84	69	33	36	68.8	85.5	58.3
85 - 89	71	32	39	120.3	158.4	100.5
90 - 94	38	11	27	154.5	♦135.8	♦163.6
95 - 99	19	6	13	♦422.2	♦545.5	♦382.4
100 +	6	2	4	♦1200.0	♦666.7	♦2000.0

19. Deaths by age and sex, age-specific death rates by sex: latest available year, 2003 - 2012
Décès et taux de mortalité selon l'âge et le sexe : dernière année disponible, 2003 - 2012 (continued - suite)

Continent, country or area, date, code and age (in years) Continent, pays ou zone, date, code et âge (en années)	Number - Nombre			Rate - Taux		
	Both sexes Les deux sexes	Male Masculin	Female Féminin	Both sexes Les deux sexes	Male Masculin	Female Féminin
EUROPE						
Finland - Finlande						
2011 (C)						
Total..........	50 585	25 335	25 250	9.4	9.6	9.3
0 - 4..........	182	104	78	0.6	0.7	0.5
0..........	143	79	64	2.4	2.6	2.2
1 - 4..........	39	25	14	0.2	♦0.2	♦0.1
5 - 9..........	28	15	13	♦0.1	♦0.1	♦0.1
10 - 14..........	30	14	16	♦0.1	♦0.1	♦0.1
15 - 19..........	118	89	29	0.4	0.5	♦0.2
20 - 24..........	201	146	55	0.6	0.9	0.3
25 - 29..........	246	191	55	0.7	1.1	0.3
30 - 34..........	267	198	69	0.8	1.1	0.4
35 - 39..........	319	228	91	1.0	1.4	0.6
40 - 44..........	492	349	143	1.4	2.0	0.8
45 - 49..........	900	632	268	2.4	3.3	1.4
50 - 54..........	1 518	1 042	476	4.1	5.6	2.6
55 - 59..........	2 368	1 635	733	6.2	8.7	3.8
60 - 64..........	3 572	2 418	1 154	9.0	12.4	5.7
65 - 69..........	3 787	2 474	1 313	13.2	18.0	8.7
70 - 74..........	4 517	2 873	1 644	19.6	27.6	13.0
75 - 79..........	6 005	3 481	2 524	33.5	46.3	24.3
80 - 84..........	8 690	4 163	4 527	61.1	80.6	50.0
85 - 89..........	9 130	3 272	5 858	113.2	139.8	102.3
90 - 94..........	5 840	1 544	4 296	205.4	241.2	195.0
95 - 99..........	2 049	409	1 640	334.3	380.5	324.5
100 +..........	326	58	268	513.0	651.7	490.4
France[36]						
2011 (C)						
Total..........	534 795	272 470	262 325	8.5	8.9	8.1
0 - 4..........	3 109	1 712	1 397	0.8	0.9	0.7
0..........	2 604	1 437	1 167	3.3	3.6	3.1
1 - 4..........	505	275	230	0.2	0.2	0.2
5 - 9..........	325	188	137	0.1	0.1	0.1
10 - 14..........	363	218	145	0.1	0.1	0.1
15 - 19..........	1 114	784	330	0.3	0.4	0.2
20 - 24..........	1 889	1 428	461	0.5	0.7	0.2
25 - 29..........	2 159	1 618	541	0.6	0.8	0.3
30 - 34..........	2 559	1 802	757	0.7	0.9	0.4
35 - 39..........	4 163	2 859	1 304	1.0	1.3	0.6
40 - 44..........	6 768	4 495	2 273	1.6	2.1	1.0
45 - 49..........	11 026	7 218	3 808	2.5	3.3	1.7
50 - 54..........	17 406	11 675	5 731	4.1	5.7	2.7
55 - 59..........	24 547	16 791	7 756	6.0	8.5	3.7
60 - 64..........	32 765	22 297	10 468	8.1	11.4	5.0
65 - 69..........	30 542	20 449	10 093	11.7	16.4	7.4
70 - 74..........	38 580	24 669	13 911	16.2	22.9	10.7
75 - 79..........	60 226	35 352	24 874	27.0	37.8	19.2
80 - 84..........	87 574	44 799	42 775	49.1	66.6	38.5
85 - 89..........	105 961	44 421	61 540	92.0	119.8	78.8
90 - 94..........	64 912	21 578	43 334	176.0	217.0	160.8
95 - 99..........	30 931	7 006	23 925	271.2	322.0	259.2
100 +..........	7 876	1 111	6 765	441.5	471.8	436.9
Germany - Allemagne						
2011 (C)						
Total..........	852 328	407 628	444 700	10.4	10.2	10.7
0 - 4..........	2 871	1 603	1 268	0.8	0.9	0.8
0..........	2 408	1 347	1 061	3.6	3.9	3.2
1 - 4..........	463	256	207	0.2	0.2	0.2
5 - 9..........	311	163	148	0.1	0.1	0.1
10 - 14..........	395	229	166	0.1	0.1	0.1
15 - 19..........	1 034	718	316	0.3	0.3	0.2
20 - 24..........	1 922	1 430	492	0.4	0.6	0.2
25 - 29..........	2 031	1 425	606	0.4	0.6	0.2
30 - 34..........	2 607	1 775	832	0.5	0.7	0.3
35 - 39..........	3 564	2 314	1 250	0.7	0.9	0.5
40 - 44..........	7 946	5 106	2 840	1.2	1.5	0.9
45 - 49..........	15 378	9 849	5 529	2.2	2.7	1.6

19. Deaths by age and sex, age-specific death rates by sex: latest available year, 2003 - 2012

Décès et taux de mortalité selon l'âge et le sexe : dernière année disponible, 2003 - 2012 (continued - suite)

Continent, country or area, date, code and age (in years) / Continent, pays ou zone, date, code et âge (en années)	Number - Nombre			Rate - Taux		
	Both sexes Les deux sexes	Male Masculin	Female Féminin	Both sexes Les deux sexes	Male Masculin	Female Féminin
EUROPE						
Germany - Allemagne						
2011 (C)						
50 - 54	24 003	15 653	8 350	3.8	4.9	2.7
55 - 59	33 128	21 702	11 426	6.0	7.9	4.1
60 - 64	43 196	27 804	15 392	9.0	11.9	6.3
65 - 69	56 554	36 262	20 292	13.4	17.9	9.3
70 - 74	99 375	61 228	38 147	20.0	26.6	14.3
75 - 79	117 121	66 126	50 995	35.1	45.6	27.0
80 - 84	151 448	71 693	79 755	64.1	79.6	54.6
85 - 89	158 614	52 563	106 051	116.2	135.6	108.6
90 - 94	88 324	22 529	65 795	201.0	214.4	196.8
95 - 99	35 783	6 545	29 238	316.7	224.4	348.8
100 +	6 590	846	5 744	87.2	28.9	124.0
Unknown - Inconnu	133	65	68	..	..	..
Greece - Grèce						
2011 (C)						
Total	111 099	57 999	53 100	9.8	10.4	9.3
0 - 4	437	247	190	0.8	0.8	0.7
0	357	197	160	3.2	3.5	3.0
1 - 4	80	50	30	0.2	0.2	♦0.1
5 - 9	55	34	21	0.1	0.1	♦0.1
10 - 14	73	37	36	0.1	0.1	0.1
15 - 19	186	129	57	0.3	0.4	0.2
20 - 24	364	280	84	0.6	0.9	0.3
25 - 29	429	341	88	0.6	0.9	0.3
30 - 34	574	410	164	0.7	0.9	0.4
35 - 39	727	491	236	0.8	1.1	0.6
40 - 44	1 143	810	333	1.3	1.8	0.8
45 - 49	1 747	1 198	549	2.2	3.0	1.4
50 - 54	2 648	1 832	816	3.4	4.7	2.0
55 - 59	3 794	2 653	1 141	5.3	7.6	3.1
60 - 64	5 071	3 469	1 602	7.6	10.8	4.6
65 - 69	6 404	4 339	2 065	11.6	16.8	7.0
70 - 74	10 238	6 416	3 822	18.4	26.2	12.2
75 - 79	16 923	9 484	7 439	33.3	43.5	25.7
80 - 84	23 684	11 426	12 258	65.4	75.4	58.2
85 - 89	20 497	8 528	11 969	126.4	124.3	128.0
90 - 94	10 955	4 141	6 814	229.5	169.8	291.8
95 - 99	4 314	1 510	2 804	843.2	461.4	1521.4
100 +	836	224	612	248.0	104.4	499.2
Unknown - Inconnu	-	-	-	..	..	..
Hungary - Hongrie						
2011 (C)						
Total	128 795	63 883	64 912	12.9	13.5	12.4
0 - 4	523	273	250	1.1	1.1	1.1
0	433	240	193	4.9	5.3	4.5
1 - 4	90	33	57	0.2	0.2	0.3
5 - 9	47	28	19	0.1	♦0.1	♦0.1
10 - 14	60	37	23	0.1	0.1	♦0.1
15 - 19	199	134	65	0.3	0.5	0.2
20 - 24	288	215	73	0.4	0.7	0.2
25 - 29	333	242	91	0.5	0.7	0.3
30 - 34	563	397	166	0.7	1.0	0.4
35 - 39	930	629	301	1.2	1.5	0.8
40 - 44	1 704	1 154	550	2.4	3.2	1.6
45 - 49	2 973	2 015	958	5.0	6.9	3.2
50 - 54	5 806	4 007	1 799	8.9	12.9	5.3
55 - 59	9 863	6 746	3 117	13.1	19.3	7.7
60 - 64	11 319	7 461	3 858	18.0	26.8	11.1
65 - 69	12 131	7 451	4 680	23.7	34.7	15.7
70 - 74	14 426	7 895	6 531	34.4	49.4	25.1
75 - 79	18 124	8 633	9 491	54.3	74.1	43.7
80 - 84	20 988	8 182	12 806	88.8	109.2	79.3
85 - 89	18 286	5 798	12 488	146.7	167.3	138.8
90 +	10 223	2 579	7 644	209.9	192.2	216.6
90 - 94	7 645	1 986	5 659	...	...	...
95 - 99	2 239	525	1 714	...	...	...

Continent, country or area, date, code and age (in years) Continent, pays ou zone, date, code et âge (en années)	Number - Nombre			Rate - Taux		
	Both sexes Les deux sexes	Male Masculin	Female Féminin	Both sexes Les deux sexes	Male Masculin	Female Féminin
EUROPE						
Hungary - Hongrie						
2011 (C)						
100 +	339	68	271	...	...	...
Unknown - Inconnu	9	7	2	..	..	..
Iceland - Islande[37]						
2011 (C)						
Total	1 986	999	987	6.2	6.2	6.2
0 - 4	7	5	2	♦0.3	♦0.4	♦0.2
0	4	3	1	♦0.9	♦1.2	♦0.4
1 - 4	3	2	1	♦0.2	♦0.2	♦0.1
5 - 9	4	3	1	♦0.2	♦0.3	♦0.1
10 - 14	4	2	2	♦0.2	♦0.2	♦0.2
15 - 19	6	4	2	♦0.3	♦0.3	♦0.2
20 - 24	9	5	4	♦0.4	♦0.4	♦0.3
25 - 29	11	9	2	♦0.5	♦0.8	♦0.2
30 - 34	8	7	1	♦0.4	♦0.6	♦0.1
35 - 39	13	9	4	♦0.6	♦0.8	♦0.4
40 - 44	20	13	7	♦1.0	♦1.3	♦0.7
45 - 49	34	22	12	1.5	♦2.0	♦1.1
50 - 54	44	24	20	2.1	♦2.2	♦1.9
55 - 59	69	34	35	3.7	3.6	3.7
60 - 64	105	61	44	6.6	7.5	5.6
65 - 69	129	77	52	10.5	12.6	8.5
70 - 74	160	96	64	18.4	22.9	14.2
75 - 79	272	150	122	35.6	42.5	29.7
80 - 84	353	185	168	57.5	69.2	48.5
85 - 89	361	167	194	104.5	124.9	91.7
90 - 94	259	97	162	204.9	234.3	190.6
95 - 99	100	27	73	383.1	♦394.2	379.2
100 +	18	2	16	♦423.5	♦285.7	♦450.7
Unknown - Inconnu	-	-	-	..	..	..
Ireland - Irlande[38]						
2011 (I)						
Total	27 880	14 211	13 669	6.1	6.3	5.9
0	251	140	111	3.5	3.8	3.1
1 - 4	38	24	14	0.1	♦0.2	♦0.1
5 - 9	27	15	12	♦0.1	♦0.1	♦0.1
10 - 14	21	13	8	♦0.1	♦0.1	♦0.1
15 - 19	97	68	29	0.3	0.5	♦0.2
20 - 24	163	128	35	0.5	0.9	0.2
25 - 29	197	150	47	0.5	0.8	0.2
30 - 34	237	170	67	0.6	0.9	0.3
35 - 39	327	220	107	0.9	1.2	0.6
40 - 44	425	273	152	1.3	1.7	0.9
45 - 49	608	372	236	2.0	2.5	1.5
50 - 54	808	470	338	3.0	3.5	2.5
55 - 59	1 113	686	427	4.6	5.6	3.5
60 - 64	1 710	1 074	636	7.9	9.9	5.9
65 - 69	2 192	1 325	867	12.9	15.7	10.2
70 - 74	2 710	1 634	1 076	20.9	26.1	16.1
75 - 79	3 713	2 069	1 644	36.8	44.8	30.0
80 - 84	4 546	2 296	2 250	65.6	82.1	54.4
85 - 89	4 744	1 915	2 829	119.6	142.4	108.0
90 - 94	2 861	912	1 949	196.8	226.1	185.5
95 - 99	946	227	719	293.5	343.4	280.6
100 +	146	30	116	402.2	♦566.0	374.2
Isle of Man - Île de Man						
2004 (+C)						
Total	798	390	408	10.3	10.2	10.3
0	2	1	1	♦2.3	♦2.3	♦2.4
1 - 4	-	-	-	-	-	-
5 - 9	-	-	-	-	-	-
10 - 14	1	1	-	♦0.2	♦0.4	-
15 - 19	3	3	-	♦0.6	♦1.3	-
20 - 24	5	4	1	♦1.1	♦1.8	♦0.4
25 - 29	3	3	-	♦0.7	♦1.4	-
30 - 34	3	1	2	♦0.6	♦0.4	♦0.7

19. Deaths by age and sex, age-specific death rates by sex: latest available year, 2003 - 2012
Décès et taux de mortalité selon l'âge et le sexe : dernière année disponible, 2003 - 2012 (continued - suite)

Continent, country or area, date, code and age (in years) Continent, pays ou zone, date, code et âge (en années)	Number - Nombre			Rate - Taux		
	Both sexes Les deux sexes	Male Masculin	Female Féminin	Both sexes Les deux sexes	Male Masculin	Female Féminin
EUROPE						
Isle of Man - Île de Man						
2004 (+C)						
35 - 39	6	5	1	♦1.0	♦1.7	♦0.3
40 - 44	7	4	3	♦1.2	♦1.3	♦1.0
45 - 49	11	5	6	♦2.0	♦1.9	♦2.2
50 - 54	17	8	9	♦3.3	♦3.0	♦3.5
55 - 59	31	18	13	5.7	♦6.4	♦5.0
60 - 64	33	19	14	7.8	♦9.1	♦6.6
65 - 69	60	45	15	16.4	25.0	♦8.1
70 - 74	82	46	36	27.1	33.4	21.8
75 - 79	118	59	59	46.0	55.6	39.2
80 - 84	169	77	92	80.5	98.2	70.0
85 - 89	111	43	68	112.2	126.5	104.7
90 +	136	48	88	208.7	278.5	183.6
90 - 94	96	36	60	...	...	...
95 +	40	12	28	...	...	...
Italy - Italie						
2010 (C)						
Total	581 307	282 866	298 441	9.6	9.6	9.6
0 - 4	2 098	1 163	935	0.7	0.8	0.7
0	1 773	992	781	3.2	3.5	2.9
1 - 4	325	171	154	0.1	0.1	0.1
5 - 9	209	119	90	0.1	0.1	0.1
10 - 14	268	149	119	0.1	0.1	0.1
15 - 19	772	548	224	0.3	0.4	0.2
20 - 24	1 039	794	245	0.3	0.5	0.2
25 - 29	1 233	928	305	0.4	0.5	0.2
30 - 34	1 855	1 310	545	0.4	0.6	0.3
35 - 39	2 932	1 912	1 020	0.6	0.8	0.4
40 - 44	4 889	3 044	1 845	1.0	1.2	0.7
45 - 49	7 695	4 776	2 919	1.6	2.0	1.2
50 - 54	10 888	6 707	4 181	2.7	3.3	2.0
55 - 59	15 655	9 992	5 663	4.2	5.5	3.0
60 - 64	25 393	16 488	8 905	6.8	9.1	4.6
65 - 69	33 555	21 519	12 036	10.8	14.7	7.3
70 - 74	53 563	33 319	20 244	17.5	23.8	12.1
75 - 79	78 959	44 619	34 340	31.2	41.4	23.6
80 - 84	111 302	55 468	55 834	58.2	76.4	47.1
85 - 89	123 528	49 725	73 803	106.5	133.9	93.6
90 - 94	63 635	20 295	43 340	188.4	225.2	175.0
95 - 99	35 629	8 916	26 713	295.1	333.6	284.2
100 +	6 210	1 075	5 135	399.1	361.8	407.9
Latvia - Lettonie						
2011 (C)						
Total	28 540	13 857	14 683	13.8	14.6	13.0
0 - 4	152	85	67	1.4	1.5	1.3
0	124	68	56	6.4	6.8	6.0
1 - 4	28	17	11	♦0.3	♦0.4	♦0.3
5 - 9	25	17	8	♦0.3	♦0.3	♦0.2
10 - 14	13	9	4	♦0.1	♦0.2	♦0.1
15 - 19	59	43	16	0.5	0.7	♦0.3
20 - 24	118	89	29	0.8	1.1	♦0.4
25 - 29	175	140	35	1.2	1.9	0.5
30 - 34	246	195	51	1.8	2.9	0.8
35 - 39	350	259	91	2.4	3.7	1.3
40 - 44	501	357	144	3.6	5.2	2.0
45 - 49	863	605	258	5.8	8.5	3.3
50 - 54	1 253	907	346	8.2	12.8	4.2
55 - 59	1 688	1 155	533	12.7	19.8	7.2
60 - 64	2 157	1 429	728	18.1	28.8	10.5
65 - 69	2 706	1 687	1 019	25.4	41.3	15.5
70 - 74	3 735	2 072	1 663	34.2	54.1	23.4
75 - 79	4 128	1 904	2 224	53.9	81.0	41.9
80 - 84	4 786	1 742	3 044	85.8	119.4	73.8
85 - 89	3 595	788	2 807	140.9	168.2	134.7
90 - 94	1 427	281	1 146	247.0	259.9	244.0
95 - 99	487	83	404	339.8	353.2	337.2

19. Deaths by age and sex, age-specific death rates by sex: latest available year, 2003 - 2012
Décès et taux de mortalité selon l'âge et le sexe : dernière année disponible, 2003 - 2012 (continued - suite)

Continent, country or area, date, code and age (in years) / Continent, pays ou zone, date, code et âge (en années)	Number - Nombre			Rate - Taux		
	Both sexes Les deux sexes	Male Masculin	Female Féminin	Both sexes Les deux sexes	Male Masculin	Female Féminin
EUROPE						
Latvia - Lettonie						
2011 (C)						
100 +	76	10	66	493.5	♦526.3	488.9
Unknown - Inconnu	-	-	-	..	..	..
Liechtenstein						
2011 (C)						
Total	248	126	122	6.8	7.0	6.7
0 - 4	1	-	1	♦0.5	-	♦1.1
0	1	-	1	♦2.8	-	♦5.6
1 - 4	-	-	-	-	-	-
5 - 9	-	-	-	-	-	-
10 - 14	-	-	-	-	-	-
15 - 19	-	-	-	-	-	-
20 - 24	2	1	1	♦0.9	♦0.9	♦0.9
25 - 29	-	-	-	-	-	-
30 - 34	-	-	-	-	-	-
35 - 39	2	2	-	♦0.8	♦1.6	-
40 - 44	2	2	-	♦0.6	♦1.3	-
45 - 49	8	6	2	♦2.6	♦4.0	♦1.3
50 - 54	5	4	1	♦1.7	♦2.8	♦0.7
55 - 59	10	5	5	♦4.0	♦4.0	♦4.0
60 - 64	20	11	9	♦9.0	♦9.5	♦8.4
65 - 69	25	17	8	♦13.6	♦18.9	♦8.5
70 - 74	25	19	6	♦19.4	♦30.7	♦8.9
75 - 79	20	13	7	♦23.4	♦36.4	♦14.1
80 - 84	37	16	21	61.5	♦66.7	♦58.0
85 - 89	55	20	35	145.1	♦190.5	127.7
90 - 94	29	9	20	♦210.1	♦187.5	♦222.2
95 - 99	6	1	5	♦166.7	♦71.4	♦227.3
100 +	1	-	1	♦500.0	...	♦500.0
Lithuania - Lituanie						
2011 (C)						
Total	41 037	20 944	20 093	13.5	15.0	12.3
0 - 4	178	101	77	1.2	1.3	1.1
0	144	80	64	4.4	4.8	4.1
1 - 4	34	21	13	0.3	♦0.3	♦0.2
5 - 9	26	18	8	♦0.2	♦0.3	♦0.1
10 - 14	36	24	12	0.2	♦0.3	♦0.2
15 - 19	122	100	22	0.6	0.9	♦0.2
20 - 24	227	189	38	1.0	1.7	0.4
25 - 29	283	230	53	1.5	2.3	0.6
30 - 34	367	278	89	2.0	3.0	1.0
35 - 39	593	445	148	3.0	4.6	1.4
40 - 44	951	719	232	4.4	6.9	2.1
45 - 49	1 497	1 105	392	6.6	10.1	3.3
50 - 54	2 060	1 472	588	8.8	13.5	4.7
55 - 59	2 392	1 698	694	12.9	20.4	6.8
60 - 64	3 005	2 089	916	18.2	30.0	9.6
65 - 69	3 550	2 313	1 237	24.3	40.5	13.9
70 - 74	4 538	2 623	1 915	31.4	50.0	20.8
75 - 79	5 766	2 773	2 993	48.7	71.7	37.5
80 - 84	6 870	2 606	4 264	82.3	107.7	72.0
85 - 89	5 471	1 421	4 050	138.0	160.7	131.5
90 - 94	2 192	540	1 652	224.3	263.7	213.9
95 - 99	726	148	578	332.1	323.1	334.5
100 +	186	51	135	467.3	435.9	480.4
Unknown - Inconnu	1	1	-	..	..	..
Luxembourg						
2011 (C)						
Total	3 819	1 895	1 924	7.5	7.4	7.5
0 - 4	27	18	9	♦0.9	♦1.2	♦0.6
0	24	16	8	♦4.1	♦5.4	♦2.8
1 - 4	3	2	1	♦0.1	♦0.2	♦0.1
5 - 9	2	1	1	♦0.1	♦0.1	♦0.1
10 - 14	1	-	1	-	-	♦0.1
15 - 19	8	3	5	♦0.3	♦0.2	♦0.3
20 - 24	14	10	4	♦0.5	♦0.6	♦0.3

19. Deaths by age and sex, age-specific death rates by sex: latest available year, 2003 - 2012
Décès et taux de mortalité selon l'âge et le sexe : dernière année disponible, 2003 - 2012 (continued - suite)

Continent, country or area, date, code and age (in years) / Continent, pays ou zone, date, code et âge (en annèes)	Number - Nombre			Rate - Taux		
	Both sexes Les deux sexes	Male Masculin	Female Féminin	Both sexes Les deux sexes	Male Masculin	Female Féminin
EUROPE						
Luxembourg						
2011 (C)						
25 - 29	15	10	5	♦0.4	♦0.6	♦0.3
30 - 34	14	9	5	♦0.4	♦0.5	♦0.3
35 - 39	26	15	11	♦0.7	♦0.8	♦0.6
40 - 44	38	24	14	0.9	♦1.1	♦0.7
45 - 49	89	53	36	2.2	2.5	1.8
50 - 54	130	83	47	3.6	4.5	2.6
55 - 59	159	109	50	5.2	7.0	3.3
60 - 64	243	151	92	9.4	11.5	7.2
65 - 69	259	166	93	13.1	17.3	9.2
70 - 74	366	228	138	20.9	28.4	14.5
75 - 79	486	261	225	33.1	41.2	26.9
80 - 84	738	378	360	64.3	85.0	51.2
85 - 89	655	245	410	115.0	160.0	98.5
90 - 94	375	95	280	225.2	307.4	206.5
95 - 99	145	30	115	555.6	♦3000.0	458.2
100 +	29	6	23	♦743.6	...	♦589.7
Unknown - Inconnu	-	-	-	..	..	..
Malta - Malte						
2011 (C)						
Total	3 290	1 671	1 619	7.9	8.1	7.7
0 - 4	30	13	17	♦1.5	♦1.3	♦1.8
0	27	13	14	♦6.7	♦6.4	♦7.1
1 - 4	3	-	3	♦0.2	-	♦0.4
5 - 9	2	1	1	♦0.1	♦0.1	♦0.1
10 - 14	1	-	1	-	-	♦0.1
15 - 19	11	9	2	♦0.4	♦0.7	♦0.2
20 - 24	8	7	1	♦0.3	♦0.5	♦0.1
25 - 29	20	11	9	♦0.7	♦0.7	♦0.6
30 - 34	15	11	4	♦0.5	♦0.7	♦0.3
35 - 39	20	13	7	♦0.7	♦0.9	♦0.5
40 - 44	26	15	11	♦1.0	♦1.2	♦0.9
45 - 49	45	30	15	1.6	♦2.2	♦1.1
50 - 54	83	52	31	2.7	3.4	2.0
55 - 59	118	72	46	4.1	4.9	3.2
60 - 64	225	147	78	7.3	9.7	5.0
65 - 69	271	165	106	11.9	15.1	9.0
70 - 74	330	209	121	20.2	28.0	13.6
75 - 79	491	265	226	37.5	48.7	29.5
80 - 84	601	287	314	71.7	90.9	60.1
85 - 89	587	238	349	128.9	147.6	118.6
90 - 94	291	95	196	190.7	202.1	185.6
95 - 99	97	27	70	320.1	♦337.5	313.9
100 +	18	4	14	♦400.0	♦266.7	♦466.7
Unknown - Inconnu	-	-	-	..	..	..
Montenegro - Monténégro						
2011 (C)						
Total	5 847	3 090	2 757	9.4	10.1	8.8
0 - 4	41	28	13	1.1	♦1.4	♦0.7
0	32	21	11	4.0	♦5.1	♦2.8
1 - 4	9	7	2	♦0.3	♦0.4	♦0.1
5 - 9	4	2	2	♦0.1	♦0.1	♦0.1
10 - 14	10	6	4	♦0.2	♦0.3	♦0.2
15 - 19	10	7	3	♦0.2	♦0.3	♦0.1
20 - 24	17	11	6	♦0.4	♦0.5	♦0.3
25 - 29	25	19	6	♦0.5	♦0.8	♦0.3
30 - 34	33	19	14	0.7	♦0.9	♦0.6
35 - 39	61	43	18	1.5	2.1	♦0.8
40 - 44	78	54	24	1.9	2.7	♦1.2
45 - 49	142	91	51	3.3	4.2	2.4
50 - 54	242	163	79	5.5	7.5	3.6
55 - 59	400	272	128	9.7	13.3	6.2
60 - 64	483	328	155	14.5	21.1	8.7
65 - 69	494	306	188	21.9	30.8	14.9
70 - 74	833	434	399	33.1	39.8	28.0
75 - 79	1 038	538	500	61.0	74.7	50.9

19. Deaths by age and sex, age-specific death rates by sex: latest available year, 2003 - 2012
Décès et taux de mortalité selon l'âge et le sexe : dernière année disponible, 2003 - 2012 (continued - suite)

Continent, country or area, date, code and age (in years) Continent, pays ou zone, date, code et âge (en années)	Number - Nombre			Rate - Taux		
	Both sexes Les deux sexes	Male Masculin	Female Féminin	Both sexes Les deux sexes	Male Masculin	Female Féminin

EUROPE

Montenegro - Monténégro
2011 (C)

80 - 84	1 055	464	591	106.5	116.8	99.6
85 - 89	595	221	374	163.4	172.7	158.3
90 - 94	210	59	151	244.8	214.5	259.0
95 - 99	61	22	39	293.3	♦372.9	261.7
100 +	15	3	12	♦51.4	♦28.8	♦63.8
Unknown - Inconnu	-	-	-	..	..	..

Netherlands - Pays-Bas[39]
2011 (C)

Total	135 741	65 259	70 482	8.1	7.9	8.4
0 - 4	758	440	318	0.8	0.9	0.7
0	654	375	279	3.6	4.0	3.1
1 - 4	104	65	39	0.1	0.2	0.1
5 - 9	73	48	25	0.1	0.1	♦0.1
10 - 14	106	64	42	0.1	0.1	0.1
15 - 19	217	145	72	0.2	0.3	0.1
20 - 24	327	232	95	0.3	0.4	0.2
25 - 29	356	228	128	0.4	0.5	0.3
30 - 34	445	272	173	0.4	0.5	0.3
35 - 39	754	434	320	0.7	0.8	0.6
40 - 44	1 378	755	623	1.1	1.2	1.0
45 - 49	2 426	1 318	1 108	1.9	2.0	1.7
50 - 54	3 756	2 031	1 725	3.1	3.4	2.9
55 - 59	5 635	3 250	2 385	5.2	5.9	4.4
60 - 64	8 474	5 007	3 467	7.7	9.0	6.3
65 - 69	10 299	6 207	4 092	13.0	15.9	10.2
70 - 74	12 940	7 729	5 211	20.3	25.5	15.6
75 - 79	17 849	10 107	7 742	35.7	46.1	27.6
80 - 84	23 554	11 602	11 952	65.3	83.3	54.0
85 - 89	24 463	9 546	14 917	115.4	142.6	102.8
90 - 94	15 620	4 573	11 047	205.0	243.1	192.5
95 +	6 311	1 271	5 040	341.7	396.7	330.1
95 - 99	5 442	1 127	4 315	...	...	...
100 +	869	144	725	...	...	...

Norway - Norvège[40]
2011 (C)

Total	41 393	20 069	21 324	8.4	8.1	8.6
0 - 4	176	109	67	0.6	0.7	0.4
0	142	92	50	2.3	2.9	1.7
1 - 4	34	17	17	0.1	♦0.1	♦0.1
5 - 9	20	13	7	♦0.1	♦0.1	-
10 - 14	34	14	20	0.1	♦0.1	♦0.1
15 - 19	153	96	57	0.5	0.6	0.4
20 - 24	168	128	40	0.5	0.8	0.3
25 - 29	170	121	49	0.5	0.7	0.3
30 - 34	222	156	66	0.7	0.9	0.4
35 - 39	265	181	84	0.7	1.0	0.5
40 - 44	380	252	128	1.0	1.3	0.7
45 - 49	640	404	236	1.8	2.3	1.4
50 - 54	895	539	356	2.8	3.3	2.3
55 - 59	1 436	857	579	4.8	5.6	3.9
60 - 64	2 133	1 289	844	7.4	8.8	5.9
65 - 69	2 803	1 759	1 044	11.8	14.9	8.7
70 - 74	3 141	1 930	1 211	19.0	24.7	13.9
75 - 79	4 508	2 552	1 956	34.6	44.1	27.0
80 - 84	6 781	3 494	3 287	62.6	79.6	51.0
85 - 89	8 495	3 585	4 910	115.0	141.3	101.2
90 - 94	6 377	1 982	4 395	201.2	232.6	189.6
95 - 99	2 163	504	1 659	322.7	379.8	308.6
100 +	342	51	291	492.1	459.5	498.3
Unknown - Inconnu	91	53	38	..	..	..

Poland - Pologne
2011 (C)

Total	375 501	198 178	177 323	9.7	10.6	8.9
0 - 4	2 168	1 214	954	1.0	1.1	0.9
0	1 836	1 027	809	4.6	5.0	4.2

Continent, country or area, date, code and age (in years) Continent, pays ou zone, date, code et âge (en années)	Number - Nombre			Rate - Taux		
	Both sexes Les deux sexes	Male Masculin	Female Féminin	Both sexes Les deux sexes	Male Masculin	Female Féminin
EUROPE						
Poland - Pologne						
2011 (C)						
1 - 4	332	187	145	0.2	0.2	0.2
5 - 9	214	130	84	0.1	0.1	0.1
10 - 14	289	164	125	0.1	0.2	0.1
15 - 19	1 060	773	287	0.4	0.6	0.2
20 - 24	1 853	1 531	322	0.7	1.1	0.2
25 - 29	2 316	1 866	450	0.7	1.1	0.3
30 - 34	2 968	2 363	605	0.9	1.5	0.4
35 - 39	4 249	3 268	981	1.5	2.3	0.7
40 - 44	5 924	4 462	1 462	2.5	3.7	1.2
45 - 49	9 761	7 212	2 549	4.0	5.9	2.1
50 - 54	19 296	13 861	5 435	6.7	9.7	3.7
55 - 59	28 768	20 246	8 522	9.9	14.6	5.6
60 - 64	34 263	23 142	11 121	14.2	20.8	8.6
65 - 69	28 257	18 252	10 005	20.0	29.6	12.6
70 - 74	38 447	22 720	15 727	28.7	41.9	19.7
75 - 79	51 386	26 547	24 839	44.9	62.7	34.4
80 - 84	61 785	25 903	35 882	75.3	96.9	64.9
85 - 89	52 399	16 851	35 548	128.4	154.0	119.0
90 - 94	21 624	5 811	15 813	208.3	232.2	200.7
95 - 99	7 253	1 612	5 641	306.6	342.5	297.7
100 +	1 221	250	971	891.2	1201.9	835.6
Portugal[15]						
2011 (C)						
Total	102 845	52 544	50 301	9.7	10.4	9.1
0 - 4	371	219	152	0.8	0.9	0.6
0	301	175	126	3.1	3.6	2.7
1 - 4	70	44	26	0.2	0.2	♦0.1
5 - 9	65	36	29	0.1	0.1	♦0.1
10 - 14	53	39	14	0.1	0.1	♦0.1
15 - 19	163	104	59	0.3	0.4	0.2
20 - 24	259	181	78	0.4	0.6	0.3
25 - 29	308	218	90	0.5	0.7	0.3
30 - 34	521	375	146	0.7	1.0	0.4
35 - 39	843	601	242	1.0	1.5	0.6
40 - 44	1 348	922	426	1.7	2.5	1.1
45 - 49	2 134	1 511	623	2.8	4.1	1.6
50 - 54	3 090	2 204	886	4.3	6.4	2.3
55 - 59	3 881	2 670	1 211	5.7	8.3	3.4
60 - 64	5 018	3 386	1 632	7.9	11.3	4.8
65 - 69	6 448	4 223	2 225	11.6	16.5	7.4
70 - 74	9 624	5 828	3 796	19.4	26.4	13.8
75 - 79	14 901	8 195	6 706	34.3	45.0	26.6
80 - 84	19 239	9 273	9 966	63.9	80.5	53.5
85 +	34 567	12 549	22 018	142.2	158.1	134.4
85 - 89	19 277	7 855	11 422	...	...	...
90 - 94	10 821	3 586	7 235	...	...	...
95 - 99	3 806	991	2 815	...	...	...
100 +	663	117	546	...	...	...
Unknown - Inconnu	12	10	2	..	..	..
Republic of Moldova - République de Moldova[41]						
2011 (C)						
Total	39 249	20 578	18 671	11.0	12.0	10.1
0 - 4	525	327	198	2.7	3.3	2.1
0	431	278	153	10.9	13.8	8.0
1 - 4	94	49	45	0.6	0.6	0.6
5 - 9	40	21	19	0.2	♦0.2	♦0.2
10 - 14	53	35	18	0.3	0.3	♦0.2
15 - 19	137	103	34	0.5	0.7	0.3
20 - 24	267	209	58	0.8	1.2	0.3
25 - 29	347	263	84	1.0	1.6	0.5
30 - 34	453	347	106	1.6	2.4	0.8
35 - 39	642	465	177	2.6	3.8	1.4
40 - 44	1 011	751	260	4.5	6.9	2.2
45 - 49	1 575	1 174	401	6.4	10.0	3.1
50 - 54	2 708	1 883	825	9.9	14.8	5.6

19. Deaths by age and sex, age-specific death rates by sex: latest available year, 2003 - 2012
Décès et taux de mortalité selon l'âge et le sexe : dernière année disponible, 2003 - 2012 (continued - suite)

Continent, country or area, date, code and age (in years) Continent, pays ou zone, date, code et âge (en années)	Number - Nombre			Rate - Taux		
	Both sexes Les deux sexes	Male Masculin	Female Féminin	Both sexes Les deux sexes	Male Masculin	Female Féminin
EUROPE						
Republic of Moldova - République de Moldova[41]						
2011 (C)						
55 - 59	3 364	2 219	1 145	14.5	21.1	9.0
60 - 64	3 984	2 445	1 539	24.1	33.6	16.6
65 - 69	3 395	1 910	1 485	31.3	41.9	23.6
70 - 74	5 075	2 541	2 534	50.3	66.6	40.4
75 - 79	5 658	2 473	3 185	78.3	95.3	68.7
80 - 84	5 450	2 043	3 407	117.1	133.8	108.9
85 - 89	3 257	1 000	2 257	160.8	167.1	158.2
90 - 94	1 071	317	754	244.2	242.4	244.9
95 - 99	203	49	154	173.4	128.4	195.2
100 +	34	3	31	98.8	◆25.5	136.9
Romania - Roumanie						
2011 (C)						
Total	251 439	132 180	119 259	11.8	12.7	10.9
0 - 4	2 264	1 303	961	2.1	2.4	1.9
0	1 850	1 067	783	9.3	10.4	8.0
1 - 4	414	236	178	0.5	0.5	0.4
5 - 9	206	134	72	0.2	0.2	0.1
10 - 14	259	164	95	0.2	0.3	0.2
15 - 19	547	394	153	0.5	0.7	0.3
20 - 24	999	746	253	0.6	0.9	0.3
25 - 29	976	689	287	0.6	0.8	0.4
30 - 34	1 607	1 136	471	0.9	1.3	0.5
35 - 39	2 390	1 714	676	1.4	2.0	0.8
40 - 44	4 464	3 211	1 253	2.4	3.5	1.4
45 - 49	5 349	3 844	1 505	4.6	6.6	2.6
50 - 54	10 631	7 604	3 027	7.5	11.1	4.2
55 - 59	16 034	11 256	4 778	11.0	16.4	6.2
60 - 64	19 470	13 061	6 409	15.9	23.3	9.7
65 - 69	20 149	12 463	7 686	22.8	32.3	15.5
70 - 74	32 043	17 909	14 134	35.9	48.9	26.8
75 - 79	41 509	20 519	20 990	57.9	73.0	48.1
80 - 84	44 918	19 171	25 747	99.4	114.3	90.6
85 - 89	33 575	12 406	21 169	170.6	183.1	164.1
90 - 94	10 489	3 334	7 155	268.4	260.3	272.4
95 - 99	3 145	986	2 159	331.3	282.4	359.8
100 +	415	136	279	94.0	82.7	100.8
Russian Federation - Fédération de Russie[20]						
2011 (C)						
Total	1 925 720	997 494	928 226	13.5	15.1	12.1
0 - 4	16 465	9 472	6 993	2.1	2.3	1.8
0	13 168	7 572	5 596	8.0	9.0	7.0
1 - 4	3 297	1 900	1 397	0.5	0.6	0.5
5 - 9	1 972	1 160	812	0.3	0.3	0.2
10 - 14	2 006	1 249	757	0.3	0.4	0.2
15 - 19	6 656	4 634	2 022	0.8	1.1	0.5
20 - 24	18 666	14 374	4 292	1.5	2.3	0.7
25 - 29	32 160	24 684	7 476	2.7	4.1	1.3
30 - 34	45 451	34 852	10 599	4.1	6.4	1.9
35 - 39	50 630	38 270	12 360	5.0	7.7	2.4
40 - 44	55 007	40 708	14 299	6.0	9.1	3.0
45 - 49	81 813	60 225	21 588	7.7	12.0	3.8
50 - 54	124 961	89 971	34 990	10.9	17.1	5.6
55 - 59	156 587	108 205	48 382	15.6	24.9	8.5
60 - 64	177 990	118 728	59 262	22.7	36.6	12.9
65 - 69	111 156	66 246	44 910	27.8	44.4	17.9
70 - 74	263 633	136 875	126 758	40.8	62.8	29.6
75 - 79	232 616	99 250	133 366	65.5	92.9	53.7
80 - 84	290 314	94 614	195 700	101.1	129.8	91.4
85 - 89	172 178	35 533	136 645	166.8	187.8	162.0
90 - 94	56 714	9 585	47 129	244.6	241.3	245.3
95 - 99	18 647	2 652	15 995	320.7	294.4	325.5
100 +	2 562	320	2 242	352.6	232.1	380.8
Unknown - Inconnu	7 536	5 887	1 649	..	..	..

19. Deaths by age and sex, age-specific death rates by sex: latest available year, 2003 - 2012
Décès et taux de mortalité selon l'âge et le sexe : dernière année disponible, 2003 - 2012 (continued - suite)

Continent, country or area, date, code and age (in years) / Continent, pays ou zone, date, code et âge (en années)	Number - Nombre			Rate - Taux		
	Both sexes Les deux sexes	Male Masculin	Female Féminin	Both sexes Les deux sexes	Male Masculin	Female Féminin
EUROPE						
San Marino - Saint-Marin						
2012 (+C)						
Total	237	110	127	...	...	...
0 - 20	-	-	-	...	...	...
21 - 25	-	-	-	...	...	...
26 - 30	-	-	-	...	...	...
31 - 35	-	-	-	...	...	...
36 - 40	1	1	-	...	...	...
41 - 45	5	1	4	...	...	...
46 - 50	1	1	-	...	...	...
51 - 55	5	5	-	...	...	...
56 - 60	8	4	4	...	...	...
61 - 65	9	4	5	...	...	...
66 - 70	14	9	5	...	...	...
71 - 75	21	8	13	...	...	...
76 - 80	34	22	12	...	...	...
81 - 85	44	25	19	...	...	...
86 - 90	53	17	36	...	...	...
91 - 95	26	9	17	...	...	...
96 - 100	15	4	11	...	...	...
Serbia - Serbie[42]						
2011 (+C)						
Total	102 935	52 114	50 821	14.2	14.8	13.6
0 - 4	469	264	205	1.4	1.5	1.2
0	414	231	183	6.2	6.7	5.7
1 - 4	55	33	22	0.2	0.2	♦0.2
5 - 9	46	19	27	0.1	♦0.1	♦0.1
10 - 14	56	29	27	0.2	♦0.2	♦0.2
15 - 19	153	102	51	0.4	0.5	0.3
20 - 24	237	171	66	0.5	0.7	0.3
25 - 29	341	240	101	0.7	0.9	0.4
30 - 34	462	324	138	0.9	1.2	0.5
35 - 39	625	412	213	1.2	1.6	0.9
40 - 44	971	633	338	2.1	2.7	1.4
45 - 49	1 910	1 282	628	3.9	5.4	2.5
50 - 54	3 488	2 340	1 148	6.7	9.3	4.3
55 - 59	6 160	4 125	2 035	10.6	14.7	6.8
60 - 64	8 126	5 249	2 877	16.3	22.4	10.9
65 - 69	8 115	4 897	3 218	25.3	34.0	18.2
70 - 74	13 996	7 586	6 410	40.9	51.4	32.9
75 - 79	20 360	9 717	10 643	70.8	81.7	63.0
80 - 84	20 718	8 739	11 979	118.4	126.5	113.2
85 - 89	12 617	4 541	8 076	178.4	178.4	178.4
90 - 94	3 366	1 193	2 173	170.7	167.4	172.6
95 - 99	588	193	395	153.2	135.3	163.8
100 +	94	34	60	43.2	42.3	43.7
Unknown - Inconnu	37	24	13	..	..	..
Slovakia - Slovaquie						
2011 (C)						
Total	51 903	26 797	25 106	9.6	10.2	9.1
0 - 4	363	206	157	1.3	1.4	1.1
0	300	172	128	5.1	5.7	4.4
1 - 4	63	34	29	0.3	0.3	♦0.3
5 - 9	52	32	20	0.2	0.2	♦0.2
10 - 14	43	27	16	0.2	♦0.2	♦0.1
15 - 19	139	99	40	0.4	0.6	0.2
20 - 24	200	148	52	0.5	0.7	0.3
25 - 29	294	226	68	0.7	1.0	0.3
30 - 34	369	272	97	0.8	1.2	0.4
35 - 39	531	388	143	1.2	1.8	0.7
40 - 44	793	578	215	2.2	3.2	1.2
45 - 49	1 380	990	390	3.7	5.3	2.1
50 - 54	2 535	1 772	763	6.6	9.4	3.9
55 - 59	3 705	2 646	1 059	9.6	14.3	5.3
60 - 64	4 502	3 157	1 345	14.4	21.9	8.0
65 - 69	4 591	2 900	1 691	20.9	31.0	13.4
70 - 74	5 456	3 154	2 302	31.3	46.1	21.8

19. Deaths by age and sex, age-specific death rates by sex: latest available year, 2003 - 2012
Décès et taux de mortalité selon l'âge et le sexe : dernière année disponible, 2003 - 2012 (continued - suite)

Continent, country or area, date, code and age (in years) Continent, pays ou zone, date, code et âge (en années)	Number - Nombre			Rate - Taux		
	Both sexes Les deux sexes	Male Masculin	Female Féminin	Both sexes Les deux sexes	Male Masculin	Female Féminin
EUROPE						
Slovakia - Slovaquie						
2011 (C)						
75 - 79	7 285	3 544	3 741	53.6	73.0	42.8
80 - 84	8 726	3 387	5 339	93.1	113.6	83.5
85 - 89	7 390	2 308	5 082	157.3	174.6	150.6
90 - 94	2 708	772	1 936	234.8	248.0	229.9
95 - 99	750	166	584	322.3	270.6	340.8
100 +	91	25	66	327.3	♦378.8	311.3
Slovenia - Slovénie						
2011 (C)						
Total	18 699	9 235	9 464	9.1	9.1	9.1
0 - 4	82	48	34	0.8	0.9	0.6
0	64	41	23	2.9	3.6	♦2.1
1 - 4	18	7	11	♦0.2	♦0.2	♦0.3
5 - 9	7	4	3	♦0.1	♦0.1	♦0.1
10 - 14	9	6	3	♦0.1	♦0.1	♦0.1
15 - 19	27	22	5	♦0.3	♦0.4	♦0.1
20 - 24	59	44	15	0.5	0.7	♦0.2
25 - 29	54	44	10	0.4	0.6	♦0.1
30 - 34	87	73	14	0.6	0.9	♦0.2
35 - 39	119	82	37	0.8	1.0	0.5
40 - 44	248	171	77	1.7	2.2	1.1
45 - 49	379	250	129	2.4	3.1	1.7
50 - 54	613	412	201	4.0	5.3	2.7
55 - 59	1 022	728	294	6.7	9.4	3.9
60 - 64	1 216	832	384	9.5	13.2	5.9
65 - 69	1 373	892	481	14.7	20.6	9.6
70 - 74	1 914	1 226	688	21.7	31.6	14.0
75 - 79	2 797	1 486	1 311	38.5	52.8	29.4
80 - 84	3 420	1 494	1 926	65.8	88.2	55.0
85 - 89	3 262	942	2 320	122.4	145.8	114.9
90 - 94	1 419	363	1 056	207.4	253.1	195.3
95 - 99	509	107	402	341.4	436.7	322.6
100 +	83	9	74	365.6	♦225.0	395.7
Unknown - Inconnu	-	-	-	..	..	..
Spain - Espagne						
2011 (C)						
Total	386 017	198 528	187 489	8.4	8.8	8.0
0 - 4	1 795	981	814	0.7	0.8	0.7
0	1 477	804	673	3.0	3.2	2.8
1 - 4	318	177	141	0.2	0.2	0.1
5 - 9	198	118	80	0.1	0.1	0.1
10 - 14	233	129	104	0.1	0.1	0.1
15 - 19	479	303	176	0.2	0.3	0.2
20 - 24	733	550	183	0.3	0.4	0.1
25 - 29	1 018	714	304	0.3	0.5	0.2
30 - 34	1 692	1 149	543	0.4	0.6	0.3
35 - 39	2 643	1 743	900	0.7	0.8	0.5
40 - 44	4 378	2 860	1 518	1.2	1.5	0.8
45 - 49	6 998	4 667	2 331	2.0	2.7	1.3
50 - 54	10 384	7 054	3 330	3.3	4.6	2.1
55 - 59	13 030	9 066	3 964	4.9	7.0	2.9
60 - 64	17 278	12 203	5 075	7.1	10.4	4.0
65 - 69	22 314	15 474	6 840	10.4	15.3	6.1
70 - 74	29 676	19 531	10 145	17.1	24.7	10.7
75 - 79	51 739	30 668	21 071	30.4	42.0	21.6
80 - 84	72 134	37 140	34 994	56.4	74.1	45.0
85 - 89	77 205	32 605	44 600	105.1	127.3	93.2
90 - 94	48 746	15 880	32 866	177.4	195.9	169.6
95 - 99	19 578	4 926	14 652	290.5	296.3	288.6
100 +	3 766	767	2 999	422.8	325.1	457.9
Unknown - Inconnu	-	-	-	..	..	..
Sweden - Suède						
2011 (C)						
Total	89 938	43 594	46 344	9.5	9.3	9.8
0 - 4	295	165	130	0.5	0.6	0.5
0	235	128	107	2.1	2.2	1.9

517

19. Deaths by age and sex, age-specific death rates by sex: latest available year, 2003 - 2012
Décès et taux de mortalité selon l'âge et le sexe : dernière année disponible, 2003 - 2012 (continued - suite)

Continent, country or area, date, code and age (in years) / Continent, pays ou zone, date, code et âge (en annèes)	Number - Nombre			Rate - Taux		
	Both sexes Les deux sexes	Male Masculin	Female Féminin	Both sexes Les deux sexes	Male Masculin	Female Féminin
EUROPE						
Sweden - Suède						
2011 (C)						
1 - 4	60	37	23	0.1	0.2	♦0.1
5 - 9	47	22	25	0.1	♦0.1	♦0.1
10 - 14	43	22	21	0.1	♦0.1	♦0.1
15 - 19	171	112	59	0.3	0.4	0.2
20 - 24	281	204	77	0.4	0.6	0.2
25 - 29	287	198	89	0.5	0.7	0.3
30 - 34	307	204	103	0.5	0.7	0.4
35 - 39	390	239	151	0.6	0.7	0.5
40 - 44	588	378	210	0.9	1.1	0.7
45 - 49	1 021	642	379	1.6	1.9	1.2
50 - 54	1 526	912	614	2.6	3.1	2.1
55 - 59	2 521	1 567	954	4.4	5.4	3.3
60 - 64	4 213	2 526	1 687	7.0	8.4	5.5
65 - 69	6 427	4 010	2 417	11.4	14.3	8.5
70 - 74	7 397	4 340	3 057	18.7	22.8	14.9
75 - 79	10 106	5 761	4 345	33.2	41.9	26.0
80 - 84	14 991	7 570	7 421	61.1	75.2	51.3
85 - 89	18 981	8 217	10 764	115.5	138.2	102.6
90 - 94	14 399	5 095	9 304	203.3	240.2	187.5
95 - 99	5 125	1 282	3 843	334.4	380.5	321.4
100 +	822	128	694	479.4	491.4	477.3
Unknown - Inconnu	-	-	-	..	..	..
Switzerland - Suisse						
2011 (C)						
Total	62 091	30 094	31 997	7.8	7.7	8.0
0 - 4	347	190	157	1.0	1.0	0.9
0	305	168	137	7.8	8.3	7.2
1 - 4	42	22	20	0.1	♦0.1	♦0.1
5 - 9	40	24	16	0.1	♦0.1	♦0.1
10 - 14	40	24	16	0.1	♦0.1	♦0.1
15 - 19	107	78	29	0.2	0.3	♦0.1
20 - 24	182	132	50	0.4	0.5	0.2
25 - 29	191	125	66	0.4	0.5	0.3
30 - 34	244	150	94	0.5	0.6	0.3
35 - 39	327	219	108	0.6	0.8	0.4
40 - 44	589	358	231	0.9	1.1	0.7
45 - 49	1 081	675	406	1.6	2.0	1.2
50 - 54	1 466	936	530	2.5	3.2	1.8
55 - 59	1 981	1 254	727	4.0	5.0	2.9
60 - 64	2 979	1 869	1 110	6.5	8.2	4.8
65 - 69	4 199	2 614	1 585	10.2	13.0	7.4
70 - 74	4 912	2 964	1 948	15.6	20.4	11.5
75 - 79	7 313	4 176	3 137	27.8	36.4	21.1
80 - 84	10 348	5 142	5 206	51.1	64.8	42.2
85 - 89	12 587	5 195	7 392	97.3	118.8	86.4
90 - 94	8 910	2 951	5 959	165.4	190.2	155.4
95 - 99	3 598	896	2 702	269.7	288.1	264.1
100 +	650	122	528	357.3	402.6	348.3
Unknown - Inconnu	-	-	-	..	..	..
TFYR of Macedonia - L'ex-R. y. de Macédoine						
2011 (C)						
Total	19 465	10 204	9 261	9.5	9.9	9.0
0 - 4	196	113	83	1.7	1.9	1.5
0	172	95	77	7.4	7.9	6.8
1 - 4	24	18	6	♦0.3	♦0.4	♦0.1
5 - 9	15	10	5	♦0.1	♦0.2	♦0.1
10 - 14	21	10	11	♦0.2	♦0.2	♦0.2
15 - 19	43	28	15	0.3	♦0.4	♦0.2
20 - 24	58	45	13	0.4	0.5	♦0.2
25 - 29	60	37	23	0.4	0.4	♦0.3
30 - 34	93	60	33	0.6	0.7	0.4
35 - 39	162	110	52	1.1	1.4	0.7
40 - 44	231	152	79	1.6	2.0	1.1
45 - 49	455	304	151	3.1	4.1	2.1
50 - 54	765	520	245	5.4	7.2	3.5

19. Deaths by age and sex, age-specific death rates by sex: latest available year, 2003 - 2012
Décès et taux de mortalité selon l'âge et le sexe : dernière année disponible, 2003 - 2012 (continued - suite)

Continent, country or area, date, code and age (in years) Continent, pays ou zone, date, code et âge (en annèes)	Number - Nombre			Rate - Taux		
	Both sexes Les deux sexes	Male Masculin	Female Féminin	Both sexes Les deux sexes	Male Masculin	Female Féminin
EUROPE						
TFYR of Macedonia - L'ex-R. y. de Macédoine						
2011 (C)						
55 - 59	1 171	752	419	8.9	11.4	6.3
60 - 64	1 524	971	553	13.9	18.6	9.7
65 - 69	1 917	1 127	790	23.8	30.0	18.3
70 - 74	2 748	1 474	1 274	40.1	47.5	34.0
75 - 79	3 647	1 767	1 880	68.4	76.2	62.5
80 - 84	3 486	1 575	1 911	129.8	142.9	120.7
85 - 89	2 091	833	1 258	214.3	219.8	210.9
90 - 94	633	261	372	294.9	332.3	273.3
95 - 99	131	47	84	168.4	185.4	160.2
100 +	18	8	10	...	...	...
Unknown - Inconnu	-	-	-	..	..	..
Ukraine[43]						
2011 (+C)						
Total	664 588	325 482	339 106	14.6	15.5	13.8
0 - 4	5 373	3 087	2 286	2.2	2.4	1.9
0	4 511	2 603	1 908	9.1	10.2	7.9
1 - 4	862	484	378	0.4	0.5	0.4
5 - 9	492	299	193	0.2	0.3	0.2
10 - 14	547	332	215	0.3	0.3	0.2
15 - 19	1 557	1 110	447	0.6	0.8	0.4
20 - 24	3 702	2 831	871	1.1	1.6	0.5
25 - 29	6 367	4 830	1 537	1.7	2.5	0.8
30 - 34	9 739	7 374	2 365	2.9	4.3	1.4
35 - 39	12 743	9 489	3 254	3.9	5.9	2.0
40 - 44	15 213	11 144	4 069	5.0	7.6	2.6
45 - 49	21 997	16 010	5 987	6.7	10.5	3.4
50 - 54	33 289	23 774	9 515	9.5	15.0	5.0
55 - 59	42 062	28 920	13 142	13.8	21.8	7.6
60 - 64	53 506	34 934	18 572	20.4	32.1	12.0
65 - 69	47 307	27 638	19 669	28.4	44.2	18.9
70 - 74	105 422	54 279	51 143	43.8	64.6	32.7
75 - 79	85 959	37 471	48 488	67.5	89.8	56.6
80 - 84	113 904	38 786	75 118	109.2	133.1	99.9
85 - 89	74 167	17 266	56 901	167.1	178.0	164.0
90 - 94	23 098	4 427	18 671	240.6	216.3	247.2
95 - 99	6 833	1 113	5 720	359.1	299.8	373.4
100 +	635	98	537	327.4	218.3	360.3
Unknown - Inconnu	676	270	406	..	..	..
United Kingdom of Great Britain and Northern Ireland - Royaume-Uni de Grande-Bretagne et d'Irlande du Nord[44]						
2011 (+C)						
Total	552 232	267 491	284 741	8.8	8.7	8.9
0 - 4	4 002	2 323	1 679	1.0	1.2	0.9
0	3 386	1 975	1 411	4.2	4.8	3.6
1 - 4	616	348	268	0.2	0.2	0.2
5 - 9	285	175	110	0.1	0.1	0.1
10 - 14	314	177	137	0.1	0.1	0.1
15 - 19	913	619	294	0.2	0.3	0.2
20 - 24	1 576	1 102	474	0.4	0.5	0.2
25 - 29	2 009	1 356	653	0.5	0.6	0.3
30 - 34	2 658	1 729	929	0.7	0.9	0.5
35 - 39	3 960	2 534	1 426	1.0	1.3	0.7
40 - 44	6 619	4 078	2 541	1.4	1.8	1.1
45 - 49	9 683	5 758	3 925	2.1	2.5	1.7
50 - 54	13 534	7 948	5 586	3.3	3.9	2.7
55 - 59	18 826	11 275	7 551	5.2	6.4	4.1
60 - 64	30 585	18 203	12 382	8.2	10.0	6.5
65 - 69	38 788	22 897	15 891	12.6	15.4	9.9
70 - 74	52 159	30 333	21 826	21.1	26.1	16.7
75 - 79	70 517	38 304	32 213	34.9	42.1	28.9
80 - 84	93 465	46 032	47 433	61.6	73.8	53.1
85 - 89	100 412	42 103	58 309	106.7	126.0	96.0
90 +	100 863	29 838	71 025	197.7	202.3	195.8
90 - 94	67 910	22 554	45 356	...	...	...

19. Deaths by age and sex, age-specific death rates by sex: latest available year, 2003 - 2012
Décès et taux de mortalité selon l'âge et le sexe : dernière année disponible, 2003 - 2012 (continued - suite)

Continent, country or area, date, code and age (in years) Continent, pays ou zone, date, code et âge (en années)	Number - Nombre			Rate - Taux		
	Both sexes Les deux sexes	Male Masculin	Female Féminin	Both sexes Les deux sexes	Male Masculin	Female Féminin
EUROPE						
United Kingdom of Great Britain and Northern Ireland - Royaume-Uni de Grande-Bretagne et d'Irlande du Nord[44]						
2011 (+C)						
95 - 99	27 619	6 483	21 136	...	...	...
100 +	5 334	801	4 533	...	...	...
Unknown - Inconnu	1 064	707	357	..	..	..
OCEANIA - OCÉANIE						
American Samoa - Samoas américaines						
2006 (C)						
Total	267	156	111	...	...	...
0	17	9	8	...	...	...
1 - 4	7	3	4	...	...	...
5 - 9	1	1	-	...	...	...
10 - 14	5	2	3	...	...	...
15 - 19	3	-	3	...	...	...
20 - 24	5	4	1	...	...	...
25 - 29	4	3	1	...	...	...
30 - 34	5	5	-	...	...	...
35 - 39	10	6	4	...	...	...
40 - 44	9	4	5	...	...	...
45 - 49	19	10	9	...	...	...
50 - 54	18	11	7	...	...	...
55 - 59	21	13	8	...	...	...
60 - 64	23	15	8	...	...	...
65 - 69	27	18	9	...	...	...
70 - 74	31	22	9	...	...	...
75 - 79	28	19	9	...	...	...
80 - 84	13	6	7	...	...	...
85 +	21	5	16	...	...	...
Australia - Australie						
2011 (+C)						
Total	146 932	75 330	71 602	6.6	6.8	6.4
0	1 140	638	502	3.9	4.2	3.5
1 - 4	202	109	93	0.2	0.2	0.2
5 - 9	147	83	64	0.1	0.1	0.1
10 - 14	132	73	59	0.1	0.1	0.1
15 - 19	477	310	167	0.3	0.4	0.2
20 - 24	741	521	220	0.5	0.6	0.3
25 - 29	871	624	247	0.5	0.7	0.3
30 - 34	1 027	708	319	0.7	0.9	0.4
35 - 39	1 395	887	508	0.9	1.1	0.6
40 - 44	1 896	1 163	733	1.2	1.5	0.9
45 - 49	2 828	1 715	1 113	1.8	2.2	1.4
50 - 54	4 108	2 488	1 620	2.7	3.4	2.1
55 - 59	5 546	3 485	2 061	4.2	5.3	3.1
60 - 64	7 865	4 971	2 894	6.3	8.1	4.6
65 - 69	9 533	5 964	3 569	10.0	12.6	7.5
70 - 74	12 493	7 569	4 924	17.4	21.7	13.3
75 - 79	16 498	9 748	6 750	29.6	37.8	22.5
80 - 84	24 322	12 946	11 376	54.8	68.0	44.9
85 - 89	27 843	12 393	15 450	102.3	122.9	90.2
90 - 94	18 890	6 711	12 179	182.6	211.7	169.8
95 - 99	7 614	1 986	5 628	307.5	339.2	297.6
100 +	1 361	235	1 126	446.4	424.2	451.3
Unknown - Inconnu	3	3	-	..	..	..
Cook Islands - Îles Cook[45]						
2009 (+C)						
Total	67	37	30	...	...	...
0	2	1	1	...	...	...
1 - 4	1	1	-	...	...	...
5 - 9	-	-	-	...	...	...
10 - 14	-	-	-	...	...	...
15 - 19	3	2	1	...	...	...

19. Deaths by age and sex, age-specific death rates by sex: latest available year, 2003 - 2012
Décès et taux de mortalité selon l'âge et le sexe : dernière année disponible, 2003 - 2012 (continued - suite)

Continent, country or area, date, code and age (in years) / Continent, pays ou zone, date, code et âge (en années)	Number - Nombre			Rate - Taux		
	Both sexes Les deux sexes	Male Masculin	Female Féminin	Both sexes Les deux sexes	Male Masculin	Female Féminin
OCEANIA - OCÉANIE						
Cook Islands - Îles Cook[45]						
2009 (+C)						
20 - 24	3	3	-	...	...	...
25 - 29	1	1	-	...	...	...
30 - 34	2	1	1	...	...	...
35 - 39	4	3	1	...	...	...
40 - 44	-	-	-	...	...	...
45 - 49	2	1	1	...	...	...
50 - 54	3	1	2	...	...	...
55 - 59	1	1	-	...	...	...
60 - 64	6	3	3	...	...	...
65 - 69	8	4	4	...	...	...
70 - 74	9	1	8	...	...	...
75 - 79	8	5	3	...	...	...
80 +	14	9	5	...	...	...
Fiji - Fidji						
2004 (C)						
Total	5 628	3 150	2 478	6.8	7.5	6.1
0	316	180	136	18.8	20.6	16.9
1 - 4	83	53	30	1.2	1.5	◆0.9
5 - 9	47	27	20	0.6	◆0.6	◆0.5
10 - 14	51	24	27	0.6	◆0.5	◆0.7
15 - 19	100	61	39	1.2	1.4	1.0
20 - 24	103	58	45	1.4	1.5	1.2
25 - 29	116	71	45	1.7	2.0	1.4
30 - 34	124	64	60	2.0	2.0	2.0
35 - 39	140	89	51	2.4	3.0	1.8
40 - 44	247	138	109	4.7	5.1	4.3
45 - 49	371	232	139	8.1	10.0	6.2
50 - 54	463	267	196	12.3	14.1	10.6
55 - 59	527	321	206	18.0	22.0	13.9
60 - 64	641	366	275	29.5	34.7	24.5
65 - 69	569	323	246	36.1	43.5	29.4
70 - 74	597	311	286	56.4	64.8	49.4
75 +	1 133	565	568	85.3	103.0	72.9
75 - 79	414	219	195	...	...	...
80 - 84	361	191	170	...	...	...
85 - 89	223	97	126	...	...	...
90 - 94	81	40	41	...	...	...
95 +	54	18	36	...	...	...
Guam[46]						
2004 (C)						
Total	691	426	265	4.4	5.3	3.4
0	42	25	17	...	...	...
1 - 4	4	1	3	...	...	...
5 - 9	3	3	-	◆0.2	◆0.4	-
10 - 14	5	3	2	◆0.3	◆0.4	◆0.3
15 - 19	13	9	4	◆1.0	◆1.3	◆0.6
20 - 24	16	12	4	◆1.4	◆2.1	◆0.7
25 - 29	12	7	5	◆1.1	◆1.2	◆0.9
30 - 34	20	16	4	◆1.6	◆2.6	◆0.7
35 - 39	19	17	2	◆1.6	◆2.7	◆0.3
40 - 44	39	30	9	3.3	◆4.9	◆1.6
45 - 49	37	24	13	3.9	◆4.9	◆2.8
50 - 54	52	40	12	6.3	9.5	◆2.9
55 - 59	60	36	24	9.3	11.1	◆7.5
60 - 64	56	29	27	12.5	◆12.9	◆12.0
65 - 69	59	32	27	15.3	17.4	◆13.4
70 - 74	65	40	25	23.6	31.0	◆17.0
75 - 79	77	47	30	47.7	59.6	◆36.3
80 - 84	53	31	22	55.7	72.8	◆41.8
85 +	59	24	35	99.2	◆109.1	93.3
Marshall Islands - Îles Marshall						
2006 (+U)						
Total	318	171	147	...	...	...
0	27	17	10	...	...	...
1 - 4	13	7	6	...	...	...

Continent, country or area, date, code and age (in years) Continent, pays ou zone, date, code et âge (en années)	Number - Nombre			Rate - Taux		
	Both sexes Les deux sexes	Male Masculin	Female Féminin	Both sexes Les deux sexes	Male Masculin	Female Féminin
OCEANIA - OCÉANIE						
Marshall Islands - Îles Marshall						
2006 (+U)						
5 - 9	4	3	1	...	...	...
10 - 14	1	1	-	...	...	...
15 - 19	11	7	4	...	...	...
20 - 24	8	4	4	...	...	...
25 - 29	6	5	1	...	...	...
30 - 34	10	4	6	...	...	...
35 - 39	15	10	5	...	...	...
40 - 44	20	10	10	...	...	...
45 - 49	16	11	5	...	...	...
50 - 54	26	11	15	...	...	...
55 - 59	38	26	12	...	...	...
60 - 64	21	9	12	...	...	...
65 +	102	46	56	...	...	...
Micronesia (Federated States of) - Micronésie (États fédérés de)						
2003 (U)						
Total	427	...	...	...	...	...
0	21	...	...	...	...	...
1 - 4	20	...	...	...	...	...
5 - 9	8	...	...	...	...	...
10 - 14	4	...	...	...	...	...
15 - 19	14	...	...	...	...	...
20 - 24	8	...	...	...	...	...
25 - 29	13	...	...	...	...	...
30 - 34	6	...	...	...	...	...
35 - 39	10	...	...	...	...	...
40 - 44	19	...	...	...	...	...
45 - 49	21	...	...	...	...	...
50 - 54	47	...	...	...	...	...
55 - 59	33	...	...	...	...	...
60 - 64	32	...	...	...	...	...
65 - 69	50	...	...	...	...	...
70 +	121	...	...	...	...	...
New Caledonia - Nouvelle-Calédonie						
2010 (C)						
Total	1 191	701	490	4.8	5.5	4.0
0	19	9	10	...	...	...
1 - 4	3	1	2	...	...	...
5 - 9	9	8	1	♦0.5	♦0.8	♦0.1
10 - 14	1	1	-	-	♦0.1	-
15 - 19	14	11	3	♦0.6	♦1.0	♦0.3
20 - 24	23	17	6	♦1.2	♦1.7	♦0.6
25 - 29	32	23	9	1.7	♦2.5	♦1.0
30 - 34	20	14	6	♦1.1	♦1.5	♦0.6
35 - 39	42	32	10	2.1	3.1	♦1.0
40 - 44	34	25	9	1.8	♦2.6	♦1.0
45 - 49	46	33	13	2.8	3.9	♦1.6
50 - 54	77	46	31	5.6	6.6	4.6
55 - 59	68	49	19	6.0	8.5	♦3.4
60 - 64	114	86	28	11.6	16.6	♦6.0
65 - 69	114	74	40	15.9	20.3	11.4
70 - 74	130	79	51	23.6	29.9	17.8
75 - 79	131	67	64	36.6	39.4	34.1
80 +	314	126	188	80.9	81.4	80.6
80 - 84	132	60	72	...	...	...
85 - 89	97	43	54	...	...	...
90 - 94	52	17	35	...	...	...
95 +	33	6	27	...	...	...
New Zealand - Nouvelle-Zélande[15]						
2012 (+C)						
Total	30 099	15 056	15 043	6.8	6.9	6.7
0	256	142	114	4.2	4.6	3.9
1 - 4	64	35	29	0.3	0.3	♦0.2
5 - 9	31	17	14	0.1	♦0.1	♦0.1
10 - 14	46	29	17	0.2	♦0.2	♦0.1

Continent, country or area, date, code and age (in years) Continent, pays ou zone, date, code et âge (en annèes)	Number - Nombre			Rate - Taux		
	Both sexes Les deux sexes	Male Masculin	Female Féminin	Both sexes Les deux sexes	Male Masculin	Female Féminin
OCEANIA - OCÉANIE						
New Zealand - Nouvelle-Zélande[15]						
2012 (+C)						
15 - 19	172	118	54	0.6	0.7	0.4
20 - 24	191	137	54	0.6	0.8	0.3
25 - 29	152	118	34	0.5	0.8	0.2
30 - 34	173	94	79	0.6	0.7	0.6
35 - 39	232	146	86	0.8	1.1	0.6
40 - 44	419	238	181	1.3	1.6	1.1
45 - 49	665	367	298	2.1	2.4	1.8
50 - 54	934	530	404	3.1	3.6	2.6
55 - 59	1 131	676	455	4.3	5.2	3.4
60 - 64	1 632	962	670	6.9	8.3	5.5
65 - 69	2 157	1 291	866	11.3	13.8	8.9
70 - 74	2 824	1 660	1 164	18.5	22.7	14.7
75 - 79	3 430	1 905	1 525	31.7	37.9	26.3
80 - 84	4 799	2 541	2 258	57.4	68.9	48.3
85 - 89	5 419	2 413	3 006	107.3	124.1	96.7
90 +	5 372	1 637	3 735	237.7	270.1	226.0
90 - 94	3 733	1 251	2 482	...	...	...
95 - 99	1 414	352	1 062	...	...	...
100 +	225	34	191	...	...	...
Niue - Nioué[47]						
2009 (C)						
Total	12	6	6	...	...	...
0	-	-	-	...	...	...
1 - 4	-	-	-	...	...	...
5 - 9	-	-	-	...	...	...
10 - 14	-	-	-	...	...	...
15 - 19	-	-	-	...	...	...
20 - 24	-	-	-	...	...	...
25 - 29	-	-	-	...	...	...
30 - 34	-	-	-	...	...	...
35 - 39	-	-	-	...	...	...
40 - 44	-	-	-	...	...	...
45 - 49	-	-	-	...	...	...
50 - 54	-	-	-	...	...	...
55 - 59	2	2	-	...	...	...
60 - 64	-	-	-	...	...	...
65 - 69	-	-	-	...	...	...
70 - 74	1	-	1	...	...	...
75 - 79	1	1	-	...	...	...
80 +	8	3	5	...	...	...
Northern Mariana Islands - Îles Mariannes septentrionales						
2005 (U)						
Total	188	107	81	...	...	...
0	5	1	4	...	...	...
1 - 4	4	3	1	...	...	...
5 - 9	-	-	-	...	...	...
10 - 14	3	2	1	...	...	...
15 - 19	1	-	1	...	...	...
20 - 24	3	2	1	...	...	...
25 - 29	10	3	7	...	...	...
30 - 34	11	9	2	...	...	...
35 - 39	7	4	3	...	...	...
40 - 44	11	6	5	...	...	...
45 - 49	7	6	1	...	...	...
50 - 54	17	13	4	...	...	...
55 - 59	19	11	8	...	...	...
60 - 64	20	9	11	...	...	...
65 - 69	20	14	6	...	...	...
70 - 74	20	11	9	...	...	...
75 - 79	13	6	7	...	...	...
80 - 84	8	5	3	...	...	...
85 - 89	5	1	4	...	...	...
90 - 94	2	-	2	...	...	...

19. Deaths by age and sex, age-specific death rates by sex: latest available year, 2003 - 2012
Décès et taux de mortalité selon l'âge et le sexe : dernière année disponible, 2003 - 2012 (continued - suite)

Continent, country or area, date, code and age (in years) Continent, pays ou zone, date, code et âge (en années)	Number - Nombre			Rate - Taux		
	Both sexes Les deux sexes	Male Masculin	Female Féminin	Both sexes Les deux sexes	Male Masculin	Female Féminin
OCEANIA - OCÉANIE						
Northern Mariana Islands - Îles Mariannes septentrionales						
2005 (U)						
95 - 99	2	1	1	...	...	...
100 + ...	-	-	-	...	...	...
Palau - Palaos						
2003 (C)						
Total..	136	79	57	...	...	...
0	3	1	2	...	...	...
1 - 14	5	4	1	...	...	...
15 - 24	7	4	3	...	...	...
25 - 44	17	12	5	...	...	...
45 - 64	33	29	4	...	...	...
65 + ...	71	29	42	...	...	...
2005 (C)						
Total..	134	...	...	6.7	...	...
0	5	...	...	♦18.5	...	...
1 - 4	1	...	...	♦0.9	...	...
5 - 9	-	...	...	-	...	...
10 - 14	-	...	...	-	...	...
15 - 19	2	...	...	♦1.4	...	...
20 - 24	1	...	...	♦0.8	...	...
25 - 29	5	...	...	♦3.2	...	...
30 - 34	4	...	...	♦2.2	...	...
35 - 39	6	...	...	♦3.1	...	...
40 - 44	9	...	...	♦4.8	...	...
45 - 49	13	...	...	♦8.5	...	...
50 - 54	14	...	...	♦11.8	...	...
55 - 59	9	...	...	♦12.3	...	...
60 - 64	10	...	...	♦19.8	...	...
65 - 69	8	...	...	♦21.4	...	...
70 - 74	11	...	...	♦42.8	...	...
75 + ...	36	...	...	71.1	...	...
Pitcairn						
2007 (C)						
Total..	1	...	...	...	...	...
0	-	...	...	...	...	...
1 - 4	-	...	...	...	...	...
5 - 9	-	...	...	...	...	...
10 - 14	-	...	...	...	...	...
15 - 19	-	...	...	...	...	...
20 - 24	-	...	...	...	...	...
25 - 29	-	...	...	...	...	...
30 - 34	-	...	...	...	...	...
35 - 39	-	...	...	...	...	...
40 - 44	-	...	...	...	...	...
45 - 49	-	...	...	...	...	...
50 - 54	-	...	...	...	...	...
55 - 59	-	...	...	...	...	...
60 - 64	-	...	...	...	...	...
65 - 69	-	...	...	...	...	...
70 - 74	-	...	...	...	...	...
75 - 79	1	...	...	...	...	...
80 - 84	-	...	...	...	...	...
85 - 89	-	...	...	...	...	...
90 + ...	-	...	...	...	...	...
Samoa[48]						
2011 (I)						
Total..	812	427	385	4.3	4.4	4.2
0	78	51	27	...	...	...
1 - 4	14	7	7	...	...	...
5 - 9	4	1	3	♦0.2	♦0.1	♦0.3
10 - 14	2	-	2	♦0.1	-	♦0.2
15 - 19	10	7	3	♦0.5	♦0.7	♦0.3
20 - 24	12	5	7	♦0.8	♦0.6	♦1.0
25 - 29	10	8	2	♦0.8	♦1.2	♦0.3
30 - 34	6	4	2	♦0.5	♦0.7	♦0.4

19. Deaths by age and sex, age-specific death rates by sex: latest available year, 2003 - 2012
Décès et taux de mortalité selon l'âge et le sexe : dernière année disponible, 2003 - 2012 (continued - suite)

Continent, country or area, date, code and age (in years) Continent, pays ou zone, date, code et âge (en années)	Number - Nombre			Rate - Taux		
	Both sexes Les deux sexes	Male Masculin	Female Féminin	Both sexes Les deux sexes	Male Masculin	Female Féminin

OCEANIA - OCÉANIE

Samoa[48]
2011 (|)

35 - 39	20	8	12	♦1.8	♦1.4	♦2.3
40 - 44	19	12	7	♦1.8	♦2.1	♦1.4
45 - 49	38	20	18	4.3	♦4.4	♦4.2
50 - 54	48	28	20	6.3	♦7.1	♦5.5
55 - 59	49	22	27	8.3	♦7.3	♦9.3
60 - 64	69	37	32	17.3	18.5	16.2
65 - 69	76	36	40	22.5	22.4	22.6
70 - 74	101	59	42	39.5	49.7	30.7
75 +	250	120	130	74.5	92.2	63.4
75 - 79	80	45	35	...	...	...
80 - 84	84	37	47	...	...	...
85 - 89	62	30	32	...	...	...
90 - 94	17	6	11	...	...	...
95 - 99	7	2	5	...	...	...
100 +	-	-	-	...	...	...
Unknown - Inconnu	6	2	4	..	..	..

Tonga[49]
2006 (|)

Total	709	402	307	6.9	7.6	6.1
0 - 4	61	38	24	5.1	6.2	♦4.1
0	53	32	21	...	...	...
1 - 4	8	6	3	...	...	...
5 - 9	10	5	4	♦0.9	♦0.8	♦0.7
10 - 14	7	4	4	♦0.6	♦0.6	♦0.7
15 - 19	12	8	3	♦1.1	♦1.3	♦0.6
20 - 24	11	9	2	♦1.0	♦1.6	♦0.4
25 - 29	7	5	2	♦0.9	♦1.2	♦0.5
30 - 34	12	9	4	♦2.1	♦3.2	♦1.4
35 - 39	12	7	5	♦2.1	♦2.4	♦1.8
40 - 44	19	11	8	♦3.8	♦4.4	♦3.2
45 - 49	29	18	11	♦6.8	♦8.8	♦4.9
50 - 54	29	16	13	♦7.7	♦8.9	♦6.5
55 - 59	37	23	15	11.8	♦15.6	♦9.0
60 - 64	53	33	20	18.5	23.9	♦13.5
65 - 69	49	28	21	20.2	♦22.5	♦17.7
70 - 74	70	38	32	37.5	39.7	35.2
75 +	288	149	139	135.1	141.2	129.2
75 - 79	95	54	41	...	...	...
80 +	193	95	98	...	...	...

Tuvalu
2005 (U)

Total	59	33	26	...	...	...
0	6	5	1	...	...	...
1 - 4	2	1	1	...	...	...
5 - 9	-	-	-	...	...	...
10 - 14	-	-	-	...	...	...
15 - 19	-	-	-	...	...	...
20 - 24	1	1	-	...	...	...
25 - 29	-	-	-	...	...	...
30 - 34	1	1	-	...	...	...
35 - 39	2	2	-	...	...	...
40 - 44	2	2	-	...	...	...
45 - 49	3	3	-	...	...	...
50 - 54	6	3	3	...	...	...
55 - 59	4	3	1	...	...	...
60 - 64	7	2	5	...	...	...
65 - 69	6	2	4	...	...	...
70 - 74	1	-	1	...	...	...
75 - 79	8	4	4	...	...	...
80 - 84	8	3	5	...	...	...
85 - 89	2	1	1	...	...	...
Unknown - Inconnu	-	-	-	..	..	..

19. Deaths by age and sex, age-specific death rates by sex: latest available year, 2003 - 2012
Décès et taux de mortalité selon l'âge et le sexe : dernière année disponible, 2003 - 2012 (continued - suite)

Continent, country or area, date, code and age (in years) / Continent, pays ou zone, date, code et âge (en années)	Number - Nombre			Rate - Taux		
	Both sexes Les deux sexes	Male Masculin	Female Féminin	Both sexes Les deux sexes	Male Masculin	Female Féminin
OCEANIA - OCÉANIE						
Wallis and Futuna Islands - Îles Wallis et Futuna						
2008 (C)						
Total	90	51	39	...	...	...
0 - 4	1	1	-	...	...	...
5 - 9	-	-	-	...	...	...
10 - 14	1	1	-	...	...	...
15 - 19	2	1	1	...	...	...
20 - 24	4	3	1	...	...	...
25 - 29	4	4	-	...	...	...
30 - 34	3	3	-	...	...	...
35 - 39	2	1	1	...	...	...
40 - 44	-	-	-	...	...	...
45 - 49	2	1	1	...	...	...
50 - 54	2	1	1	...	...	...
55 - 59	4	2	2	...	...	...
60 - 64	5	4	1	...	...	...
65 - 69	12	8	4	...	...	...
70 - 74	15	9	6	...	...	...
75 - 79	13	4	9	...	...	...
80 - 84	11	4	7	...	...	...
85 - 89	5	3	2	...	...	...
90 - 94	4	1	3	...	...	...
95 - 99	-	-	-	...	...	...
100 +	-	-	-	...	...	...

FOOTNOTES - NOTES

♦ Rates based on 30 or fewer deaths. - Taux basés sur 30 décès ou moins.

Italics: estimates which are less reliable. - Italiques : estimations moins sûres.

* Provisional. - Données provisoires.

'Code' indicates the source of data, as follows:
C - Civil registration, estimated over 90% complete
U - Civil registration, estimated less than 90% complete
| - Other source, estimated reliable
+ - Data tabulated by date of registration rather than occurence
... - Information not available

Le 'Code' indique la source des données, comme suit :
C - Registres de l'état civil considérés complets à 90 p. 100 au moins
U - Registres de l'état civil qui ne sont pas considérés complets à 90 p. 100 au moins
| - Autre source, considérée pas douteuses
+ - Données exploitées selon la date de l'enregistrement et non la date de l'événement
... - Information pas disponible

[1] Data from Health Statistics Reports since 1998, due to incompleteness of civil registration. - Données provenant des "Health Statistics Reports" (bulletins statistiques de santé) depuis 1998, en raison des déficiences de l'état civil.
[2] Data refer to the 12 months preceding the census in June. - Les données se raportent aux 12 mois précédant le recensement de juin.
[3] Excludes the islands of St. Brandon and Agalega. - Non compris les îles St. Brandon et Agalega.
[4] Data refer to the 12 months preceding the census in April. The figures in this table are derived from survey data. They are representative only of private households, internally displaced persons, refugees and nomads, and do not include cattle camps, institutional households, homeless people or overnight travelers. - Les données se rapportent aux douze mois précédant le recensement d'avril. Les chiffres de ce tableau proviennent de données d'enquête. Ils représentent exclusivement les ménages privés et les déplacés, réfugiés et nomades; ils ne comprennent ni les personnes se trouvant dans des camps pastoraux et des établissements collectifs, ni les sans-abri, ni les voyageurs.

[5] Data refer to the 12 months preceding the census in December. - Les données se rapportent aux 12 mois précédant le recensement de décembre.
[6] Data refer to the 12 months preceding the census in October. - Les données se rapportent aux 12 mois précédant le recensement de octobre.
[7] Data refer to the 12 months preceding the census in May. - Les données se rapportent aux 12 mois précédant le recensement de mai.
[8] Excluding visitors. - Ne comprend pas les visiteurs.
[9] Reason for discrepancy between these figures and corresponding figures shown elsewhere not ascertained. - On ne sait pas comment s'explique la divergence entre ces chiffres et les chiffres correspondants indiqués ailleurs.
[10] Excluding non-residents and foreign service personnel and their dependants. - À l'exclusion des non-résidents et du personnel diplomatique et de leurs charges de famille.
[11] Including Canadian residents temporarily in the United States, but excluding United States residents temporarily in Canada. - Y compris les résidents canadiens se trouvant temporairement aux Etats-Unis, mais ne comprenant pas les résidents des Etats-Unis se trouvant temporairement au Canada.
[12] Excluding live-born infants who died before their birth was registered. - Non compris les enfants nés vivants décédés avant l'enregistrement de leur naissance.
[13] Source: World Health Organization. - Source : Organisation mondiale de la santé.
[14] Data have been adjusted for undercoverage of infant deaths and sudden and violent deaths. - Ajusté pour la sous-estimation de la mortalité infantile, du nombre de morts soudaines et de morts violentes.
[15] Data refer to resident population only. - Pour la population résidante seulement.
[16] Figures for male and female do not add up to the total, since they do not include the category "Unknown". - La somme des chiffres indiqués pour les sexes masculin et féminin n'est pas égale au total parce qu'elle n'inclut pas la catégorie " inconnue ".
[17] Excludes nomadic Indian tribes. - Non compris les tribus d'Indiens nomades.
[18] Source: Reports of the Ministry of Health. - Source: Rapports du Ministère de la Santé.
[19] Including non-residents. - Y compris les non-résidents.
[20] Excluding infants born alive of less than 28 weeks' gestation, of less than 1 000 grams in weight and 35 centimeters in length, who die within seven days of birth. - Non compris les enfants nés vivants après moins de 28 semaines de gestation, pesant moins de 1 000 grammes, mesurant moins de 35 centimètres et décédés dans les sept jours qui ont suivi leur naissance.

[21] For statistical purposes, the data for China do not include those for the Hong Kong Special Administrative Region (Hong Kong SAR), Macao Special Administrative Region (Macao SAR) and Taiwan province of China. Data refer to the 12 months preceding the census in November. - Pour la présentation des statistiques, les données pour la Chine ne comprennent pas la Région Administrative Spéciale de Hong Kong (Hong Kong RAS), la Région Administrative Spéciale de Macao (Macao RAS) et Taïwan province de Chine. Données se rapportant aux 12 mois précédant le recensement de novembre.

[22] Data refer to government controlled areas. - Les données se rapportent aux zones contrôlées par le Gouvernement.

[23] Data refer to the Iranian Year which begins on 21 March and ends on 20 March of the following year. - Les données concernent l'année iranienne, qui commence le 21 mars et se termine le 20 mars de l'année suivante.

[24] Includes data for East Jerusalem and Israeli residents in certain other territories under occupation by Israeli military forces since June 1967. Including deaths abroad of Israeli residents who were out of the country for less than a year. - Y compris les données pour Jérusalem-Est et les résidents israéliens dans certains autres territoires occupés depuis 1967 par les forces armées israéliennes. Y compris les décès à l'étranger de résidents israéliens qui ont quitté le pays depuis moins d'un an.

[25] Data refer to Japanese nationals in Japan only. - Les données se raportent aux nationaux japonais au Japon seulement.

[26] Data refer to urban areas only. - Données ne concernant que les zones urbaines.

[27] Data from Births and Deaths Notification System (Ministry of Health and all health care providers). - Les données proviennent du système de notification des naissances et des décès (Ministère de la santé et tous prestataires de soins de santé).

[28] Excluding unknown sex. - Non compris le sexe inconnu.

[29] Excluding data for the Pakistan-held part of Jammu and Kashmir, the final status of which has not yet been determined. Based on the results of the Pakistan Demographic Survey. - Non compris les données concernant la partie du Jammu et Cachemire occupée par le Pakistan dont le statut définitif n'a pas été déterminé. Données extraites de l'enquête démographique effectuée par le Pakistan.

[30] Excluding alien armed forces, civilian aliens employed by armed forces, and foreign diplomatic personnel and their dependants. - Non compris les militaires étrangers, les civils étrangers employés par les forces armées ni le personnel diplomatique étranger et les membres de leur famille les accompagnant.

[31] The registration of births and deaths is conducted by the Ministry of Health. An estimate of completeness is not provided. - L'enregistrement des naissances et des décès est mené par le Ministère de la Santé. Le degré estimatif de complétude n'est pas fourni.

[32] Excluding data from Mulative and Killnochchi districts. - À l'exclusion des données des districts de Mulative et Killnochchi.

[33] Including deaths of nationals abroad. - Y compris les décès des nationaux survenus à l'étranger.

[34] Including armed forces stationed outside the country, but excluding alien armed forces stationed in the area. - Y compris les militaires nationaux hors du pays, mais non compris les militaires étrangers en garnison sur le territoire.

[35] Excluding Faeroe Islands and Greenland shown separately, if available. - Non compris les Iles Féroé et le Groenland, qui font l'objet de rubriques distinctes, si disponible.

[36] Including armed forces stationed outside the country. - Y compris les militaires nationaux hors du pays.

[37] Definition of localities was revised from 2011 causing a break with the previous series. - La rupture par rapport aux séries précédentes s'explique par le fait que la définition des localités a été révisée depuis 2011.

[38] Data refer to the 12 months preceding the census in April. - Les données se rapportent aux douze mois précédant le recensement d'avril.

[39] Including residents outside the country if listed in a Netherlands population register. - Englobe les résidents se trouvant à l'étranger à condition qu'ils soient inscrits sur le registre de population des Pays-Bas.

[40] Including residents temporarily outside the country. - Y compris les résidents se trouvant temporairement hors du pays.

[41] Excluding Transnistria and the municipality of Bender. - Les données ne tiennent pas compte de l'information sur la Transnistria et la municipalité de Bender.

[42] Excludes data for Kosovo and Metohia. - Sans les données pour le Kosovo et Metohie.

[43] Data includes deaths resulting from births with weight 500g and more (if weight is unknown - with length 25 centimeters and more, or with gestation during 22 weeks or more). - Y compris les décès de nouveau-nés de 500 grammes ou plus (si le poids est inconnu – de 25 centimètres de long ou plus, ou après une grossesse de 22 semaines ou plus).

[44] Excluding Channel Islands (Guernsey and Jersey) and Isle of Man, shown separately, if available. - Non compris les îles Anglo-Normandes (Guernesey et Jersey) et l'île de Man, qui font l'objet de rubriques distinctes, si disponible.

[45] Excluding Niue, shown separately, which is part of Cook Islands, but because of remoteness is administered separately. - Non compris Nioué, qui fait l'objet d'une rubrique distincte et qui fait partie des îles Cook, mais qui, en raison de son éloignement, est administrée séparément.

[46] Including United States military personnel, their dependants and contract employees. - Y compris les militaires des Etats-Unis, les membres de leur famille les accompagnant et les agents contractuels des Etats-Unis.

[47] Includes deaths occurred in New Zealand but buried in Niue and deaths occurred in Niue but buried elsewhere. - Y compris les personnes décédées en Nouvelle-Zélande qui sont enterrées à Nioué et les personnes décédées à Nioué qui sont enterrées ailleurs.

[48] Data refer to the 12 months preceding the census in November. - Données se rapportant aux 12 mois précédant le recensement de novembre.

[49] Estimate based on results of the Population Census. - Estimation fondeé sur les résultats du recensement de la population.

Table 20 - *Demographic Yearbook 2012*

Table 20 presents the life tables' probabilities of dying in the five year interval following specified ages ($_5q_x$), for each sex, for the latest available year between 2000 and 2012. The probabilities are multiplied by a thousand, that is, the values presented in the table are 1000*$_5q_x$.

Male and female probabilities of dying are shown separately for selected ages beginning at birth and proceeding at every fifth age thereafter up to age 100.

The values presented in the table are derived by the United Nations Statistics Division from the official complete life tables reported by the countries or areas.

Data are shown with one decimal regardless of the number of digits provided in the original computation.

The life table is a statistical device for summarizing the mortality experience of a population, from which the probability of dying, survivorship and expectation of life can be calculated. It is based on the assumption that the theoretical cohort is subject, throughout its existence, to the age-specific mortality rates observed at a particular time. Thus, levels of mortality prevailing at the time a life table is constructed are assumed to remain unchanged into the future until all members of the cohort have died.

Reliability of data: The values shown in this table are derived from official complete life tables. It is assumed that, if necessary, the basic data (population and deaths classified by age and sex) have been adjusted for deficiencies before their use in constructing the complete life tables.

Limitations: The life tables' probabilities of dying are subject to the same qualifications as have been set forth for population statistics in general and death statistics in particular, as discussed in sections 3 and 4, respectively, of the Technical Notes. They must be interpreted strictly using the underlying assumption that surviving cohorts are subjected to the same age-specific mortality rates of the period to which the life table refers.

Earlier data: The life tables' probabilities of dying at specified ages, for each sex, have been shown in previous issues of the *Demographic Yearbook*. For information on specific years covered, the reader should consult the Historical Index.

Tableau 20 – *Annuaire démographique 2012*

Le tableau 20 donne les probabilités de décès dans l'intervalle de cinq ans que suit l'âge spécifié ($_5q_x$), pour chaque sexe, pour la dernière année disponible entre 2000 et 2012. Les probabilités sont multipliées par mille, c'est-à-dire que les valeurs indiquées dans le tableau sont égales à $1000*_5q_x$.

Les probabilités de décès sont indiquées séparément pour les hommes et les femmes pour différents âges, depuis la naissance puis tous les cinq ans jusqu'à 100 ans.

Les chiffres indiqués dans ce tableau ont été calculés par la Division de statistique de l'Organisation des Nations Unies à partir des tables de mortalité complètes communiquées par les pays ou zones.

Les données sont arrondies à la première décimale, indépendamment du nombre de décimales qui figurent dans le calcul initial.

La table de mortalité est un moyen statistique que s'utilise pour donner un aperçu complet de la mortalité d'une population incluant les probabilités de décès et l'espérance de vie à chaque âge. Les tables de mortalité reposent sur l'hypothèse que chaque cohorte théoriquement distinguée connaît, pendant toute son existence, les taux de mortalité par âge observé à un moment donné. Les taux de mortalité correspondant à l'époque à laquelle sont calculées les tables de mortalité sont ainsi censés demeurer inchangées dans l'avenir jusqu'au décès de tous les membres de la cohorte.

Fiabilité des donnés : Les chiffres indiqués dans ce tableau ont été calculés à partir des tables officielles de mortalité complètes. En ce qui concerne les chiffres extraits de tables officielles de mortalité, on part du principe que les données de base (effectif de la population et nombre de décès selon l'âge et le sexe) ont été ajustées, en tant que de besoin, avant de servir à l'établissement de la table de mortalité.

Insuffisance des données : Les probabilités de décès appellent les mêmes réserves que celles qui ont été formulées à propos des statistiques de la population en général et des statistiques de mortalité en particulier (voir les sections 3 et 4 des Notes techniques). Lorsque l'on interprète les données, il ne faut jamais perdre de vue que, par hypothèse, les cohortes de survivants sont soumises, pour chaque âge, aux conditions de mortalité de la période visée par la table de mortalité.

Données publiées antérieurement : Les probabilités de décès pour chaque sexe figuraient déjà dans des éditions antérieures de *l'Annuaire démographique*. Pour plus de précisions concernant les années pour lesquelles ces données ont été publiées, se reporter à l'index historique.

20. Probability of dying in the five year interval following specified age (5qx), by sex, latest available year: 2000 - 2012
Probabilité de décès dans l'intervalle de cinq ans qui suit un âge donné (5qx), par sexe, dernière année disponible : 2000 - 2012

Continent, country or area and date / Continent, pays ou zone et date	Age (in years) - Age (en années)																				
	0	5	10	15	20	25	30	35	40	45	50	55	60	65	70	75	80	85	90	95	100

AFRICA - AFRIQUE

Zimbabwe
2001 - 2002

| Male - Hommes | 116.9 | 18.0 | 12.8 | 12.2 | 30.6 | 70.9 | 129.9 | 193.2 | 193.5 | 186.2 | 175.7 | 177.3 | 167.1 | 186.5 | 197.2 | 270.7 | 297.7 | 432.4 | 545.1 | ... | ... |
| Female - Femmes | 100.5 | 15.2 | 10.8 | 15.2 | 46.7 | 97.4 | 141.4 | 159.8 | 125.9 | 122.9 | 101.0 | 99.6 | 100.9 | 122.5 | 128.8 | 161.1 | 223.5 | 304.5 | 438.0 | ... | ... |

AMERICA, NORTH - AMÉRIQUE DU NORD

Canada
2000 - 2002

| Male - Hommes | 6.9 | 0.5 | 1.3 | 3.6 | 4.2 | 4.2 | 4.9 | 6.0 | 9.8 | 14.2 | 23.1 | 35.7 | 58.9 | 93.6 | 147.5 | 232.0 | 356.1 | 522.1 | 699.2 | 832.4 | ... |
| Female - Femmes | 5.5 | 0.4 | 0.7 | 1.5 | 1.7 | 1.7 | 2.3 | 3.6 | 5.5 | 8.8 | 13.9 | 22.4 | 35.1 | 55.7 | 88.8 | 145.8 | 244.8 | 402.2 | 576.2 | 750.4 | ... |

Costa Rica
2007

| Male - Hommes | 12.6 | 0.8 | 1.2 | 4.2 | 5.3 | 6.8 | 7.9 | 9.0 | 10.5 | 16.8 | 24.2 | 35.4 | 54.0 | 83.4 | 126.3 | 208.9 | 323.3 | 458.3 | 637.4 | 793.5 | *1000 |
| Female - Femmes | 10.2 | 0.6 | 0.8 | 1.5 | 1.9 | 1.9 | 3.0 | 4.3 | 5.4 | 8.9 | 13.2 | 20.5 | 33.2 | 58.2 | 83.7 | 147.7 | 240.8 | 407.6 | 563.5 | 791.3 | *1000 |

Cuba
2005 - 2007

| Male - Hommes | 7.5 | 1.2 | 1.5 | 2.7 | 3.9 | 4.8 | 5.8 | 7.7 | 11.7 | 19.1 | 30.0 | 45.4 | 67.1 | 100.4 | 153.8 | 231.5 | 340.6 | 482.1 | 616.8 | 675.5 | *1000 |
| Female - Femmes | 6.5 | 0.7 | 0.8 | 1.4 | 2.0 | 2.5 | 3.1 | 4.5 | 7.3 | 12.3 | 19.4 | 29.6 | 45.0 | 70.9 | 112.1 | 174.8 | 276.2 | 420.9 | 573.8 | 657.2 | *1000 |

Curaçao[1]
2008 - 2010

| Male - Hommes | 12.6 | 0.0 | 0.6 | 3.1 | 10.3 | 9.0 | 8.4 | 10.7 | 15.7 | 21.7 | 33.8 | 55.6 | 87.9 | 136.6 | 186.1 | 308.6 | 396.9 | 546.1 | 765.7 | 906.0 | ... |
| Female - Femmes | 11.3 | 2.0 | 1.6 | 3.7 | 8.8 | 3.7 | 3.2 | 4.1 | 7.4 | 15.0 | 14.6 | 27.3 | 41.1 | 60.0 | 101.2 | 163.0 | 280.0 | 415.0 | 685.4 | 883.2 | ... |

Greenland - Groenland
2007 - 2011

| Male - Hommes | 0.0 | 0.0 | 0.0 | 0.0 | 0.0 | 0.0 | 0.0 | 0.0 | 0.0 | 0.0 | 0.0 | 0.1 | 0.1 | 0.2 | 0.4 | 0.6 | 1.1 | 1.5 | 2.4 | 1.0 | ... |
| Female - Femmes | 0.0 | 0.0 | 0.0 | 0.0 | 0.0 | 0.0 | 0.0 | 0.0 | 0.0 | 0.0 | 0.0 | 0.1 | 0.1 | 0.2 | 0.2 | 0.4 | 0.8 | 0.9 | 1.6 | 3.5 | ... |

Guadeloupe
2002

| Male - Hommes | 8.7 | 1.1 | 2.1 | 4.6 | 9.3 | 11.1 | 10.0 | 12.7 | 14.6 | 24.3 | 31.1 | 45.3 | 68.9 | 95.0 | 141.6 | 219.3 | 290.6 | 421.7 | 994.4 | *1000 | ... |
| Female - Femmes | 6.0 | 0.3 | 0.3 | 1.2 | 2.9 | 1.4 | 4.3 | 5.8 | 8.0 | 8.1 | 10.9 | 22.1 | 39.9 | 55.5 | 87.1 | 112.0 | 212.4 | 331.5 | 984.3 | *1000 | ... |

Jamaica - Jamaïque
2006

| Male - Hommes | 31.7 | 2.8 | 2.5 | 4.5 | 6.5 | 6.5 | 7.0 | 9.4 | 14.5 | 23.2 | 37.5 | 60.5 | 96.9 | 153.2 | 236.8 | 353.8 | 502.7 | 667.6 | 817.2 | 921.8 | *1000 |
| Female - Femmes | 18.0 | 1.3 | 1.1 | 1.7 | 2.6 | 3.4 | 4.3 | 5.9 | 8.7 | 13.9 | 22.8 | 38.0 | 63.2 | 104.5 | 169.8 | 268.2 | 405.3 | 574.1 | 747.0 | 883.6 | *1000 |

Martinique
2007

| Male - Hommes | 11.6 | 1.0 | 1.1 | 4.2 | 8.8 | 7.5 | 8.8 | 8.5 | 10.4 | 13.5 | 26.7 | 28.9 | 42.2 | 87.6 | 122.7 | 202.9 | 325.3 | 532.7 | 663.7 | 834.4 | *1000 |
| Female - Femmes | 7.8 | 0.4 | 0.7 | 0.6 | 2.1 | 2.9 | 4.6 | 4.1 | 4.8 | 5.3 | 11.3 | 14.8 | 28.6 | 45.6 | 76.8 | 135.3 | 216.7 | 362.2 | 508.4 | 810.4 | *1000 |

Mexico - Mexique
2005

| Male - Hommes | 21.6 | 1.7 | 2.2 | 4.3 | 7.4 | 9.9 | 12.0 | 15.1 | 20.3 | 28.7 | 41.3 | 59.9 | 86.6 | 124.3 | 176.5 | 246.8 | 337.7 | 448.7 | 574.2 | 702.2 | *1000 |
| Female - Femmes | 17.4 | 1.3 | 1.2 | 1.8 | 2.4 | 3.1 | 4.3 | 6.4 | 9.9 | 15.4 | 23.9 | 37.2 | 57.5 | 88.4 | 134.4 | 201.1 | 293.6 | 414.1 | 557.1 | 705.8 | *1000 |

Panama[2]
2012

| Male - Hommes | 22.7 | 2.1 | 2.6 | 7.4 | 13.4 | 15.1 | 13.9 | 13.3 | 15.2 | 20.1 | 28.8 | 42.4 | 62.8 | 92.7 | 135.7 | 196.2 | 278.2 | 384.0 | 510.7 | 647.7 | *1000 |
| Female - Femmes | 17.2 | 1.3 | 1.5 | 2.5 | 3.5 | 4.6 | 5.6 | 6.9 | 8.8 | 11.9 | 17.1 | 25.4 | 39.0 | 60.6 | 94.7 | 147.0 | 224.5 | 333.1 | 472.9 | 631.7 | *1000 |

United States of America - États-Unis d'Amérique
2008

| Male - Hommes | 8.4 | 0.7 | 0.9 | 4.0 | 6.9 | 6.8 | 7.3 | 9.0 | 13.2 | 20.7 | 31.7 | 45.5 | 64.8 | 95.5 | 142.5 | 218.0 | 332.4 | 498.7 | 684.3 | 835.2 | *1000 |
| Female - Femmes | 7.0 | 0.6 | 0.6 | 1.6 | 2.3 | 2.8 | 3.5 | 5.1 | 8.3 | 12.9 | 18.8 | 26.6 | 41.0 | 63.2 | 98.3 | 155.8 | 250.9 | 405.6 | 604.2 | 786.9 | *1000 |

AMERICA, SOUTH - AMÉRIQUE DU SUD

Brazil - Brésil[2]
2009

| Male - Hommes | 31.2 | 1.9 | 2.1 | 8.1 | 12.9 | 13.9 | 15.7 | 19.3 | 25.3 | 34.9 | 47.3 | 67.9 | 93.6 | 131.7 | 190.7 | 266.8 | *1000 | ... | ... | ... | ... |
| Female - Femmes | 22.5 | 1.3 | 1.2 | 2.2 | 3.0 | 4.0 | 5.4 | 7.7 | 11.9 | 17.9 | 26.4 | 38.8 | 57.9 | 85.5 | 130.1 | 197.2 | *1000 | ... | ... | ... | ... |

20. Probability of dying in the five year interval following specified age (5qx), by sex, latest available year: 2000 - 2012
Probabilité de décès dans l'intervalle de cinq ans qui suit un âge donné (5qx), par sexe, dernière année disponible : 2000 - 2012 (continued - suite)

Continent, country or area and date / Continent, pays ou zone et date	0	5	10	15	20	25	30	35	40	45	50	55	60	65	70	75	80	85	90	95	100
AMERICA, SOUTH - AMÉRIQUE DU SUD																					
Chile - Chili 2011																					
Male - Hommes	9.2	0.8	1.0	3.4	5.3	6.0	6.5	8.5	11.7	17.6	24.9	37.9	62.8	97.3	149.4	261.7	360.2	533.5	931.4	*1000	...
Female - Femmes	7.7	0.6	0.7	1.4	1.8	2.0	2.6	3.6	5.9	8.9	14.1	21.6	36.9	56.8	90.7	161.3	268.4	454.7	814.4	*1000	...
French Guiana - Guyane française 2007																					
Male - Hommes	16.3	1.5	2.1	4.9	7.7	8.1	10.0	14.0	17.2	29.4	16.0	32.3	52.4	79.5	135.5	261.3	306.7	474.0	733.7	...	...
Female - Femmes	15.1	1.9	1.3	1.4	1.2	3.0	4.6	4.2	11.9	11.0	10.4	11.6	26.7	85.4	77.4	203.8	253.1	321.1	434.3	...	...
Uruguay 2004																					
Male - Hommes	20.0	1.3	1.3	3.5	5.8	6.8	7.2	9.0	12.8	21.2	36.4	62.2	95.4	145.2	204.6	305.7	430.5	610.5	776.7	862.5	*1000
Female - Femmes	15.5	1.0	1.1	1.6	1.9	2.7	3.8	5.2	7.9	12.5	19.4	30.5	41.2	63.4	97.2	177.7	292.9	472.0	654.3	820.5	*1000
ASIA - ASIE																					
Armenia - Arménie 2006 - 2007																					
Male - Hommes	15.3	1.1	1.1	2.9	3.9	4.9	7.3	11.4	20.4	28.6	45.0	68.2	112.2	173.3	246.9	350.8	495.4	691.9	870.7	975.9	...
Female - Femmes	11.9	1.0	0.9	0.9	1.6	1.8	2.7	4.4	7.8	11.3	18.4	29.4	52.7	95.7	158.1	254.3	413.9	670.0	851.3	957.0	...
Azerbaijan - Azerbaïdjan 2010																					
Male - Hommes	15.2	2.0	1.6	3.5	4.2	5.5	7.8	10.8	15.7	24.9	41.5	71.5	102.3	165.9	242.3	344.6	458.4	507.0	635.5	735.6	...
Female - Femmes	14.5	1.5	1.2	1.7	2.3	2.6	3.7	4.9	7.1	11.9	20.0	34.4	59.0	96.5	175.1	286.6	402.4	500.4	588.3	646.1	...
China, Hong Kong SAR - Chine, Hong Kong RAS 2011																					
Male - Hommes	2.6	0.4	0.5	1.0	1.7	2.2	3.2	4.7	6.4	10.5	17.3	26.8	43.6	71.1	107.0	180.0	300.5	454.6	631.7	799.8	*1000
Female - Femmes	2.2	0.4	0.3	0.6	1.0	1.0	1.4	2.4	3.5	5.7	9.2	13.3	19.8	29.7	51.8	99.0	176.6	285.4	436.7	623.4	*1000
China, Macao SAR - Chine, Macao RAS 2002 - 2005																					
Male - Hommes	7.2	0.6	0.4	1.7	3.9	5.4	6.2	7.6	9.0	13.6	17.8	25.8	43.1	72.1	128.9	239.9	369.5	574.4	841.2	991.4	*1000
Female - Femmes	5.2	0.4	0.2	0.9	1.5	1.9	2.3	3.8	4.7	5.9	7.4	10.9	19.3	33.3	70.4	186.2	317.0	485.2	717.3	923.7	*1000
Israel - Israël[3] 2007 - 2011																					
Male - Hommes	4.7	0.7	0.7	2.0	3.3	3.1	3.5	4.7	7.1	11.3	18.4	29.7	47.2	74.5	118.1	189.8	305.1	468.8	642.4	749.6	*1000
Female - Femmes	4.3	0.5	0.5	0.7	0.9	1.2	1.7	2.5	4.0	6.5	10.6	17.2	27.9	45.9	77.7	136.4	243.8	419.1	633.4	793.7	*1000
Japan - Japon 2010																					
Male - Hommes	3.4	0.5	0.6	1.3	3.0	3.3	3.7	5.0	7.6	12.0	19.1	30.4	47.3	70.0	108.1	183.7	306.5	473.8	658.4	820.7	...
Female - Femmes	2.9	0.4	0.4	0.8	1.3	1.5	2.0	2.8	4.2	6.4	9.6	13.6	19.9	29.1	48.0	86.8	161.1	302.6	506.4	721.5	...
Kazakhstan 2005																					
Male - Hommes	21.2	2.9	3.3	7.8	17.2	27.1	34.1	41.8	55.6	75.9	105.2	141.1	191.0	256.5	329.2	413.6	513.6	662.0	795.9	896.1	...
Female - Femmes	16.8	1.9	1.9	3.3	5.3	7.5	10.5	13.3	17.9	26.0	38.8	58.0	83.8	125.4	194.3	297.4	433.3	608.9	783.7	914.7	...
Kyrgyzstan - Kirghizstan 2011																					
Male - Hommes	26.6	1.9	2.0	4.0	5.8	10.2	18.1	25.6	34.4	45.7	67.4	98.6	137.6	204.4	274.3	384.5	507.4	613.4	822.3	905.9	*1000
Female - Femmes	21.4	1.2	1.3	2.8	3.6	4.6	7.6	9.0	13.2	18.6	28.6	42.3	69.2	110.0	167.9	288.0	413.1	569.5	777.3	821.4	*1000
Qatar 2006																					
Male - Hommes	10.2	0.8	1.8	9.4	8.9	6.5	5.6	6.6	7.1	9.0	16.1	22.1	42.2	88.0	167.5	248.6	376.7	*1000	...	...	...
Female - Femmes	9.0	1.3	0.9	2.2	1.4	2.4	1.2	1.8	3.8	6.7	9.8	22.1	76.0	120.2	253.6	354.1	348.3	*1000	...	...	...
Republic of Korea - République de Corée 2011																					
Male - Hommes	4.3	0.6	0.7	1.8	2.7	3.7	4.4	6.2	9.9	16.2	25.1	35.7	51.6	79.6	135.6	221.3	357.5	530.7	693.0	818.6	*1000
Female - Femmes	3.5	0.4	0.5	0.9	1.5	2.1	2.8	3.3	4.5	6.3	8.6	12.1	18.9	32.4	59.2	118.1	226.9	390.3	576.6	741.8	*1000

20. Probability of dying in the five year interval following specified age (5qx), by sex, latest available year: 2000 - 2012
Probabilité de décès dans l'intervalle de cinq ans qui suit un âge donné (5qx), par sexe, dernière année disponible : 2000 - 2012 (continued - suite)

Continent, country or area and date / Continent, pays ou zone et date	0	5	10	15	20	25	30	35	40	45	50	55	60	65	70	75	80	85	90	95	100
ASIA - ASIE																					
Singapore - Singapour[4]																					
2012																					
Male - Hommes	3.2	0.6	0.7	1.2	2.2	2.1	2.3	3.4	5.8	10.3	17.1	28.7	45.9	74.0	124.8	201.5	297.9	441.1	614.2	786.7	*1000
Female - Femmes	2.3	0.5	0.4	0.8	0.9	1.2	1.7	2.3	3.8	6.6	10.2	15.7	25.7	42.3	73.0	131.8	213.1	339.8	507.4	694.0	*1000
EUROPE																					
Austria - Autriche																					
2011																					
Male - Hommes	5.3	0.4	0.4	2.4	3.7	3.2	3.8	4.7	7.5	12.9	22.8	36.3	59.9	85.5	118.1	198.9	329.3	509.8	706.0	...	...
Female - Femmes	3.3	0.5	0.4	1.1	1.4	1.6	1.7	2.3	3.8	7.5	11.9	18.9	29.0	44.4	64.7	116.9	230.0	414.3	639.5	...	...
Belarus - Bélarus																					
2011																					
Male - Hommes	5.8	1.4	1.2	3.9	8.3	14.0	22.2	31.7	43.6	59.5	87.5	125.5	177.7	224.8	289.4	388.7	505.3	632.3	757.4	864.6	...
Female - Femmes	4.4	0.8	0.8	1.6	2.2	3.5	6.3	8.3	12.4	16.8	26.1	42.7	60.9	84.4	137.0	233.3	370.4	545.8	735.9	892.7	...
Belgium - Belgique																					
2006																					
Male - Hommes	4.4	0.6	0.7	2.6	4.6	4.4	5.6	7.1	10.7	17.3	27.2	42.4	65.1	93.3	149.7	248.7	387.2	570.9	751.3	886.0	...
Female - Femmes	3.9	0.5	0.6	1.3	1.1	1.8	2.4	3.8	5.8	10.2	16.3	22.5	33.8	48.2	79.3	149.1	270.8	466.0	663.7	835.2	...
Bulgaria - Bulgarie																					
2009 - 2011																					
Male - Hommes	11.9	1.3	1.7	3.3	5.0	5.8	7.5	10.1	18.2	33.1	52.8	80.6	116.3	158.1	226.4	322.6	473.3	633.5	780.6	927.7	...
Female - Femmes	8.8	0.9	1.0	1.8	2.1	2.3	3.5	5.5	9.0	14.3	21.0	32.2	47.3	75.5	129.9	234.2	398.1	588.2	754.4	905.3	...
Czech Republic - République tchèque																					
2011																					
Male - Hommes	3.9	0.5	0.5	2.4	4.0	4.0	4.7	6.6	10.9	17.9	33.3	54.8	85.8	125.0	175.9	264.5	403.0	586.6	785.6	933.7	...
Female - Femmes	2.9	0.3	0.6	1.2	1.4	1.2	1.9	3.1	5.4	8.6	14.1	23.8	37.7	61.0	98.0	170.1	308.9	515.7	765.0	945.6	...
Denmark - Danemark[5]																					
2010 - 2011																					
Male - Hommes	4.2	0.4	0.6	1.4	3.2	2.7	4.1	5.8	8.8	14.4	25.9	40.5	59.9	89.3	141.7	227.6	351.7	535.9	720.3	871.0	...
Female - Femmes	3.5	0.5	0.3	0.8	1.3	0.9	1.5	2.1	4.8	8.9	16.9	25.6	37.4	56.5	93.5	164.2	265.8	428.9	624.6	803.1	...
Estonia - Estonie																					
2011																					
Male - Hommes	2.9	1.2	1.8	3.0	5.9	9.9	13.3	16.8	22.5	32.1	47.4	70.2	103.7	151.6	218.2	307.4	420.1	551.4	688.3	811.7	...
Female - Femmes	2.4	0.0	0.4	1.5	3.2	4.6	5.3	5.6	6.1	7.5	10.7	17.3	30.2	54.3	97.8	173.2	295.0	469.8	676.0	855.4	...
Finland - Finlande[6]																					
2010																					
Male - Hommes	3.2	0.5	0.5	2.4	5.7	5.7	5.9	7.3	11.0	17.1	28.0	44.0	64.1	89.7	134.4	216.2	355.6	521.4	723.7	872.6	...
Female - Femmes	2.6	0.5	0.3	0.9	1.8	2.0	2.1	2.8	5.0	8.4	13.4	18.7	28.1	41.4	66.9	123.1	231.6	420.1	642.0	832.5	...
France																					
2008 - 2010																					
Male - Hommes	4.7	0.5	0.6	2.2	3.8	4.3	4.9	7.1	10.9	17.8	29.4	42.8	57.5	78.6	115.9	185.5	303.7	480.8	687.9	856.1	...
Female - Femmes	3.9	0.4	0.4	0.9	1.2	1.5	2.0	3.3	5.6	9.0	13.7	18.5	25.1	36.0	56.0	99.3	188.0	350.4	569.2	776.0	...
Germany - Allemagne																					
2009 - 2011																					
Male - Hommes	4.7	0.5	0.5	1.7	2.7	3.0	3.6	4.9	7.9	14.3	25.2	39.8	58.9	86.4	131.1	216.1	344.3	519.4	704.8	848.0	...
Female - Femmes	3.8	0.4	0.4	0.9	1.1	1.3	1.7	2.6	4.5	8.1	13.5	20.3	31.1	45.0	71.7	134.3	250.2	441.8	654.2	814.0	...
Greece - Grèce																					
2011																					
Male - Hommes	4.3	0.6	0.8	2.2	3.7	4.2	4.4	5.3	8.8	14.6	23.1	36.5	53.6	80.8	124.5	201.4	329.7	473.7	620.3	774.2	...
Female - Femmes	3.6	0.5	0.7	1.0	1.3	1.4	1.9	2.7	4.1	6.8	10.2	15.7	23.4	36.4	66.2	137.5	287.0	464.0	617.0	772.8	...
Hungary - Hongrie																					
2011																					
Male - Hommes	6.0	0.6	0.7	2.1	3.2	3.6	4.8	7.7	16.2	34.3	61.9	93.2	125.1	162.5	221.4	316.9	426.6	626.1	873.3	991.8	...
Female - Femmes	5.7	0.4	0.5	1.0	1.2	1.5	2.1	3.9	7.7	15.7	26.6	37.9	53.7	75.8	118.6	201.2	330.5	559.2	838.4	985.5	...
Iceland - Islande																					
2010 - 2011																					
Male - Hommes	2.7	0.7	0.7	2.1	2.6	3.7	4.4	4.6	5.6	10.3	12.9	20.4	35.7	69.6	108.3	192.3	323.0	522.4	744.2	906.6	*1000
Female - Femmes	2.2	0.2	0.9	1.5	1.3	0.6	1.4	2.4	3.3	6.1	8.2	15.7	28.4	43.0	71.4	132.7	229.6	409.6	645.1	811.4	*1000
Ireland - Irlande																					
2005 - 2007																					
Male - Hommes	4.9	0.6	0.8	3.6	5.4	4.7	5.1	5.7	8.6	13.3	21.1	33.3	54.5	88.7	148.8	247.0	395.4	567.3	730.3	919.0	...
Female - Femmes	4.5	0.4	0.7	1.6	1.5	1.6	2.0	3.0	5.2	9.2	13.6	21.3	33.8	53.6	90.1	153.4	284.4	460.3	643.4	800.7	...

20. Probability of dying in the five year interval following specified age (5qx), by sex, latest available year: 2000 - 2012
Probabilité de décès dans l'intervalle de cinq ans qui suit un âge donné (5qx), par sexe, dernière année disponible : 2000 - 2012 (continued - suite)

Continent, country or area and date / Continent, pays ou zone et date	Age (in years) - Age (en années)																					
	0	5	10	15	20	25	30	35	40	45	50	55	60	65	70	75	80	85	90	95	100	

EUROPE

	0	5	10	15	20	25	30	35	40	45	50	55	60	65	70	75	80	85	90	95	100
Italy - Italie																					
2009																					
Male - Hommes	4.3	0.5	0.7	2.2	3.1	3.3	3.6	4.5	6.9	10.6	17.4	29.0	46.8	75.3	117.9	200.8	333.8	500.6	721.1	818.2	...
Female - Femmes	3.7	0.4	0.4	0.9	1.0	1.0	1.4	2.2	3.8	6.3	10.4	15.6	24.3	38.5	63.8	117.1	221.2	389.2	629.0	778.3	...
Latvia - Lettonie																					
2006																					
Male - Hommes	10.5	1.4	1.6	3.0	6.2	11.3	18.6	28.3	40.6	56.3	76.6	104.3	143.2	199.8	282.1	397.7	547.0	712.6	...	...	...
Female - Femmes	12.7	1.3	1.2	1.5	2.2	3.2	4.8	7.3	11.2	17.3	26.7	41.0	63.0	96.1	145.1	215.5	312.2	436.5	...	...	...
Lithuania - Lituanie																					
2011																					
Male - Hommes	6.1	1.3	1.4	4.4	8.2	11.6	15.0	22.3	34.3	48.7	66.0	98.0	140.4	181.4	225.1	304.1	422.8	572.9	745.5	839.8	*1000
Female - Femmes	5.0	0.6	0.8	0.6	1.9	2.6	4.7	6.9	10.4	16.0	23.1	33.6	46.6	67.5	99.2	173.1	308.3	495.1	681.6	835.7	*1000
Luxembourg																					
2005 - 2007																					
Male - Hommes	4.2	0.4	0.5	1.3	4.5	3.5	5.2	6.3	8.6	16.2	25.5	39.7	65.9	94.7	151.9	231.1	361.3	563.3	867.2	*1000	...
Female - Femmes	3.5	0.1	0.5	1.1	1.7	2.6	1.8	3.5	5.4	8.6	14.6	21.7	34.1	52.2	80.3	149.2	258.5	447.8	734.9	*1000	...
Malta - Malte																					
2011																					
Male - Hommes	6.4	0.5	0.0	2.5	3.0	3.2	3.2	5.1	5.2	10.8	15.6	24.6	44.0	78.6	130.6	222.1	388.8	572.2	785.0	925.1	...
Female - Femmes	8.7	0.5	0.0	1.2	0.3	3.0	1.4	1.5	4.4	6.3	9.1	16.4	22.8	44.1	64.5	132.0	264.3	496.5	688.5	918.8	...
Netherlands - Pays-Bas																					
2009																					
Male - Hommes	4.8	0.5	0.6	1.4	2.3	2.4	3.0	4.1	6.6	10.7	18.7	30.3	49.9	79.1	132.1	225.2	363.5	539.8	738.0	...	...
Female - Femmes	4.1	0.4	0.5	0.8	1.0	1.3	1.7	2.9	5.0	8.9	15.0	21.5	32.5	47.8	76.4	136.1	249.6	428.5	644.7	...	...
Norway - Norvège																					
2011																					
Male - Hommes	3.5	0.5	0.4	2.9	3.9	3.7	4.8	5.0	6.7	11.3	16.4	27.9	43.2	73.6	117.9	199.4	335.5	518.6	713.4	858.9	...
Female - Femmes	2.2	0.2	0.7	1.8	1.3	1.6	2.1	2.4	3.5	7.1	11.3	19.3	29.0	43.5	67.8	126.8	227.6	404.2	631.4	795.2	...
Poland - Pologne																					
2011																					
Male - Hommes	6.0	0.7	0.8	3.2	5.3	5.6	7.6	11.7	18.4	29.9	48.0	71.8	101.6	138.7	190.7	272.9	389.5	531.0	682.4	818.6	...
Female - Femmes	5.0	0.5	0.6	1.2	1.2	1.4	2.1	3.6	6.1	10.6	18.0	28.2	42.1	60.7	93.0	161.5	281.1	440.6	620.8	787.6	...
Portugal																					
2009 - 2011																					
Male - Hommes	3.9	0.6	0.8	1.9	3.3	3.5	4.9	7.8	13.2	19.9	30.0	41.6	58.9	84.8	133.8	218.9	376.6	643.7	861.4	970.3	...
Female - Femmes	3.3	0.5	0.4	1.0	1.5	1.5	2.3	3.6	5.6	8.3	12.4	16.5	25.1	39.1	69.9	130.6	265.5	540.6	801.0	952.2	...
Republic of Moldova - République de Moldova																					
2010																					
Male - Hommes	16.1	1.5	1.6	3.9	6.9	9.5	16.5	27.1	39.2	60.0	86.0	121.9	156.5	219.7	308.9	408.1	510.7	590.1	*1000	...	...
Female - Femmes	11.1	1.4	1.5	1.8	1.8	2.9	5.1	8.1	12.2	22.9	33.7	53.4	87.5	135.4	201.3	311.1	441.6	580.0	*1000	...	...
Romania - Roumanie																					
2009 - 2011																					
Male - Hommes	13.1	1.4	1.5	3.3	4.8	4.9	7.2	11.4	20.1	36.1	58.9	84.7	115.3	158.7	224.0	314.4	450.6	612.0	764.6	883.1	...
Female - Femmes	10.5	1.0	1.0	1.6	1.7	1.9	2.7	4.7	7.9	13.9	21.7	32.8	49.6	78.6	129.9	224.6	380.0	571.7	751.8	886.6	...
Russian Federation - Fédération de Russie																					
2011																					
Male - Hommes	10.5	1.6	1.9	5.6	11.8	20.2	31.6	37.6	44.6	60.1	82.4	116.9	163.6	201.8	275.9	371.7	485.3	575.6	698.0	781.9	*1000
Female - Femmes	8.2	1.2	1.2	2.6	3.6	6.2	9.5	11.7	14.9	19.6	27.7	41.5	60.7	87.5	139.3	235.2	375.7	542.8	712.8	827.3	*1000
Serbia - Serbie																					
2001 - 2003																					
Male - Hommes	13.7	1.2	1.5	3.1	5.0	5.9	6.8	9.8	17.3	31.7	53.4	83.0	115.8	173.6	258.6	378.2	514.5	674.0	800.7	884.7	*1000
Female - Femmes	9.9	0.8	0.8	1.5	1.7	2.2	3.4	5.4	9.3	17.0	26.0	39.6	64.1	107.2	187.2	310.3	479.8	648.8	805.4	867.7	*1000
Slovakia - Slovaquie																					
2011																					
Male - Hommes	6.8	1.2	1.0	2.7	3.7	5.1	5.8	8.8	15.9	26.1	45.6	68.9	105.0	143.7	210.4	306.7	445.0	618.3	798.0	931.2	...
Female - Femmes	5.5	0.7	0.6	1.2	1.3	1.6	2.2	3.3	6.2	10.3	19.4	26.1	39.3	64.3	105.8	195.3	350.2	589.2	844.6	980.2	...
Slovenia - Slovénie																					
2011																					
Male - Hommes	4.3	0.4	0.6	2.1	3.4	2.9	4.4	5.2	11.0	15.5	26.1	45.9	65.6	96.4	147.8	235.7	363.7	537.3	758.5	882.7	...
Female - Femmes	3.2	0.3	0.3	0.5	1.2	0.7	0.9	2.6	5.3	8.3	13.3	19.5	29.6	46.1	68.0	137.3	245.5	456.6	655.4	818.1	...

20. Probability of dying in the five year interval following specified age (5qx), by sex, latest available year: 2000 - 2012
Probabilité de décès dans l'intervalle de cinq ans qui suit un âge donné (5qx), par sexe, dernière année disponible : 2000 - 2012 (continued - suite)

Continent, country or area and date / Continent, pays ou zone et date	0	5	10	15	20	25	30	35	40	45	50	55	60	65	70	75	80	85	90	95	100
EUROPE																					
Spain - Espagne 2011																					
Male - Hommes	3.9	0.5	0.6	1.3	2.2	2.2	2.9	4.2	7.5	13.2	22.6	34.3	50.6	74.0	116.6	190.7	315.6	483.0	645.7	787.9	*1000
Female - Femmes	3.4	0.3	0.5	0.8	0.7	1.0	1.4	2.3	4.1	6.7	10.5	14.5	19.8	30.0	52.0	102.9	205.1	383.4	593.1	783.7	*1000
Sweden - Suède 2011																					
Male - Hommes	2.9	0.4	0.4	1.7	3.1	3.3	3.4	3.7	5.7	9.7	15.3	26.9	40.8	70.0	109.0	191.4	320.1	510.6	714.1	852.4	...
Female - Femmes	2.4	0.5	0.4	1.0	1.2	1.5	1.8	2.4	3.3	5.9	10.5	16.6	27.3	42.4	72.3	122.5	228.8	410.1	627.9	789.6	...
Switzerland - Suisse 2011																					
Male - Hommes	4.6	0.5	0.6	1.5	2.8	2.3	2.8	3.9	5.8	9.5	16.0	25.8	40.3	64.0	103.8	170.1	289.1	496.9	706.0	814.3	...
Female - Femmes	4.0	0.4	0.4	0.5	1.0	1.1	1.4	2.2	3.6	5.9	9.4	15.0	23.8	36.5	57.9	102.5	197.4	374.7	610.1	802.0	...
TFYR of Macedonia - L'ex-R. y. de Macédoine 2009																					
Male - Hommes	12.1	0.9	0.7	2.3	3.2	3.5	4.3	6.6	10.8	21.3	37.0	58.9	90.1	143.4	216.1	343.7	501.0	701.0	832.1	...	...
Female - Femmes	9.9	0.6	0.4	1.2	1.0	1.4	2.2	3.8	6.3	10.9	19.7	32.2	50.3	88.8	159.1	283.8	471.8	661.9	737.7	...	...
Ukraine 2011																					
Male - Hommes	11.9	1.4	1.6	4.0	7.9	12.5	21.5	29.2	37.3	50.9	72.5	103.8	150.5	197.5	276.7	368.0	494.0	593.0	698.0	793.0	...
Female - Femmes	9.4	1.0	1.1	1.7	2.5	4.1	7.0	9.7	12.8	17.0	24.7	37.4	59.3	89.3	150.8	251.2	399.4	568.7	740.9	882.9	...
United Kingdom of Great Britain and Northern Ireland - Royaume-Uni de Grande-Bretagne et d'Irlande du Nord[7] 2006 - 2008																					
Male - Hommes	6.3	0.6	0.7	2.4	3.5	4.1	5.3	6.9	9.4	14.1	22.4	34.4	54.8	86.9	136.5	222.9	353.3	502.9	684.7	836.1	...
Female - Femmes	5.2	0.4	0.5	1.1	1.3	1.7	2.4	3.7	5.8	9.2	14.7	22.1	34.9	55.1	90.9	155.8	265.4	419.9	627.3	801.1	...
OCEANIA - OCÉANIE																					
Australia - Australie 2009 - 2011																					
Male - Hommes	5.8	0.5	0.6	2.2	3.2	3.7	4.7	6.0	8.0	11.6	17.7	26.4	40.6	65.5	106.2	175.8	296.7	465.6	638.9	772.1	...
Female - Femmes	4.2	0.4	0.4	1.1	1.3	1.5	2.0	3.0	4.8	7.4	11.0	15.9	24.1	38.2	65.2	111.5	208.1	372.8	580.9	755.2	...
New Zealand - Nouvelle-Zélande 2010 - 2012																					
Male - Hommes	6.1	0.5	0.8	3.4	4.6	3.5	4.0	5.7	8.1	11.8	18.0	27.1	41.8	67.1	109.4	179.5	298.0	478.1	665.0	835.4	...
Female - Femmes	4.9	0.3	0.6	1.6	1.9	1.9	2.5	3.6	5.4	8.6	12.4	17.8	28.7	46.7	73.7	123.9	222.0	394.3	608.0	811.8	...

FOOTNOTES - NOTES

* Open-ended group (e.g. 80+). - Groupe d'âge ouvert (par exemple, 80 ans et plus).

[1] Because of the small population and the resulting small numbers of deaths, the data for the calendar years 2008-2010 have been aggregated to construct a more reliable life table. - La population étant peu élevée et, par conséquent, le nombre de décès aussi, les données des années civiles 2008, 2009 et 2010 ont été agrégées afin d'améliorer la fiabilité de la table de mortalité.

[2] Excluding Indian jungle population. - Non compris les Indiens de la jungle.

[3] Includes data for East Jerusalem and Israeli residents in certain other territories under occupation by Israeli military forces since June 1967. - Y compris les données pour Jérusalem-Est et les résidents israéliens dans certains autres territoires occupés depuis 1967 par les forces armées israéliennes.

[4] Data refer to resident population which comprises Singapore citizens and permanent residents. Provisional. - Les données se rapportent à la population résidente composé des citoyens de Singapour et des résidents permanents. Données provisoires.

[5] Excluding Faeroe Islands and Greenland shown separately, if available. - Non compris les Iles Féroé et le Groenland, qui font l'objet de rubriques distinctes, si disponible.

[6] Excluding Åland Islands. - Non compris les Îles d'Åland.

[7] Excluding Channel Islands (Guernsey and Jersey) and Isle of Man, shown separately, if available. - Non compris les îles Anglo-Normandes (Guernesey et Jersey) et l'île de Man, qui font l'objet de rubriques distinctes, si disponible.

Table 21 - *Demographic Yearbook 2012*

Table 21 presents life expectancy at specified ages for each sex for the latest available year between 1993 and 2012.

Description of variables: Life expectancy at age x, e_x is defined as the average number of years of life remaining to persons who have reached age *x* if they continue to be subject to the mortality conditions of the period indicated in the life table.

Male and female life expectancy values are shown separately at selected ages beginning at birth and proceeding at every fifth age thereafter up to age 100.

The table shows life expectancy derived from a complete or abridged life table as reported by the country or area.

Data are shown with one decimal regardless of the number of digits provided in the original computation.

The life table is a statistical device for summarizing the mortality experience of a population, from which the probability of dying, survivorship and life expectancy can be calculated. It is based on the assumption that the theoretical cohort is subject, throughout its existence, to the age-specific mortality rates observed at a particular time. Thus, levels of mortality prevailing at the time a life table is constructed are assumed to remain unchanged into the future until all members of the cohort have died.

Reliability of data: The values shown in this table come from official life tables. It is assumed that, if necessary, the basic data (population and deaths classified by age and sex) have been adjusted for deficiencies before their use in constructing the life tables.

Limitations: Life expectancy values are subject to the same qualifications as have been set forth for population statistics in general and death statistics in particular, as discussed in sections 3 and 4, respectively, of the Technical Notes. They must be interpreted strictly using the underlying assumption that surviving cohorts are subjected to the same age-specific mortality rates of the period to which the life table refers.

Earlier data: Life expectancy values at specified ages for each sex have been shown in previous issues of the *Demographic Yearbook*. For information on specific years covered, the reader should consult the Historical Index.

Tableau 21 – *Annuaire démographique 2012*

Le tableau 21 présente les espérances de vie à des âges déterminés, pour chaque sexe, pour la dernière année disponible entre 1993 et 2012.

Description des variables : L'espérance de vie à l'âge x, e_x, se définit comme le nombre moyen d'années restant à vivre aux hommes et aux femmes qui ont atteint l'âge x, à supposer qu'ils continuent de connaître les mêmes conditions de mortalité observées pendant la période sur laquelle porte la table de mortalité.

Les chiffres sont présentés séparément pour chaque sexe à partir de la naissance et puis tous les cinq ans jusqu'à 100 ans.

Dans le tableau figurent les espérances de vie calculées selon les tables de mortalité complètes ou abrégées communiquées par les pays et les zones.

Les données sont arrondies à la première décimale, indépendamment du nombre de décimales qui figurent dans le calcul initial.

La table de mortalité est un moyen statistique que s'utilise pour donner un aperçu complet de la mortalité d'une population incluant les probabilités de décès et l'espérance de vie à chaque âge. Les tables de mortalité reposent sur l'hypothèse que chaque cohorte théoriquement distinguée connaît, pendant toute son existence, les taux de mortalité par âge observé à un moment donné. Les taux de mortalité correspondant à l'époque à laquelle sont calculées les tables de mortalité sont ainsi censés demeurer inchangées dans l'avenir jusqu'au décès de tous les membres de la cohorte.

Fiabilité des donnés : Les chiffres figurant dans ce tableau proviennent de tables officielles de mortalité. En ce qui concerne les chiffres extraits de tables officielles de mortalité, on part du principe que les données de base (effectif de la population et nombre de décès selon l'âge et le sexe) ont été ajustées, en tant que de besoin, avant de servir à l'établissement de la table de mortalité.

Insuffisance des données : les espérances de vie appellent les mêmes réserves que celles qui ont été formulées à propos des statistiques de la population en général et des statistiques de mortalité en particulier (voir les sections 3 et 4 des Notes techniques). Lorsque l'on interprète les données, il ne faut jamais perdre de vue que, par hypothèse, les cohortes de survivants sont soumises, pour chaque âge, aux conditions de mortalité de la période visée par la table de mortalité.

Données publiées antérieurement : les espérances de vie à des âges déterminés pour chaque sexe figuraient déjà dans des éditions antérieures de *l'Annuaire démographique*. Pour plus de précisions concernant les années pour lesquelles ces données ont été publiées, se reporter à l'index historique.

21. Life expectancy at specified ages for each sex: latest available year, 1993 - 2012
Espérance de vie à un âge donné pour chaque sexe : dernière année disponible, 1993 - 2012

Continent, country or area and date / Continent, pays ou zone et date	Age (in years) - Age (en années)																					
	0	5	10	15	20	25	30	35	40	45	50	55	60	65	70	75	80	85	90	95	100
AFRICA - AFRIQUE																						
Algeria - Algérie[1]																						
2010																						
Male - Hommes	75.6	72.8	68.0	63.1	58.3	53.6	48.8	44.1	39.4	34.7	30.2	25.8	21.6	17.7	14.0	10.6	7.7	5.2	...	...	...
Female - Femmes	77.0	74.1	69.2	64.3	59.5	54.6	49.8	45.0	40.3	35.6	31.0	26.5	22.2	18.1	14.2	10.6	7.6	5.0	...	...	...
Benin - Bénin[2]																						
2002																						
M~le - Hommes	57.2	63.4	59.1	54.7	50.2	45.9	41.8	37.8	33.8	30.0	26.2	22.7	19.4	16.2	13.2	10.6	8.1	5.5	3.8	...	...
Female - Femmes	61.3	65.4	61.2	56.7	52.3	48.1	43.9	39.9	36.0	32.1	28.3	24.6	21.2	18.0	14.2	10.8	7.7	4.8	2.9	...	...
Botswana[3]																						
2006																						
Male - Hommes	54.0	57.6	54.0	49.7	45.6	41.8	37.9	34.0	30.0	26.2	22.4	19.9	15.4	12.3	9.4	7.0	4.8	...	...	...	...
Female - Femmes	66.0	65.7	61.4	56.8	52.3	47.8	43.4	39.1	34.7	30.4	26.2	22.1	18.2	14.5	11.2	8.3	5.8	...	...	...	...
Burkina Faso[4]																						
2006																						
Male - Hommes	55.8	60.0	55.9	51.3	46.9	42.8	38.6	34.5	30.5	26.6	22.8	19.3	16.0	12.9	10.3	8.1	6.2	4.8	...	...	...
Female - Femmes	57.5	61.6	57.6	53.1	48.6	44.4	40.2	36.1	32.0	28.0	24.1	20.3	16.8	13.5	10.7	8.4	6.4	4.9	...	...	...
Côte d'Ivoire[5]																						
1998																						
Male - Hommes	49.2	...	...	...	...	...	...	...	...	...	...	...	...	...	...	...	...	...	...	...	...
Female - Femmes	52.7	...	...	...	...	...	...	...	...	...	...	...	...	...	...	...	...	...	...	...	...
Djibouti																						
1998																						
Male - Hommes	49.0	...	...	...	...	...	...	...	...	...	...	...	...	...	...	...	...	...	...	...	...
Female - Femmes	52.0	...	...	...	...	...	...	...	...	...	...	...	...	...	...	...	...	...	...	...	...
Egypt - Égypte																						
2011																						
Male - Hommes	68.6	65.5	60.6	55.7	50.9	46.1	41.4	36.6	31.9	27.3	23.1	19.2	15.7	12.2	9.1	6.4	3.4	...	...	...	...
Female - Femmes	71.4	68.1	63.2	58.2	53.3	48.4	43.5	38.7	33.9	29.1	24.5	20.1	16.1	12.3	8.8	5.7	2.4	...	...	...	...
Ethiopia - Éthiopie																						
1994																						
Male - Hommes	49.8	55.2	51.2	46.8	42.7	38.9	35.0	31.1	27.4	23.7	20.2	16.9	13.8	11.0	8.6	6.5	5.0	...	...	...	...
Female - Femmes	51.8	56.9	53.0	48.8	44.8	40.9	37.1	33.4	29.6	25.9	22.1	18.6	15.2	12.1	9.4	7.1	5.4	...	...	...	...
Ghana																						
2005																						
Male - Hommes	58.3	...	...	...	...	...	...	...	...	...	...	...	...	...	...	...	...	...	...	...	...
Female - Femmes	62.0	...	...	...	...	...	...	...	...	...	...	...	...	...	...	...	...	...	...	...	...
Guinea-Bissau - Guinée-Bissau																						
2006																						
Male - Hommes	43.4	...	...	...	...	...	...	...	...	...	...	...	...	...	...	...	...	...	...	...	...
Female - Femmes	46.2	...	...	...	...	...	...	...	...	...	...	...	...	...	...	...	...	...	...	...	...
Kenya																						
1989 - 1999																						
Male - Hommes	52.9	54.8	51.1	46.6	42.3	38.3	34.5	31.0	27.7	24.4	21.0	17.7	14.5	11.6	8.9	6.7	5.0	3.8	3.1	2.5	...
Female - Femmes	60.4	63.0	59.0	54.3	49.9	45.9	42.2	38.6	34.8	30.9	27.0	23.1	19.3	15.6	12.2	9.2	6.7	4.8	3.6	2.5	...
Lesotho																						
2001																						
Male - Hommes	48.7	...	...	...	...	...	...	...	...	...	...	...	...	...	...	...	...	...	...	...	...
Female - Femmes	56.3	...	...	...	...	...	...	...	...	...	...	...	...	...	...	...	...	...	...	...	...
Madagascar																						
1993																						
Male - Hommes	51.3	56.1	52.7	48.8	44.9	41.0	37.2	33.3	29.6	26.0	22.6	19.2	16.1	13.0	10.3	7.6	4.6	...	...	...	...
Female - Femmes	53.2	58.1	54.6	50.5	46.7	43.0	39.4	35.8	32.3	28.7	25.2	21.6	18.1	14.7	11.9	9.0	5.8	...	...	...	...
Malawi																						
1992 - 1997																						
Male - Hommes	43.5	52.1	49.5	45.7	41.9	38.4	34.8	31.2	27.6	24.0	20.6	17.3	14.1	11.2	8.6	6.3	4.4	...	...	...	...
Female - Femmes	46.8	54.5	52.0	48.2	44.4	40.6	36.9	33.2	29.6	25.9	22.2	18.6	15.1	11.9	9.2	6.8	4.6	...	...	...	...
2007[6]																						
Male - Hommes	45.7	...	...	...	...	...	...	...	...	...	...	...	...	...	...	...	...	...	...	...	...
Female - Femmes	48.3	...	...	...	...	...	...	...	...	...	...	...	...	...	...	...	...	...	...	...	...
Mauritius - Maurice[7]																						
2009 - 2011																						
Male - Hommes	69.7	65.8	60.9	56.0	51.2	46.5	41.8	37.3	32.8	28.6	24.5	20.8	17.2	14.1	11.3	8.7	6.5	4.6	...	...	...
Female - Femmes	77.0	73.0	68.1	63.1	58.2	53.4	48.5	43.7	39.0	34.3	29.9	25.5	21.4	17.6	14.1	10.9	8.2	5.9	...	...	...

Continent, country or area and date / Continent, pays ou zone et date	Age (in years) - Age (en années)																				
	0	5	10	15	20	25	30	35	40	45	50	55	60	65	70	75	80	85	90	95	100
AFRICA - AFRIQUE																					
Namibia - Namibie																					
2001																					
Male - Hommes	47.6	54.0	50.1	45.8	41.7	38.0	34.2	30.5	26.8	23.2	19.8	16.6	13.5	10.8	8.4	6.4	4.9	...	...	...	...
Female - Femmes	50.2	56.1	52.2	48.1	44.1	40.3	36.6	32.9	29.2	25.5	21.8	18.3	14.9	12.0	9.3	7.0	5.3	...	...	...	...
Réunion																					
2009																					
Male - Hommes	74.9	...	...	...	...	...	...	...	...	...	...	...	20.3	...	...	...	...	...	...	...	...
Female - Femmes	82.7	...	...	...	...	...	...	...	...	...	...	...	25.6	...	...	...	...	...	...	...	...
Rwanda																					
2002																					
Male - Hommes	48.4	58.4	54.4	49.9	45.6	41.6	37.5	33.5	29.4	25.4	21.6	17.9	14.5	11.4	8.6	6.3	4.6	...	...	...	...
Female - Femmes	53.8	63.1	58.8	54.3	49.9	45.7	41.4	37.2	32.9	28.7	24.5	20.4	16.5	12.9	9.8	7.1	5.1	...	...	...	...
2009																					
Male - Hommes	49.4	...	...	...	...	...	...	...	...	...	...	...	...	...	...	...	...	...	...	...	...
Female - Femmes	53.3	...	...	...	...	...	...	...	...	...	...	...	...	...	...	...	...	...	...	...	...
Saint Helena ex. dep. - Sainte-Hélène sans dép.																					
2003 - 2012																					
Male - Hommes	72.0	68.1	63.4	...	53.9	...	44.2	...	35.5	...	27.1	...	19.3	...	12.5	...	7.2	...	...	...	...
Female - Femmes	79.7	75.3	70.3	...	60.3	...	51.0	...	41.8	...	32.0	...	23.0	...	15.5	...	8.6	...	...	...	...
Sao Tome and Principe - Sao Tomé-et-Principe																					
2001																					
Male - Hommes	61.3	63.1	59.2	55.0	50.5	46.1	41.5	37.5	33.5	29.8	25.5	22.2	18.3	15.1	13.1	10.6	8.4	6.5	...	...	...
Female - Femmes	66.5	68.1	64.1	59.8	55.2	50.8	46.1	41.6	37.5	33.0	28.6	25.0	21.1	17.3	14.4	12.0	9.5	8.1	...	...	...
Senegal - Sénégal[6]																					
2011																					
Male - Hommes	56.9	...	...	...	...	...	...	...	...	...	...	...	...	...	...	...	...	...	...	...	...
Female - Femmes	59.8	...	...	...	...	...	...	...	...	...	...	...	...	...	...	...	...	...	...	...	...
Seychelles																					
2007																					
Male - Hommes	68.9	65.0	60.2	55.3	50.5	45.9	41.6	37.0	32.7	28.7	24.4	20.9	17.1	14.1	11.0	9.0	7.4	...	...	...	...
Female - Femmes	77.7	73.3	68.5	63.5	58.5	53.7	48.9	44.3	39.5	35.3	31.0	26.4	22.2	18.5	15.1	12.1	9.2	...	...	...	...
2011																					
Male - Hommes	67.7	...	...	...	...	...	...	...	...	...	...	...	...	...	...	...	...	...	...	...	...
Female - Femmes	78.1	...	...	...	...	...	...	...	...	...	...	...	...	...	...	...	...	...	...	...	...
Sierra Leone																					
2004																					
Male - Hommes	47.5	...	...	...	...	...	...	...	...	...	...	...	...	...	...	...	...	...	...	...	...
Female - Femmes	49.4	...	...	...	...	...	...	...	...	...	...	...	...	...	...	...	...	...	...	...	...
South Africa - Afrique du Sud																					
2009																					
Male - Hommes	53.5	...	...	...	...	...	...	...	...	...	...	...	...	...	...	...	...	...	...	...	...
Female - Femmes	57.2	...	...	...	...	...	...	...	...	...	...	...	...	...	...	...	...	...	...	...	...
Swaziland[5]																					
2007																					
Male - Hommes	42.2	...	...	...	...	...	...	...	...	...	...	...	...	...	...	...	...	...	...	...	...
Female - Femmes	43.1	...	...	...	...	...	...	...	...	...	...	...	...	...	...	...	...	...	...	...	...
Tunisia - Tunisie																					
1995																					
Male - Hommes	69.6	67.5	62.7	57.9	53.1	48.4	43.8	39.2	34.6	30.1	25.8	21.6	17.7	14.1	10.8	7.9	5.2	3.5	...	...	...
Female - Femmes	73.1	70.7	65.9	61.0	56.2	51.3	46.5	41.7	37.0	32.4	27.8	23.3	19.1	15.0	11.3	7.8	4.8	2.9	...	...	...
2011																					
Male - Hommes	72.9	...	...	...	...	...	...	...	...	...	...	...	...	...	...	...	...	...	...	...	...
Female - Femmes	76.9	...	...	...	...	...	...	...	...	...	...	...	...	...	...	...	...	...	...	...	...
Uganda - Ouganda[8]																					
2002																					
Male - Hommes	48.8	53.0	49.2	44.8	40.5	36.6	33.6	31.0	28.4	25.8	23.2	20.4	17.2	14.4	11.6	9.2	6.7	4.1	...	...	...
Female - Femmes	52.0	56.0	52.1	47.6	43.3	39.6	36.7	34.2	31.5	28.6	25.6	22.3	18.9	15.7	12.6	9.9	7.0	4.2	...	...	...
Zimbabwe																					
2001 - 2002																					
Male - Hommes	45.8	44.2	40.0	35.4	30.9	26.8	23.8	22.1	21.8	21.3	20.4	19.2	17.7	15.7	13.7	11.4	9.5	7.5	6.2	5.2	...
Female - Femmes	50.3	48.6	44.2	39.7	35.3	32.1	30.4	30.1	30.2	29.0	27.6	25.3	22.9	20.2	17.6	14.8	12.2	9.9	8.1	7.3	...

21. Life expectancy at specified ages for each sex: latest available year, 1993 - 2012
Espérance de vie à un âge donné pour chaque sexe : dernière année disponible, 1993 - 2012 (continued - suite)

Continent, country or area and date / Continent, pays ou zone et date	Age (in years) - Age (en années)																				
	0	5	10	15	20	25	30	35	40	45	50	55	60	65	70	75	80	85	90	95	100
AMERICA, NORTH - AMÉRIQUE DU NORD																					
Anguilla																					
2000 - 2002																					
Male - Hommes	76.5	72.1	67.1	62.1	57.3	53.1	48.4	43.7	39.4	34.7	30.2	25.4	21.1	16.5	12.7	10.0	8.0	6.9	...	...	...
Female - Femmes	81.1	76.4	71.4	66.4	61.4	57.1	52.7	47.7	42.7	38.3	33.5	28.7	24.0	19.4	15.3	10.8	8.3	7.6	...	...	...
Antigua and Barbuda - Antigua-et-Barbuda																					
2010																					
Male - Hommes	74.0	...	...	...	...	...	...	...	...	...	...	...	...	...	...	...	...	...	...	...	...
Female - Femmes	79.7	...	...	...	...	...	...	...	...	...	...	...	...	...	...	...	...	...	...	...	...
Aruba																					
2000																					
Male - Hommes	70.0	65.4	60.5	55.6	50.9	46.7	42.3	37.7	33.0	28.5	24.2	20.1	16.3	13.1	10.4	8.1	5.7	3.9	4.0	3.2	...
Female - Femmes	76.0	71.9	67.0	62.0	57.2	52.5	47.7	43.0	38.3	33.6	28.9	24.4	20.5	16.7	13.1	10.4	7.5	5.5	4.7	3.6	...
Bahamas																					
1999 - 2001																					
Male - Hommes	69.9	...	...	...	...	...	...	...	...	...	...	...	...	...	...	...	...	...	...	...	...
Female - Femmes	76.4	...	...	...	...	...	...	...	...	...	...	...	...	...	...	...	...	...	...	...	...
Bermuda - Bermudes																					
2012																					
Male - Hommes	77.2	72.2	67.2	62.2	57.4	52.6	47.7	42.8	38.0	33.2	28.7	24.2	20.1	16.2	12.7	9.6	7.1	5.1	...	...	...
Female - Femmes	82.4	77.6	72.6	67.6	62.6	57.6	52.7	47.7	43.0	38.2	33.5	28.9	24.4	20.2	16.1	12.5	9.1	6.4	...	...	...
British Virgin Islands - Îles Vierges britanniques																					
2004																					
Male - Hommes	69.9	...	...	...	...	...	...	...	...	...	...	...	...	...	...	...	...	...	...	...	...
Female - Femmes	78.5	...	...	...	...	...	...	...	...	...	...	...	...	...	...	...	...	...	...	...	...
Canada																					
2006 - 2008																					
Male - Hommes	78.5	74.0	69.1	64.1	59.3	54.5	49.7	44.9	40.2	35.5	30.9	26.5	22.3	18.3	14.7	11.4	8.5	6.2	4.5	...	...
Female - Femmes	83.2	78.6	73.6	68.7	63.8	58.9	53.9	49.1	44.2	39.4	34.7	30.2	25.7	21.5	17.4	13.7	10.4	7.5	5.4	...	...
Cayman Islands - Îles Caïmanes[9]																					
2006																					
Male - Hommes	76.3	72.1	67.1	62.1	57.7	53.3	48.9	44.0	39.3	34.5	29.8	25.3	20.8	17.1	13.6	10.2	8.2	6.4	3.3	5.3	2.5
Female - Femmes	83.8	79.8	74.8	69.8	65.1	60.1	55.2	50.2	45.3	40.4	35.7	30.9	26.1	21.9	17.5	13.9	10.4	6.9	7.0	3.1	2.5
Costa Rica																					
2010																					
Male - Hommes	76.8	72.8	67.8	62.9	58.2	53.5	48.8	44.2	39.5	34.9	30.5	26.2	22.0	18.1	14.5	11.2	8.5	6.3	4.5	3.2	...
Female - Femmes	81.8	77.6	72.7	67.7	62.8	57.9	53.0	48.2	43.4	38.6	33.9	29.3	24.9	20.6	16.7	13.0	9.8	7.1	5.1	3.5	...
Cuba																					
2005 - 2007																					
Male - Hommes	76.0	71.6	66.7	61.8	56.9	52.1	47.4	42.6	37.9	33.4	29.0	24.8	20.8	17.1	13.7	10.8	8.2	6.2	4.7	3.6	1.8
Female - Femmes	80.0	75.5	70.6	65.6	60.7	55.8	51.0	46.1	41.3	36.6	32.0	27.6	23.4	19.3	15.6	12.3	9.3	6.9	5.1	3.7	1.9
Curaçao[10]																					
2008 - 2010																					
Male - Hommes	72.0	68.4	63.4	58.5	53.6	49.2	44.6	39.9	35.3	30.9	26.5	22.3	18.5	15.0	12.0	9.1	7.0	5.0	3.3	2.7	2.8
Female - Femmes	78.8	75.1	70.3	65.4	60.6	56.2	51.4	46.5	41.7	37.0	32.5	28.0	23.7	19.6	15.6	12.1	8.9	6.4	4.1	2.8	2.4
Dominica - Dominique																					
2008																					
Male - Hommes	73.8	...	...	...	...	...	...	...	...	...	...	...	...	...	...	...	...	...	...	...	...
Female - Femmes	78.2	...	...	...	...	...	...	...	...	...	...	...	...	...	...	...	...	...	...	...	...
Dominican Republic - République dominicaine																					
2005 - 2010																					
Male - Hommes	69.2	66.8	62.0	57.2	52.6	48.3	44.1	39.9	35.7	31.6	27.6	23.7	20.1	16.8	13.9	11.3	9.3	...	...	...	...
Female - Femmes	75.5	72.6	67.8	62.9	58.1	53.3	48.7	44.2	39.6	35.2	30.9	26.7	22.7	19.0	15.6	12.7	10.3	...	...	...	...
El Salvador[11]																					
2000 - 2005																					
Male - Hommes	65.4	62.6	57.8	52.9	48.7	45.0	41.5	37.8	34.1	30.4	26.8	23.3	20.0	16.7	13.8	11.1	9.0	...	...	...	...
Female - Femmes	74.9	72.0	67.1	62.3	57.5	52.9	48.2	43.6	39.0	34.6	30.3	26.1	22.1	18.4	15.0	12.0	9.6	...	...	...	...

Continent, country or area and date / Continent, pays ou zone et date	0	5	10	15	20	25	30	35	40	45	50	55	60	65	70	75	80	85	90	95	100
AMERICA, NORTH - AMÉRIQUE DU NORD																					
Greenland - Groenland 2007 - 2011																					
Male - Hommes	68.2	64.5	59.6	54.7	50.5	46.6	42.2	37.8	33.4	28.9	24.5	20.2	16.4	12.7	9.6	7.0	5.3	3.9	3.1	2.4	...
Female - Femmes	72.9	68.8	63.8	58.9	54.5	50.0	45.2	40.4	35.7	31.0	26.6	22.4	18.4	14.8	11.8	9.0	6.6	5.3	4.1	2.4	...
Guadeloupe 2002																					
Male - Hommes	74.6	70.2	65.3	60.5	55.7	51.2	46.8	42.2	37.7	33.2	29.0	24.8	20.9	17.3	13.8	10.6	7.9	5.1	2.0	0.5	...
Female - Femmes	81.5	77.0	72.1	67.1	62.1	57.3	52.4	47.6	42.9	38.2	33.5	28.8	24.4	20.3	16.4	12.7	9.0	5.7	2.3	0.5	...
Guatemala 1995 - 2000																					
Male - Hommes	61.4	60.6	56.0	51.2	46.8	42.7	38.8	34.9	31.2	27.4	23.7	20.1	16.8	13.6	10.7	8.2	6.1	...	...	...	...
Female - Femmes	67.2	66.2	62.6	56.9	52.3	47.7	43.3	38.9	34.6	30.4	26.3	22.3	18.6	15.2	12.0	9.2	6.9	...	...	...	...
Jamaica - Jamaïque 2006																					
Male - Hommes	69.7	67.0	62.2	57.3	52.6	47.9	43.2	38.5	33.8	29.3	24.9	20.8	16.9	13.5	10.4	7.8	5.8	4.1	2.9	2.1	1.5
Female - Femmes	75.2	71.6	66.7	61.7	56.8	52.0	47.1	42.3	37.6	32.9	28.3	23.9	19.7	15.9	12.4	9.4	6.9	5.0	3.5	2.4	1.7
Martinique 2007																					
Male - Hommes	76.5	72.4	67.5	62.6	57.8	53.3	48.7	44.1	39.5	34.9	30.3	26.1	21.8	17.6	14.1	10.7	7.7	5.2	3.7	1.8	...
Female - Femmes	82.9	78.5	73.6	68.6	63.7	58.8	54.0	49.2	44.4	39.6	34.8	30.1	25.6	21.2	17.1	13.4	10.0	7.1	4.6	1.9	...
Mexico - Mexique 2008																					
Male - Hommes	72.8	69.2	64.3	59.4	54.7	50.0	45.5	40.9	36.5	32.1	27.9	23.9	20.2	16.8	13.7	11.0	8.7	6.6	4.9	3.5	2.6
Female - Femmes	77.5	73.8	68.9	63.9	59.0	54.2	49.3	44.5	39.7	35.1	30.6	26.2	22.1	18.3	14.8	11.7	9.0	6.8	4.9	3.5	2.6
Nicaragua 2005 - 2010																					
Male - Hommes	63.4	47.9	44.2	40.5	36.5	32.5	28.6	24.9	21.3	17.7	14.6	11.6	9.0	6.5	...	...	...	...	...	...	...
Female - Femmes	68.9	52.1	47.6	43.0	38.5	34.1	29.8	25.7	21.9	18.1	14.9	11.8	9.3	6.9	...	...	...	...	...	...	...
Panama[12] 2012																					
Male - Hommes	74.1	70.8	66.0	61.1	56.6	52.3	48.1	43.7	39.3	34.8	30.5	26.3	22.4	18.7	15.3	12.3	9.7	7.5	5.7	4.1	2.5
Female - Femmes	80.4	76.8	71.9	67.0	62.1	57.3	52.6	47.9	43.2	38.5	34.0	29.5	25.2	21.1	17.3	13.9	10.8	8.2	6.0	4.2	2.5
Puerto Rico - Porto Rico 2004 - 2006																					
Male - Hommes	74.1	69.8	64.9	59.9	55.2	50.9	46.5	42.0	37.6	33.3	29.1	25.1	21.3	17.7	14.4	11.3	8.7	6.5	4.8	3.4	2.3
Female - Femmes	81.5	77.2	72.3	67.3	62.4	57.5	52.7	47.9	43.1	38.4	33.8	29.3	24.9	20.8	16.9	13.3	10.1	7.4	5.2	3.7	3.1
Saint Kitts and Nevis - Saint-Kitts-et-Nevis 1998																					
Male - Hommes	68.2	65.0	60.1	55.3	50.5	45.8	41.1	36.5	32.7	28.5	24.3	20.6	16.6	13.3	11.0	9.1	6.6	4.7	3.4	2.2	0.4
Female - Femmes	70.7	67.5	62.5	57.6	52.7	48.0	43.4	38.8	34.4	29.8	25.4	21.3	17.6	14.3	11.3	8.9	6.3	4.6	3.3	2.2	0.4
Saint Lucia - Sainte-Lucie 2005																					
Male - Hommes	69.9	66.4	61.5	56.6	52.0	47.4	43.1	38.6	34.3	30.1	25.9	21.7	17.9	14.7	11.8	9.0	7.2	5.2	...	...	...
Female - Femmes	75.7	72.2	67.3	62.4	57.5	52.6	47.8	43.2	38.4	33.8	29.2	25.0	20.8	17.2	13.8	10.4	7.7	4.8	...	...	...
Saint Vincent and the Grenadines - Saint-Vincent-et-les Grenadines 2001																					
Male - Hommes	66.9	63.9	59.2	54.3	49.6	45.1	40.7	36.5	32.3	28.2	24.1	19.9	16.2	12.8	9.7	7.3	4.3	4.1	...	...	...
Female - Femmes	72.9	69.3	64.5	59.5	54.7	49.8	45.2	40.7	36.1	31.7	27.3	23.0	19.0	14.6	10.8	7.3	4.1	3.6	...	...	...
Trinidad and Tobago - Trinité-et-Tobago 2000																					
Male - Hommes	68.3	65.2	60.3	55.5	50.7	46.1	41.7	37.3	33.1	29.0	24.9	21.2	17.9	14.7	12.0	9.7	7.8	...	...	...	...
Female - Femmes	73.7	70.2	65.3	60.4	55.6	50.9	46.2	41.7	37.1	32.7	28.4	24.4	20.7	17.4	14.4	11.7	9.6	...	...	...	...

21. Life expectancy at specified ages for each sex: latest available year, 1993 - 2012
Espérance de vie à un âge donné pour chaque sexe : dernière année disponible, 1993 - 2012 (continued - suite)

Continent, country or area and date / Continent, pays ou zone et date	Age (in years) - Age (en années)																				
	0	5	10	15	20	25	30	35	40	45	50	55	60	65	70	75	80	85	90	95	100
AMERICA, NORTH - AMÉRIQUE DU NORD																					
Turks and Caicos Islands - Îles Turques et Caïques 2001																					
Male - Hommes	79.0	75.3	70.3	65.3	60.3	55.8	50.8	46.0	41.2	37.1	33.0	28.4	24.3	20.8	17.5	12.5	7.5	4.1	...	...	...
Female - Femmes	77.4	72.5	67.5	62.5	57.5	52.9	48.2	43.4	38.6	33.8	29.6	25.0	20.0	17.0	13.2	11.7	10.3	8.8	...	...	...
United States of America - États-Unis d'Amérique 2008																					
Male - Hommes	75.6	71.2	66.3	61.3	56.6	52.0	47.3	42.6	38.0	33.5	29.1	25.0	21.0	17.3	13.9	10.7	8.0	5.7	4.0	2.8	2.0
Female - Femmes	80.6	76.1	71.2	66.2	61.3	56.5	51.6	46.8	42.0	37.3	32.8	28.4	24.1	20.0	16.2	12.6	9.5	6.8	4.7	3.2	2.2
AMERICA, SOUTH - AMÉRIQUE DU SUD																					
Argentina - Argentine 2000 - 2001																					
Male - Hommes	70.0	66.6	61.7	56.8	52.1	47.4	42.8	38.2	33.7	29.3	25.0	21.1	17.4	14.1	11.1	8.6	6.5	4.9	3.7	2.9	...
Female - Femmes	77.5	73.9	69.0	64.1	59.2	54.4	49.5	44.7	40.0	35.4	30.9	26.5	22.3	18.4	14.7	11.3	8.4	6.2	4.6	3.5	...
2006 - 2010[6]																					
Male - Hommes	71.6	...	...	...	...	...	...	...	...	...	...	...	...	...	...	...	...	...	...	...	...
Female - Femmes	79.1	...	...	...	...	...	...	...	...	...	...	...	...	...	...	...	...	...	...	...	...
Bolivia (Plurinational State of) - Bolivie (État plurinational de) 1995 - 2000																					
Male - Hommes	59.8	60.8	56.7	52.2	48.0	43.7	39.5	35.3	31.2	27.1	23.2	19.5	15.9	12.7	9.8	7.5	5.9	...	...	...	...
Female - Femmes	63.2	63.8	59.7	55.2	50.8	46.5	42.1	37.8	33.6	29.4	25.3	21.4	17.6	14.0	10.8	8.3	6.5	...	...	...	...
2011																					
Male - Hommes	64.6	...	...	...	...	...	...	...	...	...	...	...	...	...	...	...	...	...	...	...	...
Female - Femmes	68.9	...	...	...	...	...	...	...	...	...	...	...	...	...	...	...	...	...	...	...	...
Brazil - Brésil[12] 2009																					
Male - Hommes	69.4	66.6	61.8	56.9	52.3	48.0	43.6	39.3	35.0	30.8	26.9	23.1	19.5	16.3	13.4	10.9	9.0	...	...	...	...
Female - Femmes	77.0	73.8	68.9	63.9	59.1	54.2	49.5	44.7	40.0	35.5	31.1	26.9	22.8	19.1	15.6	12.6	10.0	...	...	...	...
Chile - Chili 2011																					
Male - Hommes	75.6	71.3	66.3	61.4	56.6	51.9	47.2	42.5	37.8	33.2	28.8	24.4	20.3	16.5	13.0	9.8	7.3	5.1	3.1	4.7	...
Female - Femmes	80.9	76.5	71.6	66.6	61.7	56.8	51.9	47.0	42.2	37.4	32.7	28.2	23.7	19.5	15.6	11.8	8.6	5.8	3.5	3.0	...
Colombia - Colombie[13] 2005 - 2010																					
Male - Hommes	70.7	67.7	62.9	58.0	53.5	49.4	45.2	40.9	36.5	32.2	27.8	23.7	19.7	16.0	12.7	9.8	7.4	...	...	...	...
Female - Femmes	77.5	74.1	69.2	64.3	59.5	54.7	49.9	45.1	40.4	35.7	31.2	26.7	22.5	18.5	14.8	11.5	8.6	...	...	...	...
Ecuador - Équateur[14] 2005 - 2010																					
Male - Hommes	72.1	69.3	64.5	59.7	55.2	50.9	46.6	42.3	38.1	33.8	29.7	25.7	21.7	18.0	14.6	11.3	8.2	...	...	...	...
Female - Femmes	78.0	74.8	69.9	65.1	60.4	55.6	50.9	46.2	41.6	37.0	32.6	28.2	24.1	20.0	16.1	12.5	9.1	...	...	...	...
French Guiana - Guyane française 2007																					
Male - Hommes	75.1	71.3	66.4	61.5	56.8	52.2	47.7	43.1	38.7	34.3	30.3	25.7	21.5	17.5	13.8	10.5	8.2	5.7	3.6	2.1	...
Female - Femmes	80.8	77.0	72.1	67.2	62.3	57.4	52.6	47.8	43.0	38.5	33.9	29.2	24.5	19.9	16.6	12.7	10.2	7.8	5.1	2.2	...
Paraguay 1990 - 1995																					
Male - Hommes	66.3	65.5	60.8	56.0	51.3	46.7	42.1	37.5	32.9	28.5	24.2	20.2	16.5	13.2	10.2	7.7	5.6	...	...	...	...
Female - Femmes	70.8	69.3	64.5	59.7	54.9	50.1	45.4	40.7	36.0	31.5	27.0	22.8	18.7	14.9	11.5	8.5	6.3	...	...	...	...
2005 - 2010																					
Male - Hommes	69.7	...	...	...	...	...	...	...	...	...	...	...	...	...	...	...	...	...	...	...	...
Female - Femmes	73.9	...	...	...	...	...	...	...	...	...	...	...	...	...	...	...	...	...	...	...	...

Continent, country or area and date / Continent, pays ou zone et date	Age (in years) - Age (en années)																				
	0	5	10	15	20	25	30	35	40	45	50	55	60	65	70	75	80	85	90	95	100
AMERICA, SOUTH - AMÉRIQUE DU SUD																					
Peru - Pérou[12]																					
1995 - 2000																					
Male - Hommes	65.9	65.9	61.4	56.6	52.0	47.4	42.9	38.5	34.1	29.8	25.7	21.7	18.1	14.7	11.7	9.2	7.0	...	...	...	...
Female - Femmes	70.9	70.2	65.6	60.7	55.9	51.2	46.5	41.9	37.3	32.9	28.5	24.3	20.3	16.5	13.3	10.4	7.8	...	...	...	...
2000 - 2005																					
Male - Hommes	69.0	...	...	...	...	...	...	...	...	...	...	...	...	...	...	...	...	...	...	...	...
Female - Femmes	74.3	...	...	...	...	...	...	...	...	...	...	...	...	...	...	...	...	...	...	...	...
Suriname																					
2006																					
Male - Hommes	68.0	60.4	55.5	50.6	46.0	41.5	37.0	32.8	28.6	24.6	20.7	16.9	13.5	10.5	8.1	7.1	6.5	...	...	...	...
Female - Femmes	73.7	66.0	61.1	56.2	51.5	46.8	42.3	37.7	33.2	28.8	24.5	20.3	16.4	12.9	9.9	8.0	8.5	...	...	...	...
Uruguay																					
2006																					
Male - Hommes	72.1	68.5	63.6	58.7	53.8	49.1	44.4	39.7	35.0	30.5	26.0	21.9	18.1	14.7	11.7	9.0	6.7	4.8	3.4	2.7	...
Female - Femmes	79.5	75.7	70.8	65.8	60.9	56.1	51.2	46.3	41.6	36.8	32.3	27.8	23.6	19.4	15.5	11.9	8.8	6.3	4.4	3.1	...
2008																					
Male - Hommes	72.4	...	...	...	...	...	...	...	...	...	...	...	...	...	...	...	...	...	...	...	...
Female - Femmes	79.7	...	...	...	...	...	...	...	...	...	...	...	...	...	...	...	...	...	...	...	...
Venezuela (Bolivarian Republic of) - Venezuela (République bolivarienne du)																					
1995 - 2000																					
Male - Hommes	68.6	66.6	61.8	56.9	52.3	47.8	43.3	38.8	34.3	29.9	25.6	21.6	17.9	14.5	11.4	8.6	5.9	...	...	...	...
Female - Femmes	74.5	72.1	67.2	62.3	57.5	52.6	47.8	43.1	38.4	33.7	29.2	24.9	20.8	16.9	13.3	9.9	6.9	...	...	...	...
2007																					
Male - Hommes	70.7	...	...	...	...	...	...	...	...	...	...	...	...	...	...	...	...	...	...	...	...
Female - Femmes	76.6	...	...	...	...	...	...	...	...	...	...	...	...	...	...	...	...	...	...	...	...
ASIA - ASIE																					
Afghanistan																					
2004																					
Male - Hommes	45.0	...	...	...	...	...	...	...	...	...	...	...	...	...	...	...	...	...	...	...	...
Female - Femmes	44.0	...	...	...	...	...	...	...	...	...	...	...	...	...	...	...	...	...	...	...	...
Armenia - Arménie																					
2006 - 2007																					
Male - Hommes	70.2	66.3	61.4	56.4	51.6	46.8	42.0	37.3	32.7	28.3	24.1	20.1	16.4	13.1	10.3	7.8	5.7	3.9	2.6	1.6	0.7
Female - Femmes	76.6	72.5	67.6	62.7	57.7	52.8	47.9	43.0	38.2	33.5	28.8	24.3	20.0	15.9	12.4	9.2	6.4	4.1	2.7	1.8	0.7
Azerbaijan - Azerbaïdjan																					
2010																					
Male - Hommes	70.9	67.0	62.2	57.2	52.4	47.7	42.9	38.2	33.6	29.1	24.8	20.7	17.1	13.8	11.0	8.7	6.9	5.8	4.4	3.0	0.8
Female - Femmes	76.1	72.2	67.4	62.4	57.5	52.7	47.8	43.0	38.1	33.4	28.8	24.3	20.1	16.2	12.6	9.7	7.6	6.0	4.8	3.5	0.9
Bahrain - Bahreïn																					
2001																					
Male - Hommes	73.2	69.3	64.4	59.5	54.7	49.9	45.2	40.4	35.6	30.9	26.4	22.0	17.8	14.1	11.3	9.5	...	...	...	...	...
Female - Femmes	76.2	72.0	67.1	62.1	57.2	52.3	47.4	42.5	37.7	32.9	28.2	23.7	19.6	15.9	12.9	10.9	...	...	...	...	...
2005																					
Male - Hommes	73.1	...	...	...	...	...	...	...	...	...	...	...	...	...	...	...	...	...	...	...	...
Female - Femmes	77.3	...	...	...	...	...	...	...	...	...	...	...	...	...	...	...	...	...	...	...	...
Bangladesh																					
2011																					
Male - Hommes	67.9	65.5	60.8	56.1	51.3	46.5	41.8	37.1	32.6	28.2	24.1	20.2	16.6	13.2	10.0	6.7	4.4	...	...	...	...
Female - Femmes	70.3	67.8	63.1	58.3	53.6	48.8	44.0	39.3	34.7	30.1	25.6	21.4	17.4	13.8	10.3	6.7	5.6	...	...	...	...
Bhutan - Bhoutan																					
2005																					
Male - Hommes	65.7	...	...	...	...	...	...	...	...	...	...	...	...	...	...	...	...	...	...	...	...
Female - Femmes	66.9	...	...	...	...	...	...	...	...	...	...	...	...	...	...	...	...	...	...	...	...
Brunei Darussalam - Brunéi Darussalam																					
2008																					
Male - Hommes	76.6	...	...	...	...	...	...	...	...	...	...	...	...	...	...	...	...	...	...	...	...
Female - Femmes	79.8	...	...	...	...	...	...	...	...	...	...	...	...	...	...	...	...	...	...	...	...

Continent, country or area and date / Continent, pays ou zone et date	Age (in years) - Age (en années)																				
	0	5	10	15	20	25	30	35	40	45	50	55	60	65	70	75	80	85	90	95	100
ASIA - ASIE																					
China - Chine[15]																					
2010																					
Male - Hommes	66.8	...	...	...	...	...	...	...	...	...	...	...	...	...	...	...	...	...	...	...	...
Female - Femmes	70.5	...	...	...	...	...	...	...	...	...	...	...	...	...	...	...	...	...	...	...	...
China, Hong Kong SAR - Chine, Hong Kong RAS																					
2011																					
Male - Hommes	80.3	75.5	70.5	65.6	60.6	55.7	50.8	46.0	41.2	36.5	31.8	27.3	23.0	18.9	15.2	11.7	8.7	6.3	4.4	3.1	2.1
Female - Femmes	86.7	81.9	76.9	71.9	67.0	62.0	57.1	52.2	47.3	42.5	37.7	33.0	28.4	23.9	19.6	15.5	11.9	8.9	6.4	4.5	3.0
China, Macao SAR - Chine, Macao RAS																					
2009 - 2012																					
Male - Hommes	79.1	74.5	69.5	64.6	59.7	54.8	50.1	45.3	40.7	36.1	31.6	27.2	23.0	19.0	15.2	12.0	9.4	7.1	...	...	...
Female - Femmes	85.7	80.9	75.9	71.0	66.1	61.2	56.3	51.4	46.6	41.7	37.0	32.3	27.8	23.3	19.0	15.1	11.8	9.1	...	...	...
Cyprus - Chypre[16]																					
2010 - 2011																					
Male - Hommes	79.0	74.3	69.3	64.4	59.5	54.7	49.9	45.1	40.3	35.6	31.0	26.4	22.0	17.8	13.9	10.3	7.1	4.3	2.7	...	...
Female - Femmes	82.9	78.2	73.2	68.2	63.3	58.3	53.4	48.5	43.6	38.7	33.9	29.2	24.6	20.0	15.5	11.4	7.7	4.6	2.7	...	...
Democratic People's Republic of Korea - République populaire démocratique de Corée																					
2008																					
Male - Hommes	65.6	...	...	...	...	...	...	...	...	...	...	...	...	...	...	...	...	...	...	...	...
Female - Femmes	72.7	...	...	...	...	...	...	...	...	...	...	...	...	...	...	...	...	...	...	...	...
Georgia - Géorgie																					
2010																					
Male - Hommes	70.2	66.3	61.3	56.4	51.6	46.9	42.2	37.6	33.0	28.7	24.7	20.9	17.4	14.2	11.5	9.2	7.5	6.5	...	...	...
Female - Femmes	78.6	74.5	69.6	64.6	59.7	54.8	49.9	45.0	40.2	35.5	30.8	26.3	22.0	18.0	14.3	11.1	8.8	7.5	...	...	...
India - Inde[17]																					
2002 - 2006																					
Male - Hommes	62.6	63.8	59.3	54.6	49.9	45.4	40.9	36.5	32.2	28.0	24.0	20.2	16.7	13.6	10.9	...	...	...	...	...	...
Female - Femmes	64.2	67.4	62.9	58.2	53.7	49.2	44.8	40.2	35.7	31.3	26.9	22.7	18.9	15.4	12.4	...	...	...	...	...	...
Indonesia - Indonésie																					
2010																					
Male - Hommes	68.7	...	...	...	...	...	...	...	...	...	...	...	...	...	...	...	...	...	...	...	...
Female - Femmes	72.6	...	...	...	...	...	...	...	...	...	...	...	...	...	...	...	...	...	...	...	...
Iran (Islamic Republic of) - Iran (République islamique d')																					
1996																					
Male - Hommes	66.1	64.6	59.9	55.1	50.5	46.0	41.4	36.8	32.3	27.9	23.7	19.8	16.2	12.9	10.1	7.7	5.7	4.2	3.1	...	...
Female - Femmes	68.4	66.8	62.1	57.3	52.7	48.0	43.5	39.0	34.5	30.1	25.8	21.7	17.8	14.3	11.1	8.4	6.2	4.5	3.2	...	...
2006																					
Male - Hommes	71.1	...	...	...	...	...	...	...	...	...	...	...	...	...	...	...	...	...	...	...	...
Female - Femmes	73.1	...	...	...	...	...	...	...	...	...	...	...	...	...	...	...	...	...	...	...	...
Iraq																					
1997																					
Male - Hommes	58.0	...	...	...	...	...	...	...	...	...	...	...	...	...	...	...	...	...	...	...	...
Female - Femmes	59.0	...	...	...	...	...	...	...	...	...	...	...	...	...	...	...	...	...	...	...	...
Israel - Israël[18]																					
2007 - 2011																					
Male - Hommes	79.4	74.7	69.8	64.8	60.0	55.1	50.3	45.5	40.7	36.0	31.3	26.9	22.6	18.6	14.9	11.5	8.6	6.3	4.6	3.8	4.3
Female - Femmes	83.1	78.5	73.5	68.5	63.6	58.7	53.7	48.8	43.9	39.1	34.3	29.7	25.1	20.8	16.6	12.8	9.4	6.6	4.5	3.3	3.3
Japan - Japon[19]																					
2011																					
Male - Hommes	79.4	74.7	69.8	64.8	59.9	55.1	50.3	45.5	40.7	36.0	31.4	27.0	22.7	18.7	14.9	11.4	8.4	6.0	4.1	2.8	1.9
Female - Femmes	85.9	81.2	76.2	71.3	66.4	61.5	56.6	51.7	46.8	42.1	37.3	32.7	28.1	23.7	19.3	15.2	11.4	8.1	5.5	3.6	2.3
Jordan - Jordanie[20]																					
2011																					
Male - Hommes	71.6	...	...	...	...	...	...	...	...	...	...	...	...	...	...	...	...	...	...	...	...
Female - Femmes	74.4	...	...	...	...	...	...	...	...	...	...	...	...	...	...	...	...	...	...	...	...

21. Life expectancy at specified ages for each sex: latest available year, 1993 - 2012
Espérance de vie à un âge donné pour chaque sexe : dernière année disponible, 1993 - 2012 (continued - suite)

Continent, country or area and date / Continent, pays ou zone et date	0	5	10	15	20	25	30	35	40	45	50	55	60	65	70	75	80	85	90	95	100
ASIA - ASIE																					
Kazakhstan 2008																					
Male - Hommes	61.9	58.6	53.8	48.9	44.2	39.8	35.6	31.7	27.8	24.0	20.5	17.2	14.1	11.5	9.2	7.2	5.7	4.3	3.1	2.4	1.8
Female - Femmes	72.4	69.0	64.1	59.3	54.4	49.7	45.0	40.5	35.9	31.5	27.1	22.9	18.9	15.3	11.9	8.9	6.5	4.5	3.0	2.2	1.7
Kuwait - Koweït 1992 - 1993																					
Male - Hommes	71.8	67.9	63.0	58.2	53.6	48.9	44.2	39.4	34.7	30.1	25.6	21.4	17.3	14.1	10.8	7.8	4.4	2.5	...	...	...
Female - Femmes	73.3	69.2	64.3	59.4	54.5	49.6	44.7	39.8	35.0	30.2	25.5	21.1	16.8	13.3	10.0	7.4	4.3	2.6	...	...	...
1990 - 1995																					
Male - Hommes	73.3	...	...	...	...	...	...	...	...	...	...	...	...	...	...	...	...	...	...	...	...
Female - Femmes	77.2	...	...	...	...	...	...	...	...	...	...	...	...	...	...	...	...	...	...	...	...
Kyrgyzstan - Kirghizstan 2011																					
Male - Hommes	65.7	62.5	57.6	52.7	47.9	43.2	38.6	34.2	30.1	26.1	22.2	18.6	15.3	12.4	9.9	7.6	5.9	4.5	3.0	2.2	1.7
Female - Femmes	73.7	70.3	65.4	60.5	55.6	50.8	46.1	41.4	36.7	32.2	27.8	23.5	19.4	15.7	12.3	9.2	6.9	5.0	3.4	2.6	1.8
Lao People's Democratic Republic - République démocratique populaire lao[21] 2005																					
Male - Hommes	59.0	...	...	...	...	...	...	...	...	...	...	...	...	...	...	...	...	...	...	...	...
Female - Femmes	63.0	...	...	...	...	...	...	...	...	...	...	...	...	...	...	...	...	...	...	...	...
Malaysia - Malaisie 2009																					
Male - Hommes	71.6	67.0	62.1	57.2	52.4	47.7	43.1	38.5	33.9	29.5	25.2	21.1	17.2	13.7	10.5	8.1	5.8	...	...	...	...
Female - Femmes	76.5	71.9	67.0	62.0	57.1	52.3	47.4	42.6	37.8	33.0	28.4	24.0	19.8	15.8	12.2	9.1	6.6	...	...	...	...
Maldives 2009																					
Male - Hommes	72.5	68.7	63.8	59.0	54.1	49.2	44.4	39.5	34.7	29.9	25.2	20.6	16.3	12.3	8.8	6.1	...	...	...	...	...
Female - Femmes	74.2	70.2	65.3	60.4	55.5	50.6	45.6	40.8	35.8	31.0	26.3	21.6	17.1	12.9	9.1	6.0	...	...	...	...	...
2011																					
Male - Hommes	72.8	...	...	...	...	...	...	...	...	...	...	...	...	...	...	...	...	...	...	...	...
Female - Femmes	74.8	...	...	...	...	...	...	...	...	...	...	...	...	...	...	...	...	...	...	...	...
Mongolia - Mongolie 1998 - 2007																					
Male - Hommes	63.1	61.3	56.5	51.6	46.9	42.3	38.0	33.7	29.7	25.9	22.4	19.2	16.1	13.7	12.0	...	...	...	...	...	...
Female - Femmes	70.2	68.9	64.0	59.1	54.2	49.5	44.8	40.2	35.7	31.3	27.2	23.3	19.7	16.7	14.3	...	...	...	...	...	...
2010																					
Male - Hommes	64.9	...	...	...	...	...	...	...	...	...	...	...	...	...	...	...	...	...	...	...	...
Female - Femmes	72.3	...	...	...	...	...	...	...	...	...	...	...	...	...	...	...	...	...	...	...	...
Myanmar[22] 2010																					
Male - Hommes	64.6	64.0	59.3	54.5	49.8	45.1	40.4	35.8	31.3	26.9	22.6	18.7	15.7	12.7	10.2	7.7	6.3	5.6	...	...	...
Female - Femmes	68.6	68.0	63.6	58.8	54.1	49.4	44.6	39.8	35.1	30.4	25.8	21.5	17.8	14.2	11.1	8.2	5.7	4.3	...	...	...
Nepal - Népal 2008																					
Male - Hommes	63.6	...	...	...	...	...	...	...	...	...	...	...	...	...	...	...	...	...	...	...	...
Female - Femmes	64.5	...	...	...	...	...	...	...	...	...	...	...	...	...	...	...	...	...	...	...	...
Oman 2008																					
Male - Hommes	72.2	68.1	63.2	58.3	53.6	48.8	44.1	39.3	34.6	29.9	25.2	20.9	16.8	13.2	10.1	7.8	7.2	...	...	...	...
Female - Femmes	75.7	71.5	66.6	61.7	56.7	51.8	46.9	42.0	37.2	32.4	27.7	23.3	19.3	15.8	12.6	10.3	9.3	...	...	...	...
2011																					
Male - Hommes	73.1	...	...	...	...	...	...	...	...	...	...	...	...	...	...	...	...	...	...	...	...
Female - Femmes	77.7	...	...	...	...	...	...	...	...	...	...	...	...	...	...	...	...	...	...	...	...
Pakistan[23] 2007																					
Male - Hommes	63.6	65.3	60.7	55.9	51.3	46.7	42.2	37.7	33.3	29.0	25.0	21.3	18.1	15.2	12.7	10.8	9.2	7.3	...	...	...
Female - Femmes	67.6	68.6	64.1	59.5	54.9	50.3	45.7	41.1	36.5	32.1	27.7	23.5	19.6	16.2	13.4	10.9	8.6	6.1	...	...	...
Qatar 2008																					
Male - Hommes	77.9	73.7	68.8	63.9	59.1	54.3	49.4	44.6	39.8	35.0	30.3	25.6	21.2	17.0	13.3	9.9	7.1	...	...	...	...
Female - Femmes	78.1	73.9	68.9	64.0	59.1	54.1	49.2	44.3	39.3	34.5	29.6	24.9	20.5	16.6	13.2	10.0	7.8	...	...	...	...

Continent, country or area and date / Continent, pays ou zone et date	Age (in years) - Age (en années)																				
	0	5	10	15	20	25	30	35	40	45	50	55	60	65	70	75	80	85	90	95	100
ASIA - ASIE																					
2011																					
Male - Hommes	76.5	...	...	...	...	...	...	...	...	...	...	...	...	...	...	...	...	...	...	...	...
Female - Femmes	81.0	...	...	...	...	...	...	...	...	...	...	...	...	...	...	...	...	...	...	...	...
Republic of Korea - République de Corée																					
2011																					
Male - Hommes	77.7	73.0	68.0	63.1	58.2	53.3	48.5	43.7	39.0	34.3	29.9	25.6	21.4	17.4	13.7	10.4	7.7	5.5	4.0	2.9	2.3
Female - Femmes	84.5	79.8	74.8	69.8	64.9	60.0	55.1	50.2	45.4	40.6	35.8	31.1	26.5	21.9	17.6	13.5	10.0	7.1	5.0	3.6	2.7
Saudi Arabia - Arabie saoudite[24]																					
2012																					
Male - Hommes	72.8	...	...	...	...	...	...	...	...	...	...	...	...	...	...	...	...	...	...	...	...
Female - Femmes	75.2	...	...	...	...	...	...	...	...	...	...	...	...	...	...	...	...	...	...	...	...
Singapore - Singapour[25]																					
2012																					
Male - Hommes	79.9	75.1	70.2	65.2	60.3	55.4	50.5	45.7	40.8	36.0	31.4	26.9	22.6	18.5	14.8	11.5	8.8	6.4	4.6	3.2	2.2
Female - Femmes	84.5	79.7	74.7	69.7	64.8	59.8	54.9	50.0	45.1	40.3	35.5	30.9	26.3	21.9	17.8	14.0	10.7	7.9	5.6	3.9	2.6
State of Palestine - État de Palestine																					
2001																					
Male - Hommes	70.5	67.5	62.7	57.8	53.1	48.4	43.6	38.9	34.2	29.6	25.2	21.1	17.2	13.8	10.7	8.1	6.1	...	...	...	...
Female - Femmes	73.6	70.3	65.5	60.5	55.7	50.9	46.1	41.3	36.6	32.0	27.5	23.2	19.0	15.2	11.7	8.8	6.4	...	...	...	...
2012																					
Male - Hommes	71.3	...	...	...	...	...	...	...	...	...	...	...	...	...	...	...	...	...	...	...	...
Female - Femmes	74.1	...	...	...	...	...	...	...	...	...	...	...	...	...	...	...	...	...	...	...	...
Tajikistan - Tadjikistan																					
2008																					
Male - Hommes	69.7	67.9	63.0	58.1	53.3	48.5	43.7	39.1	34.6	30.1	25.7	21.6	17.9	14.7	12.2	10.4	9.2	...	...	...	...
Female - Femmes	74.8	72.5	67.6	62.7	57.8	52.9	48.1	43.4	38.6	33.9	29.4	25.0	21.0	17.5	14.7	12.5	11.1	...	...	...	...
2011																					
Male - Hommes	70.9	...	...	...	...	...	...	...	...	...	...	...	...	...	...	...	...	...	...	...	...
Female - Femmes	74.1	...	...	...	...	...	...	...	...	...	...	...	...	...	...	...	...	...	...	...	...
Thailand - Thaïlande																					
2005 - 2006																					
Male - Hommes	69.9	...	...	...	...	...	...	...	...	...	...	...	...	...	...	...	...	...	...	...	...
Female - Femmes	77.6	...	...	...	...	...	...	...	...	...	...	...	...	...	...	...	...	...	...	...	...
Turkey - Turquie																					
2011																					
Male - Hommes	72.0	...	...	...	...	...	...	...	...	...	...	...	...	...	...	...	...	...	...	...	...
Female - Femmes	77.1	...	...	...	...	...	...	...	...	...	...	...	...	...	...	...	...	...	...	...	...
United Arab Emirates - Émirats arabes unis																					
2006																					
Male - Hommes	76.7	72.5	67.6	62.7	57.9	53.1	48.3	43.5	38.7	33.9	29.3	24.8	20.7	16.9	13.8	11.3	10.2	...	...	...	...
Female - Femmes	78.8	74.5	69.5	64.6	59.7	54.8	49.8	44.9	40.0	35.2	30.4	25.8	21.6	18.0	15.4	14.0	14.5	...	...	...	...
Viet Nam																					
2012																					
Male - Hommes	70.4	67.6	62.8	57.9	53.2	48.5	43.8	39.1	34.4	30.0	25.7	21.8	18.2	15.0	12.2	10.0	8.3	...	...	...	...
Female - Femmes	75.8	72.0	67.1	62.2	57.3	52.4	47.6	42.7	38.0	33.4	28.9	24.6	20.5	16.8	13.6	11.0	8.9	...	...	...	...
Yemen - Yémen																					
2004																					
Male - Hommes	60.2	...	...	...	...	...	...	...	...	...	...	...	...	...	...	...	...	...	...	...	...
Female - Femmes	62.0	...	...	...	...	...	...	...	...	...	...	...	...	...	...	...	...	...	...	...	...
EUROPE																					
Åland Islands - Îles d'Åland																					
2011																					
Male - Hommes	79.5	74.5	69.5	64.5	59.8	54.8	49.8	45.1	40.6	35.6	30.7	26.3	22.1	17.7	13.7	10.4	7.7	5.3	4.2	1.6	1.0
Female - Femmes	84.8	79.8	74.8	69.8	64.8	59.8	54.8	49.8	44.8	39.8	34.8	29.9	25.5	21.3	17.5	13.3	9.6	6.4	4.3	3.0	1.8
Albania - Albanie																					
2004																					
Male - Hommes	72.5	69.5	64.8	59.9	55.1	50.4	45.8	41.1	36.4	31.8	27.3	22.9	18.6	14.8	11.3	8.4	6.0	3.8	...	...	...
Female - Femmes	77.3	74.4	69.5	64.7	59.8	54.9	50.0	45.2	40.3	35.5	30.8	26.1	21.6	17.3	13.2	9.6	6.4	3.8	...	...	...

Continent, country or area and date / Continent, pays ou zone et date	Age (in years) - Age (en années)																				
	0	5	10	15	20	25	30	35	40	45	50	55	60	65	70	75	80	85	90	95	100
EUROPE																					
Austria - Autriche 2011																					
Male - Hommes	78.1	73.5	68.6	63.6	58.7	53.9	49.1	44.3	39.5	34.8	30.2	25.8	21.7	17.9	14.3	10.9	8.0	5.6	3.8	2.8	...
Female - Femmes	83.4	78.7	73.8	68.8	63.9	58.9	54.0	49.1	44.2	39.4	34.7	30.0	25.6	21.3	17.1	13.1	9.5	6.5	4.3	2.9	...
Belarus - Bélarus 2011																					
Male - Hommes	64.7	60.1	55.2	50.2	45.4	40.8	36.3	32.1	28.0	24.2	20.6	17.3	14.4	11.9	9.7	7.6	5.9	4.5	3.4	2.5	1.8
Female - Femmes	76.7	72.1	67.1	62.2	57.3	52.4	47.6	42.9	38.2	33.6	29.2	24.9	20.9	17.1	13.4	10.1	7.4	5.2	3.5	2.3	1.4
Belgium - Belgique 2006																					
Male - Hommes	77.0	71.4	66.5	61.5	56.7	51.9	47.1	42.4	37.7	33.1	28.6	24.3	20.3	16.5	12.9	9.7	7.1	5.0	3.4	2.5	...
Female - Femmes	82.7	77.0	72.1	67.1	62.2	57.3	52.4	47.5	42.6	37.9	33.2	28.7	24.3	20.1	16.0	12.1	8.8	6.1	4.1	2.8	...
Bosnia and Herzegovina - Bosnie-Herzégovine 2003																					
Male - Hommes	71.3	...	...	...	...	...	...	...	...	...	...	...	...	...	...	...	...	...	...	...	...
Female - Femmes	76.7	...	...	...	...	...	...	...	...	...	...	...	...	...	...	...	...	...	...	...	...
Bulgaria - Bulgarie 2009 - 2011																					
Male - Hommes	70.4	66.2	61.3	56.4	51.6	46.8	42.1	37.4	32.7	28.3	24.2	20.3	16.9	13.8	10.9	8.3	6.1	4.4	3.0	1.9	0.5
Female - Femmes	77.4	73.1	68.1	63.2	58.3	53.4	48.5	43.7	38.9	34.2	29.7	25.3	21.0	16.9	13.1	9.7	6.8	4.7	3.0	1.9	0.5
Czech Republic - République tchèque 2011																					
Male - Hommes	74.7	70.0	65.0	60.0	55.2	50.4	45.6	40.8	36.1	31.4	26.9	22.8	18.9	15.5	12.3	9.4	6.8	4.8	3.2	2.0	1.3
Female - Femmes	80.7	76.0	71.0	66.0	61.1	56.2	51.3	46.4	41.5	36.7	32.0	27.4	23.0	18.8	14.9	11.2	7.9	5.3	3.3	2.0	1.1
Denmark - Danemark[26] 2010 - 2011																					
Male - Hommes	77.3	72.6	67.7	62.7	57.8	53.0	48.1	43.3	38.5	33.8	29.3	25.0	20.9	17.1	13.5	10.3	7.6	5.3	3.7	2.5	...
Female - Femmes	81.6	76.9	71.9	67.0	62.0	57.1	52.2	47.2	42.3	37.5	32.8	28.3	24.0	19.8	15.9	12.2	9.1	6.5	4.4	3.0	...
Estonia - Estonie 2011																					
Male - Hommes	71.2	66.4	61.4	56.6	51.7	47.0	42.4	38.0	33.6	29.3	25.2	21.3	17.7	14.5	11.6	9.1	7.0	5.3	4.0	3.0	2.2
Female - Femmes	81.1	76.3	71.3	66.3	61.4	56.6	51.9	47.1	42.4	37.6	32.9	28.2	23.7	19.3	15.3	11.6	8.5	5.9	4.0	2.6	1.7
Faeroe Islands - Îles Féroé 2008																					
Male - Hommes	76.8	72.5	67.7	62.7	57.9	53.0	48.1	43.3	38.5	33.9	29.3	24.8	20.8	17.0	13.4	10.1	7.6	6.0	4.6	3.2	...
Female - Femmes	82.3	77.8	72.8	67.8	62.9	57.9	53.0	48.1	43.2	38.2	33.4	28.7	24.3	20.0	15.9	12.5	9.2	6.6	4.4	3.3	...
Finland - Finlande[27] 2010																					
Male - Hommes	76.7	71.9	67.0	62.0	57.2	52.5	47.8	43.0	38.3	33.7	29.2	25.0	21.0	17.3	13.7	10.5	7.6	5.4	3.7	2.5	1.8
Female - Femmes	83.2	78.4	73.5	68.5	63.6	58.7	53.8	48.9	44.0	39.2	34.5	30.0	25.5	21.2	17.0	13.0	9.4	6.5	4.3	2.8	1.7
France 2008 - 2010																					
Male - Hommes	77.8	73.2	68.2	63.2	58.4	53.6	48.8	44.0	39.3	34.7	30.3	26.2	22.2	18.4	14.8	11.3	8.3	5.8	4.0	2.7	...
Female - Femmes	84.5	79.8	74.9	69.9	65.0	60.0	55.1	50.2	45.4	40.6	36.0	31.4	27.0	22.6	18.4	14.3	10.6	7.4	4.9	3.3	...
Germany - Allemagne 2009 - 2011																					
Male - Hommes	77.7	73.1	68.1	63.1	58.3	53.4	48.6	43.7	38.9	34.2	29.7	25.4	21.3	17.5	13.9	10.6	7.8	5.5	3.8	2.7	2.0
Female - Femmes	82.7	78.0	73.1	68.1	63.2	58.2	53.3	48.4	43.5	38.7	34.0	29.4	25.0	20.7	16.5	12.6	9.1	6.3	4.3	3.0	2.1
Gibraltar 2001																					
Male - Hommes	78.5	73.5	68.5	63.5	58.5	53.5	...	43.5	...	33.9	...	25.8	...	17.9	...	11.3	...	...	...	...	...
Female - Femmes	83.3	79.5	75.0	70.0	65.0	60.0	...	50.3	...	40.3	...	30.3	...	20.6	...	13.7	...	...	...	...	...
Greece - Grèce 2011																					
Male - Hommes	78.3	73.6	68.6	63.7	58.8	54.0	49.2	44.5	39.7	35.0	30.5	26.1	22.0	18.1	14.5	11.2	8.3	6.2	4.6	3.3	2.3
Female - Femmes	83.1	78.4	73.4	68.5	63.6	58.6	53.7	48.8	43.9	39.1	34.3	29.7	25.1	20.6	16.3	12.3	8.8	6.3	4.6	3.3	2.3
Hungary - Hongrie 2011																					
Male - Hommes	70.9	66.4	61.4	56.4	51.6	46.7	41.9	37.1	32.3	27.8	23.7	20.1	16.9	13.9	11.1	8.6	6.4	4.3	2.6	1.4	0.6
Female - Femmes	78.2	73.7	68.7	63.7	58.8	53.9	48.9	44.0	39.2	34.5	30.0	25.7	21.6	17.7	14.0	10.5	7.5	4.8	2.8	1.5	0.6

21. Life expectancy at specified ages for each sex: latest available year, 1993 - 2012
Espérance de vie à un âge donné pour chaque sexe : dernière année disponible, 1993 - 2012 (continued - suite)

Continent, country or area and date / Continent, pays ou zone et date	0	5	10	15	20	25	30	35	40	45	50	55	60	65	70	75	80	85	90	95	100
EUROPE																					
Iceland - Islande																					
2010 - 2011																					
Male - Hommes	79.9	75.1	70.1	65.2	60.3	55.5	50.7	45.9	41.1	36.3	31.6	27.0	22.5	18.3	14.4	10.8	7.8	5.3	3.4	2.2	1.5
Female - Femmes	82.8	77.8	72.8	67.9	63.0	58.1	53.1	48.2	43.3	38.5	33.7	29.0	24.4	20.2	16.1	12.3	8.9	6.0	3.9	2.5	1.5
Ireland - Irlande																					
2005 - 2007																					
Male - Hommes	76.8	72.2	67.2	62.3	57.5	52.8	48.0	43.3	38.5	33.8	29.2	24.8	20.6	16.6	13.0	9.8	7.1	5.1	3.6	2.6	1.9
Female - Femmes	81.6	76.9	72.0	67.0	62.1	57.2	52.3	47.4	42.5	37.7	33.1	28.5	24.0	19.8	15.8	12.1	8.8	6.2	4.3	3.1	2.1
Isle of Man - Île de Man																					
1996																					
Male - Hommes	73.6	68.6	63.6	58.6	53.6	49.1	44.6	40.2	35.8	31.2	26.7	22.4	18.4	15.1	12.0	9.3	7.5	5.2	4.7	3.2	0.5
Female - Femmes	79.9	75.1	70.1	65.1	60.1	55.1	50.1	45.1	40.2	35.4	30.7	26.2	22.0	18.3	14.5	11.3	8.6	5.9	3.7	2.0	1.5
Italy - Italie																					
2009																					
Male - Hommes	79.0	74.4	69.4	64.4	59.6	54.7	49.9	45.1	40.3	35.5	30.9	26.4	22.1	18.1	14.3	10.9	7.9	5.6	3.8	2.9	2.0
Female - Femmes	84.1	79.4	74.5	69.5	64.6	59.6	54.7	49.8	44.9	40.0	35.3	30.6	26.0	21.6	17.4	13.4	9.8	6.8	4.5	3.2	2.1
Latvia - Lettonie																					
2010																					
Male - Hommes	68.8	64.3	59.4	54.4	49.6	44.9	40.2	35.6	31.2	27.0	23.0	19.4	16.1	13.2	10.6	8.3	6.3	4.8	3.6	3.1	2.5
Female - Femmes	78.4	73.9	69.0	64.1	59.2	54.3	49.4	44.5	39.8	35.1	30.6	26.2	22.0	18.1	14.3	10.9	7.8	5.4	3.6	2.6	2.0
Lithuania - Lituanie																					
2011																					
Male - Hommes	68.1	63.5	58.5	53.6	48.8	44.2	39.7	35.3	31.0	27.0	23.3	19.7	16.6	13.9	11.4	9.0	6.8	5.0	3.6	2.9	2.3
Female - Femmes	79.1	74.5	69.6	64.6	59.7	54.8	49.9	45.1	40.4	35.8	31.4	27.0	22.9	18.9	15.1	11.4	8.2	5.8	4.0	2.8	2.1
Luxembourg																					
2005 - 2007																					
Male - Hommes	77.6	72.9	67.9	63.0	58.0	53.3	48.5	43.7	39.0	34.3	29.8	25.4	21.3	17.6	14.1	10.9	8.1	5.7	3.7	0.4	...
Female - Femmes	82.7	78.0	73.0	68.1	63.1	58.2	53.4	48.5	43.6	38.9	34.2	29.6	25.2	20.9	16.9	13.1	9.7	6.8	4.5	2.2	...
Malta - Malte																					
2011																					
Male - Hommes	78.4	73.9	69.0	64.0	59.1	54.3	49.5	44.6	39.8	35.0	30.4	25.8	21.4	17.2	13.4	10.0	7.0	4.9	3.0	1.3	1.5
Female - Femmes	82.7	78.4	73.4	68.4	63.5	58.5	53.7	48.8	43.8	39.0	34.2	29.5	25.0	20.5	16.3	12.2	8.6	5.8	3.7	1.9	0.8
Netherlands - Pays-Bas																					
2009																					
Male - Hommes	78.5	73.8	68.8	63.9	59.0	54.1	49.2	44.4	39.5	34.8	30.1	25.6	21.4	17.3	13.6	10.3	7.5	5.3	3.6	2.6	...
Female - Femmes	82.7	77.8	72.8	67.9	62.9	58.0	53.1	48.2	43.3	38.5	33.8	29.3	24.9	20.6	16.5	12.7	9.2	6.4	4.3	2.9	...
2011																					
Male - Hommes	79.2	...	...	...	...	...	...	...	...	...	...	...	...	...	...	...	...	...	...	...	...
Female - Femmes	82.8	...	...	...	...	...	...	...	...	...	...	...	...	...	...	...	...	...	...	...	...
Norway - Norvège																					
2011																					
Male - Hommes	79.0	74.3	69.3	64.3	59.5	54.7	49.9	45.2	40.4	35.6	31.0	26.5	22.2	18.0	14.3	10.8	7.9	5.5	3.8	2.6	2.1
Female - Femmes	83.5	78.6	73.7	68.7	63.8	58.9	54.0	49.1	44.2	39.4	34.6	30.0	25.5	21.2	17.1	13.1	9.6	6.6	4.4	3.0	2.0
Poland - Pologne																					
2011																					
Male - Hommes	72.4	67.9	62.9	58.0	53.2	48.4	43.7	39.0	34.4	30.0	25.9	22.0	18.5	15.3	12.4	9.7	7.4	5.5	4.0	2.9	2.1
Female - Femmes	80.9	76.3	71.3	66.4	61.5	56.5	51.6	46.7	41.9	37.1	32.5	28.0	23.8	19.7	15.8	12.1	9.0	6.4	4.5	3.2	2.2
Portugal																					
2009 - 2011																					
Male - Hommes	76.4	71.7	66.8	61.8	56.9	52.1	47.3	42.5	37.8	33.3	28.9	24.7	20.7	16.8	13.1	9.8	6.8	4.3	2.6	1.7	1.1
Female - Femmes	82.3	77.6	72.6	67.6	62.7	57.8	52.9	48.0	43.2	38.4	33.7	29.1	24.5	20.1	15.8	11.8	8.1	5.1	3.1	1.9	1.2
Republic of Moldova - République de Moldova[28]																					
2010																					
Male - Hommes	65.0	61.1	56.2	51.2	46.4	41.7	37.1	32.7	28.5	24.6	21.0	17.7	14.8	12.1	9.8	8.0	6.8	6.6	7.6	...	...
Female - Femmes	73.4	69.2	64.3	59.4	54.5	49.6	44.8	40.0	35.3	30.7	26.3	22.2	18.2	14.8	11.7	8.9	6.8	5.3	4.2	...	...
Romania - Roumanie																					
2009 - 2011																					
Male - Hommes	70.1	66.0	61.1	56.2	51.4	46.6	41.9	37.1	32.5	28.1	24.1	20.4	17.1	14.0	11.1	8.6	6.4	4.7	3.4	2.4	1.8
Female - Femmes	77.5	73.3	68.4	63.5	58.6	53.7	48.8	43.9	39.1	34.4	29.8	25.4	21.2	17.2	13.4	10.0	7.2	5.0	3.5	2.4	1.7

21. Life expectancy at specified ages for each sex: latest available year, 1993 - 2012
Espérance de vie à un âge donné pour chaque sexe : dernière année disponible, 1993 - 2012 (continued - suite)

Continent, country or area and date / Continent, pays ou zone et date	Age (in years) - Age (en années)																				
	0	5	10	15	20	25	30	35	40	45	50	55	60	65	70	75	80	85	90	95	100
EUROPE																					
Russian Federation - Fédération de Russie 2011																					
Male - Hommes	64.0	59.7	54.8	49.9	45.2	40.7	36.5	32.6	28.8	25.0	21.4	18.1	15.1	12.6	10.1	8.0	6.3	5.1	3.9	2.9	1.4
Female - Femmes	75.6	71.2	66.3	61.4	56.6	51.7	47.1	42.5	38.0	33.5	29.1	24.9	20.8	17.0	13.4	10.1	7.4	5.3	3.8	2.8	1.8
San Marino - Saint-Marin 2000																					
Male - Hommes	78.0	73.6	68.6	63.7	59.1	54.4	49.6	44.7	39.9	35.0	30.4	25.9	21.5	17.3	13.6	10.6	7.7	5.5	3.8	2.5	...
Female - Femmes	84.6	80.1	75.2	70.2	65.2	60.2	55.3	50.4	45.5	40.7	35.9	31.1	26.4	22.0	17.7	13.5	9.6	6.7	4.6	2.5	...
Serbia - Serbie[29] 2011																					
Male - Hommes	71.6	67.2	62.2	57.3	52.4	47.6	42.8	38.0	33.3	28.8	24.5	20.5	16.9	13.6	10.7	8.1	6.0	4.2	...	...	...
Female - Femmes	76.8	72.3	67.4	62.4	57.5	52.6	47.7	42.8	38.0	33.2	28.6	24.2	19.9	15.9	12.2	9.0	6.4	4.4	...	...	...
Slovakia - Slovaquie 2011																					
Male - Hommes	72.2	67.7	62.7	57.8	52.9	48.1	43.4	38.6	33.9	29.4	25.1	21.2	17.6	14.4	11.3	8.7	6.4	4.5	3.1	2.0	0.7
Female - Femmes	79.4	74.8	69.8	64.9	60.0	55.0	50.1	45.2	40.4	35.6	30.9	26.5	22.1	17.9	14.0	10.3	7.2	4.6	2.8	1.6	0.7
Slovenia - Slovénie 2011																					
Male - Hommes	76.6	71.9	67.0	62.0	57.1	52.3	47.5	42.7	37.9	33.3	28.7	24.4	20.5	16.7	13.2	10.1	7.4	5.2	3.5	2.5	2.0
Female - Femmes	82.9	78.2	73.2	68.2	63.2	58.3	53.4	48.4	43.5	38.7	34.0	29.5	25.0	20.7	16.5	12.6	9.1	6.2	4.3	3.1	2.1
Spain - Espagne 2011																					
Male - Hommes	79.2	74.5	69.5	64.5	59.6	54.7	49.9	45.0	40.2	35.5	30.9	26.6	22.4	18.5	14.7	11.3	8.4	6.0	4.4	3.2	2.9
Female - Femmes	85.0	80.3	75.3	70.3	65.4	60.4	55.5	50.6	45.7	40.8	36.1	31.5	26.9	22.4	18.0	13.8	10.1	7.0	4.7	3.1	2.0
Sweden - Suède 2011																					
Male - Hommes	79.8	75.0	70.1	65.1	60.2	55.4	50.6	45.7	40.9	36.1	31.4	26.9	22.5	18.4	14.6	11.0	8.0	5.5	3.8	2.7	1.9
Female - Femmes	83.7	78.9	73.9	69.0	64.0	59.1	54.2	49.3	44.4	39.5	34.8	30.1	25.6	21.2	17.0	13.1	9.6	6.7	4.5	3.2	2.3
Switzerland - Suisse 2011																					
Male - Hommes	80.3	75.7	70.7	65.8	60.9	56.0	51.1	46.3	41.4	36.7	32.0	27.5	23.1	19.0	15.1	11.6	8.4	5.7	3.9	2.9	1.8
Female - Femmes	84.7	80.1	75.1	70.1	65.2	60.2	55.3	50.4	45.5	40.6	35.9	31.2	26.6	22.2	17.9	13.9	10.2	7.0	4.6	3.1	2.1
TFYR of Macedonia - L'ex-R. y. de Macédoine 2009																					
Male - Hommes	72.5	68.4	63.4	58.5	53.6	48.8	43.9	39.1	34.4	29.7	25.3	21.2	17.3	13.8	10.6	7.9	5.6	3.9	2.8	2.4	...
Female - Femmes	76.7	72.5	67.5	62.6	57.6	52.7	47.8	42.9	38.0	33.2	28.6	24.1	19.8	15.7	12.0	8.7	6.1	4.4	3.5	2.7	...
Ukraine 2011																					
Male - Hommes	66.0	61.8	56.9	51.9	47.1	42.5	38.0	33.8	29.7	25.8	22.0	18.5	15.4	12.6	10.1	8.0	6.2	5.0	3.9	3.1	2.1
Female - Femmes	75.9	71.6	66.7	61.7	56.8	52.0	47.2	42.5	37.9	33.3	28.9	24.5	20.4	16.5	12.9	9.7	7.0	5.0	3.5	2.4	1.6
United Kingdom of Great Britain and Northern Ireland - Royaume-Uni de Grande-Bretagne et d'Irlande du Nord[30] 2006 - 2008																					
Male - Hommes	77.4	72.9	67.9	63.0	58.1	53.3	48.5	43.8	39.1	34.4	29.9	25.5	21.3	17.4	13.8	10.5	7.8	5.7	4.0	2.8	2.0
Female - Femmes	81.6	77.1	72.1	67.1	62.2	57.3	52.4	47.5	42.7	37.9	33.2	28.7	24.3	20.0	16.0	12.4	9.2	6.5	4.5	3.1	2.2
OCEANIA - OCÉANIE																					
American Samoa - Samoas américaines 2006																					
Male - Hommes	68.5	...	...	...	...	...	...	...	...	...	...	...	...	...	...	...	...	...	...	...	...
Female - Femmes	76.2	...	...	...	...	...	...	...	...	...	...	...	...	...	...	...	...	...	...	...	...
Australia - Australie 2009 - 2011																					
Male - Hommes	79.8	75.2	70.3	65.3	60.4	55.6	50.8	46.0	41.3	36.6	32.0	27.5	23.2	19.1	15.2	11.7	8.7	6.2	4.5	3.3	2.7
Female - Femmes	84.2	79.6	74.6	69.6	64.7	59.8	54.9	50.0	45.1	40.3	35.6	31.0	26.4	22.0	17.8	13.8	10.2	7.2	4.9	3.5	2.7

21. Life expectancy at specified ages for each sex: latest available year, 1993 - 2012
Espérance de vie à un âge donné pour chaque sexe : dernière année disponible, 1993 - 2012 (continued - suite)

Continent, country or area and date / Continent, pays ou zone et date	0	5	10	15	20	25	30	35	40	45	50	55	60	65	70	75	80	85	90	95	100
OCEANIA - OCÉANIE																					
Cook Islands - Îles Cook[31]																					
2006																					
Male - Hommes	69.5	66.0	61.3	56.5	52.0	47.4	42.8	38.1	33.6	29.1	24.8	20.9	17.5	14.3	11.4	9.0	7.3	...	...	...	...
Female - Femmes	76.2	72.4	67.4	62.4	57.4	52.7	48.0	43.2	38.4	33.6	29.1	24.7	20.4	16.4	12.6	9.5	6.9	...	...	...	...
Fiji - Fidji																					
1996																					
Male - Hommes	64.5	...	...	...	...	42.4	...	...	...	...	...	...	...	10.7	...	...	...	...	...	...	...
Female - Femmes	68.7	...	...	...	...	46.4	...	...	...	...	...	...	...	13.0	...	...	...	...	...	...	...
2007																					
Male - Hommes	65.3	...																			
Female - Femmes	69.6	...																			
French Polynesia - Polynésie française																					
2010																					
Male - Hommes	73.2	69.1	64.1	59.3	54.6	50.0	45.3	40.6	35.8	31.2	26.8	22.7	19.0	15.4	12.4	9.9	7.2	5.1	...	...	...
Female - Femmes	78.3	74.2	69.3	64.3	59.4	54.4	49.6	44.8	40.0	35.3	30.6	26.3	22.1	17.8	14.3	11.1	7.8	5.2	...	...	...
Guam																					
2008																					
Male - Hommes	75.9	...																			
Female - Femmes	82.2	...																			
Kiribati																					
2005																					
Male - Hommes	58.9	58.2	53.6	48.9	44.4	40.0	35.6	31.3	27.1	23.1	19.4	16.0	13.0	10.4	8.3	6.6	5.3	4.2	...	...	...
Female - Femmes	63.1	62.6	57.9	53.1	48.6	44.1	39.7	35.4	31.2	27.1	23.2	19.5	16.1	13.1	10.4	8.1	6.2	4.7	...	...	...
Marshall Islands - Îles Marshall																					
2004																					
Male - Hommes	67.0	...	...	...	...	...	...	...	...	...	...	...	...	...	...	...	...	...	...	...	...
Female - Femmes	70.6	...	...	...	...	...	...	...	...	...	...	...	...	...	...	...	...	...	...	...	...
Micronesia (Federated States of) - Micronésie (États fédérés de)																					
2000																					
Male - Hommes	66.5	...	...	...	...	...	...	...	...	...	...	...	...	...	...	...	...	...	...	...	...
Female - Femmes	67.5	...	...	...	...	...	...	...	...	...	...	...	...	...	...	...	...	...	...	...	...
Nauru																					
2006																					
Male - Hommes	55.2	...	...	...	...	...	...	...	...	...	...	...	...	...	...	...	...	...	...	...	...
Female - Femmes	57.1	...	...	...	...	...	...	...	...	...	...	...	...	...	...	...	...	...	...	...	...
New Caledonia - Nouvelle-Calédonie																					
2010																					
Male - Hommes	74.4	69.8	65.0	60.0	55.3	50.8	46.3	41.7	37.3	32.8	28.4	24.3	20.3	17.0	13.9	11.0	8.3	6.1	4.7	5.0	...
Female - Femmes	80.7	76.2	71.2	66.2	61.3	56.5	51.8	46.9	42.1	37.3	32.6	28.4	23.9	19.6	15.6	12.0	9.0	6.6	4.7	3.1	...
New Zealand - Nouvelle-Zélande																					
2010 - 2012																					
Male - Hommes	79.3	74.8	69.9	64.9	60.1	55.4	50.6	45.8	41.0	36.3	31.7	27.3	23.0	18.8	15.0	11.5	8.5	5.9	4.1	2.8	1.9
Female - Femmes	83.0	78.4	73.4	68.5	63.6	58.7	53.8	48.9	44.1	39.3	34.7	30.1	25.6	21.2	17.1	13.3	9.8	6.8	4.6	3.0	2.0
Niue - Nioué																					
2006																					
Male - Hommes	67.0	...	...	...	...	...	...	...	...	...	...	...	...	...	...	...	...	...	...	...	...
Female - Femmes	76.0	...	...	...	...	...	...	...	...	...	...	...	...	...	...	...	...	...	...	...	...
Northern Mariana Islands - Îles Mariannes septentrionales																					
2009																					
Male - Hommes	74.5	...	...	...	...	...	...	...	...	...	...	...	...	...	...	...	...	...	...	...	...
Female - Femmes	79.9	...	...	...	...	...	...	...	...	...	...	...	...	...	...	...	...	...	...	...	...
Palau - Palaos																					
2005																					
Male - Hommes	66.3	...	...	...	...	...	...	...	...	...	...	...	...	...	...	...	...	...	...	...	...
Female - Femmes	72.1	...	...	...	...	...	...	...	...	...	...	...	...	...	...	...	...	...	...	...	...

21. Life expectancy at specified ages for each sex: latest available year, 1993 - 2012
Espérance de vie à un âge donné pour chaque sexe : dernière année disponible, 1993 - 2012 (continued - suite)

Continent, country or area and date / Continent, pays ou zone et date	Age (in years) - Age (en années)																				
	0	5	10	15	20	25	30	35	40	45	50	55	60	65	70	75	80	85	90	95	100
OCEANIA - OCÉANIE																					
Papua New Guinea - Papouasie-Nouvelle-Guinée																					
2000																					
Male - Hommes	53.7	54.1	50.2	45.7	41.6	37.7	33.7	29.8	25.9	22.1	18.5	15.0	11.9	9.2	6.9	5.0	3.6	2.6	1.7	0.6	...
Female - Femmes	54.8	54.7	50.8	46.3	42.1	38.1	34.1	30.1	26.2	22.3	18.6	15.2	12.0	9.2	6.8	5.0	3.6	2.5	1.6	0.6	...
Samoa																					
2006																					
Male - Hommes	71.5	...	...	...	...	...	...	...	...	...	...	...	...	...	...	...	...	...	...	...	...
Female - Femmes	74.2	...	...	...	...	...	...	...	...	...	...	...	...	...	...	...	...	...	...	...	...
Solomon Islands - Îles Salomon																					
1999																					
Male - Hommes	60.6	...	...	...	...	...	...	...	...	...	...	...	...	...	...	...	...	...	...	...	...
Female - Femmes	61.6	...	...	...	...	...	...	...	...	...	...	...	...	...	...	...	...	...	...	...	...
Tonga																					
2006																					
Male - Hommes	67.3	64.1	59.3	54.5	49.9	45.4	40.7	36.2	31.6	27.2	23.4	19.4	15.9	13.0	9.4	6.3	4.0	...	...	...	...
Female - Femmes	73.0	69.3	64.6	59.8	55.0	50.1	45.2	40.4	35.7	31.3	27.1	23.0	19.0	15.3	11.6	8.6	6.1	...	...	...	...
Tuvalu																					
1997 - 2002																					
Male - Hommes	61.7	59.5	54.8	50.0	45.2	40.6	35.9	32.1	28.0	24.1	20.0	17.1	13.7	10.8	9.0	6.9	5.4	...	...	...	...
Female - Femmes	65.1	62.6	57.7	53.7	50.0	45.3	40.9	36.6	32.2	28.1	23.8	20.3	16.9	13.2	10.6	7.9	6.4	...	...	...	...
Vanuatu																					
1999																					
Male - Hommes	65.6	...	...	...	...	...	...	...	...	...	...	...	...	...	...	...	...	...	...	...	...
Female - Femmes	69.0	...	...	...	...	...	...	...	...	...	...	...	...	...	...	...	...	...	...	...	...
Wallis and Futuna Islands - Îles Wallis et Futuna																					
2003																					
Male - Hommes	73.1	...	...	...	...	...	...	...	...	...	...	...	...	...	...	...	...	...	...	...	...
Female - Femmes	75.5	...	...	...	...	...	...	...	...	...	...	...	...	...	...	...	...	...	...	...	...

FOOTNOTES - NOTES

[1] Data refer to Algerian population only. - Les données ne concernent que la population algérienne.

[2] Based on the results of the Population Census. - D'après les résultats du recensement de la population.

[3] Based on the results of the Botswana Demographic Survey. - Données extraites de l'enquête démographique effectuée par le Botswana.

[4] Based on the results of the 2006 Population and Housing Census. - Données fondées sur les résultats du recensement de la population et de l'habitat de 2006.

[5] Based on the population census of the same year. - Sur la base du recensement de la population de la même année.

[6] Data refer to national projections. - Les données se réfèrent aux projections nationales.

[7] Excludes the islands of St. Brandon and Agalega. - Non compris les îles St. Brandon et Agalega.

[8] Based on underlying data of the 2002 census. - Données fondées sur le recensement de 2002.

[9] Data are based on a small number of deaths. - Les données sont basées sur un nombre limité de décès.

[10] Because of the small population and the resulting small numbers of deaths, the data for the calendar years 2008-2010 have been aggregated to construct a more reliable life table. - La population étant peu élevée et, par conséquent, le nombre de décès aussi, les données des années civiles 2008, 2009 et 2010 ont été agrégées afin d'améliorer la fiabilité de la table de mortalité.

[11] Data refer to projections based on the 1992 Population Census. - Les données se réfèrent aux projections basées sur le recensement de la population de 1992.

[12] Excluding Indian jungle population. - Non compris les Indiens de la jungle.

[13] Data refer to projections based on the 2005 Population Census. - Les données se réfèrent aux projections basées sur le recensement de la population de 2005.

[14] Data refer to national projections. Excludes nomadic Indian tribes. - Les données se réfèrent aux projections nationales. Non compris les tribus d'Indiens nomades.

[15] For statistical purposes, the data for China do not include those for the Hong Kong Special Administrative Region (Hong Kong SAR), Macao Special Administrative Region (Macao SAR) and Taiwan province of China. - Pour la présentation des statistiques, les données pour la Chine ne comprennent pas la Région Administrative Spéciale de Hong Kong (Hong Kong RAS), la Région Administrative Spéciale de Macao (Macao RAS) et Taïwan province de Chine.

[16] Data refer to government controlled areas. - Les données se rapportent aux zones contrôlées par le Gouvernement.

[17] Includes data for the Indian-held part of Jammu and Kashmir, the final status of which has not yet been determined. - Y compris les données pour la partie du Jammu et du Cachemire occupée par l'Inde dont le statut définitif n'a pas encore été déterminé.

[18] Includes data for East Jerusalem and Israeli residents in certain other territories under occupation by Israeli military forces since June 1967. - Y compris les données pour Jérusalem-Est et les résidents israéliens dans certains autres territoires occupés depuis 1967 par les forces armées israéliennes.

[19] Data refer to Japanese nationals in Japan only. - Les données se raportent aux nationaux japonais au Japon seulement.

[20] Excluding data for Jordanian territory under occupation since June 1967 by Israeli military forces. Excluding foreigners, including registered Palestinian refugees. - Non compris les données pour le territoire jordanien occupé depuis juin 1967 par les forces armées israéliennes. Non compris les étrangers, mais y compris les réfugiés de Palestine enregistrés.

[21] Based on the results of the 2005 Population and Housing Census. - Données fondées sur les résultats du recensement de la population et de l'habitat de 2005.

[22] Data refer to urban areas only. - Données ne concernant que les zones urbaines.

[23] Excluding data for the Pakistan-held part of Jammu and Kashmir, the final status of which has not yet been determined. Based on the results of the Pakistan Demographic Survey. - Non compris les données concernant la partie du Jammu et Cachemire occupée par le Pakistan dont le statut définitif n'a pas été déterminé. Données extraites de l'enquête démographique effectuée par le Pakistan.

[24] Projections based on the final results of the 2004 Population and Housing Census. - Projections basées sur les résultats définitifs du recensement de la population et de l'habitat de 2004.

[25] Data refer to resident population which comprises Singapore citizens and permanent residents. Provisional. - Les données se rapportent à la population résidente composé des citoyens de Singapour et des résidents permanents. Données provisoires.

[26] Excluding Faeroe Islands and Greenland shown separately, if available. - Non compris les Iles Féroé et le Groenland, qui font l'objet de rubriques distinctes, si disponible.

[27] Excluding Åland Islands. - Non compris les Îles d'Åland.

[28] Excluding Transnistria and the municipality of Bender. - Les données ne tiennent pas compte de l'information sur la Transnistria et la municipalité de Bender.

[29] Excludes data for Kosovo and Metohia. - Sans les données pour le Kosovo et Metohie.

[30] Excluding Channel Islands (Guernsey and Jersey) and Isle of Man, shown separately, if available. - Non compris les îles Anglo-Normandes (Guernesey et Jersey) et l'île de Man, qui font l'objet de rubriques distinctes, si disponible.

[31] Excluding Niue, shown separately, which is part of Cook Islands, but because of remoteness is administered separately. - Non compris Nioué, qui fait l'objet d'une rubrique distincte et qui fait partie des îles Cook, mais qui, en raison de son éloignement, est administrée séparément.

Table 22 - Demographic Yearbook 2012

Table 22 presents the number of marriages and crude marriage rates by urban/rural residence for every year with available data between 2008 and 2012.

Description of variables: Marriage is defined as the act, ceremony or process by which the legal relationship of husband and wife is constituted. The legality of the union may be established by civil, religious or other means as recognized by the laws of each country[1].

Marriage statistics in this table, therefore, include both first marriages and remarriages after divorce, widowhood or annulment. They do not, unless otherwise noted, include resumption of marriage ties after legal separation. These statistics refer to the number of marriages performed, and not to the number of persons marrying.

Statistics shown are obtained from civil registers of marriage. Exceptions, such as data from church registers, are identified in footnotes.

The urban/rural classification of marriages is that provided by each country or area; it is presumed to be based on the national census definitions of urban population which have been set forth at the end of the notes for table 6.

For certain countries, there is a discrepancy between the total number of marriages shown in this table and those shown in subsequent tables for the same year. Usually this discrepancy arises because the total number of marriages occurring in a given year is revised although the remaining tabulations are not.

Rate computation: Crude marriage rates are the annual number of marriages per 1 000 mid-year population. Rates by urban/rural residence are the annual number of marriages, in the appropriate urban or rural category, per 1 000 corresponding mid-year population. Rates presented in this table have been limited to those for countries or areas having at least a total of 30 marriages in a given year. These rates are calculated by the Statistics Division of the United Nations based on the appropriate reference population (for example: total population, nationals only, etc.) if known and available. If the reference population is not known or unavailable the total population is used to calculate the rates. Therefore, if the population that is used to calculate the rates is different from the correct reference population, the rates presented might under- or overstate the true situation in a country or area.

Reliability of data: Each country or area has been asked to indicate the estimated completeness of the number of marriages recorded in its civil register. These national assessments are indicated by the quality codes "C" and "U" that appear in the first column of this table.

"C" indicates that the data are estimated to be virtually complete, that is, representing at least 90 per cent of the marriages occurring each year, while "U" indicates that data are estimated to be incomplete, that is, representing less than 90 per cent of the marriages occurring each year. The code "..." indicates that no information was provided regarding completeness.

Data from civil registers which are reported as incomplete or of unknown completeness (coded "U" or "...") are considered unreliable. They appear in italics in this table; rates are not computed for these data.

These quality codes apply only to data from civil registers. For more information about the quality of vital statistics data in general, see section 4.2 of the Technical Notes.

Limitations: Statistics on marriages are subject to the same qualifications that have been set forth for vital statistics in general and marriage statistics in particular as discussed in section 4 of the Technical Notes.

The fact that marriage is a legal event, unlike birth and death that are biological events, has implications for international comparability of data. Marriage has been defined, for statistical purposes, in terms of the laws of individual countries or areas. These laws vary throughout the world. In addition, comparability is further limited because some countries or areas compile statistics only for civil marriages although religious marriages may also be legally recognized; in other countries or areas, the only available records are church registers and, therefore, the statistics may not reflect marriages that are civil marriages only.

Because in many countries or areas marriage is a civil legal contract which, to establish its legality, must be celebrated before a civil officer, it follows that for these countries or areas registration would tend to be almost automatic at the time of, or immediately following, the marriage ceremony. This factor should be kept in mind when considering the reliability of data, described above. For this reason the practice of tabulating data by date of registration does not generally pose serious problems of comparability as it does in the case of birth and death statistics.

As indicators of family formation, the statistics on the number of marriages presented in this table are bound to be deficient to the extent that they do not include either customary unions, which are not registered even though they are considered legal and binding under customary law, or consensual unions (also known as extra-legal or de facto unions). In general, lower marriage rates over a period of years are an indication of higher incidence of customary or consensual unions.

In addition, rates are affected also by the quality and limitations of the population estimates that are used in their computation. The problems of under-enumeration or over-enumeration and, to some extent, the differences in definition of total population have been discussed in section 3 of the Technical Notes dealing with population data in general, and specific information pertaining to individual countries or areas is given in the footnotes to table 3.

Strict correspondence between the numerator of the rate and the denominator is not always obtained; for example, marriages among civilian and military segments of the population may be related to civilian population. The effect of this may be to increase the rates, but, in most cases, this effect is negligible.

It should be emphasized that crude marriage rates like crude birth, death and divorce rates, may be seriously affected by the age-sex-marital structure of the population to which they relate. Crude marriage rates do, however, provide a simple measure of the level and changes in marriage.

The comparability of data by urban/rural residence is affected by the national definitions of urban and rural used in tabulating these data. It is assumed, in the absence of specific information to the contrary, that the definitions of urban and rural used in connection with the national population census were also used in the compilation of the vital statistics for each country or area. However, it cannot be excluded that, for a given country or area, different definitions of urban and rural are used for the vital statistics data and the population census data respectively. When known, the definitions of urban in national population censuses are presented at the end of the technical notes for table 6. As discussed in detail in the notes, these definitions vary considerably from one country or area to another.

In addition to problems of comparability, marriage rates classified by urban/rural residence are also subject to certain special types of bias. If, when calculating marriage rates, different definitions of urban are used in connection with the vital events and the population data, and if this results in a net difference between the numerator and denominator of the rate in the population at risk, then the marriage rates would be biased. Urban/rural differentials in marriage rates may also be affected by whether the vital events have been tabulated in terms of place of occurrence or place of usual residence. This problem is discussed in more detail in section 4.1.4.1 of the Technical Notes.

Earlier data: Marriages and crude marriage rates have been shown in each issue of the *Demographic Yearbook*. For more information on specific topics, and years for which data are reported, readers should consult the Historical Index.

NOTES

[1] *Principles and Recommendations for a Vital Statistics System Revision 2*, Sales No. E. 01.XVII.10, United Nations, New York, 2001

Tableau 22 – *Annuaire démographique 2012*

Le tableau 22 présente des données sur les mariages et les taux bruts de nuptialité selon le lieu de résidence (zone urbaine ou rurale) pour les années où l'information est disponible entre 2008 et 2012.

Description des variables : le mariage désigne l'acte, la cérémonie ou la procédure qui établit un rapport légal entre mari et femme. L'union peut être rendue légale par une procédure civile ou religieuse, ou par toute autre procédure, conformément à la législation du pays[1].

Les statistiques de la nuptialité présentées dans ce tableau comprennent donc les premiers mariages et les remariages faisant suite à un divorce, un veuvage ou une annulation. Toutefois, sauf indication contraire, elles ne comprennent pas les unions reconstituées après une séparation légale. Ces statistiques se rapportent au nombre de mariages célébrés, non au nombre de personnes qui se marient.

Les statistiques présentées reposent sur l'enregistrement des mariages par les services de l'état civil. Les exceptions (données provenant des registres des églises, par exemple) font l'objet d'une note à la fin du tableau.

La classification des mariages selon le lieu de résidence (zone urbaine ou rurale) est celle qui a été communiquée par chaque pays ou zone ; on part du principe qu'elle repose sur les définitions de la population urbaine utilisées pour les recensements nationaux telles qu'elles sont reproduites à la fin des notes se rapportant au tableau 6.

Pour quelques pays il y a une discordance entre le nombre total de mariages présenté dans ce tableau et ceux présentés après pour la même année. Habituellement ces différences apparaissent lorsque le nombre total des mariages pour une certaine année a été révisé alors que les autres tabulations ne l'ont pas été.

Calcul des taux : les taux bruts de nuptialité représentent le nombre annuel de mariages pour 1 000 habitants au milieu de l'année. Les taux selon le lieu de résidence (zone urbaine ou rurale) représentent le nombre annuel de mariages, classés selon la catégorie urbaine ou rurale appropriée, pour 1 000 habitants au milieu de l'année. Les taux de ce tableau ne se rapportent qu'aux pays ou zones où l'on a enregistré un total d'au moins 30 mariages pendant une année donnée. Ces taux sont calculés par la division de statistique des Nations Unies sur la base de la population de référence adéquate (par exemple : population totale, nationaux seulement, etc.) si connue et disponible. Si la population de référence n'est pas connue ou n'est pas disponible, la population totale est utilisée pour calculer les taux. Par conséquent, si la population utilisée pour calculer les taux est différente de la population de référence adéquate, les taux présentés sont susceptibles de sous ou sur estimer la situation réelle d'un pays ou d'un territoire.

Fiabilité des données : il a été demandé à chaque pays ou zone d'indiquer le degré estimatif de complétude des données sur les mariages figurant dans ses registres d'état civil. Ces évaluations nationales sont signalées par les codes de qualité "C" et "U" qui apparaissent dans la deuxième colonne du tableau.

La lettre "C" indique que les données sont jugées à peu près complètes, c'est-à-dire qu'elles représentent au moins 90 p. 100 des mariages survenus chaque année ; la lettre "U" signale que les données sont jugées incomplètes, c'est-à-dire qu'elles représentent moins de 90 p. 100 des mariages survenus chaque année. Le code "..." indique qu'aucun renseignement n'a été communiqué quant à la complétude des données.

Les données issues des registres de l'état civil qui sont déclarées incomplètes ou dont le degré de complétude n'est pas connu (code "U" ou "...") sont jugées douteuses. Elles apparaissent en italique dans le tableau et les taux correspondants n'ont pas été calculés.

Les codes de qualité ne s'appliquent qu'aux données provenant des registres de l'état civil. Pour plus de précisions sur la qualité des données reposant sur les statistiques de l'état civil en général, voir la section 4.2 des Notes techniques.

Insuffisance des données : les statistiques relatives aux mariages appellent les mêmes réserves que celles qui ont été formulées à propos des statistiques de l'état civil en général et des statistiques concernant la nuptialité en particulier (voir la section 4 des Notes techniques).

Le fait que le mariage soit un acte juridique, à la différence de la naissance et du décès, qui sont des faits biologiques, a des répercussions sur la comparabilité internationale des données. Aux fins de la statistique, le mariage est défini par la législation de chaque pays ou zone. Cette législation varie d'un pays à l'autre. La comparabilité est limitée en outre du fait que certains pays ou zones ne réunissent des statistiques que pour les mariages civils, bien que les mariages religieux y soient également reconnus par la loi ; dans d'autres, les seuls relevés disponibles sont les registres des églises et, en conséquence, les statistiques peuvent ne pas rendre compte des mariages exclusivement civils.

Étant donné que, dans de nombreux pays ou zones, le mariage est un contrat juridique civil qui, pour être légal, doit être conclu devant un officier d'état civil, il s'ensuit que dans ces pays ou zones l'enregistrement se fait à peu près systématiquement au moment de la cérémonie ou immédiatement après. Il faut tenir compte de cet élément lorsque l'on évalue la fiabilité des données, dont il est question plus haut. C'est pourquoi la pratique consistant à exploiter les données selon la date de l'enregistrement ne pose généralement pas les graves problèmes de comparabilité auxquels on se heurte dans le cas des statistiques concernant les naissances et les décès.

Les statistiques relatives au nombre des mariages présentées dans ce tableau donnent une idée forcément trompeuse de la formation des familles, dans la mesure où elles ne tiennent compte ni des mariages coutumiers, qui ne sont pas enregistrés bien qu'ils soient considérés comme légaux et créateurs d'obligations en vertu du droit coutumier, ni des unions consensuelles (appelées également unions non légalisées ou unions de fait). En général, une diminution du taux de nuptialité pendant un certain nombre d'années indique une augmentation des mariages coutumiers ou des unions consensuelles.

L'exactitude des taux dépend également de la qualité et des insuffisances des estimations de population qui sont utilisées pour leur calcul. Le problème des erreurs par excès ou par défaut commises lors du dénombrement et, dans une certaine mesure, le problème de l'hétérogénéité des définitions de la population totale ont été examinés à la section 3 des Notes techniques relative à la population en général ; des indications concernant les différents pays ou zones sont données en note à la fin du tableau 3.

Il n'a pas toujours été possible d'obtenir une correspondance rigoureuse entre le numérateur et le dénominateur pour le calcul des taux. Par exemple, les mariages parmi la population civile et les militaires sont parfois rapportés à la population civile. Cela peut avoir pour effet d'accroître les taux, mais, dans la plupart des cas, il est probable que la différence sera négligeable.

Il faut souligner que les taux bruts de nuptialité, de même que les taux bruts de natalité, de mortalité et de divortialité, peuvent varier sensiblement selon la structure par âge et par sexe de la population à laquelle ils se rapportent. Les taux bruts de nuptialité offrent néanmoins un moyen simple de mesurer la fréquence et l'évolution des mariages.

La comparabilité des données selon le lieu de résidence (zone urbaine ou rurale) peut être limitée par les définitions nationales des termes « urbain » et « rural » utilisées pour le classement de ces données. En l'absence d'indications contraires, on a supposé que les mêmes définitions avaient servi pour le recensement national de la population et pour l'établissement des statistiques de l'état civil pour chaque pays ou zone. Toutefois, il n'est pas exclu que, pour une zone ou un pays donné, des définitions différentes aient été retenues. Les définitions du terme « urbain » utilisées pour les recensements nationaux de population ont été présentées à la fin des notes techniques du tableau 6 lorsqu'elles étaient connues. Comme on l'a précisé dans les notes techniques relatives au tableau 6, ces définitions varient considérablement d'un pays ou d'une zone à l'autre.

Outre les problèmes de comparabilité, les taux de nuptialité classés selon le lieu de résidence (zone urbaine ou rurale) sont également sujets à des distorsions particulières. Si l'on utilise des définitions différentes du terme « urbain » pour classer les faits d'état civil et les données relatives à la population lors du calcul des taux et qu'il en résulte une différence nette entre le numérateur et le dénominateur pour le taux de la population exposée au risque, les taux de nuptialité s'en trouveront faussés. La différence entre ces taux pour les zones urbaines et rurales pourra aussi être faussée selon que les faits d'état civil auront été classés d'après le lieu où ils se sont produits ou d'après le lieu de résidence habituel. Ce problème est examiné plus en détail à la section 4.1.4.1 des Notes techniques.

Données publiées antérieurement : les différentes éditions de l'*Annuaire démographique* regroupent des données sur le nombre des mariages. Pour plus de précisions concernant les années et les sujets pour lesquels des données ont été publiées, se reporter à l'index historique.

NOTE

[1] *Principes et recommandations pour un système de statistiques de l'état civil, deuxième révision*, numéro de vente : F.01.XVII.10, publication des Nations Unies, New York, 2003.

22. Marriages and crude marriage rates, by urban/rural residence: 2008 - 2012
Mariages et taux bruts de nuptialité, selon la résidence, urbaine/rurale : 2008 - 2012

Continent, country or area, and urban/rural residence / Continent, pays ou zone et résidence, urbaine/rurale	Code[a]	Number - Nombre					Rate - Taux				
		2008	2009	2010	2011	2012	2008	2009	2010	2011	2012
AFRICA - AFRIQUE											
Algeria - Algérie[1]											
Total	...	331 190	341 321	344 819	369 031	371 280	...	...	...	...	...
Botswana											
Total	+U	5 037	4 521	4 416	...	...	...	...	...	...	...
Egypt - Égypte[2]											
Total	+C	660 159	759 004	864 857	897 969	...	8.8	9.9	11.0	11.2	...
Urban - Urbaine	+C	216 120	282 598	354 223	353 048	...	6.7	8.5	10.5	10.2	...
Rural - Rurale	+C	444 039	476 406	510 634	544 921	...	10.3	10.9	11.4	11.9	...
Lesotho											
Total	+U	...	2 662	8 342	...	...	...	...	...	...	...
Libya - Libye[3]											
Total	+U	65 326	66 551	...	...	...	...	...	...	...	...
Mauritius - Maurice[4]											
Total	+C	11 197	10 619	10 555	10 499	*10 382	8.8	8.3	8.2	8.2	*8.0
Urban - Urbaine	+C	3 440	3 372	3 174	3 195	...	6.5	6.3	5.9	6.0	...
Rural - Rurale	+C	7 757	7 247	7 381	7 304	...	10.5	9.8	9.9	9.7	...
Réunion											
Total	C	3 149	2 919	...	...	...	3.9	3.6	...	...	...
Saint Helena ex. dep. - Sainte-Hélène sans dép.											
Total	C	9	14	8	15	12	...	...	...	...	...
Seychelles[5]											
Total	+C	1 248	1 208	1 440	1 525	...	14.4	13.8	16.0	17.4	...
South Africa - Afrique du Sud											
Total	...	186 522	171 989	170 826	...	...	...	...	...	...	...
Tunisia - Tunisie											
Total	...	78 748	81 605	87 081	91 590	...	...	...	...	...	...
AMERICA, NORTH - AMÉRIQUE DU NORD											
Anguilla[6]											
Total	C	54	58	62	47	...	3.5	3.6	3.8	2.8	...
Aruba[7]											
Total	C	*405	...	...	...	...	*3.8	...	...	...	...
Bahamas											
Total	+C	1 969	1 977	1 939	*3 915[8]	...	5.8	5.8	5.6	*11.2	...
Bermuda - Bermudes											
Total	C	721	683	619	555	...	11.2	10.6	9.6	8.6	...
Canada[9]											
Total	C	147 288	...	...	...	...	4.4	...	...	...	...
Cayman Islands - Îles Caïmanes[10]											
Total	+C	487	556	530	533	473	8.7	10.5	9.7	9.6	8.3
Costa Rica[11]											
Total	C	25 034	23 920	*23 955	*25 013	*26 112	5.6	5.3	*5.2	*5.4	*5.6
Urban - Urbaine	C	12 918	12 628	*12 564	...	...	...	...	...	...	...
Rural - Rurale	C	12 116	11 292	*11 391	...	...	...	...	...	...	...
Cuba[12]											
Total	C	61 852	54 969	58 490	59 676	...	5.5	4.9	5.2	5.3	...
Urban - Urbaine	C	58 336	51 396	54 300	54 847	...	6.9	6.1	6.4	6.5	...
Rural - Rurale	C	3 516	3 573	4 190	4 829	...	1.3	1.3	1.5	1.7	...
Curaçao											
Total	C	829	837	874	859	...	5.7	5.7	5.9	5.7	...
Dominican Republic - République dominicaine											
Total	+C	38 310	40 040	43 797	44 253	...	4.0	4.1	4.4	4.4	...
El Salvador[13]											
Total	...	27 714	28 048	30 279	31 220	...	...	...	...	...	...
Urban - Urbaine	...	10 632	10 642	10 905	11 702	...	...	...	...	...	...
Rural - Rurale	...	17 082	17 406	19 374	19 518	...	...	...	...	...	...
Guadeloupe											
Total	C	1 502	1 440	1 402	...	...	3.7	3.6	3.5	...	...

22. Marriages and crude marriage rates, by urban/rural residence: 2008 - 2012
Mariages et taux bruts de nuptialité, selon la résidence, urbaine/rurale : 2008 - 2012 (continued - suite)

Continent, country or area, and urban/rural residence / Continent, pays ou zone et résidence, urbaine/rurale	Co-de[a]	Number - Nombre					Rate - Taux				
		2008	2009	2010	2011	2012	2008	2009	2010	2011	2012

AMERICA, NORTH - AMÉRIQUE DU NORD

Guatemala											
Total	C	52 315	62 104	73 124	78 285	...	3.8	4.4	5.1	...	...
Urban - Urbaine[14]	C	15 442	...	...	...	...	...	...	...	...	...
Rural - Rurale[14]	C	10 324	...	...	...	...	...	...	...	...	...
Jamaica - Jamaïque											
Total	+C	22 152	21 692	20 910	20 685	20 175	8.2	8.0	7.7	7.7	7.5
Martinique											
Total	C	1 395	1 357	1 279	...	...	3.5	3.4	3.2	...	...
Mexico - Mexique											
Total	+C	589 352	558 913	567 943	570 152	...	5.5	5.2	5.1	...	...
Urban - Urbaine[15]	+C	443 959	408 656	421 265	411 883	...	5.4	4.9	...	...	...
Rural - Rurale[15]	+C	125 479	122 798	118 146	126 737	...	5.1	5.0	...	...	...
Montserrat											
Total	+...	18	15	17	19	...	...	...	...	...	...
Nicaragua											
Total	+U	16 542	...	...	...	...	...	...	...	...	...
Panama[11]											
Total	C	11 508	12 273	12 981	...	...	3.4	3.6	3.7	...	...
Urban - Urbaine	C	9 490	9 689	9 753	...	...	4.4	4.4	4.3	...	...
Rural - Rurale	C	2 018	2 584	3 228	...	...	1.7	2.1	2.6	...	...
Puerto Rico - Porto Rico											
Total	C	18 620	...	...	...	...	4.7	...	...	...	...
Saint Vincent and the Grenadines - Saint-Vincent-et-les Grenadines											
Total	+C	588	573	...	...	...	5.9	5.7	...	...	...
Sint Maarten (Dutch part) - Saint-Martin (partie néerlandaise)											
Total	+C	232	...	...	...	...	5.8	...	...	...	...
Turks and Caicos Islands - Îles Turques et Caïques											
Total	C	486	...	...	...	...	13.3	...	...	...	...
United States of America - États-Unis d'Amérique											
Total	C	2 157 000	2 077 000	2 096 000	2 118 000	...	7.1	6.8	6.8	6.8	...

AMERICA, SOUTH - AMÉRIQUE DU SUD

Argentina - Argentine											
Total	C	133 060	126 081	123 208	128 797	...	3.3	3.1	3.0	3.1	...
Bolivia (Plurinational State of) - Bolivie (État plurinational de)											
Total	U	40 633	...	...	...	...	...	...	...	...	...
Brazil - Brésil											
Total	U	959 901	935 116	977 620	1 026 736	...	...	...	...	...	...
Chile - Chili											
Total	+C	56 112	56 127	60 362	...	...	3.3	3.3	3.5	...	...
Urban - Urbaine[16]	+C	51 133	50 679	54 747	...	...	3.5	3.4	3.7	...	...
Rural - Rurale[16]	+C	4 979	5 448	5 615	...	...	2.3	2.5	2.5	...	...
Ecuador - Équateur[17]											
Total	U	76 354	76 892	74 800	...	...	...	...	...	...	...
French Guiana - Guyane française											
Total	C	619	611	581	...	...	2.8	2.7	2.5	...	...
Guyana[18]											
Total	C	3 233	4 342	4 239	...	...	4.2	5.6	5.4	...	...
Paraguay											
Total	U	18 832	...	...	...	...	...	...	...	...	...
Peru - Pérou[19]											
Total	+C	94 971	87 561	82 043	97 693	...	3.3	3.0	2.8	3.3	...
Uruguay											
Total	C	12 180	11 080	10 629	9 604	9 631	3.7	3.3	3.2	2.9	2.8

22. Marriages and crude marriage rates, by urban/rural residence: 2008 - 2012
Mariages et taux bruts de nuptialité, selon la résidence, urbaine/rurale : 2008 - 2012 (continued - suite)

Continent, country or area, and urban/rural residence / Continent, pays ou zone et résidence, urbaine/rurale	Code[a]	Number - Nombre					Rate - Taux				
		2008	2009	2010	2011	2012	2008	2009	2010	2011	2012
AMERICA, SOUTH - AMÉRIQUE DU SUD											
Venezuela (Bolivarian Republic of) - Venezuela (République bolivarienne du)[20]											
Total	C	93 741	94 870	94 977	103 004	...	3.4	3.3	3.3	3.5	...
ASIA - ASIE											
Armenia - Arménie											
Total	+C	18 465	18 773	16 904	19 706	...	5.7	5.8	5.2	6.0	...
Urban - Urbaine	+C	12 198	12 441	...	...	...	5.9	6.0	...	...	...
Rural - Rurale	+C	6 267	6 332	...	...	...	5.4	5.4	...	...	...
Azerbaijan - Azerbaïdjan											
Total	+C	79 964	78 072	79 172	88 145	79 065	9.0	8.7	8.7	9.6	8.5
Urban - Urbaine	+C	40 996	40 708	41 592	...	...	8.7	8.6	8.7	...	...
Rural - Rurale	+C	38 968	37 364	37 580	...	...	9.4	8.9	8.8	...	...
Bahrain - Bahreïn											
Total	...	4 896	5 067	4 960	...	...	...	...	...	...	...
Bangladesh											
Total	...	...	...	1 885 109	2 066 820	...	...	...	...	...	...
Urban - Urbaine	...	...	...	416 761	443 040	...	...	...	...	...	...
Rural - Rurale	...	...	...	1 468 348	1 623 780	...	...	...	...	...	...
Brunei Darussalam - Brunéi Darussalam											
Total	...	2 391	...	...	...	...	...	...	...	...	...
China - Chine[21]											
Total	+C	10 980 000	12 120 000	12 410 000	12 471 000	12 971 000	8.3	9.1	9.3	9.3	9.6
China, Hong Kong SAR - Chine, Hong Kong RAS											
Total	C	47 331	51 175	52 558	58 369	...	6.8	7.3	7.5	8.3	...
China, Macao SAR - Chine, Macao RAS											
Total	+C	2 778	3 035	3 103	3 545	3 783	5.1	5.7	5.8	6.5	6.7
Cyprus - Chypre[22]											
Total	C	6 115	6 327	6 081	6 210	...	7.8	7.8	7.3	7.3	...
Georgia - Géorgie[11]											
Total	C	31 414	31 752	34 675	30 863	30 412	7.2	7.2	7.8	6.9	6.8
Urban - Urbaine	C	21 028	17 859	18 563	17 625	...	9.1	7.7	7.9	7.4	...
Rural - Rurale	C	10 386	13 893	16 112	13 238	...	5.0	6.7	7.7	6.3	...
Indonesia - Indonésie											
Total	U	2 195 037	2 162 115	2 207 224	2 319 821	...	...	...	...	...	...
Iran (Islamic Republic of) - Iran (République islamique d')[23]											
Total	+C	881 592	890 208	891 627	874 792	...	12.2	12.2	12.0	11.6	...
Urban - Urbaine	+C	633 179	629 893	622 397	...	...	12.8	12.5	12.1	...	...
Rural - Rurale	+C	248 413	260 315	269 230	...	...	11.0	11.4	11.7	...	...
Israel - Israël[24]											
Total	C	50 038	48 997	47 855	...	...	6.8	6.5	6.3	...	...
Urban - Urbaine[25]	C	44 967	43 902	43 035	...	...	6.7	6.4	6.2	...	...
Rural - Rurale[25]	C	3 801	3 830	3 736	...	...	6.3	6.2	5.9	...	...
Japan - Japon[26]											
Total	+C	726 106	707 734	700 214	661 895	...	5.8	5.5	5.5	5.2	...
Urban - Urbaine	+C	666 651	650 746	647 127	613 035	...	...	...	...	...	...
Rural - Rurale	+C	59 455	56 988	53 087	48 860	...	...	...	...	...	...
Jordan - Jordanie[27]											
Total	+C	60 922	63 389	62 107	64 665	...	10.4	10.6	10.2	10.3	...
Kazakhstan											
Total	C	135 280	140 785	146 443	160 494	...	8.6	8.7	9.0	9.7	...
Urban - Urbaine	C	82 235	...	...	...	...	9.9	...	...	...	...
Rural - Rurale	C	53 045	...	...	...	...	7.2	...	...	...	...
Kuwait - Koweït											
Total	C	14 709	14 526	13 993	19 860	...	5.9	5.2	4.8	6.4	...

22. Marriages and crude marriage rates, by urban/rural residence: 2008 - 2012
Mariages et taux bruts de nuptialité, selon la résidence, urbaine/rurale : 2008 - 2012 (continued - suite)

Continent, country or area, and urban/rural residence / Continent, pays ou zone et résidence, urbaine/rurale	Code[a]	Number - Nombre					Rate - Taux				
		2008	2009	2010	2011	2012	2008	2009	2010	2011	2012
ASIA - ASIE											
Kyrgyzstan - Kirghizstan											
Total	C	44 258	47 567	50 362	56 509	...	8.7	9.3	9.7	10.7	...
Urban - Urbaine	C	13 400	14 442	15 198	15 930	...	7.5	8.0	8.3	8.6	...
Rural - Rurale	C	30 858	33 125	35 164	40 579	...	9.4	10.0	10.5	11.9	...
Lebanon - Liban											
Total	C	37 593	40 565	41 758	42 500	38 691	...	...	...	...	...
Mongolia - Mongolie											
Total	+C	32 982	34 071	9 349	...	...	12.4	12.6	3.4	...	...
Urban - Urbaine	+C	23 582	24 748	...	...	...	14.5	14.7	...	...	...
Rural - Rurale	+C	9 400	9 323	...	...	...	9.1	9.1	...	...	...
Oman[28]											
Total	+U	...	25 608	20 820	26 540	...	...	...	...	...	...
Philippines											
Total	U	486 514	492 254	482 480	...	...	...	...	...	...	...
Qatar											
Total	C	3 235	3 153	2 977	3 293	...	2.2	1.9	1.7	1.9	...
Republic of Korea - République de Corée[29]											
Total	+C	327 715	309 759	326 104	329 087	...	6.6	6.2	6.5	6.6	...
Urban - Urbaine[14]	+C	262 357	248 050	261 077	266 713	...	6.5	6.2	6.5	6.6	...
Rural - Rurale[14]	+C	57 035	52 918	56 502	54 441	...	6.1	5.6	6.0	5.8	...
Singapore - Singapour[30]											
Total	+C	24 596	26 081	24 363	27 258	27 936	6.8	7.0	6.5	7.2	7.3
Sri Lanka											
Total	+U	*198 578	*194 970	*200 985	*200 314	...	...	...	...	...	...
State of Palestine - État de Palestine											
Total	C	35 777	38 316	37 228	36 284	...	9.4	9.7	9.2	8.7	...
Syrian Arab Republic - République arabe syrienne[31]											
Total	+U	379 319	241 422	227 808	...	...	...	...	...	...	...
Tajikistan - Tadjikistan											
Total	+C	106 388	100 678	100 759	94 730	...	14.6	13.7	13.4	12.3	...
Urban - Urbaine	+C	25 718	25 322	25 624	25 068	...	13.4	13.0	12.8	12.3	...
Rural - Rurale	+C	80 670	75 356	75 135	69 662	...	15.0	14.0	13.6	12.3	...
Turkey - Turquie											
Total	C	641 973	591 742	582 715	592 775	603 751	9.0	8.2	8.0	8.0	8.0
United Arab Emirates - Émirats arabes unis[32]											
Total	...	15 041	...	...	...	...	...	...	...	...	...
Uzbekistan - Ouzbékistan											
Total	C	250 200	272 100	292 300	287 800	299 000	9.2	9.9	10.4	9.9	10.1
EUROPE											
Åland Islands - Îles d'Åland											
Total	C	139	120	143	113[33]	*137	5.1	4.3	5.1	4.0	*4.8
Urban - Urbaine	C	66	54	50	44[33]	*54	6.0	4.9	4.5	3.9	*4.8
Rural - Rurale	C	73	66	93	69[33]	*83	4.5	4.0	5.6	4.1	*4.8
Albania - Albanie											
Total	C	21 299	...	...	25 303	...	7.3	...	...	8.9	...
Andorra - Andorre											
Total	C	260	265	287	283	288	3.1	3.1	3.4	3.6	3.7
Austria - Autriche[34]											
Total	C	35 223	35 469	37 545	36 426	38 592	4.2	4.2	4.5	4.3	4.6
Belarus - Bélarus											
Total	C	77 201	78 800	76 978	86 785	76 245	8.0	8.2	8.1	9.2	8.1
Urban - Urbaine	C	64 281	65 149	63 813	71 795	...	...	...	...	10.0	...
Rural - Rurale	C	12 920	13 651	13 165	14 990	...	...	...	...	6.4	...
Belgium - Belgique[35]											
Total	C	45 613	43 303	42 159	*45 000	*40 500	4.3	4.0	3.9	*4.1	*3.6
Urban - Urbaine	C	45 040	42 673	...	...	...	4.3	4.0	...	...	...
Rural - Rurale	C	573	630	...	...	...	3.7	4.1	...	...	...
Bosnia and Herzegovina - Bosnie-Herzégovine											
Total	C	22 151	20 633	19 541	...	*18 980	5.8	5.4	5.1	...	*4.9

22. Marriages and crude marriage rates, by urban/rural residence: 2008 - 2012
Mariages et taux bruts de nuptialité, selon la résidence, urbaine/rurale : 2008 - 2012 (continued - suite)

Continent, country or area, and urban/rural residence / Continent, pays ou zone et résidence, urbaine/rurale	Co-de[a]	Number - Nombre					Rate - Taux				
		2008	2009	2010	2011	2012	2008	2009	2010	2011	2012
EUROPE											
Bulgaria - Bulgarie[36]											
Total	C	27 722	25 923	24 286	21 448	21 167	3.6	3.4	3.2	2.9	2.9
Urban - Urbaine	C	21 844	20 592	19 262	16 704	...	4.0	3.8	3.6	3.1	...
Rural - Rurale	C	5 878	5 331	5 024	4 744	...	2.6	2.4	2.3	2.4	...
Croatia - Croatie											
Total	C	23 373	22 382	21 294	20 211	...	5.3	5.1	4.8	4.6	...
Urban - Urbaine	C	13 048	12 637	11 964	...	...	...	...	...	...	...
Rural - Rurale	C	10 325	9 745	9 330	...	...	...	...	...	...	...
Czech Republic - République tchèque											
Total	C	52 457	47 862	46 746	45 137	45 206	5.0	4.6	4.4	4.3	4.3
Urban - Urbaine	C	39 602	35 882	35 007	33 601	...	5.1	4.6	4.5	4.4	...
Rural - Rurale	C	12 855	11 980	11 739	11 536	...	4.7	4.3	4.2	4.1	...
Denmark - Danemark[37]											
Total	C	37 376	32 934	30 949	27 198	28 503	6.8	6.0	5.6	4.9	5.1
Estonia - Estonie											
Total	C	6 127	5 362	5 066	5 499	5 888	4.6	4.0	3.8	4.1	4.4
Urban - Urbaine[38]	C	4 218	3 693	3 515	3 837	...	4.5	4.0	3.8	4.1	...
Rural - Rurale[38]	C	1 687	1 456	1 352	1 396	...	4.1	3.6	3.3	3.4	...
Finland - Finlande[39]											
Total	C	31 014	29 716[40]	29 809[40]	28 295[40]	28 741[40]	5.8	5.6	5.6	5.3	5.3
Urban - Urbaine	C	23 189	22 437[40]	22 403[40]	21 331[40]	...	6.4	6.2	6.2	5.8	...
Rural - Rurale	C	7 825	7 279[40]	7 406[40]	6 964[40]	...	4.6	4.3	4.4	4.1	...
France[41]											
Total	C	258 739	245 151	245 334	*231 100	*235 000	4.2	3.9	3.9	*3.7	*3.7
Urban - Urbaine[42]	C	190 122	181 876	190 401	...	...	...	...	...	...	...
Rural - Rurale[42]	C	63 935	58 391	51 644	...	...	...	...	...	...	...
Germany - Allemagne											
Total	C	376 998	378 439	382 047	377 816	*386 000	4.6	4.6	4.7	4.6	*4.7
Gibraltar[43]											
Total	+C	158	188	198	176	...	5.4	6.4	6.7	5.9	...
Greece - Grèce											
Total	C	53 500	59 212	56 338	55 099	...	4.8	5.2	5.0	4.9	...
Urban - Urbaine	C	37 500	41 719	39 903	39 624	...	...	...	...	...	...
Rural - Rurale	C	16 000	17 493	16 435	15 475	...	...	...	...	...	...
Guernsey - Guernesey											
Total	C	300	332	334	340	325	4.9	5.3	5.3	5.4	5.2
Hungary - Hongrie											
Total	C	40 105[12]	36 730[12]	35 520[12]	35 812[12]	*36 200	4.0	3.7	3.6	3.6	*3.6
Urban - Urbaine[44]	C	29 228	27 066	26 288	26 793	...	4.3	3.9	3.8	3.9	...
Rural - Rurale[44]	C	10 306	9 157	8 775	8 607	...	3.2	2.9	2.9	2.8	...
Iceland - Islande											
Total	C	1 642	1 480	1 547	1 456[45]	...	5.1	4.6	4.9	4.6	...
Urban - Urbaine[45]	C	...	...	...	1 432	...	...	...	...	4.6	...
Rural - Rurale[45]	C	...	...	...	24	...	...	...	...	...	...
Ireland - Irlande											
Total	+C	22 187	21 627	20 594	*19 879	*21 245	5.0	4.9	4.6	*4.4	*4.6
Italy - Italie											
Total	C	246 613	230 613	217 700	204 830	*208 947	4.1	3.8	3.6	3.4	*3.4
Latvia - Lettonie[11]											
Total	C	12 946	9 925	9 290	10 760	11 244	5.7	4.4	4.1	5.2	5.5
Urban - Urbaine	C	9 117	7 105	6 516	...	...	5.9	4.7	4.3	...	...
Rural - Rurale	C	3 829	2 820	2 774	...	...	5.3	3.9	3.8	...	...
Liechtenstein[11]											
Total	C	205	154	186	*163	*185	5.8	4.3	5.2	*4.5	*5.1
Lithuania - Lituanie											
Total	C	24 063	20 542	18 688	19 221	20 660	7.2	6.2	5.7	6.3	6.5
Urban - Urbaine	C	16 420	14 471	13 110	13 546	...	7.3	6.5	6.0	6.7	...
Rural - Rurale	C	7 643	6 071	5 578	5 675	...	6.9	5.5	5.1	5.6	...
Luxembourg[43]											
Total	C	1 917	1 739	1 749	1 714	1 782	3.9	3.5	3.5	3.3	3.4
Malta - Malte											
Total	C	2 482	2 353	2 596	2 562	...	6.1	5.7	6.3	6.1	...
Montenegro - Monténégro											
Total	C	3 445	3 829	3 675	3 528	3 305	5.5	6.1	6.0	5.7	5.3
Urban - Urbaine	C	2 708	3 517	...	...	...	6.8	8.8	...	...	...
Rural - Rurale	C	737	312	...	...	...	3.2	1.4	...	...	...

Continent, country or area, and urban/rural residence / Continent, pays ou zone et résidence, urbaine/rurale	Co-de[a]	Number - Nombre					Rate - Taux				
		2008	2009	2010	2011	2012	2008	2009	2010	2011	2012
EUROPE											
Netherlands - Pays-Bas[46]											
Total	C	74 030	72 119	75 399	71 572	*70 315	4.5	4.4	4.5	4.3	*4.2
Norway - Norvège											
Total	C	25 125	24 582[47]	23 577[47]	23 135[47]	24 346[47]	5.3	5.1	4.8	4.7	4.9
Poland - Pologne											
Total	C	257 744	250 794	228 337	206 471	203 850	6.8	6.6	5.9	5.4	5.3
Urban - Urbaine	C	154 936	152 651	137 218	122 737	...	6.6	6.6	5.9	5.2	...
Rural - Rurale	C	102 808	98 143	91 119	83 734	...	6.9	6.6	6.0	5.5	...
Portugal											
Total	C	43 228	40 391	39 993	36 035	34 423	4.1	3.8	3.8	3.4	3.3
Republic of Moldova - République de Moldova											
Total	C	26 666	26 781	26 483	25 900	24 262	7.5	7.5	7.4	7.3	6.8
Urban - Urbaine	C	13 368	13 360	13 242	...	...	9.1	9.0	9.0	...	...
Rural - Rurale	C	13 298	13 421	13 241	...	...	6.3	6.4	6.4	...	...
Romania - Roumanie											
Total	C	149 439	134 275	115 778	105 599	107 760	6.9	6.3	5.4	4.9	5.0
Urban - Urbaine	C	96 963	86 363	74 787	67 962	...	8.2	7.3	6.3	5.8	...
Rural - Rurale	C	52 476	47 912	40 991	37 637	...	5.4	5.0	4.3	3.9	...
Russian Federation - Fédération de Russie											
Total	C	1 179 007	1 199 446	1 215 066	1 316 011	...	8.3	8.4	8.5	9.2	...
Urban - Urbaine	C	...	...	...	978 039	...	...	...	...	9.3	...
Rural - Rurale	C	...	...	...	337 972	...	...	...	...	9.0	...
San Marino - Saint-Marin[48]											
Total	C	202	238	213	205	203	6.4	7.2	6.7	6.1	6.1
Serbia - Serbie[49]											
Total	+C	38 285	36 853	35 815	35 808	34 639	5.2	5.0	4.9	4.9	4.8
Urban - Urbaine	+C	24 537	24 051	23 633	23 564	...	5.7	5.6	5.5	5.5	...
Rural - Rurale	+C	13 748	12 802	12 182	12 244	...	4.5	4.2	4.1	4.1	...
Slovakia - Slovaquie[11]											
Total	C	28 293	26 356	25 415	25 621	26 006	5.2	4.9	4.7	4.7	4.8
Urban - Urbaine	C	16 355	15 094	14 528	14 608	...	5.5	5.1	4.9	5.0	...
Rural - Rurale	C	11 938	11 262	10 887	11 013	...	4.9	4.6	4.4	4.5	...
Slovenia - Slovénie[50]											
Total	C	6 703	6 542	6 528	6 671	*7 043	3.3	3.2	3.2	3.3	*3.4
Urban - Urbaine	C	3 460	3 337	3 274	3 430	...	3.4	3.3	3.2	3.4	...
Rural - Rurale	C	3 243	3 205	3 254	3 241	...	3.2	3.1	3.2	3.2	...
Spain - Espagne											
Total	C	194 022	172 357	165 641	158 220	*163 074	4.3	3.8	3.6	3.4	*3.5
Sweden - Suède[47]											
Total	C	50 332	47 259	50 028	47 564	50 616	5.5	5.1	5.3	5.0	5.3
Switzerland - Suisse[51]											
Total	C	41 534	41 918	43 257	42 083	*42 650	5.4	5.4	5.5	5.3	*5.3
Urban - Urbaine	C	31 883	32 130	33 328	32 279	...	5.7	5.6	...	5.5	...
Rural - Rurale	C	9 651	9 788	9 929	9 804	...	4.8	4.8	...	4.7	...
TFYR of Macedonia - L'ex-R. y. de Macédoine											
Total	C	14 695	14 923	14 155	*14 797	13 991	7.2	7.3	6.9	*7.2	6.8
Urban - Urbaine	C	7 696	8 067	7 750	...	...	...	...	...	...	...
Rural - Rurale	C	6 999	6 856	6 405	...	...	...	...	...	...	...
Ukraine											
Total	+C	321 992	318 198	305 933	355 880	278 276	7.0	6.9	6.7	7.8	6.1
Urban - Urbaine	+C	244 832	239 277	231 680	270 245	...	7.7	7.6	...	...	...
Rural - Rurale	+C	77 160	78 921	74 253	85 635	...	5.3	5.4	...	...	...
United Kingdom of Great Britain and Northern Ireland - Royaume-Uni de Grande-Bretagne et d'Irlande du Nord[52]											
Total	C	273 207	267 898	*277 740	...	...	4.4	4.3	*4.5	...	...
OCEANIA - OCÉANIE											
Australia - Australie											
Total	+C	118 756	120 118	121 176	121 752	...	5.6	5.5	5.5	5.5	...

Continent, country or area, and urban/rural residence / Continent, pays ou zone et résidence, urbaine/rurale	Co-de[a]	Number - Nombre					Rate - Taux				
		2008	2009	2010	2011	2012	2008	2009	2010	2011	2012
OCEANIA - OCÉANIE											
Cook Islands - Îles Cook[53]											
Total	+C	702	817	846	*918	*894	32.1	36.2	35.8	*44.1	...
French Polynesia - Polynésie française											
Total	C	1 178	1 229	1 330	...	...	4.5	4.6	5.0	...	...
Guam											
Total	C	...	1 394	...	...	...	...	8.7	...	...	...
New Caledonia - Nouvelle-Calédonie											
Total	C	975	961	908	...	...	4.0	3.9	3.6	...	...
New Zealand - Nouvelle-Zélande[11]											
Total	+C	21 948	21 628	20 940	20 231	...	5.1	5.0	4.8	4.6	...
Niue - Nioué											
Total	C	13	12	...	...	...	...	...	...	...	...
Norfolk Island - Île Norfolk[54]											
Total	+C	32	...	...	...	...	...	...	...	...	...
Samoa											
Total	U	*1 052*	*953*	...	...	...	...	...	...	...	...
Wallis and Futuna Islands - Îles Wallis et Futuna											
Total	C	53	...	...	...	...	3.9	...	...	...	...

FOOTNOTES - NOTES

Italics: data from civil registers which are incomplete or of unknown completeness. - Italiques : données incomplètes ou dont le degré d'exactitude n'est pas connu, provenant des registres de l'état civil.

* Provisional. - Données provisoires.

[a] 'Code' indicates the source of data, as follows:
C - Civil registration, estimated over 90% complete
U - Civil registration, estimated less than 90% complete
| - Other source, estimated reliable
+ - Data tabulated by date of registration rather than occurence
... - Information not available

Le 'Code' indique la source des données, comme suit :
C - Registres de l'état civil considérés complèts à 90 p. 100 au moins
U - Registres de l'état civil qui ne sont pas considérés complèts à 90 p. 100 au moins
| - Autre source, considérée pas douteuses
+ - Données exploitées selon la date de l'enregistrement et non la date de l'événement
... - Information pas disponible

[1] Data refer to Algerian population only. - Les données ne concernent que la population algérienne.
[2] Including marriages resumed after 'revocable divorce' (among Moslem population), which approximates legal separation. - Y compris les unions reconstituées après un 'divorce révocable' (parmi la population musulmane), qui est à peu près l'équivalent d'une séparation légale.
[3] Data refer to Libyan nationals only. - Les données se raportent aux nationaux libyens seulement.
[4] Excludes the islands of St. Brandon and Agalega. - Non compris les îles St. Brandon et Agalega.
[5] Including visitors. - Y compris les visiteurs.
[6] Excluding visitors. - Ne comprend pas les visiteurs.
[7] Data refer to resident population only. - Pour la population résidante seulement.
[8] Including non-residents. - Y compris les non-résidents.
[9] Since 2003, definition of marriage has been changed in some provinces and territories to include the legal union of two persons of the same sex. - Depuis 2003, la définition du mariage a changé dans certaines provinces et certains territoires afin d'englober les unions légales entre deux personnes du même sexe.
[10] Either bride or groom or both are residents. - Le marié, la mariée ou les deux sont résidents.
[11] Data refer to marriages registered at the place of residence of the groom. - Correspond aux mariages enregistrés dans le lieu de résidence du marié.
[12] Marriages registered by residence of bride. - Les mariages sont enregistrés selon le lieu de résidence de la mariée.
[13] Including marriages where bride/groom are non-residents. - Y compris les mariages pour lesquels le marié et la mariée sont des non-résidents.
[14] The total number includes 'Unknown residence', but the categories urban and rural do not. - Le nombre total englobe les personnes dont la résidence n'est pas connue, à l'inverse des catégories de population urbaine et rurale.
[15] The difference between 'Total' and the sum of urban and rural is due to the unknown place of residence of bride/wife. Urban and rural distribution refers to the usual residence of the bride/wife. - La différence entre le « Total » et la somme des chiffres urbains et ruraux s'explique par le fait que le lieu de résidence de la mariée ou de la femme n'est pas toujours connu. La répartition entre résidence urbaine et résidence rurale fait référence au lieu de résidence habituel de la mariée ou de la femme.
[16] Urban and rural distribution refers to the usual residence of the groom/husband. - La répartition entre résidence urbaine et résidence rurale fait référence au lieu de résidence habituel du marié ou du mari.
[17] Excludes nomadic Indian tribes. - Non compris les tribus d'Indiens nomades.
[18] Excluding Amerindians. - Non compris les Amérindiens.
[19] Source: The National Registers of Identification and Civil Status (RENIEC). - Source : Les Registres Nationaux d'Identification et d'État Civil (RENIEC).
[20] Residence established by place where marriage took place. - La résidence est déterminée par rapport au lieu où le mariage a été célébré.
[21] For statistical purposes, the data for China do not include those for the Hong Kong Special Administrative Region (Hong Kong SAR), Macao Special Administrative Region (Macao SAR) and Taiwan province of China. - Pour la présentation des statistiques, les données pour la Chine ne comprennent pas la Région Administrative Spéciale de Hong Kong (Hong Kong RAS), la Région Administrative Spéciale de Macao (Macao RAS) et Taïwan province de Chine.
[22] Data refer to government controlled areas. Data refer to marriages of residents only. - Les données se rapportent aux zones contrôlées par le Gouvernement. Les données ne portent que sur les mariages de résidents.
[23] Data refer to the Iranian Year which begins on 21 March and ends on 20 March of the following year. - Les données concernent l'année iranienne, qui commence le 21 mars et se termine le 20 mars de l'année suivante.
[24] Includes data for East Jerusalem and Israeli residents in certain other territories under occupation by Israeli military forces since June 1967. - Y

compris les données pour Jérusalem-Est et les résidents israéliens dans certains autres territoires occupés depuis 1967 par les forces armées israéliennes.

[25] The total number includes 'Unknown residence', but the categories urban and rural do not. Urban and rural distribution refers to the usual residence of the groom/husband. - Le nombre total englobe les personnes dont la résidence n'est pas connue, à l'inverse des catégories de population urbaine et rurale. La répartition entre résidence urbaine et résidence rurale fait référence au lieu de résidence habituel du marié ou du mari.

[26] Data refer to residence of groom. Data refer to Japanese nationals in Japan only. - Données relatives au lieu de résidence du marié. Les données se raportent aux nationaux japonais au Japon seulement.

[27] Excluding data for Jordanian territory under occupation since June 1967 by Israeli military forces. Excluding foreigners, including registered Palestinian refugees. - Non compris les données pour le territoire jordanien occupé depuis juin 1967 par les forces armées israéliennes. Non compris les étrangers, mais y compris les réfugiés de Palestine enregistrés.

[28] Data refer to registered events only. - Les données ne concernent que les événements enregistrés.

[29] Excluding alien armed forces, civilian aliens employed by armed forces, and foreign diplomatic personnel and their dependants. Data refer to residence of groom. - Non compris les militaires étrangers, les civils étrangers employés par les forces armées ni le personnel diplomatique étranger et les membres de leur famille les accompagnant. Données relatives au lieu de résidence du marié.

[30] Excluding marriages previously officiated outside Singapore or under religious and customary rites. - Ne comprend pas les mariages prononcés ailleurs qu'à Singapour ni les mariages religieux ou coutumiers.

[31] Excluding nomad population. - Non compris les nomades.

[32] As published by the United Nations Economic and Social Commission for Western Asia. - Publié par la Commission économique et sociale des Nations Unies pour l'Asie occidentale.

[33] Only marriages in which the bride was resident of Åland Islands. - Ne porte que sur les mariages pour lesquels la mariée réside des Îles Åland.

[34] Excluding aliens temporarily in the area. - Non compris les étrangers se trouvant temporairement dans le territoire.

[35] Including armed forces stationed outside the country and alien armed forces in the area, if the marriage is performed by local authority. - Y compris les militaires nationaux hors du pays et les militaires étrangers en garnison sur le territoire, si le mariage a été célébré par l'autorité locale.

[36] Including nationals outside the country, but excluding foreigners in the country. - Y compris les nationaux à l'étranger, mais non compris les étrangers sur le territoire.

[37] Excluding Faeroe Islands and Greenland shown separately, if available. - Non compris les Iles Féroé et le Groenland, qui font l'objet de rubriques distinctes, si disponible.

[38] Urban and rural distribution of marriages and divorces is displayed by place of residence of groom/husband. The difference between 'Total' and the sum of urban and rural is due to the unknown place of residence of grooms/husbands and to grooms/husbands living outside country. - La répartition des mariages et des divorces entre zones urbaines et zones rurales est fondée sur le lieu de résidence du marié ou du mari. La différence entre le « Total » et la somme des chiffres urbains et ruraux s'explique par le fait que la résidence du marié ou du mari n'est pas toujours connue ou est située à l'étranger.

[39] Only marriages in which the bride was resident in Finland. - Ne porte que sur les mariages pour lesquels la mariée réside en Finlande.

[40] Excluding Åland Islands. - Non compris les Îles d'Åland.

[41] Including armed forces stationed outside the country. - Y compris les militaires nationaux hors du pays.

[42] The data for urban and rural exclude the nationals outside the country. - Les données relatives à la population urbaine et rurale n'englobent pas les nationaux se trouvant à l'étranger.

[43] Data refer to marriages where one or both partners are residents. - Les données portent sur les mariages pour lesquels l'un des deux partenaires ou les deux sont résidents.

[44] Marriages registered by residence of bride. Total includes the data of foreigners, persons of unknown residence and homeless, but the categories urban and rural do not. - Les mariages sont enregistrés selon le lieu de résidence de la mariée. Le total englobe les données relatives aux étrangers, aux personnes dont la résidence n'est pas connue et aux personnes sans domicile fixe, à l'inverse des chiffres portant sur la population urbaine et rurale.

[45] Definition of localities was revised from 2011 causing a break with the previous series. Data for residence abroad are excluded. Data refer to common residence after marriage. - La rupture par rapport aux séries précédentes s'explique par le fait que la définition des localités a été révisée depuis 2011. Les données relatives aux résidents à l'étranger sont exclues. Données se rapportant à la résidence commune après le mariage.

[46] Includes same sex marriages. Marriages of couples of which at least one partner is recorded in a Dutch municipal register, irrespective of the country where the marriage was performed. Including residents outside the country if listed in a Netherlands population register. - Y compris les mariages entre personnes du même sexe. Correspond aux mariages pour lesquels au moins l'un des partenaires est inscrit sur un registre municipal néerlandais, quel que soit le pays dans lequel le mariage est célébré. Englobe les résidents se trouvant à l'étranger à condition qu'ils soient inscrits sur le registre de population des Pays-Bas.

[47] Includes same sex marriages. - Y compris les mariages entre personnes du même sexe.

[48] Includes civil and religious marriages as well as not specified. - Englobe les mariages civils et religieux et ceux pour lesquels rien n'a été indiqué.

[49] Excludes data for Kosovo and Metohia. - Sans les données pour le Kosovo et Metohie.

[50] Data refer to residence of groom or bride before marriage. - Données relatives au lieu de résidence du marié ou de la mariée avant le mariage.

[51] Data based on the residence of groom if he has permanent address in the country, otherwise, based on the residence of bride. If neither partner is a permanent resident, the marriage is not included in the official statistics. - Les données sont fondées sur la résidence du marié si celui-ci a une adresse permanente dans le pays, sinon elles sont fondées sur la résidence de la mariée. Si aucun des deux partenaires n'est un résident permanent, le mariage n'apparaît pas dans les statistiques officielles.

[52] Marriages registered by place of occurrence of marriage. Excluding Channel Islands (Guernsey and Jersey) and Isle of Man, shown separately, if available. - Mariages enregistrés en fonction du lieu de l'événement. Non compris les îles Anglo-Normandes (Guernesey et Jersey) et l'île de Man, qui font l'objet de rubriques distinctes, si disponible.

[53] Excluding Niue, shown separately, which is part of Cook Islands, but because of remoteness is administered separately. A high percentage of marriages are non resident marriages, therefore the rates do not reflect the crude marriage rate of resident population. - Non compris Nioué, qui fait l'objet d'une rubrique distincte et qui fait partie des îles Cook, mais qui, en raison de son éloignement, est administrée séparément. Un pourcentage élevé de mariages correspond à des mariages de non-résidents; les taux ne reflètent donc pas le taux brut de nuptialité de la population résidente.

[54] Data cover the period from 1 July of the previous year to 30 June of the present year. - Pour la période allant du 1er juillet de l'année précédente au 30 juin de l'année en cours.

Table 23 - *Demographic Yearbook 2012*

Table 23 presents the marriages cross-classified by age of groom and age of bride for the latest available year between 2003 and 2012.

Description of variables: Marriage is defined as the act, ceremony or process by which the legal relationship of husband and wife is constituted. The legality of the union may be established by civil, religious or other means as recognized by the laws of each country[1].

Marriage statistics in this table, therefore, include both first marriages and remarriages after divorce, widowhood or annulment. They do not, unless otherwise noted, include resumption of marriage ties after legal separation. These statistics refer to the number of marriages performed, and not to the number of persons marrying.

Age is defined as age at last birthday, that is, the difference between the date of birth and the date of the occurrence of the event, expressed in completed solar years. The age classification used for brides in this table is the following: under 15 years, 5-year age groups through 90-94, and 95 years and over, depending on the availability of data. Age classification for grooms is restricted to: under 15 years, 5-year age groups from 15 to 59, and 60 years and over.

In an effort to provide interpretation of these statistics, countries or areas providing data on marriages by age of groom and bride have been requested to specify "the minimum legal age at which marriage can take place with and without parental consent". This information is presented in the table 23-1 below.

Reliability of data: Data from civil registers of marriages that are reported as incomplete (less than 90 per cent completeness) or of unknown completeness are considered unreliable and are set in *italics* rather than in roman type. Table 23 and the technical notes for that table provide more detailed information on the completeness of marriage registration. For more information about the quality of vital statistics data in general, see Section 4.2 of the Technical Notes.

Limitations: Statistics on marriages by age of groom and age of bride are subject to the same qualifications as have been set forth for vital statistics in general and marriage statistics in particular as discussed in Section 4 of the Technical Notes.

The fact that marriage is a legal event, unlike birth and death that are biological events, has implications for international comparability of data. Marriage has been defined, for statistical purposes, in terms of the laws of individual countries or areas. These laws vary throughout the world. In addition, comparability is further limited because some countries or areas compile statistics only for civil marriages although religious marriages may also be legally recognized; in other countries or areas, the only available records are church registers and, therefore, the statistics may not reflect marriages that are civil marriages only.

Because in many countries or areas marriage is a civil legal contract which, to establish its legality, must be celebrated before a civil officer, it follows that for these countries or areas registration would tend to be almost automatic at the time of, or immediately following, the marriage ceremony. This factor should be kept in mind when considering the reliability of data, described above. For this reason the practice of tabulating data by date of registration does not generally pose serious problems of comparability as it does in the case of birth and death statistics.

Because these statistics are classified according to age, they are subject to the limitations with respect to accuracy of age reporting similar to those already discussed in connection with Section 3.1.3 of the Technical Notes. It is probable that biases are less pronounced in marriage statistics, because information is obtained from the persons concerned and since marriage is a legal act, the participants are likely to give correct information. However, in some countries or areas, there appears to be a concentration of marriages at the legal minimum age for marriage and at the age at which valid marriage may be contracted without parental consent, indicating perhaps an overstatement in some cases to comply with the law.

Aside from the possibility of age misreporting, it should be noted that marriage patterns at younger ages, that is, for ages up to 24 years, are influenced to a large extent by laws regarding the minimum age for marriage.

Factors that may influence age reporting, particularly at older ages include an inclination to understate the age of the bride in order that it may be equal to or less than that of the groom.

The absence of data in the unknown age group does not necessarily indicate completely accurate reporting and tabulation of the age item. It is sometimes an indication that the unknowns have been eliminated by assigning ages to them before tabulation, or by proportionate distribution after tabulation.

Another age-reporting factor that must be kept in mind in using these data is the variation that may result from calculating age at marriage from year of birth rather than from day, month and year of birth. Information on this factor is given in footnotes when known.

Earlier data: Marriages by age of groom and age of bride have been shown for the latest available year in most issues of the *Demographic Yearbook*. Data cross-classified by age of groom and bride have been presented in previous issues featuring marriage and divorce statistics. For information on the specific topics and the years covered, readers should consult the Historical Index.

23-1 Minimum legal age at which marriage can take place

Country or area	With parental consent		Without parental consent	
	Groom	*Bride*	*Groom*	*Bride*
Africa				
Botswana	18	18	21	21
Burkina Faso[2]	18	15	20	17
Egypt	18	16	21	21
Ghana			18	18
Liberia	16	16	21	18
Libya[3]	18	18		
Malawi[4]			18	18
Mauritius	16	16	18	18
Morocco[4]			18	18
Namibia	18	18	21	21
Saint Helena ex. dep.	16	16	21	21
Senegal	Under 18	Under 18	18	18
Seychelles	16	16	18	18
Sierra Leone[4]			18	18
South Africa	18	15	21	21
Uganda[4, 5]			18	18
Zimbabwe	16	16	18	18
America, North				
Anguilla			18	18
Aruba	18	15	18	18
Bermuda[4]			18	18
Canada[6]	16	16	18	18
Cayman Islands	16	16	18	18
Costa Rica	15	15	18	18
Cuba	16	14	18	16
Dominican Republic	17	16	18	18
El Salvador	15	14	18	18
Greenland[7]	16	15	18	18

Country or area	With parental consent		Without parental consent	
	Groom	Bride	Groom	Bride
Jamaica	16	16	18	18
Mexico[8]	16	14	18	18
Montserrat[9]	16	16	18	18
Netherlands Antilles			18	18
Panama	16	14	18	18
Puerto Rico	18	16	21	21
Trinidad and Tobago[10]	Under 18	Under 18	18	18
America, South				
Brazil	16	16	18	18
Chile	16	16	18	18
Colombia	14	14	18	18
Ecuador	Under 18	Under 18	18	18
Suriname	17	15	21	21
Uruguay	14	12	18	18
Venezuela (Bolivarian Republic of)[4]			12	12
Asia				
Armenia			18	17
Azerbaijan	18	17		
Bahrain			15	
Cambodia			18	18
China, Hong Kong SAR	16	16	21	21
China, Macao SAR	16	16	18	18
Cyprus	16	16	18	18
Georgia	16	16	18	18
Indonesia			19	16
Iran	18	15		
Israel[4]			17	17
Japan	18	16	20	20
Kazakhstan	16	16	18	17
Kyrgyzstan	16	16	18	18
Malaysia[11]	18	16	18 and 21	16 and 21
Nepal	18	18	20	20
Occupied Palestinian Territory[12]		14.5	15.5	
Oman[4]			18	18
Philippines	18	18	21	21
Republic of Korea	18	18	20	20
Singapore[13]	Under 21	Under 21	21	21
Tajikistan	17	17	18	18
Turkey	16	16	18	18

Country or area	With parental consent		Without parental consent	
	Groom	Bride	Groom	Bride
Uzbekistan			17	17
Europe				
Åland Islands[4]			18	18
Albania	18	16		
Austria[14]	16	16	18	18
Belarus[15]			18	18
Belgium	Under 18	Under 18	18	18
Bosnia and Herzegovina			18	18
Bulgaria	16	16	18	18
Croatia	16	16	18	18
Czech Republic	16	16	18	18
Denmark	15	15	18	18
Estonia	15	15	18	18
Finland[16]			18	18
France[4]			18	18
Germany[17]	16	16	18	18
Gibraltar	16	16	18	18
Greece[18]			18	18
Hungary	16	16	18	18
Iceland[4]			18	18
Ireland[4, 19]			18	18
Isle of Man	16	16	18	18
Italy	16	16	18	18
Jersey	16	16	18	18
Latvia	16	16	18	18
Liechtenstein[14]			18	18
Lithuania[20]	15	15	18	18
Luxembourg			18	16
Malta			16	16
Montenegro	16	16	18	18
Netherlands	16	16	18	18
Norway	16	16	18	18
Poland[21]			18	18
Portugal	16	16	18	18
Republic of Moldova			18	16
Romania[4]			18	18
Russian Federation	16	16	18	18
Serbia	16	16	18	18
Slovakia[22]			16	16

Country or area	With parental consent		Without parental consent	
	Groom	Bride	Groom	Bride
Slovenia	15	15	18	18
Spain	14	14	18	18
Sweden [23]			18	18
Switzerland	16	16	18	18
TFYR of Macedonia	16	16	18	18
Ukraine	15	15	18	17
United Kingdom of Great Britain and Northern Ireland	16	16	18	18
Oceania				
Australia	16	16	18	18
Cook Islands	16	16	21	21
New Caledonia			18	18
New Zealand	16	16	18	18

NOTES

[1] *Principles and Recommendations for a Vital Statistics System Revision 2,* Sales No. 01.XVII.10, United Nations, New York, 2001.

[2] In addition, an age waiver may be granted by a civil court for a serious reason from 15 years for women and 18 years for men.

[3] According to the Islamic law, marriage requires parental consent. Consent of the bride herself, as well as the guardian's consent are fundamental in the marriage contract. Young men usually choose the consent of the parents. Minimum age at marriage is usually 18 years. According to the law, marriage is not restricted to individuals over the age of 18 years.

[4] The minimum legal age at which marriage can take place is the same respectively for bride and groom with or without parental consent.

[5] As reported by Uganda Bureau of Statistics, marriages with or without parental consent may occur much earlier than 18 years of age.

[6] Marriage is under provincial and territory legislations. Without parental consent, the minimum legal age at which marriage can take place is 18 years of age in all provinces and territories in Canada except in British Columbia, Newfoundland and Labrador, Nova Scotia, Nunavut, and Yukon where the minimum legal age is 19 years. With parental consent, the minimum legal age is 16 years in all provinces except in Northwest Territories, Nunavut, and Yukon. With parental consent, in Northwest Territories, and Yukon the minimum legal age is 15 years whereas in Nunavut, the minimum legal age is 18 years.

[7] To marry at age younger than 18 years, both parental and official consent are needed. Pregnancy is one of the very few reasons to get official consent.

[8] Each of the 31 Federal States and the Federal District has its own civil code for marriage. Exceptions to ages given in the table are as follows: without parental consent, the minimum legal age at which marriage can take place in Baja California and Tlaxcala is 16 years for males and 14 years for females whereas in Baja California Sur, it is 16 years for females. With parental consent, the minimum legal age for marriage is 16 years for both males and females in Aguascalientes, Campeche, Chiapas, Distrito Federal, Guerrero, Jalisco, Morelos, Puebla, Quintana Roo, Querétaro, San Luis Potosí, and Sonora. With parental consent, the minimum legal age for marriage is under 18 years for both males and females in Coahuila, Hidalgo, and Zacatecas. The Minimum legal age for marriage remains the same respectively for bride and groom with or without parental consent in Baja California, Baja California Sur and Tlaxcala.

[9] Consent can be given by a guardian or a person who has custody of the child wishing to marry. Also the Governor has discretion to permit persons as young as 15 years and 1 day old to marry, if he thinks that getting married is in the best interest of the persons who are intending to marry and the persons in this instance must have also received the necessary consent.

[10] With parental consent, age for marriage is 14 years for males and 12 years for females in a civil marriage; 16 years for males and 12 years for females in a Muslim marriage; 18 years for males and 14 years for females in a Hindu marriage; and 18 years for males and 16 for females in Orisa marriage.

[11] Without parental consent, it is 21 years of age for non-Muslim males and 18 years of age for Muslim males whereas it is 21 years of age for non-Muslim females and 16 years of age for Muslim females. For marriage with parental consent, approval of relevant authorities is required.

[12] The legal marriage age for females is 14 years, 6 months and 22 days. There must be parental consent (father or brother if the father is dead). The legal marriage age for males is 15 years, 6 months and 21 days. Parental consent is not required.

[13] Specified minimum legal marriage age refers to marriages contracted under the Women's Charter. For Muslim marriages under the Administration of Muslim Law Act, no marriage shall be solemnised when either party is below the age of 18 years. Notwithstanding that, Muslim women below the age of 18 years who have attained the age of puberty may be married under the Administration of the Muslim Law Act.

[14] Persons less than 18 years old need a decision of the court.

[15] In compliance with the Marriage and Family Code of the Republic of Belarus, in the exclusive cases related to pregnancy, childbirth, and in case of acquiring by a juvenile of a full legal capacity under lawful age, the civil registration offices are in a position to reduce the marriage age of espousing persons, but not more than by 3 years. The marriage age is to be reduced by an application of espousing persons; the parental consent is not required.

[16] Persons less than 18 years old need the permission of the Ministry of Justice.

[17] Marriage at 16-17 years of age requires that the other spouse be an adult already betrothed (18 years) and an exemption from the requirement of majority by a competent family court.

[18] Under some conditions (e.g. pregnancy) the marriage can take place without age restrictions.

[19] An exemption on the minimum age can be granted by court order if granting of such an exemption is in the best interests of the parties to the intended marriage and good reasons for the application can be demonstrated.

[20] In addition to parental consent, persons less than 18 years old need judicial approval. In case of pregnancy, marriage can be allowed below 15 years of age.

[21] Females can marry at the age of 16 or 17 years with parental and court consent.

[22] A marriage cannot be entered into by a minor. The court may exceptionally and for important reasons approve of entrance into marriage by a minor older than sixteen years. Without this approval, the marriage is invalid and the court shall declare the invalidity even without a petition.

[23] With parental consent, no limit but authorities must approve; without parental consent, 18 years of age for Swedish citizens.

Tableau 23 – *Annuaire démographique 2012*

Le tableau 23 présente des statistiques concernant les mariages classés selon l'âge de l'époux et selon l'âge de l'épouse pour les années où les données sont disponibles entre 2003 et 2012.

Description des variables : le mariage désigne l'acte, la cérémonie ou la procédure qui établit un rapport légal entre mari et femme. L'union peut être rendue légale par une procédure civile ou religieuse, ou par toute autre procédure, conformément à la législation du pays[1].

Les statistiques de la nuptialité présentées dans ce tableau comprennent donc les premiers mariages et les remariages faisant suite à un divorce, un veuvage ou une annulation. Toutefois, sauf indication contraire, elles ne comprennent pas les unions reconstituées après une séparation légale. Ces statistiques se rapportent au nombre de mariages célébrés, non au nombre de personnes qui se marient.

L'âge désigne l'âge au dernier anniversaire, c'est-à-dire la différence entre la date de naissance et la date de l'événement, exprimée en années solaires révolues. Le classement par âge pour l'épouse utilisé dans ce tableau comprend les groupes suivants : moins de 15 ans, groupes quinquennaux jusqu'à 90-94 ans, et 95 ans et plus, selon la disponibilité des données. Le classement par âge pour l'époux est : moins de 15 ans, groupes quinquennal de 15 jusqu' à 59 ans et 60 ans et plus.

Dans un effort de fournir l'interprétation de ces statistiques, les pays ou les zones fournissant des données sur les mariages par l'âge de l'épouse et de par l'âge de l'époux ont été demandés d'indiquer "l'âge légal minimum avec auquel le mariage peut avoir lieu avec et sans consentement parental". Cette information est présentée dans le tableau 23-1 ci-dessous.

Fiabilité des données : les données sur les mariages issues des registres de l'état civil qui sont déclarées incomplètes (degré de complétude inférieur à 90 p. 100) ou dont le degré de complétude n'est pas connu sont jugées douteuses et apparaissent en italique et non en caractères romains. Le tableau 23 et les notes techniques s'y rapportant présentent des renseignements plus détaillés sur le degré de complétude de l'enregistrement des mariages. Pour plus de précisions sur la qualité des données reposant sur les statistiques de l'état civil en général, voir la section 4.2 des notes techniques.

Insuffisance des données : les statistiques des mariages selon l'âge de l'époux et selon l'âge de l'épouse appellent les mêmes réserves que celles formulées à propos des statistiques de l'état civil en général et des statistiques de la nuptialité en particulier (voir la section 4 des Notes techniques).

Le fait que le mariage soit un acte juridique, à la différence de la naissance et du décès, qui sont des faits biologiques, a des répercussions sur la comparabilité internationale des données. Aux fins de la statistique, le mariage est défini par la législation de chaque pays ou zone. Cette législation varie d'un pays à l'autre. La comparabilité est limitée en outre du fait que certains pays et zones ne réunissent des statistiques que pour les mariages civils, bien que les mariages religieux y soient également reconnus par la loi ; dans d'autres, les seuls relevés disponibles sont les registres des églises et, en conséquence, les statistiques peuvent ne pas rendre compte des mariages exclusivement civils.

Le mariage étant, dans de nombreux pays ou zones, un contrat juridique civil qui, pour être légal, doit être conclu devant un officier d'état civil, il s'ensuit que, dans ces pays ou zones, l'enregistrement se fait à peu près systématiquement au moment de la cérémonie ou immédiatement après. Il faut tenir compte de cet élément lorsque l'on évalue la fiabilité des données, dont il est question plus haut. C'est pourquoi la pratique consistant à exploiter les données selon la date de l'enregistrement ne pose généralement pas les graves problèmes de comparabilité auxquels on se heurte dans le cas des statistiques des naissances et des décès.

Étant donné que ces statistiques sont classées selon l'âge, elles appellent les mêmes réserves concernant l'exactitude des déclarations d'âge que celles dont il a déjà été question à la section 3.1.3 des Notes techniques. Il est probable que les statistiques de la nuptialité sont moins faussées par ce genre d'erreur, car les renseignements sont donnés par les intéressés eux-mêmes, et, comme le mariage est un acte juridique, il y a toutes chances que leurs déclarations soient exactes. Toutefois, dans certains pays ou zones, il semble y avoir une concentration de mariages à l'âge minimal légal de nubilité ainsi qu'à l'âge auquel le mariage peut être valablement contracté sans le consentement des parents, ce qui peut indiquer que certains déclarants se vieillissent pour se conformer à la loi.

Outre la possibilité d'erreurs dans les déclarations d'âge, il convient de noter que la législation fixant l'âge minimal de nubilité influe notablement sur les caractéristiques de la nuptialité pour les premiers âges, c'est-à-dire jusqu'à 24 ans.

Parmi les facteurs pouvant exercer une influence sur les déclarations d'âge, en particulier celles qui sont faites par des personnes plus âgées, il faut citer la tendance à diminuer l'âge de l'épouse de façon qu'il soit égal ou inférieur à celui de l'époux.

Si aucun nombre ne figure dans la rangée réservée aux âges inconnus, cela ne signifie pas nécessairement que les déclarations d'âge et l'exploitation des données par âge aient été tout à fait exactes. C'est parfois une indication que l'on a attribué un âge aux personnes d'âge inconnu avant l'exploitation des données ou qu'elles ont été réparties proportionnellement entre les différents groupes après cette opération.

Il importe de ne pas oublier non plus, lorsque l'on utilisera ces données, que l'on calcule parfois l'âge des conjoints au moment du mariage sur la base de l'année de naissance seulement et non d'après la date exacte (jour, mois et année) de naissance. Des renseignements à ce sujet sont donnés en note chaque fois que possible.

Donnés publiées antérieurement : on trouve dans la plupart des éditions de l'*Annuaire démographique* des statistiques concernant les mariages selon l'âge de l'époux et selon l'âge de l'épouse qui ont été établies à partir des données les plus récentes dont on disposait à l'époque. Des données croisant l'âge des époux ont été présentées dans des éditions antérieurs, plus particulièrement consacrées aux statistiques de la nuptialité et de la divortialité. Pour plus de précisions concernant les années et les sujets pour lesquels des données ont été publiées, se reporter à l'index historique.

23-1 L'âge légal minimum avec auquel le mariage peut avoir lieu

Pays ou zone	Avec consentement parental		Sans consentement parental	
	Epoux	Epouse	Epoux	Epouse
Afrique				
Afrique du Sud	18	15	21	21
Botswana	18	18	21	21
Burkina Faso[2]	18	15	20	17
Egypte	18	16	21	21
Ghana			18	18
Libéria	16	16	21	18
Libye[3]	18	18		
Malawi[4]			18	18
Maurice	16	16	18	18
Maroc[4]			18	18
Namibie	18	18	21	21
Ouganda[4, 5]			18	18
Sainte-Hélène sans dép.	16	16	21	21
Sénégal	moins de 18	moins de 18	18	18
Seychelles	16	16	18	18
Sierra Leone[4]			18	18
Zimbabwe	16	16	18	18
Amérique du Nord				
Anguilla			18	18
Antilles néerlandaises			18	18

Pays ou zone	Avec consentement parental		Sans consentement parental	
	Epoux	Epouse	Epoux	Epouse
Aruba	18	15	18	18
Bermudes[4]			18	18
Canada[6]	16	16	18	18
Costa Rica	15	15	18	18
Cuba	16	14	18	16
El Salvador	15	14	18	18
Groenland[7]	16	15	18	18
Îles Caïmanes	16	16	18	18
Jamaïque	16	16	18	18
Mexique[8]	16	14	18	18
Montserrat[9]	16	16	18	18
Panama	16	14	18	18
Porto Rico	18	16	21	21
République dominicaine	17	16	18	18
Trinité-et-Tobago[10]	moins de 18	moins de 18	18	18
Amérique du Sud				
Brésil	16	16	18	18
Chili	16	16	18	18
Colombie	14	14	18	18
Equateur	moins de 18	moins de 18	18	18
Suriname	17	15	21	21
Uruguay	14	12	18	18
Venezuela (République bolivarienne du)[4]			12	12
Asie				
Arménie			18	17
Azerbaïdjan	18	17		
Bahreïn			15	
Cambodge			18	18
Chine, Hong Kong RAS	16	16	21	21
Chine, Macao RAS	16	16	18	18
Géorgie	16	16	18	18
Indonésie			19	16
Iran (République islamique d')	18	15		
Israël[4]			17	17
Japon	18	16	20	20
Kazakhstan	16	16	18	17
Kirghizistan	16	16	18	18
Malaisie[11]	18	16	18 et 21	16 et 21

Pays ou zone	Avec consentement parental		Sans consentement parental	
	Epoux	Epouse	Epoux	Epouse
Népal	18	18	20	20
Oman[4]			18	18
Ouzbékistan			17	17
Philippines	18	18	21	21
République de Corée	18	18	20	20
Singapour[12]	moins de 21	moins de 21	21	21
Tadjikistan	17	17	18	18
Territoire palestinien occupé[13]		14.5	15.5	
Turquie	16	16	18	18
Europe				
Albanie	18	16		
Allemagne[14]	16	16	18	18
Autriche[15]	16	16	18	18
Bélarus[16]			18	18
Belgique	moins de 18	moins de 18	18	18
Bosnie-Herzégovine			18	18
Bulgarie	16	16	18	18
Croatie	16	16	18	18
Danemark	15	15	18	18
Espagne	14	14	18	18
Estonie	15	15	18	18
Fédération de Russie	16	16	18	18
Finlande[17]			18	18
France[4]			18	18
Gibraltar	16	16	18	18
Grèce[18]			18	18
Hongrie	16	16	18	18
Île de Man	16	16	18	18
Îles d'Åland[4]			18	18
Irlande[4, 19]			18	18
Islande[4]			18	18
Italie	16	16	18	18
Jersey	16	16	18	18
L'ex-R. y. de Macédoine	16	16	18	18
Lettonie	16	16	18	18
Liechtenstein[15]			18	18

Pays ou zone	Avec consentement parental		Sans consentement parental	
	Epoux	Epouse	Epoux	Epouse
Lituanie[20]	15	15	18	18
Luxembourg			18	16
Malte			16	16
Monténégro	16	16	18	18
Norvège	16	16	18	18
Pays-Bas	16	16	18	18
Pologne[21]			18	18
Portugal	16	16	18	18
République de Moldova			18	16
République tchèque	16	16	18	18
Roumanie[4]			18	18
Royaume-Uni de Grande-Bretagne et d'Irlande du Nord	16	16	18	18
Serbie	16	16	18	18
Slovaque[22]			16	16
Slovénie	15	15	18	18
Suede[23]			18	18
Suisse	16	16	18	18
Ukraine	15	15	18	17
Océanie				
Australie	16	16	18	18
Îles Cook	16	16	21	21
Nouvelle-Calédonie			18	18
Nouvelle-Zélande	16	16	18	18

NOTES

[1] *Principes et recommandations pour un système de statistiques de l'état civil, deuxième révision,* numéro de vente F.01.XVII.10, publication des Nations Unies, New York, 2003.

[2] De plus, une dispense d'âge peut être accordée par un tribunal civil pour motif grave à partir de 15 ans pour les femmes et de 18 ans pour les hommes.

[3] Conformément à la loi islamique, le mariage requiert le consentement parental. Le consentement de la mariée, elle-même ainsi que le consentement du tuteur sont fondamentaux dans le contrat de mariage. Les jeunes hommes choisissent habituellement le consentement des parents. L'âge minimum du mariage est généralement 18 ans. Conformément à la loi, le mariage n'est pas limité aux individus âgés de plus de 18 ans.

[4] L'âge minimum légal du mariage est le même respectivement pour le marié et la mariée, avec ou sans le consentement parental.

[5] Tel que le signale l' "Uganda Bureau of Statistics", les mariages avec ou sans le consentement parental peuvent se produire beaucoup plus tôt que 18 ans.

[6] Le mariage est en vertu des législations provinciales et territoriales. Sans le consentement des parents, l'âge minimum légal du mariage est de 18 ans dans toutes les provinces et territoires du Canada sauf en Colombie-Britannique, Terre-Neuve-et-Labrador, la Nouvelle-Écosse, du Nunavut et du Yukon, où l'âge minimum légal est de 19 ans. Avec le consentement des parents, l'âge minimum légal est de

16 ans dans toutes les provinces sauf dans les Territoires du Nord-Ouest, Nunavut et Yukon. Avec le consentement des parents, dans les Territoires du Nord-Ouest et le Yukon l'âge minimum légal est de 15 ans alors que dans le Nunavut, l'âge minimum légal est de 18 ans.

[7] Pour se marier à un âge inférieur à 18 ans, les consentements à la fois des parents et des autorités sont nécessaires. La maternité est l'une des rares raisons permettant d'obtenir le consentement officiel des autorités.

[8] Chacun des 31 Etats fédéraux et du District fédéral a son propre code civil pour le mariage. Les exceptions aux âges figurant sur le tableau sont les suivantes : sans le consentement des parents, l'âge minimum légal du mariage en Basse-Californie et au Tlaxcala est de 16 ans pour les hommes et 14 ans pour les femmes alors que dans la Basse-Californie du Sud, il est de 16 ans pour les femmesfemelles. Avec le consentement des parents, l'âge minimum légal du mariage est de 16 ans pour les hommes et les femmes les femelles à Aguascalientes, Campeche, Chiapas, Distrito Federal, Guerrero, Jalisco, Morelos, Puebla, Quintana Roo, Querétaro, San Luis Potosí et Sonora. Avec le consentement des parents, l'âge minimum légal du mariage est en-dessous de 18 ans pour les hommes et femmes à Coahuila, Hidalgo, et Zacatecas. L'âge minimum légal du mariage reste le même, respectivement pour les mariés avec ou sans le consentement parental en Basse-Californie, Basse Californie du Sud et Tlaxcala.

[9] Le consentement peut être donné par un tuteur ou une personne qui a la garde de l'enfant qui souhaitent se marier. En outre, le gouverneur a la faculté de permettre aux personnes âgés d'au moins 15 ans et 1 jour de se marier, s'il pense que le mariage est dans le meilleur intérêt des personnes qui ont l'intention de s'unir et que les personnes concernées aient également reçu le consentement nécessaire.

[10] Avec l'âge du le consentement parental, l'âge minimum du mariage pour se marier est de 14 ans pour les hommes et de 12 ans pour les femmes pour un mariage civil ; de 16 ans pour les hommes et de 12 ans pour les femmes pour un mariage musulman ; de 18 ans pour les hommes et de 14 ans pour les femmes pour un mariage hindou, et de18 ans pour les hommes et de 16 pour les femmes pour un mariage orisa.

[11] Sans le consentement parental, il est de 21 ans pour les hommes non-musulmans et de 18 ans pour les hommes musulmans alors qu'il est de 21 ans pour les femmes non-musulmanes et il est de 16 ans pour les femmes musulmanes. Pour le mariage avec le consentement parental, l'accord des autorités compétentes est nécessaire.

[12] L'âge minimum légal du mariage spécifié correspond à des mariages contractés en vertu de la Charte des femmes. Pour les mariages musulmans sous l'administration de la « Loi sur le Droit Musulman », aucun mariage ne doit être célébré lorsque l'une des parties est en dessous de l'âge de 18 ans. Néanmoins, les femmes musulmanes en dessous de l'âge de 18 ans qui ont atteint l'âge de la puberté peuvent être mariées dans le cadre de l'administration de la « Loi sur le Droit Musulman ».

[13] L'âge légal du mariage pour les femmes est de 14 ans, 6 mois et 22 jours. Le consentement parental (du père ou du frère si le père est mort) est requis. L'âge légal du mariage pour les hommes est de 15 ans, 6 mois et 21 jours. Le consentement parental n'est pas nécessaire.

[14] Le mariage à 16-17 ans exige que l'autre conjoint soit un adulte déjà fiancée (18 ans) ainsi qu'une exemption de l'obligation de la majorité par un juge aux affaires familiales.

[15] Les personnes âgées de moins de 18 ans doivent obtenir l'autorisation de la justice.

[16] En conformité avec le Code du mariage et la famille de la République du Bélarus, dans les cas exclusifs liés à la maternité, l'accouchement et en cas d'acquisition par un mineur d'une pleine capacité juridique en vertu de l'âge légal, les bureaux d'état civil sont en mesure de de réduire l'âge du mariage des personnes souhaitant se marier, de 3 ans au plus. L'âge du mariage est abaissé suite à une demande des personnes se mariant, le consentement parental n'est pas nécessaire.

[17] Les personnes âgées de moins de 18 ans doivent obtenir l'autorisation du ministère de la justice.

[18] Dans certaines conditions (par exemple la grossesse), le mariage peut avoir lieu sans restriction d'âge.

[19] Une exemption sur l'âge minimum peut être accordée par ordonnance du tribunal si l'octroi d'une telle exemption est dans le meilleur intérêt des parties ayant l'intention de se marier et si la demande est appuyée par de bonnes raisons.

[20] En plus du consentement parental, les personnes de moins de 18 ans doivent obtenir l'autorisation du tribunall'approbation judiciaire. En cas de grossesse, le mariage peut être autorisé en dessous de 15 ans.

[21] Les femmes peuvent se marier à l'âge de 16 ou 17 ans avec l'autorisation des parents et du tribunal de la cour.

[22] Un mariage ne peut être conclu par un mineur. Le tribunal peut, exceptionnellement et pour des raisons importantes approuver l'entrée en mariage par un mineur de plus de seize ans. Sans cet accord, le mariage est invalide et le tribunal est en mesure de prononcer sa nullité, même sans une demande explicite.

[23] Avec le consentement des parents, aucune limite mais les autorités doivent approuver. Sans le consentement parental, l'âge minimum légal du mariage est de 18 ans pour les citoyens suédois.

23. Marriages by age of groom and by age of bride: latest available year, 2003 - 2012
Mariages selon l'âge de l'époux et selon l'âge de l'épouse : dernière année disponible, 2003 - 2012

Continent, country or area, year, code and age of bride / Continent, pays ou zone, date, code et âge de l'épouse	Total	0-14	15-19	20-24	25-29	30-34	35-39	40-44	45-49	50-54	55-59	60+	Unknown Inconnu
AFRICA - AFRIQUE													
Botswana													
2010 (+U)													
Total	4 416	-	-	42	598	1 194	1 005	610	392	243	160	172	...
0 - 14	-	-	-	-	-	-	-	-	-	-	-	-	...
15 - 19	6	-	-	2	1	3	-	-	-	-	-	-	...
20 - 24	361	-	-	29	155	107	41	19	6	4	-	-	...
25 - 29	1 511	-	-	8	353	622	331	131	42	17	2	5	...
30 - 34	1 209	-	-	2	67	397	428	172	88	38	12	5	...
35 - 39	593	-	-	1	15	46	173	186	105	38	22	7	...
40 - 44	335	-	-	-	3	10	28	75	97	67	32	23	...
45 - 49	206	-	-	-	3	4	3	20	47	56	41	32	...
50 - 54	109	-	-	-	1	4	-	5	6	18	39	36	...
55 - 59	45	-	-	-	-	1	1	-	1	5	9	28	...
60 - 64	24	-	-	-	-	-	-	1	-	-	3	20	...
65 +	17	-	-	-	-	-	-	1	-	-	-	16	...
Egypt - Égypte[1]													
2011 (+C)													
Total	897 969	...	12 618[i]	202 662	385 585	164 706	51 432	27 503	18 050	12 343	8 965	11 932	2 173
18 - 19	206 495	...	7 157[i]	78 146	93 041	23 198	3 180	1 185	269	140	82	85	12
20 - 24	398 188	...	4 429[i]	106 584	199 434	67 535	12 510	4 469	1 578	737	466	422	24
25 - 29	178 484	...	774[i]	14 802	80 903	52 037	16 563	6 339	3 305	1 729	996	1 027	9
30 - 34	58 330	...	145[i]	2 103	9 220	17 708	12 401	7 026	4 298	2 364	1 446	1 619	-
35 - 39	24 995	...	41[i]	512	1 738	2 966	4 960	5 056	3 818	2 423	1 710	1 770	1
40 - 44	13 617	...	26[i]	189	573	749	1 169	2 373	2 732	2 275	1 537	1 993	1
45 - 49	8 280	...	13[i]	116	296	305	440	767	1 522	1 701	1 309	1 811	-
50 - 54	4 125	...	14[i]	75	161	113	134	200	401	777	908	1 342	-
55 - 59	1 752	...	3[i]	32	55	30	30	46	90	140	395	930	1
60 - 64	725	...	2[i]	5	21	15	22	17	22	34	82	505	-
65 - 69	296	...	-[i]	9	10	2	7	8	7	7	17	229	-
70 - 74	138	...	2[i]	5	10	3	3	5	1	7	5	97	-
75 +	193	...	9[i]	27	41	7	2	3	2	4	2	96	-
Unknown - Inconnu	2 351	...	3[i]	57	82	38	11	9	5	5	10	6	2 125
Mauritius - Maurice[2]													
2011 (+C)													
Total	10 499	-	136	1 372	2 999	2 701	1 212	780	535	360	202	200	2
0 - 14	-	-	-	-	-	-	-	-	-	-	-	-	-
15 - 19	1 090	-	89	471	340	159	21	6	1	2	-	1	-
20 - 24	2 878	-	38	707	1 284	695	106	31	10	3	3	1	-
25 - 29	2 797	-	6	147	1 123	1 066	301	96	35	17	4	2	-
30 - 34	1 641	-	1	34	196	631	433	220	79	32	6	8	1
35 - 39	774	-	2	7	40	105	240	198	120	42	14	6	-
40 - 44	539	-	-	3	6	22	72	144	165	84	29	14	-
45 - 49	406	-	-	-	4	18	32	60	96	110	51	35	-
50 - 54	209	-	-	-	3	2	7	20	23	48	52	54	-
55 - 59	96	-	-	-	-	2	-	4	2	15	37	36	-
60 +	60	-	-	-	1	-	-	1	3	7	5	43	-
Unknown - Inconnu	9	-	-	3	2	1	-	-	1	-	1	-	1
Réunion													
2008 (C)													
Total	3 149	-	15	338	787	681	514	306	185	150	62	111	-
0 - 14	1	-	1	-	-	-	-	-	-	-	-	-	-
15 - 19	91	-	8	45	26	7	2	2	1	-	-	-	-
20 - 24	679	-	4	235	296	99	28	13	3	-	1	-	-
25 - 29	858	-	2	42	391	264	117	30	7	4	1	-	-
30 - 34	584	-	-	12	52	232	185	56	29	10	4	4	-
35 - 39	384	-	-	3	16	55	134	106	38	25	4	3	-
40 - 44	234	-	-	-	4	16	34	77	49	28	13	13	-
45 - 49	144	-	-	1	1	7	11	18	34	40	18	14	-
50 - 54	94	-	-	-	1	1	3	4	19	30	12	24	-
55 - 59	39	-	-	-	-	-	-	-	3	10	7	19	-
60 - 64	16	-	-	-	-	-	-	-	2	2	1	11	-
65 - 69	16	-	-	-	-	-	-	-	-	1	1	14	-
70 - 74	7	-	-	-	-	-	-	-	-	-	-	7	-
75 +	2	-	-	-	-	-	-	-	-	-	-	2	-

Continent, country or area, year, code and age of bride / Continent, pays ou zone, date, code et âge de l'épouse	Total	Age of groom - âge de l'époux											Unknown Inconnu
		0-14	15-19	20-24	25-29	30-34	35-39	40-44	45-49	50-54	55-59	60+	
AFRICA - AFRIQUE													
Seychelles[3]													
2011 (+C)													
Total	1 525	-	3	68	293	381	270	207	145	86	39	33	-
0 - 14	-	-	-	-	-	-	-	-	-	-	-	-	-
15 - 19	18	-	1	7	8	2	-	-	-	-	-	-	-
20 - 24	148	-	1	36	65	32	9	4	1	-	-	-	-
25 - 29	418	-	1	19	162	155	38	28	12	1	1	1	-
30 - 34	384	-	-	3	48	153	103	40	24	10	3	-	-
35 - 39	236	-	-	1	9	29	95	64	24	9	4	1	-
40 - 44	138	-	-	1	1	7	19	45	35	20	6	4	-
45 - 49	94	-	-	1	-	3	5	19	34	18	8	6	-
50 - 54	55	-	-	-	-	-	1	5	11	20	11	7	-
55 - 59	23	-	-	-	-	-	-	2	2	7	5	7	-
60 - 64	5	-	-	-	-	-	-	-	1	1	1	2	-
65 - 69	3	-	-	-	-	-	-	-	1	-	-	2	-
70 - 74	3	-	-	-	-	-	-	-	-	-	-	3	-
75 +	-	-	-	-	-	-	-	-	-	-	-	-	-
South Africa - Afrique du Sud													
2010 (...)													
Total	170 826	3	196	9 391	37 196	39 243	30 562	20 183	12 930	8 431	5 194	...	7 497
0 - 14	5	-	-	5	-	-	-	-	-	-	-	...	-
15 - 19	2 338	-	99	1 059	759	274	98	29	12	7	-	...	1
20 - 24	27 238	1	74	6 078	13 192	5 359	1 674	540	193	77	26	...	24
25 - 29	51 052	-	12	1 783	19 316	18 931	7 532	2 236	787	281	100	...	74
30 - 34	35 295	-	8	328	3 092	11 671	12 272	5 112	1 781	634	251	...	146
35 - 39	22 385	-	2	102	607	2 303	7 100	7 101	3 180	1 224	439	...	327
40 - 44	13 476	-	1	22	183	540	1 436	3 926	3 969	2 005	822	...	572
45 - 49	8 380	-	-	8	35	121	345	945	2 286	2 434	1 217	...	989
50 - 54	5 033	1	-	4	10	31	85	231	577	1 378	1 374	...	1 342
55 - 59	2 631	1	-	1	2	10	17	41	109	292	707	...	1 451
60 - 64	1 512	-	-	1	-	2	3	20	25	79	203	...	1 179
65 - 69	764	-	-	-	-	1	-	1	6	11	33	...	712
70 - 74	717	-	-	-	-	-	1	5	9	22	...	680	
Tunisia - Tunisie													
2011 (...)													
Total	91 590	...	228[e]	5 724	24 725	30 919	15 770	5 904	2 881	4 652[r]	...	...	787
0 - 19	6 504	...	...	...	...	...	...	...	...	...	...	...	...
20 - 24	24 862	...	...	...	...	...	...	...	...	...	...	...	...
25 - 29	31 959	...	...	...	...	...	...	...	...	...	...	...	...
30 - 34	15 109	...	...	...	...	...	...	...	...	...	...	...	...
35 - 39	6 123	...	...	...	...	...	...	...	...	...	...	...	...
40 - 44	3 104	...	...	...	...	...	...	...	...	...	...	...	...
45 - 49	1 744	...	...	...	...	...	...	...	...	...	...	...	...
50 +	1 267	...	...	...	...	...	...	...	...	...	...	...	...
Unknown - Inconnu	918	...	...	...	...	...	...	...	...	...	...	...	...
AMERICA, NORTH - AMÉRIQUE DU NORD													
Anguilla													
2008[4] (C)													
Total	54	...	...	...	...	...	...	...	...	...	...	...	...
0 - 17	-	...	...	...	...	...	...	...	...	...	...	...	...
18 - 23	8	...	...	...	...	...	...	...	...	...	...	...	...
24 - 29	15	...	...	...	...	...	...	...	...	...	...	...	...
30 - 35	16	...	...	...	...	...	...	...	...	...	...	...	...
36 - 41	5	...	...	...	...	...	...	...	...	...	...	...	...
42 - 47	7	...	...	...	...	...	...	...	...	...	...	...	...
48 - 53	1	...	...	...	...	...	...	...	...	...	...	...	...
54	2	...	...	...	...	...	...	...	...	...	...	...	...
Aruba[5,6]													
2007 (C)													
Total	532	-	7	53	94	89	77	71	44	34	30	20	13
0 - 14	-	-	-	-	-	-	-	-	-	-	-	-	-
15 - 19	27	-	3	16	4	2	1	-	-	-	-	-	1
20 - 24	71	-	3	17	29	12	7	2	-	-	1	-	-
25 - 29	93	-	-	7	39	27	9	6	1	1	1	-	2

Continent, country or area, year, code and age of bride — Continent, pays ou zone, date, code et âge de l'épouse	Age of groom - âge de l'époux											
	Total	0-14	15-19	20-24	25-29	30-34	35-39	40-44	45-49	50-54	55-59	60+	Unknown Inconnu

AMERICA, NORTH - AMÉRIQUE DU NORD

Aruba[5,6]
2007

	Total	0-14	15-19	20-24	25-29	30-34	35-39	40-44	45-49	50-54	55-59	60+	Unknown Inconnu
30 - 34	97	-	-	5	15	25	28	12	6	2	-	-	4
35 - 39	63	-	-	3	1	12	12	15	8	5	4	2	1
40 - 44	55	-	-	-	1	6	8	19	10	6	1	4	-
45 - 49	45	-	-	-	-	1	5	10	8	7	7	3	4
50 - 54	21	-	-	-	-	-	1	2	4	3	7	4	-
55 - 59	17	-	-	-	-	-	-	-	3	1	9	3	1
60 - 64	4	-	-	-	-	-	-	-	-	2	-	2	-
65 +	2	-	-	-	-	-	-	-	-	-	-	2	-
Unknown - Inconnu	37	-	1	5	5	4	6	5	4	7	-	-	-

Bahamas
2010 (+C)

	Total	0-14	15-19	20-24	25-29	30-34	35-39	40-44	45-49	50-54	55-59	60+	Unknown Inconnu
Total	1 939	-	10	209	462	432	289	200	136	87	40	...	4
0 - 14	-	-	-	-	-	-	-	-	-	-	-	...	-
15 - 19	54	-	3	26	12	7	1	1	1	-	1	...	1
20 - 24	385	-	4	116	153	74	26	6	5	-	1	...	-
25 - 29	515	-	2	44	199	156	56	36	14	5	-	...	1
30 - 34	369	-	-	12	74	131	78	37	19	13	2	...	-
35 - 39	221	-	-	3	13	31	80	40	29	12	6	...	1
40 - 44	161	-	-	2	5	22	28	49	29	14	6	...	-
45 - 49	111	-	-	1	2	5	15	18	24	22	10	...	-
50 - 54	60	-	-	1	1	1	2	9	9	14	7	...	-
55 - 59	26	-	-	-	-	1	1	3	5	4	5	...	-
60 - 64	24	-	-	1	-	1	1	1	-	3	2	...	-
Unknown - Inconnu	13	...	1	3	3	3	1	-	1	-	-	...	1

Bermuda - Bermudes
2011 (C)

	Total	0-14	15-19	20-24	25-29	30-34	35-39	40-44	45-49	50-54	55-59	60+	Unknown Inconnu
Total	555	-	-	18	107	119	84	65	57	44	28	33	...
0 - 14	-	-	-	-	-	-	-	-	-	-	-	-	...
15 - 19	-	-	-	-	-	-	-	-	-	-	-	-	...
20 - 24	37	-	-	11	18	5	3	-	-	-	-	-	...
25 - 29	148	-	-	5	63	47	18	9	4	1	1	-	...
30 - 34	125	-	-	2	16	52	26	18	9	2	-	-	...
35 - 39	83	-	-	-	6	10	30	16	10	7	3	1	...
40 - 44	55	-	-	-	3	5	5	14	14	9	4	1	...
45 - 49	45	-	-	-	1	-	-	6	12	14	9	3	...
50 - 54	29	-	-	-	-	-	2	1	6	11	4	5	...
55 - 59	19	-	-	-	-	-	-	-	2	-	5	12	...
60 - 64	8	-	-	-	-	-	-	1	-	-	2	5	...
65 - 69	3	-	-	-	-	-	-	-	-	-	-	3	...
70 - 74	2	-	-	-	-	-	-	-	-	-	-	2	...
75 +	1	-	-	-	-	-	-	-	-	-	-	1	...

Costa Rica[7]
2011* (C)

	Total	0-14	15-19	20-24	25-29	30-34	35-39	40-44	45-49	50-54	55-59	60+	Unknown Inconnu
Total	25 013	-	504	4 567	6 708	4 897	2 665	1 719	1 165	2 211[r]	...	...	577
0 - 14	4	-	2	1	-	1	-	-	-	-[r]	...	...	-
15 - 19	2 293	-	288	1 221	522	162	37	24	14	13[r]	...	...	12
20 - 24	6 207	-	171	2 253	2 445	852	270	111	48	48[r]	...	...	9
25 - 29	6 522	-	25	758	2 659	1 936	642	279	123	87[r]	...	...	13
30 - 34	3 949	-	8	205	756	1 373	858	403	181	154[r]	...	...	11
35 - 39	1 996	-	3	65	201	373	538	369	210	231[r]	...	...	6
40 - 44	1 231	-	2	24	59	106	182	306	233	315[r]	...	...	4
45 - 49	889	-	-	8	21	38	83	139	212	385[r]	...	...	3
50 +	1 230	-	-	4	9	18	34	69	134	953[r]	...	...	9
Unknown - Inconnu	692	-	5	28	36	38	21	19	10	25[r]	...	...	510

Cuba[8]
2011 (C)

	Total	0-14	15-19	20-24	25-29	30-34	35-39	40-44	45-49	50-54	55-59	60+	Unknown Inconnu
Total	59 676	2	1 173	7 778	10 136	7 352	8 210	7 159	6 376	3 623	2 579	5 286	2
0 - 14	79	-	22	39	11	3	3	-	1	-	-	-	-
15 - 19	4 711	2	686	2 189	1 127	350	191	81	48	13	2	22	-
20 - 24	11 792	-	339	3 659	4 070	1 665	1 020	503	273	112	47	104	-
25 - 29	9 705	-	85	1 178	2 901	2 249	1 616	874	455	163	78	106	-
30 - 34	6 391	-	17	378	996	1 339	1 658	997	582	196	88	140	-
35 - 39	7 016	-	10	188	538	934	1 760	1 656	1 104	412	210	204	-
40 - 44	6 477	-	7	83	276	471	1 106	1 640	1 551	615	365	363	-
45 - 49	5 767	-	4	39	131	233	579	951	1 505	1 035	579	711	-

23. Marriages by age of groom and by age of bride: latest available year, 2003 - 2012
Mariages selon l'âge de l'époux et selon l'âge de l'épouse : dernière année disponible, 2003 - 2012 (continued - suite)

Continent, country or area, year, code and age of bride / Continent, pays ou zone, date, code et âge de l'épouse	Total	0-14	15-19	20-24	25-29	30-34	35-39	40-44	45-49	50-54	55-59	60+	Unknown Inconnu
AMERICA, NORTH - AMÉRIQUE DU NORD													
Cuba[8]													
2011													
50 - 54	3 121	-	1	11	48	68	168	287	547	631	598	762	-
55 - 59	2 017	-	1	6	19	25	65	94	202	274	391	940	-
60 - 64	1 314	-	-	3	11	7	24	45	72	108	162	882	-
65 - 69	692	-	-	4	3	6	10	18	21	40	43	547	-
70 - 74	360	-	-	-	3	2	5	6	8	17	13	306	-
75 +	232	-	1	1	2	-	5	7	7	7	3	199	-
Unknown - Inconnu	2	-	-	-	-	-	-	-	-	-	-	-	2
Curaçao													
2010 (C)													
Total	874	-	3	70	127	137	117	106	103	76	69	58	8
0 - 14	-	-	-	-	-	-	-	-	-	-	-	-	-
15 - 19	15	-	1	7	6	1	-	-	-	-	-	-	-
20 - 24	101	-	2	36	29	18	9	4	2	1	-	-	-
25 - 29	196	-	-	18	69	57	22	15	11	2	2	-	-
30 - 34	147	-	-	6	15	42	32	21	18	8	3	2	-
35 - 39	135	-	-	1	5	14	31	30	27	15	8	4	-
40 - 44	79	-	-	2	2	2	12	16	19	13	9	4	-
45 - 49	86	-	-	-	-	2	9	15	15	19	15	11	-
50 - 54	55	-	-	-	1	1	1	4	8	11	19	10	-
55 - 59	33	-	-	-	-	-	-	1	3	4	11	14	-
60 - 64	9	-	-	-	-	-	1	-	-	3	-	5	-
65 - 69	4	-	-	-	-	-	-	-	-	-	1	3	-
70 - 74	6	-	-	-	-	-	-	-	-	-	1	5	-
75 +	-	-	-	-	-	-	-	-	-	-	-	-	-
Unknown - Inconnu	8	-	-	-	-	-	-	-	-	-	-	-	8
Dominican Republic - République dominicaine													
2011 (+C)													
Total	44 253	1	399	5 551	9 261	7 899	5 939	4 832	3 533	2 425	1 750	2 270	393
0 - 14	6	-	1	2	1	-	1	-	1	-	-	-	-
15 - 19	2 498	-	176	1 156	656	259	113	58	35	20	13	12	-
20 - 24	9 598	1	154	2 890	3 492	1 602	681	356	203	110	49	55	5
25 - 29	9 705	-	37	928	3 399	2 668	1 205	691	358	187	111	114	7
30 - 34	7 379	-	16	341	1 034	2 087	1 736	991	530	299	171	171	3
35 - 39	5 155	-	6	134	389	714	1 336	1 180	667	338	196	193	2
40 - 44	3 764	-	3	52	156	324	512	904	834	467	265	243	4
45 - 49	2 542	-	2	21	69	157	218	405	556	524	301	287	2
50 - 54	1 548	-	-	8	26	46	87	153	225	321	350	329	3
55 - 59	867	-	2	3	16	15	33	52	74	106	204	362	-
60 - 64	422	-	-	1	3	9	8	19	26	37	59	258	2
65 - 69	197	-	-	1	1	3	3	11	9	9	23	137	-
70 - 74	82	-	1	-	-	3	1	1	7	1	4	64	-
75 +	43	-	-	-	1	-	1	1	3	-	1	36	-
Unknown - Inconnu	447	-	1	14	18	12	4	10	5	6	3	9	365
El Salvador[9]													
2011 (...)													
Total	31 220	59	4 019	8 834	6 506	4 515	2 597	1 637	1 179	678	443	...	166
0 - 14	-	-	-	-	-	-	-	-	-	-	-	...	-
15 - 19	1 171	14	637	395	92	19	6	2	3	1	-	...	2
20 - 24	7 084	26	2 034	3 640	1 015	247	67	23	7	1	2	...	20
25 - 29	7 224	6	828	2 822	2 481	791	179	57	17	6	1	...	29
30 - 34	5 508	7	296	1 182	1 747	1 542	493	140	58	14	-	...	24
35 - 39	3 336	3	127	422	637	1 018	725	257	90	24	9	...	21
40 - 44	2 210	-	52	194	266	482	522	427	175	56	18	...	10
45 - 49	1 505	2	21	102	120	209	308	337	291	67	31	...	8
50 - 54	1 037	1	11	32	73	104	138	198	241	159	50	...	6
55 - 59	729	-	2	18	41	54	79	83	119	170	107	...	3
60 - 64	493	-	2	10	10	21	39	55	84	87	103	...	-
65 - 69	839	-	4	9	10	21	37	56	92	93	121	...	5
70 - 74	-	-	-	-	-	-	-	-	-	-	-	...	-
75 +	-	-	-	-	-	-	-	-	-	-	-	...	-
Unknown - Inconnu	84	-	5	8	14	7	4	2	2	-	1	...	38

23. Marriages by age of groom and by age of bride: latest available year, 2003 - 2012
Mariages selon l'âge de l'époux et selon l'âge de l'épouse : dernière année disponible, 2003 - 2012 (continued - suite)

Continent, country or area, year, code and age of bride / Continent, pays ou zone, date, code et âge de l'épouse	Total	\multicolumn{12}{c}{Age of groom - âge de l'époux}											
		0-14	15-19	20-24	25-29	30-34	35-39	40-44	45-49	50-54	55-59	60+	Unknown Inconnu

AMERICA, NORTH - AMÉRIQUE DU NORD

	Total	0-14	15-19	20-24	25-29	30-34	35-39	40-44	45-49	50-54	55-59	60+	Unknown Inconnu
Guadeloupe 2003 (C)													
Total	1 701	-	3	49	320	437	328	197	121	74	63	109	-
0 - 14	-	-	-	-	-	-	-	-	-	-	-	-	-
15 - 19	28	-	1	8	13	4	2	-	-	-	-	-	-
20 - 24	226	-	2	24	116	56	19	5	4	-	-	-	-
25 - 29	423	-	-	14	139	169	74	19	4	1	2	1	-
30 - 34	412	-	-	2	46	159	128	46	18	3	6	4	-
35 - 39	238	-	-	-	4	33	79	69	35	8	7	3	-
40 - 44	122	-	-	-	-	14	19	35	23	18	6	7	-
45 - 49	94	-	-	1	2	-	6	18	22	25	13	7	-
50 - 54	61	-	-	-	-	-	-	4	9	10	18	20	-
55 - 59	35	-	-	-	-	2	1	-	6	6	5	15	-
60 - 64	29	-	-	-	-	-	-	1	-	3	5	20	-
65 - 69	11	-	-	-	-	-	-	-	-	-	-	11	-
70 +	22	-	-	-	-	-	-	-	-	-	1	21	-
Guatemala 2011 (C)													
Total	78 286	17	9 779	27 197	18 081	9 430	4 619	2 550	1 635	1 375	1 126	2 362	115
0 - 14	1 122	4	513	458	109	31	5	1	1	-	-	-	-
15 - 19	22 191	12	6 733	11 231	3 124	788	191	52	27	9	6	6	12
20 - 24	25 037	1	2 199	12 176	7 600	2 137	592	162	69	39	16	25	21
25 - 29	13 633	-	267	2 705	5 632	3 393	1 009	338	135	61	39	42	12
30 - 34	6 599	-	46	494	1 284	2 336	1 504	497	192	115	64	63	4
35 - 39	3 263	-	11	83	240	588	933	780	283	165	77	96	7
40 - 44	1 869	-	2	19	49	112	266	504	401	255	116	144	1
45 - 49	1 436	-	1	8	17	31	78	156	373	379	184	205	4
50 - 54	1 094	-	-	1	6	8	26	41	107	260	335	306	4
55 - 59	760	-	-	-	1	-	8	13	32	70	225	410	1
60 - 64	511	-	-	2	-	-	1	2	8	15	44	438	1
65 - 69	332	-	1	-	1	1	-	2	2	3	14	308	-
70 - 74	183	-	-	-	-	-	-	-	-	2	2	178	1
75 +	139	-	-	-	-	-	-	-	-	1	1	137	-
Unknown - Inconnu	117	-	6	20	18	5	6	2	5	1	3	4	47
Jamaica - Jamaïque 2006 (+C)													
Total	23 181	-	70	2 153	5 477	4 987	3 749	2 672	1 676	1 032	568	797	-
0 - 14	-	-	-	-	-	-	-	-	-	-	-	-	-
15 - 19	368	-	31	168	89	35	23	11	6	1	1	3	-
20 - 24	3 726	-	22	1 251	1 579	531	195	86	31	19	4	8	-
25 - 29	6 263	-	11	501	2 670	1 870	742	277	108	43	15	26	-
30 - 34	4 635	-	4	136	715	1 660	1 242	525	199	86	41	27	-
35 - 39	3 194	-	1	62	266	571	940	765	360	123	55	51	-
40 - 44	2 190	-	1	18	105	221	402	635	440	202	102	64	-
45 - 49	1 452	-	-	15	35	75	147	273	364	292	133	118	-
50 - 54	708	-	-	1	15	18	39	63	122	200	105	145	-
55 - 59	327	-	-	1	-	5	17	24	28	45	71	136	-
60 - 64	179	-	-	-	2	1	1	10	15	15	27	108	-
65 - 69	84	-	-	-	1	-	-	2	1	4	10	66	-
70 - 74	35	-	-	-	-	-	-	1	2	1	3	28	-
75 +	20	-	-	-	-	-	1	-	-	1	1	17	-
Martinique 2007 (C)													
Total	1 341	-	19	128	297	284	185	155	117	63	32	61	-
0 - 14	-	-	-	-	-	-	-	-	-	-	-	-	-
15 - 19	55	-	11	35	8	1	-	-	-	-	-	-	-
20 - 24	217	-	4	63	108	25	13	4	-	-	-	-	-
25 - 29	273	-	3	20	123	99	16	7	1	4	-	-	-
30 - 34	243	-	1	4	38	97	65	24	11	2	1	-	-
35 - 39	173	-	-	4	12	42	54	49	9	3	-	-	-
40 - 44	146	-	-	1	3	11	26	47	45	10	3	-	-
45 - 49	84	-	-	1	3	6	6	19	29	14	5	1	-
50 - 54	53	-	-	-	2	3	3	3	15	11	10	6	-
55 - 59	31	-	-	-	-	-	1	-	7	12	3	8	-
60 - 64	24	-	-	-	-	-	-	1	-	4	8	11	-
65 - 69	12	-	-	-	-	1	-	-	-	2	-	9	-

23. Marriages by age of groom and by age of bride: latest available year, 2003 - 2012
Mariages selon l'âge de l'époux et selon l'âge de l'épouse : dernière année disponible, 2003 - 2012 (continued - suite)

Continent, country or area, year, code and age of bride / Continent, pays ou zone, date, code et âge de l'épouse	Age of groom - âge de l'époux												
	Total	0-14	15-19	20-24	25-29	30-34	35-39	40-44	45-49	50-54	55-59	60+	Unknown Inconnu
AMERICA, NORTH - AMÉRIQUE DU NORD													
Martinique													
2007													
70 - 74	16	-	-	-	-	-	-	1	-	1	2	12	-
75 +	14	-	-	-	-	-	-	-	-	-	-	14	-
Mexico - Mexique													
2011 (+C)													
Total	570 152	81	52 632	168 077	152 706	83 789	42 423	22 403	13 960	9 869	7 203	16 329	680
0 - 14	2 443	18	1 343	777	203	66	24	9	1	1	-	1	-
15 - 19	121 304	40	38 792	59 716	16 795	4 193	1 142	367	122	54	29	36	18
20 - 24	175 992	14	11 104	85 558	57 089	15 670	4 325	1 331	469	202	91	125	14
25 - 29	129 629	1	1 089	18 128	62 759	32 738	9 929	2 997	1 098	438	204	232	16
30 - 34	60 852	2	220	3 003	12 556	23 354	13 296	4 849	1 870	895	376	423	8
35 - 39	31 093	2	39	638	2 505	5 904	9 907	6 262	2 868	1 505	699	756	8
40 - 44	17 161	1	17	128	534	1 366	2 736	4 557	3 485	1 982	1 061	1 292	2
45 - 49	11 356	2	6	43	135	340	763	1 485	2 812	2 411	1 447	1 912	-
50 - 54	7 626	1	3	15	31	74	209	407	891	1 700	1 710	2 580	5
55 - 59	5 213	-	1	10	13	22	40	75	233	470	1 147	3 199	3
60 - 64	3 143	-	1	6	6	8	13	32	70	144	305	2 558	-
65 - 69	1 791	-	-	2	3	4	2	12	21	34	97	1 616	-
70 - 74	960	-	1	-	1	-	1	4	6	10	23	914	-
75 +	707	-	1	3	2	6	2	-	4	8	7	673	1
Unknown - Inconnu	882	-	15	50	74	44	34	16	10	15	7	12	605
Montserrat													
2011 (+...)													
Total	19	-	-	1	3	5	6	1	1	1	-	1	...
0 - 14	-	-	-	-	-	-	-	-	-	-	-	-	...
15 - 19	-	-	-	-	-	-	-	-	-	-	-	-	...
20 - 24	2	-	-	1	1	-	-	-	-	-	-	-	...
25 - 29	4	-	-	-	1	2	1	-	-	-	-	-	...
30 - 34	2	-	-	-	1	-	1	-	-	-	-	-	...
35 - 39	4	-	-	-	-	2	2	-	-	-	-	-	...
40 - 44	1	-	-	-	-	-	1	-	-	-	-	-	...
45 - 49	2	-	-	-	-	-	-	1	-	1	-	-	...
50 - 54	2	-	-	-	-	1	1	-	-	-	-	-	...
55 - 59	2	-	-	-	-	-	-	-	1	-	-	1	...
60 - 64	-	-	-	-	-	-	-	-	-	-	-	-	...
65 - 69	-	-	-	-	-	-	-	-	-	-	-	-	...
70 - 74	-	-	-	-	-	-	-	-	-	-	-	-	...
75 +	-	-	-	-	-	-	-	-	-	-	-	-	...
Panama[7]													
2010 (C)													
Total	12 981	-	75	1 552	2 974	2 611	1 715	2 070[m]	...	969[n]	...	841	174
0 - 14	7	-	1	4	-	1	-	1[m]	...	-[n]	...	-	-
15 - 19	470	-	21	219	122	46	20	24[m]	...	5[n]	...	-	13
20 - 24	2 551	-	40	791	937	412	174	131[m]	...	29[n]	...	16	21
25 - 29	3 507	-	8	445	1 422	943	350	230[m]	...	36[n]	...	20	53
30 - 34	2 312	-	1	59	396	816	565	341[m]	...	84[n]	...	20	30
35 - 39	1 295	-	-	31	56	228	338	479[m]	...	104[n]	...	39	20
40 - 49	1 525	-	-	-	-	122	165	681[m]	...	375[n]	...	161	21
50 - 59	698	-	-	-	-	11	19	115[m]	...	250[n]	...	294	9
60 - 69	259	-	-	-	-	-	4	8[m]	...	37[n]	...	209	1
70 +	64	-	-	-	-	-	-	-[m]	...	3[n]	...	61	-
Unknown - Inconnu	293	-	4	3	41	32	80	60[m]	...	46[n]	...	21	6
Puerto Rico - Porto Rico													
2008 (C)													
Total	18 620	-	734	3 690	4 638	2 960	1 933	1 287	999	732	1 646[s]	...	1
0 - 14	27	-	14	12	1	-	-	-	-	-	-[s]	...	-
15 - 19	1 820	-	535	947	249	61	19	9	-	-	-[s]	...	-
20 - 24	4 360	-	154	2 074	1 516	404	140	41	18	10	2[s]	...	1
25 - 29	4 484	-	27	512	2 194	1 120	413	133	50	17	18[s]	...	-
30 - 34	2 589	-	4	113	515	929	587	262	106	42	31[s]	...	-
35 - 39	1 649	-	-	20	111	313	513	348	188	85	71[s]	...	-
40 - 44	1 136	-	-	6	38	86	175	266	251	149	165[s]	...	-
45 - 49	945	-	-	5	10	32	61	160	259	193	225[s]	...	-
50 - 54	626	-	-	1	2	8	22	50	92	151	300[s]	...	-
55 +	984	-	-	-	2	7	3	18	35	85	834[s]	...	-

23. Marriages by age of groom and by age of bride: latest available year, 2003 - 2012
Mariages selon l'âge de l'époux et selon l'âge de l'épouse : dernière année disponible, 2003 - 2012 (continued - suite)

Continent, country or area, year, code and age of bride / Continent, pays ou zone, date, code et âge de l'épouse	Total	0-14	15-19	20-24	25-29	30-34	35-39	40-44	45-49	50-54	55-59	60+	Unknown Inconnu
AMERICA, NORTH - AMÉRIQUE DU NORD													
Saint Lucia - Sainte-Lucie													
2003* (C)													
Total	489	-	1	31	114	103	95	61	34	18	9	23	-
0 - 14	-	-	-	-	-	-	-	-	-	-	-	-	-
15 - 19	8	-	-	6	2	-	-	-	-	-	-	-	-
20 - 24	84	-	1	17	41	17	7	1	-	-	-	-	-
25 - 29	128	-	-	8	41	47	23	4	3	1	-	1	-
30 - 34	102	-	-	-	23	30	30	11	5	2	1	-	-
35 - 39	71	-	-	-	4	6	26	22	8	5	-	-	-
40 - 44	41	-	-	-	2	1	7	16	10	2	2	1	-
45 - 49	23	-	-	-	1	-	2	3	7	5	2	3	-
50 - 54	13	-	-	-	-	2	-	3	1	2	1	4	-
55 - 59	8	-	-	-	-	-	-	-	-	1	1	6	-
60 - 64	4	-	-	-	-	-	-	-	-	-	1	3	-
65 +	7	-	-	-	-	-	-	1	-	-	1	5	-
Saint Vincent and the Grenadines - Saint-Vincent-et-les Grenadines													
2009 (+C)													
Total	573	...	...	...	...	...	...	...	...	...	...	...	...
0 - 14	-	...	...	...	...	...	...	...	...	...	...	...	...
15 - 19	3	...	...	...	...	...	...	...	...	...	...	...	...
20 - 24	48	...	...	...	...	...	...	...	...	...	...	...	...
25 - 29	134	...	...	...	...	...	...	...	...	...	...	...	...
30 - 34	120	...	...	...	...	...	...	...	...	...	...	...	...
35 - 39	84	...	...	...	...	...	...	...	...	...	...	...	...
40 - 44	59	...	...	...	...	...	...	...	...	...	...	...	...
45 - 49	48	...	...	...	...	...	...	...	...	...	...	...	...
50 - 54	28	...	...	...	...	...	...	...	...	...	...	...	...
55 - 59	16	...	...	...	...	...	...	...	...	...	...	...	...
60 - 64	15	...	...	...	...	...	...	...	...	...	...	...	...
65 +	8	...	...	...	...	...	...	...	...	...	...	...	...
Unknown - Inconnu	10	...	...	...	...	...	...	...	...	...	...	...	...
Trinidad and Tobago - Trinité-et-Tobago													
2005 (C)													
Total	8 144	-	122	1 350	2 247	1 591	927	703	458	297	180	269	-
0 - 14	3	-	1	-	1	1	-	-	-	-	-	-	-
15 - 19	623	-	72	300	178	50	14	7	1	-	-	1	-
20 - 24	2 285	-	39	794	907	355	120	43	16	7	2	2	-
25 - 29	2 127	-	9	197	911	629	234	89	36	12	7	3	-
30 - 34	1 177	-	-	38	186	376	288	179	62	21	11	16	-
35 - 39	716	-	-	15	45	125	189	187	90	36	16	13	-
40 - 44	503	-	1	4	15	45	61	130	131	58	32	26	-
45 - 49	330	-	-	-	2	8	10	49	90	80	39	52	-
50 - 54	188	-	-	2	1	2	6	10	24	59	44	40	-
55 - 59	92	-	-	-	-	-	1	6	5	19	15	46	-
60 - 64	56	-	-	-	-	-	3	3	2	5	10	33	-
65 +	43	-	-	-	-	-	1	-	1	-	4	37	-
Unknown - Inconnu	1	-	-	-	1	-	-	-	-	-	-	-	-
Turks and Caicos Islands - Îles Turques et Caïques													
2005 (C)													
Total	489	-	-	19	88	149	95	69	34	20	6	8	1
0 - 14	-	-	-	-	-	-	-	-	-	-	-	-	-
15 - 19	3	-	-	1	1	1	-	-	-	-	-	-	-
20 - 24	40	-	-	12	18	8	1	1	-	-	-	-	-
25 - 29	120	-	-	4	45	48	14	5	2	1	-	1	-
30 - 34	142	-	-	2	19	69	31	13	5	3	-	-	-
35 - 39	103	-	-	-	5	18	37	28	9	5	1	-	-
40 - 44	37	-	-	-	-	1	9	15	7	2	1	2	-
45 - 49	31	-	-	-	-	4	3	5	7	7	4	1	-
50 - 54	8	-	-	-	-	-	-	2	2	2	-	2	-
55 - 59	3	-	-	-	-	-	-	-	1	-	-	2	-
60 - 64	1	-	-	-	-	-	-	-	1	-	-	-	-

23. Marriages by age of groom and by age of bride: latest available year, 2003 - 2012
Mariages selon l'âge de l'époux et selon l'âge de l'épouse : dernière année disponible, 2003 - 2012 (continued - suite)

Continent, country or area, year, code and age of bride / Continent, pays ou zone, date, code et âge de l'épouse	Total	0-14	15-19	20-24	25-29	30-34	35-39	40-44	45-49	50-54	55-59	60+	Unknown Inconnu
AMERICA, NORTH - AMÉRIQUE DU NORD													
Turks and Caicos Islands - Îles Turques et Caïques													
2005													
65 +	-	-	-	-	-	-	-	-	-	-	-	-	-
Unknown - Inconnu	1	-	-	-	-	-	-	-	-	-	-	-	1
2008 (C)													
Total	486	...	-	20	110	114	94	63	51	17	10	7	-
15 - 19	2	...	...	...	...	...	...	...	...	...	...	...	...
20 - 24	47	...	...	...	...	...	...	...	...	...	...	...	...
25 - 29	134	...	...	...	...	...	...	...	...	...	...	...	...
30 - 34	127	...	...	...	...	...	...	...	...	...	...	...	...
35 - 39	94	...	...	...	...	...	...	...	...	...	...	...	...
40 - 44	37	...	...	...	...	...	...	...	...	...	...	...	...
45 - 49	26	...	...	...	...	...	...	...	...	...	...	...	...
50 - 54	12	...	...	...	...	...	...	...	...	...	...	...	...
55 - 59	6	...	...	...	...	...	...	...	...	...	...	...	...
60 - 64	-	...	...	...	...	...	...	...	...	...	...	...	...
65 +	1	...	...	...	...	...	...	...	...	...	...	...	...
Unknown - Inconnu	-	...	...	...	...	...	...	...	...	...	...	...	...
AMERICA, SOUTH - AMÉRIQUE DU SUD													
Brazil - Brésil													
2011 (U)													
Total	1026736	42	30 080	214 598	284 470	196 327	107 569	65 892	44 003	29 063	20 023	34 047	622
0 - 14	438	10	138	166	71	28	8	5	8	1	-	3	-
15 - 19	131 178	14	19 211	69 708	30 264	8 344	2 393	741	284	113	45	57	4
20 - 24	260 618	5	8 110	99 376	101 540	35 467	10 009	3 551	1 457	583	248	267	5
25 - 29	257 197	3	1 837	32 906	107 183	74 233	25 237	8 893	3 903	1 564	739	694	5
30 - 34	159 743	7	524	8 880	33 719	54 494	34 600	14 982	6 748	3 131	1 395	1 254	9
35 - 39	85 379	1	166	2 443	8 201	16 478	22 503	17 322	9 184	4 528	2 281	2 271	1
40 - 44	52 221	1	54	746	2 401	4 957	8 474	12 276	10 376	6 070	3 251	3 614	1
45 - 49	34 659	-	23	216	735	1 624	3 041	5 377	7 617	6 463	4 292	5 269	2
50 - 54	21 060	1	6	79	226	477	919	1 888	2 997	4 240	4 137	6 089	1
55 - 59	11 530	-	2	28	71	119	250	579	984	1 567	2 449	5 480	1
60 - 64	6 166	-	4	6	21	46	76	178	307	539	792	4 196	1
65 +	5 926	-	5	36	35	51	55	99	138	264	394	4 849	...
Unknown - Inconnu	621	-	-	8	3	9	4	1	-	-	-	4	592
Chile - Chili													
2010 (+C)													
Total	60 362	-	759	8 605	17 040	12 783	7 234	3 956	2 799	2 104	1 594	3 488	...
0 - 14	-	-	-	-	-	-	-	-	-	-	-	-	...
15 - 19	2 709	-	415	1 478	581	156	51	21	5	2	-	-	...
20 - 24	12 721	-	288	5 063	5 174	1 549	468	119	39	12	8	1	...
25 - 29	18 168	-	43	1 656	8 784	5 367	1 677	422	141	50	15	13	...
30 - 34	10 331	-	8	316	1 990	4 248	2 384	844	334	122	51	34	...
35 - 39	5 583	-	3	69	399	1 085	1 815	1 159	583	253	107	110	...
40 - 44	3 296	-	2	10	87	284	571	786	697	406	231	222	...
45 - 49	2 755	-	-	12	22	78	209	400	599	561	396	478	...
50 - 54	1 964	-	-	-	3	15	47	149	260	426	386	678	...
55 - 59	1 233	-	-	-	-	-	11	33	98	174	251	666	...
60 - 64	798	-	-	1	-	-	1	14	30	68	104	580	...
65 - 69	427	-	-	-	-	-	-	7	7	20	31	362	...
70 - 74	229	-	-	-	-	-	-	2	4	8	12	203	...
75 +	148	-	-	-	-	1	-	-	2	2	2	141	...
Ecuador - Équateur[10]													
2010 (U)													
Total	74 800	12	5 890	20 849	20 366	11 757	5 769	3 414	2 247	1 505	971	1 926	94
0 - 14	578	5	263	217	56	27	7	2	-	-	1	-	-
15 - 19	14 673	4	4 029	7 385	2 374	629	164	50	17	12	-	4	5
20 - 24	23 210	2	1 335	10 244	8 173	2 452	671	203	72	29	11	14	4
25 - 29	16 769	-	211	2 356	7 475	4 547	1 410	431	185	62	41	41	10
30 - 34	8 413	-	33	449	1 704	3 060	1 865	777	282	135	58	46	4
35 - 39	4 207	1	10	114	395	726	1 141	952	503	191	80	89	5
40 - 44	2 502	-	3	26	82	187	346	668	601	300	139	149	1
45 - 49	1 703	-	-	12	40	71	116	220	411	399	205	228	1

584

23. Marriages by age of groom and by age of bride: latest available year, 2003 - 2012
Mariages selon l'âge de l'époux et selon l'âge de l'épouse : dernière année disponible, 2003 - 2012 (continued - suite)

Continent, country or area, year, code and age of bride / Continent, pays ou zone, date, code et âge de l'épouse	Total	0-14	15-19	20-24	25-29	30-34	35-39	40-44	45-49	50-54	55-59	60+	Unknown Inconnu
AMERICA, SOUTH - AMÉRIQUE DU SUD													
Ecuador - Équateur[10]													
2010													
50 - 54	998	-	1	4	12	19	23	72	121	263	237	245	1
55 - 59	613	-	1	2	4	3	12	18	40	77	141	315	-
60 - 64	376	-	-	-	2	1	1	5	8	21	35	303	-
65 - 69	264	-	-	-	1	1	1	3	2	7	13	235	1
70 +	282	-	1	5	4	2	-	2	1	5	7	255	1
Unknown - Inconnu	212	-	3	35	44	32	12	11	4	4	3	2	62
French Guiana - Guyane française													
2007 (C)													
Total	667	...	5	48	123	150	108	79	47	48	26	33	-
15 - 19	30	...	-	10	13	4	-	1	1	-	1	-	-
20 - 24	93	...	3	22	33	15	8	7	-	1	2	2	-
25 - 29	151	...	1	5	51	57	17	7	5	2	6	-	-
30 - 34	135	...	1	8	16	41	35	18	7	7	2	-	-
35 - 39	98	...	-	3	6	20	27	20	11	2	6	3	-
40 - 44	62	...	-	-	4	7	10	15	10	9	2	5	-
45 - 49	55	...	-	-	-	3	5	9	10	16	4	8	-
50 - 54	23	...	-	-	-	2	4	2	3	6	2	4	-
55 - 59	13	...	-	-	-	1	2	-	-	3	1	6	-
60 - 64	2	...	-	-	-	-	-	-	-	1	-	1	-
65 - 69	4	...	-	-	-	-	-	-	-	1	-	3	-
70 - 74	1	...	-	-	-	-	-	-	-	-	-	1	-
75 - 79	-	...	-	-	-	-	-	-	-	-	-	-	-
80 - 84	-	...	-	-	-	-	-	-	-	-	-	-	-
85 +	-	...	-	-	-	-	-	-	-	-	-	-	-
Paraguay													
2008 (U)													
Total	18 832	-	583	5 084	6 143	3 229	1 516	826	516	337	212	376	10
0 - 14	9	-	2	4	3	-	-	-	-	-	-	-	-
15 - 19	3 668	-	391	1 879	999	276	77	27	11	4	2	2	-
20 - 24	5 912	-	158	2 340	2 336	736	207	79	26	19	5	6	-
25 - 29	4 722	-	21	691	2 194	1 219	367	112	60	31	13	14	-
30 - 34	2 075	-	6	112	460	729	404	222	83	33	13	12	1
35 - 39	1 009	-	4	28	102	182	317	195	89	45	21	25	1
40 - 44	560	-	1	16	30	52	95	118	128	60	36	24	-
45 - 49	345	-	-	6	13	17	30	49	79	74	36	41	-
50 - 54	205	-	-	1	2	8	12	18	25	40	46	53	-
55 - 59	135	-	-	2	2	4	2	2	10	18	27	68	-
60 - 64	69	-	-	1	-	2	3	2	2	10	7	42	-
65 - 69	41	-	-	-	-	1	1	-	1	2	3	32	1
70 - 74	32	-	-	-	-	-	1	1	2	1	2	25	1
75 +	33	-	-	-	-	-	-	-	-	-	1	32	-
Unknown - Inconnu	17	-	-	4	2	3	-	1	-	-	-	-	7
Peru - Pérou[11,12]													
2010 (+C)													
Total	25 907	-	239	2 913	6 562	6 610	3 921	2 227	1 224	2 211[r]	...	...	...
0 - 14	6	-	5	-	-	-	-	1	-	-[r]	...	...	...
15 - 19	939	-	136	491	191	74	31	9	3	4[r]	...	...	...
20 - 24	4 805	-	82	1 694	1 880	766	254	86	21	22[r]	...	...	...
25 - 29	7 793	-	11	529	3 342	2 576	894	264	86	91[r]	...	...	...
30 - 34	5 669	-	4	134	900	2 445	1 346	538	180	122[r]	...	...	...
35 - 39	2 976	-	-	34	168	551	1 051	685	286	201[r]	...	...	...
40 - 44	1 520	-	-	9	39	116	248	459	328	321[r]	...	...	...
45 - 49	864	-	-	1	9	27	65	127	234	401[r]	...	...	...
50 +	1 335	-	1	21	33	55	32	58	86	1 049[r]	...	...	...
Venezuela (Bolivarian Republic of) - Venezuela (République bolivarienne du)[13]													
2011 (C)													
Total	103 004	56	3 163	20 727	29 040	20 127	11 423	7 083	4 441	2 698	1 692	2 554	...
0 - 14	299	3	80	125	48	22	9	6	2	1	1	2	...
15 - 19	11 549	14	2 046	5 828	2 456	784	247	95	34	17	5	23	...
20 - 24	26 604	20	748	10 475	10 087	3 556	1 071	366	159	55	26	41	...
25 - 29	27 226	8	188	3 185	11 916	7 545	2 731	978	387	153	56	79	...

23. Marriages by age of groom and by age of bride: latest available year, 2003 - 2012
Mariages selon l'âge de l'époux et selon l'âge de l'épouse : dernière année disponible, 2003 - 2012 (continued - suite)

Continent, country or area, year, code and age of bride / Continent, pays ou zone, date, code et âge de l'épouse	Total	0-14	15-19	20-24	25-29	30-34	35-39	40-44	45-49	50-54	55-59	60+	Unknown Inconnu
AMERICA, SOUTH - AMÉRIQUE DU SUD													
Venezuela (Bolivarian Republic of) - Venezuela (République bolivarienne du)[13]													
2011													
30 - 34	16 183	5	56	771	3 335	5 715	3 492	1 610	692	268	136	103	...
35 - 39	8 668	-	20	211	781	1 679	2 539	1 876	851	395	158	158	...
40 - 44	5 315	2	8	74	260	563	911	1 420	1 073	524	271	209	...
45 - 49	3 210	3	4	30	91	174	285	501	800	654	356	312	...
50 - 54	1 809	1	3	5	24	49	92	156	303	412	343	421	...
55 - 59	1 052	-	5	5	13	12	25	41	92	146	232	481	...
60 +	1 089	-	5	18	29	28	21	34	48	73	108	725	...
ASIA - ASIE													
Armenia - Arménie													
2009 (+C)													
Total	18 773	...	153	4 608	7 796	3 482	1 313	560	325	208	132	196	-
15 - 19	2 010	...	122	928	825	124	11	-	-	-	-	-	-
20 - 24	9 521	...	28	3 366	4 655	1 278	170	19	2	3	-	-	-
25 - 29	4 516	...	2	282	2 151	1 474	478	95	27	7	-	-	-
30 - 34	1 467	...	-	26	130	539	455	215	76	17	9	-	-
35 - 39	528	...	-	4	20	47	165	154	92	32	10	4	-
40 - 44	238	...	-	2	8	13	22	52	72	42	16	11	-
45 - 49	161	...	1	-	2	4	6	14	39	53	20	22	-
50 - 54	153	...	-	-	4	3	4	8	8	45	47	34	-
55 - 59	101	...	-	-	-	-	1	2	4	5	25	64	-
60 +	78	...	-	-	1	-	1	1	5	4	5	61	-
Azerbaijan - Azerbaïdjan													
2009 (+C)													
Total	78 072	...	950	26 010	28 589	12 723	4 899	2 266	1 107	603	364	561	-
15 - 19	20 753	...	642	10 257	7 780	1 797	216	43	13	1	2	2	-
20 - 24	35 222	...	267	13 852	14 624	5 203	1 039	177	33	10	9	8	-
25 - 29	12 668	...	30	1 590	5 320	3 668	1 509	405	108	21	8	9	-
30 - 34	4 954	...	4	225	704	1 645	1 327	694	247	69	22	17	-
35 - 39	2 034	...	5	46	104	285	597	551	252	111	48	35	-
40 - 44	1 260	...	-	20	44	98	174	312	260	168	88	96	-
45 - 49	691	...	2	11	4	18	30	69	151	152	91	163	-
50 - 54	307	...	-	-	7	6	6	15	36	51	71	115	-
55 - 59	97	...	-	3	1	1	1	-	5	17	20	49	-
60 +	86	...	-	6	1	2	-	-	2	3	5	67	-
2010 (+C)													
Total	79 172	-	857	26 434	29 773	12 524	4 607	2 317	1 097	638	378	547	-
0 - 14	-	...	...	...	...	...	...	...	...	...	...	...	...
15 - 19	20 657	...	...	...	...	...	...	...	...	...	...	...	...
20 - 24	36 217	...	...	...	...	...	...	...	...	...	...	...	...
25 - 29	13 008	...	...	...	...	...	...	...	...	...	...	...	...
30 - 34	4 875	...	...	...	...	...	...	...	...	...	...	...	...
35 - 39	1 996	...	...	...	...	...	...	...	...	...	...	...	...
40 - 44	1 165	...	...	...	...	...	...	...	...	...	...	...	...
45 - 49	718	...	...	...	...	...	...	...	...	...	...	...	...
50 - 54	305	...	...	...	...	...	...	...	...	...	...	...	...
55 - 59	121	...	...	...	...	...	...	...	...	...	...	...	...
60 +	110	...	...	...	...	...	...	...	...	...	...	...	...
Bahrain - Bahreïn													
2010 (...)													
Total	4 960	-	130	1 735	1 752	619	268	190	99	159ʳ	...	...	8
0 - 14	13	-	4	7	1	1	-	-	-	-ʳ	...	...	-
15 - 19	1 146	-	100	661	340	34	6	3	1	-ʳ	...	...	1
20 - 24	2 176	-	23	954	957	171	47	11	5	7ʳ	...	...	1
25 - 29	871	-	2	86	387	260	75	36	9	15ʳ	...	...	1
30 - 34	364	-	1	15	45	114	83	64	24	18ʳ	...	...	-
35 - 39	170	-	-	4	13	24	34	40	23	32ʳ	...	...	-
40 - 44	107	-	-	1	3	10	15	22	23	31ʳ	...	...	2
45 - 49	56	-	-	1	2	3	4	10	8	28ʳ	...	...	-

23. Marriages by age of groom and by age of bride: latest available year, 2003 - 2012
Mariages selon l'âge de l'époux et selon l'âge de l'épouse : dernière année disponible, 2003 - 2012 (continued - suite)

Continent, country or area, year, code and age of bride / Continent, pays ou zone, date, code et âge de l'épouse	Total	0-14	15-19	20-24	25-29	30-34	35-39	40-44	45-49	50-54	55-59	60+	Unknown Inconnu
ASIA - ASIE													
Bahrain - Bahreïn													
2010													
50 +	38	-	-	-	1	2	2	2	4	27ʳ	...	...	-
Unknown - Inconnu	19	-	-	6	3	-	2	2	2	1ʳ	...	...	3
Brunei Darussalam - Brunéi Darussalam													
2008 (...)													
Total	2 391	-	68	527	870	534	177	73	53	40	23	26	-
0 - 14	6	...	...	...	...	...	...	...	...	...	...	...	...
15 - 19	205	...	...	...	...	...	...	...	...	...	...	...	...
20 - 24	701	...	...	...	...	...	...	...	...	...	...	...	...
25 - 29	954	...	...	...	...	...	...	...	...	...	...	...	...
30 - 34	403	...	...	...	...	...	...	...	...	...	...	...	...
35 - 39	66	...	...	...	...	...	...	...	...	...	...	...	...
40 - 44	37	...	...	...	...	...	...	...	...	...	...	...	...
45 - 49	15	...	...	...	...	...	...	...	...	...	...	...	...
50 - 54	3	...	...	...	...	...	...	...	...	...	...	...	...
55 - 59	1	...	...	...	...	...	...	...	...	...	...	...	...
60 - 64	-	...	...	...	...	...	...	...	...	...	...	...	...
65 - 69	-	...	...	...	...	...	...	...	...	...	...	...	...
70 - 74	-	...	...	...	...	...	...	...	...	...	...	...	...
75 +	-	...	...	...	...	...	...	...	...	...	...	...	...
Unknown - Inconnu	-	...	...	...	...	...	...	...	...	...	...	...	...
China, Hong Kong SAR - Chine, Hong Kong RAS													
2011 (C)													
Total	58 369	...	174ᵍ	4 081	14 202	15 890	8 964	5 017	3 628	2 585	1 649	2 179	...
16 - 19	696	...	78ᵍ	336	171	54	28	17	6	2	3	1	...
20 - 24	8 686	...	77ᵍ	2 862	3 092	1 340	677	334	165	80	38	21	...
25 - 29	20 253	...	16ᵍ	680	8 952	6 428	2 183	946	574	280	128	66	...
30 - 34	14 911	...	3ᵍ	138	1 664	6 864	3 297	1 355	748	441	226	175	...
35 - 39	7 056	...	-ᵍ	45	220	967	2 189	1 323	912	670	385	345	...
40 - 44	3 462	...	-ᵍ	14	71	173	443	772	670	513	350	456	...
45 - 49	1 768	...	-ᵍ	5	22	40	113	199	396	364	241	388	...
50 - 54	776	...	-ᵍ	1	6	16	22	52	118	167	149	245	...
55 - 59	396	...	-ᵍ	-	3	7	12	13	28	57	92	184	...
60 - 64	166	...	-ᵍ	-	1	1	-	2	10	7	26	119	...
65 - 69	75	...	-ᵍ	-	-	-	-	3	1	1	10	60	...
70 - 74	60	...	-ᵍ	-	-	-	-	1	-	3	-	56	...
75 +	64	...	-ᵍ	-	-	-	-	-	-	-	1	63	...
China, Macao SAR - Chine, Macao RAS													
2009 (+C)													
Total	3 035	-	18	608	1 023	697	286	157	98	68	39	41	-
0 - 14	-	-	-	-	-	-	-	-	-	-	-	-	-
15 - 19	66	-	5	40	17	3	1	-	-	-	-	-	-
20 - 24	993	-	12	445	353	125	36	14	5	3	-	-	-
25 - 29	1 166	-	1	109	575	313	94	42	13	11	7	1	-
30 - 34	444	-	-	10	62	212	83	33	25	12	5	2	-
35 - 39	195	-	-	4	9	30	62	41	26	8	8	7	-
40 - 44	72	-	-	-	5	8	9	17	12	9	6	6	-
45 - 49	58	-	-	-	1	4	1	7	16	14	8	7	-
50 - 54	20	-	-	-	1	2	-	3	1	9	2	2	-
55 - 59	11	-	-	-	-	-	-	-	-	1	2	8	-
60 - 64	4	-	-	-	-	-	-	-	-	1	1	2	-
65 - 69	1	-	-	-	-	-	-	-	-	-	-	1	-
70 +	5	-	-	-	-	-	-	-	-	-	-	5	-
2012 (+C)													
Total	3 783	...	...	575ᶠ	...	...	...	...	397�q	...	...	...	...
0 - 24	1 023	...	...	...	...	...	...	...	...	...	...	...	...
25 - 34	2 229	...	...	...	...	...	...	...	...	...	...	...	...
35 - 44	371	...	...	...	...	...	...	...	...	...	...	...	...
45 +	160	...	...	...	...	...	...	...	...	...	...	...	...

Continent, country or area, year, code and age of bride / Continent, pays ou zone, date, code et âge de l'épouse	Age of groom - âge de l'époux												
	Total	0-14	15-19	20-24	25-29	30-34	35-39	40-44	45-49	50-54	55-59	60+	Unknown Inconnu
ASIA - ASIE													
Cyprus - Chypre													
2006[14],[15] (C)													
Total	4 887	...	13	645	1 813	1 117	559	302	151	97	70	117	3
15 - 19	131	...	7	84	31	7	2	-	-	-	-	-	-
20 - 24	1 302	...	4	449	627	145	42	23	7	4	1	-	-
25 - 29	1 931	...	-	83	985	573	178	71	21	10	7	3	-
30 - 34	838	...	2	21	134	319	214	93	29	15	4	7	-
35 - 39	313	...	-	5	24	50	91	60	42	16	7	18	-
40 - 44	155	...	-	3	10	14	23	36	23	18	14	14	-
45 - 49	107	...	-	-	2	6	9	17	24	15	13	21	-
50 - 54	54	...	-	-	-	3	-	1	3	15	14	18	-
55 - 59	31	...	-	-	-	-	-	1	2	4	8	16	-
60 - 64	13	...	-	-	-	-	-	-	-	-	1	12	-
65 - 69	6	...	-	-	-	-	-	-	-	-	1	5	-
70 - 74	2	...	-	-	-	-	-	-	-	-	-	2	-
75 - 79	1	...	-	-	-	-	-	-	-	-	-	1	-
80 +	-	...	-	-	-	-	-	-	-	-	-	-	-
Unknown - Inconnu	3	...	-	-	-	-	-	-	-	-	-	-	3
Georgia - Géorgie[7]													
2011 (C)													
Total	30 863	...	1 013[9]	7 972	8 522	5 705	3 513	1 915	1 047	534	285	353	4
16 - 19	4 554	...	...	...	...	...	...	...	...	...	...	...	...
20 - 24	10 875	...	...	...	...	...	...	...	...	...	...	...	...
25 - 29	7 155	...	...	...	...	...	...	...	...	...	...	...	...
30 - 34	4 052	...	...	...	...	...	...	...	...	...	...	...	...
35 - 39	2 053	...	...	...	...	...	...	...	...	...	...	...	...
40 - 44	1 040	...	...	...	...	...	...	...	...	...	...	...	...
45 - 49	567	...	...	...	...	...	...	...	...	...	...	...	...
50 - 54	280	...	...	...	...	...	...	...	...	...	...	...	...
55 - 59	145	...	...	...	...	...	...	...	...	...	...	...	...
60 +	142	...	...	...	...	...	...	...	...	...	...	...	...
Unknown - Inconnu	-	...	...	...	...	...	...	...	...	...	...	...	...
Iran (Islamic Republic of) - Iran (République islamique d')[16]													
2011 (+C)													
Total	874 792	39 831	281 747	302 991	157 519	51 587	18 736	8 816	5 054	3 240	1 897	2 660	714
15 - 19	48 144	7 440	30 404	8 329	1 535	304	75	24	13	3	1	10	6
20 - 24	340 400	23 612	160 108	127 786	24 155	3 665	671	164	54	42	16	73	54
25 - 29	311 973	7 619	79 344	131 627	78 474	12 339	1 847	421	129	46	20	63	44
30 - 34	98 393	804	9 785	28 837	38 242	16 856	3 126	559	106	27	10	25	16
35 - 39	29 653	186	1 248	4 184	9 669	9 423	3 907	835	146	24	13	11	7
40 - 44	14 061	80	387	1 173	3 017	4 422	3 190	1 319	361	78	16	14	4
45 - 49	8 379	36	177	437	1 111	1 991	2 203	1 466	708	180	41	25	4
50 - 54	6 446	17	97	242	546	1 060	1 389	1 285	1 027	548	181	53	1
55 - 59	4 674	6	47	97	278	594	859	946	808	671	276	92	-
60 - 64	3 253	7	27	68	156	296	536	639	531	484	293	213	3
65 - 69	2 467	4	25	51	99	210	340	427	400	327	297	286	1
70 - 74	2 440	10	28	53	82	184	292	347	345	323	282	493	1
75 +	3 723	5	47	76	121	201	277	365	411	480	450	1 288	2
Unknown - Inconnu	786	5	23	31	34	42	24	19	15	7	1	14	571
Israel - Israël[17]													
2010 (C)													
Total	47 855	...	1 743	11 711	17 471	9 631	3 134	1 241	665	415	292	498	1 054
15 - 19	7 233	...	1 243	3 657	1 693	303	30	4	2	3	-	-	298
20 - 24	16 870	...	440	7 302	6 708	1 704	262	48	9	3	-	1	393
25 - 29	14 590	...	6	490	8 128	4 682	885	160	44	14	1	1	179
30 - 34	5 074	...	1	33	686	2 506	1 210	384	96	36	14	9	99
35 - 39	1 728	...	1	5	65	287	595	411	196	74	22	25	47
40 - 44	617	...	-	-	4	18	67	157	170	98	44	40	19
45 - 49	359	...	-	-	-	2	10	33	104	91	53	56	10
50 - 54	281	...	-	-	1	1	2	10	16	62	88	96	5
55 - 59	158	...	-	-	-	-	-	2	1	13	42	97	3
60 - 64	79	...	-	-	-	1	-	-	-	-	7	71	-
65 - 69	27	...	-	-	-	-	-	-	-	-	1	26	-
70 - 74	21	...	-	-	-	-	-	-	-	-	-	20	1

23. Marriages by age of groom and by age of bride: latest available year, 2003 - 2012
Mariages selon l'âge de l'époux et selon l'âge de l'épouse : dernière année disponible, 2003 - 2012 (continued - suite)

Continent, country or area, year, code and age of bride / Continent, pays ou zone, date, code et âge de l'épouse	Total	0-14	15-19	20-24	25-29	30-34	35-39	40-44	45-49	50-54	55-59	60+	Unknown Inconnu
ASIA - ASIE													
Israel - Israël[17]													
2010													
75 +	20	...	-	-	-	-	-	-	-	-	-	20	-
Unknown - Inconnu	798	...	52	224	186	127	73	32	27	21	20	36	-
Japan - Japon[18]													
2011 (+C)													
Total	550 248	-	5 021	60 720	181 897	138 721	84 034	38 372	16 968	9 049	6 115	9 351	-
0 - 14	-	-	-	-	-	-	-	-	-	-	-	-	-
15 - 19	10 910	-	3 727	4 651	1 475	608	245	93	46	32	20	13	-
20 - 24	91 473	-	1 127	41 212	31 858	10 976	4 075	1 219	505	226	141	134	-
25 - 29	210 632	-	126	12 125	121 173	53 595	16 927	4 345	1 310	521	278	232	-
30 - 34	126 347	-	31	2 126	22 569	58 587	29 948	8 947	2 517	911	411	300	-
35 - 39	65 115	-	6	486	4 130	12 833	26 989	13 702	4 423	1 460	661	425	-
40 - 44	23 544	-	3	93	595	1 817	4 902	8 214	4 539	1 893	847	641	-
45 - 49	9 410	-	1	24	84	256	770	1 507	2 831	1 945	1 083	909	-
50 - 54	5 174	-	-	2	8	39	155	288	636	1 594	1 247	1 205	-
55 - 59	3 170	-	-	-	3	7	18	47	123	345	1 063	1 564	-
60 - 64	2 401	-	-	1	2	3	3	9	35	97	302	1 949	-
65 - 69	1 154	-	-	-	-	-	1	1	3	19	51	1 079	-
70 - 74	556	-	-	-	-	-	-	-	-	2	10	544	-
75 +	362	-	-	-	-	-	1	-	-	4	1	356	-
Unknown - Inconnu	-	-	-	-	-	-	-	-	-	-	-	-	-
Jordan - Jordanie													
2010[19] (+C)													
Total	62 107	...	16 151	25 559	12 760	4 002	1 795	1 151	437	252[r]	...	...	-
18 - 19	1 262	...	1 017	191	40	11	1	2	-	-[r]	...	...	-
20 - 24	14 272	...	6 768	6 453	835	139	42	20	7	8[r]	...	...	-
25 - 29	25 434	...	6 276	12 608	5 720	633	120	45	16	16[r]	...	...	-
30 - 34	11 523	...	1 603	4 782	3 679	1 153	197	70	25	14[r]	...	...	-
35 - 39	4 064	...	299	1 043	1 434	819	350	92	19	8[r]	...	...	-
40 - 44	2 365	...	99	321	681	647	358	217	35	7[r]	...	...	-
45 - 49	1 139	...	35	81	220	283	249	196	57	18[r]	...	...	-
50 - 54	639	...	14	37	73	152	169	121	53	20[r]	...	...	-
55 - 59	425	...	12	18	35	80	95	107	56	22[r]	...	...	-
60 - 64	318	...	11	7	21	40	66	97	39	37[r]	...	...	-
65 +	666	...	17	18	22	45	148	184	130	102[r]	...	...	-
Kazakhstan													
2008 (C)													
Total	135 280	120	3 870	50 022	44 135	18 895	8 267	4 159	2 485	1 427	851	1 048	1
0 - 14	1 691	39	409	982	225	30	4	1	1	-	-	-	-
15 - 19	17 070	53	2 113	10 510	3 670	618	78	17	7	1	2	1	-
20 - 24	68 159	27	1 242	34 207	25 518	5 809	1 047	217	68	16	7	-	1
25 - 29	26 297	1	90	3 755	12 348	7 129	2 144	588	168	50	16	8	-
30 - 34	11 205	-	13	459	1 969	4 251	2 790	1 100	422	133	49	19	-
35 - 39	5 092	-	1	81	325	873	1 743	1 222	541	195	61	50	-
40 - 44	2 363	-	2	21	55	151	362	732	609	243	120	68	-
45 - 49	1 545	-	-	4	19	29	81	231	480	405	167	129	-
50 - 54	880	-	-	1	5	4	15	43	137	293	221	161	-
55 - 59	498	-	-	2	-	1	3	6	42	72	162	210	-
60 +	480	-	-	-	1	-	-	2	10	19	46	402	-
Unknown - Inconnu	-	-	-	-	-	-	-	-	-	-	-	-	-
Kuwait - Koweït													
2011 (C)													
Total	19 860	...	547[e]	5 136	5 790	3 750	2 054	1 096	662	332	192	210	91
0 - 14	51	...	15[e]	22	11	-	1	-	-	-	1	-	1
15 - 19	3 118	...	402[e]	1 863	675	109	27	10	5	1	3	-	23
20 - 24	6 899	...	108[e]	2 825	2 798	846	195	54	28	5	4	4	32
25 - 29	4 826	...	13[e]	335	1 851	1 603	635	214	101	27	7	19	21
30 - 34	2 574	...	-[e]	39	320	906	704	319	152	60	41	27	6
35 - 39	1 224	...	1[e]	12	80	190	354	278	158	75	46	27	3
40 - 44	653	...	-[e]	6	26	66	107	157	131	77	38	44	1
45 - 49	275	...	-[e]	2	12	14	18	51	67	57	25	29	-
50 - 54	90	...	-[e]	-	1	2	6	5	16	21	19	20	-
55 - 59	52	...	-[e]	-	1	1	1	6	4	8	7	24	-
60 +	16	...	-[e]	-	-	-	-	-	-	-	-	15	1
Unknown - Inconnu	82	...	8[e]	32	15	13	6	2	-	1	1	1	3

23. Marriages by age of groom and by age of bride: latest available year, 2003 - 2012
Mariages selon l'âge de l'époux et selon l'âge de l'épouse : dernière année disponible, 2003 - 2012 (continued - suite)

Continent, country or area, year, code and age of bride / Continent, pays ou zone, date, code et âge de l'épouse	Total	0-14	15-19	20-24	25-29	30-34	35-39	40-44	45-49	50-54	55-59	60+	Unknown Inconnu
ASIA - ASIE													
Kyrgyzstan - Kirghizstan													
2011 (C)													
Total	56 509	-	983	19 895	20 892	7 268	3 378	1 758	1 019	600	348	368	...
0 - 14	-	-	-	-	-	-	-	-	-	-	-	-	...
15 - 19	11 307	-	779	7 016	3 191	269	30	10	8	3	-	1	...
20 - 24	28 007	-	187	12 048	12 854	2 469	357	65	17	6	3	1	...
25 - 29	9 527	-	15	751	4 464	3 001	982	232	55	16	7	4	...
30 - 34	3 704	-	-	73	316	1 299	1 255	502	178	57	14	10	...
35 - 39	1 944	-	2	7	60	189	651	613	263	100	35	24	...
40 - 44	918	-	-	-	6	33	83	288	273	123	75	37	...
45 - 49	564	-	-	-	1	7	17	40	182	171	75	71	...
50 - 54	306	-	-	-	-	-	3	8	38	103	81	73	...
55 - 59	130	-	-	-	-	-	-	-	5	14	50	61	...
60 - 64	66	-	-	-	-	-	-	-	-	5	8	53	...
65 - 69	12	-	-	-	-	-	-	-	-	2	-	10	...
70 - 74	18	-	-	-	-	1	-	-	-	-	-	17	...
75 +	6	-	-	-	-	-	-	-	-	-	-	6	...
Mongolia - Mongolie													
2009 (+C)													
Total	34 071	...	1 742[i]	15 582	10 852	4 219	1 057	369	147	103[r]	...	...	-
18 - 19	3 283	...	...	...	...	...	...	...	...	...	...	...	...
20 - 24	17 343	...	...	...	...	...	...	...	...	...	...	...	...
25 - 29	8 841	...	...	...	...	...	...	...	...	...	...	...	...
30 - 34	3 187	...	...	...	...	...	...	...	...	...	...	...	...
35 - 39	1 003	...	...	...	...	...	...	...	...	...	...	...	...
40 - 44	274	...	...	...	...	...	...	...	...	...	...	...	...
45 - 49	95	...	...	...	...	...	...	...	...	...	...	...	...
50 +	45	...	...	...	...	...	...	...	...	...	...	...	...
Philippines													
2007 (U)													
Total	490 054	...	15 312[e]	144 422	169 845	80 840	35 320	17 335	10 279	16 599[r]	...	...	102
0 - 19	69 052	...	8 734[e]	37 433	16 524	4 113	1 309	460	232	242[r]	...	...	5
20 - 24	186 012	...	5 726[e]	82 967	68 408	18 887	5 458	2 047	1 072	1 428[r]	...	...	19
25 - 29	136 584	...	700[e]	20 075	68 381	31 528	9 390	3 129	1 514	1 860[r]	...	...	7
30 - 34	52 437	...	110[e]	2 936	12 993	19 841	9 766	3 605	1 492	1 687[r]	...	...	7
35 - 39	22 507	...	27[e]	683	2 644	4 879	6 768	4 011	1 808	1 682[r]	...	...	5
40 - 44	8 081	...	5[e]	138	434	794	1 300	2 120	1 683	1 605[r]	...	...	2
45 - 49	5 985	...	3[e]	59	163	315	555	879	1 568	2 440[r]	...	...	3
50 +	6 562	...	5[e]	48	77	126	172	337	534	5 262[r]	...	...	1
Unknown - Inconnu	2 834	...	2[e]	83	221	357	602	747	376	393[r]	...	...	53
Qatar													
2011 (C)													
Total	3 293	...	35	841	1 235	601	262	160	80	38	23	17	...
15 - 19	412	...	20	224	136	25	6	1	-	-	-	-	...
20 - 24	1 325	...	13	518	616	155	15	4	2	1	1	-	...
25 - 29	838	...	2	77	390	230	88	32	8	6	3	2	...
30 - 34	427	...	-	19	72	148	95	49	27	8	4	4	...
35 - 39	178	...	-	3	13	31	45	45	22	8	7	4	...
40 - 44	60	...	-	-	7	7	10	17	10	6	2	1	...
45 - 49	34	...	-	-	-	4	-	7	10	7	5	1	...
50 - 54	16	...	-	-	1	1	3	5	1	2	1	2	...
55 - 59	1	...	-	-	-	-	-	-	-	-	-	1	...
60 +	2	...	-	-	-	-	-	-	-	-	-	2	...
Republic of Korea - République de Corée[20,21]													
2011 (+C)													
Total	329 087	8	5 132	30 519	141 801	89 898	26 345	13 529	9 845	6 844	3 092	2 074	-
0 - 14	-	-	-	-	-	-	-	-	-	-	-	-	-
15 - 19	813	5	581	194	27	4	2	-	-	-	-	-	-
20 - 24	9 438	2	809	6 213	2 031	316	58	8	1	-	-	-	-
25 - 29	93 613	1	668	12 715	68 046	11 297	765	89	23	6	2	1	-
30 - 34	123 390	-	697	5 889	60 207	52 158	3 824	522	78	13	1	1	-
35 - 39	49 120	-	1 356	2 872	8 527	21 330	12 462	2 153	362	48	9	1	-
40 - 44	21 513	-	845	1 878	1 898	3 442	6 584	5 186	1 354	286	36	4	-
45 - 49	12 267	-	155	608	728	829	1 709	3 498	3 579	988	153	20	-
50 - 54	8 905	-	15	113	253	361	661	1 420	3 004	2 593	415	70	-
55 - 59	5 098	-	5	30	70	124	191	452	1 017	1 932	1 105	172	-

Mariages selon l'âge de l'époux et selon l'âge de l'épouse : dernière année disponible, 2003 - 2012 (continued - suite)

Continent, country or area, year, code and age of bride / Continent, pays ou zone, date, code et âge de l'épouse	Total	0-14	15-19	20-24	25-29	30-34	35-39	40-44	45-49	50-54	55-59	60+	Unknown Inconnu
ASIA - ASIE													
Republic of Korea - République de Corée[20,21]													
2011													
60 - 64	2 634	-	-	6	10	28	67	139	297	739	905	443	-
65 - 69	1 279	-	1	1	3	7	14	46	96	174	333	604	-
70 - 74	621	-	-	-	1	1	7	11	22	46	100	433	-
75 +	396	-	-	-	-	1	1	5	12	19	33	325	-
Unknown - Inconnu	-	-	-	-	-	-	-	-	-	-	-	-	-
Singapore - Singapour[22]													
2012 (+C)													
Total	27 936	-	84	1 907	9 429	8 012	3 744	1 907	1 201	794	438	420	...
0 - 14	-	-	-	-	-	-	-	-	-	-	-	-	...
15 - 19	386	-	62	172	70	37	21	9	7	3	-	5	...
20 - 24	4 622	-	20	1 216	2 041	772	286	135	81	42	23	6	...
25 - 29	12 213	-	1	400	6 251	3 798	1 037	380	195	97	39	15	...
30 - 34	6 308	-	-	87	879	2 880	1 461	546	247	121	59	28	...
35 - 39	2 358	-	-	20	152	447	763	465	261	134	70	46	...
40 - 44	1 071	-	1	4	25	61	139	278	230	168	80	85	...
45 - 49	542	-	-	6	6	15	33	70	134	133	73	72	...
50 - 54	244	-	-	2	4	1	3	21	37	68	58	50	...
55 - 59	115	-	-	-	1	1	1	2	8	23	23	56	...
60 +	77	-	-	-	-	-	-	1	1	5	13	57	...
Sri Lanka													
2007 (+U)													
Total	196 236	-	4 874	50 475	77 223	37 758	13 636	5 693	3 065	1 585	988	939	-
0 - 14	20	-	7	7	5	1	-	-	-	-	-	-	-
15 - 19	35 127	-	3 814	19 794	10 010	1 301	168	27	6	3	1	3	-
20 - 24	73 649	-	899	26 759	35 730	8 980	1 043	174	44	12	4	4	-
25 - 29	55 088	-	135	3 335	29 096	18 013	3 732	560	160	29	16	12	-
30 - 34	17 764	-	15	432	1 881	8 373	5 319	1 316	310	74	29	15	-
35 - 39	7 468	-	3	123	400	864	2 930	2 070	815	185	47	31	-
40 - 44	3 529	-	-	10	74	184	350	1 307	1 008	389	157	50	-
45 - 49	1 852	-	-	8	14	31	74	194	600	536	278	117	-
50 - 54	958	-	1	5	8	8	18	39	98	299	294	188	-
55 - 59	471	-	-	1	5	2	2	6	17	43	138	257	-
60 - 64	193	-	-	1	-	1	-	-	6	13	21	151	-
65 - 69	71	-	-	-	-	-	-	-	1	1	1	68	-
70 - 74	31	-	-	-	-	-	-	-	-	1	2	28	-
75 +	15	-	-	-	-	-	-	-	-	-	-	15	-
State of Palestine - État de Palestine													
2011 (C)													
Total	36 284	...	2 694	14 463	12 246	3 536	1 214	668	476	329	218	435	...
12 - 14	611	...	159	351	95	5	-	-	-	-	-	-	...
15 - 19	16 323	...	2 248	8 688	4 492	737	96	38	12	3	1	5	...
20 - 24	13 565	...	264	5 061	5 997	1 642	375	121	65	24	6	9	...
25 - 29	3 598	...	19	323	1 497	873	436	201	135	65	27	22	...
30 - 34	1 160	...	2	34	126	231	225	182	137	98	55	70	...
35 - 39	583	...	1	1	35	41	64	82	77	77	74	131	...
40 - 44	265	...	1	3	4	5	16	29	33	34	39	101	...
45 - 49	121	...	-	2	-	2	1	14	10	21	9	62	...
50 - 54	42	...	-	-	-	-	1	1	4	7	3	26	...
55 - 59	14	...	-	-	-	-	-	-	2	-	4	8	...
60 +	2	...	-	-	-	-	-	-	1	-	-	1	...
Tajikistan - Tadjikistan													
2011 (+C)													
Total	94 730	-	2 820	44 216	26 305	10 755	5 652	2 443	1 062	546	357	478	96
0 - 14	-	-	-	-	-	-	-	-	-	-	-	-	-
15 - 19	31 474	-	2 295	22 041	6 666	384	44	10	3	1	1	2	27
20 - 24	38 590	-	483	21 026	13 991	2 547	405	75	23	10	5	1	24
25 - 29	13 929	-	32	953	5 270	5 513	1 642	328	107	34	13	22	15
30 - 34	6 317	-	3	120	310	2 120	2 486	745	281	117	56	71	8
35 - 39	2 776	-	2	14	22	142	993	933	320	146	98	101	5
40 - 44	954	-	-	5	10	23	66	312	237	115	80	105	1
45 - 49	359	-	1	5	9	7	9	28	78	84	53	84	1
50 - 54	137	-	1	-	1	4	-	3	12	35	36	44	1
55 - 59	50	-	-	1	2	-	-	2	1	4	8	32	-

Continent, country or area, year, code and age of bride — Continent, pays ou zone, date, code et âge de l'épouse	Total	0-14	15-19	20-24	25-29	30-34	35-39	40-44	45-49	50-54	55-59	60+	Unknown Inconnu
ASIA - ASIE													
Tajikistan - Tadjikistan													
2011													
60 - 64	17	-	-	-	-	-	-	-	-	-	6	11	-
65 - 69	5	-	-	-	-	-	-	-	-	-	1	4	-
70 - 74	1	-	-	-	-	-	-	-	-	-	-	1	-
75 +	-	-	-	-	-	-	-	-	-	-	-	-	-
Unknown - Inconnu	121	-	3	51	24	15	7	7	-	-	-	-	14
Turkey - Turquie													
2011 (C)													
Total	592 775	...	14 217[e]	162 204	238 572	97 512	31 881	14 600	10 300	6 616	5 283	8 299	3 291
0 - 19	130 647	...	10 073[e]	62 617	47 547	8 811	1 003	182	40	13	11	5	345
20 - 24	214 283	...	3 339[e]	79 781	100 261	25 308	3 752	652	236	69	23	23	839
25 - 29	136 540	...	451[e]	14 864	73 390	35 949	7 964	1 962	712	233	111	79	825
30 - 34	49 768	...	97[e]	1 933	10 940	19 528	10 224	3 689	1 626	576	286	240	629
35 - 39	20 800	...	17[e]	339	1 651	3 986	5 751	4 230	2 397	1 061	592	443	333
40 - 44	10 039	...	3[e]	65	254	590	1 281	2 261	2 528	1 361	732	792	172
45 - 49	6 848	...	-[e]	18	63	130	234	554	1 683	1 694	1 129	1 246	97
50 - 54	3 941	...	-[e]	1	8	19	46	61	332	908	1 190	1 342	34
55 - 59	2 465	...	-[e]	-	4	3	8	22	67	200	708	1 444	9
60 - 64	1 275	...	-[e]	2	2	-	3	3	6	38	135	1 081	5
65 - 69	563	...	-[e]	-	-	2	-	1	-	2	25	530	3
70 - 74	295	...	-[e]	-	1	-	1	-	-	-	3	290	-
75 +	153	...	-[e]	-	-	-	-	-	1	-	1	151	-
Unknown - Inconnu	15 158	...	237[e]	2 584	4 451	3 186	1 614	983	672	461	337	633	-
EUROPE													
Åland Islands - Îles d'Åland[23]													
2011 (C)													
Total	113	-	-	1	19	24	25	13	19	5	3	4	...
0 - 14	-	-	-	-	-	-	-	-	-	-	-	-	...
15 - 19	-	-	-	-	-	-	-	-	-	-	-	-	...
20 - 24	10	-	-	1	5	2	1	-	1	-	-	-	...
25 - 29	32	-	-	-	13	9	8	1	1	-	-	-	...
30 - 34	16	-	-	-	1	7	5	3	-	-	-	-	...
35 - 39	21	-	-	-	-	6	8	4	3	-	-	-	...
40 - 44	13	-	-	-	-	-	2	4	7	-	-	-	...
45 - 49	9	-	-	-	-	-	1	1	3	2	2	-	...
50 - 54	8	-	-	-	-	-	-	-	4	3	-	1	...
55 - 59	2	-	-	-	-	-	-	-	-	-	1	1	...
60 - 64	2	-	-	-	-	-	-	-	-	-	-	2	...
65 - 69	-	-	-	-	-	-	-	-	-	-	-	-	...
70 - 74	-	-	-	-	-	-	-	-	-	-	-	-	...
75 +	-	-	-	-	-	-	-	-	-	-	-	-	...
Albania - Albanie													
2007 (C)													
Total	22 371	...	257[e]	4 716	10 147	4 648	1 540	509	272	282[r]	...	...	...
0 - 19	6 383	...	...	...	...	...	...	...	...	...	...	...	...
20 - 24	10 194	...	...	...	...	...	...	...	...	...	...	...	...
25 - 29	3 833	...	...	...	...	...	...	...	...	...	...	...	...
30 - 34	1 103	...	...	...	...	...	...	...	...	...	...	...	...
35 - 39	476	...	...	...	...	...	...	...	...	...	...	...	...
40 - 44	212	...	...	...	...	...	...	...	...	...	...	...	...
45 - 49	110	...	...	...	...	...	...	...	...	...	...	...	...
50 +	60	...	...	...	...	...	...	...	...	...	...	...	...
Austria - Autriche[24]													
2011 (C)													
Total	36 426	-	185	2 742	7 421	8 518	5 959	4 118	2 884	1 977	1 119	1 503	...
0 - 14	-	-	-	-	-	-	-	-	-	-	-	-	...
15 - 19	726	-	109	431	123	39	12	7	4	1	-	-	...
20 - 24	4 944	-	62	1 713	2 145	667	212	87	34	14	6	4	...
25 - 29	9 985	-	10	452	4 082	3 667	1 158	380	133	57	30	16	...
30 - 34	7 927	-	3	94	872	3 283	2 298	889	314	109	37	28	...
35 - 39	4 710	-	-	29	144	684	1 650	1 316	563	206	67	51	...
40 - 44	3 028	-	1	14	31	136	451	930	839	384	156	86	...

23. Marriages by age of groom and by age of bride: latest available year, 2003 - 2012
Mariages selon l'âge de l'époux et selon l'âge de l'épouse : dernière année disponible, 2003 - 2012 (continued - suite)

Continent, country or area, year, code and age of bride / Continent, pays ou zone, date, code et âge de l'épouse	Total	0-14	15-19	20-24	25-29	30-34	35-39	40-44	45-49	50-54	55-59	60+	Unknown Inconnu
				Age of groom - âge de l'époux									

EUROPE

Austria - Autriche[24]
2011

45 - 49	2 330	-	-	5	16	28	139	387	681	574	248	252	...
50 - 54	1 477	-	-	4	7	11	31	96	239	450	317	322	...
55 - 59	735	-	-	-	1	1	5	24	60	131	194	319	...
60 - 64	312	-	-	-	-	2	2	1	13	44	50	200	...
65 - 69	163	-	-	-	-	-	-	1	2	3	9	148	...
70 - 74	67	-	-	-	-	-	-	-	1	2	4	60	...
75 +	22	-	-	-	-	-	1	-	1	2	1	17	...

Belarus - Bélarus
2011 (C)

Total	86 785	68[c]	1 449[i]	28 211	28 630	11 278	6 134	3 770	2 747	2 040	1 185	1 273	...
0 - 17	882	38[c]	197[i]	518	112	11	3	1	2	-	-	-	...
18 - 19	6 188	14[c]	633[i]	4 078	1 263	171	19	6	4	-	-	-	...
20 - 24	37 227	12[c]	520[i]	19 156	14 233	2 529	562	145	46	19	4	1	...
25 - 29	21 133	4[c]	75[i]	3 783	10 426	4 592	1 534	499	149	51	12	8	...
30 - 34	8 705	-[c]	15[i]	542	2 034	2 864	1 929	844	313	123	31	10	...
35 - 39	4 642	-[c]	7[i]	121	445	831	1 409	1 037	512	190	65	25	...
40 - 44	2 814	-[c]	2[i]	9	95	214	477	830	691	326	126	44	...
45 - 49	2 045	-[c]	-[i]	2	18	51	154	298	709	552	166	95	...
50 - 54	1 557	-[c]	-[i]	2	3	12	36	89	257	587	375	196	...
55 - 59	854	-[c]	-[i]	-	-	2	8	18	49	159	305	313	...
60 +	738	-[c]	-[i]	-	1	1	3	3	15	33	101	581	...

Belgium - Belgique[25,26]
2009 (C)

Total	43 303	-	119	3 550	12 333	8 750	5 728	4 065	3 235	2 353	1 501	1 660	9
0 - 14	-	-	-	-	-	-	-	-	-	-	-	-	-
15 - 19	787	-	58	372	248	67	26	10	4	1	1	-	-
20 - 24	7 511	-	42	2 313	3 744	953	282	103	49	21	2	2	-
25 - 29	13 267	-	11	697	6 918	3 801	1 181	385	173	57	29	13	2
30 - 34	7 227	-	2	108	1 042	2 847	1 856	811	351	129	51	29	1
35 - 39	4 813	-	2	37	231	736	1 587	1 174	599	284	113	50	-
40 - 44	3 402	-	-	13	75	207	519	996	861	438	187	106	-
45 - 49	2 757	-	2	4	48	95	194	417	808	655	320	214	-
50 - 54	1 812	-	1	2	15	27	64	129	303	528	400	343	-
55 - 59	966	-	-	2	8	12	11	31	68	176	292	366	-
60 - 64	451	-	1	1	-	2	2	6	14	51	77	297	-
65 - 69	164	-	-	1	1	2	-	2	3	8	23	124	-
70 - 74	76	-	-	-	-	1	-	-	-	3	2	70	-
75 +	50	-	-	-	-	-	1	-	-	1	2	46	-
Unknown - Inconnu	20	-	-	-	3	-	5	1	2	1	2	-	6

Bosnia and Herzegovina - Bosnie-Herzégovine
2010 (C)

Total	19 541	-	248	4 381	7 262	3 932	1 613	793	447	289	189	385	2
0 - 14	1	-	-	1	-	-	-	-	-	-	-	-	-
15 - 19	2 408	-	149	1 392	701	142	18	4	2	-	-	-	-
20 - 24	6 887	-	91	2 465	3 266	864	141	45	12	2	1	-	-
25 - 29	5 848	-	5	465	2 900	1 864	487	84	20	11	5	7	-
30 - 34	2 158	-	1	42	335	895	566	210	76	26	4	2	1
35 - 39	910	-	1	5	38	127	321	254	112	32	14	6	-
40 - 44	473	-	-	7	5	26	57	150	116	66	17	29	-
45 - 49	324	-	1	-	3	8	15	39	79	77	59	43	-
50 - 54	214	-	-	1	1	-	3	6	22	51	50	80	-
55 - 59	148	-	-	1	-	1	-	-	7	20	31	88	-
60 - 64	82	-	-	-	2	1	1	-	1	1	3	73	-
65 - 69	42	-	-	-	3	1	-	-	-	2	2	34	-
70 - 74	21	-	-	1	1	-	-	-	-	1	1	17	-
75 +	11	-	-	1	1	-	2	-	-	-	1	6	-
Unknown - Inconnu	14	-	-	-	6	3	2	1	-	-	1	-	1

Bulgaria - Bulgarie[27]
2011 (C)

Total	21 448	-	181	2 992	7 607	5 348	2 434	1 102	549	411	306	518	...
0 - 14	-	-	-	-	-	-	-	-	-	-	-	-	...
15 - 19	1 290	-	135	732	337	65	19	1	1	-	-	-	...
20 - 24	6 252	-	40	1 785	3 050	1 104	211	41	11	6	2	2	...

23. Marriages by age of groom and by age of bride: latest available year, 2003 - 2012
Mariages selon l'âge de l'époux et selon l'âge de l'épouse : dernière année disponible, 2003 - 2012 (continued - suite)

Continent, country or area, year, code and age of bride / Continent, pays ou zone, date, code et âge de l'épouse	Total	0-14	15-19	20-24	25-29	30-34	35-39	40-44	45-49	50-54	55-59	60+	Unknown Inconnu
EUROPE													
Bulgaria - Bulgarie[27]													
2011													
25 - 29	7 351	-	4	405	3 624	2 462	671	133	31	17	3	1	...
30 - 34	3 353	-	1	50	518	1 454	903	277	88	39	14	9	...
35 - 39	1 438	-	1	17	61	220	508	394	132	68	31	6	...
40 - 44	621	-	-	3	13	31	89	191	143	86	41	24	...
45 - 49	380	-	-	-	3	9	21	47	103	95	53	49	...
50 - 54	334	-	-	-	1	2	10	15	34	82	91	99	...
55 - 59	204	-	-	-	-	1	1	2	4	16	58	122	...
60 - 64	122	-	-	-	-	-	-	1	2	2	12	105	...
65 - 69	53	-	-	-	-	-	1	-	-	-	1	51	...
70 - 74	34	-	-	-	-	-	-	-	-	-	-	34	...
75 +	16	-	-	-	-	-	-	-	-	-	-	16	...
Croatia - Croatie													
2010 (C)													
Total	21 294	-	178	3 018	7 994	5 587	2 244	892	472	260	216	430	3
0 - 14	-	-	-	-	-	-	-	-	-	-	-	-	-
15 - 19	1 136	-	117	622	313	61	16	4	1	2	-	-	-
20 - 24	5 783	-	55	1 795	2 861	863	161	37	6	2	1	1	1
25 - 29	7 963	-	5	513	4 016	2 598	632	147	32	13	5	2	-
30 - 34	3 849	-	-	71	714	1 781	888	265	93	24	11	2	-
35 - 39	1 198	-	-	10	82	235	440	265	101	37	18	9	1
40 - 44	516	-	-	3	5	41	95	134	118	67	22	31	-
45 - 49	271	-	1	-	-	3	9	23	86	48	47	54	-
50 - 54	230	-	-	1	1	2	3	11	24	49	57	82	-
55 - 59	140	-	-	-	-	-	-	2	7	11	39	81	-
60 - 64	107	-	-	-	-	-	-	3	2	5	11	86	-
65 - 69	46	-	-	-	-	-	-	1	-	1	3	41	-
70 - 74	27	-	-	-	-	-	-	-	1	-	1	25	-
75 +	17	-	-	-	-	-	-	-	1	1	1	14	-
Unknown - Inconnu	11	-	-	3	2	3	-	-	-	-	-	2	1
Czech Republic - République tchèque													
2011 (C)													
Total	45 137	-	113	2 804	12 212	13 354	7 021	3 243	2 266	1 497	1 223	1 404	...
0 - 14	-	-	-	-	-	-	-	-	-	-	-	-	...
15 - 19	475	-	56	223	121	51	13	9	-	1	1	-	...
20 - 24	6 907	-	45	1 687	3 235	1 352	426	107	40	9	3	3	...
25 - 29	16 170	-	5	671	7 028	6 107	1 738	420	140	36	17	8	...
30 - 34	10 371	-	4	161	1 468	4 676	2 713	806	347	122	51	23	...
35 - 39	4 589	-	3	45	272	903	1 561	961	496	209	90	49	...
40 - 44	2 345	-	-	14	64	211	417	607	546	274	135	77	...
45 - 49	1 700	-	-	3	17	44	111	252	485	394	253	141	...
50 - 54	1 093	-	-	-	4	8	32	57	145	306	310	231	...
55 - 59	827	-	-	-	1	2	7	16	48	109	278	366	...
60 - 64	408	-	-	-	2	-	2	7	17	31	69	280	...
65 - 69	148	-	-	-	-	-	-	1	1	5	13	128	...
70 - 74	70	-	-	-	-	-	1	-	-	1	3	65	...
75 +	34	-	-	-	-	-	-	-	1	-	-	33	...
Denmark - Danemark[28]													
2011 (C)													
Total	27 198	-	22	1 035	4 854	6 778	4 535	2 863	2 234	1 551	1 124	1 594	608
0 - 14	-	-	-	-	-	-	-	-	-	-	-	-	-
15 - 19	129	-	8	72	22	7	1	2	1	-	-	-	16
20 - 24	2 181	-	12	678	979	285	69	19	13	4	1	2	119
25 - 29	6 676	-	-	191	2 944	2 505	606	155	59	21	6	7	182
30 - 34	6 275	-	-	33	616	3 081	1 715	517	144	51	12	8	98
35 - 39	3 592	-	-	12	78	527	1 517	878	356	111	31	22	60
40 - 44	2 273	-	-	1	20	81	355	817	599	237	76	44	43
45 - 49	1 779	-	-	-	2	15	78	247	682	441	187	88	39
50 - 54	1 305	-	-	-	-	7	11	74	185	430	354	218	26
55 - 59	795	-	-	1	-	-	1	3	41	127	273	337	12
60 - 64	499	-	-	-	-	-	-	4	10	15	83	378	9
65 - 69	256	-	-	-	-	-	-	-	-	4	23	227	2
70 - 74	117	-	-	-	-	-	-	-	-	1	3	111	2
75 +	72	-	-	-	-	-	-	-	-	-	-	72	-
Unknown - Inconnu	1 249	-	2	47	193	270	182	147	144	109	75	80	-

23. Marriages by age of groom and by age of bride: latest available year, 2003 - 2012
Mariages selon l'âge de l'époux et selon l'âge de l'épouse : dernière année disponible, 2003 - 2012 (continued - suite)

Continent, country or area, year, code and age of bride / Continent, pays ou zone, date, code et âge de l'épouse	Total	0-14	15-19	20-24	25-29	30-34	35-39	40-44	45-49	50-54	55-59	60+	Unknown Inconnu
EUROPE													
Estonia - Estonie													
2011 (C)													
Total	5 499	-	32	646	1 534	1 170	847	481	296	230	129	134	...
0 - 14	-	-	-	-	-	-	-	-	-	-	-	-	...
15 - 19	137	-	14	77	38	7	-	1	-	-	-	-	...
20 - 24	1 187	-	17	420	523	163	44	6	7	4	2	1	...
25 - 29	1 669	-	1	116	777	491	201	52	26	4	1	-	...
30 - 34	1 003	-	-	27	149	379	277	113	31	18	5	4	...
35 - 39	590	-	-	5	30	92	238	133	56	24	8	4	...
40 - 44	379	-	-	1	15	28	70	129	77	45	10	4	...
45 - 49	220	-	-	-	2	7	12	37	62	59	28	13	...
50 - 54	164	-	-	-	-	1	3	7	30	58	41	24	...
55 - 59	84	-	-	-	-	2	2	3	6	14	29	28	...
60 - 64	40	-	-	-	-	-	-	-	1	3	5	31	...
65 - 69	13	-	-	-	-	-	-	-	-	1	-	12	...
70 - 74	8	-	-	-	-	-	-	-	-	-	-	8	...
75 +	5	-	-	-	-	-	-	-	-	-	-	5	...
Finland - Finlande[29,30]													
2011 (C)													
Total	28 295	-	237	2 511	7 041	6 478	3 830	2 573	2 289	1 342	949	1 045	...
0 - 14	-	-	-	-	-	-	-	-	-	-	-	-	...
15 - 19	640	-	155	366	88	15	8	5	-	2	1	-	...
20 - 24	3 988	-	68	1 609	1 722	409	113	47	13	5	2	-	...
25 - 29	8 159	-	11	431	4 116	2 629	710	172	59	19	12	-	...
30 - 34	5 786	-	3	69	879	2 664	1 474	462	174	38	11	12	...
35 - 39	3 076	-	-	25	150	573	1 093	798	291	102	31	13	...
40 - 44	2 096	-	-	5	55	130	313	678	596	211	77	31	...
45 - 49	2 149	-	-	3	19	40	86	322	898	472	207	102	...
50 - 54	1 067	-	-	2	8	11	28	72	200	338	267	141	...
55 - 59	677	-	-	1	3	5	3	13	42	127	252	231	...
60 - 64	392	-	-	-	1	1	2	3	14	18	77	276	...
65 - 69	167	-	-	-	-	1	-	1	2	8	10	145	...
70 - 74	61	-	-	-	-	-	-	-	-	2	2	57	...
75 +	37	-	-	-	-	-	-	-	-	-	-	37	...
France[31]													
2010 (C)													
Total	245 334	1	397	13 870	62 783	57 423	36 751	23 894	16 655	13 076	9 212	11 272	...
0 - 14	22	-	-	13	6	1	1	-	-	-	-	1	...
15 - 19	1 957	-	108	894	630	216	69	20	13	5	-	2	...
20 - 24	30 181	-	137	9 340	15 051	4 040	1 070	309	135	58	17	24	...
25 - 29	74 758	-	63	3 016	39 144	23 927	5 961	1 707	548	214	97	81	...
30 - 34	49 947	-	33	407	6 317	23 335	13 267	4 202	1 432	573	234	147	...
35 - 39	30 619	-	23	111	1 136	4 520	11 883	7 714	3 079	1 308	497	348	...
40 - 44	20 191	-	11	63	323	980	3 308	6 879	4 748	2 329	931	619	...
45 - 49	14 453	1	13	10	94	277	873	2 191	4 396	3 586	1 762	1 250	...
50 - 54	10 905	-	3	8	53	87	241	661	1 702	3 463	2 664	2 023	...
55 - 59	6 415	-	3	4	12	23	57	161	448	1 159	2 092	2 456	...
60 - 64	3 577	-	1	1	5	9	17	41	122	302	732	2 347	...
65 - 69	1 269	-	-	-	3	2	1	4	28	53	139	1 039	...
70 - 74	598	-	1	1	4	2	1	2	1	19	36	531	...
75 +	442	-	1	2	5	4	2	3	3	7	11	404	...
Germany - Allemagne													
2011 (C)													
Total	377 816	-	898	24 392	81 500	89 269	54 393	41 621	32 146	22 591	14 048	16 958	...
0 - 14	-	-	-	-	-	-	-	-	-	-	-	-	...
15 - 19	4 661	-	473	2 666	1 060	294	78	43	34	8	3	2	...
20 - 24	50 314	-	342	15 978	23 296	7 594	1 901	755	285	105	37	21	...
25 - 29	106 664	-	52	4 681	46 195	38 980	11 117	3 781	1 288	346	135	89	...
30 - 34	81 147	-	17	772	9 148	35 132	22 506	9 165	3 041	912	277	177	...
35 - 39	40 697	-	9	191	1 295	5 715	13 946	11 987	4 958	1 645	593	358	...
40 - 44	30 234	-	2	65	335	1 129	3 529	10 285	8 799	3 879	1 383	828	...
45 - 49	27 214	-	1	35	113	298	987	4 100	9 349	7 268	3 172	1 891	...
50 - 54	18 903	-	1	2	44	95	268	1 213	3 418	6 137	4 456	3 269	...
55 - 59	9 747	-	1	1	9	25	41	236	782	1 745	2 982	3 925	...
60 - 64	4 705	-	-	1	3	6	15	43	156	436	827	3 218	...
65 - 69	1 967	-	-	-	2	-	4	10	23	73	133	1 722	...

595

23. Marriages by age of groom and by age of bride: latest available year, 2003 - 2012

Mariages selon l'âge de l'époux et selon l'âge de l'épouse : dernière année disponible, 2003 - 2012 (continued - suite)

Continent, country or area, year, code and age of bride / Continent, pays ou zone, date, code et âge de l'épouse	Total	Age of groom - âge de l'époux											
		0-14	15-19	20-24	25-29	30-34	35-39	40-44	45-49	50-54	55-59	60+	Unknown Inconnu
EUROPE													
Germany - Allemagne													
2011													
70 - 74	1 112	-	-	-	-	-	1	2	11	23	39	1 036	...
75 +	451	-	-	-	-	1	-	1	2	14	11	422	...
Greece - Grèce													
2011 (C)													
Total	55 099	1	216	2 477	12 950	19 199	10 504	4 653	2 147	1 210	707	1 035	-
0 - 14	29	-	19	9	1	-	-	-	-	-	-	-	-
15 - 19	1 005	1	147	400	282	125	33	12	4	1	-	-	-
20 - 24	6 800	-	37	1 337	3 056	1 714	485	133	21	13	3	1	-
25 - 29	19 563	-	6	520	7 257	8 123	2 739	655	173	58	20	12	-
30 - 34	16 393	-	6	149	1 961	7 748	4 399	1 474	440	140	38	38	-
35 - 39	6 272	-	1	38	308	1 226	2 294	1 453	575	237	85	55	-
40 - 44	2 428	-	-	16	55	204	439	693	501	298	129	93	-
45 - 49	1 193	-	-	7	18	36	80	177	322	239	167	147	-
50 - 54	764	-	-	-	9	15	26	42	83	177	162	250	-
55 - 59	374	-	-	1	2	8	8	9	23	35	74	214	-
60 - 64	187	-	-	-	1	-	1	5	3	10	23	144	-
65 - 69	57	-	-	-	-	-	-	-	-	2	4	51	-
70 - 74	21	-	-	-	-	-	-	-	2	-	-	19	-
75 +	13	-	-	-	-	-	-	-	-	-	2	11	-
Hungary - Hongrie[8,32]													
2011 (C)													
Total	35 812	-	222	2 010	8 642	11 052	6 246	2 862	1 465	999	1 042	1 272	-
0 - 14	-	-	-	-	-	-	-	-	-	-	-	-	-
15 - 19	818	-	163	388	168	60	24	5	6	-	2	2	-
20 - 24	4 803	-	38	1 011	2 131	1 118	369	83	28	13	8	4	-
25 - 29	11 902	-	8	460	4 786	4 675	1 492	325	91	37	22	6	-
30 - 34	8 804	-	9	109	1 270	3 939	2 384	722	213	95	43	20	-
35 - 39	4 347	-	3	36	223	1 040	1 522	936	342	117	85	43	-
40 - 44	1 918	-	1	5	48	167	348	577	367	197	129	79	-
45 - 49	1 086	-	-	-	7	38	78	170	274	240	159	120	-
50 - 54	844	-	-	1	6	13	25	30	95	225	281	168	-
55 - 59	657	-	-	-	1	-	2	11	34	57	232	320	-
60 - 64	370	-	-	-	2	2	2	2	14	12	62	274	-
65 - 69	149	-	-	-	-	-	-	-	-	5	17	127	-
70 - 74	83	-	-	-	-	-	-	1	-	1	1	80	-
75 +	31	-	-	-	-	-	-	-	1	-	1	29	-
Unknown - Inconnu	-	-	-	-	-	-	-	-	-	-	-	-	-
Iceland - Islande[33,34,35]													
2011 (C)													
Total	1 458	-	3	77	302	334	272	161	111	74	64	55	5
0 - 14	-	-	-	-	-	-	-	-	-	-	-	-	-
15 - 19	6	-	-	2	4	-	-	-	-	-	-	-	-
20 - 24	152	-	3	52	69	21	1	3	1	1	-	-	1
25 - 29	371	-	-	19	173	115	44	9	5	3	1	1	1
30 - 34	350	-	-	3	43	157	104	25	9	3	4	1	1
35 - 39	243	-	-	1	7	33	101	62	22	9	6	1	1
40 - 44	113	-	-	-	3	6	14	44	28	11	3	4	-
45 - 49	94	-	-	-	1	-	6	15	36	24	7	4	1
50 - 54	68	-	-	-	-	1	1	2	9	18	25	12	-
55 - 59	30	-	-	-	-	-	1	-	1	4	15	9	-
60 - 64	18	-	-	-	-	-	-	1	-	1	2	14	-
65 - 69	7	-	-	-	-	-	-	-	-	-	1	6	-
70 - 74	2	-	-	-	-	-	-	-	-	-	-	2	-
75 +	1	-	-	-	-	-	-	-	-	-	-	1	-
Unknown - Inconnu	3	-	-	-	2	1	-	-	-	-	-	-	-
Ireland - Irlande													
2009 (+C)													
Total	21 627	-	106	720	5 881	7 960	3 745	1 486	731	442	263	293	-
0 - 14	-	-	-	-	-	-	-	-	-	-	-	-	-
15 - 19	275	-	77	99	69	24	4	1	-	-	1	-	-
20 - 24	1 556	-	24	374	769	266	84	28	8	1	2	-	-
25 - 29	7 794	-	5	184	3 800	2 964	673	129	28	7	4	-	-
30 - 34	7 320	-	-	52	1 072	3 997	1 639	413	100	33	11	3	-
35 - 39	2 612	-	-	7	141	609	1 071	503	180	68	27	6	-
40 - 44	1 016	-	-	-	19	75	215	307	226	104	50	20	-

Continent, country or area, year, code and age of bride / Continent, pays ou zone, date, code et âge de l'épouse	Total	0-14	15-19	20-24	25-29	30-34	35-39	40-44	45-49	50-54	55-59	60+	Unknown Inconnu
EUROPE													
Ireland - Irlande													
2009													
45 - 49	510	-	-	3	8	17	44	84	129	127	56	42	-
50 - 54	280	-	-	1	3	4	12	20	40	78	62	60	-
55 - 59	133	-	-	-	-	2	3	1	16	18	35	58	-
60 - 64	67	-	-	-	-	1	-	-	4	4	11	47	-
65 - 69	45	-	-	-	-	1	-	-	-	1	3	40	-
70 - 74	12	-	-	-	-	-	-	-	-	1	1	10	-
75 +	7	-	-	-	-	-	-	-	-	-	-	7	-
Unknown - Inconnu	-	-	-	-	-	-	-	-	-	-	-	-	-
Isle of Man - Île de Man													
2005 (C)													
Total	404	-	6	42	72	87	63	51	26	22	17	18	-
0 - 14	-	...	...	...	...	...	...	...	...	...	...	...	...
15 - 19	5	...	...	...	...	...	...	...	...	...	...	...	...
20 - 24	65	...	...	...	...	...	...	...	...	...	...	...	...
25 - 29	98	...	...	...	...	...	...	...	...	...	...	...	...
30 - 34	79	...	...	...	...	...	...	...	...	...	...	...	...
35 - 39	61	...	...	...	...	...	...	...	...	...	...	...	...
40 - 44	40	...	...	...	...	...	...	...	...	...	...	...	...
45 - 49	26	...	...	...	...	...	...	...	...	...	...	...	...
50 - 54	16	...	...	...	...	...	...	...	...	...	...	...	...
55 - 59	5	...	...	...	...	...	...	...	...	...	...	...	...
60 - 64	7	...	...	...	...	...	...	...	...	...	...	...	...
65 - 69	1	...	...	...	...	...	...	...	...	...	...	...	...
70 - 74	-	...	...	...	...	...	...	...	...	...	...	...	...
75 - 79	1	...	...	...	...	...	...	...	...	...	...	...	...
Italy - Italie													
2010 (C)													
Total	217 700	...	418	8 962	47 871	69 828	43 980	19 670	10 511	5 936	4 097	6 427	...
0 - 14	-	...	-	-	-	-	-	-	-	-	-	-	...
15 - 19	2 818	...	266	1 608	685	189	49	16	1	1	...	-	...
20 - 24	24 494	...	129	5 369	12 408	4 921	1 267	270	78	29	13	...	...
25 - 29	70 274	...	15	1 639	27 686	29 747	8 802	1 718	440	119	59	49	...
30 - 34	60 721	...	6	269	6 069	28 594	18 658	4 963	1 408	436	176	142	...
35 - 39	30 212	...	1	53	845	5 545	12 257	7 080	2 739	972	423	297	...
40 - 44	13 278	...	1	21	123	689	2 396	4 232	3 150	1 503	645	518	...
45 - 49	7 106	...	...	1	35	117	470	1 101	1 970	1 539	922	951	...
50 - 54	4 314	...	...	1	13	19	63	243	566	992	1 024	1 393	...
55 - 59	2 365	...	...	...	5	4	14	40	122	281	593	1 306	...
60 - 64	1 210	...	...	1	1	1	4	5	30	54	195	919	...
65 - 69	480	...	...	...	...	...	...	1	4	8	33	434	...
70 - 74	248	...	...	...	...	1	...	1	1	...	11	234	...
75 +	180	...	...	...	1	1	...	...	2	2	3	171	...
Latvia - Lettonie[7]													
2010 (C)													
Total	9 290	-	65	1 455	2 865	1 816	1 044	655	470	305	189	426	-
0 - 14	-	-	-	-	-	-	-	-	-	-	-	-	-
15 - 19	274	-	37	159	53	22	3	-	-	-	-	-	-
20 - 24	2 402	-	25	978	1 013	280	79	18	6	2	-	1	-
25 - 29	2 872	-	2	269	1 438	764	265	100	21	7	3	3	-
30 - 34	1 410	-	1	33	275	543	331	146	53	20	6	2	-
35 - 39	812	-	-	14	65	163	247	180	94	37	8	4	-
40 - 44	502	-	-	2	17	35	87	139	129	56	20	17	-
45 - 49	344	-	-	-	3	9	24	51	103	75	41	38	-
50 - 54	244	-	-	-	1	-	7	18	45	75	46	52	-
55 - 59	163	-	-	-	-	-	1	1	13	28	39	81	-
60 - 64	129	-	-	-	-	-	-	1	3	4	20	101	-
65 - 69	65	-	-	-	-	-	-	-	2	-	3	60	-
70 - 74	45	-	-	-	-	-	-	1	1	-	2	41	-
75 +	28	-	-	-	-	-	-	-	-	1	1	26	-
Unknown - Inconnu	-	-	-	-	-	-	-	-	-	-	-	-	-

23. Marriages by age of groom and by age of bride: latest available year, 2003 - 2012
Mariages selon l'âge de l'époux et selon l'âge de l'épouse : dernière année disponible, 2003 - 2012 (continued - suite)

Continent, country or area, year, code and age of bride / Continent, pays ou zone, date, code et âge de l'épouse	Total	0-14	15-19	20-24	25-29	30-34	35-39	40-44	45-49	50-54	55-59	60+	Unknown Inconnu
EUROPE													
Liechtenstein[7]													
2011* (C)													
Total	163	-	-	8	32	40	26	21	14	13	6	3	...
Lithuania - Lituanie													
2011 (C)													
Total	19 221	-	146	3 068	7 315	3 724	1 920	1 061	761	517	293	416	-
0 - 14	2	-	1	-	-	1	-	-	-	-	-	-	-
15 - 19	733	-	83	434	180	32	2	2	-	-	-	-	-
20 - 24	5 567	-	52	2 035	2 711	583	137	34	9	5	1	-	-
25 - 29	6 952	-	9	515	3 846	1 771	567	159	51	21	8	5	-
30 - 34	2 550	-	1	63	478	1 005	618	232	104	30	11	8	-
35 - 39	1 378	-	-	15	85	263	431	319	153	72	23	17	-
40 - 44	754	-	-	6	12	50	118	212	182	114	36	24	-
45 - 49	542	-	-	-	1	15	33	75	177	134	66	41	-
50 - 54	351	-	-	-	1	3	11	21	68	105	74	68	-
55 - 59	193	-	-	-	1	1	2	6	15	27	53	88	-
60 - 64	99	-	-	-	-	-	1	1	2	8	18	69	-
65 - 69	53	-	-	-	-	-	-	-	-	1	1	51	-
70 - 74	30	-	-	-	-	-	-	-	-	-	2	28	-
75 +	17	-	-	-	-	-	-	-	-	-	-	17	-
Unknown - Inconnu	-	-	-	-	-	-	-	-	-	-	-	-	-
Luxembourg[36]													
2011 (C)													
Total	1 714	-	20	206	489	445	206	136	93	72	34	13	-
0 - 14	-	-	-	-	-	-	-	-	-	-	-	-	-
15 - 19	4	-	1	1	2	-	-	-	-	-	-	-	-
20 - 24	102	-	11	54	28	6	1	1	1	-	-	-	-
25 - 29	394	-	6	100	209	62	8	7	1	-	1	-	-
30 - 34	435	-	2	33	162	190	34	8	4	1	1	-	-
35 - 39	263	-	-	10	58	103	61	19	7	4	-	1	-
40 - 44	200	-	-	3	18	55	53	41	22	5	3	-	-
45 - 49	117	-	-	2	3	18	28	28	19	16	3	-	-
50 - 54	96	-	-	3	7	8	13	19	22	19	4	1	-
55 - 59	61	-	-	-	2	1	3	9	14	20	10	2	-
60 - 64	23	-	-	-	-	2	2	4	2	4	6	3	-
65 - 69	7	-	-	-	-	-	-	-	-	1	2	4	-
70 - 74	10	-	-	-	-	-	1	-	1	2	4	2	-
75 +	2	-	-	-	-	-	2	-	-	-	-	-	-
Unknown - Inconnu	-	-	-	-	-	-	-	-	-	-	-	-	-
Malta - Malte													
2011 (C)													
Total	2 562	-	2	200	958	756	285	130	81	62	36	49	3
0 - 14	-	-	-	-	-	-	-	-	-	-	-	-	-
15 - 19	23	-	1	11	6	5	-	-	-	-	-	-	-
20 - 24	460	-	1	122	252	75	7	3	-	-	-	-	-
25 - 29	1 128	-	-	49	592	390	76	16	1	2	2	-	-
30 - 34	506	-	-	14	93	232	113	30	13	5	4	2	-
35 - 39	205	-	-	2	9	47	75	48	10	8	3	3	-
40 - 44	91	-	-	1	4	6	10	24	21	13	7	5	-
45 - 49	63	-	-	-	2	1	2	7	28	14	4	5	-
50 - 54	44	-	-	-	-	-	1	2	7	18	6	10	-
55 - 59	18	-	-	1	-	-	1	-	1	2	7	6	-
60 - 64	14	-	-	-	-	-	-	-	-	-	3	11	-
65 - 69	4	-	-	-	-	-	-	-	-	-	-	4	-
70 - 74	1	-	-	-	-	-	-	-	-	-	-	1	-
75 +	2	-	-	-	-	-	-	-	-	-	-	2	-
Unknown - Inconnu	3	-	-	-	-	-	-	-	-	-	-	-	3
Montenegro - Monténégro													
2009 (C)													
Total	3 829	...	26	619	1 371	876	425	232	131	66	31	52	-
0 - 14	-	...	-	-	-	-	-	-	-	-	-	-	...
15 - 19	376	...	15	172	131	41	11	4	1	-	-	1	-
20 - 24	1 268	...	9	358	600	217	53	22	6	2	1	-	-
25 - 29	1 243	...	1	75	549	406	151	47	12	1	1	-	-
30 - 34	517	...	-	8	81	176	135	79	33	5	-	-	-
35 - 39	203	...	-	3	8	32	60	47	33	16	2	2	-
40 - 44	96	...	-	2	1	2	15	25	31	10	7	3	-

23. Marriages by age of groom and by age of bride: latest available year, 2003 - 2012
Mariages selon l'âge de l'époux et selon l'âge de l'épouse : dernière année disponible, 2003 - 2012 (continued - suite)

Continent, country or area, year, code and age of bride / Continent, pays ou zone, date, code et âge de l'épouse	Total	0-14	15-19	20-24	25-29	30-34	35-39	40-44	45-49	50-54	55-59	60+	Unknown Inconnu
EUROPE													
Montenegro - Monténégro													
2009													
45 - 49	55	...	1	1	-	1	-	7	12	15	7	11	-
50 - 54	34	...	-	-	1	1	-	1	1	15	6	9	-
55 - 59	22	...	-	-	-	-	-	-	2	1	5	14	-
60 - 64	8	...	-	-	-	-	-	-	-	1	2	5	-
65 - 69	7	...	-	-	-	-	-	-	-	-	-	7	-
70 - 74	-	...	-	-	-	-	-	-	-	-	-	-	-
75 +	-	...	-	-	-	-	-	-	-	-	-	-	-
Netherlands - Pays-Bas													
2009[37,38,39] (C)													
Total	72 119	...	85	4 976	16 276	17 802	11 712	7 321	4 939	3 443	2 300	3 265	-
0 - 14	-	-	-	-	-	-	-	-	-	-	-	-	...
15 - 19	687	...	47	385	178	49	17	8	3	-	-	-	-
20 - 24	11 006	...	32	3 710	5 283	1 374	408	120	56	14	5	4	-
25 - 29	20 820	...	4	735	8 958	7 932	2 233	615	211	87	26	19	-
30 - 34	15 428	...	2	108	1 548	6 998	4 516	1 456	522	162	66	50	-
35 - 39	8 770	...	-	24	239	1 136	3 385	2 481	947	347	118	93	-
40 - 44	5 477	...	-	10	47	232	843	1 888	1 455	646	211	145	-
45 - 49	3 879	...	-	3	13	54	239	575	1 193	1 035	482	285	-
50 - 54	2 754	...	-	1	7	19	57	136	436	884	707	507	-
55 - 59	1 553	...	-	-	-	6	10	35	83	213	501	705	-
60 - 64	962	...	-	-	2	2	3	5	26	42	146	736	-
65 - 69	489	...	-	-	1	-	-	2	7	12	32	435	-
70 - 74	170	...	-	-	-	-	1	-	-	1	3	165	-
75 +	124	...	-	-	-	-	-	-	-	-	3	121	-
Norway - Norvège													
2011 (C)													
Total	22 876	2	46	1 437	4 755	5 039	3 760	2 719	1 871	1 293	949	1 005	...
0 - 14	2	2	-	-	-	-	-	-	-	-	-	-	...
15 - 19	356	-	26	175	88	40	18	7	1	-	-	1	...
20 - 24	3 154	-	17	1 000	1 351	463	166	74	46	19	8	10	...
25 - 29	6 382	-	2	213	2 732	2 125	760	286	138	66	40	20	...
30 - 34	4 970	-	1	35	481	1 991	1 404	587	258	107	55	51	...
35 - 39	3 095	-	-	11	81	349	1 124	866	374	145	88	57	...
40 - 44	1 899	-	-	3	17	56	234	664	468	248	115	94	...
45 - 49	1 361	-	-	-	5	12	46	198	435	357	199	109	...
50 - 54	861	-	-	-	-	1	6	30	119	273	256	176	...
55 - 59	437	-	-	-	-	1	2	5	28	62	149	190	...
60 - 64	229	-	-	-	-	-	-	1	3	12	32	181	...
65 - 69	89	-	-	-	-	1	-	1	1	2	6	78	...
70 - 74	30	-	-	-	-	-	-	-	-	2	1	27	...
75 +	11	-	-	-	-	-	-	-	-	-	-	11	...
Poland - Pologne													
2011 (C)													
Total	206 471	-	1 090	37 920	92 002	41 100	14 770	5 974	3 668	3 085	2 501	4 361	-
0 - 14	-	-	-	-	-	-	-	-	-	-	-	-	-
15 - 19	7 300	-	709	4 618	1 646	243	67	12	-	5	-	-	-
20 - 24	68 913	-	341	26 759	34 522	6 113	915	165	58	18	13	9	-
25 - 29	81 181	-	29	5 901	49 626	20 452	4 013	748	267	92	34	19	-
30 - 34	25 874	-	8	536	5 436	11 869	5 598	1 504	543	235	101	44	-
35 - 39	9 321	-	1	93	670	2 061	3 299	1 853	749	374	151	70	-
40 - 44	3 999	-	1	9	78	280	656	1 147	909	536	231	152	-
45 - 49	2 833	-	-	3	18	62	160	377	724	724	459	306	-
50 - 54	2 707	-	-	-	3	13	50	132	299	770	713	727	-
55 - 59	1 961	-	-	1	2	7	9	27	87	232	591	1 005	-
60 - 64	1 261	-	-	-	-	-	3	8	24	72	163	991	-
65 - 69	567	-	-	-	1	-	-	1	7	12	31	515	-
70 - 74	349	-	1	-	-	-	-	-	1	8	13	326	-
75 +	205	-	-	-	-	-	-	-	-	7	1	197	-
Unknown - Inconnu	-	-	-	-	-	-	-	-	-	-	-	-	-
Portugal													
2011 (C)													
Total	36 035	-	190	3 547	10 763	9 568	4 587	2 375	1 551	1 123	808	1 523	-
0 - 14	-	-	-	-	-	-	-	-	-	-	-	-	-
15 - 19	52	-	14	27	5	5	1	-	-	-	-	-	-
20 - 24	829	-	90	494	168	53	17	3	1	-	1	2	-

23. Marriages by age of groom and by age of bride: latest available year, 2003 - 2012
Mariages selon l'âge de l'époux et selon l'âge de l'épouse : dernière année disponible, 2003 - 2012 (continued - suite)

Continent, country or area, year, code and age of bride / Continent, pays ou zone, date, code et âge de l'épouse	Total	Age of groom - âge de l'époux											Unknown Inconnu
		0-14	15-19	20-24	25-29	30-34	35-39	40-44	45-49	50-54	55-59	60+	
EUROPE													
Portugal													
2011													
25 - 29	5 870	-	64	2 034	2 689	791	188	62	24	12	5	1	-
30 - 34	12 208	-	17	779	6 118	3 954	933	265	81	33	12	16	-
35 - 39	7 918	-	2	142	1 471	3 684	1 711	520	231	89	38	30	-
40 - 44	3 735	-	2	50	237	861	1 211	748	338	158	82	48	-
45 - 49	1 949	-	1	17	55	156	376	511	393	236	107	97	-
50 - 54	1 307	-	-	2	15	48	99	186	329	272	173	183	-
55 - 59	895	-	-	1	2	14	39	61	119	226	187	246	-
60 - 64	570	-	-	-	2	2	8	16	23	66	143	310	-
65 - 69	381	-	-	-	1	-	2	2	7	24	43	302	-
70 - 74	178	-	-	-	-	-	2	-	2	4	13	157	-
75 +	83	-	-	-	-	-	-	1	2	2	3	75	-
Unknown - Inconnu	60	-	-	1	-	-	-	-	1	1	1	56	-
Republic of Moldova - République de Moldova[40]													
2010 (C)													
Total	20 347	-	398	8 790	8 159	2 217	523	136	65	22	13	23	1
0 - 14	2	-	-	2	-	-	-	-	-	-	-	-	-
15 - 19	3 213	-	237	2 070	797	95	10	1	2	1	-	-	-
20 - 24	11 651	-	148	5 900	4 659	818	99	18	7	1	1	-	-
25 - 29	4 298	-	10	760	2 425	878	186	30	7	1	1	-	-
30 - 34	883	-	3	52	248	379	147	38	12	2	2	-	-
35 - 39	184	-	-	6	27	42	69	25	10	4	1	1	-
40 - 44	50	-	-	-	2	2	7	21	15	1	1	1	-
45 - 49	25	-	-	-	1	1	4	3	10	3	2	1	-
50 - 54	17	-	-	-	-	-	1	-	2	8	2	4	-
55 - 59	6	-	-	-	-	2	-	-	-	1	1	2	-
60 - 64	7	-	-	-	-	-	-	-	-	-	2	5	-
65 - 69	4	-	-	-	-	-	-	-	-	-	-	4	-
70 - 74	-	-	-	-	-	-	-	-	-	-	-	-	-
75 +	6	-	-	-	-	-	-	-	-	-	-	6	-
Unknown - Inconnu	1	-	-	-	-	-	-	-	-	-	-	-	1
Romania - Roumanie													
2011 (C)													
Total	105 599	...	599	18 236	38 670	25 303	10 304	5 571	2 247	1 781	1 336	1 552	...
0 - 14	-	...	-	-	-	-	-	-	-	-	-	-	...
15 - 19	7 909	...	384	4 219	2 451	710	114	21	5	5	-	9	...
20 - 24	36 214	...	185	11 282	17 206	6 099	1 117	253	41	15	7	14	...
25 - 29	31 770	...	22	2 324	15 832	10 134	2 514	689	146	68	27	14	...
30 - 34	15 016	...	7	334	2 669	6 519	3 567	1 332	355	135	63	35	...
35 - 39	6 679	...	-	61	406	1 462	2 200	1 635	485	253	109	68	...
40 - 44	3 855	...	-	14	90	323	657	1 258	708	448	222	135	...
45 - 49	1 608	...	-	2	9	42	107	290	366	409	242	141	...
50 - 54	1 111	...	-	-	5	12	22	73	103	299	346	251	...
55 - 59	773	...	1	-	2	1	4	16	31	112	242	364	...
60 +	664	...	-	-	-	1	2	4	7	37	78	535	...
Russian Federation - Fédération de Russie													
2011 (C)													
Total	1316011	...	18 234	363 320	431 438	201 922	110 629	65 217	46 555	35 018	21 203	22 423	52
15 - 19	92 860	...	10 709	58 239	20 103	2 930	617	174	59	16	7	5	1
20 - 24	493 272	...	6 266	237 067	195 704	41 258	9 254	2 446	821	307	84	61	4
25 - 29	355 022	...	936	56 734	171 233	83 247	28 820	9 273	3 152	1 112	337	175	3
30 - 34	159 317	...	214	8 935	34 874	53 550	36 210	15 653	6 345	2 434	767	331	4
35 - 39	84 678	...	68	1 770	7 598	16 014	25 371	18 382	9 521	4 121	1 263	567	3
40 - 44	45 247	...	21	390	1 473	3 656	7 509	12 827	10 791	5 664	2 001	914	1
45 - 49	32 808	...	12	106	315	983	2 126	4 616	10 464	8 701	3 680	1 803	2
50 - 54	24 985	...	5	45	80	200	564	1 464	4 128	9 078	5 981	3 438	2
55 - 59	14 771	...	2	10	21	51	117	299	1 029	2 803	5 327	5 112	-
60 +	13 016	...	-	16	32	31	39	81	244	782	1 755	10 014	22
Unknown - Inconnu	35	...	1	8	5	2	2	2	1	-	1	3	10
San Marino - Saint-Marin[41]													
2004 (C)													
Total	207	-	-	9	56	59	30	14	7	3	8	4	17
0 - 14	-	-	-	-	-	-	-	-	-	-	-	-	-
15 - 19	-	-	-	-	-	-	-	-	-	-	-	-	-

23. Marriages by age of groom and by age of bride: latest available year, 2003 - 2012
Mariages selon l'âge de l'époux et selon l'âge de l'épouse : dernière année disponible, 2003 - 2012 (continued - suite)

Continent, country or area, year, code and age of bride / Continent, pays ou zone, date, code et âge de l'épouse	Total	\multicolumn{12}{c}{Age of groom - âge de l'époux}											
		0-14	15-19	20-24	25-29	30-34	35-39	40-44	45-49	50-54	55-59	60+	Unknown Inconnu
EUROPE													
San Marino - Saint-Marin[41]													
2004													
20 - 24	16	-	-	4	4	1	-	2	-	-	1	-	4
25 - 29	63	-	-	1	28	20	4	-	1	-	1	-	8
30 - 34	37	-	-	-	3	13	13	4	-	-	-	-	4
35 - 39	11	-	-	-	-	2	2	2	1	-	2	1	1
40 · 44	5	-	-	-	-	1	-	2	-	-	2	-	-
45 - 49	4	-	-	-	-	-	1	1	-	1	1	-	-
50 - 54	2	-	-	-	-	-	-	-	1	-	-	1	-
55 - 59	1	-	-	-	-	-	-	-	-	1	-	-	-
60 +	-	-	-	-	-	-	-	-	-	-	-	-	-
Unknown - Inconnu	68	-	-	4	21	22	10	3	4	1	1	2	-
Serbia - Serbie[42]													
2011 (+C)													
Total	35 808	-	260	4 521	11 929	9 625	3 996	1 889	1 067	728	596	1 119	78
0 - 14	-	-	-	-	-	-	-	-	-	-	-	-	-
15 - 19	2 104	-	162	1 052	661	167	42	11	3	-	-	4	2
20 - 24	8 935	-	79	2 678	4 186	1 557	333	68	22	3	3	2	4
25 - 29	12 152	-	12	659	5 835	4 241	1 019	253	75	30	8	9	11
30 - 34	6 490	-	1	93	1 041	3 057	1 507	517	169	55	26	16	8
35 - 39	2 545	-	1	15	111	472	893	590	257	108	48	43	7
40 - 44	1 121	-	-	3	26	64	145	323	267	158	68	66	1
45 - 49	802	-	1	1	10	17	22	79	201	203	112	153	3
50 - 54	572	-	-	1	4	8	8	25	46	117	147	213	3
55 - 59	457	-	-	-	4	2	4	8	15	32	133	259	-
60 - 64	243	-	-	2	3	-	1	3	7	15	30	181	1
65 - 69	102	-	-	-	1	1	-	2	-	2	8	88	-
70 - 74	64	-	-	-	1	1	1	-	-	2	6	53	-
75 +	33	-	-	1	-	-	1	-	-	-	2	29	-
Unknown - Inconnu	188	-	4	16	46	38	20	10	5	3	5	3	38
Slovakia - Slovaquie[7]													
2011 (C)													
Total	25 621	-	437	2 688	8 671	7 447	3 008	1 272	755	468	366	509	...
0 - 14	-	-	-	-	-	-	-	-	-	-	-	-	...
15 - 19	1 191	-	330	613	187	44	10	5	-	-	2	-	...
20 - 24	5 439	-	84	1 519	2 652	933	187	36	18	8	1	1	...
25 - 29	10 147	-	20	455	4 863	3 623	830	224	83	34	9	6	...
30 - 34	5 082	-	1	77	825	2 346	1 225	391	133	48	19	17	...
35 - 39	1 789	-	1	15	114	418	599	348	171	70	31	22	...
40 - 44	733	-	-	8	25	66	120	186	154	90	52	32	...
45 - 49	444	-	1	1	2	12	28	56	124	106	70	44	...
50 - 54	329	-	-	-	3	5	6	21	48	78	90	78	...
55 - 59	252	-	-	-	-	-	3	4	18	30	69	128	...
60 - 64	140	-	-	-	-	-	-	1	6	4	18	111	...
65 - 69	53	-	-	-	-	-	-	-	-	-	5	48	...
70 - 74	14	-	-	-	-	-	-	-	-	-	-	14	...
75 +	8	-	-	-	-	-	-	-	-	-	-	8	...
Slovenia - Slovénie[43]													
2011 (C)													
Total	6 671	-	26	521	1 880	2 087	1 017	448	259	163	105	165	-
0 - 14	-	-	-	-	-	-	-	-	-	-	-	-	-
15 - 19	91	-	10	48	25	8	-	-	-	-	-	-	-
20 - 24	1 071	-	9	325	491	200	30	11	2	2	1	-	-
25 - 29	2 437	-	2	119	1 082	904	247	49	24	9	1	-	-
30 - 34	1 661	-	2	19	240	792	442	113	34	11	5	3	-
35 - 39	659	-	1	8	29	142	227	153	57	27	9	6	-
40 - 44	306	-	1	-	6	30	56	87	69	37	10	10	-
45 - 49	186	-	-	-	6	8	12	31	47	31	25	26	-
50 - 54	120	-	-	2	-	2	1	2	19	35	31	28	-
55 - 59	71	-	1	-	-	-	1	1	4	9	17	38	-
60 - 64	38	-	-	-	1	1	1	-	2	1	4	28	-
65 - 69	16	-	-	-	-	-	-	-	-	1	2	13	-
70 - 74	8	-	-	-	-	-	-	-	-	-	-	8	-
75 +	7	-	-	-	-	-	-	1	1	-	-	5	-
Unknown - Inconnu	-	-	-	-	-	-	-	-	-	-	-	-	-

Continent, country or area, year, code and age of bride / Continent, pays ou zone, date, code et âge de l'épouse	Total	0-14	15-19	20-24	25-29	30-34	35-39	40-44	45-49	50-54	55-59	60+	Unknown Inconnu
EUROPE													
Spain - Espagne													
2011 (C)													
Total	158 220	-	215	4 865	32 291	54 830	30 901	14 402	7 876	5 011	3 267	4 562	-
0 - 14	1	-	-	1	-	-	-	-	-	-	-	-	-
15 - 19	1 111	-	72	490	339	144	36	23	4	3	-	-	-
20 - 24	11 030	-	80	2 430	5 182	2 302	674	208	79	34	27	14	-
25 - 29	45 733	-	44	1 351	19 667	18 757	4 239	1 050	366	145	63	51	-
30 - 34	51 222	-	11	390	5 767	27 230	12 973	3 158	979	393	187	134	-
35 - 39	24 538	-	4	133	948	5 140	10 137	5 126	1 798	718	303	231	-
40 - 44	11 134	-	2	42	245	896	2 196	3 483	2 306	1 046	508	410	-
45 - 49	6 176	-	2	23	99	255	500	998	1 645	1 317	727	610	-
50 - 54	3 875	-	-	4	29	75	118	277	556	1 010	823	983	-
55 - 59	1 927	-	-	-	14	22	22	66	119	277	492	915	-
60 - 64	872	-	-	-	1	9	6	10	16	58	115	657	-
65 - 69	365	-	-	-	-	-	-	3	6	8	20	328	-
70 - 74	135	-	-	-	-	-	-	-	1	1	2	131	-
75 +	101	-	-	1	-	-	-	-	1	1	-	98	-
Unknown - Inconnu	-	-	-	-	-	-	-	-	-	-	-	-	-
Sweden - Suède													
2011 (C)													
Total	46 922	-	59	1 663	7 268	10 118	8 172	5 124	3 777	2 608	1 840	2 338	3 955
0 - 14	-	-	-	-	-	-	-	-	-	-	-	-	-
15 - 19	621	-	32	126	90	14	9	1	2	-	-	1	346
20 - 24	4 381	-	25	1 117	1 615	534	165	44	26	12	3	1	839
25 - 29	10 720	-	2	331	4 257	3 801	1 064	290	121	40	11	13	790
30 - 34	10 699	-	-	61	1 074	4 653	3 036	825	245	89	34	23	659
35 - 39	7 302	-	-	20	179	890	2 992	1 783	638	202	84	51	463
40 - 44	4 637	-	-	4	31	170	738	1 614	1 143	407	150	66	314
45 - 49	3 524	-	-	2	14	40	140	472	1 172	862	362	178	282
50 - 54	2 278	-	-	2	7	10	20	78	359	749	560	338	155
55 - 59	1 373	-	-	-	-	4	8	14	60	198	486	540	63
60 - 64	785	-	-	-	1	2	-	2	10	40	116	588	26
65 - 69	410	-	-	-	-	-	-	1	1	7	32	360	9
70 - 74	116	-	-	-	-	-	-	-	-	2	1	108	5
75 +	76	-	-	-	-	-	-	-	-	-	1	71	4
Switzerland - Suisse[44]													
2011 (C)													
Total	42 083	-	89	2 788	8 747	11 219	7 267	4 462	2 832	1 866	1 219	1 594	-
0 - 14	-	-	-	-	-	-	-	-	-	-	-	-	-
15 - 19	562	-	38	327	143	36	8	7	2	1	-	-	-
20 - 24	5 351	-	36	1 785	2 375	752	218	111	44	12	8	10	-
25 - 29	11 371	-	11	505	4 515	4 152	1 369	470	192	92	31	34	-
30 - 34	11 301	-	2	114	1 276	4 960	3 023	1 166	443	172	68	77	-
35 - 39	5 812	-	-	28	280	996	1 982	1 447	636	233	126	84	-
40 - 44	3 039	-	-	18	79	198	457	866	739	376	167	139	-
45 - 49	2 010	-	2	5	44	66	137	267	529	481	256	223	-
50 - 54	1 391	-	-	5	24	41	55	96	195	370	304	301	-
55 - 59	701	-	-	1	9	12	13	24	42	100	192	308	-
60 - 64	312	-	-	-	2	3	4	5	8	19	46	225	-
65 - 69	134	-	-	-	-	2	1	2	-	8	16	105	-
70 - 74	60	-	-	-	1	-	1	1	1	1	5	51	-
75 +	39	-	-	-	-	-	-	-	1	1	-	37	-
Unknown - Inconnu	-	-	-	-	-	-	-	-	-	-	-	-	-
TFYR of Macedonia - L'ex-R. y. de Macédoine													
2010 (C)													
Total	14 155	-	329	3 640	5 299	2 831	1 039	472	211	131	81	122	-
0 - 14	-	-	-	-	-	-	-	-	-	-	-	-	-
15 - 19	1 957	-	230	1 206	418	83	14	5	-	-	-	1	-
20 - 24	5 315	-	93	2 136	2 420	551	99	14	1	1	-	-	-
25 - 29	4 183	-	4	268	2 191	1 355	292	56	12	3	1	1	-
30 - 34	1 596	-	1	24	242	728	425	123	41	9	2	1	-
35 - 39	516	-	-	-	25	94	175	154	45	15	1	7	-
40 - 44	262	-	1	2	2	19	30	95	53	31	19	10	-
45 - 49	157	-	-	1	-	1	4	18	47	45	20	21	-
50 - 54	83	-	-	-	1	-	-	5	11	22	18	26	-
55 - 59	43	-	-	1	-	-	-	2	-	4	17	19	-

23. Marriages by age of groom and by age of bride: latest available year, 2003 - 2012
Mariages selon l'âge de l'époux et selon l'âge de l'épouse : dernière année disponible, 2003 - 2012 (continued - suite)

Continent, pays ou zone, date, code et âge de l'épouse	Total	0-14	15-19	20-24	25-29	30-34	35-39	40-44	45-49	50-54	55-59	60+	Unknown Inconnu
EUROPE													
TFYR of Macedonia - L'ex-R. y. de Macédoine													
2010													
60 - 64	24	-	-	-	-	-	-	-	-	-	3	21	-
65 - 69	11	-	-	-	-	-	-	-	1	1	-	9	-
70 - 74	3	-	-	-	-	-	-	-	-	-	-	3	-
75 +	5	-	-	2	-	-	-	-	-	-	-	3	-
Ukraine													
2011 (+C)													
Total	355 880	3[a]	7 733[g]	109 720	116 183	50 245	26 138	15 101	10 468	8 146	5 099	7 044	...
0 - 15	229	1[a]	80[g]	122	23	2	1	-	-	-	-	-	...
16 - 19	40 799	2[a]	4 948[g]	25 178	9 074	1 299	212	58	18	6	3	1	...
20 - 24	145 609	-[a]	2 379[g]	69 619	57 360	12 503	2 762	682	193	71	32	8	...
25 - 29	84 630	-[a]	265[g]	12 724	40 353	20 578	7 340	2 234	735	263	85	53	...
30 - 34	34 562	-[a]	42[g]	1 670	7 507	11 499	8 004	3 658	1 353	553	175	101	...
35 - 39	18 475	-[a]	12[g]	327	1 512	3 353	5 522	4 146	2 212	910	321	160	...
40 - 44	10 537	-[a]	5[g]	59	268	806	1 651	2 853	2 549	1 519	570	257	...
45 - 49	7 673	-[a]	2[g]	11	60	160	515	1 072	2 283	2 067	914	589	...
50 - 54	5 931	-[a]	-[g]	6	16	34	106	313	887	2 022	1 474	1 073	...
55 - 59	3 490	-[a]	-[g]	2	8	6	18	73	179	570	1 154	1 480	...
60 +	3 945	-[a]	-[g]	2	2	5	7	12	59	165	371	3 322	...
United Kingdom of Great Britain and Northern Ireland - Royaume-Uni de Grande-Bretagne et d'Irlande du Nord[45,46]													
2008 (C)													
Total	273 207	-	1 122	21 050	67 546	61 496	42 280	27 710	19 554	12 624	8 524	11 301	-
0 - 14	-	-	-	-	-	-	-	-	-	-	-	-	-
15 - 19	3 671	-	680	1 752	811	242	105	38	29	8	4	2	-
20 - 24	38 193	-	328	13 302	16 575	5 180	1 767	625	263	96	30	27	-
25 - 29	80 982	-	66	4 604	39 104	24 714	8 533	2 605	892	279	109	76	-
30 - 34	54 770	-	30	942	8 411	23 192	14 217	5 199	1 860	577	216	126	-
35 - 39	34 732	-	15	300	1 938	6 234	12 069	8 193	3 846	1 357	443	337	-
40 - 44	22 820	-	2	104	492	1 455	4 057	7 170	5 381	2 484	1 033	642	-
45 - 49	16 193	-	1	35	164	344	1 186	2 899	4 958	3 676	1 790	1 140	-
50 - 54	9 852	-	-	7	38	107	259	744	1 777	2 843	2 323	1 754	-
55 - 59	5 600	-	-	2	9	22	67	186	397	947	1 747	2 223	-
60 - 64	3 599	-	-	1	2	5	15	45	126	290	651	2 464	-
65 - 69	1 552	-	-	1	-	-	3	5	23	55	142	1 323	-
70 - 74	769	-	-	-	2	-	2	1	1	10	26	727	-
75 +	474	-	-	-	-	1	-	-	1	2	10	460	-
Unknown - Inconnu	-	-	-	-	-	-	-	-	1	2	10	460	-
OCEANIA - OCÉANIE													
Australia - Australie[47]													
2011 (+C)													
Total	121 752	-	471	13 576	37 099	28 143	15 275	9 001	6 267	4 616	3 140	4 164	-
0 - 14	-	-	-	-	-	-	-	-	-	-	-	-	-
15 - 19	2 078	-	247	1 202	461	111	33	10	7	5	-	-	-
20 - 24	22 235	-	185	9 152	9 452	2 323	655	227	115	71	27	27	-
25 - 29	42 073	-	31	2 587	22 340	12 046	3 338	1 034	355	166	104	74	-
30 - 34	24 245	-	6	436	3 959	10 921	5 637	1 993	753	295	145	101	-
35 - 39	11 812	-	-	114	661	2 204	4 095	2 646	1 207	499	226	157	-
40 - 44	6 954	-	-	49	146	385	1 153	2 109	1 658	837	363	253	-
45 - 49	4 998	-	-	23	56	105	274	725	1 482	1 264	665	404	-
50 - 54	3 496	-	-	9	19	32	75	190	540	1 091	854	686	-
55 - 59	1 854	-	-	3	5	6	10	53	123	304	562	788	-
60 - 64	1 081	-	-	-	-	6	4	11	21	68	165	805	-
65 - 69	492	-	-	-	-	3	-	3	5	13	20	448	-
70 - 74	244	-	-	-	-	-	-	-	-	3	5	236	-
75 +	190	-	-	-	-	3	-	-	-	-	3	184	-
Unknown - Inconnu	-	-	-	-	-	-	-	-	-	-	-	-	-

23. Marriages by age of groom and by age of bride: latest available year, 2003 - 2012
Mariages selon l'âge de l'époux et selon l'âge de l'épouse : dernière année disponible, 2003 - 2012 (continued - suite)

Continent, country or area, year, code and age of bride / Continent, pays ou zone, date, code et âge de l'épouse	Total	_____ Age of groom - âge de l'époux _____											
		0-14	15-19	20-24	25-29	30-34	35-39	40-44	45-49	50-54	55-59	60+	Unknown Inconnu
OCEANIA - OCÉANIE													
Fiji - Fidji													
2004 (+C)													
Total	7 076	-	125	2 060	2 429	1 113	522	334	217	125	74	77	-
0 - 14	-	...	...	...	...	...	...	...	...	...	...	...	...
15 - 19	1 176	...	...	...	...	...	...	...	...	...	...	...	...
20 - 24	2 990	...	...	...	...	...	...	...	...	...	...	...	...
25 - 29	1 438	...	...	...	...	...	...	...	...	...	...	...	...
30 - 34	656	...	...	...	...	...	...	...	...	...	...	...	...
35 - 39	367	...	...	...	...	...	...	...	...	...	...	...	...
40 - 44	204	...	...	...	...	...	...	...	...	...	...	...	...
45 - 49	128	...	...	...	...	...	...	...	...	...	...	...	...
50 - 54	62	...	...	...	...	...	...	...	...	...	...	...	...
55 - 59	35	...	...	...	...	...	...	...	...	...	...	...	...
60 - 64	13	...	...	...	...	...	...	...	...	...	...	...	...
65 +	7	...	...	...	...	...	...	...	...	...	...	...	...
Guam													
2003 (C)													
Total	1 334	...	41^e	268	353	240	171	110	55	46	14	36	-
0 - 19	96	...	23^e	49	18	3	-	3	-	-	-	-	-
20 - 24	334	...	14^e	164	102	34	14	2	3	1	-	-	-
25 - 29	374	...	2^e	36	180	104	24	15	6	4	1	2	-
30 - 34	230	...	1^e	15	38	69	63	27	6	8	2	1	-
35 - 39	140	...	1^e	4	12	26	48	32	11	4	1	1	-
40 - 44	74	...	-^{e}	-	3	4	13	21	12	13	2	6	-
45 - 49	42	...	-^{e}	-	-	-	7	10	10	8	4	3	-
50 - 54	23	...	-^{e}	-	-	-	-	-	7	6	3	7	-
55 - 59	10	...	-^{e}	-	-	-	-	-	-	2	-	8	-
60 - 69	8	...	-^{e}	-	-	-	1	-	-	-	1	6	-
70 +	3	...	-^{e}	-	-	-	1	-	-	-	-	2	-
New Caledonia - Nouvelle-Calédonie													
2010 (C)													
Total	908	...	2^e	62	149	200	171	169^m	...	90^n	...	65	-
0 - 19	13	...	1^e	6	2	2	1	1^m	...	-^{n}	...	-	-
20 - 24	118	...	-^{e}	36	51	18	10	2^m	...	1^n	...	-	-
25 - 29	194	...	1^e	16	77	63	20	13^m	...	3^n	...	1	-
30 - 34	205	...	-^{e}	4	14	94	62	27^m	...	4^n	...	-	-
35 - 39	139	...	-^{e}	-	3	19	55	52^m	...	7^n	...	3	-
40 - 49	150	...	-^{e}	-	2	4	22	65^m	...	41^n	...	16	-
50 - 59	59	...	-^{e}	-	-	-	1	9^m	...	30^n	...	19	-
60 +	30	...	-^{e}	-	-	-	-	-^{m}	...	4^n	...	26	-
New Zealand - Nouvelle-Zélande[7]													
2011 (+C)													
Total	20 231	170	2 419	5 401	4 264	2 623	1 736	1 235	895	604	430	454	...
0 - 14	-	-	-	-	-	-	-	-	-	-	-	-	...
15 - 19	513	103	285	95	20	5	4	1	-	-	-	-	...
20 - 24	3 515	59	1 624	1 363	315	102	28	12	7	1	2	2	...
25 - 29	6 089	5	414	3 245	1 734	464	153	48	19	3	2	2	...
30 - 34	3 866	1	67	568	1 754	933	369	110	36	11	6	11	...
35 - 39	2 180	2	18	98	342	788	507	266	101	32	17	9	...
40 - 44	1 444	-	8	23	76	264	453	341	173	60	30	16	...
45 - 49	1 058	-	3	5	17	58	163	327	284	119	58	24	...
50 - 54	710	-	-	4	4	6	47	100	200	191	108	50	...
55 - 59	394	-	-	-	2	2	11	25	58	138	97	61	...
60 - 64	227	-	-	-	-	1	1	4	14	40	78	89	...
65 - 69	117	-	-	-	-	-	-	1	2	7	22	85	...
70 - 74	75	-	-	-	-	-	-	-	1	2	9	63	...
75 +	43	-	-	-	-	-	-	-	-	-	1	42	...
Unknown - Inconnu	-	-	-	-	-	-	-	-	-	-	-	-	...
Niue - Nioué													
2009 (C)													
Total	12	...	-	2	3	4	-	1	1	-	1	-	-
15 - 19	-	...	...	...	...	...	...	...	...	...	...	...	...
20 - 24	-	...	...	...	...	...	...	...	...	...	...	...	...
25 - 29	3	...	...	...	...	...	...	...	...	...	...	...	...

Continent, country or area, year, code and age of bride / Continent, pays ou zone, date, code et âge de l'épouse	Total	Age of groom - âge de l'époux											
		0-14	15-19	20-24	25-29	30-34	35-39	40-44	45-49	50-54	55-59	60+	Unknown Inconnu
OCEANIA - OCÉANIE													
Niue - Nioué													
2009													
30 - 34	4	...	...	...	...	...	...	...	...	...	...	...	...
35 - 39	3	...	...	...	...	...	...	...	...	...	...	...	...
40 - 44	-	...	...	...	...	...	...	...	...	...	...	...	...
45 - 49	1	...	...	...	...	...	...	...	...	...	...	...	...
50 - 54	1	...	...	...	...	...	...	...	...	...	...	...	...
55 - 59	-	...	...	...	...	...	...	...	...	...	...	...	...
60 - 64	-	...	...	...	...	...	...	...	...	...	...	...	...
65 +	-	...	...	...	...	...	...	...	...	...	...	...	...
Tonga[48]													
2004* (+C)													
Total	677	-	34	237	203	83	59	27	14	20[r]	...	...	-
0 - 14	-	...	...	...	...	...	...	...	...	...	...	...	...
15 - 19	107	...	...	...	...	...	...	...	...	...	...	...	...
20 - 24	262	...	...	...	...	...	...	...	...	...	...	...	...
25 - 29	161	...	...	...	...	...	...	...	...	...	...	...	...
30 - 34	76	...	...	...	...	...	...	...	...	...	...	...	...
35 - 39	44	...	...	...	...	...	...	...	...	...	...	...	...
40 - 44	17	...	...	...	...	...	...	...	...	...	...	...	...
45 - 49	6	...	...	...	...	...	...	...	...	...	...	...	...
50 +	4	...	...	...	...	...	...	...	...	...	...	...	...
Unknown - Inconnu	-	...	...	...	...	...	...	...	...	...	...	...	...
Wallis and Futuna Islands - Îles Wallis et Futuna													
2008 (C)													
Total	53	-	1	14	23	8	3	2	-	2	-	-	-
0 - 14	-	...	...	...	...	...	...	...	...	...	...	...	...
15 - 19	9	...	...	...	...	...	...	...	...	...	...	...	...
20 - 24	18	...	...	...	...	...	...	...	...	...	...	...	...
25 - 29	12	...	...	...	...	...	...	...	...	...	...	...	...
30 - 34	7	...	...	...	...	...	...	...	...	...	...	...	...
35 - 39	5	...	...	...	...	...	...	...	...	...	...	...	...
40 - 44	-	...	...	...	...	...	...	...	...	...	...	...	...
45 - 49	1	...	...	...	...	...	...	...	...	...	...	...	...
50 - 54	-	...	...	...	...	...	...	...	...	...	...	...	...
55 - 59	-	...	...	...	...	...	...	...	...	...	...	...	...
60 - 64	1	...	...	...	...	...	...	...	...	...	...	...	...
65 - 69	-	...	...	...	...	...	...	...	...	...	...	...	...
70 - 74	-	...	...	...	...	...	...	...	...	...	...	...	...
75 +	-	...	...	...	...	...	...	...	...	...	...	...	...

FOOTNOTES - NOTES

Italics: data from civil registers which are incomplete or of unknown completeness. - Italiques : données incomplètes ou dont le degré d'exactitude n'est pas connu, provenant des registres de l'état civil.

* Provisional. - Données provisoires.

'Code' indicates the source of data, as follows:
C - Civil registration, estimated over 90% complete
U - Civil registration, estimated less than 90% complete
| - Other source, estimated reliable
+ - Data tabulated by date of registration rather than occurence
... - Information not available

Le 'Code' indique la source des données, comme suit :
C - Registres de l'état civil considérés complèts à 90 p. 100 au moins
U - Registres de l'état civil qui ne sont pas considérés complèts à 90 p. 100 au moins
| - Autre source, considérée pas douteuses
+ - Données exploitées selon la date de l'enregistrement et non la date de l'événement
... - Information pas disponible

a Refers to 0-15 years of age. - Données se raportent au groupe d'âges 0-15.
b Refers to 0-16 years of age. - Données se raportent au groupe d'âges 0-16.
c Refers to 0-17 years of age. - Données se raportent au groupe d'âges 0-17.
d Refers to 0-18 years of age. - Données se raportent au groupe d'âges 0-18.
e Refers to 0-19 years of age. - Données se raportent au groupe d'âges 0-19.
f Refers to 0-24 years of age. - Données se raportent au groupe d'âges 0-24.
g Refers to 16-19 years of age. - Données se raportent au groupe d'âges 16-19.
h Refers to 17-19 years of age. - Données se raportent au groupe d'âges 17-19.
i Refers to 18-19 years of age. - Données se raportent au groupe d'âges 18-19.
j Refers to 19-24 years of age. - Données se raportent au groupe d'âges 19-24.
k Refers to 20-29 years of age. - Données se raportent au groupe d'âges 20-29.
l Refers to 30-39 years of age. - Données se raportent au groupe d'âges 30-39.
m Refers to 40-49 years of age. - Données se raportent au groupe d'âges 40-49.
n Refers to 50-59 years of age. - Données se raportent au groupe d'âges 50-59.
o Refers to 35+ years of age. - Données se raportent au groupe d'âges 35+.
p Refers to 40+ years of age. - Données se raportent au groupe d'âges 40+.
q Refers to 45+ years of age. - Données se raportent au groupe d'âges 45+.
r Refers to 50+ years of age. - Données se raportent au groupe d'âges 50+.
s Refers to 55+ years of age. - Données se raportent au groupe d'âges 55+.

1 Including marriages resumed after 'revocable divorce' (among Moslem population), which approximates legal separation. - Y compris les unions reconstituées après un 'divorce révocable' (parmi la population musulmane), qui est à peu près l'équivalent d'une séparation légale.

2 Excludes the islands of St. Brandon and Agalega. - Non compris les îles St. Brandon et Agalega.

3 Including visitors. - Y compris les visiteurs.

4 Excluding visitors. - Ne comprend pas les visiteurs.

5 As reported by the country. Reasons for discrepancy with other tables not ascertained. - Comme indiqué par le pays. L'on ne connaît pas la raison des écarts avec d'autres tableaux.

6 Data refer to resident population only. - Pour la population résidante seulement.

7 Data refer to marriages registered at the place of residence of the groom. - Correspond aux mariages enregistrés dans le lieu de résidence du marié.

8 Marriages registered by residence of bride. - Les mariages sont enregistrés selon le lieu de résidence de la mariée.

9 Including marriages where bride/groom are non-residents. - Y compris les mariages pour lesquels le marié et la mariée sont des non-résidents.

10 Excludes nomadic Indian tribes. - Non compris les tribus d'Indiens nomades.

11 Source: The National Registers of Identification and Civil Status (RENIEC). - Source : Les Registres Nationaux d'Identification et d'État Civil (RENIEC).

12 Data refers to metropolitan Lima and Callao. - Les données font référence à la région métropolitaine de Lima et Callao.

13 Residence established by place where marriage took place. - La résidence est déterminée par rapport au lieu où le mariage a été célébré.

14 Data refer to marriages of residents only. - Les données ne portent que sur les mariages de résidents.

15 Data refer to government controlled areas. - Les données se rapportent aux zones contrôlées par le Gouvernement.

16 Data refer to the Iranian Year which begins on 21 March and ends on 20 March of the following year. - Les données concernent l'année iranienne, qui commence le 21 mars et se termine le 20 mars de l'année suivante.

17 Includes data for East Jerusalem and Israeli residents in certain other territories under occupation by Israeli military forces since June 1967. - Y compris les données pour Jérusalem-Est et les résidents israéliens dans certains autres territoires occupés depuis 1967 par les forces armées israéliennes.

18 Data refer to Japanese nationals in Japan only; and to grooms and brides married for the first time whose marriages occurred and were registered in the same year. - Les données se raportent aux nationaux japonais au Japon seulement; et aux époux et épouses mariés pour la première fois, dont le mariage a été célébré et enregistré la même année.

19 Excluding data for Jordanian territory under occupation since June 1967 by Israeli military forces. Excluding foreigners, including registered Palestinian refugees. - Non compris les données pour le territoire jordanien occupé depuis juin 1967 par les forces armées israéliennes. Non compris les étrangers, mais y compris les réfugiés de Palestine enregistrés.

20 Data refer to residence of groom. - Données relatives au lieu de résidence du marié.

21 Excluding alien armed forces, civilian aliens employed by armed forces, and foreign diplomatic personnel and their dependants. - Non compris les militaires étrangers, les civils étrangers employés par les forces armées ni le personnel diplomatique étranger et les membres de leur famille les accompagnant.

22 Excluding marriages previously officiated outside Singapore or under religious and customary rites. - Ne comprend pas les mariages prononcés ailleurs qu'à Singapour ni les mariages religieux ou coutumiers.

23 Only marriages in which the bride was resident of Åland Islands. - Ne porte que sur les mariages pour lesquels la mariée réside des Îles Åland.

24 Excluding aliens temporarily in the area. - Non compris les étrangers se trouvant temporairement dans le territoire.

25 Since 2003, marriage between persons of the same sex is authorized in Belgium, but the sex of spouses is not revealed. In this table, husband is used for first spouse, whereas wife is used for second spouse. - Depuis 2003, le mariage entre personnes de même sexe est autorisé en Belgique, mais le sexe des conjoints n'est pas indiqué. Dans ce tableau, la mention "époux" est utilisée pour le premier conjoint et la mention "épouse" pour le second conjoint.

26 Including armed forces stationed outside the country and alien armed forces in the area, if the marriage is performed by local authority. - Y compris les militaires nationaux hors du pays et les militaires étrangers en garnison sur le territoire, si le mariage a été célébré par l'autorité locale.

27 Including nationals outside the country, but excluding foreigners in the country. - Y compris les nationaux à l'étranger, mais non compris les étrangers sur le territoire.

28 Excluding Faeroe Islands and Greenland shown separately, if available. - Non compris les Iles Féroé et le Groenland, qui font l'objet de rubriques distinctes, si disponible.

29 Excluding Åland Islands. - Non compris les Îles d'Åland.

30 Only marriages in which the bride was resident in Finland. - Ne porte que sur les mariages pour lesquels la mariée réside en Finlande.

31 Including armed forces stationed outside the country. - Y compris les militaires nationaux hors du pays.

32 Total is including the data of foreigners, persons of unknown residence and homeless. - Le total comprend les données relatives aux étrangers, aux personnes n'ayant pas de lieu de résidence connu et aux sans-abri.

33 Definition of localities was revised from 2011 causing a break with the previous series. - La rupture par rapport aux séries précédentes s'explique par le fait que la définition des localités a été révisée depuis 2011.

34 Data for residence abroad are excluded. - Les données relatives aux résidents à l'étranger sont exclues.

35 Data refer to common residence after marriage. - Données se rapportant à la résidence commune après le mariage.

36 Data refer to marriages where one or both partners are residents. - Les données portent sur les mariages pour lesquels l'un des deux partenaires ou les deux sont résidents.

37 Marriages of couples of which at least one partner is recorded in a Dutch municipal register, irrespective of the country where the marriage was performed. - Correspond aux mariages pour lesquels au moins l'un des partenaires est inscrit sur un registre municipal néerlandais, quel que soit le pays dans lequel le mariage est célébré.

38 Including residents outside the country if listed in a Netherlands population register. - Englobe les résidents se trouvant à l'étranger à condition qu'ils soient inscrits sur le registre de population des Pays-Bas.

39 Includes same sex marriages. - Y compris les mariages entre personnes du même sexe.

40 Data refer to first marriages only. - Données se rapportent aux premiers mariages seulement.

41 Includes civil and religious marriages as well as not specified. - Englobe les mariages civils et religieux et ceux pour lesquels rien n'a été indiqué.

42 Excludes data for Kosovo and Metohia. - Sans les données pour le Kosovo et Metohie.

43 Data refer to residence of groom or bride before marriage. - Données relatives au lieu de résidence du marié ou de la mariée avant le mariage.

44 Data based on the residence of groom if he has permanent address in the country, otherwise, based on the residence of bride. If neither partner is a permanent resident, the marriage is not included in the official statistics. - Les données sont fondées sur la résidence du marié si celui-ci a une adresse permanente dans le pays, sinon elles sont fondées sur la résidence de la mariée. Si aucun des deux partenaires n'est un résident permanent, le mariage n'apparaît pas dans les statistiques officielles.

45 Marriages registered by place of occurrence of marriage. - Mariages enregistrés en fonction du lieu de l'événement.

46 Excluding Channel Islands (Guernsey and Jersey) and Isle of Man, shown separately, if available. - Non compris les îles Anglo-Normandes (Guernesey et Jersey) et l'île de Man, qui font l'objet de rubriques distinctes, si disponible.

47 Data for certain cells suppressed by national statistical office for confidentiality reasons. - Les données pour certaines cases ont été supprimées par le bureau national de statistiques pour des raisons de confidentialité.

48 Data refer to the island of Tongatapu only. - Les données se réfèrent uniquement à l'île de Tongatapu.

Table 24 - *Demographic Yearbook 2012*

Table 24 presents the number of divorces and crude divorce rates for as many years as possible between 2008 and 2012.

Description of variables: Divorce is defined as a final legal dissolution of a marriage, that is, the separation of husband and wife which confers on the parties the right to remarriage under civil, religious and/or other provisions, according to the laws of each country[1].

Unless otherwise noted, divorce statistics exclude legal separations that do not allow remarriage. These statistics refer to the number of divorces granted, and not to the number of persons divorcing.

Divorce statistics are obtained from court records and/or civil registers according to national practice. The actual compilation of these statistics may be the responsibility of the civil registrar, the national statistical office or other government offices.

The urban/rural classification of divorces is that provided by each country or area; it is presumed to be based on the national census definitions of urban population, which have been set forth at the end of the technical notes for table 6.

Rate computation: Crude divorce rates by urban/rural residence are the annual number of divorces per 1 000 mid-year population. Rates presented in this table have been limited to those countries or areas having at least a total of 30 divorces in a given year. These rates are calculated by the Statistics Division of the United Nations based on the appropriate reference population (for example: total population, nationals only etc.) if known and available. If the reference population is not known or unavailable the total population is used to calculate the rates. Therefore, if the population that is used to calculate the rates is different from the correct reference population, the rates presented might under- or overstate the true situation in a country or area.

Reliability of data: Each country or area has been asked to indicate the estimated completeness of the divorces recorded in its civil register. These national assessments are indicated by the quality codes "C" and "U" that appear in the first column of this table.

"C" indicates that the data are estimated to be virtually complete, that is, representing at least 90 per cent of the divorces that occur each year, while "U" indicates that data are estimated to be incomplete, that is, representing less than 90 per cent of the divorces occurring each year. The code "..." indicates that no information was provided regarding completeness.

Data from civil registers that are reported as incomplete or of unknown completeness (coded "U" or "...") are considered unreliable. They appear in *italics* in this table and the rates were not computed on data so coded. These quality codes apply only to data from civil registers. For more information about the quality of vital statistics data in general, see section 4.2 of the Technical Notes.

Limitations: Statistics on divorces are subject to the same qualifications as have been set forth for vital statistics in general and divorce statistics in particular as discussed in section 4 of the Technical Notes.

Divorce, like marriage, is a legal event, and this has implications for international comparability of data. Divorce has been defined, for statistical purposes, in terms of the laws of individual countries or areas. The laws pertaining to divorce vary considerably from one country or area to another. This variation in the legal provision for divorce also affects the incidence of divorce, which is relatively low in countries or areas where divorce decrees are difficult to obtain.

Since divorces are granted by courts and statistics on divorce refer to the actual divorce decree, effective as of the date of the decree, marked year-to-year fluctuations may reflect court delays and clearances rather than trends in the incidence of divorce. The comparability of divorce statistics may also be affected by tabulation procedures. In some countries or areas annulments and/or legal separations may be included. This practice is more common for countries or areas in which the number of divorces is small. Information on this practice is given in the footnotes when known.

The registration of a divorce in many countries or areas is the responsibility solely of the court or the authority which granted it. Since the registration recording such cases is part of the records of the court proceedings, divorces are likely to be registered soon after the decree is granted. For this reason the practice of tabulating data by date of registration does not generally pose serious problems of comparability as it does in the case of birth and death statistics.

As noted briefly above, the incidence of divorce is affected by the relative ease or difficulty of obtaining a divorce according to the laws of individual countries or areas. The incidence of divorce is also affected by the ability of individuals to meet financial and other costs of the court procedures. Connected with this aspect is the influence of certain religious faiths on the incidence of divorce. For all these reasons, divorce statistics are not strictly comparable as measures of family dissolution by legal means. Furthermore, family dissolution by other than legal means, such as separation, is not measured in statistics for divorce.

For certain countries or areas there is or was no legal provision for divorce in the sense used here, and therefore no data for these countries or areas appear in this table.

In addition, it should be noted that rates are affected also by the quality and limitations of the population estimates that are used in their computation. The problems of under-enumeration or over-enumeration, and to some extent, the differences in definition of total population, have been discussed in section 3 of the Technical Notes dealing with population data in general, and specific information pertaining to individual countries or areas is given in the footnotes to table 3.

As will be seen from the footnotes, strict correspondence between the numerator of the rate and the denominator is not always obtained; for example, divorces among civilian plus military segments of the population may be related to civilian population only. The effect of this may be to increase the rates but, in most cases, the effect is negligible.

As mentioned above, data for some countries or areas may include annulments and/or legal separations. This practice affects the comparability of the crude divorce rates. For example, inclusion of annulments in the numerator of the rates produces a negligible effect on the rates, but inclusion of legal separations may have a measurable effect on the level.

It should be emphasized that crude divorce rates like crude birth, death and marriage rates may be seriously affected by age-sex structure of the populations to which they relate. Like crude marriage rates, they are also affected by the existing distribution of the population by marital status. Nevertheless, crude divorce rates provide a simple measure of the level and changes in divorces.

The comparability of data by urban/rural residence is affected by the national definitions of urban and rural used in tabulating these data. It is assumed, in the absence of specific information to the contrary, that the definitions of urban and rural used in connection with the national population census were also used in the compilation of the vital statistics for each country or area. However, it cannot be excluded that, for a given country or area, different definitions of urban and rural are used for the vital statistics data and the population census data respectively. When known, the definitions of urban in national population censuses are presented at the end of the technical notes for table 6. As discussed in detail in the notes, these definitions vary considerably from one country or area to another.

In addition to problems of comparability, divorce rates classified by urban/rural residence are also subject to certain special types of bias. If, when calculating divorce rates, different definitions of urban are used in connection with the vital events and the population data, and if this results in a net difference between the numerator and denominator of the rate in the population at risk, then the divorce rates would be biased. Urban/rural differentials in divorce rates may also be affected by whether the vital events have been tabulated in terms of place of occurrence or place of usual residence. This problem is discussed in more detail in section 4.1.4.1 of the Technical Notes.

Earlier data: Divorces have been shown in previous issues of the Demographic Yearbook. The earliest data, which were for 1935, appeared in the 1951 issue. For more information on specific topics and years for which data are reported, readers should consult the Historical Index.

NOTES

[1] For definition, please see section 4.1.1 of the Technical Notes.

Tableau 24 – *Annuaire démographique 2012*

Le tableau 24 présente des statistiques concernant les divorces et les taux bruts de divortialité pour le plus grand nombre d'années possible entre 2008 et 2012.

Description des variables : le divorce est la dissolution légale et définitive des liens du mariage, c'est-à-dire la séparation de l'époux et de l'épouse qui confère aux parties le droit de se remarier civilement ou religieusement, ou selon toute autre procédure, conformément à la législation du pays[1].

Sauf indication contraire, les statistiques de la divortialité n'englobent pas les séparations légales qui excluent un remariage. Ces statistiques se rapportent aux jugements de divorce prononcés, non aux personnes divorcées.

Les statistiques de la divortialité proviennent, selon la pratique suivie par chaque pays, des actes des tribunaux et/ou des registres de l'état civil. L'officier d'état civil, les services nationaux de statistique ou d'autres services gouvernementaux peuvent être chargés d'établir ces statistiques.

La classification des divorces selon le lieu de résidence (zone urbaine ou rurale) est celle qui a été communiquée par chaque pays ou zone ; on part du principe qu'elle repose sur les définitions de la population urbaine utilisées pour les recensements nationaux, qui sont reproduites à la fin des notes techniques du tableau 6.

Calcul des taux : les taux bruts de divortialité selon le lieu de résidence (zone urbaine ou rurale) représentent le nombre annuel de divorces enregistrés pour 1 000 habitants au milieu de l'année. Les taux de ce tableau ne se rapportent qu'aux pays ou zones où l'on a enregistré un total d'au moins 30 divorces pendant une année donnée. Ces taux sont calculés par la division de statistique des Nations Unies sur la base de la population de référence adéquate (par exemple : population totale, nationaux seulement, etc.) si connue et disponible. Si la population de référence n'est pas connue ou n'est pas disponible, la population totale est utilisée pour calculer les taux. Par conséquent, si la population utilisée pour calculer les taux est différente de la population de référence adéquate, les taux présentés sont susceptibles de sous ou sur estimer la situation réelle d'un pays ou d'un territoire.

Fiabilité des données : il a été demandé à chaque pays ou zone d'indiquer le degré estimatif de complétude des données sur les divorces figurant dans ses registres d'état civil. Ces évaluations nationales sont désignées par les codes de qualité "C" et "U" qui apparaissent dans la deuxième colonne du tableau.

La lettre "C" indique que les données sont jugées à peu près complètes, c'est-à-dire qu'elles représentent au moins 90 p. 100 des divorces survenus chaque année ; la lettre "U" signale que les données sont jugées incomplètes, c'est-à-dire qu'elles représentent moins de 90 p. 100 des divorces survenus chaque année. Le code "..." indique qu'aucun renseignement n'a été communiqué quant à la complétude des données.

Les données issues des registres de l'état civil qui sont déclarées incomplètes ou dont le degré de complétude n'est pas connu (code "U" ou "...") sont jugées douteuses. Elles apparaissent en italique dans le tableau et les taux correspondants n'ont pas été calculés. Les codes de qualité ne s'appliquent qu'aux données extraites des registres de l'état civil. Pour plus de précisions sur la qualité des données reposant sur les statistiques de l'état civil en général, voir la section 4.2 des notes techniques.

Insuffisance des données : les statistiques des divorces appellent les mêmes réserves que celles formulées à propos des statistiques de l'état civil en général et des statistiques de divortialité en particulier (voir la section 4 des notes techniques).

Le divorce est, comme le mariage, un acte juridique, et ce fait influe sur la comparabilité internationale des données. Aux fins de la statistique, le divorce est défini par la législation de chaque pays ou zone. La législation sur le divorce varie considérablement d'un pays ou d'une zone à l'autre, ce qui influe aussi sur la fréquence des divorces, laquelle est relativement faible dans les pays ou zones où le jugement de divorce est difficile à obtenir.

Du fait que les divorces sont prononcés par les tribunaux et que les statistiques de la divortialité se rapportent aux jugements de divorce proprement dits, qui prennent effet à la date où ces jugements sont rendus, il se peut que des fluctuations annuelles accusées traduisent le rythme plus ou moins rapide auquel les affaires sont jugées plutôt que l'évolution de la fréquence des divorces. Les méthodes d'exploitation des données peuvent aussi influer sur la comparabilité des statistiques de la divortialité. Dans certains pays ou zones, ces statistiques peuvent comprendre les annulations et/ou les séparations légales. C'est notamment le cas dans les pays ou zones où les divorces sont peu nombreux. Lorsqu'ils sont connus, des renseignements à ce propos sont donnés en note à la fin du tableau.

Étant donné que dans de nombreux pays ou zones, le tribunal ou l'autorité qui a prononcé le divorce est seul habilité à enregistrer cet acte, et, comme l'acte d'enregistrement figure alors sur les registres du tribunal, l'enregistrement suit généralement de peu le jugement. C'est pourquoi la pratique consistant à exploiter les données selon la date de l'enregistrement ne pose généralement pas les graves problèmes de comparabilité auxquels on se heurte dans le cas des statistiques des naissances et des décès.

Comme on l'a brièvement mentionné ci-dessus, la fréquence des divorces est fonction notamment de la facilité relative avec laquelle la législation de chaque pays ou zone permet d'obtenir le divorce. Elle dépend également de la capacité des intéressés à supporter les frais de procédure. Il faut aussi citer l'influence de certaines religions sur la fréquence des divorces. Pour toutes ces raisons, les statistiques de divortialité ne sont pas rigoureusement comparables et ne permettent pas de mesurer exactement la fréquence des dissolutions légales des mariages. De plus, elles ne rendent pas compte des cas de dissolution extrajudiciaire du mariage, comme la séparation.

Dans certains pays ou zones, il n'existe ou il n'existait pas de législation sur le divorce selon l'acception retenue aux fins de ce tableau, si bien que l'on ne dispose pas de données les concernant.

De surcroît, il convient de noter que l'exactitude des taux dépend également de la qualité et des insuffisances des estimations de population qui sont utilisées pour leur calcul. Le problème des erreurs par excès ou par défaut commises lors du dénombrement et, dans une certaine mesure, le problème de l'hétérogénéité des définitions de la population totale ont été examinés à la section 3 des notes techniques, relative à la population en général ; des explications concernant les différents pays ou zones sont données en note à la fin du tableau 3.

Comme on le verra dans les notes, il n'a pas toujours été possible d'obtenir une correspondance rigoureuse entre le numérateur et le dénominateur pour le calcul des taux. Par exemple, les divorces parmi la population civile et les militaires sont parfois rapportés à la population civile seulement. Cela peut avoir pour effet d'accroître les taux, mais, dans la plupart des cas, il est probable que la différence sera négligeable.

Comme indiqué plus haut, les données concernant certains pays ou zones peuvent comprendre les annulations et/ou les séparations légales. Cette pratique influe sur la comparabilité des taux bruts de divortialité. Par exemple, l'inclusion des annulations dans le numérateur a une influence négligeable, mais l'inclusion des séparations légales peut avoir un effet appréciable.

Il faut souligner que les taux bruts de divortialité, de même que les taux bruts de natalité, de mortalité et de nuptialité, peuvent varier sensiblement selon la structure par âge et par sexe. Comme les taux bruts de nuptialité, ils peuvent également varier en raison de la répartition de la population selon l'état matrimonial. Les taux bruts de divortialité offrent néanmoins un moyen simple de mesurer la fréquence et l'évolution des divorces.

La comparabilité des données selon le lieu de résidence (zone urbaine ou rurale) peut être limitée par les définitions nationales des termes « urbain » et « rural » utilisées pour la mise en tableaux de ces données. En l'absence d'indications contraires, on a supposé que les mêmes définitions avaient servi pour le recensement national de la population et pour l'établissement des statistiques de l'état civil pour chaque pays ou zone. Toutefois, il n'est pas exclu que, pour une zone ou un pays donné, des définitions différentes aient été retenues. Les définitions du terme « urbain » utilisées pour les recensements nationaux de population ont été présentées à la fin des notes techniques du tableau 6 lorsqu'elles étaient connues. Comme on l'a précisé dans les notes techniques relatives au tableau 6, ces définitions varient considérablement d'un pays ou d'une zone à l'autre.

Outre les problèmes de comparabilité, les taux de divortialité classés selon le lieu de résidence (zone urbaine ou rurale) sont également sujets à des distorsions particulières. Si l'on utilise des définitions différentes du terme « urbain » pour classer les faits d'état civil et les données relatives à la population lors du calcul des taux et qu'il en résulte une différence nette entre le numérateur et le dénominateur pour le taux de la population exposée au risque, les taux de divortialité s'en trouveront faussés. La différence entre ces taux pour les zones urbaines et rurales pourra aussi être faussée selon que les faits d'état civil auront été classés d'après le lieu de l'événement ou d'après le lieu de résidence habituel. Ce problème est examiné plus en détail à la section 4.1.4.1 des notes techniques.

Données publiées antérieurement : des statistiques concernant les divorces ont déjà été présentées dans des éditions antérieures de l'*Annuaire démographique*. Les plus anciennes, qui portaient sur 1935, ont été publiées dans l'édition de 1951. Pour plus de précisions concernant les années et les sujets pour lesquels des données ont été publiées, se reporter à l'index historique.

NOTE

[1] Pour la définition, voir la section 4.1.1 des Notes techniques.

24. Divorces and crude divorce rates by urban/rural residence: 2008 - 2012
Divorces et taux bruts de divortialité selon la résidence, urbaine/rurale : 2008 - 2012

Continent, country or area, and urban/rural residence / Continent, pays ou zone et résidence, urbaine/rurale	Co-de	Number - Nombre					Rate - Taux				
		2008	2009	2010	2011	2012	2008	2009	2010	2011	2012
AFRICA - AFRIQUE											
Egypt - Égypte[1]											
Total	+C	84 430	141 467	149 376	151 933	...	1.1	1.8	1.9	1.9	...
Urban - Urbaine	+C	44 593	75 134	85 686	87 091	...	1.4	2.3	2.5	2.5	...
Rural - Rurale	+C	39 837	66 333	63 690	64 842	...	0.9	1.5	1.4	1.4	...
Lesotho											
Total	+U	...	236	127	...	...	...	...	...	...	...
Libya - Libye[2]											
Total	+U	2 989	3 691	...	...	...	...	...	...	...	...
Mauritius - Maurice[3]											
Total	+C	1 569	2 154	1 837	1 788		1.2	1.7	1.4	1.4	
Mozambique											
Total	+U	849	936	869	...	...	...	...	...	...	...
Saint Helena ex. dep. - Sainte-Hélène sans dép.											
Total	C	6	5	...	1	5	...	...	...	...	...
Seychelles											
Total	+C	145	145	156	165	...	1.7	1.7	1.7	1.9	...
South Africa - Afrique du Sud											
Total	...	28 924	30 763	22 936	...	...	...	...	...	...	...
Tunisia - Tunisie											
Total	...	12 035	12 822	12 871	12 651	...	...	...	...	...	...
AMERICA, NORTH - AMÉRIQUE DU NORD											
Anguilla											
Total	+C	-	-	...	...	...	...	...	...	...	...
Aruba											
Total	C	*391	*410	*433	...	...	*3.7	*3.8	*4.3	...	...
Bahamas											
Total	+C	*688	*603[4]	*399	...	...	*2.0	*1.8	*1.2	...	...
Bermuda - Bermudes											
Total	C	229	177	210	177	...	3.6	2.7	3.3	2.7	...
Canada											
Total	C	70 226	...	...	...	...	2.1	...	...	...	...
Cayman Islands - Îles Caïmanes											
Total	+C	196	*93	...	...	...	3.5	*1.8	...	...	...
Costa Rica											
Total	C	...	11 580	*11 556[5]	...	...	...	2.6	*2.5	...	...
Cuba											
Total	C	35 882	35 034	32 318[6]	29 712[6]	...	3.2	3.1	2.9	2.6	...
Urban - Urbaine	C	33 627	32 772	30 181[6]	27 654[6]	...	4.0	3.9	3.6	3.3	...
Rural - Rurale	C	2 255	2 262	2 137[6]	2 058[6]	...	0.8	0.8	0.8	0.7	...
Curaçao											
Total	C	397	413	393	396	...	2.7	2.8	2.6	2.6	...
Dominican Republic - République dominicaine											
Total	+C	17 181	16 408	17 674	17 927	...	1.8	1.7	1.8	1.8	...
El Salvador											
Total	...	6 201	6 019	6 103	6 053	...	...	...	...	...	...
Urban - Urbaine[7]	...	3 033	3 002	3 003	3 022	...	...	...	...	...	...
Rural - Rurale[7]	...	3 168	3 017	3 100	3 031	...	...	...	...	...	...
Guatemala											
Total	C	2 834	...	...	...	...	0.2	...	...	...	...
Jamaica - Jamaïque											
Total	+C	1 654	1 853	2 371	1 960	2 409	0.6	0.7	0.9	0.7	0.9
Mexico - Mexique											
Total	+C	81 851	84 302	86 042	91 285	...	0.8	0.8	0.8	...	...
Urban - Urbaine[8]	+C	74 050	76 193	77 951	82 623	...	0.9	0.9	...	...	...
Rural - Rurale[8]	+C	3 765	3 943	3 733	4 122	...	0.2	0.2	...	...	...
Nicaragua											
Total	+U	2 843	...	...	...	...	...	...	...	...	...

24. Divorces and crude divorce rates by urban/rural residence: 2008 - 2012
Divorces et taux bruts de divortialité selon la résidence, urbaine/rurale : 2008 - 2012 (continued - suite)

Continent, country or area, and urban/rural residence / Continent, pays ou zone et résidence, urbaine/rurale	Co-de	Number - Nombre					Rate - Taux				
		2008	2009	2010	2011	2012	2008	2009	2010	2011	2012
AMERICA, NORTH - AMÉRIQUE DU NORD											
Panama											
Total	C	2 997	3 469	3 583	...	...	0.9	1.0	1.0	...	...
Urban - Urbaine	C	2 656	2 926	3 078	...	...	1.2	1.3	1.4	...	...
Rural - Rurale	C	341	543	505	...	...	0.3	0.4	0.4	...	...
Puerto Rico - Porto Rico											
Total	C	14 849	...	...	...	...	3.8	...	...	...	...
Sint Maarten (Dutch part) - Saint-Martin (partie néerlandaise)											
Total	+C	108	...	...	...	...	2.7	...	...	...	...
Turks and Caicos Islands - Îles Turques et Caïques											
Total	C	8	...	...	...	...	...	...	...	...	...
United States of America - États-Unis d'Amérique[9]											
Total	C	844 000	840 000	872 000	877 000	...	2.8	2.7	2.8	2.8	...
AMERICA, SOUTH - AMÉRIQUE DU SUD											
Brazil - Brésil											
Total	...	188 090	174 747	239 070	347 583	...	...	...	...	...	...
Chile - Chili											
Total	C	2 013[10]	2 068[10]	1 558	...	...	0.1	0.1	0.1	...	...
Ecuador - Équateur[11]											
Total	U	17 111	17 117	18 231	...	...	...	...	...	...	...
Peru - Pérou											
Total	+C	6 750[12]	8 702[12]	9 016[12]	5 625[13]	...	0.2	0.3	0.3	0.2	...
Venezuela (Bolivarian Republic of) - Venezuela (République bolivarienne du)											
Total	...	29 044	...	...	28 653	...	...	...	...	...	...
ASIA - ASIE											
Armenia - Arménie											
Total	+C	3 031	2 829	10 425	3 188	...	0.9	0.9	3.2	1.0	...
Urban - Urbaine	+C	2 370	2 237	...	...	...	1.1	1.1	...	...	...
Rural - Rurale	+C	661	592	...	...	...	0.6	0.5	...	...	...
Azerbaijan - Azerbaïdjan											
Total	+C	7 933	7 784	9 061	10 747	11 087	0.9	0.9	1.0	1.2	1.2
Urban - Urbaine	+C	5 820	5 765	6 753	...	...	1.2	1.2	1.4	...	...
Rural - Rurale	+C	2 113	2 019	2 308	...	...	0.5	0.5	0.5	...	...
Bahrain - Bahreïn											
Total	...	1 323	1 459	1 569	...	...	...	...	...	...	...
Bangladesh											
Total	...	...	...	120 395	124 110	...	...	...	...	...	...
Urban - Urbaine	...	...	...	26 587	29 250	...	...	...	...	...	...
Rural - Rurale	...	...	...	93 808	94 860	...	...	...	...	...	...
Brunei Darussalam - Brunéi Darussalam											
Total	...	534	...	...	...	...	...	...	...	...	...
China - Chine[14]											
Total	+C	2 270 000	2 470 000	2 680 000	2 111 000	2 388 000	1.7	1.9	2.0	1.6	1.8
China, Hong Kong SAR - Chine, Hong Kong RAS											
Total	...	17 771	17 002	18 167	19 597	21 125	...	...	...	...	...
China, Macao SAR - Chine, Macao RAS											
Total	+C	658	782	889	998	1 230	1.2	1.5	1.7	1.8	2.2
Cyprus - Chypre[15]											
Total	C	1 639	1 738	1 929	1 934	...	2.1	2.2	2.3	2.3	...
Urban - Urbaine[16]	C	1 256	1 393	1 471	1 518	...	...	...	...	...	...
Rural - Rurale[16]	C	304	296	396	354	...	...	...	...	...	...

24. Divorces and crude divorce rates by urban/rural residence: 2008 - 2012
Divorces et taux bruts de divortialité selon la résidence, urbaine/rurale : 2008 - 2012 (continued - suite)

Continent, country or area, and urban/rural residence / Continent, pays ou zone et résidence, urbaine/rurale	Co-de	Number - Nombre					Rate - Taux				
		2008	2009	2010	2011	2012	2008	2009	2010	2011	2012
ASIA - ASIE											
Georgia - Géorgie											
Total	C	3 189	4 030	4 726	5 850	7 136	0.7	0.9	1.1	1.3	1.6
Urban - Urbaine	C	2 665	3 249	3 636	4 384	...	1.2	1.4	1.5	1.8	...
Rural - Rurale	C	524	781	1 090	1 466	...	0.3	0.4	0.5	0.7	...
Indonesia - Indonésie											
Total	U	193 189	223 371	285 184	276 791	...	...	...	...	...	...
Iran (Islamic Republic of) - Iran (République islamique d')[17]											
Total	+C	110 510	125 747	137 200	142 841	...	1.5	1.7	1.8	1.9	...
Urban - Urbaine	+C	93 496	106 548	116 643	...	...	1.9	2.1	2.3	...	...
Rural - Rurale	+C	17 014	19 199	20 557	...	...	0.8	0.8	0.9	...	...
Israel - Israël[18]											
Total	C	13 488	13 233	13 042	...	...	1.8	1.8	1.7	...	...
Urban - Urbaine[16]	C	12 330	12 074	11 906	...	...	1.8	1.8	1.7	...	...
Rural - Rurale[16]	C	924	916	871	...	...	1.5	1.5	1.4	...	...
Japan - Japon[19]											
Total	+C	251 136	253 353	251 378	235 719	...	2.0	2.0	2.0	1.8	...
Urban - Urbaine	+C	228 233	230 655	230 064	216 337	...	...	...	...	...	...
Rural - Rurale	+C	22 903	22 698	21 314	19 382	...	...	...	...	...	...
Jordan - Jordanie[20]											
Total	+C	12 862	15 442	15 707	16 086	...	2.2	2.6	2.6	2.6	...
Kazakhstan											
Total	C	35 852	39 466	41 617	44 862	...	2.3	2.5	2.5	2.7	...
Urban - Urbaine	C	27 475	...	...	...	...	3.3	...	...	...	...
Rural - Rurale	C	8 377	...	...	...	...	1.1	...	...	...	...
Kuwait - Koweït											
Total	C	4 907	5 932	5 965	6 254	...	2.0	2.1	2.0	2.0	...
Kyrgyzstan - Kirghizstan											
Total	C	7 419	7 381	8 155	8 705	...	1.5	1.4	1.6	1.7	...
Urban - Urbaine	C	4 144	4 044	4 459	4 497	...	2.3	2.2	2.4	2.4	...
Rural - Rurale	C	3 275	3 337	3 696	4 208	...	1.0	1.0	1.1	1.2	...
Lebanon - Liban											
Total	+C	5 389	5 957	5 897	6 879	6 498	...	...	...	...	...
Mongolia - Mongolie											
Total	+C	1 901	2 399	3 054	...	...	0.7	0.9	1.1	...	...
Urban - Urbaine	+C	1 745	2 142	2 619	...	...	1.1	1.3	1.5	...	...
Rural - Rurale	+C	156	257	435	...	...	0.2	0.3	0.4	...	...
Oman[21]											
Total	+U	...	2 675	2 736	3 805	...	...	...	...	...	...
Qatar											
Total	C	939	1 108	1 172	1 108	...	0.6	0.7	0.7	0.6	...
Republic of Korea - République de Corée[22]											
Total	+C	116 535	123 999	116 858	114 284	...	2.4	2.5	2.3	2.3	...
Urban - Urbaine[23]	+C	91 986	97 501	90 708	88 273	...	2.3	2.4	2.2	2.2	...
Rural - Rurale[23]	+C	20 934	22 818	22 333	22 398	...	2.2	2.4	2.4	2.4	...
Singapore - Singapour											
Total	+C	6 771	6 927	6 969	7 234	6 893	1.9	1.9	1.8	1.9	1.8
State of Palestine - État de Palestine											
Total	C	5 009	5 761	6 150	6 155	...	1.3	1.5	1.5	1.5	...
Syrian Arab Republic - République arabe syrienne[24]											
Total	+U	22 661	29 525	28 202	...	...	...	...	...	...	...
Tajikistan - Tadjikistan											
Total	+C	5 178	5 593	6 019	6 762	...	0.7	0.8	0.8	0.9	...
Urban - Urbaine	+C	2 764	2 647	3 181	2 811	...	1.4	1.4	1.6	1.4	...
Rural - Rurale	+C	2 414	2 946	2 838	3 951	...	0.4	0.5	0.5	0.7	...
Turkey - Turquie											
Total	C	99 663[25]	114 162[25]	118 568[25]	120 117	123 325	1.4	1.6	1.6	1.6	1.6
United Arab Emirates - Émirats arabes unis[26]											
Total	...	3 855	...	...	...	...	...	...	...	...	...
Uzbekistan - Ouzbékistan											
Total	C	16 400	16 900	17 800	18 600	17 900	0.6	0.6	0.6	0.6	0.6

Continent, country or area, and urban/rural residence — Continent, pays ou zone et résidence, urbaine/rurale	Co-de	Number - Nombre					Rate - Taux				
		2008	2009	2010	2011	2012	2008	2009	2010	2011	2012
EUROPE											
Åland Islands - Îles d'Åland											
Total	C	44	53	52	53	*63	1.6	1.9	1.9	1.9	*2.2
Urban - Urbaine	C	24	29	25	26	*34	...	...	...	...	*3.0
Rural - Rurale	C	20	24	27	27	*29	...	...	...	...	...
Albania - Albanie											
Total	C	3 610	...	...	4 807	...	1.2	...	...	1.7	...
Austria - Autriche[27]											
Total	C	19 701	18 806	17 442	17 295	17 006	2.4	2.2	2.1	2.1	2.0
Belarus - Bélarus											
Total	C	36 679	35 056	36 655	38 584	39 034	3.8	3.7	3.9	4.1	4.1
Urban - Urbaine	C	31 739	30 221	31 603	33 105	...	...	...	...	4.6	...
Rural - Rurale	C	4 940	4 835	5 052	5 479	...	...	...	...	2.4	...
Belgium - Belgique[28]											
Total	C	35 366	32 606	28 903	*31 500	*27 400	3.3	3.0	2.7	*2.9	*2.5
Urban - Urbaine	C	34 967	32 251	...	...	...	3.3	3.0	...	...	...
Rural - Rurale	C	399	355	...	...	...	2.6	2.3	...	...	...
Bosnia and Herzegovina - Bosnie-Herzégovine											
Total	C	1 369	1 402	1 676	...	*1 471	0.4	0.4	0.4	...	*0.4
Bulgaria - Bulgarie[29]											
Total	C	14 104	11 662	11 012	10 581	11 947	1.9	1.5	1.5	1.4	1.6
Urban - Urbaine	C	11 515	9 640	9 254	8 849	...	2.1	1.8	1.7	1.7	...
Rural - Rurale	C	2 589	2 022	1 758	1 732	...	1.2	0.9	0.8	0.9	...
Croatia - Croatie											
Total	C	5 025	5 076	5 058	5 662	...	1.1	1.1	1.1	1.3	...
Urban - Urbaine	C	3 492	3 476	3 514	...	...	...	...	...	...	...
Rural - Rurale	C	1 533	1 600	1 544	...	...	...	...	...	...	...
Czech Republic - République tchèque											
Total	C	31 300	29 133	30 783	28 113	26 402	3.0	2.8	2.9	2.7	2.5
Urban - Urbaine	C	24 574	22 147	23 497	22 170	...	3.2	2.9	3.0	2.9	...
Rural - Rurale	C	6 726	6 986	7 286	5 943	...	2.5	2.5	2.6	2.1	...
Denmark - Danemark[30]											
Total	C	14 695	14 940	14 460	14 484	15 709	2.7	2.7	2.6	2.6	2.8
Estonia - Estonie											
Total	C	3 501	3 189	2 989	3 099	3 142	2.6	2.4	2.2	2.3	2.3
Urban - Urbaine[31]	C	2 488	2 242	2 106	2 169	...	2.7	2.4	2.3	2.3	...
Rural - Rurale[31]	C	919	856	812	848	...	2.2	2.1	2.0	2.1	...
Finland - Finlande[32]											
Total	C	13 471[33]	13 474[34]	13 567[34]	13 416[34]	12 977[34]	2.5	2.5	2.5	2.5	2.4
Urban - Urbaine	C	10 079[33]	10 071[34]	10 187[34]	10 041[34]	...	2.8	2.8	2.8	2.7	...
Rural - Rurale	C	3 392[33]	3 403[34]	3 380[34]	3 375[34]	...	2.0	2.0	2.0	2.0	...
France											
Total	C	129 379	127 578	130 810	129 802	...	2.1	2.0	2.1	2.1	...
Germany - Allemagne											
Total	C	191 948	185 817	187 027	187 640	...	2.3	2.3	2.3	2.3	...
Gibraltar											
Total	+C	78	89	93	148	...	2.7	3.0	3.2	5.0	...
Greece - Grèce											
Total	C	13 163	...	...	...	...	1.2	...	...	...	...
Hungary - Hongrie[32]											
Total	C	25 155	23 820	23 873	23 335	*22 000	2.5	2.4	2.4	2.3	*2.2
Urban - Urbaine[35]	C	18 294	17 441	17 643	17 132	...	2.7	2.5	2.5	2.5	...
Rural - Rurale[35]	C	6 689	6 216	6 043	5 998	...	2.1	2.0	2.0	2.0	...
Iceland - Islande											
Total	C	549	559[36]	571[36]	516[36]	...	1.7	1.8	1.8	1.6	...
Urban - Urbaine[37]	C	...	529	533	504	...	...	1.8	1.8	1.6	...
Rural - Rurale[37]	C	...	24	30	4	...	...	...	1.5	...	...
Ireland - Irlande											
Total	+C	3 630	*3 341	3 113	3 363	...	0.8	*0.7	0.7	0.7	...
Italy - Italie											
Total	C	54 351	54 456	54 160	...	...	0.9	0.9	0.9	...	...
Latvia - Lettonie											
Total	C	6 214	5 099	4 930	8 302	7 311	2.7	2.3	2.2	4.0	3.6
Urban - Urbaine	C	4 582	3 813	...	...	...	3.0	2.5	...	...	...
Rural - Rurale	C	1 632	1 286	...	...	...	2.2	1.8	...	...	...

24. Divorces and crude divorce rates by urban/rural residence: 2008 - 2012
Divorces et taux bruts de divortialité selon la résidence, urbaine/rurale : 2008 - 2012 (continued - suite)

Continent, country or area, and urban/rural residence / Continent, pays ou zone et résidence, urbaine/rurale	Code	Number - Nombre					Rate - Taux				
		2008	2009	2010	2011	2012	2008	2009	2010	2011	2012
EUROPE											
Liechtenstein[38]											
Total	C	98	97	87	*91	*87	2.8	2.7	2.4	*2.5	*2.4
Lithuania - Lituanie											
Total	C	10 317	9 270	10 006	10 341	10 399	3.1	2.8	3.0	3.4	3.3
Urban - Urbaine	C	7 145	6 451	6 836	7 128	...	3.2	2.9	3.1	3.5	...
Rural - Rurale	C	3 172	2 819	3 170	3 213	...	2.9	2.6	2.9	3.2	...
Luxembourg											
Total	C	977	1 052	1 083	1 275	...	2.0	2.1	2.1	2.5	...
Malta - Malte											
Total	C	...	...	...	42	...	...	...	...	0.1	...
Montenegro - Monténégro											
Total	C	460	456	520	471	515	0.7	0.7	0.8	0.8	0.8
Urban - Urbaine	C	435	440	...	...	...	1.1	1.1	...	...	...
Rural - Rurale	C	25	16	...	...	...	...	...	...	...	...
Netherlands - Pays-Bas[39]											
Total	C	32 236	30 779[41]	33 723[41]	33 755[41]	*34 317[41]	2.0	1.9	2.0	2.0	*2.1
Urban - Urbaine	C	22 607[40]	21 492[42]	...	...	...	2.1	2.0	...	...	...
Rural - Rurale	C	9 175[40]	8 802[42]	...	...	...	1.6	1.6	...	...	...
Norway - Norvège[43]											
Total	C	10 158	10 235[41]	10 228[41]	10 207[41]	9 929[41]	2.1	2.1	2.1	2.1	2.0
Poland - Pologne											
Total	C	65 475	65 345	61 300	64 594	64 432	1.7	1.7	1.6	1.7	1.7
Urban - Urbaine[44]	C	51 946	51 398	47 394	49 186	...	2.2	2.2	2.0	2.1	...
Rural - Rurale[44]	C	13 059	13 457	13 423	14 855	...	0.9	0.9	0.9	1.0	...
Portugal											
Total	C	26 394	26 464	27 903	26 750	...	2.5	2.5	2.6	2.5	...
Republic of Moldova - République de Moldova											
Total	C	12 601	11 884	11 504	11 120	10 637	3.5	3.3	3.2	3.1	3.0
Urban - Urbaine	C	10 749	10 300	10 174	...	...	7.3	7.0	6.9	...	...
Rural - Rurale	C	1 852	1 584	1 330	...	...	0.9	0.8	0.6	...	...
Romania - Roumanie											
Total	C	35 685	32 341	32 632	35 780	*31 324	1.7	1.5	1.5	1.7	*1.5
Urban - Urbaine	C	24 806	22 308	22 144	25 152	...	2.1	1.9	1.9	2.1	...
Rural - Rurale	C	10 879	10 033	10 488	10 628	...	1.1	1.0	1.1	1.1	...
Russian Federation - Fédération de Russie											
Total	C	703 412	699 430	639 321	669 376	...	4.9	4.9	4.5	4.7	...
Urban - Urbaine	C	...	...	...	523 697	...	...	...	...	5.0	...
Rural - Rurale	C	...	...	...	145 679	...	...	...	...	3.9	...
San Marino - Saint-Marin											
Total	+C	71	63	61	82	49	2.2	1.9	1.9	2.5	1.5
Serbia - Serbie[45]											
Total	+C	8 502	8 505	6 644	8 251	7 275	1.2	1.2	0.9	1.1	1.0
Urban - Urbaine	+C	6 061	5 965	4 901	6 192	...	1.4	1.4	1.1	1.4	...
Rural - Rurale	+C	2 441	2 540	1 743	2 059	...	0.8	0.8	0.6	0.7	...
Slovakia - Slovaquie											
Total	C	12 675	12 671	12 015	11 102	10 948	2.3	2.3	2.2	2.1	2.0
Urban - Urbaine	C	8 637	8 311	7 772	7 053	...	2.9	2.8	2.6	2.4	...
Rural - Rurale	C	4 038	4 360	4 243	4 049	...	1.7	1.8	1.7	1.6	...
Slovenia - Slovénie											
Total	C	2 246	2 297	2 430	2 298	*2 469	1.1	1.1	1.2	1.1	*1.2
Urban - Urbaine	C	1 266	1 290	1 416	1 308	...	1.3	1.3	1.4	1.3	...
Rural - Rurale	C	980	1 007	1 014	990	...	1.0	1.0	1.0	1.0	...
Spain - Espagne											
Total	C	109 922	98 207	102 690	103 290	...	2.4	2.1	2.2	2.2	...
Sweden - Suède											
Total	C	21 377	22 211	23 593[41]	23 389[41]	23 422[41]	2.3	2.4	2.5	2.5	2.5
Switzerland - Suisse											
Total	C	19 613	19 321	22 081	17 566	*17 550	2.6	2.5	2.8	2.2	*2.2
Urban - Urbaine[46]	C	15 285	15 069	17 095	13 603	...	2.7	2.6	...	2.3	...
Rural - Rurale[46]	C	4 328	4 252	4 986	3 963	...	2.1	2.1	...	1.9	...
TFYR of Macedonia - L'ex-R. y. de Macédoine											
Total	C	1 209	1 287	1 720	1 753	1 926	0.6	0.6	0.8	0.9	0.9
Urban - Urbaine	C	735	760	1 116	...	...	...	...	...	...	...
Rural - Rurale	C	474	527	604	...	...	...	...	...	...	...

Continent, country or area, and urban/rural residence / Continent, pays ou zone et résidence, urbaine/rurale	Co-de	Number - Nombre					Rate - Taux				
		2008	2009	2010	2011	2012	2008	2009	2010	2011	2012
EUROPE											
Ukraine											
Total	+C	166 845	145 439	126 068[47]	61 872[47]	49 807[47]	3.6	3.2	2.8	1.4	1.1
Urban - Urbaine	+C	128 909	112 681	98 568[47]	50 652[47]	...	4.1	3.6	...	...	...
Rural - Rurale	+C	37 936	32 758	27 500[47]	11 220[47]	...	2.6	2.3	...	...	...
United Kingdom of Great Britain and Northern Ireland - Royaume-Uni de Grande-Bretagne et d'Irlande du Nord[48]											
Total	C	135 942	126 520	132 338	129 764	...	2.2	2.0	2.1	2.1	...
OCEANIA - OCÉANIE											
Australia - Australie											
Total	C	47 209	49 448	50 240	48 935	...	2.2	2.3	2.3	2.2	...
Guam											
Total	C	868	868	849	...	...	5.5	5.4	5.3	...	...
New Caledonia - Nouvelle-Calédonie[49]											
Total	C	*247	*249	*305	...	...	*1.0	*1.0	*1.2	...	...
New Zealand - Nouvelle-Zélande											
Total	+C	9 713	8 737	8 874	8 551	...	2.3	2.0	2.0	1.9	...
Samoa											
Total	U	*10*	*48*	...	...	...	...	...	...	...	...

FOOTNOTES - NOTES

Italics: data from civil registers which are incomplete or of unknown completeness. - Italiques : données incomplètes ou dont le degré d'exactitude n'est pas connu, provenant des registres de l'état civil.

* Provisional. - Données provisoires.

'Code' indicates the source of data, as follows:
C - Civil registration, estimated over 90% complete
U - Civil registration, estimated less than 90% complete
| - Other source, estimated reliable
+ - Data tabulated by date of registration rather than occurence
... - Information not available

Le 'Code' indique la source des données, comme suit :
C - Registres de l'état civil considérés complets à 90 p. 100 au moins
U - Registres de l'état civil qui ne sont pas considérés complets à 90 p. 100 au moins
| - Autre source, considérée pas douteuses
+ - Données exploitées selon la date de l'enregistrement et non la date de l'événement
... - Information pas disponible

[1] Including 'revocable divorces' (among Muslim population), which approximate legal separations. - Y compris les 'divorces révocables' (parmi la population musulmane), qui sont plus au moins l'équivalent des séparations légales.
[2] Data refer to Libyan nationals only. - Les données se raportent aux nationaux libyens seulement.
[3] Excludes the islands of St. Brandon and Agalega. - Non compris les îles St. Brandon et Agalega.
[4] Excluding annulments. - Ne comprend pas les annulations.
[5] Data refer to registered divorces only. - Les données ne portent que sur les divorces enregistrés.
[6] Refer to divorces confirmed by final judgment. - Correspond aux divorces ayant fait l'objet d'un jugement.
[7] Urban and rural distribution refers to the usual residence of the bride/wife. Unrevised data. - La répartition entre résidence urbaine et résidence rurale fait référence au lieu de résidence habituel de la mariée ou de la femme. Les données n'ont pas été révisées.
[8] Urban and rural distribution refers to the usual residence of the bride/wife. The difference between 'Total' and the sum of urban and rural is due to the unknown place of residence of bride/wife. - La répartition entre résidence urbaine et résidence rurale fait référence au lieu de résidence habituel de la mariée ou de la femme. La différence entre le « Total » et la somme des chiffres urbains et ruraux s'explique par le fait que le lieu de résidence de la mariée ou de la femme n'est pas toujours connu.
[9] Excluding data for California, Georgia, Hawaii, Indiana, Louisiana, and Minnesota. - Non compris les données pour la Californie, la Géorgie, Hawaii, l'Indiana, la Louisiane et le Minnesota.
[10] Data refer exclusively to divorces collected from courts that are not in line with the judiciary power of Chile. - Données concernant exclusivement les divorces recensés dans des tribunaux sans rapport avec l'autorité judiciaire chilienne.
[11] Excludes nomadic Indian tribes. - Non compris les tribus d'Indiens nomades.
[12] Source: The National Registry of Municipalities (RENAMU). - Source : Le Registre National des Municipalités (RENAMU).
[13] Source: The National Registers of Identification and Civil Status (RENIEC). - Source : Les Registres Nationaux d'Identification et d'État Civil (RENIEC).
[14] Including annulments. For statistical purposes, the data for China do not include those for the Hong Kong Special Administrative Region (Hong Kong SAR), Macao Special Administrative Region (Macao SAR) and Taiwan province of China. - Y compris les annulations. Pour la présentation des statistiques, les données pour la Chine ne comprennent pas la Région Administrative Spéciale de Hong Kong (Hong Kong RAS), la Région Administrative Spéciale de Macao (Macao RAS) et Taïwan province de Chine.
[15] Data refer to government controlled areas. - Les données se rapportent aux zones contrôlées par le Gouvernement.
[16] The total number includes 'Unknown residence', but the categories urban and rural do not. The urban and rural residence is recorded according to the place of usual residence of husband. - Le nombre total englobe les personnes dont la résidence n'est pas connue, à l'inverse des catégories de population urbaine et rurale. Le lieu de résidence (zone urbaine ou zone rurale) correspond au lieu de résidence habituel du mari.
[17] Data refer to the Iranian Year which begins on 21 March and ends on 20 March of the following year. - Les données concernent l'année iranienne, qui commence le 21 mars et se termine le 20 mars de l'année suivante.

18 Includes data for East Jerusalem and Israeli residents in certain other territories under occupation by Israeli military forces since June 1967. - Y compris les données pour Jérusalem-Est et les résidents israéliens dans certains autres territoires occupés depuis 1967 par les forces armées israéliennes.

19 Data refer to Japanese nationals in Japan only. - Les données se raportent aux nationaux japonais au Japon seulement.

20 Excluding data for Jordanian territory under occupation since June 1967 by Israeli military forces. Excluding foreigners, including registered Palestinian refugees. - Non compris les données pour le territoire jordanien occupé depuis juin 1967 par les forces armées israéliennes. Non compris les étrangers, mais y compris les réfugiés de Palestine enregistrés.

21 Data refer to registered events only. - Les données ne concernent que les événements enregistrés.

22 Excluding alien armed forces, civilian aliens employed by armed forces, and foreign diplomatic personnel and their dependants. Data refer to residence of groom. - Non compris les militaires étrangers, les civils étrangers employés par les forces armées ni le personnel diplomatique étranger et les membres de leur famille les accompagnant. Données relatives au lieu de résidence du marié.

23 The total number includes 'Unknown residence', but the categories urban and rural do not. - Le nombre total englobe les personnes dont la résidence n'est pas connue, à l'inverse des catégories de population urbaine et rurale.

24 Excluding nomad population. - Non compris les nomades.

25 Data from MERNIS (Central Population Administrative System). - Données de MERNIS (Système central de données démographiques).

26 As published by the United Nations Economic and Social Commission for Western Asia. - Publié par la Commission économique et sociale des Nations Unies pour l'Asie occidentale.

27 Excluding aliens temporarily in the area. - Non compris les étrangers se trouvant temporairement dans le territoire.

28 Including divorces among armed forces stationed outside the country and alien armed forces in the area. - Y compris les divorces de militaires nationaux hors du pays et les militaires étrangers en garnison sur le territoire.

29 Including annulments. Including nationals outside the country, but excluding foreigners in the country. - Y compris les annulations. Y compris les nationaux à l'étranger, mais non compris les étrangers sur le territoire.

30 Excluding Faeroe Islands and Greenland shown separately, if available. - Non compris les Iles Féroé et le Groenland, qui font l'objet de rubriques distinctes, si disponible.

31 Urban and rural distribution of marriages and divorces is displayed by place of residence of groom/husband. The difference between 'Total' and the sum of urban and rural is due to the unknown place of residence of grooms/husbands and to grooms/husbands living outside country. - La répartition des mariages et des divorces entre zones urbaines et zones rurales est fondée sur le lieu de résidence du marié ou du mari. La différence entre le « Total » et la somme des chiffres urbains et ruraux s'explique par le fait que la résidence du marié ou du mari n'est pas toujours connue ou est située à l'étranger.

32 Including annulments. - Y compris les annulations.

33 Including nationals temporarily outside the country. - Y compris les nationaux se trouvant temporairement hors du pays.

34 Excluding Åland Islands. - Non compris les Îles d'Åland.

35 Total includes the data of foreigners, persons of unknown residence and homeless, but the categories urban and rural do not. - Le total englobe les données relatives aux étrangers, aux personnes dont la résidence n'est pas connue et aux personnes sans domicile fixe, à l'inverse des chiffres portant sur la population urbaine et rurale.

36 Data refers for common residence before divorce. - Données se rapportant à la résidence commune avant le divorce.

37 Data refers for common residence before divorce. Total includes residence abroad, but the categories urban and rural do not. - Données se rapportant à la résidence commune avant le divorce. Le total compris résidence à l'étranger, à l'inverse des catégories de population urbaine et rurale.

38 Data refer to residence of groom. Excluding annulments. - Données relatives au lieu de résidence du marié. Ne comprend pas les annulations.

39 Based on the general office for civil registration. - Données provenant des services généraux d'état civil.

40 The difference between 'Total' and the sum of 'urban' and 'rural' is due to divorces contracted abroad. - La différence entre le « Total » et la somme des chiffres urbains et ruraux s'explique par les divorces prononcés à l'étranger.

41 Including same sex divorces. - Y compris les divorces entre conjoints du même sexe.

42 Including same sex divorces. The difference between 'Total' and the sum of 'urban' and 'rural' is due to the cases of unknown place of residence or residence abroad. - Y compris les divorces entre conjoints du même sexe. La différence entre le « Total » et la somme des chiffres urbains et ruraux s'explique par le fait que la résidence n'est pas toujours connue ou que des personnes résident à l'étranger.

43 Data refer to male residents of Norway only. - Ces données ne concernent que les hommes habitant en Norvège.

44 Data for urban and rural exclude divorces if both persons live abroad. - Les données pour les zones urbaines et rurales excluent le divorce si les deux personnes vivent à l'étranger.

45 Excludes data for Kosovo and Metohia. - Sans les données pour le Kosovo et Metohie.

46 Urban/rural distribution is based on updated classification on December 31 2008. - La répartition entre zone urbaine et zone rurale est fondée sur la classification mise à jour le 31 décembre 2008.

47 Excluding divorces made in courts (under the Law of Ukraine "On state registration of civil status" from 1 July 2010). - Excepté les divorces prononcés par un tribunal (en vertu de la loi ukrainienne du 1er juillet 2010 sur l'enregistrement de l'état civil).

48 Excluding Channel Islands (Guernsey and Jersey) and Isle of Man, shown separately, if available. - Non compris les îles Anglo-Normandes (Guernesey et Jersey) et l'île de Man, qui font l'objet de rubriques distinctes, si disponible.

49 Based on place of residence at marriage not at divorce. - Les divorces sont comptés en fonction du lieu de résidence au mariage, et non pas au divorce.

Table 25 - *Demographic Yearbook 2012*

Table 25 presents the number of divorces according to the duration of marriage and the percentage distribution for the latest available year between 2003 and 2012.

Description of variables: Divorces are the final legal dissolutions of a marriage, which confer on the parties the right to remarry as defined by the laws of each country or area. Unless otherwise noted, divorce statistics exclude legal separations which do not allow remarriage. These statistics refer to the number of divorces granted, and not to the number of persons divorcing.

Duration of marriage is defined as the interval of time between the day, month and year of marriage and the day, month and year of divorce in completed years. This definition refers to the "legal" duration rather than the "effective" duration, it having been calculated until the day, month and year of the actual divorce decree rather than until the separation date or the date when the couple ceased to live as man and wife.

The duration of marriage classification used in this table to the extent possible, is the following: under one year, single years of duration through 9 years, 10-14 years, 15-19 years, 20 years and over and duration unknown, when appropriate.

Reliability of data: Data from civil registers of divorces which are reported as incomplete (less than 90 per cent completeness) or of unknown completeness are considered unreliable and are set in italics rather than in roman type. For more information about the quality of vital statistics data in general, see section 4.2 of the Technical Notes.

Limitations: Statistics on divorces by duration of marriage are subject to the same qualifications which have been set forth for vital statistics in general and divorce statistics in particular as discussed in Section 4 of the Technical Notes.

Earlier data: Divorces by duration by marriage, cross-classified by age of husband and by age of wife have been shown previously in issues of the Demographic Yearbook featuring marriage and divorce. For information on years covered, readers should consult the Historical Index.

Tableau 25 – *Annuaire démographique 2012*

Le tableau 25 indique le nombre de divorces selon la durée du mariage et la répartition des pourcentages, pour la dernière année disponible entre 2003 et 2012.

Description des variables : le divorce est la dissolution définitive des liens du mariage qui confère aux parties le droit de se remarier, telle qu'elle est définie par la législation de chaque pays ou zone. Sauf indication contraire, les statistiques de la divortialité n'englobent pas les séparations légales qui excluent le remariage. Ces statistiques se rapportent aux jugements de divorce prononcés, non aux personnes divorcées.

La durée du mariage correspond à l'intervalle du temps qui s'est écoulé entre la date exacte (jour, mois et année) du mariage et la date exacte (jour, mois et année) du divorce exprimé en années révolues. Cette définition est celle de la durée "légale" du mariage et non de sa durée "effective", puisque la durée est calculée jusqu'à la date (jour, mois et année) du jugement de divorce et non jusqu'à la date de la séparation ou la date à laquelle le couple a cessé de vivre comme mari et femme.

Le classement selon la durée du mariage utilisé dans ce tableau dans la mesure du possible comprend les catégories suivantes : moins d'un an, une catégorie par an jusqu'à 9 ans inclus, 10-14 ans, 15-19 ans, 20 ans et plus et, le cas échéant, une catégorie pour la durée du mariage inconnue.

Fiabilité des données : les données sur les divorces provenant des registres de l'état civil qui sont déclarées incomplètes (degré de complétude inférieur à 90 pour cent) ou dont le degré de complétude n'est pas connu, sont jugées douteuses et apparaissent en italique et non en caractères romains. Pour plus de précisions sur la qualité des données reposant sur les statistiques de l'état civil en general, voir la section 4.2 des Notes techniques.

Insuffisance des données : les statistiques des divorces selon la durée du mariage, appellent toutes les réserves qui ont été formulées à propos des statistiques de l'état civil en general et des statistiques des divorces en particulier (voir les explications figurant à la section 4 des Notes techniques).

Données publiées antérieurement : les statistiques des divorces selon la durée du mariage, classées selon l'âge de l'époux, d'une part, et selon l'âge de l'épouse, d'autre part, ont été présentées dans des éditions antérieures de l'Annuaire démographique qui avaient comme sujet spécial la nuptialité et la divortialité. Pour plus de précisions concernant les années pour lesquelles ces données ont été publiées, on se reportera à l'index historique.

25. Divorces and percentage distribution by duration of marriage, latest available year: 2003 - 2012
Divorces et répartition des pourcentages selon la durée du mariage, dernière année disponible: 2003 - 2012

Continent, country or area, year, code and duration of marriage (in years) / Continent, pays ou zone, année, code et durée du mariage (en années)	Number of divorces / Nombre de divorces	Per cent / Pour cent
AFRICA - AFRIQUE		
Egypt - Égypte[1]		
2011 (+C)		
Total	151 933	100.0
Less than 1 - Moins de 1	24 983	16.4
1	18 054	11.9
2	12 395	8.2
3	10 389	6.8
4	8 586	5.7
5	6 823	4.5
6	5 905	3.9
7	4 526	3.0
8	3 566	2.3
9	3 201	2.1
10 - 14	12 161	8.0
15 - 19	6 103	4.0
20 +	9 129	6.0
Not stated - Inconnu	26 112	17.2
Mauritius - Maurice[2]		
2011 (+C)		
Total	1 788	100.0
Less than 1 - Moins de 1	4	0.2
1	57	3.2
2	95	5.3
3	130	7.3
4	114	6.4
5	101	5.6
6	96	5.4
7	103	5.8
8	100	5.6
9	91	5.1
10 - 14	348	19.5
15 - 19	239	13.4
20 +	310	17.3
Not stated - Inconnu	-	0.0
South Africa - Afrique du Sud		
2010 (...)		
Total	22 936	100.0
Less than 1 - Moins de 1	94	0.4
1	700	3.1
2	1 115	4.9
3	1 403	6.1
4	1 420	6.2
5	1 343	5.9
6	1 366	6.0
7	1 359	5.9
8	1 133	4.9
9	1 015	4.4
10 - 14	4 267	18.6
15 - 19	2 906	12.7
20 +	3 704	16.1
Not stated - Inconnu	1 111	4.8
AMERICA, NORTH - AMÉRIQUE DU NORD		
Aruba		
2007 (C)		
Total	417	100.0
Less than 1 - Moins de 1	-	0.0
1	12	2.9
2	30	7.2
3	15	3.6
4	18	4.3
5	42	10.1
6	26	6.2
7	13	3.1
8	12	2.9

Continent, country or area, year, code and duration of marriage (in years) / Continent, pays ou zone, année, code et durée du mariage (en années)	Number of divorces / Nombre de divorces	Per cent / Pour cent
AMERICA, NORTH - AMÉRIQUE DU NORD		
Aruba		
2007 (C)		
9	25	6.0
10 - 14	84	20.1
15 - 19	61	14.6
20 +	55	13.2
Not stated - Inconnu	24	5.8
Bermuda - Bermudes		
2011 (C)		
Total	177	100.0
Less than 1 - Moins de 1	-	0.0
1	3	1.7
2	4	2.3
3	9	5.1
4	13	7.3
5	16	9.0
6	14	7.9
7	4	2.3
8	10	5.6
9	11	6.2
10 - 14	34	19.2
15 - 19	34	19.2
20 +	25	14.1
Canada		
2004 (C)		
Total	69 644	100.0
Less than 1 - Moins de 1	149	0.2
1	1 360	2.0
2	3 298	4.7
3	4 166	6.0
4	3 757	5.4
5	3 587	5.2
6	3 312	4.8
7	3 076	4.4
8	3 040	4.4
9	2 744	3.9
10 - 14	12 312	17.7
15 - 19	9 816	14.1
20 +	19 024	27.3
Not stated - Inconnu	3	0.0
Cuba[3]		
2011 (C)		
Total	29 712	100.0
Less than 1 - Moins de 1	2 006	6.8
1	2 361	7.9
2	2 346	7.9
3	2 059	6.9
4	1 735	5.8
5	1 417	4.8
6	1 150	3.9
7	1 026	3.5
8	992	3.3
9	826	2.8
10 - 14	3 662	12.3
15 - 19	4 805	16.2
20 +	5 311	17.9
Not stated - Inconnu	16	0.1
Dominican Republic - République dominicaine		
2011 (+C)		
Total	17 927	100.0
1	153	0.9
2	303	1.7
3	389	2.2
4	396	2.2
5	381	2.1
6	320	1.8
7	304	1.7

25. Divorces and percentage distribution by duration of marriage, latest available year: 2003 - 2012
Divorces et répartition des pourcentages selon la durée du mariage, dernière année disponible: 2003 - 2012 (continued - suite)

Continent, country or area, year, code and duration of marriage (in years) Continent, pays ou zone, année, code et durée du mariage (en années)	Number of divorces Nombre de divorces	Per cent Pour cent	Continent, country or area, year, code and duration of marriage (in years) Continent, pays ou zone, année, code et durée du mariage (en années)	Number of divorces Nombre de divorces	Per cent Pour cent
AMERICA, NORTH - AMÉRIQUE DU NORD			**AMERICA, NORTH - AMÉRIQUE DU NORD**		
Dominican Republic - République dominicaine			Trinidad and Tobago - Trinité-et-Tobago		
2011 (+C)			2005 (C)		
8	237	1.3	Total	2 785	100.0
9	218	1.2	Less than 1 - Moins de 1	-	0.0
10 - 14	904	5.0	1	40	1.4
15 - 19	638	3.6	2	77	2.8
20 +	687	3.8	3	80	2.9
Not stated - Inconnu	12 997	72.5	4	92	3.3
El Salvador			5	142	5.1
2011 (...)			6	149	5.4
Total	6 053	100.0	7	120	4.3
Less than 1 - Moins de 1	100	1.7	8	144	5.2
1	154	2.5	9	111	4.0
2	211	3.5	10 - 14	572	20.5
3	243	4.0	15 - 19	417	15.0
4	303	5.0	20 +	838	30.1
5	241	4.0	Not stated - Inconnu	3	0.1
6	242	4.0	Turks and Caicos Islands - Îles Turques et Caïques		
7	218	3.6	2005 (C)		
8	233	3.8	Total	24	100.0
9	265	4.4	Less than 1 - Moins de 1	-	0.0
10 - 14	1 379	22.8	1	-	0.0
15 - 19	973	16.1	2	-	0.0
20 - 24	1 396	23.1	3	-	0.0
Not stated - Inconnu	95	1.6	4	2	8.3
Jamaica - Jamaïque[4]			5	3	12.5
2007 (+C)			6	3	12.5
Total	1 140	100.0	7	2	8.3
Less than 1 - Moins de 1	-	0.0	8	4	16.7
1	1	0.1	9	1	4.2
2	3	0.3	10 - 14	5	20.8
3	22	1.9	15 - 19	2	8.3
4	42	3.7	20 +	2	8.3
5	53	4.6	Not stated - Inconnu	-	0.0
6	62	5.4			
7	89	7.8			
8	96	8.4	**AMERICA, SOUTH - AMÉRIQUE DU SUD**		
9	75	6.6			
10 - 14	294	25.8	Brazil - Brésil		
15 - 19	160	14.0	2011 (...)		
20 +	242	21.2	Total	347 583	100.0
Mexico - Mexique[5]			Less than 1 - Moins de 1	6 281	1.8
2011 (+C)			1	12 019	3.5
Total	91 285	100.0	2	16 996	4.9
Less than 1 - Moins de 1	285	0.3	3	18 714	5.4
1	4 969	5.4	4	18 191	5.2
2	5 105	5.6	5	17 232	5.0
3	5 037	5.5	6	15 541	4.5
4	4 927	5.4	7	14 272	4.1
5	4 494	4.9	8	12 670	3.6
6	4 225	4.6	9	11 958	3.4
7	3 958	4.3	10 - 14	51 103	14.7
8	3 796	4.2	15 - 19	39 270	11.3
9	3 898	4.3	20 +	111 179	32.0
10 - 14	16 602	18.2	Not stated - Inconnu	2 157	0.6
15 - 19	11 699	12.8	Chile - Chili		
20 +	21 339	23.4	2010 (C)		
Not stated - Inconnu	951	1.0	Total	1 558	100.0
Panama			Less than 1 - Moins de 1	11	0.7
2010 (C)			1	17	1.1
Total	3 583	100.0	2	36	2.3
Less than 5 - Moins de 5	759	21.2	3	35	2.2
5 - 9	753	21.0	4	36	2.3
10 - 14	722	20.2	5	32	2.1
15 - 19	452	12.6	6	28	1.8
20 +	897	25.0	7	39	2.5

25. Divorces and percentage distribution by duration of marriage, latest available year: 2003 - 2012
Divorces et répartition des pourcentages selon la durée du mariage, dernière année disponible: 2003 - 2012 (continued - suite)

Continent, country or area, year, code and duration of marriage (in years) / Continent, pays ou zone, année, code et durée du mariage (en années)	Number of divorces / Nombre de divorces	Per cent / Pour cent
AMERICA, SOUTH - AMÉRIQUE DU SUD		
Chile - Chili		
2010 (C)		
8	38	2.4
9	47	3.0
10 - 14	270	17.3
15 - 19	211	13.5
20 +	610	39.2
Not stated - Inconnu	148	9.5
Ecuador - Équateur[6]		
2010 (U)		
Total	18 231	100.0
Less than 1 - Moins de 1	198	1.1
1	643	3.5
2	792	4.3
3	858	4.7
4	906	5.0
5	792	4.3
6	777	4.3
7	759	4.2
8	734	4.0
9	754	4.1
10 - 14	3 509	19.2
15 - 19	2 546	14.0
20 +	4 963	27.2
Suriname[7]		
2005 (C)		
Total	724	100.0
Less than 1 - Moins de 1	17	2.3
1 - 3	73	10.1
4 - 6	119	16.4
7 - 9	113	15.6
10 - 12	99	13.7
13 - 15	63	8.7
16 - 18	62	8.6
19 - 21	54	7.5
22 - 24	34	4.7
25 +	90	12.4
Not stated - Inconnu	-	0.0
Venezuela (Bolivarian Republic of) - Venezuela (République bolivarienne du)		
2011 (...)		
Total	28 653	100.0
Less than 1 - Moins de 1	96	0.3
1 - 4	2 271	7.9
5 - 9	7 032	24.5
10 - 14	6 579	23.0
15 - 19	5 512	19.2
20 +	7 072	24.7
Not stated - Inconnu	91	0.3
ASIA - ASIE		
Armenia - Arménie		
2009 (+C)		
Total	2 829	100.0
Less than 1 - Moins de 1	92	3.3
1	161	5.7
2	148	5.2
3	126	4.5
4	117	4.1
5 - 9	445	15.7
10 - 14	426	15.1
15 - 19	514	18.2
20 +	800	28.3
ASIA - ASIE		
Azerbaijan - Azerbaïdjan		
2010 (+C)		
Total	9 061	100.0
Less than 1 - Moins de 1	236	2.6
1	618	6.8
2	753	8.3
3	796	8.8
4	768	8.5
5	647	7.1
6	504	5.6
7	444	4.9
8	344	3.8
9	285	3.1
10 - 14	1 266	14.0
15 - 19	1 096	12.1
20 +	1 304	14.4
Bahrain - Bahreïn		
2010 (...)		
Total	1 569	100.0
Less than 1 - Moins de 1	405	25.8
1	223	14.2
2	145	9.2
3	92	5.9
4	67	4.3
5	63	4.0
6	76	4.8
7	68	4.3
8	50	3.2
9	34	2.2
10 - 14	146	9.3
15 - 19	83	5.3
20 +	99	6.3
Not stated - Inconnu	18	1.1
Brunei Darussalam - Brunéi Darussalam		
2008 (...)		
Total	534	100.0
Less than 1 - Moins de 1	7	1.3
1	18	3.4
2	30	5.6
3	35	6.6
4	43	8.1
5	53	9.9
6	32	6.0
7	43	8.1
8	32	6.0
9	30	5.6
10 - 14	92	17.2
15 - 19	52	9.7
20 +	67	12.5
Not stated - Inconnu	-	0.0
China, Macao SAR - Chine, Macao RAS		
2012 (+C)		
Total	1 230	100.0
Less than 5 - Moins de 5	245	19.9
5 - 9	502	40.8
10 - 14	152	12.4
15 +	331	26.9
Cyprus - Chypre[8]		
2009 (C)		
Total	1 738	100.0
Less than 1 - Moins de 1	66	3.8
1	142	8.2
2	107	6.2
3	127	7.3
4	120	6.9
5	106	6.1
6	108	6.2
7	84	4.8

25. Divorces and percentage distribution by duration of marriage, latest available year: 2003 - 2012
Divorces et répartition des pourcentages selon la durée du mariage, dernière année disponible: 2003 - 2012 (continued - suite)

Continent, country or area, year, code and duration of marriage (in years) Continent, pays ou zone, année, code et durée du mariage (en années)	Number of divorces Nombre de divorces	Per cent Pour cent
ASIA - ASIE		
Cyprus - Chypre[8]		
2009 (C)		
8	80	4.6
9	60	3.5
10 - 14	267	15.4
15 - 19	167	9.6
20 +	304	17.5
Georgia - Géorgie		
2011 (C)		
Total	5 850	100.0
Less than 1 - Moins de 1	317	5.4
1	296	5.1
2	315	5.4
3	302	5.2
4	294	5.0
5	1 045	17.9
10	817	14.0
15	898	15.4
20	1 430	24.4
Not stated - Inconnu	136	2.3
Iran (Islamic Republic of) - Iran (République islamique d')[9]		
2011 (+C)		
Total	142 841	100.0
Less than 1 - Moins de 1	19 730	13.8
1	17 091	12.0
2	13 761	9.6
3	11 763	8.2
4	9 339	6.5
5	8 140	5.7
6	7 292	5.1
7	6 068	4.2
8	5 480	3.8
9	4 726	3.3
10 - 14	16 231	11.4
15 - 19	9 344	6.5
20 +	13 643	9.6
Not stated - Inconnu	233	0.2
Israel - Israël[10]		
2010 (C)		
Total	13 042	100.0
Less than 1 - Moins de 1	380	2.9
1	827	6.3
2	814	6.2
3	731	5.6
4	648	5.0
5	592	4.5
6	538	4.1
7	466	3.6
8	468	3.6
9	422	3.2
10 - 14	1 753	13.4
15 - 19	1 185	9.1
20 +	2 315	17.8
Not stated - Inconnu	1 903	14.6
Japan - Japon[11]		
2011 (+C)		
Total	235 719	100.0
Less than 1 - Moins de 1	14 594	6.2
1	16 935	7.2
2	16 563	7.0
3	14 989	6.4
4	13 812	5.9
5 - 9	49 218	20.9
10 - 14	32 978	14.0
15 - 19	24 133	10.2

Continent, country or area, year, code and duration of marriage (in years) Continent, pays ou zone, année, code et durée du mariage (en années)	Number of divorces Nombre de divorces	Per cent Pour cent
ASIA - ASIE		
Japan - Japon[11]		
2011 (+C)		
20 +	37 791	16.0
Not stated - Inconnu	14 706	6.2
Kazakhstan		
2008 (C)		
Total	35 852	100.0
Less than 1 - Moins de 1	1 647	4.6
1	2 482	6.9
2	2 690	7.5
3	2 516	7.0
4	2 373	6.6
5 - 9	7 939	22.1
10 - 14	5 756	16.1
15 - 19	4 717	13.2
20 +	5 730	16.0
Not stated - Inconnu	2	0.0
Kuwait - Koweït		
2011 (C)		
Total	6 254	100.0
Less than 1 - Moins de 1	1 403	22.4
1	809	12.9
2	581	9.3
3	434	6.9
4	389	6.2
5 - 9	1 241	19.8
10 - 14	547	8.7
15 - 19	348	5.6
20 +	499	8.0
Not stated - Inconnu	3	0.0
Kyrgyzstan - Kirghizstan		
2011 (C)		
Total	8 705	100.0
Less than 1 - Moins de 1	547	6.3
1	453	5.2
2	496	5.7
3	593	6.8
4	598	6.9
5	522	6.0
6	473	5.4
7	453	5.2
8	375	4.3
9	292	3.4
10 - 14	1 146	13.2
15 - 19	1 158	13.3
20 +	1 599	18.4
Mongolia - Mongolie		
2010 (+C)		
Total	3 054	100.0
Less than 1 - Moins de 1	101	3.3
1 - 3	576	18.9
4 - 6	601	19.7
7 - 9	395	12.9
10 +	1 381	45.2
Qatar		
2011 (C)		
Total	1 108	100.0
Less than 1 - Moins de 1	319	28.8
1	93	8.4
2	94	8.5
3	85	7.7
4	74	6.7
5 - 9	197	17.8
10 - 14	99	8.9
15 - 19	59	5.3
20 +	67	6.0
Not stated - Inconnu	21	1.9

Continent, country or area, year, code and duration of marriage (in years) Continent, pays ou zone, année, code et durée du mariage (en années)	Number of divorces Nombre de divorces	Per cent Pour cent
ASIA - ASIE		
Republic of Korea - République de Corée[12]		
2011 (+C)		
Total....................	114 284	100.0
Less than 1 - Moins de 1	5 653	4.9
1	6 587	5.8
2	6 268	5.5
3	6 173	5.4
4	6 008	5.3
5	5 491	4.8
6	5 069	4.4
7	4 134	3.6
8	3 576	3.1
9	3 430	3.0
10 - 14	17 370	15.2
15 - 19	16 226	14.2
20 - 24	28 299	24.8
Not stated - Inconnu	-	0.0
Singapore - Singapour		
2012 (+C)		
Total....................	6 893	100.0
Less than 5 - Moins de 5	1 268	18.4
5 - 9	2 084	30.2
10 - 14	1 254	18.2
15 - 19	859	12.5
20 + ...	1 428	20.7
State of Palestine - État de Palestine		
2011 (C)		
Total....................	6 155	100.0
Less than 1 - Moins de 1	2 762	44.9
1	1 021	16.6
2	460	7.5
3	311	5.1
4	209	3.4
5	151	2.5
6	141	2.3
7	157	2.6
8	106	1.7
9	82	1.3
10 - 14	345	5.6
15 - 19	158	2.6
20 + ...	252	4.1
Tajikistan - Tadjikistan		
2008 (+C)		
Total....................	5 178	100.0
Less than 1 - Moins de 1	518	10.0
1	451	8.7
2	379	7.3
3	345	6.7
4	305	5.9
5	225	4.3
6	207	4.0
7	183	3.5
8	180	3.5
9	168	3.2
10 - 14	785	15.2
15 - 19	648	12.5
20 + ...	602	11.6
Not stated - Inconnu	217	4.2
Turkey - Turquie		
2011 (C)		
Total....................	120 117	100.0
Less than 1 - Moins de 1	4 274	3.6
1	10 881	9.1
2	9 287	7.7
3	8 742	7.3
4	8 044	6.7
5	7 089	5.9
6	6 118	5.1

Continent, country or area, year, code and duration of marriage (in years) Continent, pays ou zone, année, code et durée du mariage (en années)	Number of divorces Nombre de divorces	Per cent Pour cent
ASIA - ASIE		
Turkey - Turquie		
2011 (C)		
7	5 459	4.5
8	4 683	3.9
9	4 208	3.5
10 - 14	18 891	15.7
15 - 19	13 482	11.2
20 + ...	18 636	15.5
Not stated - Inconnu	323	0.3
EUROPE		
Austria - Autriche[13]		
2011 (C)		
Total....................	17 295	100.0
Less than 1 - Moins de 1	283	1.6
1	803	4.6
2	992	5.7
3	1 069	6.2
4	924	5.3
5	997	5.8
6	945	5.5
7	844	4.9
8	731	4.2
9	656	3.8
10 - 14	2 836	16.4
15 - 19	2 315	13.4
20 + ...	3 900	22.5
Belarus - Bélarus		
2011 (C)		
Total....................	38 584	100.0
Less than 1 - Moins de 1	1 124	2.9
1	2 875	7.5
2	3 317	8.6
3	3 581	9.3
4	3 100	8.0
5 - 9	9 488	24.6
10 - 14	5 638	14.6
15 - 19	3 728	9.7
20 + ...	5 733	14.9
Belgium - Belgique[14]		
2010 (C)		
Total....................	28 903	100.0
Less than 1 - Moins de 1	61	0.2
1	721	2.5
2	1 394	4.8
3	1 683	5.8
4	1 689	5.8
5	1 543	5.3
6	1 432	5.0
7	1 241	4.3
8	1 168	4.0
9	1 132	3.9
10 - 14	4 757	16.5
15 - 19	4 028	13.9
20 + ...	8 054	27.9
Bosnia and Herzegovina - Bosnie-Herzégovine		
2010 (C)		
Total....................	1 676	100.0
Less than 1 - Moins de 1	100	6.0
1	139	8.3
2	121	7.2
3	133	7.9
4	131	7.8
5	94	5.6

25. Divorces and percentage distribution by duration of marriage, latest available year: 2003 - 2012
Divorces et répartition des pourcentages selon la durée du mariage, dernière année disponible: 2003 - 2012 (continued - suite)

Continent, country or area, year, code and duration of marriage (in years) Continent, pays ou zone, année, code et durée du mariage (en années)	Number of divorces Nombre de divorces	Per cent Pour cent
EUROPE		
Bosnia and Herzegovina - Bosnie-Herzégovine		
2010 (C)		
6	71	4.2
7	72	4.3
8	64	3.8
9	46	2.7
10 - 14	244	14.6
15 - 19	139	8.3
20 +	322	19.2
Bulgaria - Bulgarie		
2011 (C)		
Total	10 581	100.0
Less than 1 - Moins de 1	111	1.0
1	320	3.0
2	434	4.1
3	502	4.7
4	535	5.1
5	456	4.3
6	466	4.4
7	405	3.8
8	387	3.7
9	352	3.3
10 - 14	1 829	17.3
15 - 19	1 683	15.9
20 +	3 101	29.3
Croatia - Croatie		
2011 (C)		
Total	5 662	100.0
Less than 1 - Moins de 1	88	1.6
1	189	3.3
2	290	5.1
3	318	5.6
4	305	5.4
5	262	4.6
6	235	4.2
7	255	4.5
8	240	4.2
9	200	3.5
10 - 14	925	16.3
15 - 19	780	13.8
20 +	1 575	27.8
Czech Republic - République tchèque		
2011 (C)		
Total	28 113	100.0
Less than 1 - Moins de 1	226	0.8
1	924	3.3
2	1 267	4.5
3	1 456	5.2
4	1 376	4.9
5	1 242	4.4
6	1 147	4.1
7	1 106	3.9
8	1 011	3.6
9	1 071	3.8
10 - 14	4 393	15.6
15 - 19	4 127	14.7
20 +	8 337	29.7
Not stated - Inconnu	430	1.5
Denmark - Danemark[15]		
2011 (C)		
Total	14 484	100.0
Less than 1 - Moins de 1	147	1.0
1	504	3.5
2	851	5.9
3	922	6.4
4	845	5.8
5	830	5.7

Continent, country or area, year, code and duration of marriage (in years) Continent, pays ou zone, année, code et durée du mariage (en années)	Number of divorces Nombre de divorces	Per cent Pour cent
EUROPE		
Denmark - Danemark[15]		
2011 (C)		
6	794	5.5
7	787	5.4
8	693	4.8
9	754	5.2
10 - 14	2 876	19.9
15 - 19	1 901	13.1
20 +	2 441	16.9
Not stated - Inconnu	139	1.0
Estonia - Estonie		
2011 (C)		
Total	3 099	100.0
Less than 1 - Moins de 1	71	2.3
1	138	4.5
2	218	7.0
3	218	7.0
4	240	7.7
5	193	6.2
6	155	5.0
7	134	4.3
8	118	3.8
9	104	3.4
10 - 14	381	12.3
15 - 19	324	10.5
20 +	805	26.0
Finland - Finlande		
2011 (C)		
Total	13 469	100.0
Less than 1 - Moins de 1	156	1.2
1	727	5.4
2	985	7.3
3	947	7.0
4	894	6.6
5	751	5.6
6	770	5.7
7	645	4.8
8	610	4.5
9	522	3.9
10 - 14	2 012	14.9
15 - 19	1 542	11.4
20 +	2 905	21.6
Not stated - Inconnu	3	0.0
France		
2011 (C)		
Total	129 802	100.0
Less than 1 - Moins de 1	158	0.1
1	1 468	1.1
2	3 489	2.7
3	5 045	3.9
4	6 173	4.8
5	6 788	5.2
6	6 914	5.3
7	6 488	5.0
8	6 088	4.7
9	5 573	4.3
10 - 14	25 093	19.3
15 - 19	17 840	13.7
20	3 299	2.5
21	3 124	2.4
22	2 849	2.2
23	2 599	2.0
24	2 383	1.8
25	2 188	1.7
26	2 069	1.6
27	1 949	1.5
28	1 917	1.5
29	1 874	1.4

Continent, country or area, year, code and duration of marriage (in years) Continent, pays ou zone, année, code et durée du mariage (en années)	Number of divorces Nombre de divorces	Per cent Pour cent
EUROPE		
France		
2011 (C)		
30	6 633	5.1
35 +	7 801	6.0
Germany - Allemagne		
2011 (C)		
Total	187 640	100.0
Less than 1 - Moins de 1	42	0.0
1	1 271	0.7
2	5 726	3.1
3	7 808	4.2
4	7 834	4.2
5	9 936	5.3
6	10 243	5.5
7	10 072	5.4
8	9 244	4.9
9	8 741	4.7
10 - 14	36 073	19.2
15 - 19	27 959	14.9
20 +	52 691	28.1
Greece - Grèce		
2005 (C)		
Total	13 494	100.0
Less than 1 - Moins de 1	2	0.0
1	38	0.3
2	724	5.4
3	739	5.5
4	688	5.1
5	624	4.6
6	802	5.9
7	669	5.0
8	673	5.0
9	502	3.7
10 - 14	2 633	19.5
15 - 19	1 964	14.6
20 +	3 206	23.8
Not stated - Inconnu	230	1.7
Hungary - Hongrie[7]		
2011 (C)		
Total	23 335	100.0
Less than 1 - Moins de 1	253	1.1
1	658	2.8
2	1 001	4.3
3	1 135	4.9
4	1 080	4.6
5	1 086	4.7
6	1 022	4.4
7	1 023	4.4
8	1 000	4.3
9	908	3.9
10 - 14	3 988	17.1
15 - 19	3 534	15.1
20 +	6 647	28.5
Iceland - Islande[16]		
2011 (C)		
Total	516	100.0
Less than 1 - Moins de 1	6	1.2
1	16	3.1
2	20	3.9
3	37	7.2
4	36	7.0
5	38	7.4
6	28	5.4
7	20	3.9
8	33	6.4
9	16	3.1
10 - 14	101	19.6

Continent, country or area, year, code and duration of marriage (in years) Continent, pays ou zone, année, code et durée du mariage (en années)	Number of divorces Nombre de divorces	Per cent Pour cent
EUROPE		
Iceland - Islande[16]		
2011 (C)		
15 - 19	63	12.2
20 +	100	19.4
Italy - Italie		
2010 (C)		
Total	54 160	100.0
Less than 1 - Moins de 1	2	0.0
1	8	0.0
2	7	0.0
3	45	0.1
4	526	1.0
5	1 370	2.5
6	1 913	3.5
7	2 332	4.3
8	2 537	4.7
9	2 645	4.9
10 - 14	11 610	21.4
15 - 19	10 621	19.6
20 +	20 544	37.9
Latvia - Lettonie		
2011 (C)		
Total	8 302	100.0
Less than 1 - Moins de 1	26	0.3
1	147	1.8
2	344	4.1
3	535	6.4
4	712	8.6
5	627	7.6
6	519	6.3
7	376	4.5
8	352	4.2
9	341	4.1
10 - 14	1 066	12.8
15 - 19	907	10.9
20 +	2 350	28.3
Liechtenstein[17]		
2011* (C)		
Total	91	100.0
Less than 1 - Moins de 1	-	0.0
1	3	3.3
2	5	5.5
3	2	2.2
4	5	5.5
5	4	4.4
6	5	5.5
7	4	4.4
8	3	3.3
9	6	6.6
10 - 14	21	23.1
15 - 19	10	11.0
20 +	14	15.4
Not stated - Inconnu	9	9.9
Lithuania - Lituanie		
2011 (C)		
Total	10 341	100.0
Less than 1 - Moins de 1	145	1.4
1	387	3.7
2	632	6.1
3	727	7.0
4	635	6.1
5	597	5.8
6	449	4.3
7	429	4.1
8	319	3.1
9	266	2.6
10 - 14	1 376	13.3

25. Divorces and percentage distribution by duration of marriage, latest available year: 2003 - 2012
Divorces et répartition des pourcentages selon la durée du mariage, dernière année disponible: 2003 - 2012 (continued - suite)

Continent, country or area, year, code and duration of marriage (in years) / Continent, pays ou zone, année, code et durée du mariage (en années)	Number of divorces / Nombre de divorces	Per cent / Pour cent
EUROPE		
Lithuania - Lituanie		
2011 (C)		
15 - 19	1 396	13.5
20 +	2 983	28.8
Luxembourg		
2010 (C)		
Total	1 083	100.0
Less than 1 - Moins de 1	9	0.8
1	10	0.9
2	34	3.1
3	66	6.1
4	66	6.1
5	60	5.5
6	63	5.8
7	61	5.6
8	57	5.3
9	56	5.2
10 - 14	186	17.2
15 - 19	186	17.2
20 +	229	21.1
Malta - Malte		
2011 (C)		
Total	42	100.0
Less than 1 - Moins de 1	-	0.0
1	-	0.0
2	-	0.0
3	-	0.0
4	-	0.0
5	-	0.0
6	1	2.4
7	1	2.4
8	-	0.0
9	-	0.0
10 - 14	15	35.7
15 - 19	4	9.5
20 +	21	50.0
Montenegro - Monténégro		
2011 (C)		
Total	471	100.0
Less than 1 - Moins de 1	20	4.2
1	36	7.6
2	44	9.3
3	30	6.4
4	25	5.3
5	21	4.5
6	29	6.2
7	21	4.5
8	23	4.9
9	19	4.0
10 - 14	74	15.7
15 - 19	49	10.4
20 +	80	17.0
Netherlands - Pays-Bas[18]		
2011 (C)		
Total	33 755	100.0
Less than 1 - Moins de 1	398	1.2
1	1 339	4.0
2	1 681	5.0
3	1 721	5.1
4	1 645	4.9
5	1 547	4.6
6	1 515	4.5
7	1 558	4.6
8	1 553	4.6
9	1 400	4.1
10 - 14	5 946	17.6
15 - 19	4 712	14.0
20 +	8 740	25.9
EUROPE		
Norway - Norvège[19]		
2011 (C)		
Total	10 188	100.0
Less than 1 - Moins de 1	6	0.1
1	162	1.6
2	436	4.3
3	543	5.3
4	541	5.3
5	614	6.0
6	586	5.8
7	566	5.6
8	585	5.7
9	518	5.1
10 - 14	1 879	18.4
15 - 19	1 150	11.3
20 +	2 257	22.2
Not stated - Inconnu	345	3.4
Poland - Pologne		
2011 (C)		
Total	64 594	100.0
Less than 1 - Moins de 1	475	0.7
1	2 293	3.5
2	3 596	5.6
3	3 920	6.1
4	3 654	5.7
5	3 100	4.8
6	2 725	4.2
7	2 550	3.9
8	2 391	3.7
9	2 228	3.4
10 - 14	10 684	16.5
15 - 19	8 766	13.6
20 +	18 212	28.2
Portugal		
2011 (C)		
Total	26 750	100.0
Less than 1 - Moins de 1	440	1.6
1	772	2.9
2	954	3.6
3	994	3.7
4	1 149	4.3
5	1 120	4.2
6	1 027	3.8
7	972	3.6
8	1 065	4.0
9	1 067	4.0
10 - 14	4 977	18.6
15 - 19	4 007	15.0
20 +	8 134	30.4
Not stated - Inconnu	72	0.3
Republic of Moldova - République de Moldova		
2010 (C)		
Total	11 504	100.0
Less than 1 - Moins de 1	346	3.0
1	699	6.1
2	860	7.5
3	895	7.8
4	832	7.2
5	665	5.8
6	582	5.1
7	455	4.0
8	414	3.6
9	364	3.2
10	1 579	13.7
15	1 530	13.3
20	2 283	19.8

Continent, country or area, year, code and duration of marriage (in years) Continent, pays ou zone, année, code et durée du mariage (en années)	Number of divorces Nombre de divorces	Per cent Pour cent
EUROPE		
Romania - Roumanie		
2011 (C)		
Total	35 780	100.0
Less than 1 - Moins de 1	815	2.3
1	1 830	5.1
2	2 246	6.3
3	2 480	6.9
4	2 505	7.0
5	2 111	5.9
6	1 793	5.0
7	1 650	4.6
8	1 434	4.0
9	1 313	3.7
10 - 14	5 789	16.2
15 - 19	4 395	12.3
20 +	7 419	20.7
Russian Federation - Fédération de Russie		
2011 (C)		
Total	669 376	100.0
Less than 1 - Moins de 1	33 567	5.0
1	50 768	7.6
2	58 099	8.7
3	57 871	8.6
4	50 042	7.5
5 - 9	165 467	24.7
10 - 14	82 645	12.3
15 - 19	60 911	9.1
20 +	109 624	16.4
Not stated - Inconnu	382	0.1
San Marino - Saint-Marin		
2012 (+C)		
Total	49	100.0
Less than 1 - Moins de 1	-	0.0
1 - 3	9	18.4
4 - 6	10	20.4
7 - 9	3	6.1
10 - 19	14	28.6
20 +	13	26.5
Serbia - Serbie[20]		
2011 (+C)		
Total	8 251	100.0
Less than 1 - Moins de 1	217	2.6
1	428	5.2
2	498	6.0
3	499	6.0
4	493	6.0
5	457	5.5
6	401	4.9
7	355	4.3
8	371	4.5
9	287	3.5
10 - 14	1 367	16.6
15 - 19	1 072	13.0
20 +	1 806	21.9
Slovakia - Slovaquie		
2011 (C)		
Total	11 102	100.0
Less than 1 - Moins de 1	73	0.7
1	254	2.3
2	408	3.7
3	466	4.2
4	443	4.0
5	450	4.1
6	488	4.4
7	489	4.4
8	436	3.9
9	403	3.6
10 - 14	1 901	17.1

Continent, country or area, year, code and duration of marriage (in years) Continent, pays ou zone, année, code et durée du mariage (en années)	Number of divorces Nombre de divorces	Per cent Pour cent
EUROPE		
Slovakia - Slovaquie		
2011 (C)		
15 - 19	1 855	16.7
20 +	3 436	30.9
Slovenia - Slovénie		
2011 (C)		
Total	2 298	100.0
Less than 1 - Moins de 1	24	1.0
1	68	3.0
2	95	4.1
3	107	4.7
4	107	4.7
5	97	4.2
6	87	3.8
7	79	3.4
8	89	3.9
9	80	3.5
10 - 14	321	14.0
15 - 19	322	14.0
20 +	822	35.8
Spain - Espagne		
2011 (C)		
Total	103 290	100.0
Less than 1 - Moins de 1	761	0.7
1	2 600	2.5
2	4 002	3.9
3	4 930	4.8
4	5 179	5.0
5	4 950	4.8
6	4 798	4.6
7	4 422	4.3
8	4 342	4.2
9	4 075	3.9
10 - 14	17 809	17.2
15 - 19	14 243	13.8
20 +	31 179	30.2
Sweden - Suède[21]		
2011 (C)		
Total	23 389	100.0
Less than 1 - Moins de 1	420	1.8
1	1 411	6.0
2	1 848	7.9
3	2 297	9.8
4	1 961	8.4
5	1 420	6.1
6	1 266	5.4
7	1 094	4.7
8	897	3.8
9	846	3.6
10 - 14	3 249	13.9
15 - 19	2 244	9.6
20 +	4 271	18.3
Not stated - Inconnu	165	0.7
Switzerland - Suisse		
2011 (C)		
Total	17 566	100.0
Less than 1 - Moins de 1	132	0.8
1	398	2.3
2	512	2.9
3	676	3.8
4	733	4.2
5	928	5.3
6	1 179	6.7
7	1 012	5.8
8	905	5.2
9	786	4.5
10 - 14	3 059	17.4

25. Divorces and percentage distribution by duration of marriage, latest available year: 2003 - 2012
Divorces et répartition des pourcentages selon la durée du mariage, dernière année disponible: 2003 - 2012 (continued - suite)

Continent, country or area, year, code and duration of marriage (in years) / Continent, pays ou zone, année, code et durée du mariage (en années)	Number of divorces / Nombre de divorces	Per cent / Pour cent
EUROPE		
Switzerland - Suisse		
2011 (C)		
15 - 19	2 516	14.3
20 +	4 730	26.9
TFYR of Macedonia - L'ex-R. y. de Macédoine		
2011 (C)		
Total	1 753	100.0
Less than 1 - Moins de 1	80	4.6
1	186	10.6
2	145	8.3
3	110	6.3
4	112	6.4
5	100	5.7
6	83	4.7
7	76	4.3
8	64	3.7
9	51	2.9
10 - 14	267	15.2
15 - 19	195	11.1
20 +	284	16.2
Ukraine[22]		
2011 (+C)		
Total	61 872	100.0
Less than 1 - Moins de 1	3 207	5.2
1	4 654	7.5
2	4 567	7.4
3	4 818	7.8
4	4 030	6.5
5 - 9	12 838	20.7
10 - 14	7 288	11.8
15 - 19	5 949	9.6
20 +	14 521	23.5
United Kingdom of Great Britain and Northern Ireland - Royaume-Uni de Grande-Bretagne et d'Irlande du Nord[23]		
2011 (C)		
Total	129 764	100.0
Less than 1 - Moins de 1	38	0.0
1	1 863	1.4
2	4 348	3.4
3	6 343	4.9
4	7 180	5.5
5	7 245	5.6
6	7 670	5.9
7	7 771	6.0
8	6 910	5.3
9	5 989	4.6
10 - 14	24 231	18.7
15 - 19	17 386	13.4
20 +	32 790	25.3
OCEANIA - OCÉANIE		
Australia - Australie		
2011 (C)		
Total	48 935	100.0
Less than 1 - Moins de 1	-	0.0
1	593	1.2
2	2 428	5.0
3	3 019	6.2
4	3 092	6.3
5	2 694	5.5
6	2 490	5.1
7	2 233	4.6
8	2 067	4.2

Continent, country or area, year, code and duration of marriage (in years) / Continent, pays ou zone, année, code et durée du mariage (en années)	Number of divorces / Nombre de divorces	Per cent / Pour cent
OCEANIA - OCÉANIE		
Australia - Australie		
2011 (C)		
9	1 864	3.8
10 - 14	8 398	17.2
15 - 19	6 559	13.4
20 +	13 495	27.6
Not stated - Inconnu	3	0.0
New Caledonia - Nouvelle-Calédonie[24]		
2005 (C)		
Total	341	100.0
Less than 1 - Moins de 1	1	0.3
1	6	1.8
2	6	1.8
3	12	3.5
4	16	4.7
5	17	5.0
6	23	6.7
7	21	6.2
8	18	5.3
9	27	7.9
10 - 14	66	19.4
15 - 19	53	15.5
20 +	75	22.0
New Zealand - Nouvelle-Zélande		
2011 (+C)		
Total	8 551	100.0
Less than 1 - Moins de 1	-	0.0
1	-	0.0
2	179	2.1
3	361	4.2
4	472	5.5
5	420	4.9
6	403	4.7
7	420	4.9
8	424	5.0
9	370	4.3
10 - 14	1 591	18.6
15 - 19	1 253	14.7
20 +	2 658	31.1
Not stated - Inconnu	-	0.0
Northern Mariana Islands - Îles Mariannes septentrionales[25]		
2007 (U)		
Total	160	100.0
Less than 1 - Moins de 1	2	1.3
1	3	1.9
2	5	3.1
3	9	5.6
4	4	2.5
5	14	8.8
6	11	6.9
7	9	5.6
8	6	3.8
9	8	5.0
10 - 14	34	21.3
15 - 19	20	12.5
20 +	35	21.9
Samoa		
2009 (U)		
Total	48	100.0
Less than 1 - Moins de 1	-	0.0
1	-	0.0
2	-	0.0
3	2	4.2
4	-	0.0
5	1	2.1
6	2	4.2

25. Divorces and percentage distribution by duration of marriage, latest available year: 2003 - 2012
Divorces et répartition des pourcentages selon la durée du mariage, dernière année disponible: 2003 - 2012 (continued - suite)

Continent, country or area, year, code and duration of marriage (in years) Continent, pays ou zone, année, code et durée du mariage (en années)	Number of divorces Nombre de divorces	Per cent Pour cent	Continent, country or area, year, code and duration of marriage (in years) Continent, pays ou zone, année, code et durée du mariage (en années)	Number of divorces Nombre de divorces	Per cent Pour cent
OCEANIA - OCÉANIE			**OCEANIA - OCÉANIE**		
Samoa			Samoa		
2009 (U)			2009 (U)		
7	*3*	*6.3*	15 - 19	*10*	*20.8*
8	*2*	*4.2*	20 + ...	*7*	*14.6*
9	*2*	*4.2*	Not stated - Inconnu	*15*	*31.3*
10 - 14	*4*	*8.3*			

FOOTNOTES - NOTES

Italics: estimates which are less reliable. - Italiques: estimations moins sûres.

* Provisional. - Données provisoires.

'Code' indicates the source of data, as follows:
C - Civil registration, estimated over 90% complete
U - Civil registration, estimated less than 90% complete
| - Other source, estimated reliable
+ - Data tabulated by date of registration rather than occurence.
... - Information not available

Le 'Code' indique la source des données, comme suit:
C - Registres de l'état civil considérés complets à 90 p. 100 au moins.
U - Registres de l'état civil qui ne sont pas considérés complets à 90 p. 100 au moins.
| - Autre source, considérée pas douteuses.
+ - Données exploitées selon la date de l'enregistrement et non la date de l'événement.
... - Information non disponible.

[1] Including 'revocable divorces' (among Muslim population), which approximate legal separations. - Y compris les 'divorces révocables' (parmi la population musulmane), qui sont plus au moins l'équivalent des séparations légales.
[2] Excludes the islands of St. Brandon and Agalega. - Non compris les îles St. Brandon et Agalega.
[3] Refer to divorces confirmed by final judgment. - Correspond aux divorces ayant fait l'objet d'un jugement.
[4] Because of rounding, totals are not in all cases the sum of the respective components. - Les chiffres étant arrondis, les totaux ne correspondent pas toujours rigoureusement à la somme des composants respectifs.
[5] Duration of marriage is defined as the time from the day of celebration of the marriage till the day of filing of the divorce. - La durée du mariage est définie comme la période s'écoulant depuis le jour de la célébration de l'union jusqu'à la date de la demande de divorce.
[6] Excludes nomadic Indian tribes. - Non compris les tribus d'Indiens nomades.
[7] Including annulments. - Y compris les annulations.
[8] Data refer to government controlled areas. - Les données se rapportent aux zones contrôlées par le Gouvernement.
[9] Data refer to the Iranian Year which begins on 21 March and ends on 20 March of the following year. - Les données concernent l'année iranienne, qui commence le 21 mars et se termine le 20 mars de l'année suivante.
[10] Includes data for East Jerusalem and Israeli residents in certain other territories under occupation by Israeli military forces since June 1967. - Y compris les données pour Jérusalem-Est et les résidents israéliens dans certains autres territoires occupés depuis 1967 par les forces armées israéliennes.
[11] Data refer to Japanese nationals in Japan only. - Les données se raportent aux nationaux japonais au Japon seulement.
[12] Excluding alien armed forces, civilian aliens employed by armed forces, and foreign diplomatic personnel and their dependants. - Non compris les militaires étrangers, les civils étrangers employés par les forces armées ni le personnel diplomatique étranger et les membres de leur famille les accompagnant.

[13] Excluding aliens temporarily in the area. - Non compris les étrangers se trouvant temporairement dans le territoire.
[14] Including armed forces stationed outside the country, but excluding alien armed forces stationed in the area. - Y compris les militaires nationaux hors du pays, mais non compris les militaires étrangers en garnison sur le territoire.
[15] Excluding Faeroe Islands and Greenland shown separately, if available. - Non compris les Iles Féroé et le Groenland, qui font l'objet de rubriques distinctes, si disponible.
[16] Data refers for common residence before divorce. - Données se rapportant à la résidence commune avant le divorce.
[17] Data refer to residence of groom. Excluding annulments. - Données relatives au lieu de résidence du marié. Ne comprend pas les annulations.
[18] Based on the general office for civil registration. Including same sex divorces. - Données provenant des services généraux d'état civil. Y compris les divorces entre conjoints du même sexe.
[19] Data refer to male residents of Norway only. - Ces données ne concernent que les hommes habitant en Norvège.
[20] Excludes data for Kosovo and Metohia. - Sans les données pour le Kosovo et Metohie.
[21] Including same sex divorces. - Y compris les divorces entre conjoints du même sexe.
[22] Excluding divorces made in courts (under the Law of Ukraine "On state registration of civil status" from 1 July 2010). - Excepté les divorces prononcés par un tribunal (en vertu de la loi ukrainienne du 1er juillet 2010 sur l'enregistrement de l'état civil).
[23] Excluding Channel Islands (Guernsey and Jersey) and Isle of Man, shown separately, if available. - Non compris les îles Anglo-Normandes (Guernesey et Jersey) et l'île de Man, qui font l'objet de rubriques distinctes, si disponible.
[24] Based on place of residence at marriage not at divorce. - Les divorces sont comptés en fonction du lieu de résidence au mariage, et non pas au divorce.
[25] Data refer to the islands of Saipan, Tinian and Rota only. - Les données se réfèrent uniquement aux îles de Saipan, Tinian et Rota.

Continent and country or area Continent et pays ou zone	Population estimates (in thousands) - Estimations de population (en milliers)[1]									
	2003	2004	2005	2006	2007	2008	2009	2010	2011	2012

AFRICA - AFRIQUE

	2003	2004	2005	2006	2007	2008	2009	2010	2011	2012
Algeria - Algérie	33 003	33 461	33 961	34 507	35 097	35 725	36 383	37 063	37 763	38 482
Angola	15 421	15 977	16 544	17 122	17 713	18 314	18 927	19 549	20 180	20 821
Benin - Bénin	7 666	7 923	8 182	8 444	8 707	8 973	9 241	9 510	9 780	10 051
Botswana	1 833	1 855	1 876	1 896	1 915	1 934	1 952	1 969	1 987	2 004
Burkina Faso	12 659	13 034	13 422	13 822	14 235	14 660	15 095	15 540	15 995	16 460
Burundi	7 264	7 511	7 770	8 043	8 328	8 624	8 927	9 233	9 540	9 850
Cabo Verde	467	474	479	482	484	485	486	488	491	494
Cameroon - Cameroun	17 223	17 675	18 138	18 612	19 098	19 595	20 104	20 624	21 156	21 700
Central African Republic - République centrafricaine	3 830	3 894	3 961	4 032	4 107	4 185	4 266	4 350	4 436	4 525
Chad - Tchad	9 311	9 665	10 014	10 357	10 694	11 031	11 371	11 721	12 080	12 448
Comoros - Comores	570	585	601	617	633	649	666	683	700	718
Congo	3 363	3 449	3 543	3 647	3 759	3 876	3 995	4 112	4 225	4 337
Côte d'Ivoire	16 910	17 144	17 394	17 662	17 949	18 260	18 601	18 977	19 390	19 840
Democratic Republic of the Congo - République démocratique du Congo	50 972	52 487	54 028	55 591	57 188	58 819	60 486	62 191	63 932	65 705
Djibouti	755	766	777	788	799	810	822	834	847	860
Egypt - Égypte	69 432	70 591	71 778	72 991	74 230	75 492	76 775	78 076	79 392	80 722
Equatorial Guinea - Guinée équatoriale	569	586	604	622	640	658	677	696	716	736
Eritrea - Érythrée	4 473	4 666	4 854	5 035	5 210	5 382	5 558	5 741	5 933	6 131
Ethiopia - Éthiopie	71 990	74 066	76 167	78 291	80 441	82 621	84 838	87 095	89 393	91 729
Gabon	1 316	1 347	1 379	1 413	1 447	1 483	1 519	1 556	1 594	1 633
Gambia - Gambie	1 349	1 392	1 437	1 482	1 529	1 578	1 628	1 681	1 735	1 791
Ghana	20 302	20 836	21 384	21 948	22 526	23 110	23 692	24 263	24 821	25 366
Guinea - Guinée	9 205	9 380	9 576	9 799	10 047	10 315	10 593	10 876	11 162	11 451
Guinea-Bissau - Guinée-Bissau	1 361	1 391	1 422	1 453	1 484	1 517	1 551	1 587	1 624	1 664
Kenya	33 905	34 835	35 786	36 757	37 752	38 773	39 825	40 909	42 028	43 178
Lesotho	1 899	1 912	1 926	1 940	1 956	1 972	1 990	2 009	2 030	2 052
Liberia - Libéria	3 124	3 185	3 270	3 385	3 522	3 673	3 821	3 958	4 080	4 190
Libya - Libye	5 423	5 507	5 594	5 686	5 782	5 877	5 964	6 041	6 103	6 155
Madagascar	17 245	17 763	18 290	18 826	19 371	19 927	20 496	21 080	21 679	22 294
Malawi	12 239	12 569	12 925	13 308	13 714	14 138	14 573	15 014	15 458	15 906
Mali	11 220	11 573	11 941	12 326	12 726	13 138	13 559	13 986	14 417	14 854
Mauritania - Mauritanie	2 966	3 055	3 146	3 238	3 330	3 423	3 516	3 609	3 703	3 796
Mauritius - Maurice[2]	1 204	1 209	1 213	1 217	1 220	1 223	1 227	1 231	1 235	1 240
Mayotte	164	170	175	181	186	192	198	204	210	216
Morocco - Maroc	29 587	29 856	30 125	30 395	30 667	30 955	31 277	31 642	32 059	32 521
Mozambique	19 873	20 439	21 010	21 587	22 171	22 763	23 361	23 967	24 581	25 203
Namibia - Namibie	1 981	2 003	2 027	2 053	2 081	2 111	2 143	2 179	2 218	2 259
Niger	12 254	12 709	13 184	13 680	14 197	14 738	15 303	15 894	16 511	17 157
Nigeria - Nigéria	132 550	135 999	139 586	143 315	147 187	151 208	155 381	159 708	164 193	168 834
Republic of South Sudan - République de Soudan du Sud	7 450	7 730	8 039	8 377	8 737	9 118	9 521	9 941	10 381	10 838
Réunion	770	780	791	802	813	823	834	845	855	865
Rwanda	9 126	9 254	9 429	9 661	9 928	10 223	10 530	10 837	11 144	11 458
Sao Tome and Principe - Sao Tomé-et-Principe	147	151	155	159	163	168	173	178	183	188
Senegal - Sénégal	10 674	10 968	11 271	11 583	11 905	12 239	12 587	12 951	13 331	13 726
Seychelles	84	86	87	88	89	90	91	91	92	92
Sierra Leone	4 713	4 928	5 120	5 281	5 416	5 532	5 641	5 752	5 865	5 979
Somalia - Somalie	8 038	8 250	8 467	8 688	8 911	9 140	9 381	9 636	9 908	10 195
South Africa - Afrique du Sud	46 869	47 553	48 235	48 919	49 603	50 267	50 890	51 452	51 949	52 386
Sudan - Soudan	29 974	30 779	31 586	32 398	33 218	34 040	34 853	35 652	36 431	37 195
Swaziland	1 088	1 095	1 105	1 118	1 135	1 154	1 174	1 193	1 212	1 231
Togo	5 259	5 398	5 540	5 686	5 835	5 987	6 144	6 306	6 472	6 643
Tunisia - Tunisie	9 847	9 947	10 051	10 160	10 274	10 391	10 511	10 632	10 753	10 875
Uganda - Ouganda	26 838	27 767	28 725	29 711	30 729	31 779	32 864	33 987	35 148	36 346
United Republic of Tanzania - République Unie de Tanzanie	36 761	37 765	38 824	39 942	41 120	42 354	43 640	44 973	46 355	47 783
Western Sahara - Sahara occidental	378	404	428	448	466	482	498	515	532	549
Zambia - Zambie	10 895	11 175	11 470	11 782	12 110	12 457	12 825	13 217	13 634	14 075
Zimbabwe	12 673	12 693	12 711	12 724	12 740	12 784	12 889	13 077	13 359	13 724

AMERICA, NORTH - AMÉRIQUE DU NORD

	2003	2004	2005	2006	2007	2008	2009	2010	2011	2012
Anguilla	12	12	13	13	13	13	14	14	14	14
Antigua and Barbuda - Antigua-et-Barbuda	81	82	83	83	84	85	86	87	88	89
Aruba	97	99	100	101	101	101	101	102	102	102
Bahamas	316	322	329	336	342	348	354	360	366	372
Barbados - Barbade	271	272	274	275	276	278	279	280	282	283

Continent and country or area Continent et pays ou zone	Population estimates (in thousands) - Estimations de population (en milliers)[1]									
	2003	2004	2005	2006	2007	2008	2009	2010	2011	2012

AMERICA, NORTH - AMÉRIQUE DU NORD

	2003	2004	2005	2006	2007	2008	2009	2010	2011	2012
Belize...............	258	265	272	279	286	294	301	309	316	324
Bermuda - Bermudes	64	64	64	64	65	65	65	65	65	65
Bonaire, Saba and Sint Eustatius - Bonaire, Saba et Saint-Eustache...............	14	14	14	15	15	16	17	18	18	19
British Virgin Islands - Îles Vierges britanniques	22	23	23	24	25	26	27	27	28	28
Canada	31 592	31 914	32 253	32 611	32 986	33 370	33 753	34 126	34 487	34 838
Cayman Islands - Îles Caïmanes	46	47	49	50	51	53	54	56	57	58
Costa Rica	4 171	4 246	4 320	4 392	4 463	4 533	4 601	4 670	4 738	4 805
Cuba...............	11 246	11 273	11 292	11 301	11 302	11 296	11 289	11 282	11 276	11 271
Curaçao...............	128	128	129	132	135	139	143	148	152	155
Dominica - Dominique...............	70	70	71	71	71	71	71	71	71	72
Dominican Republic - République dominicaine...............	9 071	9 207	9 343	9 479	9 615	9 750	9 884	10 017	10 148	10 277
El Salvador	6 029	6 050	6 073	6 097	6 123	6 152	6 183	6 218	6 256	6 297
Greenland - Groenland...............	57	57	57	57	57	57	57	57	57	57
Grenada - Grenade	102	103	103	103	104	104	104	105	105	105
Guadeloupe[3]	437	441	444	447	450	453	456	459	461	464
Guatemala...............	12 063	12 368	12 679	12 995	13 318	13 648	13 989	14 342	14 707	15 083
Haiti - Haïti...............	8 996	9 130	9 261	9 389	9 514	9 638	9 765	9 896	10 033	10 174
Honduras...............	6 628	6 762	6 899	7 037	7 178	7 322	7 470	7 621	7 777	7 936
Jamaica - Jamaïque...............	2 647	2 666	2 682	2 696	2 708	2 719	2 730	2 741	2 755	2 769
Martinique...............	392	394	396	398	399	399	400	401	402	403
Mexico - Mexique...............	108 056	109 382	110 732	112 117	113 530	114 968	116 423	117 886	119 361	120 847
Montserrat...............	4	5	5	5	5	5	5	5	5	5
Nicaragua...............	5 318	5 386	5 455	5 525	5 596	5 668	5 743	5 822	5 905	5 992
Panama...............	3 241	3 303	3 366	3 429	3 491	3 553	3 616	3 678	3 740	3 802
Puerto Rico - Porto Rico...............	3 785	3 773	3 761	3 750	3 739	3 729	3 719	3 710	3 701	3 694
Saint Kitts and Nevis - Saint-Kitts-et-Nevis...............	48	48	49	50	50	51	52	52	53	54
Saint Lucia - Sainte-Lucie...............	162	163	165	168	170	173	175	177	179	181
Saint Pierre and Miquelon - Saint Pierre-et-Miquelon...............	6	6	6	6	6	6	6	6	6	6
Saint Vincent and the Grenadines - Saint-Vincent-et-les Grenadines...............	108	109	109	109	109	109	109	109	109	109
Sint Maarten (Dutch part) - Saint-Martin (partie néerlandaise)...............	34	36	37	39	40	41	42	43	43	44
Trinidad and Tobago - Trinité-et-Tobago	1 284	1 290	1 297	1 303	1 310	1 316	1 323	1 328	1 333	1 337
Turks and Caicos Islands - Îles Turques et Caïques...............	23	25	26	28	29	29	30	31	32	32
United States of America - États-Unis d'Amérique...............	292 883	295 487	298 166	300 943	303 787	306 657	309 492	312 247	314 912	317 505
United States Virgin Islands - Îles Vierges américaines...............	108	108	108	107	107	107	107	106	106	106

AMERICA, SOUTH - AMÉRIQUE DU SUD

	2003	2004	2005	2006	2007	2008	2009	2010	2011	2012
Argentina - Argentine...............	37 970	38 309	38 648	38 989	39 331	39 676	40 024	40 374	40 729	41 087
Bolivia (Plurinational State of) - Bolivie (État plurinational de)...............	9 017	9 188	9 355	9 517	9 676	9 834	9 993	10 157	10 324	10 496
Brazil - Brésil...............	181 753	184 010	186 142	188 134	189 997	191 766	193 491	195 210	196 935	198 656
Chile - Chili...............	15 996	16 168	16 338	16 505	16 669	16 831	16 992	17 151	17 308	17 465
Colombia - Colombie...............	41 872	42 528	43 184	43 841	44 498	45 153	45 803	46 445	47 079	47 704
Ecuador - Équateur...............	13 280	13 529	13 777	14 024	14 268	14 512	14 756	15 001	15 246	15 492
Falkland Islands (Malvinas) - Îles Falkland (Malvinas)...............	3	3	3	3	3	3	3	3	3	3
French Guiana - Guyane française...............	187	195	202	208	214	220	225	231	237	243
Guyana...............	754	757	761	765	770	776	781	786	791	795
Paraguay...............	5 682	5 793	5 904	6 015	6 125	6 236	6 347	6 460	6 573	6 687
Peru - Pérou...............	27 073	27 404	27 723	28 031	28 328	28 626	28 934	29 263	29 615	29 988
Suriname...............	487	493	500	505	510	515	520	525	530	535
Uruguay...............	3 325	3 324	3 325	3 330	3 338	3 349	3 360	3 372	3 383	3 395
Venezuela (Bolivarian Republic of) - Venezuela (République bolivarienne du)...............	25 797	26 261	26 726	27 191	27 656	28 120	28 583	29 043	29 501	29 955

ASIA - ASIE

	2003	2004	2005	2006	2007	2008	2009	2010	2011	2012
Afghanistan...............	23 116	24 019	24 861	25 631	26 349	27 032	27 708	28 398	29 105	29 825
Armenia - Arménie...............	3 036	3 026	3 015	3 003	2 990	2 977	2 968	2 963	2 964	2 969
Azerbaijan - Azerbaïdjan[4]...............	8 370	8 465	8 563	8 665	8 770	8 878	8 986	9 095	9 202	9 309
Bahrain - Bahreïn...............	772	821	880	951	1 032	1 116	1 192	1 252	1 293	1 318
Bangladesh...............	139 186	141 235	143 135	144 869	146 457	147 970	149 503	151 125	152 862	154 695
Bhutan - Bhoutan...............	616	634	650	666	679	692	705	717	729	742
Brunei Darussalam - Brunéi Darussalam...............	354	361	368	375	381	388	394	401	407	412

Continent and country or area / Continent et pays ou zone	Population estimates (in thousands) - Estimations de population (en milliers)[1]									
	2003	2004	2005	2006	2007	2008	2009	2010	2011	2012
ASIA - ASIE										
Cambodia - Cambodge	12 934	13 149	13 356	13 555	13 747	13 941	14 144	14 365	14 606	14 865
China - Chine[5]	1 302 810	1 310 414	1 318 177	1 326 146	1 334 344	1 342 733	1 351 248	1 359 821	1 368 440	1 377 065
China, Hong Kong SAR - Chine, Hong Kong RAS	6 907	6 897	6 897	6 911	6 935	6 968	7 007	7 050	7 096	7 148
China, Macao SAR - Chine, Macao RAS	451	459	468	480	493	508	522	535	546	557
Cyprus - Chypre[6]	998	1 016	1 033	1 048	1 063	1 077	1 091	1 104	1 117	1 129
Democratic People's Republic of Korea - République populaire démocratique de Corée	23 449	23 639	23 813	23 970	24 112	24 244	24 372	24 501	24 631	24 763
Georgia - Géorgie[7]	4 565	4 515	4 475	4 446	4 426	4 413	4 401	4 389	4 374	4 358
India - Inde	1 093 787	1 110 626	1 127 144	1 143 289	1 159 095	1 174 662	1 190 138	1 205 625	1 221 156	1 236 687
Indonesia - Indonésie	218 146	221 294	224 481	227 710	230 973	234 243	237 487	240 676	243 802	246 864
Iran (Islamic Republic of) - Iran (République islamique d')...	68 543	69 342	70 152	70 977	71 809	72 661	73 543	74 462	75 424	76 424
Iraq	25 960	26 674	27 377	28 064	28 741	29 430	30 163	30 962	31 837	32 778
Israel - Israël	6 349	6 468	6 604	6 759	6 930	7 107	7 274	7 420	7 542	7 644
Japan - Japon	126 524	126 773	126 979	127 136	127 249	127 319	127 353	127 353	127 319	127 250
Jordan - Jordanie	4 984	5 092	5 239	5 429	5 656	5 911	6 181	6 455	6 731	7 009
Kazakhstan	14 748	14 902	15 064	15 227	15 396	15 568	15 744	15 921	16 098	16 271
Kuwait - Koweït	2 116	2 196	2 296	2 417	2 555	2 702	2 850	2 992	3 125	3 250
Kyrgyzstan - Kirghizstan	5 009	5 019	5 042	5 082	5 134	5 197	5 265	5 334	5 403	5 474
Lao People's Democratic Republic - République démocratique populaire lao	5 619	5 699	5 791	5 896	6 013	6 139	6 268	6 396	6 521	6 646
Lebanon - Liban	3 690	3 854	3 987	4 080	4 140	4 186	4 247	4 341	4 478	4 647
Malaysia - Malaisie[8]	24 891	25 365	25 843	26 327	26 814	27 302	27 790	28 276	28 759	29 240
Maldives	288	293	298	303	308	314	320	326	332	338
Mongolia - Mongolie	2 469	2 496	2 527	2 559	2 595	2 633	2 672	2 713	2 754	2 796
Myanmar	49 577	49 875	50 181	50 500	50 829	51 174	51 540	51 931	52 351	52 797
Nepal - Népal	24 526	24 922	25 292	25 634	25 950	26 249	26 545	26 846	27 156	27 474
Oman	2 389	2 464	2 522	2 555	2 570	2 594	2 663	2 803	3 025	3 314
Pakistan	152 420	155 151	157 971	160 906	163 928	167 008	170 094	173 149	176 166	179 160
Philippines	82 605	84 231	85 821	87 367	88 876	90 371	91 886	93 444	95 053	96 707
Qatar	660	720	821	968	1 152	1 359	1 564	1 750	1 911	2 051
Republic of Korea - République de Corée	46 592	46 801	47 033	47 291	47 573	47 868	48 165	48 454	48 733	49 003
Saudi Arabia - Arabie saoudite	22 852	23 839	24 690	25 372	25 916	26 366	26 796	27 258	27 762	28 288
Singapore - Singapour	4 255	4 375	4 496	4 614	4 732	4 849	4 964	5 079	5 192	5 303
Sri Lanka	19 502	19 738	19 951	20 138	20 302	20 452	20 602	20 759	20 926	21 098
State of Palestine - État de Palestine	3 427	3 490	3 560	3 639	3 725	3 818	3 914	4 013	4 114	4 219
Syrian Arab Republic - République arabe syrienne	17 298	17 676	18 167	18 805	19 561	20 346	21 032	21 533	21 804	21 890
Tajikistan - Tadjikistan	6 530	6 664	6 806	6 955	7 111	7 275	7 447	7 627	7 815	8 009
Thailand - Thaïlande	64 488	65 087	65 559	65 884	66 077	66 185	66 277	66 402	66 576	66 785
Timor-Leste	933	967	996	1 018	1 036	1 050	1 064	1 079	1 096	1 114
Turkey - Turquie	65 938	66 846	67 743	68 626	69 497	70 364	71 241	72 138	73 059	73 997
Turkmenistan - Turkménistan	4 648	4 697	4 748	4 802	4 858	4 918	4 979	5 042	5 107	5 173
United Arab Emirates - Émirats arabes unis	3 369	3 659	4 149	4 876	5 797	6 799	7 718	8 442	8 925	9 206
Uzbekistan - Ouzbékistan	25 554	25 784	26 044	26 341	26 669	27 023	27 393	27 769	28 152	28 541
Viet Nam	83 353	84 151	84 948	85 748	86 553	87 369	88 200	89 047	89 914	90 796
Yemen - Yémen	19 081	19 613	20 140	20 662	21 182	21 704	22 230	22 763	23 304	23 852
EUROPE										
Albania - Albanie	3 239	3 216	3 196	3 180	3 166	3 157	3 151	3 150	3 154	3 162
Andorra - Andorre	76	79	81	82	81	80	79	78	78	78
Austria - Autriche	8 142	8 193	8 239	8 277	8 311	8 342	8 372	8 402	8 433	8 464
Belarus - Bélarus	9 784	9 720	9 665	9 620	9 585	9 556	9 526	9 491	9 450	9 405
Belgium - Belgique	10 385	10 441	10 508	10 588	10 678	10 773	10 862	10 941	11 007	11 060
Bosnia and Herzegovina - Bosnie-Herzégovine	3 896	3 887	3 880	3 875	3 869	3 861	3 853	3 846	3 839	3 834
Bulgaria - Bulgarie	7 807	7 745	7 683	7 623	7 563	7 504	7 446	7 389	7 333	7 278
Croatia - Croatie	4 411	4 400	4 389	4 379	4 369	4 360	4 350	4 338	4 324	4 307
Czech Republic - République tchèque	10 204	10 208	10 231	10 275	10 338	10 412	10 486	10 554	10 611	10 660
Denmark - Danemark	5 383	5 399	5 418	5 441	5 468	5 496	5 524	5 551	5 575	5 598
Estonia - Estonie	1 339	1 332	1 325	1 319	1 313	1 308	1 303	1 299	1 294	1 291
Faeroe Islands - Îles Féroé	48	49	49	49	50	50	50	50	50	50
Finland - Finlande[9]	5 213	5 228	5 246	5 268	5 292	5 318	5 344	5 368	5 389	5 408
France	60 528	61 003	61 445	61 845	62 211	62 553	62 888	63 231	63 582	63 937
Germany - Allemagne	83 788	83 849	83 836	83 740	83 579	83 380	83 183	83 017	82 893	82 800
Gibraltar	28	29	29	29	29	29	29	29	29	29
Greece - Grèce	11 032	11 035	11 042	11 053	11 067	11 083	11 098	11 110	11 119	11 125
Holy See - Saint-Siège	1	1	1	1	1	1	1	1	1	1
Hungary - Hongrie	10 142	10 118	10 096	10 077	10 061	10 046	10 031	10 015	9 996	9 976

Continent and country or area Continent et pays ou zone	Population estimates (in thousands) - Estimations de population (en milliers)[1]									
	2003	2004	2005	2006	2007	2008	2009	2010	2011	2012
EUROPE										
Iceland - Islande	290	293	297	301	305	309	314	318	322	326
Ireland - Irlande	4 011	4 086	4 158	4 226	4 291	4 352	4 410	4 468	4 523	4 576
Isle of Man - Île de Man	79	80	80	81	82	83	83	84	85	85
Italy - Italie	57 868	58 267	58 672	59 078	59 486	59 874	60 220	60 509	60 729	60 885
Latvia - Lettonie	2 288	2 258	2 228	2 197	2 167	2 138	2 112	2 091	2 073	2 060
Liechtenstein	34	34	35	35	35	36	36	36	36	37
Lithuania - Lituanie	3 378	3 333	3 287	3 239	3 190	3 143	3 102	3 068	3 044	3 028
Luxembourg	447	452	458	466	476	487	498	508	516	524
Malta - Malte	412	413	415	417	419	421	423	425	426	428
Monaco	33	33	34	34	35	36	36	37	37	38
Montenegro - Monténégro	613	615	616	617	618	619	619	620	621	621
Netherlands - Pays-Bas	16 134	16 221	16 302	16 376	16 443	16 504	16 561	16 615	16 666	16 714
Norway - Norvège[10]	4 560	4 588	4 624	4 669	4 721	4 778	4 836	4 891	4 944	4 994
Poland - Pologne	38 250	38 225	38 206	38 194	38 189	38 190	38 194	38 199	38 205	38 211
Portugal	10 439	10 478	10 511	10 537	10 556	10 570	10 581	10 590	10 598	10 604
Republic of Moldova - République de Moldova[11]	3 896	3 828	3 767	3 716	3 673	3 637	3 604	3 573	3 543	3 514
Romania - Roumanie	22 202	22 158	22 113	22 065	22 016	21 965	21 913	21 861	21 809	21 755
Russian Federation - Fédération de Russie	144 880	144 331	143 933	143 715	143 652	143 677	143 690	143 618	143 438	143 170
San Marino - Saint-Marin	29	29	30	30	30	31	31	31	31	31
Serbia - Serbie[12]	10 090	10 024	9 956	9 889	9 824	9 761	9 702	9 647	9 597	9 553
Slovakia - Slovaquie	5 387	5 388	5 391	5 397	5 406	5 415	5 425	5 433	5 440	5 446
Slovenia - Slovénie	1 991	1 995	2 000	2 009	2 020	2 032	2 044	2 054	2 062	2 068
Spain - Espagne[13]	42 016	42 710	43 387	44 038	44 664	45 243	45 754	46 182	46 514	46 755
Sweden - Suède	8 942	8 981	9 030	9 090	9 159	9 235	9 310	9 382	9 449	9 511
Switzerland - Suisse	7 289	7 345	7 409	7 482	7 565	7 653	7 743	7 831	7 915	7 997
TFYR of Macedonia - L'ex-R. y. de Macédoine	2 081	2 086	2 090	2 094	2 097	2 099	2 101	2 102	2 104	2 106
Ukraine	47 807	47 450	47 136	46 871	46 653	46 461	46 267	46 050	45 803	45 530
United Kingdom of Great Britain and Northern Ireland - Royaume-Uni de Grande-Bretagne et d'Irlande du Nord	59 698	59 984	60 291	60 621	60 970	61 333	61 701	62 066	62 427	62 783
OCEANIA - OCÉANIE										
American Samoa - Samoas américaines	59	59	59	59	58	57	56	56	55	55
Australia - Australie[14]	19 953	20 218	20 521	20 866	21 246	21 645	22 037	22 404	22 741	23 050
Cook Islands - Îles Cook	19	19	19	20	20	20	20	20	20	21
Fiji - Fidji	817	819	822	828	835	844	852	861	868	875
French Polynesia - Polynésie française	249	252	255	258	260	263	265	268	271	274
Guam	158	158	158	158	158	158	159	159	161	163
Kiribati	87	89	90	92	93	95	96	98	99	101
Marshall Islands - Îles Marshall	52	52	52	52	52	52	52	52	52	53
Micronesia (Federated States of) - Micronésie (États fédérés de)	107	107	106	106	105	104	104	104	103	103
Nauru	10	10	10	10	10	10	10	10	10	10
New Caledonia - Nouvelle-Calédonie	221	225	229	232	236	239	243	246	250	253
New Zealand - Nouvelle-Zélande	4 021	4 079	4 134	4 185	4 233	4 278	4 323	4 368	4 414	4 460
Niue - Nioué	2	2	2	2	2	2	2	1	1	1
Northern Mariana Islands - Îles Mariannes septentrionales	68	66	64	62	60	57	55	54	53	53
Palau - Palaos	20	20	20	20	20	20	20	20	21	21
Papua New Guinea - Papouasie-Nouvelle-Guinée	5 803	5 948	6 096	6 246	6 398	6 551	6 705	6 859	7 013	7 167
Samoa	178	179	180	181	182	183	185	186	187	189
Solomon Islands - Îles Salomon	446	458	469	481	492	504	515	526	538	550
Tokelau - Tokélaou	1	1	1	1	1	1	1	1	1	1
Tonga	100	100	101	102	102	103	104	104	105	105
Tuvalu	10	10	10	10	10	10	10	10	10	10
Vanuatu	199	204	209	215	220	225	231	236	242	247
Wallis and Futuna Islands - Îles Wallis et Futuna	14	14	14	14	14	14	14	14	13	13

SOURCE

United Nations, Department of Economic and Social Affairs, Population Division (2013). World Population Prospects: The 2012 Revision. Extended dataset in Excel and ASCII formats, DVD-ROM edition (United Nations publication, ST/ESA/SER.A/334). - Organisation des Nations Unies, Département des affaires économiques et sociales, Division de la population (2013). Perspectives de la population mondiale : La révision de 2012. Ensemble de données étendues en formats Excel et ASCII, edition DVD-ROM (publication des Nations Unies, ST/ESA/SER.A/334).

FOOTNOTES - NOTES

[1] All data refer to annual interpolated estimates of mid-year population. - Les données sont des estimations interpolées de population au milieu de l'année.

[2] Including Agalega, Rodrigues and Saint Brandon. - Y compris Agalega, Rodrigues et Saint Brandon.

[3] Including Saint-Barthélemy and Saint-Martin (French part). - Y compris Saint-Barthélemy et Saint-Martin (partie française).

[4] Including Nagorno-Karabakh. - Y compris le Haut-Karabakh.

[5] For statistical purposes, the data for China do not include Hong Kong and Macao Special Administrative Regions (SAR) of China. - A des fins statistiques, les données pour la Chine ne comprennent pas les Régions Administratives Spéciales (SAR) de Hong Kong et Macao.

[6] Including Northern-Cyprus. - Y compris Chypre-Nord.

[7] Including Abkhazia and South Ossetia. - Y compris l'Abkhazie et l'Ossétie du Sud.

[8] Including Sabah and Sarawak. - Y compris le Sabah et le Sarawak.

[9] Including Åland Islands. - Y compris les îles Åland.

[10] Including Svalbard and Jan Mayen Islands. - Y compris Svalbard et l'île Jan Mayen.

[11] Including Transnistria. - Y compris la Transnistrie.

[12] Including Kosovo. - Y compris le Kosovo.

[13] Including Canary Islands, Ceuta and Melilla. - Y compris les îles Canaries, Ceuta et Melilla.

[14] Including Christmas Island, Cocos (Keeling) Islands and Norfolk Island. - Y compris les îles Christmas, Cocos (Keeling) et Norfolk.

Annex II: Vital statistics summary, United Nations medium variant projections: 2010-2015
Annexe II: Aperçu des statistiques de l'état civil, variante moyenne, projections des Nations Unies : 2010-2015

Continent and country or area Continent et pays ou zone	Crude birth rate - Taux bruts de natalité[1]	Crude death rate - Taux bruts de mortalité[1]	Infant mortality rate - Décès d'enfants de moins d'un an[1]	Life expectancy at birth - Espérance de vie à la naissance[1]		Total fertility rate - Indice synthétique de fécondité[1]	Natural increase - Accroissement naturel[1]
				Male - Masculin	Female - Féminin		

AFRICA - AFRIQUE

Algeria - Algérie	24.6	5.9	26.4	69.4	72.6	2.82	18.6
Angola	44.3	14.1	96.2	50.2	53.2	5.90	30.3
Benin - Bénin	36.6	9.6	68.7	57.8	60.6	4.89	27.1
Botswana	23.7	17.0	31.8	48.0	46.5	2.64	6.7
Burkina Faso	41.1	11.2	69.8	55.5	56.7	5.65	29.9
Burundi	44.8	12.9	87.0	52.0	55.8	6.08	31.9
Cabo Verde	20.4	5.1	17.2	70.9	78.7	2.33	15.2
Cameroon - Cameroun	37.5	11.9	73.5	53.7	56.0	4.82	25.6
Central African Republic - République centrafricaine	34.4	15.0	93.3	48.0	51.8	4.41	19.4
Chad - Tchad	46.1	14.5	95.8	50.1	51.9	6.31	31.7
Comoros - Comores	35.5	8.8	67.2	59.4	62.2	4.74	26.7
Congo	37.9	10.3	63.6	57.2	60.1	5.00	27.5
Côte d'Ivoire	36.9	14.3	75.3	49.7	51.4	4.92	22.5
Democratic Republic of the Congo - République démocratique du Congo	42.9	15.5	108.6	48.1	51.6	5.98	27.4
Djibouti	27.6	8.8	55.3	60.0	63.2	3.42	18.8
Egypt - Égypte	23.3	6.5	18.9	68.7	73.5	2.79	16.8
Equatorial Guinea - Guinée équatoriale	35.6	13.3	88.9	51.5	54.5	4.89	22.3
Eritrea - Érythrée	37.0	6.8	41.8	60.2	64.9	4.74	30.2
Ethiopia - Éthiopie	33.3	7.7	49.7	61.7	65.0	4.59	25.6
Gabon	32.1	9.2	43.3	62.3	64.3	4.12	23.0
Gambia - Gambie	42.9	9.8	55.3	57.4	60.1	5.78	33.2
Ghana	31.1	9.1	51.1	60.0	61.9	3.89	22.0
Guinea - Guinée	37.1	11.6	73.5	55.2	56.7	4.95	25.5
Guinea-Bissau - Guinée-Bissau	37.7	12.6	93.9	52.7	55.7	4.96	25.0
Kenya	35.1	8.3	51.6	59.7	63.5	4.41	26.9
Lesotho	27.6	14.9	60.1	49.2	49.6	3.07	12.7
Liberia - Libéria	35.7	9.0	61.2	59.3	61.2	4.83	26.7
Libya - Libye	20.9	4.2	13.8	73.4	77.2	2.38	16.7
Madagascar	34.8	6.9	36.8	63.0	66.0	4.50	27.9
Malawi	39.9	11.5	86.1	54.9	55.2	5.42	28.4
Mali	47.3	13.2	86.7	54.9	54.7	6.86	34.1
Mauritania - Mauritanie	34.3	8.7	71.7	59.9	63.0	4.70	25.5
Mauritius - Maurice[2]	11.6	7.9	11.5	70.2	77.0	1.52	3.7
Mayotte	29.1	2.0	4.2	76.0	82.9	3.83	27.0
Morocco - Maroc	23.2	6.3	26.3	69.0	72.6	2.78	16.8
Mozambique	39.1	14.2	74.3	49.2	51.1	5.22	24.9
Namibia - Namibie	26.2	7.2	33.5	61.6	67.0	3.08	19.0
Niger	49.8	11.1	53.6	58.0	58.4	7.58	38.7
Nigeria - Nigéria	41.5	13.4	76.3	52.0	52.6	6.01	28.1
Republic of South Sudan - République de Soudan du Sud	36.3	12.0	78.0	53.9	56.0	4.97	24.4
Réunion	16.8	5.2	4.2	76.0	82.9	2.24	11.6
Rwanda	35.4	7.3	49.8	61.9	65.3	4.56	28.1
Sao Tome and Principe - Sao Tomé-et-Principe	34.2	6.9	43.5	64.2	68.2	4.10	27.4
Senegal - Sénégal	38.1	7.7	49.3	61.8	64.7	4.98	30.3
Seychelles	16.7	7.8	8.2	68.9	78.0	2.18	8.9
Sierra Leone	36.9	17.4	116.7	45.1	45.6	4.75	19.5
Somalia - Somalie	43.9	12.4	79.5	53.3	56.5	6.61	31.5
South Africa - Afrique du Sud	21.0	12.9	38.3	54.9	59.1	2.40	8.2
Sudan - Soudan	33.7	8.4	55.0	60.2	63.8	4.46	25.3
Swaziland	30.0	14.1	64.6	49.7	48.5	3.36	15.9
Togo	36.7	10.7	66.4	55.5	57.3	4.68	26.0
Tunisia - Tunisie	17.3	5.7	15.5	73.5	78.2	2.02	11.6
Uganda - Ouganda	43.4	9.4	57.0	57.8	60.2	5.91	34.0
United Republic of Tanzania - République Unie de Tanzanie	39.3	8.6	48.7	60.0	62.7	5.24	30.7
Western Sahara - Sahara occidental	20.7	5.6	37.2	65.9	69.8	2.38	15.1
Zambia - Zambie	43.0	10.4	65.5	55.9	59.5	5.71	32.6
Zimbabwe	31.3	9.0	37.2	58.8	60.8	3.51	22.3

AMERICA, NORTH - AMÉRIQUE DU NORD

Antigua and Barbuda - Antigua-et-Barbuda	16.5	6.1	8.5	73.4	78.2	2.10	10.4
Aruba	10.3	8.3	14.8	72.9	77.8	1.68	2.0
Bahamas	15.3	6.1	9.1	72.0	78.1	1.89	9.3
Barbados - Barbade	12.7	9.1	10.1	72.9	77.7	1.85	3.6
Belize	23.6	4.5	12.9	70.8	77.0	2.70	19.1

Annex II: Vital statistics summary, United Nations medium variant projections: 2010-2015

Annexe II: Aperçu des statistiques de l'état civil, variante moyenne, projections des Nations Unies : 2010-2015 (continued - suite)

Continent and country or area Continent et pays ou zone	Crude birth rate - Taux bruts de natalité[1]	Crude death rate - Taux bruts de mortalité[1]	Infant mortality rate - Décès d'enfants de moins d'un an[1]	Life expectancy at birth - Espérance de vie à la naissance[1]		Total fertility rate - Indice synthétique de fécondité[1]	Natural increase - Accroissement naturel[1]
				Male - Masculin	Female - Féminin		
AMERICA, NORTH - AMÉRIQUE DU NORD							
Canada...	11.2	7.5	4.4	79.3	83.5	1.66	3.7
Costa Rica..	15.3	4.2	8.5	77.7	82.1	1.81	11.1
Cuba..	9.6	7.7	4.5	77.2	81.2	1.45	1.9
Curaçao..	12.0	8.4	11.2	73.6	80.1	1.92	3.7
Dominican Republic - République dominicaine.....................	21.0	6.0	25.6	70.3	76.6	2.50	15.0
El Salvador...	20.2	6.5	17.3	67.7	77.0	2.20	13.7
Grenada - Grenade	19.4	7.5	8.9	70.2	75.2	2.18	11.9
Guadeloupe[3]...	13.3	6.8	5.6	77.4	84.0	2.08	6.5
Guatemala...	31.2	5.2	23.4	68.4	75.5	3.82	26.0
Haiti - Haïti..	25.8	8.6	40.2	61.1	64.9	3.18	17.2
Honduras..	26.0	4.7	22.3	71.3	76.2	3.03	21.3
Jamaica - Jamaïque	18.1	7.1	20.9	70.9	76.0	2.27	10.9
Martinique...	11.3	7.8	6.2	77.9	84.4	1.83	3.4
Mexico - Mexique	18.6	4.5	14.2	74.9	79.7	2.20	14.1
Nicaragua...	22.9	4.6	16.6	71.6	77.7	2.52	18.4
Panama..	19.6	4.9	14.6	74.7	80.4	2.48	14.7
Puerto Rico - Porto Rico..	12.1	8.1	6.3	75.0	82.5	1.64	4.0
Saint Lucia - Sainte-Lucie	15.5	7.2	10.5	72.1	77.4	1.92	8.3
Saint Vincent and the Grenadines - Saint-Vincent-et-les Grenadines...	16.4	7.2	16.9	70.3	74.7	2.01	9.3
Trinidad and Tobago - Trinité-et-Tobago	14.6	9.6	24.1	66.3	73.6	1.80	5.0
United States of America - États-Unis d'Amérique................	13.2	8.3	6.1	76.4	81.2	1.97	4.9
United States Virgin Islands - Îles Vierges américaines.........	15.2	7.4	9.4	77.2	82.9	2.49	7.7
AMERICA, SOUTH - AMÉRIQUE DU SUD							
Argentina - Argentine	16.8	7.7	11.4	72.5	79.8	2.18	9.1
Bolivia (Plurinational State of) - Bolivie (État plurinational de)..	25.9	7.1	39.1	64.9	69.3	3.25	18.8
Brazil - Brésil..	15.1	6.5	19.5	70.2	77.5	1.82	8.7
Chile - Chili...	14.0	5.5	5.9	77.0	82.6	1.83	8.5
Colombia - Colombie...	18.9	5.6	16.3	70.3	77.6	2.30	13.4
Ecuador - Équateur	21.0	4.9	17.0	73.6	79.3	2.58	16.1
French Guiana - Guyane française	23.6	3.6	12.2	73.8	80.8	3.08	19.9
Guyana..	20.3	6.7	28.5	63.5	68.9	2.55	13.6
Paraguay..	23.9	5.7	30.4	70.0	74.5	2.89	18.2
Peru - Pérou...	19.8	5.3	16.6	72.0	77.4	2.43	14.6
Suriname..	17.9	7.3	17.4	67.8	74.2	2.28	10.6
Uruguay...	14.5	9.4	11.5	73.6	80.5	2.05	5.2
Venezuela (Bolivarian Republic of) - Venezuela (République bolivarienne du)..	19.9	5.3	15.0	71.7	77.6	2.41	14.6
ASIA - ASIE							
Afghanistan	34.5	8.0	67.3	59.5	62.0	5.00	26.5
Armenia - Arménie	13.8	8.7	19.0	71.2	77.9	1.74	5.1
Azerbaijan - Azerbaïdjan[4]...	18.0	6.9	39.6	67.5	73.8	1.93	11.1
Bahrain - Bahreïn	15.5	2.3	6.9	75.8	77.4	2.10	13.2
Bangladesh...	20.3	5.7	32.3	69.8	71.3	2.20	14.5
Bhutan - Bhoutan...	19.8	6.6	30.7	67.7	68.4	2.26	13.3
Brunei Darussalam - Brunéi Darussalam	15.8	3.1	4.2	76.6	80.4	2.01	12.6
Cambodia - Cambodge	25.8	6.0	40.6	68.8	74.2	2.89	19.8
China - Chine[5]..	13.4	7.2	13.0	74.0	76.6	1.66	6.3
China, Hong Kong SAR - Chine, Hong Kong RAS................	9.4	6.2	1.9	80.3	86.4	1.13	3.2
China, Macao SAR - Chine, Macao RAS	10.1	4.8	4.1	78.1	82.5	1.07	5.3
Cyprus - Chypre[6]...	11.5	6.9	3.7	77.8	81.8	1.46	4.6
Democratic People's Republic of Korea - République populaire démocratique de Corée	14.4	9.2	22.0	66.3	73.3	2.00	5.3
Georgia - Géorgie[7]...	13.4	11.5	19.4	70.5	77.7	1.81	1.9
India - Inde...	20.7	7.9	43.8	64.6	68.1	2.50	12.7
Indonesia - Indonésie..	18.9	6.3	25.6	68.7	72.8	2.35	12.7
Iran (Islamic Republic of) - Iran (République islamique d').....	19.0	5.2	15.7	72.1	75.9	1.93	13.8
Iraq..	31.3	5.2	28.1	66.0	73.1	4.06	26.1
Israel - Israël..	20.5	5.5	3.3	79.8	83.5	2.91	15.0
Japan - Japon...	8.4	9.8	2.2	80.0	86.9	1.41	-1.4

Annex II: Vital statistics summary, United Nations medium variant projections: 2010-2015
Annexe II: Aperçu des statistiques de l'état civil, variante moyenne, projections des Nations Unies : 2010-2015 (continued - suite)

Continent and country or area / Continent et pays ou zone	Crude birth rate - Taux bruts de natalité[1]	Crude death rate - Taux bruts de mortalité[1]	Infant mortality rate - Décès d'enfants de moins d'un an[1]	Life expectancy at birth - Espérance de vie à la naissance[1] Male - Masculin	Female - Féminin	Total fertility rate - Indice synthétique de fécondité[1]	Natural increase - Accroissement naturel[1]
ASIA - ASIE							
Jordan - Jordanie	27.3	3.7	17.1	72.2	75.5	3.27	23.6
Kazakhstan	20.5	10.1	24.6	60.9	72.3	2.44	10.4
Kuwait - Koweït	20.7	2.9	8.6	73.4	75.5	2.60	17.8
Kyrgyzstan - Kirghizstan	27.4	7.5	33.1	63.4	71.8	3.10	19.9
Lao People's Democratic Republic - République démocratique populaire lao	26.9	6.0	36.2	66.7	69.4	3.05	20.8
Lebanon - Liban	13.5	4.4	8.3	77.9	82.1	1.51	9.0
Malaysia - Malaisie[8]	17.7	4.7	4.1	72.7	77.3	1.98	13.1
Maldives	22.3	3.4	10.4	76.7	78.8	2.29	18.9
Mongolia - Mongolie	22.8	6.8	25.8	63.6	71.5	2.44	16.0
Myanmar	17.3	8.5	48.9	63.0	67.1	1.95	8.8
Nepal - Népal	21.1	6.7	35.5	67.1	69.3	2.32	14.4
Oman	21.4	2.8	7.3	74.7	78.9	2.91	18.7
Pakistan	25.4	7.0	65.1	65.6	67.4	3.22	18.4
Philippines	24.6	6.0	21.0	65.3	72.2	3.07	18.6
Qatar	11.2	1.4	6.5	77.7	79.4	2.05	9.8
Republic of Korea - République de Corée	9.6	5.6	3.4	77.9	84.6	1.32	4.1
Saudi Arabia - Arabie saoudite	19.6	3.3	11.2	73.8	77.5	2.68	16.4
Singapore - Singapour	9.9	4.7	1.8	79.7	84.6	1.28	5.2
Sri Lanka	18.1	7.0	9.0	71.1	77.4	2.35	11.0
State of Palestine - État de Palestine	30.6	3.5	19.2	71.4	74.9	4.05	27.1
Syrian Arab Republic - République arabe syrienne	24.3	3.9	17.7	71.6	77.6	3.00	20.4
Tajikistan - Tadjikistan	33.3	6.6	56.8	64.0	70.7	3.85	26.7
Thailand - Thaïlande	10.4	7.7	9.9	71.0	77.7	1.41	2.7
Timor-Leste	35.7	5.8	39.3	65.8	68.9	5.91	29.9
Turkey - Turquie	17.0	5.7	12.0	71.7	78.5	2.05	11.3
Turkmenistan - Turkménistan	21.5	7.8	46.7	61.3	69.7	2.34	13.7
United Arab Emirates - Émirats arabes unis	14.8	1.0	5.7	76.1	78.1	1.82	13.8
Uzbekistan - Ouzbékistan	21.6	6.7	44.0	64.9	71.6	2.32	14.9
Viet Nam	15.6	5.7	14.1	71.2	80.4	1.75	10.0
Yemen - Yémen	31.4	7.3	56.2	61.7	64.4	4.15	24.1
EUROPE							
Albania - Albanie	13.0	6.9	14.4	74.5	80.5	1.79	6.1
Austria - Autriche	9.5	9.4	3.1	78.5	83.5	1.47	0.1
Belarus - Bélarus	11.0	15.7	5.6	64.1	75.7	1.48	-4.7
Belgium - Belgique	11.7	10.0	3.2	77.9	83.0	1.85	1.7
Bosnia and Herzegovina - Bosnie-Herzégovine	8.9	10.0	7.6	73.7	78.8	1.28	-1.1
Bulgaria - Bulgarie	9.6	15.8	9.0	69.9	77.2	1.53	-6.2
Croatia - Croatie	9.5	12.4	5.1	73.6	80.3	1.50	-2.9
Czech Republic - République tchèque	11.0	10.6	2.6	74.5	80.6	1.55	0.4
Denmark - Danemark	11.3	10.1	3.4	77.2	81.4	1.88	1.3
Estonia - Estonie	10.8	13.6	4.2	68.9	79.5	1.59	-2.8
Finland - Finlande[9]	11.2	9.6	2.3	77.3	83.6	1.85	1.6
France	12.3	8.9	3.2	78.2	85.1	1.98	3.4
Germany - Allemagne	8.5	10.9	3.1	78.2	83.1	1.42	-2.4
Greece - Grèce	9.8	10.4	3.6	78.3	83.0	1.52	-0.6
Hungary - Hongrie	9.9	13.4	4.8	70.4	78.5	1.41	-3.6
Iceland - Islande	14.5	6.4	1.8	80.2	83.8	2.08	8.1
Ireland - Irlande	15.5	6.4	2.9	78.4	82.7	2.00	9.1
Italy - Italie	9.2	10.1	2.8	79.5	84.9	1.48	-0.9
Latvia - Lettonie	10.9	15.7	7.3	66.6	77.5	1.60	-4.8
Lithuania - Lituanie	11.2	13.9	5.4	66.0	78.1	1.51	-2.7
Luxembourg	11.6	7.9	2.0	77.9	83.0	1.67	3.7
Malta - Malte	9.2	8.3	4.8	77.4	82.0	1.36	0.9
Montenegro - Monténégro	11.7	10.4	9.6	72.4	77.1	1.67	1.3
Netherlands - Pays-Bas	10.7	8.6	3.6	78.9	82.8	1.77	2.1
Norway - Norvège[10]	12.4	8.4	2.6	79.3	83.5	1.93	4.1
Poland - Pologne	10.8	10.5	5.5	72.2	80.5	1.41	0.3
Portugal	8.8	10.3	2.8	76.8	82.8	1.32	-1.5
Republic of Moldova - République de Moldova[11]	12.2	14.1	14.0	64.9	72.8	1.46	-1.9
Romania - Roumanie	10.3	12.5	10.5	70.2	77.4	1.41	-2.2
Russian Federation - Fédération de Russie	11.8	15.5	9.7	61.7	74.3	1.53	-3.7
Serbia - Serbie[12]	9.8	12.4	10.9	71.2	76.8	1.37	-2.6
Slovakia - Slovaquie	10.7	10.3	5.4	71.5	79.2	1.39	0.3

639

Annex II: Vital statistics summary, United Nations medium variant projections: 2010-2015

Annexe II: Aperçu des statistiques de l'état civil, variante moyenne, projections des Nations Unies : 2010-2015 (continued - suite)

Continent and country or area Continent et pays ou zone	Crude birth rate - Taux bruts de natalité[1]	Crude death rate - Taux bruts de mortalité[1]	Infant mortality rate - Décès d'enfants de moins d'un an[1]	Life expectancy at birth - Espérance de vie à la naissance[1]		Total fertility rate - Indice synthétique de fécondité[1]	Natural increase - Accroissement naturel[1]
				Male - Masculin	Female - Féminin		
EUROPE							
Slovenia - Slovénie..	10.0	9.8	2.8	76.2	82.7	1.50	0.3
Spain - Espagne[13]	10.5	8.7	3.1	78.8	85.2	1.50	1.8
Sweden - Suède...	11.9	9.6	2.3	79.7	83.8	1.92	2.3
Switzerland - Suisse...	10.4	8.2	3.6	80.1	84.9	1.53	2.2
TFYR of Macedonia - L'ex-R. y. de Macédoine....................	10.7	9.6	10.1	72.9	77.5	1.44	1.1
Ukraine..	10.8	16.8	11.7	62.8	74.3	1.46	-6.0
United Kingdom of Great Britain and Northern Ireland - Royaume-Uni de Grande-Bretagne et d'Irlande du Nord	12.2	9.4	4.2	78.5	82.4	1.89	2.8
OCEANIA - OCÉANIE							
Australia - Australie[14]	13.2	6.6	3.9	80.2	84.7	1.88	6.6
Fiji - Fidji	20.7	6.8	16.0	66.9	72.9	2.61	13.9
French Polynesia - Polynésie française	16.5	5.5	6.9	74.0	78.6	2.07	11.0
Guam...	17.5	4.8	9.7	76.1	81.5	2.42	12.7
Kiribati..	23.3	6.0	34.3	65.9	71.6	2.98	17.3
Micronesia (Federated States of) - Micronésie (États fédérés de)	23.6	6.2	32.7	68.0	69.9	3.33	17.4
New Caledonia - Nouvelle-Calédonie	15.7	6.9	13.1	73.6	79.3	2.13	8.7
New Zealand - Nouvelle-Zélande	13.8	7.0	4.3	79.1	82.9	2.05	6.8
Papua New Guinea - Papouasie-Nouvelle-Guinée	29.1	7.7	47.6	60.3	64.5	3.81	21.3
Samoa...	26.4	5.4	19.7	70.0	76.4	4.16	21.0
Solomon Islands - Îles Salomon...................................	31.1	5.9	38.0	66.2	69.0	4.06	25.2
Tonga..	25.7	6.1	20.4	69.7	75.6	3.79	19.7
Vanuatu	26.9	4.8	23.9	69.6	73.6	3.41	22.1

SOURCE

United Nations, Department of Economic and Social Affairs, Population Division (2013). World Population Prospects: The 2012 Revision. Extended dataset in Excel and ASCII formats, DVD-ROM edition (United Nations publication, ST/ESA/SER.A/334). - Organisation des Nations Unies, Département des affaires économiques et sociales, Division de la population (2013). Perspectives de la population mondiale : La révision de 2012. Ensemble de données étendues en formats Excel et ASCII, edition DVD-ROM (publication des Nations Unies, ST/ESA/SER.A/334).

FOOTNOTES - NOTES

[1] All data are mid-year medium variant projections. - Toutes ces données sont des projections de la population au milieu de l'année de variante moyenne.

[2] Including Agalega, Rodrigues and Saint Brandon. - Y compris Agalega, Rodrigues et Saint Brandon.

[3] Including Saint-Barthélemy and Saint-Martin (French part). - Y compris Saint-Barthélemy et Saint-Martin (partie française).

[4] Including Nagorno-Karabakh. - Y compris le Haut-Karabakh.

[5] For statistical purposes, the data for China do not include Hong Kong and Macao Special Administrative Regions (SAR) of China. - A des fins statistiques, les données pour la Chine ne comprennent pas les Régions Administratives Spéciales (SAR) de Hong Kong et Macao.

[6] Including Northern-Cyprus. - Y compris Chypre-Nord.

[7] Including Abkhazia and South Ossetia. - Y compris l'Abkhazie et l'Ossétie du Sud.

[8] Including Sabah and Sarawak. - Y compris le Sabah et le Sarawak.

[9] Including Åland Islands. - Y compris les îles Åland.

[10] Including Svalbard and Jan Mayen Islands. - Y compris Svalbard et l'île Jan Mayen.

[11] Including Transnistria. - Y compris la Transnistrie.

[12] Including Kosovo. - Y compris le Kosovo.

[13] Including Canary Islands, Ceuta and Melilla. - Y compris les îles Canaries, Ceuta et Melilla.

[14] Including Christmas Island, Cocos (Keeling) Islands and Norfolk Island. - Y compris les îles Christmas, Cocos (Keeling) et Norfolk.

Subject-matter	Year of issue	Time coverage	Subject-matter	Year of issue	Time coverage
	1985	1981-85		1969	1963-68
	1986	1967-86		1970-1974	Latest
	1987	1983-87		1975	1966-74
	1988	1984-88		1976-1978	Latest
	1989	1985-89		1978HS[ii]	1948-77
	1990	1986-90		1979-1980	Latest
	1991	1987-91		1981	1972-80
	1992	1983-92		1982-1985	Latest
	1993	1989-93		1986	1977-85
	1994	1990-94		1987-1991	Latest
	1995	1991-95		1992	1983-92
	1996	1992-96		1993-1997	Latest
	1997	1993-97		1997HS[iii] [3]	1948-96
	1997HS[iii]	1948-97		1998-99	Latest
	1998	1994-98		1999CD[iv]	1990-98
	1999	1995-99		2000-2012	Latest
	1999CD[iv]	1980-99			
	2000	1996-00	- by age of mother and birth order	1949/50	1936-47
	2001	1997-01		1954	Latest
	2002	1998-02		1959	1949-58
	2003	1999-03		1965	1955-64
	2004	2000-04		1969	1963-68
	2005	2001-05		1975	1966-74
	2006	2002-06		1981	1972-80
	2007	2003-07		1986	1977-85
	2008	2004-08		1999CD[iv]	1990-98
	2009-2010	2006-10			
	2011	2007-11	- by age of mother and sex of child	1965-1968	Latest
	2012	2008-12		1969	1963-68
				1970-1974	Latest
- by age of father	1949/50	1942-49		1975	1966-74
	1954	1936-53		1976-1978	Latest
	1959	1949-58		1978HS[ii]	1948-77
	1965	1955-64		1979-1980	Latest
	1969	1963-68		1981	1972-80
	1975	1966-74		1982-1985	Latest
	1981	1972-80		1986	1977-85
	1999CD[iv]	1990-98		1987-1991	Latest
	2007-2012	Latest		1992	1983-92
				1993-1997	Latest
- by age of mother	1948	1936-47		1997HS[iii]	1948-96
	1949/50	1936-49		1998-99	Latest
	1954	1936-53		1999CD[iv]	1990-98
	1955-1956	Latest			
	1958	Latest			
	1959	1949-58			
	1960-1964	Latest			
	1965	1955-64			
	1966-1968	Latest			

Subject-matter	Year of issue	Time coverage	Subject-matter	Year of issue	Time coverage
	2000-2012	Latest		1967-1968	Latest
				1969	1963-68
- by age of mother and urban/rural residence (see: by urban/rural residence, below)				1970-1974	Latest
				1975	1956-75
				1976-1980	Latest
				1981	1962-81
				1982-1985	Latest
- by birth order	1948	1936-47		1986	1967-86
	1949/50	1936-49		1987-1991	Latest
	1954	1936-53		1992	1983-92
	1955	Latest		1993-1999	Latest
	1959	1949-58		1999CD[iv]	1990-98
	1965	1955-64		2000-2012	Latest
	1969	1963-68			
	1975	1966-74	- by plurality	1965	Latest
	1981	1972-80		1969	Latest
	1986	1977-85		1975	Latest
	1999CD[iv]	1990-98		1981	1972-80
				1986	1977-85
- by birth weight	1975	Latest		1999CD[iv]	1990-98
	1981	1972-80			
	1986	1977-85	- by urban/rural residence		
	1999CD[iv]	1990-98		1965	Latest
				1967	Latest
- by gestational	1975	Latest		1968	1964-68
	1981	1972-80		1969	1964-68
	1986	1977-85		1970	1966-70
	1999CD[iv]	1990-98		1971	1967-71
				1972	1968-72
- by legitimacy status				1973	1969-73
	1959	1949-58		1974	1970-74
	1965	1955-64		1975	1956-75
	1969	1963-68		1976	1972-76
	1975	1966-74		1977	1973-77
	1981	1972-80		1978	1974-78
	1986	1977-85		1979	1975-79
	1999CD[iv]	1990-98		1980	1976-80
				1981	1962-81
- by month	2002	1980-02		1982	1978-82
				1983	1979-83
- by occupation of father				1984	1980-84
	1965	Latest		1985	1981-85
	1969	Latest		1986	1967-86
				1987	1983-87
- by sex	1959	1949-58		1988	1984-88
	1965	1955-64		1989	1985-89
				1990	1986-90
				1991	1987-91
				1992	1983-92

Subject-matter	Year of issue	Time coverage	Subject-matter	Year of issue	Time coverage
	1993	1989-93		1954	1936-53
	1994	1990-94		1959	1949-58
	1995	1991-95		1965	1955-64
	1996	1992-96		1969	1963-68
	1997	1993-97		1975	1966-74
	1998	1994-98		1981	1972-80
	1999	1995-99		1986	1977-85
	1999CD[iv]	1980-99		1999CD[iv]	1990-98
	2000	1996-00			
	2001	1997-01	- legitimate, by age of father	1959	1949-58
	2002	1998-02		1965	1955-64
	2003	1999-03		1969	1963-68
	2004	2000-04		1975	1966-74
	2005	2001-05		1981	1972-80
	2006	2002-06		1986	1977-85
	2007	2003-07	- legitimate, by age of mother	1954	1936-53
	2008	2004-08		1959	1949-58
	2009-2010	2006-10		1965	1955-64
	2011	2007-11		1969	1963-68
	2012	2008-12		1975	1966-74
				1981	1972-80
- by urban/rural residence and age of mother	1965	Latest		1986	1977-85
	1969-1974	Latest	- legitimate, by duration of marriage	1948	1936-47
	1975	1966-74		1949/50	1936-49
	1976-1980	Latest		1954	1936-53
	1981	1972-80		1959	1949-58
	1982-1985	Latest		1965	1955-64
	1986	1977-85		1969	1963-68
	1987-1991	Latest		1975	1966-74
	1992	1983-92		1981	1972-80
	1993-1997	Latest		1986	1977-85
	1997HS[iii]	1948-96		1999CD[iv]	1990-98
	1998-1999	Latest			
	1999CD[iv]	1990-98	**Birth rates**	1948	1932-47
	2000-2006	Latest		1949/50	1932-49
				1951	1905-30[v]
- illegitimate	1959	1949-58			1930-50
	1965	1955-64		1952	1920-34[v]
	1969	1963-68			1934-51
	1975	1966-74		1953	1920-39[v]
	1981	1972-80			1940-52
	1986	1977-85		1954	1920-39[v]
	1999CD[iv]	1990-98			1939-53
				1955	1920-34[v]
- legitimate	1948	1936-47			1946-54
	1949/50	1936-49		1956	1947-55

Subject-matter	Year of issue	Time coverage	Subject-matter	Year of issue	Time coverage
for continents	1949/50	1947		1969	Latest
	1956-1977	Latest		1975	Latest
	1978-1979	1970-75		1981	Latest
	1980-1983	1975-80		1986	Latest
	1984-1986	1980-85	- legitimate by age of father	1959	1949-58
	1987-1992	1985-90		1965	Latest
	1993-1997	1990-95		1969	Latest
	1998-2000	1995-00		1975	Latest
	2001-2005	2000-05		1981	Latest
	2006-2010	2005-10		1986	Latest
	2011-2012	2010-15	- legitimate by age of mother	1954	1936-53
for macro regions	1964-1977	Latest		1959	1949-58
	1978-1979	1970-75		1965	Latest
	1980-1983	1975-80		1969	Latest
	1984-1986	1980-85		1975	Latest
	1987-1992	1985-90		1981	Latest
	1993-1997	1990-95		1986	Latest
	1998-2000	1995-00	- legitimate by duration of marriage	1959	1950-57
	2001-2005	2000-05		1965	Latest
	2006-2010	2005-10		1969	Latest
	2011-2012	2010-15		1975	Latest
for regions	1949/1950	1947	**Birth Ratios**		
	1956-1977	Latest	- fertility	1949/1950	Latest
	1978-1979	1970-75		1954	Latest
	1980-1983	1975-80		1959	1949-58
	1984-1986	1980-85		1965	1955-65
	1987-1992	1985-90		1969	1963-68
	1993-1997	1990-95		1975	1965-74
	1998-2000	1995-00		1978HS[ii]	1948-77
	2001-2005	2000-05		1981	1972-80
	2006-2010	2005-10		1986	1977-85
	2011-2012	2010-15		1997HS[iii]	1948-96
				1999CD[iv]	1980-99
for the world	1949/50	1947	- illegitimate	1959	1949-58
	1956-1977	Latest		1965	1955-64
	1978-1979	1970-75		1969	1963-68
	1980-1983	1975-80		1975	1965-74
	1984-1986	1980-85		1981	1972-80
	1987-1992	1985-90		1986	1977-85
	1993-1997	1990-95			
	1998-2000	1995-00	**Birth to women under 20 by single years of age of mother**		
	2001-2005	2000-05			
	2006-2010	2005-10			
	2011-2012	2010-15	- by urban/rural residence	1986	1970-85
- illegitimate	1959	1949-58			
- legitimate	1954	1936-53			
	1959	1949-58			
	1965	Latest			

Subject-matter	Year of issue	Time coverage	Subject-matter	Year of issue	Time coverage
	1982	1978-82			
	1983	1979-83	- by age and sex and urban/rural residence		
	1984	1980-84			
	1985	1976-85		1967-1973	Latest
	1986	1982-86		1974	1965-73
	1987	1983-87		1975-1979	Latest
	1988	1984-88		1980	1971-79
	1989	1985-89		1981-1984	Latest
	1990	1986-90		1985	1976-84
	1991	1987-91		1986-1991	Latest
	1992	1983-92		1992	1983-92
	1993	1989-93		1993-1995	Latest
	1994	1990-94		1996	1987-95
	1995	1991-95		1997	Latest
	1996	1987-96		1997HS[iii]	1948-96
	1997	1993-97		1998-2006	Latest
	1997HS[iii]	1948-97			
	1998	1994-98	- by cause	1951	1947-50
	1999	1995-99		1952	1947-51[vi]
	2000	1996-00		1953	Latest
	2001	1997-01		1954	1945-53
	2002	1998-02		1955-1956	Latest
	2003	1999-03		1957	1952-56
	2004	2000-04		1958-1960	Latest
	2005	2001-05		1961	1955-60
	2006	2002-06		1962-1965	Latest
	2007	2003-07		1966	1960-65
	2008	2004-08		1967-1973	Latest
	2009-2010	2006-10		1974	1965-73
	2011	2007-11		1975-1979	Latest
				1980	1971-79
	2012	2008-12		1981-1984	Latest
- by age and sex	1948	1936-47		1985	1976-84
	1951	1936-50		1986-1991	Latest
	1955-1956	Latest		1991PA[vii]	1960-90
	1957	1948-56		1992-1995	Latest
	1958-1960	Latest		1996	1987-95
	1961	1955-60		1997-2000	Latest
	1962-1965	Latest		2002	1995-02
	1966	1961-65		2004	1995-04
	1967-1973	Latest		2006	2002-06
	1974	1965-73		2008	2004-08
	1975-1979	Latest		2011	2006-10
	1978HS[ii]	1948-77			
	1980	1971-79	- by cause, age and sex	1951	Latest
	1981-1984	Latest			
	1985	1976-84		1952	Latest
	1986-1991	Latest		1957	Latest
	1992	1983-92		1961	Latest
	1993-1995	Latest		1967	Latest
	1996	1987-95		1974	Latest
	1997	Latest		1980	Latest
	1997HS[iii]	1948-96		1985	Latest
	1998-2012	Latest		1991PA[vii]	1960-90

Subject-matter	Year of issue	Time coverage	Subject-matter	Year of issue	Time coverage
	1953	1920-39[v]		1998	1994-98
		1940-52		1999	1995-99
	1954	1920-39[v]		2000	1996-00
		1946-53		2001	1997-01
	1955	1920-34[v]		2002	1998-02
		1946-54		2003	1999-03
	1956	1947-55		2004	2000-04
	1957	1930-56		2005	2001-05
	1958	1948-57		2006	2002-06
	1959	1949-58		2007	2003-07
	1960	1950-59		2008	2004-08
	1961	1945-59[v]		2009-2010	2006-10
		1952-61		2011	2007-11
	1962	1945-54[v]			
		1952-62		2012	2008-12
	1963	1945-59[v]	- by age and sex	1948	1935-47
		1954-63		1949/50	1936-49
	1964	1960-64		1951	1936-50
	1965	1961-65		1952	1936-51
	1966	1920-64[v]		1953	1940-52
		1951-66		1954	1946-53
	1967	1963-67		1955-1956	Latest
	1968	1964-68		1957	1948-56
	1969	1965-69		1961	1952-60
	1970	1966-70		1966	1950-65
	1971	1967-71		1972	Latest
	1972	1968-72		1974	1965-73
	1973	1969-73		1975-1979	Latest
	1974	1965-74		1978HS[ii]	1948-77
	1975	1971-75		1980	1971-79
	1976	1972-76		1981-1984	Latest
	1977	1973-77		1985	1976-84
	1978	1974-78		1986-1991	Latest
	1978HS[ii]	1948-78		1991PA[vii]	1950-1990
	1979	1975-79		1992	1983-1992
	1980	1971-80		1993-1995	Latest
	1981	1977-81		1996	1987-95
	1982	1978-82		1997	Latest
	1983	1979-83		1997HS[iii]	1948-96
	1984	1980-84		1998-2012	Latest
	1985	1976-85			
	1986	1982-86	- by age and sex and urban/rural residence		
	1987	1983-87		1967	Latest
	1988	1984-88		1972	Latest
	1989	1985-89		1974	1965-73
	1990	1986-90		1975-1979	Latest
	1991	1987-91		1980	1971-79
	1992	1983-92		1981-1984	Latest
	1993	1989-93		1985	1976-84
	1994	1990-94		1986-1991	Latest
	1995	1991-95		1991PA[vii]	1950-1990
	1996	1987-96		1992	1983-1992
	1997	1993-97		1993-1995	Latest
	1997HS[iii]	1948-97			

Subject-matter	Year of issue	Time coverage	Subject-matter	Year of issue	Time coverage
	2002	1998-02		1987-1992	1985-90
	2003	1999-03		1993-1997	1990-95
	2004	2000-04		1998-2000	1995-00
	2005	2001-05		2001-2005	2000-05
	2006	2002-06		2006-2010	2005-10
	2007	2003-07		2011-2012	2010-15
	2008	2004-08			
	2009-2010	2006-10	- of infants (see: Infant deaths)		
	2011	2007-11			
	2012	2008-12	Density of population:		
- estimated			- of continents	1949/50	1920-49
for continents	1949/50	1947		1951-1999	Latest
	1956-1977	Latest		2000	2000
	1978-1979	1970-75		2001	2001
	1980-1983	1975-80		2002	2002
	1984-1986	1980-85		2003	2003
	1984-1986	1980-85		2004	2004
	1987-1992	1985-90		2005	2005
	1993-1997	1990-95		2006	2006
	1998-2000	1995-00		2007	2007
	2001-2005	2000-05		2008	2008
	2006-2010	2005-10		2009-2010	2010
	2011-2012	2010-15		2011	2011
for macro regions	1964-1977	Latest		2012	2012
	1978-1979	1970-75	- of countries	1948-1999	Latest
	1980-1983	1975-80		2000	2000
	1984-1986	1980-85		2001	2001
	1987-1992	1985-90		2002	2002
	1993-1997	1990-95		2003	2003
	1998-2000	1995-00		2004	2004
	2001-2005	2000-05		2005	2005
	2006-2010	2005-10		2006	2006
	2011-2012	2010-15		2007	2007
for regions	1949/50	1947		2008	2008
	1956-1977	Latest		2009-2010	2010
	1978-1979	1970-75		2011	2011
	1980-1983	1975-80		2012	2012
	1984-1986	1980-85	- of major areas	1964-1999	Latest
	1987-1992	1985-90		2000	2000
	1993-1997	1990-95		2001	2001
	1998-2000	1995-00		2002	2002
	2001-2005	2000-05		2003	2003
	2006-2010	2005-10		2004	2004
	2011-2012	2010-15		2005	2005
for the world	1949/50	1947		2006	2006
	1956-1977	Latest		2007	2007
	1978-1979	1970-75		2008	2008
	1980-1983	1975-80		2009-2010	2010
	1984-1986	1980-85			

Subject-matter	Year of issue	Time coverage	Subject-matter	Year of issue	Time coverage
	2011	2011		1968	1949-68
				1969	1965-69
	2012	2012		1970	1966-70
				1971	1967-71
- of regions	1949/50	1920-49		1972	1968-72
	1952-1999	Latest		1973	1969-73
	2000	2000		1974	1970-74
	2001	2001		1975	1971-75
	2002	2002		1976	1957-76
	2003	2003		1977	1973-77
	2004	2004		1978	1974-78
	2005	2005		1979	1975-79
	2006	2006		1980	1976-80
	2007	2007		1981	1977-81
	2008	2008		1982	1963-82
	2009-2010	2010		1983	1979-83
	2011	2011		1984	1980-84
				1985	1981-85
	2012	2012		1986	1982-86
- of the world	1949/50	1920-49		1987	1983-87
	1952-1999	Latest		1988	1984-88
	2000	2000		1989	1985-89
	2001	2001		1990	1971-90
	2002	2002		1991	1987-91
	2003	2003		1992	1988-92
	2004	2004		1993	1989-93
	2005	2005		1994	1990-94
	2006	2006		1995	1991-95
	2007	2007		1996	1992-96
	2008	2008		1997	1993-97
	2009-2010	2010		1998	1994-98
	2011	2011		1999	1995-99
				2000	1996-00
	2012	2012		2001	1997-01
				2002	1998-02
Disability (see: Population)				2003	1999-03
				2004	2000-04
Divorces	1951	1935-50		2005	2001-05
	1952	1936-51		2006	2002-06
	1953	1950-52		2007	2003-07
	1954	1946-53		2008	2004-08
	1955	1946-54			
	1956	1947-55		2009-2010	2006-10
	1957	1948-56		2011	2007-11
	1958	1940-57			
	1959	1949-58		2012	2008-12
	1960	1950-59	- by age of		
	1961	1952-61	husband	1968	1958-67
	1962	1953-62		1976	1966-75
	1963	1954-63		1982	1972-81
	1964	1960-64		1987	1975-86
	1965	1961-65		1990	1980-89
	1966	1962-66			
	1967	1963-67	- by age of wife	1968	1958-67

Subject-matter	Year of issue	Time coverage	Subject-matter	Year of issue	Time coverage
	1992	1983-92		1975	1966-74
	1993-1997	Latest		1980	1971-79
	1997HS[iii]	1948-96		1981	1972-80
	1998-2012	Latest		1985	1976-84
				1986	1977-85
- total	1986	1967-85		1996	1987-95
	1987-1997	Latest		1999CD[iv]	1990-98
	1997HS[iii]	1948-96			
	1998	1995-98	Foetal deaths, late...............	1951	1935-50
	1999	1996-99		1952	1936-51
	1999CD[iv]	1980-99		1953	1936-52
	2000	1995-00		1954	1938-53
	2001	1997-01		1955	1946-54
	2002	1998-02		1956	1947-55
	2003	1999-03		1957	1948-56
	2004	2000-04		1958	1948-57
	2005	2001-05		1959	1949-58
	2006	2002-06		1960	1950-59
	2007	2003-07		1961	1952-60
	2008	2004-08		1962	1953-61
	2009-2010	2006-10		1963	1953-62
	2011	2007-11		1964	1959-63
				1965	1955-64
	2012	2008-12		1966	1947-65
				1967	1962-66
Fertility ratios	1949/50	1900-50		1968	1963-67
	1954	1900-52		1969	1959-68
	1955	1945-54		1970	1965-69
	1959	1935-59		1971	1966-70
	1963	1955-63		1972	1967-71
	1965	1955-65		1973	1968-72
	1969	Latest		1974	1965-73
	1975	1966-74		1975	1966-74
	1978HS[ii]	1948-77		1976	1971-75
	1981	1962-80		1977	1972-76
	1986	1967-85		1978	1973-77
	1997HS[iii]	1948-96		1979	1974-78
	1999CD[iv]	1980-99		1980	1971-79
				1981	1972-80
Foetal deaths				1982	1977-81
- by period of gestation	1957	1950-56		1983	1978-82
	1959	1949-58		1984	1979-83
	1961	1952-60		1985	1975-84
	1965	5-Latest		1986	1977-85
	1966	1956-65		1987	1982-86
	1967-1968	Latest		1988	1983-87
	1969	1963-68		1989	1984-88
	1974	1965-73		1990	1985-89
				1991	1986-90
				1992	1987-91

Subject-matter	Year of issue	Time coverage	Subject-matter	Year of issue	Time coverage
	2011	2007-11			
	2012	2008-12	**Foetal death ratios, late**	1951	1935-50
				1952	1935-51
				1953	1936-52
- illegitimate	1961	1952-60		1954	1938-53
	1965	5-Latest		1955	1946-54
	1969	1963-68		1956	1947-55
	1975	1966-74		1957	1948-56
	1981	1972-80		1958	1948-57
	1986	1977-85		1959	1920-54[v]
					1953-58
- illegitimate, percent				1960	1950-59
	1961	1952-60		1961	1945-49[v]
	1965	5-Latest			1952-60
	1969	1963-68		1962	1945-54[v]
	1975	1966-74			1952-61
	1981	1972-80		1963	1945-59[v]
	1986	1977-85			1953-62
				1964	1959-63
- legitimate	1959	1949-58		1965	1950-64[v]
	1965	1955-64			1955-64
	1969	1963-68		1966	1950-64[v]
	1975	1966-74			1956-65
	1981	1972-80		1967	1962-66
	1986	1977-85		1968	1963-67
- legitimate by age of mother	1959	1949-58		1969	1950-64[v]
	1965	1955-64			1959-68
	1969	1963-68		1970	1965-69
	1975	1966-74		1971	1966-70
	1981	1972-80		1972	1967-71
	1986	1977-85		1973	1968-72
	1996	1987-95		1974	1965-73
				1975	1966-74
Foetal Death Ratios				1976	1971-75
- by period of gestation				1977	1972-76
	1957	1950-56		1978	1973-77
	1959	1949-58		1979	1974-78
	1961	1952-60		1980	1971-79
	1965	5-Latest		1981	1972-80
	1966	1956-65		1982	1977-81
	1967-1968	Latest		1983	1978-82
	1969	1963-68		1984	1979-83
	1974	1965-73		1985	1975-84
	1975	1966-74		1986	1977-85
	1980	1971-79		1987	1982-86
	1981	1972-80		1988	1983-87
	1985	1976-84		1989	1984-88
	1986	1977-85		1990	1985-89
	1996	1987-95		1991	1986-90
	1999CD[iv]	1990-98		1992	1987-91
				1993	1988-92
				1994	1989-93
				1995	1990-94
				1996	1987-95

Subject-matter	Year of issue	Time coverage	Subject-matter	Year of issue	Time coverage
	1997	1992-96		1980	1971-79
	1998	1993-97		1981	1972-80
	1999	1994-98		1985	1976-84
	1999CD[iv]	1990-98		1986	1977-85
	2000	1995-99	- by urban/rural residence		
	2001	1997-01		1971	1966-70
	2002	1998-02		1972	1967-71
	2003	1999-03		1973	1968-72
	2004	2000-04		1974	1965-73
	2005	2001-05		1975	1966-74
	2006	2002-06		1976	1971-75
	2007	2003-07		1977	1972-76
	2008	2004-08		1978	1973-77
	2009-2010	2006-10		1979	1974-78
	2011	2007-11		1980	1971-79
				1981	1972-80
	2012	2008-12		1982	1977-81
				1983	1978-82
- by age of mother	1954	1936-53		1984	1979-83
	1959	1949-58		1985	1975-84
	1965	1955-64		1986	1977-85
	1969	1963-68		1987	1982-86
	1975	1966-74		1988	1983-87
	1981	1972-80		1989	1984-88
	1986	1977-85		1990	1985-89
	1996	1987-95		1991	1986-90
	1999CD[iv]	1990-98		1992	1987-91
				1993	1988-92
- by age of mother and birth order	1954	Latest		1994	1989-93
	1959	1949-58		1995	1990-94
	1965	3-Latest		1996	1987-95
	1969	1963-68		1997	1992-96
	1975	1966-74		1998	1993-97
	1981	1972-80		1999	1994-98
	1986	1977-85		1999CD[iv]	1990-98
	1999CD[iv]	1990-98		2000	1995-99
				2001	1997-01
- by period of gestation				2002	1998-02
	1957	1950-56		2003	1999-03
	1959	1949-58		2004	2000-04
	1961	1952-60		2005	2001-05
	1965	5-Latest		2006	2002-06
	1966	1956-65		2007	2003-07
	1967-1968	Latest		2008	2004-08
	1969	1963-68		2009-2010	2006-10
	1974	1965-73		2011	2007-11
	1975	1966-74			
				2012	2008-12
			- illegitimate	1961	1952-60

Subject-matter	Year of issue	Time coverage		Subject-matter	Year of issue	Time coverage
	1991PA[vii]	Latest			1999CD[iv]	1990-98
- by sex and persons 60 +	1991PA[vii]	Latest		- foetal death(s),	1961	1952-60
- population in each type of	1955	1945-54			1965	5-Latest
	1962	1955-62			1969	1963-68
	1963	1955-63[vi]			1975	1966-74
	1968	Latest			1981	1972-80
	1971	1962-71			1986	1977-85
	1973	1965-73[vi]		- foetal death ratios, late	1961	1952-60
	1976	Latest			1965	5-Latest
	1982	Latest			1969	1963-68
	1987	1975-86			1975	1966-74
	1990	1980-89			1981	1972-80
	1995	1985-95			1986	1977-85

Illiteracy rates(see: Population)

Illegitimacy rates and ratios

Immigrants (see : Migration)

Subject-matter	Year of issue	Time coverage		Subject-matter	Year of issue	Time coverage
- of births	1959	1949-58		**Infant deaths**	1948	1932-47
	1965	1955-64			1949/50	1934-49
	1969	1963-68			1951	1935-50
	1975	1966-74			1952	1936-51
	1981	1972-80			1953	1950-52
	1986	1977-85			1954	1946-53
	1999CD[iv]	1990-98			1955	1946-54
- of foetal deaths, late	1961	1952-60			1956	1947-55
	1965	5-Latest			1957	1948-56
	1969	1963-68			1958	1948-57
	1975	1966-74			1959	1949-58
	1981	1972-80			1960	1950-59
	1986	1977-85			1961	1952-61
					1962	1953-62
Illegitimate (see also: Births and Foetal deaths, late)					1963	1954-63
- birth(s)	1959	1949-58			1964	1960-64
	1965	1955-64			1965	1961-65
	1969	1963-68			1966	1947-66
	1975	1966-74			1967	1963-67
	1981	1972-80			1968	1964-68
	1986	1977-85			1969	1965-69
	1999CD[iv]	1990-98			1970	1966-70
					1971	1967-71
- birth ratios	1959	1949-58			1972	1968-72
	1965	1955-64			1973	1969-73
	1969	1963-68			1974	1965-74
	1975	1966-74			1975	1971-75
	1981	1972-80			1976	1972-76
	1986	1977-85			1977	1973-77
					1978	1974-78
					1978HS[ii]	1948-78

Subject-matter	Year of issue	Time coverage	Subject-matter	Year of issue	Time coverage
	1979	1975-79			
	1980	1971-80	- by age and sex and urban/rural residence	1967-1973	Latest
	1981	1977-81		1974	1965-73
	1982	1978-82		1975-1979	Latest
	1983	1979-83		1980	1971-79
	1984	1980-84		1981-1984	Latest
	1985	1976-85		1985	1976-84
	1986	1982-86		1986-1991	Latest
	1987	1983-87		1992	1983-92
	1988	1984-88		1993-1995	Latest
	1989	1985-89		1996	1987-95
	1990	1986-90		1997-1999	Latest
	1991	1987-91			
	1992	1983-92	- by month	1967	1962-66
	1993	1989-93		1974	1965-73
	1994	1990-94		1980	1971-79
	1995	1991-95		1985	1976-84
	1996	1987-96			
	1997	1993-97	- by urban/rural residence	1967	Latest
	1997HS[iii]	1948-97		1968	1964-68
	1998	1994-98		1969	1965-69
	1999	1995-99		1970	1966-70
	2000	1996-00		1971	1967-71
	2001	1997-01		1972	1968-72
	2002	1998-02		1973	1969-73
	2003	1999-03		1974	1965-74
	2004	2000-04		1975	1971-75
	2005	2001-05		1976	1972-76
	2006	2002-06		1977	1973-77
	2007	2003-07		1978	1974-78
	2008	2004-08		1979	1975-79
	2009-2010	2006-10		1980	1971-80
	2011	2007-11		1981	1977-81
	2012	2008-12		1982	1978-82
- by age and sex	1948	1936-47		1983	1979-83
	1951	1936-49		1984	1980-84
	1957	1948-56		1985	1976-85
	1961	1952-60		1986	1982-86
	1962-1965	Latest		1987	1983-87
	1966	1956-65		1988	1984-88
	1967-1973	Latest		1989	1985-89
	1974	1965-73		1990	1986-90
	1975-1979	Latest		1991	1987-91
	1980	1971-79		1992	1983-92
	1981-1984	Latest		1993	1989-93
	1985	1976-84		1994	1990-94
	1986-1991	Latest		1995	1991-95
	1992	1983-92		1996	1987-96
	1993-1995	Latest		1997	1993-97
	1996	1987-95		1998	1994-98
	1997-2004	Latest		1999	1995-99
	2005	1996-05		2000	1996-00
	2006-2012	Latest			

Subject-matter	Year of issue	Time coverage	Subject-matter	Year of issue	Time coverage
	1975-1979	Latest		2011	2007-11
	1980	1971-79		2012	2008-12
	1981-1984	Latest	**Intercensal rates of**		
	1985	1976-84	**population increase**	1948	1900-48
	1986-1991	Latest		1949/50	1900-50
	1992	1983-92		1951	1900-51
	1993-1995	Latest		1952	1850-1952
	1996	1987-95		1953	1850-1953
	1997-1999	Latest		1955	1850-1954
				1960	1900-61
				1962	1900-62
- by urban/rural				1964	1955-64
residence	1967	Latest		1970	1900-70
	1968	1964-68		1978HS[ii]	1948-78
	1969	1965-69		1997HS[iii]	1948-97
	1970	1966-70			
	1971	1967-71			
	1972	1968-72	**International migration (see:**		
	1973	1969-73	**Migration)**		
	1974	1965-74			
	1975	1971-75	**L**		
	1976	1972-76			
	1977	1973-77	**Late foetal deaths(see:**		
	1978	1974-78	**Foetal deaths, late)**		
	1979	1975-79			
	1980	1971-80	**Life tables**		
	1981	1977-81	- life expectancy		
	1982	1978-82	at birth, by sex	1959-1973	Latest
	1983	1979-83		1974	2-Latest
	1984	1980-84		1975-1978	Latest
	1985	1976-85		1978HS[ii]	1948-77
	1986	1982-86		1979	Latest
	1987	1983-87		1980	2-Latest
	1988	1984-88		1981-1984	Latest
	1989	1985-89		1985	2-Latest
	1990	1986-90		1986-1991	Latest
	1991	1987-91		1991PA[vii]	1950-90
	1992	1983-92		1992-1995	Latest
	1993	1989-93		1996	2-Latest
	1994	1990-94		1997	Latest
	1995	1991-95		1997HS[iii]	1948-96
	1996	1987-96		1998	1995-98
	1997	1993-97		1999	1995-99
	1998	1994-98		2000	1995-00
	1999	1995-99		2001	1997-01
	2000	1996-00		2002	1998-02
	2001	1997-01		2003	1999-03
	2002	1998-02		2004	2000-04
	2003	1999-03		2005	2001-05
	2004	2000-04		2006	2002-06
	2005	2001-05		2007	2003-07
	2006	2002-06		2008	2004-08
	2007	2003-07		2009-10	2006-10
	2008	2004-08		2011	2007-11
	2009-2010	2006-10		2012	2008-12

Subject-matter	Year of issue	Time coverage	Subject-matter	Year of issue	Time coverage
	1981	1977-81		2006-2012	Latest
	1982	1963-82			
	1983	1979-83	- by age of bride classified by age of groom		
	1984	1980-84		1958	1948-57
	1985	1981-85		1968	Latest
	1986	1982-86		1976	Latest
	1987	1983-87		1982	Latest
	1988	1984-88		1990	Latest
	1989	1985-89		2006-2012	Latest
	1990	1971-90			
	1991	1987-91	- by age of bride and previous marital status		
	1992	1988-92		1958	1948-57
	1993	1989-93		1968	Latest
	1994	1990-94		1976	Latest
	1995	1991-95		1982	Latest
	1996	1992-96		1990	Latest
	1997	1993-97	- by age of groom	1948	1936-47
	1998	1994-98		1949/50	1936-49
	1999	1995-99		1958	1948-57
	2000	1996-00		1959-1967	Latest
	2001	1997-01		1968	1958-67
	2002	1998-02		1969-1975	Latest
	2003	1999-03		1976	1966-75
	2004	2000-04		1977-1981	Latest
	2005	2001-05		1982	1972-81
	2006	2002-06		1983-1986	Latest
	2007	2003-07		1987	1975-86
	2008	2004-08		1988-1989	Latest
	2009-2010	2006-10		1990	1980-1989
	2011	2007-11		1990-1997	Latest
	2012	2008-12		1998	1993-97
				1999	1994-98
- by age of bride	1948	1936-47		2000	1995-99
	1949/50	1936-49		2001	1997-01
	1958	1948-57		2002	1998-02
	1959-1967	Latest		2003	1999-03
	1968	1958-67		2004	2000-04
	1969-1975	Latest		2005	2001-05
	1976	1966-75		2006-2012	Latest
	1977-1981	Latest			
	1982	1972-81	- by age of groom classified by age of bride		
	1983-1986	Latest			
	1987	1975-86		1958	1948-57
	1988-1989	Latest		1968	Latest
	1990	1980-1989		1976	Latest
	1991-1997	Latest		1982	Latest
	1998	1993-97		1990	Latest
	1999	1994-98		2006-2012	Latest
	2000	1995-99			
	2001	1997-01	- by age of groom and previous	1958	1948-57
	2002	1998-02			
	2003	1999-03			
	2004	2000-04			
	2005	2001-05			

Subject-matter	Year of issue	Time coverage	Subject-matter	Year of issue	Time coverage
marital status				1982	1963-82
	1968	Latest		1983	1979-83
	1976	Latest		1984	1980-84
	1982	Latest		1985	1981-85
	1990	Latest		1986	1982-86
				1987	1983-87
- by month	1968	1963-67		1988	1984-88
				1989	1985-89
- by previous marital status of bride:				1990	1971-90
				1991	1987-91
				1992	1988-92
and age	1958	1946-57		1993	1989-93
	1968	Latest		1994	1990-94
	1976	Latest		1995	1991-95
	1982	Latest		1996	1992-96
	1990	Latest		1997	1993-97
and previous marital status of groom				1998	1994-98
				1999	1995-99
	1949/50	Latest		2000	1996-00
	1958	1948-57		2001	1997-01
	1968	1958-67		2002	1998-02
	1976	1966-75		2003	1999-03
	1982	1972-81		2004	2000-04
	1990	1980-89		2005	2001-05
- by previous marital status of groom:				2006	2002-06
				2007	2003-07
and age	1958	1946-57		2008	2004-08
	1968	Latest		2009-2010	2006-10
	1976	Latest		2011	2007-11
	1982	Latest		2012	2008-12
	1990	Latest			
and previous marital status of bride			**Marriage, first**		
	1949/50	Latest	- by detailed age of groom and bride	1976	Latest
	1958	1948-57			
	1968	1958-67		1982	1972-81
	1976	1966-75		1990	1980-89
	1982	1972-81			
	1990	1980-89	**Marriage rates**	1948	1932-47
-by urban/rural residence	1968	Latest		1949/50	1932-49
	1969	1965-69		1951	1930-50
	1970	1966-70		1952	1920-34[v]
	1971	1967-71			1934-51
	1972	1968-72		1953	1920-39[v]
	1973	1969-73			1940-52
	1974	1970-74		1954	1920-39[v]
	1975	1971-75			1946-53
	1976	1957-76		1955	1920-34[v]
	1977	1973-77			1946-54
	1978	1974-78		1956	1947-55
	1979	1975-79		1957	1948-56
	1980	1976-80		1958	1930-57
	1981	1977-81		1959	1949-58
				1960	1950-59
				1961	1952-61

Subject-matter	Year of issue	Time coverage	Subject-matter	Year of issue	Time coverage
	1962	1953-62		1953	1936-51
	1963	1954-63		1954	1936-52
	1964	1960-64		1958	1935-56
	1965	1956-65		1968	1955-67
	1966	1962-66		1976	1966-75
	1967	1963-67		1982	1972-81
	1968	1920-64ᵛ		1987	1975-86
		1953-68		1990	1980-89
	1969	1965-69	- by sex among		
	1970	1966-70	marriageable		
	1971	1967-71	population	1958	1935-56
	1972	1968-72		1968	1935-67
	1973	1969-73		1976	1966-75
	1974	1970-74		1982	1972-81
	1975	1971-75		1990	1980-89
	1976	1957-76	- by urban/rural		
	1977	1973-77	residence	1968	Latest
	1978	1974-78		1969	1965-69
	1979	1975-79		1970	1966-70
	1980	1976-80		1971	1967-71
	1981	1977-81		1972	1968-72
	1982	1963-82		1973	1969-73
	1983	1979-83		1974	1970-74
	1984	1980-84		1975	1971-75
	1985	1981-85		1976	1957-76
	1986	1982-86		1977	1973-77
	1987	1983-87		1978	1974-78
	1988	1984-88		1979	1975-79
	1989	1985-89		1980	1976-80
	1990	1971-90		1981	1977-81
	1991	1987-91		1982	1963-82
	1992	1988-92		1983	1979-83
	1993	1989-93		1984	1980-84
	1994	1990-94		1985	1981-85
	1995	1991-95		1986	1982-86
	1996	1992-96		1987	1983-87
	1997	1993-97		1988	1984-88
	1998	1994-98		1989	1985-89
	1999	1995-99		1990	1971-90
	2000	1996-00		1991	1987-91
	2001	1997-01		1992	1988-92
	2002	1998-02		1993	1989-93
	2003	1999-03		1994	1990-94
	2004	2000-04		1995	1991-95
	2005	2001-05		1996	1992-96
	2006	2002-06		1997	1993-97
	2007	2003-07		1998	1994-98
	2008	2004-08		1999	1995-99
	2009-2010	2006-10		2000	1996-00
	2011	2007-11		2001	1997-01
	2012	2008-12		2002	1998-02
				2003	1999-03
- by age and sex	1948	1936-46		2004	2000-04
	1949/50	1936-49		2005	2001-05

Subject-matter	Year of issue	Time coverage	Subject-matter	Year of issue	Time coverage
	2006	2002-06		2005	1995-04
	2007	2003-07		2006	1997-06
	2008	2004-08		2007	1997-06
	2009-2010	2006-10		2008	1999-08
	2011	2007-11		2009-2010	1999-08
	2012	2008-12		2011-2012	2001-10
Marriage rates, first			- by age	1951	Latest
-by detailed age of				1952	Latest[vi]
groom and bride	1982	1972-81		1957	Latest
	1990	1980-89		1961	Latest
				1967	Latest
Married population by age and sex (see: Population by marital status)				1974	Latest
				1980	Latest
				1985	Latest
Maternal death	1951	1947-50	**Maternal mortality rates**	1951	1947-50
	1952	1947-51		1952	1947-51
	1953	Latest		1953	Latest
	1954	1945-53		1954	1945-53
	1955-1956	Latest		1955-1956	Latest
	1957	1952-56		1957	1952-62
	1958-1960	Latest		1958-1960	Latest
	1961	1955-60		1961	1955-60
	1962-1965	Latest		1962-1965	Latest
	1966	1960-65		1966	1960-65
	1967-1973	Latest		1967-1973	Latest
	1974	1965-73		1974	1965-73
	1975-1979	Latest		1975	1966-74
	1980	1971-79		1976	1966-75
	1981	1972-80		1977	1967-76
	1982	1972-81		1978	1968-77
	1983	1973-82		1979	1969-78
	1984	1974-83		1980	1971-79
	1985	1975-84		1981	1972-80
	1986	1976-85		1982	1972-81
	1987	1977-86		1983	1973-82
	1988	1978-87		1984	1974-83
	1989	1979-88		1985	1975-84
	1990	1980-89		1986	1976-85
	1991	1981-90		1987	1977-86
	1992	1982-91		1988	1978-87
	1993	1983-92		1989	1979-88
	1994	1984-93		1990	1980-89
	1995	1985-94		1991	1981-90
	1996	1986-95		1992	1982-91
	1997	1987-96		1993	1983-92
	1998	1988-97		1994	1984-93
	1999	1989-98		1995	1985-94
	2000	1991-00		1996	1986-95
	2001	1991-00		1997	1987-96
	2002	1995-02		1998	1988-97
	2003	1995-02		1999	1989-98
	2004	1995-04		2000	1991-00

Subject-matter	Year of issue	Time coverage	Subject-matter	Year of issue	Time coverage
	2001	1991-00		1962	1956-61
	2002	1995-02		1966	1960-65
	2003	1995-02		1968	1966-67
	2004	1995-04		1977	1967-76
	2006	1997-06		1985	1975-84
	2007	1997-06		1989	1979-88
	2008	1999-08		1996	1986-95
	2009-2010	1999-08			
	2011-2012	2001-10	- emigrants, long term:		
			by age and sex	1948	1945-47
Migration (international):				1949/50	1946-48
- arrivals	1970	1963-69		1951	1948-50
	1972	1965-71		1952	1949-51
	1974	1967-73		1954	1950-53
	1976	1969-75		1957	1953-56
	1977	1967-76		1959	1955-58
	1985	1975-84		1962	1958-61
	1989	1979-88		1966	1960-65
	1996	1986-95		1970	1962-69
	1972	1965-71		1977	1967-76
	1974	1967-73		1989	1975-88
	1976	1969-75			
- arrivals, by major categories	1949/50	1945-49	by country or area of intended residence	1948	1945-47
	1951	1946-50		1949/50	1945-48
	1952	1947-51		1951	1948-50
	1954	1948-53		1952	1949-51
	1957	1951-56		1954	1950-53
	1959	1953-58		1957	1953-56
	1962	1956-61		1959	1956-58
	1966	1960-65		1977	1958-76
	1968	1966-67		1989	1975-88
	1977	1967-76			
	1985	1975-84	- immigrants, long term		
	1989	1979-88	by age and sex	1948	1945-47
	1996	1986-95		1949/50	1946-48
- continental and inter-continental	1948	1936-47		1951	1948-50
	1977	1967-76		1952	1949-51
				1954	1950-53
- departures	1970	1963-69		1957	1953-56
	1972	1965-71		1959	1955-58
	1974	1967-73		1962	1958-61
	1976	1969-75		1966	1960-65
	1977	1967-76		1970	1962-69
	1985	1975-84		1977	1967-76
	1989	1979-88		1989	1975-88
	1996	1986-95	by country or area of last residence	1948	1945-47
- departures, by major categories	1949/50	1945-49		1949/50	1945-48
	1951	1946-50			
	1952	1947-51			
	1954	1948-53			
	1957	1951-56			
	1959	1953-58			

Subject-matter	Year of issue	Time coverage	Subject-matter	Year of issue	Time coverage
	1951	1948-50		2004	2000-04
	1952	1949-51		2005	2001-05
	1954	1950-53		2006	2002-06
	1957	1953-56		2007	2003-07
	1959	1956-58		2008	2004-08
	1977	1958-76		2009-2010	2006-10
	1989	1975-88		2011	2007-11
	1948	1945-47		2012	2008-12
	1949/50	1945-48	**Neo-natal mortality**		
- refugees, by country or area of destination:			- by sex	1948	1936-47
repatriated by the International Refugee Organization	1952	1947-51		1951	1936-50
				1957	1948-56
				1961	1952-60
				1963-1965	Latest
				1966	1961-65
				1967	1962-66
resettled by the International Refugee Organization	1952	1947-51		2000-2012	Latest
			- by sex and urban/rural residence	1968-1973	Latest
				1974	1965-73
Mortality [see: Death(s), Death rates, infant deaths, infant mortality rates, Foetal death(s), Foetal death ratios, Life tables, Maternal deaths, Maternal mortality rates, Neonatal deaths, Neo-natal mortality rates, Perinatal mortality, Post-neo-natal deaths, Post-neo-natal mortality rates]				1975-1979	Latest
				1980	1971-79
				1981-1984	Latest
				1985	1976-84
				1986-1991	Latest
				1992	1983-92
				1993-1995	Latest
				1996	1987-95
				1997	Latest
				1997HS[iii]	1948-96
				1998-1999	Latest

N

Natality (see: Births and Birth rates)

Subject-matter	Year of issue	Time coverage	Subject-matter	Year of issue	Time coverage
Natural increase rate	1958-1978	Latest	**Neo-natal mortality rates**		
	1978HS[ii]	1948-78	- by sex	1948	1936-47
	1979-1997	Latest		1951	1936-50
	1998	1995-98		1957	1948-56
	1999	1996-99		1961	1952-60
	2000	1995-00		1966	1956-65
	2001	1997-01		1967	1962-66
	2002	1998-02		2000-2012	Latest
	2003	1999-03	- by sex and urban/rural residence	1971-1973	Latest
				1974	1965-73
				1975-1979	Latest
				1980	1971-79
				1981-1984	Latest
				1985	1976-84
				1986-1991	Latest
				1992	1983-92
				1993-1995	Latest

Subject-matter	Year of issue	Time coverage
	1963	1955-63
	1964	1955-64[vi]
	1971	1962-71
	1973	1965-73[vi]
	1979	1970-79[vi]
	1983	1974-83
	1988	1980-88[vi]
	1993	1985-93
- by households, number and size (see also: Households)	1955	1945-54
	1962	1955-62
	1963	1955-63[vi]
	1968	Latest
	1971	1962-71
	1973	1965-73[vi]
	1976	Latest
	1982	Latest
	1987	1975-86
	1990	1980-89
	1995	1985-95
- by language and sex	1956	1945-55
	1963	1955-63
	1964	1955-64[vi]
	1971	1962-71
	1973	1965-73[vi]
	1979	1970-79[vi]
	1983	1974-83
	1988	1980-88[vi]
	1993	1985-93
- by level of education, age and sex	1956	1945-55
	1963	1955-63
	1964	1955-64[vi]
	1971	1962-71
	1973	1965-73[vi]
	1979	1970-79[vi]
	1983	1974-83
	1988	1980-88[vi]
	1993	1985-93
- by literacy, age and sex (see also: illiteracy, below)	1948	Latest
	1955	1945-54
	1963	1955-63
	1964	1955-64[vi]
	1971	1962-71
- by literacy, age and sex and urban/rural residence	1973	1965-73[vi]
	1979	1970-79[vi]
	1983	1974-83

Subject-matter	Year of issue	Time coverage
	1988	1980-88[vi]
	1993	1985-93
- by localities of: 100000 + inhabitants	1948	Latest
	1952	Latest
	1955	1945-54
	1960	1920-61
	1962	1955-62
	1963	1955-63[vi]
	1970	1950-70
	1971	1962-71
	1973	1965-73[vi]
	1979	1970-79[vi]
	1983	1974-83
	1988	1980-88[vi]
	1993	1985-93
20000 + inhabitants	1948	Latest
	1952	Latest
	1955	1945-54
	1960	1920-61
	1962	1955-62
	1963	1955-63[vi]
	1970	1950-70
	1971	1962-71
	1973	1965-73[vi]
	1979	1970-79[vi]
	1983	1974-83
	1988	1980-88[vi]
	1993	1985-93
- by locality size-classes and sex	1948	Latest
	1952	Latest
	1955	1945-54
	1962	1955-62
	1963	1955-63[vi]
	1971	1962-71
	1973	1965-73[vi]
	1979	1970-79[vi]
	1983	1974-83
	1988	1980-88[vi]
	1993	1985-93
- by major civil divisions	1952	Latest
	1955	1945-54
	1962	1955-62
	1963	1955-63[vi]
	1971	1962-71
	1973	1965-73[vi]
	1979	1970-79[vi]
	1983	1974-83
	1988	1980-88[vi]
	1993	1985-93

Subject-matter	Year of issue	Time coverage	Subject-matter	Year of issue	Time coverage
- density (see: Density)			by industry, status and sex and urban/rural residence	1973	1965-73[vi]
				1979	1970-79[vi]
- Disabled	1991PA[vii]	Latest		1984	1974-84
- economically active:				1988	1980-88[vi]
by age and sex	1945	1945-54		1994	1985-94
	1956	1945-55	by living arrangements, age, sex and urban/rural residence	1987	1975-86
	1964	1955-64		1995	1985-95
	1972	1962-72	by occupation, age and sex	1956	1945-55
by age and sex and urban/rural residence	1973	1965-73[vi]		1964	1955-64
	1979	1970-79[vi]		1972	1962-72
	1984	1974-84	by occupation, age and sex and urban/rural residence	1973	1965-73[vi]
	1988	1980-88[vi]		1979	1970-79[vi]
	1994	1985-94		1984	1974-84
by age and sex, per cent	1949/50	1930-48		1988	1980-88[vi]
	1954	Latest		1994	1985-94
	1955	1945-54	by occupation, status and sex	1956	1945-55
	1956	1945-55		1964	1955-64
	1964	1955-64		1972	1962-72
	1972	1962-72	by occupation, status and sex and urban/rural residence	1973	1965-73[vi]
by age and sex, per cent and urban/rural residence	1973	1965-73[vi]		1979	1970-7vi[vi]
	1979	1970-79[vi]		1984	1974-84
	1984	1974-84		1988	1980-88[vi]
	1988	1980-88[vi]		1994	1985-94
	1994	1985-94	by sex	1948	Latest
by industry, age and sex	1956	1945-55		1949/50	1926-48
	1964	1955-64		1955	1945-54
	1972	1962-72		1956	1945-55
by industry, age, sex and urban/rural residence	1973	1965-74[vi]		1960	1920-60
	1979	1970-79[vi]		1963	1955-63
	1984	1974-84		1964	1955-64
	1988	1980-88[vi]		1970	1950-70
	1994	1985-94		1972	1962-72
by industry, status and sex	1948	Latest			
	1949/50	Latest			
	1955	1945-54			
	1964	1955-64			
	1972	1962-72			

Subject-matter	Year of issue	Time coverage	Subject-matter	Year of issue	Time coverage
	1965	1955-65		1965	1958-64
	1969	Latest		1966	1958-66
	1971	1962-71		1967	1963-67
	1973	1965-73[vi]		1968	1963-68
	1975	1965-74		1969	1963-69
	1978HS[ii]	1948-77		1970	1963-70
	1981	1972-80		1971	1963-71
	1986	1977-85		1972	1963-72
	1997HS[iii]	1948-96		1973	1970-73
by number of children living and age				1974	1970-74
				1975	1970-75
	1949/50	Latest		1976	1970-76
	1954	1930-53		1977	1970-77
	1955	1945-54		1978	1975-78
	1959	1949-58		1979	1975-79
	1963	1955-63		1980	1975-80
	1965	1955-65		1981	1975-81
	1968-1969	Latest		1982	1975-82
	1971	1962-71		1983	1980-83
	1973	1965-73[vi]		1984	1980-84
	1975	1965-74		1985	1980-85
	1978HS[ii]	1948-77		1986	1980-86
	1981	1972-80		1987	1980-87
	1986	1977-85		1988	1985-88
	1997HS[iii]	1948-96		1989	1985-89
in households by age, sex of householder, size and relationship to householder and urban/rural residence				1990	1985-90
				1991	1985-91
				1992	1985-92
				1993	1990-93
				1994	1990-94
				1995	1990-95
				1996	1990-96
				1997	1990-97
				1998	1993-98
				1999	1995-99
	1987	1975-86		2000	1995-00
	1995	1991-95		2001	1995-01
institutional, by age, sex and urban/rural residence				2002	1995-02
				2003	2000-03
				2004	2000-04
				2005	2000-05
	1987	1875-86		2006	2000-06
	1995	1991-95		2007	2005-07
-growth rates: average annual for countries or areas				2008	2005-08
				2009-2010	2005-10
				2011	2005-11
				2012	2005-12
	1957	1953-56			
	1958	1953-57	average annual for the world, macro-regions (continents) and regions		
	1959	1953-58			
	1960	1953-59			
	1961	1953-60			
	1962	1958-61			
	1963	1958-62			
	1964	1958-63		1957	1950-56

Subject-matter	Year of issue	Time coverage	Subject-matter	Year of issue	Time coverage
sex (see also: illiteracy rates, above)				1979	1970-79[vi]
				1984	1974-84
				1988	1980-88[vi]
				1994	1985-94
- literacy rates, by sex and age	1955	1945-54	- of cities: capital city	1952	Latest
				1955	1945-54
				1957	Latest
- literate, by sex and age (see also: illiterate, above)	1948	Latest		1960	1939-61
	1955	1945-54		1962	1955-62
	1963	1955-63		1963	1955-63
	1964	1955-64[vi]		1964-1969	Latest
- literate, by sex and age by urban/rural residence				1970	1950-70
				1971	1962-71
				1972	Latest
	1971	1962-71		1973	1965-73
	1973	1965-73[vi]		1974-2012	Latest
	1979	1970-74[vi]			
	1983	1974-83	of 100000 + inhabitants	1952	Latest
	1988	1980-88[vi]		1955	1945-54
	1993	1985-93		1957	Latest
	1987	1975-86		1960	1939-61
- living arrangements	1991PA[vii]	1950-90		1962	1955-62
	1995	1985-95		1963	1955-63
- localities (see: by localities, above)				1964-1969	Latest
				1970	1950-70
- major civil divisions (see: by major civil divisions, above)				1971	1962-71
				1972	Latest
				1973	1965-73
				1974-2012	Latest
- married by age and sex (see also: by marital status, above): numbers and percent	1954	1926-52	- of continents (see: of macro regions, below) - of countries or areas (totals): enumerated	1948	1900-48
	1960	1920-60		1949/50	1900-50
	1970	1950-70		1951	1900-51
- married female by percentage and duration of marriage	1968	Latest		1952	1850-1952
				1953	1850-1953
				1954	Latest
				1955	1850-1954
- never married proportion by sex, selected ages	1976	1966-75		1956-1961	Latest
	1978HS[ii]	1948-77		1962	1900-62
	1982	1972-81		1963	Latest
	1990	1980-89		1964	1955-64
- not economically active	1972	1962-72		1965-1978	Latest
				1978HS[ii]	1948-78
				1979-1997	Latest
- not economically active by urban/rural residence				1997HS[iii]	1948-97
				1998-2012	Latest
	1973	1965-73[vi]	estimated	1948	1932-47

Subject-matter	Year of issue	Time coverage	Subject-matter	Year of issue	Time coverage
	1949/50	1932-49		2002	1993-02
	1951	1930-50		2003	1994-03
	1952	1920-51		2004	1995-04
	1953	1920-53		2005	1996-05
	1954	1920-54		2006	1997-06
	1955	1920-55		2007	1998-07
	1956	1920-56		2008	1999-08
	1957	1940-57		2009-2010	2001-10
	1958	1939-58		2011	2002-11
	1959	1940-59		2012	2003-12
	1960	1920-60			
	1961	1941-61	- of major regions	1949/50	1920-49
	1962	1942-62		1951	1950
	1963	1943-63		1952	1920-51
	1964	1955-64		1953	1920-52
	1965	1946-65		1954	1920-53
	1966	1947-66		1955	1920-54
	1967	1958-67		1956	1920-55
	1968	1959-68		1957	1920-56
	1969	1960-69		1958	1920-57
	1970	1950-70		1959	1920-58
	1971	1962-71		1960	1920-59
	1972	1963-72		1961	1920-60
	1973	1964-73		1962	1920-61
	1974	1965-74		1963	1930-62
	1975	1966-75		1964	1930-63
	1976	1967-76		1965	1930-65
	1977	1968-77		1966	1930-66
	1978	1969-78		1967	1930-67
	1978HS[ii]	1948-78		1968	1930-68
	1979	1970-79		1969	1930-69
	1980	1971-80		1970	1950-70
	1981	1972-81		1971	1950-71
	1982	1973-82		1972	1950-72
	1983	1974-83		1973	1950-73
	1984	1975-84		1974	1950-74
	1985	1976-85		1975	1950-75
	1986	1977-86		1976	1950-76
	1987	1978-87		1977	1950-77
	1988	1979-88		1978	1950-78
	1989	1980-89		1979	1950-79
	1990	1981-90		1980	1950-80
	1991	1982-91		1981	1950-81
	1992	1983-92		1982	1950-82
	1993	1984-93		1983	1950-83
	1994	1985-94		1984	1950-84
	1995	1986-95		1985	1950-85
	1996	1987-96		1986	1950-86
	1997	1988-97		1987	1950-87
	1997HS[iii]	1948-97		1988	1950-88
	1998	1989-98		1989	1950-89
	1999	1990-99		1990	1950-90
	2000	1991-00		1991	1950-91
	2001	1992-01		1992	1950-92

Index
Historical index
(See notes at end of index)

Subject-matter	Year of issue	Time coverage
	1993	1950-93
	1994	1950-94
	1995	1950-95
	1996	1950-96
	1997	1950-97
	1998-1999	1950-00
	2000	1950-00
	2001	1950-01
	2002	1950-02
	2003	1950-03
	2004	1950-04
	2005	1950-05
	2006	1950-06
	2007	1950-07
	2008	1950-08
	2009-2010	1950-10
	2011	1960-11
	2012	1960-12
- of regions	1949/50	1920-49
	1952	1920-51
	1953	1920-52
	1954	1920-53
	1955	1920-54
	1956	1920-55
	1957	1920-56
	1958	1920-57
	1959	1920-58
	1960	1920-59
	1961	1920-60
	1962	1920-61
	1963	1930-62
	1964	1930-63
	1965	1930-65
	1966	1930-66
	1967	1930-67
	1968	1930-68
	1969	1930-69
	1970	1950-70
	1971	1950-71
	1972	1950-72
	1973	1950-73
	1974	1950-74
	1975	1950-75
	1976	1950-76
	1977	1950-77
	1978	1950-78
	1979	1950-79
	1980	1950-80
	1981	1950-81
	1982	1950-82
	1983	1950-83
	1984	1950-84
	1985	1950-85

Subject-matter	Year of issue	Time coverage
	1986	1950-86
	1987	1950-87
	1988	1950-88
	1989	1950-89
	1990	1950-90
	1991	1950-91
	1992	1950-92
	1993	1950-93
	1994	1950-94
	1995	1950-95
	1996	1950-96
	1997	1950-97
	1998-1999	1950-00
	2000	1950-00
	2001	1950-01
	2002	1950-02
	2003	1950-03
	2004	1950-04
	2005	1950-05
	2006	1950-06
	2007	1950-07
	2008	1950-08
	2009-2010	1950-10
	2011	1960-11
	2012	1960-12
- of the world	1949/50	1920-49
	1951	1950
	1952	1920-51
	1953	1920-52
	1954	1920-53
	1955	1920-54
	1956	1920-55
	1957	1920-56
	1958	1920-57
	1959	1920-58
	1960	1920-59
	1961	1920-60
	1962	1920-61
	1963	1930-62
	1964	1930-63
	1965	1930-65
	1966	1930-66
	1967	1930-67
	1968	1930-68
	1969	1930-69
	1970	1950-70
	1971	1950-71
	1972	1950-72
	1973	1950-73
	1974	1950-74
	1975	1950-75
	1976	1950-76
	1977	1950-77

Subject-matter	Year of issue	Time coverage	Subject-matter	Year of issue	Time coverage
	1978	1950-78		1975	1967-75
	1979	1950-79		1976	1967-76
	1980	1950-80		1977	1968-77
	1981	1950-81		1978	1969-78
	1982	1950-82		1979	1970-79
	1983	1950-83		1980	1971-80
	1984	1950-84		1981	1972-81
	1985	1950-85		1982	1973-82
	1986	1950-86		1983	1974-83
	1987	1950-87		1984	1975-84
	1988	1950-88		1985	1976-85
	1989	1950-89		1986	1977-86
	1990	1950-90		1987	1978-87
	1991	1950-91		1988	1979-88
	1992	1950-92		1989	1980-89
	1993	1950-93		1990	1981-90
	1994	1950-94		1991	1982-91
	1995	1950-95		1992	1983-92
	1996	1950-96		1993	1984-93
	1997	1950-97		1994	1985-94
	1998-1999	1950-00		1995	1986-95
	2000	1950-00		1996	1987-96
	2001	1950-01		1997	1988-97
	2002	1950-02		1998	1989-98
	2003	1950-03		1999	1990-99
	2004	1950-04		2000	1991-00
	2005	1950-05		2001	1992-01
	2006	1950-06		2002	1993-02
	2007	1950-07		2003	1994-03
	2008	1950-08		2004	1995-04
	2009-2010	1950-10		2005	1996-05
	2011	1960-11		2006	1997-06
	2012	1960-12		2007	1998-07
				2008	1999-08
- rural residence (see: urban/rural residence, below)				2009-2010	2001-10
				2011	2002-11
				2012	2003-12
- single, by age and sex (see also: by marital status, above):			by age and sex:		
			enumerate	1963	1955-63
				1964	1955-64[vi]
numbers	1960	1920-60		1967	Latest
	1970	1950-70		1970	1950-70
percent	1949/50	1926-48		1971	1962-71
	1960	1920-60		1972	Latest
	1970	1950-70		1973	1965-73
- urban/rural residence				1974-1978	Latest
	1968	1964-68		1978HS[ii]	1948-77
	1969	1965-69		1979-1996	Latest
	1970	1950-70		1979-1997	Latest
	1971	1962-71		1997HS[iii]	1948-96
	1972	1968-72		1998-2012	Latest
	1973	1965-73			
	1974	1966-74			

Subject-matter		Year of issue	Time coverage	Subject-matter		Year of issue	Time coverage
	estimated	1963	Latest			1983	1974-83
		1967	Latest			1988	1980-88[vi]
		1970	1950-70			1993	1985-93
		1971-1997	Latest		by literacy,		
		1997HS[iii]	1948-96		age and sex	1971	1962-71
		1998-2012	Latest			1973	1965-73[vi]
						1979	1970-79[vi]
	by country or					1983	1974-83
	area of birth					1988	1980-88[vi]
	and sex	1971	1962-71			1993	1985-93
		1973	1965-73[vi]		by major civil		
	by country or				divisions	1971	1962-71
	area of birth					1973	1965-73[vi]
	and sex and					1979	1970-79[vi]
	age	1977	Latest			1983	1974-83
						1988	1980-88[vi]
	by citizenship					1993	1985-93
	and sex	1971	1962-71		by marital		
		1973	1965-73[vi]		status, age		
	by citizenship				and sex	1971	1962-71
	and sex and					1973	1965-73[vi]
	age	1977	Latest		by religion		
		1983	1974-83		and sex	1971	1962-71
		1989	1980-88			1973	1965-73[vi]
	by ethnic					1979	1970-79[vi]
	composition					1983	1974-83
	and sex	1971	Latest			1988	1980-88[vi]
		1973	1965-73[vi]			1993	1985-93
		1979	1970-79[vi]		by school		
		1983	1974-83		attendance,		
		1988	1980-88[vi]		age and sex	1971	1962-71
		1993	1985-93			1973	1965-73[vi]
	by					1979	1970-79[vi]
	households,					1983	1974-83
	number and					1988	1980-88[vi]
	size (see also:					1993	1985-93
	Households)	1968	Latest		by sex:		
		1971	1962-71		numbers	1948	Latest
		1973	1965-73[vi]			1952	1900-51
		1976	Latest			1955	1945-54
		1982	Latest			1960	1920-60
		1987	1975-86			1962	1955-62
		1990	1980-89			1963	1955-63
		1995	1985-95			1964	1955-64[vi]
	by language	1971	1962-71			1967	Latest
	and sex					1970	1950-70
		1973	1965-73[vi]			1971	1962-71
		1979	1970-79[vi]			1972	Latest
		1983	1974-83			1973	1965-73
		1988	1980-88[vi]			1974	1966-74
		1993	1985-93			1975	1967-75
	by level of					1976	1967-76
	education,					1977	1968-77
	age and sex	1971	1962-71			1978	1969-78
		1973	1965-73[vi]			1979	1970-79
		1979	1970-79[vi]				

Subject-matter	Year of issue	Time coverage	Subject-matter	Year of issue	Time coverage
	1980	1971-80		1987	1978-87
	1981	1972-81		1988	1979-88
	1982	1973-82		1989	1980-89
	1983	1974-83		1990	1981-90
	1984	1975-84		1991	1982-91
	1985	1976-85		1992	1983-92
	1986	1977-86		1993	1984-93
	1987	1978-87		1994	1985-94
	1988	1979-88		1995	1986-95
	1989	1980-89		1996	1987-96
	1990	1981-90		1997	1988-97
	1991	1982-91		1998	1989-98
	1992	1983-92		1999	1990-99
	1993	1984-93		2000	1991-00
	1994	1985-94		2001	1992-01
	1995	1986-95		2002	1993-02
	1996	1987-96		2003	1994-03
	1997	1988-97		2004	1995-04
	1998	1989-98		2005	1996-05
	1999	1990-99		2006	1997-06
	2000	1991-00		2007	1998-07
	2001	1992-01		2008	1999-08
	2002	1993-02		2009-2010	2001-10
	2003	1994-03		2011	2002-11
	2004	1995-04		2012	2003-12
	2005	1996-05			
	2006	1997-06	by single		
	2007	1998-07	years of age		
	2008	1999-08	and sex	1971	1962-71
	2009-2010	2001-10		1973	1965-73[vi]
	2011	2002-11		1979	1970-79[vi]
	2012	2003-12		1983	1974-83
				1993	1985-93
percent	1948	Latest	female:		
	1952	1900-51	by number of		
	1955	1945-54	children		
	1960	1920-60	born alive and		
	1962	1955-62	age	1971	1962-71
	1970	1950-70		1973	1965-73[vi]
	1971	1962-71		1975	1965-74
	1973	1965-73		1978HS[ii]	1948-77
	1974	1966-74		1981	1972-80
	1975	1967-75		1986	1977-85
	1976	1967-76		1997HS[iii]	1948-96
	1977	1968-77			
	1978	1969-78	female:		
	1979	1970-79	by number of		
	1980	1971-80	children		
	1981	1972-81	living and age	1971	1962-71
	1982	1973-82		1973	1965-73[vi]
	1983	1974-83		1975	1965-74
	1984	1975-84		1978HS[ii]	1948-77
	1985	1976-85		1981	1972-80
	1986	1977-86		1986	1977-85
				1997HS[iii]	1948-96

Subject-matter	Year of issue	Time coverage	Subject-matter	Year of issue	Time coverage
Post-neo-natal deaths:				1993-1995	Latest
- by sex	1948	1936-47		1996	1987-95
	1951	1936-50		1997	Latest
	1957	1948-56		1997HS [ii]	1948-96
	1961	1952-60		1998-2012	Latest
	1963-1965	Latest			
	1966	1961-65	- by urban/rural residence	1971-1973	Latest
	1967	1962-66		1974	1965-73
	1968-1973	Latest		1975-1979	Latest
	1974	1965-73		1980	1971-79
	1975-1979	Latest		1981-1984	Latest
	1980	1971-79		1985	1976-84
	1981-1984	Latest		1986-1991	Latest
	1985	1976-84		1992	1983-92
	1986-1991	Latest		1993-1995	Latest
	1992	1983-92		1996	1987-95
	1993-1995	Latest		1997	Latest
	1996	1987-95		1997HS [ii]	1948-96
	1997	Latest		1998-1999	Latest
	1997HS [ii]	1948-96			
	1998-2012	Latest			

R

Rates (see under following subject-matter headings: Annulments, Births, Deaths, Divorces, Fertility, Illiteracy, Infant Mortality, Intercensal, Life Tables, Literacy Marriages, Maternal mortality, Natural increase, Neo-natal mortality, Population growth, Post-neo-natal mortality, Reproduction)

Subject-matter	Year of issue	Time coverage
- by urban/rural residence	1971-1973	Latest
	1974	1965-73
	1975-1979	Latest
	1980	1971-79
	1981-1984	Latest
	1985	1976-84
	1986-1991	Latest
	1992	1983-92
	1993-1995	Latest
	1996	1987-95
	1997	Latest
	1997 HS [ii]	1948-96
	1998-1999	Latest

Ratios (see under following subject matter headings: Births, Child-woman, Fertility, Foetal deaths, Perinatal mortality)

Subject-matter	Year of issue	Time coverage
Post-neo-natal mortality rates:		
- by sex	1948	1936-47
	1951	1936-50
	1957	1948-56
	1961	1952-60
	1966	1956-65
	1967	1962-66
	1968-1973	Latest
	1974	1965-73
	1975-1979	Latest
	1980	1971-79
	1981-1984	Latest
	1985	1976-84
	1986-1991	Latest
	1992	1983-92

Subject-matter	Year of issue	Time coverage
Refugees, by country or area of destination:		
- repatriated by the International Refugee Organization	1952	1947-51
- resettled by the International Refugee Organization	1952	1947-51
Religion and sex (see: Population)		
Reproduction rates,	1948	1920-47

Subject-matter	Year of issue	Time coverage	Subject-matter	Year of issue	Time coverage
	2004	2004		1975	1956-75
	2005	2005		1981	1962-81
	2006	2006		1986	1967-86
	2007	2007		1992	1983-92
	2008	2008		1999CD[iv]	1980-99
	2009-2010	2010	- Nuptiality (see: Marriage and Divorce, above)		
	2011	2011			
	2012	2012			
Survivors (see: Life tables)			- Population Ageing and the Situation of Elderly Persons	1991PA[vii]	1950-90
T			- Population Census:		
Text (see separate listing in Appendix to this Index)			Economic characteristics	1956	1945-55
				1964	1955-64
Topic of each Demographic Yearbook				1972	1962-72
- Divorce (see: Marriage and Divorce, below)				1973	1965-73[vi]
				1979	1970-79[vi]
				1984	1974-84
- General demography	1948	1900-48		1988	1980-88[vi]
	1953	1850 -1953		1994	1985-94
- Historical Supplement	1978HS[ii]	1948-78	Educational characteristics	1955	1945-54
	1997HS[iii]	1948-97		1956	1945-55
- Marriage and Divorce	1958	1930-57		1963	1955-63
	1968	1920-68		1964	1955-64[vi]
	1976	1957-76		1971	1962-71
	1982	1963-82		1973	1965-73[vi]
	1990	1971-90		1979	1970-79[vi]
- Migration (international)	1977	1958-76		1983	1974-83
	1989	1975-88		1988	1980-88[vi]
				1993	1985-93
- Mortality	1951	1905-50	Ethnic characteristics	1956	1945-55
	1957	1930-56		1963	1955-63
	1961	1945-61		1964	1955-64[vi]
	1966	1920-66		1971	1962-71
	1967	1900-67		1973	1965-73[vi]
	1974	1965-74		1979	1970-79[vi]
	1980	1971-80		1983	1974-83
	1985	1976-85		1988	1980-88[vi]
	1992	1983-92		1993	1985-93
	1996	1987-96	Fertility characteristics	1940/50	1900-50
- Natality	1949/50	1932-49		1954	1900-53
	1954	1920-53		1955	1945-54
	1959	1920-58		1959	1935-59
	1965	1920-65		1963	1955-63
	1969	1925-69		1965	1955-65
				1969	Latest
				1971	1962-71
				1973	1965-73[vi]

Subject-matter	Year of issue	Time coverage	Subject-matter	Year of issue	Time coverage
	1975	1965-75		1971	1962-71
	1981	1972-81		1973	1965-73[vi]
	1986	1977-86		1979	1970-79[vi]
	1992	1983-92		1983	1974-83
Geographic				1988	1980-88[vi]
characteristics	1952	1900-51		1993	1985-93
	1955	1945-54	-Population trends	1960	1920-60
	1962	1955-62		1970	1950-70
	1964	1955-64[vi]			
	1971	1962-71			
	1973	1965-73[vi]			
	1979	1970-79[vi]			
	1983	1974-83			
	1988	1980-88[vi]			
	1993	1985-93			
Household					
characteristics	1955	1945-54			
	1962	1955-62			
	1963	1955-63[vi]			
	1971	1962-71			
	1973	1965-73[vi]			
	1976	1966-75			
	1983	1974-83			
	1987	1975-86			
	1995	1985-95			
Personal					
characteristics	1955	1945-54			
	1962	1955-62			

U

Urban/rural births
(see: Births)

Urban/rural deaths
(see: Deaths)

Urban/rural infant deaths
(see: Infant deaths)

Urban/rural population
(see: Population:
urban/rural residence)

**Urban/rural population
by average size of
households** (see:
Households)

APPENDIX

Special text of each Demographic Yearbook:

Divorce:

'Uses of Marriage and Divorce Statistics', 1958.

Marriage:

'Uses of Marriage and Divorce Statistics', 1958.

Households:

'Concepts and definitions of households, householder and institutional population', 1987.

Migration:

'Statistics of International Migration', 1977.

Mortality:

'Recent Mortality Trends', 1951.
'Development of Statistics of Causes of Death', 1951.
'Factors in Declining Mortality', 1957.
'Notes on Methods of Evaluating the Reliability of Conventional Mortality Statistics', 1961.
'Recent Trends of Mortality', 1966.
'Mortality Trends among Elderly Persons', 1991PA[vii].

Natality:

'Graphic Presentation of Trends in Fertility', 1959.
'Recent Trends in Birth Rates', 1965.
'Recent Changes in World Fertility', 1969.

Population

'World Population Trends, 1920-1949', 1949/50.
'Urban Trends and Characteristics', 1952.
'Background to the 1950 Censuses of Population', 1955.
'The World Demographic Situation', 1956.
'How Well Do We Know the Present Size and Trend of the World's Population?', 1960.
'Notes on Availability of National Population Census Data and Methods of Estimating their Reliability', 1962.
'Availability and Adequacy of Selected Data Obtained from Population Censuses Taken 1955-1963', 1963.
'Availability of Selected Population Census Statistics: 1955-1964', 1964.
'Statistical Concepts and Definitions of Urban and Rural Population', 1967.
'Statistical Concepts and Definitions of Household', 1968.
'How Well Do We Know the Present Size and Trend of the World's Population?', 1970.
'United Nations Recommendations on Topics to be Investigated in a Population Census
Compared with Country Practice in National Censuses taken 1965-1971', 1971.
'Statistical Definitions of Urban Population and their Use in Applied Demography', 1972.
'Dates of National Population and Housing Census carried out during the decade 1965-1974', 1974.
'Dates of National Population and/or Housing Censuses taken or anticipated during the decade 1975-1984', 1979.
'Dates of National Population and/or Housing Censuses taken during the decade 1965-1974 and taken or anticipated during the decade 1975-1984', 1983.
'Dates of National Population and/or Housing Censuses taken during the decade 1975-1984 and taken or anticipated during the decade 1985-1994', 1988 and 1993.
'Statistics Concerning the Economically Active Population: An Overview', 1984.

'Disability', 1991PA[vii].
'Population Ageing', 1991PA[vii].
'Special Needs for the Study of Population Ageing and Elderly Persons', 1991PA[vii].

General Notes

This cumulative index covers the contents of each of the 63 issues of the Demographic Yearbook. 'Year of issue' stands for the particular issue in which the indicated subject-matter appears. Unless otherwise specified, 'Time coverage' designates the years for which annual statistics are shown in the Demographic Yearbook referred to in 'Year of issue' column. 'Latest' or '2-Latest' indicates that data are for latest available year(s) only.

---

[i] Only titles not available for preceding bibliography.

[ii] Historical Supplement to the 30th DYB published in a separate volume in year 1979.

[iii] Historical Supplement to the 49th DYB published in a separate volume (CD-ROM) in year 2000.

[iv] Supplement to the 51st DYB focusing on natality published in a separate volume (CD-ROM) in year 2002.

[v] Five-year average rates.

[vi] Only data not available for preceding issue.

[vii] Population ageing published in separate volume.

Index
Index historique (suite)
(Voir notes à la fin de l'index)

Index
Index historique (suite)
(Voir notes à la fin de l'index)

Index
Index historique (suite)
(Voir notes à la fin de l'index)

Sujet	Année de l'édition	Période considérée	Sujet	Année de l'édition	Période considérée
	1985	1976-84		1970	1966-70
	1986-1991	Dernière		1971	1967-71
	1992	1983-92		1972	1968-72
	1993-1995	Dernière		1973	1969-73
	1996	1987-95		1974	1965-74
	1997	Dernière		1975	1971-75
	1997SR [ii]	1948-96		1976	1972-76
	1998-2006	Dernière		1977	1973-77
				1978	1974-78
-selon la cause	1951	1947-50		1979	1975-79
	1952	1947-51 [iii]		1980	1971-80
	1953	Dernière		1981	1977-81
	1954	1945-53		1982	1978-82
	1955-1956	Dernière		1983	1979-83
	1957	1952-56		1984	1980-84
	1958-1960	Dernière		1985	1976-85
	1961	1955-60		1986	1982-86
	1962-1965	Dernière		1987	1983-87
	1966	1960-65		1988	1984-88
	1967-1973	Dernière		1989	1985-89
	1974	1965-73		1990	1986-90
	1975-1979	Dernière		1991	1987-91
	1980	1971-79		1992	1983-92
	1981-1984	Dernière		1993	1989-93
	1985	1976-84		1994	1990-94
	1986-1995	Dernière		1995	1991-95
	1996	1987-95		1996	1987-96
	1997-2000	Dernière		1997	1993-97
	2002	1995-02		1998	1994-98
	2004	1995-04		1999	1995-99
	2006	2002-06		2001	1997-01
	2008	2004-08		2002	1998-02
	2011	2006-10		2003	1999-03
				2004	2000-04
-selon la cause, l'âge et le sexe	1951	Dernière		2005	2001-05
	1952	Dernière [iii]		2006	2002-06
	1957	Dernière		2007	2003-07
	1961	Dernière		2008	2004-08
	1967	Dernière		2009-2010	2006-10
	1974	Dernière		2011	2007-11
	1980	Dernière		2012	2008-12
	1985	Dernière			
	1991 VP [v]	1960-90	-selon l'état matrimonial, l'âge et le sexe	1958	Dernière
	1996	Dernière		1961	Dernière
-selon la cause, l'âge et le sexe et la résidence (urbaine/rurale)	1967	Dernière		1967	Dernière
				1974	Dernière
-selon la cause et le sexe	1967	Dernière		1980	Dernière
	1974	Dernière		1985	Dernière
	1980	Dernière		1991 VP [v]	1950-90
	1985	Dernière		1996	Dernière
	1991VP [v]	1960-90		2003	Dernière
	1996	Dernière			
	2006	2002-06	-selon le mois	1951	1946-50
	2008	2004-08		1967	1962-66
	2011	2006-10		1974	1965-73
				1980	1971-79
-selon la résidence (urbaine/rurale)	1967	Dernière		1985	1976-84
	1968	1964-68		2001	1985-00
	1969	1965-69		2005	2001-05
			-selon la profession et l'âge (sexe masculin)	1957	Dernière

Index
Index historique (suite)
(Voir notes à la fin de l'index)

Sujet	Année de l'édition	Période considérée	Sujet	Année de l'édition	Période considérée
	1961	1957-60		1986	1982-86
	1967	1962-66		1987	1983-87
-selon le type de certification et la cause:				1988	1984-88
				1989	1985-89
nombres	1957	Dernière		1990	1986-90
	1974	1965-73		1991	1987-91
	1980	1971-79		1992	1983-92
	1985	1976-84		1993	1989-93
pourcentage	1957	Dernière		1994	1990-94
	1961	1955-60		1995	1991-95
	1966	1960-65		1996	1987-96
	1974	1965-73		1997	1993-97
	1980	1971-79		1997SR [ii]	1948-97
	1985	1976-84		1998	1994-98
				1999	1995-99
Décès, taux de..........................	1948	1932-47		2000	1996-00
	1949/50	1932-49		2001	1997-01
	1951	1905-30 [vi]		2002	1998-02
		1930-50		2003	1999-03
	1952	1920-34 [vi]		2004	2000-04
		1934-51		2005	2001-05
	1953	1920-39 [vi]		2006	2002-06
		1940-52		2007	2003-07
	1954	1920-39 [vi]		2008	2004-08
		1946-53		2009-2010	2006-10
	1955	1920-34 [vi]		2011	2007-11
		1946-54		2012	2008-12
	1956	1947-55			
	1957	1930-56	-d'enfants de moins d'un an (voir: Mortalités infantile)		
	1958	1948-57			
	1959	1949-58	-estimatifs:		
	1960	1950-59	pour les continents	1949/50	1947
	1961	1945-59 [vi]		1956-1977	Dernière
		1952-61		1978-1979	1970-75
	1962	1945-54 [vi]		1980-1983	1975-80
		1952-62		1984-1986	1980-85
	1963	1945-59 [vi]		1987-1992	1985-90
		1954-63		1993-1997	1990-95
	1964	1960-64		1998-2000	1995-00
	1965	1961-65		2001-2005	2000-05
	1966	1920-64 [vi]		2006-2010	2005-10
		1951-66		2011-2012	2010-15
	1967	1963-67			
	1968	1964-68	pour les grandes régions (continentales)	1964-1977	Dernière
	1969	1965-69		1978-1979	1970-75
	1970	1966-70		1980-1983	1975-80
	1971	1967-71		1984-1986	1980-85
	1972	1968-72		1987-1992	1985-90
	1973	1969-73		1993-1997	1990-95
	1974	1965-74		1998-2000	1995-00
	1975	1971-75		2001-2005	2000-05
	1976	1972-76		2006-2010	2005-10
	1977	1973-77		2011-2012	2010-15
	1978	1974-78			
	1978SR [i]	1948-78	pour les régions	1949/50	1947
	1979	1975-79		1956-1977	Dernière
	1980	1971-80		1978-1979	1970-75
	1981	1977-81		1980-1983	1975-80
	1982	1978-82		1984-1986	1980-85
	1983	1979-83			
	1984	1980-84			
	1985	1976-85			

Index
Index historique (suite)
(Voir notes à la fin de l'index)

Index
Index historique (suite)
(Voir notes à la fin de l'index)

Index
Index historique (suite)
(Voir notes à la fin de l'index)

Index
Index historique (suite)
(Voir notes à la fin de l'index)

Index
Index historique (suite)
(Voir notes à la fin de l'index)

Sujet	Année de l'édition	Période considérée
-selon la résidence (urbaine/rurale)	2002	1998-02
	2003	1999-03
	2004	2000-04
	2005	2001-05
	2006	2002-06
	2007	2003-07
	2008	2004-08
	2009-2010	2006-10
	2011	2007-11
	2012	2008-12

Durée du mariage (voir: Divorces)

E

Emigrants (voir: Migration internationale)

Enfants, nombre:

Sujet	Année de l'édition	Période considérée
-dont il est tenu compte dans les divorces	1958	1948-57
	1968	1958-67
	1976	1966-75
	1982	1972-81
	1990	1980-89
-mis au monde, selon l'âge de la mère	1949/50	Dernière
	1954	1930-53
	1955	1945-54
	1959	1949-58
	1963	1955-63
	1965	1955-65
	1969	Dernière
	1971	1962-71
	1973	1965-73 [iii]
	1975	1965-74
	1978SR [i]	1948-77
	1981	1972-80
	1986	1977-85
	1997SR [ii]	1948-96
-vivants, selon l'âge de la mère	1940/50	Dernière
	1954	1930-53
	1955	1945-54
	1959	1949-58
	1963	1955-63
	1965	1955-65
	1968	1955-67
	1969	Dernière
	1971	1962-71
	1973	1965-73 [iii]
	1975	1965-74
	1978SR [i]	1948-77
	1981	1972-80
	1986	1977-85
	1997SR [ii]	1948-96

Espérance de vie (voir: Mortalité, tables de)

Etat matrimonial (voir la rubrique appropriée par sujet, p.ex., Décès, Population, etc.)

F

Sujet	Année de l'édition	Période considérée
Fécondité, indice synthétique de	1987-1997	Dernière
	1997SR [ii]	1948-96
	1998	1995-98
	1999	1996-99
	1999CD [vii]	1980-99
	2000	1995-00
	2001	1997-01
	2002	1998-02
	2003	1999-03
	2004	2000-04
	2005	2001-05
	2006	2002-06
	2007	2003-07
	2008	2004-08
	2009-2010	2006-10
	2011	2007-11
	2012	2008-12
Fécondité proportionnelle	1949/50	1900-50
	1954	1900-52
	1955	1945-54
	1959	1935-59
	1963	1955-63
	1965	1955-65
	1969	Dernière
	1975	1966-74
	1978SR [i]	1948-77
	1981	1962-80
	1986	1967-85
	1997SR [ii]	1948-96
	1999CD [vii]	1980-99
Fécondité, taux global de	1948	1936-47
	1949/50	1936-49
	1951	1936-50
	1952	1936-50
	1953	1936-52
	1954	1936-53
	1955-1956	Dernière
	1959	1949-58
	1960-1964	Dernière
	1965	1955-64
	1966-1974	Dernière
	1975	1966-74
	1976-1978	Dernière
	1978SR [i]	1948-77
	1979-1980	Dernière
	1981	1962-80
	1982-1985	Dernière
	1986	1977-85
	1987-1991	Dernière
	1992	1983-92
	1993-1997	Dernière

Sujet	Année de l'édition	Période considérée	Sujet	Année de l'édition	Période considérée
	1997SR [ii]	1948-96		1956	1947-55
	1998-2012	Dernière		1957	1948-56
				1958	1940-57
I				1959	1949-58
				1960	1950-59
Illégitime (voir également: Naissances et morts fœtales tardives):				1961	1952-61
				1962	1953-62
				1963	1954-63
-morts fœtales tardives	1961	1952-60		1964	1960-64
	1965	5-Dernières		1965	1956-65
	1969	1963-68		1966	1962-66
	1975	1966-74		1967	1963-67
	1981	1972-80		1968	1949-68
	1986	1977-85		1969	1965-69
-morts fœtales tardives, rapports de				1970	1966-70
				1971	1967-71
	1961	1952-60		1972	1968-72
	1965	5-Dernières		1973	1969-73
	1969	1963-68		1974	1970-74
	1975	1966-74		1975	1971-75
	1981	1972-80		1976	1957-76
	1986	1977-85		1977	1973-77
				1978	1974-78
-naissances	1959	1949-58		1979	1975-79
	1965	1955-64		1980	1976-80
	1969	1963-68		1981	1977-81
	1975	1966-74		1982	1963-82
	1981	1972-80		1983	1979-83
	1986	1977-85		1984	1980-84
	1999CD [vii]	1990-98		1985	1981-85
-naissances, rapports de	1959	1949-58		1986	1982-86
	1965	1955-64		1987	1983-87
	1969	1963-68		1988	1984-88
	1975	1966-74		1989	1985-89
	1981	1972-80		1990	1971-90
	1986	1977-85		1991	1987-91
	1999CD [vii]	1990-98		1992	1988-92
Immigrants (voir: Migration internationale)				1993	1989-93
				1994	1990-94
				1995	1991-95
Instruction, degré d' (voir: Population)				1996	1992-96
				1997	1993-97
				1998	1994-98
L				1999	1995-99
				2000	1996-00
				2001	1997-01
				2002	1998-02
Langue et sexe (voir: Population)				2003	1999-03
				2004	2000-04
Localités (voir: Population)				2005	2001-05
				2006	2002-06
				2007	2003-07
M				2008	2004-08
				2009-2010	2006-10
				2011	2007-11
Mariages	1948	1932-47		2012	2008-12
	1949/50	1934-49			
	1951	1935-50	-selon l'âge de l'épouse		
	1952	1936-51		1948	1936-47
	1953	1950-52		1949/50	1936-49
	1954	1946-53		1958	1948-57
	1955	1946-54		1959-1967	Dernière

Index
Index historique (suite)
(Voir notes à la fin de l'index)

Sujet	Année de l'édition	Période considérée	Sujet	Année de l'édition	Période considérée
	1968	1958-67		1976	Dernière
	1969-1975	Dernière		1982	Dernière
	1976	1966-75		1990	Dernière
	1977-1981	Dernière		2006-2012	Dernière
	1982	1972-81			
	1983-1986	Dernière	-selon l'âge de l'époux et		
	1987	1975-86	l'état matrimonial antérieur	1958	1946-57
	1988-1989	Dernière		1968	Dernière
	1990	1980-89		1976	Dernière
	1991-1997	Dernière		1982	Dernière
	1998	1993-97		1990	Dernière
	1999	1994-98	-selon l'état matrimonial		
	2000	1995-99	antérieur de l'épouse: et		
	2001	1997-01	l'âge	1958	1946-57
	2002	1998-02		1968	Dernière
	2003	1999-03		1976	Dernière
	2004	2000-04		1982	Dernière
	2005	2001-05		1990	Dernière
	2006-2012	Dernière	-selon l'état matrimonial		
			antérieur de l'épouse		
-selon l'âge de l'épouse et			(suite): et l'état matrimonial		
l'âge de l'époux	1958	1948-57	antérieur de l'époux	1949/50	Dernière
	1968	Dernière		1958	1948-57
	1976	Dernière		1968	1958-67
	1982	Dernière		1976	1966-75
	1990	Dernière		1982	1972-81
	2006-2012	Dernière		1990	1980-89
			-selon l'état matrimonial		
-selon l'âge de l'épouse et			antérieur de l'époux		
l'état matrimonial antérieur	1958	1948-57	et l'âge	1958	1946-57
	1968	Dernière		1968	Dernière
	1976	Dernière		1976	Dernière
	1982	Dernière		1982	Dernière
	1990	Dernière		1990	Dernière
			et l'état matrimonial		
-selon l'âge de l'époux	1948	1936-47	antérieur de l'épouse	1949/50	Dernière
	1949/50	1936-49		1958	1948-57
	1958	1948-57		1968	1958-67
	1959-1967	Dernière		1976	1966-75
	1968	1958-67		1982	1972-81
	1969-1975	Dernière		1990	1980-89
	1976	1966-75	-selon la résidence		
	1977-1981	Dernière	(urbaine/rurale)	1968	Dernière
	1982	1972-81		1969	1965-69
	1983-1986	Dernière		1970	1966-70
	1987	1975-86		1971	1967-71
	1988-1989	Dernière		1972	1968-72
	1990	1980-89		1973	1969-73
	1991-1997	Dernière		1974	1970-74
	1998	1993-97		1975	1971-75
	1999	1994-98		1976	1957-76
	2000	1995-99		1977	1973-77
	2001	1997-01		1978	1974-78
	2002	1998-02		1979	1975-79
	2003	1999-03		1980	1976-80
	2004	2000-04		1981	1977-81
	2005	2001-05		1982	1963-82
	2006-2012	Dernière		1983	1979-83
				1984	1980-84
-selon l'âge de l'époux et				1985	1981-85
l'âge de l'épouse	1958	1948-57		1986	1982-86
	1968	Dernière		1987	1983-87

Index
Index historique (suite)
(Voir notes à la fin de l'index)

703

Index
Index historique (suite)
(Voir notes à la fin de l'index)

Index
Index historique (suite)
(Voir notes à la fin de l'index)

Index
Index historique (suite)
(Voir notes à la fin de l'index)

Index
Index historique (suite)
(Voir notes à la fin de l'index)

Sujet	Année de l'édition	Période considérée	Sujet	Année de l'édition	Période considérée
	1997	1993-97		1978	1974-78
	1997SR [ii]	1948-97		1979	1975-79
	1998	1994-98		1980	1971-80
	1999	1995-99		1981	1977-81
	2000	1996-00		1982	1978-82
	2001	1997-01		1983	1979-83
	2002	1998-02		1984	1980-84
	2003	1999-03		1985	1976-85
	2004	2000-04		1986	1982-86
	2005	2001-05		1987	1983-87
	2006	2002-06		1988	1984-88
	2007	2003-07		1989	1985-89
	2008	2004-08		1990	1986-90
	2009-2010	2006-10		1991	1987-91
	2011	2007-11		1992	1983-92
	2012	2008-12		1993	1989-93
				1994	1990-94
-selon l'âge et le sexe	1948	1936-47		1995	1991-95
	1951	1936-49		1996	1987-96
	1957	1948-56		1997	1993-97
	1961	1952-60		1998	1994-98
	1962-1965	Dernière		1999	1995-99
	1966	1956-65		2000	1996-00
	1967-1973	Dernière		2001	1997-01
	1974	1965-73		2002	1998-02
	1975-1979	Dernière		2003	1999-03
	1980	1971-79		2004	2000-04
	1981-1984	Dernière		2005	2001-05
	1985	1976-84		2006	2002-06
	1986-1991	Dernière		2007	2003-07
	1992	1983-92		2008	2004-08
	1993-1995	Dernière		2009-2010	2006-10
	1996	1987-95		2011	2007-11
	1997-2004	Dernière		2012	2008-12
	2005	1996-05	-selon le mois	1967	1962-66
	2006-2012	Dernière		1974	1965-73
				1980	1971-79
-selon l'âge et le sexe et la résidence (urbaine/rurale)	1968-1973	Dernière		1985	1976-84
	1974	1965-73	**Mortalité infantile, taux de**	1948	1932-47
	1975-1979	Dernière		1949/50	1932-49
	1980	1971-79		1951	1930-50
	1981-1984	Dernière		1952	1920-34 [vi]
	1985	1976-84			1934-51
	1986-1991	Dernière		1953	1920-39 [vi]
	1992	1983-92			1940-52
	1993-1995	Dernière		1954	1920-39 [vi]
	1996	1987-95			1946-53
	1997-1999	Dernière		1955	1920-34 [vi]
					1946-54
-selon la résidence (urbaine/rurale)	1967	Dernière		1956	1947-55
	1968	1964-68		1957	1948-56
	1969	1965-69		1958	1948-57
	1970	1966-70		1959	1949-58
	1971	1967-71		1960	1950-59
	1972	1968-72		1961	1945-59 [vi]
	1973	1969-73			1952-61
	1974	1965-74		1962	1945-59 [vi]
	1975	1971-75			1952-62
	1976	1972-76		1963	1945-59 [vi]
	1977	1973-77			1954-63

Index
Index historique (suite)
(Voir notes à la fin de l'index)

Sujet	Année de l'édition	Période considérée	Sujet	Année de l'édition	Période considérée
	1964	1960-64		1980	1971-79
	1965	1961-65		1981-1984	Dernière
	1966	1920-64 [vi]		1985	1976-84
		1951-66		1986-1991	Dernière
	1967	1963-67		1992	1983-92
	1968	1964-68		1993-1995	Dernière
	1969	1965-69		1996	1987-95
	1970	1966-70		1997-2012	Dernière
	1971	1967-71			
	1972	1968-72	-selon l'âge et le sexe et la résidence (urbaine/rurale)		
	1973	1969-73		1971-1973	Dernière
	1974	1965-74		1974	1965-73
	1975	1971-75		1975-1979	Dernière
	1976	1972-76		1980	1971-79
	1977	1973-77		1981-1984	Dernière
	1978	1974-78		1985	1976-84
	1978SR [i]	1948-78		1986-1991	Dernière
	1979	1975-79		1992	1983-92
	1980	1971-80		1993-1995	Dernière
	1981	1977-81		1996	1987-95
	1982	1978-82		1997-1999	Dernière
	1983	1979-83	-selon la résidence (urbaine/rurale)		
	1984	1980-84		1967	Dernière
	1985	1976-85		1968	1964-68
	1986	1982-86		1969	1965-69
	1987	1983-87		1970	1966-70
	1988	1984-88		1971	1967-71
	1989	1985-89		1972	1968-72
	1990	1986-90		1973	1969-73
	1991	1987-91		1974	1965-74
	1992	1983-92		1975	1971-75
	1993	1989-93		1976	1972-76
	1994	1990-94		1977	1973-77
	1995	1991-95		1978	1974-78
	1996	1987-96		1979	1975-79
	1997	1993-97		1980	1971-80
	1997SR [ii]	1948-97		1981	1977-81
	1998	1994-98		1982	1978-82
	1999	1995-99		1983	1979-83
	2000	1996-00		1984	1980-84
	2001	1997-01		1985	1976-85
	2002	1998-02		1986	1982-86
	2003	1999-03		1987	1983-87
	2004	2000-04		1988	1984-88
	2005	2001-05		1989	1985-89
	2006	2002-06		1990	1986-90
	2007	2003-07		1991	1987-91
	2008	2004-08		1992	1983-92
	2009-2010	2006-10		1993	1989-93
	2011	2007-11		1994	1990-94
	2012	2008-12		1995	1991-95
				1996	1987-96
-selon l'âge et le sexe	1948	1936-47		1997	1993-97
	1951	1936-49		1998	1994-98
	1957	1948-56		1999	1995-99
	1961	1952-60		2000	1996-00
	1966	1956-65		2001	1997-01
	1967	1962-66		2002	1998-02
	1971-1973	Dernière		2003	1999-03
	1974	1965-73		2004	2000-04
	1975-1979	Dernière		2005	2001-05

Index
Index historique (suite)
(Voir notes à la fin de l'index)

Index
Index historique (suite)
(Voir notes à la fin de l'index)

Sujet	Année de l'édition	Période considérée	Sujet	Année de l'édition	Période considérée
-selon le sexe et la résidence (urbaine/rurale)	1968-1973	Dernière	-selon la résidence (urbaine/rurale)	1971	1966-70
	1974	1965-73		1974	1965-73
	1975-1979	Dernière		1980	1971-79
	1980	1971-79		1985	1976-84
	1981-1984	Dernière		1996	1987-95
	1985	1976-84			
	1986-1991	Dernière	**Mortalité post-néonatale (nombres):**		
	1992	1983-92	-selon le sexe	1948	1936-47
	1993-1995	Dernière		1951	1936-50
	1996	1987-95		1957	1948-56
	1997	Dernière		1961	1952-60
	1997SR [ii]	1948-96		1963-1965	Dernière
	1998-1999	Dernière		1966	1961-65
				1967	1962-66
Mortalité néonatale, taux de				1968-1973	Dernière
-selon le sexe	1948	1936-47		1974	1965-73
	1951	1936-50		1975-1979	Dernière
	1957	1948-56		1980	1971-79
	1961	1952-60		1981-1984	Dernière
	1966	1956-65		1985	1976-84
	1967	1962-66		1986-1991	Dernière
	2000-2012	Dernière		1992	1983-92
-selon le sexe et la résidence (urbaine/rurale)	1968	Dernière		1993-1995	Dernière
	1971-1973	Dernière		1996	1987-95
	1974	1965-73		1997	Dernière
	1975-1979	Dernière		1997SR [ii]	1948-96
	1980	1971-79		1998-2012	Dernière
	1981-1984	Dernière	-selon la résidence (urbaine/rurale)	1971-1973	Dernière
	1985	1976-84		1974	1965-73
	1986-1991	Dernière		1975-1979	Dernière
	1992	1983-92		1980	1971-79
	1993-1995	Dernière		1981-1984	Dernière
	1996	1987-95		1985	1976-84
	1997	Dernière		1986-1991	Dernière
	1997SR [ii]	1948-96		1992	1983-92
	1998-1999	Dernière		1993-1995	Dernière
Mortalité périnatale (nombres) .	1961	1952-60		1996	1987-95
	1966	1956-65		1997	Dernière
	1971	1966-70		1997SR [ii]	1948-96
	1974	1965-73		1998-1999	Dernière
	1980	1971-79			
	1985	1976-84	**Mortalité post-néonatale, taux de:**		
	1996	1987-95	-selon le sexe	1948	1936-47
-selon la résidence (urbaine/rurale)	1971	1966-70		1951	1936-50
	1974	1965-73		1957	1948-56
	1980	1971-79		1961	1952-60
	1985	1976-84		1966	1956-65
	1996	1987-95		1967	1962-66
				1968-1973	Dernière
Mortalité périnatale, rapports de	1961	1952-60		1974	1965-73
	1966	1956-65		1975-1979	Dernière
	1971	1966-70		1980	1971-79
	1974	1965-73		1981-1984	Dernière
	1980	1971-79		1985	1976-84
	1985	1976-84		1986-1991	Dernière
	1996	1987-95		1992	1983-92
				1993-1995	Dernière

Index
Index historique (suite)
(Voir notes à la fin de l'index)

Sujet	Année de l'édition	Période considérée	Sujet	Année de l'édition	Période considérée
	1996	1987-95		1966	2-Dernières
	1997	Dernière		1967	1900-66
	1997SR [ii]	1948-96		1968-1973	Dernière
	1998-2012	Dernière		1974	2-Dernières
				1975-1978	Dernière
-selon la résidence (urbaine/rurale)	1971-1973	Dernière		1978HS [i]	1948-77
	1974	1965-73		1979	Dernière
	1975-1979	Dernière		1980	2-Dernières
	1980	1971-79		1981-1984	Dernière
	1981-1984	Dernière		1985	2-Dernières
	1985	1976-84		1986-1991	Dernière
	1986-1991	Dernière		1991 VP [v]	1950-90
	1992	1983-92		1992-1994	Dernière
	1993-1995	Dernière		1996	2-Dernières
	1996	1987-95		1997	Dernière
	1997	Dernière		1997SR [ii]	1948-96
	1997SR [ii]	1948-96		1998-2012	Dernière
	1998-1999	Dernière			
			- probabilité de décès à un âge donné selon le sexe	1948	1891-1945
Mortalité, tables de:				1951	1891-1950
-espérance de vie à la naissance selon le sexe	1959-1973	Dernière		1952	1891-1951 [iii]
	1974	2-Dernière		1953	1891-1952
	1975-1978	Dernière		1954	1891-1953 [iii]
	1978SR [i]	1948-77		1957	1900-56
	1979	Dernière		1961	1940-60
	1980	2-Dernières		1966	2-Dernières
	1981-1984	Dernière		1974	2-Dernières
	1985	2-Dernières		1980	2-Dernières
	1986-1991	Dernière		1985	2-Dernières
	1991 VP [v]	1950-90		1996	2-Dernières
	1992-1995	Dernière		2008-2012	Dernière
	1996	2-Dernières			
	1997	Dernière	-survivants à un âge donné selon le sexe	1948	1891-1945
	1997SR [ii]	1948-1996		1951	1891-1950
	1998	1995-98		1952	1891-1951 [iii]
	1999	1995-99		1953	1891-1952
	2000	1995-00		1954	1891-1953 [iii]
	2001	1997-01		1957	1900-56
	2002	1998-02		1961	1940-60
	2003	1999-03		1966	2-Dernières
	2004	2000-04		1974	2-Dernières
	2005	2001-05		1980	2-Dernières
	2006	2002-06		1985	2-Dernières
	2007	2003-07		1996	2-Dernières
	2008	2004-08			
	2009-10	2006-10	**Mort-nés** (voir: Morts fœtales tardives)		
	2011	2007-11			
	2012	2008-12	**Morts fœtales:**		
			-selon la période de gestation	1957	1950-56
-espérance de vie à un âge donné selon le sexe	1948	1891-1945		1959	1949-58
	1951	1891-1950		1961	1952-60
	1952	1891-1951 [iii]		1965	5-Dernières
	1953	1891-1952		1966	1956-65
	1954	1891-1953 [iii]		1967-1968	Dernière
	1955-1956	Dernière		1969	1963-68
	1957	1900-56		1974	1965-73
	1958-1960	Dernière		1975	1966-74
	1961	1940-60		1980	1971-79
	1962-64	Dernière			

Index
Index historique (suite)
(Voir notes à la fin de l'index)

Index
Index historique (suite)
(Voir notes à la fin de l'index)

Sujet	Année de l'édition	Période considérée
	1975	1966-74
	1980	1971-79
	1981	1972-80
	1985	1976-84
	1986	1977-85
	1996	1987-95
-selon la résidence (urbaine/rurale)	1971	1966-70
	1972	1967-71
	1973	1968-72
	1974	1965-73
	1975	1966-74
	1976	1971-75
	1977	1972-76
	1978	1973-77
	1979	1974-78
	1980	1971-79
	1981	1972-80
	1982	1977-81
	1983	1978-82
	1984	1979-83
	1985	1975-84
	1986	1977-85
	1987	1982-86
	1988	1983-87
	1989	1984-88
	1990	1985-89
	1991	1986-90
	1992	1987-91
	1993	1988-92
	1994	1989-93
	1995	1990-94
	1996	1987-95
	1997	1992-96
	1998	1993-97
	1999	1994-98
	1999CD [vii]	1990-98
	2000	1995-99
	2001	1997-01
	2002	1998-02
	2003	1999-03
	2004	2000-04
	2005	2001-05
	2006	2002-06
	2007	2003-07
	2008	2004-08
	2009-2010	2006-10
	2011	2007-11
	2012	2008-12
-selon le sexe	1961	1952-60
	1965	5-Dernières
	1969	1963-68
	1975	1966-74
	1981	1972-80
	1986	1977-85

Mortinatalité, rapports de (voir: Mortalité fœtale tardive)

Morts néonatales, selon le

Sujet	Année de l'édition	Période considérée
sexe (voir: Mortalité post-néonatale)		
Morts post-néonatales, selon le sexe (voir: Mortalité post-néonatale)		

N

Naissances	Année de l'édition	Période considérée
Naissances	1948	1932-47
	1949/50	1934-49
	1951	1935-50
	1952	1936-51
	1953	1950-52
	1954	1938-53
	1955	1946-54
	1956	1947-55
	1957	1948-56
	1958	1948-57
	1959	1949-58
	1960	1950-59
	1961	1952-61
	1962	1953-62
	1963	1954-63
	1964	1960-64
	1965	1946-65
	1966	1957-66
	1967	1963-67
	1968	1964-68
	1969	1950-69
	1970	1966-70
	1971	1967-71
	1972	1968-72
	1973	1969-73
	1974	1970-74
	1975	1956-75
	1976	1972-76
	1977	1973-77
	1978	1974-78
	1978SR [i]	1948-78
	1979	1975-79
	1980	1976-80
	1981	1962-81
	1982	1978-82
	1983	1979-83
	1984	1980-84
	1985	1981-85
	1986	1967-86
	1987	1983-87
	1988	1984-88
	1989	1985-89
	1990	1986-90
	1991	1987-91
	1992	1983-92
	1993	1989-93
	1994	1990-94
	1995	1991-95
	1996	1992-96
	1997	1993-97
	1997SR [ii]	1948-97
	1998	1994-98
	1999	1995-99

Index
Index historique (suite)
(Voir notes à la fin de l'index)

Sujet	Année de l'édition	Période considérée	Sujet	Année de l'édition	Période considérée
	1999CD [vii]	1980-99		1955-1956	Dernière
	2000	1996-00		1958	Dernière
	2001	1997-01		1959	1949-58
	2002	1998-02		1960-1964	Dernière
	2003	1999-03		1965	1955-64
	2004	2000-04		1966-1968	Dernière
	2005	2001-05		1969	1963-68
	2006	2002-06		1970-1974	Dernière
	2007	2003-07		1975	1966-74
	2008	2004-08		1976-1978	Dernière
	2009-2010	2006-10		1978SR [i]	1948-77
	2011	2007-11		1979-1980	Dernière
	2012	2008-12		1981	1972-80
				1982-1985	Dernière
-illégitimes (voir également: légitimes)				1986	1977-85
	1959	1949-58		1987-1991	Dernière
	1965	1955-64		1992	1983-92
	1969	1963-68		1993-1997	Dernière
	1975	1966-74		1997SR [ii]	1948-96'
	1981	1972-80		1998-1999	Dernière
	1986	1977-85		1999CD [vii]	1990-98
	1999CD [vii]	1990-98		2000-2012	Dernière
-légitimes	1948	1936-47	-selon l'âge de la mère et le rang de naissance	1949/50	1936-47
	1949/50	1936-49		1954	Dernière
	1954	1936-53		1959	1949-58
	1959	1949-58		1965	1955-64
	1965	1955-64		1969	1963-68
	1969	1963-68		1975	1966-74
	1975	1966-74		1981	1972-80
	1981	1972-80		1986	1977-85
	1986	1977-85		1999CD [vii]	1990-98
	1999CD [vii]	1990-98			
-légitimes selon l'âge de la mère	1954	1936-53	-selon l'âge de la mère et la résidence (urbaine/rurale) (voir: selon la résidence (urbaine/rurale), ci-dessous)		
	1959	1949-58			
	1965	1955-64			
	1969	1963-68			
	1975	1966-74	-selon l'âge de la mère et le sexe	1965-1968	Dernière
	1981	1972-80		1969	1963-68
	1986	1977-85		1970-1974	Dernière
-légitimes selon l'âge du père	1959	1949-58		1975	1966-74
	1965	1955-64		1976-1978	Dernière
	1969	1963-68		1978SR [i]	1948-77
	1975	1966-74		1979-1980	Dernière
	1981	1972-80		1981	1972-80
	1986	1977-85		1982-1985	Dernière
-légitimes selon la durée du mariage	1948	1936-47		1986	1977-85
	1949/50	1936-49		1987-1991	Dernière
	1954	1936-53		1992	1983-92
	1959	1949-58		1993-1997	Dernière
	1965	1955-64		1997SR [ii]	1948-96
	1969	1963-68		1998-1999	Dernière
	1975	1966-74		1999CD [vii]	1990-98
	1981	1972-80		2000-2012	Dernière
	1986	1977-85	-selon l'âge du père	1949/50	1942-49
	1999CD [vii]	1990-98		1954	1936-53
-selon l'âge de la mère	1948	1936-47		1959	1949-58
	1949/50	1936-49		1965	1955-64
	1954	1936-53			

Index
Index historique (suite)
(Voir notes à la fin de l'index)

Index
Index historique (suite)
(Voir notes à la fin de l'index)

Index
Index historique (suite)
(Voir notes à la fin de l'index)

Index
Index historique (suite)
(Voir notes à la fin de l'index)

Index
Index historique (suite)
(Voir notes à la fin de l'index)

Sujet	Année de l'édition	Période considérée	Sujet	Année de l'édition	Période considérée
	1994	1990-94		1972	1968-72
	1995	1991-95		1973	1969-73
	1996	1992-96		1974	1970-74
	1997	1993-97		1975	1971-75
	1998	1994-98		1976	1957-76
	1999	1995-99		1977	1973-77
	1972	1968-72		1978	1974-78
	1973	1969-73		1979	1975-79
	1974	1970-74		1980	1976-80
	1975	1971-75		1981	1977-81
	1976	1957-76		1982	1963-82
	1977	1973-77		1983	1979-83
	1978	1974-78		1984	1980-84
	1979	1975-79		1985	1981-85
	1980	1976-80		1986	1982-86
	1981	1977-81		1987	1983-87
	1982	1963-82		1988	1984-88
	1983	1979-83		1989	1985-89
	1984	1980-84		1990	1971-90
	1985	1981-85		1991	1987-91
	1986	1982-86		1992	1988-92
	1987	1983-87		1993	1989-93
	1988	1984-88		1994	1990-94
	1989	1985-89		1995	1991-95
	1990	1971-90		1996	1992-96
	1991	1987-91		1997	1993-97
	1992	1988-92		1998	1994-98
	1993	1989-93		1999	1995-99
	1994	1990-94		2000	1996-00
	1995	1991-95		2001	1997-01
	1996	1992-96		2002	1998-02
	1997	1993-97		2003	1999-03
	1998	1994-98		2004	2000-04
	1999	1995-99		2005	2001-05
	2000	1996-00		2006	2002-06
	2001	1997-01		2007	2003-07
	2002	1998-02		2008	2004-08
	2003	1999-03		2009-2010	2006-10
	2004	2000-04		2011	2007-11
	2005	2001-05		2012	2008-12
	2006	2002-06	-selon le sexe et la population mariable	1958	1935-56
	2007	2003-07		1968	1935-67
	2008	2004-08		1976	1966-75
	2009-2010	2006-10		1982	1972-81
	2011	2007-11		1990	1980-89
	2012	2008-12			
-selon l'âge et le sexe	1948	1936-46	**Nuptialité au premier mariage, taux de, classification détaillée selon l'âge de l'épouse et de l'époux**	1982	1972-81
	1949/50	1936-49		1990	1980-89
	1953	1936-51			
	1954	1936-52			
	1958	1935-56	**P**		
	1968	1955-67			
	1976	1966-75			
	1982	1972-81			
	1987	1975-86	**Population:**		
	1990	1980-89	-accroissement, taux d'......:		
-selon la résidence (urbaine/rurale)	1968	Dernière	annuels moyens pour les pays ou zones	1957	1953-56
	1969	1965-69		1958	1953-57
	1970	1966-70			
	1971	1967-71			

Index
Index historique (suite)
(Voir notes à la fin de l'index)

Index
Index historique (suite)
(Voir notes à la fin de l'index)

Index
Index historique (suite)
(Voir notes à la fin de l'index)

Sujet	Année de l'édition	Période considérée	Sujet	Année de l'édition	Période considérée
	1964	1955-64		1970	1950-70
	1972	1962-72	-analphabète selon le sexe et l'âge et la résidence (urbaine/rurale)		
selon la situation dans la profession, la profession et le sexe et la résidence (urbaine/rurale)				1973	1965-73
	1973	1965-73 [iii]		1979	1970-79 [iii]
	1979	1970-79 [iii]		1983	1974-83
	1984	1974-84		1988	1980-88 [iii]
	1988	1980-88 [iii]		1993	1985-93 [iii]
	1994	1985-94	-analphabète selon le sexe, taux d'......	1948	Dernière
				1955	1945-54
selon le sexe	1948	Dernière		1960	1920-60
	1949/50	1926-48		1963	1955-63
	1955	1945-54		1964	1955-64 [iii]
	1956	1945-55		1970	1950-70
	1960	1920-60	-analphabète selon le sexe, taux d'...... et la résidence (urbaine/rurale)		
	1963	1955-63		1973	1965-73
	1964	1955-64		1979	1970-79 [iii]
	1970	1950-70		1983	1974-83
	1972	1962-72		1988	1980-88 [iii]
	1973	1965-73 [iii]		1993	1985-93 [iii]
	1979	1970-79 [iii]	-analphabète selon le sexe et l'âge, taux d'......	1948	Dernière
	1984	1974-84		1955	1945-54
	1988	1980-88 [iii]		1960	1920-60
	1994	1985-94		1963	1955-63 [iii]
-alphabète selon l'âge et le sexe (voir également: analphabète, ci-dessous)				1964	1955-64 [iii]
	1948	Dernière		1970	1950-70
	1955	1945-54	-analphabète selon le sexe et l'âge, taux d'...... et la résidence (urbaine/rurale)		
	1963	1955-63		1973	1965-73
	1964	1955-64 [iii]		1979	1970-79 [iii]
	1971	1962-71		1983	1974-83
-alphabète selon l'âge et le sexe et la résidence (urbaine/rurale)				1988	1980-88 [iii]
	1973	1965-73 [iii]		1993	1985-93 [iii]
	1979	1970-79 [iii]	-célibataire selon l'âge et le sexe (voir également: selon l'état matrimonial, ci-dessous):		
	1984	1974-84	nombres	1960	1920-60
	1988	1980-88 [iii]		1970	1950-70
	1993	1985-93	pourcentages	1949/50	1926-48
-alphabétisme selon le sexe, taux d'...... (voir également: analphabétisme, taux d', ci-dessous)				1960	1920-60
	1955	1945-54		1970	1950-70
-alphabétisme selon le sexe et l'âge, taux d'......	1955	1945-54	-chômeurs selon l'âge et le sexe	1949/50	1946-49
-analphabète selon le sexe	1948	Dernière	-dans les localités (voir: selon l'importance des localités, ci-dessous)		
	1955	1945-54	des collectivités, âge et sexe et résidence urbaine/rurale		
	1960	1920-60		1987	1975-86
	1963	1955-63		1995	1985-95
	1964	1955-64 [iii]	-dans les ménages selon le type et la dimension des ménages privés (voir également: Ménages)		
	1970	1950-70			
-analphabète selon le sexe et la résidence (urbaine/rurale)				1955	1945-54
	1973	1965-73		1962	1955-62
	1979	1970-79 [iii]		1963	1955-63 [iii]
	1983	1974-83	-dans les logements collectifs et sans abri	1991VP [v]	Dernière
	1988	1980-88 [iii]			
-analphabète selon le sexe et l'âge	1948	Dernière			
	1955	1945-54			
	1963	1955-63			
	1964	1955-64 [iii]			

Index
Index historique (suite)
(Voir notes à la fin de l'index)

Index
Index historique (suite)
(Voir notes à la fin de l'index)

Index
Index historique (suite)
(Voir notes à la fin de l'index)

Index
Index historique (suite)
(Voir notes à la fin de l'index)

Index
Index historique (suite)
(Voir notes à la fin de l'index)

Sujet	Année de l'édition	Période considérée	Sujet	Année de l'édition	Période considérée
	1960	1920-61	naissance et le sexe et l'âge		
	1962	1955-62		1983	1974-83
	1963	1955-63 [iii]		1989	1980-88
	1970	1950-70	-selon la nationalité		
	1971	1962-71	juridique et le sexe	1956	1945-55
	1973	1965-73 [iii]		1963	1955-63
	1979	1970-79 [iii]		1964	1955-64 [iii]
	1983	1974-83		1971	1962-71
	1988	1980-88 [iii]		1973	1965-73 [iii]
	1993	1985-93	-selon la nationalité		
de 20 000 habitants et			juridique et le sexe et l'âge	1977	Dernière
plus	1948	Dernière		1983	1974-83
	1952	Dernière		1989	1980-88
	1955	1945-54	-selon les principales		
	1960	1920-61	divisions administratives		
	1962	1955-62	(voir: des principales		
	1963	1955-63 [iii]	divisions administratives, ci-		
	1970	1950-70	dessus)		
	1971	1962-71	-selon la religion et le sexe	1956	1945-55
	1973	1965-73 [iii]		1963	1955-63
	1979	1970-79 [iii]		1964	1955-64 [iii]
	1983	1974-83		1971	1962-71
	1988	1980-88 [iii]		1973	1965-73 [iii]
	1993	1985-93		1979	1970-79 [iii]
-selon l'importance des				1983	1974-83
localités et le sexe	1948	Dernière		1988	1980-88 [iii]
	1952	Dernière		1993	1985-93
	1955	1945-54	-selon la résidence		
	1962	1955-62	(urbaine/rurale) (voir:		
	1963	1955-63 [iii]	urbaine/rurale (résidence),		
	1971	1962-71	ci-dessous)		
	1973	1965-73 [iii]	-selon le sexe:		
	1979	1970-79 [iii]	dénombrée	1948-1952	Dernière
	1983	1974-83		1953	1950-52
	1988	1980-88 [iii]		1954-1959	Dernière
	1993	1985-93		1960	1900-61
-selon la langue et le sexe	1956	1945-55		1961	Dernière
	1963	1955-63		1962	1900-62
	1964	1955-64 [iii]		1963	1955-63
	1971	1962-71		1964	1955-64
	1973	1965-73 [iii]		1965-1969	Dernière
	1979	1970-79 [iii]		1970	1950-70
	1983	1974-83		1971	1962-71
	1988	1980-88 [iii]		1972	Dernière
	1993	1985-93		1973	1965-73
-selon le niveau				1974-1978	Dernière
d'instruction, l'âge et le sexe	1956	1945-55		1978SR [i]	1948-78
	1963	1955-63		1979-1982	Dernière
	1964	1955-64 [iii]		1983	1974-83
	1971	1962-71		1984-1991	Dernière
	1973	1965-73 [iii]		1991 VP [v]	1950-90
	1979	1970-79 [iii]		1992-1997	Dernière
	1983	1974-83		1997SR [ii]	1948-97
	1988	1980-88 [iii]		1998-2012	Dernière
	1993	1985-93			
-selon le pays ou zone de			estimée	1948-	
naissance et le sexe	1956	1945-55		1949/50	1945 et
	1963	1955-63			Dernière
	1964	1955-64 [iii]		1951-1954	Dernière [iii]
	1971	1962-71		1955-1959	Dernière
	1973	1965-73 [iii]		1960	1940-60
-selon le pays ou zone de	1977	Dernière		1961-1969	Dernière

Index
Index historique (suite)
(Voir notes à la fin de l'index)

Index
Index historique (suite)
(Voir notes à la fin de l'index)

Index
Index historique (suite)
(Voir notes à la fin de l'index)

Index
Index historique (suite)
(Voir notes à la fin de l'index)

Index
Index historique (suite)
(Voir notes à la fin de l'index)

Sujet	Année de l'édition	Période considérée	Sujet	Année de l'édition	Période considérée
			Taux (voir: Accroissement intercensitaire de la population; Accroissement naturel; Alphabétisme; Analphabétisme; Annulation; Divortialité; Fécondité Intercensitaire; Mortalité Infantile, Mortalité maternelle; Mortalité néonatale; Mortalité post-néonatale; Mortalité, tables de; Mortalité; Natalité; Nuptialité; Reproduction; taux bruts et nets de)		
-des régions	1952-1999	Dernière			
	2000	2000			
	2001	2001			
	2002	2002			
	2003	2003			
	2004	2004			
	2005	2005			
	2006	2006			
	2007	2007			
	2008	2008			
	2009-2010	2010			
	2011	2011			
	2012	2012			
-du monde	1949/50-1999	Dernière	**Taux bruts de reproduction** (voir: Reproduction)		
	2000	2000			
	2001	2001			
	2004	2004	**Taux nets de reproduction** (voir: Reproduction)		
	2005	2005			
	2006	2006	**Texte spécial** (voir liste détaillée dans l'Appendice de cet index)		
	2007	2007			
	2008	2008			
	2009-2010	2010			
	2011	2011			
	2012	2012			

-Vieillissement de la population et situation des personnes âgées 1991VP [v] 1950-90

Survivants (voir: Mortalité, tables de)

Tables de mortalité (voir: Mortalité, tables de)

Urbaine/rurale (décès) (voir: Décès)

Urbaine/rurale (ménages: dimension moyenne des) (voir: Ménages)

Urbaine/rurale (mortalité infantile) (voir: Mortalité infantile)

Urbaine/rurale(naissances) (voir: Naissances)

Urbaine/rurale(population) (voir: Population selon la résidence (urbaine/rurale))

Vieillissement (voir: Population)

Villes (voir: Population)

Index
Index historique (suite)
(Voir notes à la fin de l'index)

APPENDICE

Texte spécial de chaque Annuaire démographique

Divorce:

"Application des statistiques de la nuptialité et de la divortialité", 1958.

Mariage:

"Application des statistiques de la nuptialité et de la divortialité", 1958.

Ménages:

"Concepts et définitions des ménages, du chef de ménage et de la population des collectivités", 1987.

Migration:

"'Statistiques des migrations internationales",1977.

Mortalité:

"Tendances récentes de la mortalité", 1951.
"Développement des statistiques des causes de décès",1951.
"Les facteurs du fléchissement de la mortalité",1957.
"Notes sur les méthodes d'évaluation de la fiabilité des statistiques classiques de la mortalité",1961.
"Mortalité: Tendances récentes",1966.
"Tendances de la mortalité chez les personnes âgées",1991VP [v].

Natalité:

"Présentation graphiques des tendances de la fécondité",1959.

"Taux de natalité: Tendances récentes",1965.

Population: ..

"Tendances démo-graphiques mondiales,1920-1949",1949/50.
"Mouvements d'urbanisation et ses caractéristiques",1952.
"Les recensements de population de 1950",1955.
"Situation démographique mondiale",1956.
"Ce que nous savons de l'état et de l'évolution de la population mondiale",1960.
"Notes sur les statistiques disponibles des recensements nationaux de population et méthodes d'évaluation de leur exactitude",1962.
"Disponibilité et qualité de certaines données statistiques fondées sur les recensements de population effectués entre 1955 et 1963",1963.
"Disponibilité de certaines statistiques fondées sur les recensements de population: 1955-1964",1964.

"Définitions et concepts statistiques de la population urbaine et de la population rurale",1967.
"Application des statistiques de la nuptialité et de la divortialité",1958.
"Ce que nous savons de l'état et de l'évolution de la population mondiale",1970.
"Recommandations de l'Organisation des Nations Unies quant aux sujets sur lesquels doit porter un recensement de population, en regard de la pratique adoptée par les différents pays dans les recensements nationaux effectués de 1965 à 1971",1971.
"Les définitions statistiques de la population urbaine et leurs usages en démographie appliquée",1972.

"Evolution récente de la fécondité dans le monde",1969.
"Dates des recensements nationaux de la population et de l'habitation effectués au cours de la décennie

Index
Index historique (suite)
(Voir notes à la fin de l'index)

1965-1974", 1974.

"Dates des recensements nationaux de la population et de l'habitation effectués ou prévus, au cours de la décennie 1975-1984",1979.

"Dates des recensements nationaux de la population et/ou de l'habitation effectués au cours de la décennie 1965-1974 et effectués ou prévus au cours de la décennie1975-1984",1983.

"Définitions et concepts statistiques du ménage",1968.

"Dates des recensements nationaux de la population et/ou de l'habitation effectués au cours de la décennie 1975-1984 et effectués ou prévus au cours de la décennie1985-1994", 1988, 1993.

"Statistiques concernant la population active: un aperçu",1984.

"'Etude du vieillissement et de la situation des personnes âgées: Besoins particuliers",1991VP [v].

"Les incapacités", 1991VP [v].

"Le vieillissement", 1991VP [v].

Notes générales

Cet index alphabétique donne la liste des sujets traités dans chacune de 63 éditions de l'Annuaire démographique. La colonne "Année de l'édition" indique l'édition spécifique dans laquelle le sujet a été traité. Sauf indication contraire, la colonne "Période considérée" désigne les années pour lesquelles les statistiques annuelles apparaissant dans l'Annuaire démographique sont indiquées sous la colonne "Année de l'édition". La rubrique "Dernière" ou " 2-Dernières" indique que les données représentent la ou les dernières années disponibles seulement.

---

[i] Le Supplément rétrospectif du 30ème Annuaire Démographique fait l'objet d'un tirage spécial publié en 1979.

[ii] Le Supplément rétrospectif du 49ème Annuaire Démographique fait l'objet d'un tirage spécial (CD-ROM) publié en 2000

[iii] Données non disponibles dans l'édition précédente seulement.

[iv] Titres non disponibles dans la bibliographie précédente seulement.

[v] Taux moyens pour 5 ans.

[vi] Vieillissement de la population.

[vii] Le Supplément du 51 Annuaire Démographique, ayant comme suject la natalité, fait l'objet d'un tirage spécial (CD-ROM) publié en 2002.